STREET Cheshire

Chester, Crewe, Macclesfield, Northwich, Warrington

First published in 1995 by

Philip's, a division of
Octopus Publishing Group Ltd
2-4 Heron Quays, London E14 4JP
An Hachette Livre UK Company

Fourth colour edition 2007
Second impression 2009
CHEDA

ISBN-13 978-0-540-09163-8 (spiral)

To the best of the Publishers' knowledge, the information in this atlas was correct at the time of going to press. No responsibility can be accepted for any errors or their consequences.

The representation in this atlas of a road, track or path is no evidence of the existence of a right of way.

Data for the speed cameras provided by PocketGPSWorld.com Ltd.

Printed by Toppan, China

Contents

II **List of mobile speed cameras**

III **Key to map symbols**

IV **Key to map pages**

VI **Route planning**

VIII **Administrative and Postcode boundaries**

1 **Street maps** at 3½ inches to 1 mile

237 **Street map of Chester city centre** at 7 inches to 1 mile

238 **Index** of towns, villages, streets, hospitals, industrial estates, railway stations, schools, shopping centres, universities and places of interest

Digital Data

The exceptionally high-quality mapping found in this atlas is available as digital data in TIFF format, which is easily convertible to other bitmapped (raster) image formats.

The index is also available in digital form as a standard database table. It contains all the details found in the printed index together with the National Grid reference for the map square in which each entry is named.

For further information, please contact victoria.dawbarn@philips-maps.co.uk

Mobile speed cameras

The vast majority of speed cameras used on Britain's roads are operated by safety camera partnerships. These comprise local authorities, the police, Her Majesty's Court Service (HMCS) and the Highways Agency.

This table lists the sites where each safety camera partnership may enforce speed limits through the use of mobile cameras or detectors. These are usually set up on the roadside or a bridge spanning the road and operated by a police or civilian enforcement officer. The speed limit at each site (if available) is shown in red type, followed by the approximate location in black type.

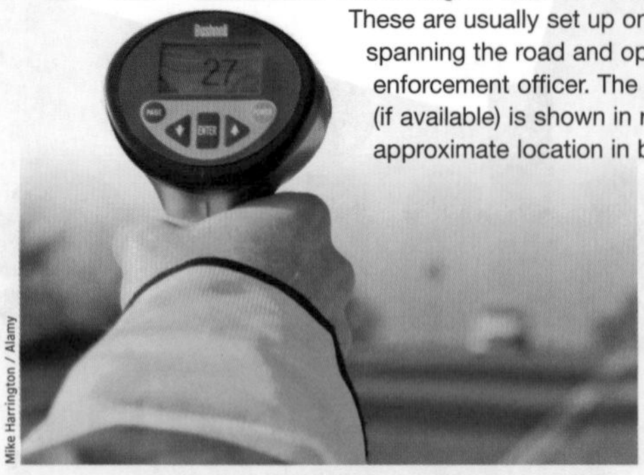

Mike Harrington / Alamy

M6
- 70 Bradwell, northbound
- 70 Northwich, northbound
- 50 Woolston near Warrington, northbound

M62
- 70 Croft, eastbound and westbound

A50
- 30 Grappenhall, Knutsford Rd
- 30 Knutsford, Manchester/Toft Rd
- 30 Warrington, Long Lane

A54
- 60&70 Ashton, Kelsall Rd

A56
- 40 Lymm, Camsley Lane

A57
- 40 Paddington, New Manchester Rd

A523
- 30 Poynton, London Rd

A532
- 30 Crewe, West St

A533
- 40 Middlewich, Booth Lane

A537
- 50 Macclesfield, Buxton Rd nr Wildboarclough

A5019
- 30 Crewe, Mill St

A5032
- 30 Whitby, Chester Rd

A5034
- 60 Mere, Mereside Rd

A5104
- 30 Chester, Hough Green

B5071
- 30 Crewe, Gresty Rd

B5078
- 30 Alsager, Sandbach Rd North

B5082
- 30 Northwich, Middlewich Rd

B5132
- 30 Ellesmere Port, Overpool Rd

B5153
- 30 Mill Lane/Hollow Lane (speed indicator sign)

B5463
- 30 Little Sutton, Station Rd

B5470
- 30 Macclesfield, Rainow Rd

Key to map symbols

22a	**Motorway** with junction number
	Primary route – dual/single carriageway
	A road – dual/single carriageway
	B road – dual/single carriageway
	Minor road – dual/single carriageway
	Other minor road – dual/single carriageway
	Road under construction
	Tunnel, covered road
30 30	**Speed cameras - single, multiple**
	Rural track, private road or narrow road in urban area
	Gate or obstruction to traffic (restrictions may not apply at all times or to all vehicles)
	Path, bridleway, byway open to all traffic, road used as a public path
	Pedestrianised area
DY7	**Postcode boundaries**
	County and unitary authority boundaries
	Railway, tunnel, railway under construction
	Tramway, tramway under construction
	Miniature railway
Walsall	**Railway station**
	Private railway station
South Shields	**Metro station**
	Tram stop, tram stop under construction
	Bus, coach station
	Ambulance station
	Coastguard station
	Fire station
	Police station
	Accident and Emergency entrance to hospital
H	**Hospital**
+	**Place of worship**
i	**Information Centre** (open all year)
	Shopping Centre
P P&R	**Parking, Park and Ride**
PO	**Post Office**
	Camping site, caravan site
	Golf course, picnic site
Prim Sch	**Important buildings, schools, colleges, universities and hospitals**
	Built up area
	Woods
River Medway	**Water name**
	River, weir, stream
	Canal, lock, tunnel
	Water
	Tidal water
Church	**Non-Roman antiquity**
ROMAN FORT	**Roman antiquity**
87 237	**Adjoining page indicators and overlap bands** The colour of the arrow and the band indicates the scale of the adjoining or overlapping page (see scales below)

Enlarged mapping only

	Railway or bus station building
	Place of interest
	Parkland

Acad	**Academy**	Inst	**Institute**	Recn Gd	**Recreation Ground**
Allot Gdns	**Allotments**	Ct	**Law Court**	Resr	**Reservoir**
Cemy	**Cemetery**	L Ctr	**Leisure Centre**	Ret Pk	**Retail Park**
C Ctr	**Civic Centre**	LC	**Level Crossing**	Sch	**School**
CH	**Club House**	Liby	**Library**	Sh Ctr	**Shopping Centre**
Coll	**College**	Mkt	**Market**	TH	**Town Hall/House**
Crem	**Crematorium**	Meml	**Memorial**	Trad Est	**Trading Estate**
Ent	**Enterprise**	Mon	**Monument**	Univ	**University**
Ex H	**Exhibition Hall**	Mus	**Museum**	W Twr	**Water Tower**
Ind Est	**Industrial Estate**	Obsy	**Observatory**	Wks	**Works**
IRB Sta	**Inshore Rescue Boat Station**	Pal	**Royal Palace**	YH	**Youth Hostel**
		PH	**Public House**		

■ The small numbers around the edges of the maps identify the 1 kilometre National Grid lines

■ The dark grey border on the inside edge of some pages indicates that the mapping does not continue onto the adjacent page

The scale of the maps on the pages numbered in blue is 5.52 cm to 1 km • 3½ inches to 1 mile • 1: 18103

0 ¼ ½ ¾ 1 mile
0 250 m 500 m 750 m 1 kilometre

The scale of the maps on pages numbered in red is 11.04 cm to 1 km • 7 inches to 1 mile • 1: 9051

0 220 yards 440 yards 660 yards ½ mile
0 125 m 250 m 375 m ½ kilometre

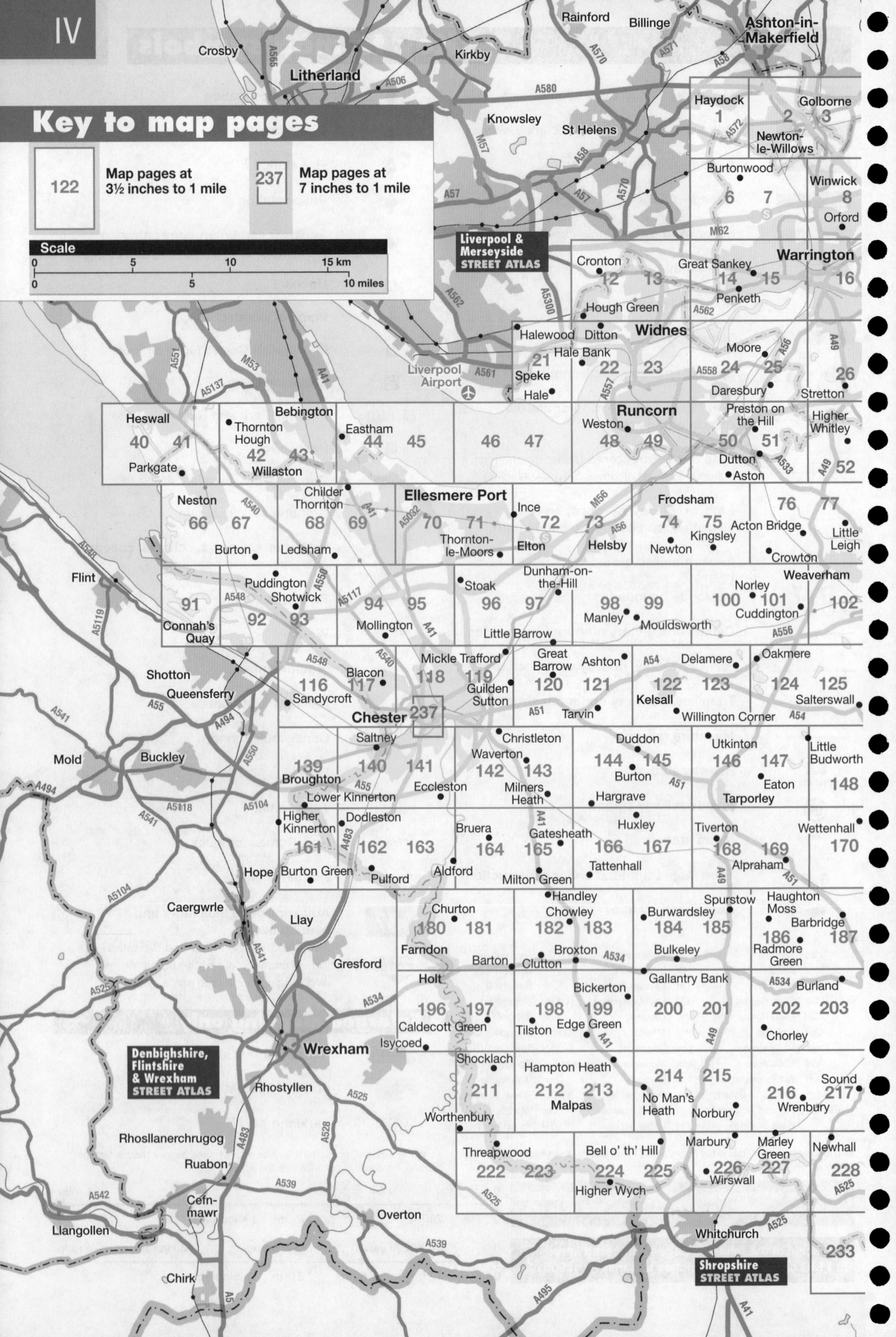
Key to map pages
122
Map pages at 3½ inches to 1 mile
237
Map pages at 7 inches to 1 mile
Scale
0 5 10 15 km
0 5 10 miles
Liverpool & Merseyside STREET ATLAS
Denbighshire, Flintshire & Wrexham STREET ATLAS
Shropshire STREET ATLAS
Crosby
Litherland
Rainford
Billinge
Ashton-in-Makerfield
Kirkby
Knowsley
St Helens
Haydock 1
Golborne 2 3
Newton-le-Willows
Burtonwood 6 7
Winwick 8
Orford
Cronton 12 13
Great Sankey 14 15
Warrington 16
Penketh
Hough Green
Halewood
Ditton
Widnes
Moore
21 22 23 24 25 26
Hale Bank
Speke
Hale
Liverpool Airport
Daresbury
Stretton
Heswall 40 41
Thornton Hough 42 43
Bebington
Eastham 44 45
46 47
Weston 48 49
Runcorn
Preston on the Hill 50 51
Higher Whitley
Parkgate
Willaston
Dutton
Aston
52
Neston 66 67
Childer Thornton 68 69
Ellesmere Port 70 71
Ince 72
73
Frodsham 74 75
76 77
Acton Bridge
Kingsley
Little Leigh
Burton
Ledsham
Thornton-le-Moors
Elton
Helsby
Newton
Crowton
Flint
Puddington
Shotwick
Stoak
Dunham-on-the-Hill
Norley
Weaverham
91 92 93 94 95 96 97 98 99 100 101 102
Connah's Quay
Mollington
Manley
Mouldsworth
Cuddington
Little Barrow
Mickle Trafford
Great Barrow
Ashton
Delamere
Oakmere
Shotton
Blacon
116 117 118 119 120 121 122 123 124 125
Guilden Sutton
Kelsall
Salterswall
Queensferry
Sandycroft
Chester 237
Tarvin
Willington Corner
Mold
Buckley
Saltney
Christleton
Duddon
Utkinton
Little Budworth
139 140 141 142 143 144 145 146 147 148
Broughton
Waverton
Burton
Eaton
Lower Kinnerton
Eccleston
Milners Heath
Hargrave
Tarporley
Higher Kinnerton
Dodleston
Bruera
Gatesheath
Huxley
Tiverton
Wettenhall
161 162 163 164 165 166 167 168 169 170
Hope
Burton Green
Pulford
Aldford
Milton Green
Tattenhall
Alpraham
Handley
Spurstow
Haughton Moss
Caergwrle
Churton
Chowley
Burwardsley
Barbridge
180 181 182 183 184 185 186 187
Llay
Farndon
Radmore Green
Gresford
Barton
Clutton
Broxton
Bulkeley
Holt
Gallantry Bank
Burland
Bickerton
196 197 198 199 200 201 202 203
Caldecott Green
Tilston
Edge Green
Chorley
Isycoed
Wrexham
Shocklach
Hampton Heath
214 215
Sound
211 212 213 216 217
Malpas
No Man's Heath
Norbury
Wrenbury
Rhostyllen
Worthenbury
Rhosllanerchrugog
Threapwood
Bell o' th' Hill
Marbury
Marley Green
Newhall
222 223 224 225 226 227 228
Ruabon
Higher Wych
Wirswall
Cefn-mawr
Overton
Llangollen
Whitchurch
233
Chirk
A565 A506 A580 A570 A571 A58 A572 M57 A57 M62 A562 A5300 A561 A558 A56 A49 A557 A533 M53 A551 A5137 A41 A540 A5032 M56 A548 A550 A5117 A5119 A556 A54 A51 A55 A541 A494 A5118 A5104 A483 A534 A525 A528 A539 A542 A495 A5

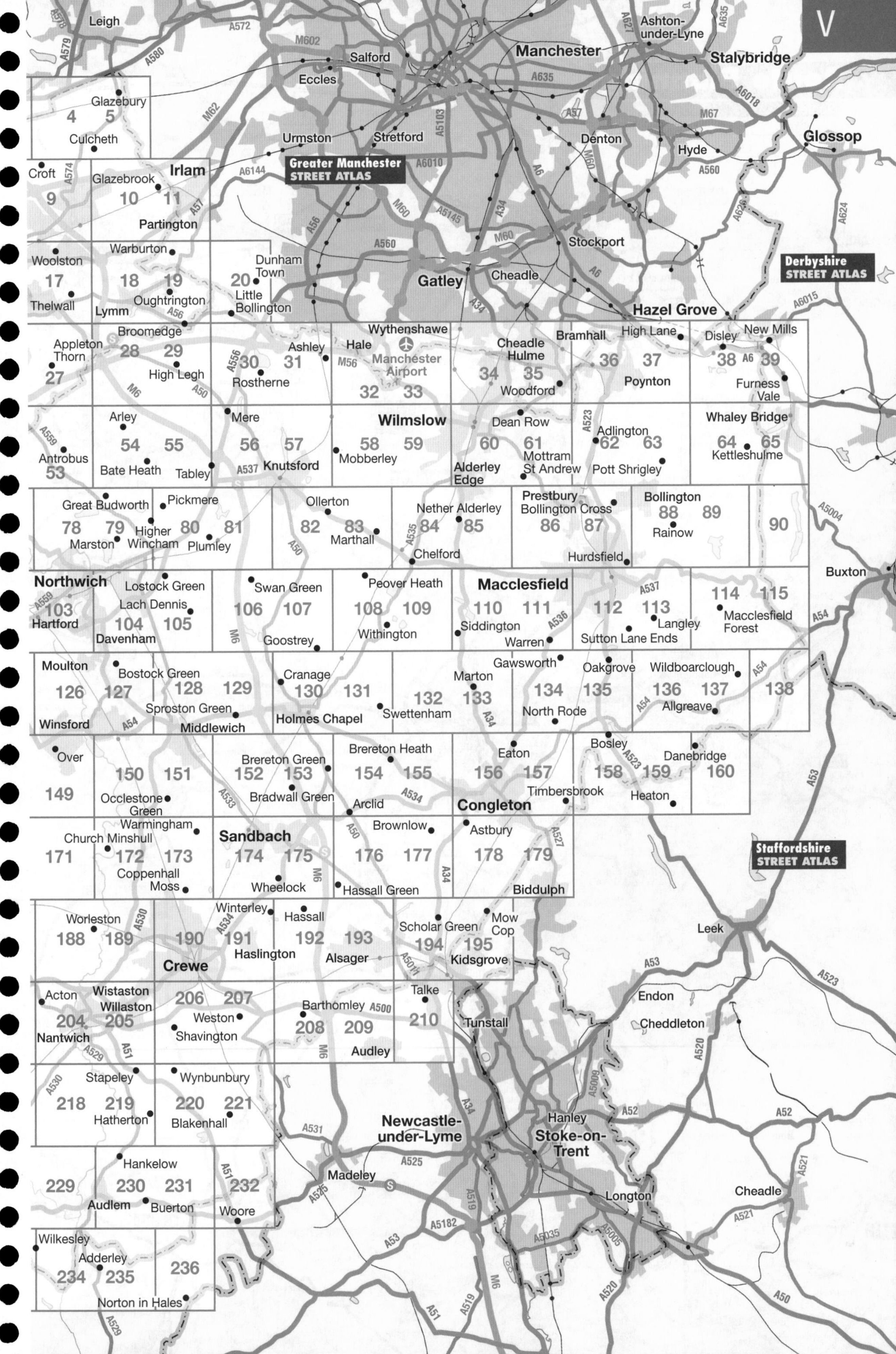

Leigh
A579
A578
A572
M602
A580
Salford
Manchester
Ashton-under-Lyne
A627
A635
Stalybridge
Eccles
A635
A6018
Glazebury
4
5
Culcheth
M62
A57
M67
Urmston
Stretford
A5103
Denton
Hyde
Glossop
Croft
A574
Glazebrook
Irlam
Greater Manchester STREET ATLAS
A6144
A6010
M60
A560
9
10
11
A57
Partington
A56
M60
A5145
A34
A6
A624
A626
Warburton
Woolston
17
18
19
Dunham Town
20
A560
M60
Stockport
Derbyshire STREET ATLAS
Thelwall
Lymm
Oughtrington
A56
Little Bollington
Gatley
Cheadle
A34
A6
Hazel Grove
A6015
Appleton Thorn
Broomedge
28
29
27
High Legh
M6
A50
A556
30
31
Ashley
Rostherne
Wythenshawe
Hale
M56
Manchester Airport
32
33
Cheadle Hulme
34
35
Woodford
Bramhall
36
37
High Lane
Poynton
Disley
38
A6
39
New Mills
Furness Vale
Arley
A559
Antrobus
53
54
55
Bate Heath
Tabley
Mere
56
57
A537
Knutsford
Wilmslow
58
59
Mobberley
60
61
Dean Row
Alderley Edge
Mottram St Andrew
A523
Adlington
62
63
Pott Shrigley
Whaley Bridge
64
65
Kettleshulme
Great Budworth
Pickmere
78
79
80
81
Higher Wincham
Marston
Plumley
Ollerton
82
83
Marthall
A50
Nether Alderley
A535
84
85
Chelford
Prestbury
Bollington Cross
86
87
Hurdsfield
Bollington
88
89
Rainow
90
A5004
Buxton
Northwich
A559
103
Hartford
Lostock Green
Lach Dennis
104
105
Davenham
Swan Green
106
107
M6
Goostrey
Peover Heath
108
109
Withington
Macclesfield
110
111
Siddington
A536
Warren
A537
112
113
Langley
Sutton Lane Ends
114
115
Macclesfield Forest
A54
Moulton
Bostock Green
126
127
128
129
Sproston Green
Winsford
A54
Middlewich
Cranage
130
131
Holmes Chapel
Swettenham
132
133
Marton
A34
Gawsworth
134
135
North Rode
Oakgrove
Wildboarclough
136
137
Allgreave
A54
A54
138
Over
149
150
151
Occlestone Green
Brereton Green
152
153
A533
Bradwall Green
Brereton Heath
154
155
Arclid
A534
Eaton
156
157
Congleton
Timbersbrook
Bosley
A523
158
159
Danebridge
160
Heaton
A53
Warmingham
Church Minshull
171
172
173
Coppenhall Moss
Sandbach
174
175
M6
Wheelock
A50
Brownlow
176
177
Hassall Green
A34
Astbury
178
179
A527
Biddulph
Staffordshire STREET ATLAS
Worleston
188
189
A530
190
191
A534
Winterley
Crewe
Haslington
Hassall
192
193
Alsager
A5011
Scholar Green
194
195
Mow Cop
Kidsgrove
Leek
A53
A523
Acton
Wistaston
Willaston
204
205
Nantwich
A529
A51
206
207
Weston
Shavington
Barthomley
A500
208
209
M6
Audley
Talke
210
Tunstall
Endon
Cheddleton
A520
A530
Stapeley
218
219
Hatherton
Wynbunbury
220
221
Blakenhall
A531
Newcastle-under-Lyme
A34
A5009
Hanley
Stoke-on-Trent
A52
A52
A521
Hankelow
229
230
231
A51
232
Audlem
Buerton
Woore
Madeley
A525
A525
A519
Longton
Cheadle
A521
Wilkesley
Adderley
234
235
236
Norton in Hales
A529
A53
A5182
A5035
A5005
M6
A51
A519
A520
A50

VI
Route Planning
Scale
0
5
10 km
0
5 miles
Merseyside
LIVERPOOL
Birkenhead
Wallasey
HOYLAKE
BEBINGTON
St Helens
Huyton
Prescot
Knowsley
Kirkby
Widnes
Runcorn
Halton
Speke
Garston
Liverpool Airport
Ellesmere Port
Warrington
Newton-le-Willows
ASHTON-IN-MAKERFIELD
Haydock
Golborne
Frodsham
Helsby
Neston
Heswall
Willaston
Flint (Y Fflint)
Connah's Quay
Queensferry
Shotton
Hawarden (Penarlâg)
Buckley (Bwcle)
Mold (Yr Wyddgrug)
Chester
Delamere Forest
Kelsall
Tarporley
Hope (Yr Hôb)
Caergwrle
Wrexham (Wrecsam)
Rhosllanerchrugog
Ruabon (Rhiwabon)
Chirk (Y Waun)
Overton (Owrtyn)
Farndon
Holt
Malpas
Whitchurch
Shropshire Union Canal
Llangollen Canal
Cheshire

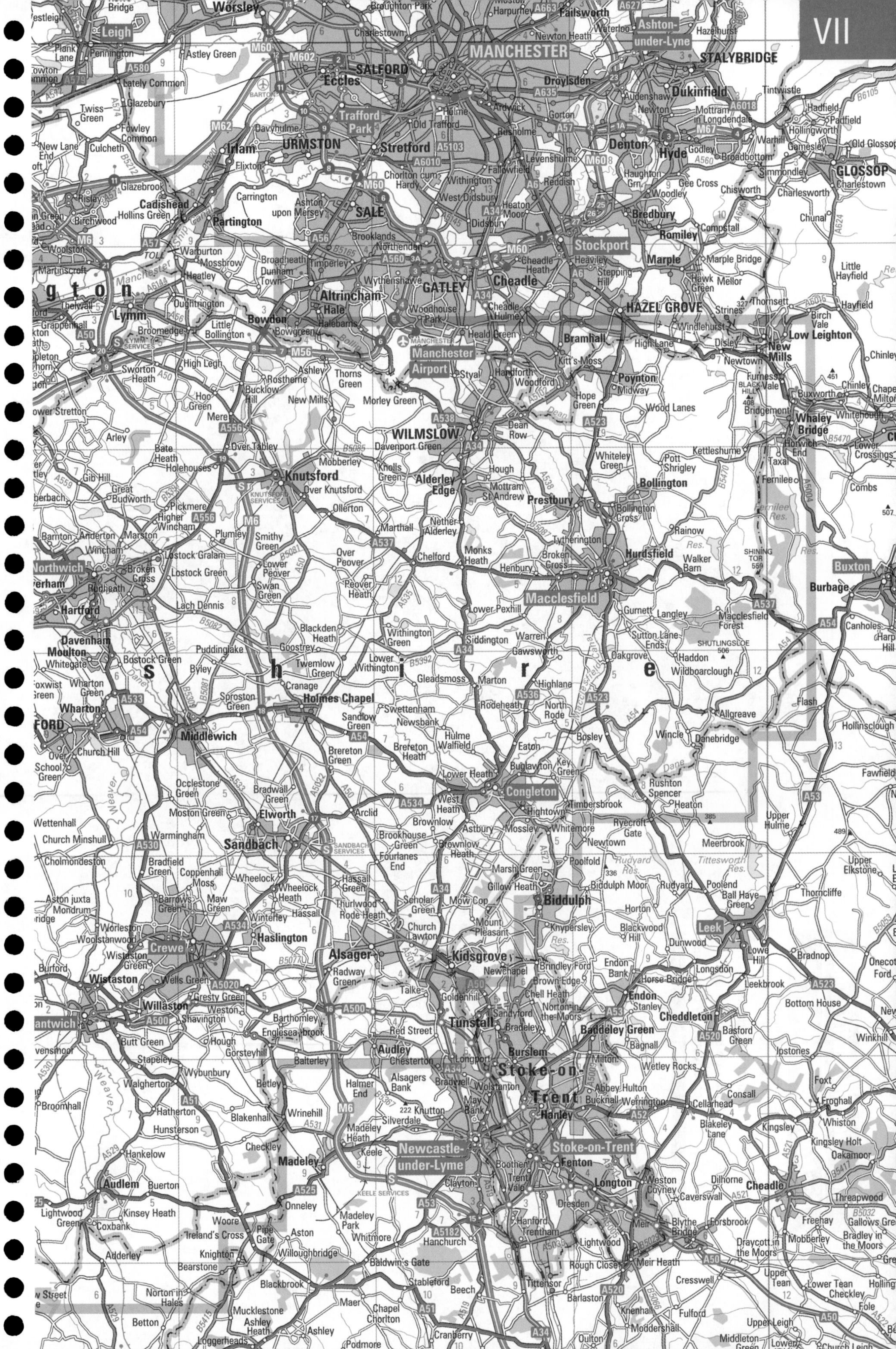
Worsley
Leigh
MANCHESTER
Ashton-under-Lyne
STALYBRIDGE
SALFORD
Eccles
Trafford Park
URMSTON
Stretford
Droylsden
Dukinfield
Denton
Hyde
GLOSSOP
Irlam
Cadishead
Partington
SALE
Stockport
Bredbury
Romiley
Marple
Cheadle
GATLEY
Altrincham
Hale
Bowdon
HAZEL GROVE
Lymm
Manchester Airport
Bramhall
Poynton
New Mills
Low Leighton
Whaley Bridge
WILMSLOW
Alderley Edge
Knutsford
Prestbury
Bollington
Macclesfield
Buxton
Burbage
Northwich
Hartford
Davenham
Moulton
Holmes Chapel
Middlewich
Congleton
Biddulph
Sandbach
Elworth
Alsager
Kidsgrove
Crewe
Haslington
Wistaston
Willaston
Leek
Tunstall
Burslem
Stoke-on-Trent
Hanley
Newcastle-under-Lyme
Fenton
Longton
Cheadle
Audley
Madeley
Audlem
Baddeley Green
Cheddleton
Endon
Shining Tor 559
Shutlingsloe 506
Macclesfield Forest
Wincle
Danebridge
Rushton Spencer
Allgreave
Flash
Keele
Trentham
Meir Heath
Blythe Bridge
Barlaston
Tittensor

Major administrative and Postcode boundaries

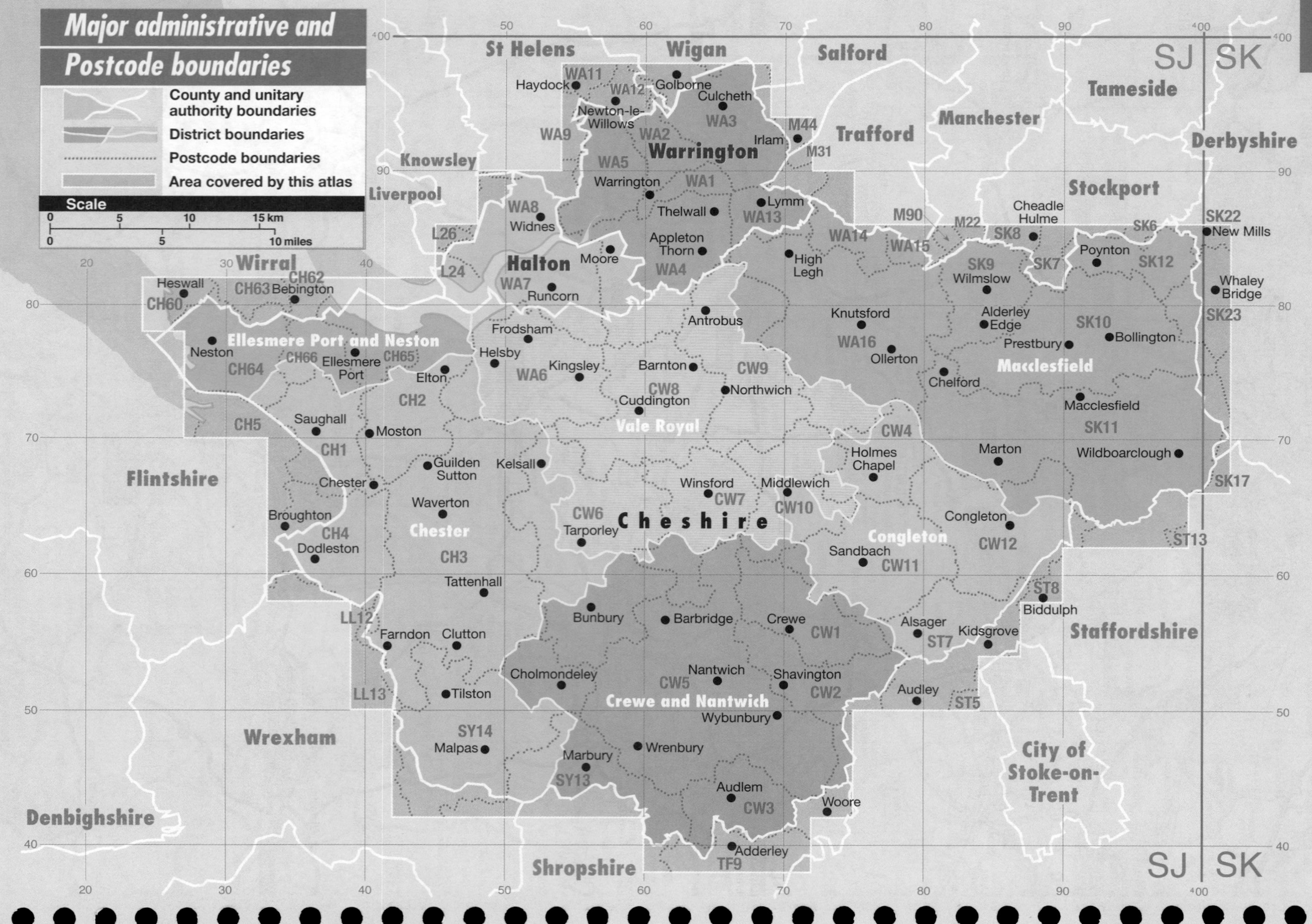

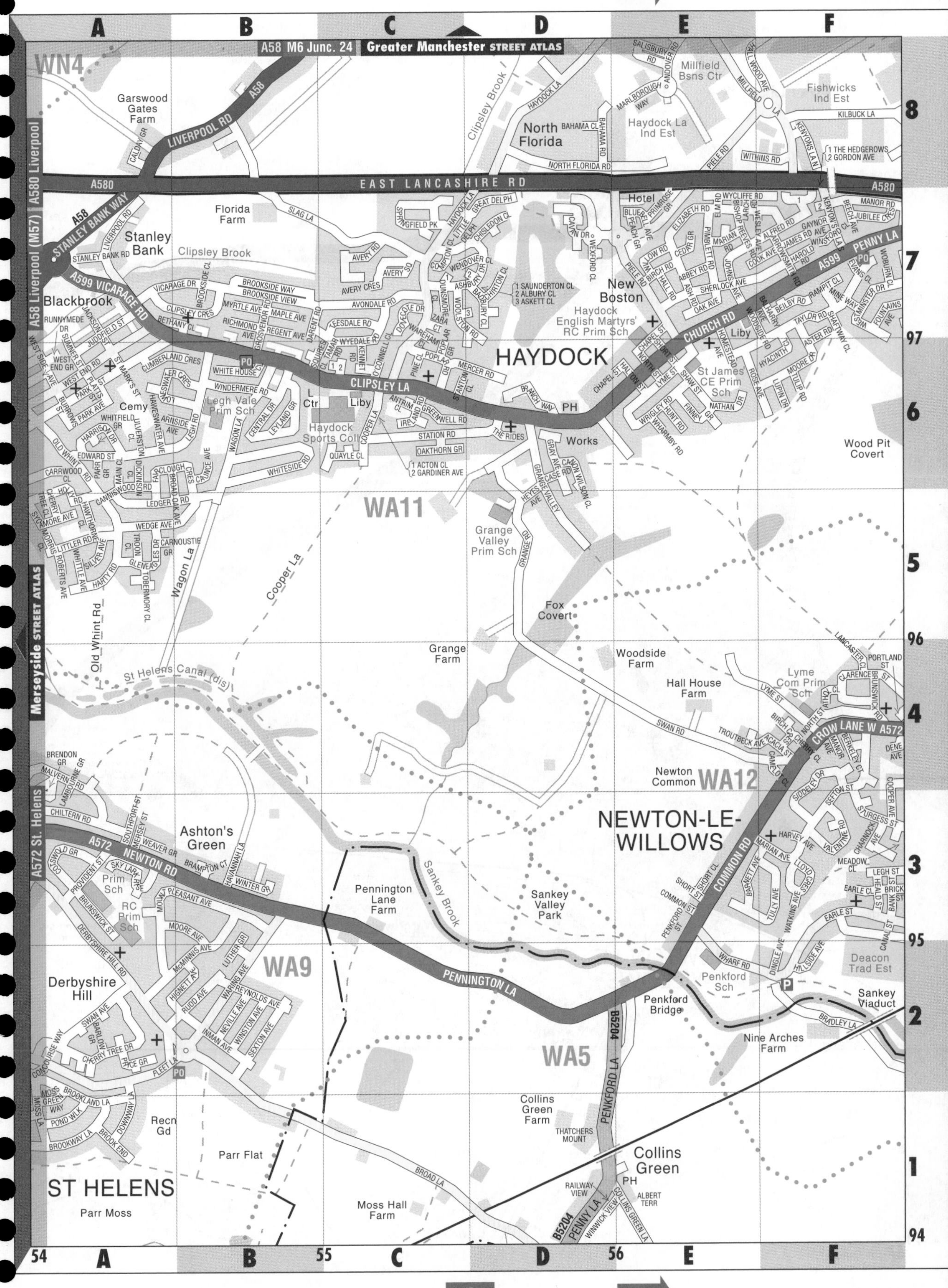

Greater Manchester STREET ATLAS
A58 M6 Junc. 24
Merseyside STREET ATLAS
WN4
Garswood Gates Farm
LIVERPOOL RD
A580
EAST LANCASHIRE RD
North Florida
Haydock La Ind Est
Millfield Bsns Ctr
Fishwicks Ind Est
Florida Farm
Stanley Bank
Clipsley Brook
Blackbrook
HAYDOCK
New Boston
Haydock English Martyrs' RC Prim Sch
St James' CE Prim Sch
CLIPSLEY LA
CHURCH RD
PENNY LA
A599 VICARAGE RD
Cemy
Legh Vale Prim Sch
Haydock Sports Coll
Works
Wood Pit Covert
WA11
Grange Valley Prim Sch
Cooper La
Wagon La
Old Whint Rd
Fox Covert
Grange Farm
Woodside Farm
Hall House Farm
Lyme Com Prim Sch
St Helens Canal (dis)
Newton Common
WA12
NEWTON-LE-WILLOWS
CROW LANE W A572
COMMON RD
Ashton's Green
A572 NEWTON RD
Pennington Lane Farm
Sankey Brook
Sankey Valley Park
Prim Sch
RC Prim Sch
Derbyshire Hill
WA9
PENNINGTON LA
Penkford Sch
Penkford Bridge
Deacon Trad Est
Sankey Viaduct
Nine Arches Farm
WA5
PENKFORD LA
B5204
Collins Green Farm
Collins Green
Recn Gd
Parr Flat
ST HELENS
Parr Moss
Moss Hall Farm
BROAD LA
A58 Liverpool
A580 Liverpool
A58 Liverpool (M57)
A572 St. Helens
2
6

1

A B C D E F
M6 Preston A49 Wigan
Greater Manchester STREET ATLAS
Yew Tree Farm Trad Est
HAYDOCK
Old Boston Trad Est
Old Boston
Hotel
Haydock Park Racecourse
WA4
White Door Covert
GOLBORNE
WA3
White Door Dam
Haydock Park
Lady Hill Plantation
SPRINGFIELD AVE 1
HIGHFIELD AVE 2
CLIFTONMILL MDWS 3
A580
A599
EAST LANCASHIRE RD
23
LODGE LA
PENNY LA
KILBUCK LA
B5209
Haydock Park Farm
Fox Covert
Dean Dam
Dean Dam Farm
WA11
Ellam's Brook
Ellam's Rough
Newton-Haydock Bridge
Woodlands Ind Est
Lawson's Farm
Hollows Bridge
NEWTON LA
VISTA RD
L Ctr
CH
ASHTON RD
Newton-le-Willows Com High Sch
WA12
LANGTON CL 1
GLADSTONE WAY 2
BROTHERTON WAY 3
Newton Bank Sch
HIGH ST
Newton Lake
CROW LANE W
CROW LANE E
A572
CHURCH ST
SOUTHWORTH RD
Liby
St Helens Coll Newton Campus
The District CE Prim Sch
St Mary's RC Jun Sch
Inf Sch
St Aelred's RC Tech Coll
St Peter's CE Prim Sch
MILLBRIDGE GDNS 4
ARCHWAY WLK 5
Newton-le-Willows Prim Sch
Newton-le-Willows
Stones Crossing
Mill Green Sch
MILL LA
WARGRAVE RD
Wargrave
Earlestown
Newton Park Farm
NEWTON PARK DR
1 PARK VIEW
2 CRABTREE CL
3 OWLSFIELD
Deacon Trad Est
NEWTON-LE-WILLOWS
Mast
WELLINGTON GDNS 1
WELLINGTON CL 2
WOODS CT 3
GRAFTON ST 4
BACK BRIDGE ST 5
THE WARREN 6
Sankey Valley Ind Est
Earlestown
Newton Community
Cemy
Newton Brook
WINWICK RD
Wargrave House Sch
Sch
Sankey Canal (dis)
Sankey Brook
HAVERTY PREC 1
NOON CT 2
CAUNCE AVE 3
LANGLEY AVE 4
SCOTT WLK 5
THOMPSON CL 6
INGHAM AVE 7
FEARNLEY WAY 8
KENT WAY 9
OLD HEY WLK 10
WA5
Vulcan Ind Est
Works
Red Bank
New Hey Farm
WA2
A49
8 7 97 6 5 96 4 3 95 2 1 94
57 58 59

1

7

D8
1 SARSFIELD AVE
2 FOXGLOVE CL
3 GROSVENOR AVE
4 RIDGEWELL AVE

E8
1 TURRET HALL DR
2 ROYSTON CL
3 SANDFIELD CL
4 ARIEL WLK
5 BALLANTYNE WAY
6 BUNTING CL
7 REDSTART CL
8 WILD ARUM CL
9 HUDSON GR
10 STONECHAT CL
11 SPEEDWELL CL
12 LUNEHURST
13 CONINGSBY GDNS

F8
1 SCOTIA WLK
2 TYRER WLK
3 ROBSON WAY
4 HORNCASTLE CL
5 HOPWOOD CL
6 BIRCH TREE RD

4

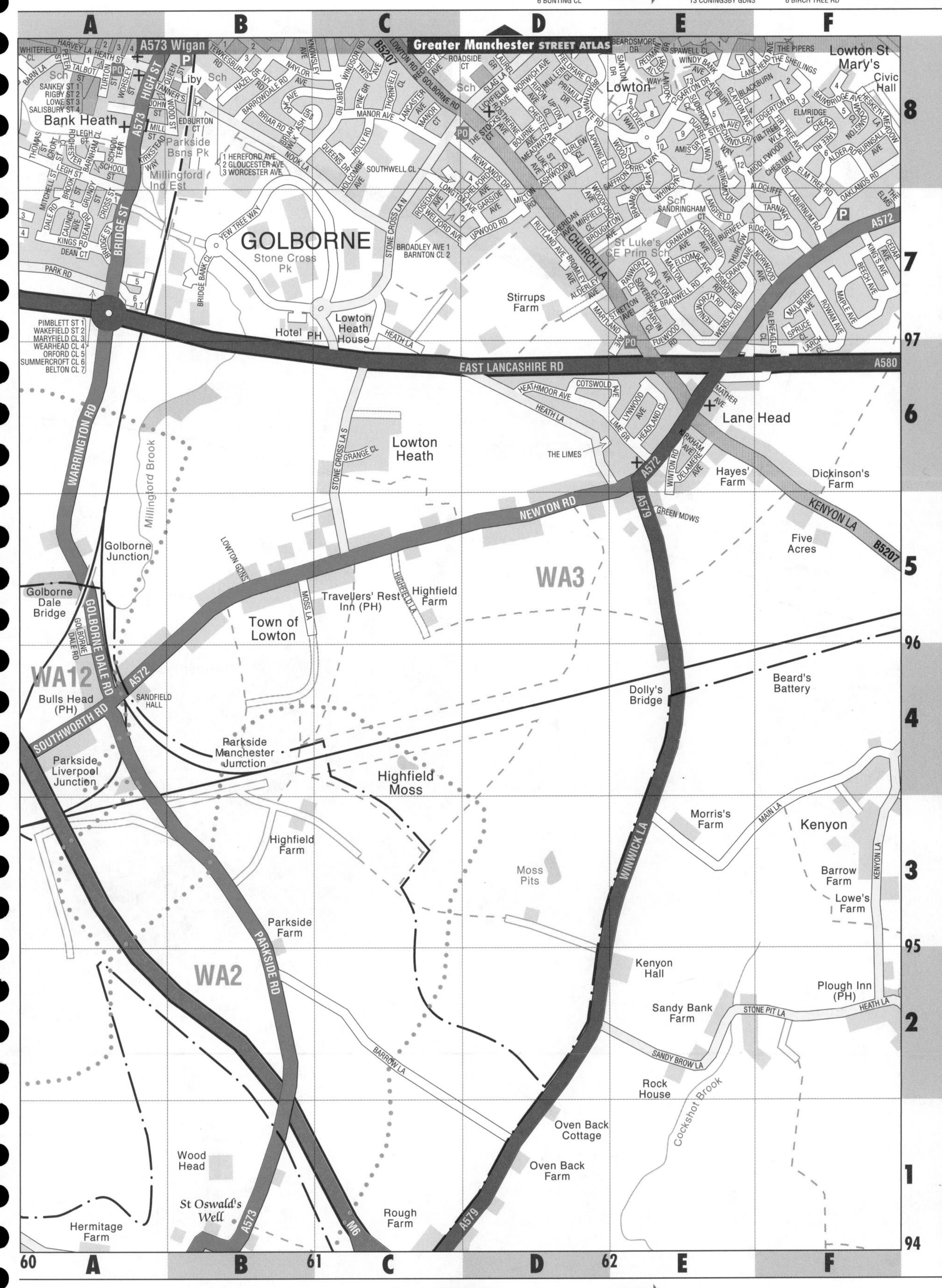

8
4

3

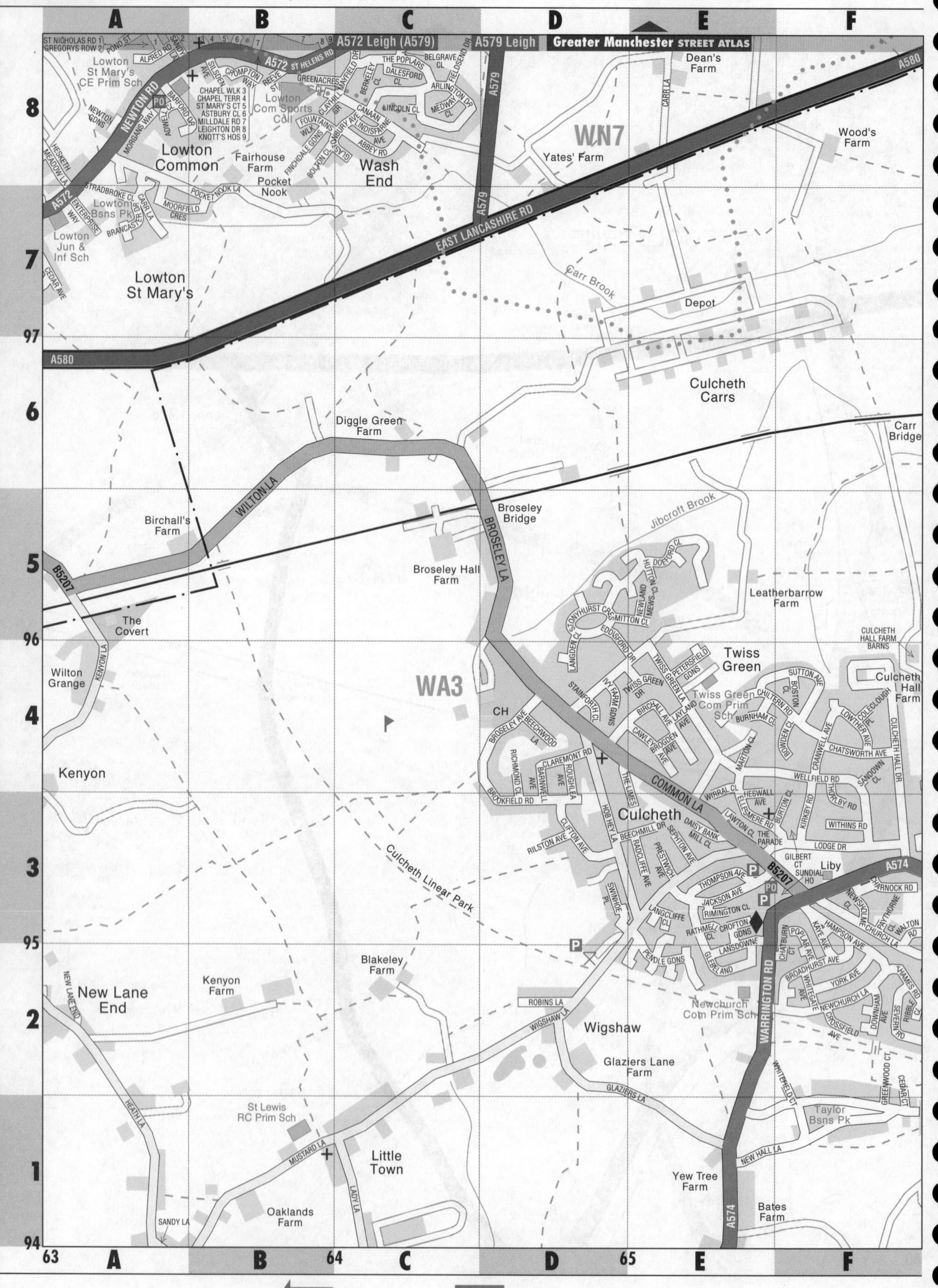
A
B
C
D
E
F
8
7
97
6
5
96
4
3
95
2
1
94
63
64
65
A572 Leigh (A579)
A579 Leigh
Greater Manchester STREET ATLAS
ST NICHOLAS RD 1
GREGORYS ROW 2
POND ST
ALFRED RD
SANDY LA
A572
ST HELENS RD
CROMPTON WAY
REEVE ST
GREENACRES CL
THE POPLARS
BELGRAVE CL
DALESFORD CL
BERKELEY CL
ARLINGTON DR
FIELDSEND DR
LINCOLN CL
MEDWAY CL
CANAAN
LINDISFARNE AVE
ABBEY RD
FOUNTAINS WLK
GLASTONBURY AVE
FINCHDALE GDNS
BOLTON CL
CHAPEL WLK 3
CHAPEL TERR 4
ST MARY'S CT 5
ASTBURY CL 6
MILLDALE RD 7
LEIGHTON DR 8
KNOTT'S HOS 9
Lowton St Mary's CE Prim Sch
Lowton Com Sports Coll
NEWTON RD
NEWTON GDNS
MORGANS WAY
BARFORD DR
ADWELL CL
PO
HESKETH MEADOW LA
Lowton Common
Fairhouse Farm
Pocket Nook
Wash End
POCKET NOOK LA
MOORFIELD CRES
STRADBROKE CL
CARR LA
BRANCASTER DR
ENTERPRISE WAY
Lowton Bsns Pk
Lowton Jun & Inf Sch
CEDAR AVE
Lowton St Mary's
A580
A579
EAST LANCASHIRE RD
Dean's Farm
CARR LA
WN7
Yates' Farm
Wood's Farm
Carr Brook
Depot
Culcheth Carrs
Carr Bridge
Diggle Green Farm
WILTON LA
Birchall's Farm
Broseley Bridge
BROSELEY LA
Broseley Hall Farm
Jibcroft Brook
B5207
The Covert
Wilton Grange
KENYON LA
DOEFORD CL
HUTTON CL
NEWLAND MEWS
STONYHURST CRES
MITTON CL
LANGDEN CL
EDISFORD DR
Leatherbarrow Farm
CULCHETH HALL FARM BARNS
Twiss Green
PETERSFIELD GDNS
TWISS GREEN LA
TWISS GREEN DR
IVY FARM GDNS
STAINFORTH CL
BIRCHALL AVE
LAYLAND AVE
Twiss Green Com Prim Sch
SUTTON AVE
CHILTERN RD
BOSTON CL
BURNHAM CL
Culcheth Hall Farm
WA3
CH
BROSELEY AVE
BEECHWOOD LA
CAWLEY AVE
BROGDEN AVE
MARTON CL
BOWDEN CL
CRANWELL AVE
LOWTHER AVE
COLECLOUGH PL
CULCHETH HALL DR
CHATSWORTH AVE
Kenyon
RICHMOND CL
BARNWELL AVE
CLAREMONT RD
ROUGHLEA AVE
BROOKFIELD RD
THE LIMES
COMMON LA
WELLFIELD RD
SANDOWN CL
THORPLBY RD
WITHINS RD
WIRRAL CL
HESWALL AVE
ELLESMERE RD
BURTON CL
KIRKBY RD
Culcheth
HOB HEY LA
BEECHMILL DR
SEPHTON AVE
DAISY BANK MILL CL
LAWTON CL
THE PARADE
LODGE DR
CLIFTON AVE
RILSTON AVE
RADCLIFFE AVE
PRESTWICH AVE
GILBERT CT
SUNDIAL HO
Liby
A574
CHARNOCK RD
Culcheth Linear Park
SWINNOE PL
THOMPSON AVE
JACKSON AVE
RIMINGTON CL
LANGCLIFFE CL
RATHMELL CL
CROFTON GDNS
LANSDOWNE
NEWSHOLME CL
PAYTHORNE CL
CHURCH LA
WALTON CL
HAMPSON AVE
CHATBURN CT
POPLAR AVE
KAYE AVE
PENDLE GDNS
GLENDALE
P
Blakeley Farm
Kenyon Farm
NEW LANE END
New Lane End
ROBINS LA
WARRINGTON RD
BROADHURST AVE
WHITEGATE AVE
YORK AVE
NEWCHURCH LA
DOWNHAM AVE
SEVERN RD
RIBBLE CL
THAMES RD
CROSSFIELD AVE
Newchurch Com Prim Sch
WIGSHAW LA
Wigshaw
Glaziers Lane Farm
GLAZIERS LA
WHITEFIELD CT
GREENWOOD CT
CEDAR CT
HEATH LA
St Lewis RC Prim Sch
Taylor Bsns Pk
MUSTARD LA
Little Town
NEW HALL LA
Yew Tree Farm
LADY LA
SANDY LA
Oaklands Farm
Bates Farm

3

9

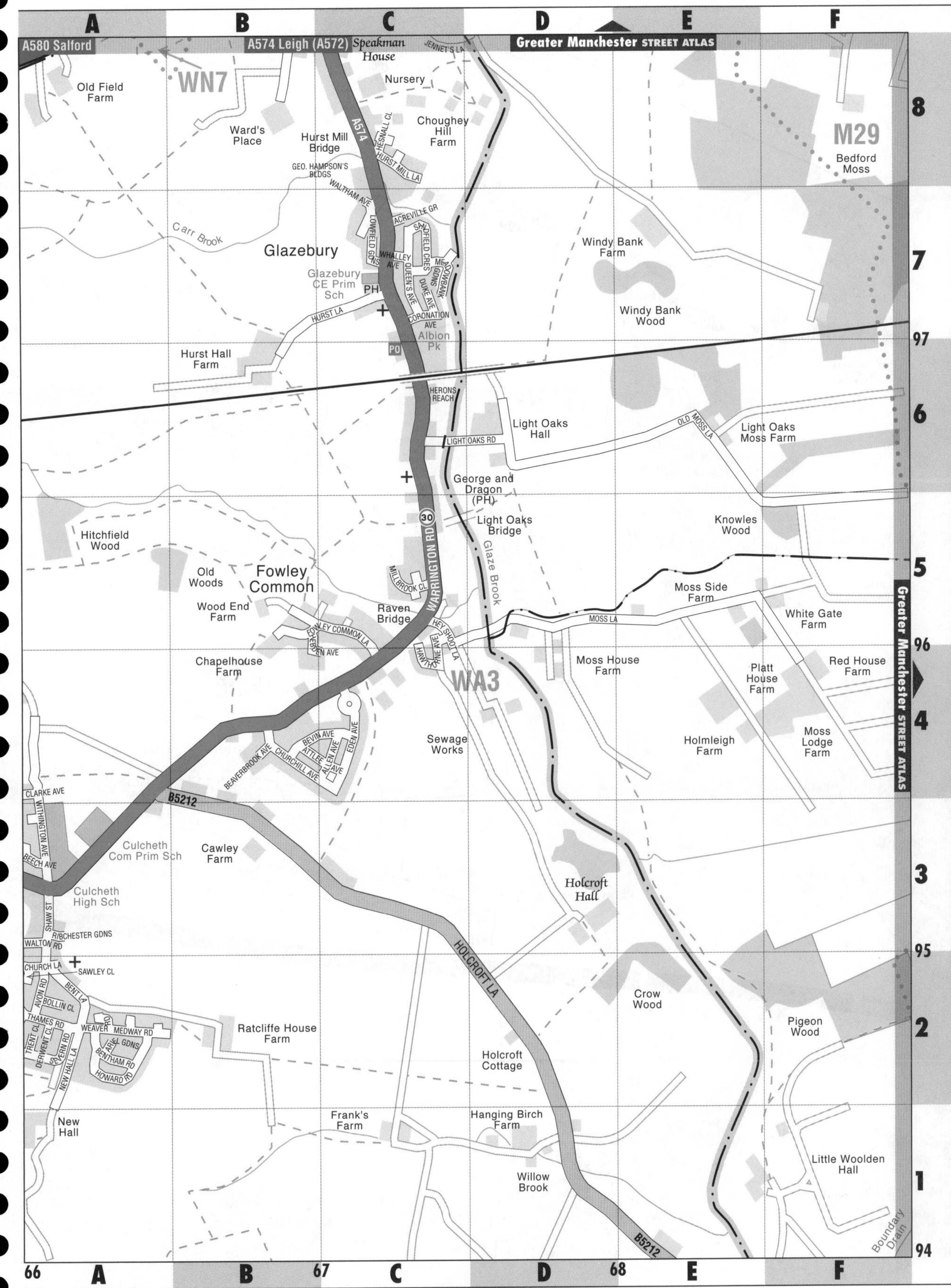
A580 Salford
A574 Leigh (A572)
Speakman House
Greater Manchester STREET ATLAS
WN7
Old Field Farm
Nursery
Ward's Place
Hurst Mill Bridge
Choughey Hill Farm
M29
Bedford Moss
Carr Brook
Glazebury
Glazebury CE Prim Sch
Windy Bank Farm
Windy Bank Wood
Albion Pk
Hurst Hall Farm
Light Oaks Hall
Light Oaks Moss Farm
George and Dragon (PH)
Light Oaks Bridge
Knowles Wood
Hitchfield Wood
Glaze Brook
Old Woods
Fowley Common
Wood End Farm
Raven Bridge
Moss Side Farm
White Gate Farm
Chapelhouse Farm
Moss House Farm
Red House Farm
Platt House Farm
WA3
Sewage Works
Holmleigh Farm
Moss Lodge Farm
Culcheth Com Prim Sch
Cawley Farm
Culcheth High Sch
Holcroft Hall
Crow Wood
Pigeon Wood
Ratcliffe House Farm
Holcroft Cottage
New Hall
Frank's Farm
Hanging Birch Farm
Willow Brook
Little Woolden Hall
Boundary Drain
WARRINGTON RD
HOLCROFT LA
B5212
MOSS LA
LIGHT OAKS RD
HURST LA
OLD MOSS LA
A B C D E F
66 67 68
94 95 96 97
1 2 3 4 5 6 7 8

10

1

A B C D E F
8
7
93
6
5
92
4
3
91
2
1
90
54 55 56
Sutton Moss
Burtonwood Moss
White House Farm
B5204
Higher Farm
COLLINS GREEN LA
FORSHAW'S LA
BROAD LA
Bold Moss
Burtonwood Brewery
Yew Tree Farm
LUMBER LA
Burtonwood Com Prim Sch
Derby Farm
GREEN LA
BOLD LA
BACK LA
Bold Bsns Ctr
DAHLIA CL
DAFFODIL GDNS
EVERGREEN WAY
SAMPHIRE GDNS
JAPONICA GDNS
PRIMULA CL
MARIGOLD WAY
THE PASTURES
PETUNIA CL
ANDROMEDA WAY
ORCHID WAY
COLUMBINE WAY
CROCUS GDNS
LOTUS GDNS
BEGONIA GDNS
JASMINE GDNS
ANEMONE WAY
CELANDINE WAY
1 PEONY GDNS
2 ARABIS GDNS
3 CAMELLIA GDNS
B5204
TRAVERS' ENTRY
AZALEA GDNS 1
IBERIS GDNS 2
HYDRANGEA WAY 3
LAVENDER GDNS 4
SUNFLOWER CL 5
NEW BOLD CT
OLLERTON PK
PHIPPS' LA
WINSFORD DR
RUSHTON CL
EPWORTH CL 1
ARNCLIFFE DR 2
ARUNDELL CL 3
DORCHESTER WAY 4
CHEDDAR
MELROSE AVE
EASTWOOD
ALDRIDGE DR
Phipps' Bridge
Burtonwood Ind Ctr
KINNOCK PK
SUNNINGDALE CL
SHAFTESBURY WAY
WEYMOUTH RD
PINEWOOD
CAMBOURNE RD
Bold
Haley Head Farm
Travers' Farm
Wheatacre Farm
EXMOUTH WAY
SHERBOURNE WAY
COLNE RD
KAREN CL
BROOKDALE CL
CHAPEL LA
Bold Ind Pk
NEILLS RD
PO
Sch
Liby
Cemy
MERCER ST
FAIRCLOUGH ST
JACKSON ST
SHERWOOD CRES
MILNTHORPE RD
SEDGEWICK CRES
NORCOTT DR
KILSHAW RD
WEBB DR
ALMOND DR
SPURLING RD
GLEAVE RD
PERRINS RD
KNIGHT RD
GREEN JONES BROW
HERBERT ST
HAWKSHEAD RD
Rose Hill Farm
ACTON RD
THE MEWS
DOUGLAS AVE
Burtonwood
HALEY RD N
ROSEHILL AVE
GORSEY LA
MITCHELL AVE
HALEY RD S
Ashton's Farm
Northfield Riding Ctr
WA9
Moat House
Old Lodge Farm
Lodge Wood
Clay Lane Farm
CLAY LA
Abbotsfield Farm
Park Cottage
Maypole Farm
Moat House Farm
WA5
Nursery
Hollin Wood
Ivy Cottage
Highfield
Joy Lane Farm
BURTONWOOD RD
HALL LA
JOY LA
Finger Post
Home Farm
LIMEKILN LA
WRIGHT'S LA
Limekiln Farm
Dog Kennel Plantation
M62
M62
M62 Liverpool
Merseyside STREET ATLAS
WA8
Booth's Wood
ORION BVD
Old Hall Farm
OMEGA BVD
Duck Wood

A B C D E F

8

Bradlegh Old Hall
BRADLEY LA
New Bradlegh Hall Farm
HEY LOCK CL
TYRER RD
KIRKACRE AVE
CONROY WAY
HEY WOOD CL
LONDON ROW
CHESTER ROW
SHEFFIELD ROW
LIVERPOOL ROW
DERBY ROW
WARGRAVE RD
MANCHESTER ROW
Vulcan Village
Sankey Canal (dis)
WA12
Newton Brook
Cop Holt Farm
A49
NEWTON RD
HALL LA

7

THE BRAMBLES
LUMBER LA
Boarded Barn Farm
Hall Lane Farm
MELROSE AVE
BAKEWELL RD
FIR TREE LA
The Old Vicarage
Red House Farm
CH
ALDER ROOT LA
WA2
Stoneyard Cottage
Alder Root Farm
Asps Wood

93

PINEWOOD RD
ALDER LA
ROXBOROUGH CL
CAMBOURNE RD
KAREN CL
CHAPEL LA
Clayton's House Farm
The Fiddle i'th Bag Inn
Lower Alder Root Farm
Primrose Hill Farm
HOLLINS LA

6

FARMER'S LA
Tan House Farm
BROWNING DR
WA5
Sankey Brook
Sankey Valley Park
WASHERY LA
Hollins Park
BROWNING DR
Phipps' Brook
OLD ALDER LA

5

Brook Head Farm
Causey Bridge
TAN HOUSE LA
Forest Farm
Causeway Bridges Farm

92

DELPH LA
M62
MILL LA
CRAVEN CT
CLARENDON CT
CALVER RD
BISHOPS CT

4

Dial Post Farm
TAURUS PK
Gemini
WARRINGTON
Burtonwood Service Area
EUROPA BVD
Superstore
Gemini Bsns Pk
WEST QUAY RD
WILLOW CT
Superstores

3

8
CROMWELL AVE
CHARON WAY
BUTTS GN
ARCHERS GREEN RD
PETERSTONE CL
GOLDCLIFF CL
HOLYHEAD CL
FAIRBOURNE CL
ST ASAPH DR
RUTHIN CL
CHEPSTOW CL
WELSHPOOL CL
LAMPETER CL
BALA CL

91

KINGSWOOD
KINGSWOOD RD
FALCONERS GN
EASTER CT
NEWBRIDGE CL
Little Moss Wood
CRESSWELL CL
HARLECH CL
BRECON CT
COLWYN CL
TENBY CL
LYDSTEP CT
A574
BURTONWOOD RD
TOURNEY GN
DELTA CRES
PENMARK CL
STANNER CL
Callands Prim Sch
PO
GRANSTON CL
CARTMEL CL
ST DAVIDS CL
SUMMERFIELD AVE
RUTTER AVE
PHOENIX AVE
DAGNALL AVE
CONWAY AVE

2

CASTLE GN
CARDIGAN CL
PENSARN GDNS
RIDGEBORNE CL
NEWBOROUGH CL
BARMOUTH CL
ROSSETT CL
SAUNDERSFOOT CL
LANGLAND CL
LEWIS AVE
HERALDS GN
WESTBROOK CRES
PENDINE CL
CARMARTHEN CL
CALLANDS RD
LYD CL
BURY CL
KILFORD CL
TINTERN CL
BOULTING AVE
CALDWELL AVE
MARSHALL AVE
BARDSLEY AVE
Dallam
DOVECOTE GN
Kingswood
Callands
WREXHAM CL
CORWEN CL
NORTH PARK BROOK RD
Dallam Com Prim Sch
PO
HARRISON SQ
LONGSHAW ST
MULLEN CL
COPPICE GN
WESTBROOK WAY
Calland's Farmhouse
WILLOUGHBY CL
GRANT CL
GRESFORD CL
MARCROSS CL
HODGSON AVE
GALE AVE
HAWLEY'S LA
St Philip (Westbrook) CE Prim Sch
Superstore
Liby
WESTBROOK CTR
RALEIGH CL
LADYWOOD RD
BOVERTON CL
ABERDARE CL
CANDLESTON CL
HIGHAM AVE

1

MATLOCK CL 1
TENBURY CL 2
Westbrook Centre
WARD CL
BLACKSHAW DR
Big Wood
HAYSCASTLE CL
HINDLE AVE
HAWLEY'S CL
MULLEN CL
TA AVE
BURTONWOOD RD
NARES CL
CABOT CL
DRAKE CL
PURDY CL
BEECROFT CL
WHITTLE AVE
HARROGATE CL
FIRMAN CL
P
BARFORD CL
GARWOOD CL
GARWOOD CL
GARWOOD CL
CARTER CL
A574
BRISTOW CL
SHACKLETON CL
Gullivers World Theme Park

90

57 A B 58 C D 59 E F

7
3

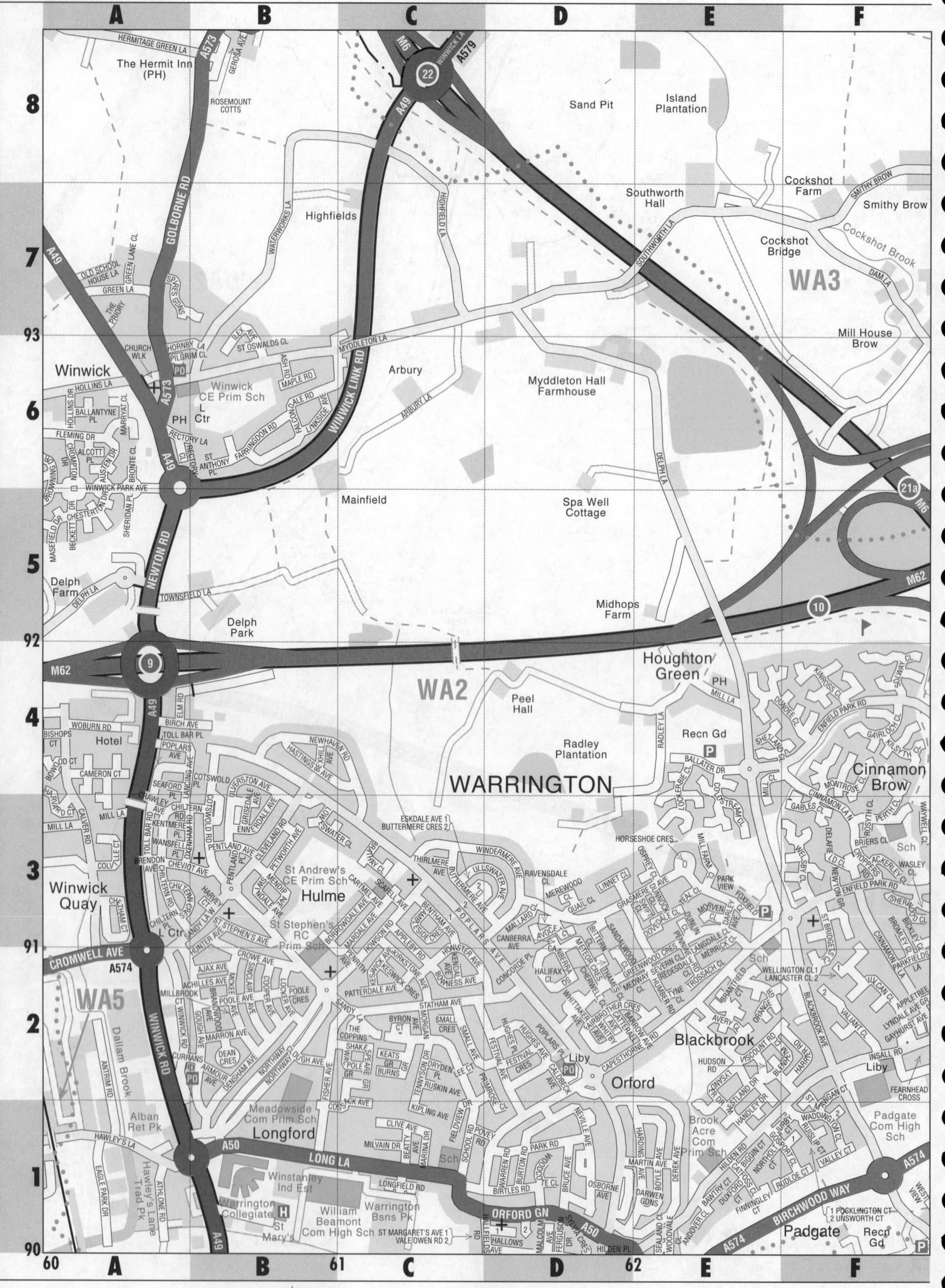
A
B
C
D
E
F
8
7
93
6
5
92
4
3
91
2
1
90
60
61
62
The Hermit Inn (PH)
HERMITAGE GREEN LA
A573
GEROSA AVE
ROSEMOUNT COTTS
M6
WINWICK LA
A579
22
A49
Sand Pit
Island Plantation
Southworth Hall
Cockshot Farm
SMITHY BROW
Smithy Brow
Cockshot Bridge
Cockshot Brook
WA3
DAM LA
Mill House Brow
Highfields
HIGHFIELD LA
WATERWORKS LA
GOLBORNE RD
SOUTHWORTH LA
OLD SCHOOL HOUSE LA
GREEN LANE CL
GREEN LA
THE PRIORY
SPIRES GDNS
MYDDLETON LA
WINWICK LINK RD
Arbury
ARBURY LA
Myddleton Hall Farmhouse
Winwick
HOLLINS LA
CHURCH WLK
HORNBY LA
PILGRIM CL
ST OSWALDS CL
ILEX AVE
ASH RD
MAPLE RD
Winwick CE Prim Sch
L Ctr
PH
BALLANTYNE PL
HOLLINS DR
MARRYAT CL
FLEMING DR
ALCOTT PL
CROMPTON DR
AUSTEN DR
BRONTE CL
RECTORY LA
FARRINGDON RD
FALCONDALE RD
LINKSIDE AVE
ST ANTHONY PL
WINWICK PARK AVE
BROWNING DR
BECKETT DR
CHESTERTON DR
SHERIDAN PL
MASEFIELD DR
Mainfield
Spa Well Cottage
DELPH LA
21a
M62
10
Delph Farm
DELPH LA
NEWTON RD
TOWNSFIELD LA
Delph Park
Midhops Farm
9
Houghton Green
PH
MILL LA
WA2
Peel Hall
Radley Plantation
RADLEY LA
Recn Gd
BALLATER DR
WARRINGTON
ELM RD
BIRCH AVE
WOBURN RD
Hotel
BISHOPS CT
TOLL BAR PL
POPLARS AVE
CAMERON CT
SEAFORD PL
LANCING AVE
COTSWOLD PL
ULVERSTON AVE
CRAWLEY AVE
MILL LA
CALVER RD
NEWHAVEN RD
HASTINGS AVE
BEXHILL AVE
ESKDALE AVE 1
BUTTERMERE CRES 2
HORSESHOE CRES
MILL FARM CL
LOCKERBIE CL
COLDSTREAM CL
SHETLAND CL
MILL CL
KINROSS CL
DUNDEE CL
ENFIELD PARK RD
SOLWAY CL
GAIRLOCH CL
KILSYTH CL
Cinnamon Brow
CINNAMON LA N
MONTROSE CL
GABLES CL
PERTH CL
ROSYTH CL
WAYWELL CL
BRIERS CL
Sch
WASLEY CL
Winwick Quay
Hulme
St Andrew's CE Prim Sch
St Stephen's RC Prim Sch
WINDERMERE AVE
THIRLMERE AVE
ULLSWATER AVE
RAVENSDALE CL
MEREWOOD
QUAIL CL
LINNET CL
POPLARS AVE
CANBERRA AVE
MALLARD CL
CONCORDE PL
HALIFAX CL
PARK VIEW
FOXFIELD
DOVEDALE CL
GREENWOOD CRES
MEDWAY
SEVERN CL
TRENT CL
LANGDALE CL
MERRICK CL
TROSSACH CL
WELLINGTON CL 1
LANCASTER CL 2
ST BRIDGETS CL
CROMWELL AVE
A574
L Ctr
WA5
Dallam Brook
ANTRIM RD
Alban Ret Pk
HAWLEY'S LA
EAGLE PARK DR
Hawley's Lane Trad Pk
ATHLONE RD
WINWICK RD
POOLE CRES
PATTERDALE AVE
SANDY LA
STATHAM AVE
BYRON CT
SMALL CRES
THE COPPINS
KEATS GR
BURNS GR
DRYDEN PL
RUSKIN AVE
KIPLING AVE
TENNYSON DR
Meadowside Com Prim Sch
Longford
CLIVE AVE
MILVAIN DR
FISHER AVE
FIELDVIEW DR
Liby
Orford
CAPESTHORNE RD
Blackbrook
HUDSON RD
BLACKBROOK AVE
VALIANT CL
APPLETREE GR
LYNDALE AVE
GAYHURST AVE
INSALL RD
Liby
FEARNHEAD CROSS
Padgate Com High Sch
A50
LONG LA
Winstanley Ind Est
LONGFIELD RD
Warrington Collegiate
St Mary's
William Beamont Com High Sch
Warrington Bsns Pk
ST MARGARET'S AVE 1
VALE OWEN RD 2
ORFORD GN
HALLOWS AVE
MALCOLM AVE
FERGUSON DR
SYKES CRES
HILDEN PL
Brook Acre Com Prim Sch
SEALAND CL
WOODVALE CL
DEREK AVE
BOYLE AVE
DARWEN GDNS
MARTIN AVE
HARDING AVE
OSBORNE AVE
BURTON RD
PARK RD
WARREN RD
BIRTLES RD
ANDOVER CL
BAWTRY CT
DUXFORD CT
FINNINGLEY CT
RUDLOE CT
VALLEY CT
BIRCHWOOD WAY
1 POCKLINGTON CT
2 UNSWORTH CT
Padgate
Recn Gd
WEST VIEW
Sch
P

7
16

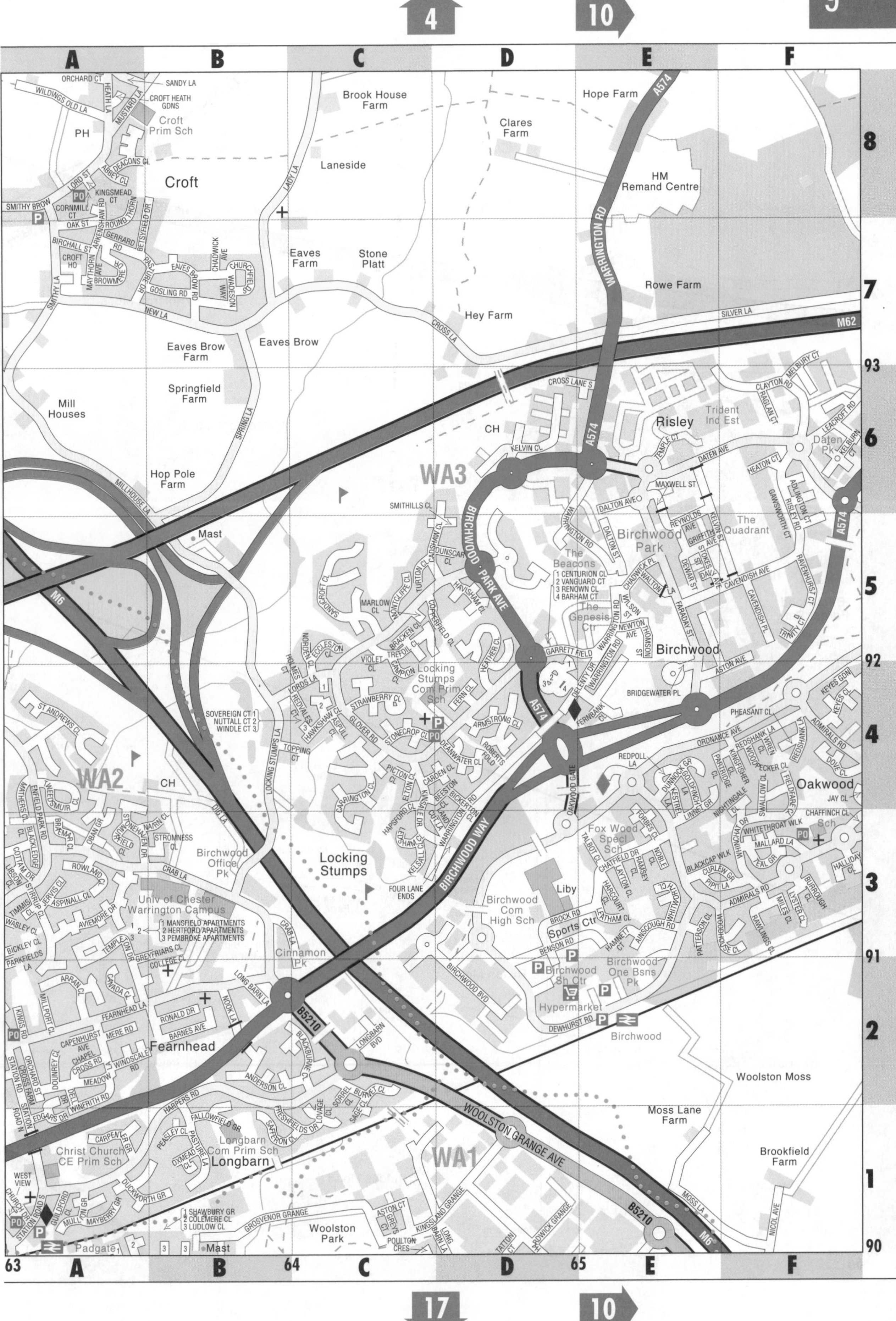

4
10
A
B
C
D
E
F
Croft
Croft Prim Sch
Brook House Farm
Hope Farm
Clares Farm
Laneside
HM Remand Centre
Eaves Farm
Stone Platt
Rowe Farm
Hey Farm
Eaves Brow Farm
Eaves Brow
Springfield Farm
Mill Houses
Hop Pole Farm
Risley
Trident Ind Est
WA3
Birchwood Park
The Quadrant
The Beacons
The Genesis Ctr
Birchwood
Locking Stumps Com Prim Sch
Locking Stumps
WA2
Birchwood Office Pk
Univ of Chester Warrington Campus
Cinnamon Pk
Fox Wood Specl Sch
Oakwood
Liby
Birchwood Com High Sch
Sports Ctr
Birchwood Sh Ctr
Birchwood One Bsns Pk
Hypermarket
Woolston Moss
Moss Lane Farm
Brookfield Farm
Fearnhead
Longbarn Com Prim Sch
Longbarn
Christ Church CE Prim Sch
WA1
Woolston Park
Padgate
Mast
M62
M6
A574
B5210
WARRINGTON RD
BIRCHWOOD PARK AVE
BIRCHWOOD WAY
WOOLSTON GRANGE AVE
8
7
6
5
4
3
2
1
93
92
91
90
63
64
65
17
10

9
5

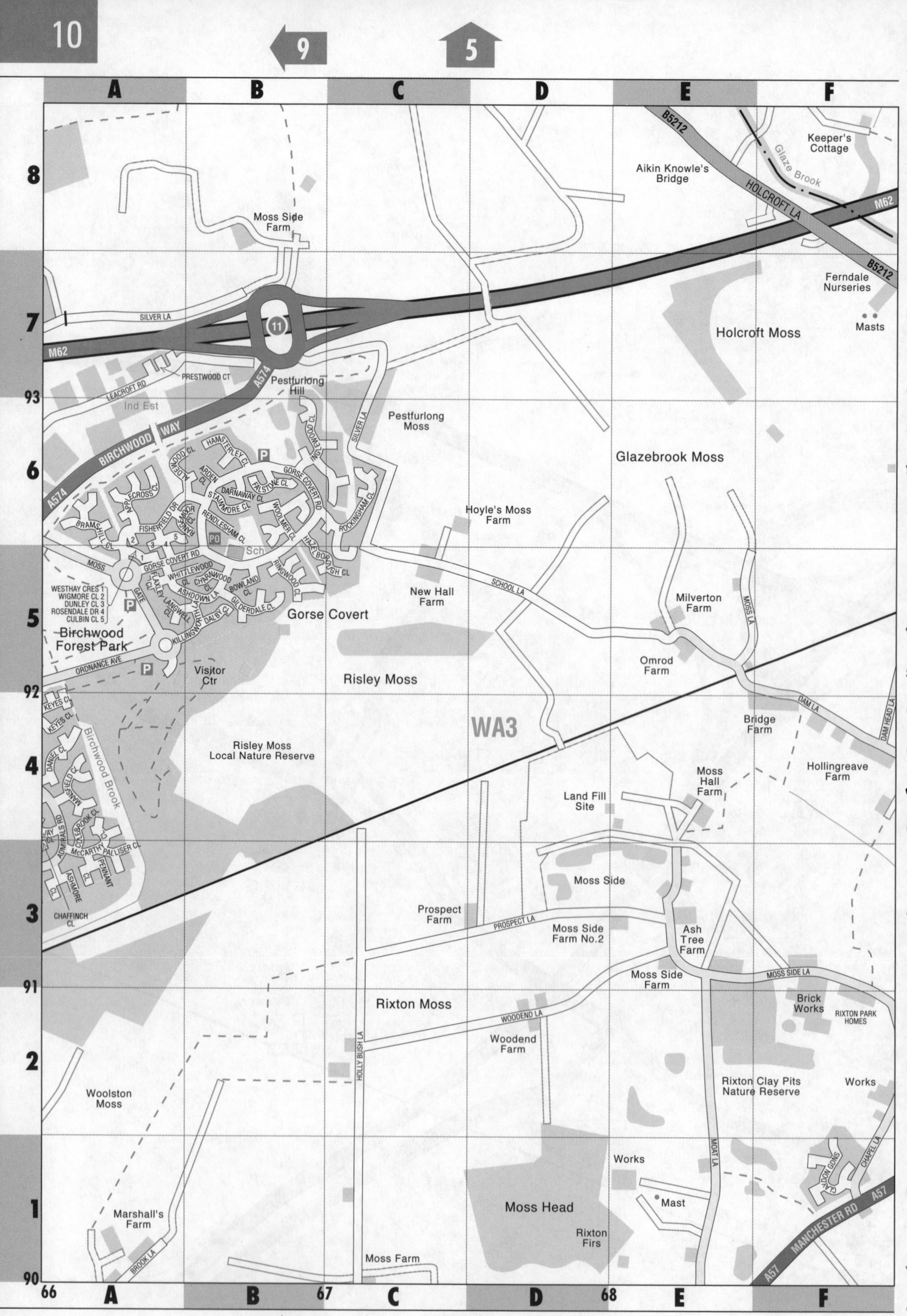
A
B
C
D
E
F
8
7
93
6
5
92
4
3
91
2
1
90
66
67
68
B5212
Keeper's Cottage
Aikin Knowle's Bridge
Glaze Brook
HOLCROFT LA
M62
Moss Side Farm
Ferndale Nurseries
Masts
SILVER LA
11
Holcroft Moss
M62
PRESTWOOD CT
LEACROFT RD
A574
Pestfurlong Hill
Ind Est
Pestfurlong Moss
SILVER LA
BIRCHWOOD WAY
A574
HAMSTERLEY CL
ALDERWOOD CL
GORSE COVERT RD
ARDEN CL
DARNAWAY CL
FALSTONE CL
APPLECROSS CL
STANMORE CL
WOOLMER CL
ROCKINGHAM CL
Glazebrook Moss
Hoyle's Moss Farm
BRAMSHILL CL
FISHERFIELD DR
RENDLESHAM CL
PO
Sch
HAZELBOROUGH CL
MOSS
GORSE COVERT RD
WHITTLEWOOD CL
CHARNWOOD CL
RINGWOOD CL
SCHOOL LA
WESTHAY CRES 1
WIGMORE CL 2
DUNLEY CL 3
ROSENDALE DR 4
CULBIN CL 5
ASHDOWN LA
BOWLAND CL
New Hall Farm
Milverton Farm
MOSS LA
GATE
LANGWELL CL
GILDERDALE CL
DALBY CL
KILLINGWORTH LA
Gorse Covert
Birchwood Forest Park
ORDNANCE AVE
Visitor Ctr
Omrod Farm
Risley Moss
KEYES CL
Birchwood Brook
WA3
DAM LA
Bridge Farm
DAM HEAD LA
Risley Moss Local Nature Reserve
DANIEL CL
MANSFIELD CL
Hollingreave Farm
Moss Hall Farm
Land Fill Site
COLEBROOK CL
ADMIRALS RD
McCARTHY CL
PALLISER CL
PENNANT
ASHMORE
Moss Side
CHAFFINCH CL
Prospect Farm
PROSPECT LA
Moss Side Farm No.2
Ash Tree Farm
Moss Side Farm
MOSS SIDE LA
Brick Works
RIXTON PARK HOMES
Rixton Moss
WOODEND LA
Woodend Farm
HOLLY BUSH LA
Rixton Clay Pits Nature Reserve
Works
Woolston Moss
MOAT LA
CHAPEL LA
Works
CLAYDON GDNS
Mast
Moss Head
Marshall's Farm
A57
MANCHESTER RD
Rixton Firs
BROOK LA
Moss Farm
A57

9
18

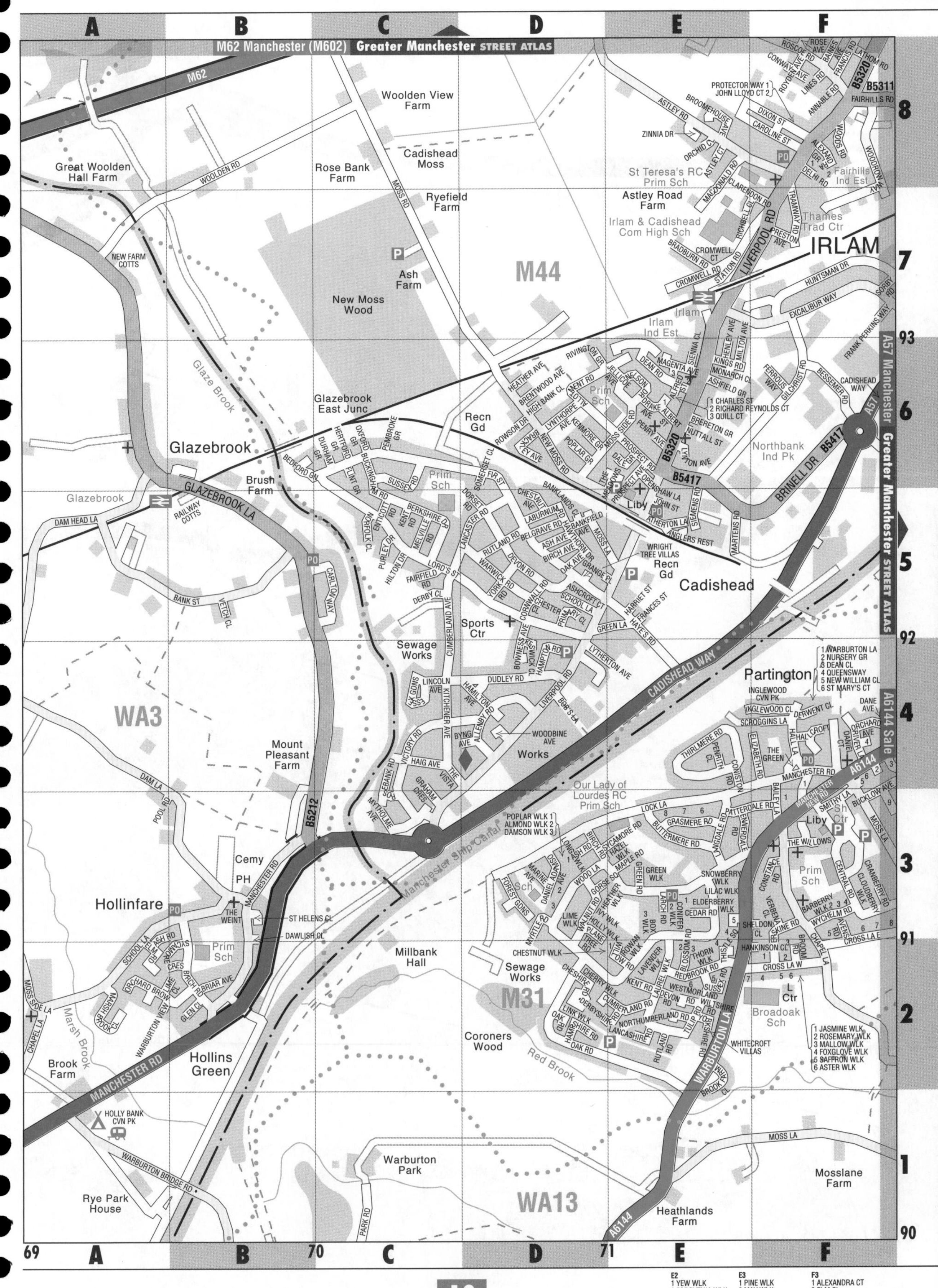

E2
1 YEW WLK
2 FORSYTHIA WLK
3 BLACKTHORN WLK
4 THISTLE WLK
5 MAGNOLIA CL
6 LOBELIA WLK
7 IRIS WLK

E3
1 PINE WLK
2 MAY WLK
3 HAWTHORN WLK
4 ROSE WLK
5 CARMICHAEL CL
6 MEADOW WLK
7 FIELD WLK
8 GARDEN WLK

F3
1 ALEXANDRA CT
2 ELM CL
3 WINTERGREEN WLK
4 BEECH CL
5 CAMOMILE WLK
6 CHARLOCK WLK
7 WOODRUFF WLK
8 COLUMBINE WLK
9 WORTHINGTON AVE

19

Merseyside STREET ATLAS
A57 Liverpool, A570 Southport
M62 Manchester (M602)
L35
WA8
Mill Wood
Higher Shaw Farm
Rough Head
Cronton Wood
Pex Hill Visitor Ctr
Pex Hill
Town End
Penny Lane Farm
Holy Family RC Prim Sch
Cronton CE Prim Sch
Nursery
Mast
Cronton Farm
Smaller Gorse Farm
Caxton Lodge
Cronton
Hotel
The Globe (PH)
Nicolford Hall
Sandhill Farm
Upton Rocks
Rose Farm
Holly Farm
Upton
Stock's Well House
All Saints Upton CE Prim Sch
St Basil's RC Prim Sch
Hough Green
Rugby Football Ground
Ball o' Ditton
WIDNES
Saints Peter & Paul RC High Sch
The Bankfield Sch
Ditton CE Prim Sch
Ditton Prim Sch
Ashley Sch
Chestnut Lodge Specl Sch
Cemy
CRONTON RD
CRONTON LA
LIVERPOOL RD
WARRINGTON RD
WATKINSON WAY
Fox's Bank Brook

14

A1	B1	B2	C1	C2	D1
1 CLAYTON CRES 2 HENDERSON RD 3 SQUIRES AVE 4 BRUNNER RD 5 MOND RD	1 ALBERT SQ 2 ALBERT RD 3 BROOK ST 4 SAXON TERR	1 HAWTHORN AVE 2 WILLOW AVE 3 LIME AVE 4 PINE AVE 5 MAPLE AVE 6 PLUMPTON CROSS	1 PARR ST 2 RUNNYMEDE CT 3 CLIFFE ST 4 HENRY ST 5 RUNNYMEDE GDNS	1 BROOKLANDS PK 2 KNOWLES ST 3 RUNNYMEDE WLK	1 ASHFORD WAY 2 MELVILLE CL 3 KINGHAM CL 4 WILSON CL 5 HARGREAVES HO

23

14

A B C D E F

8
7
89
6
5
88
4
3
87
2
1
86

Eccles Plantation
Finch's Plantation
South Park Plantation
Lingley Mere Bsns Pk
Lingley Mere
Lingley Green Ave
Billington Cl
Bainbridge Cres
Stockdale Dr
Lonsdale Cl
Whittle Ave
Wensleydale Cl
L Ctr
Whittle Brook
Great Sankey High Sch
Malham Cl
Barrow Hall La
Blue Ridge Cl
Brow Farm
Barrow Hall Com Prim Sch
Thorntondale Dr
Farndale Cl
Bransdale Cl
Gordale Cl
Widdale Cl
Woodale Cl
Barrondale Cl
Coverdale Cl
Airedale Cl
Bishopdale Cl
Kingsdale Cl
Alverstone Cl
Bembridge Cl
Goodshill Cl
Park Farm
Foreland Cl
Park Rd
Whitwell Cl
Freshwater Cl
Shorwell Cl
Totland Cl
Ventnor Cl
Mayfair Cl
Cronulla Dr
York Ave
Coogee Ave
Clovelly Ave
Mill Ave
North View
Bargyloo
A57
Warrington Rd
Lingley Green
Dawson House
Ruscolm Cl
Muriel Cl
Audre Cl
Pycroft Rd
Fraser Rd
Warwick Ave
Stanley Ave
Lingley Rd
Princess Ave
Park Rd
Greenway
Hall Terr
Phillips Dr
Sunnyside
Snowdon Cl
Chestnut Ave
Conifer Gr
Woodside Rd
Swaledale Cl
Teesdale Cl
Littledale
Deep Dale
Rowan Cl
Cedar Ave
Vine Cres
Charles Ave
Lilford Dr
Palin Dr
Wilmot Ave
Garsdale Cl
Alderbank Rd
Halton Rd
South Lane Entry
Hayfield Farm
Sandy La
Shanklin Cl
Pycroft Cl
Hilary Cl
Paul Cl
Sanderson Cl
Kintore Dr
Kirkcaldy Ave
Cromdale Ave
Wroxham Rd
George's Cres
PH
The Trigger Pond (PH)
Park Road Com Prim Sch
Victoria Ave
Keith Ave
Rhona Dr
Duncansby Cres
Ranworth Rd
Thetford Rd
Sheringham Rd
Norfolk Dr
Wednesbury Dr
Lingwood Rd
Yarmouth Rd
Conway Cl
Campbell Cres
Hawthorne Ave
Whittle Hall La
Belmont Cres
Greenside Farm
Liverpool Rd
Henderson Cl
Edward Rd
Clarence Ave
Laburnum Farm
Friends La
Laburnum La
Albert Dr
Holbrook Cl
Southwold Cres
Hadleigh Cl
Elmsett Cl
Brightwell Cl
Kingston Ave
Southfields Ave
Chapelside Cl
Beechwood Ave
Sankey for Penketh
Forge Rd
Cunningham
The Dale
Whitethorn Ave
The Willows
PO
Sandy Lane Farm
WA8
Friars Ave
Walton Ave
St Joseph's Cl
Sch
Susan Dr
Denise Ave
Groarke Dr
Kenyon Ave
Norton Ave
Larch Ave
Windmill La
St Albans Rd
Walsingham Rd
Holly Rd
St Vincent Rd
St Stephens
South Dale
St Mary's Rd
Burnham Cl
Upton Cl
Stocks La
Helston Cl
Meeting La
Heath Rd
Harford Cl
Holly Terr
Phythian Cres
Camp (dis)
A5080
Sunny Bank Cotts
Coniston Ave
Barnacombe Rd
Paignton Cl
Bideford Rd
Lynton Cl
Sidmouth Cl
Jubilee Ave
Tiverton Sq
William Penn Cl
Liby
Honiton Way
Barnstaple Way
Porlock Cl
Avon Ave
Greystone Rd
Cherry Tree Ave
Hillside Gr
Formby Cl
Ainsdale Cl
Hesketh Cl
Birkdale Ave
Coronation Dr
The Grove
Recn Gd
Daisy Bank Rd
Denehurst Cl
Broad Oak Ave
Arlington Dr
Penketh Com Prim Sch
Withycombe Rd
Tavistock Rd
Oaks Gdns
Haslemere Dr
Victoria Rd
Bank Gdns
Lamerton Cl
Greenall Ave
Four Top'd Oak
Brook Farm
South La
Farnworth Rd
Penketh
Penketh Ct
A562
Vauxhall Cl
Ash Rd
Maple Cres
Inglenook Rd
Elm Rd
Padstow Cl
Penryn Cl
Launceston Dr
Fenham Dr
Beadnell Dr
Poplar Ave
Woodley Fold
Hall Nook
Oak Rd
Oakmere Dr
Southlands Ave
Thorn Cl
Doe Green
Cuerdley Rd
Beech Ave
Tregan Dr
Station Rd
The Park
St Austel Cl
St Brides Cl
Bramble Cl
Well La
Manston Rd
Fowl Farm
Widnes Rd
Newlyn Gdns
Harlyn Gdns
Penrose Gdns
Rothay Dr
Roeburn Way
Tannery La
Radlett Cl
Falmouth Dr
Buckfast Cl
Chapel Rd
Ditchfield Rd
Finlay Ave
St Vincent's RC Prim Sch
Penketh South Com Prim Sch
Stanstead Ave
Hamble Dr
Mowcroft La
Back La
Newspaper House
Polperro Cl
Walkers La
Calstock Cl
Shaftesbury Ave
Brimelow Cres
LC
Cuerdley Gn
Cuerdley Cross
Cross Lane Farm Cottages
WA5
A562
PH
Taylor's La
Wrights La
CH
Trans Pennine Trail
Ferry Inn (PH)
River Mersey
Marsh End Farm
Marsh La
Swing Bridge
Power Station
Fiddler's Ferry Reach
Riverside Trad Est
Fiddler's Ferry
St Helens Canal (disused)
WA4

54 A B 55 C D 56 E F

B7
1 MANHATTAN GDNS
2 CAROLINA RD
3 SEATTLE CL
4 KENNEDY CT
5 LINCOLN CT
6 TRUMAN CT
7 NEW HAMPSHIRE CL
8 MILLENIUM WAY
9 MIAMI CL
C7
1 SUMMERVILLE WLK
2 LEXINGTON WLK
3 MONTANA CL
4 WOODROW CT
5 SAVANNAH PL
6 CHARLOTTE GR

7
16

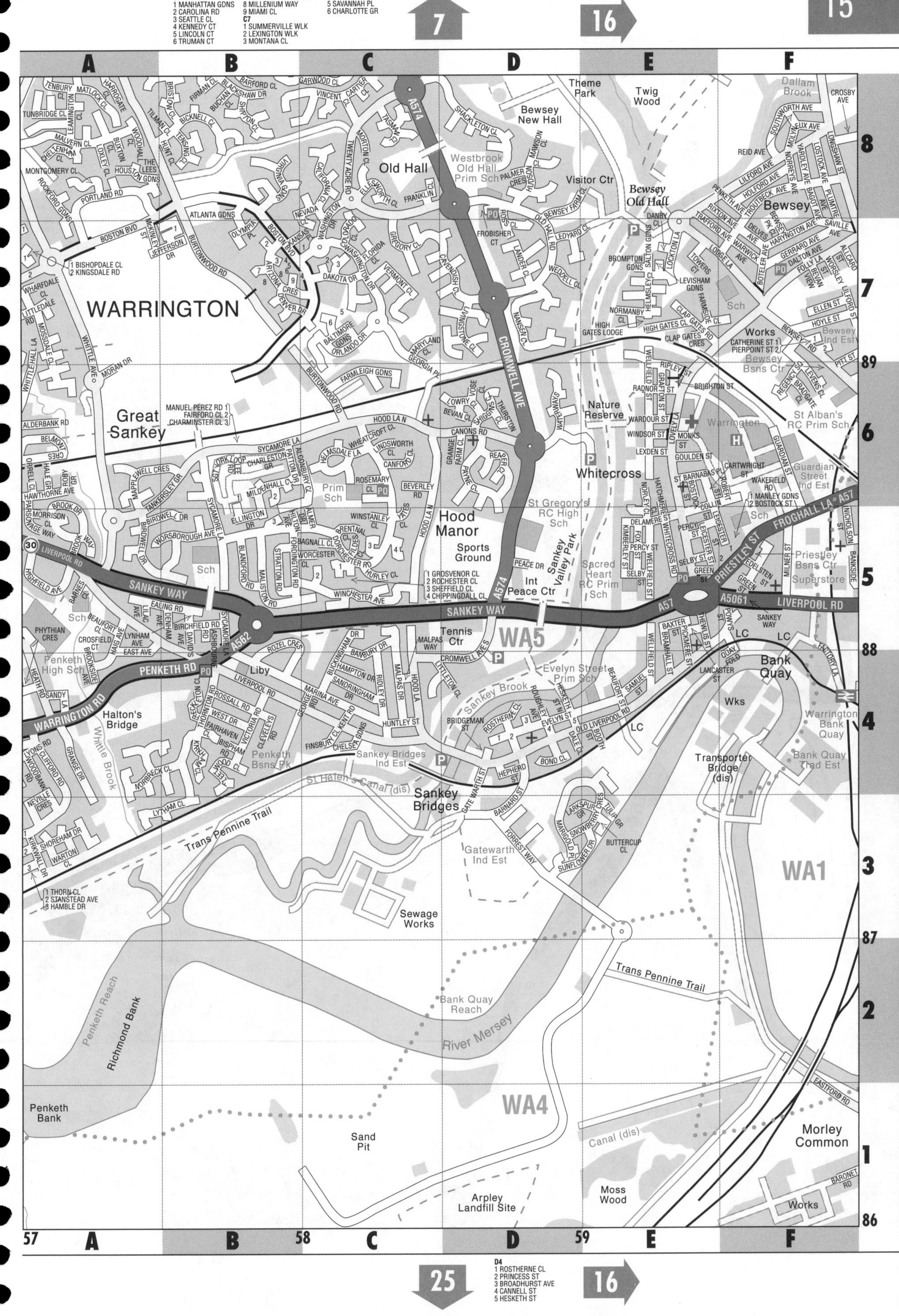

25
16

D4
1 ROSTHERNE CL
2 PRINCESS ST
3 BROADHURST AVE
4 CANNELL ST
5 HESKETH ST

A5
1 PARK CT
2 CROMWELL CT
3 EGYPT ST

B5
1 WESTMINSTER PL
2 CROWN ST
3 PRINCE HENRY SQ
4 THE COURTYARD
5 JAMES ST
6 ACADEMY PL
7 CHARLES FORBES CT
8 BANK ST
9 DOLMANS LA
10 NEW MARKET WLK
11 FRIARS CT
12 OLD MARKET PL
13 LYME ST
14 Warrington Bsns Ctr

15

8

C5
1 AMPLEFORTH HO
2 BRANDWOOD HO
3 TANNING CT
4 Wellington St Wrkshps
5 ELLESMERE ST

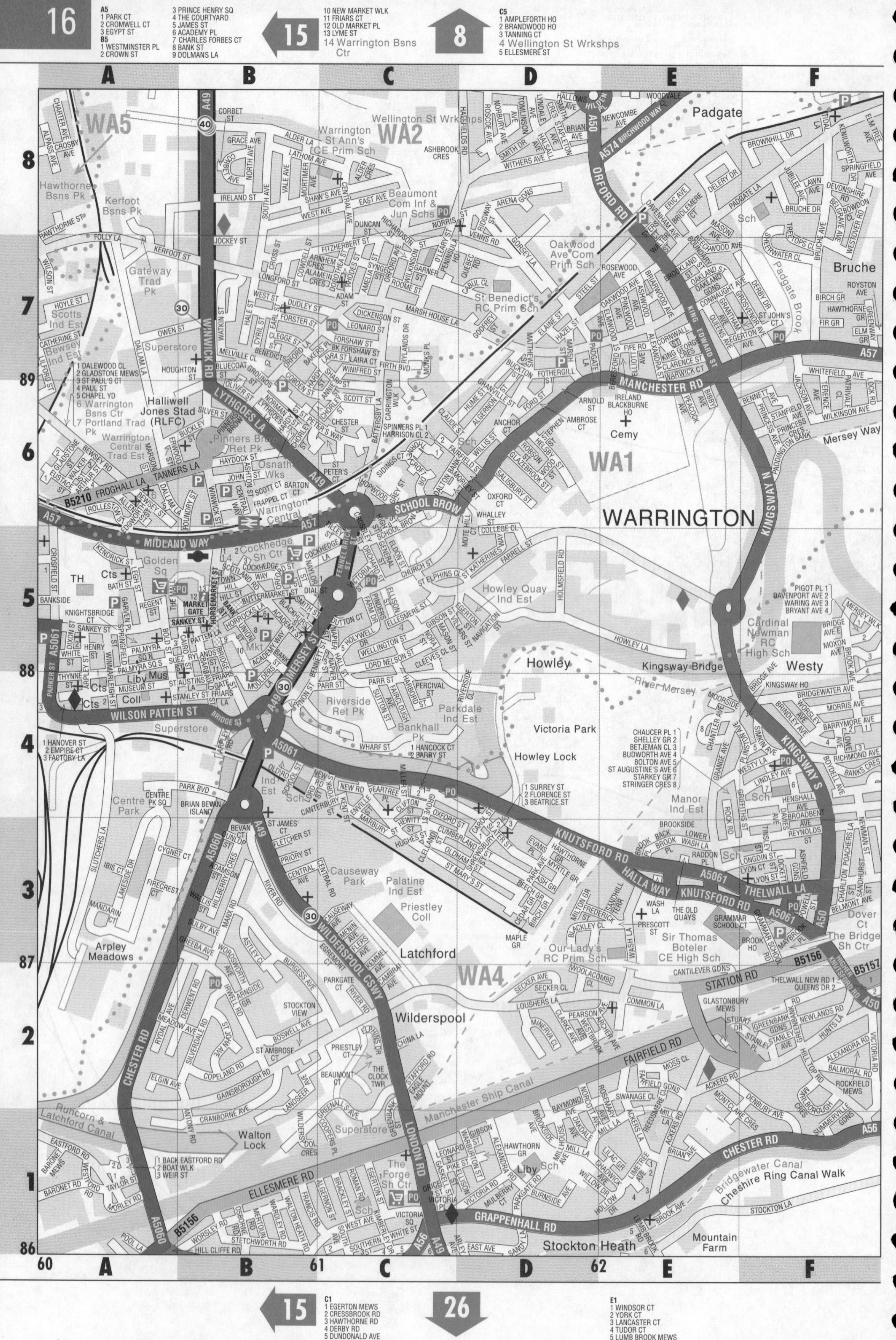

15

26

C1
1 EGERTON MEWS
2 CRESSBROOK RD
3 HAWTHORNE RD
4 DERBY RD
5 DUNDONALD AVE
6 THE VILLAGE TERR

E1
1 WINDSOR CT
2 YORK CT
3 LANCASTER CT
4 TUDOR CT
5 LUMB BROOK MEWS
6 WHARFSIDE CT

9
18

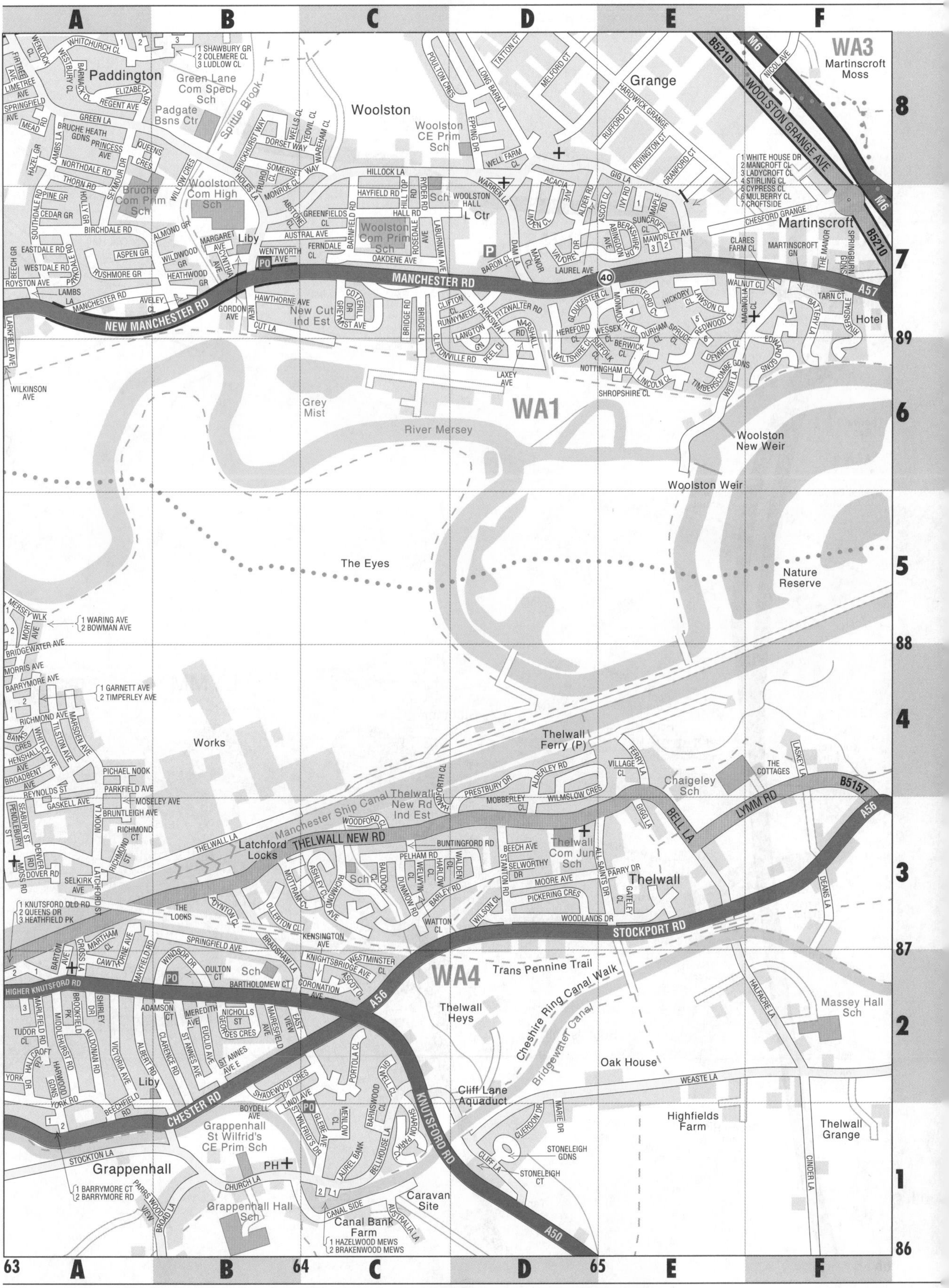

A B C D E F

WA3
Martinscroft Moss
Paddington
Green Lane Com Specl Sch
Padgate Bsns Ctr
Spittle Brook
Woolston
Woolston CE Prim Sch
Grange
Woolston Com High Sch
Bruche Com Prim Sch
Woolston Com Prim Sch
Woolston Hall
L Ctr
Liby
PO
Martinscroft
Hotel
New Cut Ind Est
MANCHESTER RD
NEW MANCHESTER RD
WOOLSTON GRANGE AVE
B5210
M6
A57
40

1 SHAWBURY GR
2 COLEMERE CL
3 LUDLOW CL

1 WHITE HOUSE DR
2 MANCROFT CL
3 LADYCROFT CL
4 STIRLING CL
5 CYPRESS CL
6 MULBERRY CL
7 CROFTSIDE

WA1
Grey Mist
River Mersey
Woolston New Weir
Woolston Weir
The Eyes
Nature Reserve

1 WARING AVE
2 BOWMAN AVE

1 GARNETT AVE
2 TIMPERLEY AVE

Works
Thelwall Ferry (P)
Chaigeley Sch
THE COTTAGES
Manchester Ship Canal
Thelwall New Rd Ind Est
Latchford Locks
THELWALL NEW RD
Thelwall Com Jun Sch
Thelwall
LYMM RD
BELL LA
B5157
A56
STOCKPORT RD
THE LOCKS

1 KNUTSFORD OLD RD
2 QUEENS DR
3 HEATHFIELD PK

WA4
Trans Pennine Trail
Cheshire Ring Canal Walk
Bridgewater Canal
Thelwall Heys
Massey Hall Sch
Oak House
Cliff Lane Aquaduct
HIGHER KNUTSFORD RD
CHESTER RD
KNUTSFORD RD
WEASTE LA
Highfields Farm
Thelwall Grange
Grappenhall St Wilfrid's CE Prim Sch
PH
Grappenhall
Grappenhall Hall Sch
Caravan Site
Canal Bank Farm
A50

1 BARRYMORE CT
2 BARRYMORE RD

1 HAZELWOOD MEWS
2 BRAKENWOOD MEWS

STONELEIGH GDNS
STONELEIGH CT

8
7
89
6
5
88
4
3
87
2
1
86

63 A B 64 C D 65 E F

27
18

17
10

17
28

C3
1 THORNLEY CL
2 WATERBRIDGE CT
3 BRIDGEWATER CT

D3
1 THE ANCHORAGE
2 BROOKFIELD COTTS
3 BOOTHS HILL HO

E3
1 LYMM BROOK
2 HENRY ST
3 LEGH ST
4 BRIDGEWATER ST
5 THIRLMERE LODGE
6 THE SQUARE
7 DUKESBRIDGE CT

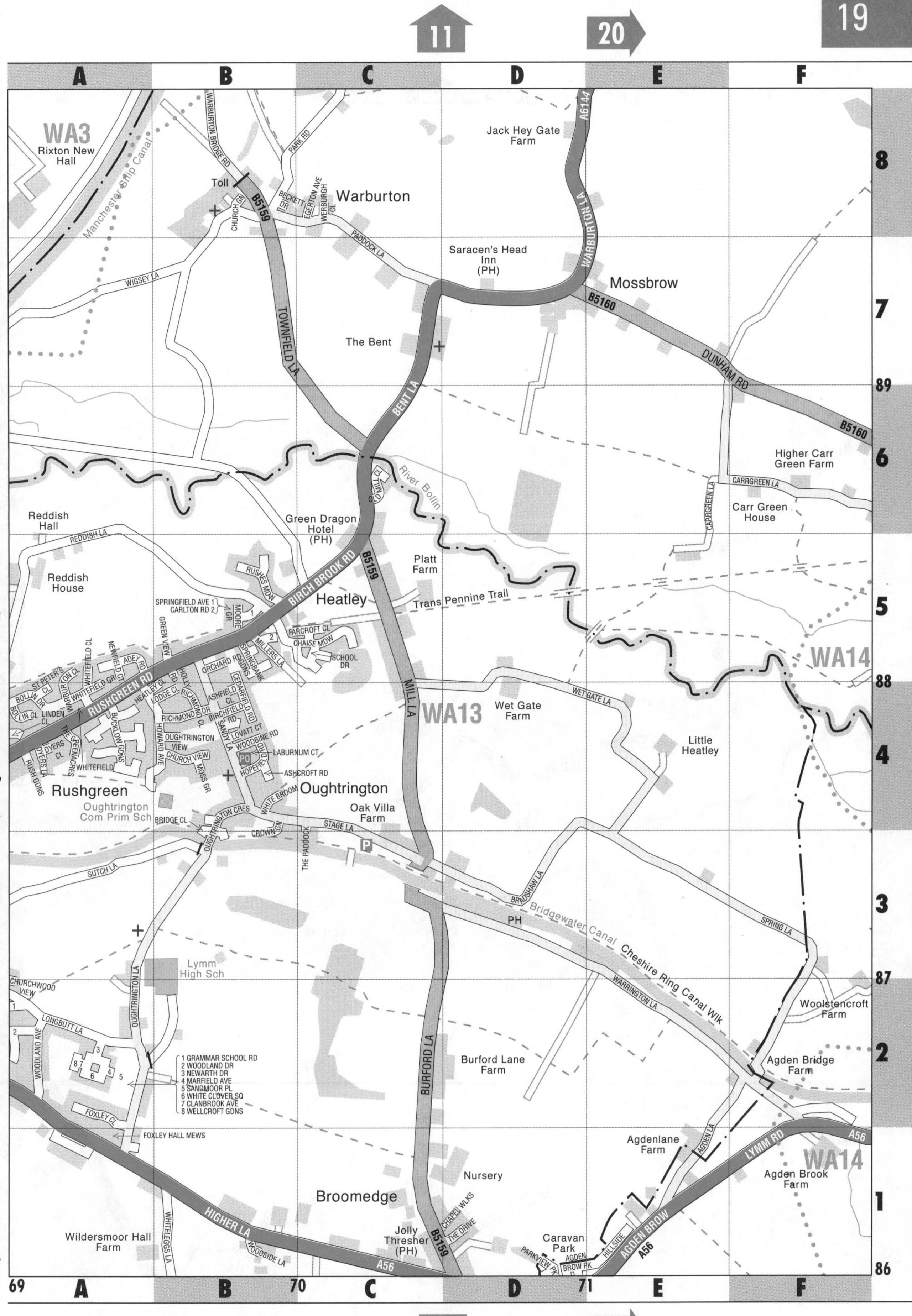
11
20
A
B
C
D
E
F
WA3
Rixton New Hall
Manchester Ship Canal
Toll
Warburton
Jack Hey Gate Farm
Saracen's Head Inn (PH)
Mossbrow
The Bent
Reddish Hall
Green Dragon Hotel (PH)
Platt Farm
Reddish House
Heatley
Trans Pennine Trail
Higher Carr Green Farm
Carr Green House
River Bollin
WA14
WA13
Wet Gate Farm
Little Heatley
Rushgreen
Oughtrington
Oughtrington Com Prim Sch
Oak Villa Farm
Bridgewater Canal
Cheshire Ring Canal Wlk
Lymm High Sch
Woolstencroft Farm
Burford Lane Farm
Agden Bridge Farm
Agdenlane Farm
Agden Brook Farm
Nursery
Broomedge
Wildersmoor Hall Farm
Jolly Thresher (PH)
Caravan Park
WARBURTON BRIDGE RD
PARK RD
BECKETT DR
EGERTON AVE
WERBURGH CL
CHURCH GN
PADDOCK LA
WIGSEY LA
TOWNFIELD LA
BENT LA
WARBURTON LA
DUNHAM RD
CARRGREEN LA
REDDISH LA
BIRCH BROOK RD
RUSHES MDW
MILL CL
SPRINGFIELD AVE 1
CARLTON RD 2
MOORE GR
FARCROFT CL
CHAISE MDW
SCHOOL DR
MILLERS LA
SPRINGBANK
ORCHARD RD
MILL LA
WET GATE LA
RUSHGREEN RD
ST PETER'S CL
BOLLIN DR
BOLLIN CL
LINDEN CL
WHITEFIELD CL
WHITEFIELD GR
NEWFIELD CT
ADEY RD
HEATLEY CL
LODGE CL
HOLLY RD
RICHMOND RD
RICHMOND DR
ASHFIELD CL
CEDARFIELD RD
BIRCHFIELD RD
SANDY LA
LOVATT CT
WOODBINE RD
LABURNUM CT
HOPEFIELD RD
ASHCROFT RD
OUGHTRINGTON VIEW
CHURCH VIEW
MOSS GR
HOWARD AVE
BUCKLOW GDNS
GREEN VIEW
THE GREENACRES
DYERS CL
DYERS LA
RUSH GDNS
WHITEFIELD
WHITE BROOM
OUGHTRINGTON CRES
BRIDGE CL
CROWN GN
STAGE LA
THE PADDOCK
SUTCH LA
BRADSHAW LA
PH
SPRING LA
WARRINGTON LA
OUGHTRINGTON LA
CHURCHWOOD VIEW
LONGBUTT LA
WOODLAND AVE
1 GRAMMAR SCHOOL RD
2 WOODLAND DR
3 NEWARTH DR
4 MARFIELD AVE
5 SANDMOOR PL
6 WHITE CLOVER SQ
7 CLANBROOK AVE
8 WELLCROFT GDNS
FOXLEY CL
FOXLEY HALL MEWS
BURFORD LA
HIGHER LA
WHITELEGGS LA
WOODSIDE LA
CHAPEL WLKS
THE DRIVE
PARKVIEW PK
AGDEN BROW PK
HILLSIDE
AGDEN LA
AGDEN BROW
LYMM RD
A56
A6144
B5159
B5160
8
7
89
6
5
88
4
3
87
2
1
86
69
70
71
29
20

19

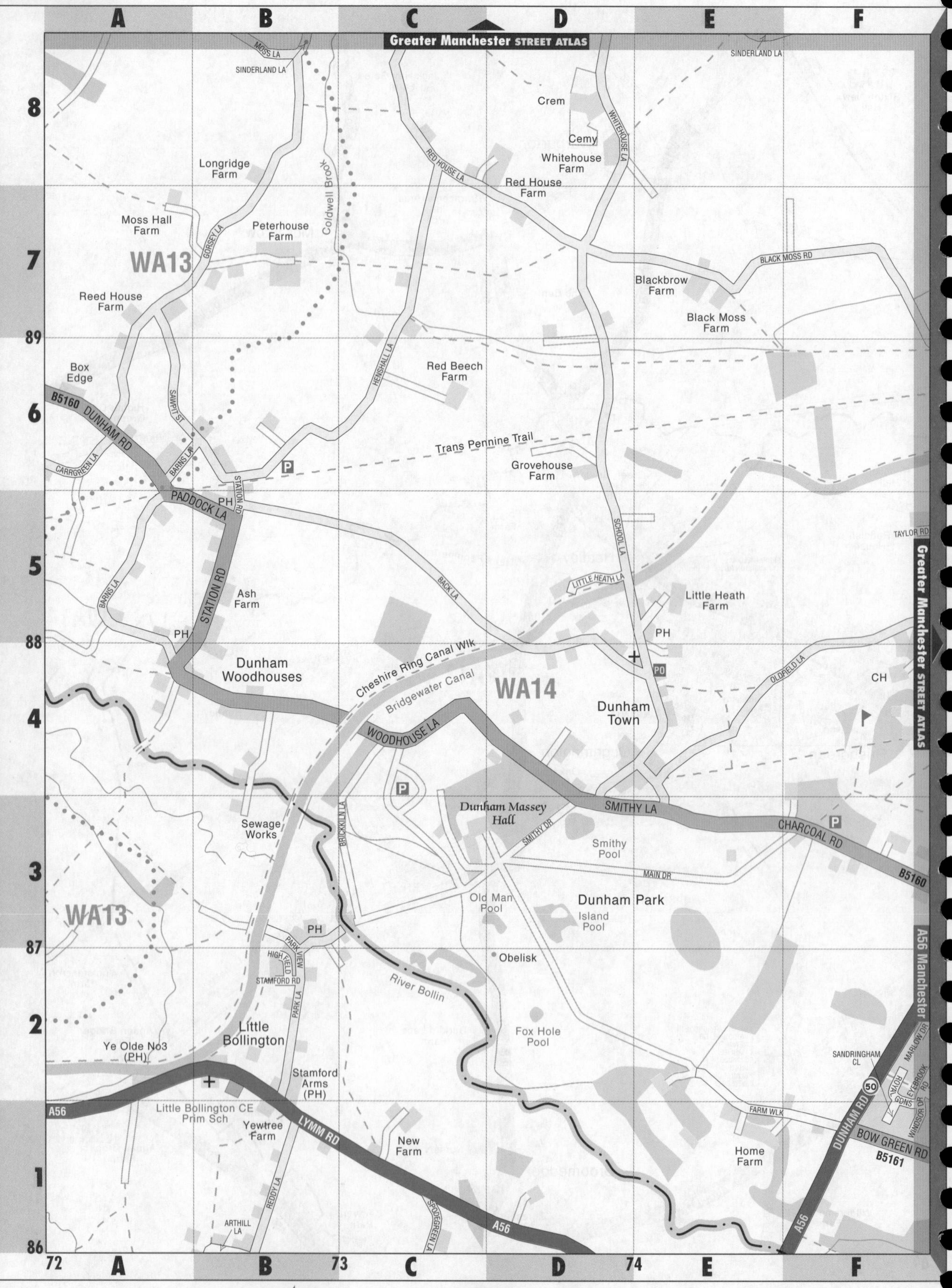

A
B
C
D
E
F
Greater Manchester STREET ATLAS
8
7
89
6
5
88
4
3
87
2
1
86
72
73
74
MOSS LA
SINDERLAND LA
Crem
Cemy
WHITEHOUSE LA
Whitehouse Farm
Red House Farm
RED HOUSE LA
Longridge Farm
Coldwell Brook
Moss Hall Farm
Peterhouse Farm
WA13
GORSEY LA
BLACK MOSS RD
Blackbrow Farm
Black Moss Farm
Reed House Farm
Red Beech Farm
HENSHALL LA
Box Edge
B5160
DUNHAM RD
SAWPIT ST
Trans Pennine Trail
Grovehouse Farm
CARRGREEN LA
BARNS LA
PADDOCK LA
STATION RD
PH
SCHOOL LA
TAYLOR RD
BACK LA
LITTLE HEATH LA
Little Heath Farm
Ash Farm
BARNS LA
STATION RD
PH
PH
Dunham Woodhouses
Cheshire Ring Canal Wlk
Bridgewater Canal
WA14
PO
OLDFIELD LA
CH
Dunham Town
WOODHOUSE LA
Greater Manchester STREET ATLAS
Dunham Massey Hall
SMITHY LA
Sewage Works
BRICKKILN LA
SMITHY DR
Smithy Pool
CHARCOAL RD
MAIN DR
B5160
WA13
Old Man Pool
Dunham Park
Island Pool
PH
PARK VIEW
HIGH FIELD
STAMFORD RD
Obelisk
A56 Manchester
River Bollin
PARK LA
Little Bollington
Ye Olde No3 (PH)
Fox Hole Pool
SANDRINGHAM CL
MARLOW DR
ROYAL GDNS
EYEBROOK RD
WINDSOR DR
50
Stamford Arms (PH)
A56
Little Bollington CE Prim Sch
LYMM RD
FARM WLK
DUNHAM RD
BOW GREEN RD
B5161
Yewtree Farm
New Farm
Home Farm
REDDY LA
SPODEGREEN LA
A56
ARTHILL LA
A56

19

30

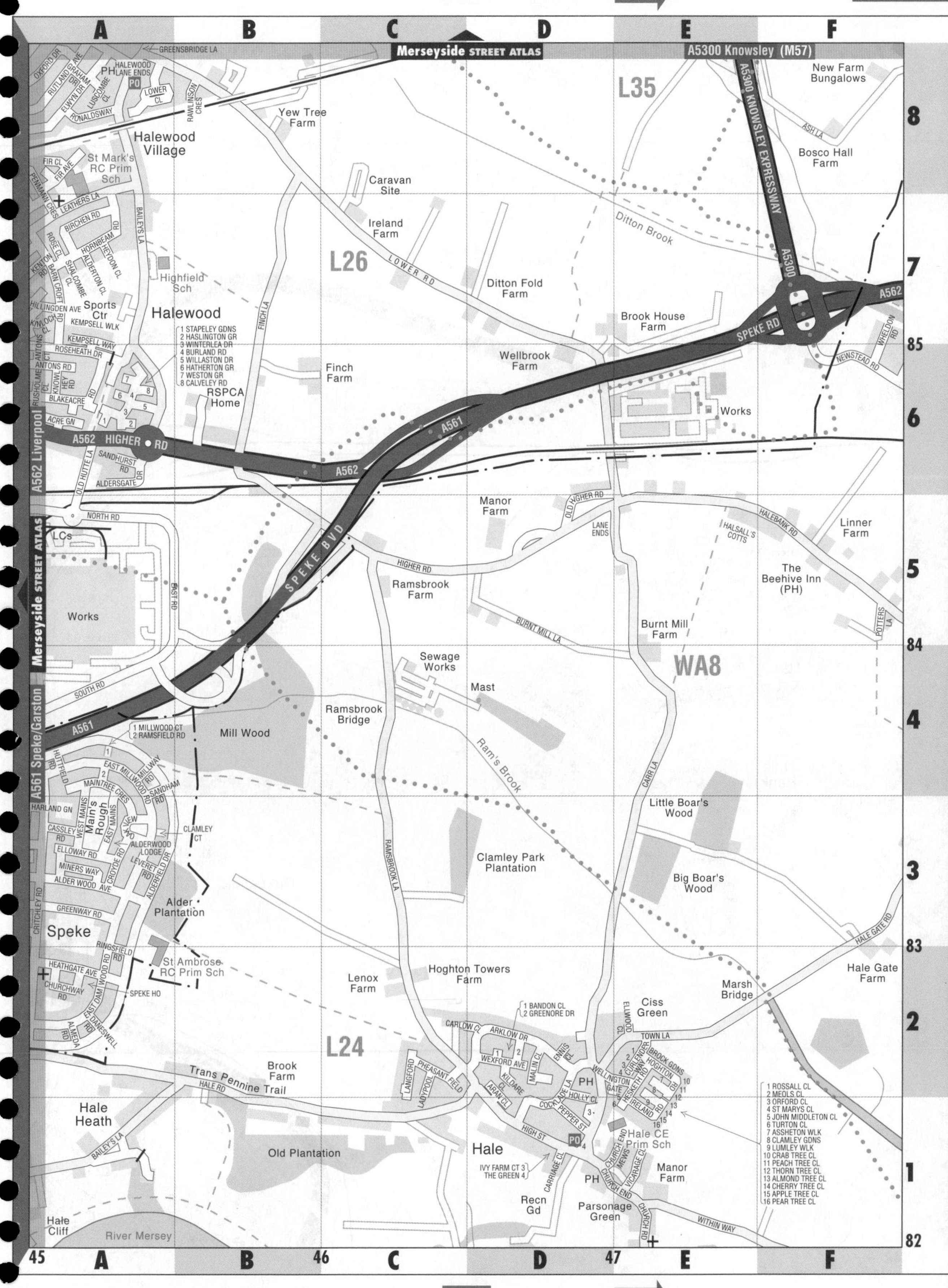
22
A
B
C
D
E
F
Merseyside STREET ATLAS
A5300 Knowsley (M57)
GREENSBRIDGE LA
PH
HALEWOOD LANE ENDS
PO
LOWER CL
RAWLINSON CRES
OXFORD DR
RUTLAND AVE
GRAHAM DR
ELWYN DR
LUSCOMBE CL
RONALDSWAY
Yew Tree Farm
L35
New Farm Bungalows
A5300 KNOWSLEY EXPRESSWAY
ASH LA
8
Bosco Hall Farm
Halewood Village
St Mark's RC Prim Sch
FIR CL
FIR AVE
PENMANN CRES
LEATHERS LA
BIRCHEN RD
BAILEYS LA
Caravan Site
Ireland Farm
Ditton Brook
HORNBEAM RD
HEYTON CL
ALDERTON CL
KENTON RD
ROSE CL
BARN CROFT
SHALCOMBE CL
Highfield Sch
L26
LOWER RD
FINCH LA
Ditton Fold Farm
A5300
7
A562
HILLINGDEN AVE
Sports Ctr
KEMPSELL WLK
Halewood
1 STAPELEY GDNS
2 HASLINGTON GR
3 WINTERLEA DR
4 BURLAND RD
5 WILLASTON DR
6 HATHERTON GR
7 WESTON GR
8 CALVELEY RD
Brook House Farm
SPEKE RD
WHELDON RD
85
KEMPSELL WAY
ROSEHEATH DR
ANTONS RD
RUSHOLME CL
KNOWL HEY RD
BLAKEACRE RD
ACRE GN
Finch Farm
Wellbrook Farm
NEWSTEAD RD
RSPCA Home
Works
A561
6
A562 HIGHER RD
SANDHURST DR
ALDERSGATE DR
OLD HUTTE LA
A562
A562 Liverpool
NORTH RD
LCs
Manor Farm
OLD HIGHER RD
LANE ENDS
HALSALL'S COTTS
HALEBANK RD
Linner Farm
SPEKE BVD
HIGHER RD
Ramsbrook Farm
The Beehive Inn (PH)
5
Works
EAST RD
BURNT MILL LA
Burnt Mill Farm
POTTERS LA
84
Merseyside STREET ATLAS
Sewage Works
WA8
SOUTH RD
Mast
Ramsbrook Bridge
Mill Wood
A561
1 MILLWOOD CT
2 RAMSFIELD RD
4
Ram's Brook
A561 Speke/Garston
HUTTFIELD RD
EAST MILLWOOD RD
MILLWAY
SANDHAM RD
MAINTREE CRES
HARLAND GN
WEST MAINS
Main's Rough
EAST MAINS
NEW LODGE
CLAMLEY CT
CARR LA
Little Boar's Wood
CASSLEY RD
ELLOWAY RD
CROYDE RD
ALDERWOOD LODGE
LEVERET RD
ALDERFIELD DR
RAMSBROOK LA
Clamley Park Plantation
MINERS WAY
ALDER WOOD AVE
3
Big Boar's Wood
CRITCHLEY RD
GREENWAY RD
Alder Plantation
Speke
RINGSFIELD RD
St Ambrose RC Prim Sch
HALE GATE RD
83
HEATHGATE AVE
CHURCHWAY RD
EAST DAM WOOD RD
SPEKE HO
Lenox Farm
Hoghton Towers Farm
Hale Gate Farm
Marsh Bridge
1 BANDON CL
2 GREENORE DR
Ciss Green
2
ALMEDA RD
DANESWELL
ELLWOOD CL
CARLOW CL
ARKLOW DR
ENNIS CL
TOWN LA
L24
WEXFORD AVE
MALIN CL
BROCK GDNS
HOGHTON RD
Brook Farm
Trans Pennine Trail
HALE RD
LANGFORD
PHEASANT FIELD
LADYPOOL
KILDARE
ARAN CL
PH
WELLINGTON GATE
CURLENDER WAY
HESKETH RD
IRELAND RD
1 ROSSALL CL
2 MEOLS CL
3 ORFORD CL
4 ST MARYS CL
5 JOHN MIDDLETON CL
6 TURTON CL
7 ASSHETON WLK
8 CLAMLEY GDNS
9 LUMLEY WLK
10 CRAB TREE CL
11 PEACH TREE CL
12 THORN TREE CL
13 ALMOND TREE CL
14 CHERRY TREE CL
15 APPLE TREE CL
16 PEAR TREE CL
Hale Heath
COCKLADE LA
HOLLY CL
PEPPER ST
HIGH ST
Hale CE Prim Sch
BAILEY'S LA
Old Plantation
Hale
PO
CHURCH END MEWS
VICARAGE CL
Manor Farm
1
IVY FARM CT 3
THE GREEN 4
CARRIAGE CL
PH
CHURCH END
Recn Gd
Parsonage Green
CHURCH RD
WITHIN WAY
Hale Cliff
River Mersey
82
45
46
47
47
22

21
12

C8
1 LEVENS WAY
2 RIDSDALE
3 LONSDALE CL
4 LEIGH GREEN CL
5 APPLEBY WLK
6 AYCLIFFE WLK

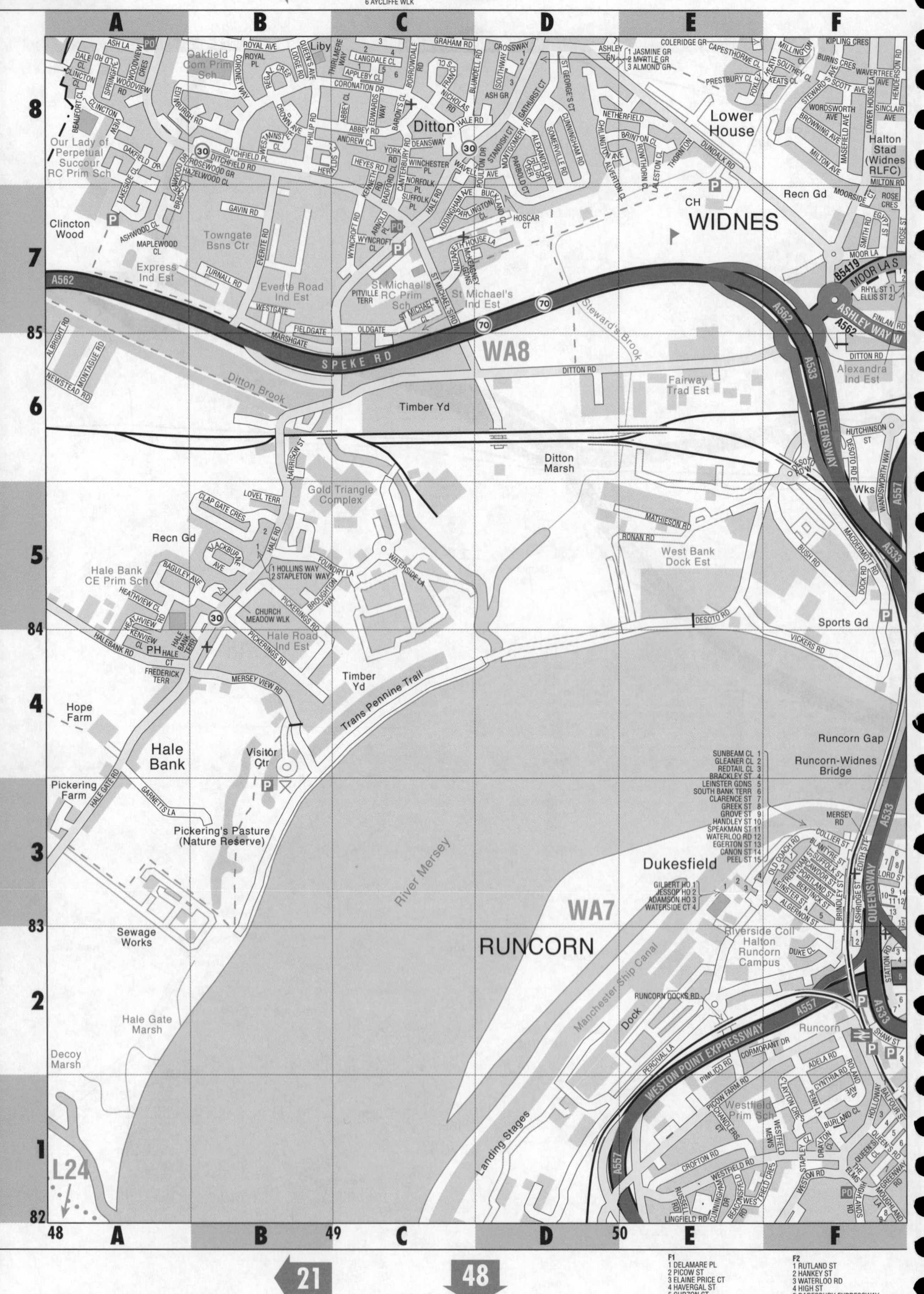

21
48

F1
1 DELAMARE PL
2 PICOW ST
3 ELAINE PRICE CT
4 HAVERGAL ST
5 CURZON ST
6 LIGHTBURN ST
7 STANLEY VILLAS
8 SOUTHLANDS MEWS
9 SOUTHLANDS CT

F2
1 RUTLAND ST
2 HANKEY ST
3 WATERLOO RD
4 HIGH ST
5 DARESBURY EXPRESSWAY
6 LOWLANDS RD
7 CAVENDISH ST
8 ARTHUR ST

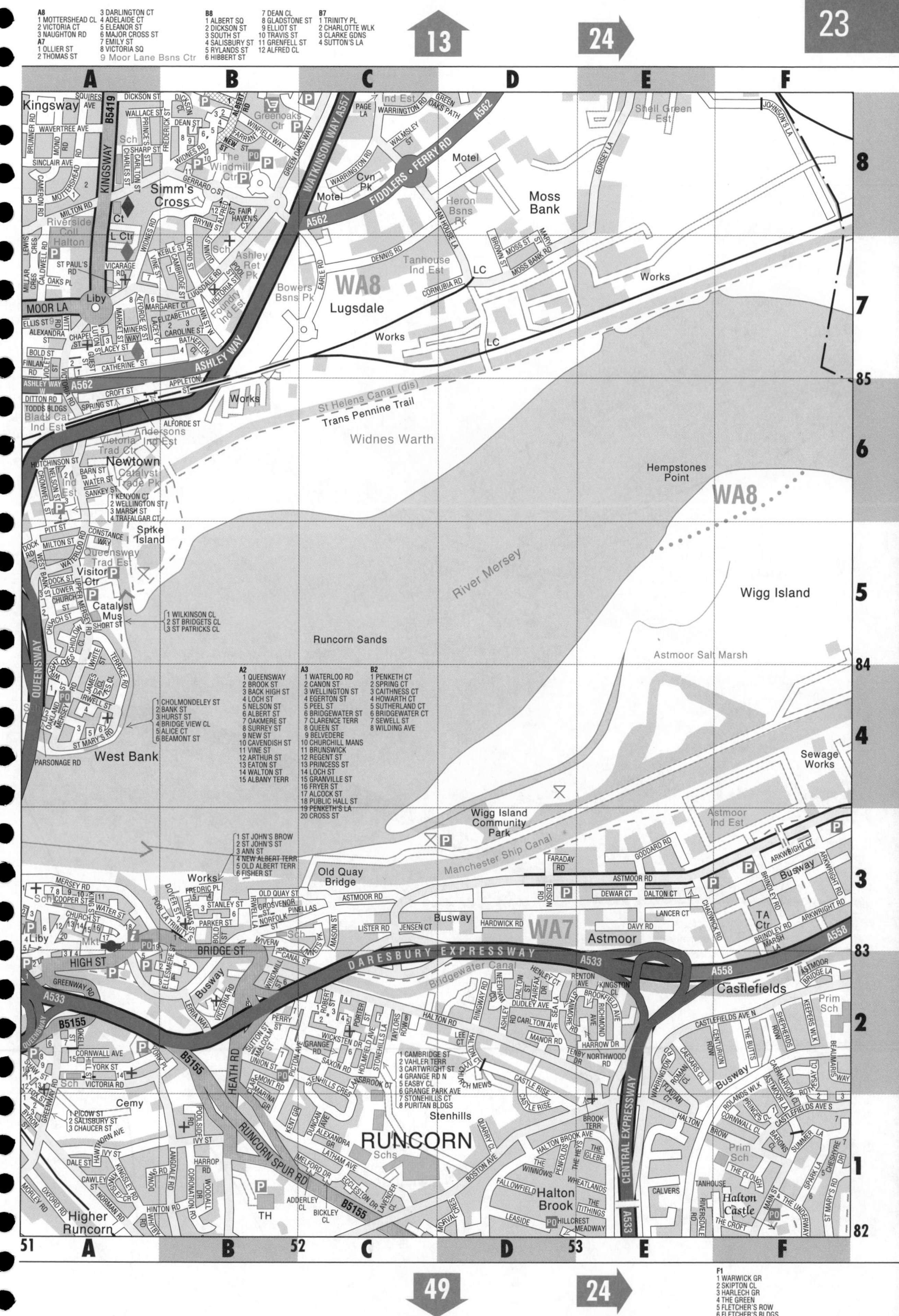

A8
1 MOTTERSHEAD CL
2 VICTORIA CT
3 NAUGHTON RD
A7
1 OLLIER ST
2 THOMAS ST
3 DARLINGTON CT
4 ADELAIDE CT
5 ELEANOR ST
6 MAJOR CROSS ST
7 EMILY ST
8 VICTORIA SQ
9 Moor Lane Bsns Ctr
B8
1 ALBERT SQ
2 DICKSON ST
3 SOUTH ST
4 SALISBURY ST
5 RYLANDS ST
6 HIBBERT ST
7 DEAN CL
8 GLADSTONE ST
9 ELLIOT ST
10 TRAVIS ST
11 GRENFELL ST
12 ALFRED CL
B7
1 TRINITY PL
2 CHARLOTTE WLK
3 CLARKE GDNS
4 SUTTON'S LA
13
24
23
A
B
C
D
E
F
Kingsway
Simm's Cross
Greenoaks Ctr
The Windmill Ctr
Riverside Coll Halton
Ashley Ret Pk
Foundry Ind Est
Bowers Bsns Pk
WA8
Lugsdale
Tanhouse Ind Est
Heron Bsns Pk
Moss Bank
Motel
Cvn Pk
Shell Green Est
Works
LC
ASHLEY WAY
WATKINSON WAY A557
FIDDLERS FERRY RD
A562
Black Cat Ind Est
Andersons Ind Est
Victoria Trad Ctr
Newtown
Catalyst Trade Pk
St Helens Canal (dis)
Trans Pennine Trail
Widnes Warth
Hempstones Point
Spike Island
Queensway Trad Est
Visitor Ctr
Catalyst Mus
River Mersey
Wigg Island
Runcorn Sands
Astmoor Salt Marsh
West Bank
QUEENSWAY
1 KENYON CT
2 WELLINGTON ST
3 MARSH ST
4 TRAFALGAR CT
1 WILKINSON CL
2 ST BRIDGETS CL
3 ST PATRICKS CL
1 CHOLMONDELEY ST
2 BANK ST
3 HURST ST
4 BRIDGE VIEW CL
5 ALICE CT
6 BEAMONT ST
A2
1 QUEENSWAY
2 BROOK ST
3 BACK HIGH ST
4 LOCH ST
5 NELSON ST
6 ALBERT ST
7 OAKMERE ST
8 SURREY ST
9 NEW ST
10 CAVENDISH ST
11 VINE ST
12 ARTHUR ST
13 EATON ST
14 WALTON ST
15 ALBANY TERR
A3
1 WATERLOO RD
2 CANON ST
3 WELLINGTON ST
4 EGERTON ST
5 PEEL ST
6 BRIDGEWATER ST
7 CLARENCE TERR
8 QUEEN ST
9 BELVEDERE
10 CHURCHILL MANS
11 BRUNSWICK
12 REGENT ST
13 PRINCESS ST
14 LOCH ST
15 GRANVILLE ST
16 FRYER ST
17 ALCOCK ST
18 PUBLIC HALL ST
19 PENKETH'S LA
20 CROSS ST
B2
1 PENKETH CT
2 SPRING CT
3 CAITHNESS CT
4 HOWARTH CT
5 SUTHERLAND CT
6 BRIDGEWATER CT
7 SEWELL ST
8 WILDING AVE
Sewage Works
Astmoor Ind Est
Wigg Island Community Park
Manchester Ship Canal
1 ST JOHN'S BROW
2 ST JOHN'S ST
3 ANN ST
4 NEW ALBERT TERR
5 OLD ALBERT TERR
6 FISHER ST
Old Quay Bridge
Busway
WA7
Astmoor
TA Ctr
DARESBURY EXPRESSWAY
A533
A558
Bridgewater Canal
Castlefields
Prim Sch
CENTRAL EXPRESSWAY
1 CAMBRIDGE ST
2 VAHLER TERR
3 CARTWRIGHT ST
4 GRANGE RD N
5 EASBY CL
6 GRANGE PARK AVE
7 STONEHILLS CT
8 PURITAN BLDGS
1 PICOW ST
2 SALISBURY ST
3 CHAUCER ST
Cemy
Stenhills
RUNCORN
Schs
Halton Brook
Halton Castle
Higher Runcorn
TH
RUNCORN SPUR RD
B5155
8
7
85
6
5
84
4
3
83
2
1
82
51
52
53
49
24
F1
1 WARWICK GR
2 SKIPTON CL
3 HARLECH GR
4 THE GREEN
5 FLETCHER'S ROW
6 FLETCHER'S BLDGS
7 SUMMER CL

23
14

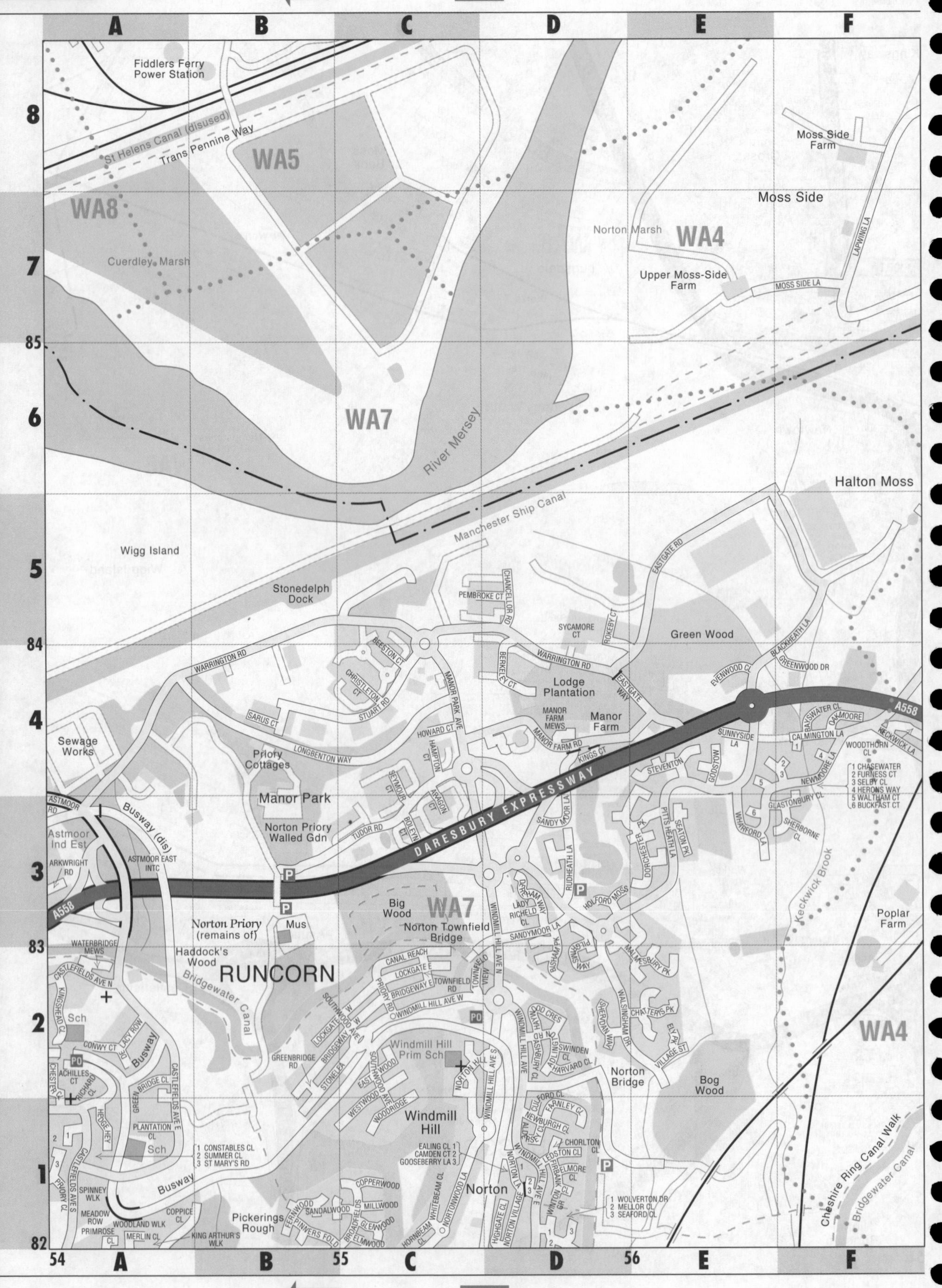
A
B
C
D
E
F
8
7
85
6
5
84
4
3
83
2
1
82
54
55
56
Fiddlers Ferry
Power Station
St Helens Canal (disused)
Trans Pennine Way
WA5
WA8
Cuerdley Marsh
Moss Side
Farm
Moss Side
Norton Marsh
WA4
Upper Moss-Side
Farm
MOSS SIDE LA
LAPWING LA
WA7
River Mersey
Halton Moss
Manchester Ship Canal
Wigg Island
Stonedelph
Dock
PEMBROKE CT
CHANCELLOR RD
EASTGATE RD
SYCAMORE
CT
ROKEBY CT
Green Wood
BLACKHEATH LA
GREENWOOD DR
EVENWOOD CL
WARRINGTON RD
BEESTON CT
CHRISTLETON
CT
STUART RD
MANOR PARK AVE
BERKELEY CT
Lodge
Plantation
EASTGATE
WAY
A558
SARUS CT
HOWARD CT
HAMPTON
CT
MANOR
FARM
MEWS
Manor
Farm
MANOR FARM RD
KINGS CT
SUNNYSIDE
LA
BAYSWATER CL
OAKMOORE
CALMINGTON LA
KECKWICK LA
WOODTHORN
CL
1 CHASEWATER
2 FURNESS CT
3 SELBY CL
4 HERONS WAY
5 WALTHAM CT
6 BUCKFAST CT
NEWMOORE LA
Sewage
Works
Priory
Cottages
LONGBENTON WAY
STEVENTON
GODSTOW
GLASTONBURY CL
SHERBORNE
CL
WHARFORD LA
ASTMOOR
RD
Astmoor
Ind Est
Busway (dis)
Manor Park
SEYMOUR
CT
ARAGON
CT
DARESBURY EXPRESSWAY
SANDY MOOR LA
PITTS HEATH LA
SEATON PK
DORCHESTER PK
Norton Priory
Walled Gdn
TUDOR RD
BOLEYN
CT
ARKWRIGHT
RD
ASTMOOR EAST
INTC
RUDHEATH LA
Keckwick Brook
HOLFORD MOSS
DERHAM WAY
LADY
RICHELD
CL
Big
Wood
WA7
Norton Townfield
Bridge
WINDMILL HILL AVE N
SANDYMOOR LA
Poplar
Farm
Norton Priory
(remains of)
Mus
Haddock's
Wood
WATERBRIDGE
MEWS
CASTLEFIELDS AVE N
KINGSHEAD CL
RUNCORN
Bridgewater Canal
CANAL REACH
LOCKGATE E
BRIDGEWAY E
TOWNFIELD
RD
PRIORY RD
WINDMILL HILL AVE W
SOUTHWOOD AVE
LOCKGATE W
BRIDGEWAY W
BISHAM PK
PILGRIMS
WAY
MALMESBURY PK
CHATERIS PK
ELY PK
VILLAGE ST
WALSINGHAM DR
SHERIDAN WAY
WA4
Sch
DE LACY ROW
CONWY CT
Busway
PO
ACHILLES
CT
CHESTER CL
RICHARD CL
GREENBRIDGE
RD
STONE LA
Windmill Hill
Prim Sch
NORTON HILL AVE S
WINDMILL HILL AVE
COD CRES
HAWORTH RD
ASHBURY CL
DITTON
CL
SWINDEN
CL
HARVARD CL
Norton
Bridge
Bog
Wood
HEDGE HEY
GREENBRIDGE CL
CASTLEFIELDS AVE E
PLANTATION
CL
EAST WOOD
SOUTHWOOD AVE
WESTWOOD
WOODRIDGE
Windmill
Hill
CLIFFORD CL
FARNLEY CL
NEWBURGH CL
CHORLTON
CL
Cheshire Ring Canal Walk
Bridgewater Canal
CASTLEFIELDS AVE S
PRIORY CL
1 CONSTABLES CL
2 SUMMER CL
3 ST MARY'S RD
Sch
EALING CL 1
CAMDEN CT 2
GOOSEBERRY LA 3
EDSTON CL
ELMORE
CL
SPINNEY
WLK
Busway
COPPERWOOD
SANDALWOOD
MILLWOOD
WHITEBEAM CL
NORTONWOOD LA
Norton
NORTON LA
WINDMILL HILL AVE E
FIRBANK
1 WOLVERTON DR
2 MELLOR CL
3 SEAFORD CL
MEADOW
ROW
PRIMROSE
CL
WOODLAND WLK
MERLIN CL
COPPICE
CL
KING ARTHUR'S
WLK
Pickerings
Rough
FERNWOOD
PINNERS FOLD
BROADFIELDS
GLENWOOD
ELMWOOD
HORNBEAM CL
HIGHGATE CL
NORTON VILLAGE

23
50

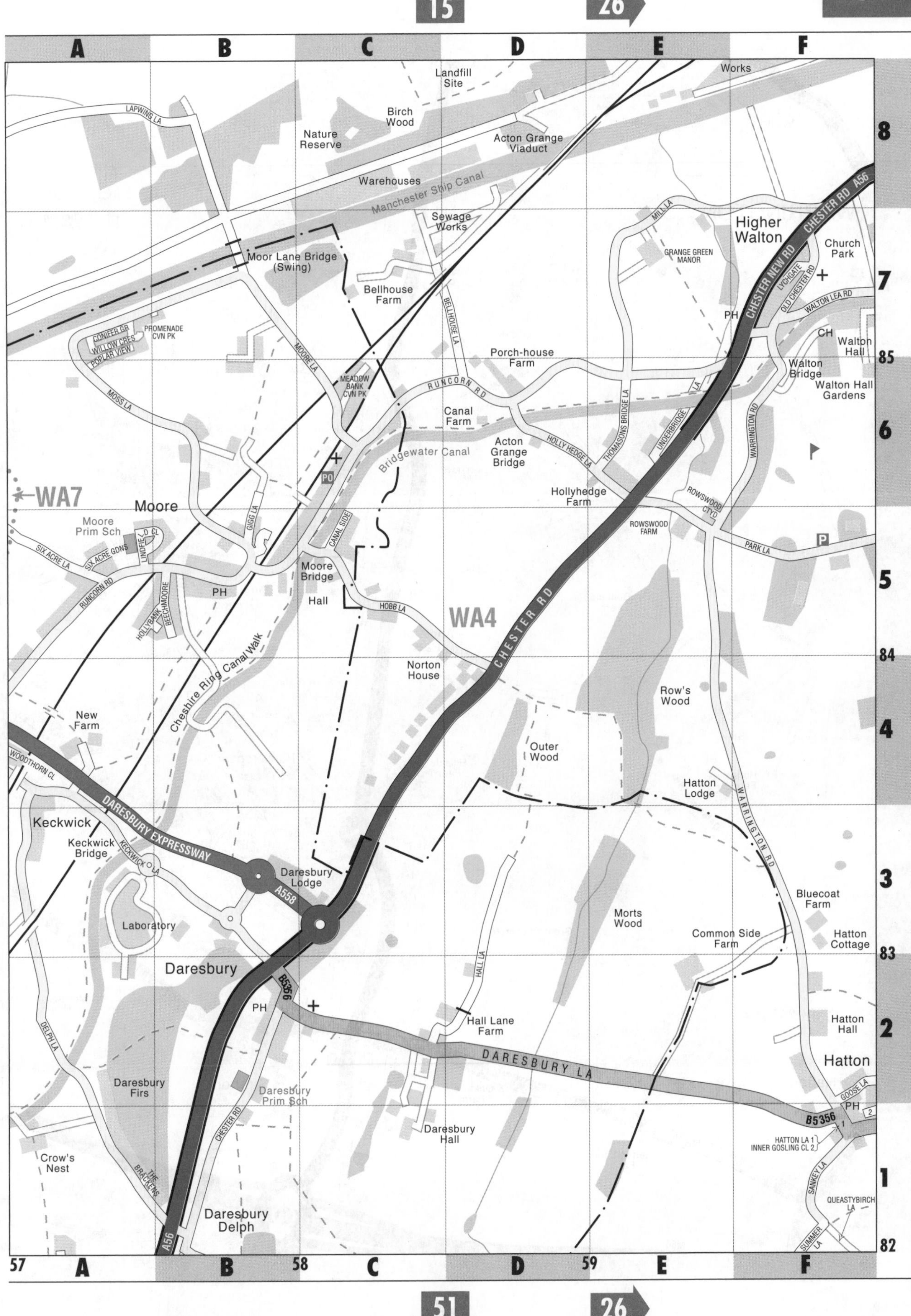

15
26
A
B
C
D
E
F
8
7
85
6
5
84
4
3
83
2
1
82
57
58
59
51
26
Landfill Site
Works
Birch Wood
Nature Reserve
Acton Grange Viaduct
Warehouses
Manchester Ship Canal
Sewage Works
Higher Walton
Church Park
Moor Lane Bridge (Swing)
Bellhouse Farm
GRANGE GREEN MANOR
LAPWING LA
MILL LA
CHESTER NEW RD
CHESTER RD
A56
LYCHGATE
OLD CHESTER RD
WALTON LEA RD
CONIFER GR
WILLOW CRES
POPLAR VIEW
PROMENADE CVN PK
MOORE LA
BELLHOUSE LA
Porch-house Farm
Walton Hall
Walton Bridge
Walton Hall Gardens
MEADOW BANK CVN PK
RUNCORN RD
Canal Farm
Acton Grange Bridge
Bridgewater Canal
HOLLY HEDGE LA
THOMASONS BRIDGE LA
UNDERBRIDGE LA
WARRINGTON RD
MOSS LA
PO
WA7
Moore
Moore Prim Sch
GIGG LA
Hollyhedge Farm
ROWSWOOD CTYD
ROWSWOOD FARM
PARK LA
P
SIX ACRE LA
SIX ACRE GDNS
CANAL SIDE
Moore Bridge
Hall
HOBB LA
WA4
RUNCORN RD
HOLLYBANK
BEECHMOORE
PH
Cheshire Ring Canal Walk
Norton House
Row's Wood
New Farm
Outer Wood
WOODTHORN CL
Hatton Lodge
DARESBURY EXPRESSWAY
Keckwick
Keckwick Bridge
KECKWICK LA
Daresbury Lodge
A558
Bluecoat Farm
Laboratory
Morts Wood
Common Side Farm
Hatton Cottage
Daresbury
HALL LA
B5356
Hall Lane Farm
Hatton Hall
DELPH LA
DARESBURY LA
Hatton
Daresbury Firs
Daresbury Prim Sch
GOOSE LA
CHESTER RD
Daresbury Hall
HATTON LA 1
INNER GOSLING CL 2
Crow's Nest
THE BRACKENS
SANKEY LA
QUEASTYBIRCH LA
Daresbury Delph
SUMMER LA

25
16

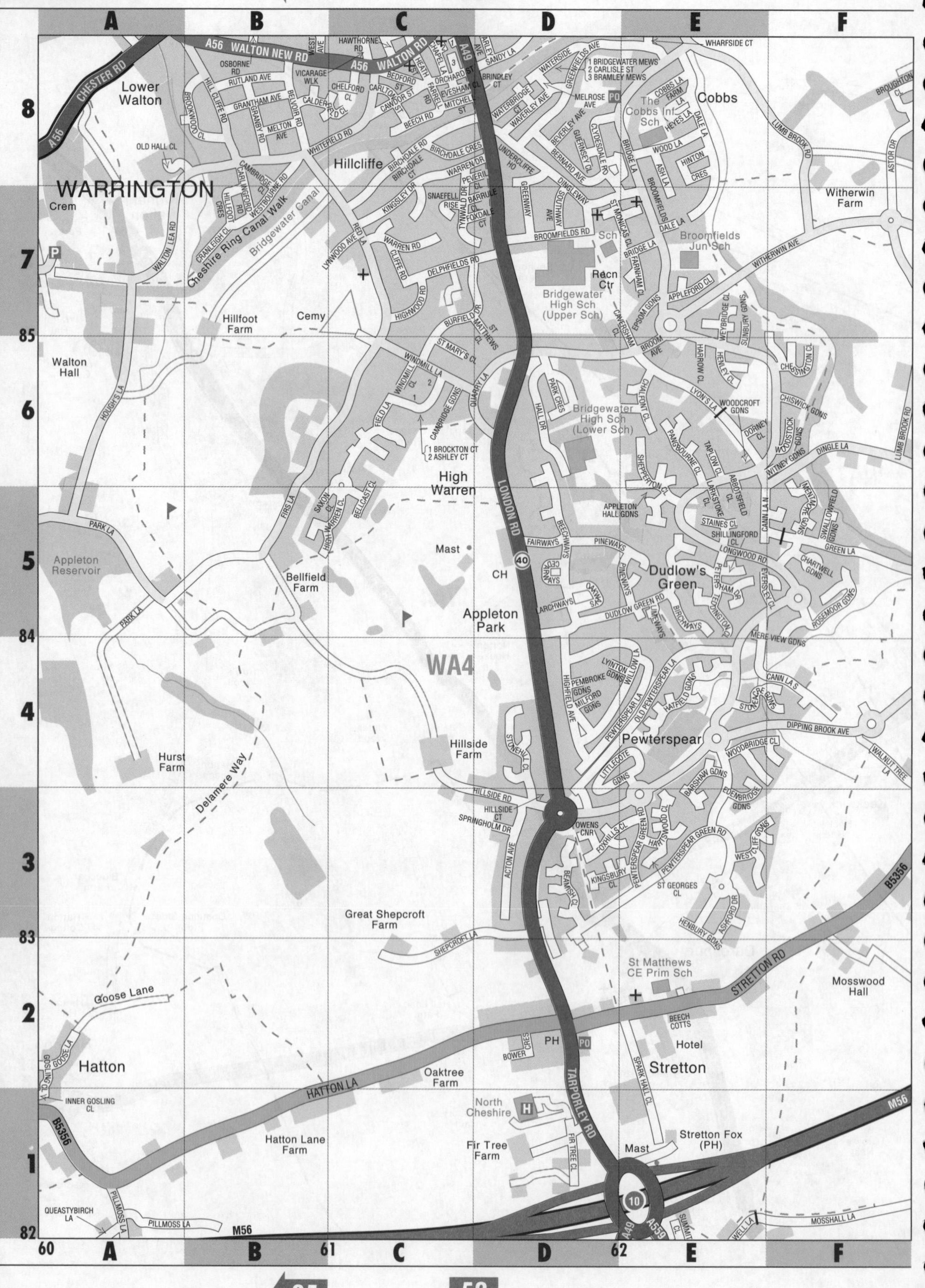
WARRINGTON
Lower Walton
Hillcliffe
Cobbs
Witherwin Farm
Hillfoot Farm
Cemy
Walton Hall
Bridgewater High Sch (Upper Sch)
Bridgewater High Sch (Lower Sch)
High Warren
Appleton Reservoir
Bellfield Farm
Dudlow's Green
Appleton Park
WA4
LONDON RD
Hurst Farm
Hillside Farm
Delamere Way
Pewterspear
Great Shepcroft Farm
St Matthews CE Prim Sch
Mosswood Hall
Hatton
Oaktree Farm
Stretton
STRETTON RD
TARPORLEY RD
HATTON LA
North Cheshire
Hatton Lane Farm
Fir Tree Farm
Stretton Fox (PH)
M56
A56 WALTON NEW RD
A56 CHESTER RD
A49
B5356
A559
Bridgewater Canal
Cheshire Ring Canal Walk
Goose Lane
WITHERWIN AVE
Broomfields Jun Sch
Cobbs Inf Sch
Recn Ctr
Mast
CH
PH
Hotel

25
52

17
28

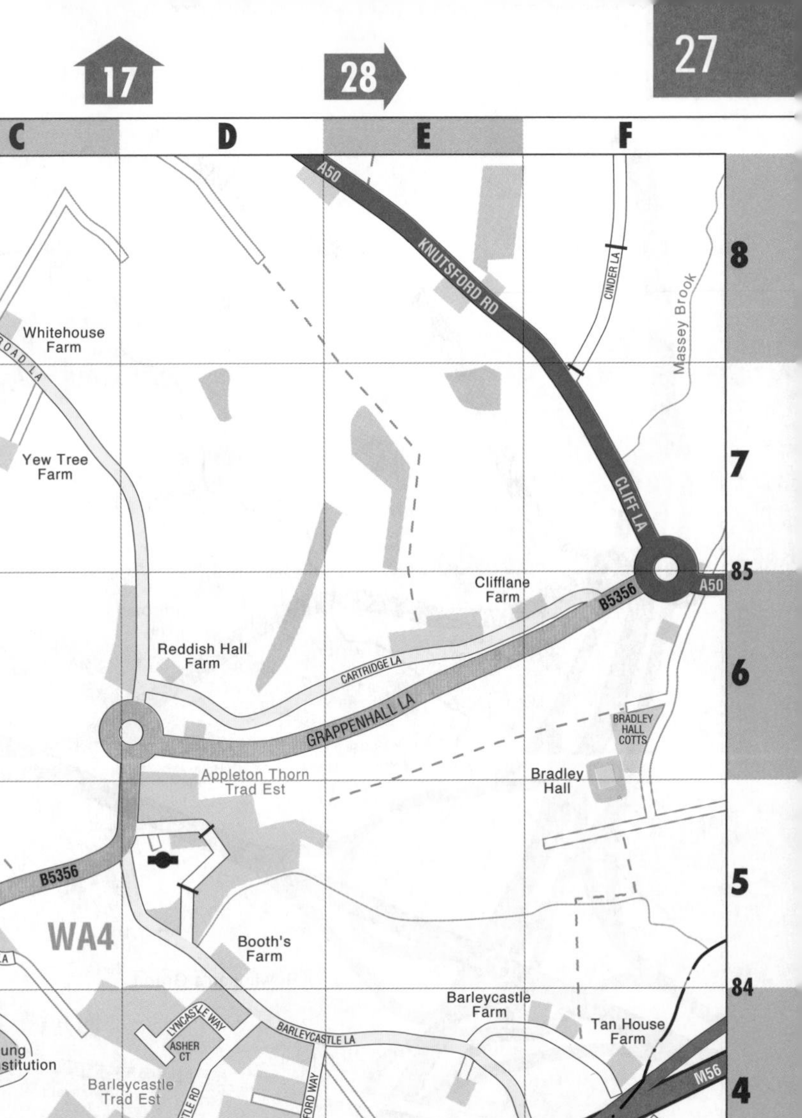
A
B
C
D
E
F
8
7
85
6
5
84
4
3
83
2
1
82
63
64
65
Grappenhall Heys
TRESHAM DR
ASTOR DR
WOLFE CL
BOURCHIER WAY
BROUGHTON CL
HALL LA
CHICHESTER CL
DASHWOOD CL
LICHFIELD AVE
STRICKLAND CL
CROFT GDNS
CURZON DR
WITHERWIN AVE
Dairy Farm
BRETLAND DR
STANSFIELD DR
KEEPER'S RD
BODDINGTON DR
JODRELL DR
LUMB BROOK RD
Com Prim Sch
Wright's Green
BROAD LA
Whitehouse Farm
Yew Tree Farm
A50
KNUTSFORD RD
CINDER LA
Massey Brook
CLIFF LA
Clifflane Farm
B5356
Reddish Hall Farm
CARTRIDGE LA
GRAPPENHALL LA
BRADLEY HALL COTTS
Bradley Hall
Appleton Thorn Trad Est
DOOD'S LA
NEW LA
GREEN LA
WA4
YEW TREE LA
ASHBERRY DR
THORNTREE GN
CROFTON CL
Booth's Farm
Thorn Inn (PH)
Greenlane Farm
SPINNEY GDNS
PARKLAND CL
HM Young Offender Institution
LYNCASTLE WAY
ASHER CT
BARLEYCASTLE LA
Barleycastle Farm
Tan House Farm
Appleton Thorn
STRETTON RD
Barleycastle Trad Est
LYNCASTLE RD
LANGFORD WAY
M56
SWINEYARD LA
BLACKCAP RD
Cross Farm
HATCHERY CL
MARSH RD
CHAPEL LA
Appleton Thorn Prim Sch
BURLEY LA
Old Farm
WALNUT TREE LA
AMBERLEIGH CL
BARLEY CASTLE CL
RED GABLES
PEPPER ST
ARLEY RD
Mast
Sewage Works
Airfield (disused)
Burleyheyes
Appleton Moss
New Farm
CW9
Stretton Moss
Fairbank Farm
REEDGATE LA
Reedgate Farm
Whitley Reed
NEW RD
Laurel Farm
MOSSHALL LA
Moss Hall

53
28

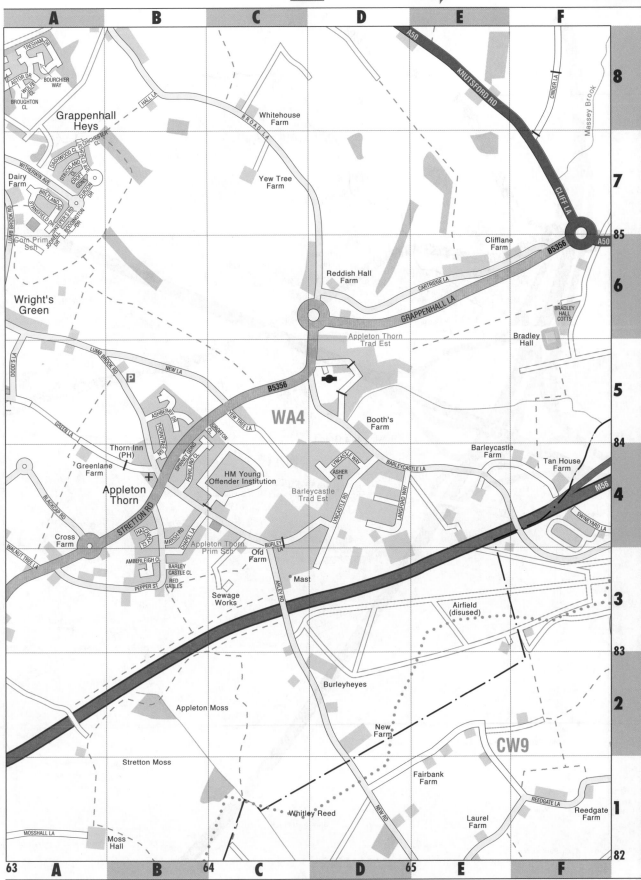

27
18

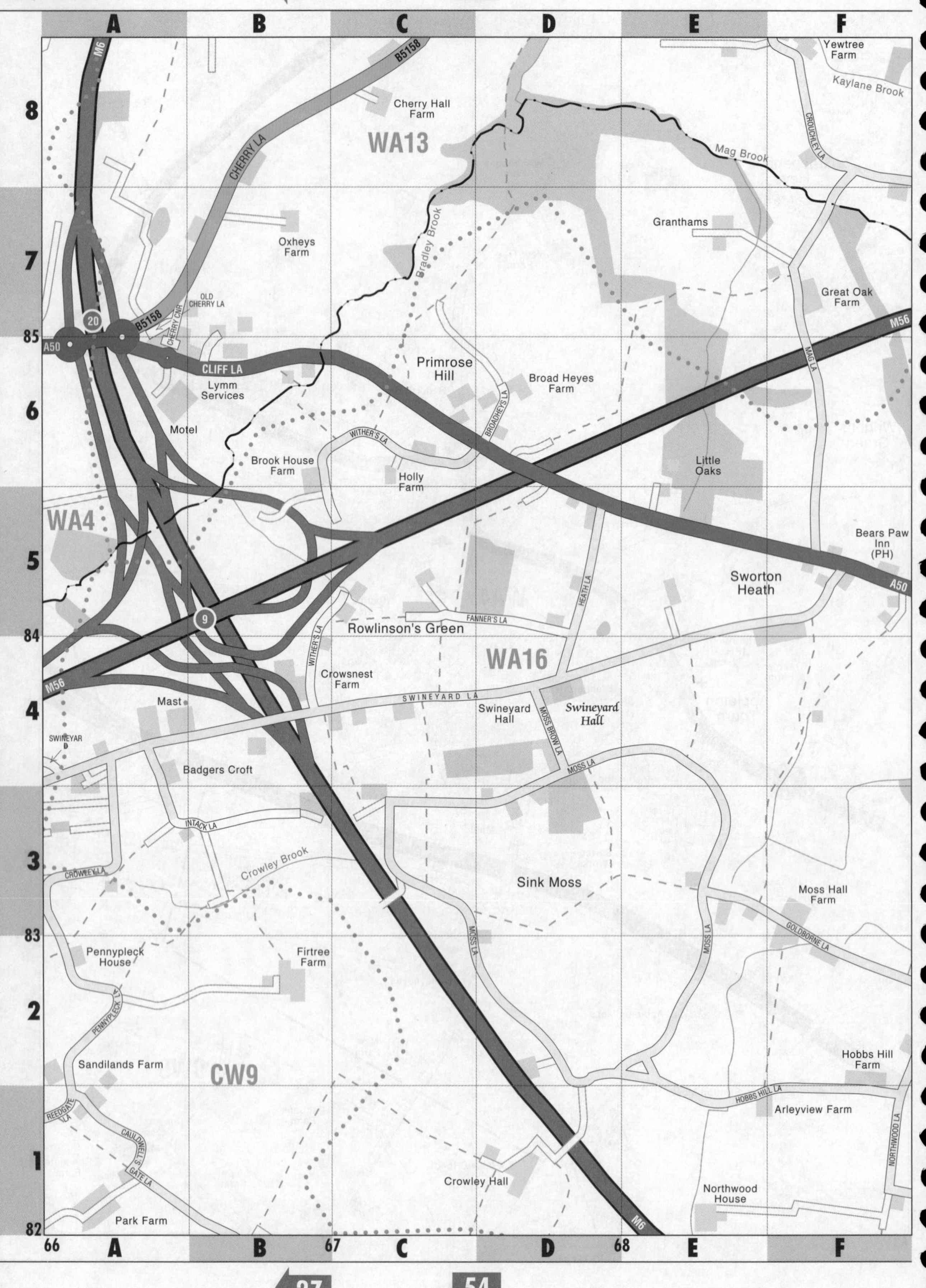
A
B
C
D
E
F
8
7
85
6
5
84
4
3
83
2
1
82
66
67
68
M6
B5158
Cherry Hall Farm
WA13
CHERRY LA
Yewtree Farm
Kaylane Brook
CROUCHLEY LA
Mag Brook
Granthams
Oxheys Farm
Bradley Brook
Great Oak Farm
OLD CHERRY LA
20
B5158
CHERRY CNR
A50
CLIFF LA
M56
Primrose Hill
Broad Heyes Farm
MAG LA
Lymm Services
Motel
WITHER'S LA
BROADHEYS LA
Brook House Farm
Holly Farm
Little Oaks
WA4
Bears Paw Inn (PH)
Sworton Heath
A50
9
FANNER'S LA
HEATH LA
Rowlinson's Green
WA16
WITHER'S LA
M56
Crowsnest Farm
SWINEYARD LA
Mast
Swineyard Hall
MOSS BROW LA
Swineyard Hall
Badgers Croft
MOSS LA
INTACK LA
Crowley Brook
CROWLEY LA
Sink Moss
Moss Hall Farm
MOSS LA
GOLDBORNE LA
Pennypleck House
Firtree Farm
PENNYPLECK LA
Sandilands Farm
CW9
Hobbs Hill Farm
HOBBS HILL LA
Arleyview Farm
REEDGATE LA
CAULDWELL'S GATE LA
NORTHWOOD LA
Crowley Hall
Northwood House
Park Farm
M6

27
54

19 30

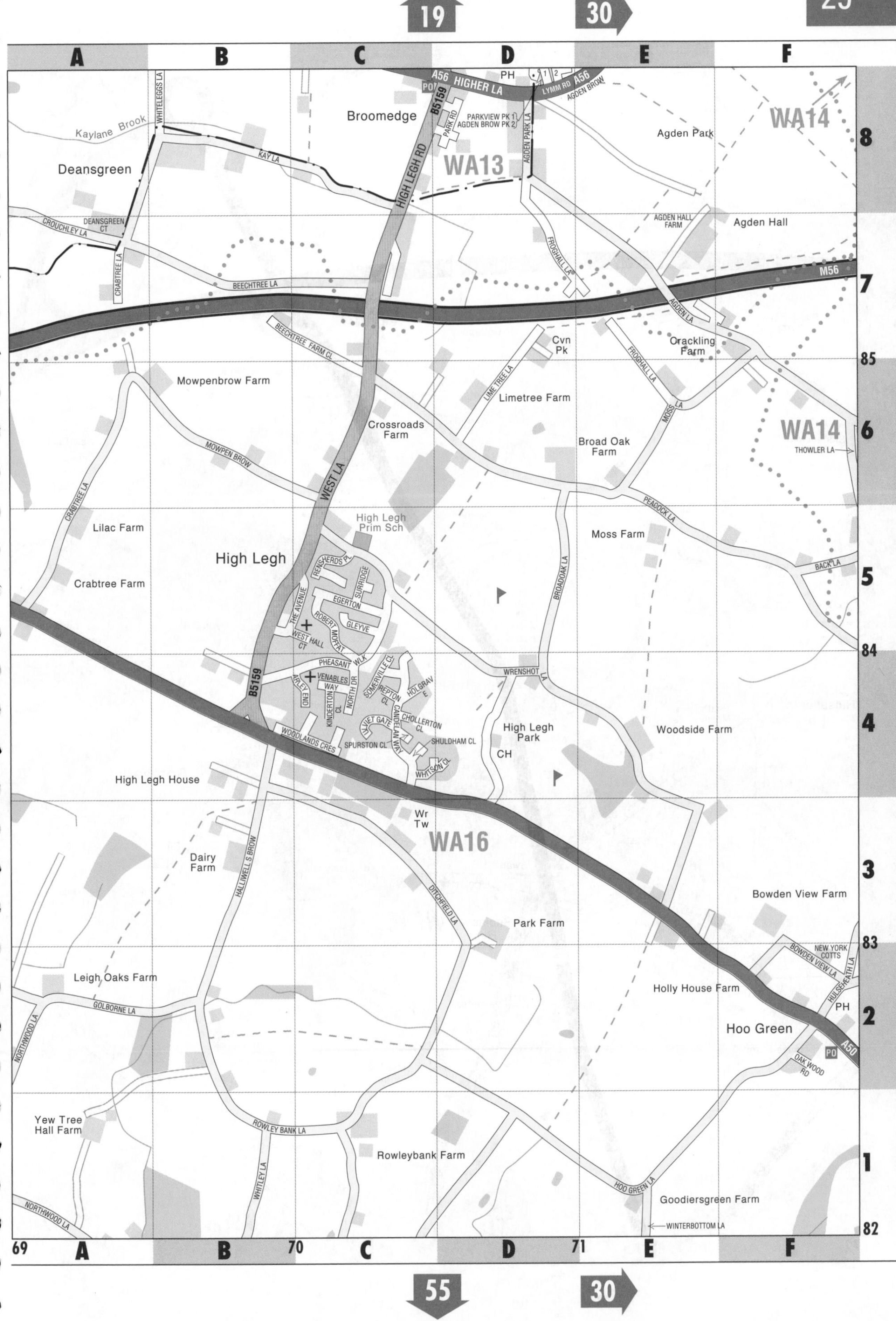
A
B
C
D
E
F
A56 HIGHER LA
LYMM RD A56
AGDEN BROW
PH
PO
B5159
Broomedge
PARKVIEW PK 1
AGDEN BROW PK 2
PARK RD
AGDEN PARK LA
WA13
WA14
Agden Park
8
Kaylane Brook
WHITELEGGS LA
KAY LA
Deansgreen
HIGH LEGH RD
DEANSGREEN CT
CROUCHLEY LA
CRABTREE LA
AGDEN HALL FARM
Agden Hall
FROGHALL LA
BEECHTREE LA
M56
7
AGDEN LA
BEECHTREE FARM CL
Cvn Pk
Crackling Farm
85
Mowpenbrow Farm
LIME TREE LA
Limetree Farm
FROGHALL LA
MOSS LA
Crossroads Farm
Broad Oak Farm
WA14
6
THOWLER LA
MOWPEN BROW
WEST LA
PEACOCK LA
CRABTREE LA
Lilac Farm
High Legh Prim Sch
Moss Farm
High Legh
RENSHERDS PL
SURRIDGE
BROADOAK LA
BACK LA
5
Crabtree Farm
EGERTON
THE AVENUE
ROBERT MOFFAT
GLEYVE
WEST HALL CT
84
PHEASANT WLK
B5159
WRENSHOT LA
ARLEY END
VENABLES WAY
KINDERTON CL
NORTH DR
SOMERVILLE CL
REPTON CL
HOLGRAVE
CHOLLERTON CL
TIL VIET GATE
CANDELAN WAY
SHULDHAM CL
High Legh Park
Woodside Farm
4
WOODLANDS CRES
SPURSTON CL
CH
WHITSON CL
High Legh House
Wr Tw
WA16
Dairy Farm
HALLIWELL'S BROW
3
DITCHFIELD LA
Bowden View Farm
Park Farm
83
NEW YORK COTTS
BOWDEN VIEW LA
Leigh Oaks Farm
HULSEHEATH LA
Holly House Farm
GOLBORNE LA
PH
2
NORTHWOOD LA
Hoo Green
A50
PO
OAK WOOD RD
Yew Tree Hall Farm
ROWLEY BANK LA
Rowleybank Farm
1
HOO GREEN LA
Goodiersgreen Farm
NORTHWOOD LA
WHITLEY LA
WINTERBOTTOM LA
82
69
70
71

55 30

29
20

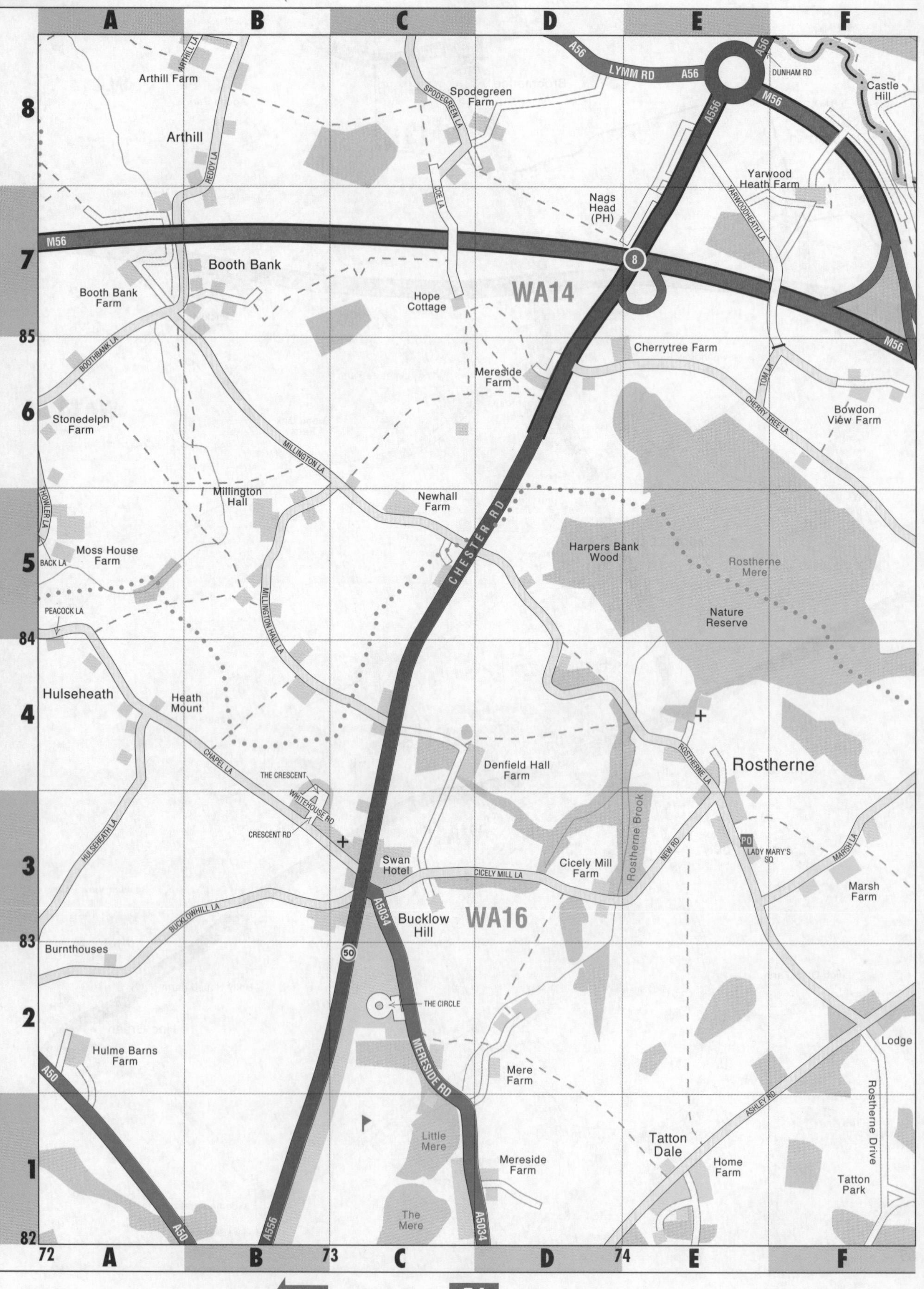
A B C D E F
8
7
85
6
5
84
4
3
83
2
1
82
72 73 74
Arthill Farm
ARTHILL LA
Arthill
REDDY LA
Spodegreen Farm
SPODEGREEN LA
DOE LA
A56
LYMM RD
A56
A556
M56
DUNHAM RD
Castle Hill
Yarwood Heath Farm
YARWOODHEATH LA
Nags Head (PH)
M56
8
Booth Bank
Booth Bank Farm
Hope Cottage
WA14
Cherrytree Farm
BOOTHBANK LA
Mereside Farm
TOM LA
CHERRY TREE LA
Bowdon View Farm
Stonedelph Farm
MILLINGTON LA
Millington Hall
Newhall Farm
CHESTER RD
THOWLER LA
Moss House Farm
BACK LA
Harpers Bank Wood
Rostherne Mere
Nature Reserve
MILLINGTON HALL LA
PEACOCK LA
Hulseheath
Heath Mount
Rostherne
ROSTHERNE LA
Denfield Hall Farm
CHAPEL LA
THE CRESCENT
WHITEHOUSE RD
CRESCENT RD
HULSEHEATH LA
Swan Hotel
CICELY MILL LA
Cicely Mill Farm
Rostherne Brook
NEW RD
PO
LADY MARY'S SQ
MARSH LA
Marsh Farm
BUCKLOWHILL LA
A5034
Bucklow Hill
WA16
Burnthouses
50
THE CIRCLE
Lodge
Hulme Barns Farm
A50
MERESIDE RD
Mere Farm
ASHLEY RD
Rostherne Drive
Little Mere
Tatton Dale
Mereside Farm
Home Farm
Tatton Park
The Mere
A50
A556
A5034

29
56

32

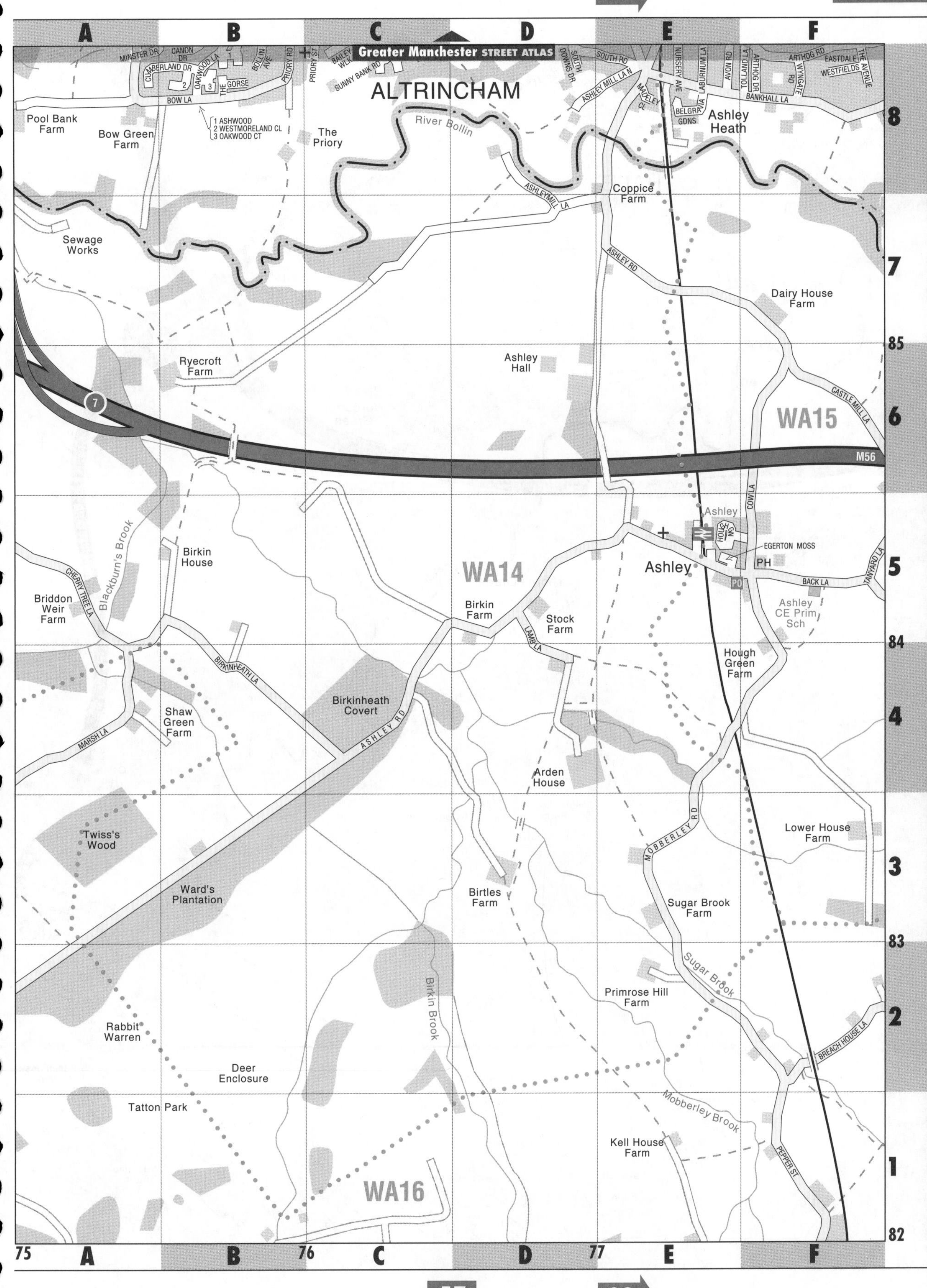
Greater Manchester STREET ATLAS
ALTRINCHAM
Pool Bank Farm
Bow Green Farm
The Priory
River Bollin
Ashley Heath
Coppice Farm
Sewage Works
Dairy House Farm
Ryecroft Farm
Ashley Hall
WA15
M56
Ashley
Birkin House
Briddon Weir Farm
WA14
Birkin Farm
Stock Farm
Ashley CE Prim Sch
Hough Green Farm
Birkinheath Covert
Shaw Green Farm
Arden House
Lower House Farm
Twiss's Wood
Ward's Plantation
Birtles Farm
Sugar Brook Farm
Primrose Hill Farm
Rabbit Warren
Deer Enclosure
Tatton Park
Kell House Farm
WA16
Birkin Brook
Sugar Brook
Mobberley Brook
Blackburn's Brook
ASHLEY RD
MOBBERLEY RD
BIRKINHEATH LA
CHERRY TREE LA
MARSH LA
LAMB LA
COW LA
BACK LA
TANYARD LA
CASTLE MILL LA
ASHLEYMILL LA
PEPPER ST
BREACH HOUSE LA
EGERTON MOSS
PH
PO
BOW LA
MINSTER DR
CANON DR
CUMBERLAND DR
OAKWOOD LA
THE GORSE
BOLLIN AVE
PRIORY RD
PRIORY ST
BAILEY WLK
SUNNY BANK RD
SOUTH DOWNS DR
SOUTH RD
ASHLEY MILL LA N
MAUDSLEY CL
NURSERY AVE
LABURNUM LA
BELGRAVIA GDNS
AVON RD
TOLLAND LA
ARTHOG DR
ARTHOG RD
WYNGATE RD
EASTDALE
WESTFIELDS
THE AVENUE
BANKHALL LA
1 ASHWOOD
2 WESTMORELAND CL
3 OAKWOOD CT
A
B
C
D
E
F
1
2
3
4
5
6
7
8
75
76
77
82
83
84
85

57

32

31

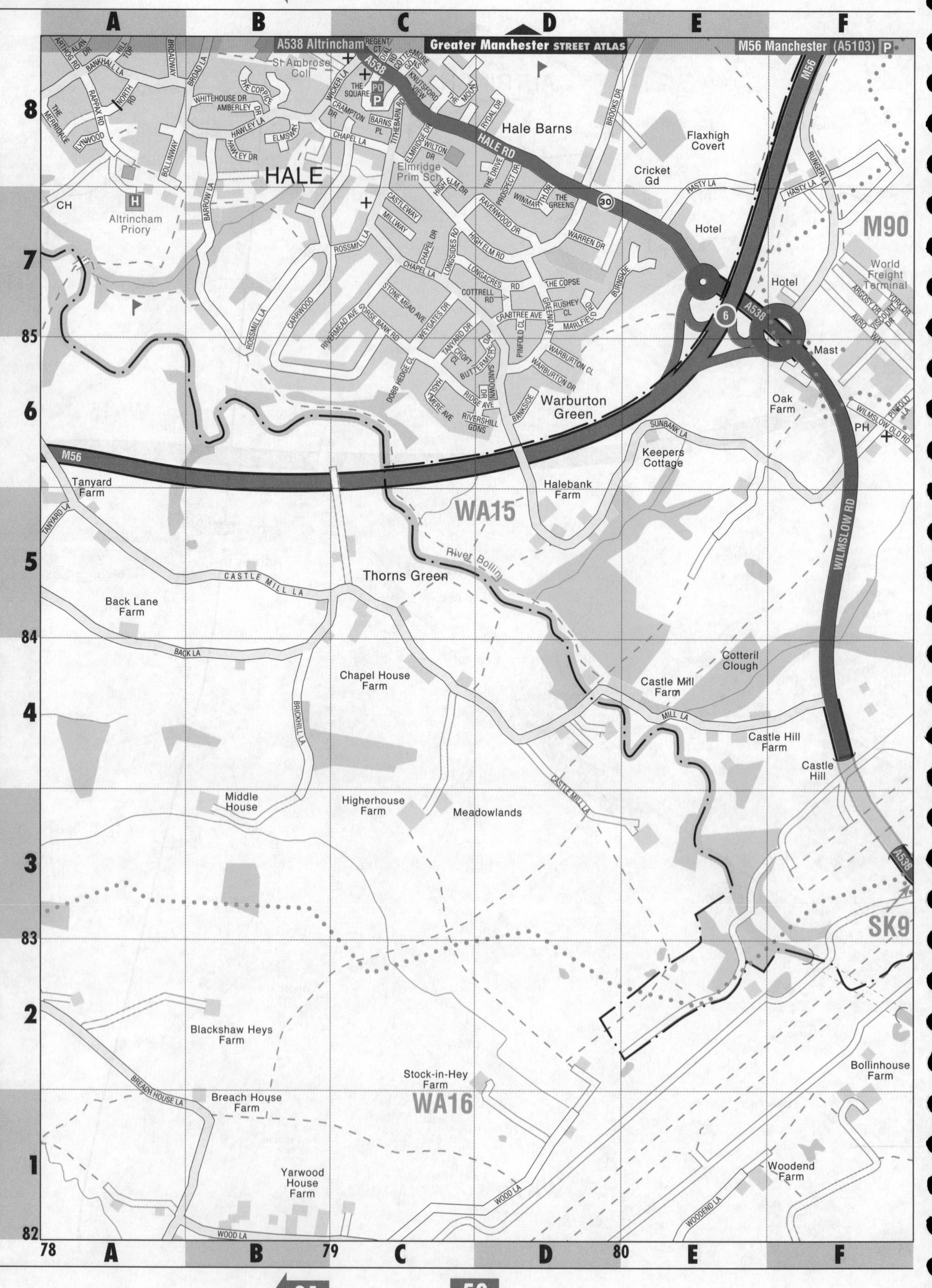
A538 Altrincham
Greater Manchester STREET ATLAS
M56 Manchester (A5103)
St Ambrose Coll
HALE
Hale Barns
Flaxhigh Covert
Cricket Gd
Altrincham Priory
Elmridge Prim Sch
HALE RD
Hotel
M90
World Freight Terminal
Warburton Green
Oak Farm
Mast
PH
Keepers Cottage
Tanyard Farm
Halebank Farm
WA15
River Bollin
Thorns Green
Back Lane Farm
CASTLE MILL LA
BACK LA
Chapel House Farm
Cotteril Clough
Castle Mill Farm
MILL LA
Castle Hill Farm
Castle Hill
WILMSLOW RD
BRICKHILL LA
Middle House
Higherhouse Farm
Meadowlands
SK9
Blackshaw Heys Farm
Breach House Farm
BREACH HOUSE LA
Stock-in-Hey Farm
WA16
Bollinhouse Farm
Yarwood House Farm
Woodend Farm
WOODEND LA
WOOD LA

31
58

34

D8
1 ROSSETT AVE
2 WHITEFRIARS WLK
3 AUSTELL RD

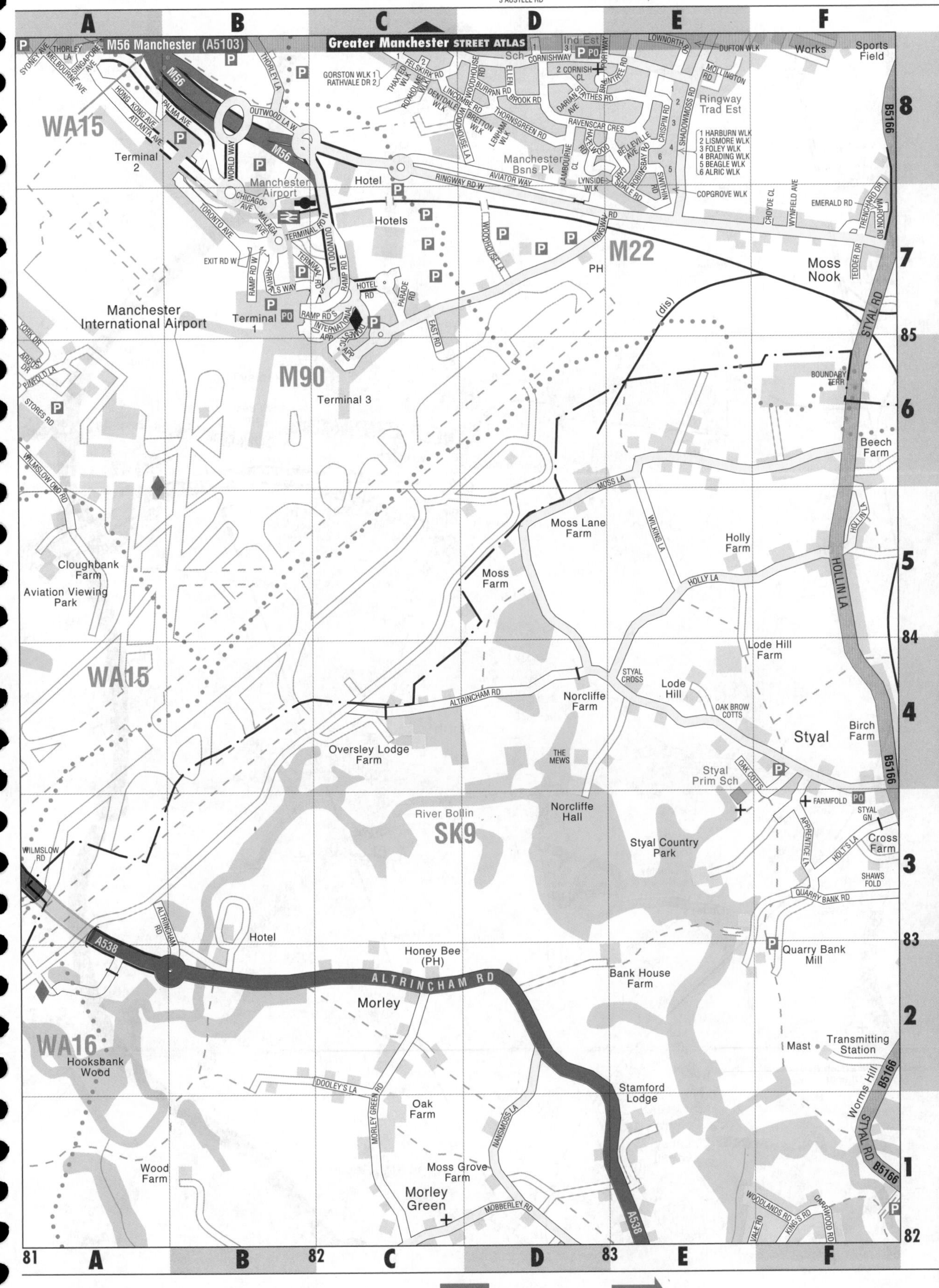

59

34

33

D5
1 TARVIN WAY
2 OVERTON WAY
3 STRETTON WAY
4 BIRTLES WAY
5 PEACOCK WAY
6 KELSALL WAY

D5
7 CUDDINGTON WAY
8 WILLASTON WAY
9 NORBURY WAY
10 PICKMERE CT
11 EASTHAM WAY
12 UPTON WAY

D5
13 ASTON WAY
14 HOOTON WAY
15 CHRISTLETON WAY
16 CRANAGE WAY
E5
1 SUTTON WAY
2 JUBILEE CT
3 SOMERFORD WAY
4 TATTON CT
5 MARTON WAY
6 NANTWICH WAY
7 HASSALL WAY
8 MARTHALL WAY

D1
1 MILLBROOK GR
2 REDBROOK GR
3 SHELLBROOK GR
4 WADEBROOK GR
5 DINGLEBROOK GR
6 LIME WLK
7 CROWBROOK GR
8 VILLAGE CT
9 DEAN ROW CT

D1
10 Summerfields Ctr
11 VILLAGE WAY
12 DRAYTON CL
13 KNIGHTSBRIDGE CL
14 KINGSBURY DR
15 QUEENSBURY CL
16 WESTBOURNE DR

D2
1 TORBROOK GR
2 CLIFFBROOK GR
3 BENSON WLK
4 CARDENBROOK GR
5 TIMBERSBROOK GR
6 LADYBROOK GR
7 FODEN WLK
8 TAME WLK
9 DE TRAFFORD MEWS

D4
1 HILLBRE WAY
2 SEALAND WAY
3 ECCLESTON WAY
4 HELSBY WAY
5 HEATLEY WAY
6 ELWORTH WAY
7 PARKGATE WAY

E1
1 BUDWORTH WLK
2 EDLESTONE GR
3 WOODCOTT GR
4 KETTLESHULME WLK
5 TILSTON WLK
6 SNAPEBROOK GR
7 DAIRYBROOK GR
8 APPLETON WLK
9 MOORSBROOK GR
10 RAINOW WAY
11 PECKFORTON WLK
12 SALTERSBROOK GR
13 PINWOOD CT
14 KINGSTON CT
15 MELROSE CT
16 SEYMOUR HO
17 HAZELDEAN CT

33

60

36

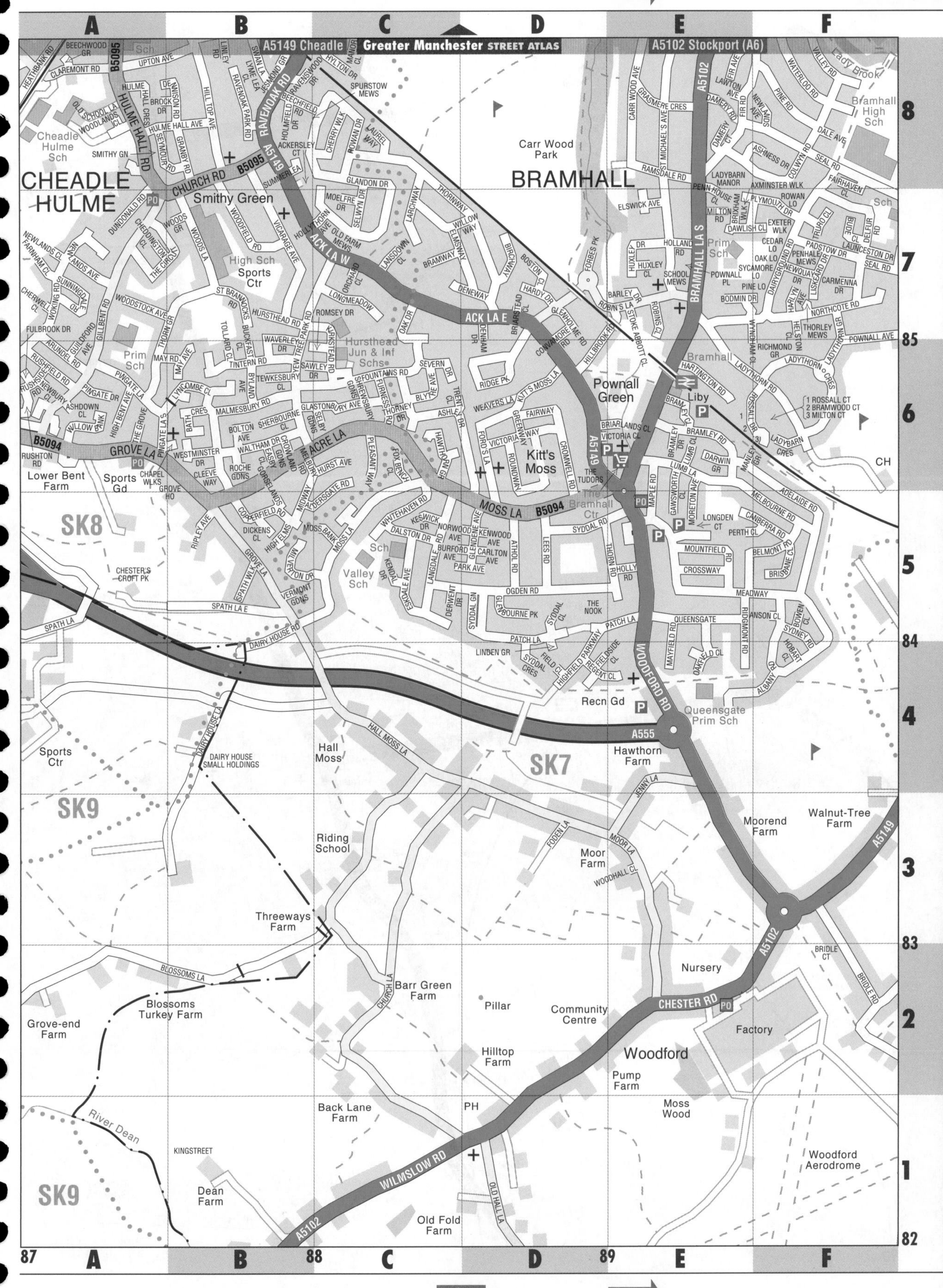

A5149 Cheadle
Greater Manchester STREET ATLAS
A5102 Stockport (A6)
A
B
C
D
E
F
8
7
85
6
5
84
4
3
83
2
1
82
87
88
89
CHEADLE HULME
Cheadle Hulme Sch
Smithy Green
High Sch
Sports Ctr
Prim Sch
Lower Bent Farm
Sports Gd
SK8
CHESTER'S CROFT PK
Hursthead Jun & Inf Schs
Valley Sch
Carr Wood Park
BRAMHALL
Bramhall High Sch
Prim Sch
Bramhall
Pownall Green
Liby
Kitt's Moss
The Bramhall Ctr
THE TUDORS
THE NOOK
Recn Gd
Queensgate Prim Sch
Hawthorn Farm
Hall Moss
SK7
Sports Ctr
SK9
DAIRY HOUSE SMALL HOLDINGS
Riding School
Moor Farm
Moorend Farm
Walnut-Tree Farm
Threeways Farm
Nursery
Barr Green Farm
Pillar
Community Centre
Blossoms Turkey Farm
Grove-end Farm
Factory
Woodford
Hilltop Farm
Pump Farm
Moss Wood
Back Lane Farm
PH
River Dean
KINGSTREET
Dean Farm
Old Fold Farm
Woodford Aerodrome
SK9
CH
A5149
A5102
A555
B5095
B5094
HULME HALL RD
CHURCH RD
RAVENOAK RD
ACK LANE W
ACK LA E
GROVE LA
ACRE LA
MOSS LA
BRAMHALL LA S
WOODFORD RD
CHESTER RD
WILMSLOW RD
HALL MOSS LA
DAIRY HOUSE RD
DAIRY HOUSE LA
SPATH LA E
SPATH LA
MOOR LA
JENNY LA
FODEN LA
WOODHALL CL
CHURCH LA
BLOSSOMS LA
OLD HALL LA
BRIDLE RD
BRIDLE CT
1 ROSSALL CT
2 BRAMWOOD CT
3 MILTON CT

61
36

35

Greater Manchester STREET ATLAS
A5143 Stockport (A5102/A6)
A523 Manchester (A6)
A
B
C
D
E
F
8
7
85
6
5
84
4
3
83
2
1
82
90
91
92
Wall Bank Farm
Dingle Farm
Hazel Grove High Sch
Lady Brook
A5143
JACKSON'S LA
Norbury Farm
Denbigh Farm
DEAN LA
A5143
FIVEWAYS PAR
PO
MACCLESFIELD RD
A523
30
CHARNWOOD CRES
TIDESWELL RD
CAVENDISH RD
LAVENHAM CL
ROWLEY RD
BAKEWELL RD
DEVONSHIRE RD
CHATSWORTH RD
PEVERIL DR
CAPESTHORNE RD
ALDERLEY CL
MILL LA
ASHBOURNE RD
DARLEY RD
CHESTER RD
WINSFIELD RD
MATLOCK DR
SUDBURY RD
LONGNOR RD
WENSLEY DR
MALTON DR
BELVOIR AVE
Further Dairyground
SK7
NEVIN CL
WARTON CL
AINSDALE CL
TROON CL
SEAL RD
CAMBERLEY CL
HILLSIDE CL
WENTWORTH DR
1 BIRKDALE CL
2 PRINCESS WLK
3 CHEVIN GDNS
POWNALL AVE
Dairyground
Norbury Hall
Millhill Bridge
Norbury Brook
Brookside Miniature Rly
Towers Farm
MILL HILL AVE
MILL HILL HOLLOW
Barlowfold
Serpentine Wood
Mill Hill Farm
LOWER PARK CRES
ANGLESEY WATER
REDACRE
ANGLESEY DR
PADDOCK CHASE
LONDON RD N
P
Birch Hall
Hill Green Farm
WOODFORD RD
Park House Farm
Poynton Lake
Poynton Park
SK12
TOWERS CL
TOWERS RD
Phillip's Bridge
GLASTONBURY DR
DUNDRENNAN CL
LOWER PARK RD
Lower Park Lodge
ABBOTSBURY CL
NEWSTEAD CL
TINTERN CL
VICARAGE LA
SOUTH PARK DR
LAKESIDE DR
WATERS REACH
WARREN LEA
MILLSTONE CL
TOWERS YARD BARNS
Distaff Farm
SOUTH MEAD
MEADWAY
DISTAFF RD
WARREN CL
MERTON RD
Lower Park Prim Sch
WHITBY CL
FURNESS CL
BOLTON CL
OAKLAND CT
MILTON DR
MALMESBURY CL
KIRKSTALL CL
LAMBOURN CL
WOODSIDE LA
CAPENHURST CL
HOLKER CL
SULGRAVE AVE
WOODSIDE
HIGHFIELD RD
DEVA CL
CHESTER RD
Poynton
SILK MILL
SPINNERS LA
WAYSIDE DR
HAZELBADGE RD
HAZELBADGE CL
ORCHARD PL
OAK GR
FOUNTAIN PL
BURTON DR
PARK AVE
Liby
PARK VIEW CT
TH
OAKFIELD RD
HARDWICKE RD
BLENHEIM CL
A5149
A5149
WEST PARK AVE
ROCHARD DR
MALLARD CRES
TERN DR
BRENT CL
GREBE CL
LOSTOCK AVE
WIGWAM CL
WOODFORD LODGE
ASH LODGE
FOUNTAIN CL
PARKLANDS WAY
SOMERFORD HO
SCHOOL CL
PARK LA
HOCKLEY PADDOCK
WOBURN
DUNLIN CL
BITTERN CL
PUFFIN AVE
SWAN CL
GILL CL
HERON DR
LOSTOCK HALL RD
Wigwam Wood
GLOUCESTER RD
BUCKINGHAM RD
ABBEY CT
GEORGE'S RD W
GEORGE'S RD E
GRANARY MEWS
VENTURE WAY
Lostock Hall Prim Sch
Nursery
BROOKFIELD AVE
CLIFFORD RD
QUEENSWAY
Schs
MAPLE AVE
BROOKSIDE AVE
ALDER AVE
LARCH CL
CHESTNUT DR
Poynton Brook
GROSVENOR DR
ARLINGTON DR
LONDON RD S
PICKWICK RD
STYPERSON WAY
CLUMBER RD
CLUMBER CL
HOLLY RD
IVY RD
FIR CL
YEW TREE LA
CHERRY TREE AVE
ELM CL
PINE RD
Worth Prim Sch
BIRCH RD
Lostockhall Farm
Upper Swineseye Farm
BRIDLE WAY
VARDEN RD
MARLEY RD
BARDELL CL
COPPERFIELDS
DOMBEY RD
ADAMS CL
BAGSTOCK AVE
DICKENS LA
L Ctr
Poynton High Sch
ADLINGTON CL
GAWSWORTH CL
WORTH CT
LOSTOCK RD
WELLER AVE
Sch
CURZON RD
BROWNLOW CL
WINCLE AVE
ALDERLEY CL
SK7
MICAWBER RD
FIELDING AVE
BARCLAY RD
DORRIT CL
GRAYMARSH DR
SPRING RD
COPPICE HO
VERNON RD
Sprink Farm
BRIDLE RD
HOPE GREEN WAY
Midway
THIRD AVE
SPENLOW CL
FIRST AVE
Woodford Aerodrome
Shirdfold Farm
SK10
Adlington Est
Hope Green
ADLINGTON PK
SECOND AVE
Poynton Ind Est
Works
HOPE LA
LONDON RD
A523
SK10
Clayton Greaves Farm
HOPE LA
Brookside Farm
SKELLORN GREEN LA
WOOD LA W
MOGGIE LA

35
62

38

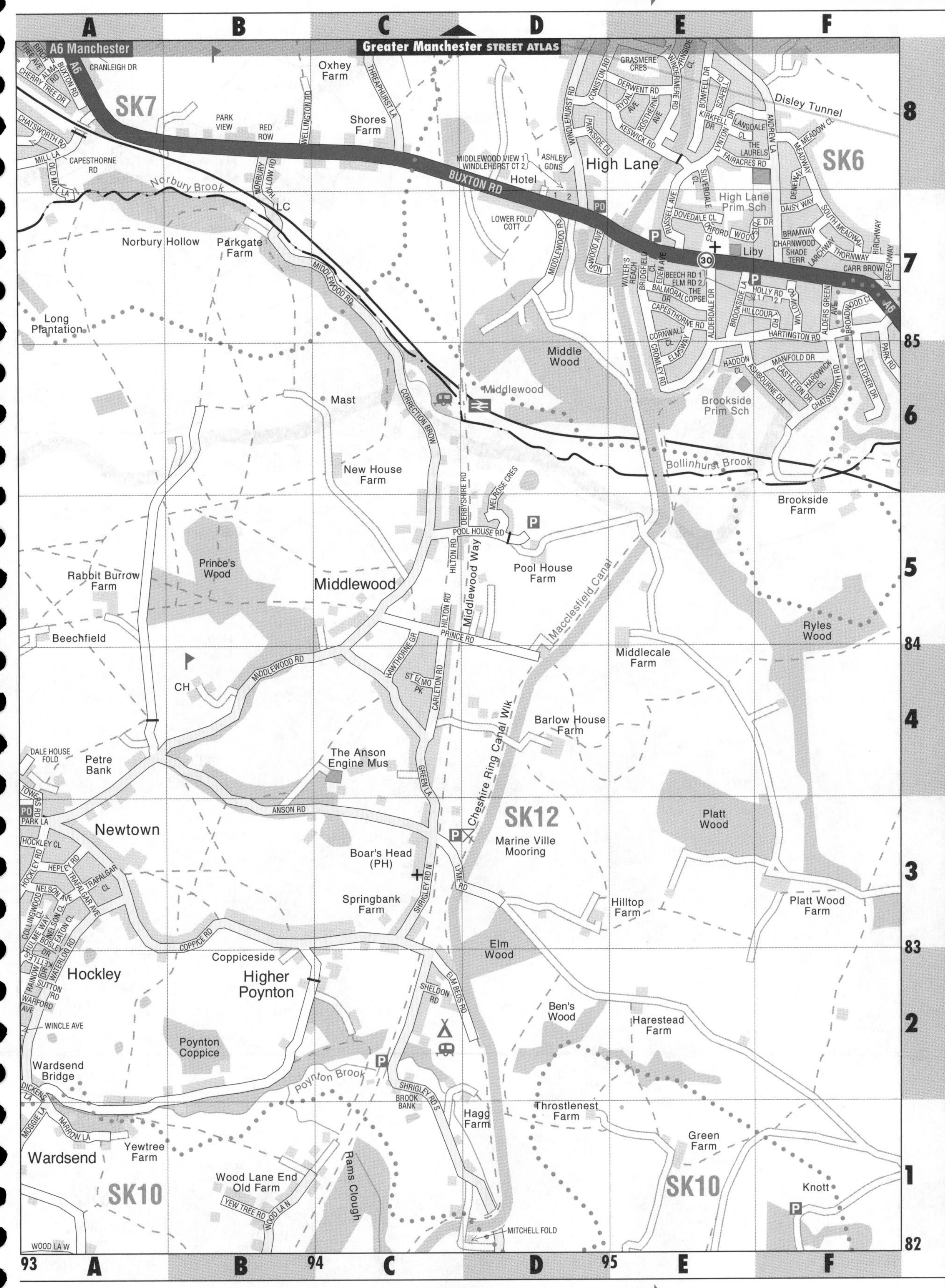
A6 Manchester
Greater Manchester STREET ATLAS
SK7
SK6
SK12
SK10
Oxhey Farm
Shores Farm
Park View
Red Row
Norbury Brook
Norbury Hollow
Parkgate Farm
Long Plantation
Mast
New House Farm
Middlewood
Rabbit Burrow Farm
Prince's Wood
Beechfield
CH
Petre Bank
Newtown
Hockley
Higher Poynton
Coppiceside
Poynton Coppice
Wardsend Bridge
Poynton Brook
Wardsend
Yewtree Farm
Wood Lane End Old Farm
Rams Clough
Hagg Farm
Throstlenest Farm
Green Farm
Knott
Ben's Wood
Harestead Farm
Elm Wood
Springbank Farm
Boar's Head (PH)
The Anson Engine Mus
Marine Ville Mooring
Cheshire Ring Canal Wlk
Macclesfield Canal
Middlewood Way
Pool House Farm
Barlow House Farm
Middlecale Farm
Hilltop Farm
Platt Wood
Platt Wood Farm
Ryles Wood
Brookside Farm
Bollinhurst Brook
Middle Wood
Brookside Prim Sch
High Lane
High Lane Prim Sch
Liby
Hotel
Disley Tunnel
BUXTON RD
MIDDLEWOOD RD
CORRECTION BROW
POOL HOUSE RD
PRINCE RD
ANSON RD
COPPICE RD
SHRIGLEY RD N
SHRIGLEY RD S
LYME RD
GREEN LA
HILTON RD
CARLETON RD
HAWTHORNE GR
DERBYSHIRE RD
MELROSE CRES
ELM BEDS RD
SHELDON RD
BROOK BANK
MITCHELL FOLD
NARROW LA
MOGGIE LA
DICKENS LA
YEW TREE RD
WOOD LA N
WOOD LA W
WINCLE AVE
DALE HOUSE FOLD
TOWERS RD
PARK LA
HOCKLEY CL
HEPLEY RD
TRAFALGAR CL
TRAFALGAR AVE
WATERLOO RD
CRANLEIGH DR
CHATSWORTH RD
MILL LA
OLD MILL LA
CAPESTHORNE RD
BUXTON RD
CHERRY TREE DR
LOWER FOLD COTT
ASHLEY GDNS
MIDDLEWOOD VIEW 1
WINDLEHURST CT 2
WINDLEHURST RD
CONISTON RD
PARKSIDE CL
GRASMERE CRES
DERWENT RD
RYDAL AVE
ROSTHERNE AVE
KESWICK RD
WINDERMERE RD
BOWFELL DR
SCAFELL CL
KIRKFELL DR
LYNTON DR
LANGDALE CL
THE LAURELS
FAIRACRES RD
ANDREW LA
MEADOWAY
MEADOW CL
DENEWAY
DAISY WAY
SOUTH MEADWAY
BRAMWAY
CHARNWOOD
SHADE TERR
LARCHWAY
THORNWAY
BIRCHWAY
BEECHWAY
CARR BROW
RUSSELL AVE
SILVERDALE CL
DOVEDALE CL
OXFORD
WATER'S REACH
BRIDGEFIELD CL
EDEN AVE
BEECH RD 1
ELM RD 2
BALMORAL CL
THE COPSE
CAPESTHORNE RD
CORNWALL CL
CROMLEY RD
ELMSWAY
ALDERDALE DR
BROOKSIDE LA
HOLLY RD
HILLCOURT RD
HARTINGTON RD
ALDERS GREEN AVE
HADDON CL
ASHBOURNE DR
MANFOLD DR
CASTLETON DR
HARDWICK CL
CHATSWORTH RD
FLETCHER DR
PARK RD
NORWOOD AVE
MIDDLEWOOD RD
LC
ST ELMO PK
A6
30
93
94
95
A
B
C
D
E
F
1
2
3
4
5
6
7
8
82
83
84
85

63

38

37

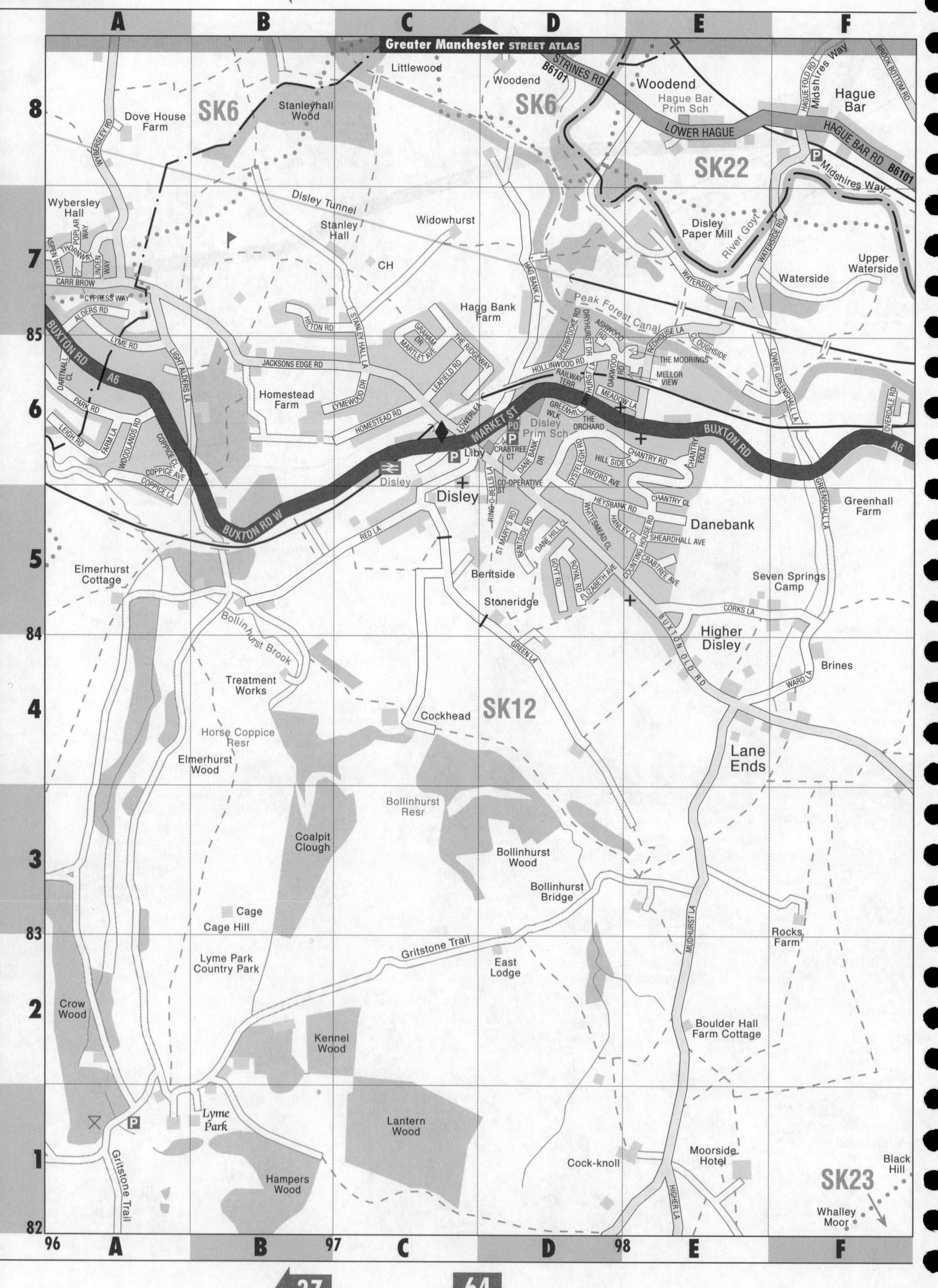

Greater Manchester STREET ATLAS
A
B
C
D
E
F
Littlewood
Woodend
Woodend
Hague Bar Prim Sch
Hague Bar
Dove House Farm
SK6
Stanleyhall Wood
SK6
SK22
STRINES RD
B6101
LOWER HAGUE
HAGUE BAR RD
B6101
Midshires Way
HAGUE FOLD RD
BROOK BOTTOM RD
Disley Tunnel
Wybersley Hall
WYBERSLEY RD
Stanley Hall
Widowhurst
Disley Paper Mill
River Goyt
Upper Waterside
Waterside
CH
ASPEN WAY
THORNWAY
POPLAR WAY
LINDEN WAY
CARR BROW
CYPRESS WAY
ALDERS RD
HILTON RD
STANLEY HALL LA
Hagg Bank Farm
HAG BANK LA
WATERSIDE
Peak Forest Canal
BUXTON RD
A6
LYME RD
GRAHAM DR
MARTLEY AVE
THE RIDGEWAY
SHERBROOKE RD
DRYHURST DR
ASHWOOD RD
REDHOUSE LA
CLOUGHSIDE
LOWER GREENSHALL LA
JACKSONS EDGE RD
LEAFIELD RD
HOLLINWOOD RD
RAILWAY TERR
OAKWOOD RD
THE MOORINGS
MELLOR VIEW
DARTNALL CL
LIGHT ALDERS LA
Homestead Farm
LYMEWOOD DR
LOWERLEA
MEADOW LA
OVERDALE RD
PARK RD
HOMESTEAD RD
MARKET ST
PO
GREENHILL WLK
DRYHURST LA
THE ORCHARD
LEIGH RD
FARM LA
WOODLANDS RD
COPPICE CL
Disley Prim Sch
Liby
CRABTREE CT
DANE BANK DR
DYSTELEGH RD
HILL SIDE CL
CHANTRY RD
CHANTRY FOLD
BUXTON RD
A6
COPPICE AVE
COPPICE LA
Disley
Disley
RING-O-BELLS LA
CO-OPERATIVE ST
ORFORD AVE
CHANTRY CL
Greenhall Farm
HEYSBANK RD
GREENSHALL LA
BUXTON RD W
RED LA
ST MARY'S RD
BENTSIDE RD
DANE HILL CL
WHITESMEAD CL
HANLEY CL
COUNTING HOUSE RD
SHEARDHALL AVE
Danebank
CRABTREE AVE
Elmerhurst Cottage
Bentside
GOYT RD
ROYAL RD
ELIZABETH AVE
Seven Springs Camp
Stoneridge
CORKS LA
Bollinhurst Brook
GREEN LA
BUXTON OLD RD
Higher Disley
Brines
Treatment Works
WARD LA
Cockhead
SK12
Horse Coppice Resr
Lane Ends
Elmerhurst Wood
Bollinhurst Resr
Coalpit Clough
Bollinhurst Wood
Bollinhurst Bridge
Cage
Cage Hill
Rocks Farm
Gritstone Trail
MUDHURST LA
East Lodge
Lyme Park Country Park
Crow Wood
Kennel Wood
Boulder Hall Farm Cottage
Lyme Park
Lantern Wood
P
Gritstone Trail
Cock-knoll
Moorside Hotel
Black Hill
SK23
Hampers Wood
HIGHER LA
Whalley Moor
8
7
85
6
5
84
4
3
83
2
1
82
96
97
98

37
64

C7
1 FOUNDRY CT
2 LOWER ROCK ST
3 BACK UNION RD
4 LEES MILL

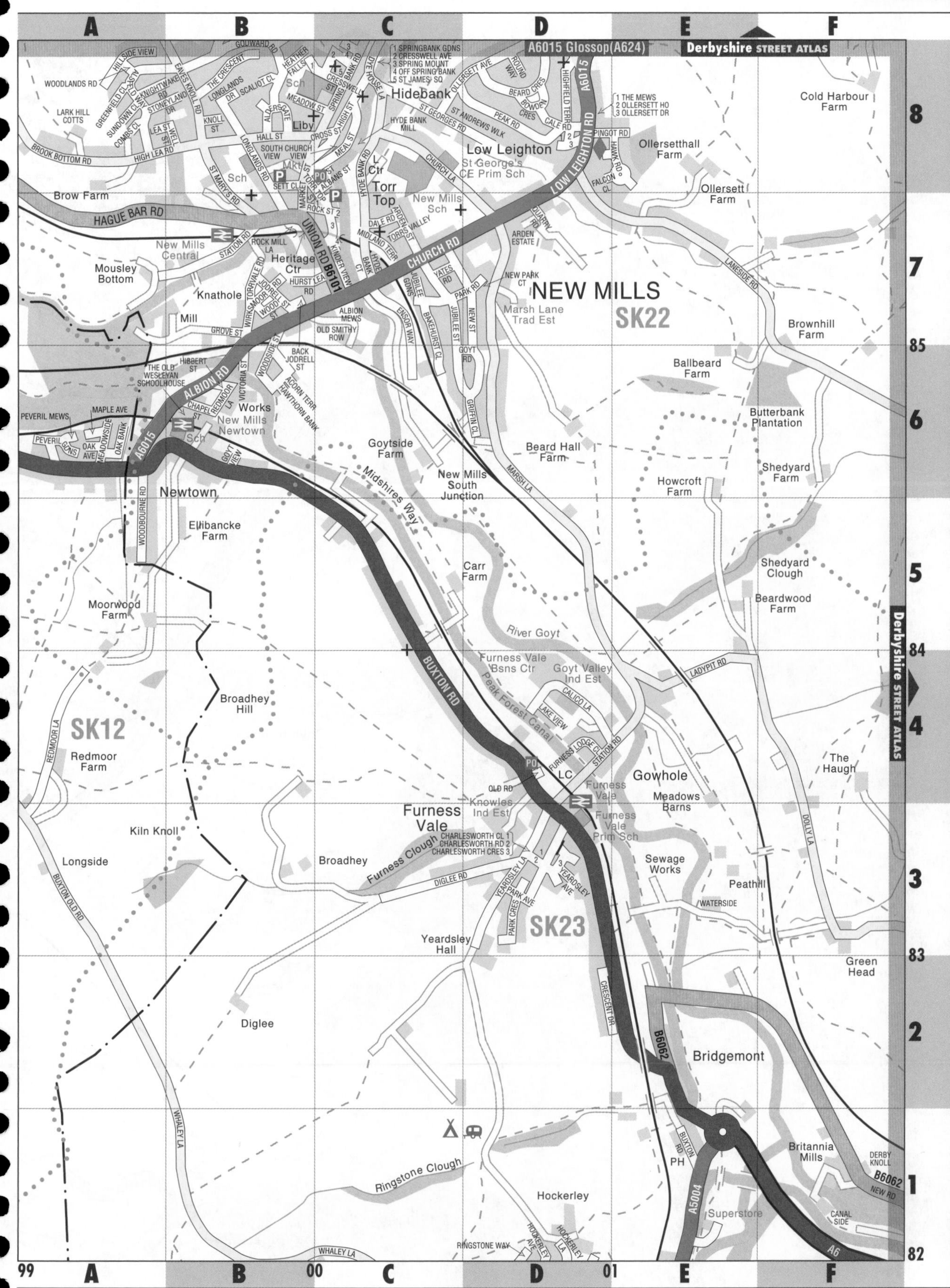

F8
1 STONEWAY CT
2 MAY RD
3 MOUNT CT
4 PYE RD

A8
1 DOWNHAM CT
2 BIRCHES HO
3 CHERRY TREE MEWS
4 BEACON CT
5 THE CHASE
6 YEW TREE CT
7 HESWALL POINT

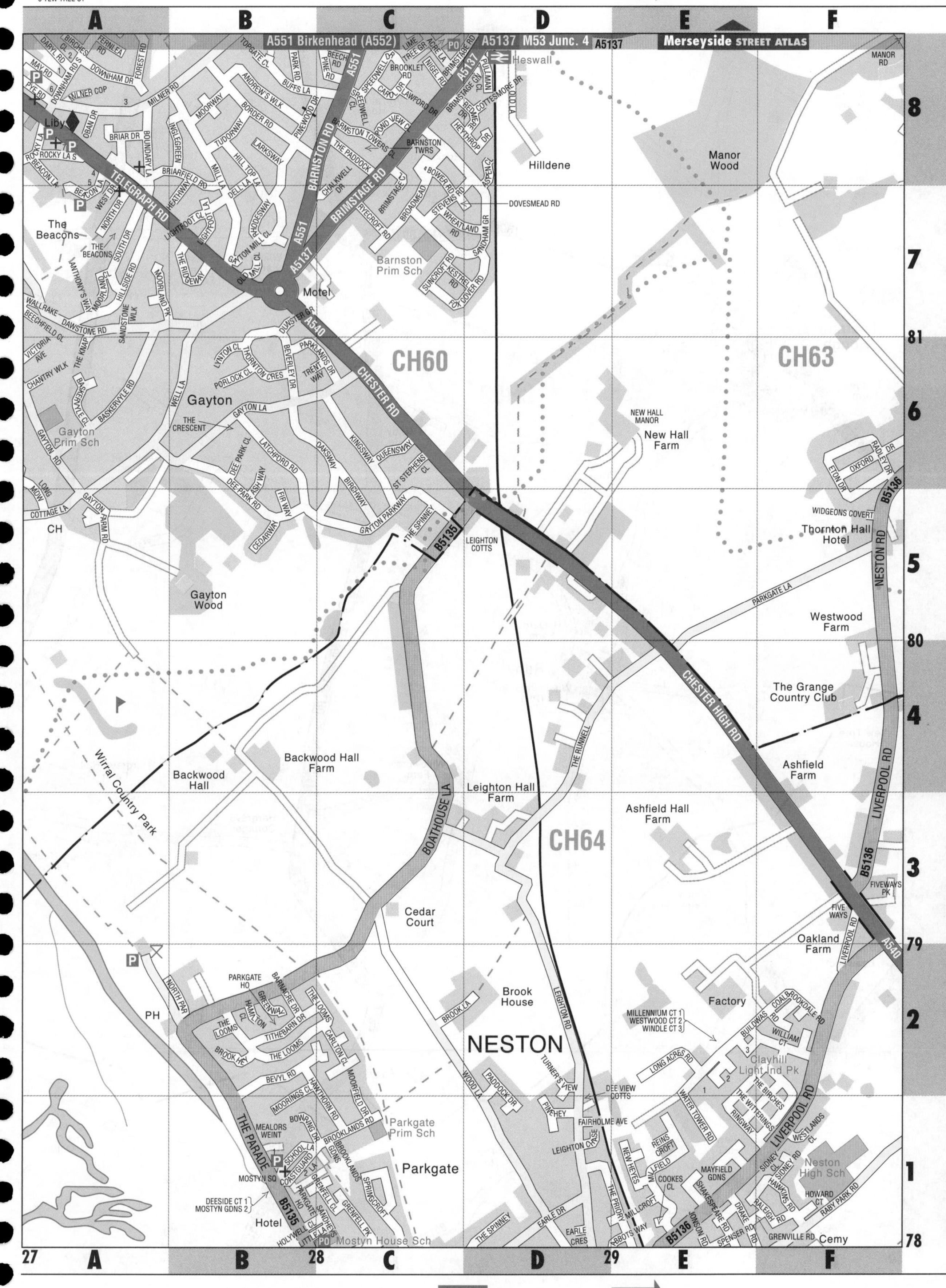

41

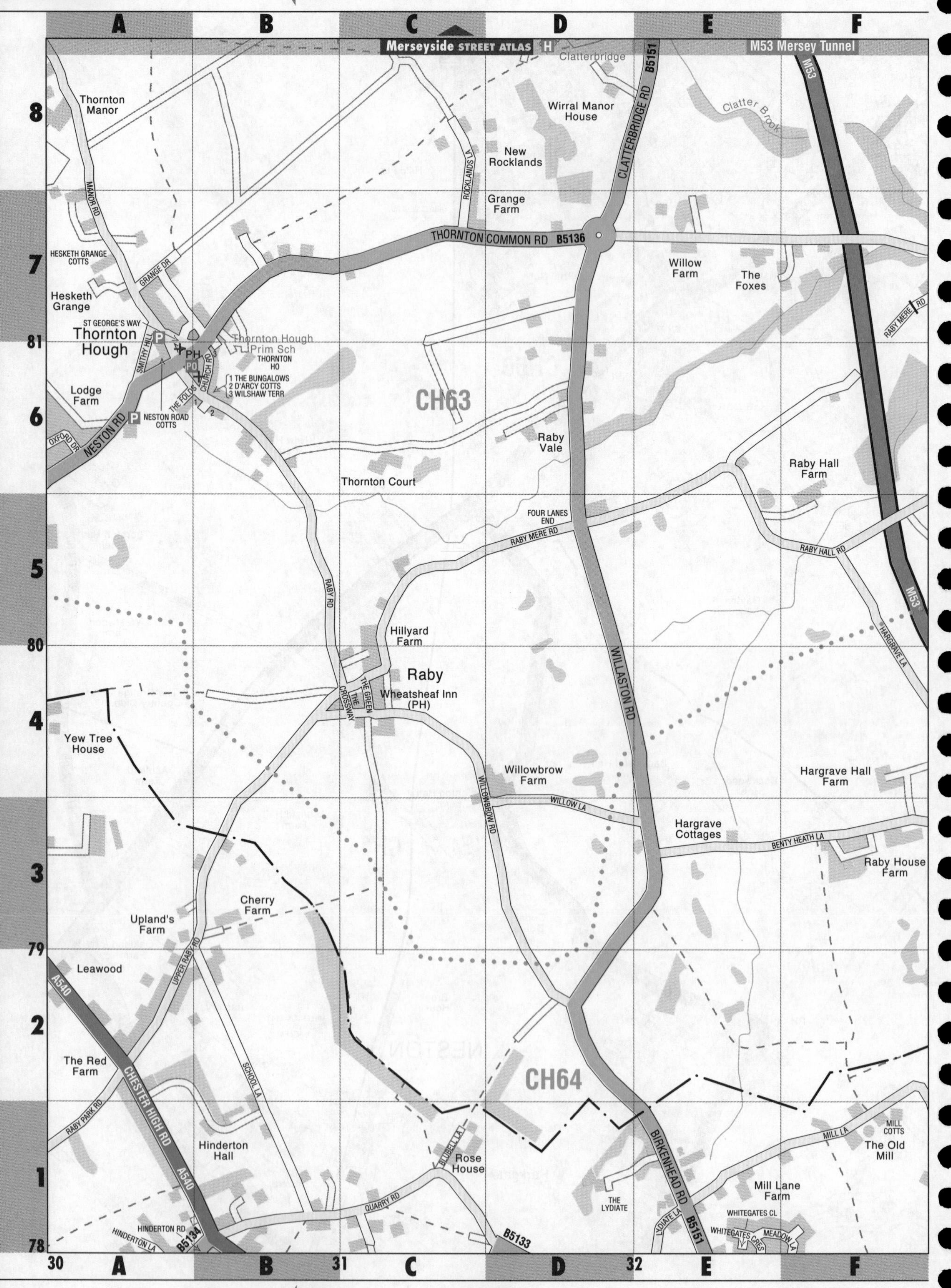

A
B
C
D
E
F
Merseyside STREET ATLAS
M53 Mersey Tunnel
Clatterbridge
Thornton Manor
Wirral Manor House
Clatter Brook
M53
New Rocklands
ROCKLANDS LA
CLATTERBRIDGE RD
B5151
Grange Farm
MANOR RD
THORNTON COMMON RD
B5136
HESKETH GRANGE COTTS
GRANGE DR
Willow Farm
The Foxes
Hesketh Grange
ST GEORGE'S WAY
RABY MERE RD
Thornton Hough
Thornton Hough Prim Sch
THORNTON HO
SMITHY HILL
CHURCH RD
1 THE BUNGALOWS
2 D'ARCY COTTS
3 WILSHAW TERR
THE FOLDS
Lodge Farm
CH63
NESTON ROAD COTTS
NESTON RD
OXFORD DR
Raby Vale
Raby Hall Farm
Thornton Court
FOUR LANES END
RABY MERE RD
RABY HALL RD
RABY RD
M53
HARGRAVE LA
Hillyard Farm
Raby
THE GREEN
THE CROSSWAY
Wheatsheaf Inn (PH)
WILLASTON RD
Yew Tree House
Willowbrow Farm
Hargrave Hall Farm
WILLOWBROW RD
WILLOW LA
Hargrave Cottages
BENTY HEATH LA
Raby House Farm
Cherry Farm
Upland's Farm
UPPER RABY RD
Leawood
A540
NESTON
CH64
The Red Farm
CHESTER HIGH RD
SCHOOL LA
RABY PARK RD
Hinderton Hall
BLUEBELL LA
Rose House
MILL LA
MILL COTTS
The Old Mill
Mill Lane Farm
THE LYDIATE
BIRKENHEAD RD
QUARRY RD
WHITEGATES CL
LYDIATE LA
B5151
WHITEGATES CRES
MEADOW LA
HINDERTON RD
HINDERTON LA
B5134
B5133
8
7
81
6
5
80
4
3
79
2
1
78
30
31
32

41
67

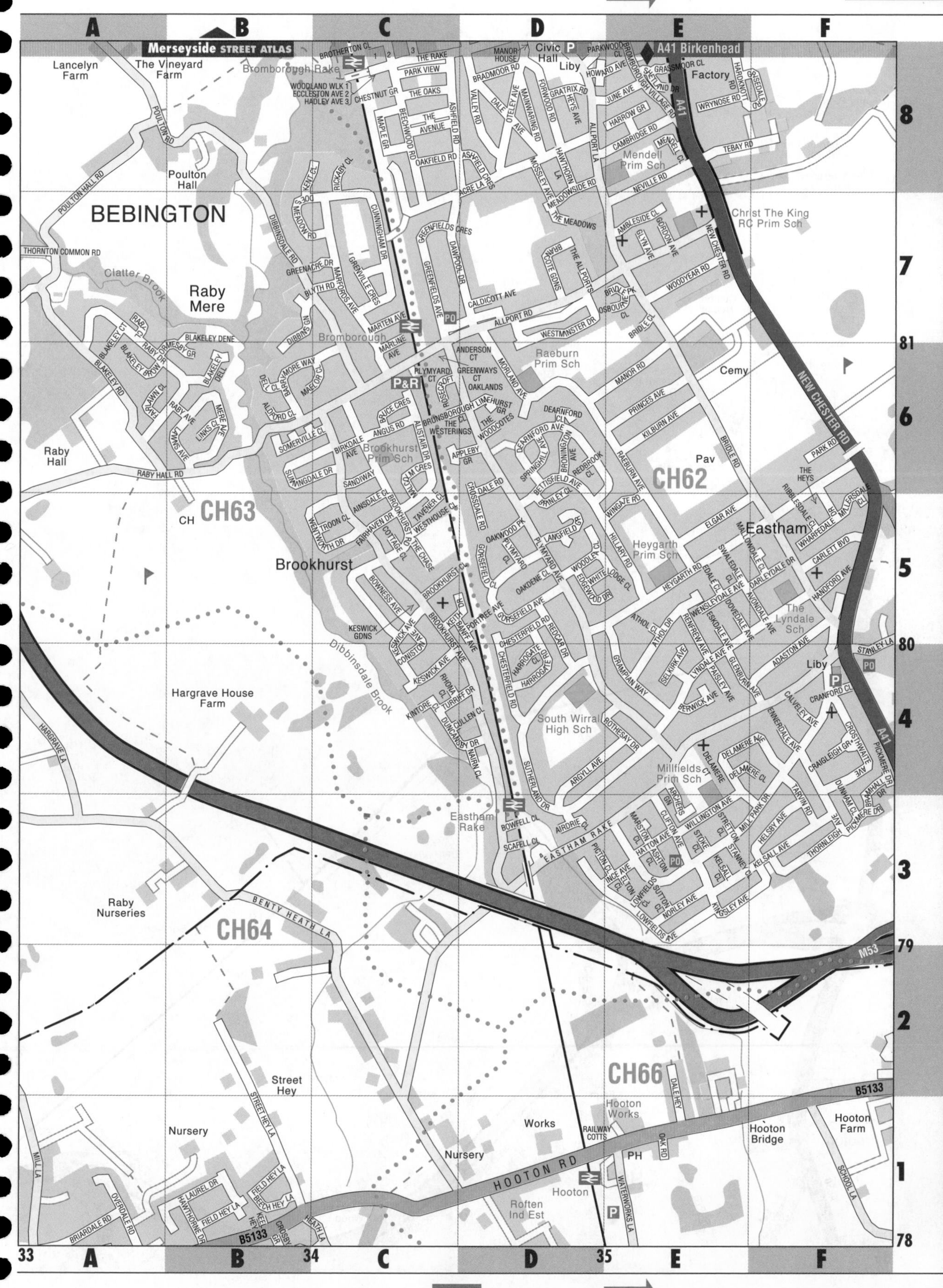

Merseyside STREET ATLAS
A41 Birkenhead
BEBINGTON
Raby Mere
Bromborough
Brookhurst
Eastham
Eastham Rake
Hooton
CH62
CH63
CH64
CH66
Poulton Hall
Lancelyn Farm
The Vineyard Farm
Raby Hall
Hargrave House Farm
Raby Nurseries
Street Hey
Nursery
Works
Hooton Works
Hooton Bridge
Hooton Farm
Roften Ind Est
South Wirral High Sch
Millfields Prim Sch
Brookhurst Prim Sch
Raeburn Prim Sch
Heygarth Prim Sch
Mendell Prim Sch
Christ The King RC Prim Sch
The Lyndale Sch
Civic Hall
Factory
Cemy
Pav
Liby
NEW CHESTER RD
HOOTON RD
BENTY HEATH LA
RABY HALL RD
EASTHAM RAKE
M53
A41
B5133

44
68
44

43

Merseyside STREET ATLAS
A
B
C
D
E
F
Eastham Country Park
Visitor Ctr
Eastham Ferry
Eastham Ferry Hotel
The Warrens Farm
River Mersey
LOCK RD
Wirral Metropolitan Coll
WOOD HEATH WAY
Custom House
Eastham Locks
CHAPEL VIEW
CH
FERRY RD
Queen Elizabeth II Dock
MAYFIELD DR
SEAVIEW AVE
CH62
ST DAVID RD
ST JOHN'S RD
CHRISTOPHER DR
Tanks
B5132
EASTHAM VILLAGE RD
Oil Storage Depot
BANKFIELDS DR
VICARAGE ROW
CHURCH LA
HALL FARM
EASTHAM HO
EASTHAM MEWS
Manchester Ship Canal
LC
Hooton Park
ERIC FOUNTAIN RD
David's Rough
CH65
A41
MERTON RD
DUDLEY CRES
NORTH RD
Booston Wood
RIVACRE RD
NEW CHESTER RD
Kennel Wood
REDVERS AVE
VERNON AVE
HOOTON WAY
HOOTON RD
B5133
HOOTON GN
CHRISTIE CL
CONISTON CL
DERWENT DR
GRANGE CRES
Park Farm
Motor Vehicle Works
HOOTON LA
Hooton
WOODCLOSE
CH66
NEW SCHOOL LA
A550
WELSH RD
CHESTER RD
M53
Rivacre Wood
SCHOOL LA
36
37
38
78
79
80
81

43

69

46

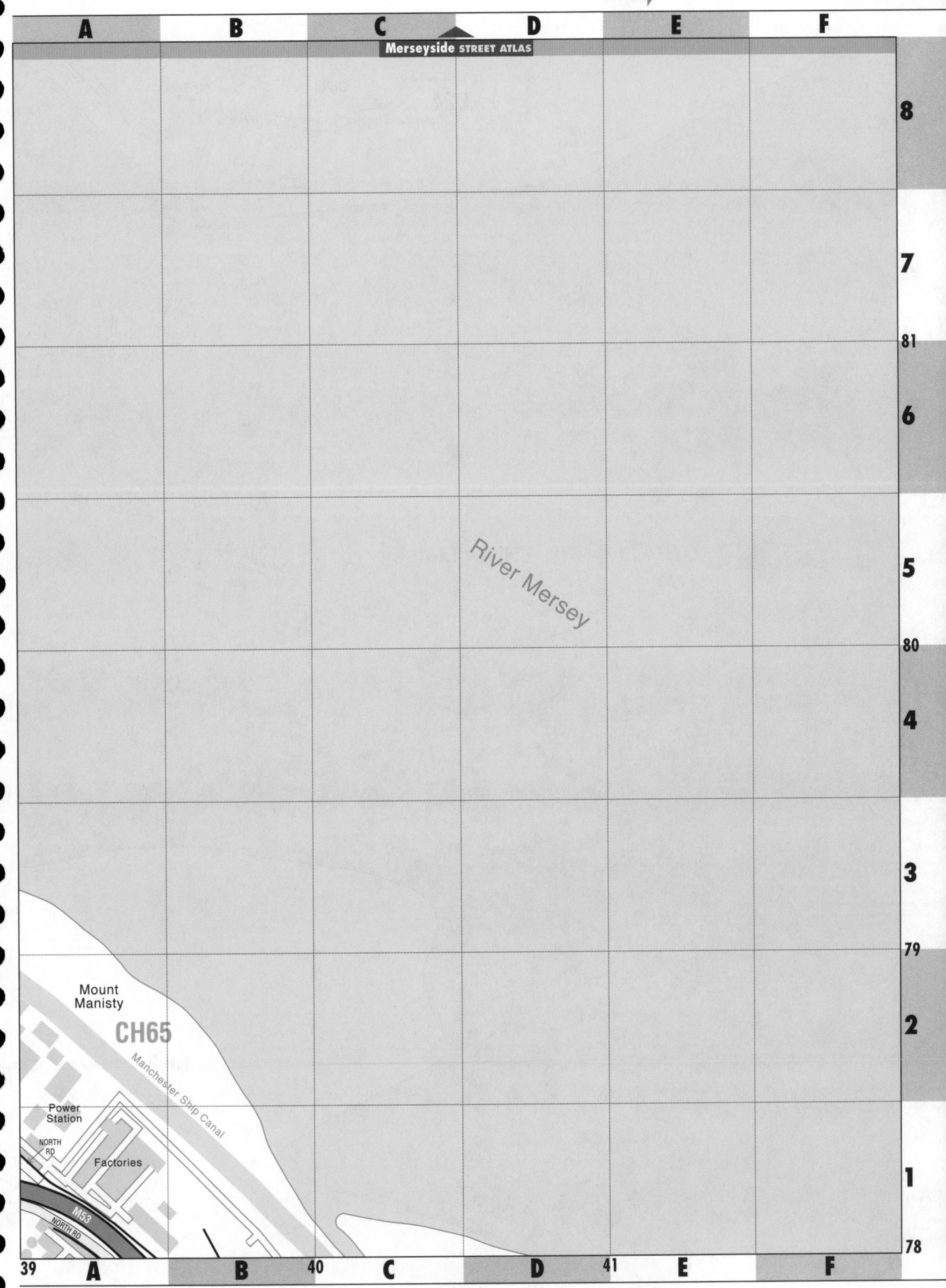

A
B
C
D
E
F
Merseyside STREET ATLAS
8
7
81
6
5
River Mersey
80
4
3
79
2
Mount Manisty
CH65
Manchester Ship Canal
Power Station
NORTH RD
Factories
M53
NORTH RD
1
78
39
40
41

70

46

45

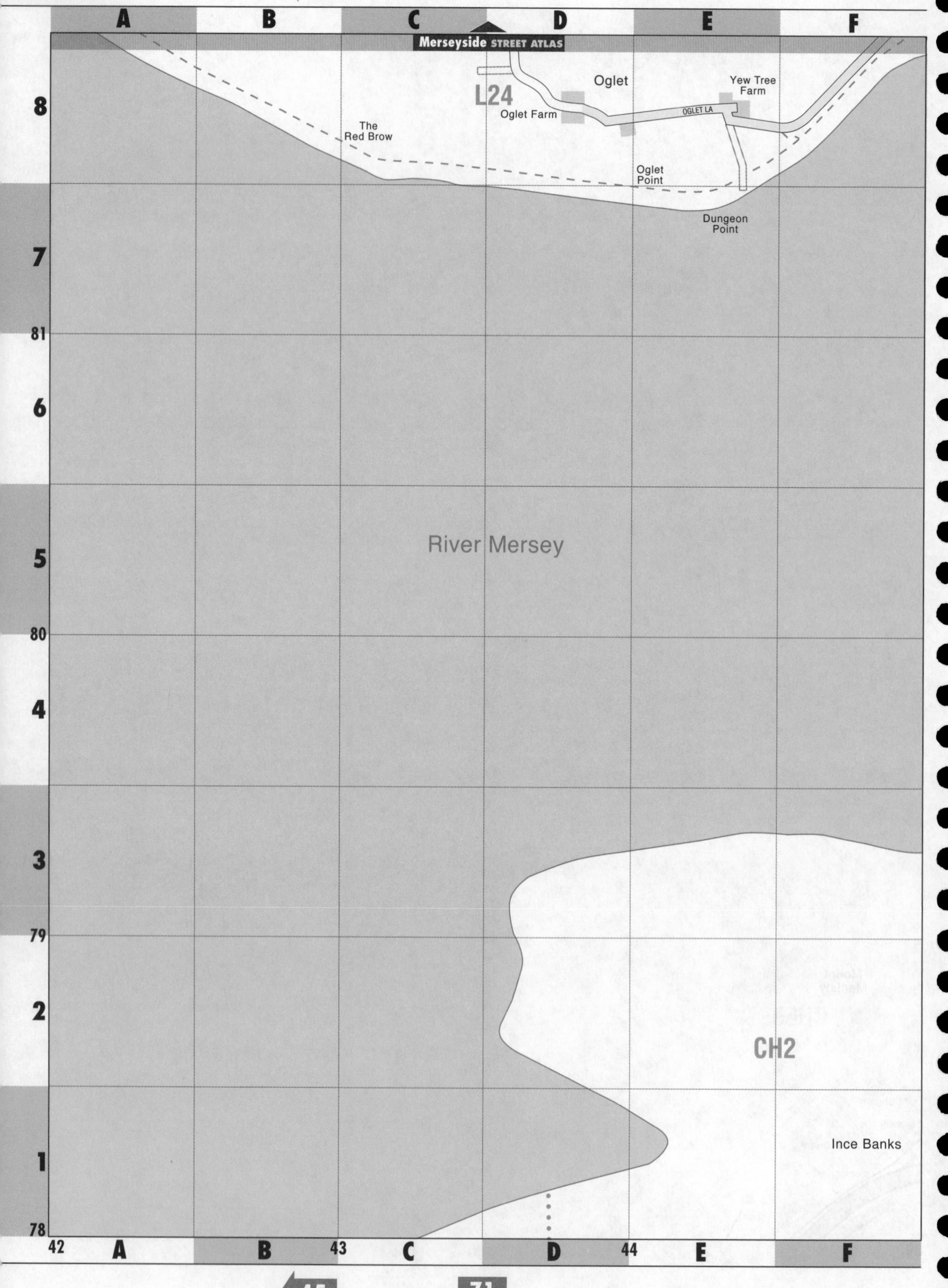
A
B
C
D
E
F
Merseyside STREET ATLAS
L24
Oglet
Yew Tree Farm
Oglet Farm
OGLET LA
The Red Brow
Oglet Point
Dungeon Point
8
7
81
6
River Mersey
5
80
4
3
79
2
CH2
1
Ince Banks
78
42
43
44

45
71

21
48

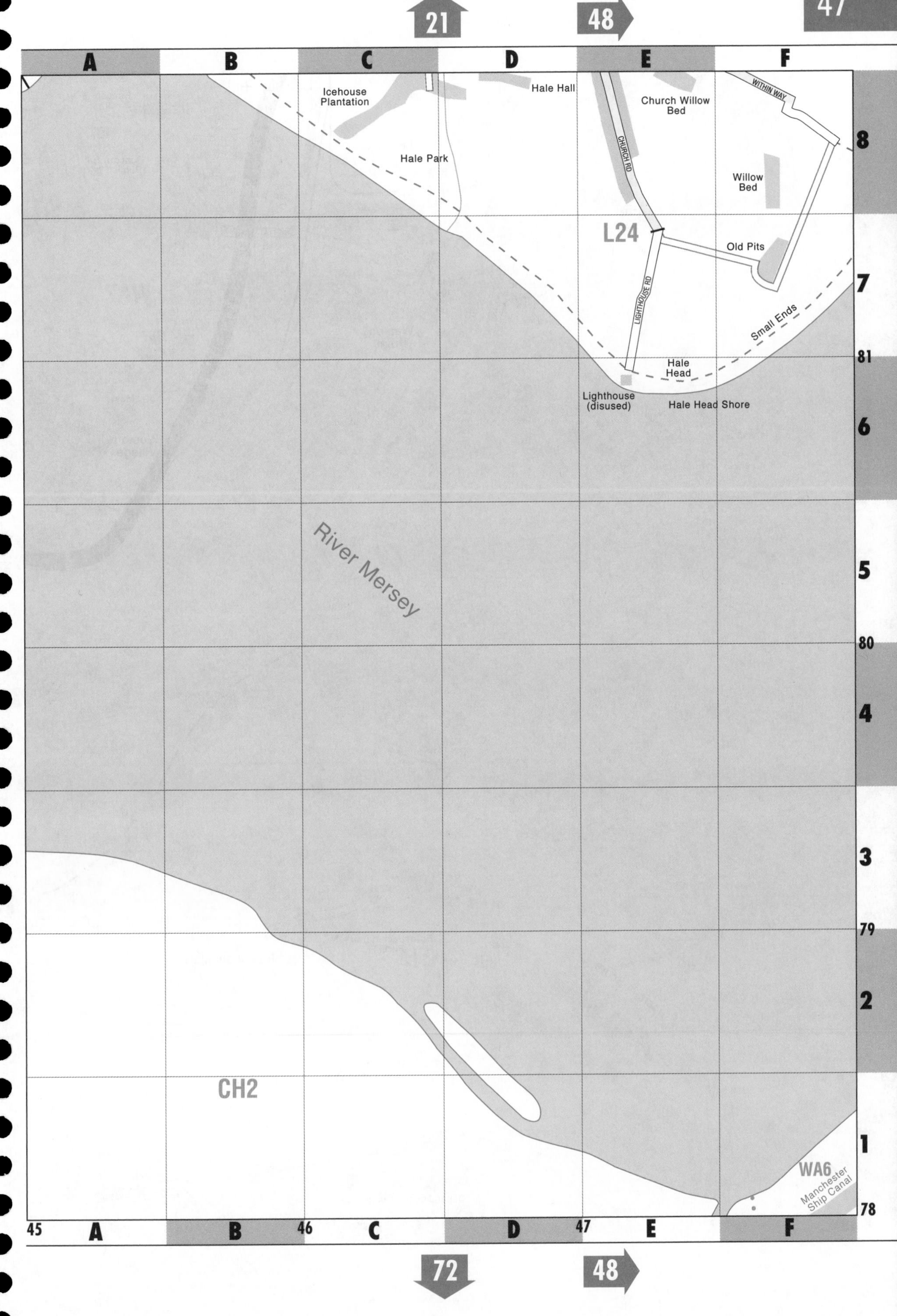
A
B
C
D
E
F
Icehouse Plantation
Hale Hall
Church Willow Bed
WITHIN WAY
8
CHURCH RD
Hale Park
Willow Bed
L24
Old Pits
7
LIGHTHOUSE RD
Small Ends
81
Hale Head
Lighthouse (disused)
Hale Head Shore
6
River Mersey
5
80
4
3
79
2
CH2
1
WA6
Manchester Ship Canal
78
45
46
47

72
48

47
22

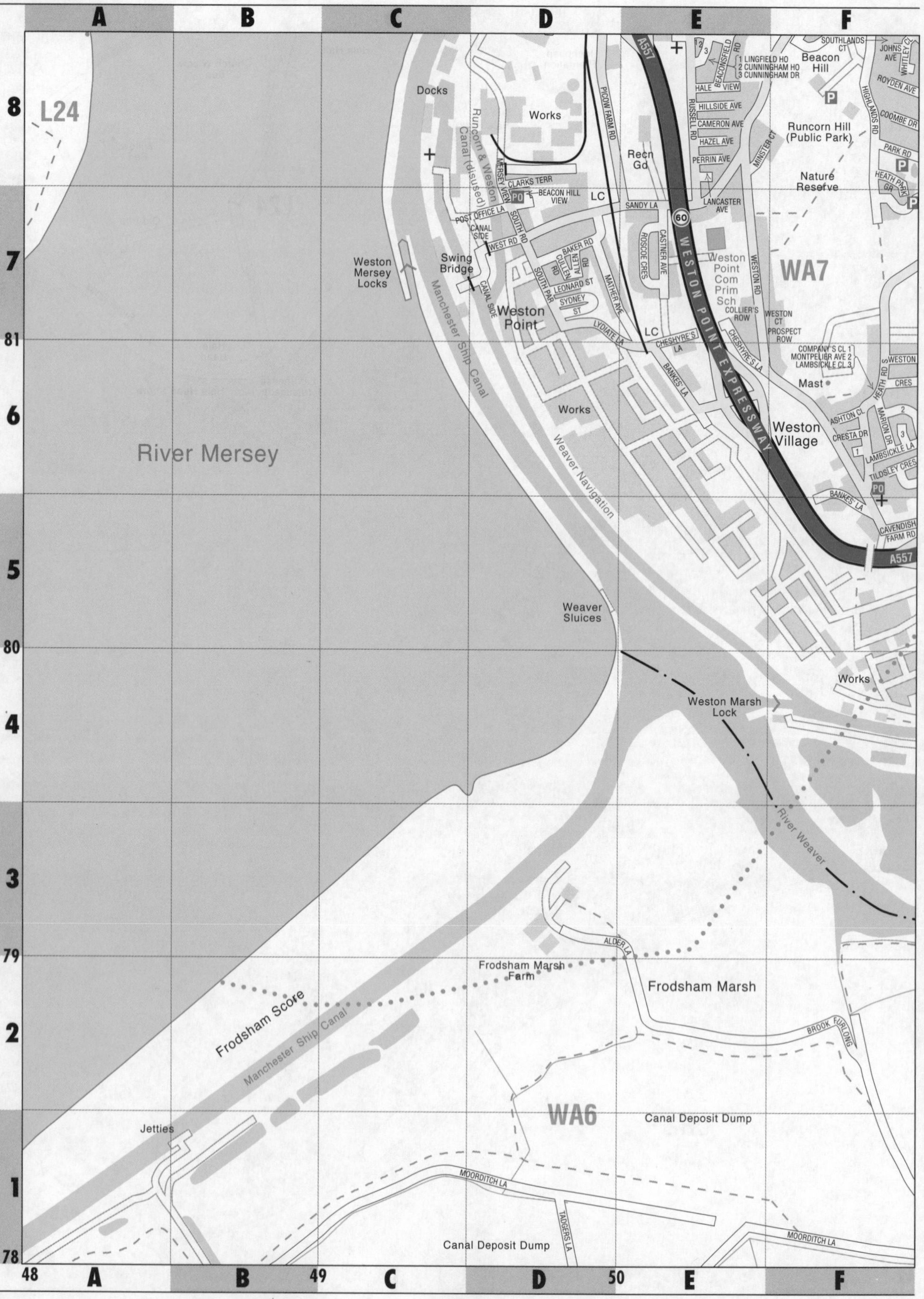
L24
River Mersey
Docks
Works
Runcorn & Weston Canal (disused)
Weston Mersey Locks
Swing Bridge
Weston Point
Manchester Ship Canal
Weaver Navigation
Works
Weaver Sluices
Recn Gd
LC
SANDY LA
PICOW FARM RD
A557
WESTON POINT EXPRESSWAY
60
Beacon Hill
SOUTHLANDS CT
JOHNS AVE
WHITLEY CL
ROYDEN AVE
HIGHLANDS RD
COOMBE DR
PARK RD
HEATH PARK GR
1 LINGFIELD HO
2 CUNNINGHAM HO
3 CUNNINGHAM DR
BEACONSFIELD RD
HALE VIEW
HILLSIDE AVE
CAMERON AVE
HAZEL AVE
PERRIN AVE
RUSSELL RD
MINSTER CT
Runcorn Hill (Public Park)
Nature Reserve
LANCASTER AVE
CASTNER AVE
ROSCOE CRES
Weston Point Com Prim Sch
WESTON RD
COLLIER'S ROW
WESTON CT
PROSPECT ROW
WA7
MERSEY VIEW
CLARKS TERR
PO
BEACON HILL VIEW
POST OFFICE LA
CANAL SIDE
SOUTH RD
WEST RD
BAKER RD
ALLEY
OLD
CULLEN RD
SOUTH PAR
LEONARD ST
SYDNEY ST
MATHER AVE
LYDIATE LA
CHESHYRE'S LA
BANKES' LA
COMPANY'S CL 1
MONTPELIER AVE 2
LAMBSICKLE CL 3
Mast
HEATH RD
WESTON CRES
ASHTON CL
MARION DR
CRESTA DR
LAMBSICKLE LA
TILDSLEY CRES
Weston Village
CAVENDISH FARM RD
Works
Weston Marsh Lock
River Weaver
ALDER LA
Frodsham Marsh Farm
Frodsham Marsh
Frodsham Score
BROOK FURLONG
WA6
Canal Deposit Dump
Jetties
MOORDITCH LA
TADGERS LA
Canal Deposit Dump
A B C D E F
8 7 81 6 5 80 4 3 79 2 1 78
48 49 50

47
73

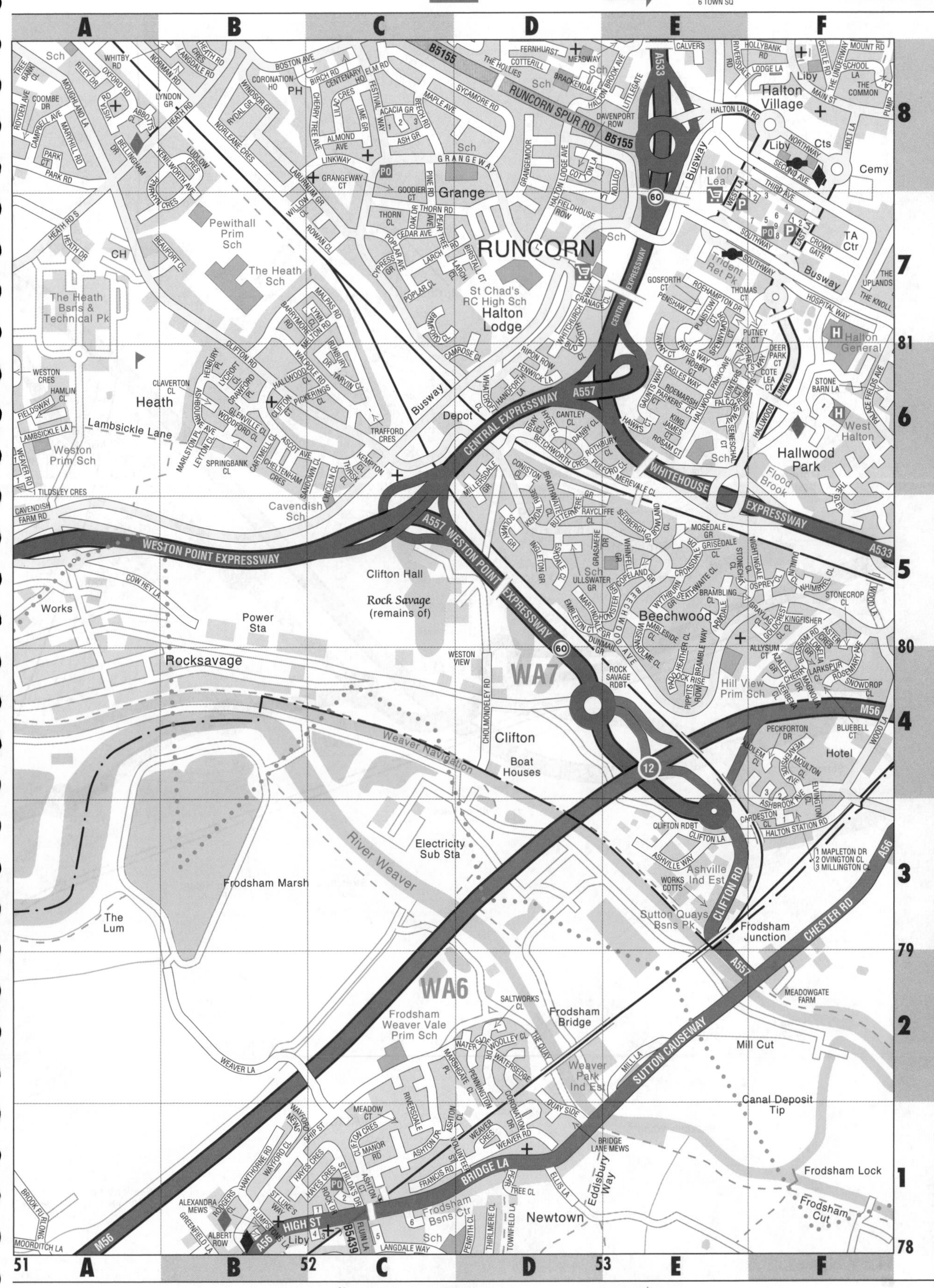
A
B
C
D
E
F
8
7
81
6
5
80
4
3
79
2
1
78
51
52
53
RUNCORN
Halton Village
Halton Lea
Grange
Halton Lodge
St Chad's RC High Sch
Pewithall Prim Sch
The Heath Sch
The Heath Bsns & Technical Pk
Heath
Weston Prim Sch
Cavendish Sch
Lambsickle Lane
CENTRAL EXPRESSWAY
WESTON POINT EXPRESSWAY
WHITEHOUSE EXPRESSWAY
RUNCORN SPUR RD
B5155
A533
A557
Busway
Trident Ret Pk
Halton General
West Halton
Hallwood Park
Flood Brook
Cemy
TA Ctr
Beechwood
Hill View Prim Sch
Clifton Hall
Rock Savage
(remains of)
Power Sta
Rocksavage
Works
WA7
Clifton
Boat Houses
Weaver Navigation
River Weaver
Electricity Sub Sta
Frodsham Marsh
The Lum
Ashville Ind Est
Sutton Quays Bsns Pk
Frodsham Junction
CLIFTON RD
CHESTER RD
SUTTON CAUSEWAY
M56
A56
WA6
Frodsham Weaver Vale Prim Sch
Frodsham Bridge
Weaver Park Ind Est
Mill Cut
Canal Deposit Tip
Frodsham Lock
Frodsham Cut
Newtown
Eddisbury Way
Frodsham Bsns Ctr
BRIDGE LA
HIGH ST
B5439
Liby
Sch
Hotel
MEADOWGATE FARM
1 MAPLETON DR
2 OVINGTON CL
3 MILLINGTON CL

49
24

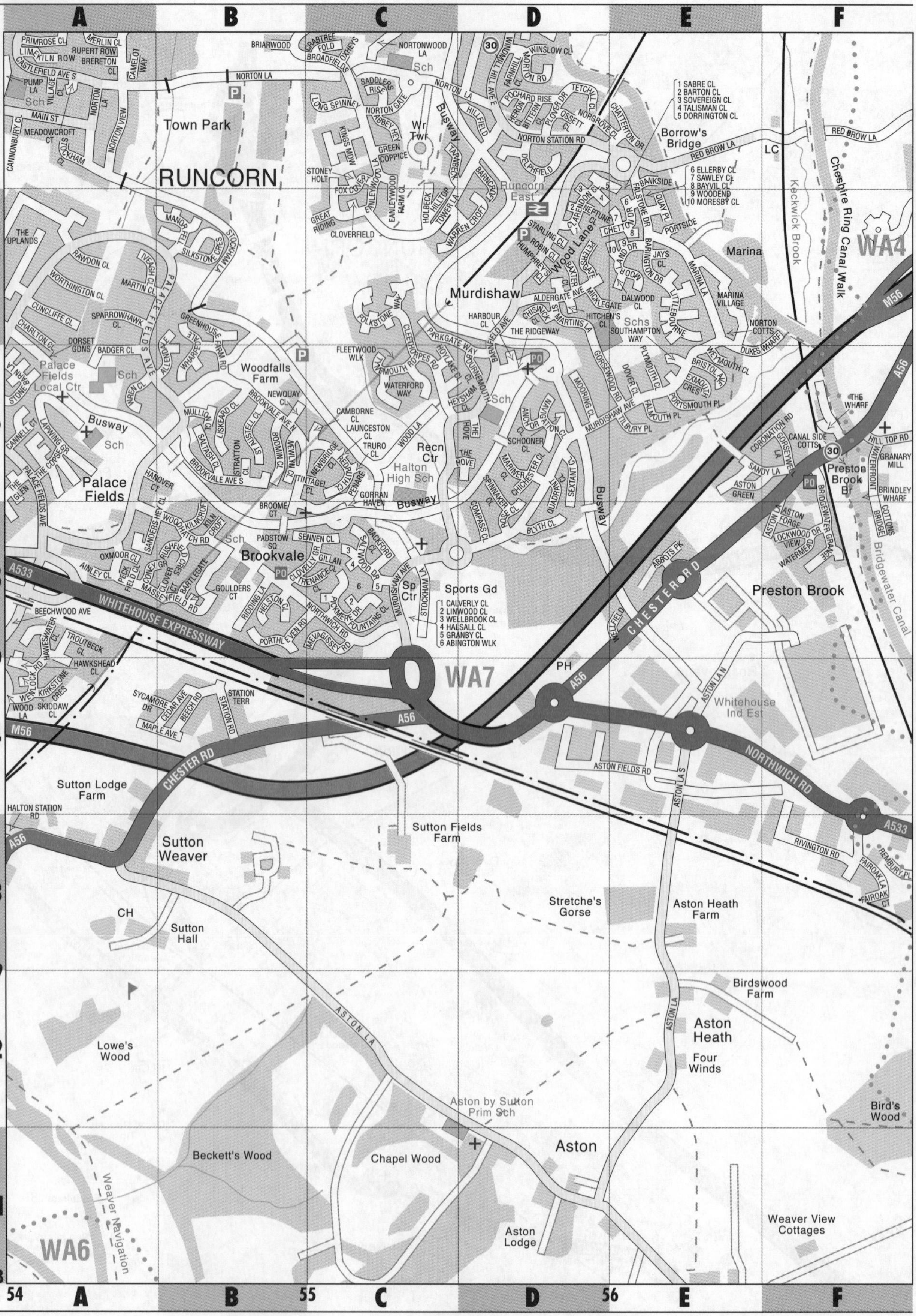
A
B
C
D
E
F
8
7
81
6
5
80
4
3
79
2
1
78
54
55
56
RUNCORN
Town Park
Runcorn East
Murdishaw
Borrow's Bridge
Marina
Marina Village
Woodfalls Farm
Palace Fields
Palace Fields Local Ctr
Brookvale
Recn Ctr
Halton High Sch
Sports Gd
Sp Ctr
Preston Brook
Preston Brook Br
Whitehouse Ind Est
Sutton Lodge Farm
Sutton Weaver
Sutton Fields Farm
Sutton Hall
Stretche's Gorse
Aston Heath Farm
Birdswood Farm
Aston Heath
Four Winds
Lowe's Wood
Beckett's Wood
Chapel Wood
Aston by Sutton Prim Sch
Aston
Aston Lodge
Weaver View Cottages
Bird's Wood
Weaver Navigation
Bridgewater Canal
Cheshire Ring Canal Walk
Keckwick Brook
WA4
WA6
WA7
M56
A56
A533
WHITEHOUSE EXPRESSWAY
CHESTER RD
NORTHWICH RD
NORTON LA
RED BROW LA
NORTON STATION RD
MURDISHAW AVE
ASTON LA
ASTON LA N
ASTON LA S
ASTON FIELDS RD
RIVINGTON RD
HALTON STATION RD
BEECHWOOD AVE
Busway
Wood Lane
1 SABRE CL
2 BARTON CL
3 SOVEREIGN CL
4 TALISMAN CL
5 DORRINGTON CL
6 ELLERBY CL
7 SAWLEY CL
8 BAYVIL CL
9 WOODEND
10 MORESBY CL
1 CALVERLY CL
2 LINWOOD CL
3 WELLBROOK CL
4 HALSALL CL
5 GRANBY CL
6 ABINGTON WLK

49
75

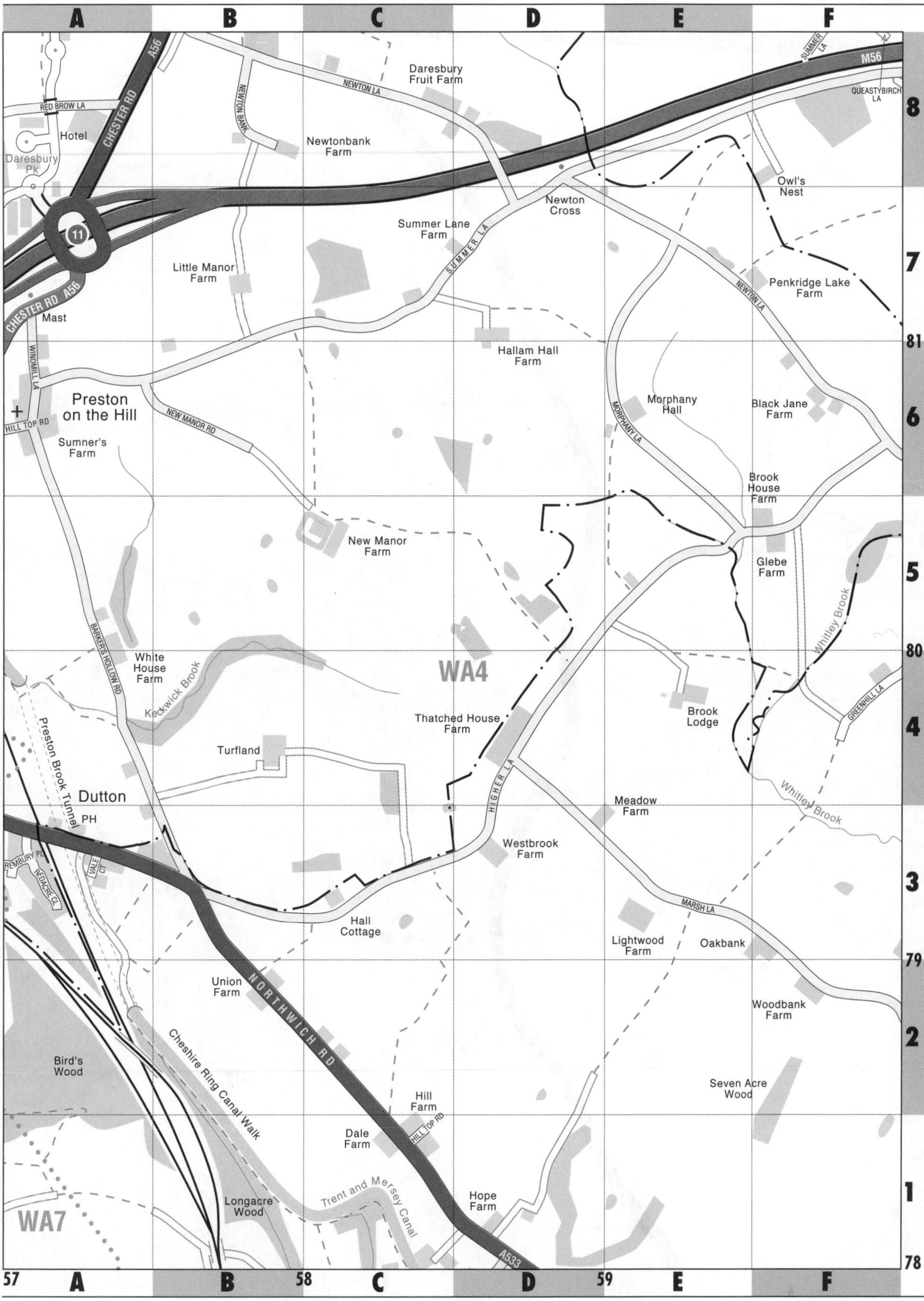

A B C D E F

Daresbury Fruit Farm
NEWTON LA
SUMMER LA
M56
QUEASTYBIRCH LA
RED BROW LA
A56
CHESTER RD
NEWTON BANK
Hotel
Daresbury Pk
Newtonbank Farm
Owl's Nest
Newton Cross
Summer Lane Farm
SUMMER LA
11
Little Manor Farm
Penkridge Lake Farm
NEWTON LA
CHESTER RD A56
Mast
WINDMILL LA
Hallam Hall Farm
Preston on the Hill
Morphany Hall
MORPHANY LA
Black Jane Farm
HILL TOP RD
NEW MANOR RD
Sumner's Farm
Brook House Farm
New Manor Farm
Glebe Farm
Whitley Brook
BARKER'S HOLLOW RD
White House Farm
Keckwick Brook
WA4
Thatched House Farm
Brook Lodge
GREENHILL LA
Preston Brook Tunnel
Turfland
HIGHER LA
Dutton
PH
Whitley Brook
Meadow Farm
Westbrook Farm
REMBURY PL
VALE CT
REDACRE CL
MARSH LA
Hall Cottage
Lightwood Farm
Oakbank
Union Farm
NORTHWICH RD
Woodbank Farm
Cheshire Ring Canal Walk
Bird's Wood
Seven Acre Wood
Hill Farm
HILL TOP RD
Dale Farm
Trent and Mersey Canal
Hope Farm
Longacre Wood
WA7
A533

8
7
81
6
5
80
4
3
79
2
1
78

57 A B 58 C D 59 E F

76
52

51
26

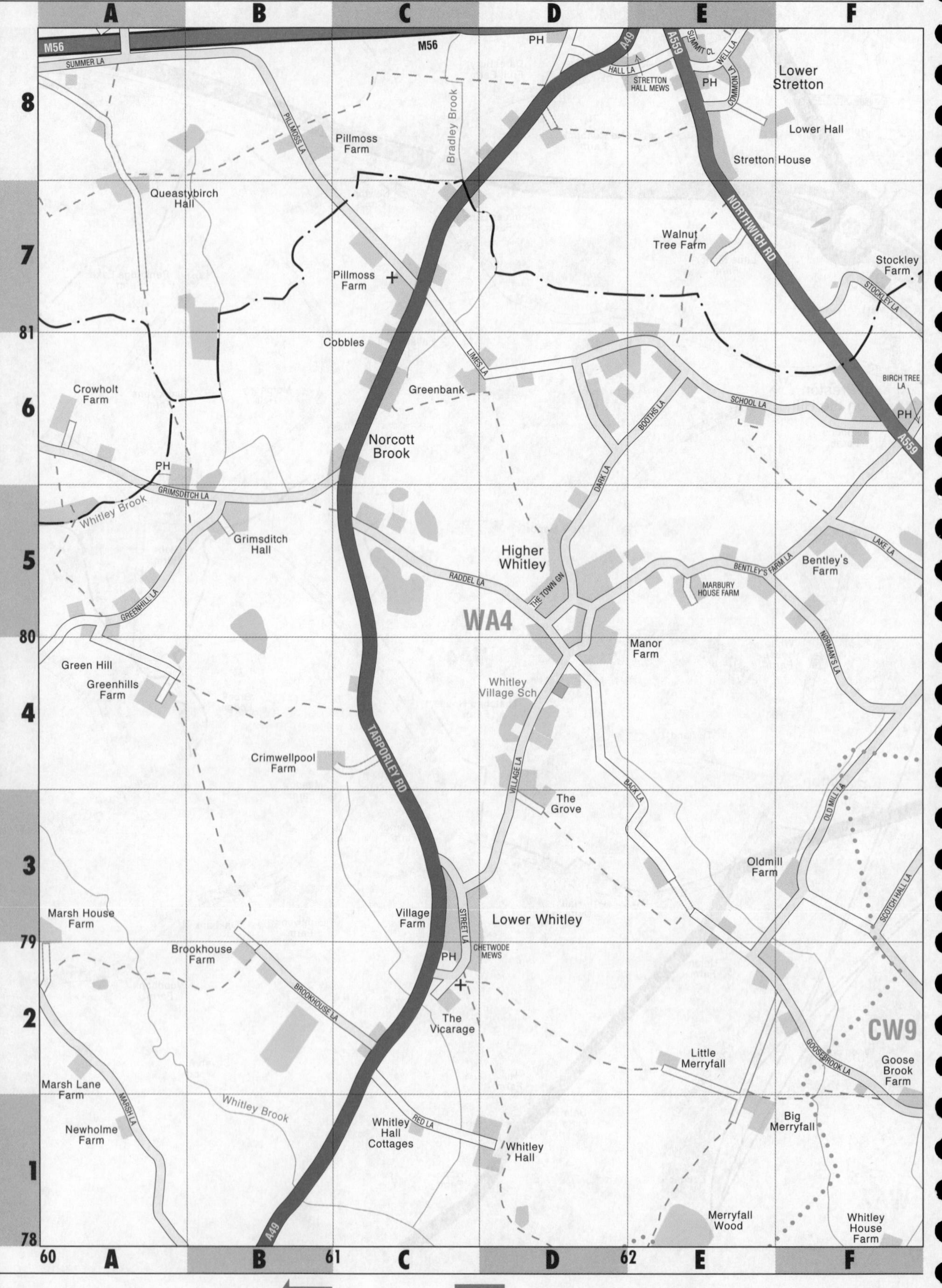
A
B
C
D
E
F
M56
SUMMER LA
PH
A49
A559
SUMMIT CL
WELL LA
HALL LA
STRETTON HALL MEWS
COMMON LA
Lower Stretton
Lower Hall
Stretton House
PILLMOSS LA
Pillmoss Farm
Bradley Brook
Queastybirch Hall
NORTHWICH RD
Walnut Tree Farm
Stockley Farm
STOCKLEY LA
Pillmoss Farm
Cobbles
LIMES LA
Crowholt Farm
Greenbank
BIRCH TREE LA
SCHOOL LA
BOOTHS LA
Norcott Brook
GRIMSDITCH LA
DARK LA
Whitley Brook
Grimsditch Hall
Higher Whitley
LAKE LA
BENTLEY'S FARM LA
Bentley's Farm
RADDEL LA
THE TOWN GN
MARBURY HOUSE FARM
GREENHILL LA
WA4
Manor Farm
NORMAN'S LA
Green Hill
Greenhills Farm
Whitley Village Sch
TARPORLEY RD
Crimwellpool Farm
VILLAGE LA
The Grove
BACK LA
OLD MILL LA
Oldmill Farm
SCOTCH HALL LA
Marsh House Farm
Village Farm
STREET LA
Lower Whitley
Brookhouse Farm
CHETWODE MEWS
BROOKHOUSE LA
The Vicarage
CW9
Little Merryfall
GOOSEBROOK LA
Goose Brook Farm
Marsh Lane Farm
MARSH LA
Whitley Brook
RED LA
Big Merryfall
Newholme Farm
Whitley Hall Cottages
Whitley Hall
Merryfall Wood
Whitley House Farm
8
7
81
6
5
80
4
3
79
2
1
78
60
61
62

51
77

27
54

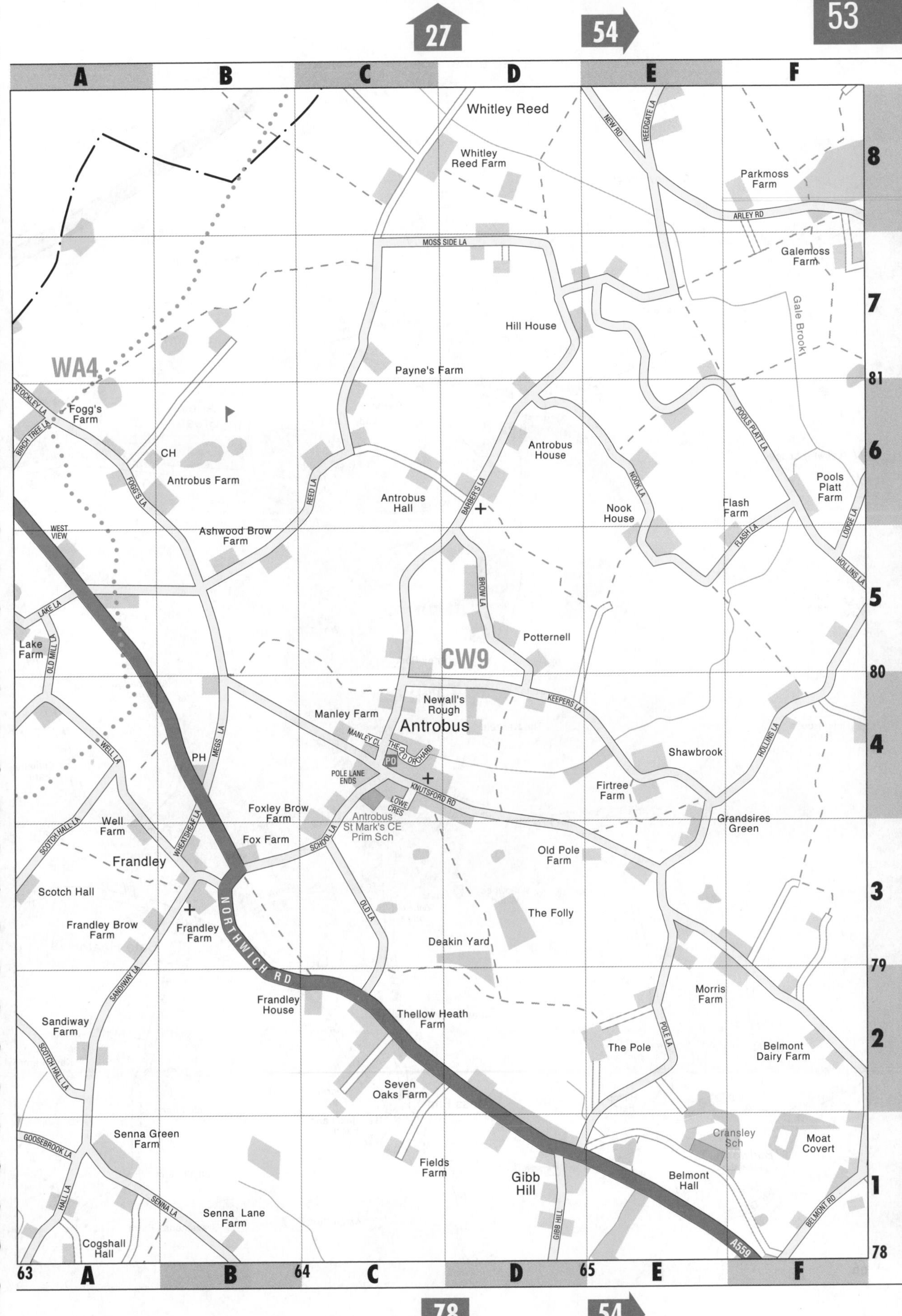
Whitley Reed
Whitley Reed Farm
Parkmoss Farm
ARLEY RD
NEW RD
REEDGATE LA
MOSS SIDE LA
Galemoss Farm
Gale Brook
Hill House
Payne's Farm
WA4
Fogg's Farm
STOCKLEY LA
BIRCH TREE LA
CH
Antrobus Farm
FOGG'S LA
REED LA
Antrobus Hall
Antrobus House
BARBER'S LA
NOOK LA
Nook House
POOLS PLATT LA
Flash Farm
FLASH LA
Pools Platt Farm
LODGE LA
HOLLINS LA
WEST VIEW
Ashwood Brow Farm
BROW LA
LAKE LA
Lake Farm
OLD MILL LA
Potternell
CW9
Newall's Rough
KEEPERS LA
Manley Farm
Antrobus
MANLEY CL
THE OLD ORCHARD
PO
WELL LA
PH
MEGS LA
POLE LANE ENDS
KNUTSFORD RD
LOWE CRES
Shawbrook
Firtree Farm
Foxley Brow Farm
Antrobus St Mark's CE Prim Sch
Grandsires Green
Well Farm
SCOTCH HALL LA
WHEATSHEAF LA
Fox Farm
SCHOOL LA
Old Pole Farm
Frandley
Scotch Hall
NORTHWICH RD
OLD LA
The Folly
Frandley Brow Farm
Frandley Farm
Deakin Yard
SANDIWAY LA
Morris Farm
Frandley House
Thellow Heath Farm
Sandiway Farm
The Pole
POLE LA
Belmont Dairy Farm
Seven Oaks Farm
Cransley Sch
Moat Covert
Senna Green Farm
GOOSEBROOK LA
Fields Farm
Gibb Hill
Belmont Hall
BELMONT RD
HALL LA
SENNA LA
Senna Lane Farm
GIBB HILL
Cogshall Hall
A559
A B C D E F
8 7 81 6 5 80 4 3 79 2 1 78
63 64 65

78
54

53
28

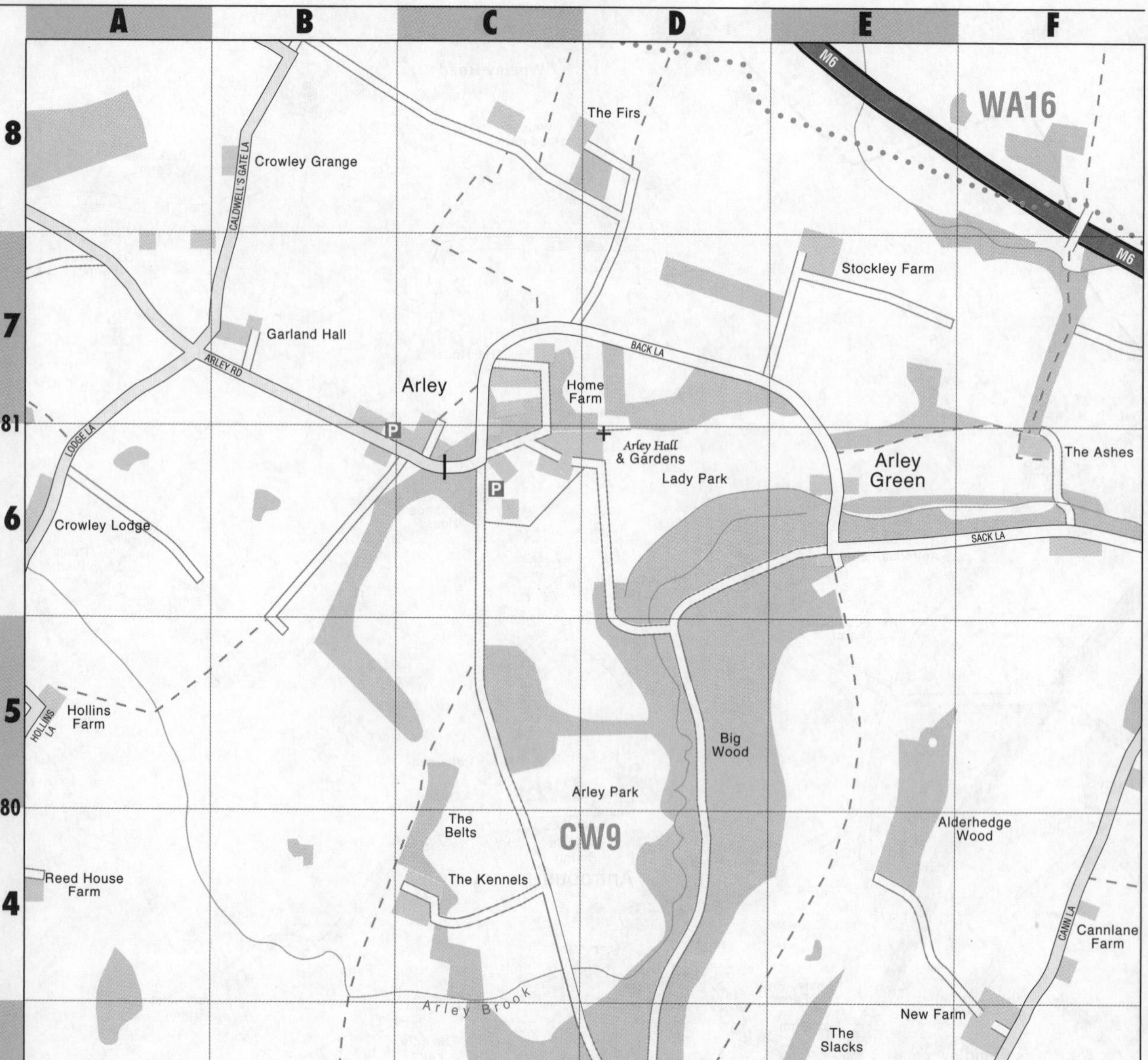

A B C D E F
8
7
81
6
5
80
4
3
79
2
1
78
66 67 68
M6
WA16
The Firs
Crowley Grange
CALDWELL'S GATE LA
Stockley Farm
Garland Hall
ARLEY RD
BACK LA
Arley
Home Farm
Arley Hall & Gardens
Lady Park
Arley Green
The Ashes
LODGE LA
Crowley Lodge
SACK LA
Hollins Farm
HOLLINS LA
Big Wood
Arley Park
The Belts
CW9
Alderhedge Wood
Reed House Farm
The Kennels
CANN LA
Cannlane Farm
Arley Brook
New Farm
The Slacks
Willowbed Wood
Willow Lodge
Bate Heath
BUDWORTH RD
COLLIERS LA
Arley Moss Farm
ARLEY MOSSEND LA
Kays Farm
KNUTSFORD RD
Hilltop Farm
Moss End
Yewtree Farm
Fields Farm
George's Lane Farm
GEORGE'S LA
Budworth Heath
BUDWORTH HEATH LA
Wathall Farm
HEATH LA
Aston Park
Gravestones Farm

53
79

29
56

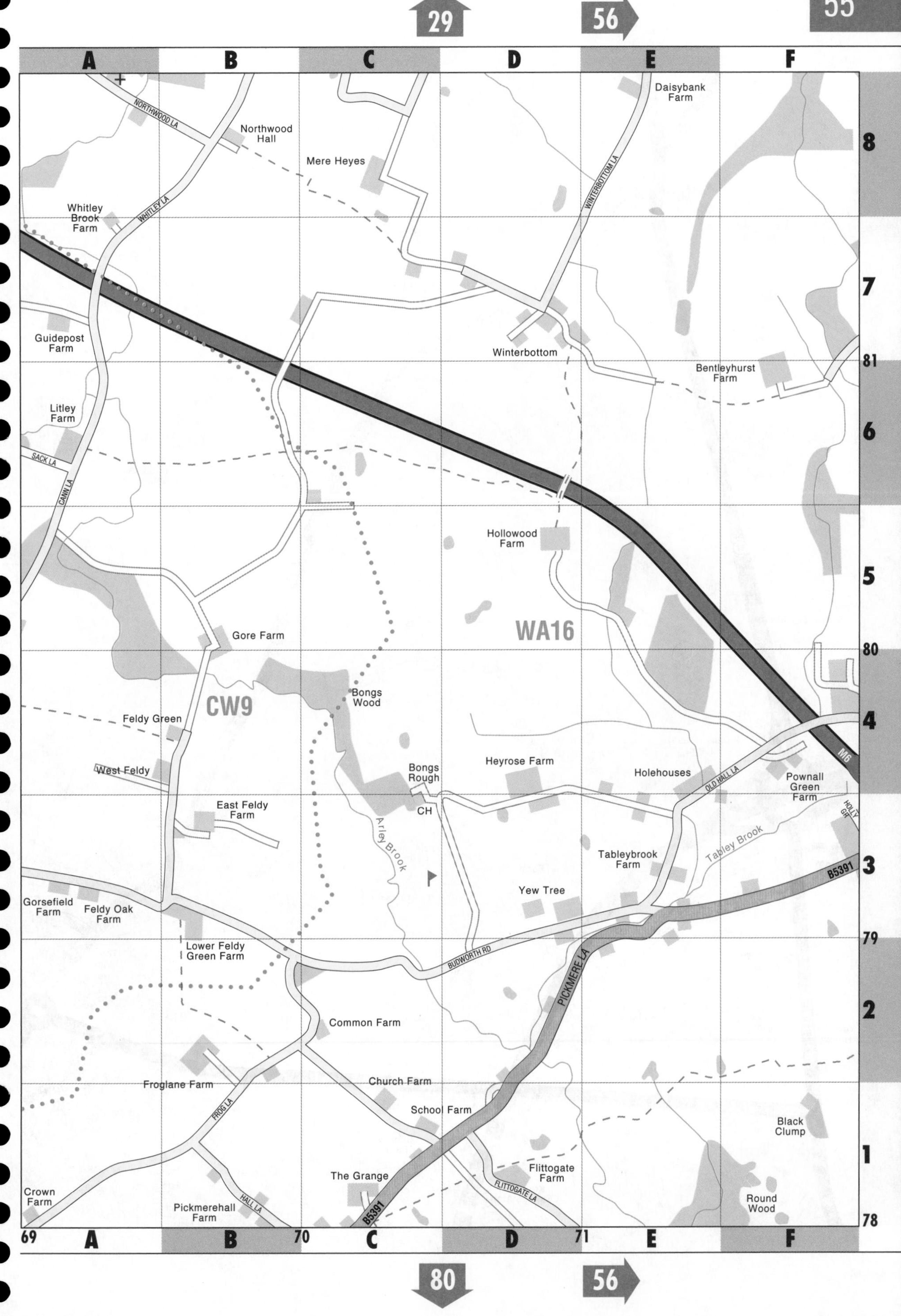
A
B
C
D
E
F
8
7
81
6
5
80
4
3
79
2
1
78
69
70
71
NORTHWOOD LA
Northwood Hall
Mere Heyes
Daisybank Farm
WINTERBOTTOM LA
Whitley Brook Farm
WHITLEY LA
Guidepost Farm
Winterbottom
Bentleyhurst Farm
Litley Farm
SACK LA
CANN LA
Hollowood Farm
WA16
Gore Farm
CW9
Bongs Wood
Feldy Green
West Feldy
Bongs Rough
Heyrose Farm
Holehouses
OLD HALL LA
Pownall Green Farm
M6
HOLLY GR
East Feldy Farm
CH
Arley Brook
Tabley Brook
Tableybrook Farm
B5391
Yew Tree
Gorsefield Farm
Feldy Oak Farm
Lower Feldy Green Farm
BUDWORTH RD
PICKMERE LA
Common Farm
Froglane Farm
Church Farm
FROG LA
School Farm
Black Clump
Flittogate Farm
FLITTOGATE LA
The Grange
Crown Farm
Pickmerehall Farm
HALL LA
Round Wood

80
56

55
30

A
B
C
D
E
F
Mere
The Mere
CH
MERE HALL
MERE HOME FARM
WARRINGTON RD
MERESIDE RD
A5034
ASHLEY RD
Mere Lodge
Lady Mary's Walk
Rostherne Drive
Tatton Hall
Tatton Park
Mereheath Drive
Lodge
The Temple
Melchett Mere
CLAMMUNGER LA
Knowlespit Farm
CHESTER RD
STEADINGS RISE
Moss Plantation
Mereheath Plantation
Moss Cottage
Gauntlet Birds of Prey Park
Hotel
MEREHEATH LA
MOSS LA
Church Farm
Over Tabley
Moss Farm
Roebuck Farm
TABLEY CT
WA16
Garage
MANCHESTER RD
Over Tabley Hall
OLD HALL LA
Bluebell Farm
GREEN LA
Dairy House Farm
Swains Walk
M6
Cemy
Playing Fields
PH
HOLLY GR
PICKMERE LA
B5391
TABLEY CL
FRESHFIELDS
QUEENSWAY
OAKWOOD 1
BEECHWOOD 2
Tabley Hill Farm
Bank Farm
Tabley Hill
TABLEY RD
SUGAR PIT LA
WILLOW GN
MEREHEATH PK
B5083
GARDEN RD
SPINNEY LA
VICTORIA ST
QUEEN ST
ALBERT ST
Burnthouse Farm
TABLEY HILL LA
Tableyvale Farm
The Heath
ELIZABETH GASKELL CT 1
WINDSOR WAY 2
ROYCE CT 3
HEATHLANDS HO 4
WINSTANLEY HO 5
A50
Tableyvale Cottages
WARREN AVE
WARREN CL
LADIES MILE
HEATH DR
Yewtree House
A5033
GASKELL AVE
Egerton Prim Sch
NORTHWICH RD
STANLEY RD
Villa Farm
HEATHFIELD SQ
SANDILEIGH AVE
WESTFIELD DR
RACEFIELD RD
CRANFORD SQ
LILAC AVE
ACACIA AVE
TABLEY GR
WESTFIELD DR
Knutsford
L Ctr
SCHOOL CL
CRANFORD AVE
ST JOHN'S AVE
ST JOHN'S RD
Belt Wood
Sudlow Farm
SUDLOW LA
MELLOR CRES
Knutsford High Sch (Lower Sch)
Knutsford High Sch (Upper Sch)
BEXTON RD
HAYTON ST
Sch
MEADOW DR
LEE CL
ST PETER'S AVE
Knutsford Service Area
FLETCHER CT 1
EAST TERR 2
MASTERS CT 3
VICTORIA CT 4
COUNTY TERR 5
ABBEYFIELD HO 6
MEAD CL
MEADOW DR
A556
8
7
81
6
5
80
4
3
79
2
1
78
72
73
74

55
81

31
58

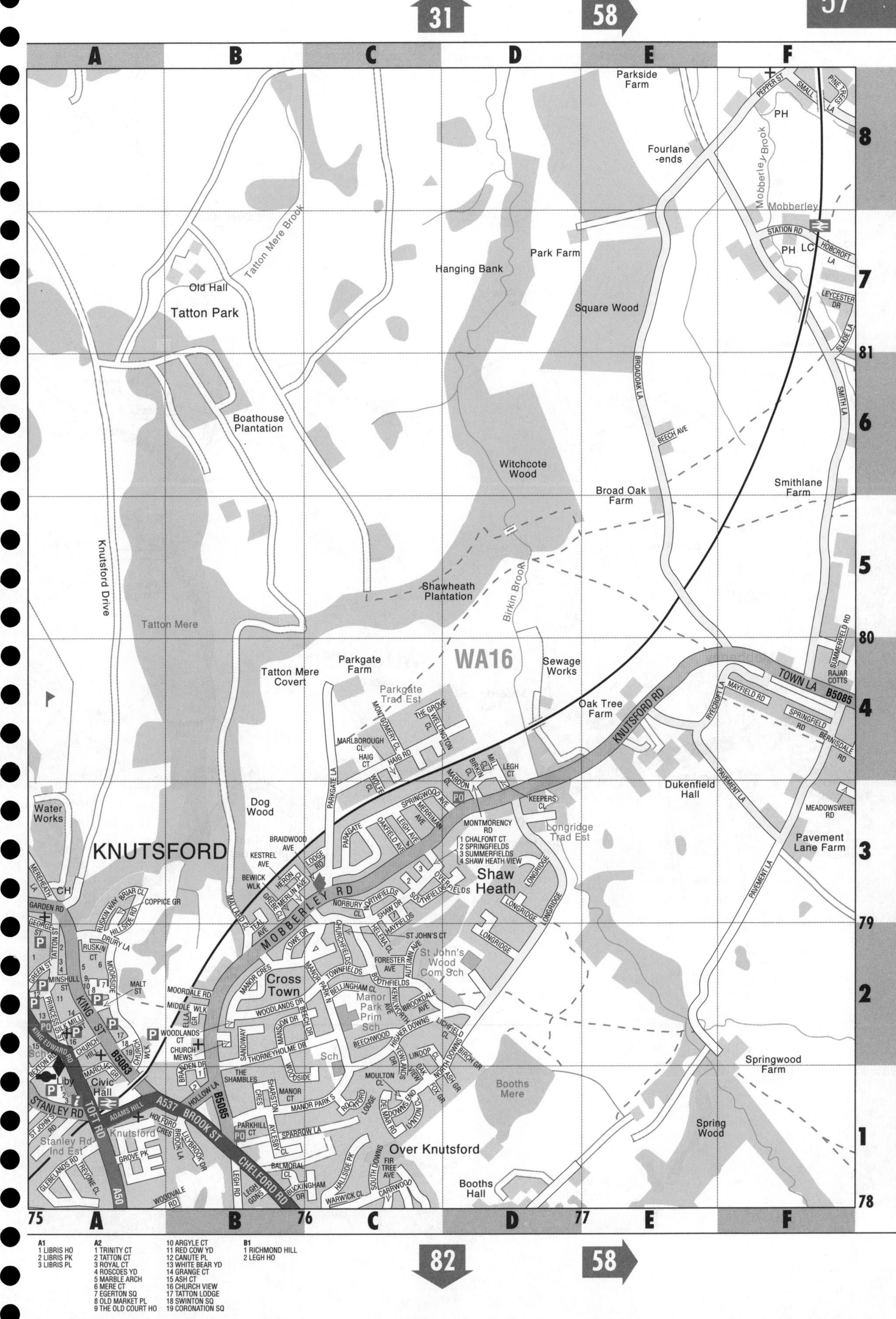

A1
1 LIBRIS HO
2 LIBRIS PK
3 LIBRIS PL

A2
1 TRINITY CT
2 TATTON CT
3 ROYAL CT
4 ROSCOES YD
5 MARBLE ARCH
6 MERE CT
7 EGERTON SQ
8 OLD MARKET PL
9 THE OLD COURT HO
10 ARGYLE CT
11 RED COW YD
12 CANUTE PL
13 WHITE BEAR YD
14 GRANGE CT
15 ASH CT
16 CHURCH VIEW
17 TATTON LODGE
18 SWINTON SQ
19 CORONATION SQ

B1
1 RICHMOND HILL
2 LEGH HO

82
58

57
32

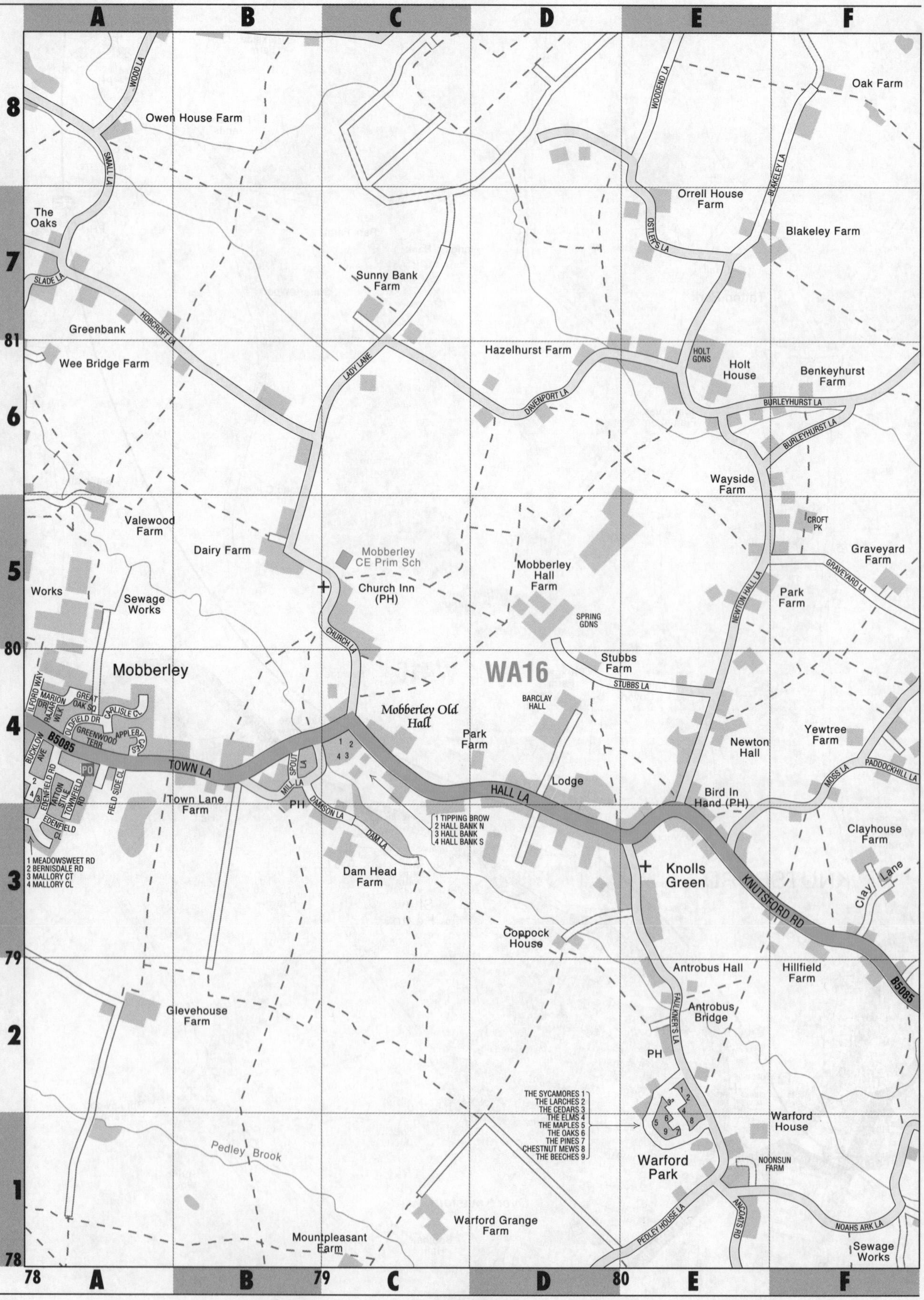

A B C D E F

8 Owen House Farm
Oak Farm
WOOD LA
SMALL LA
WOODEND LA
Orrell House Farm
BLAKELEY LA
OSTLER'S LA
The Oaks
Blakeley Farm
7
SLADE LA
Sunny Bank Farm
HOBCROFT LA
Greenbank
81
Wee Bridge Farm
Hazelhurst Farm
HOLT GDNS
Holt House
Benkeyhurst Farm
LADY LANE
DAVENPORT LA
BURLEYHURST LA
6
Wayside Farm
Valewood Farm
CROFT PK
Dairy Farm
Mobberley CE Prim Sch
Mobberley Hall Farm
Graveyard Farm
GRAVEYARD LA
5
Works
Church Inn (PH)
Sewage Works
NEWTON HALL LA
Park Farm
SPRING GDNS
CHURCH LA
80
Mobberley
WA16
Stubbs Farm
STUBBS LA
ILFORD WAY
MARION DR
RAJAH WLK
GREAT OAK SQ
OLDFIELD DR
CARLISLE CL
BARCLAY HALL
Mobberley Old Hall
4
GREENWOOD TERR
APPLEBY CRES
Park Farm
Newton Hall
Yewtree Farm
B5085
TOWN LA
PO
SPOUT LA
MOSS LA
PADDOCKHILL LA
BUCKLOW AVE
FIELD SIDE CL
Lodge
HALL LA
EDENFIELD RD
TATTON STILE
TOWNFIELD RD
MILL LA
Town Lane Farm
PH
Bird In Hand (PH)
DAMSON LA
EDENFIELD CL
1 TIPPING BROW
2 HALL BANK N
3 HALL BANK
4 HALL BANK S
Clayhouse Farm
1 MEADOWSWEET RD
2 BERNISDALE RD
3 MALLORY CT
4 MALLORY CL
DAM LA
Knolls Green
3
Dam Head Farm
KNUTSFORD RD
Clay Lane
Coppock House
79
Antrobus Hall
Hillfield Farm
B5085
Glevehouse Farm
FAULKNER'S LA
Antrobus Bridge
2
PH
THE SYCAMORES 1
THE LARCHES 2
THE CEDARS 3
THE ELMS 4
THE MAPLES 5
THE OAKS 6
THE PINES 7
CHESTNUT MEWS 8
THE BEECHES 9
Warford House
Pedley Brook
Warford Park
NOONSUN FARM
1
PEDLEY HOUSE LA
ANCOATS RD
NOAHS ARK LA
Warford Grange Farm
Mountpleasant Farm
Sewage Works
78

78 A B 79 C D 80 E F

57
83

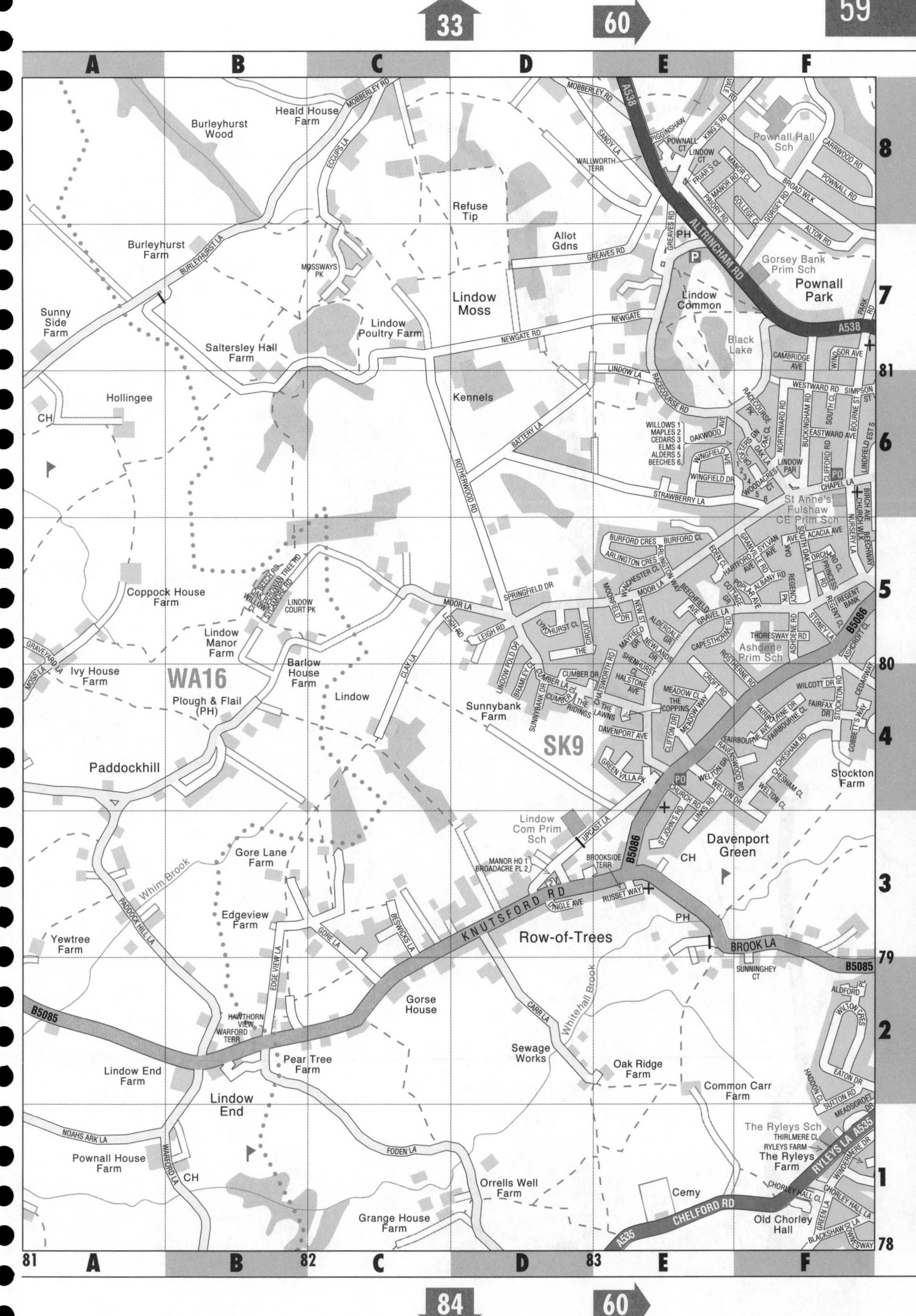
33
60
Burleyhurst Wood
Heald House Farm
Burleyhurst Farm
Sunny Side Farm
Saltersley Hall Farm
Lindow Poultry Farm
Lindow Moss
Refuse Tip
Allot Gdns
Kennels
Hollingee
CH
Coppock House Farm
Lindow Manor Farm
Lindow Court PK
Ivy House Farm
WA16
Barlow House Farm
Lindow
Plough & Flail (PH)
Paddockhill
Sunnybank Farm
SK9
Gore Lane Farm
Whim Brook
Edgeview Farm
Yewtree Farm
Row-of-Trees
Gorse House
Lindow End Farm
Lindow End
Pear Tree Farm
Pownall House Farm
Sewage Works
Oak Ridge Farm
Common Carr Farm
Orrells Well Farm
Grange House Farm
Cemy
Old Chorley Hall
The Ryleys Sch
The Ryleys Farm
Stockton Farm
Davenport Green
Lindow Com Prim Sch
Ashdene Prim Sch
St Anne's Fulshaw CE Prim Sch
Lindow Common
Black Lake
Pownall Park
Gorsey Bank Prim Sch
Pownall Hall Sch
ALTRINCHAM RD
KNUTSFORD RD
CHELFORD RD
BROOK LA
A538
B5085
B5086
A535
84
60

59
34

C8
1 GLADEWOOD CL
2 SANDHURST DR
3 CALVERLEY CL
4 DARESBURY CL

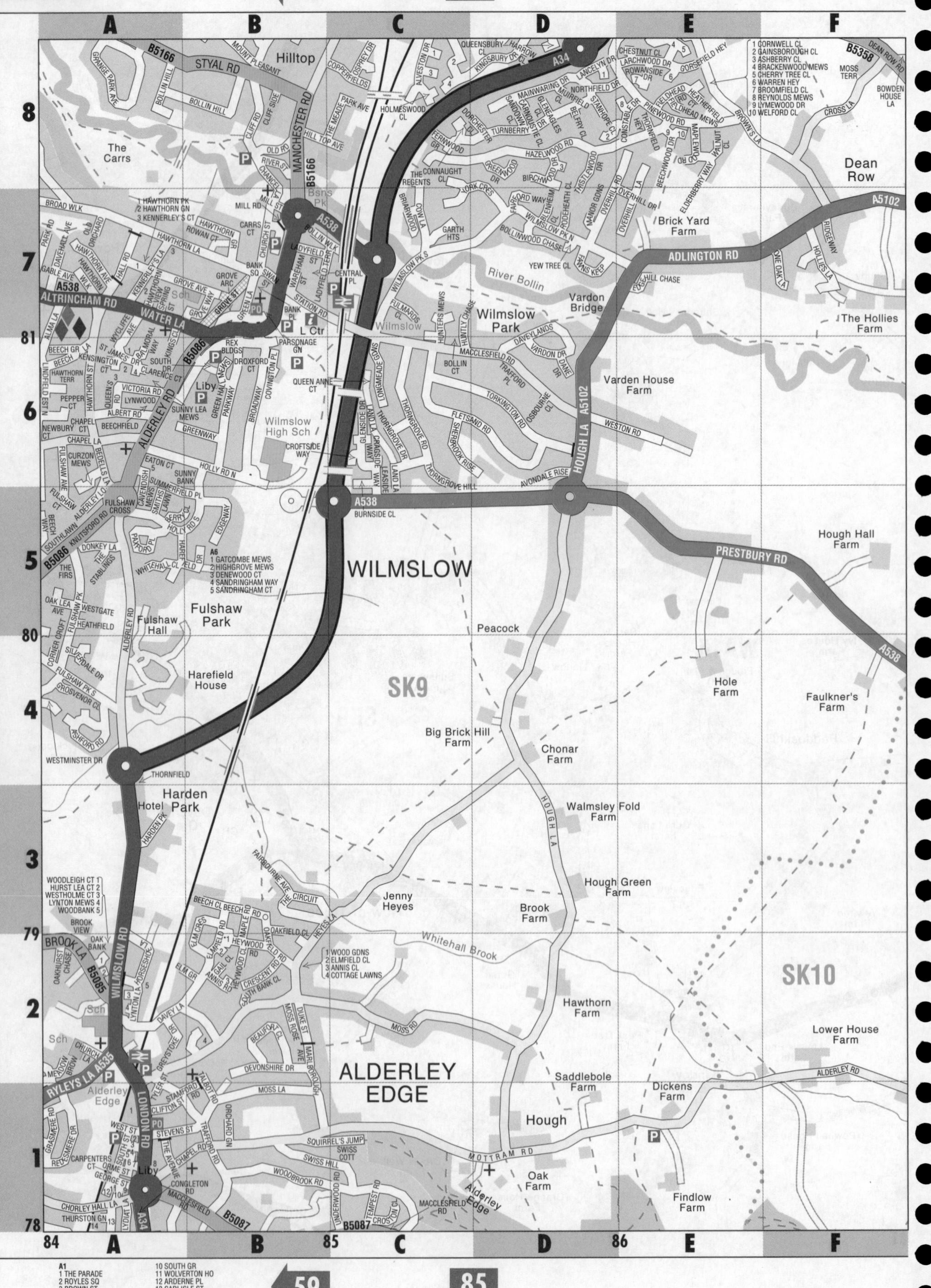

A1
1 THE PARADE
2 ROYLES SQ
3 BROWN ST
4 BERESFORD CT
5 GREEN ST
6 MASSEY ST
7 CHAPEL ST
8 CHORLEGH GRANGE
9 HUBERT WORTHINGTON HO
10 SOUTH GR
11 WOLVERTON HO
12 ARDERNE PL
13 CARLISLE ST
14 SOUTH TERR

59
85

35
62

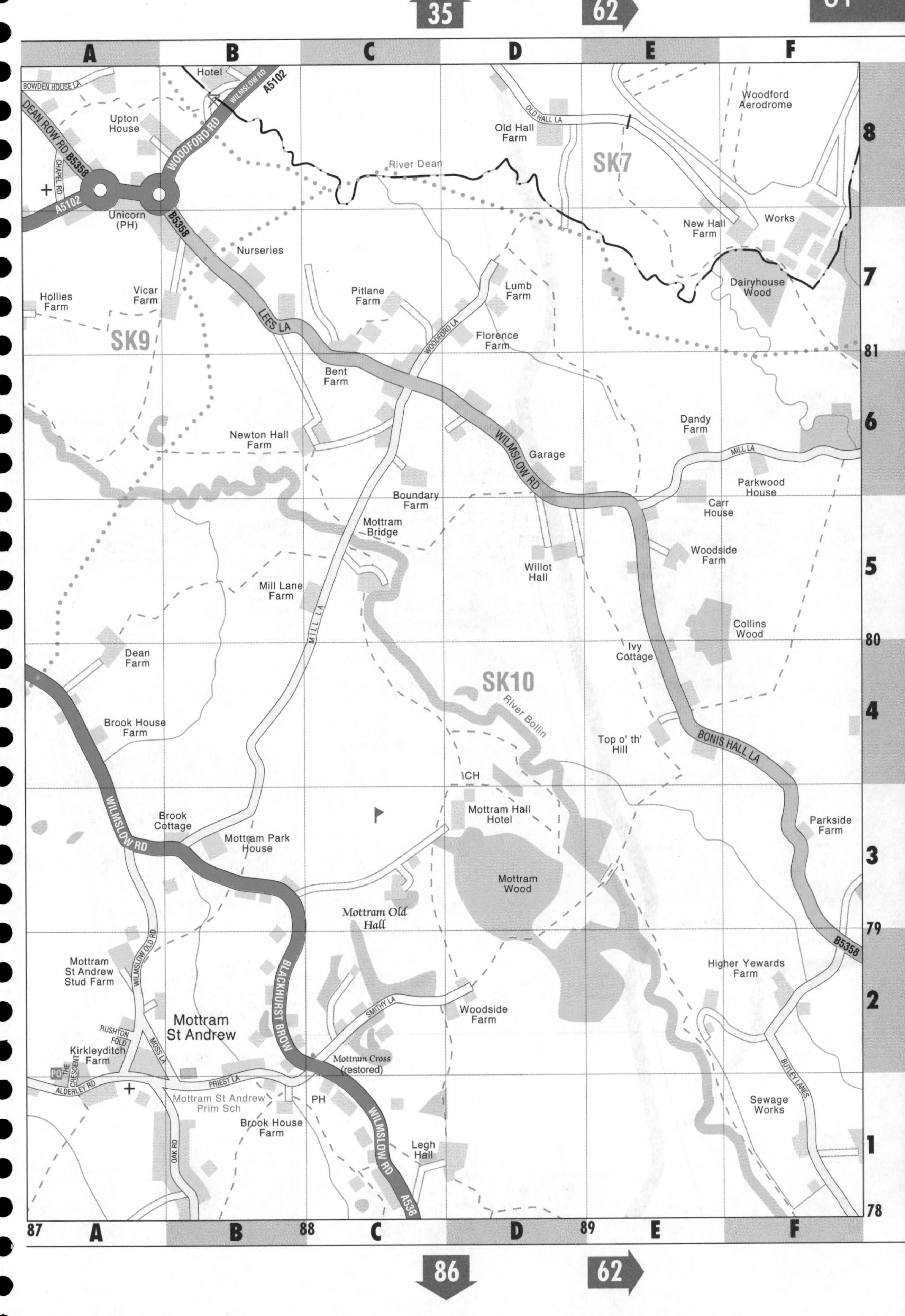
Hotel
BOWDEN HOUSE LA
DEAN ROW RD B5358
CHAPEL RD
A5102
WILMSLOW RD
WOODFORD RD
B5358
Upton House
Unicorn (PH)
River Dean
Old Hall Farm
OLD HALL LA
SK7
Woodford Aerodrome
New Hall Farm
Works
Dairyhouse Wood
Nurseries
Hollies Farm
Vicar Farm
SK9
LEES LA
Pitlane Farm
Lumb Farm
WOODFORD LA
Florence Farm
Bent Farm
Newton Hall Farm
WILMSLOW RD
Garage
Dandy Farm
MILL LA
Parkwood House
Boundary Farm
Carr House
Mottram Bridge
Woodside Farm
Willot Hall
Mill Lane Farm
MILL LA
Collins Wood
Ivy Cottage
Dean Farm
SK10
River Bollin
Brook House Farm
Top o' th' Hill
BONIS HALL LA
CH
Mottram Hall Hotel
Parkside Farm
Brook Cottage
Mottram Park House
Mottram Wood
Mottram Old Hall
B5358
Higher Yewards Farm
Mottram St Andrew Stud Farm
WILMSLOW OLD RD
BLACKHURST BROW
SMITHY LA
Woodside Farm
Mottram St Andrew
RUSHTON FOLD
MOSS LA
Kirkleyditch Farm
Mottram Cross (restored)
BUTLEY LANES
PO
THE CRESCENT
ALDERLEY RD
PRIEST LA
Mottram St Andrew Prim Sch
PH
Brook House Farm
Sewage Works
OAK RD
Legh Hall
WILMSLOW RD
A538
A
B
C
D
E
F
8
7
81
6
5
80
4
3
79
2
1
78
87
88
89

86
62

61
36

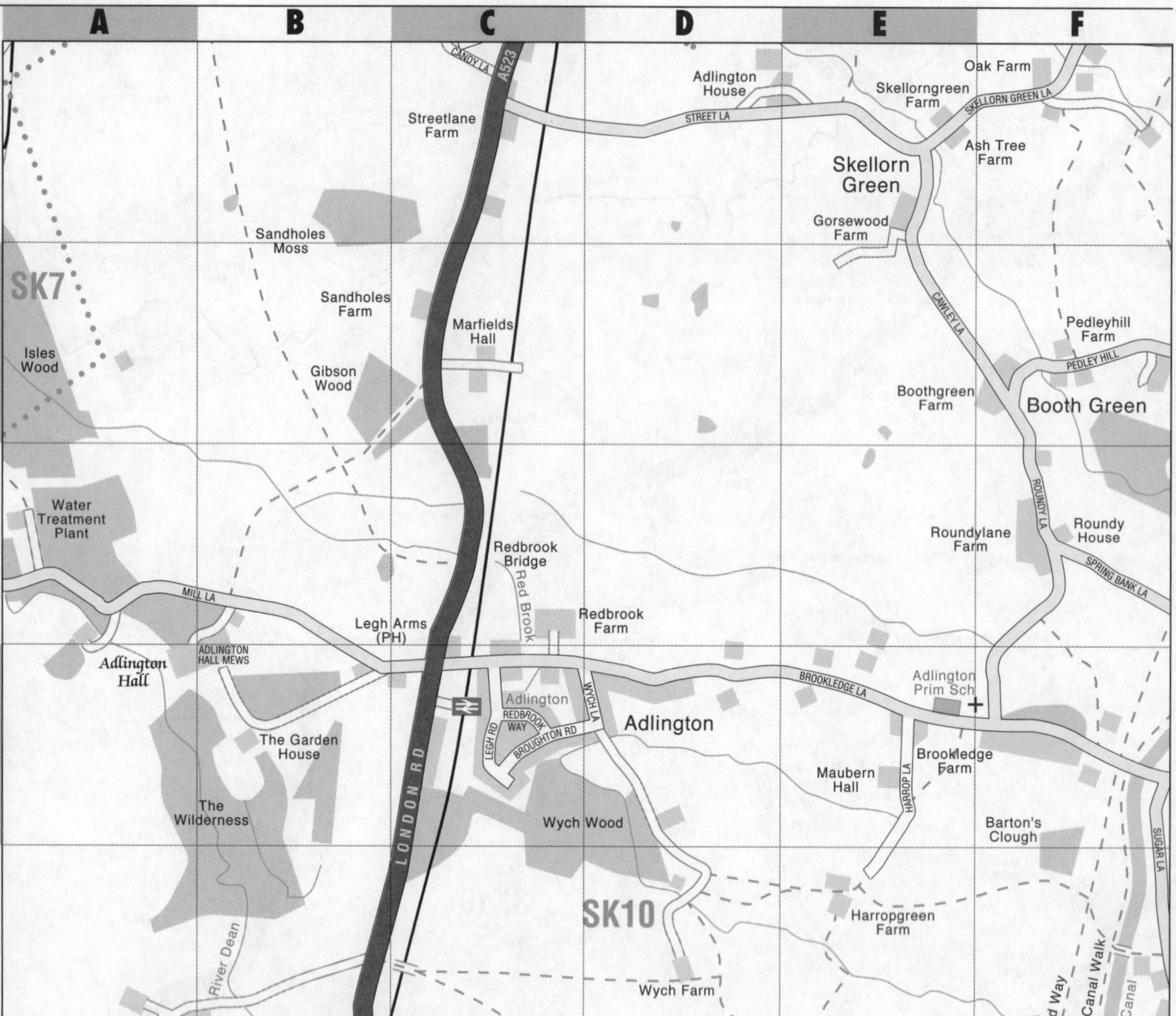

A
B
C
D
E
F
8
7
81
6
5
80
4
3
79
2
1
78
90
91
92
SK7
SK10
CANDY LA
A523
Adlington House
Skellorngreen Farm
Oak Farm
SKELLORN GREEN LA
Streetlane Farm
STREET LA
Ash Tree Farm
Skellorn Green
Gorsewood Farm
Sandholes Moss
Sandholes Farm
Marfields Hall
CAWLEY LA
Pedleyhill Farm
PEDLEY HILL
Isles Wood
Gibson Wood
Boothgreen Farm
Booth Green
Water Treatment Plant
ROUNDY LA
Roundylane Farm
Roundy House
SPRING BANK LA
Redbrook Bridge
Red Brook
MILL LA
Redbrook Farm
Legh Arms (PH)
Adlington Hall
ADLINGTON HALL MEWS
BROOKLEDGE LA
Adlington Prim Sch
Adlington
WYCH LA
LEGH RD
REDBROOK WAY
BROUGHTON RD
Adlington
The Garden House
Brookledge Farm
Maubern Hall
HARROP LA
The Wilderness
LONDON RD
Wych Wood
Barton's Clough
SUGAR LA
Harropgreen Farm
River Dean
Wych Farm
Middlewood Way
Cheshire Ring Canal Walk
Macclesfield Canal
Clark Green Farm
Brook House Farm
Issues Wood
Higher Doles Farm
Towing Path
Millhouse Bridge
Bonis Wood
Oakdene
RUSHMERE CL
Mill House
Bonis Hall
B5358
PEGGIE'S LA
Lane Head
New Mill House
Ashley Farm
Whitehall Farm
The Windmill (PH)
BONIS HALL LA
Green Farm
Whiteley Green
HOLEHOUSE LA
Whiteley Heys
Lodge Farm
B5358
Sand Pit
Plant House
Howlanehead
Sandyhead Farm
WELL LA
A523

61
87

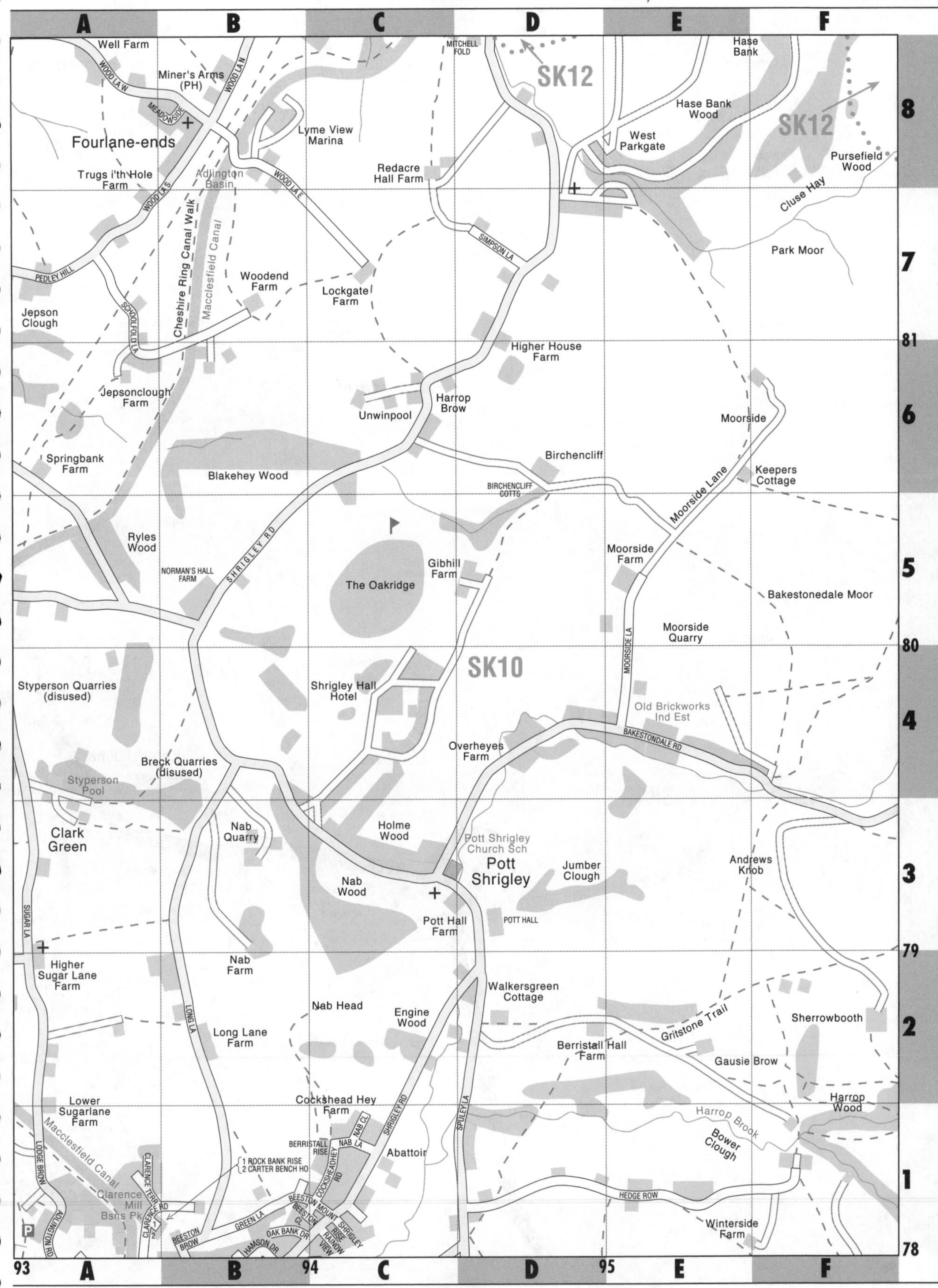

37
64
A
B
C
D
E
F
Well Farm
WOOD LA W
Miner's Arms (PH)
WOOD LAN
MEADOWSIDE
Fourlane-ends
Trugs i'th Hole Farm
Adlington Basin
WOOD LA E
WOOD LA S
Lyme View Marina
Redacre Hall Farm
MITCHELL FOLD
SK12
Hase Bank
Hase Bank Wood
West Parkgate
Pursefield Wood
Cluse Hay
Park Moor
SIMPSON LA
Cheshire Ring Canal Walk
Macclesfield Canal
PEDLEY HILL
Woodend Farm
Lockgate Farm
Jepson Clough
SCHOOLFOLD LA
Higher House Farm
Jepsonclough Farm
Harrop Brow
Unwinpool
Moorside
Springbank Farm
Blakehey Wood
Birchencliff
BIRCHENCLIFF COTTS
Keepers Cottage
Moorside Lane
Ryles Wood
NORMAN'S HALL FARM
SHRIGLEY RD
The Oakridge
Gibhill Farm
Moorside Farm
Bakestonedale Moor
Moorside Quarry
SK10
MOORSIDE LA
Styperson Quarries (disused)
Shrigley Hall Hotel
Old Brickworks Ind Est
BAKESTONDALE RD
Overheyes Farm
Breck Quarries (disused)
Styperson Pool
Clark Green
Nab Quarry
Holme Wood
Pott Shrigley Church Sch
Pott Shrigley
Jumber Clough
Andrews Knob
Nab Wood
Pott Hall Farm
POTT HALL
SUGAR LA
Higher Sugar Lane Farm
Nab Farm
Walkersgreen Cottage
Nab Head
Engine Wood
Sherrowbooth
LONG LA
Long Lane Farm
Gritstone Trail
Berristall Hall Farm
Gausie Brow
Lower Sugarlane Farm
Cockshead Hey Farm
SHRIGLEY RD
SPULEY LA
Harrop Wood
Harrop Brook
Bower Clough
Macclesfield Canal
LODGE BROW
CLARENCE TERR
BERRISTALL RISE
NAB CL
NAB LA
COCKSHEADHEY RD
Abattoir
1 ROCK BANK RISE
2 CARTER BENCH HO
Clarence Mill Bsns Pk
CLARENCE RD
HEDGE ROW
Winterside Farm
ADLINGTON RD
BEESTON BROW
GREEN LA
BEESTON MOUNT
BEESTON CL
OAK BANK DR
HAMSON DR
SHRIGLEY RISE
RAINOW VIEW
P
8
7
81
6
5
80
4
3
79
2
1
78
93
94
95
88
64

63
38

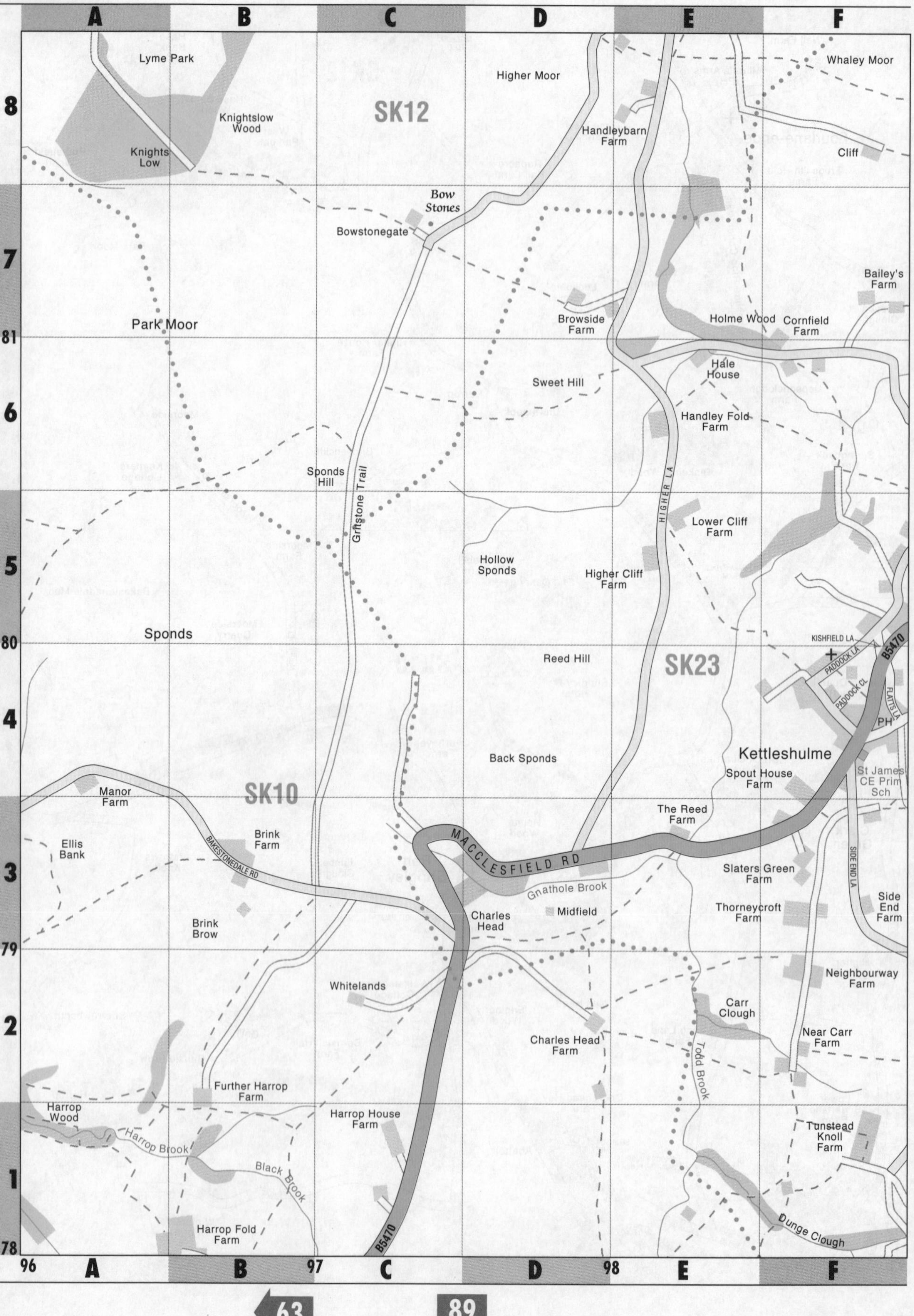

A
B
C
D
E
F
8
7
81
6
5
80
4
3
79
2
1
78
96
97
98
SK12
SK23
SK10
Lyme Park
Knightslow Wood
Knights Low
Higher Moor
Handleybarn Farm
Whaley Moor
Cliff
Bow Stones
Bowstonegate
Bailey's Farm
Park Moor
Browside Farm
Holme Wood
Cornfield Farm
Hale House
Sweet Hill
Handley Fold Farm
Sponds Hill
Gritstone Trail
Lower Cliff Farm
HIGHER LA
Hollow Sponds
Higher Cliff Farm
Sponds
KISHFIELD LA
PADDOCK LA
PADDOCK CL
B5470
RAITS LA
Reed Hill
PH
Back Sponds
Kettleshulme
Spout House Farm
St James CE Prim Sch
Manor Farm
The Reed Farm
Ellis Bank
Brink Farm
BAKESTONEDALE RD
MACCLESFIELD RD
Slaters Green Farm
SIDE END LA
Gnathole Brook
Side End Farm
Brink Brow
Charles Head
Midfield
Thorneycroft Farm
Whitelands
Neighbourway Farm
Carr Clough
Charles Head Farm
Todd Brook
Near Carr Farm
Further Harrop Farm
Harrop Wood
Harrop House Farm
Tunstead Knoll Farm
Harrop Brook
Black Brook
Harrop Fold Farm
Dunge Clough
B5470

63
89

39

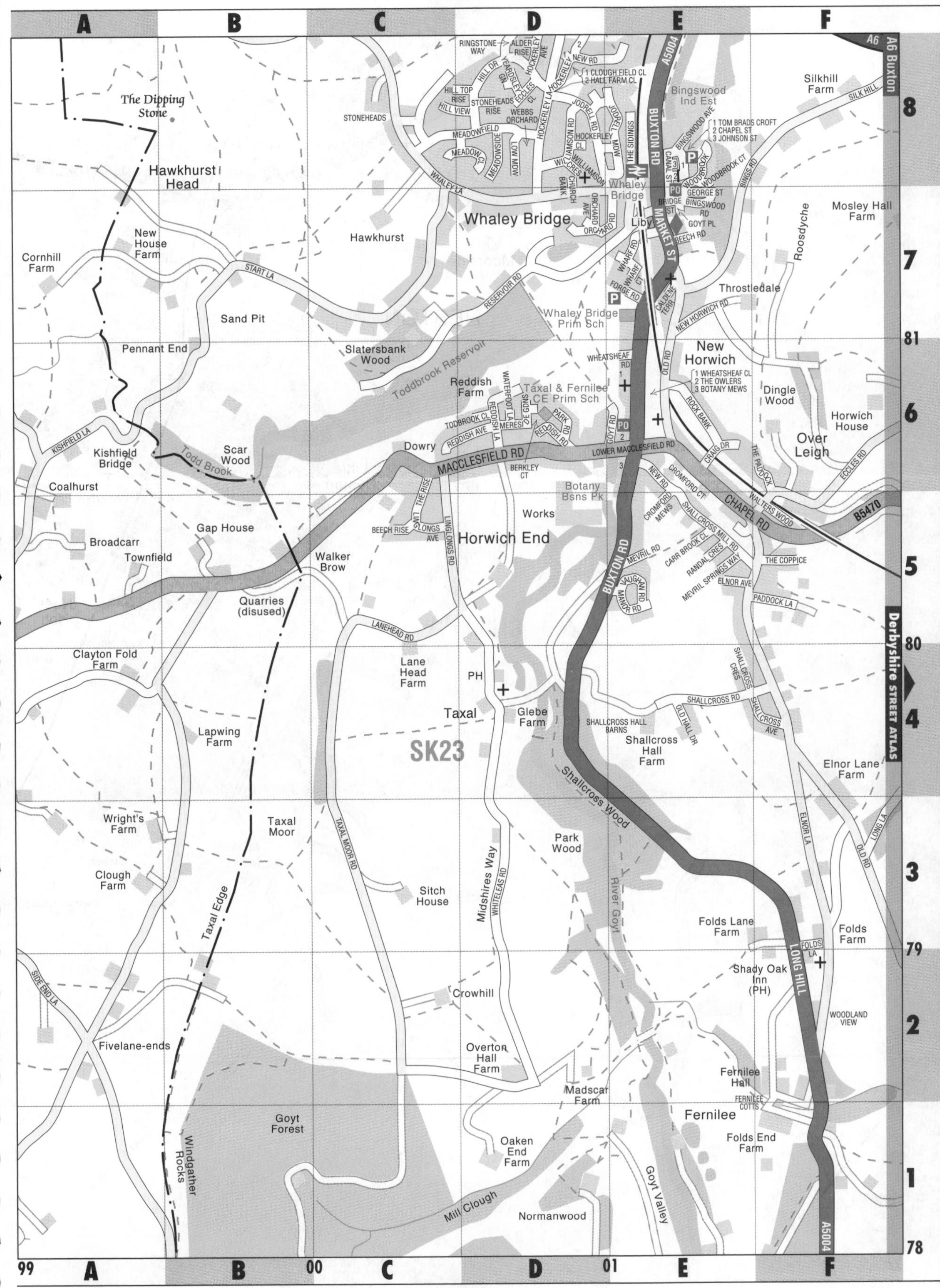

A
B
C
D
E
F
The Dipping Stone
Hawkhurst Head
New House Farm
Cornhill Farm
Hawkhurst
Whaley Bridge
Stoneheads
Sand Pit
Pennant End
Slatersbank Wood
Toddbrook Reservoir
Reddish Farm
Taxal & Fernilee CE Prim Sch
Whaley Bridge Prim Sch
Kishfield Bridge
Scar Wood
Todd Brook
Dowry
MACCLESFIELD RD
Coalhurst
Broadcarr
Gap House
Townfield
Walker Brow
Horwich End
Works
Botany Bsns Pk
Quarries (disused)
Clayton Fold Farm
Lane Head Farm
PH
Taxal
Glebe Farm
SK23
Lapwing Farm
Shallcross Hall Farm
Shallcross Wood
Wright's Farm
Taxal Moor
Park Wood
Clough Farm
Sitch House
Midshires Way
River Goyt
Taxal Edge
Folds Lane Farm
Folds Farm
Shady Oak Inn (PH)
LONG HILL
Crowhill
Fivelane-ends
Overton Hall Farm
Madscar Farm
Fernilee Hall
Fernilee
Folds End Farm
Goyt Forest
Windgather Rocks
Oaken End Farm
Mill Clough
Normanwood
Goyt Valley
Bingswood Ind Est
Silkhill Farm
Mosley Hall Farm
Roosdyche
Throstledale
New Horwich
Dingle Wood
Horwich House
Over Leigh
Elnor Lane Farm
1 TOM BRADS CROFT
2 CHAPEL ST
3 JOHNSON ST
1 CLOUGH FIELD CL
2 HALL FARM CL
1 WHEATSHEAF CL
2 THE OWLERS
3 BOTANY MEWS
BUXTON RD
MARKET ST
CHAPEL RD
B5470
A5004
A6 Buxton
Derbyshire STREET ATLAS
8
7
81
6
5
80
4
3
79
2
1
78
99
00
01

90

41

E8
1 MARLOWE RD
2 POPLAR WEINT
3 SCHOLAR'S CT
4 HADDON HO
5 DENWALL HO
6 ASHFIELD HO
7 HARGREAVE HO
8 THE CROSS
9 The Royal Sh Arc
10 ROKLIS GRANGE
F7
1 NORMANS COTTS

A B C D E F

8 7 6 5 4 3 2 1

77 76 75 74

HINDERTON LA
HINDERTON RD
B5134
A540
HANNS HALL RD
WEATHERSTONES COTTS
HANNS HALL FARM
LYDIATE LA
B5151
BIRKENHEAD RD
WHITEGATES CRES
MEADOW CROFT
MEADOW LA
MEADOW CL
Willaston CE Prim Sch
MILL GN
THE CHESTNUTS
ELM RD
ELM GN
THE COURTYARD
NESTON RD
Liby
B5133
NESS ACRE LA
BROADLAKE
PO
P
CHURCH FARM CT 1
WILLASTON FARM 2
WILLASTON GREEN MEWS 3
CHERRY BROW TERR 4
ATWORTH TERR 5
BUCKLEY LA
BUCKLEY CT
HADLOW LA
HADLOW TERR
CHERRY CL
WEATHERSTONES MEWS
University of Liverpool, Faculty of Veterinary Science (Leahurst)
Wood Park
Windle Hill
CUCKOO LA
Wirral Country Park
DAMHEAD LA
LEES LA
BENDEE RD
BENDEE AVE
RAYMOND WAY
DUNRAVEN RD
WATERFORD DR
ASHTREE DR
ASHTREE CL
SANDY LA
STONEBANK DR
BANK CL
HOWARDS WAY
ROCK FARM DR
ROCKLEE GDNS
ROCK CL
ROCK FARM CL
VICTORIA RD
ROCK FARM GR
GORSTONS LA
WOODFALL CL
WOODFALL GR
SCHOOL AVE
WOODFALL LA
Woodfall Prim Sch
CHESTER HIGH RD
FERNYESS LA
NEW HEY LA
HADLOW RD
Willaston Grange
Hyfield
Ness Wood
MILL LA
Mill Farm
Errington's Plantation
DAWN CL
CUMBERS DR
HOLT HEY
NESTON RD
CUMBERS LA
FLASHES LA
HILL CT
HILL TOP LA
HILL CL
MILL BANK
PALACE HEY
SHONES CROFT
WELL LA
WELL CL
CH64
Haddon Hall Farm
Shotwick Brook
SMITHY CL 1
LABURNHAM FARM CL 2
DIAL COTTS 3
SUNSET COTTS 4
MEALORS NEW COTTS 5
SNAB LA 6
Ness
Orchard House
Haddon Hayes
Haddon Hall Farm
WOOD END LA
Heath Farm
DUNSTAN LA
Mast
HADDON LA
Visitor Ctr
Ness Botanic Gdns
Mickwell Brow
Friends Hall
Haddon Wood
NESTON RD
Dunstan Farm
DENHALL LA
HADDON RD
Fiddleston Plantation
WOOD LA
MUDHOUSE LA
Burton Wood
VICARAGE LA
PRIESTWAY LA
MILL LA
STATION RD
THE RAKE
THE VILLAGE
Burton
Burton Marsh Farm
PUDDINGTON LA
Bishop Wilson CE Prim Sch
Burton Point Farm
Burton Manor Coll

30 A B 31 C D 32 E F

67
43

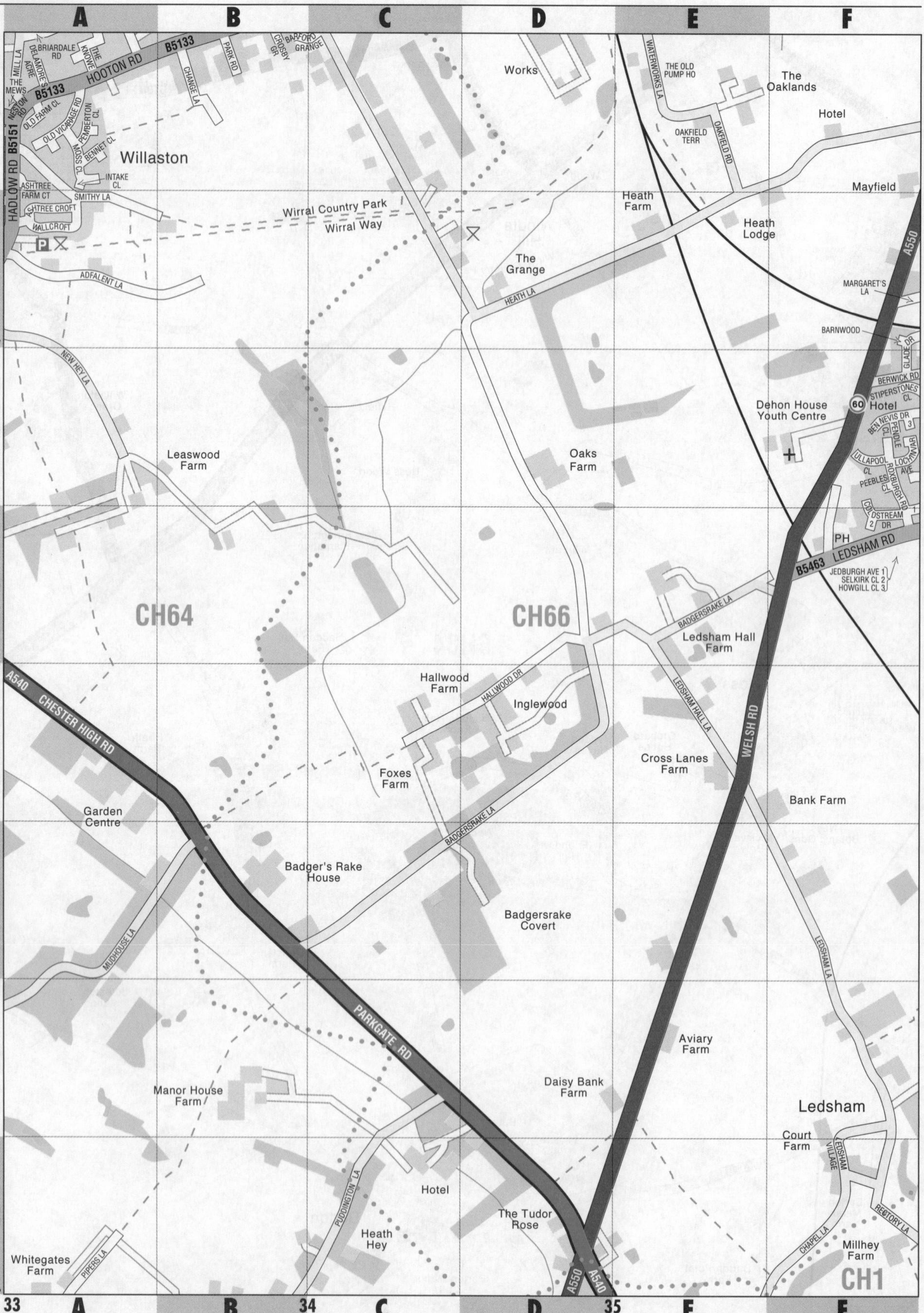
A B C D E F
8 7 6 5 4 3 2 1
77 76 75 74
33 34 35
B5133 HOOTON RD
B5151 HADLOW RD
MILL LA
THE MEWS
NESTON RD
DELAMORES ACRE
BRIARDALE RD
THE KNOWE
OLD FARM CL
OLD VICARAGE RD
PEMBERTON CL
BENNET CL
MOSS CL
INTAKE CL
ASHTREE FARM CT
SMITHY LA
CHTREE CROFT
WALLCROFT
CHANGE LA
PARK RD
CROSBY GR
BARFORD GRANGE
Willaston
Wirral Country Park
Wirral Way
ADFALENT LA
NEW HEY LA
Works
THE OLD PUMP HO
WATERWORKS LA
OAKFIELD TERR
OAKFIELD RD
The Oaklands
Hotel
Mayfield
Heath Farm
Heath Lodge
The Grange
HEATH LA
A550
MARGARET'S LA
BARNWOOD
GLADE DR
BERWICK RD
STIPERSTONES CL
Dehon House Youth Centre
60
Hotel
BEN NEVIS DR
PENDLE CL
LOCHINVAR AVE
ULLAPOOL CL
PEEBLES CL
ROXBURGH RD
COLDSTREAM DR
PH
B5463 LEDSHAM RD
JEDBURGH AVE 1
SELKIRK CL 2
HOWGILL CL 3
Leaswood Farm
Oaks Farm
CH64
CH66
BADGERSRAKE LA
Ledsham Hall Farm
Hallwood Farm
HALLWOOD DR
Inglewood
LEDSHAM HALL LA
WELSH RD
A540 CHESTER HIGH RD
Foxes Farm
Cross Lanes Farm
Bank Farm
Garden Centre
Badger's Rake House
Badgersrake Covert
MUDHOUSE LA
PARKGATE RD
Aviary Farm
Manor House Farm
Daisy Bank Farm
Ledsham
Court Farm
LEDSHAM VILLAGE
RECTORY LA
Hotel
PUDDINGTON LA
The Tudor Rose
Heath Hey
CHAPEL LA
Millhey Farm
Whitegates Farm
PIPERS LA
A550
A540
CH1
LEDSHAM LA

67
93

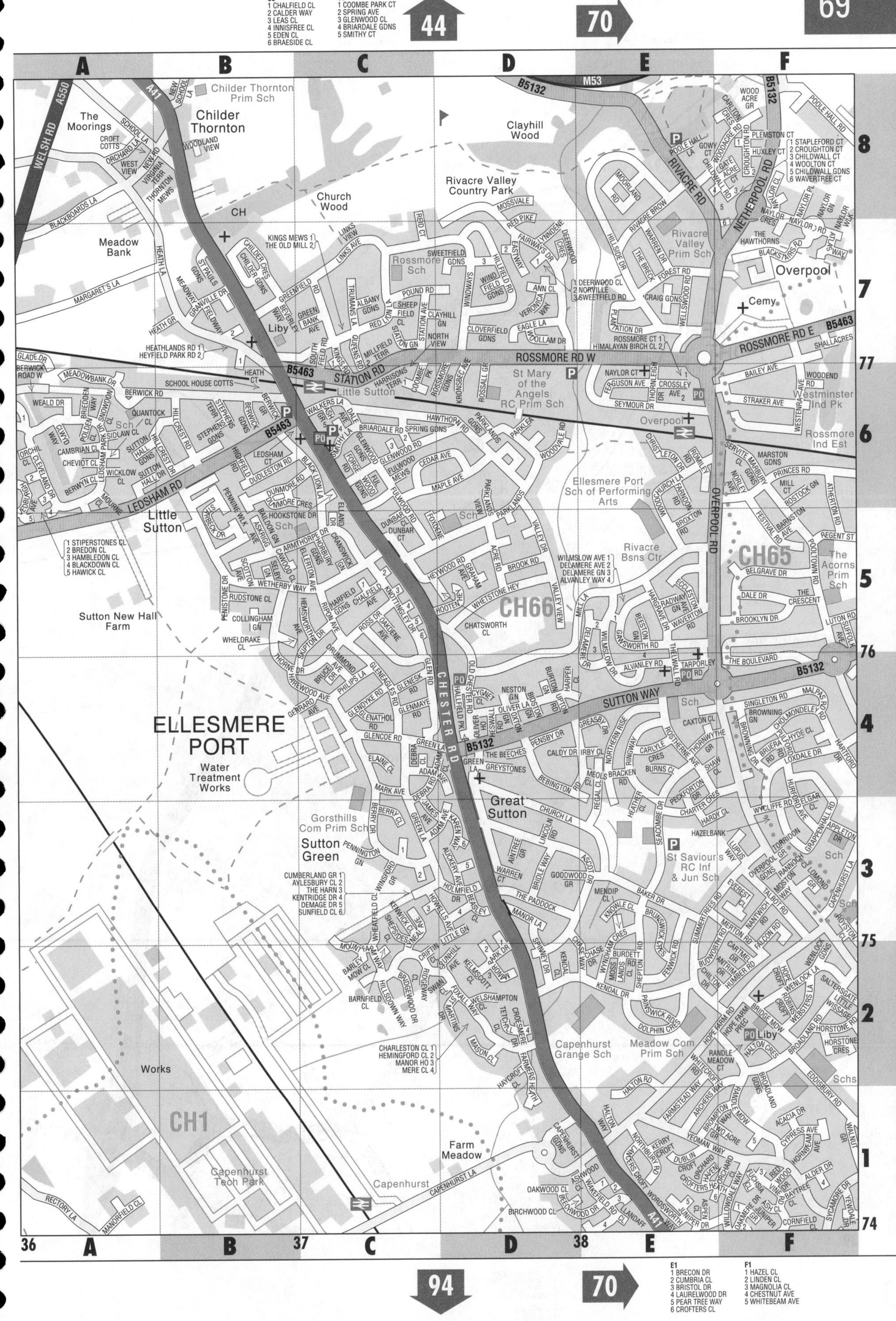

C5
1 CHALFIELD CL
2 CALDER WAY
3 LEAS CL
4 INNISFREE CL
5 EDEN CL
6 BRAESIDE CL
C6
1 COOMBE PARK CT
2 SPRING AVE
3 GLENWOOD CL
4 BRIARDALE GDNS
5 SMITHY CT
44
70
A
B
C
D
E
F
8
7
77
6
5
76
4
3
75
2
1
74
36
37
38
M53
B5132
A41
A550
WELSH RD
Childer Thornton Prim Sch
Childer Thornton
The Moorings
Clayhill Wood
Church Wood
Rivacre Valley Country Park
Meadow Bank
Rossmore Sch
Rivacre Valley Prim Sch
Overpool
Cemy
ROSSMORE RD E
B5463
ROSSMORE RD W
STATION RD
Little Sutton
St Mary of the Angels RC Prim Sch
Westminster Ind Pk
Rossmore Ind Est
Overpool
LEDSHAM RD
Little Sutton
Ellesmere Port Sch of Performing Arts
Rivacre Bsns Ctr
CH65
CH66
The Acorns Prim Sch
OVERPOOL RD
NETHERPOOL RD
RIVACRE RD
Sutton New Hall Farm
CHESTER RD
SUTTON WAY
ELLESMERE PORT
Water Treatment Works
Great Sutton
Gorsthills Com Prim Sch
Sutton Green
St Saviour's RC Inf & Jun Sch
Capenhurst Grange Sch
Meadow Com Prim Sch
Liby
Schs
Works
CH1
Capenhurst Tech Park
Capenhurst
CAPENHURST LA
Farm Meadow
1 STAPLEFORD CT
2 CROUGHTON CT
3 CHILDWALL CT
4 WOOLTON CT
5 CHILDWALL GDNS
6 WAVERTREE CT
KINGS MEWS 1
THE OLD MILL 2
1 DEERWOOD CL
2 NORVILLE
3 SWEETFIELD RD
HEATHLANDS RD 1
HEYFIELD PARK RD 2
ROSSMORE CT 1
HIMALAYAN BIRCH CL 2
1 STIPERSTONES CL
2 BREDON CL
3 HAMBLEDON CL
4 BLACKDOWN CL
5 HAWICK CL
WILMSLOW AVE 1
DELAMERE AVE 2
DELAMERE GN 3
ALVANLEY WAY 4
CUMBERLAND GR 1
AYLESBURY CL 2
THE HARN 3
KENTRIDGE DR 4
DEMAGE DR 5
SUNFIELD CL 6
CHARLESTON CL 1
HEMINGFORD CL 2
MANOR HO 3
MERE CL 4
94
70
E1
1 BRECON DR
2 CUMBRIA CL
3 BRISTOL DR
4 LAURELWOOD DR
5 PEAR TREE WAY
6 CROFTERS CL
F1
1 HAZEL CL
2 LINDEN CL
3 MAGNOLIA CL
4 CHESTNUT AVE
5 WHITEBEAM AVE

69

C6
1 WILKINSON STREET MEWS
2 CHURCH WLK
3 MARYVILLE CL
4 SUNNYSIDE
5 CHURCH PAR
6 WORCESTER WLK

C6
7 CRESSINGTON GDNS
8 CHARLES PRICE GDNS
9 THE COURT HO
10 JOSEPH GROOME TWRS
11 HIGHFIELD RD N

45

C5
1 ASHFIELD RD N
2 WOODFIELD RD N
3 WELLINGTON CL
4 SHREWSBURY RD
5 WATERLOO CL
6 WELLESLEY WLK
7 CAMBRIDGE CT

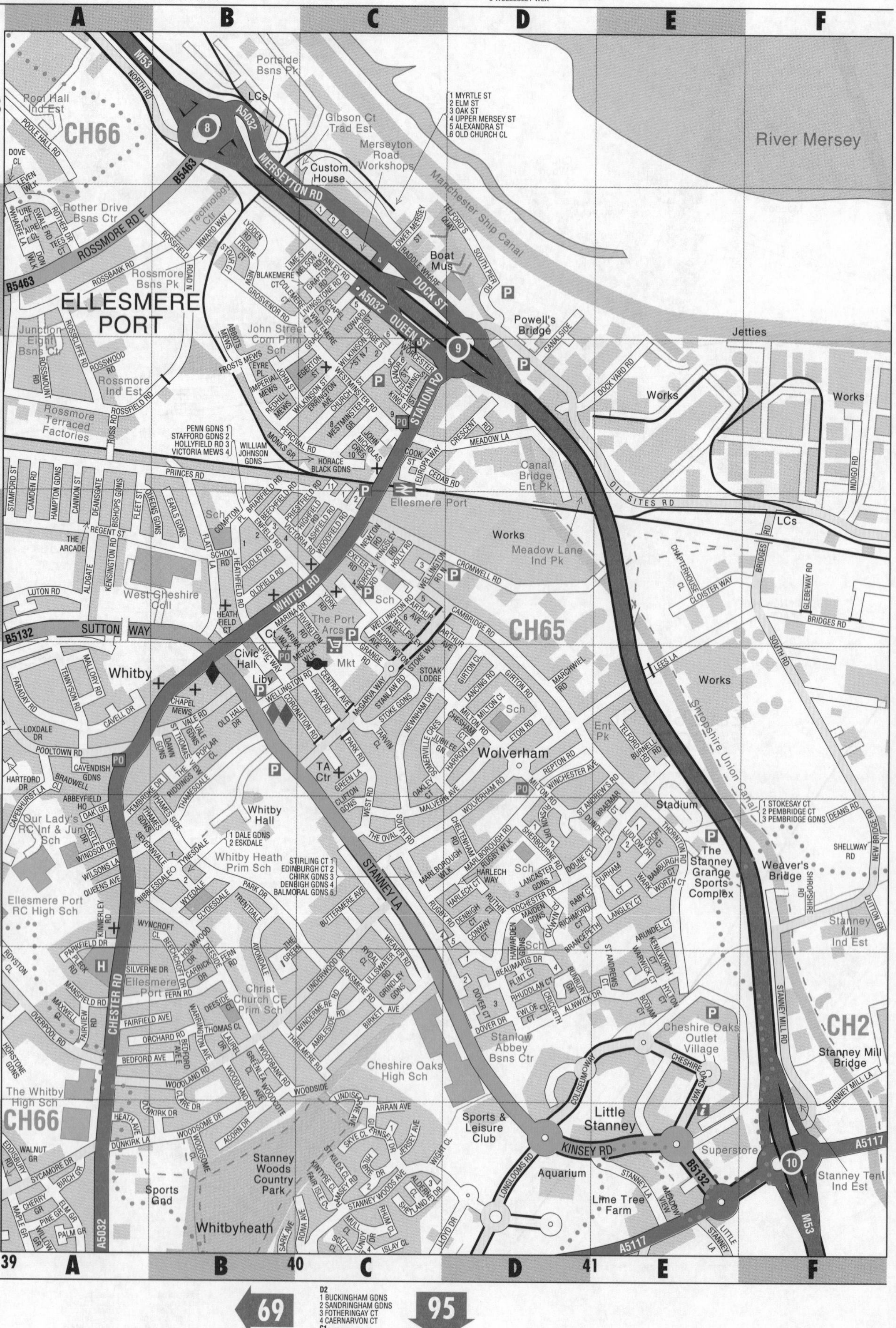

1 MYRTLE ST
2 ELM ST
3 OAK ST
4 UPPER MERSEY ST
5 ALEXANDRA ST
6 OLD CHURCH CL

PENN GDNS 1
STAFFORD GDNS 2
HOLLYFIELD RD 3
VICTORIA MEWS 4

1 STOKESAY CT
2 PEMBRIDGE CT
3 PEMBRIDGE GDNS

1 DALE GDNS
2 ESKDALE

STIRLING CT 1
EDINBURGH CT 2
CHIRK GDNS 3
DENBIGH GDNS 4
BALMORAL GDNS 5

ELLESMERE PORT

River Mersey

69

95

D2
1 BUCKINGHAM GDNS
2 SANDRINGHAM GDNS
3 FOTHERINGAY CT
4 CAERNARVON CT

C1
1 BARDSEY CL
2 ANGLESEY CL
3 ORKNEY CL
4 CUMBRAE DR

46
72

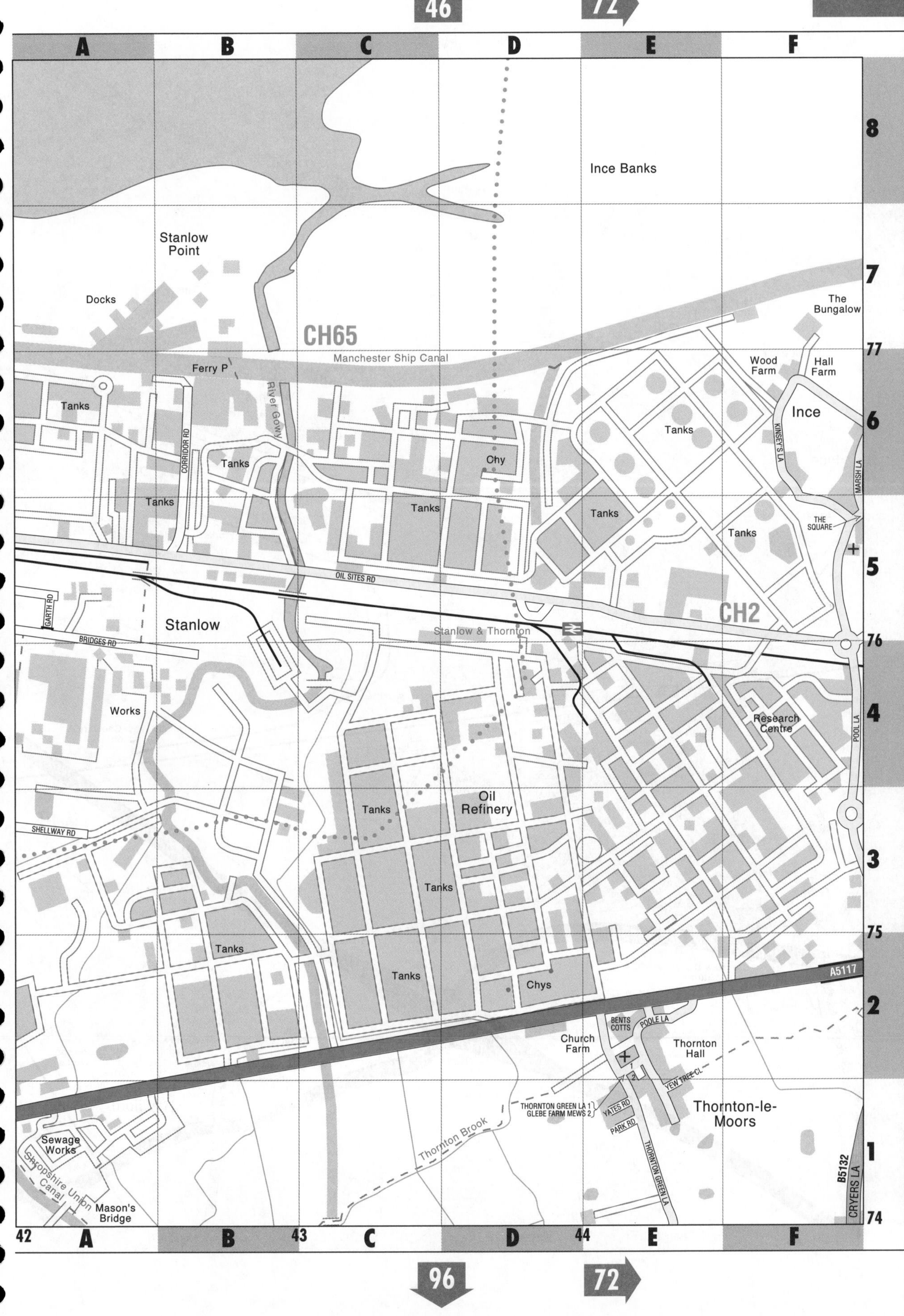
A
B
C
D
E
F
8
Ince Banks
Stanlow
Point
7
Docks
The
Bungalow
CH65
Manchester Ship Canal
77
Ferry P
Wood
Farm
Hall
Farm
River Gowy
Tanks
Ince
6
CORRIDOR RD
KINSEY'S LA
Tanks
Tanks
Chy
MARSH LA
Tanks
Tanks
Tanks
Tanks
THE
SQUARE
Tanks
5
OIL SITES RD
GARTH RD
Stanlow
CH2
BRIDGES RD
Stanlow & Thornton
76
Works
Research
Centre
4
POOL LA
Oil
Refinery
Tanks
SHELLWAY RD
3
Tanks
75
Tanks
Tanks
A5117
Chys
2
BENTS
COTTS
POOLE LA
Church
Farm
Thornton
Hall
YEW TREE CL
THORNTON GREEN LA 1
GLEBE FARM MEWS 2
YATES RD
Thornton-le-
Moors
PARK RD
Sewage
Works
Thornton Brook
1
THORNTON GREEN LA
Shropshire Union
Canal
B5132
CRYERS LA
Mason's
Bridge
74
42
A
B
43
C
D
44
E
F

96
72

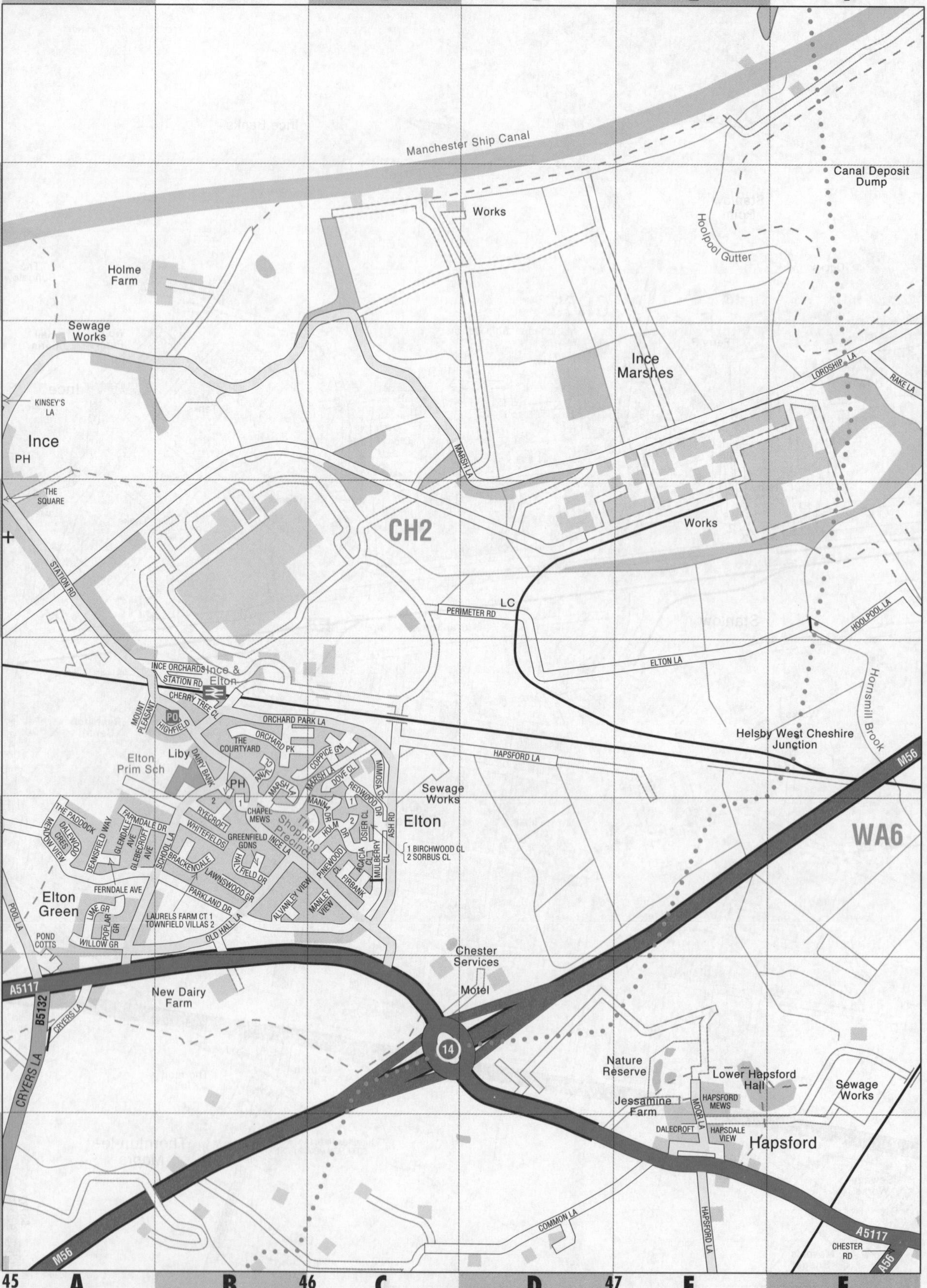

A B C D E F

8
7
77
6
5
76
4
3
75
2
1
74

45 A B 46 C D 47 E F

48
74

A B C D E F
8 7 6 5 4 3 2 1
77 76 75 74
48 49 50

98
74

B8
1 GREENFIELD LA
2 COLLINSON CT
3 SANDFIELD CT
4 DERFEL TERR
5 WHITEHALL PL

73
49

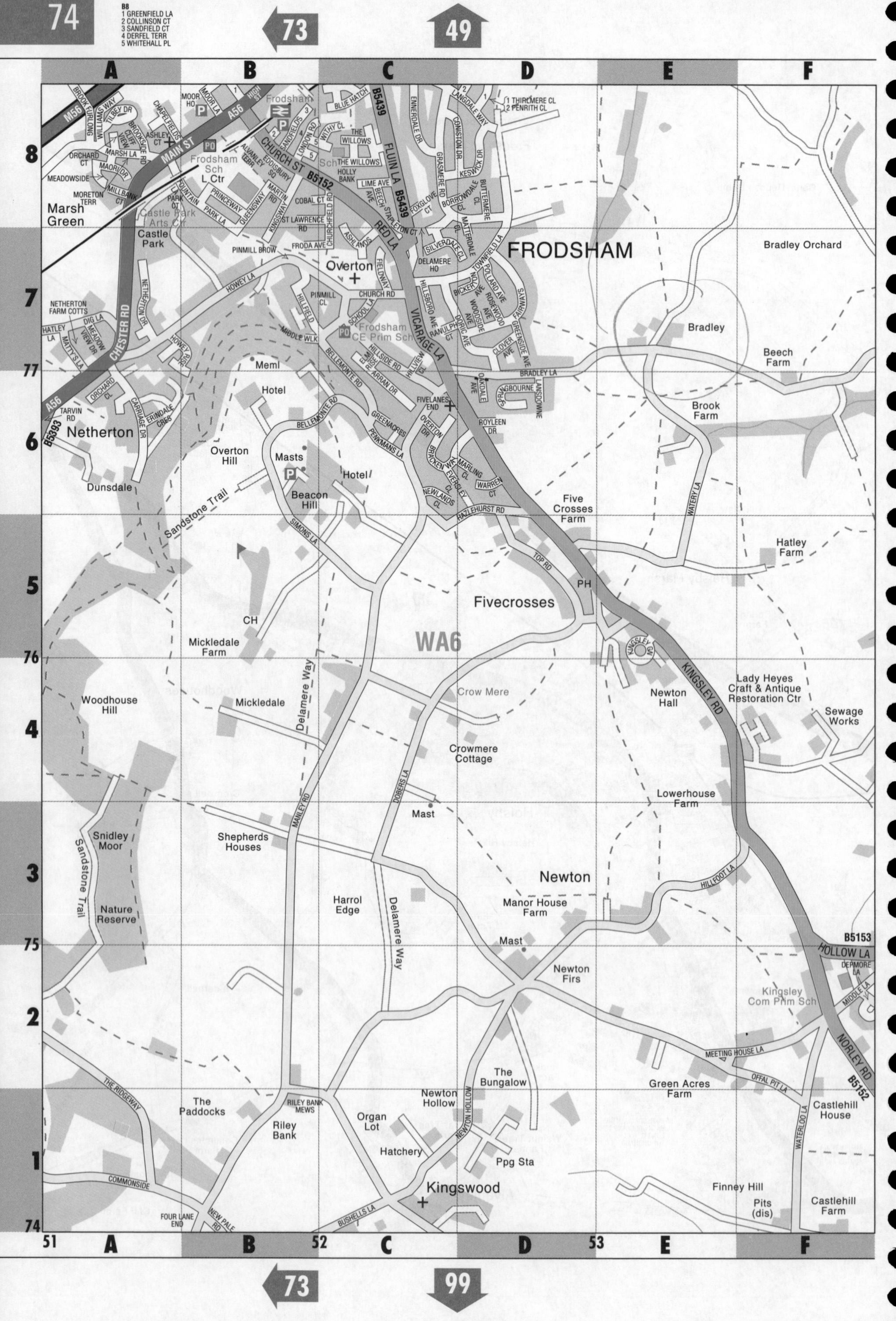

73
99

50 76

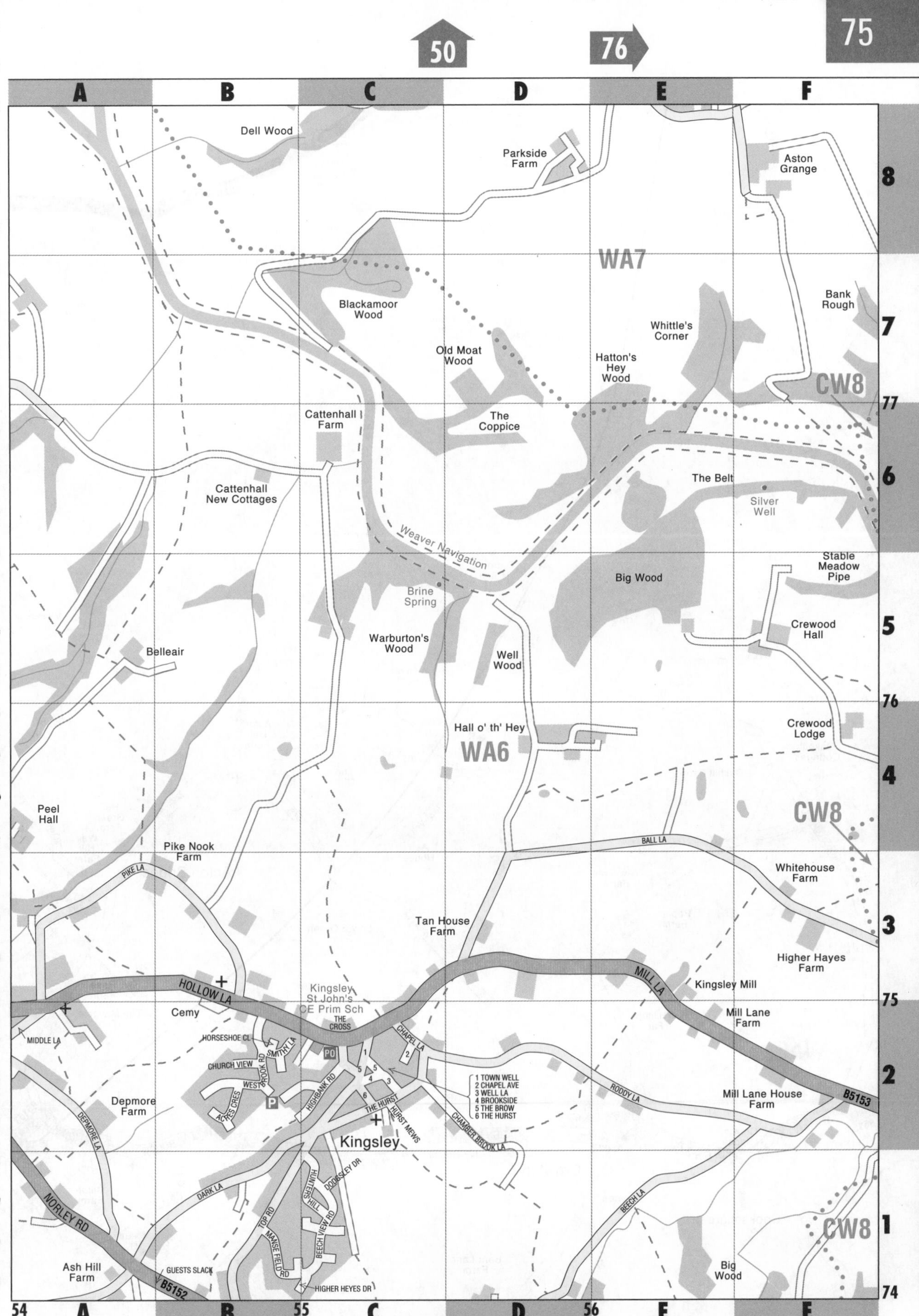
A B C D E F
8 7 77 6 5 76 4 3 75 2 1 74
54 55 56
Dell Wood
Parkside Farm
Aston Grange
WA7
Blackamoor Wood
Bank Rough
Whittle's Corner
Old Moat Wood
Hatton's Hey Wood
CW8
Cattenhall Farm
The Coppice
Cattenhall New Cottages
The Belt
Silver Well
Weaver Navigation
Stable Meadow Pipe
Big Wood
Brine Spring
Warburton's Wood
Crewood Hall
Belleair
Well Wood
Hall o' th' Hey
Crewood Lodge
WA6
Peel Hall
CW8
Pike Nook Farm
BALL LA
PIKE LA
Whitehouse Farm
Tan House Farm
Higher Hayes Farm
HOLLOW LA
MILL LA
Kingsley Mill
Kingsley St John's CE Prim Sch
Cemy
THE CROSS
Mill Lane Farm
MIDDLE LA
HORSESHOE CL
SMITHY LA
CHAPEL LA
PO
CHURCH VIEW
BROOK RD
1 TOWN WELL
2 CHAPEL AVE
3 WELL LA
4 BROOKSIDE
5 THE BROW
6 THE HURST
RODDY LA
Mill Lane House Farm
B5153
Depmore Farm
WEST
ACRES CRES
P
HIGHBANK RD
THE HURST
HURST MEWS
CHAMBER BROOK LA
DEPMORE LA
Kingsley
DODGSLEY DR
HUNTERS HILL
DARK LA
BEECH LA
NORLEY RD
TOP RD
BEECH VIEW RD
CW8
MANSE FIELD RD
Ash Hill Farm
GUESTS SLACK
B5152
HIGHER HEYES DR
Big Wood

100 76

A B C D E F

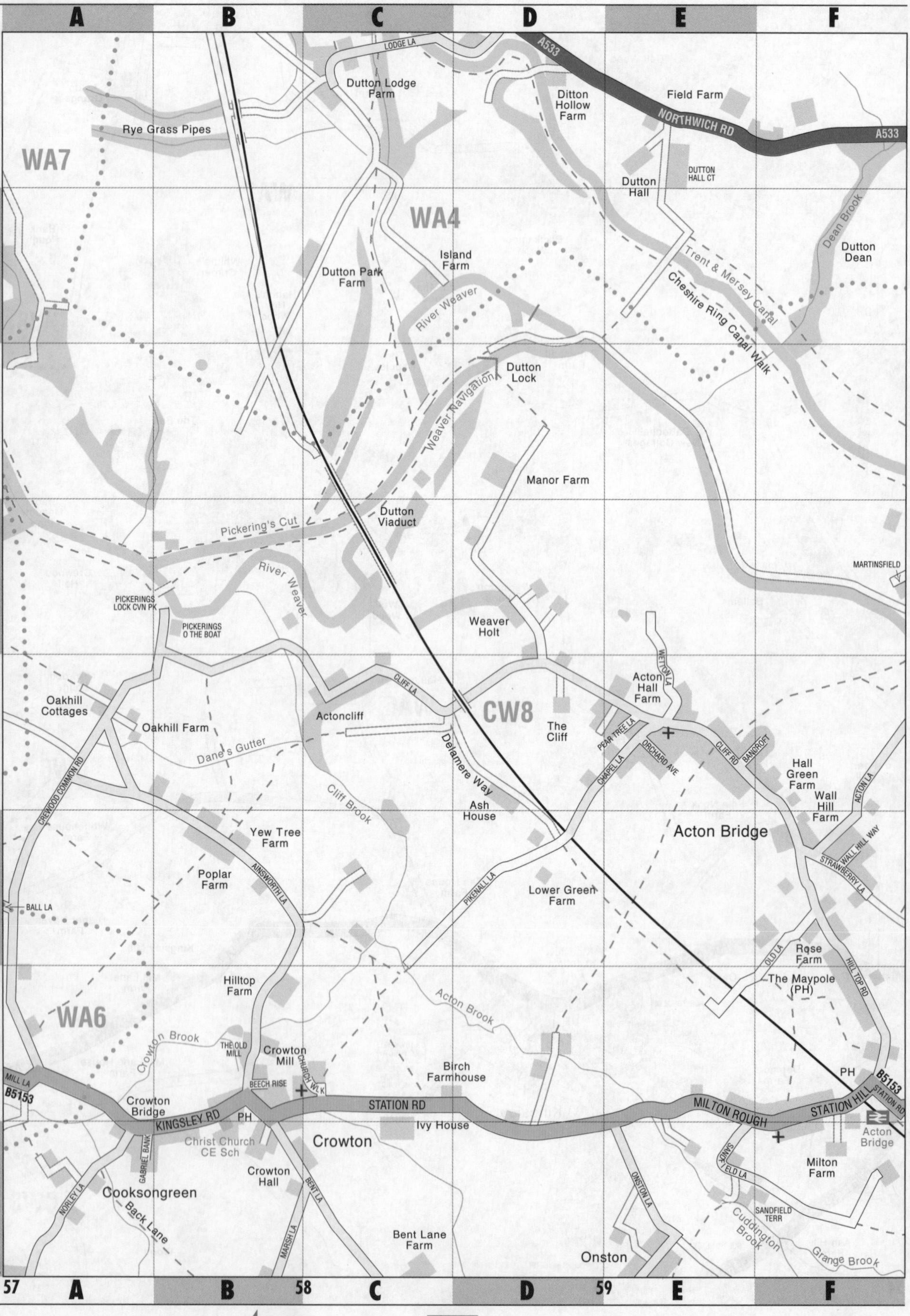

8 7 77 6 5 76 4 3 75 2 1 74

Rye Grass Pipes
WA7
Dutton Lodge Farm
LODGE LA
A533
Ditton Hollow Farm
Field Farm
NORTHWICH RD
A533
Dutton Hall
DUTTON HALL CT
WA4
Island Farm
Dutton Park Farm
Dean Brook
Dutton Dean
Trent & Mersey Canal
Cheshire Ring Canal Walk
River Weaver
Dutton Lock
Weaver Navigation
Manor Farm
Dutton Viaduct
Pickering's Cut
River Weaver
MARTINSFIELD
PICKERINGS LOCK CVN PK
PICKERINGS O THE BOAT
Weaver Holt
WETTON LA
Acton Hall Farm
CLIFF LA
Oakhill Cottages
Actoncliff
CW8
The Cliff
PEAR TREE LA
ORCHARD AVE
CLIFF RD
BANCROFT
Oakhill Farm
Dane's Gutter
Delamere Way
CHAPEL LA
Hall Green Farm
CREWOOD COMMON RD
Cliff Brook
Ash House
Wall Hill Farm
ACTON LA
WALL HILL WAY
Yew Tree Farm
Acton Bridge
STRAWBERRY LA
Poplar Farm
AINSWORTH LA
PIKENALL LA
Lower Green Farm
BALL LA
Rose Farm
OLD LA
HILL TOP RD
Hilltop Farm
The Maypole (PH)
Acton Brook
WA6
Crowton Brook
THE OLD MILL
Crowton Mill
CHURCH WLK
Birch Farmhouse
PH
MILL LA
B5153
BEECH RISE
B5153
STATION HILL
STATION RD
Crowton Bridge
KINGSLEY RD
PH
STATION RD
MILTON ROUGH
Ivy House
Acton Bridge
Christ Church CE Sch
Crowton
SANDY LA
ELD LA
Milton Farm
GABRIEL BANK
Crowton Hall
BENT LA
ONSTON LA
Cooksongreen
NORLEY LA
Back Lane
SANDFIELD TERR
MARSH LA
Bent Lane Farm
Cuddington Brook
Onston
Grange Brook

57 A B 58 C D 59 E F

52
78

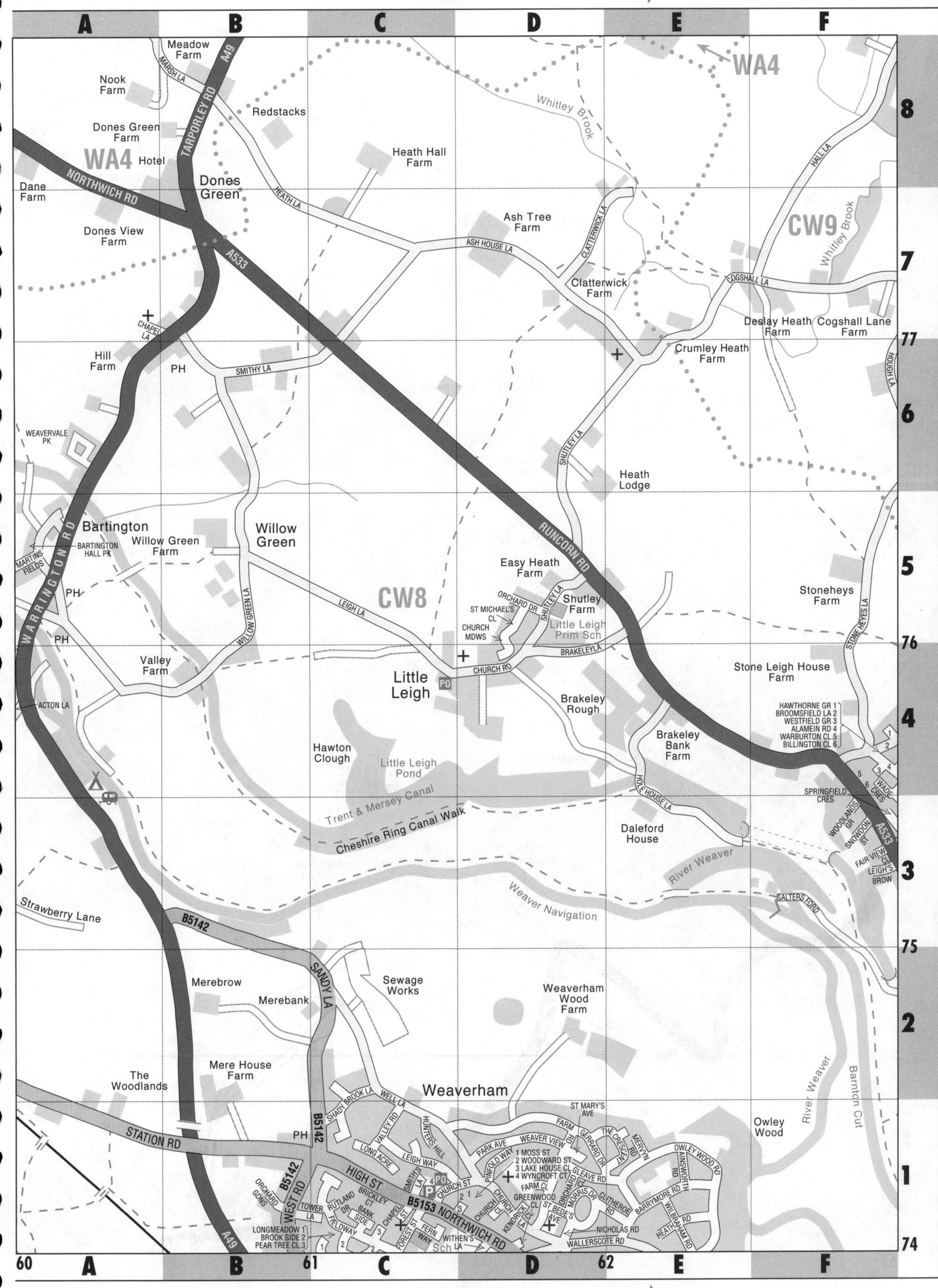
Meadow Farm
Nook Farm
Redstacks
Dones Green Farm
WA4
Hotel
Dane Farm
Dones Green
Heath Hall Farm
Dones View Farm
Ash Tree Farm
Clatterwick Farm
WA4
Whitley Brook
CW9
Deslay Heath Farm
Cogshall Lane Farm
Crumley Heath Farm
Hill Farm
PH
Heath Lodge
Bartington
Willow Green Farm
Willow Green
Easy Heath Farm
Shutley Farm
Little Leigh Prim Sch
CW8
Stoneheys Farm
Valley Farm
Little Leigh
Brakeley Rough
Stone Leigh House Farm
Hawton Clough
Little Leigh Pond
Brakeley Bank Farm
Trent & Mersey Canal
Cheshire Ring Canal Walk
Daleford House
River Weaver
Weaver Navigation
Strawberry Lane
Merebrow
Merebank
Sewage Works
Weaverham Wood Farm
The Woodlands
Mere House Farm
Weaverham
Owley Wood
Barnton Cut
HAWTHORNE GR 1
BROOMSFIELD LA 2
WESTFIELD GR 3
ALAMEIN RD 4
WARBURTON CL 5
BILLINGTON CL 6
1 MOSS ST
2 WOODWARD ST
3 LAKE HOUSE CL
4 WYNCROFT CL
LONGMEADOW 1
BROOK SIDE 2
PEAR TREE CL 3
A B C D E F
60 61 62
74 75 76 77
1 2 3 4 5 6 7 8

102
78

A
B
C
D
E
F
8
7
6
5
4
3
2
1
77
76
75
74
63
64
65
Cogshall Hall
Bogs Wood
Brook Farm
Comberbach
Comberbach Prim Sch
Brook House Farm
Avenue Farm
Brownslow Farm
PH
Cocklane Farm
Sandicroft
Brownslow House
NORTHWICH RD
A559
BELMONT RD
BUDWORTH LA
COCK LA
CROWNEST LA
THE AVENUE
GIBB HILL
BARRYMORE CRES
BURGAMOT LA
GOOSEBROOK CL
REEDSMERE WLK
BROOKFIELD RD
MATHER DR
CHAPEL CL
WARRINGTON RD
SPINNER CRES
MEADOW LA
SENNA LA
COGSHALL LA
HOUGH LA
FRESHFIELDS
BRACKEN WAY
FOXLEA
WOOD RD
KENNEL
THE MOSS
BROADACRE
Marbury Home Farm
CW9
Reed Bed
Budworth Mere
Cogshall Brook
Kennel Wood
Boat House
MARBURY RD
STONE HEYES LA
Houghlane Farm
Claycroft Farm
Marbury Park Country Park
Mill
Big Wood
MARBURY LA
Hopyards
1 SWEET BRIER CL
2 FIRTREE CL
3 MAPLE GR
4 LARCHTREE CL
CORONATION GR
Barnton Prim Sch
WHITEHALL CL
BROOMSFIELD LA
Marina
BRINE PUMP COTTS
Barnton
Anderton
UPLANDS RD
Uplands Farm
Rosebank Sch
ROSEBANK WLK
Liby
Cemy
PH
Trent and Mersey Canal
Cheshire Ring Canal Walk
Anderton Boat Lift & Nature Park
Cosgrove Bsns Pk
Haydn Pool
Weaver Navigation
A533
RUNCORN RD
Tunnel
OAKWOOD HO
Works
Ropery Farm
SHEPHERDS VIEW
1 OLD SCHOOL CL
2 THE MEWS
Slicks Bsns Ctr
River Weaver
CW8
Sewage Works
Sewage Works
Winnington
WINNINGTON LA
HOLLYBANK CL
SANDYBANK
MOSS RD
B5374
Victoria
THE WOODLANDS
BARONS QUAY RD
WEAVER WAY
WITTON ST
OLDHAMS HILL
Barnton Cut

54
80

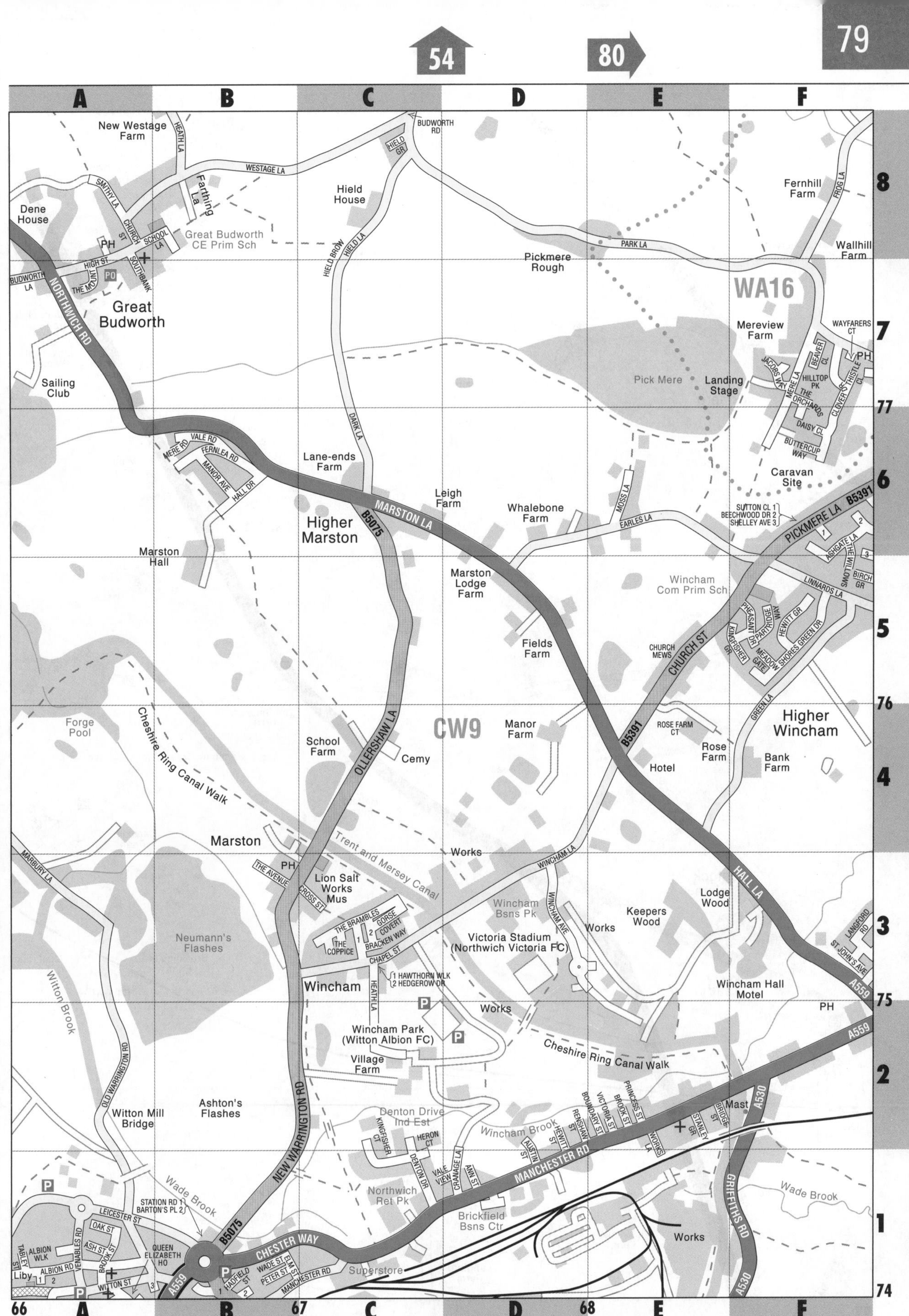

A1
1 POST OFFICE PL
2 ST PAUL'S PL
3 FOREST PL

104
80

79
55

A
B
C
D
E
F
8
7
77
6
5
76
4
3
75
2
1
74
69
70
71
Nether Tabley
Rinks Pool
Rinks Wood
Cuckoo Clock Mus
Brook Farm
Roses Farm
Pickmeremoss Wood
Clay House Farm
Tanyard Farm
Tabley Hall (rems of)
Dogkennel Wood
Providence Farm
Pickmere
Mast
The Hut
Manor Farm
Crow Wood
Tabley Grange
Smoker Hill Farm
WA16
Waterless Brook
Leonard's Wood
Home Farm
White House Farm
Smoker Brook
Smoker Wood
The Smoker (PH)
Henshaw Green Farm
Hopley's Pipes
Wincham Brook
Peas Wood
Halford Farm
Maltkiln Farm
Winnington Wood
Mill Wood
Holford Hall
Peover Eye
Lostock Gralam
Brookhouse Farm
Mushroom Farm
CW9
Long Wood
Plumley
Reservoir
Mast
Lostock Gralam
Holford Moss
Home Farm
Wade Brook
Fieldhouse Farm
Langford Farm
B5391
A556
A559
PICKMERE LA
HALL LA
MILLEY LA
FLITTOGATE LA
CHESTER RD
GREEN LA
SPINK LA
LINNARDS LA
WHITEHOUSE LA
PLUMLEY MOOR RD
MANCHESTER RD
ASCOL DR
MOSS LA
LOSTOCK HOLLOW
LOSTOCK GN
BIRCHES LA
1 CROFTERS CL
2 MEREHAVEN CL
PARK LA
MERE CL
WELLFIELD CL
PH
PO
ORCHARD CL
PEAR TREE DR
THE WOODLANDS
SHELLEY AVE
JOHN FRYER AVE
MILTON CL
KEATS LA
THE EVERGREENS
CEDAR CL
LANGFORD RD
HESKETH DR
WARREN AVE
GROVE AVE
TOWNSHEND RD
HIGHFIELD AVE
FRYER RD
GIBBON DR
WILSON CRES
HOLFORD AVE
SMITHY LA
SCHOOL LA
LODGE LA
STUBBS LA
1 AITCHISON RD
2 BATEMAN RD
FITTON ST
HERBERT ST
STATION RD
ARTHUR ST
ROBERTS RD
HARRIS RD
PAULDEN RD
ROSETREE MDW
Sch
MALT KILN RD
OAKFIELD RD 1
HAWTHORN RD 2
YEWTREE RD
HOLLYTREE RD
MOORCROFT
TROUTHALL LA
SOUTH DR

79
105

56
82

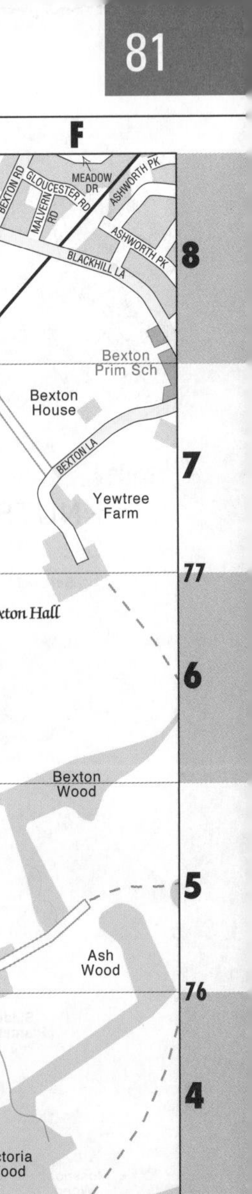
A
B
C
D
E
F
CHESTER RD
A556
TABLEY STABLES
Tabley House
Top Willowbed Wood
M6
Blackhill Farm
BEXTON RD
GLOUCESTER RD
MALVERN RD
MEADOW DR
ASHWORTH PK
BLACKHILL LA
8
Bexton Prim Sch
Bexton House
Serpentine Water
Parkgate Farm
BEXTON LA
Island Wood
7
Yewtree Farm
SUDLOW LA
Botany Bay Wood
77
Bexton Hall
Tabley Mere
6
Black Clump
Parkside Farm
Royd Wood
Bexton Wood
Parkside Cottage
5
Diamond Farm
Ullardhall Farm
Ash Wood
Nursery
WA16
76
Wash Farm
Wood's Tenement
Hucknall Farm
4
PINFOLD LA
Bucklow Farm
Victoria Wood
Plumley
Beech House Farm
3
PH
Pinfold Farm
Holly Tree Farm
The Grange
Plumleylane Farm
75
PLUMLEY MOOR RD
B5081
Beech Farm
Merry Farm
Heesom Green Farm
TROUTHALL LA
Plumley Moor
Smithy Green
2
Moss Farm
Lower Peover Hall
MIDDLEWICH RD
BROOM LA
Fields Farm
BACK LA
CH
Peover Eye
Brookfield House
CHEADLE LA
FREE GREEN LA
Lower Peover
CHURCH BARROW'S BROW
1
PH
WLK
Red Brook
The Fields Farm
THE COBBLES
CROWN LA
Lower Peover CE Prim Sch
B5081
74
72
73
74

106
82

81 57

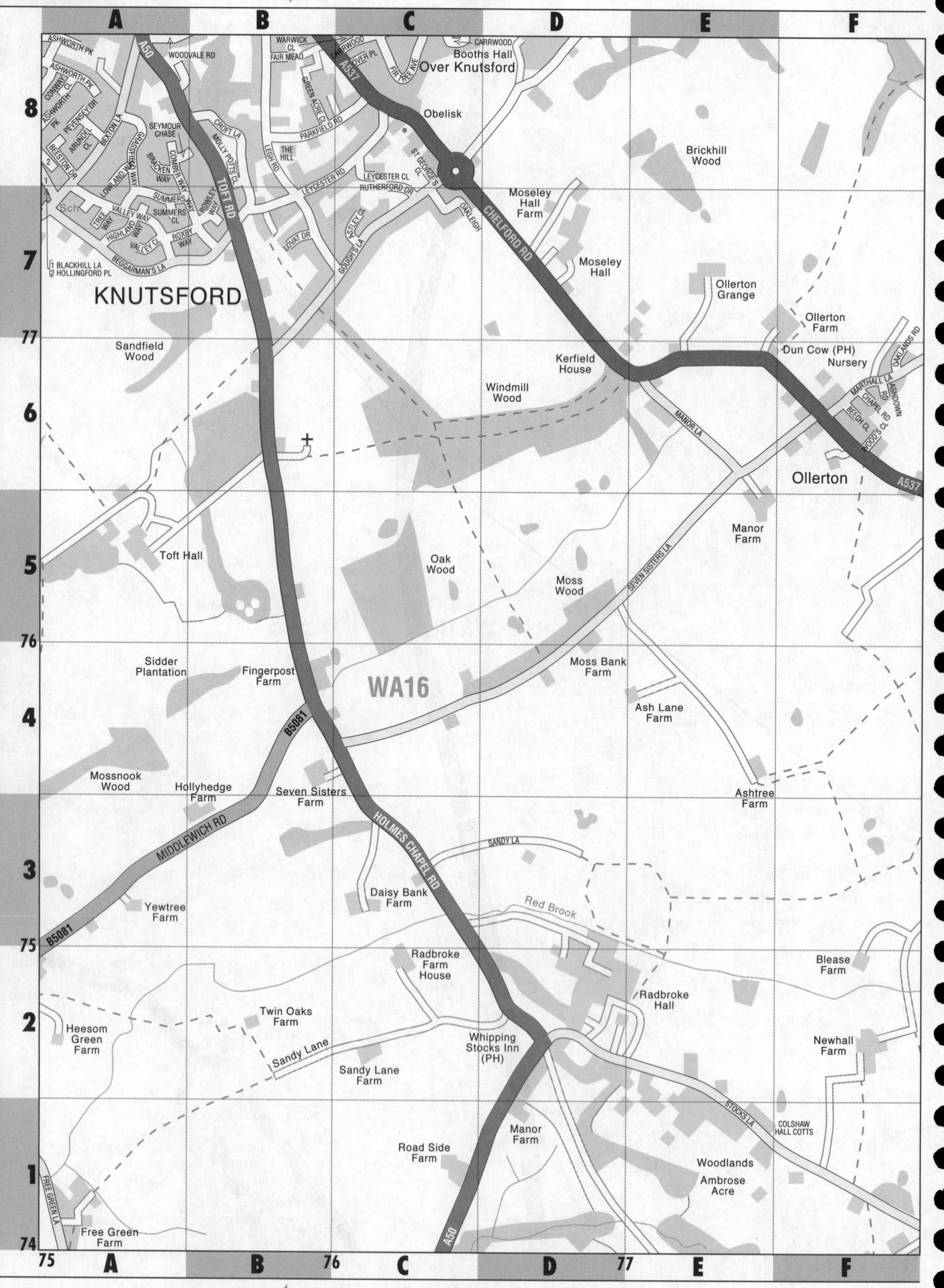

KNUTSFORD
Over Knutsford
Booths Hall
Obelisk
Brickhill Wood
Moseley Hall Farm
Moseley Hall
Ollerton Grange
Ollerton Farm
Dun Cow (PH)
Nursery
Ollerton
Kerfield House
Windmill Wood
Sandfield Wood
Toft Hall
Oak Wood
Moss Wood
Manor Farm
Sidder Plantation
Fingerpost Farm
WA16
Moss Bank Farm
Ash Lane Farm
Mossnook Wood
Hollyhedge Farm
Seven Sisters Farm
Ashtree Farm
Yewtree Farm
Daisy Bank Farm
Red Brook
Radbroke Farm House
Radbroke Hall
Blease Farm
Heesom Green Farm
Twin Oaks Farm
Whipping Stocks Inn (PH)
Sandy Lane Farm
Newhall Farm
Road Side Farm
Manor Farm
Colshaw Hall Cotts
Woodlands
Ambrose Acre
Free Green Farm
A50
A537
B5081
TOFT RD
CHELFORD RD
MANOR LA
SEVEN SISTERS LA
HOLMES CHAPEL RD
MIDDLEWICH RD
SANDY LA
Sandy Lane
STOCKS LA
FREE GREEN LA
1 BLACKHILL LA
2 HOLLINGFORD PL

81 107

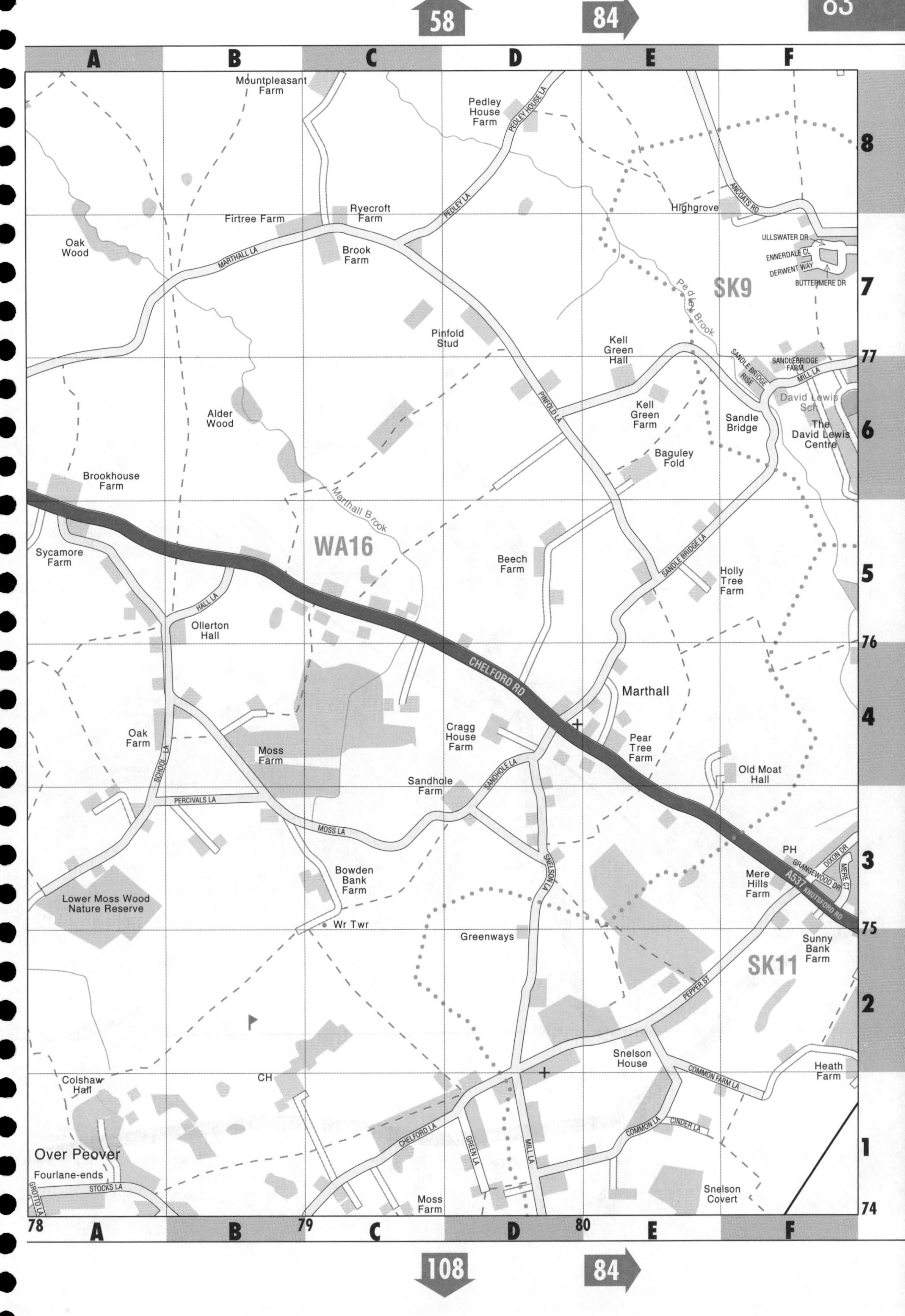
58
84
A
B
C
D
E
F
Mountpleasant Farm
Pedley House Farm
PEDLEY HOUSE LA
Oak Wood
Firtree Farm
Ryecroft Farm
Brook Farm
MARTHALL LA
PEDLEY LA
Highgrove
ANCOATS RD
ULLSWATER DR
ENNERDALE CL
DERWENT WAY
BUTTERMERE DR
SK9
Pedley Brook
Pinfold Stud
Kell Green Hall
SANDLE BRIDGE RISE
SANDLEBRIDGE FARM
MILL LA
David Lewis Sch
Alder Wood
PINFOLD LA
Kell Green Farm
Sandle Bridge
The David Lewis Centre
Baguley Fold
Brookhouse Farm
Marthall Brook
WA16
Sycamore Farm
Beech Farm
SANDLE BRIDGE LA
Holly Tree Farm
HALL LA
Ollerton Hall
CHELFORD RD
Marthall
Oak Farm
Moss Farm
SCHOOL LA
Cragg House Farm
Pear Tree Farm
SANDHOLE LA
Old Moat Hall
Sandhole Farm
PERCIVALS LA
MOSS LA
PH
GRANGEWOOD DR
DIXON DR
MERE CT
SNELSON LA
Bowden Bank Farm
Mere Hills Farm
A537 KNUTSFORD RD
Lower Moss Wood Nature Reserve
Wr Twr
Greenways
Sunny Bank Farm
SK11
PEPPER ST
Colshaw Hall
CH
Snelson House
COMMON FARM LA
Heath Farm
COMMON LA
CINDER LA
CHELFORD LA
GREEN LA
MILL LA
Over Peover
Fourlane-ends
GROTTO LA
STOCKS LA
Moss Farm
Snelson Covert
8
7
77
6
5
76
4
3
75
2
1
74
78
79
80
108
84

83
59

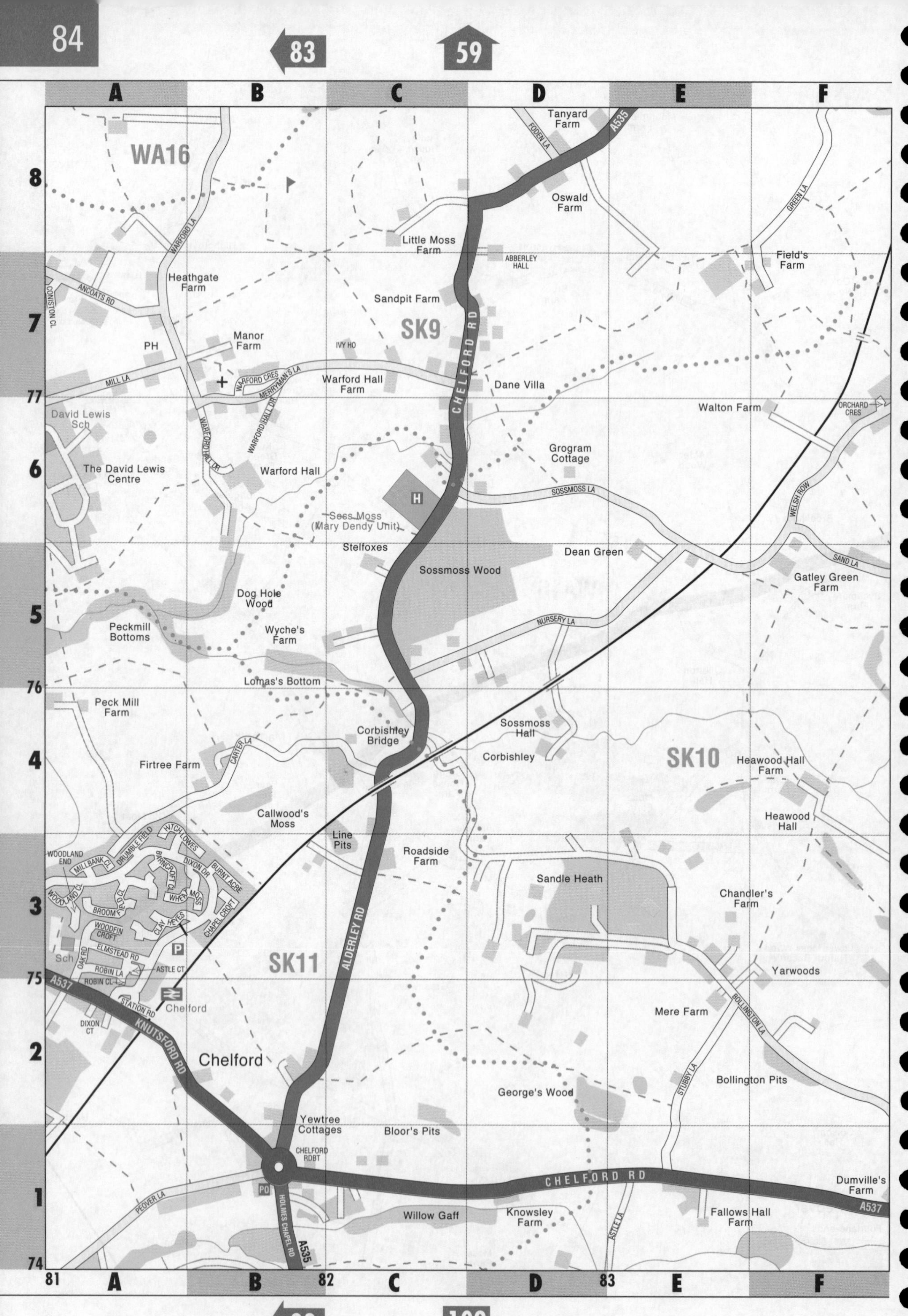
A B C D E F
8
7
77
6
5
76
4
3
75
2
1
74
81 82 83
WA16
SK9
SK10
SK11
Tanyard Farm
FODEN LA
A535
Oswald Farm
Little Moss Farm
ABBERLEY HALL
Field's Farm
GREEN LA
Heathgate Farm
ANCOATS RD
CONISTON CL
WARFORD LA
Sandpit Farm
CHELFORD RD
Manor Farm
PH
IVY HO
MILL LA
WARFORD CRES
MERRYMAN'S LA
Warford Hall Farm
Dane Villa
Walton Farm
ORCHARD CRES
David Lewis Sch
WARFORD HALL DR
Grogram Cottage
The David Lewis Centre
Warford Hall
SOSSMOSS LA
Sees Moss (Mary Dendy Unit)
WELSH ROW
Stelfoxes
Dean Green
Sossmoss Wood
SAND LA
Gatley Green Farm
Dog Hole Wood
Peckmill Bottoms
Wyche's Farm
NURSERY LA
Lomas's Bottom
Peck Mill Farm
Sossmoss Hall
Corbishley Bridge
Corbishley
CARTER LA
Firtree Farm
Heawood Hall Farm
Heawood Hall
Callwood's Moss
Line Pits
Roadside Farm
WOODLAND END
MILLBANK CL
DRUMBLE FIELD
HITCH LOWES
BRANCROFT CL
DIXON DR
BURNT ACRE
WOODLAND CL
BROOM
FIELD CL
WHEAT MOSS
CHAPEL CROFT
WOODFIN CROFT
CLAY HEYES
Sandle Heath
Chandler's Farm
Sch
OAK RD
ELMSTEAD RD
ROBIN LA
ROBIN CL
ASTLE CT
A537
STATION RD
Chelford
ALDERLEY RD
Yarwoods
DIXON CT
KNUTSFORD RD
BOLLINSTON LA
Mere Farm
STUBBY LA
Bollington Pits
George's Wood
Yewtree Cottages
Bloor's Pits
CHELFORD RDBT
PO
CHELFORD RD
Dumville's Farm
PEOVER LA
HOLMES CHAPEL RD
Willow Gaff
Knowsley Farm
ASTLE LA
Fallows Hall Farm
A535

83
109

60
86
A B C D E F 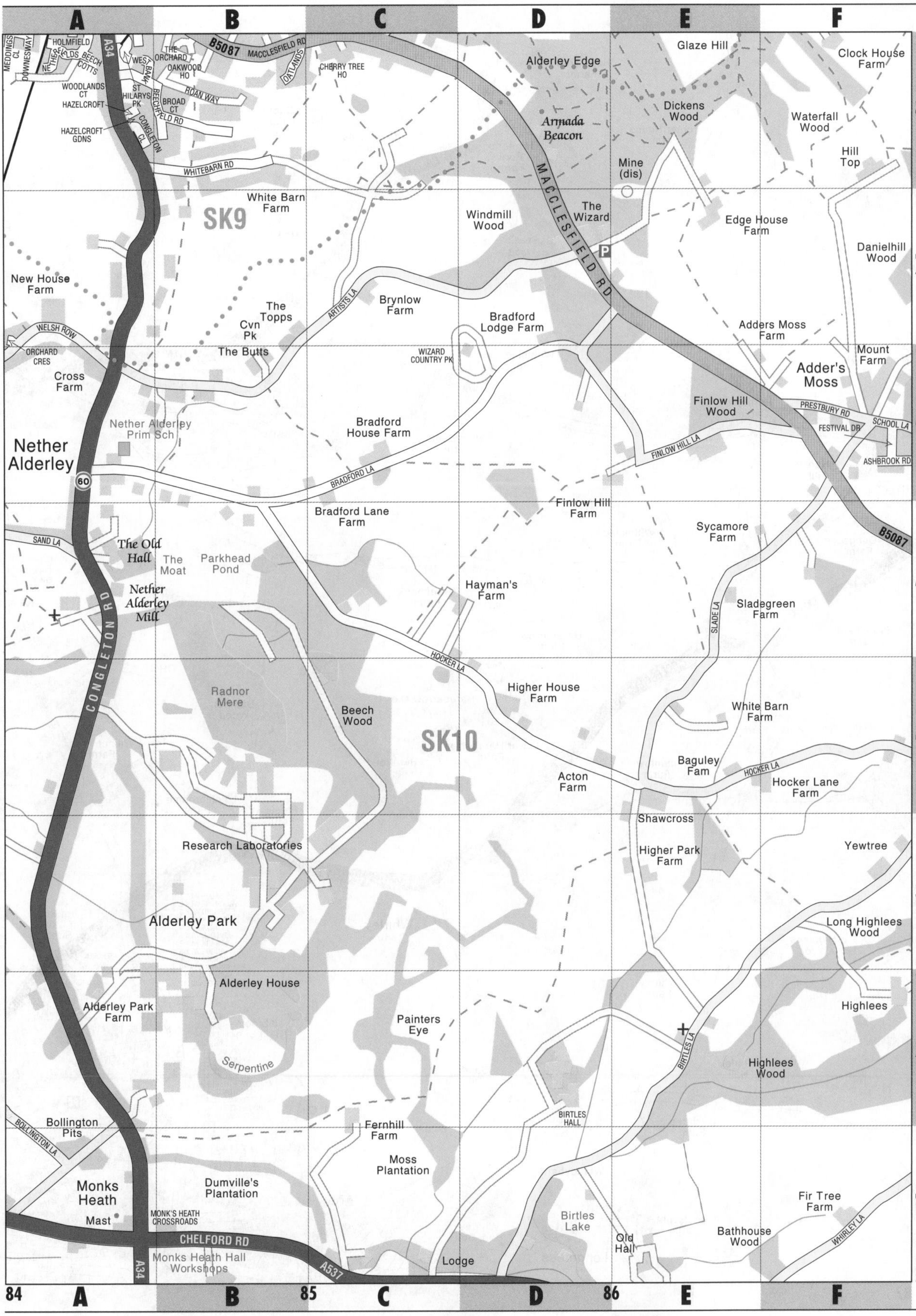
MEDDINGS CL
DOWNESWAY
HOLMFIELD
BEECH COTTS
WOODLANDS CT
HAZELCROFT
HAZELCROFT GDNS
A34
WEST BANK
THE ORCHARD
OAKWOOD HO
ST HILARYS PK
BEECHFIELD RD
BROAD CT
CONGLETON CL
B5087 MACCLESFIELD RD
ORTLANDS
CHERRY TREE HO
ROAN WAY
WHITEBARN RD
Alderley Edge
Glaze Hill
Clock House Farm
Dickens Wood
Waterfall Wood
Armada Beacon
Mine (dis)
Hill Top
White Barn Farm
SK9
Windmill Wood
The Wizard
MACCLESFIELD RD
Edge House Farm
Danielhill Wood
New House Farm
The Topps
Brynlow Farm
Cvn Pk
ARTISTS LA
Bradford Lodge Farm
Adders Moss Farm
Mount Farm
WELSH ROW
ORCHARD CRES
The Butts
WIZARD COUNTRY PK
Adder's Moss
Cross Farm
Finlow Hill Wood
PRESTBURY RD
SCHOOL LA
FESTIVAL DR
ASHBROOK RD
Nether Alderley Prim Sch
Bradford House Farm
FINLOW HILL LA
Nether Alderley
60
BRADFORD LA
Finlow Hill Farm
Bradford Lane Farm
Sycamore Farm
B5087
SAND LA
The Old Hall
The Moat
Parkhead Pond
Nether Alderley Mill
Hayman's Farm
SLADE LA
Sladegreen Farm
CONGLETON RD
HOCKER LA
Radnor Mere
Beech Wood
Higher House Farm
White Barn Farm
SK10
Baguley Fam
HOCKER LA
Acton Farm
Hocker Lane Farm
Shawcross
Research Laboratories
Higher Park Farm
Yewtree
Alderley Park
Long Highlees Wood
Alderley House
Alderley Park Farm
Painters Eye
Highlees
BIRTLES LA
Serpentine
Highlees Wood
Bollington Pits
BOLLINGTON LA
Fernhill Farm
BIRTLES HALL
Moss Plantation
Monks Heath
Dumville's Plantation
Fir Tree Farm
Mast
MONK'S HEATH CROSSROADS
Birtles Lake
CHELFORD RD
Old Hall
Bathhouse Wood
WHIRLEY LA
Monks Heath Hall Workshops
A34
A537
Lodge
8
7
77
6
5
76
4
3
75
2
1
74
84
85
86
110
86

85
61

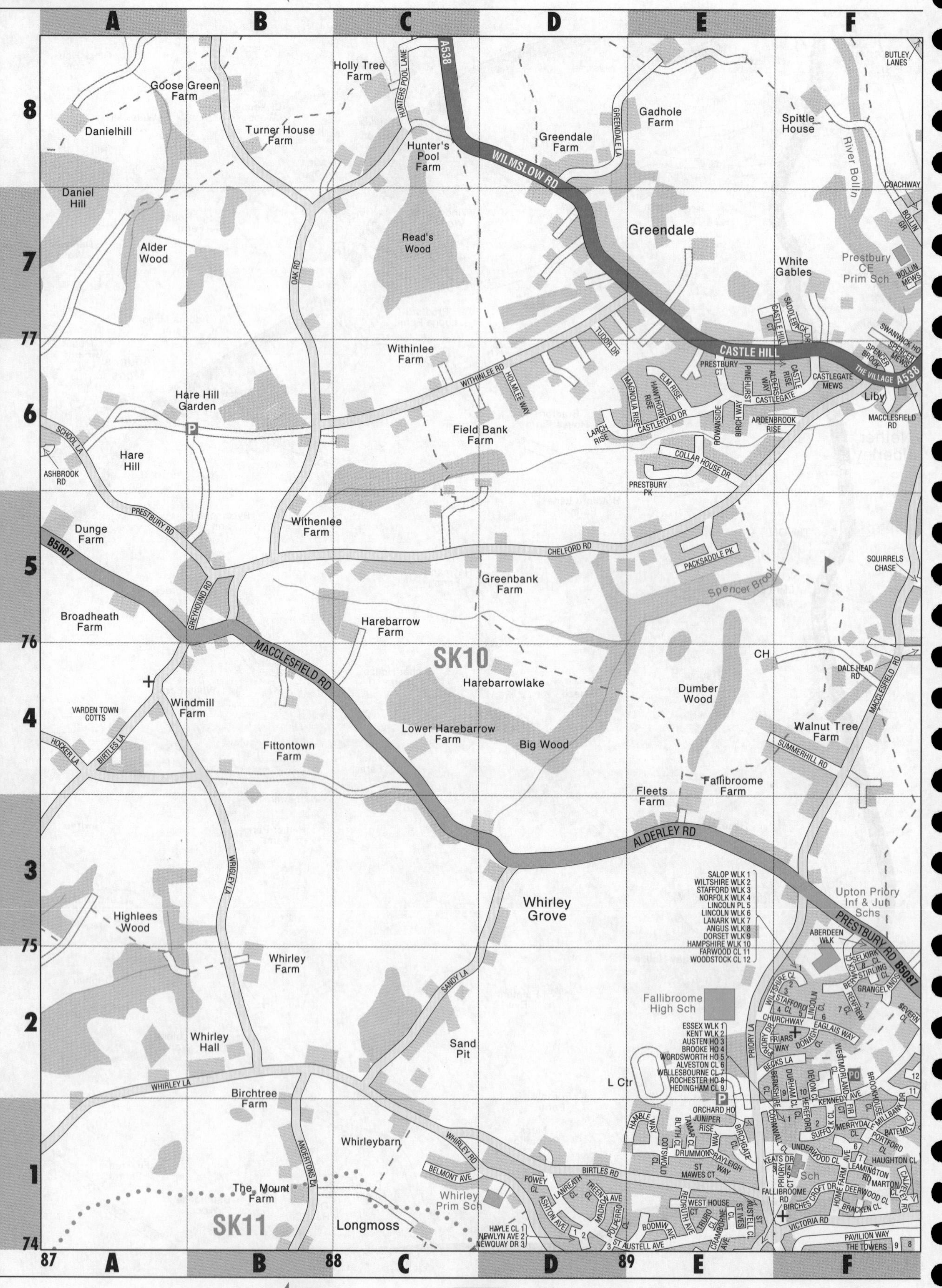
Goose Green Farm
Danielhill
Turner House Farm
Holly Tree Farm
Hunter's Pool Farm
Daniel Hill
Alder Wood
Read's Wood
Greendale Farm
Gadhole Farm
Spittle House
Greendale
White Gables
Prestbury CE Prim Sch
WILMSLOW RD
CASTLE HILL
Withinlee Farm
Hare Hill Garden
Hare Hill
Field Bank Farm
Liby
Withenlee Farm
Dunge Farm
Greenbank Farm
Broadheath Farm
Harebarrow Farm
SK10
Harebarrowlake
Dumber Wood
Windmill Farm
Lower Harebarrow Farm
Big Wood
Walnut Tree Farm
Fittontown Farm
Fallibroome Farm
Fleets Farm
ALDERLEY RD
MACCLESFIELD RD
Whirley Grove
Upton Priory Inf & Jun Schs
Highlees Wood
Whirley Farm
Fallibroome High Sch
Sand Pit
Whirley Hall
L Ctr
Birchtree Farm
Whirleybarn
The Mount Farm
Whirley Prim Sch
Longmoss
SK11
PRESTBURY RD B5087
Spencer Brook
River Bollin

62
88

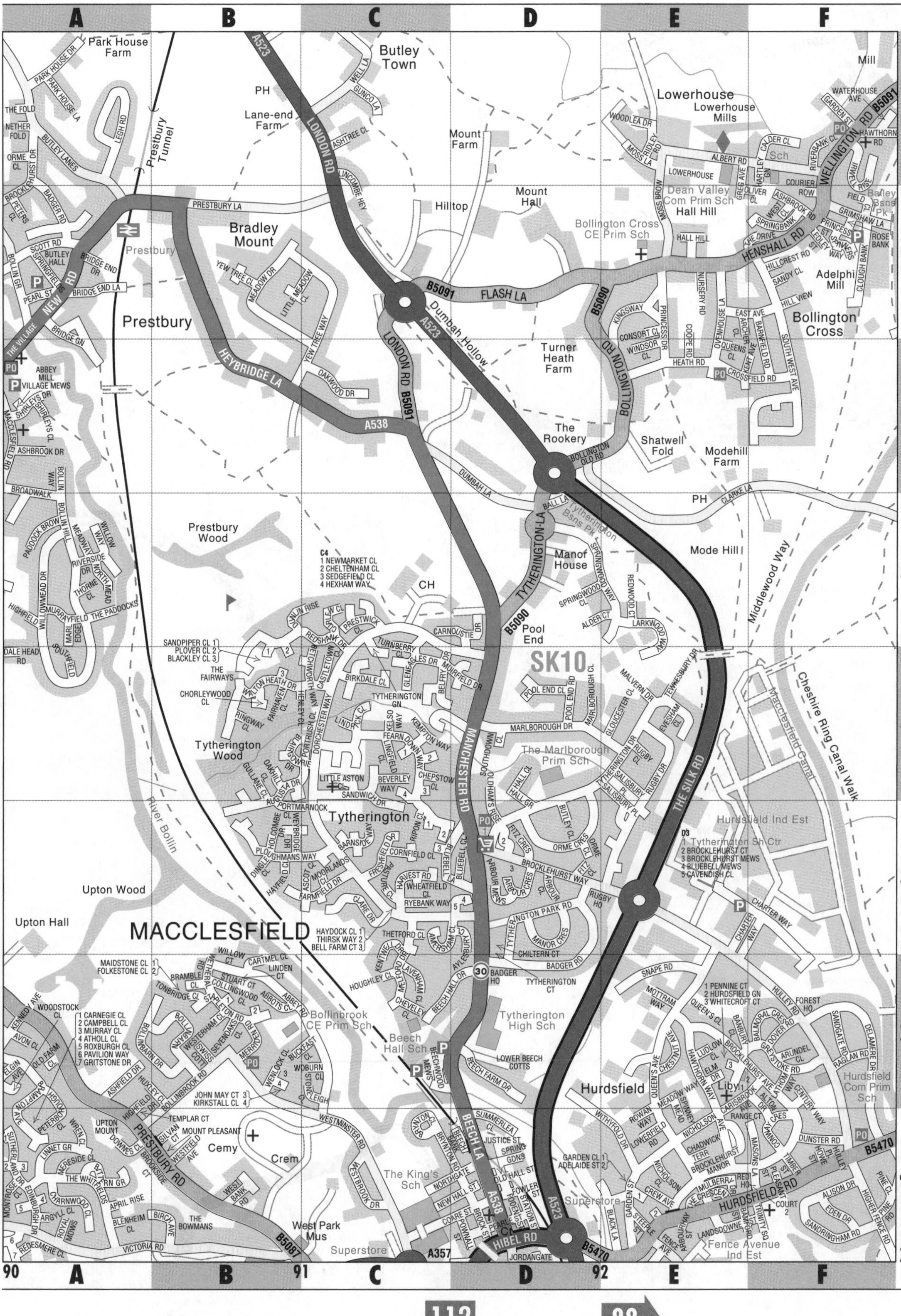

A B C D E F

Park House Farm
Butley Town
PH
Lane-end Farm
Mount Farm
Lowerhouse
Lowerhouse Mills
Mill
Prestbury Tunnel
LONDON RD
A523
PRESTBURY LA
Mount Hall
Hilltop
Dean Valley Com Prim Sch
Hall Hill
Bollington Cross CE Prim Sch
Bradley Mount
Prestbury
B5091
FLASH LA
HENSHALL RD
WELLINGTON RD
Adelphi Mill
Bollington Cross
Dumbah Hollow
Turner Heath Farm
BOLLINGTON RD
B5090
HEYBRIDGE LA
A538
The Rookery
Shatwell Fold
Modehill Farm
CLARKE LA
Prestbury Wood
TYTHERINGTON LA
Tytherington Bsns Pk
Manor House
Mode Hill
Middlewood Way
CH
Pool End
SK10
Cheshire Ring Canal Walk
Macclesfield Canal
Tytherington Wood
MANCHESTER RD
The Marlborough Prim Sch
THE SILK RD
Hurdsfield Ind Est
River Bollin
Tytherington
Upton Wood
Upton Hall
MACCLESFIELD
Tytherington High Sch
Bollinbrook CE Prim Sch
Beech Hall Sch
Hurdsfield
Hurdsfield Com Prim Sch
Cemy
Crem
PRESTBURY RD
The King's Sch
BEECH LA
HURDSFIELD RD
B5470
West Park Mus
Superstore
HIBEL RD
A357
B5087
Fence Avenue Ind Est

C4
1 NEWMARKET CL
2 CHELTENHAM CL
3 SEDGEFIELD CL
4 HEXHAM WAY

D3
1 Tytherington Sh Ctr
2 BROCKLEHURST CT
3 BROCKLEHURST MEWS
4 BLUEBELL MEWS
5 CAVENDISH CL

1 PENNINE CT
2 HURDSFIELD GN
3 WHITECROFT CT

1 CARNEGIE CL
2 CAMPBELL CL
3 MURRAY CL
4 ATHOLL CL
5 ROXBURGH CL
6 PAVILION WAY
7 GRITSTONE DR

8
7
77
6
5
76
4
3
75
2
1
74

90 A B 91 C D 92 E F

112
88

87 63

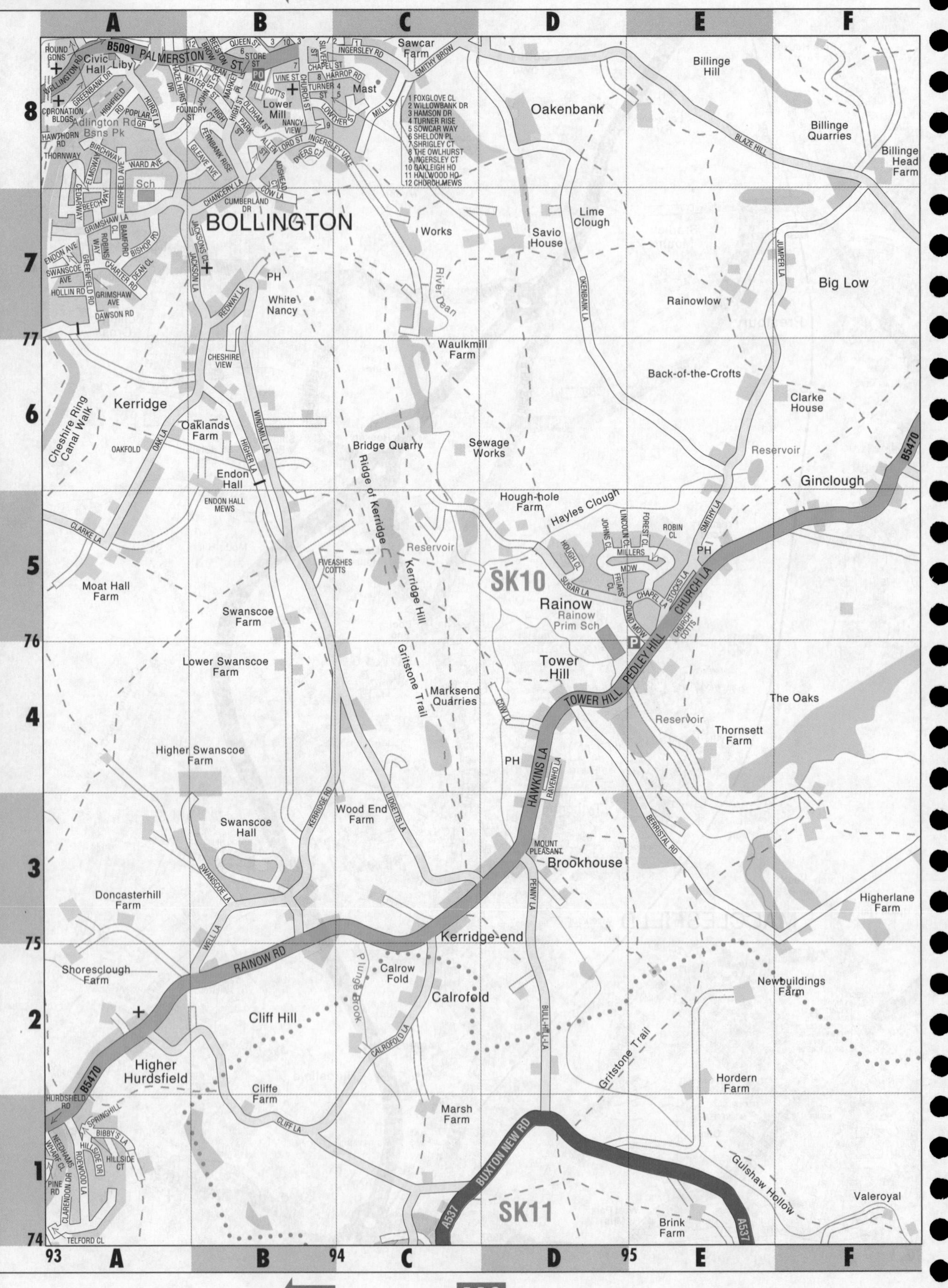
A B C D E F
8 7 6 5 4 3 2 1
77 76 75 74
93 94 95
B5091 PALMERSTON ST
BOLLINGTON
Civic Hall
Liby
Adlington Rd Bsns Pk
Sch
Lower Mill
Mast
Sawcar Farm
Works
Oakenbank
Billinge Hill
Billinge Quarries
Billinge Head Farm
Lime Clough
Savio House
Big Low
Rainowlow
White Nancy
PH
River Dean
Waulkmill Farm
Back-of-the-Crofts
Clarke House
Kerridge
Cheshire Ring Canal Walk
Oaklands Farm
OAKFOLD
Bridge Quarry
Sewage Works
Reservoir
Ginclough
B5470
Endon Hall
ENDON HALL MEWS
Ridge of Kerridge
Hough-hole Farm
Hayles Clough
Moat Hall Farm
FIVEASHES COTTS
Kerridge Hill
SK10
Rainow
Rainow Prim Sch
Swanscoe Farm
Lower Swanscoe Farm
Gritstone Trail
Tower Hill
TOWER HILL
PEDLEY HILL
CHURCH LA
Marksend Quarries
The Oaks
Thornsett Farm
Higher Swanscoe Farm
HAWKINS LA
Wood End Farm
Swanscoe Hall
MOUNT PLEASANT
Brookhouse
Doncasterhill Farm
Higherlane Farm
Kerridge-end
RAINOW RD
Shoresclough Farm
Calrow Fold
Calrofold
Plunge Brook
Newbuildings Farm
Cliff Hill
Higher Hurdsfield
Cliffe Farm
Hordern Farm
Marsh Farm
BUXTON NEW RD
A537
Gulshaw Hollow
Valeroyal
SK11
Brink Farm
TELFORD CL
1 FOXGLOVE CL
2 WILLOWBANK DR
3 HAMSON DR
4 TURNER RISE
5 SOWCAR WAY
6 SHELDON PL
7 SHRIGLEY CT
8 THE OWLHURST
9 INGERSLEY CT
10 OAKLEIGH HO
11 HALLWOOD HO
12 CHURCH MEWS

87 113

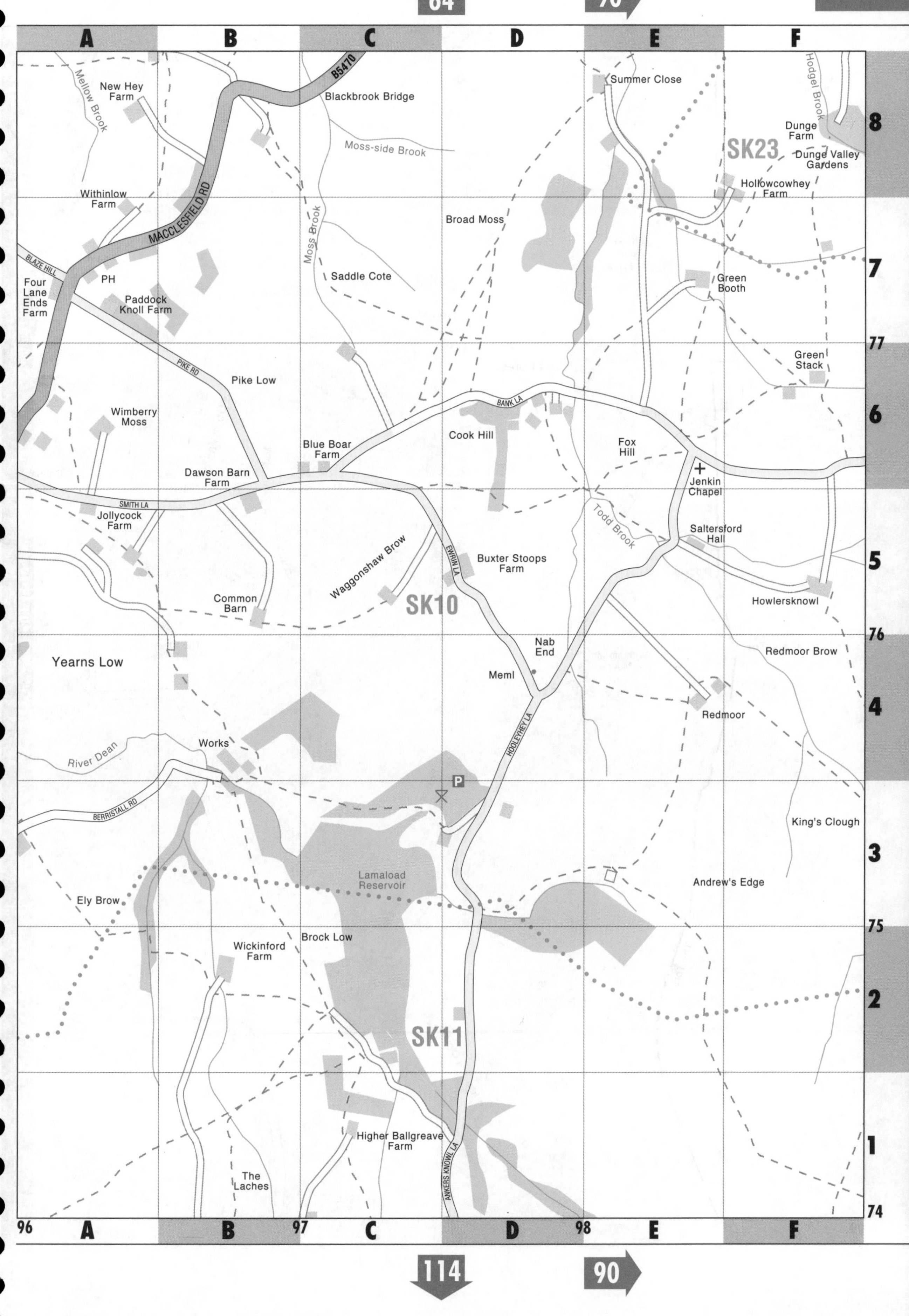
64
90
A
B
C
D
E
F
8
7
77
6
5
76
4
3
75
2
1
74
96
97
98
B5470
New Hey Farm
Mellow Brook
Blackbrook Bridge
Moss-side Brook
Summer Close
Hodgel Brook
Dunge Farm
SK23
Dunge Valley Gardens
Hollowcowhey Farm
Withinlow Farm
MACCLESFIELD RD
Moss Brook
Broad Moss
BLAZE HILL
Four Lane Ends Farm
PH
Paddock Knoll Farm
Saddle Cote
Green Booth
Green Stack
PIKE RD
Pike Low
BANK LA
Wimberry Moss
Cook Hill
Blue Boar Farm
Fox Hill
Dawson Barn Farm
Jenkin Chapel
SMITH LA
Jollycock Farm
Todd Brook
Saltersford Hall
Waggonshaw Brow
EWRIN LA
Buxter Stoops Farm
Common Barn
SK10
Howlersknowl
Yearns Low
Nab End
Redmoor Brow
Meml
Redmoor
HOOLEYHEY LA
Works
River Dean
P
BERRISTALL RD
King's Clough
Lamaload Reservoir
Andrew's Edge
Ely Brow
Brock Low
Wickinford Farm
SK11
Higher Ballgreave Farm
ANKERS KNOWL LA
The Laches
114
90

89
65

A
B
C
D
E
F
Browtop Farm
Oldfield
Works
River Goyt
A5004
LONG HILL
A5004
A5004 Buxton
8
Hodgel Brook
7
Ladbitch Wood
Hoo Moor
SK23
Goyt Forest
77
Fernilee Reservoir
P
Pym Chair
Pymchair Farm
6
Goyt Valley
Midshires Way
EMBRIDGE CSWY
Calfhay Wood
5
Oldgate Nick
Jep Clough
Derbyshire STREET ATLAS
THE STREET
76
Cats Tor
Withinleach Moor
The Street Forest Walks
SK10
4
Bunsal Cob
Sailing Club
Foxlow Edge
Errwood Reservoir
3
SK17
75
The Tors
Errwood Hall
2
GOYT'S LA
Errwood Forest Walks
Shooter's Clough
SK11
River Goyt
1
Stake Side
74
99
00
01

89
115

66
92
A
B
C
D
E
F
8
7
73
6
5
72
4
3
71
2
1
70
27
28
29
CH64
DANGER AREA
CH6
DANGER AREA
DANGER AREA
CH6
White
Sands
CH5
A548
WEIGHBRIDGE RD
WEIGHBRIDGE RD
Nature Study
Ctr
River Dee/
Afon Dyfrdwy
Power
Sta
Power
Sta
Beacon
A548 Flint
CHESTER RD
KELSTERTON RD
A548
ROCKLIFFE LA
B5129
Kelsterton Farm
Kelsterton
LLYS PERENNA/
PERENNA CT
CH5
CH6
NORTH RD
COATINGS BY-PASS RD
COATINGS
TWO
RING RD
KELSTERTON RD
Park
Farm
KELSTERTON LA
Coleg Glannau
Dyfrdwy/
Deeside Coll
Golftyn
RIVER RD
1 COLEHILL PL
2 LLYS SANT IAGO/ST JAMES CT
3 CLIFTON PARK AVE
4 TALFRYN CL
5 QUEEN'S AVE
6 ROCK COTTS
7 KINGS CROFT
8 KINGS RD
9 WILLOW CT
10 ROCK RD
CONNAH'S
QUAY
Sports
Ctr
GOLFTYN LA
COLLEGE VIEW
ROWAN GR
CEDAR AVE
YORK RD
COOPER'S LA
CHURCH ST
PO
Connah's Quay
High Sch
Top-y-fron
KELSTERTON CT
FARM DR
GOLFTYN DR
HAFOD CL
HOLLY CL
LANSDOWNE RD
DUNBAR CL
LOWER BROOK ST
HAMILTON RD
B5129
BANK RD
DEE VIEW RD
Denbighshire, Flintshire & Wrexham STREET ATLAS
92

91
67

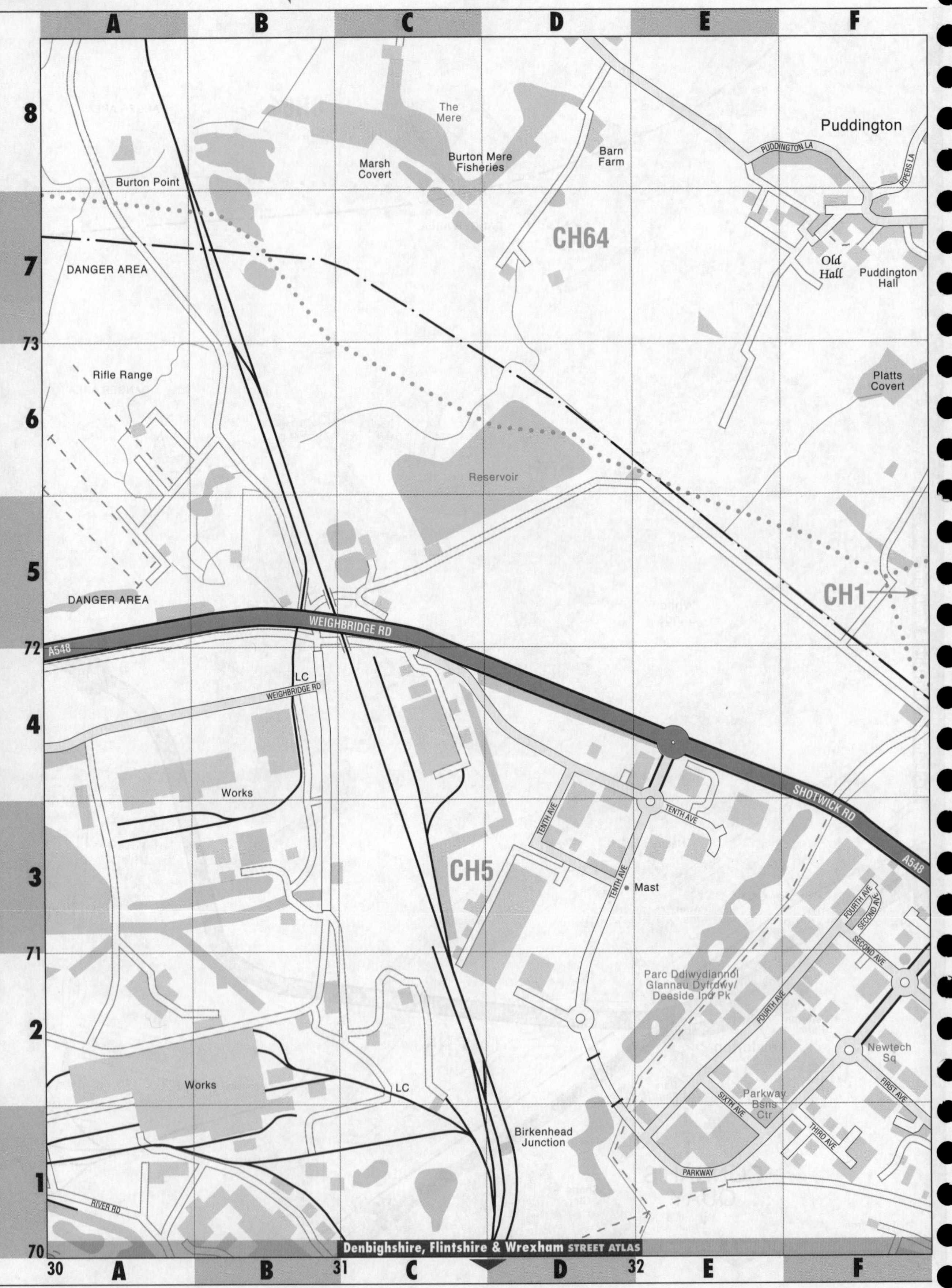
A
B
C
D
E
F
8
7
73
6
5
72
4
3
71
2
1
70
30
31
32
The Mere
Burton Mere Fisheries
Marsh Covert
Barn Farm
Puddington
PUDDINGTON LA
PIPERS LA
Burton Point
CH64
Old Hall
Puddington Hall
DANGER AREA
Rifle Range
Platts Covert
Reservoir
CH1
DANGER AREA
A548
WEIGHBRIDGE RD
LC
WEIGHBRIDGE RD
Works
SHOTWICK RD
TENTH AVE
TENTH AVE
CH5
A548
TENTH AVE
Mast
FOURTH AVE
SECOND AVE
SECOND AVE
Parc Ddiwydiannol Glannau Dyfrdwy/ Deeside Ind Pk
FOURTH AVE
Newtech Sq
Works
LC
Parkway Bsns Ctr
SIXTH AVE
FIRST AVE
THIRD AVE
Birkenhead Junction
PARKWAY
RIVER RD

91

68
94

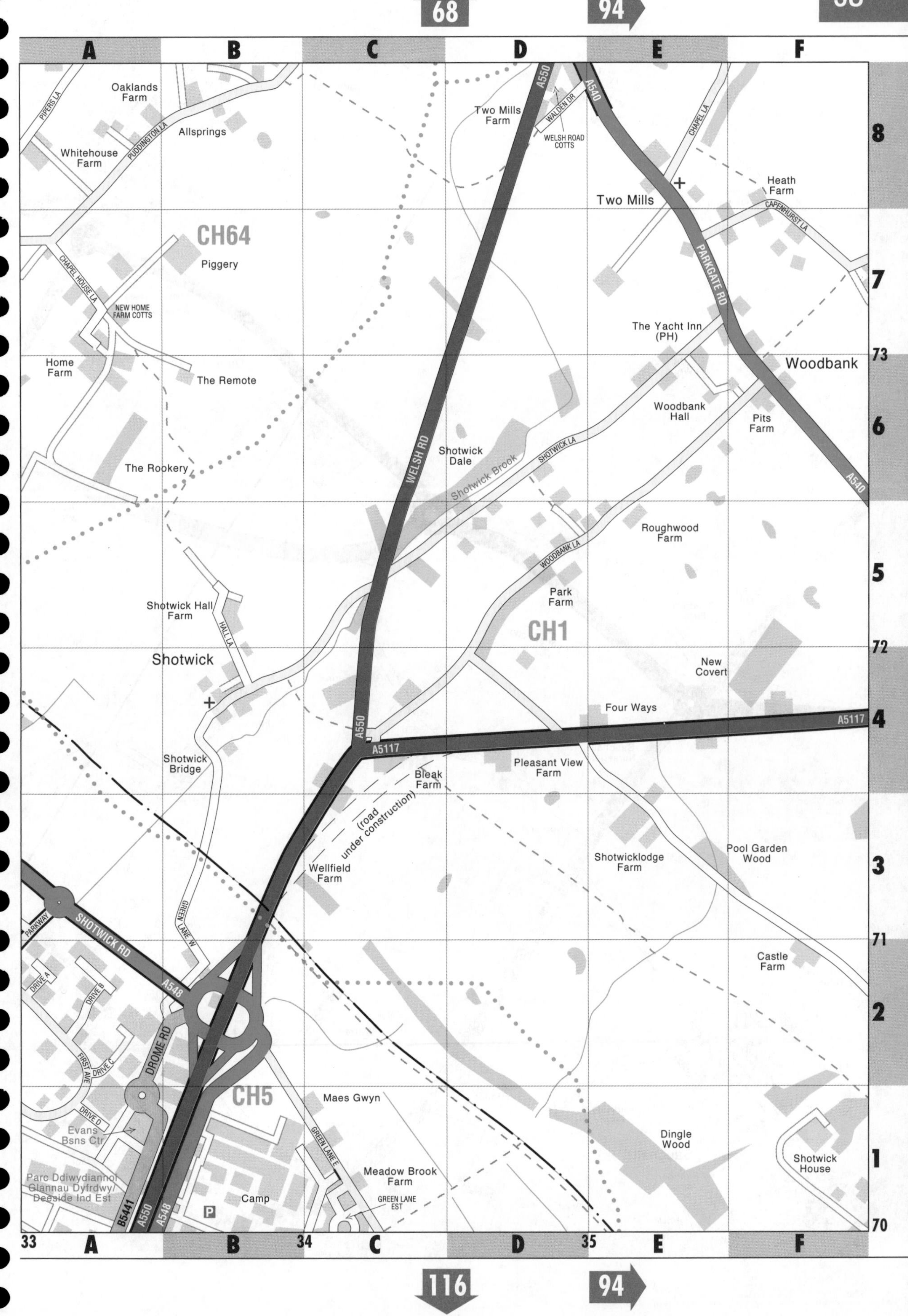
A
B
C
D
E
F
Oaklands Farm
Allsprings
Whitehouse Farm
PIPERS LA
PUDDINGTON LA
Two Mills Farm
WALDEN DR
WELSH ROAD COTTS
A550
A540
CHAPEL LA
Two Mills
Heath Farm
CAPENHURST LA
CH64
Piggery
CHAPEL HOUSE LA
NEW HOME FARM COTTS
PARKGATE RD
The Yacht Inn (PH)
Home Farm
The Remote
Woodbank
Woodbank Hall
Pits Farm
WELSH RD
Shotwick Dale
SHOTWICK LA
Shotwick Brook
The Rookery
Roughwood Farm
WOODBANK LA
Park Farm
Shotwick Hall Farm
HALL LA
CH1
Shotwick
New Covert
Four Ways
A5117
Shotwick Bridge
Pleasant View Farm
Bleak Farm
(road under construction)
Wellfield Farm
Shotwicklodge Farm
Pool Garden Wood
PARKWAY
SHOTWICK RD
GREEN LANE W
Castle Farm
A548
DRIVE A
DRIVE B
DROME RD
FIRST AVE
DRIVE C
DRIVE D
CH5
Maes Gwyn
Evans Bsns Ctr
GREEN LANE E
Dingle Wood
Shotwick House
Parc Ddiwydiannol Glannau Dyfrdwy/ Deeside Ind Est
Meadow Brook Farm
GREEN LANE EST
Camp
B5441
8
7
73
6
5
72
4
3
71
2
1
70
33
34
35

116
94

93
69

F8
1 BADGERS CL
2 BRAMLEY CL
3 HONEY SUCKLE CL
4 LAMBOURNE CL
5 SNOWBERRY WAY
6 SAXON WAY
7 WEST PARK DR
8 GREEN LAWNS DR
9 PARLIAMENT WAY
10 SALISBURY CL
11 BANGOR CL
12 ST DAVIDS DR
13 ST GEORGES AVE

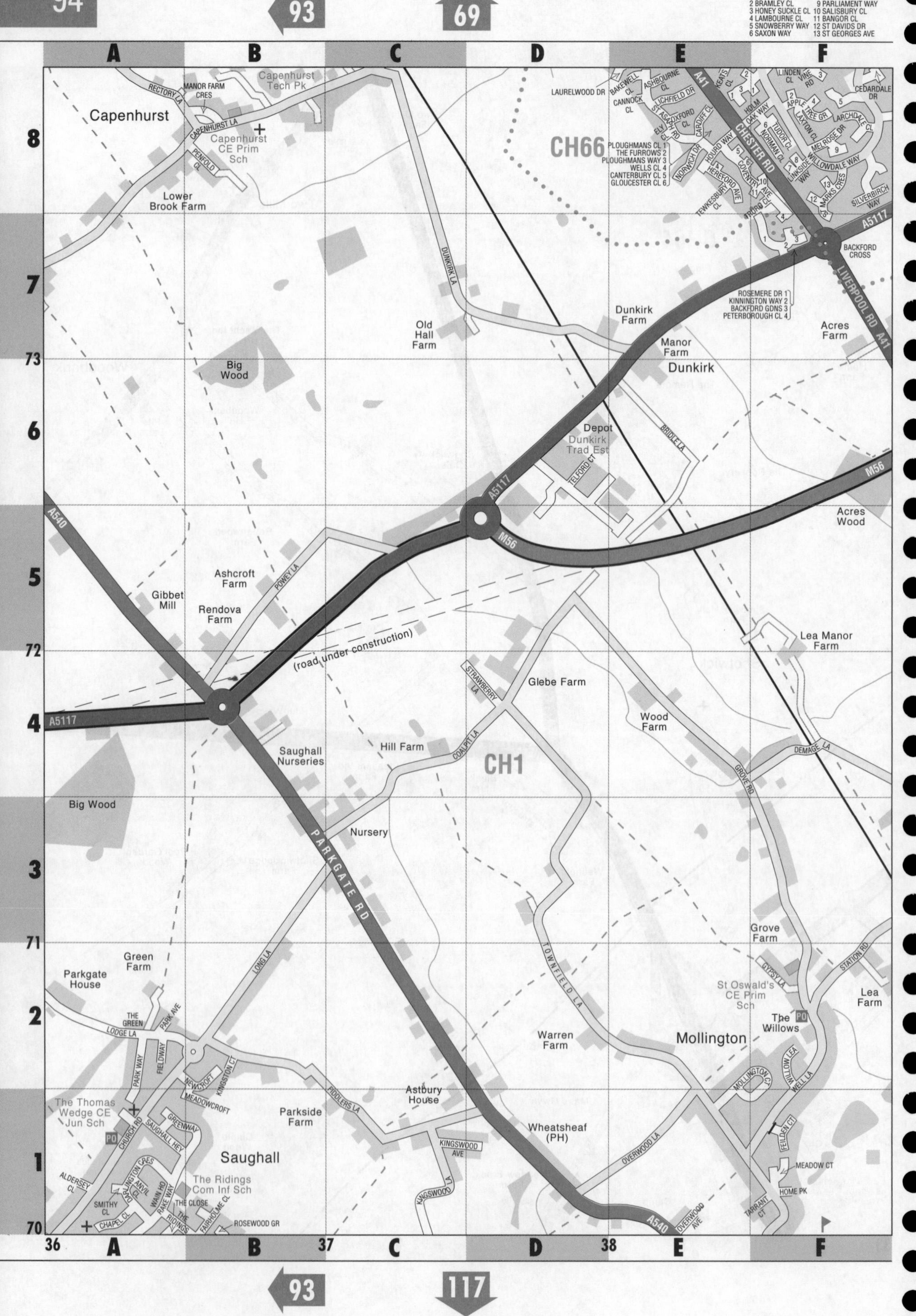

93
117

70
96
A
B
C
D
E
F
Stanney Woods Country Park
CHESTER RD
A5032
A5117
THE GROVES
LABURNUM GR
STRAWBERRY DR
WILLOW GR
ELM GR
LILAC GR
MAPLE GR
BEECH GR
BLACKTHORNE AVE
FIRTREE GR
PH
STROMA AVE
LUNDY DR
4 PUFFIN CL
5 BARRY CL
6 STANNEY WOODS AVE
7 FARNE CL
8 CUMBRIA DR
9 LEWIS CL
1 STAFFIN AVE
2 HANDA DR
3 SARK AVE
1 APPLEDALE DR
2 PINEDALE CL
3 CONIFER CL
4 LIME TREE CL
5 HEATHFIELD CT
Strawberry Farm
CH65
CH66
Sunnydale
Rake Hall (PH)
LITTLE STANNEY LA
M53
HEATH LA
Heath Farm
Heath Wood
Rosscroft
Poplarhall
M56
The Laurels
WHITBY LA
Axes Farm
MOUNT BARNS
Mount Farm
POPLAR HALL LA
RAKE LA
The Groves
The Dungeon
CROUGHTON RD
WERVIN RD
Fairfield House Farm
Croughton
Top Farm
Croughton Cottage
CH2
Chorlton Lodge Farm
LITTLE RAKE LA
GORDON LA
CH1
THE NOOK
CHURCH LA
Backford Hall
Chorlton Hall
LIVERPOOL RD
Backford Brook
THE CHANNEL
Backford
Greater Grace Sch
Rockbank
LEA HALL PK
DEMAGE LA
Lea Hall Farm
Lea Hall
STATION RD
Collinge Farm
Friars Park
Collinge Wood
Croughall Bridge
Shropshire Union Canal
Towing Path
Lea Farm
CAUGHALL RD
BADGERS WALK
Caughall Manor
Butter Hill
Moston Hall
Moston Hill Farm
Viaduct Wood
WERVIN RD
Moston
MALTA RD
1 CROOKENDEN CL
2 SIMPSON CL
3 BRODIE CL
NORMANDY RD
The Dale
A5116
MOSTON RD
P&R
PROSSER RD
ALAMEIN RD
SALERNO RD
CROOKENDEN RD
SIMPSON RD
CHARLES RD
Chester Zoo
GREENACRES CT
A41
4 DAUNCEY CL
5 HARINGTON CL
6 HARINGTON RD
FLAG LA N
ACRES LA
8
7
73
6
5
72
4
3
71
2
1
70
39
40
41
118
96

95 71

A B C D E F

8 7 73 6 5 72 4 3 71 2 1 70

Stoak Grange

Shropshire Union Canal

LITTLE STANNEY LA

PH

HEATH LA

CHURCH LA

Stoak

Densions's Bridge

CROUGHTON RD

BUNBURY CL

Stoke Bridge

M56

M53

15

ASHWOOD FARM CT

Ashwood House

Ash Wood

ASHWOOD LA

CH2

Wervin

Wervin New Hall

WERVIN RD

Woodside Farm

Ashton House

FOX COVERT LA

ACRES LA

Green La

PICTON LA

Picton

Hill Farm

GREEN LA

Picton Hall

Ash Hey Farm

ASH HAY LA

New House Farm

Mill Brook

River Gowy

Sewage Works

THE STREET

YORK DR

Cryers Farm

B5132

THORNTON GREEN LA

Thornton Green Farm

CRYERS LA

Spring Farm

HALLSGREEN LA

HOB LA

Heath Farm

Wimbolds Trafford

INCE LA

Hall Farm

Park Farm

Landfill Site

HASSALS LA

A56

PH

Trafford Bridge

The Shrewsbury Arms (PH)

WARRINGTON RD

Saw Mill

Cvn Site

1 HURLESTONE CL
2 WEAVER GR
3 DANE GR
4 ALYN RD
5 WOODLAND BANK
6 ST PETERS WAY
7 ST ANDREWS WLK

PLEMSTALL LA

GLEBE MDWS

LINDEN DR

PLEMSTALL WAY

DEE RD

GOWY RD

42 A B 43 C D 44 E F

95 119

72

98

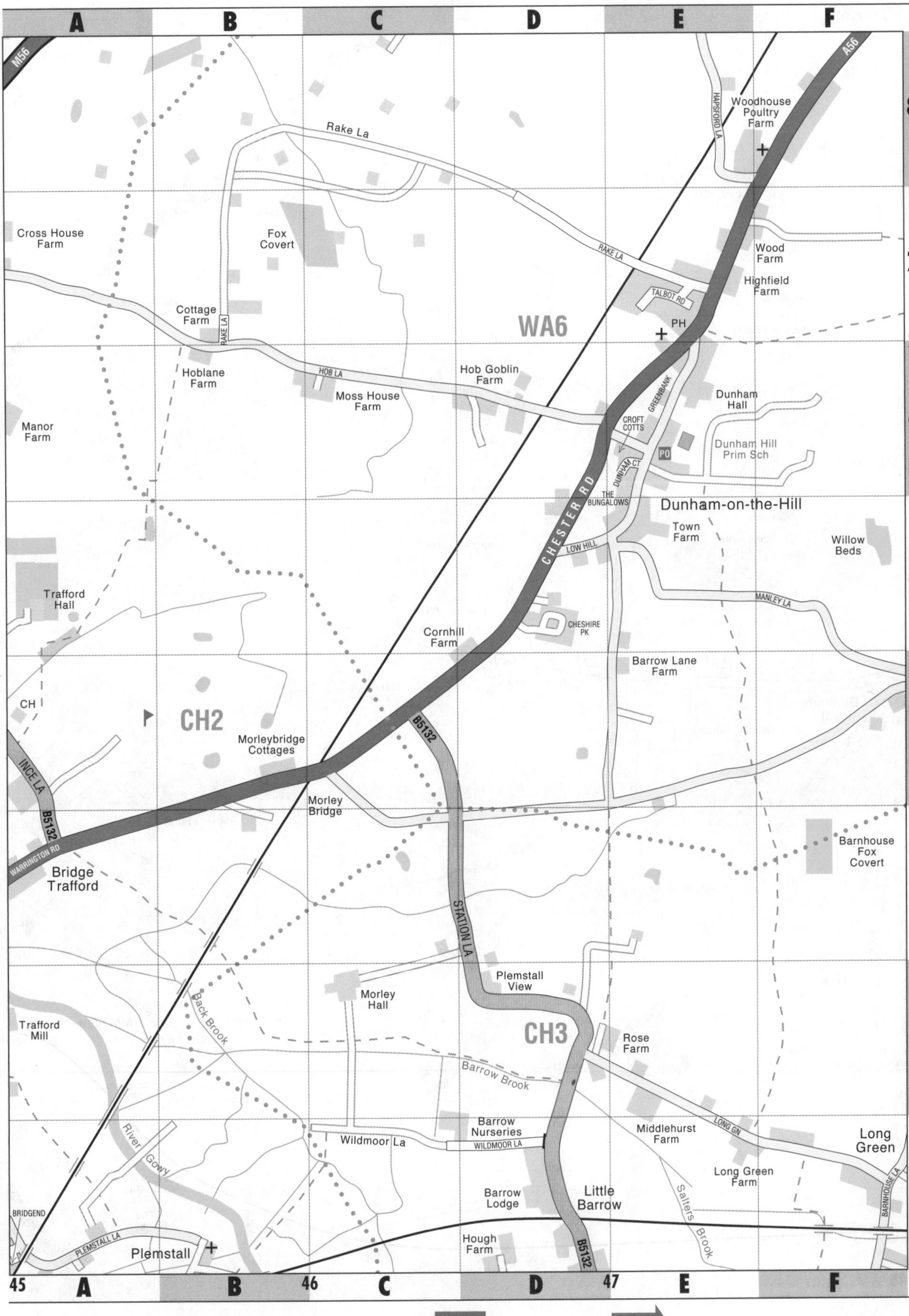

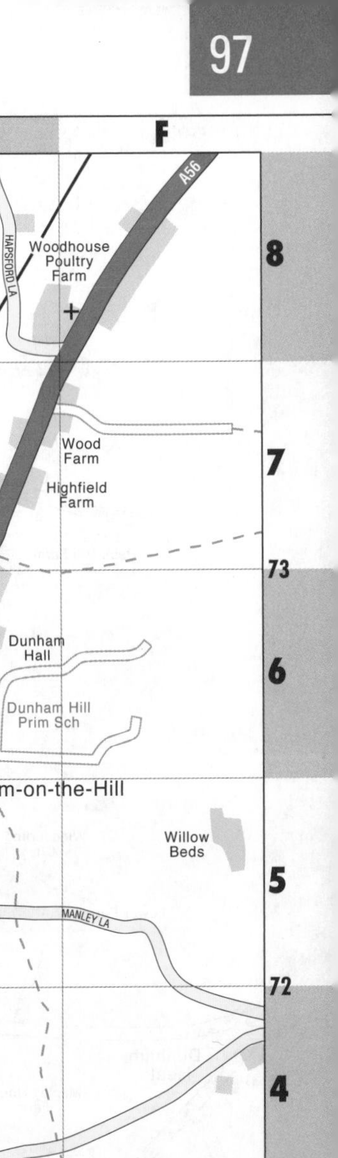
A
B
C
D
E
F
8
7
73
6
5
72
4
3
71
2
1
70
45
46
47
M56
A56
Rake La
RAKE LA
HAPSFORD LA
Woodhouse Poultry Farm
Cross House Farm
Fox Covert
Wood Farm
Highfield Farm
TALBOT RD
Cottage Farm
WA6
PH
Hoblane Farm
HOB LA
Hob Goblin Farm
Moss House Farm
Dunham Hall
GREENBANK
Manor Farm
CROFT COTTS
PO
Dunham Hill Prim Sch
DUNHAM CT
THE BUNGALOWS
Dunham-on-the-Hill
CHESTER RD
Town Farm
Willow Beds
LOW HILL
Trafford Hall
MANLEY LA
CHESHIRE PK
Cornhill Farm
Barrow Lane Farm
CH
CH2
B5132
Morleybridge Cottages
INCE LA
Morley Bridge
WARRINGTON RD
Barnhouse Fox Covert
Bridge Trafford
STATION LA
Plemstall View
Morley Hall
Trafford Mill
Back Brook
CH3
Rose Farm
Barrow Brook
Barrow Nurseries
Middlehurst Farm
LONG GN
Long Green
Wildmoor La
WILDMOOR LA
River Gowy
Long Green Farm
Barrow Lodge
Little Barrow
Salters Brook
BARNHOUSE LA
BRIDGEND
PLEMSTALL LA
Plemstall
Hough Farm

120

98

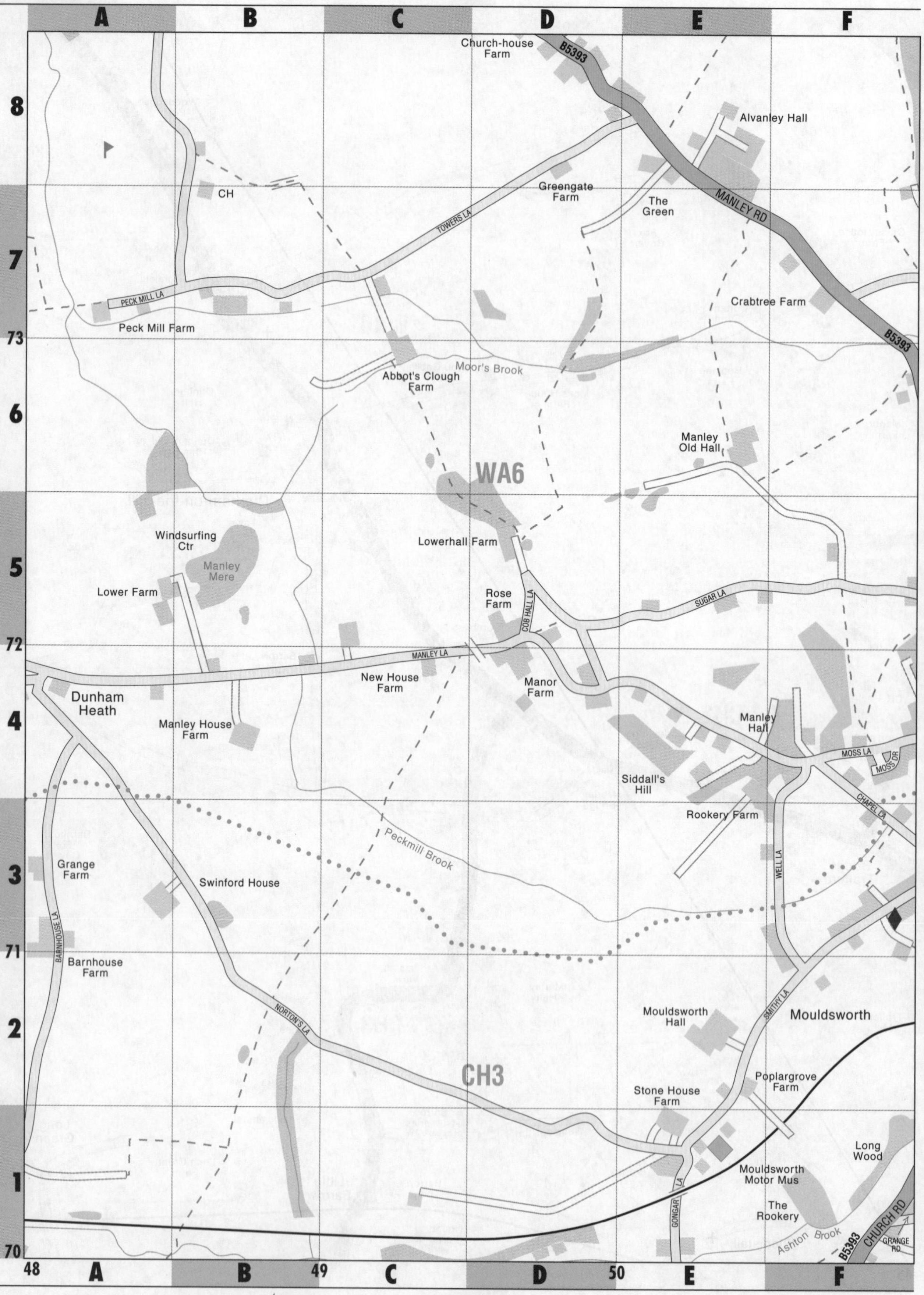

A B C D E F
8
7
73
6
5
72
4
3
71
2
1
70
48 49 50
Church-house Farm
B5393
Alvanley Hall
CH
Greengate Farm
The Green
MANLEY RD
TOWERS LA
PECK MILL LA
Peck Mill Farm
Crabtree Farm
B5393
Moor's Brook
Abbot's Clough Farm
Manley Old Hall
WA6
Lowerhall Farm
Windsurfing Ctr
Manley Mere
Lower Farm
Rose Farm
COB HALL LA
SUGAR LA
MANLEY LA
New House Farm
Manor Farm
Dunham Heath
Manley House Farm
Manley Hall
MOSS LA
MOSS DR
Siddall's Hill
CHAPEL LA
Rookery Farm
Peckmill Brook
Grange Farm
Swinford House
WELL LA
BARNHOUSE LA
Barnhouse Farm
NORTON'S LA
Mouldsworth Hall
SMITHY LA
Mouldsworth
CH3
Poplargrove Farm
Stone House Farm
Long Wood
Mouldsworth Motor Mus
GONGAR LA
The Rookery
Ashton Brook
B5393
CHURCH RD
GRANGE RD

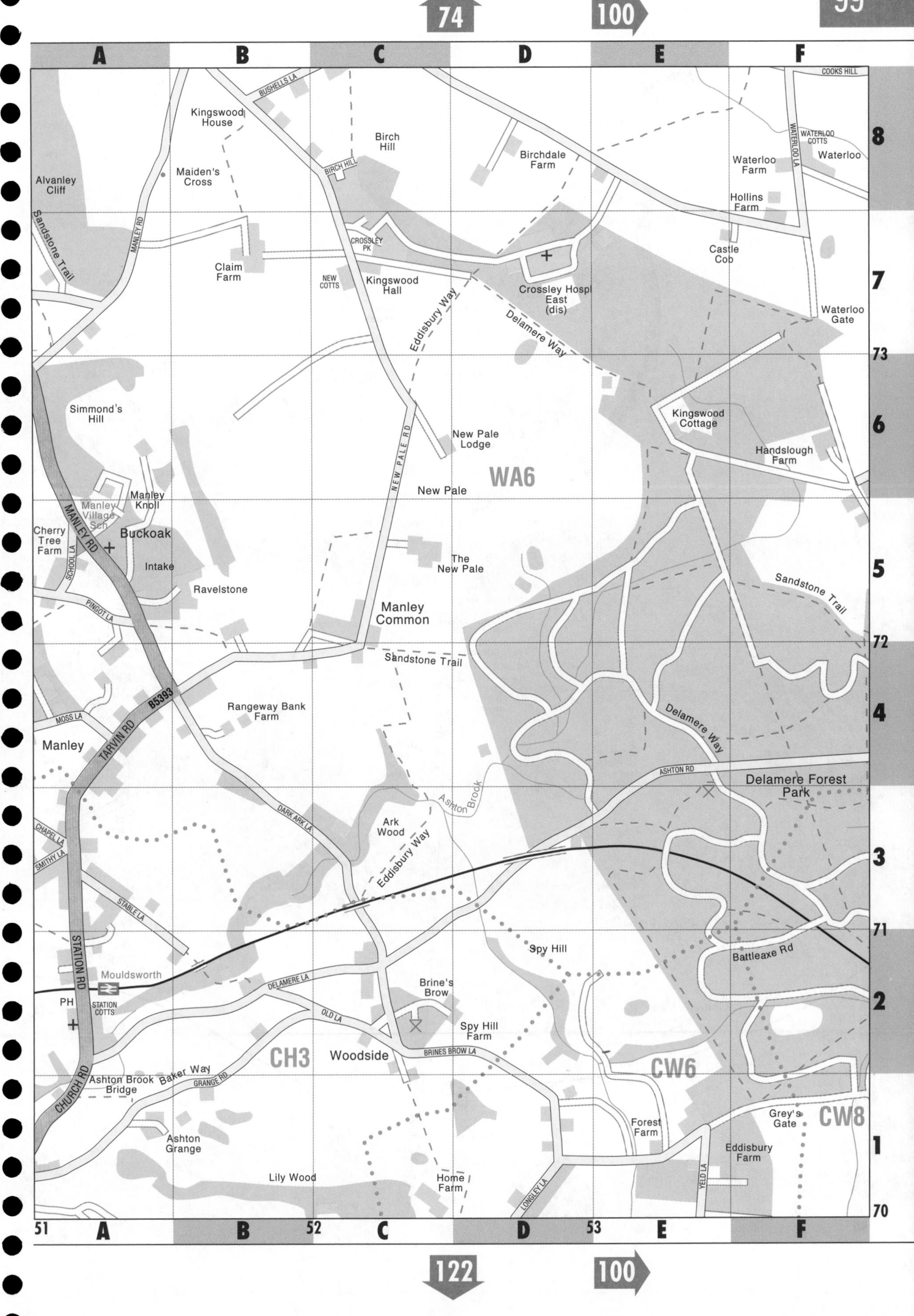

74
100
122
100
A
B
C
D
E
F
8
7
73
6
5
72
4
3
71
2
1
70
51
52
53
Alvanley Cliff
Sandstone Trail
Kingswood House
Maiden's Cross
Birch Hill
BUSHELLS LA
BIRCH HILL
Birchdale Farm
COOKS HILL
WATERLOO LA
WATERLOO COTTS
Waterloo
Waterloo Farm
Hollins Farm
Castle Cob
Claim Farm
MANLEY RD
CROSSLEY PK
NEW COTTS
Kingswood Hall
Crossley Hospl East (dis)
Eddisbury Way
Delamere Way
Waterloo Gate
Simmond's Hill
Kingswood Cottage
New Pale Lodge
NEW PALE RD
Handslough Farm
WA6
New Pale
Manley Knoll
Manley Village Sch
Cherry Tree Farm
SCHOOL LA
Buckoak
Intake
The New Pale
Sandstone Trail
Ravelstone
PINGOT LA
Manley Common
Sandstone Trail
B5393
TARVIN RD
Rangeway Bank Farm
MOSS LA
Manley
Delamere Way
ASHTON RD
Delamere Forest Park
Ashton Brook
DARK ARK LA
Ark Wood
Eddisbury Way
CHAPEL LA
SMITHY LA
STABLE LA
STATION RD
Spy Hill
Battleaxe Rd
Mouldsworth
PH
STATION COTTS
DELAMERE LA
Brine's Brow
OLD LA
Spy Hill Farm
CH3
Woodside
BRINES BROW LA
CW6
Ashton Brook Bridge
Baker Way
GRANGE RD
CHURCH RD
Forest Farm
Grey's Gate
CW8
Ashton Grange
Eddisbury Farm
YELD LA
Lily Wood
Home Farm
LONGLEY LA

99 75

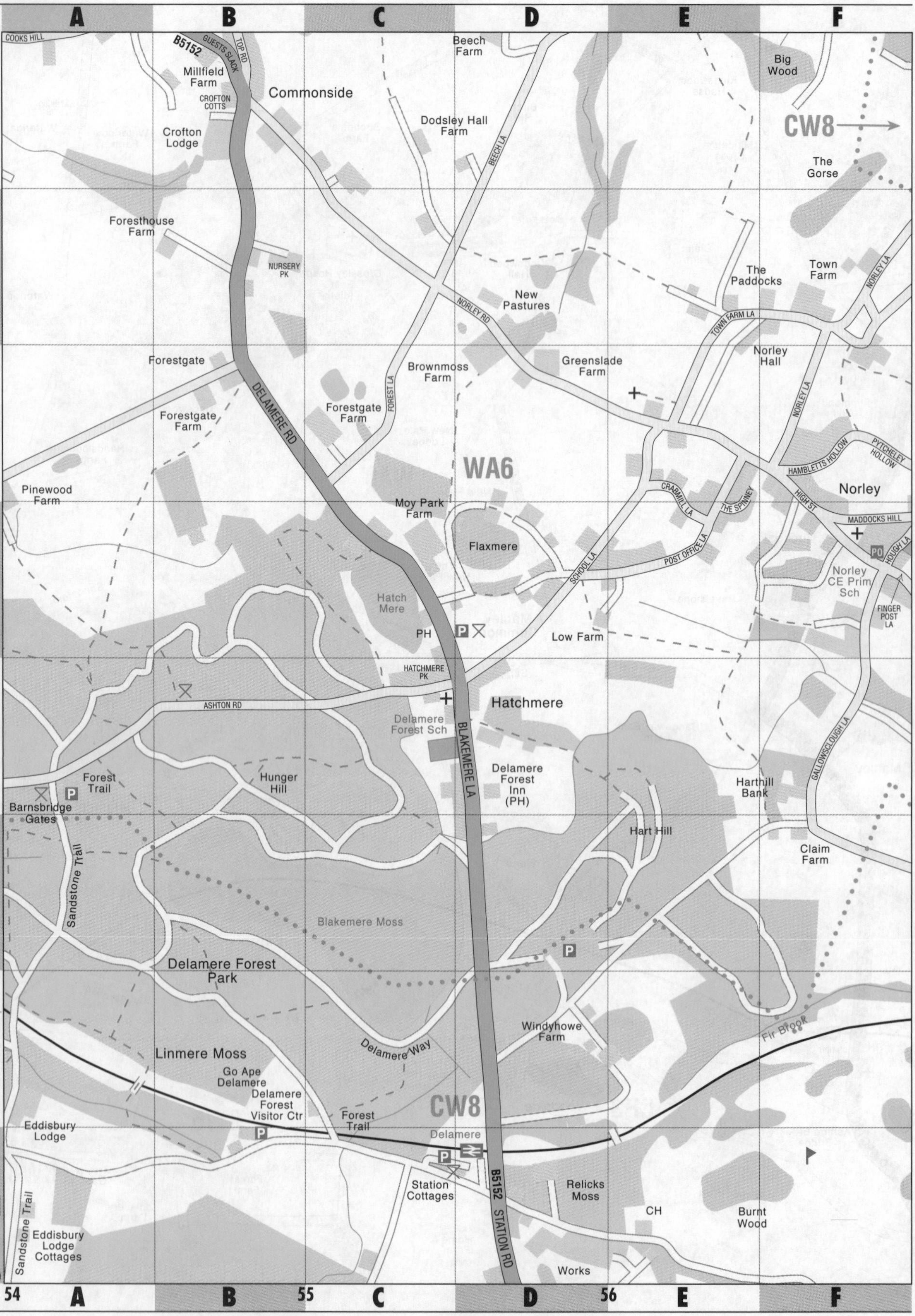

A B C D E F
8 7 73 6 5 72 4 3 71 2 1 70
COOKS HILL
B5152
GUESTS SLACK
TOP RD
Millfield Farm
CROFTON COTTS
Commonside
Beech Farm
Big Wood
Dodsley Hall Farm
CW8
Crofton Lodge
BEECH LA
The Gorse
Foresthouse Farm
NURSERY PK
The Paddocks
Town Farm
NORLEY LA
NORLEY RD
New Pastures
TOWN FARM LA
Forestgate
Brownmoss Farm
Greenslade Farm
Norley Hall
DELAMERE RD
FOREST LA
Forestgate Farm
NORLEY LA
Forestgate Farm
WA6
HAMBLETTS HOLLOW
PYTCHELEY HOLLOW
Pinewood Farm
Moy Park Farm
CRABMILL LA
THE SPINNEY
HIGH ST
Norley
MADDOCKS HILL
Flaxmere
POST OFFICE LA
SCHOOL LA
PO
HOUGH LA
Norley CE Prim Sch
Hatch Mere
FINGER POST LA
PH
Low Farm
HATCHMERE PK
Hatchmere
ASHTON RD
Delamere Forest Sch
BLAKEMERE LA
GALLOWSCLOUGH LA
Forest Trail
Hunger Hill
Delamere Forest Inn (PH)
Harthill Bank
Barnsbridge Gates
Hart Hill
Claim Farm
Sandstone Trail
Blakemere Moss
Delamere Forest Park
Windyhowe Farm
Fir Brook
Linmere Moss
Delamere Way
Go Ape Delamere
Delamere Forest Visitor Ctr
CW8
Forest Trail
Eddisbury Lodge
Delamere
B5152
STATION RD
Station Cottages
Relicks Moss
Sandstone Trail
CH
Burnt Wood
Eddisbury Lodge Cottages
Works
54 A B 55 C D 56 E F

99 123

76
102

124
102

101 77

101 125

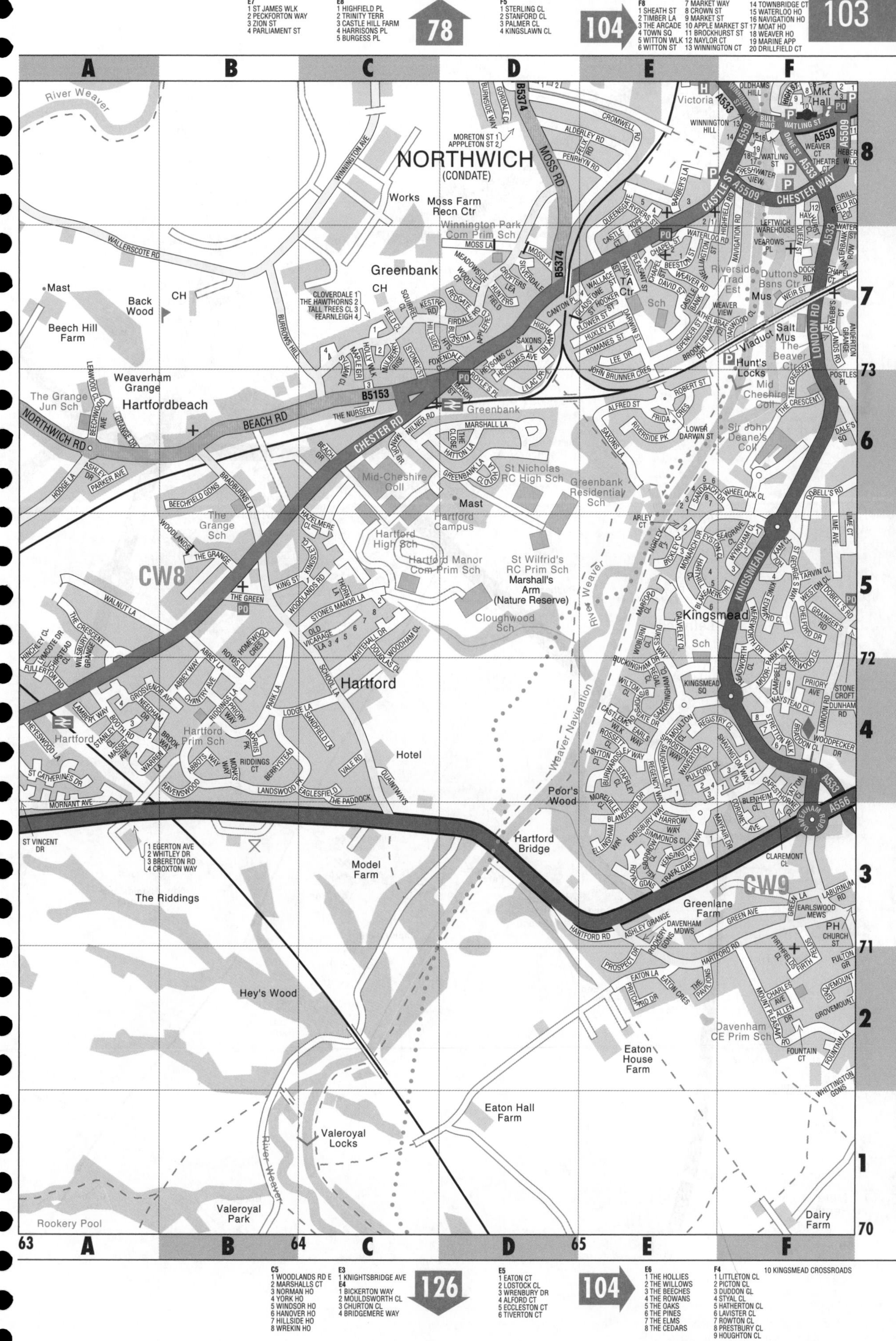

103
E7
1 ST JAMES WLK
2 PECKFORTON WAY
3 ZION ST
4 PARLIAMENT ST
E8
1 HIGHFIELD PL
2 TRINITY TERR
3 CASTLE HILL FARM
4 HARRISONS PL
5 BURGESS PL
78
F5
1 STERLING CL
2 STANFORD CL
3 PALMER CL
4 KINGSLAWN CL
104
F8
1 SHEATH ST
2 TIMBER LA
3 THE ARCADE
4 TOWN SQ
5 WITTON WLK
6 WITTON ST
7 MARKET WAY
8 CROWN ST
9 MARKET ST
10 APPLE MARKET ST
11 BROCKHURST ST
12 NAYLOR CT
13 WINNINGTON CT
14 TOWNBRIDGE CT
15 WATERLOO HO
16 NAVIGATION HO
17 MOAT HO
18 WEAVER HO
19 MARINE APP
20 DRILLFIELD CT
A
B
C
D
E
F
NORTHWICH
(CONDATE)
Greenbank
Hartfordbeach
Hartford
Kingsmead
CW8
CW9
River Weaver
Weaver Navigation
Back Wood
Beech Hill Farm
Weaverham Grange
The Grange Jun Sch
Mid-Cheshire Coll
Hartford High Sch
Hartford Manor Com Prim Sch
St Nicholas RC High Sch
Greenbank Residential Sch
St Wilfrid's RC Prim Sch
Marshall's Arm (Nature Reserve)
Cloughwood Sch
Sir John Deane's Coll
Poor's Wood
Hartford Bridge
Model Farm
The Riddings
Hey's Wood
Valeroyal Locks
Valeroyal Park
Rookery Pool
Eaton Hall Farm
Eaton House Farm
Greenlane Farm
Davenham CE Prim Sch
Dairy Farm
Moss Farm Recn Ctr
Winnington Park Com Prim Sch
Hunt's Locks
Salt Mus
The Beaver Ctr
8
7
6
5
4
3
2
1
73
72
71
70
63
64
65
C5
1 WOODLANDS RD E
2 MARSHALLS CT
3 NORMAN HO
4 YORK HO
5 WINDSOR HO
6 HANOVER HO
7 HILLSIDE HO
8 WREKIN HO
E3
1 KNIGHTSBRIDGE AVE
E4
1 BICKERTON WAY
2 MOULDSWORTH CL
3 CHURTON CL
4 BRIDGEMERE WAY
126
E5
1 EATON CT
2 LOSTOCK CL
3 WRENBURY DR
4 ALFORD CT
5 ECCLESTON CT
6 TIVERTON CT
104
E6
1 THE HOLLIES
2 THE WILLOWS
3 THE BEECHES
4 THE ROWANS
5 THE OAKS
6 THE PINES
7 THE ELMS
8 THE CEDARS
F4
1 LITTLETON CL
2 PICTON CL
3 DUDDON CL
4 STYAL CL
5 HATHERTON CL
6 LAVISTER CL
7 ROWTON CL
8 PRESTBURY CL
9 HOUGHTON CL
10 KINGSMEAD CROSSROADS

A8
1 JOHN ST
2 CRUM HILL
3 MEADOW ST
4 WESLEY PL
5 ST HELEN'S RD

B8
1 ALVINGHAM CL
2 KELSTERN CL
3 BIRKDALE CT
4 MANCHESTER RD
5 SLADE ST
6 WILLIAM ST
7 SIDDALL ST
8 SALKELD ST

103
79

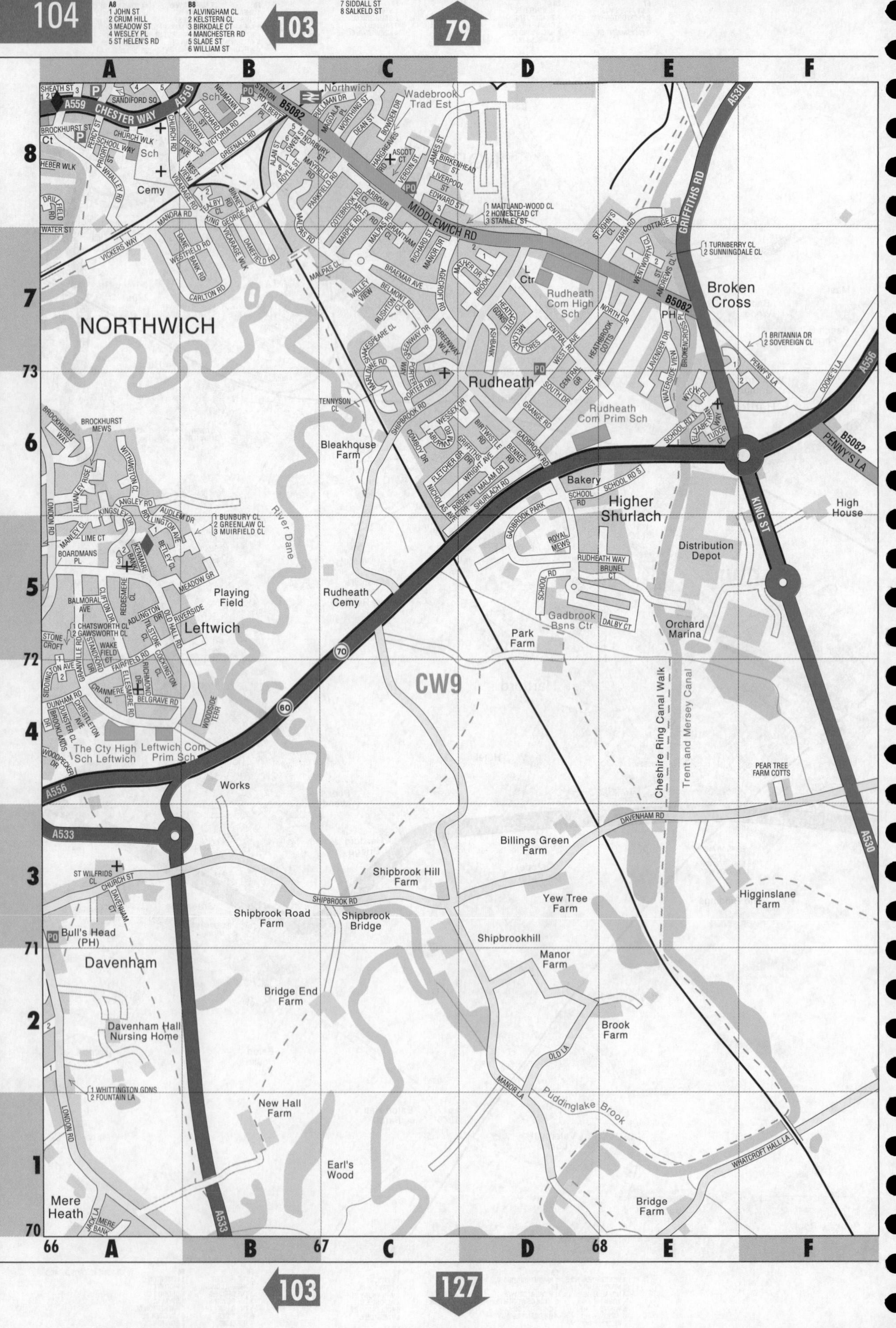

103
127

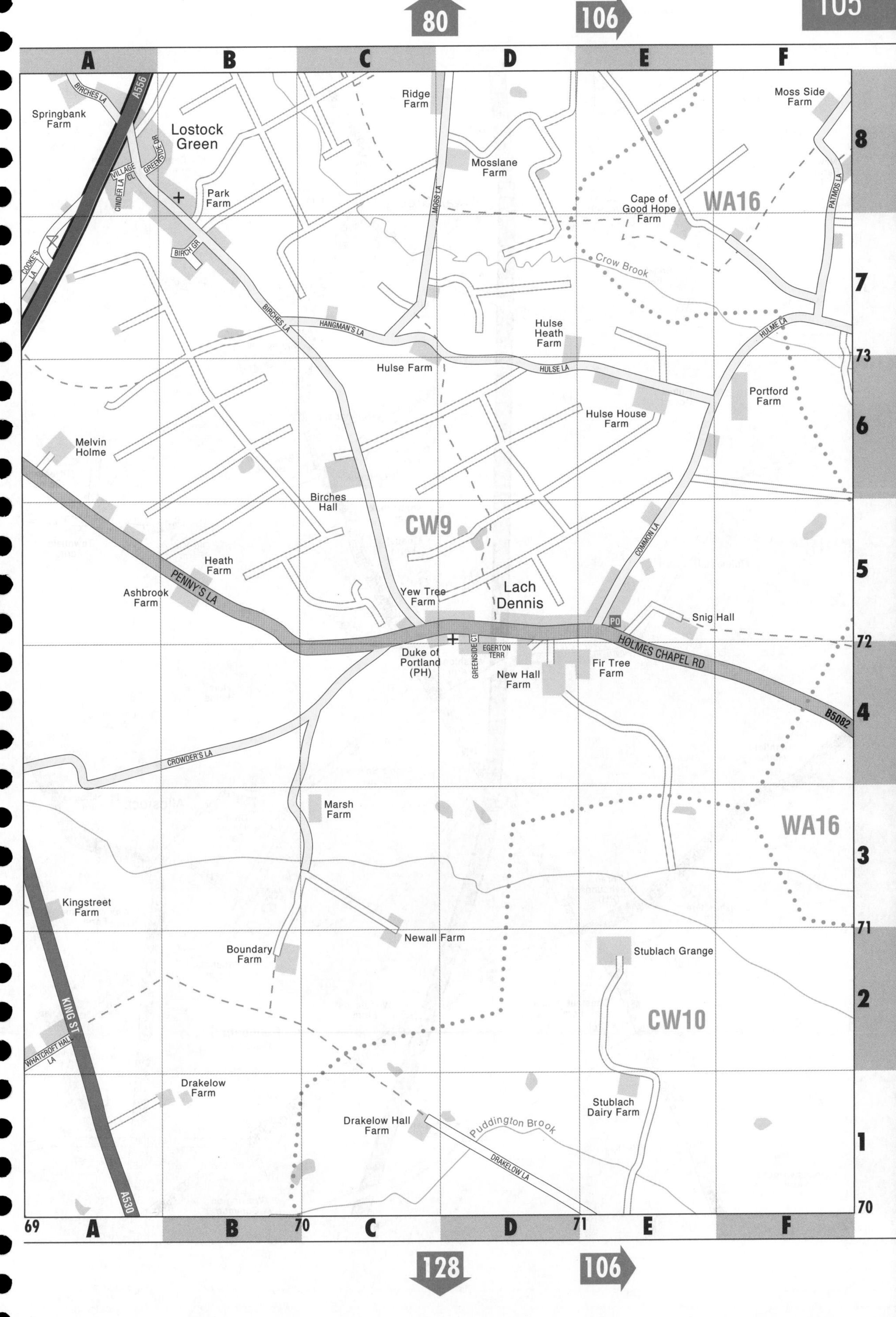
80
106
A
B
C
D
E
F
Springbank Farm
BIRCHES LA
A556
Lostock Green
GREENSIDE DR
VILLAGE CL
CINDER LA
Park Farm
COOKE'S LA
BIRCH GR
Ridge Farm
Mosslane Farm
MOSS LA
Cape of Good Hope Farm
WA16
Moss Side Farm
PATMOS LA
Crow Brook
BIRCHES LA
HANGMAN'S LA
Hulse Heath Farm
Hulse Farm
HULSE LA
HULME LA
Portford Farm
Hulse House Farm
Melvin Holme
Birches Hall
CW9
COMMON LA
Heath Farm
Ashbrook Farm
PENNY'S LA
Yew Tree Farm
Lach Dennis
PO
Snig Hall
Duke of Portland (PH)
GREENSIDE CT
EGERTON TERR
New Hall Farm
Fir Tree Farm
HOLMES CHAPEL RD
B5082
CROWDER'S LA
Marsh Farm
WA16
Kingstreet Farm
Newall Farm
Boundary Farm
Stublach Grange
CW10
KING ST
WHATCROFT HALL LA
Drakelow Farm
Drakelow Hall Farm
Puddington Brook
Stublach Dairy Farm
DRAKELOW LA
A530
8
7
73
6
5
72
4
3
71
2
1
70
69
70
71
128
106

105
81

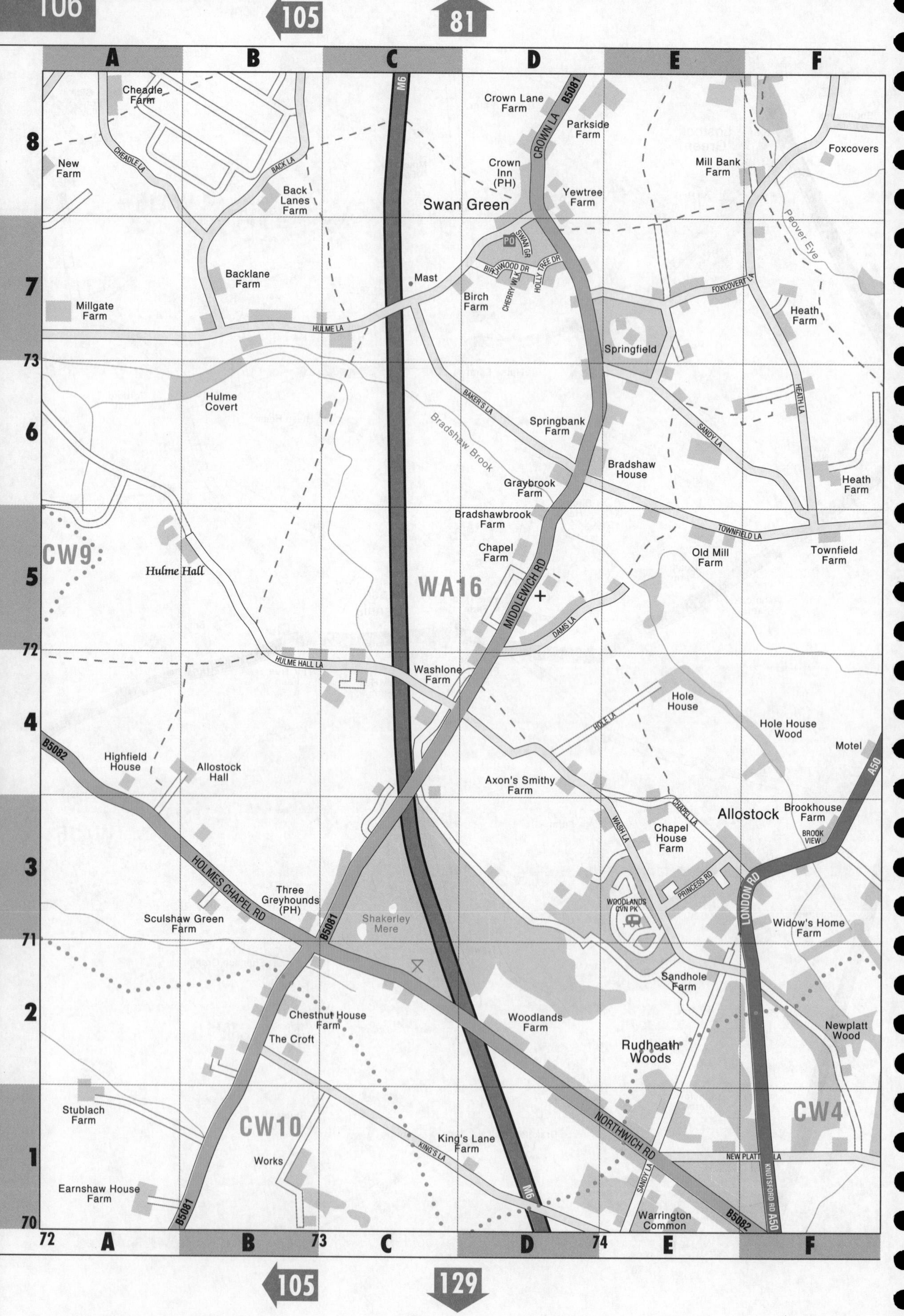

105
129

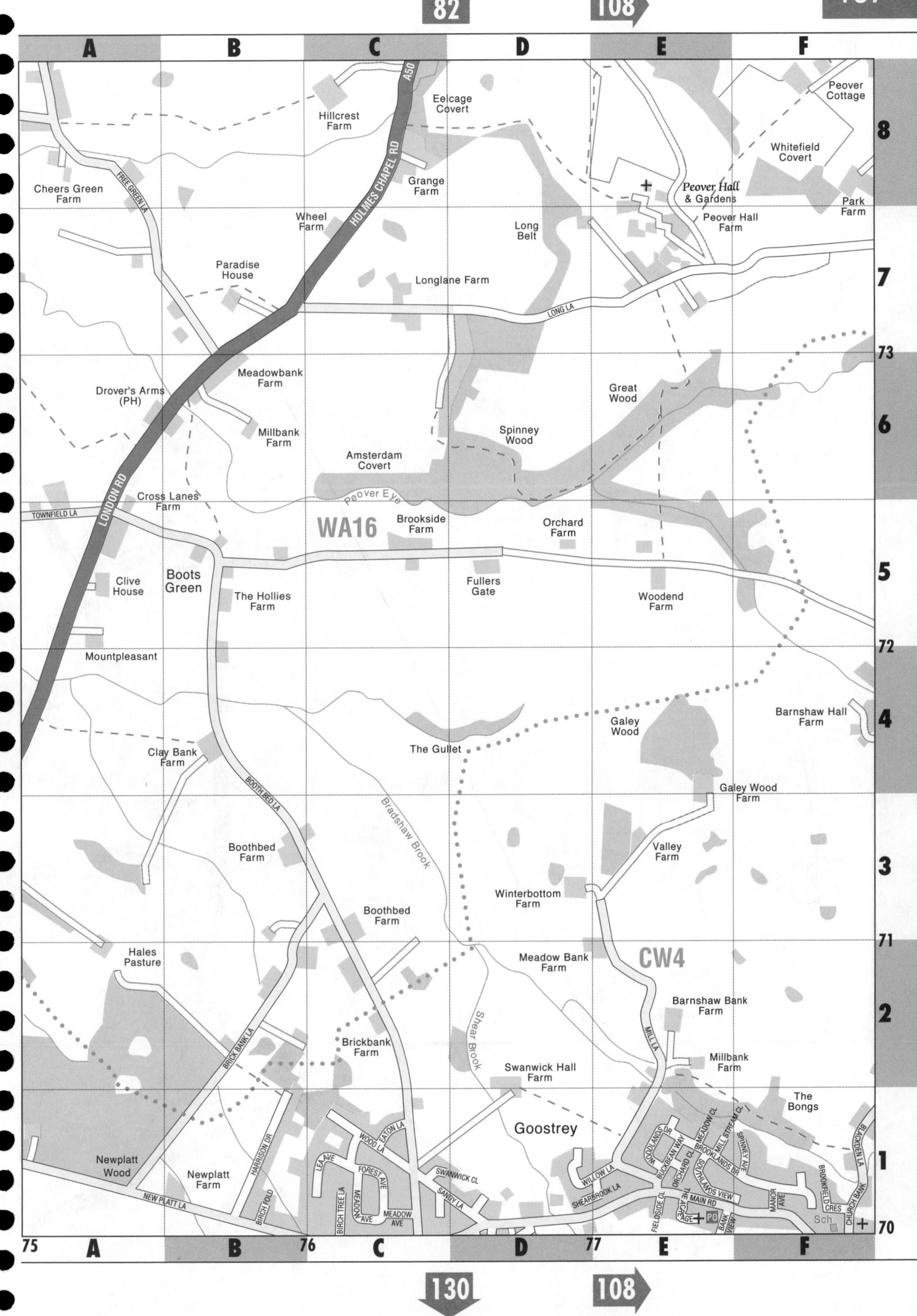

82
108
A
B
C
D
E
F
8
7
73
6
5
72
4
3
71
2
1
70
75
76
77
130
108
Eelcage Covert
Hillcrest Farm
A50
HOLMES CHAPEL RD
Peover Cottage
Whitefield Covert
Peover Hall & Gardens
Park Farm
Peover Hall Farm
Cheers Green Farm
FREE GREEN LA
Grange Farm
Wheel Farm
Long Belt
Paradise House
Longlane Farm
LONG LA
Meadowbank Farm
Drover's Arms (PH)
Millbank Farm
Great Wood
Spinney Wood
Amsterdam Covert
Peover Eye
Cross Lanes Farm
TOWNFIELD LA
LONDON RD
WA16
Brookside Farm
Orchard Farm
Clive House
Boots Green
The Hollies Farm
Fullers Gate
Woodend Farm
Mountpleasant
Barnshaw Hall Farm
Galey Wood
The Gullet
Clay Bank Farm
BOOTH BED LA
Galey Wood Farm
Bradshaw Brook
Boothbed Farm
Valley Farm
Winterbottom Farm
Boothbed Farm
Hales Pasture
Meadow Bank Farm
CW4
Barnshaw Bank Farm
Shear Brook
MILL LA
BRICK BANK LA
Brickbank Farm
Millbank Farm
Swanwick Hall Farm
The Bongs
Goostrey
Newplatt Wood
Newplatt Farm
HARRISON DR
EATON LA
WOOD LA
LEA AVE
FOREST AVE
BIRCH TREE LA
MEADOW AVE
MEADOW AVE
BIRCH FOLD
SWANWICK CL
SANBY LA
NEW PLATT LA
WILLOW LA
SHEARBROOK LA
WOODLANDS DR
BUCKBEAN WAY
ORCHARD CL
MEADOW CL
MILL STREAM CL
BROOKLANDS DR
SPINNEY AVE
BROOKLANDS VIEW
MAIN RD
THE ACREAGE
FIELDSIDE CL
BANK VIEW
PO
MANOR AVE
BROOKFIELD CRES
BLACKDEN LA
CHURCH BANK
Sch

107
83

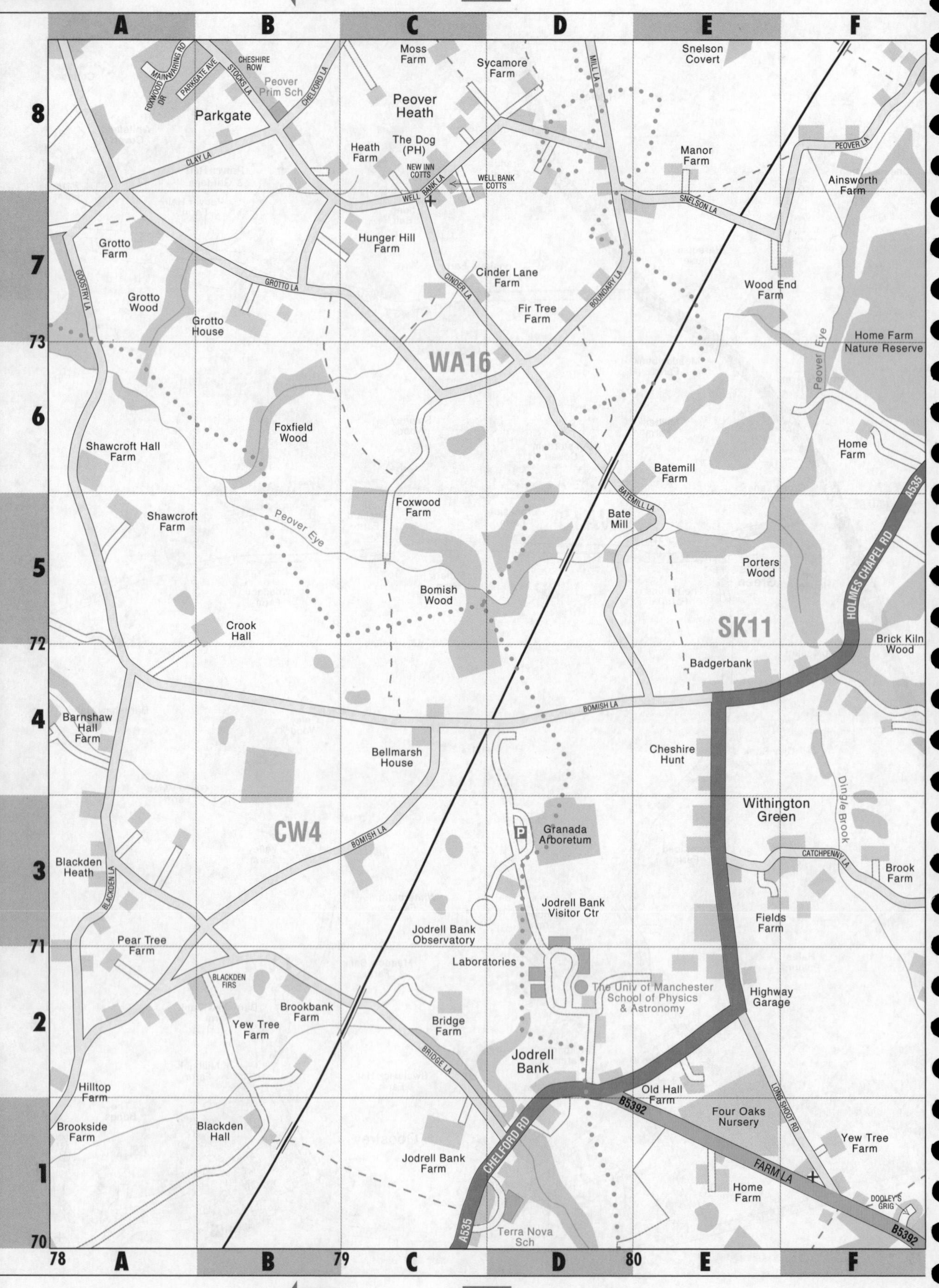

107
131

84
110

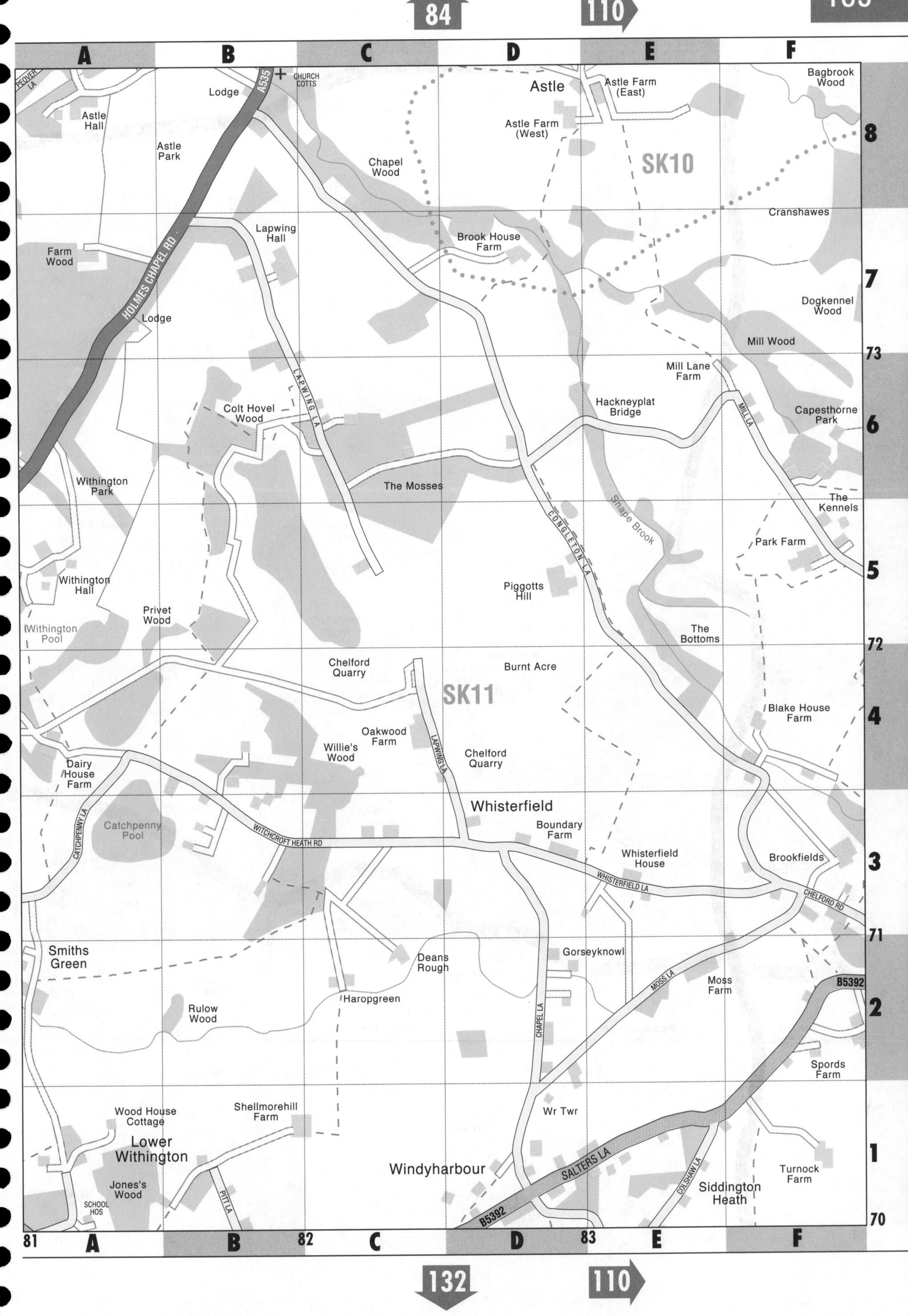

132
110

109
85

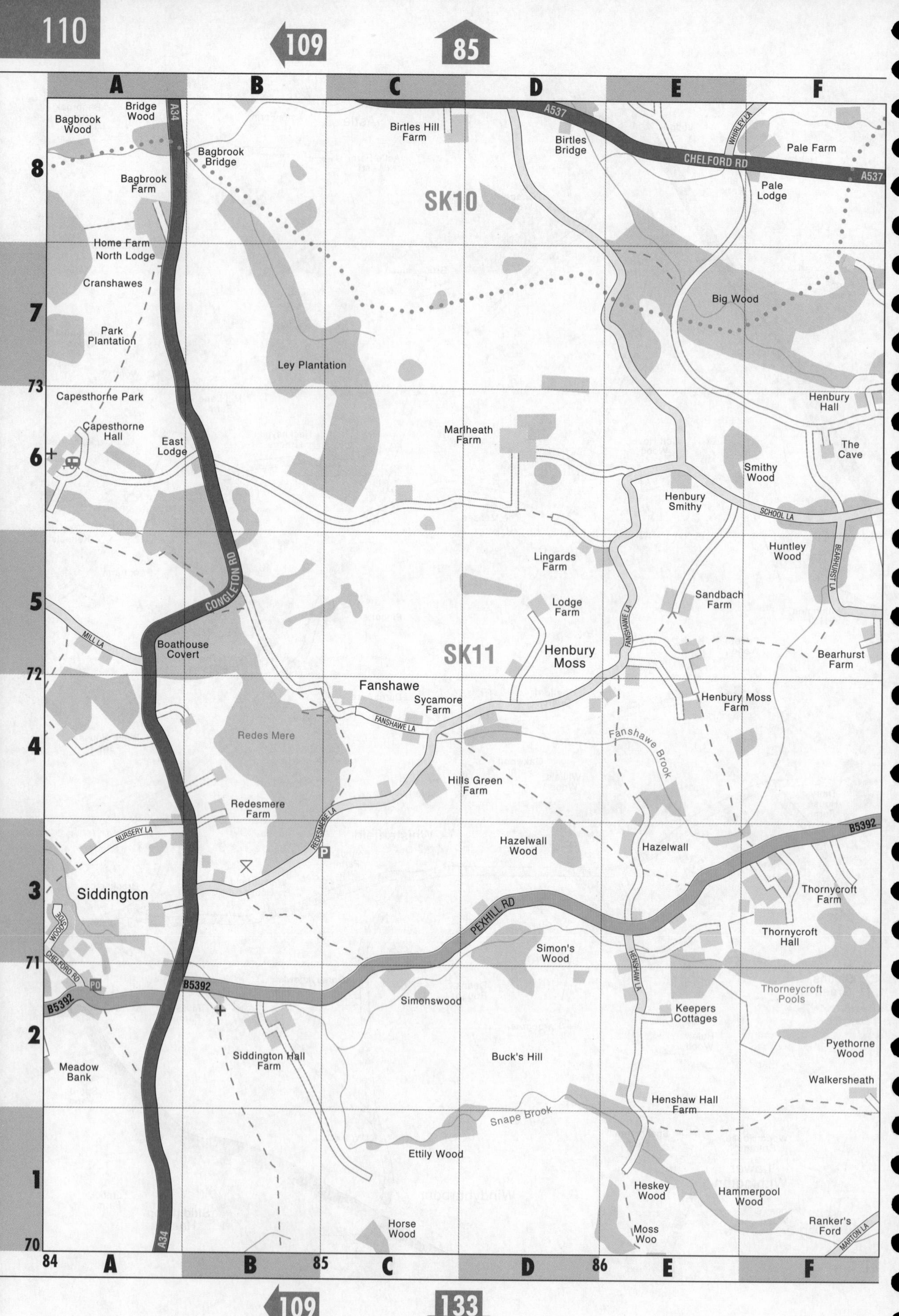

109
133

86
112

F8
1 ASHBOURNE MEWS
2 SHELBOURNE MEWS
3 ST LUKE'S HO
4 ALDERNEY CL
5 BLANDFORD DR
6 THE TOWERS
7 HEDINGHAM CL
8 MARLBOROUGH HO
9 ABINGDON CL
10 KENNET WAY
11 KENSINGTON SQ
12 WINCHESTER HO

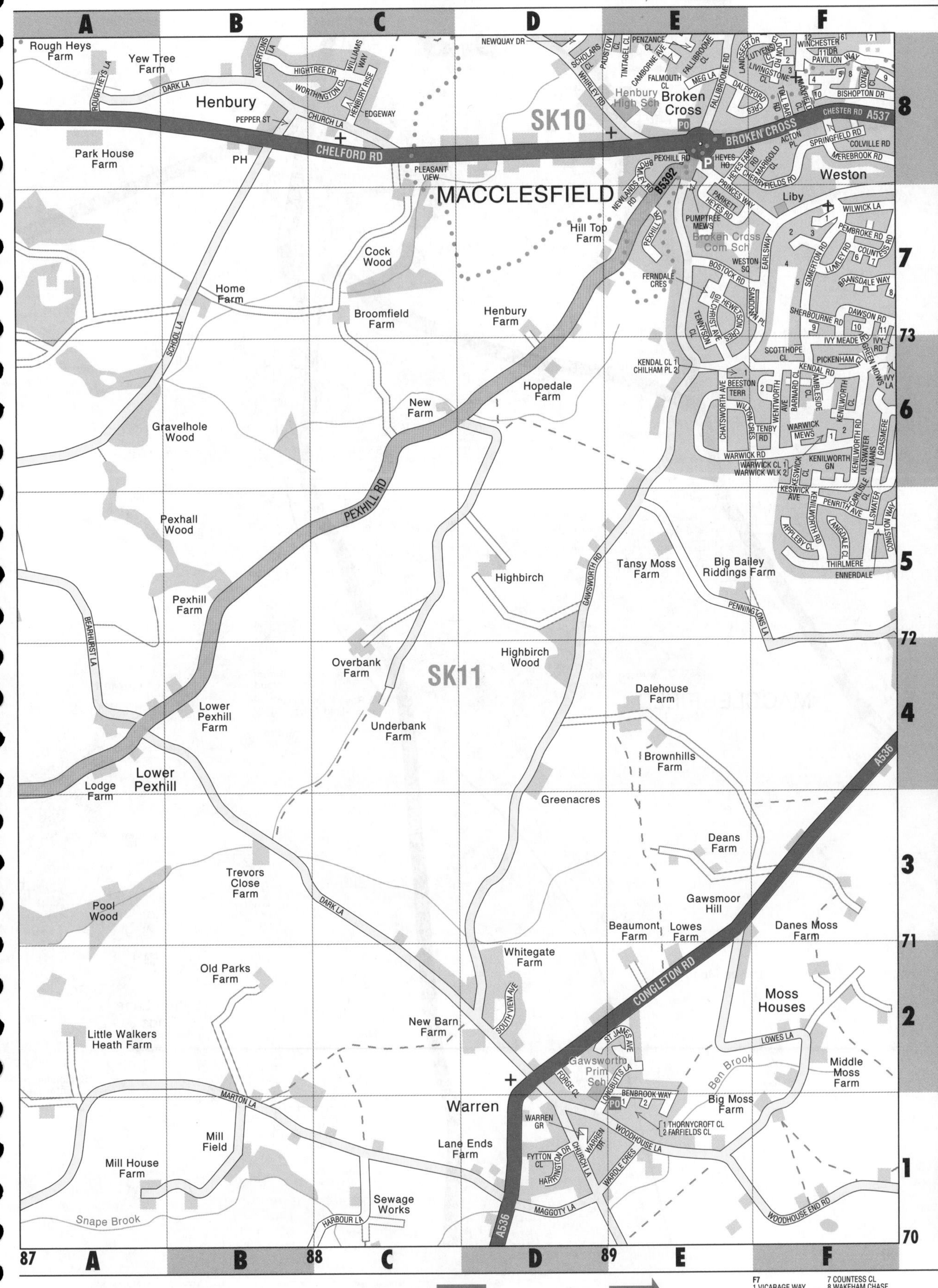

134
112

F7
1 VICARAGE WAY
2 DUDLEY WLK
3 PEVERIL WLK
4 PORTLAND WLK
5 SOMERTON CL
6 WARDOUR CL
7 COUNTESS CL
8 WAKEHAM CHASE
9 HILTON CL
10 IVY MEADE CL
11 DAWSON CL

B6
1 ARMOURY TWRS
2 EVINGTON HO
3 BARRACKS SQ
4 ARMOURY COURT MEWS
5 QUEEN ANNES CT

C7
1 PETER ST W
2 ATHEY ST MILL
3 MARSDEN TERR
4 BACK PARADISE ST
5 HOLLAND ST
6 BLACKSHAW ST

111

7 ST JOHN S RD
8 BAKER ST
D7
1 NEWGATE
2 DUKES CT
3 MARLBOROUGH CT
4 TOWNLEY ST

87

5 TOWNLEY PL
6 TOWNLEY MILL
7 WARDLE ST
8 TRAFALGAR CT
9 GRAPES ST
10 BROKEN BANKS
11 ST GEORGE S PL
12 BRUNSWICK CT
13 LOWER EXCHANGE ST
E7
1 BAILEY CT
2 ST PAUL S CT
3 ST PAUL S RD
4 HALLEFIELD DR
5 HALLEFIELD CRES
6 BROOKSIDE MILL
7 THORNYCROFT ST
8 CAWLEY ST
9 PEARSON ST
10 LOWER BANK ST
11 BUCKLOW WLK
12 KNUTSFORD ROAD WLK
13 WILMSLOW WLK
14 ALDERLEY WLK
15 ELIZABETH HO
16 PLUMLEY CL
17 STUBBS TERR
18 WINLOWE
19 BROOK STREET MILL

A B C D E F

1 GRITSTONE DR
2 BRAMHALL WAY
3 SHUTLINGSLOE WAY
4 TABLEY CL
5 ABINGDON CT
6 MEREBROOK CL

1 COMMERCIAL RD
2 PERCYVALE ST
3 WELLINGTON CIR
4 COMMONGATE
5 COOKSTOOLPIT HILL
6 FENCE CT
7 FOUNTAIN HO
8 DAINTRY TERR

BARNETT ST 1
STEVENAGE CL 2
ST ANDREWS CT 3

CHOLMONDELEY ST 1
HARPUR CL 2
SILK MILL 3
VENTURE HO 4
JACKSON ST 5
THE OLD RIBBON MILL 6
ST EDWARDS CL 7
ST BARNABAS CT 8
FARNDALE WLK 9

1 ST PETER'S HO
2 TABOR ST
3 SMITH'S TERR
4 SQUARE ST
5 HIGGINBOTHAM GN

1 MAPLEWOOD
2 LINGDALE WLK
3 SUNNY BANK
4 CHANTRY CT

Macclesfield District General
Fence Ave Ind Est
SK10
The King's Sch
Puss Bank Sch
Macclesfield
St John The Evangelist CE Prim Sch
Macclesfield Coll
Park Lane Sch
St Edward's RC Prim Sch
Cheshire Ring Canal Walk
Macclesfield Canal
SK11
Byrons Wood
The Hollins
Gurnett
MACCLESFIELD
Moss Lane
Moss Rose Football Gnd (Macclesfield Town FC)
Wood's Cut
Lyme Green Bsns Pk
Hollinhey Prim Sch
Danes Moss
Works
Lyme Green
Sutton Lane Ends
Sutton Grange
Moss Head Farm
Lyme Green Settlement
Symondley Farm
Lake House Farm
Sutton Resr

8
7
73
6
5
72
4
3
71
2
1
70

90 A B 91 C D 92 E F

111

C8
1 WILLERBY CL
2 WALKER ST
3 GROSVENOR ST
4 WESTMINSTER RD
5 STANLEY & BROCKLEHURST CT
6 COURT NO 4
7 MILLERS CT
8 MILLERS CROFT
9 BUCKDEN WAY

135

10 NEWBIGGIN WAY
11 SHARPLEY ST
12 BOOTHBY ST
13 GEORGES CT
14 WESTMINSTER ST
15 POYNTON ST
16 ANDERSON ST
17 SIMPSON S CT
18 PINFOLD ST
19 REGENT & FOUNDRY CT
20 THE TOWER HO
21 LANGFORD ST
22 CHARLOTTE STREET W
23 CHARLTON ST
24 The Crown Ctr
25 EDGAR CT
D8
1 TUNNICLIFFE ST
2 CUMBERLAND ST
3 KING EDWARD RD
4 LITTLE ST
5 BRUNSWICK ST
6 CHURCH MEWS
7 STANLEY ST
8 UNICORN GATEWAY
9 CHATHAM ST
10 ST MICHAELS TERR
11 SHORT ST
12 EXCHANGE CL
13 BACK WALLGATE
14 QUEEN VICTORIA ST
15 WELLINGTON ST
16 ALBERT PL

88
114

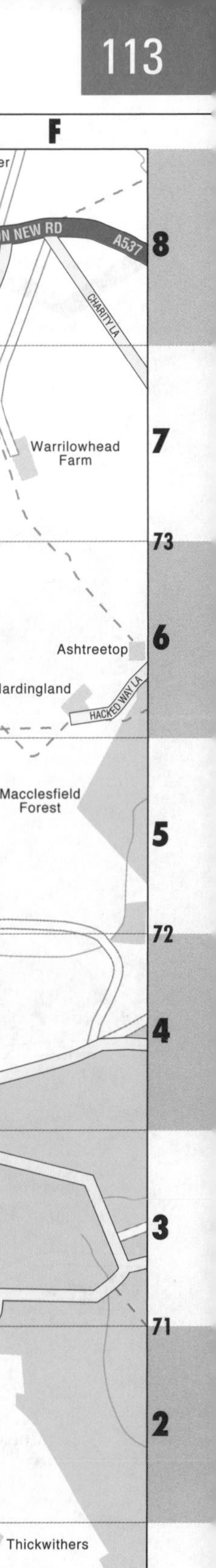

136
114

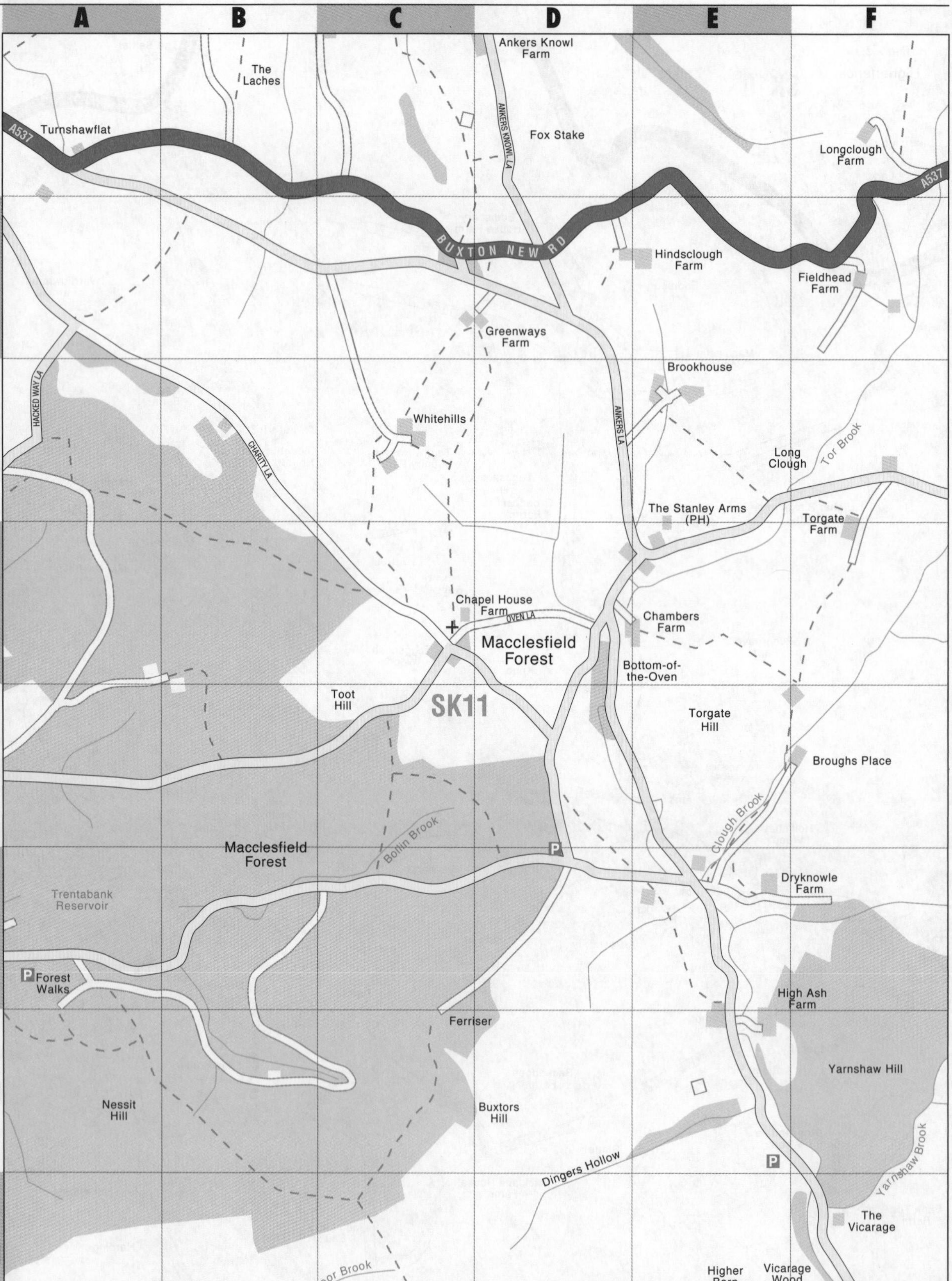

A B C D E F

8 7 73 6 5 72 4 3 71 2 1 70

Turnshawflat
A537
The Laches
Ankers Knowl Farm
ANKERS KNOWL LA
Fox Stake
Longclough Farm
A537
BUXTON NEW RD
Hindsclough Farm
Fieldhead Farm
Greenways Farm
Brookhouse
HACKED WAY LA
Whitehills
CHARITY LA
ANKERS LA
Long Clough
Tor Brook
The Stanley Arms (PH)
Torgate Farm
Chapel House Farm
OVEN LA
Macclesfield Forest
Chambers Farm
Bottom-of-the-Oven
Toot Hill
SK11
Torgate Hill
Broughs Place
Clough Brook
Bollin Brook
Macclesfield Forest
Dryknowle Farm
Trentabank Reservoir
Forest Walks
High Ash Farm
Ferriser
Yarnshaw Hill
Nessit Hill
Buxtors Hill
Dingers Hollow
Yarnshaw Brook
The Vicarage
Highmoor Brook
Higher Barn
Vicarage Wood
High Moor

96 A B 97 C D 98 E F

90

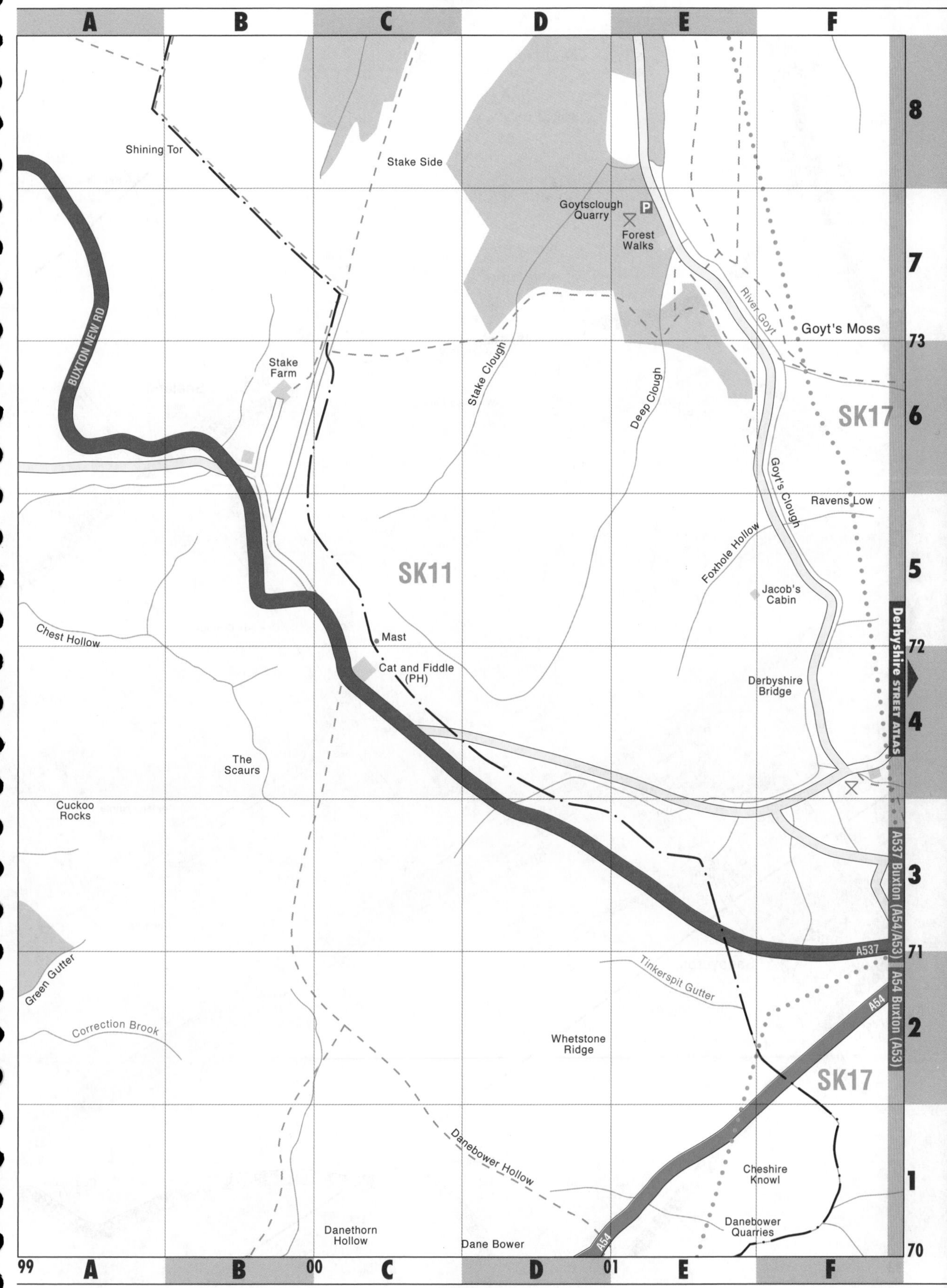

A
B
C
D
E
F
8
7
73
6
5
72
4
3
71
2
1
70
99
00
01
Shining Tor
Stake Side
Goytsclough Quarry
P
Forest Walks
River Goyt
Goyt's Moss
BUXTON NEW RD
Stake Farm
Stake Clough
Deep Clough
SK17
Goyt's Clough
Ravens Low
Foxhole Hollow
SK11
Jacob's Cabin
Chest Hollow
Mast
Cat and Fiddle (PH)
Derbyshire Bridge
Derbyshire STREET ATLAS
The Scaurs
Cuckoo Rocks
A537 Buxton (A54/A53)
A537
Green Gutter
Tinkerspit Gutter
A54 Buxton (A53)
A54
Correction Brook
Whetstone Ridge
SK17
Danebower Hollow
Cheshire Knowl
Danethorn Hollow
Dane Bower
Danebower Quarries

138

93

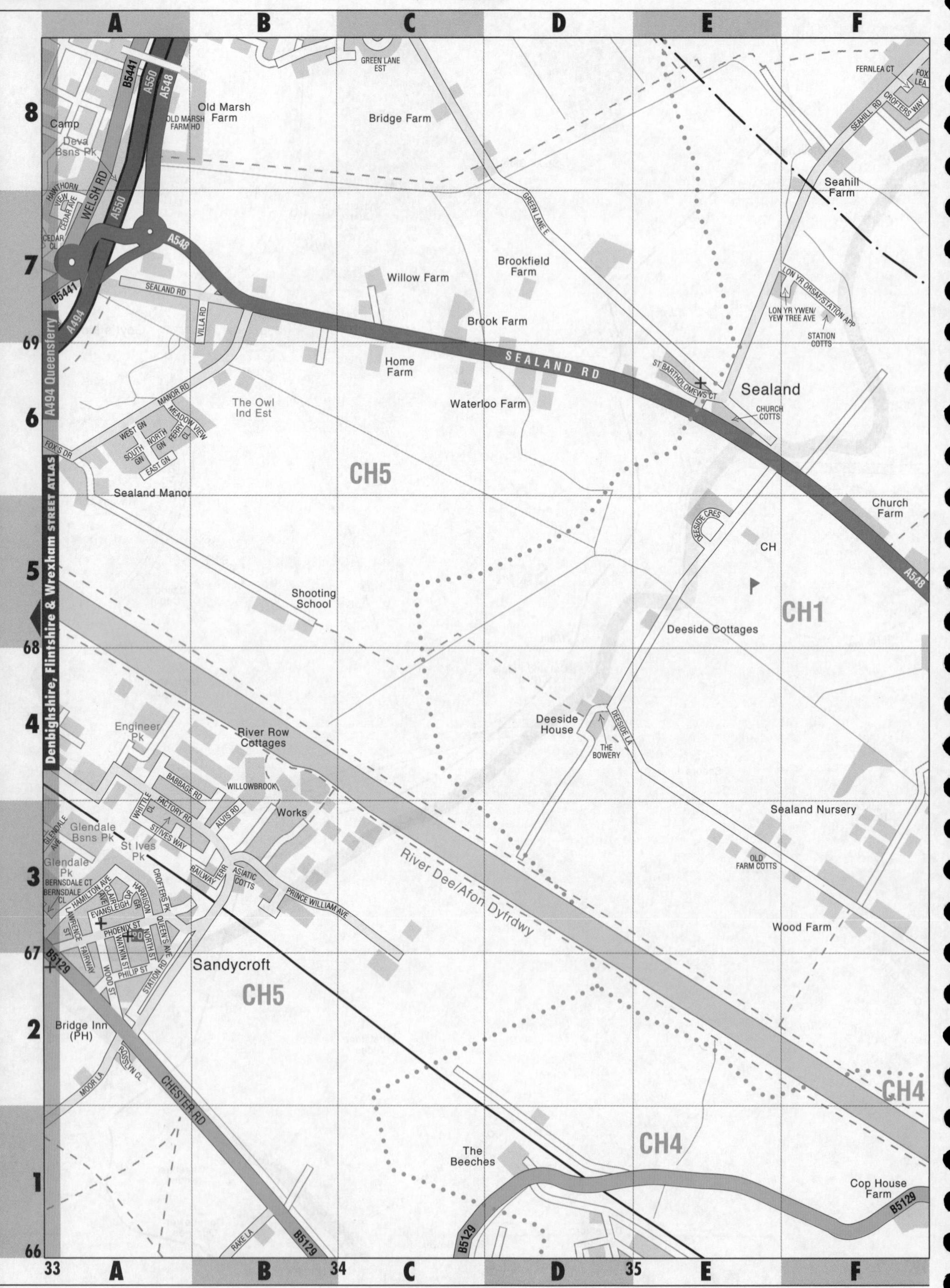

A
B
C
D
E
F
8
7
69
6
5
68
4
3
67
2
1
66
33
34
35
GREEN LANE EST
Old Marsh Farm
OLD MARSH FARM HO
Bridge Farm
Camp
Deva Bsns Pk
B5441
A550
A548
WELSH RD
HAWTHORN VIEW
CEDAR AVE
CEDAR CL
B5441
A494
SEALAND RD
VILLA RD
GREEN LANE E
Brookfield Farm
Willow Farm
Brook Farm
Home Farm
Waterloo Farm
SEALAND RD
The Owl Ind Est
MANOR RD
MEADOW VIEW
WEST GN
SOUTH GN
NORTH GN
FERRY CL
EAST GN
FOX'S DR
CH5
Sealand Manor
A494 Queensferry
Denbighshire, Flintshire & Wrexham STREET ATLAS
FERNLEA CT
FOX LEA
SEAHILL RD
CROFTERS WAY
Seahill Farm
LON YR ORSAF/STATION APP
LON YR YWEN/ YEW TREE AVE
STATION COTTS
ST BARTHOLOMEWS CT
Sealand
CHURCH COTTS
DEESIDE CRES
CH
Church Farm
A548
CH1
Shooting School
Deeside Cottages
Deeside House
DEESIDE LA
THE BOWERY
Engineer Pk
River Row Cottages
WILLOWBROOK
BABBAGE RD
FACTORY RD
WHITTLE CL
ALVIS RD
Works
ST IVES WAY
GLENDALE AVE
Glendale Bsns Pk
St Ives Pk
Glendale Pk
BERNSDALE CT
BERNSDALE CL
HAMILTON AVE
CLAIRE AVE
HARRISON DR
EVANSLEIGH DR
CROFTERS PK
RAILWAY TERR
ASIATIC COTTS
PRINCE WILLIAM AVE
River Dee/Afon Dyfrdwy
Sealand Nursery
OLD FARM COTTS
Wood Farm
LAWRENCE ST
PHOENIX ST
WATKIN ST
NORTH ST
QUEEN'S AVE
FAIRWAY
PHILIP ST
WOOD ST
STATION RD
B5129
Sandycroft
CH5
Bridge Inn (PH)
ROSSLYN CL
MOOR LA
CHESTER RD
RAKE LA
B5129
B5129
The Beeches
CH4
CH4
Cop House Farm
B5129

139

94
118

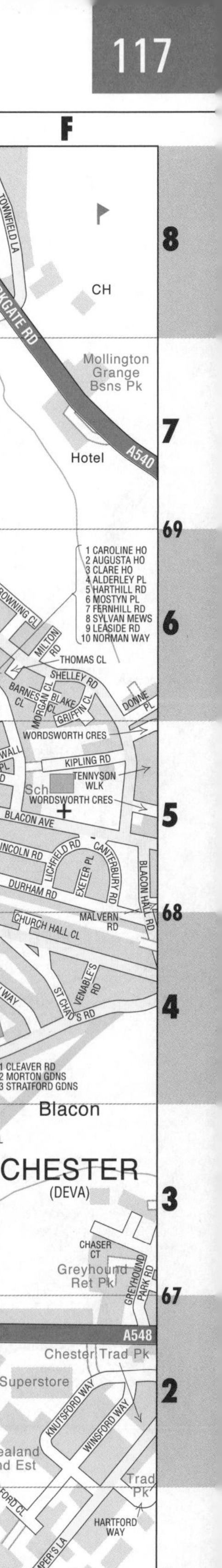

140
118

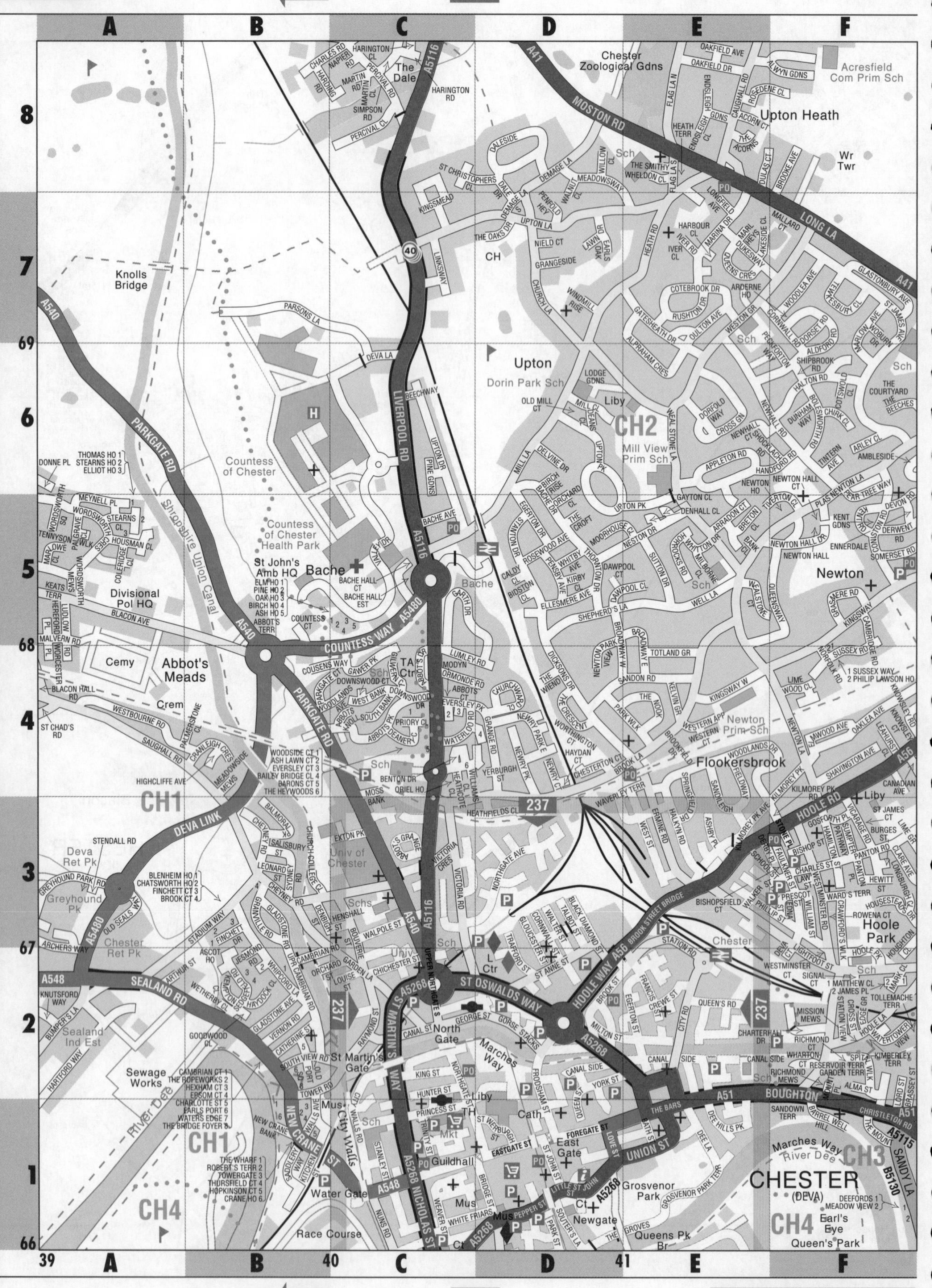

For full street detail of the highlighted area see page 237.

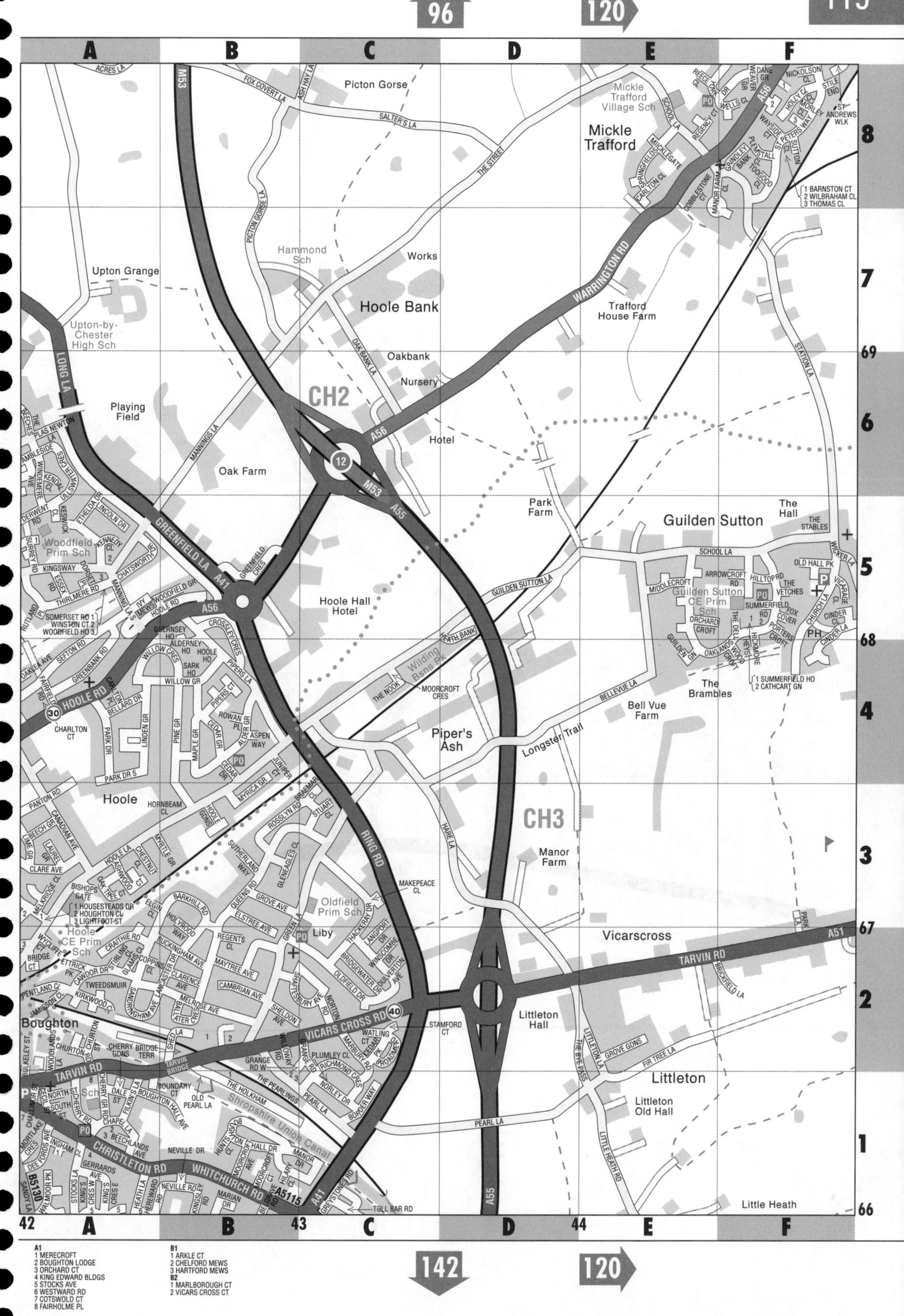

96
120
A
B
C
D
E
F
8
7
69
6
5
68
4
3
67
2
1
66
42
43
44
Picton Gorse
FOX COVERT LA
ASH HAY LA
SALTER'S LA
ACRES LA
M53
Mickle Trafford Village Sch
Mickle Trafford
SCHOOL LA
REECE CL
YORK CL
WEAVER GR
DANE GR
NICKOLSON CL
WELLS CL
A56
HOLLY CL
MORLEY CL
STILE END
ST ANDREWS WLK
REGENCY CT
MICKLEGATE
SPRINGFIELDS
CARLTON CL
COBBLESTONE CT
MANOR FARM CL
GRINDLEY BANK
PLEMSTALL CL
TOOGOOD CL
WAYSIDE CT
ST PETERS WAY
SUTTON CL
1 BARNSTON CT
2 WILBRAHAM CL
3 THOMAS CL
THE STREET
PICTON GORSE LA
Hammond Sch
Works
Upton Grange
Hoole Bank
WARRINGTON RD
Trafford House Farm
Upton-by-Chester High Sch
LONG LA
OAK BANK LA
Oakbank
Nursery
STATION LA
CH2
Playing Field
MANNINGS LA
Hotel
Oak Farm
12
M53
A55
A56
PLAS NEWTON LA
AMBLESIDE
WINDERMERE AVE
KENDAL CL
ULLSWATER CRES
DERWENT CT
KESWICK CL
ETHELDA DR
LINCOLN DR
Woodfield Prim Sch
KENNEDY CL
SURREY RD
KINGSWAY
DORSET PL
ESSEX RD
THIRLMERE RD
CHATSWORTH CL
GREENFIELD LA
A41
GREENFIELD CRES
Park Farm
Guilden Sutton
The Hall
THE STABLES
SCHOOL LA
WICKER LA
GUILDEN SUTTON LA
ARROWCROFT RD
HILLTOP RD
OLD HALL PK
MIDDLECROFT
Guilden Sutton CE Prim Sch
THE VETCHES
VICARAGE CL
SUMMERFIELD RD
FOX COVER
ORCHARD CROFT
THE DELL
CHURCH LA
CINDER CL
CINDER LA
PH
PORTERS CROFT
HICKMORE HEYS
OAKLANDS
WOOD CROFT
GUILDEN GN
1 SUMMERFIELD HO
2 CATHCART GN
Hoole Hall Hotel
RUTLAND PL
MANNING LA S
IVY MEWS
WOODFIELD GR
HOOLE RD
A56
SOMERSET RD 1
WINSTON CT 2
WOODFIELD HO 3
GUERNSEY HO
CROSSLEY CRES
ALDERNEY HO
HOOLE HO
SARK HO
WILLOW CRES
WILLOW GR
PIPERS LA
PIPERS CT
OAKLEA AVE
SEFTON RD
GREENBANK RD
FAIRFIELD RD
HOOLE RD
30
CHARLTON CT
CARLTON
BELLARD DR
LINDEN GR
PINE GR
MAPLE GR
CEDAR GR
ROWAN PL
ALDER GR
ASPEN WAY
HEATH BANK
Wilding Bsns Pk
THE NOOK
MOORCROFT CRES
The Brambles
BELLEVUE LA
Bell Vue Farm
Piper's Ash
Longster Trail
PARK DR
PARK DR S
CEDAR DR
MYRICA GR
JUNIPER
Hoole
HORNBEAM CL
HOOLE GDNS
BRAEMAR
ROSSLYN RD
STUART CL
PANTON RD
CANADIAN AVE
BEECH GR
LIME GR
LAUREL AVE
CLARE AVE
HOOLE LA
ASHWOOD
CHESTNUT CL
MYRTLE GR
SUTHERLAND WAY
GLENEAGLES CL
RING RD
HARE LA
CH3
Manor Farm
MELKRIDGE CL
BISHOPS GATE
OAK TREE CT
1 HOUSESTEADS DR
2 HOUGHTON CL
3 LIGHTFOOT ST
ELGIN CL
BARKHILL RD
QUEENS RD
GROVE AVE
MAKEPEACE CL
Oldfield Prim Sch
ELSTREE AVE
THACKERAY DR
Hoole CE Prim Sch
HOLYROOD WAY
REGENTS CL
GREEN LA
Liby
LANGPORT DR
WINSCOMBE DR
Vicarscross
A51
TARVIN RD
PARK LA
WYCLIFFE RD
CRAITHIE RD
BRIDGE CT
ETTRICK PK
STIRLING CL
GLAMIS CL
COPPINS CL
BUCKINGHAM AVE
MAYTREE AVE
SHAFTESBURY AVE
BRIDGEWATER DR
OLDFIELD DR
DULVERTON AVE
BRICKFIELD LA
CAWDOR DR
TWEEDSMUIR
CLARENCE AVE
CAMBRIAN AVE
PENTLAND CL
JAMIESON CL
KIRKWOOD CL
SANDRINGHAM AVE
LANCASTER DR
MELROSE AVE
BALLATER CRES
SHELDON AVE
NORTON RD
40
Littleton Hall
Boughton
CHURTON RD
STAMFORD CT
VICARS CROSS RD
WATLING CT
CEDAR PK
ROADWAY
CHERRY GDNS
BRIDGE TERR
SHED LA
CEDAR
GRANGE RD W
WILLOWAY RD
GRANGE RD
MARBURY RD
PLUMLEY CL
RICHMOND CRES
LITTLETON LA
THE BYE PASS
GROVE GDNS
FIR TREE LA
Littleton
BULKELEY ST
WOODLANDS
TARVIN RD
TARVIN BRIDGE
BOUNDARY CT
OLD PEARL LA
THE HOLKHAM
THE PEARLINGS
NORLEY DR
PEARL LA
BORDER WAY
Littleton Old Hall
NORTH ST
SOUTH ST
CHERRY RD
DALE ST
FILKIN'S LA
BOUGHTON HALL AVE
Shropshire Union Canal
PEARL LA
CHALLINOR ST
CHAPEL LA
BEECHLANDS AVE
MORTLAKE CRES
DEE FORDS AVE
CHRISTLETON RD
HUNTS CL
BOUGHTON HALL DR
MANOR DR
NEVILLE DR
LITTLE HEATH RD
GERRARDS AVE
HILARY CL
MOORCROFT AVE
WHITCHURCH RD
A5115
A41
GREYSTONES RD
TOLL BAR RD
A55
Little Heath
B5130
WALMOOR PK
SANDY LA
STOCKS LA
KING'S CRES W
KING'S CRES E
HEATH LA
HEREWARD RD
NEVILLE RD
KINGSLEY RD
MARIAN DR
BELGRAVE PL
142
120
A1
1 MERECROFT
2 BOUGHTON LODGE
3 ORCHARD CT
4 KING EDWARD BLDGS
5 STOCKS AVE
6 WESTWARD RD
7 COTSWOLD CT
8 FAIRHOLME PL
B1
1 ARKLE CT
2 CHELFORD MEWS
3 HARTFORD MEWS
B2
1 MARLBOROUGH CT
2 VICARS CROSS CT

119
97

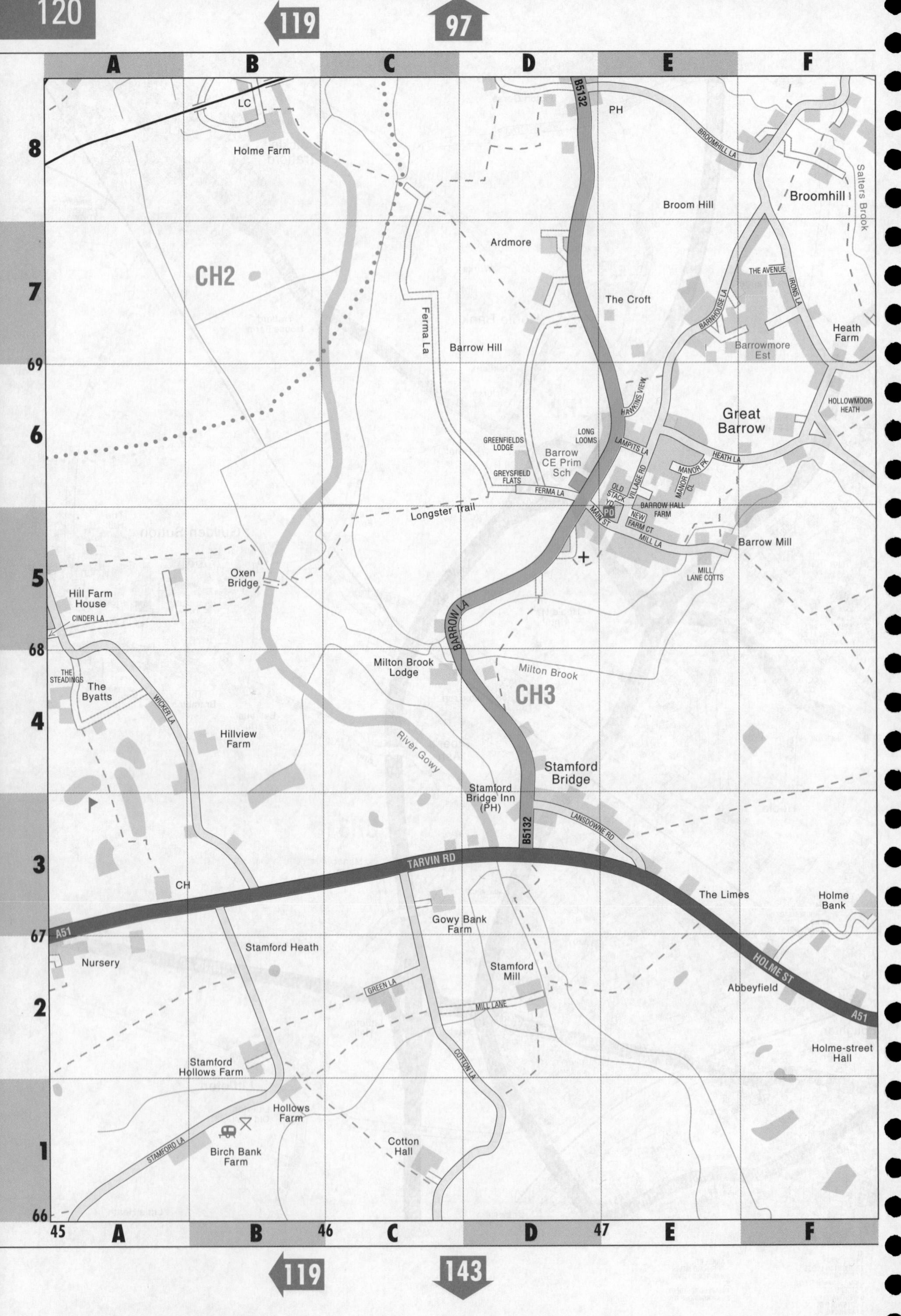

119
143

98
122

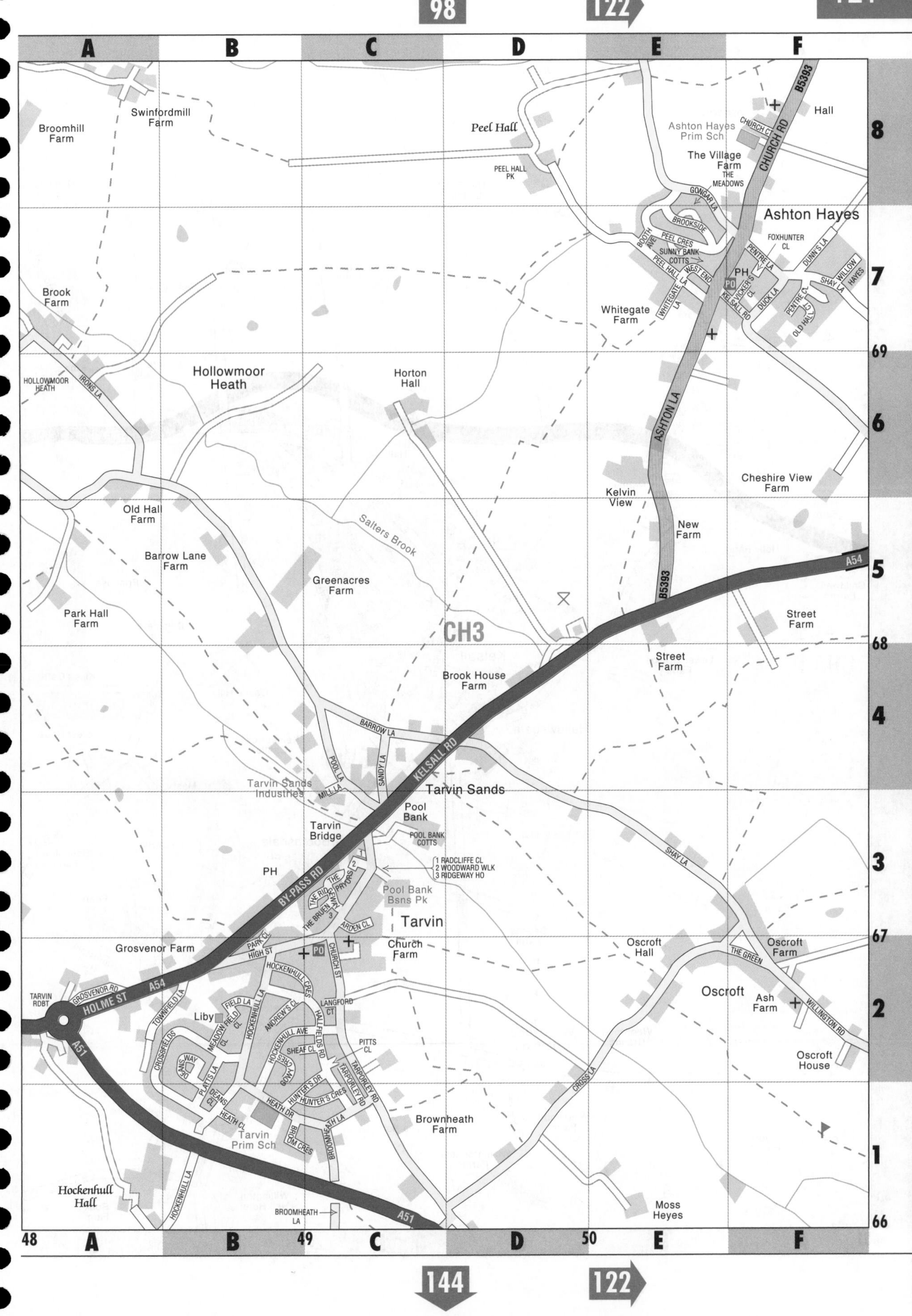

144
122

121
99

A B C D E F

Park Farm
Ashton Hayes
The Yeld Farm
CW8
Ash Wood
8
Longley Wood
YELD LA
The Top Lodge
Yeld Farm
Nettleford Wood
Dale Covert
NORTONS LA
Shay Lane
Longley Farm
The Yeld
7
Lower Longley Farm
FOREST GATE LA
Sandstone Trail
SHAY LA
MORREYS LA
69
HALL LA
Nursery
King's Chair
HILLCREST RD
DINGLE LA
CLEMLEY CL
6
PH
CHESTER RD
A54
Kelsall Hall
PRIMROSE HILL
Northwood Hall
LONGLEY AVE
BROOM'S LA
Weldon Farm
HOLLANDS LA
GRUB LA
DUTTON'S LA
OLD COACH RD
EDALE DR
CHESTER RD
SWALLOW DR
A54
Holly Farm
REDHILL RD
5
CHAPEL GN
EARLE'S LA
CHURCH BANK
ORCHARD WAY
Primrose Hill
Childwall Farm
DOG LA
PH
BRAMLEY CT
QUARRY LA
EGERTON CT
CHESTER RD
CHURCH ST N
KINGS WOOD WLK
KELSBORROW WAY
Delamere Farm
68
PO
P
THE DELL
ELIZABETH CL
CH3
Lower Grange Farm
PH
Kelsall
CHURCH ST
BROOK DR
FOX HILL
Kelsall Com Prim Sch
HALLOWS DR
CLOWS HALL
CARTER AVE
KELSBORROW WAY
Kings Gate
Castle Hill
HALLOWSGATE CT
CASTLE CL
HILLSIDE RD
FLAT LA
WASTE LA
4
Hallowsgate
MEADOW BANK
WILLINGTON LA
Forest House
Kelsborrow Castle
PASTURE CL
THE WYND
BROOKSIDE
GREEN LA
CW6
Mast
THE COMMON
WILLINGTON RD
Boothsdale
Birch Hill
TIRLEY LA
3
BOOTHSDALE
PH
Roughlow Farm
GOOSEBERRY LA
Common Farm
COMMON LA
Pearl Hole
67
Beechs Farm
CHAPEL LA
Sandstone Trail
Manor Farm
2
WILLINGTON CNR
LILAC CL
OAK TREE CT
Weetwood Grange
Weetwood Common
WILLINGTON RD
Willington Wood
WILLINGTON LA
MILL LA
Weetwood Farm
CH
Pryors Hayes
The Belt
1
Willington-mill Farm
Home Farm
Willington Hall Hotel
Rock Farm
66
51 A B 52 C D 53 E F

100

124

A
B
C
D
E
F
Coronation Farm
B5152
Golf Links Farm
FARM RD
8
Pale Heights
Masts
FRITH AVE
STATION RD
EDDISBURY HILL PK
Hall Wood
Eddisbury Hill
OLD PALE HTS
EDDISBURY HILL
ROWAN CL
7
OLD PALE COTTS
DELAMERE GR
Eddisbury Hill Farm
THE RIDGE
Hangingstone Hill
Thieves Moss
A556
69
PO
Delamere
Bowyer's Waste
WASTE LA
Lodge
Rectory Farm
Inn
6
STONEY LA
CHRIMES DR
MERE CRES
Organsdale House
PH
Works
WATLING DR
Delamere CE Prim Sch
A556
CHESTER RD
CW8
ORGANSDALE COTTS
Organsdale
ABBEY LA
5
MIDDLEWICH RD
Abbey Wood
Sand Pit
Abbey Arms Wood
Cherry Orchard Farm
68
Urchins Kitchen
Oak Tree Farm
4
Fishpool Inn (PH)
CW6
Primrosehill Wood
A54
Sandstone Trail
Harrow Hill
Fishpool Farm
Ottersbank Farm
FISHPOOL RD
3
OTTERSBANK MEWS
67
TIRLEY LA
Tirley Hollow
Tirley Farm
2
HEATHS LA
Higher Barn Farm
Hollin Hill Farm
Sidebottom Farm
Forest Farm
Monarchy Hall Farm
STABLE LA
QUARRY BANK
HOLLINS HILL
B5152
Tirley Garth
Quarry Bank House
1
KNIGHTS LA
Hollins Hill
SADLERS LA
The Willingtons
High Billinge House
66
54
A
B
55
C
D
56
E
F

146
124

123
101

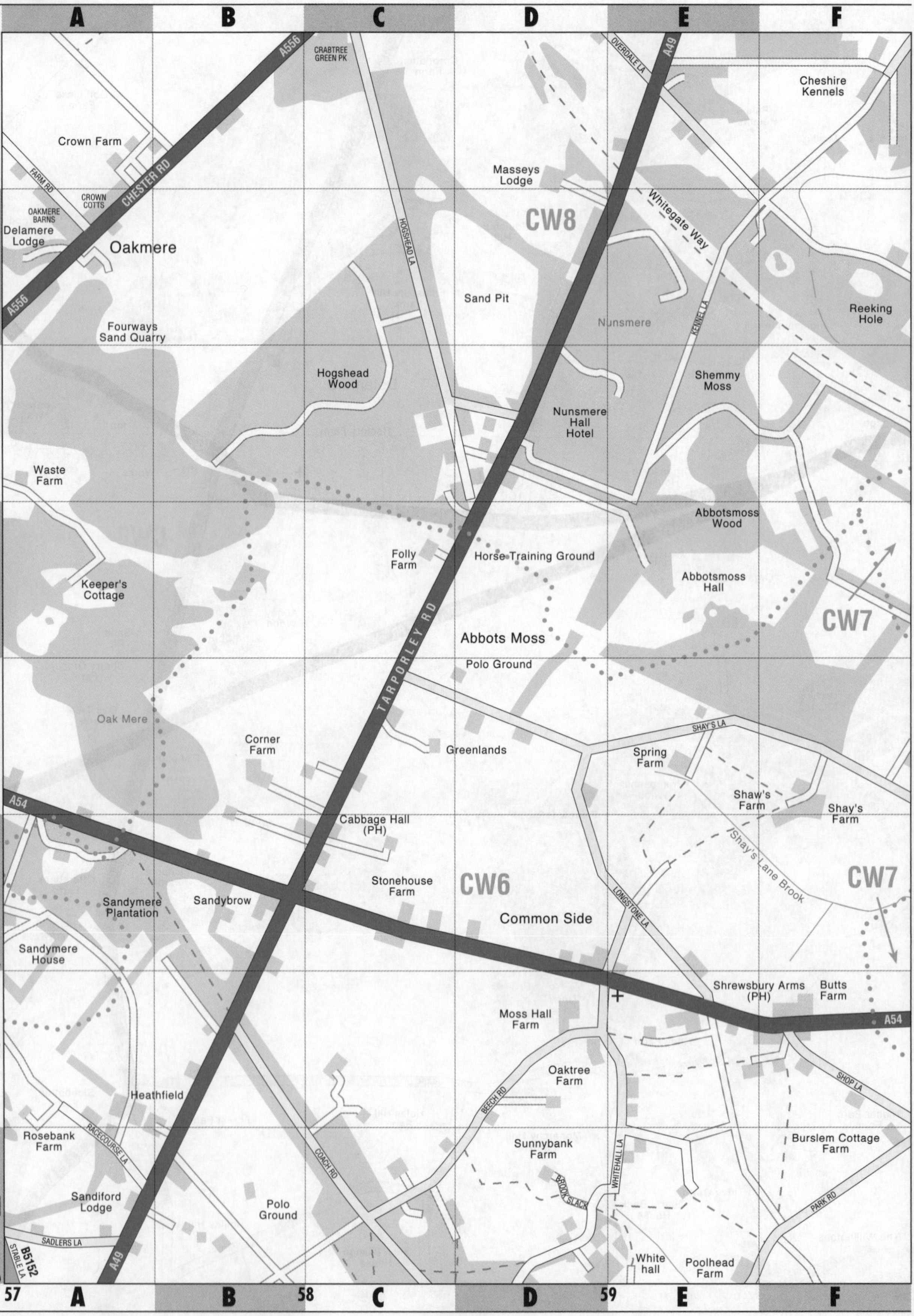

123
147

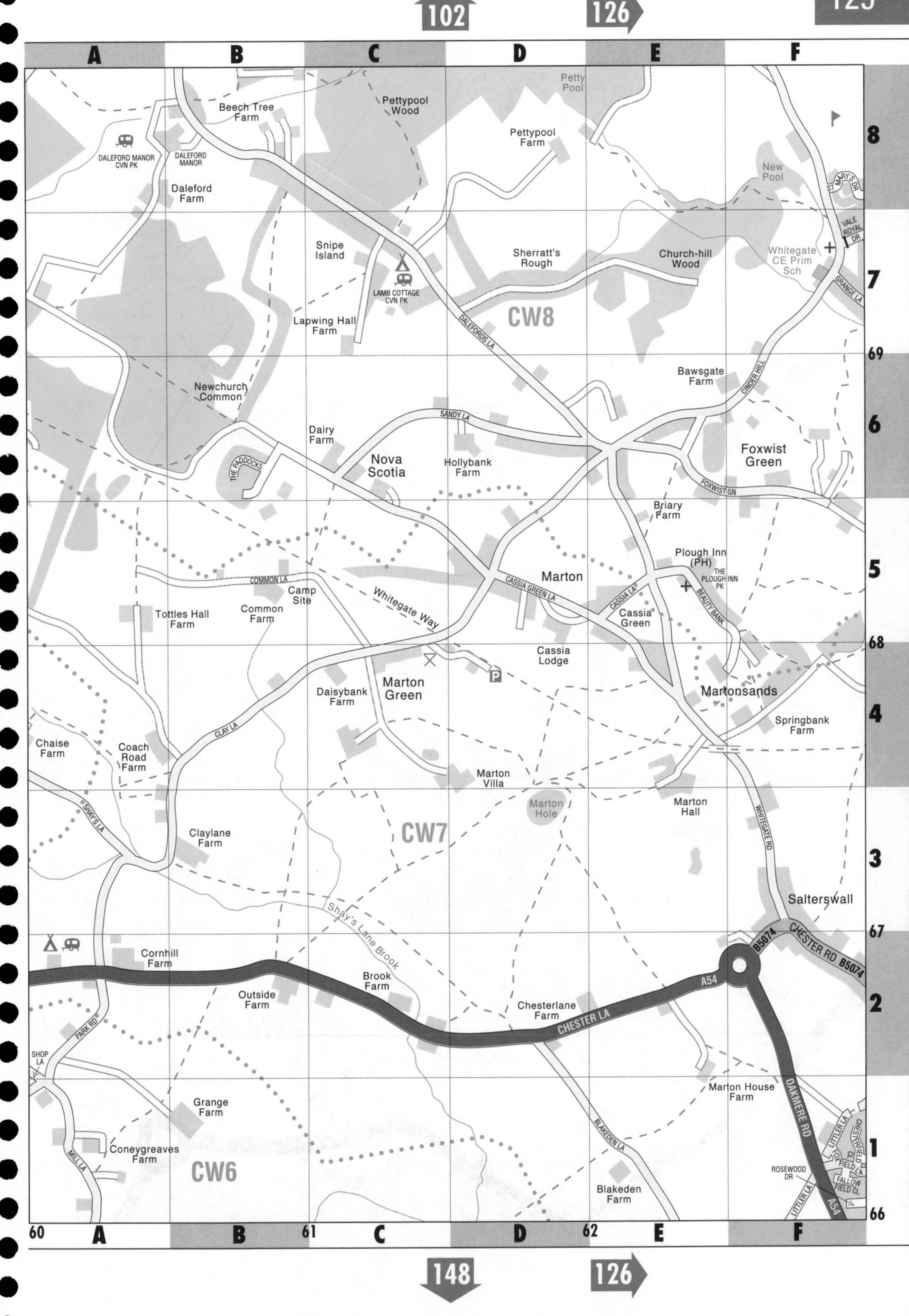
102
126
A
B
C
D
E
F
8
7
69
6
5
68
4
3
67
2
1
66
60
61
62
Petty Pool
Pettypool Wood
Beech Tree Farm
DALEFORD MANOR CVN PK
DALEFORD MANOR
Daleford Farm
Pettypool Farm
New Pool
ST MARY'S DR
VALE ROYAL DR
Whitegate CE Prim Sch
GRANGE LA
Snipe Island
Sherratt's Rough
Church-hill Wood
LAMB COTTAGE CVN PK
Lapwing Hall Farm
DALEFORDS LA
CW8
Bawsgate Farm
CINDER HILL
Newchurch Common
SANDY LA
Dairy Farm
Nova Scotia
Hollybank Farm
Foxwist Green
THE PADDOCKS
FOXWIST GN
Briary Farm
Plough Inn (PH)
THE PLOUGH INN PK
Marton
COMMON LA
Camp Site
CASSIA GREEN LA
CASSIA LA
BEAUTY BANK
Tottles Hall Farm
Common Farm
Whitegate Way
Cassia Green
Cassia Lodge
Marton Green
Daisybank Farm
Martonsands
Springbank Farm
CLAY LA
Chaise Farm
Coach Road Farm
Marton Villa
Marton Hole
Marton Hall
SHAY'S LA
Claylane Farm
CW7
WHITEGATE RD
Salterswall
Shay's Lane Brook
B5074
CHESTER RD B5074
Cornhill Farm
Brook Farm
A54
Outside Farm
Chesterlane Farm
CHESTER LA
PARK RD
SHOP LA
Marton House Farm
OAKMERE RD
Grange Farm
BLAKEDEN LA
Coneygreaves Farm
LITTLER LA
CHESTERFIELD CL
FOXFIELD LA
MILL LA
CW6
ROSEWOOD DR
FALLOW FIELD CL
Blakeden Farm
A54
148
126

125 103

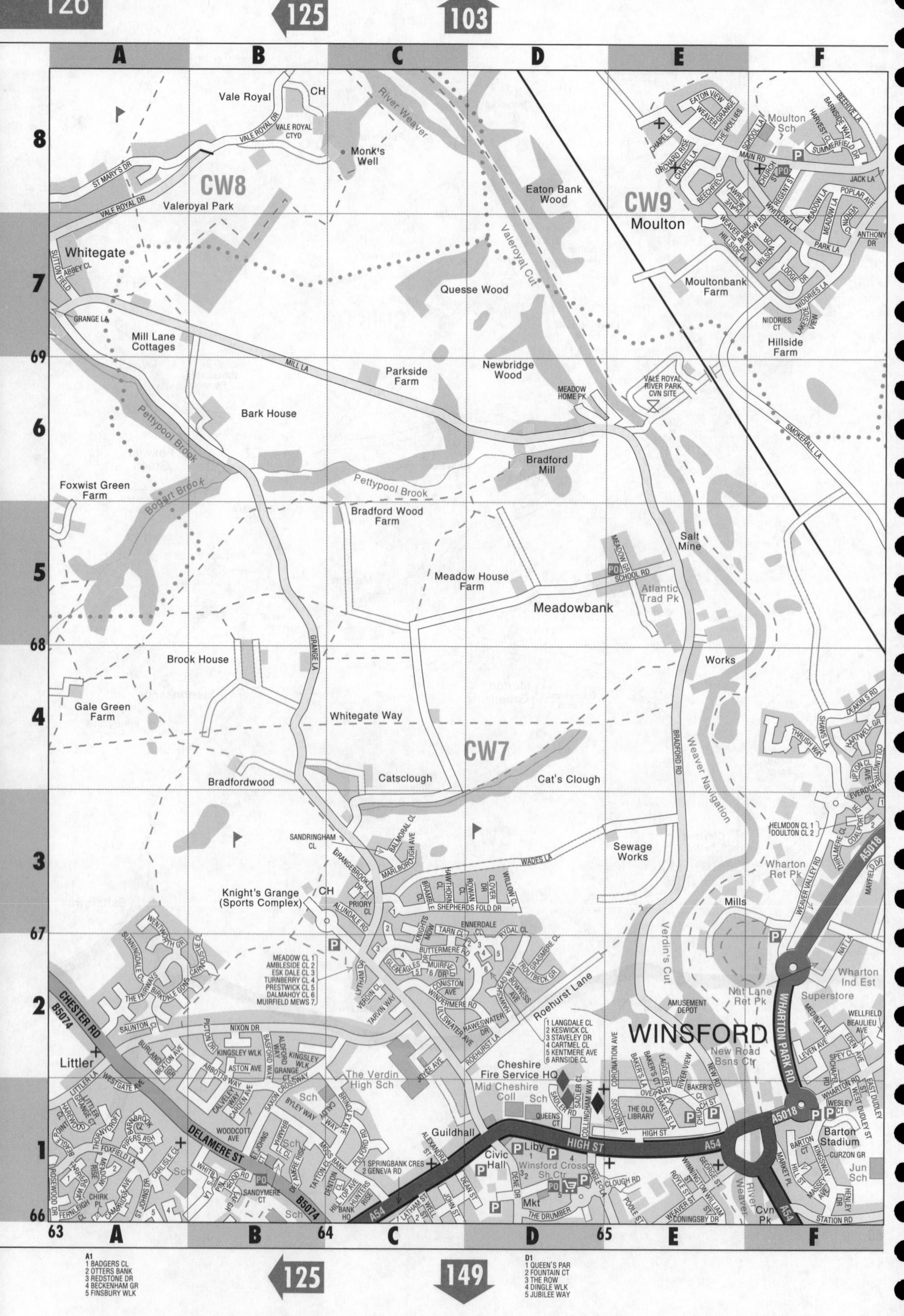

A1
1 BADGERS CL
2 OTTERS BANK
3 REDSTONE DR
4 BECKENHAM GR
5 FINSBURY WLK

125 149

D1
1 QUEEN'S PAR
2 FOUNTAIN CT
3 THE ROW
4 DINGLE WLK
5 JUBILEE WAY

104
128

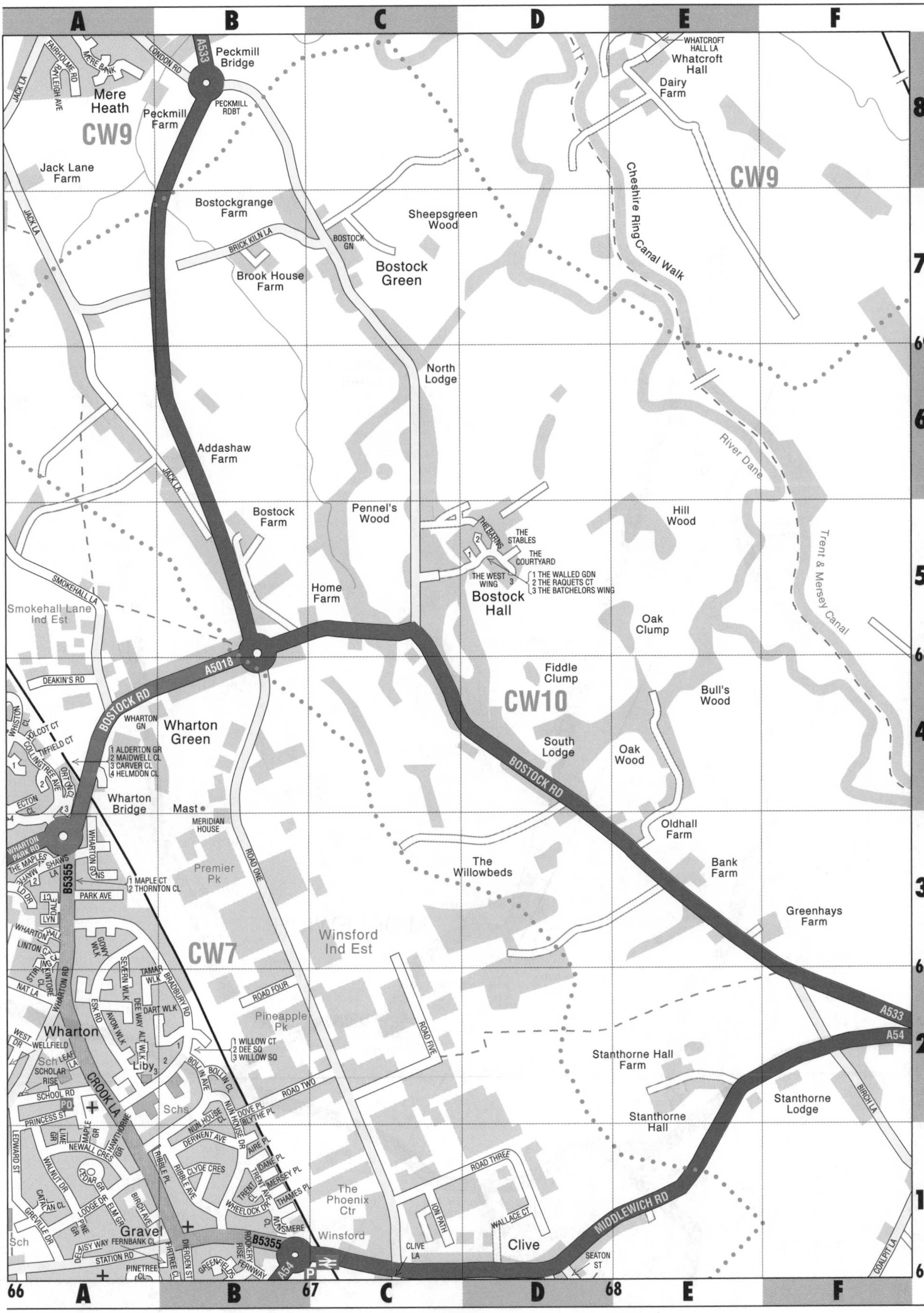

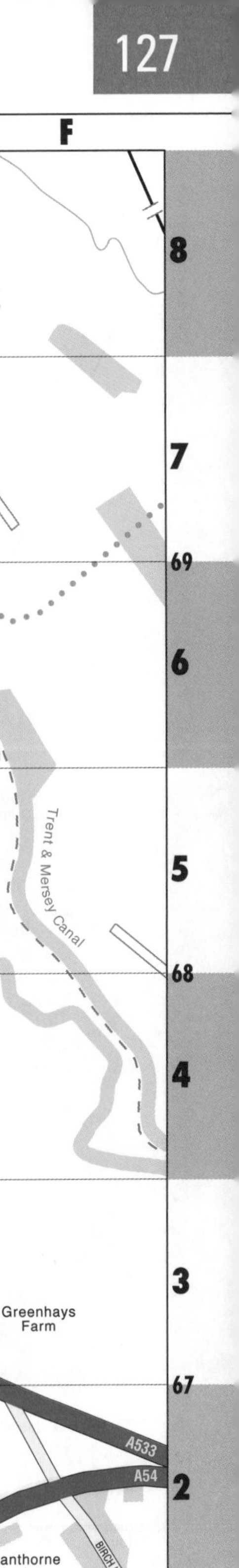

150
128

127
105

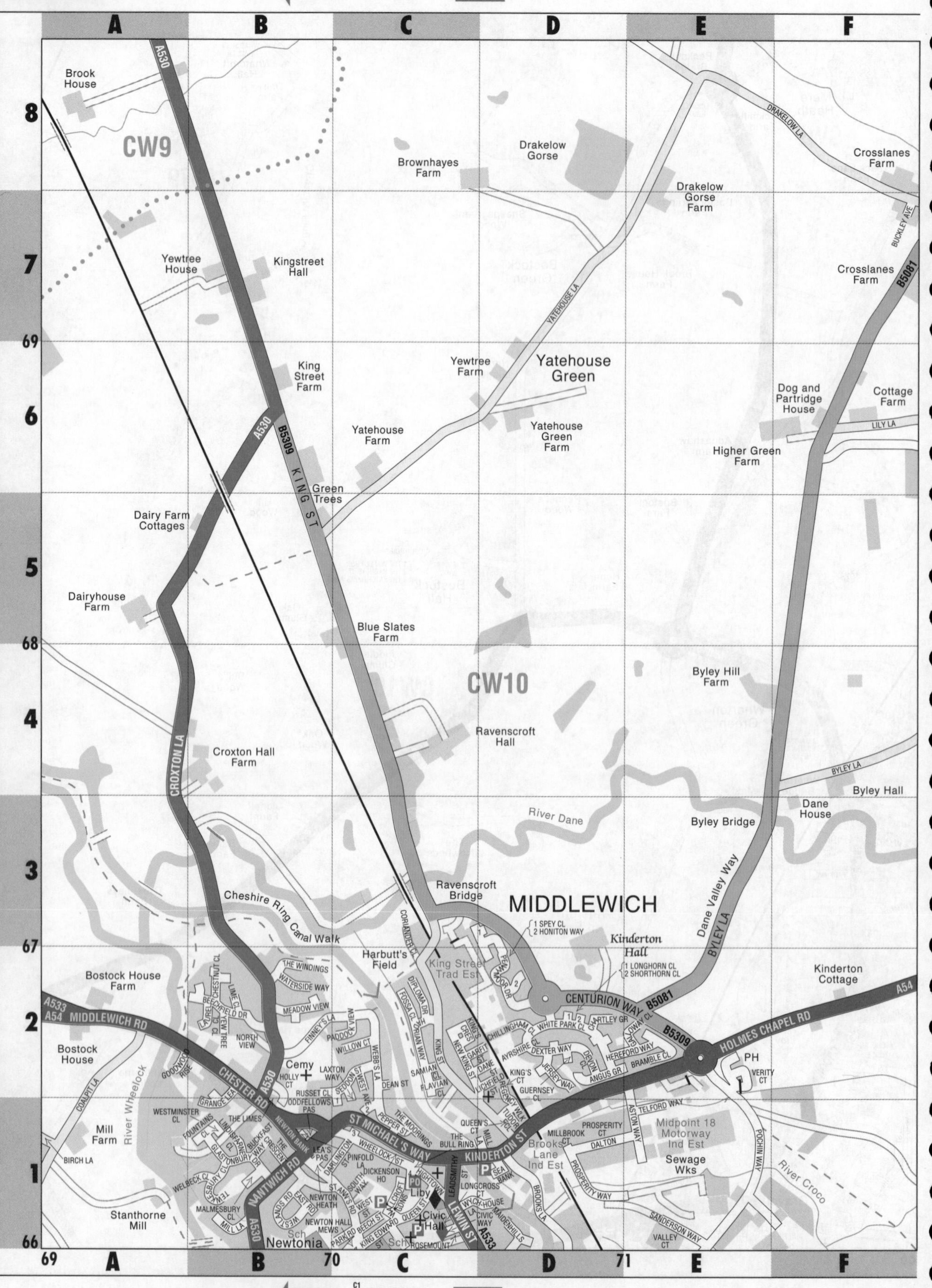

A	B	C	D	E	F

69 70 71 — 66 67 68 69 — 1 2 3 4 5 6 7 8

C1
1 LAMBOURNE GR
2 LAWRENCE AVE E
3 LAWRENCE AVE
4 DIERDENS TERR

127
151

106
130

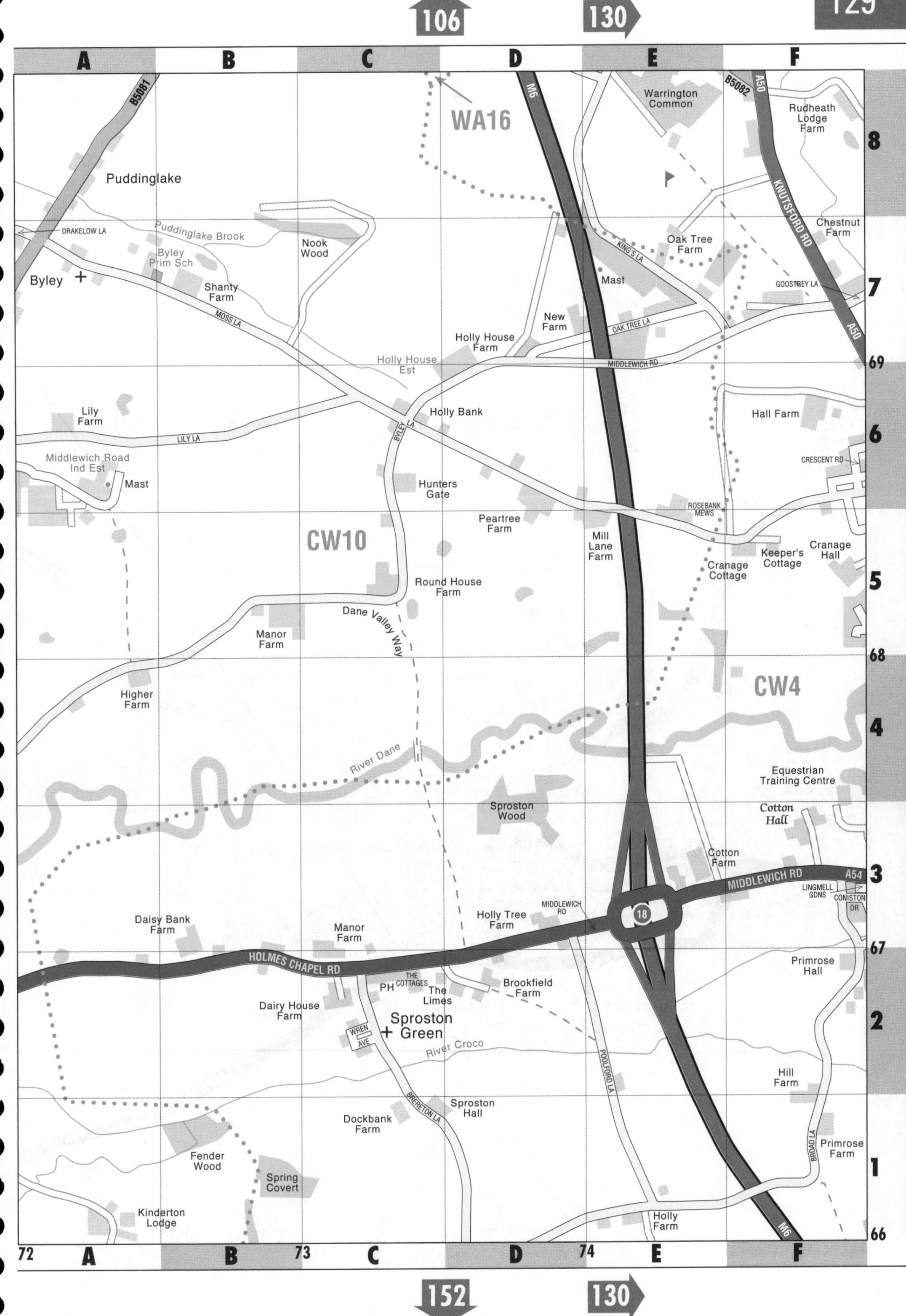

152
130

129
107

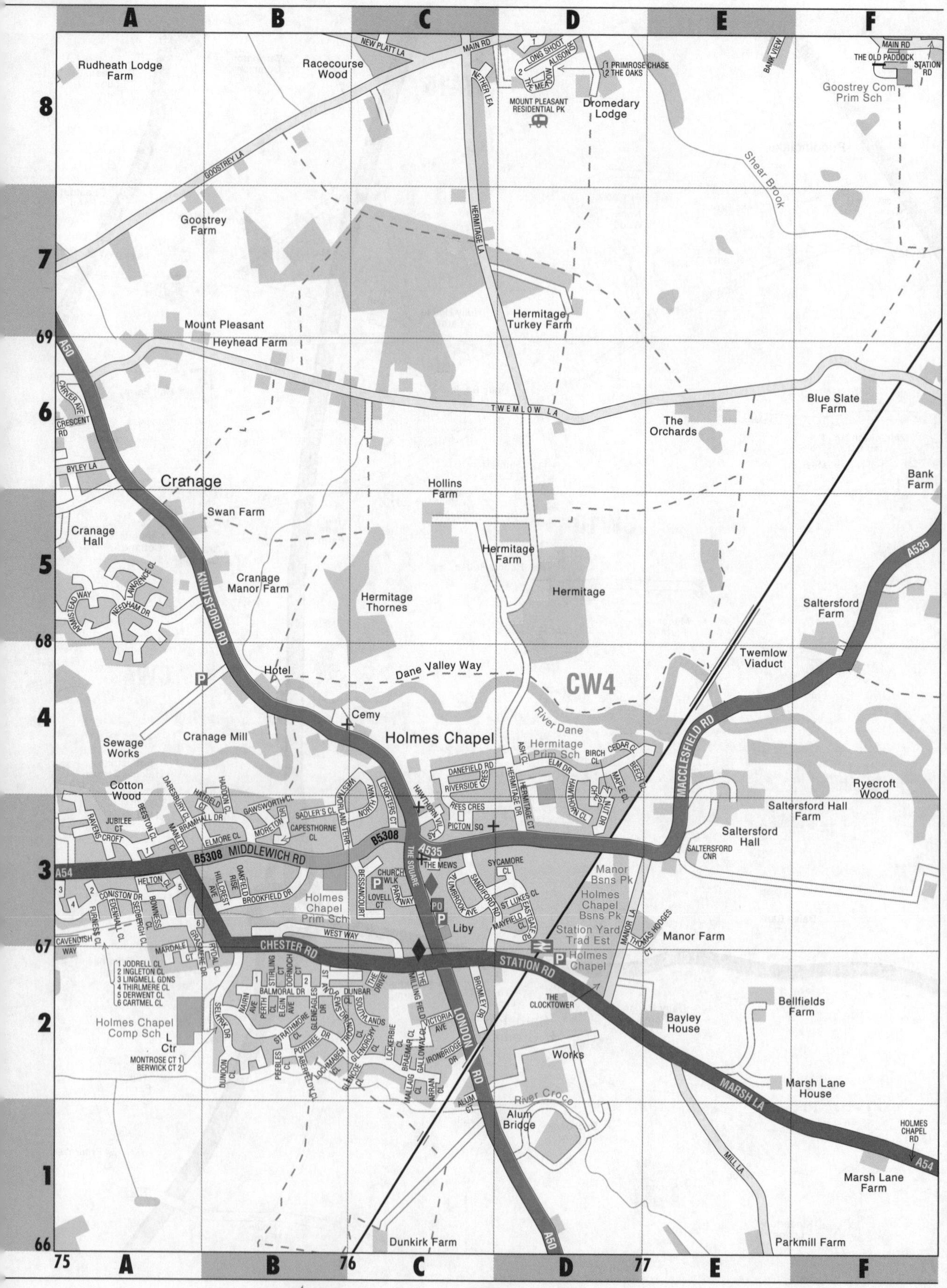

A B C D E F

8
7
69
6
5
68
4
3
67
2
1
66

Rudheath Lodge Farm
Racecourse Wood
NEW PLATT LA
MAIN RD
NETHER LEA
LONG SHOOT
ALISON DR
THE MEADOW
1 PRIMROSE CHASE
2 THE OAKS
MOUNT PLEASANT RESIDENTIAL PK
Dromedary Lodge
BANK VIEW
MAIN RD
THE OLD PADDOCK
STATION RD
Goostrey Com Prim Sch
GOOSTREY LA
Shear Brook
Goostrey Farm
HERMITAGE LA
Mount Pleasant
Heyhead Farm
Hermitage Turkey Farm
A50
CARVER AVE
CRESCENT RD
TWEMLOW LA
The Orchards
Blue Slate Farm
BYLEY LA
Cranage
Hollins Farm
Bank Farm
Swan Farm
Cranage Hall
Hermitage Farm
A535
ARMISTEAD WAY
LAWRENCE CL
NEEDHAM DR
Cranage Manor Farm
Hermitage Thornes
Hermitage
Saltersford Farm
KNUTSFORD RD
Hotel
Dane Valley Way
CW4
Twemlow Viaduct
Cemy
River Dane
Sewage Works
Cranage Mill
Holmes Chapel
Hermitage Prim Sch
ASH CL
BIRCH CL
CEDAR CL
ELM DR
BEECH CL
MACCLESFIELD RD
DANEFIELD RD
RIVERSIDE
CRES
Cotton Wood
DARESBURY CL
HATFIELD CL
HADDON CL
GAWSWORTH CL
WESTMORLAND TERR
NORTH WAY
CROFTERS CT
HAWTHORN VIL
HERMITAGE DR
HAWTHORN CL
CHASE
MAPLE CL
NUT DR
Ryecroft Wood
Saltersford Hall Farm
RAVENS CROFT
JUBILEE CT
BEESTON CL
MANLEY CL
BRAMHALL DR
ELMORE CL
MORETON DR
SADLER'S CL
CAPESTHORNE CL
REES CRES
PICTON SQ
HERMITAGE CT
Saltersford Hall
SALTERSFORD CNR
B5308
MIDDLEWICH RD
A535
THE SQUARE
THE MEWS
A54
HILLCREST AVE
OAKFIELD RISE
SYCAMORE CL
Manor Bsns Pk
HELTON CL
CONISTON DR
BOWNESS CL
EDENHALL CL
SEDBERGH CL
BROOKFIELD DR
BESSANCOURT
CHURCH WLK
LOVELL CT
PARKWAY
HOLMBROOK AVE
SANDIFORD RD
ST LUKES CL
EASTGATE RD
MAYFIELD CL
Holmes Chapel Bsns Pk
Holmes Chapel Prim Sch
PO
Liby
Station Yard Trad Est
MANOR LA
THOMAS HODGES CT
Manor Farm
FURNESS CL
CAVENDISH WAY
MARDALE CT
GRASMERE DR
RYDAL CL
WEST WAY
CHESTER RD
Holmes Chapel
STATION RD
1 JODRELL CL
2 INGLETON CL
3 LINGMELL GDNS
4 THIRLMERE CL
5 DERWENT CL
6 CARTMEL CL
NAIRN AVE
PERTH CL
STIRLING CL
ELGIN AVE
DORNOCH CT
ST ANDREWS DR
DUNBAR CL
THE DRIVE
THE MILLING FIELD
BROMLEY DR
THE CLOCKTOWER
Bellfields Farm
BALMORAL DR
GLENEAGLES DR
SOUTHLANDS
VICTORIA AVE
LONDON RD
Bayley House
Holmes Chapel Comp Sch
L Ctr
SELKIRK DR
STRATHMORE CL
PORTREE DR
GLENORCHY CL
TROON CL
LOCKERBIE CL
BRAEMAR CL
GALLOWAY CL
IRONBRIDGE DR
Works
MONTROSE CT
BERWICK CT
DUNOON CL
PEEBLES CL
ABERFELDY CL
LOCHMABEN CL
GLENCOE CL
MALLAIG CL
ARRAN CL
MARSH LA
Marsh Lane House
ALUM CT
River Croco
Alum Bridge
HOLMES CHAPEL RD
A54
MILL LA
Marsh Lane Farm
Dunkirk Farm
Parkmill Farm
A50

75 A B 76 C D 77 E F

129
153

108
132

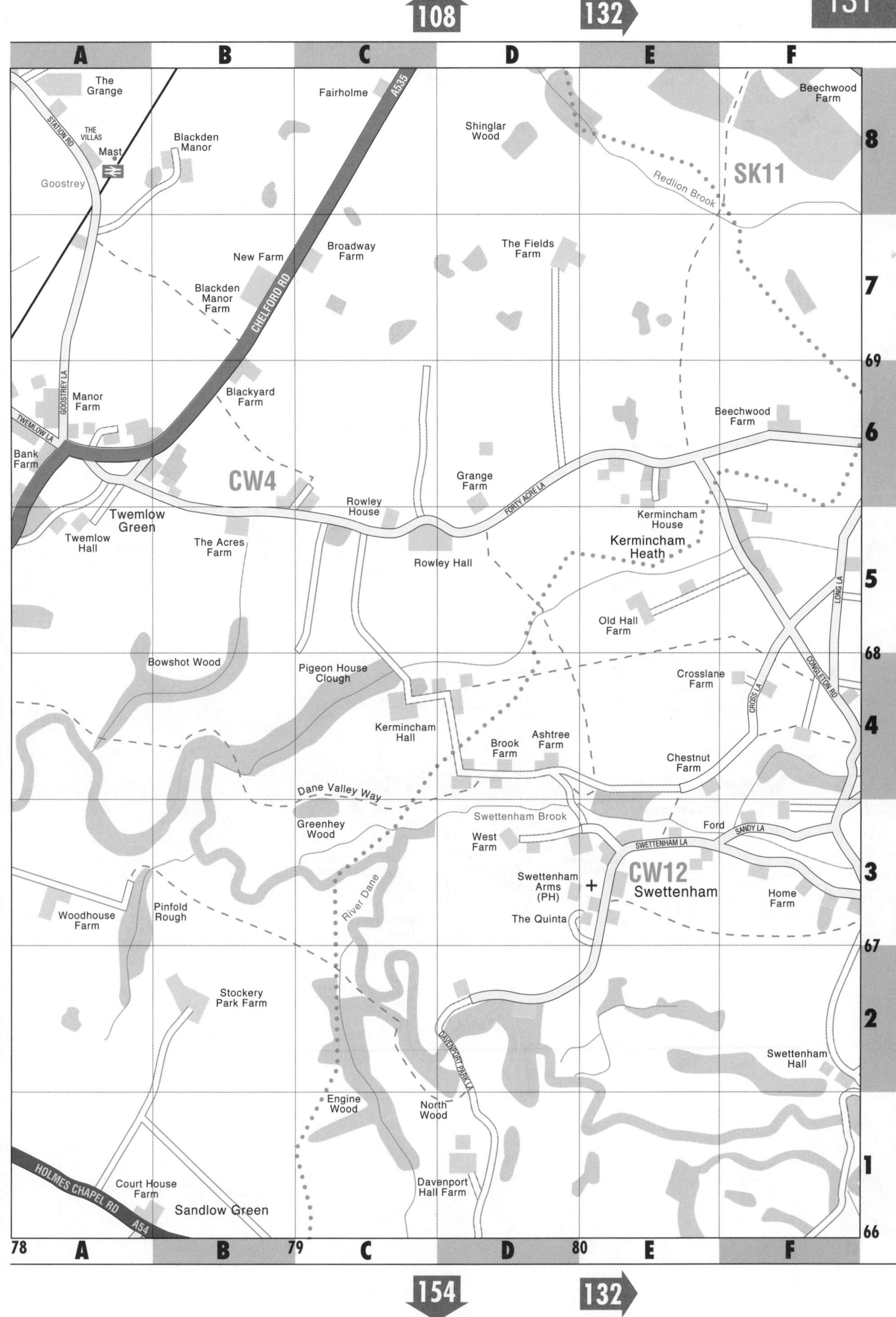

154
132

131
109

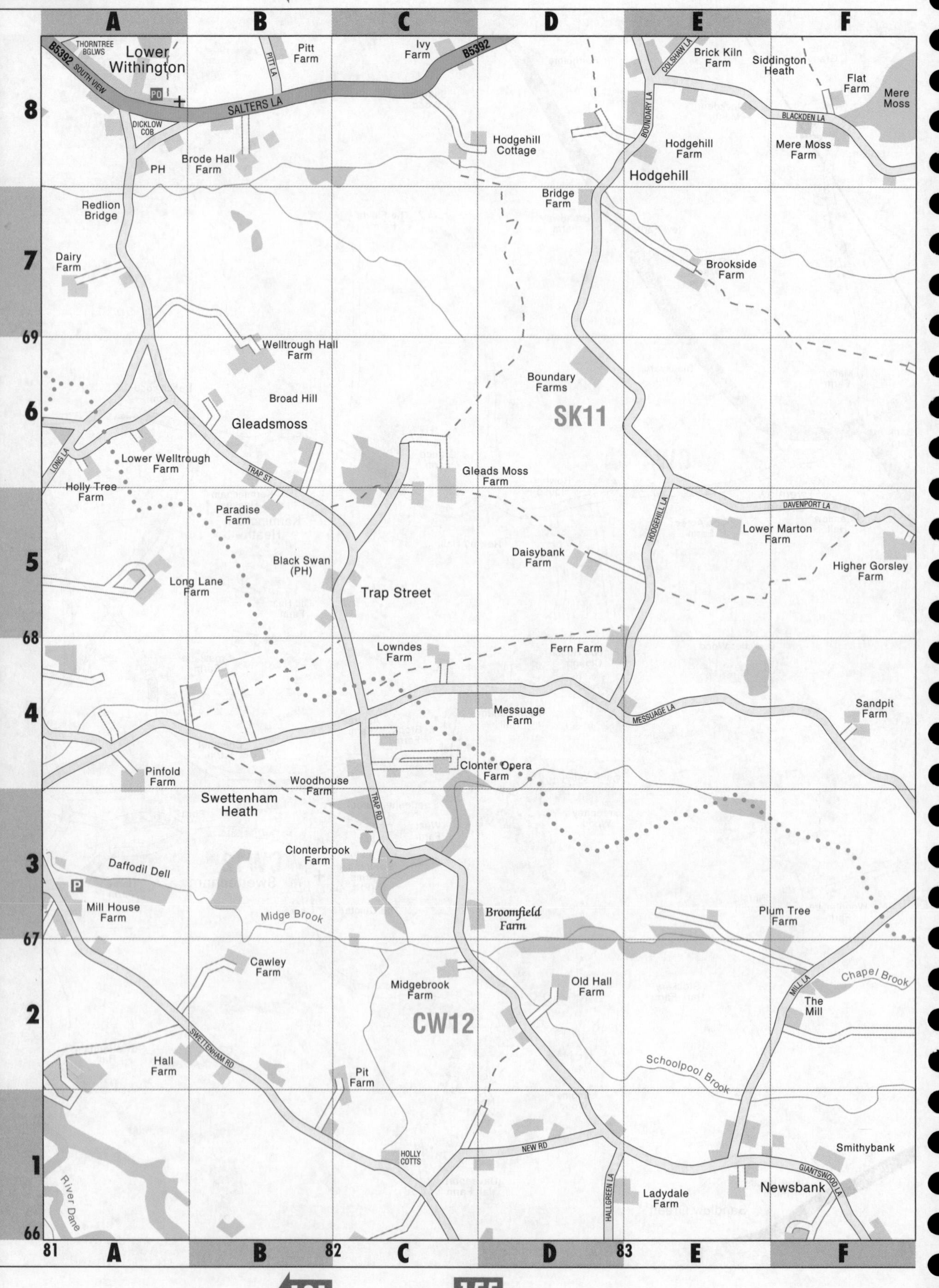

131
155

110
134

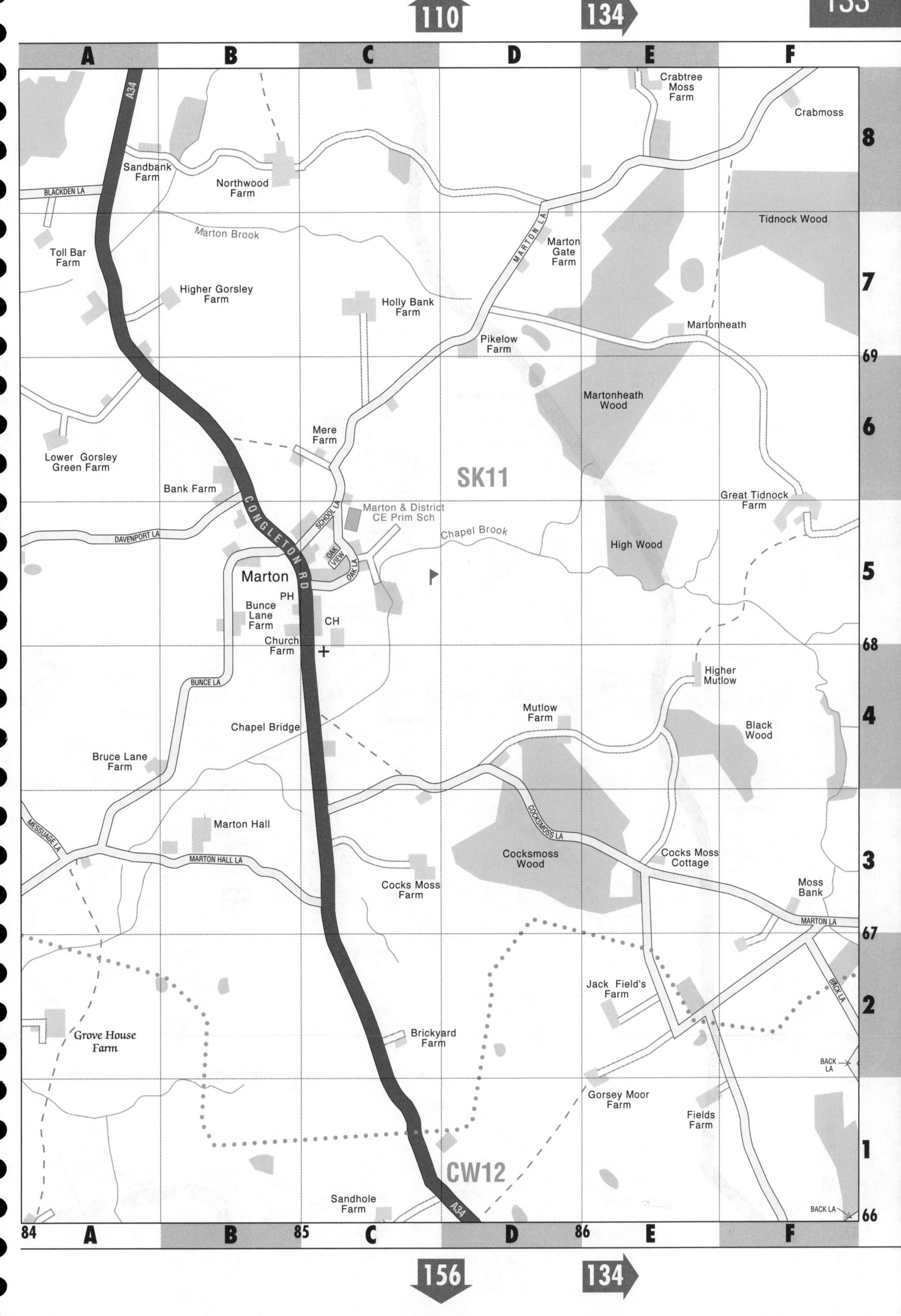

156
134

133 111

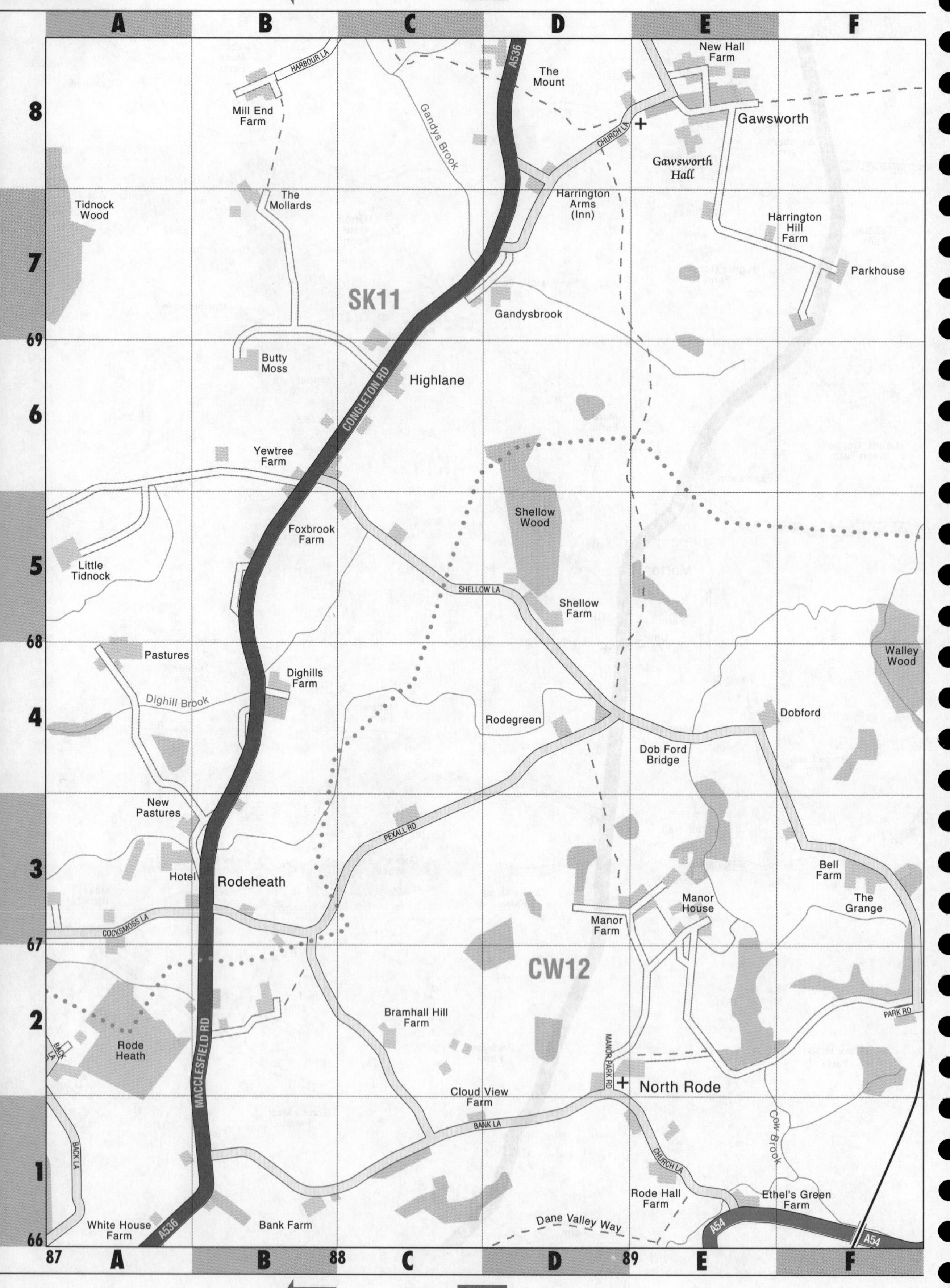

133 157

112
136

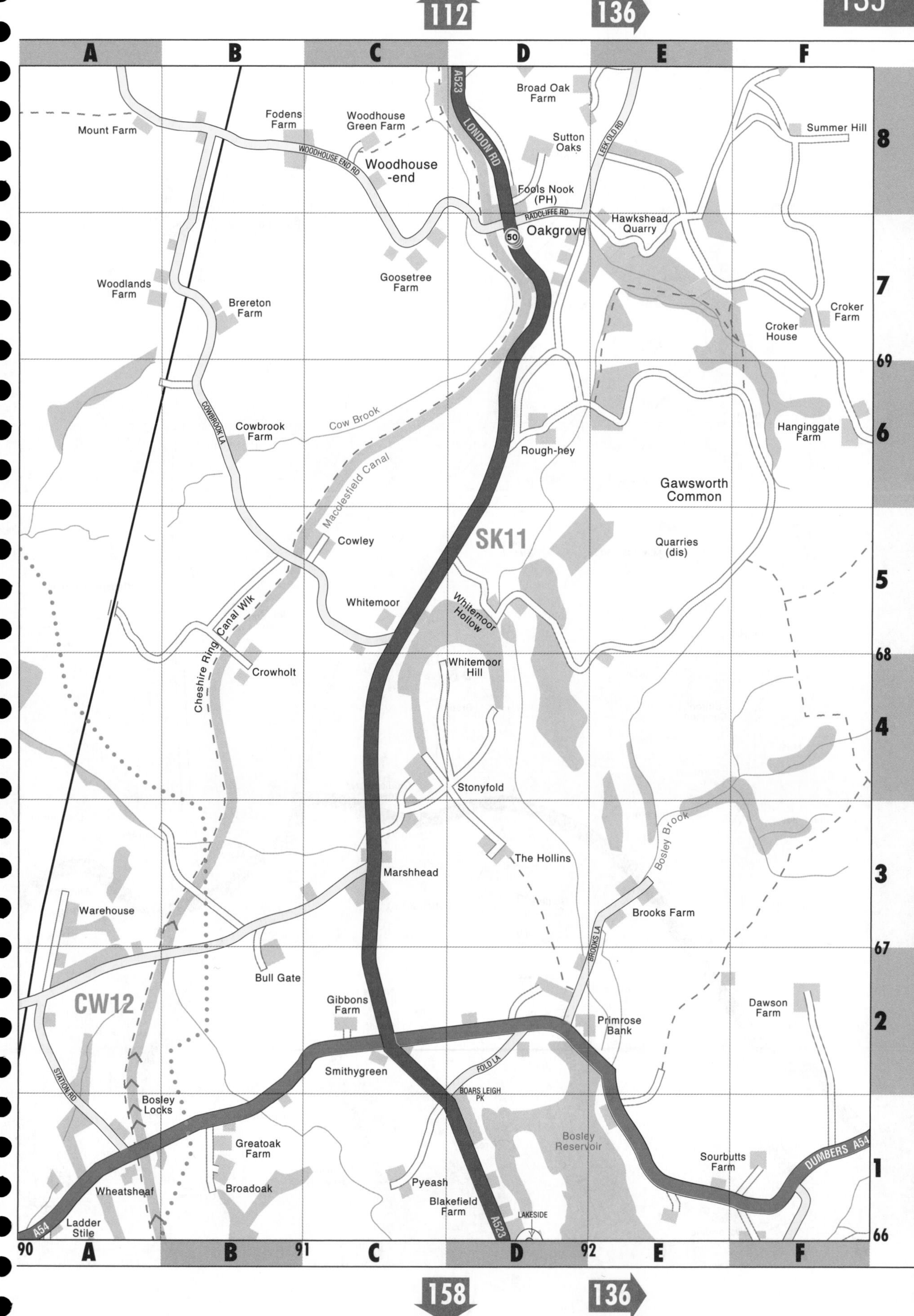

158
136

135
113

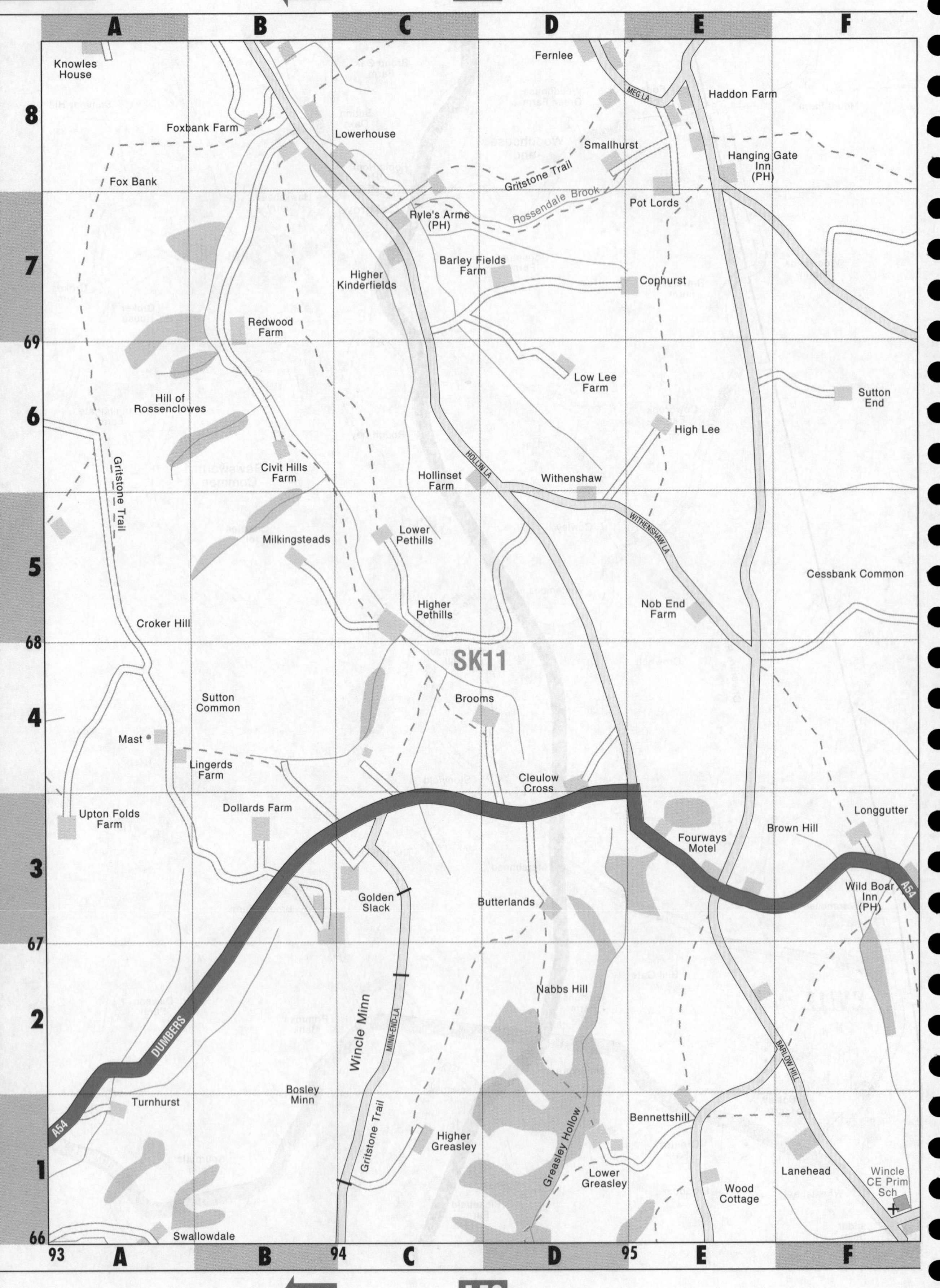

135
159

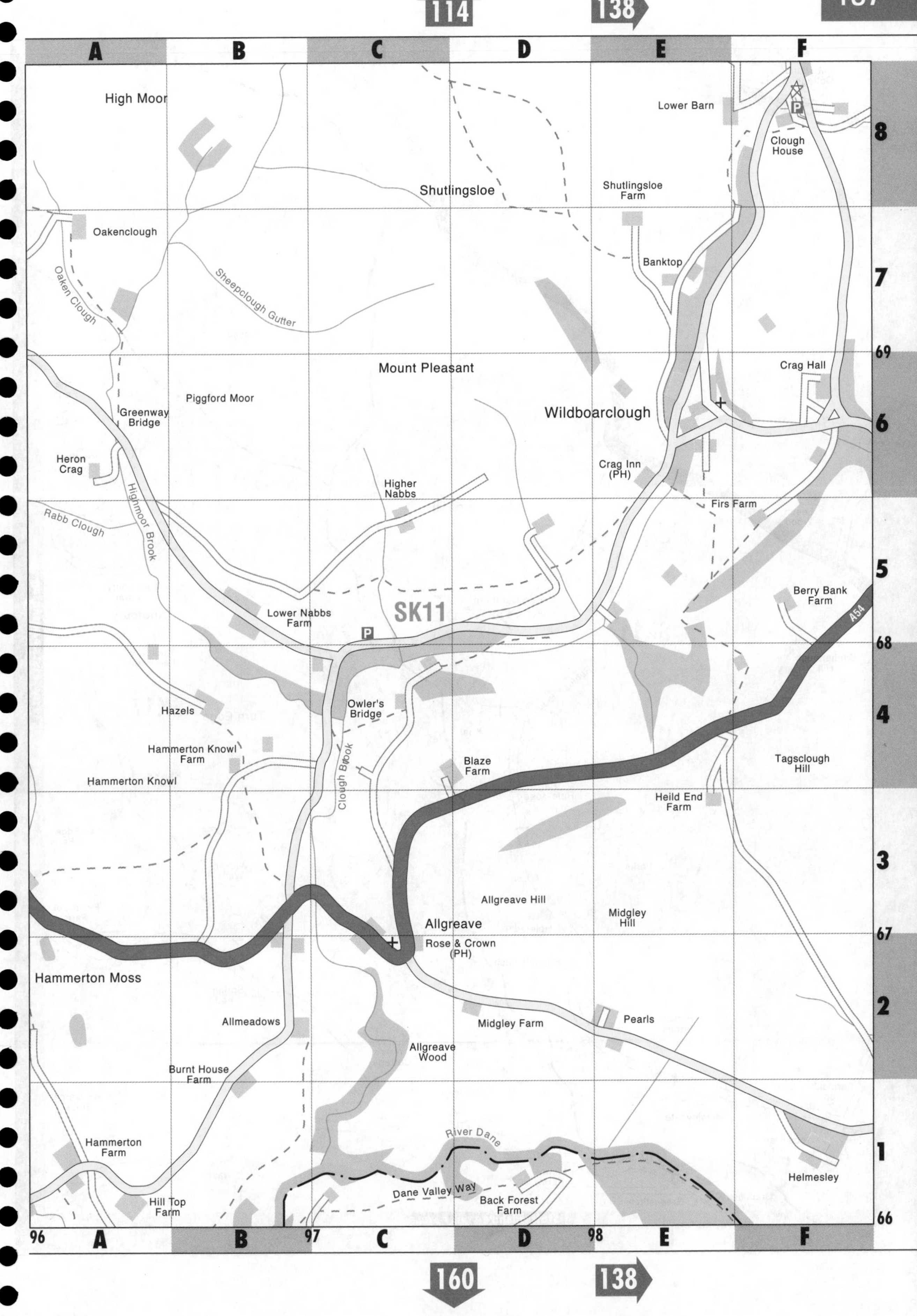
114
138
A
B
C
D
E
F
High Moor
Lower Barn
Clough House
Shutlingsloe
Shutlingsloe Farm
8
Oakenclough
Banktop
Oaken Clough
Sheepclough Gutter
7
69
Mount Pleasant
Crag Hall
Piggford Moor
Greenway Bridge
Wildboarclough
6
Heron Crag
Crag Inn (PH)
Higher Nabbs
Firs Farm
Rabb Clough
Highmoor Brook
5
Berry Bank Farm
Lower Nabbs Farm
SK11
A54
68
Hazels
Owler's Bridge
4
Hammerton Knowl Farm
Blaze Farm
Tagsclough Hill
Clough Brook
Hammerton Knowl
Heild End Farm
3
Allgreave Hill
Midgley Hill
Allgreave
67
Rose & Crown (PH)
Hammerton Moss
2
Allmeadows
Midgley Farm
Pearls
Allgreave Wood
Burnt House Farm
River Dane
Hammerton Farm
1
Helmesley
Dane Valley Way
Hill Top Farm
Back Forest Farm
66
96
97
98
160
138

137
115

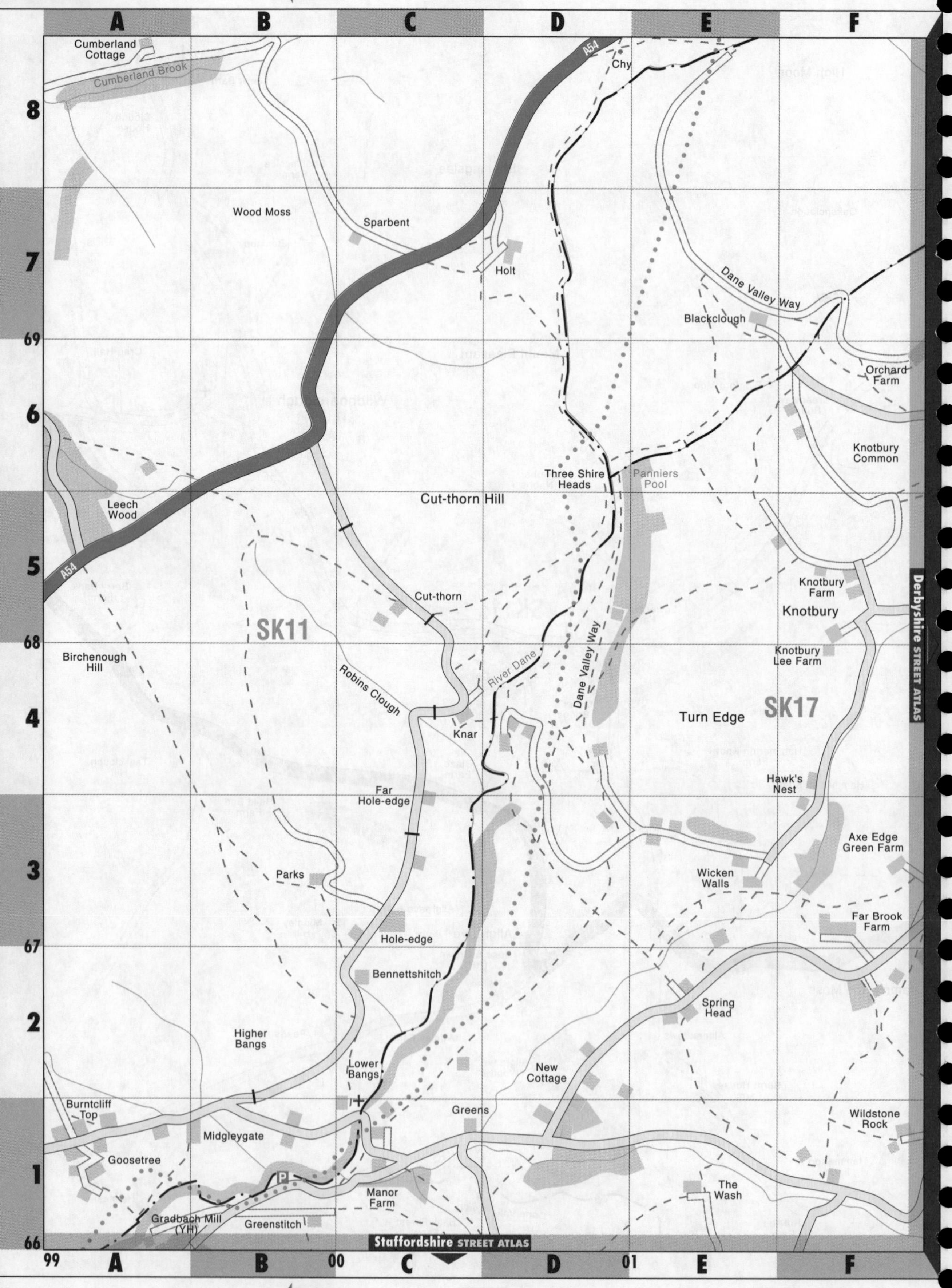
A
B
C
D
E
F
8
7
69
6
5
68
4
3
67
2
1
66
99
00
01
Cumberland Cottage
Cumberland Brook
A54
Chy
Wood Moss
Sparbent
Holt
Dane Valley Way
Blackclough
Orchard Farm
Knotbury Common
Three Shire Heads
Panniers Pool
Leech Wood
Cut-thorn Hill
Cut-thorn
SK11
Knotbury Farm
Knotbury
Knotbury Lee Farm
Birchenough Hill
Robins Clough
River Dane
Dane Valley Way
Knar
Turn Edge
SK17
Hawk's Nest
Far Hole-edge
Axe Edge Green Farm
Parks
Wicken Walls
Far Brook Farm
Hole-edge
Bennettshitch
Spring Head
Higher Bangs
Lower Bangs
New Cottage
Burntcliff Top
Greens
Wildstone Rock
Midgleygate
Goosetree
P
Manor Farm
The Wash
Gradbach Mill (YH)
Greenstitch
Staffordshire STREET ATLAS
Derbyshire STREET ATLAS

137

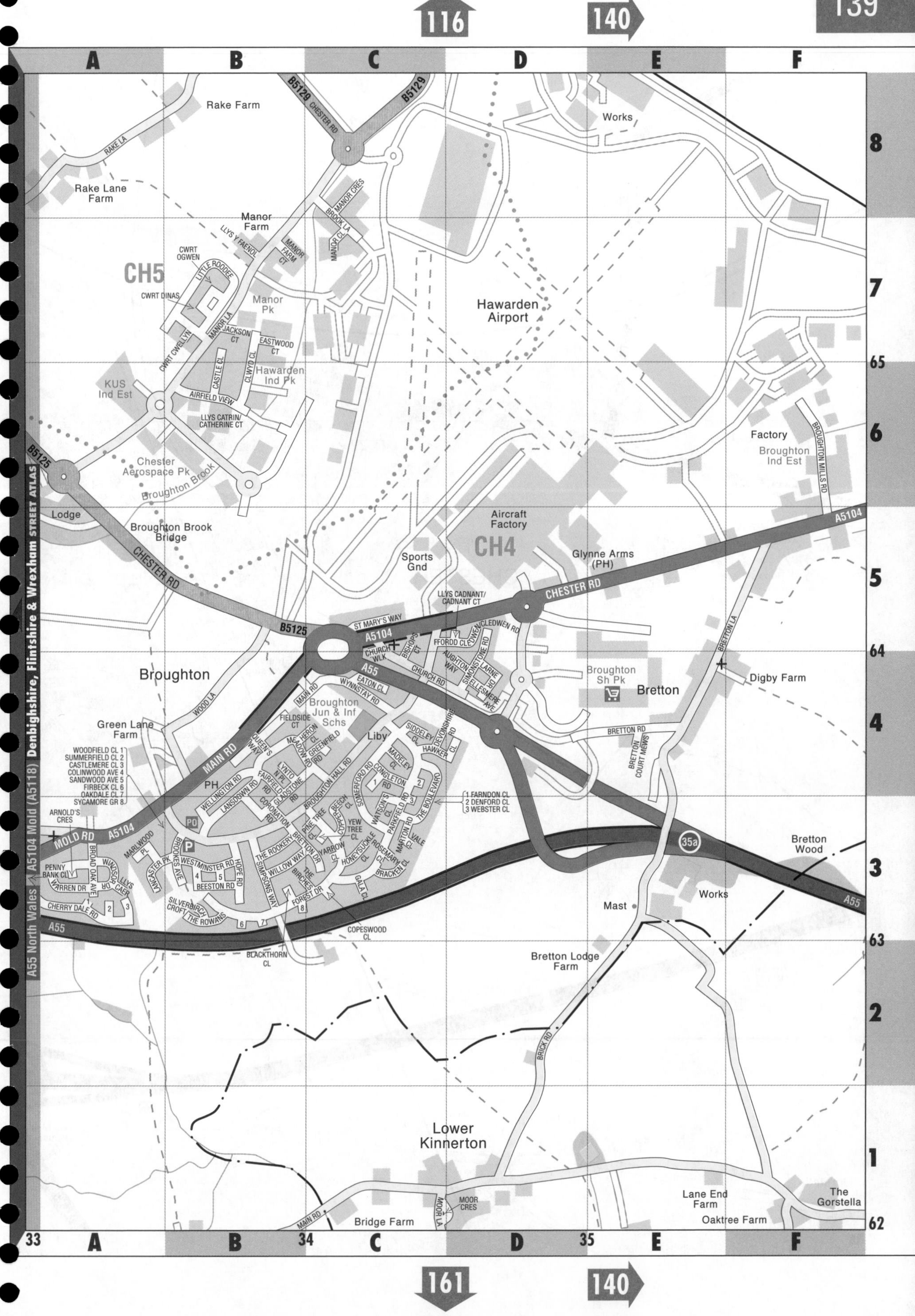
116
140
A
B
C
D
E
F
8
7
65
6
5
64
4
3
63
2
1
62
33
34
35
Rake Farm
Works
Rake Lane Farm
Manor Farm
CH5
Manor Pk
Hawarden Airport
KUS Ind Est
Hawarden Ind Pk
Chester Aerospace Pk
Broughton Brook
Lodge
Broughton Brook Bridge
Factory
Broughton Ind Est
Aircraft Factory
CH4
Sports Gnd
Glynne Arms (PH)
Broughton
Broughton Sh Pk
Bretton
Digby Farm
Broughton Jun & Inf Schs
Green Lane Farm
Liby
PH
PO
Bretton Wood
Works
Mast
Bretton Lodge Farm
Lower Kinnerton
Lane End Farm
The Gorstella
Oaktree Farm
Bridge Farm
B5129
CHESTER RD
RAKE LA
B5125
CHESTER RD
A5104
CHESTER RD
A55
MAIN RD
MOLD RD
BRETTON LA
BRETTON RD
BRICK RD
MOOR LA
MOOR CRES
BROUGHTON MILLS RD
WOOD LA
35a
WOODFIELD CL 1
SUMMERFIELD CL 2
CASTLEMERE CL 3
COLINWOOD AVE 4
SANDWOOD AVE 5
FIRBECK CL 6
OAKDALE CL 7
SYCAMORE GR 8
1 FARNDON CL
2 DENFORD CL
3 WEBSTER CL
Denbighshire, Flintshire & Wrexham STREET ATLAS
A55 North Wales A5104 Mold (A5118)
161
140

139
117

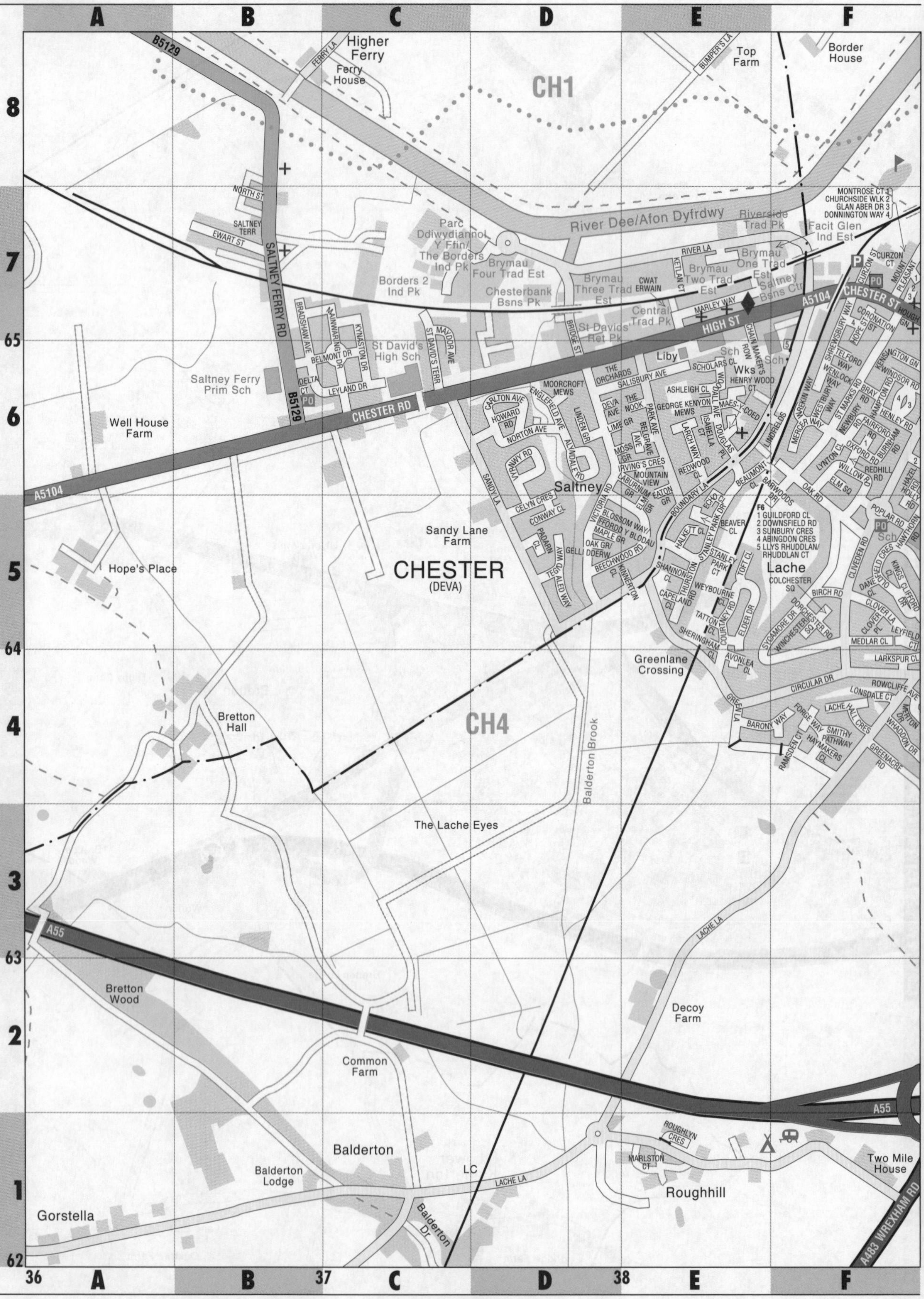

139
162

For full street detail of the highlighted area see page 237.

118 142

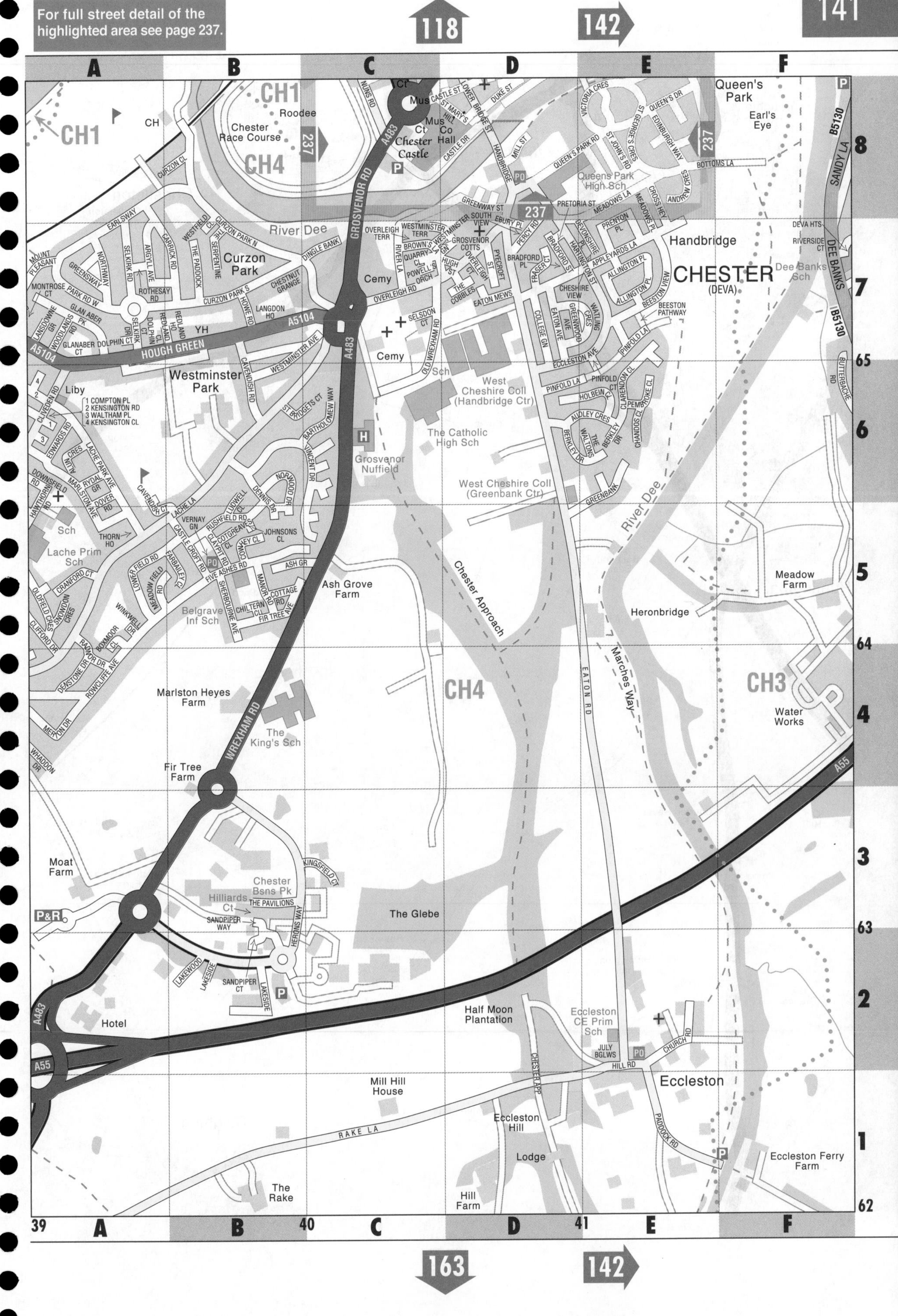

163 142

A8
1 SANDY LA
2 WALMOOR PK
3 EDGEWOOD
4 STOCKS AVE
5 DRYERSFIELD

141
119

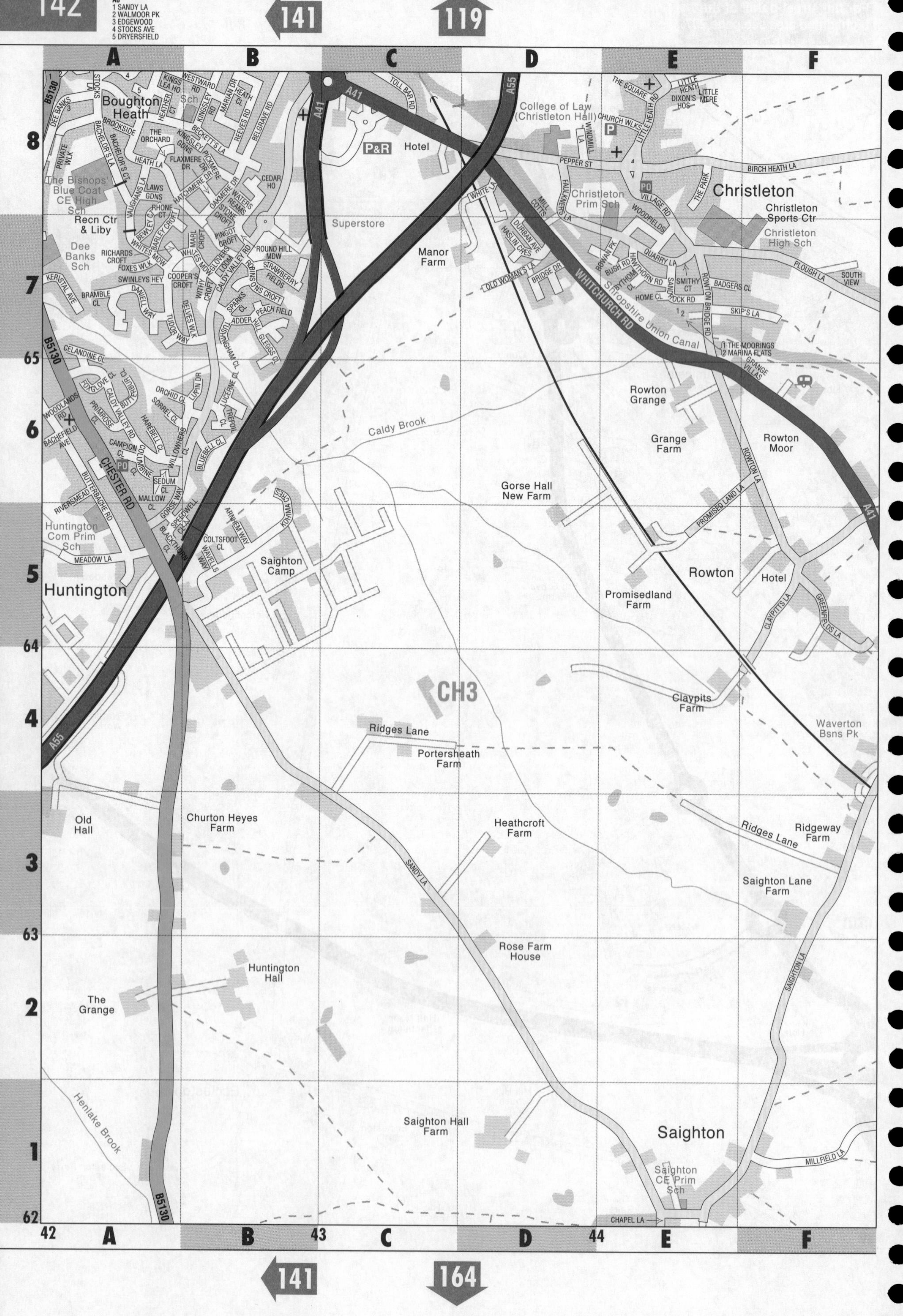

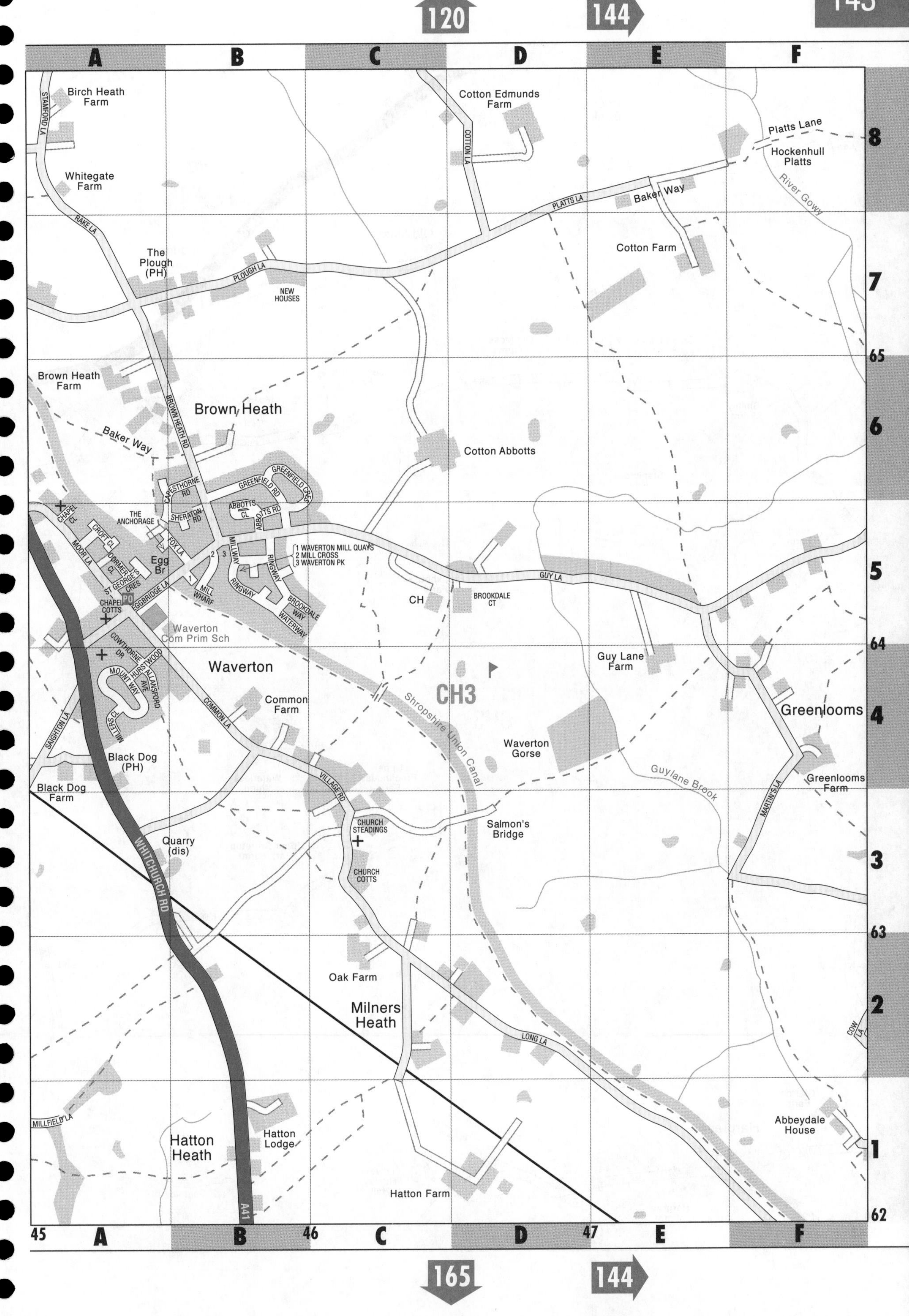
120
144
A
B
C
D
E
F
8
7
65
6
5
64
4
3
63
2
1
62
45
46
47
165
144
Birch Heath Farm
STAMFORD LA
Cotton Edmunds Farm
COTTON LA
Platts Lane
Hockenhull Platts
River Gowy
Whitegate Farm
RAKE LA
PLATTS LA
Baker Way
Cotton Farm
The Plough (PH)
PLOUGH LA
NEW HOUSES
Brown Heath Farm
Brown Heath
BROWN HEATH RD
Baker Way
Cotton Abbotts
CAPESTHORNE RD
GREENFIELD RD
GREENFIELD CRES
SHERATON RD
ABBOTTS CL
ABBOTTS RD
THE ANCHORAGE
CHAPEL CL
CROFT CL
MOOR LA
DORMER CL
ST GEORGE'S CRES
FOX LA
Egg Br
MILLWAY
RINGWAY
1 WAVERTON MILL QUAYS
2 MILL CROSS
3 WAVERTON PK
MILL WHARF
BROOKDALE WAY
WATERWAY
CHAPEL COTTS
EGGBRIDGE LA
PO
CH
BROOKDALE CT
GUY LA
Waverton Com Prim Sch
COWTHORNE DR
HURSTWOOD AVE
ALLANSFORD
MOUNT WAY
MILLERS CL
Waverton
Guy Lane Farm
CH3
Greenlooms
SAIGHTON LA
COMMON LA
Common Farm
Shropshire Union Canal
Waverton Gorse
Black Dog (PH)
Guylane Brook
Greenlooms Farm
Black Dog Farm
VILLAGE RD
MARTIN'S LA
CHURCH STEADINGS
Salmon's Bridge
Quarry (dis)
WHITCHURCH RD
CHURCH COTTS
Oak Farm
Milners Heath
COW LA
LONG LA
MILLFIELD LA
Abbeydale House
Hatton Heath
Hatton Lodge
Hatton Farm
A41

143
121

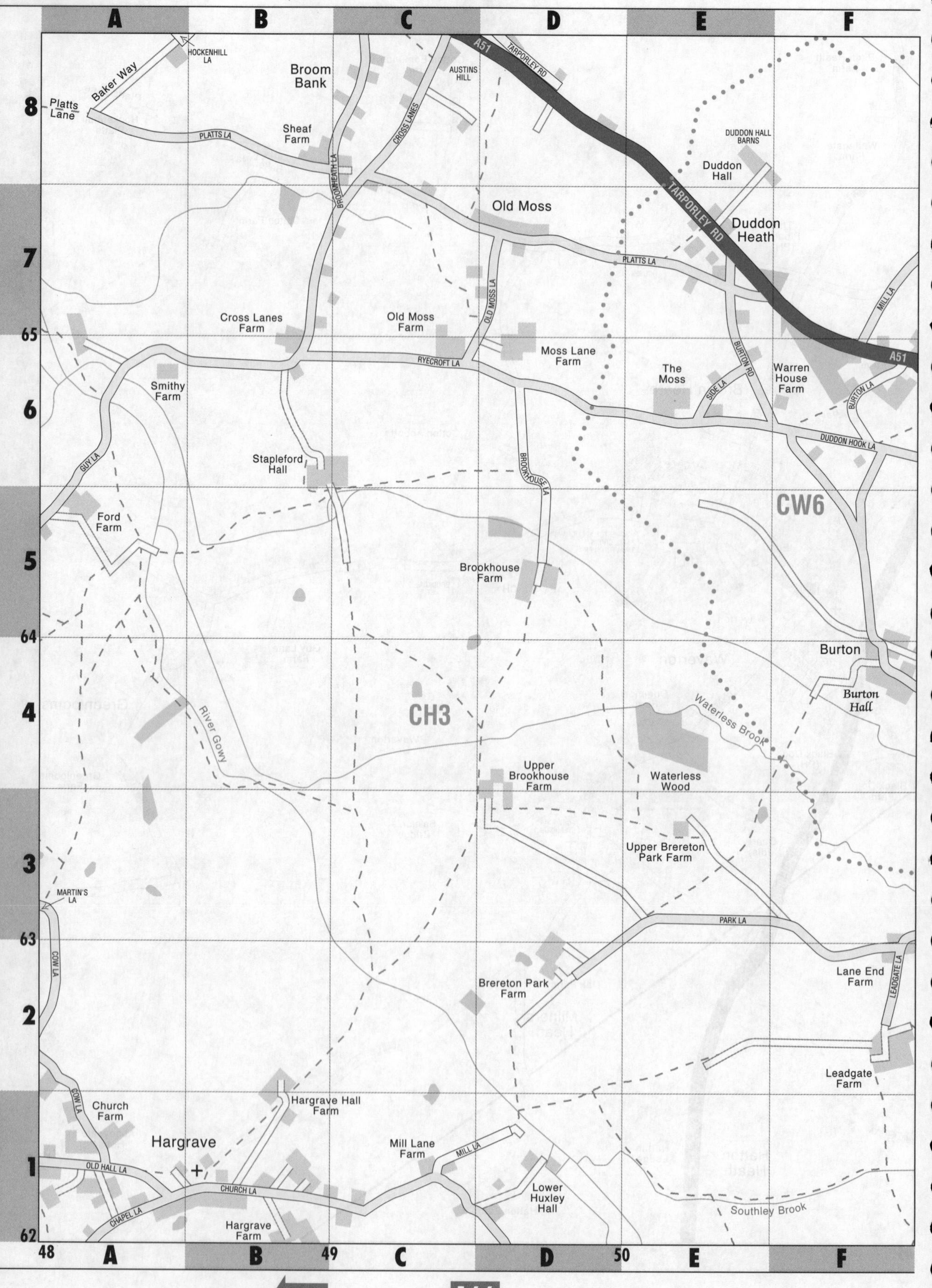

143
166

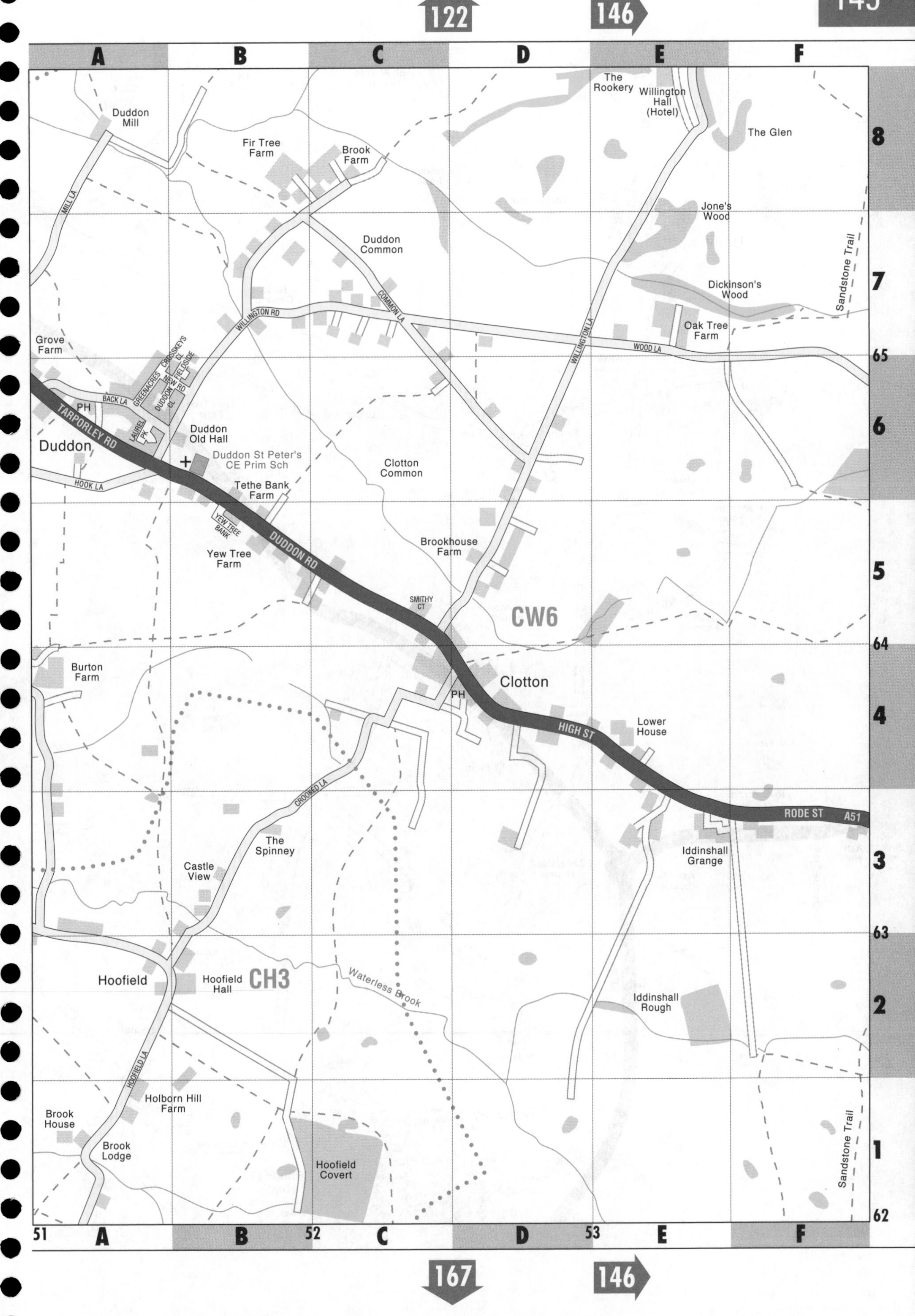
122
146
A
B
C
D
E
F
Duddon Mill
Fir Tree Farm
Brook Farm
The Rookery
Willington Hall (Hotel)
The Glen
Jone's Wood
Duddon Common
Dickinson's Wood
Sandstone Trail
Oak Tree Farm
WOOD LA
WILLINGTON LA
COMMON LA
WILLINGTON RD
MILL LA
Grove Farm
CROSSKEYS CL
NEW FIELDSIDE RD
GREENACRES
DUDDON CL
BACK LA
PH
LAUREL PK
TARPORLEY RD
Duddon
Duddon Old Hall
Duddon St Peter's CE Prim Sch
HOOK LA
Tethe Bank Farm
YEW TREE BANK
Clotton Common
Yew Tree Farm
DUDDON RD
Brookhouse Farm
SMITHY CT
CW6
Burton Farm
Clotton
PH
HIGH ST
Lower House
CROOKED LA
RODE ST
A51
The Spinney
Iddinshall Grange
Castle View
Hoofield
Hoofield Hall
CH3
Waterless Brook
Iddinshall Rough
HOOFIELD LA
Holborn Hill Farm
Brook House
Brook Lodge
Hoofield Covert
8
7
65
6
5
64
4
3
63
2
1
62
51
52
53
167
146

145
123

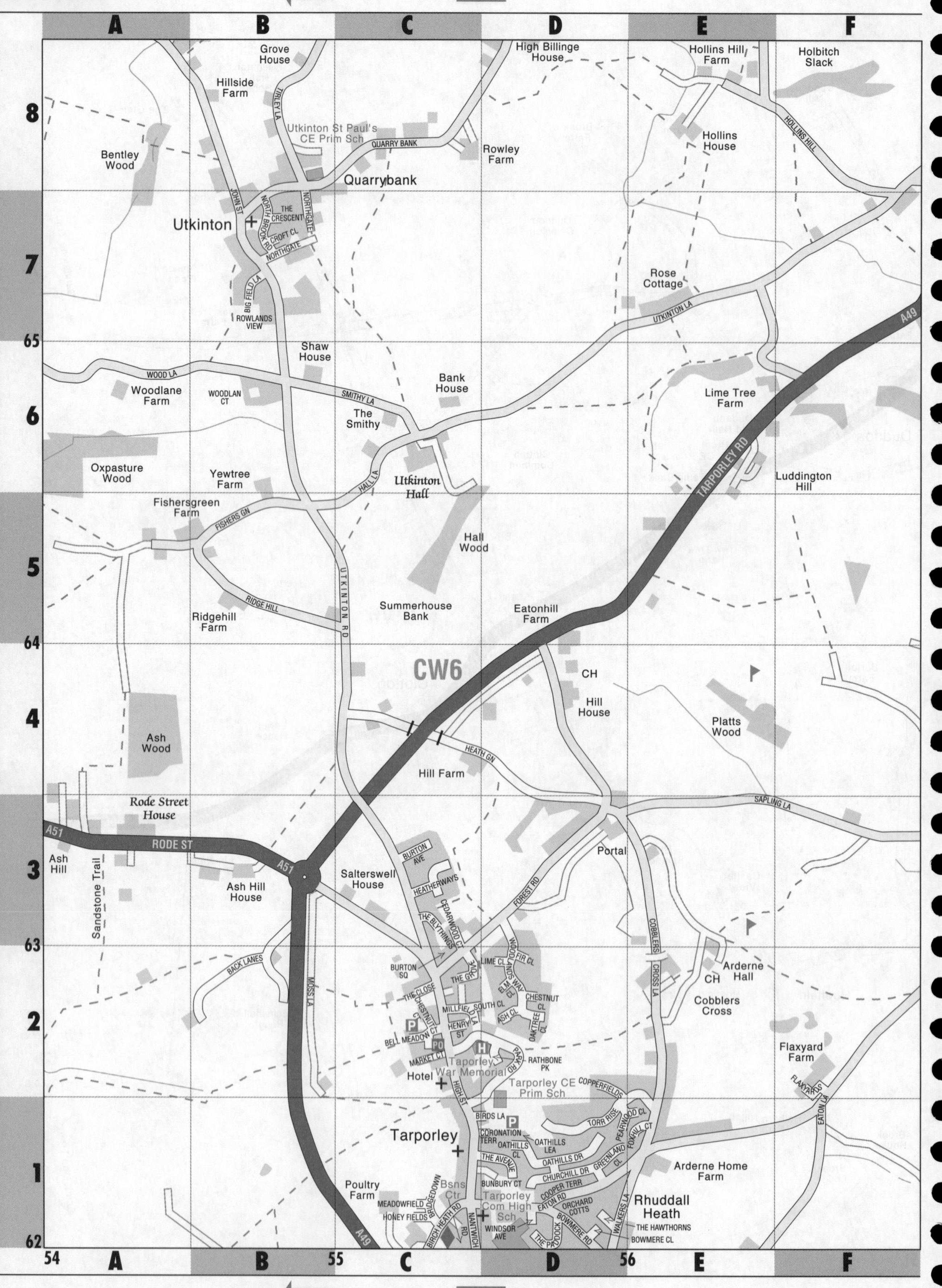

145
168

124 148

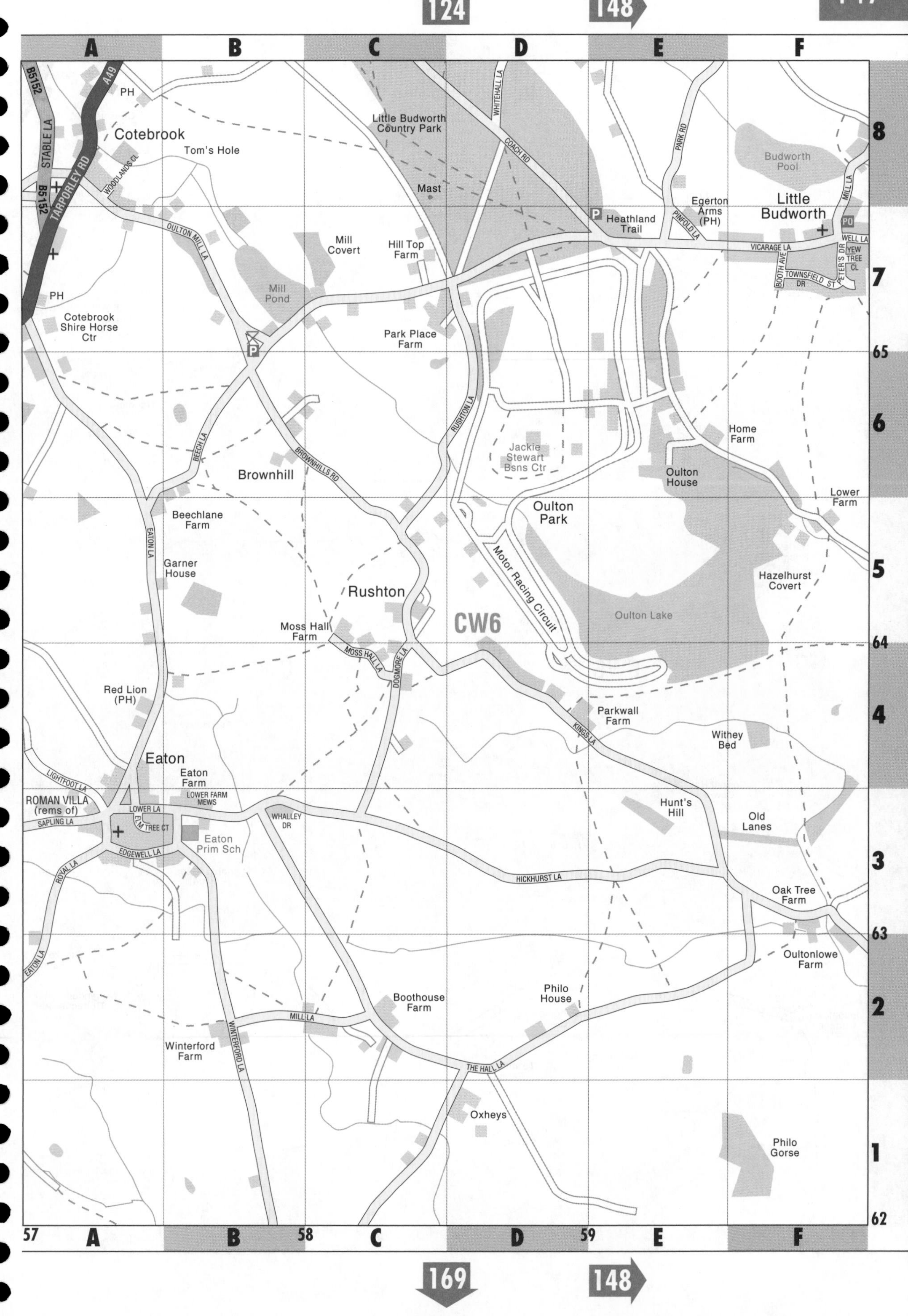

169 148

147
125

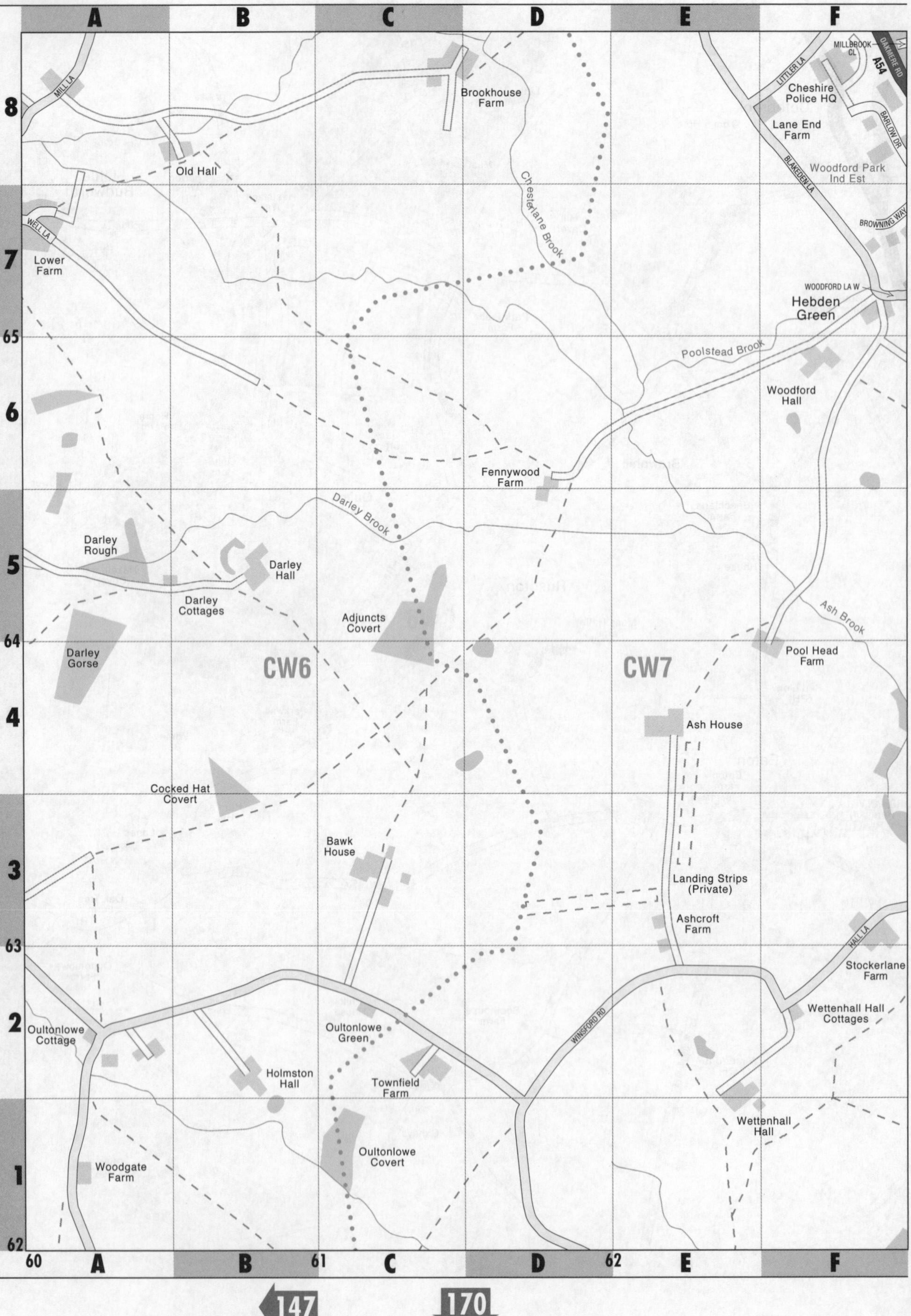

147
170

A8
1 BECKENHAM GR
2 BROCKWELL CL
3 PORTMAN PL
4 REGENTS WAY
5 NEWBURY AVE
6 ALEXANDRA SQ
7 HAMPSTEAD CT
8 WESTMINSTER GR
9 ST JAMES TERR
10 CROFTWOOD CL
11 BRACKENFIELD WAY
12 FAIROAK CL
13 BROOMFIELD CL

B8
1 GROVE CL
2 SANDHOLE COTTS
3 FOUR LANES CT

C7
1 CHEPSTOW CL
2 CALDICOTT CL
3 CARMARTHEN CL
4 CLIFFORD PL
5 BLENHEIM GDNS
6 TOWNFIELDS COTTS

C8
1 DELAMERE ST
2 HIGH ST
3 LOWER HAIGH ST

D6
1 SANDYHILL PL
2 HANOVER DR
3 PLANTAGENET CL
4 NIGHTINGALE CT
5 KINGFISHER DR
6 SWANAGE CT

D8
1 DENESGATE
2 NORMANDY AVE

126
150

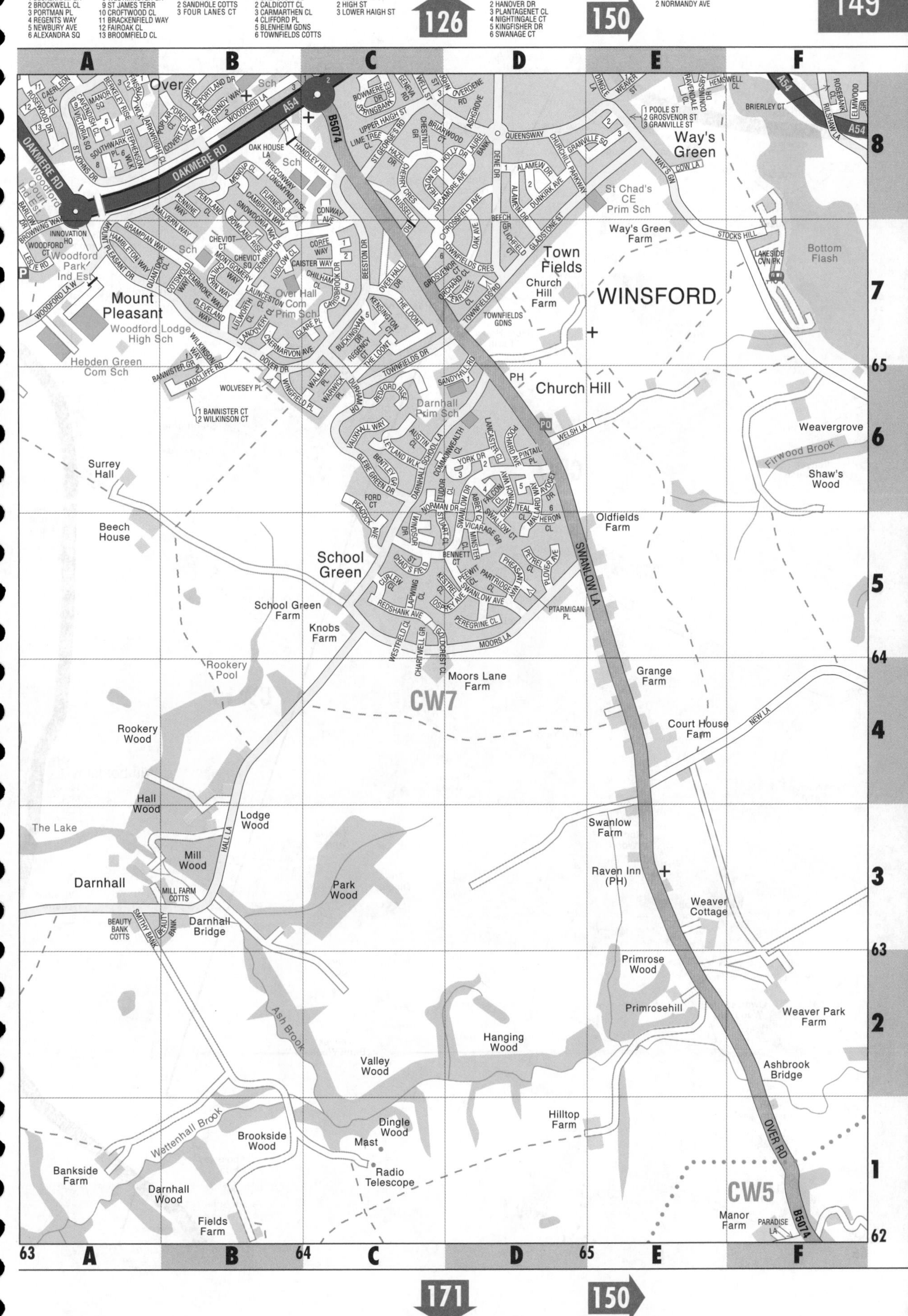

171
150

149
127

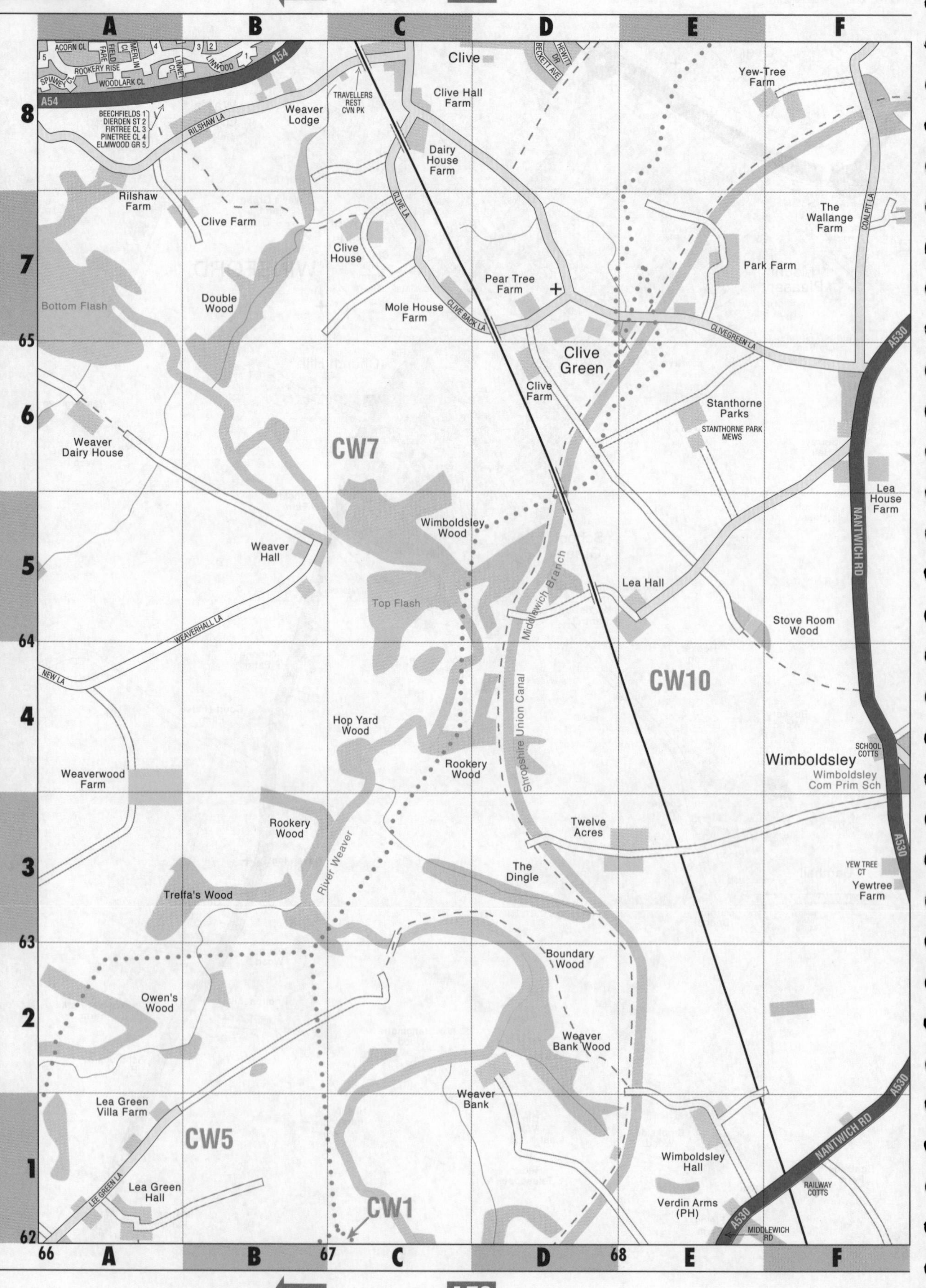

149
172

A B C D E F

8
7
65
6
5
64
4
3
63
2
1
62

MIDDLEWICH

Shropshire Union Canal Middlewich Branch
Stanthorne Lock
Middlewich Prim Sch
Sch
L Ctr
WESTBURY CL 1
SWANSCOE CL 2
NANTWICH RD
A530
A533
LEWIN ST
MAIDENHILLS
THE LOCKS
CANAL TERR
BROOKS LA
ROAD BETA
ASHFIELD ST
Brooks Lane Ind Est
VALLEY CT
POCHIN WAY
Sanderson's Brook
ERF WAY
SHROPSHIRE CL
ROYLANCE DR
BEMBRIDGE CT
VENTNOR CL
SANDOWN CL
MATHER CL
STALLARD WAY
ST ANN'S RD
HUBERT DR
WATERS EDGE MEWS
WARDLE MEWS
ST ANNE'S AVE
KITFIELD AVE
HAYHURST AVE
NORBURY DR
FARLEY CL
HILTON CL
Flea La
WALKER DR
FATON DR
LONGMOSS
KERRIDGE CL
BUCKLEY OVERTON CL
BRYNLOW DR
SIMONSWOOD CL
BLAKELOW CL
BRADLEY CL
WAVERTREE DR
ROLT CRES
LONGWOOD
LONG LA
MANOR FIELDS
THE PARKLANDS
WARREN CL
GREENDALE DR
OLD GATE CL
RYECROFT CL
RUTLAND DR
DENBIGH CRES
FALLON CT
ORCHARD CL
ELM RD
ASH GR
POPLAR DR
OAK DR
Ind Est
Manor Park
WHITLEY CL
HURDSFIELD CL
WESTON CL
RAINOW CL
WHIRLEY CL
MANOR CRES
PIPPIN CL
DUNMORE CL
BARRINGTON DR
MOTTRAM CL
RUSHTON DR
ASTLE CL
BUTLEY CL
HENBURY CL
SUTTON LA
LONG LA S
WARMINGHAM CT
DALE CT
CHADWICK CT
QUEEN'S DR
Schs
WHITEGATE CL
CRESANNE CL
WORLESTON CL
WHITEMORE RD
GEORGE VI AVE
GEORGE VI CL
CORONATION RD
CHADWICK FIELDS ORCH
PRINCESS CRES
ALEXANDRA RD
Norcroft Farm
HEATON CL
BOSLEY CL
HANKELOW CL
Keepers Cottage
P
PO
MOSS DR
REDSHAW CL
CHADWICK RD
ASHMORE CL
GORSLEY CL
EARDSWICK RD
THE GREEN
CLEDFORD LA
Works
Trent & Mersey Canal
FAULKNER DR
HUTCHINS' CL
CROSS LA
CLEDFORD CRES
TELFER CT
ROWAN CL
COPPICE DR
FERNLEIGH CL
Cledford Hall
Old Gorse
ALLGREAVE CL 1
TYTHERINGTON CL 2
WOODEND CL 3
NIGHTINGALE CL 4
BLACKWELL CL 5
TARVIN CL 6
GSTONE WAY
LINNET CL
LISTER CL
KESTREL CL
FALCON CL
BOXTON AVE
BEESTON CL
BUNBURY CL
DAVENHAM WAY
OSPREY CL
ASHTON CL
ALDINGTON DR
MILTON CL
STEELE RD
FAIRACRE DR
CEDAR CL
VENABLES WAY
SHILTON CL
BOOTH LA
BYRON CL
SYCAMORE DR
KINGSWOOD CRES
NORTHWOOD AVE
INGLEWOOD AVE
1 WOODSTOCK DR
2 CHESTERTON CL
3 SHELLEY CL
PH
Works
Cheshire Ring Canal Walk
Sutton Hall Farm
Sutton Mill
WARMINGHAM LA
Newfield Farm
CW10
A533
Sutton Lane
Saunders Field
Pettywood Farm
Fields Farm
LEA DR
Sch
River Wheelock
Tetton Hall Cottages
Occlestonegreen Farm
Tetton Hall
TETTON LA
West Farm
Manor Farm
Occlestone Green
Hopley House
NANTWICH RD
The Home Farm
New Farm
Withinstreet Farm
Bellsmithy
Forge Cottages
Forge Mill Farm
FORGE MILL LA
Sparrowgrove
Oldhough Manor
Little Hough
Denmar
DRAGON'S LA
The Bungalow
WHITE HALL LA
CW11
Fields Farm

69 A B 70 C D 71 E F

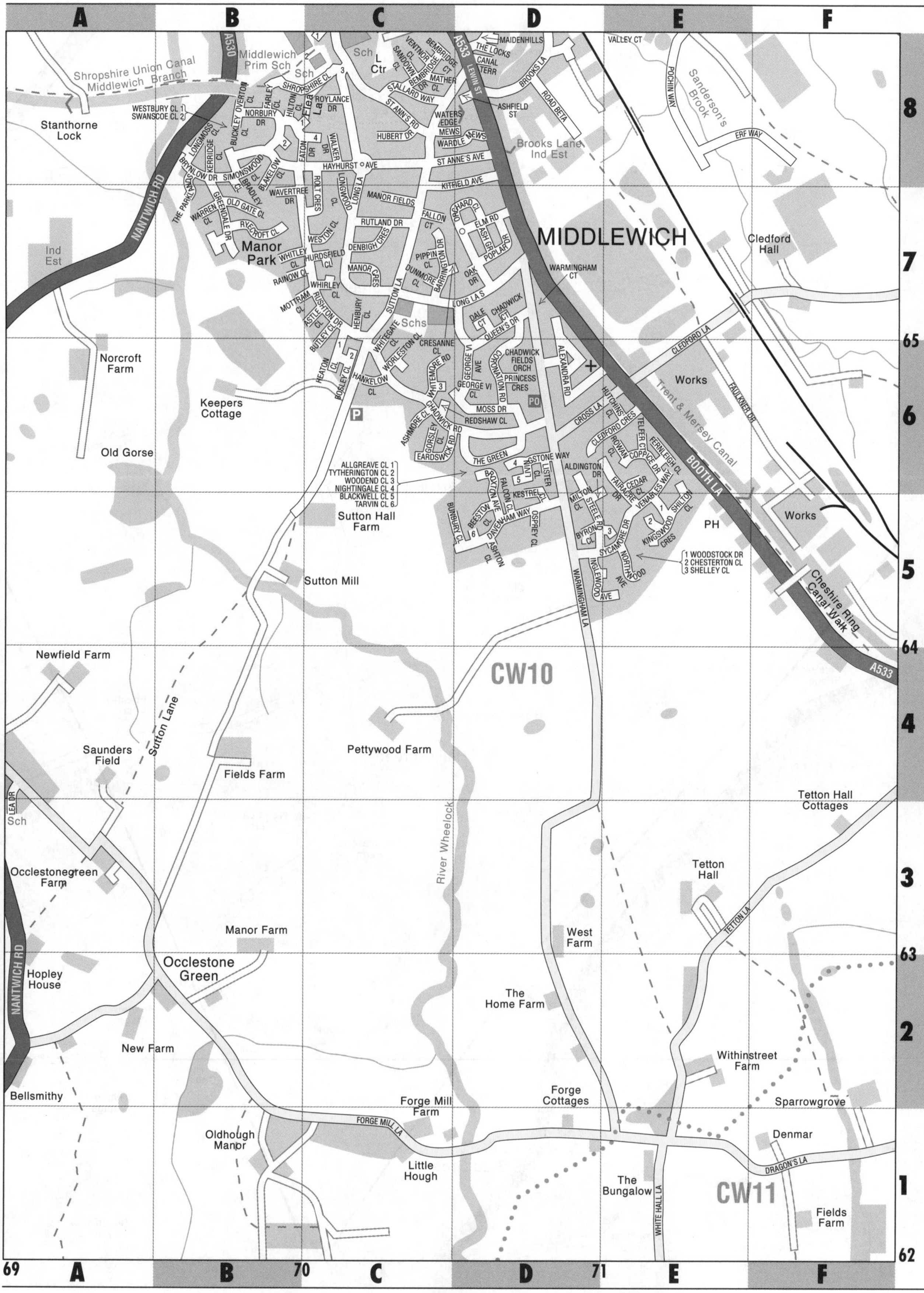

173
152

151
129

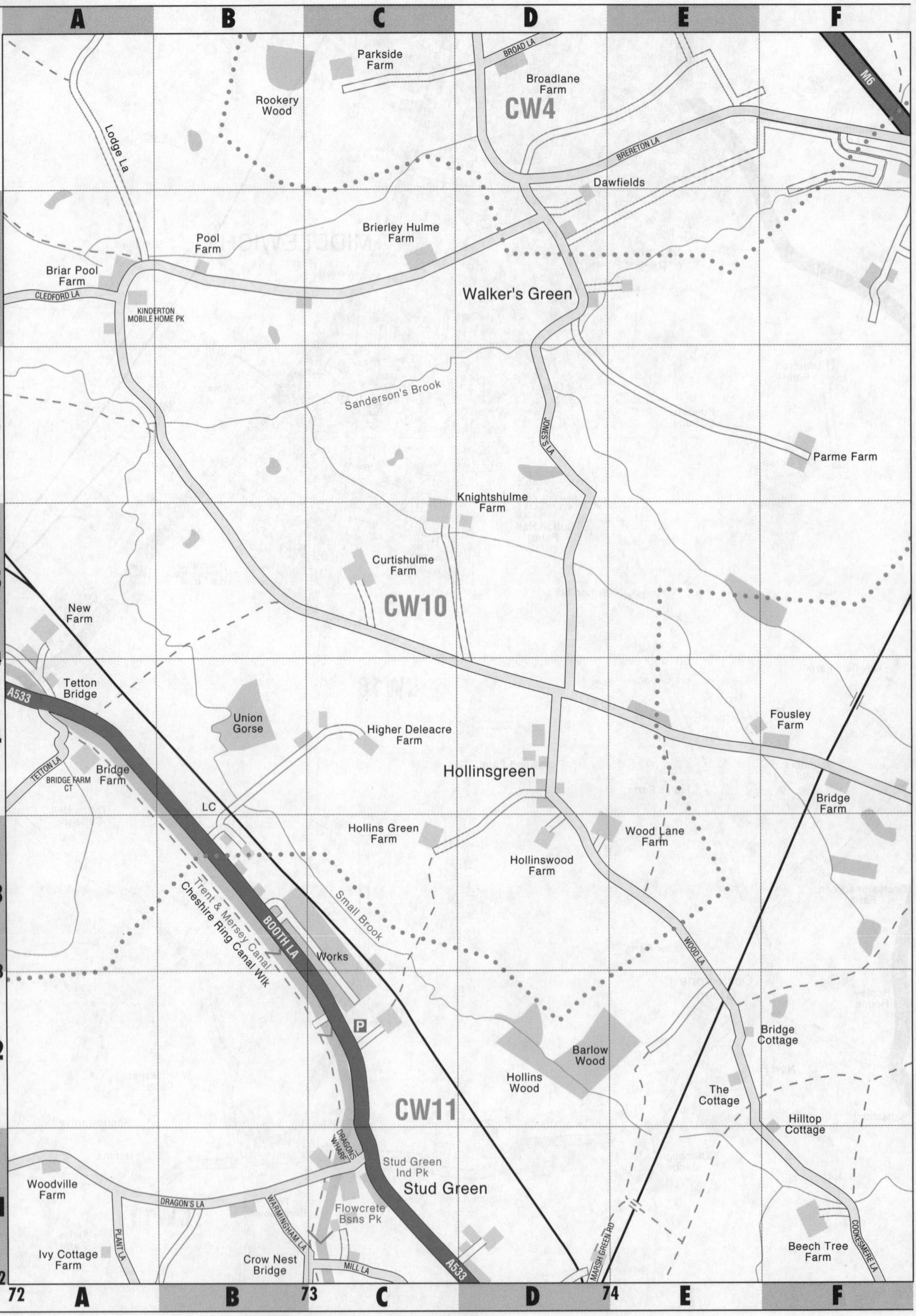

A B C D E F

8 7 65 6 5 64 4 3 63 2 1 62

Parkside Farm
Rookery Wood
BROAD LA
Broadlane Farm
CW4
M6
Lodge La
BRERETON LA
Dawfields
Pool Farm
Brierley Hulme Farm
Briar Pool Farm
CLEDFORD LA
KINDERTON MOBILE HOME PK
Walker's Green
Sanderson's Brook
JONES'S LA
Parme Farm
Knightshulme Farm
Curtishulme Farm
CW10
New Farm
Tetton Bridge
A533
Union Gorse
Higher Deleacre Farm
Fousley Farm
TETTON LA
BRIDGE FARM CT
Bridge Farm
Hollinsgreen
Bridge Farm
LC
Hollins Green Farm
Wood Lane Farm
Hollinswood Farm
Trent & Mersey Canal
Cheshire Ring Canal Wlk
BOOTH LA
Small Brook
WOOD LA
Works
P
Bridge Cottage
Barlow Wood
Hollins Wood
The Cottage
CW11
Hilltop Cottage
DRAGONS WHARF
Stud Green Ind Pk
Woodville Farm
Stud Green
DRAGON'S LA
WARMINGHAM LA
Flowcrete Bsns Pk
PLANT LA
MARSH GREEN RD
COOKESMERE LA
Beech Tree Farm
Ivy Cottage Farm
Crow Nest Bridge
MILL LA
A533

72 A B 73 C D 74 E F

151
174

130
154

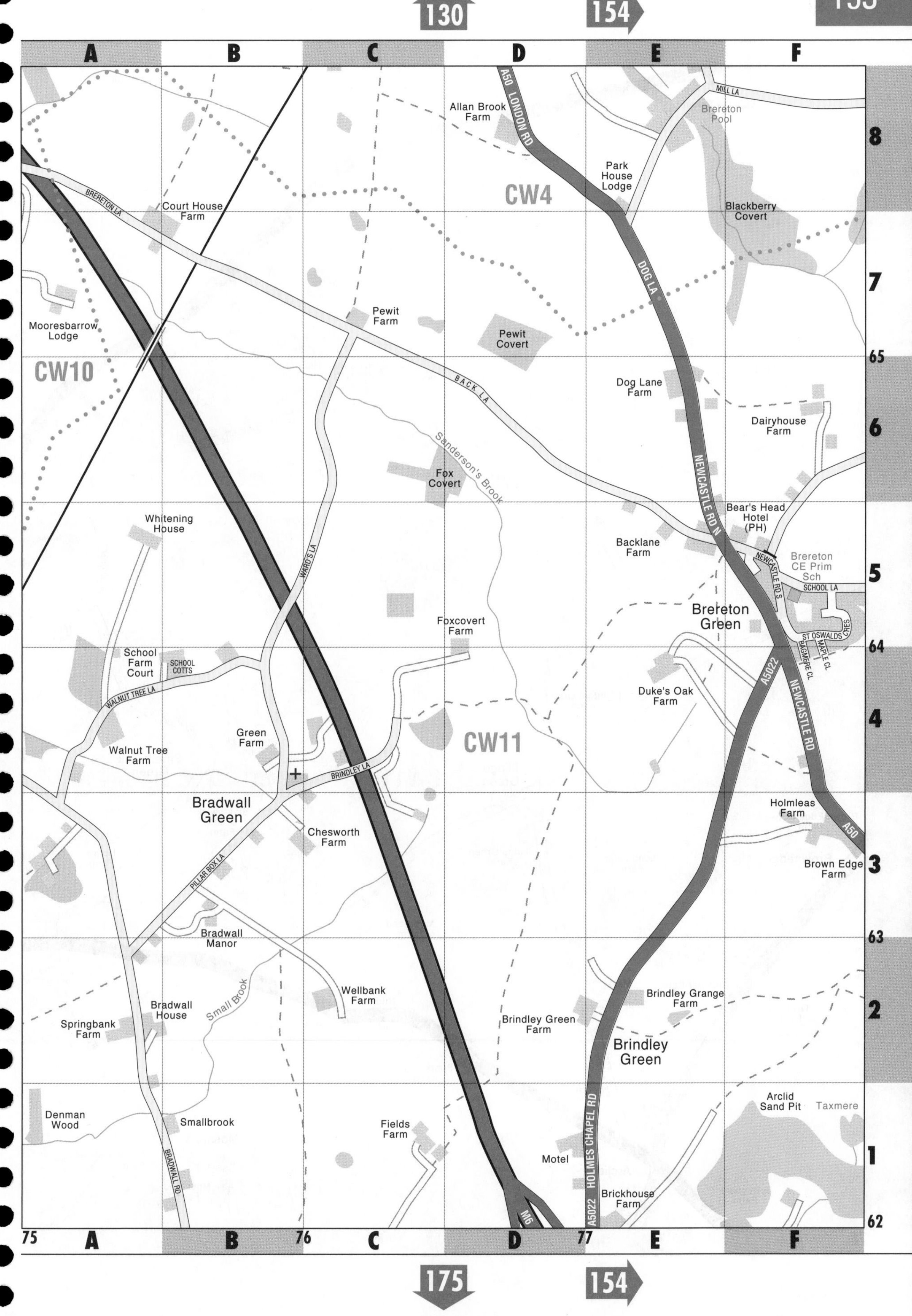

175
154

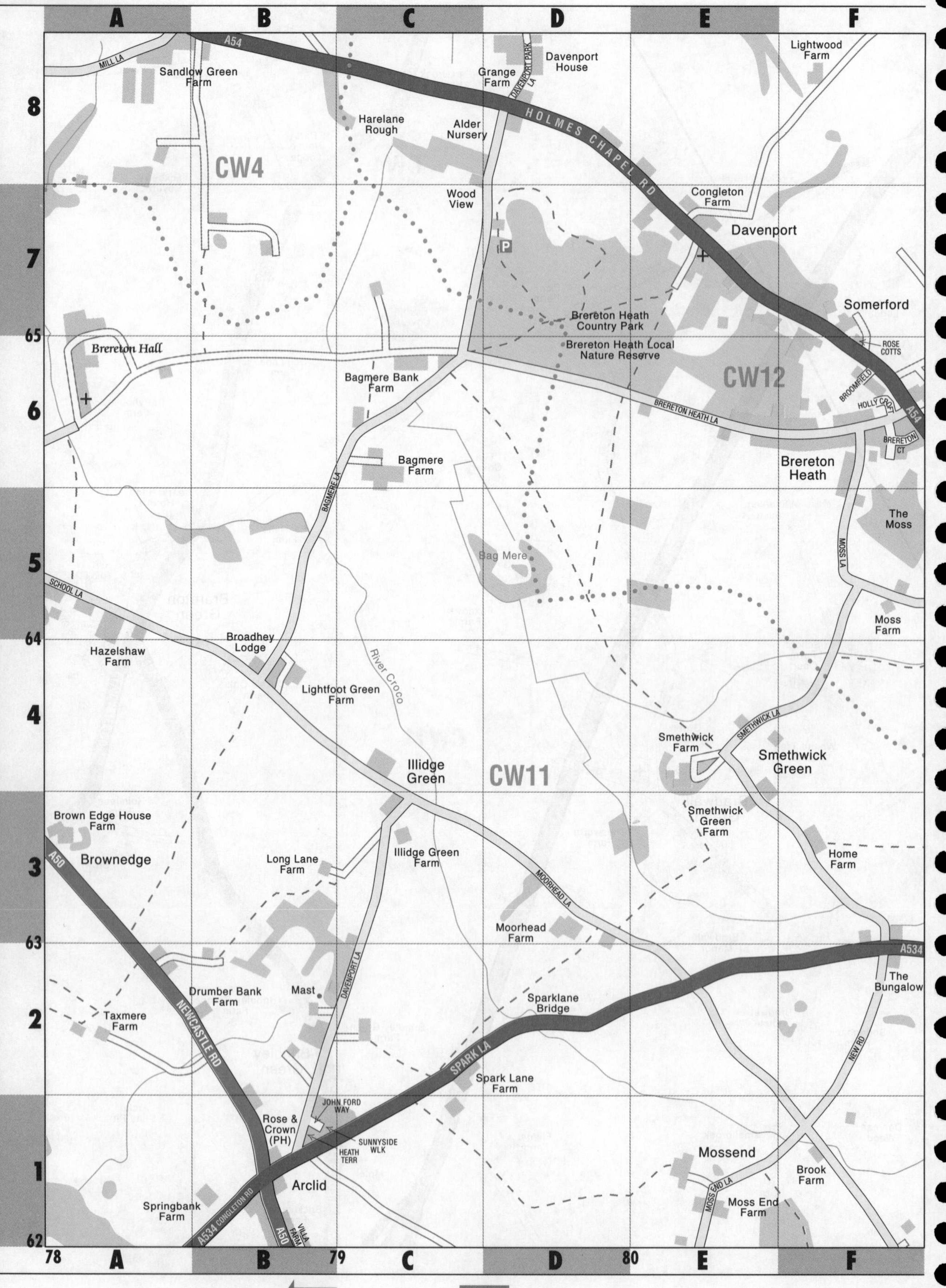
A
B
C
D
E
F
MILL LA
A54
Sandlow Green Farm
Grange Farm
DAVENPORT PARK LA
Davenport House
Lightwood Farm
8
Harelane Rough
Alder Nursery
HOLMES CHAPEL RD
CW4
Wood View
Congleton Farm
Davenport
7
P
Somerford
65
Brereton Hall
Brereton Heath Country Park
Brereton Heath Local Nature Reserve
ROSE COTTS
CW12
BROOMFIELD
Bagmere Bank Farm
HOLLY CROFT
6
BRERETON HEATH LA
A54
BRERETON CT
Bagmere Farm
Brereton Heath
BAGMERE LA
The Moss
MOSS LA
5
Bag Mere
SCHOOL LA
Moss Farm
64
Hazelshaw Farm
Broadhey Lodge
Lightfoot Green Farm
River Croco
4
SMETHWICK LA
Smethwick Farm
Smethwick Green
Illidge Green
CW11
Brown Edge House Farm
Smethwick Green Farm
A50
Brownedge
Illidge Green Farm
3
Long Lane Farm
Home Farm
MOORHEAD LA
Moorhead Farm
63
DAVENPORT LA
A534
The Bungalow
Drumber Bank Farm
Mast
Sparklane Bridge
2
Taxmere Farm
NEWCASTLE RD
SPARK LA
NEW RD
Spark Lane Farm
JOHN FORD WAY
Rose & Crown (PH)
SUNNYSIDE WLK
HEATH TERR
Mossend
1
Arclid
Brook Farm
MOSS END LA
Springbank Farm
Moss End Farm
A534 CONGLETON RD
A50
VILLA FARM
62
78
79
80

132
156

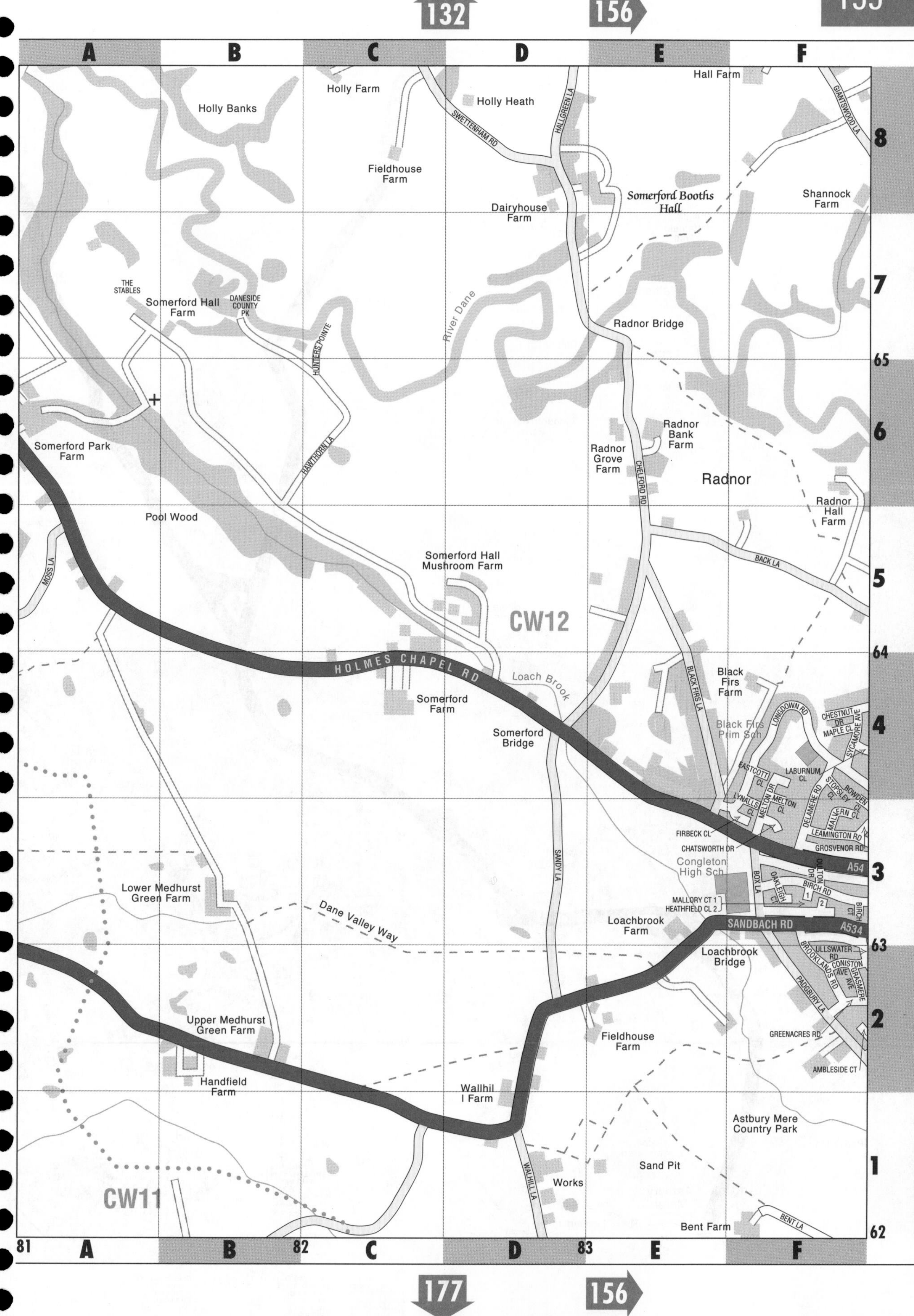

177
156

155

133

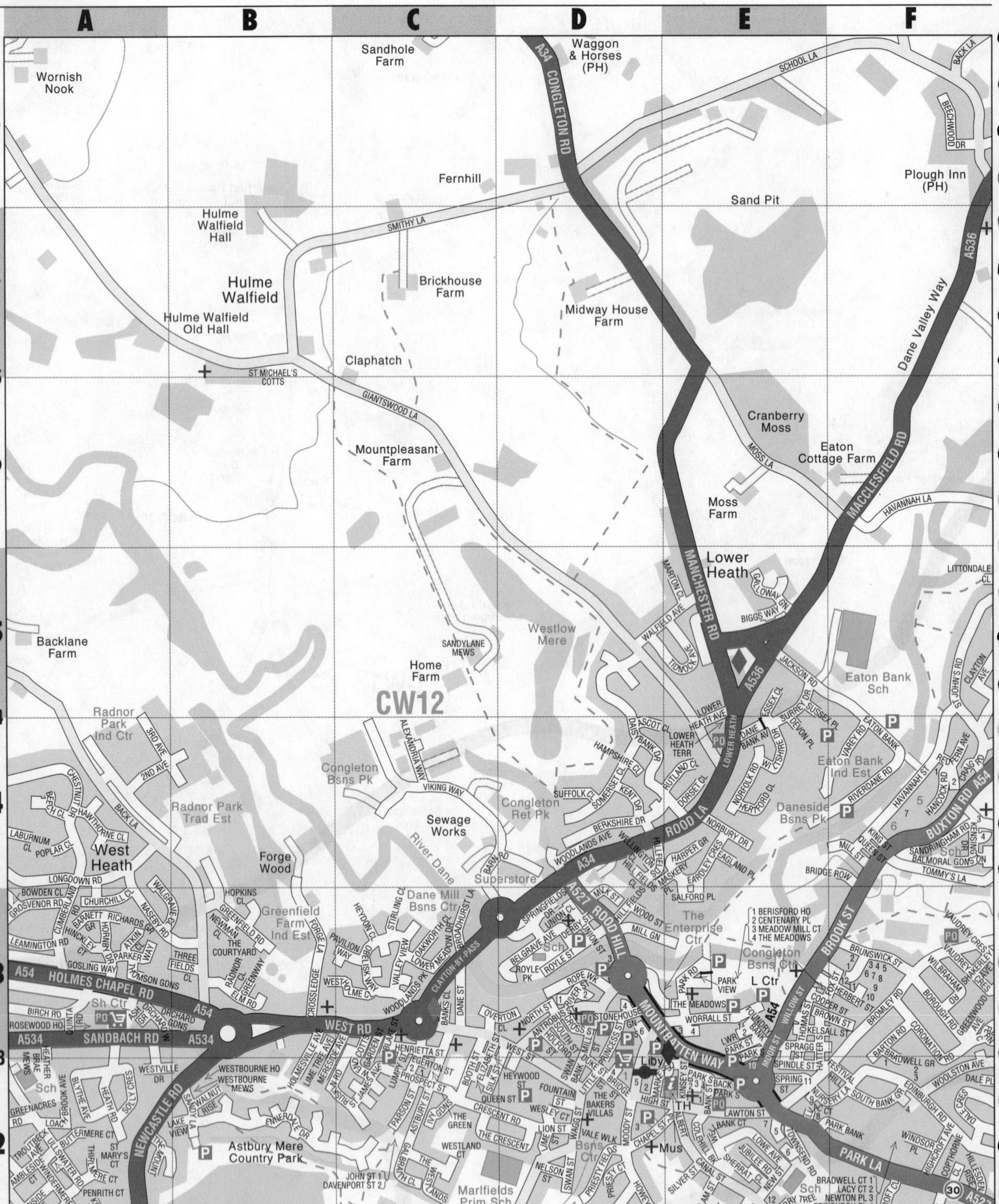

A B C D E F

Sandhole Farm
Waggon & Horses (PH)
Wornish Nook
Fernhill
Plough Inn (PH)
Sand Pit
Hulme Walfield Hall
Hulme Walfield
Brickhouse Farm
Hulme Walfield Old Hall
Midway House Farm
Claphatch
ST MICHAEL'S COTTS
Cranberry Moss
Mountpleasant Farm
Eaton Cottage Farm
Moss Farm
Lower Heath
Backlane Farm
Westlow Mere
Home Farm
Eaton Bank Sch
CW12
Radnor Park Ind Ctr
Congleton Bsns Pk
Eaton Bank Ind Est
Congleton Ret Pk
Daneside Bsns Pk
Radnor Park Trad Est
Sewage Works
West Heath
Forge Wood
River Dane
Superstore
Greenfield Farm Ind Est
Dane Mill Bsns Ctr
The Enterprise Ctr
Congleton Bsns Ctr
L Ctr
Sh Ctr
Astbury Mere Country Park
Marlfields Prim Sch
Astbury Lake
Astbury Water Park
Congleton War Memorial
Padsbridge Farm
Astbury Marsh
Lambert's Lane
Macclesfield Canal

1 BERISFORD HO
2 CENTENARY PL
3 MEADOW MILL CT
4 THE MEADOWS

JOHN ST 1
DAVENPORT ST 2

BRADSHAW PL 1
TANNER ST 2
BARK ST 3
BANK COTT 4
WALLWORTH'S BANK 5
ELVINGTON CL 6
ALBION CT 7
PARKLEIGH 8
MOUNT PLEASANT 9
PARK MILL 10
ROE ST 11
PEAR TREE BANK 12

Bridestone Sh Ctr 1
CAPITOL WLK 2
TUDOR CT 3
VICTORIA ST 4
MARKET ST 5

BRADWELL CT 1
LACY CT 2
NEWTON PL 3
EDINBURGH PL 4

62 84 A B 85 C D 86 E F

155

178

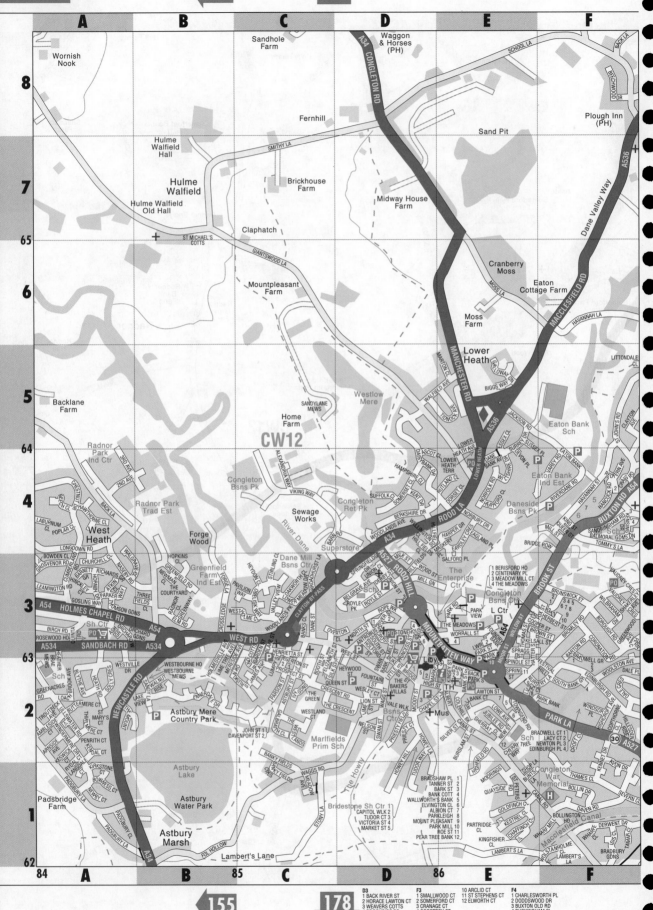

D3
1 BACK RIVER ST
2 HORACE LAWTON CT
3 WEAVERS COTTS
4 BROOKSIDE RD
5 MEADOW COTTS
6 STONEHOUSE GN

F3
1 SMALLWOOD CT
2 SOMERFORD CT
3 CRANAGE CT
4 GOOSTREY CT
5 MOSTON CT
6 BETCHTON CT
7 RODE CT
8 TETTON CT
9 NEWBOLD CT
10 ARCLID CT
11 ST STEPHENS CT
12 ELWORTH CT

F4
1 CHARLESWORTH PL
2 DODDSWOOD DR
3 BUXTON OLD RD
4 BUCKINGHAM CL
5 Buglawton Ind Est
6 Havannah Bsns Ctr
7 COUNCIL HOS

134
158

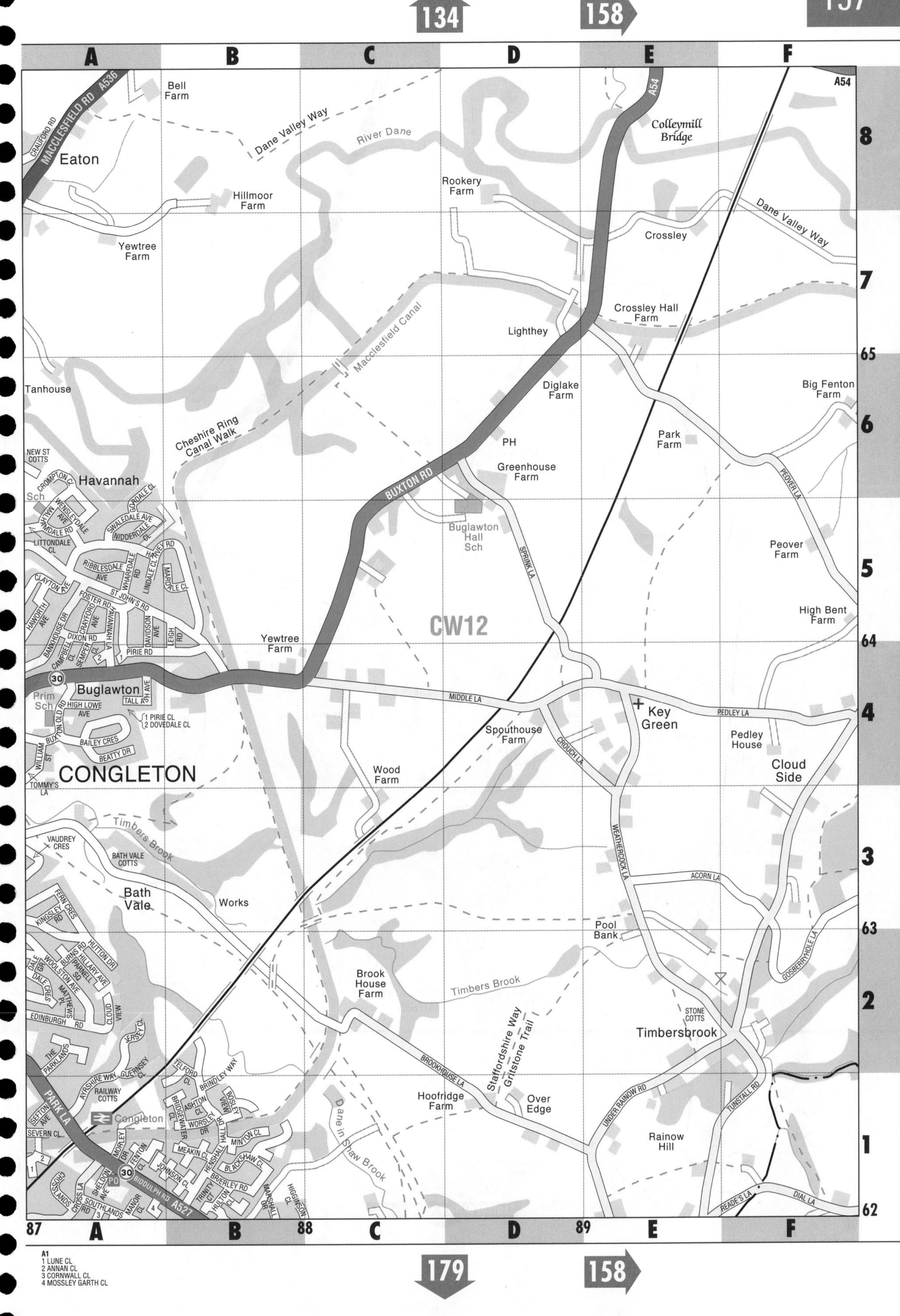

179
158

157
135

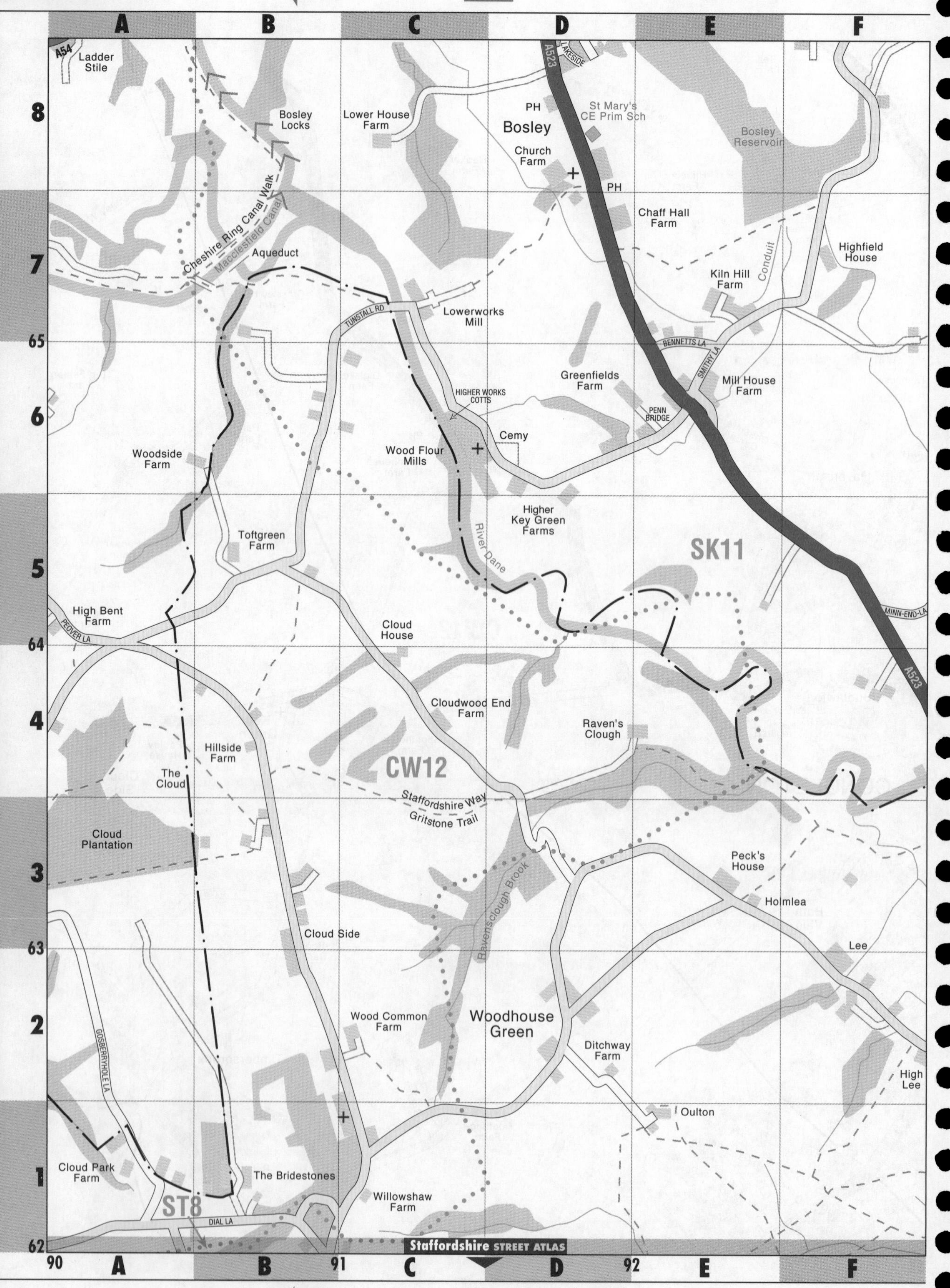
A
B
C
D
E
F
8
7
65
6
5
64
4
3
63
2
1
62
90
91
92
A54
Ladder Stile
Bosley Locks
Lower House Farm
PH
St Mary's CE Prim Sch
Bosley
Church Farm
PH
Bosley Reservoir
LAKESIDE
A523
Cheshire Ring Canal Walk
Macclesfield Canal
Aqueduct
Chaff Hall Farm
Highfield House
Kiln Hill Farm
Conduit
TUNSTALL RD
Lowerworks Mill
BENNETTS LA
SMITHY LA
Greenfields Farm
Mill House Farm
HIGHER WORKS COTTS
PENN BRIDGE
Cemy
Wood Flour Mills
Woodside Farm
Higher Key Green Farms
River Dane
Toftgreen Farm
SK11
High Bent Farm
PEOVER LA
Cloud House
MINN-END-LA
A523
Cloudwood End Farm
Raven's Clough
Hillside Farm
The Cloud
CW12
Staffordshire Way
Gritstone Trail
Cloud Plantation
Peck's House
Holmlea
Ravenscough Brook
Cloud Side
Lee
Wood Common Farm
Woodhouse Green
Ditchway Farm
High Lee
GOSBERRYHOLE LA
Oulton
Cloud Park Farm
The Bridestones
ST8
DIAL LA
Willowshaw Farm
Staffordshire STREET ATLAS

157

136
160

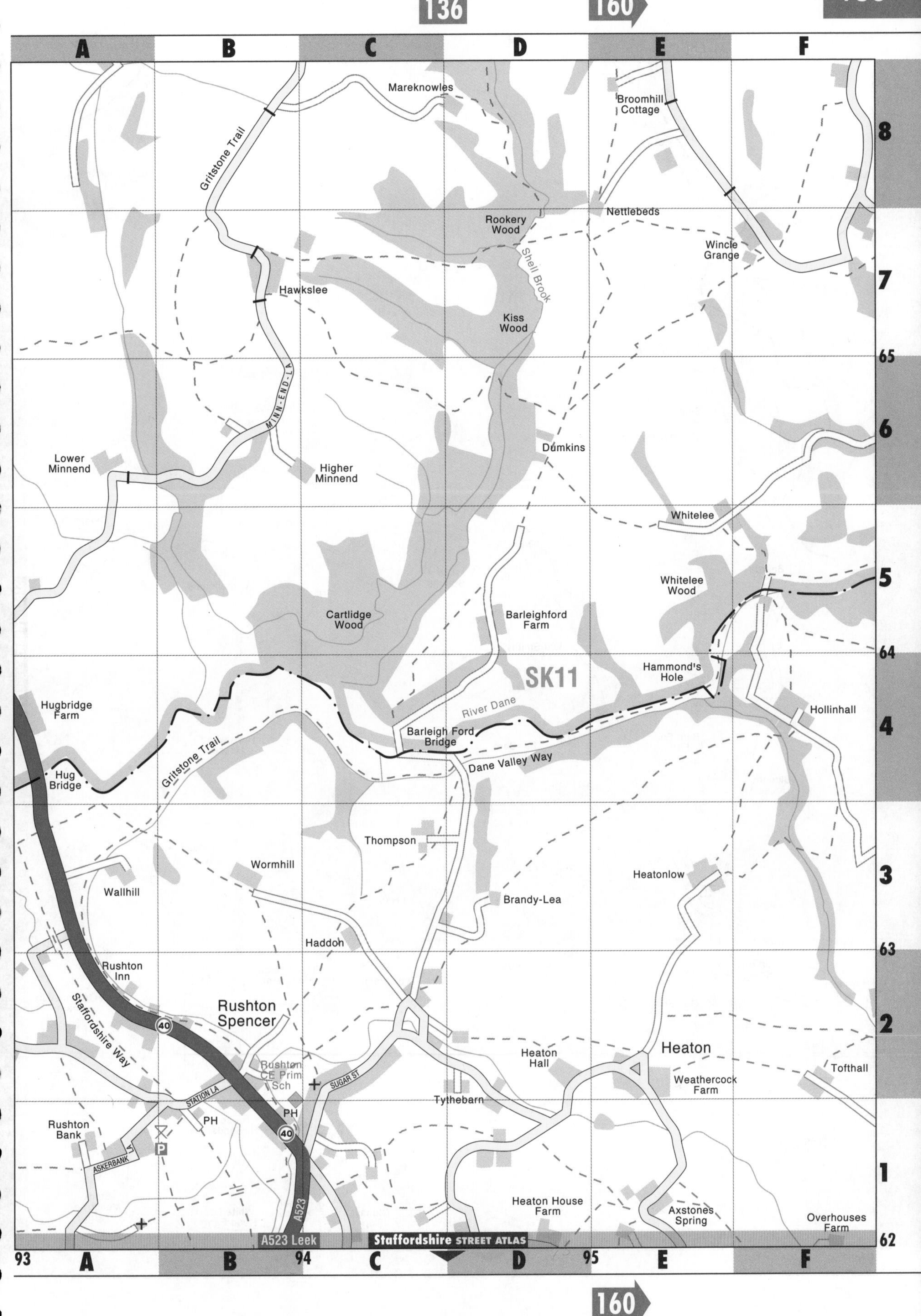
A
B
C
D
E
F
Mareknowles
Broomhill Cottage
Gritstone Trail
8
Rookery Wood
Nettlebeds
Shell Brook
Wincle Grange
7
Hawkslee
Kiss Wood
65
MINN-END-LA
6
Lower Minnend
Higher Minnend
Dumkins
Whitelee
5
Whitelee Wood
Cartlidge Wood
Barleighford Farm
64
SK11
Hammond's Hole
Hugbridge Farm
River Dane
Hollinhall
Barleigh Ford Bridge
4
Gritstone Trail
Dane Valley Way
Hug Bridge
Thompson
Wormhill
3
Heatonlow
Wallhill
Brandy-Lea
Haddon
63
Rushton Inn
Staffordshire Way
Rushton Spencer
40
2
Heaton
Heaton Hall
Rushton CE Prim Sch
Tofthall
SUGAR ST
Weathercock Farm
STATION LA
Tythebarn
PH
Rushton Bank
PH
40
ASKERBANK LA
1
Heaton House Farm
Axstones Spring
A523
Overhouses Farm
A523 Leek
Staffordshire STREET ATLAS
62
93
94
95

160

159
137

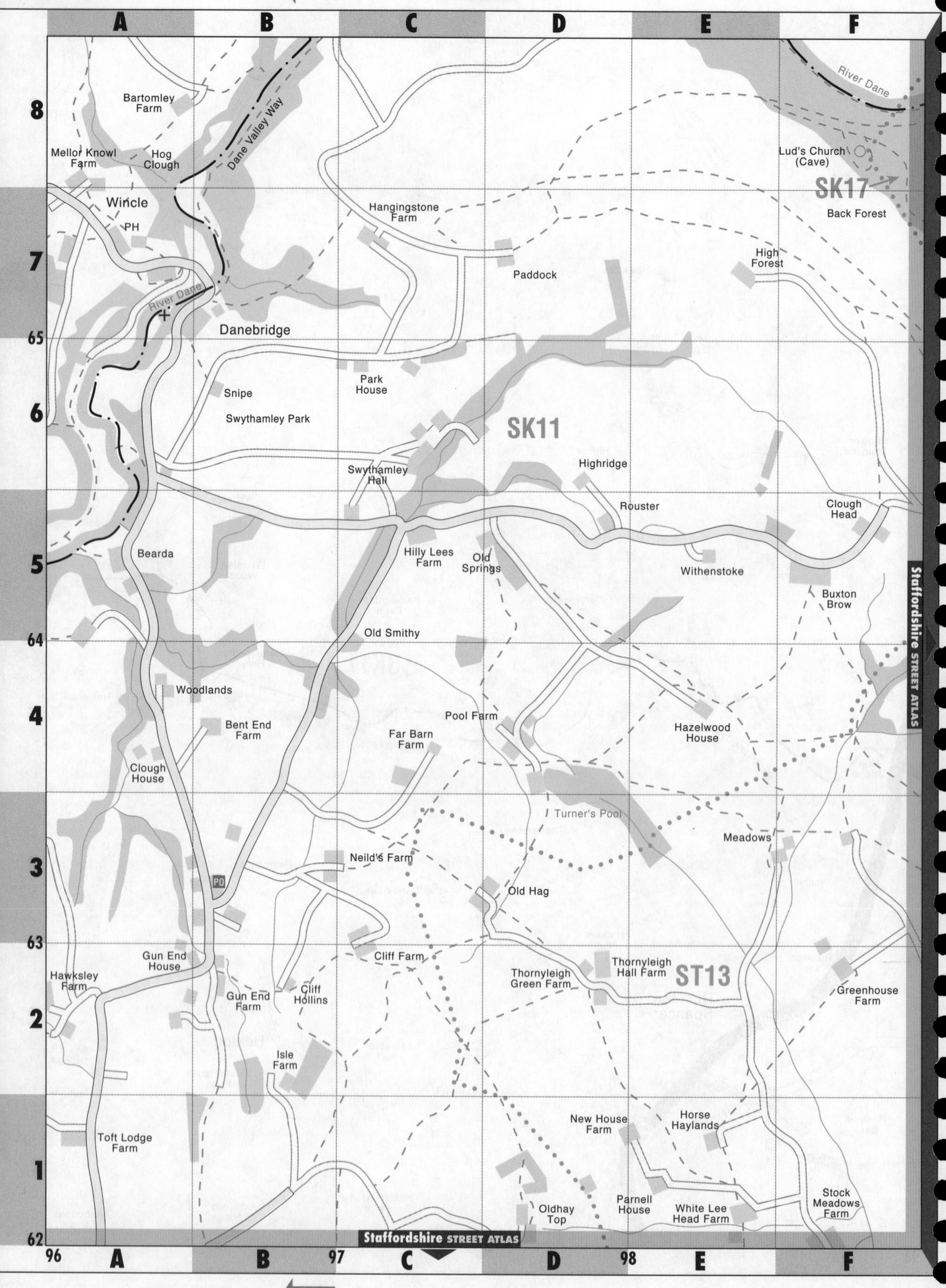
A
B
C
D
E
F
8
7
65
6
5
64
4
3
63
2
1
62
96
97
98
Bartomley Farm
Mellor Knowl Farm
Hog Clough
Dane Valley Way
Wincle
PH
River Dane
Danebridge
Hangingstone Farm
Paddock
Lud's Church (Cave)
SK17
Back Forest
High Forest
Park House
Snipe
Swythamley Park
SK11
Swythamley Hall
Highridge
Rouster
Clough Head
Bearda
Hilly Lees Farm
Old Springs
Withenstoke
Buxton Brow
Old Smithy
Woodlands
Bent End Farm
Pool Farm
Far Barn Farm
Hazelwood House
Clough House
Turner's Pool
Meadows
Neild's Farm
PO
Old Hag
Gun End House
Cliff Farm
Thornyleigh Green Farm
Thornyleigh Hall Farm
ST13
Hawksley Farm
Cliff Hollins
Gun End Farm
Greenhouse Farm
Isle Farm
New House Farm
Horse Haylands
Toft Lodge Farm
Parnell House
White Lee Head Farm
Stock Meadows Farm
Oldhay Top
Staffordshire STREET ATLAS

159

139
162

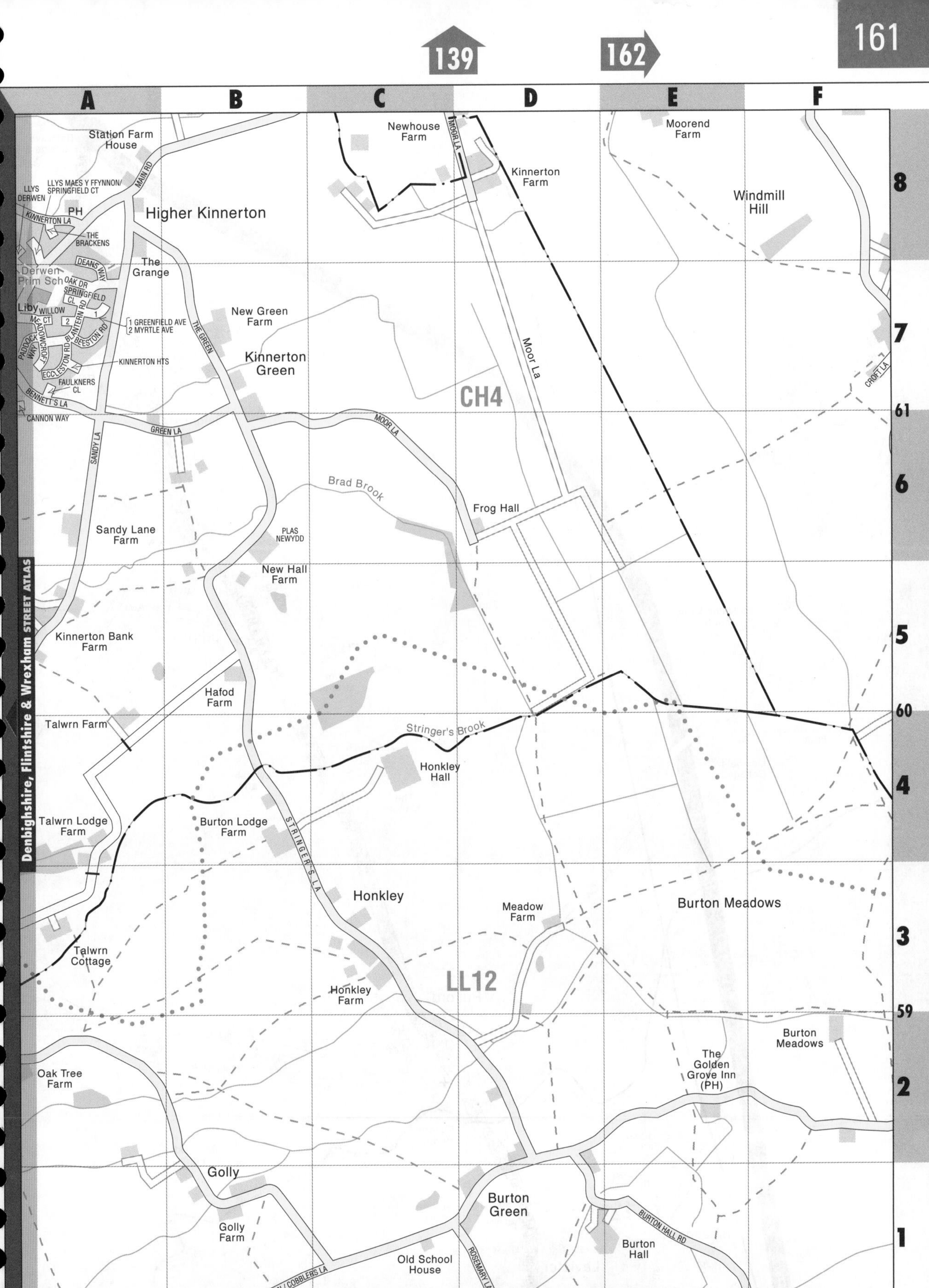
A
B
C
D
E
F
Station Farm House
Newhouse Farm
MOOR LA
Moorend Farm
Kinnerton Farm
Windmill Hill
MAIN RD
LLYS DERWEN
LLYS MAES Y FFYNNON/ SPRINGFIELD CT
PH
KINNERTON LA
Higher Kinnerton
THE BRACKENS
DEANS WAY
The Grange
Derwen Prim Sch
OAK DR
SPRINGFIELD CL
Liby
WILLOW CT
MEADOWCROFT
PADDOCK WAY
LANTERN RD
BESTON RD
1 GREENFIELD AVE
2 MYRTLE AVE
New Green Farm
THE GREEN
Kinnerton Green
ECCLESTON RD
KINNERTON HTS
FAULKNERS CL
BENNETT'S LA
CANNON WAY
GREEN LA
SANDY LA
Moor La
CH4
CROFT LA
MOOR LA
Brad Brook
Frog Hall
Sandy Lane Farm
PLAS NEWYDD
New Hall Farm
Kinnerton Bank Farm
Hafod Farm
Talwrn Farm
Stringer's Brook
Honkley Hall
Talwrn Lodge Farm
Burton Lodge Farm
STRINGER'S LA
Honkley
Meadow Farm
Burton Meadows
Talwrn Cottage
LL12
Honkley Farm
Burton Meadows
The Golden Grove Inn (PH)
Oak Tree Farm
Golly
Burton Green
Golly Farm
BURTON HALL RD
Burton Hall
ROSEMARY LA
Old School House
LON Y CRYDDION / COBBLERS LA
East View Farm
8
7
61
6
5
60
4
3
59
2
1
58
33
34
35
Denbighshire, Flintshire & Wrexham STREET ATLAS

162

161
140

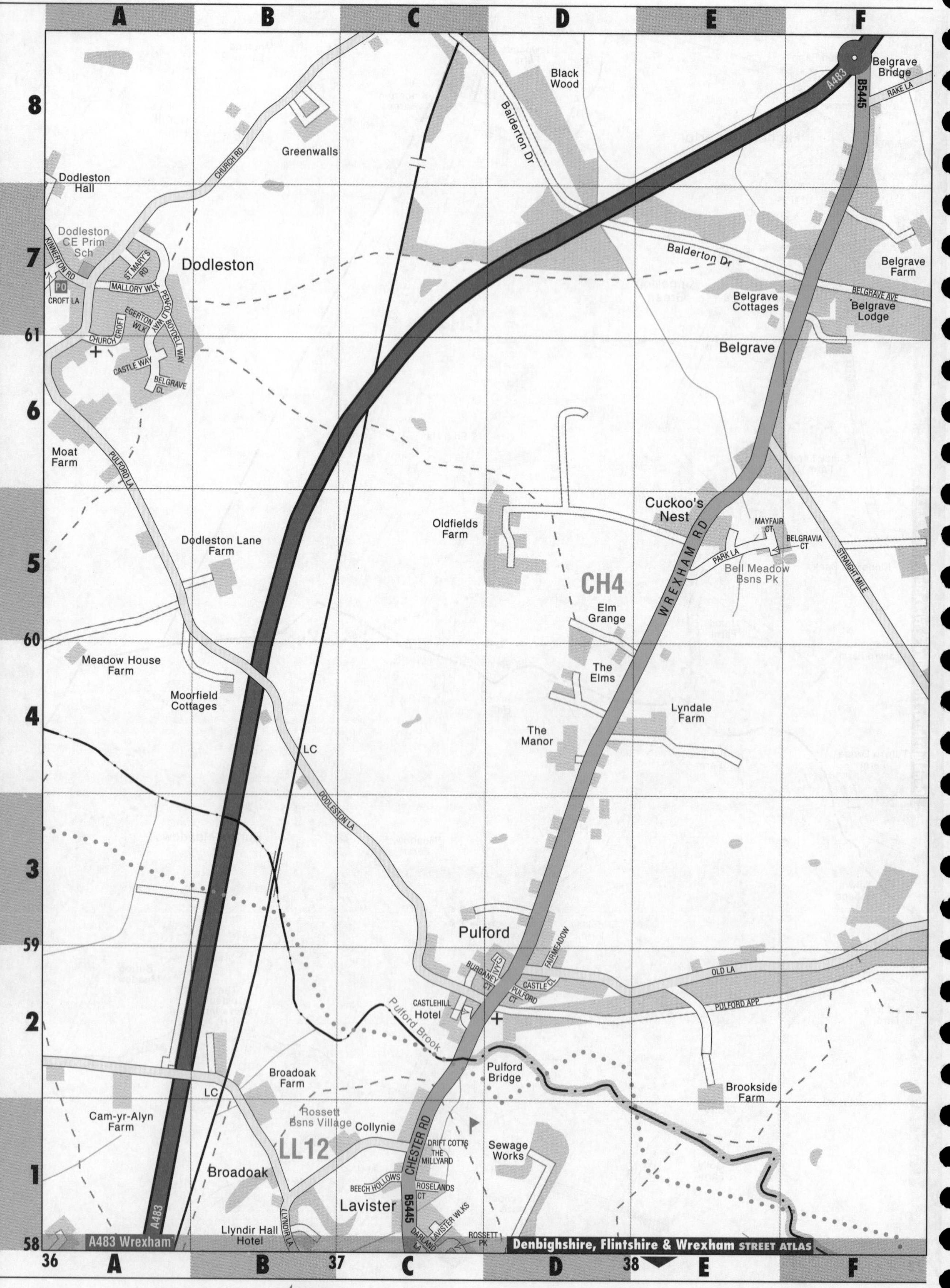
A
B
C
D
E
F
8
7
61
6
5
60
4
3
59
2
1
58
36
37
38
Black Wood
Belgrave Bridge
A483
B5445
RAKE LA
Balderton Dr
Greenwalls
CHURCH RD
Dodleston Hall
Dodleston CE Prim Sch
KINNERTON RD
ST MARY'S RD
Dodleston
MALLORY WLK
PO
CROFT LA
EGERTON WLK
CROFT
CHURCH
PENFOLD WAY
BOYDELL WAY
CASTLE WAY
BELGRAVE CL
Belgrave Farm
BELGRAVE AVE
Belgrave Cottages
Belgrave Lodge
Belgrave
Moat Farm
PULFORD LA
Oldfields Farm
Cuckoo's Nest
MAYFAIR CT
BELGRAVIA CT
PARK LA
Bell Meadow Bsns Pk
STRAIGHT MILE
WREXHAM RD
Dodleston Lane Farm
CH4
Elm Grange
Meadow House Farm
The Elms
Moorfield Cottages
Lyndale Farm
The Manor
LC
DODLESTON LA
Pulford
FAIRMEADOW
BURGANEY CT
CASTLE CL
PULFORD CT
OLD LA
PULFORD APP
CASTLEHILL
Hotel
Pulford Brook
Pulford Bridge
Broadoak Farm
LC
Brookside Farm
Cam-yr-Alyn Farm
Rossett Bsns Village
Collynie
CHESTER RD
DRIFT COTTS
THE MILLYARD
Sewage Works
LL12
Broadoak
BEECH HOLLOWS
ROSELANDS CT
Lavister
B5445
LAVISTER WLKS
Lyndir Hall Hotel
LLYNDIR LA
DARLAND LA
ROSSETT PK
A483 Wrexham

161

141
164

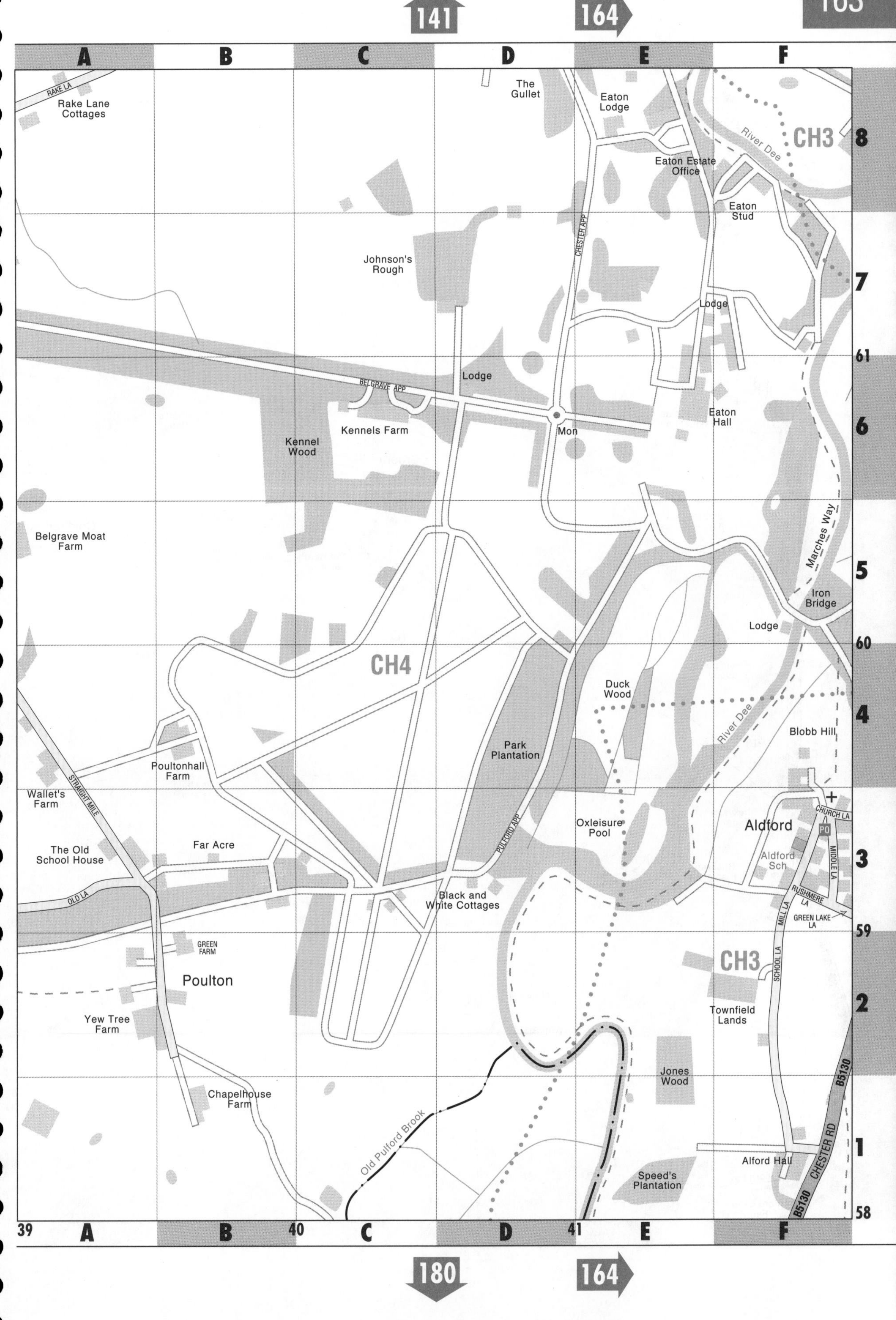

180
164

163
142

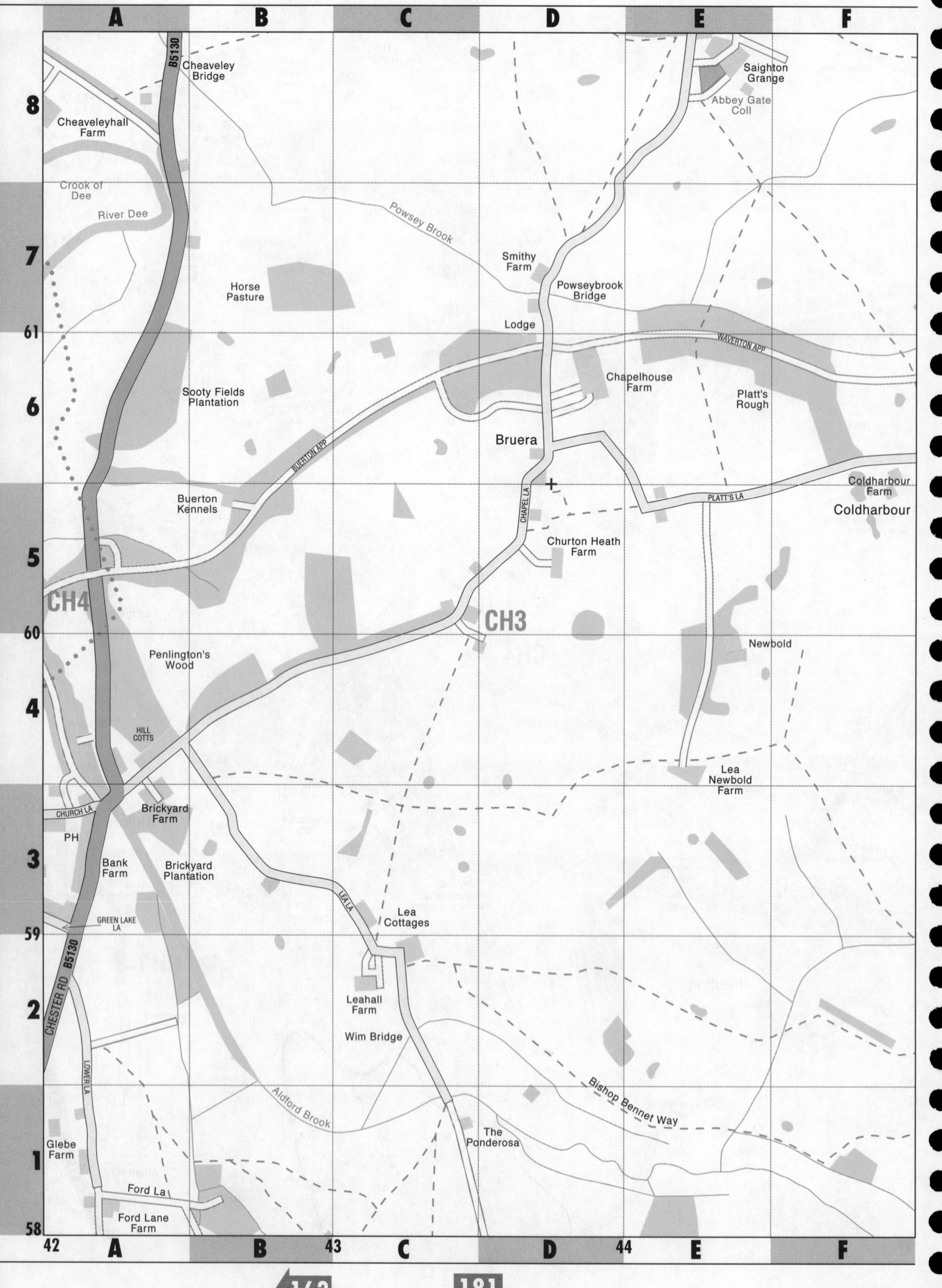

163
181

143
166

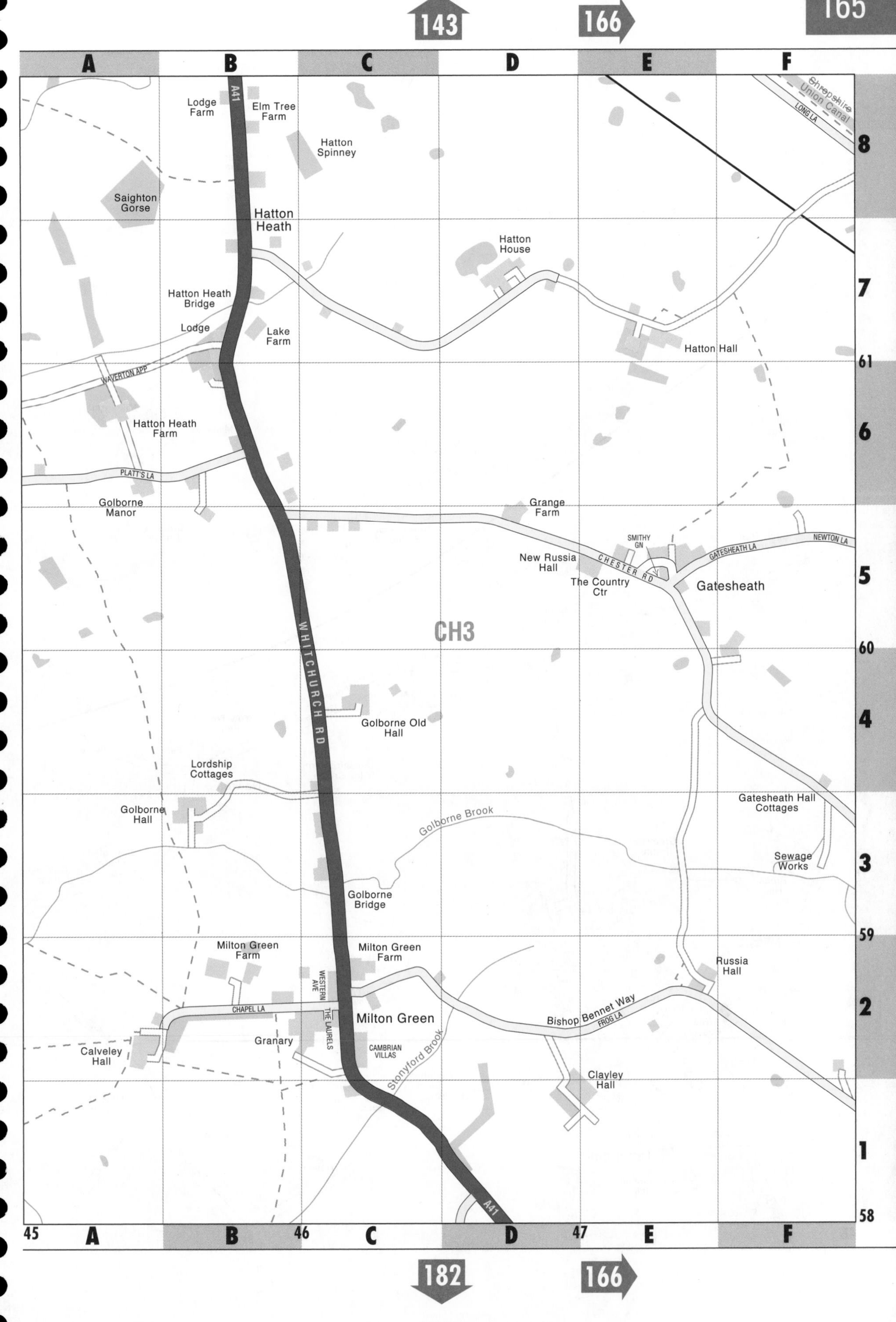
A
B
C
D
E
F
Lodge Farm
Elm Tree Farm
Hatton Spinney
Shropshire Union Canal
LONG LA
8
Saighton Gorse
Hatton Heath
Hatton House
Hatton Heath Bridge
7
Lodge
Lake Farm
Hatton Hall
61
WAVERTON APP
Hatton Heath Farm
6
PLATT'S LA
Golborne Manor
Grange Farm
SMITHY GN
NEWTON LA
GATESHEATH LA
New Russia Hall
CHESTER RD
The Country Ctr
Gatesheath
5
CH3
WHITCHURCH RD
60
Golborne Old Hall
4
Lordship Cottages
Golborne Hall
Golborne Brook
Gatesheath Hall Cottages
Sewage Works
3
Golborne Bridge
59
Milton Green Farm
Milton Green Farm
Russia Hall
WESTERN AVE
CHAPEL LA
THE LAURELS
Milton Green
Bishop Bennet Way
FROG LA
2
Calveley Hall
Granary
CAMBRIAN VILLAS
Stonyford Brook
Clayley Hall
1
A41
58
45
46
47

182
166

165
144

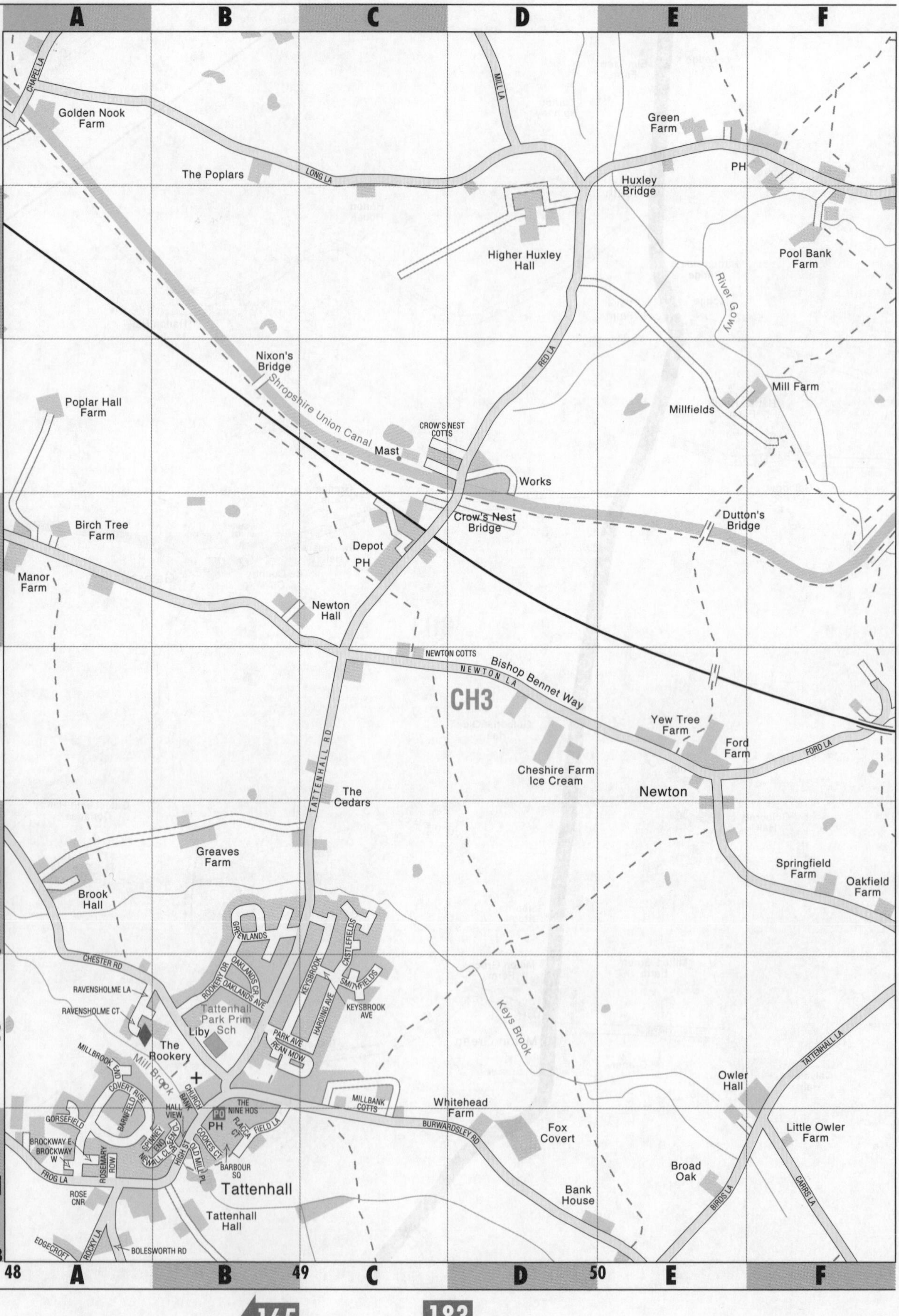

A B C D E F

8 7 61 6 5 60 4 3 59 2 1 58

CHAPEL LA
Golden Nook Farm
The Poplars
LONG LA
MILL LA
Green Farm
PH
Huxley Bridge
Higher Huxley Hall
Pool Bank Farm
River Gowy
Nixon's Bridge
Shropshire Union Canal
RED LA
Mill Farm
Millfields
Poplar Hall Farm
CROW'S NEST COTTS
Mast
Works
Crow's Nest Bridge
Dutton's Bridge
Birch Tree Farm
Depot
PH
Manor Farm
Newton Hall
NEWTON COTTS
Bishop Bennet Way
NEWTON LA
CH3
Yew Tree Farm
Ford Farm
FORD LA
Cheshire Farm Ice Cream
TATTENHALL RD
The Cedars
Newton
Greaves Farm
Springfield Farm
Oakfield Farm
Brook Hall
GREENLANDS
CASTLEFIELDS
CHESTER RD
ROOKERY DR
OAKLANDS CR
OAKLANDS AVE
KEYSBROOK
SMITHFIELDS
RAVENSHOLME LA
HARDING AVE
KEYSBROOK AVE
RAVENSHOLME CT
Tattenhall Park Prim Sch
Liby
PARK AVE
REAN MDW
Keys Brook
TATTENHALL LA
The Rookery
MILLBROOK END
Mill Brook
COVERT RISE
CHURCH BANK
THE NINE HOS
MILLBANK COTTS
Whitehead Farm
Owler Hall
GORSEFIELD
BARNFIELD
HALL VIEW
PO
PH
FLACCA CT
FIELD LA
BURWARDSLEY RD
Fox Covert
Little Owler Farm
BROCKWAY E
BROCKWAY W
ROSEMARY ROW
SPINNEY END
NEWALL CL
GLEN CL
HIGH ST
OLD MILL PL
COOKES CT
BARBOUR SQ
Broad Oak
FROG LA
ROSE CNR
Tattenhall
Bank House
BIRDS LA
CARRS LA
Tattenhall Hall
ROCKY LA
EDGECROFT
BOLESWORTH RD

48 A B 49 C D 50 E F

165
183

145
168

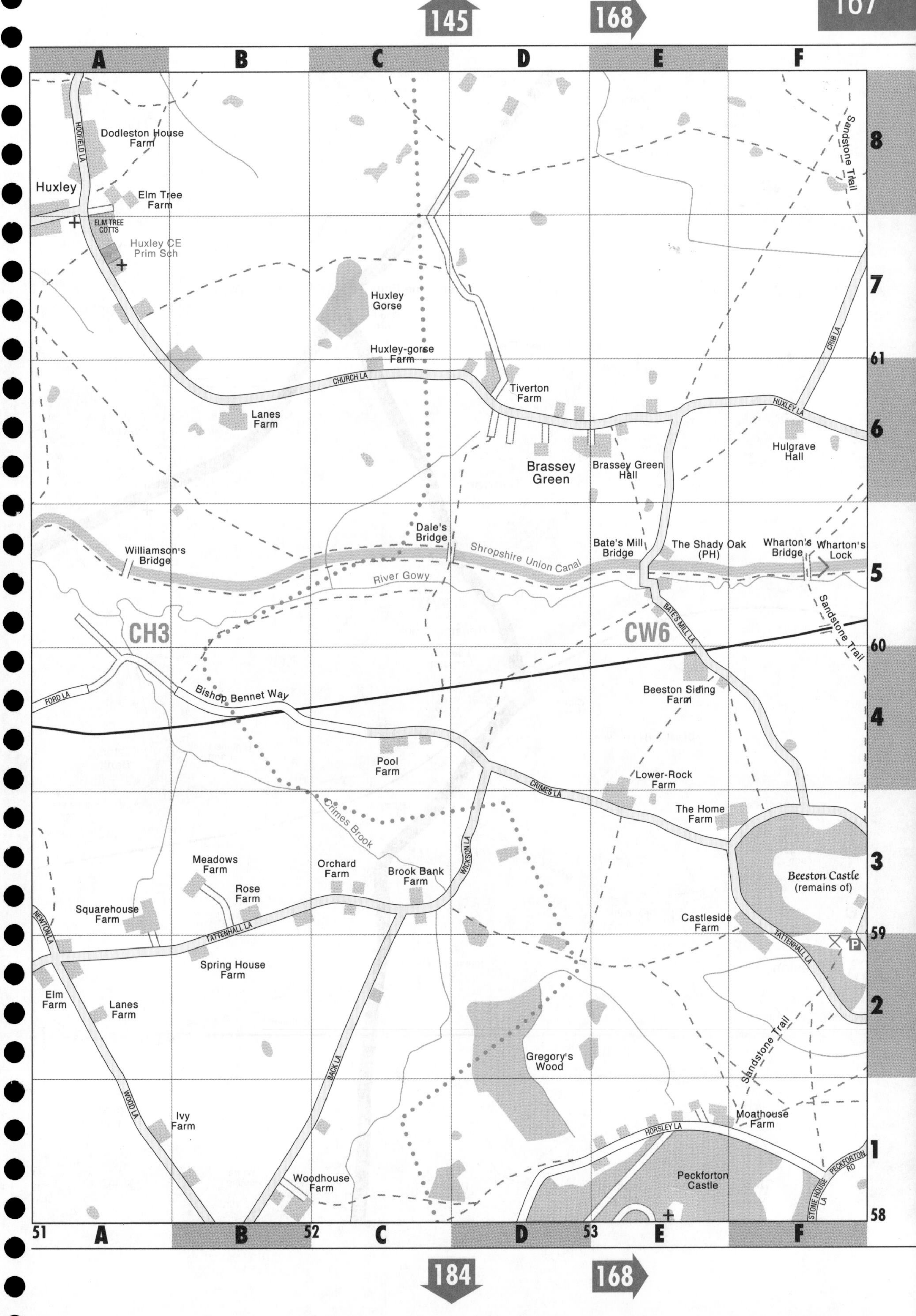

184
168

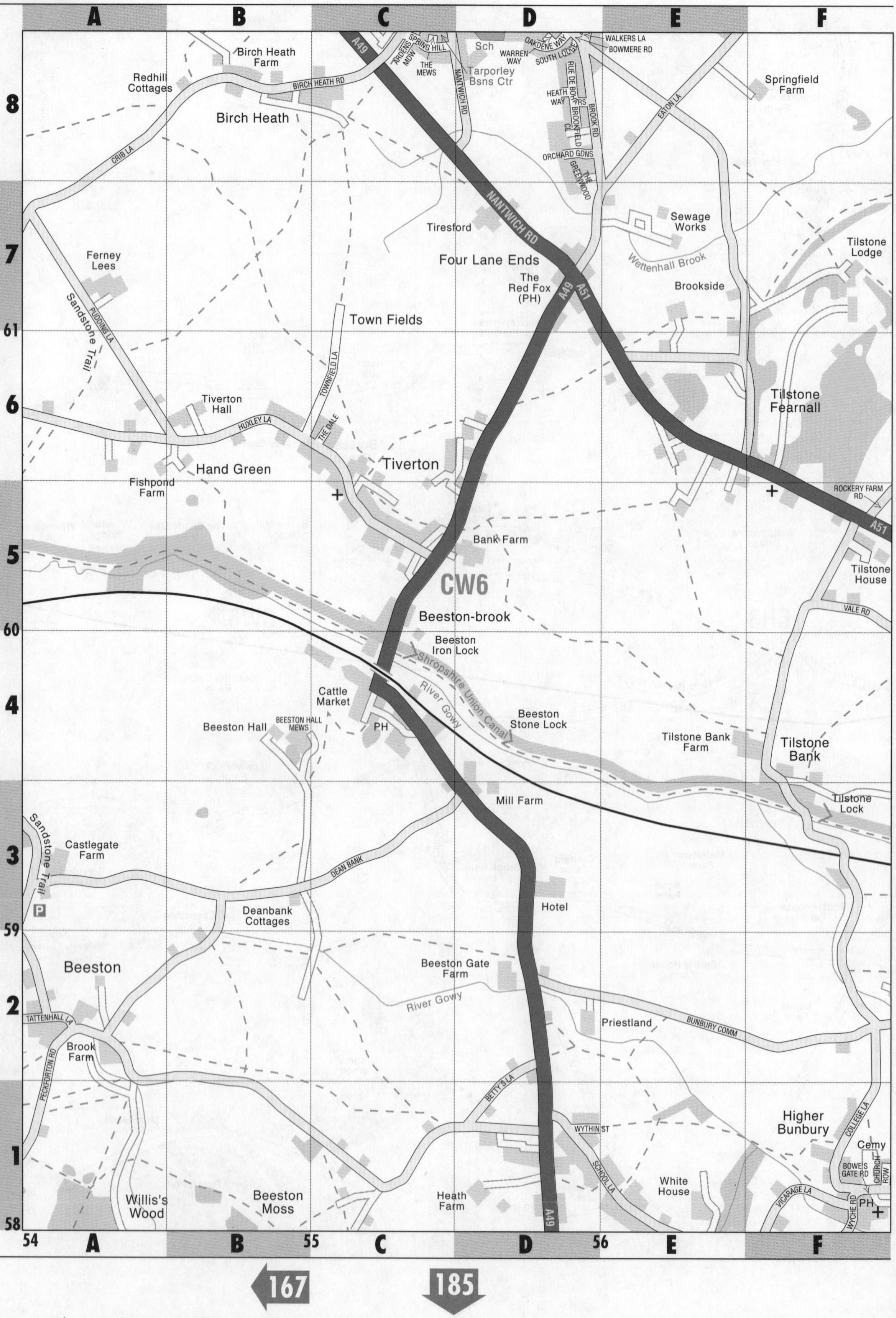

A B C D E F

8 7 61 6 5 60 4 3 59 2 1 58

54 A B 55 C D 56 E F

147
170

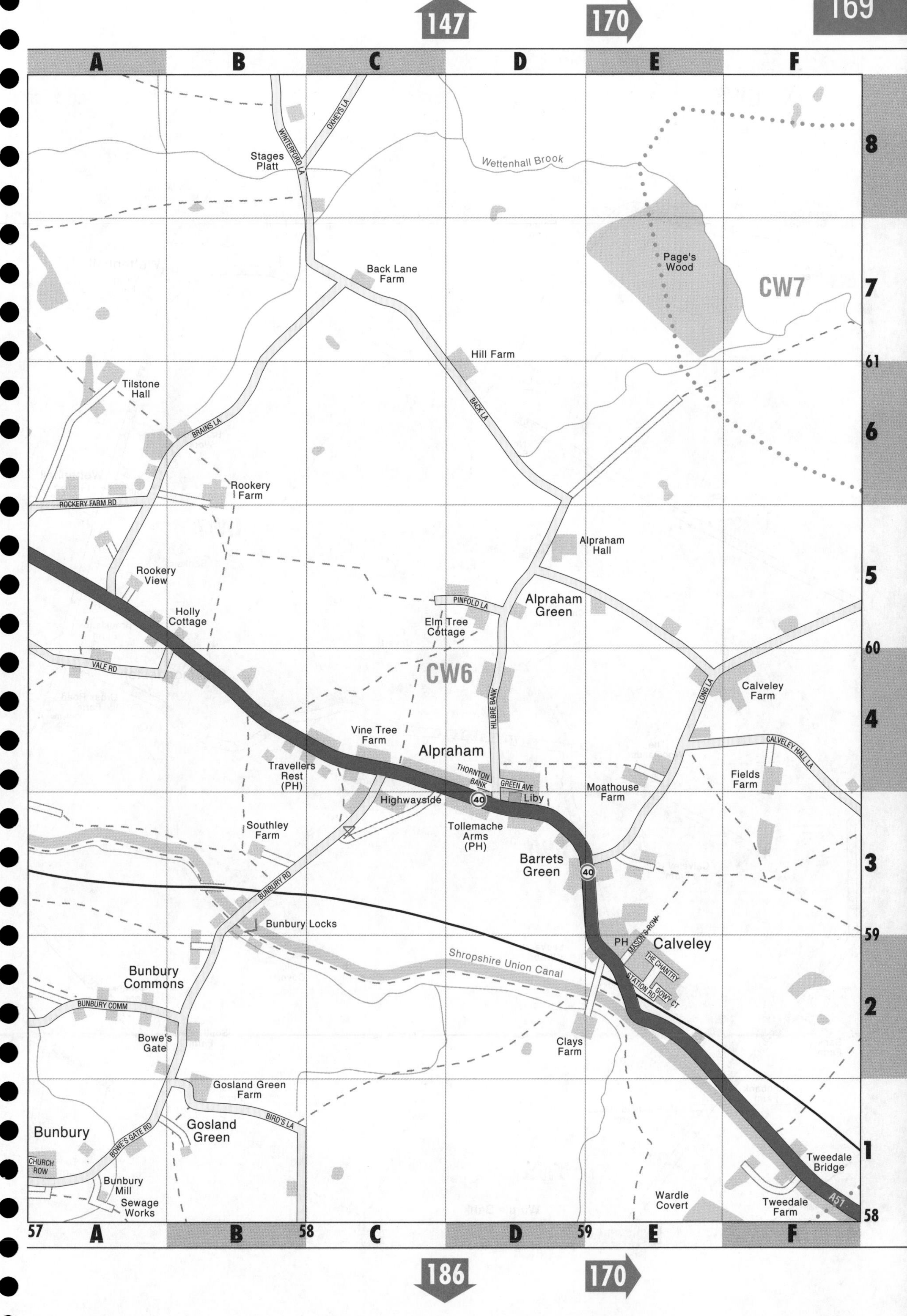

186
170

169
148

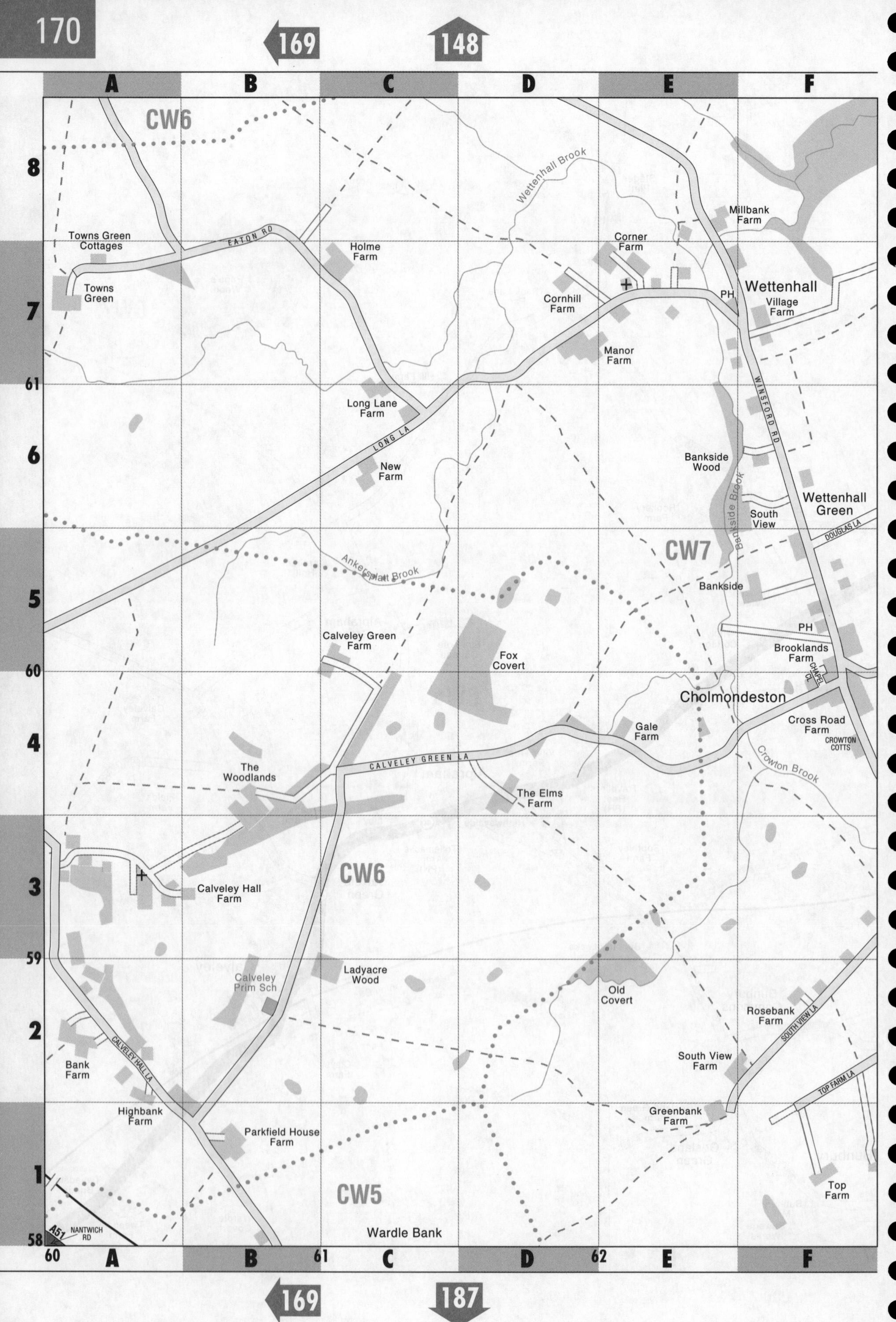

169
187

149
172

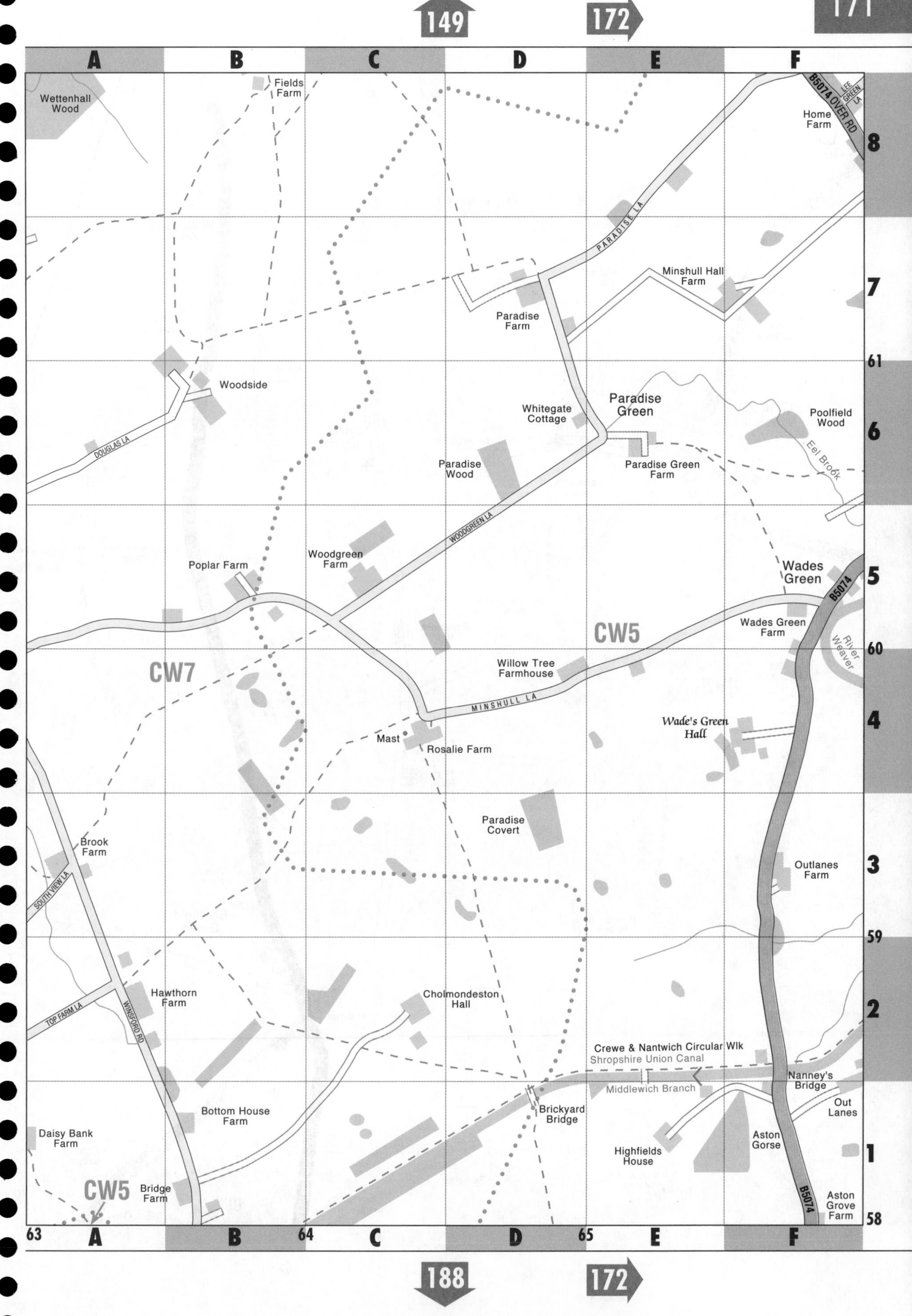
Wettenhall Wood
Fields Farm
Home Farm
B5074 OVER RD
LEE GREEN LA
PARADISE LA
Minshull Hall Farm
Paradise Farm
Woodside
DOUGLAS LA
Whitegate Cottage
Paradise Green
Poolfield Wood
Paradise Wood
Paradise Green Farm
Eel Brook
WOODGREEN LA
Poplar Farm
Woodgreen Farm
Wades Green
B5074
Wades Green Farm
CW5
River Weaver
CW7
Willow Tree Farmhouse
MINSHULL LA
Wade's Green Hall
Mast
Rosalie Farm
Paradise Covert
Brook Farm
SOUTH VIEW LA
Outlanes Farm
Hawthorn Farm
Cholmondeston Hall
TOP FARM LA
WINSFORD RD
Crewe & Nantwich Circular Wlk
Shropshire Union Canal
Nanney's Bridge
Middlewich Branch
Bottom House Farm
Brickyard Bridge
Out Lanes
Daisy Bank Farm
Aston Gorse
Highfields House
CW5
Bridge Farm
B5074
Aston Grove Farm
A B C D E F
8 7 61 6 5 60 4 3 59 2 1 58
63 64 65

188
172

171
150

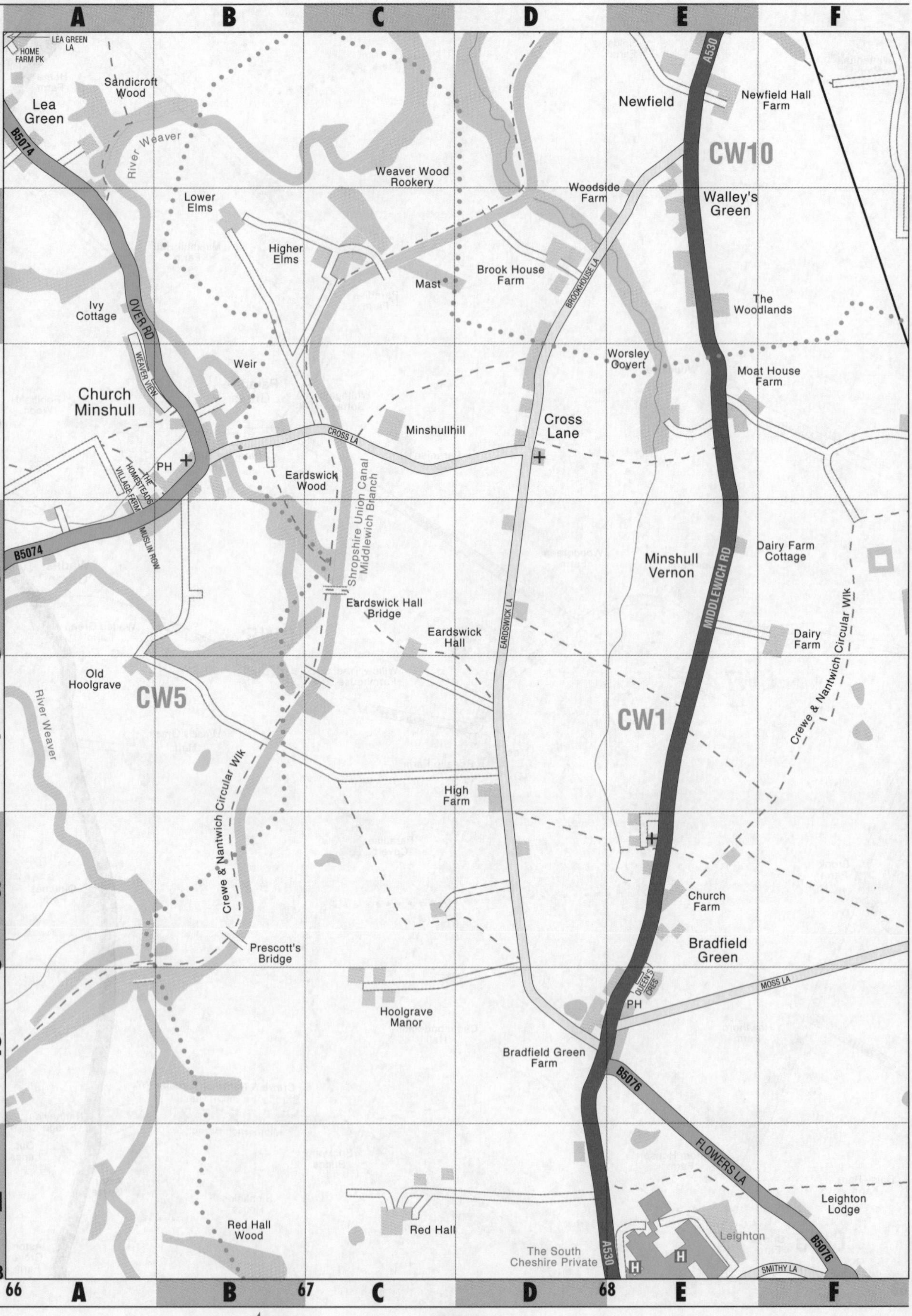

A B C D E F

8 7 61 6 5 60 4 3 59 2 1 58

LEA GREEN LA
HOME FARM PK
Sandicroft Wood
Lea Green
B5074
River Weaver
Lower Elms
Weaver Wood Rookery
Higher Elms
Mast
Brook House Farm
Woodside Farm
Newfield
Newfield Hall Farm
CW10
Walley's Green
A530
BROOKHOUSE LA
The Woodlands
Ivy Cottage
OVER RD
WEAVER VIEW
Weir
Worsley Covert
Moat House Farm
Church Minshull
CROSS LA
Minshullhill
Cross Lane
PH
THE HOMESTEADS
VILLAGE FARM
MUSLIN ROW
Eardswick Wood
Shropshire Union Canal Middlewich Branch
Minshull Vernon
MIDDLEWICH RD
Dairy Farm Cottage
Eardswick Hall Bridge
Eardswick Hall
EARDSWICK LA
Dairy Farm
Crewe & Nantwich Circular Wlk
Old Hoolgrave
CW5
CW1
River Weaver
High Farm
Crewe & Nantwich Circular Wlk
Church Farm
Prescott's Bridge
Bradfield Green
QUEEN'S CRES
MOSS LA
PH
Hoolgrave Manor
Bradfield Green Farm
B5076
FLOWERS LA
Leighton Lodge
Red Hall Wood
Red Hall
The South Cheshire Private
A530
Leighton
H
H
SMITHY LA
B5076

66 A B 67 C D 68 E F

171
189

151
174

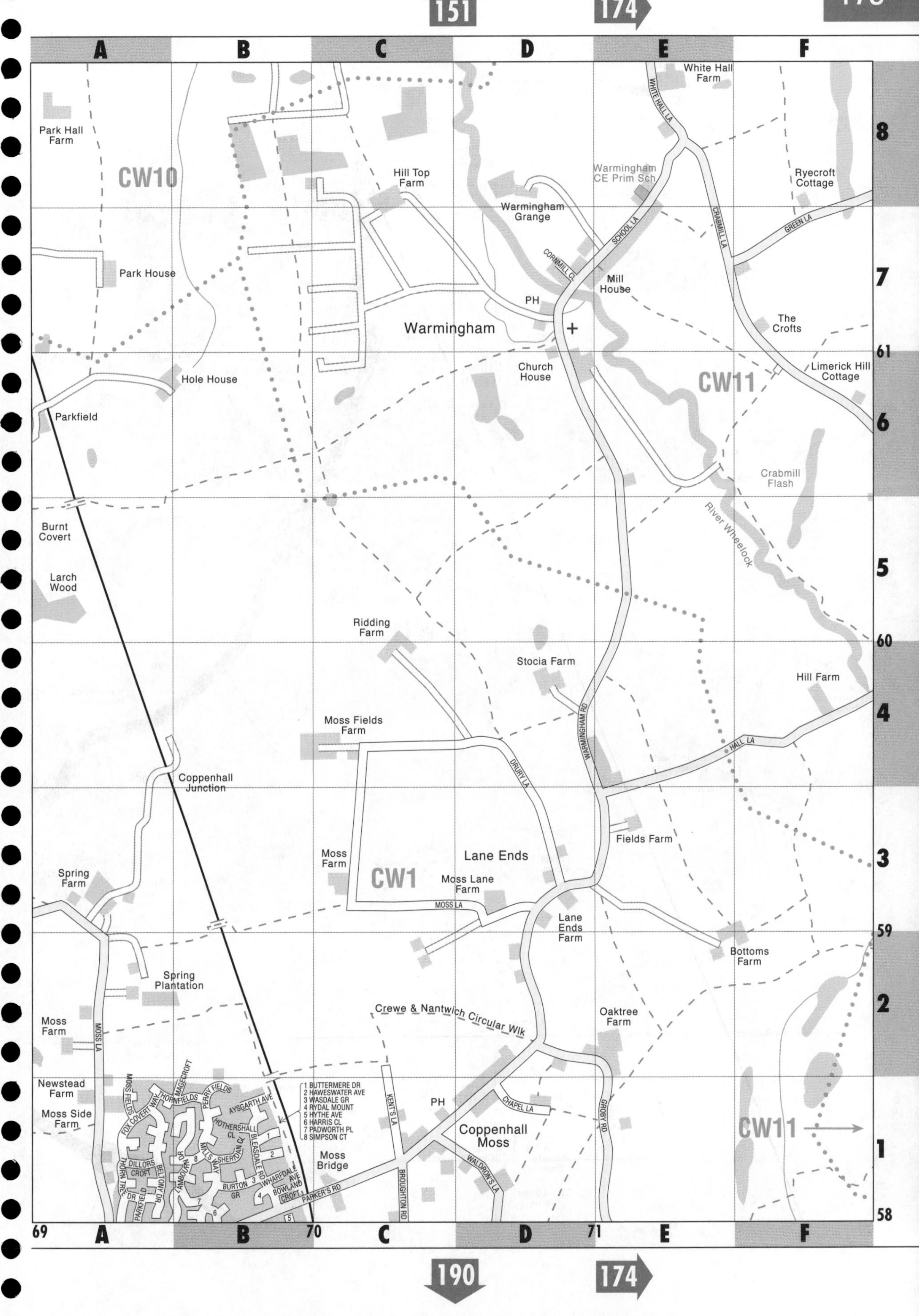
A
B
C
D
E
F
8
7
61
6
5
60
4
3
59
2
1
58
69
70
71
White Hall Farm
WHITE HALL LA
Park Hall Farm
CW10
Hill Top Farm
Warmingham CE Prim Sch
Ryecroft Cottage
Warmingham Grange
SCHOOL LA
CRABMILL LA
GREEN LA
Park House
CORNMILL CL
Mill House
PH
The Crofts
Warmingham
Church House
Limerick Hill Cottage
Hole House
CW11
Parkfield
Crabmill Flash
Burnt Covert
River Wheelock
Larch Wood
Ridding Farm
Stocia Farm
Hill Farm
Moss Fields Farm
WARMINGHAM RD
HALL LA
DRURY LA
Coppenhall Junction
Fields Farm
Moss Farm
Lane Ends
Spring Farm
CW1
Moss Lane Farm
MOSS LA
Lane Ends Farm
Bottoms Farm
Spring Plantation
Crewe & Nantwich Circular Wlk
Oaktree Farm
Moss Farm
MOSS LA
Newstead Farm
Moss Side Farm
MOSS FIELDS
FOX COVERT WAY
HORNFIELDS
MAGECROFT
PERRY FIELDS
AYSGARTH AVE
HOTHERSHALL CL
SHERIDAN CL
MILLS WAY
BLEASDALE RD
DILLORS CROFT
BELTONY DR
THORN TREE DR
PARKFIELD
TAMBOUR CR
BURTON GR
WHARFDALE AVE
BOWLAND CROFT
1 BUTTERMERE DR
2 HAWESWATER AVE
3 WASDALE GR
4 RYDAL MOUNT
5 HYTHE AVE
6 HARRIS CL
7 PADWORTH PL
8 SIMPSON CT
KENT'S LA
PH
CHAPEL LA
GROBY RD
Coppenhall Moss
Moss Bridge
PARKER'S RD
BROUGHTON RD
WALDRON'S LA
CW11

173
152

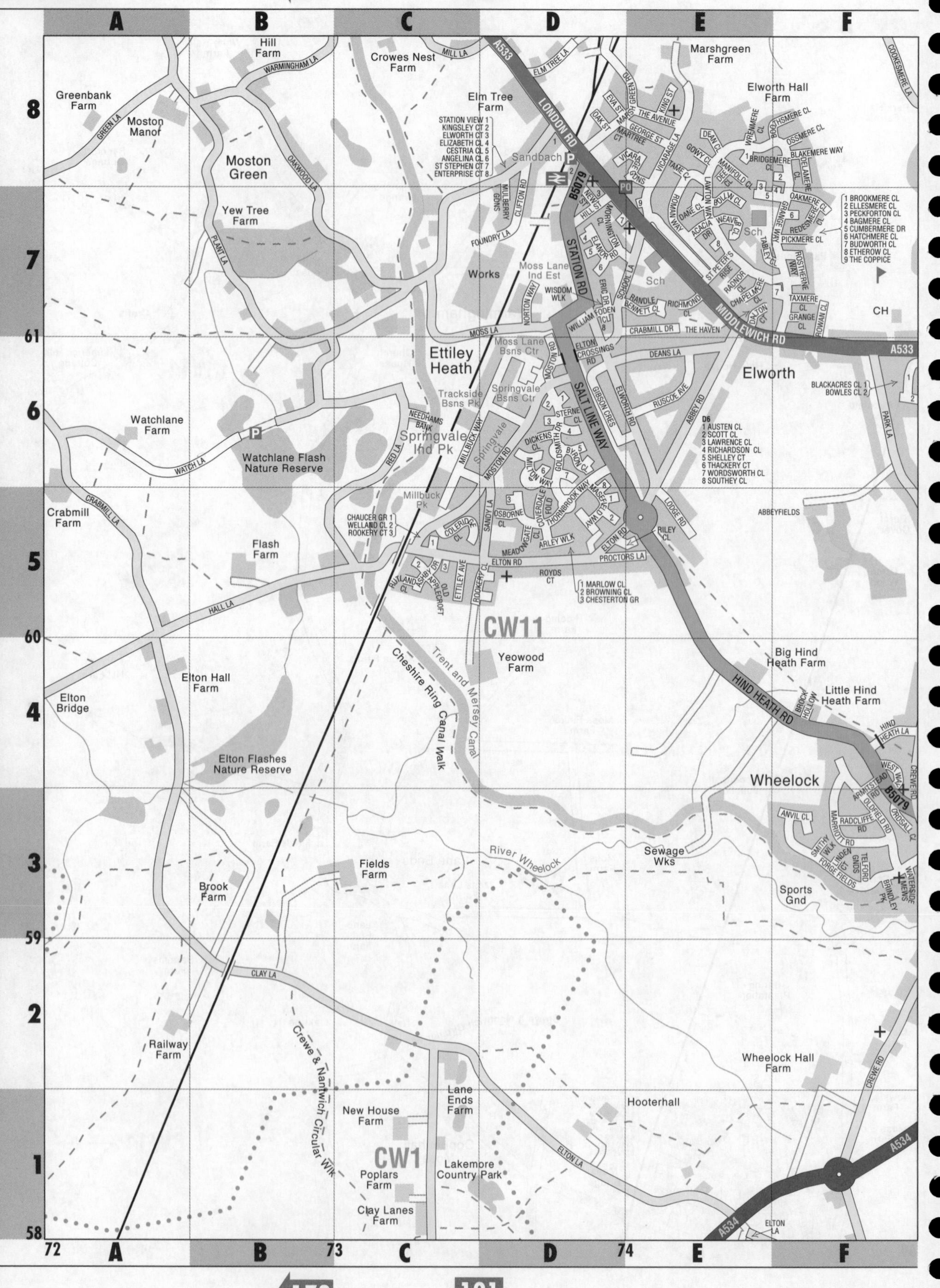

173
191

153
176

B6
1 CECIL RIGBY CL
2 WESLEY AVE
3 CROWN BANK
4 MARKET SQ
5 BROOKHOUSE RD
6 CHESTNUT HO
7 OAK HO
8 ASH HO
9 ELM HO
10 WILLIAM BARKER CT

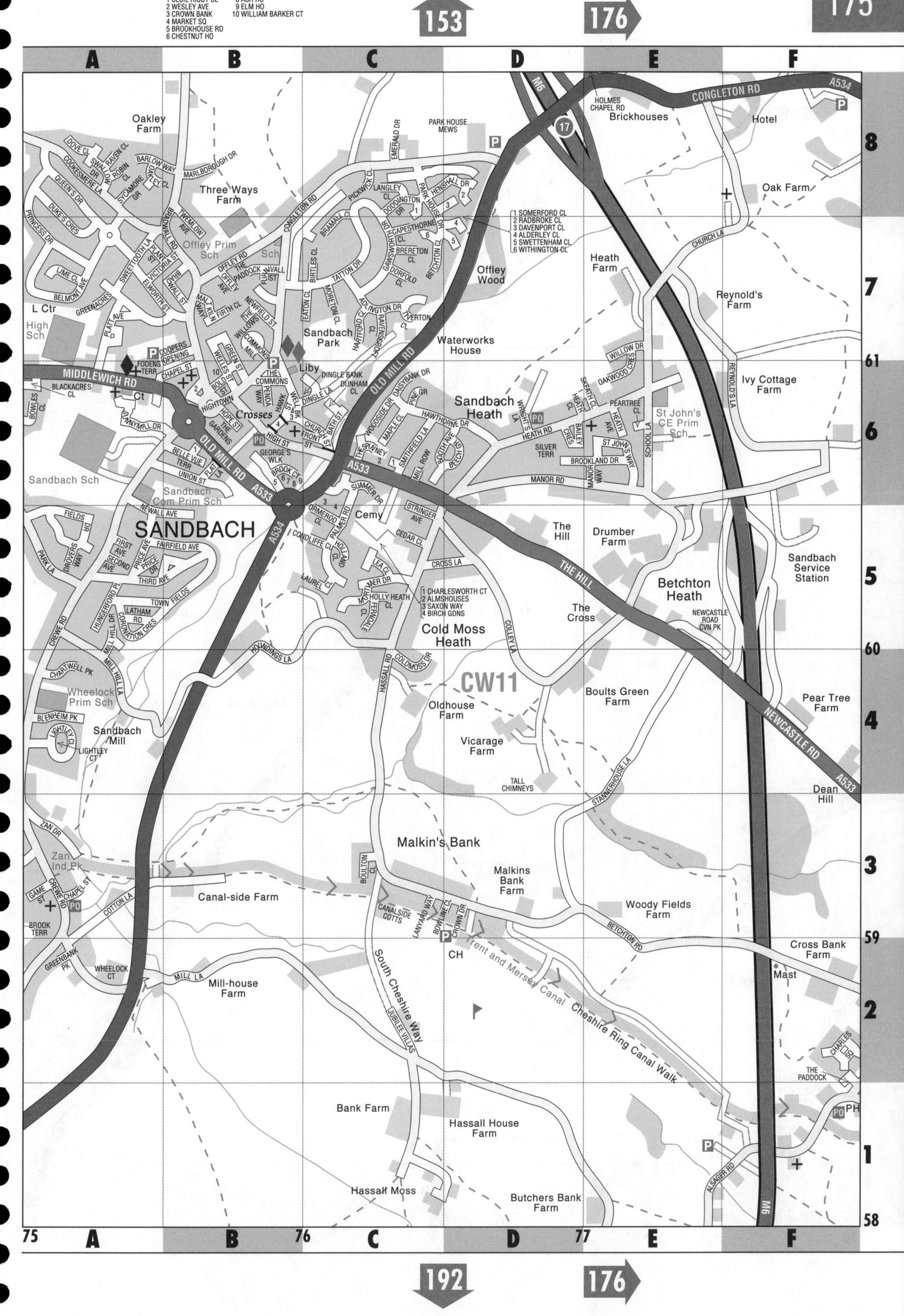

192
176

175
154

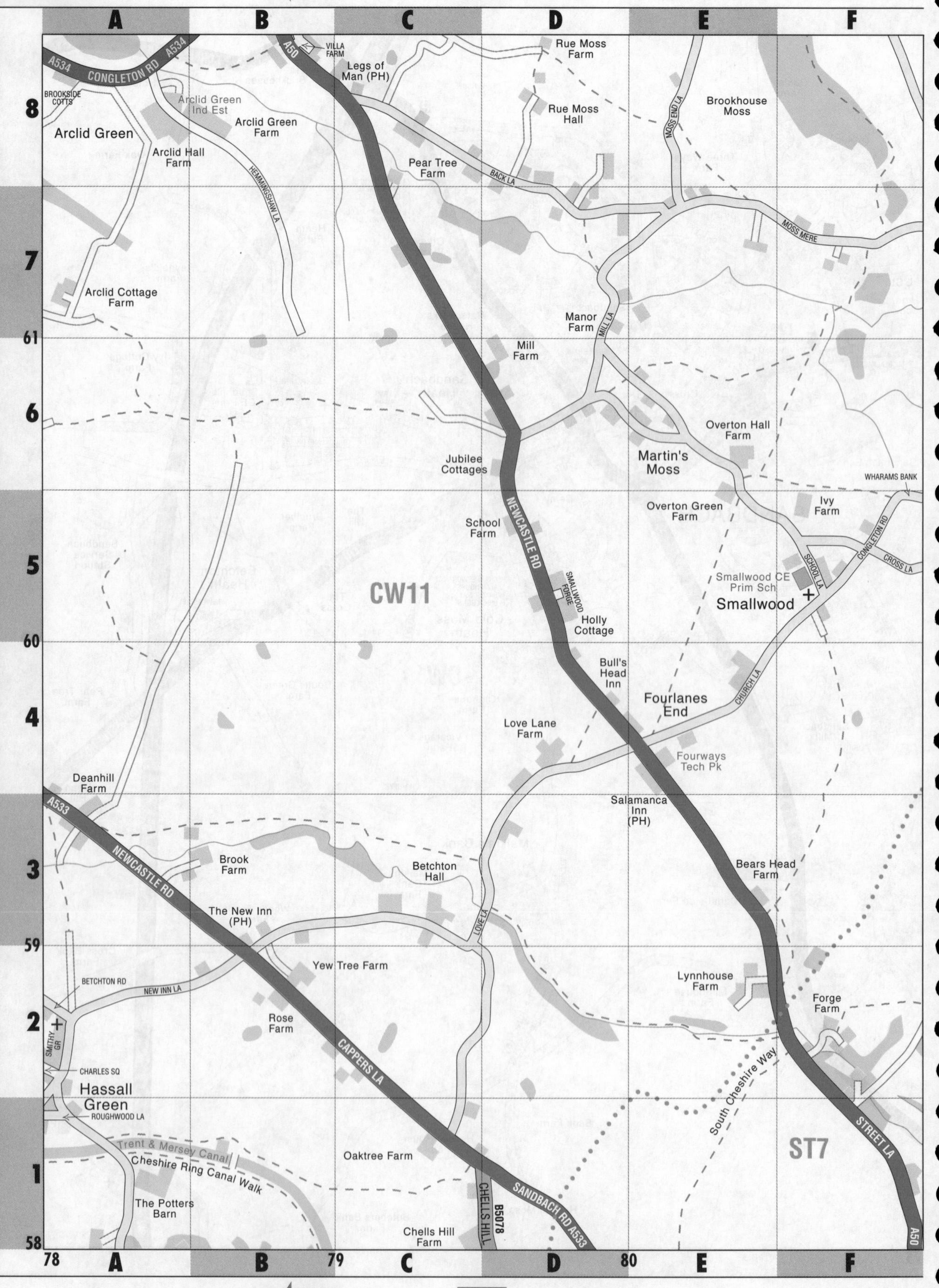

175
193

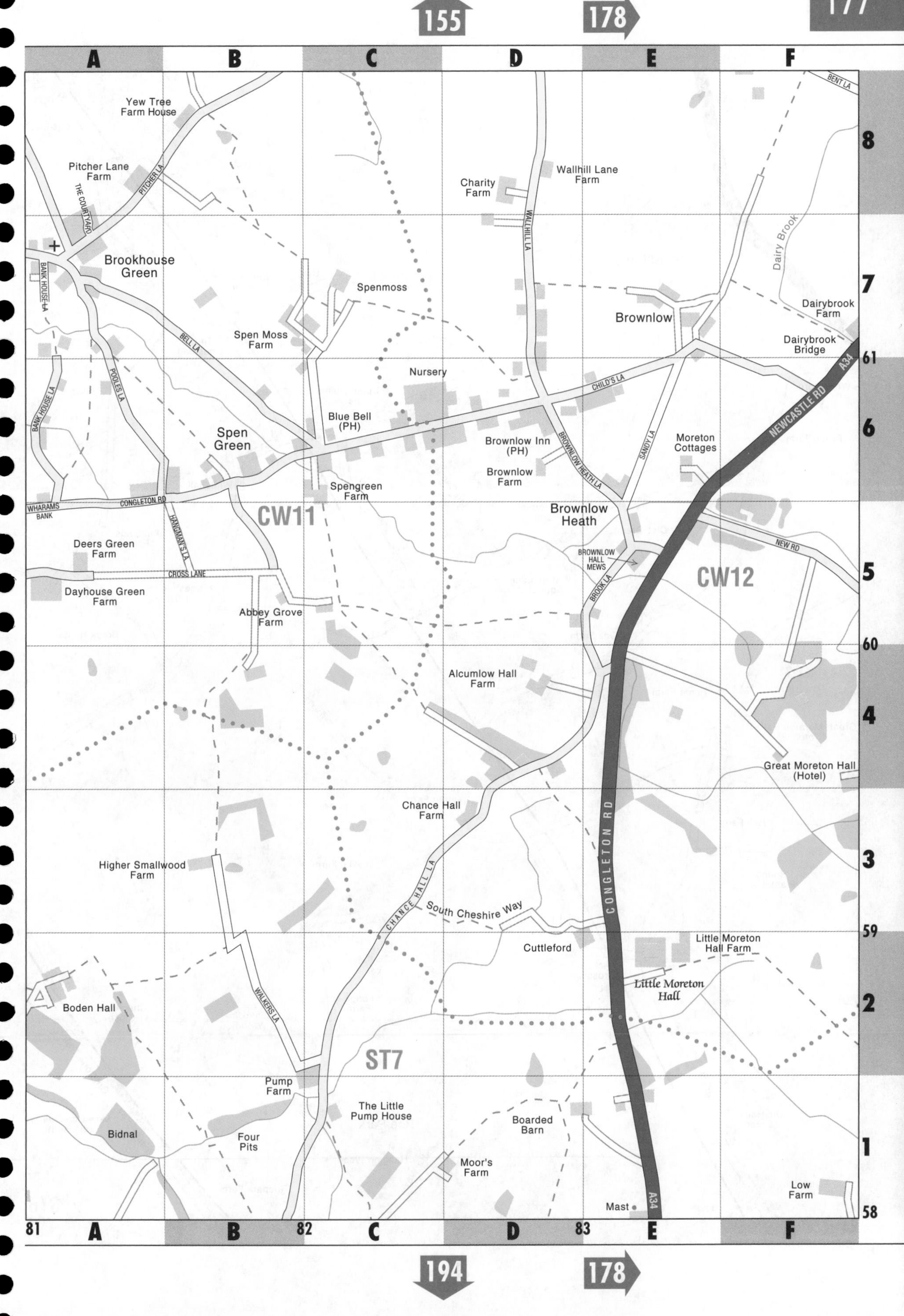
155
178
A
B
C
D
E
F
8
7
6
61
5
60
4
3
59
2
1
58
81
82
83
194
178
Yew Tree
Farm House
Pitcher Lane
Farm
PITCHER LA
THE COURTYARD
Brookhouse
Green
BANK HOUSE LA
Spenmoss
Spen Moss
Farm
BELL LA
POOLES LA
BANK HOUSE LA
Spen
Green
Blue Bell
(PH)
Nursery
Charity
Farm
Wallhill Lane
Farm
WALLHILL LA
Brownlow
Dairy Brook
Dairybrook
Farm
Dairybrook
Bridge
BENT LA
A34
NEWCASTLE RD
CHILD'S LA
Brownlow Inn
(PH)
Brownlow
Farm
BROWNLOW HEATH LA
SANDY LA
Moreton
Cottages
Spengreen
Farm
WHARAMS
BANK
CONGLETON RD
HANGMAN'S LA
CW11
Brownlow
Heath
BROWNLOW
HALL
MEWS
NEW RD
CW12
Deers Green
Farm
CROSS LANE
Dayhouse Green
Farm
Abbey Grove
Farm
BROOK LA
Alcumlow Hall
Farm
Great Moreton Hall
(Hotel)
Chance Hall
Farm
Higher Smallwood
Farm
CHANCE HALL LA
South Cheshire Way
CONGLETON RD
Cuttleford
Little Moreton
Hall Farm
Little Moreton
Hall
Boden Hall
WALKERS LA
ST7
Pump
Farm
The Little
Pump House
Bidnal
Four
Pits
Boarded
Barn
Moor's
Farm
Mast
A34
Low
Farm

A B C D E F

8
7
61
6
5
60
4
3
59
2
1
58

Caravan Park
A34
BENT LA
Astbury St Mary's CE Prim Sch
Brickhouse Farm
Cemy
PH
SCHOOL LA
THE VILLAGE
NEWCASTLE RD
PEEL DR
Astbury
The Howty
LAMBERT'S LA
FALMOUTH RD
TRURO CL
FIELDS RD
APPLETON
NEWQUAY CT
ASTBURY LANE ENDS
LENTHALL AVE
VERNON AVE
CAMBOURNE CL
LINKSWAY
SILVERGATE CT
MOSSLEY CT
PADDOCKS GN
LAMBERT'S LA
THE BRAMBLES
NEWLYN AVE
CANAL RD
CROSS LA
LEEK RD
CEDAR CT
BRADBURY GDNS 1
RUSSELL CL 2
MOSS RD
PEEL LA
Peel Farm
CH
Weld House Farm
Dubthorn
The Homestead
Whitethorn
DODDS LA
Bank Farm
Upper Hulme Farm
Brook Farm
CW12
Cheshire Ring Canal Walk
Macclesfield Canal
Whitehall
Mill House Farm
Ciss Green
WATERY LA
GORSE LA
Fairfields Farm
Watery Lane Aqueduct
Tenement Farm
Horseshoe Inn (PH)
PUDDLE BANK LA
Oak Farm
OAK LA
Brook House
Home Farm
MOW LA
FENCE LA
Great Moreton Hall (Hotel)
NEW RD
WHARF LA
Baytree Farm
Hall Farm
Limekiln Farm
Round Plantation
YEW TREE LA
Ackers Crossing LC
Lodge Farm
Limekiln Wood
Cheshire's Close
Wood Farm
ST7
STATION RD
South Cheshire Way
ROE PARK
CONGLETON RD
Gritstone Trail
Staffordshire Way
Old House Green
Roe Park
Hanging Wood
Mow Cop Quarry (disused)
Ramsdell Hall
LC
DRUMBER LA
Roepark Farm
ST8

84 A B 85 C D 86 E F

157

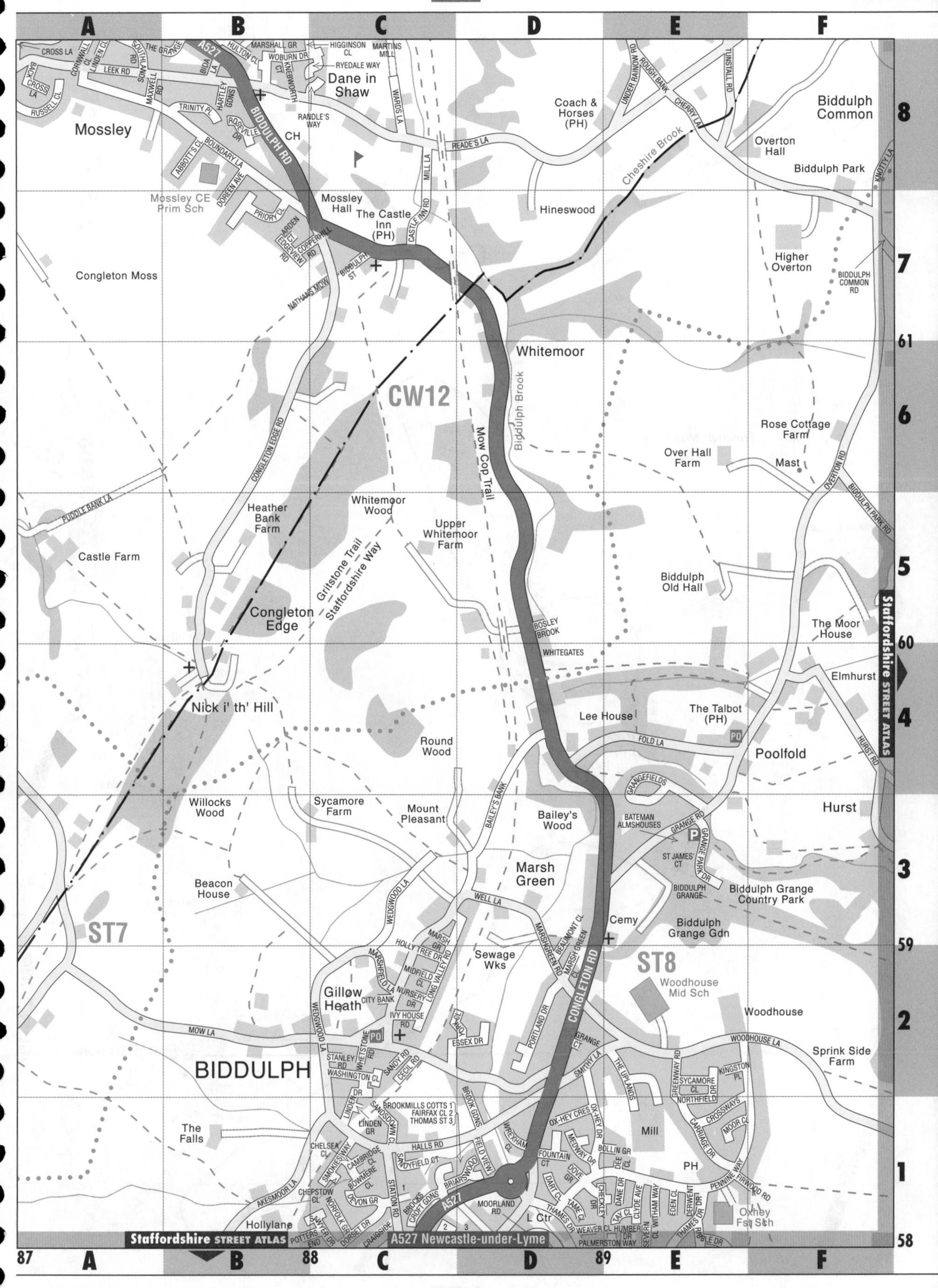

Mossley
Mossley CE Prim Sch
Dane in Shaw
Congleton Moss
Mossley Hall
The Castle Inn (PH)
Coach & Horses (PH)
Hineswood
Biddulph Common
Overton Hall
Biddulph Park
Higher Overton
Whitemoor
CW12
Rose Cottage Farm
Over Hall Farm
Mast
Heather Bank Farm
Whitemoor Wood
Upper Whitemoor Farm
Castle Farm
Biddulph Old Hall
Congleton Edge
Gritstone Trail
Staffordshire Way
Mow Cop Trail
Biddulph Brook
Cheshire Brook
The Moor House
Elmhurst
Nick i' th' Hill
Lee House
The Talbot (PH)
Round Wood
Poolfold
Willocks Wood
Sycamore Farm
Mount Pleasant
Bailey's Wood
Hurst
Biddulph Grange Country Park
Beacon House
Marsh Green
Cemy
Biddulph Grange Gdn
ST7
Sewage Wks
ST8
Woodhouse Mid Sch
Gillow Heath
Woodhouse
BIDDULPH
Sprink Side Farm
The Falls
Mill
PH
Hollylane
L Ctr
Oxhey Fst Sch
A527
BIDDULPH RD
CONGLETON RD
CONGLETON EDGE RD
MOW LA
WOODHOUSE LA
FOLD LA
READE'S LA
WELL LA
A527 Newcastle-under-Lyme
Staffordshire STREET ATLAS

163

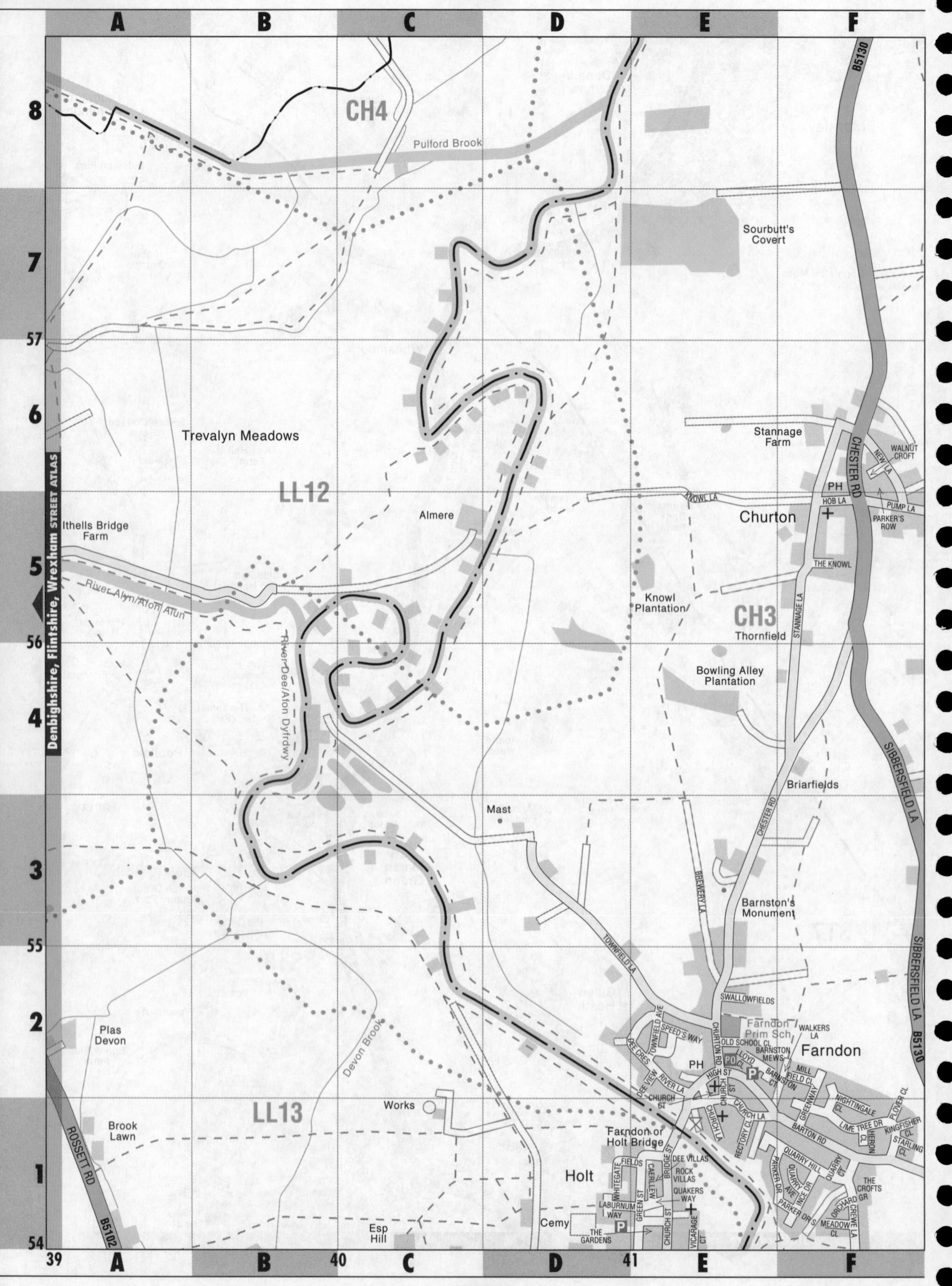

A
B
C
D
E
F
8
7
57
6
5
56
4
3
55
2
1
54
39
40
41
CH4
Pulford Brook
Sourbutt's Covert
B5130
Trevalyn Meadows
LL12
Almere
Stannage Farm
Walnut Croft
New La
PH
Hob La
Pump La
Knowl La
Churton
Parker's Row
Chester Rd
Ithells Bridge Farm
The Knowl
River Alyn/Afon Alun
River Dee/Afon Dyfrdwy
Knowl Plantation
CH3
Thornfield
Stannage La
Bowling Alley Plantation
Briarfields
Sibbersfield La
Mast
Brewery La
Barnston's Monument
Townfield La
Swallowfields
Farndon Prim Sch
Walkers La
Plas Devon
Speed's Way
Townfield Ave
Churton Rd
Old School Cl
Barnston Mews
Farndon
Dee Cres
PH
High St
Lloyd Cl
Barnston Ct
Mill Field Cl
Dee View
River La
Church St
Church
Greenway
Nightingale Cl
Plover Cl
Devon Brook
LL13
Works
Church La
Barton Rd
Lime Tree Dr
Kingfisher Cl
Brook Lawn
Farndon or Holt Bridge
Rectory Cl
Heron Cl
Starling Cl
Dee Villas
Quarry Hill
Rossett Rd
Whitegate Way
Fields
Bridge St
Rock Villas
Parker Dr
Quarry Ave
Quarry Ct
The Crofts
Holt
Caerlew
Quakers Way
Inch Dr
Orchard Gr
Laburnum Way
Green St
Church St
Parker Dr S
Crewe La
Cemy
Vicarage Ct
Meadow Cl
Esp Hill
The Gardens
B5102
Denbighshire, Flintshire, Wrexham STREET ATLAS

196

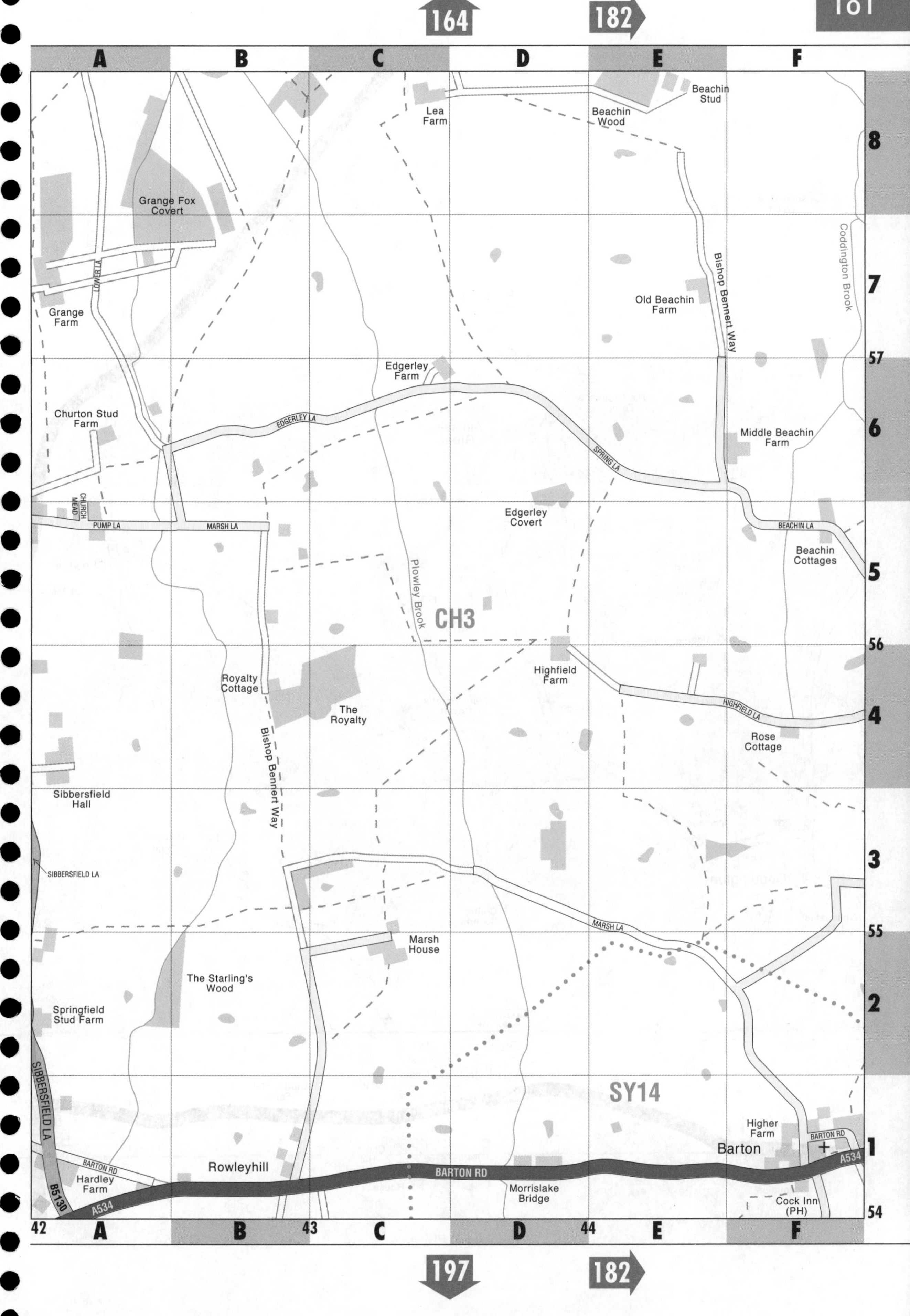
164
182
A
B
C
D
E
F
Lea Farm
Beachin Wood
Beachin Stud
8
Grange Fox Covert
LOWER LA
Grange Farm
Bishop Bennert Way
Coddington Brook
7
Old Beachin Farm
57
Edgerley Farm
Churton Stud Farm
EDGERLEY LA
Middle Beachin Farm
6
SPRING LA
CHURCH MEAD
PUMP LA
MARSH LA
Edgerley Covert
BEACHIN LA
Beachin Cottages
5
Plowley Brook
CH3
56
Royalty Cottage
Highfield Farm
The Royalty
HIGHFIELD LA
4
Rose Cottage
Bishop Bennert Way
Sibbersfield Hall
3
SIBBERSFIELD LA
MARSH LA
55
Marsh House
The Starling's Wood
Springfield Stud Farm
2
SY14
SIBBERSFIELD LA
Higher Farm
BARTON RD
1
Barton
A534
Rowleyhill
BARTON RD
BARTON RD
Hardley Farm
B5130
A534
Morrislake Bridge
Cock Inn (PH)
54
42
43
44
197
182

181
165

181
198

166

184

A B C D E F

EDGECROFT
The Righi
ROCKY LA
WORLEY CT
Worley Rise
Barrow Fork Plantation
BIRDS LA
Newtown
Cooloo Farm
CARRS LA
8
Woodlake Farm
Goshen Spinney
BURWARDSLEY RD
PLATTS LA
WOODSFIN LA
Windmill Farm
DARK LA
7
BOLESWORTH RD
Goshen Lodge
57
Dragon Hall
Oakbank Farm
Coach Drive
6
Miller's Plantation
Royal Plantation
Oaklea Plantation
The Kopje
Hatchet
GREEN LA
5
Chowley Lodge
CH3
Mickerra Farm
56
Bolesworth Castle
Burwardsley Hill
Bolesworth Hill Farm
Bolesworth Lake Farm
HARTHILL LA
Cawley's Wood
4
WHITCHURCH RD
Harthill Coombs
BOLESWORTH HILL RD
Bodnook Wood
COACH RD
Harthill
Harthill Prim Sch
Poultry Farm
THE GREEN
GARDEN LA
Harthill Pool
3
Barnhill Wood
BARNHILL GRANGE
Bankhead Farm
NEW LA
Newlane Farm
55
PADGE LA
Barnhill Wood
Raw Head
Sandstone Trail
OLD COACH RD
Park Wood
2
Bankhead Farm
The Moss
Barnhill
BARNHILL RD
Musket's Hole
Broxton
Moss Farm House
Fullersmoor Farm
BROXTON MEWS
Durham Heifer Inn (PH)
NANTWICH RD
SY14
OLD COACH RD
1
Coomb Dale
Hotel
HILL LA
Fuller's Moor
SMITHY LA
SHERRINGTON'S LA
PH
SALTER'S LA
IVY FARM LA
A534
54

48 A B 49 C D 50 E F

199
184

183
167

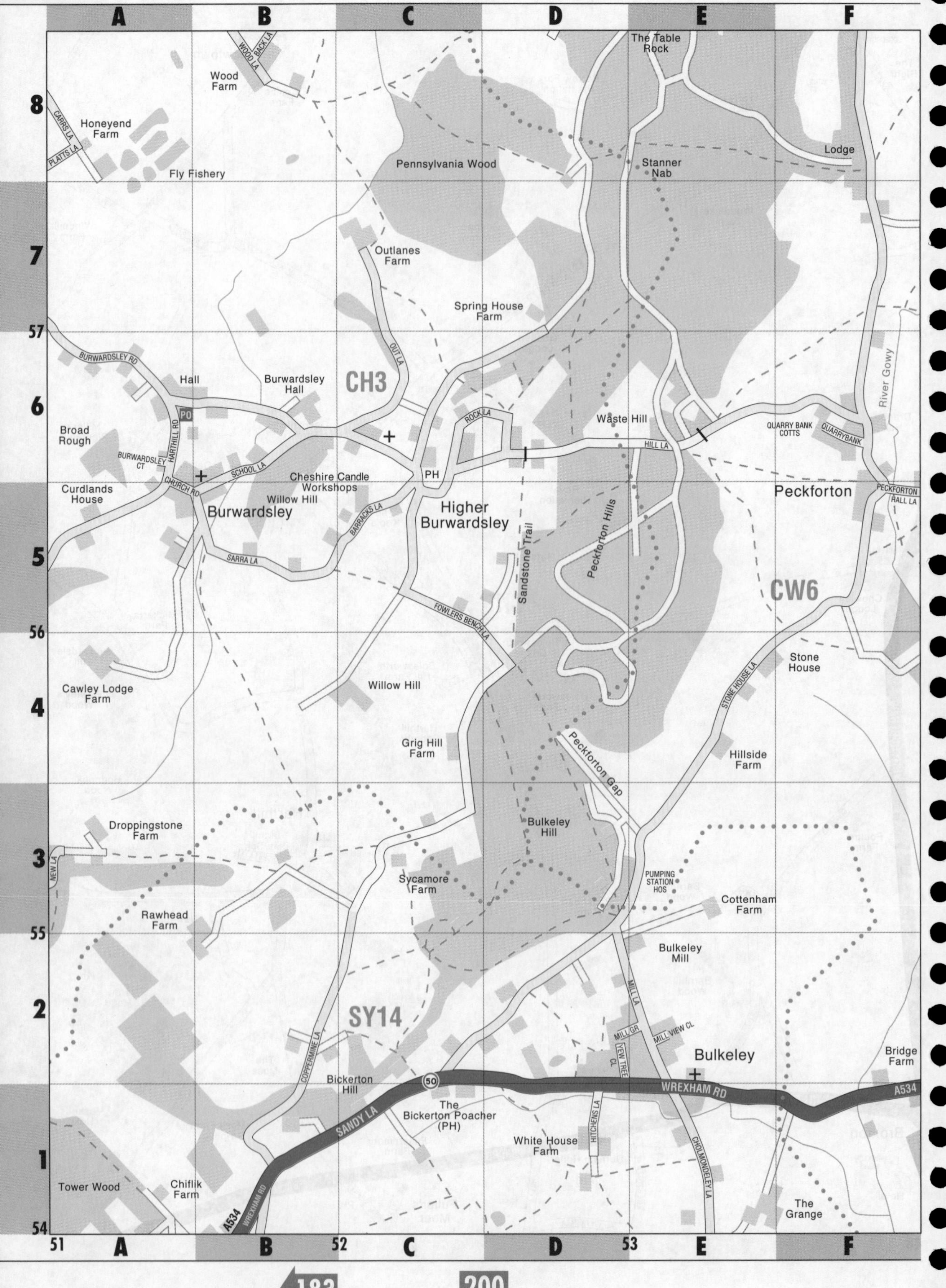

183
200

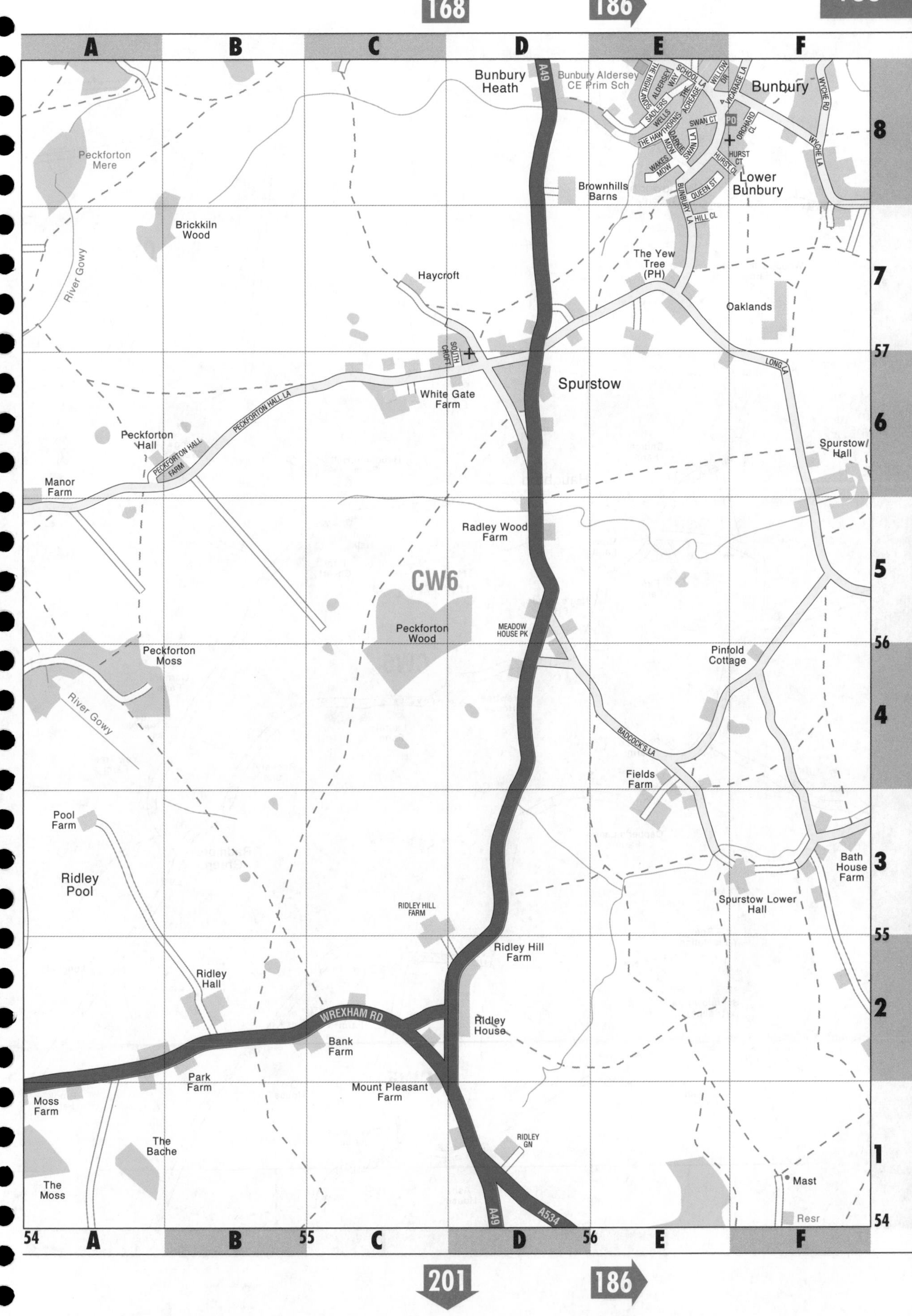
168
186
A
B
C
D
E
F
Bunbury Heath
Bunbury Aldersey CE Prim Sch
Bunbury
Lower Bunbury
Peckforton Mere
Brickkiln Wood
Brownhills Barns
River Gowy
The Yew Tree (PH)
Haycroft
Oaklands
SOUTH CROFT
LONG LA
Spurstow
White Gate Farm
PECKFORTON HALL LA
Peckforton Hall
PECKFORTON HALL FARM
Manor Farm
Spurstow Hall
Radley Wood Farm
CW6
Peckforton Wood
MEADOW HOUSE PK
Pinfold Cottage
Peckforton Moss
River Gowy
BADCOCK'S LA
Fields Farm
Pool Farm
Ridley Pool
Bath House Farm
Spurstow Lower Hall
RIDLEY HILL FARM
Ridley Hill Farm
Ridley Hall
WREXHAM RD
Ridley House
Bank Farm
Park Farm
Mount Pleasant Farm
Moss Farm
The Bache
RIDLEY GN
Mast
The Moss
Resr
A49
A534
WYCHE RD
WYCHE LA
SCHOOL LA
WILLOW DR
VICARAGE LA
ORCHARD CL
SWAN CT
SWAN LA
HURST CT
HURST CL
QUEEN ST
HILL CL
BUNBURY LA
WAKES MDW
THE HAWTHORNS
THE ACREAGE
ALDERSEY WAY
SADLERS WELLS
THE HIGHLANDS
DARKIE MDW
PO
8
7
57
6
5
56
4
3
55
2
1
54
54
55
56
201
186

185
169

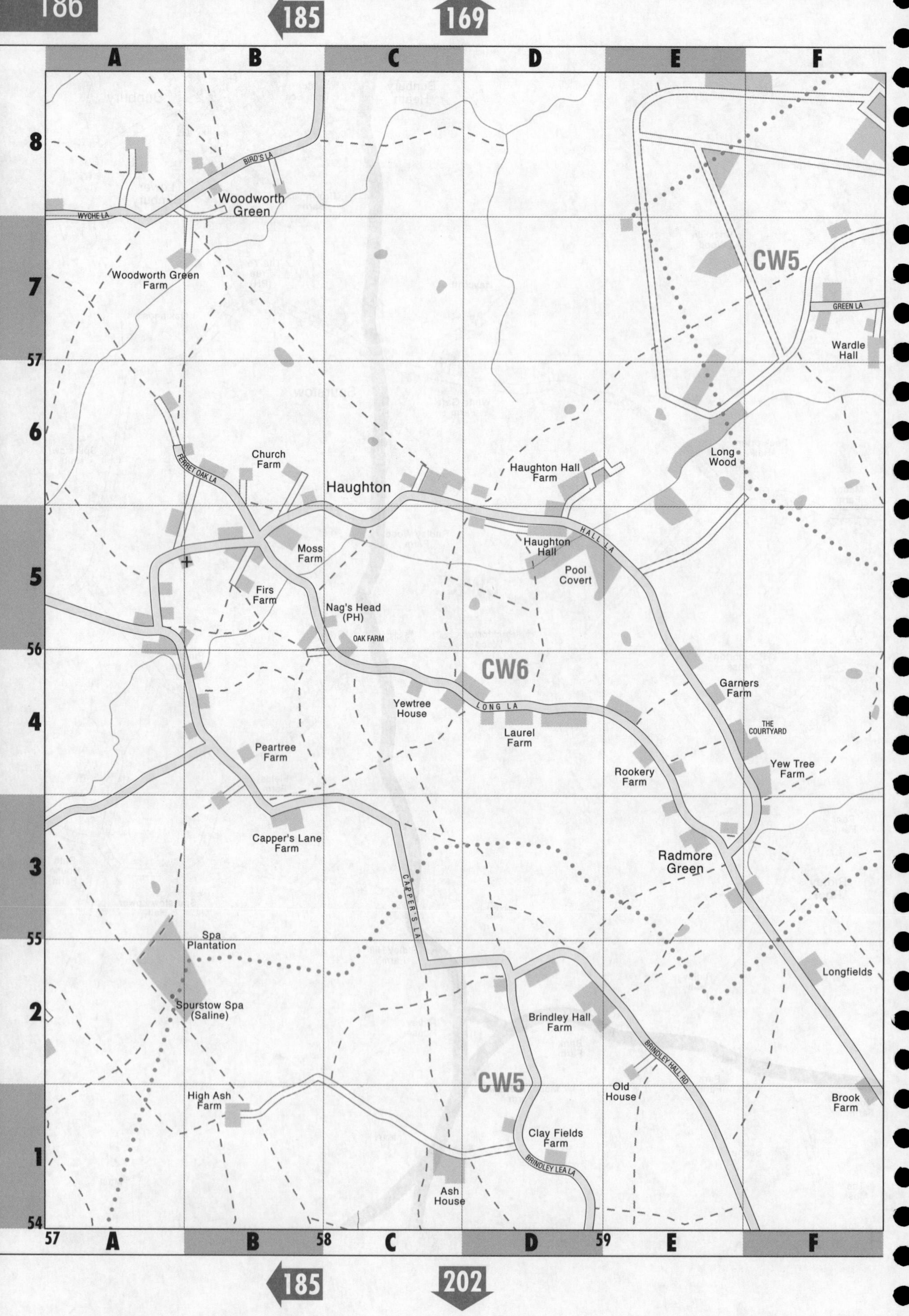

185
202

170
188

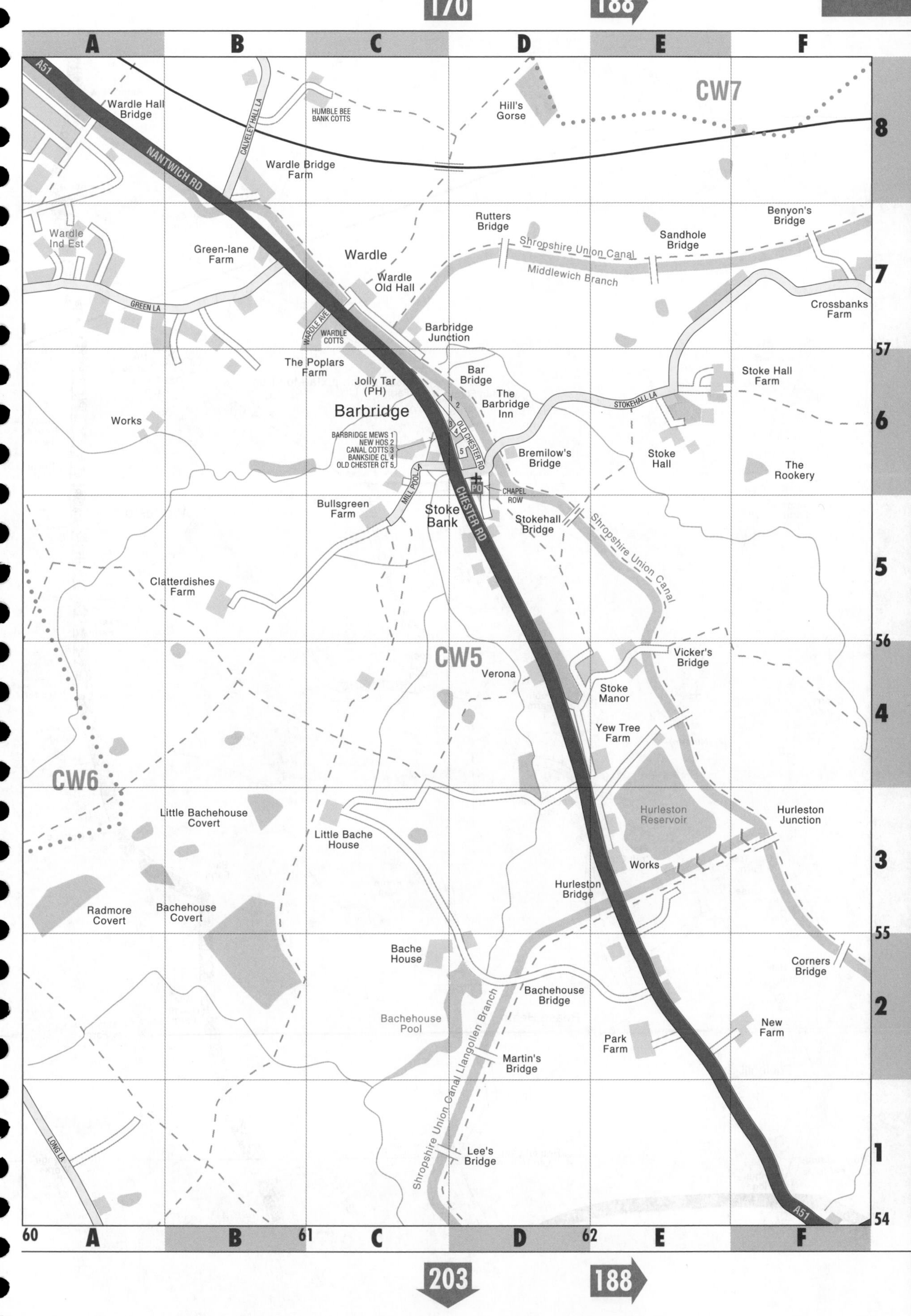

203
188

187
171

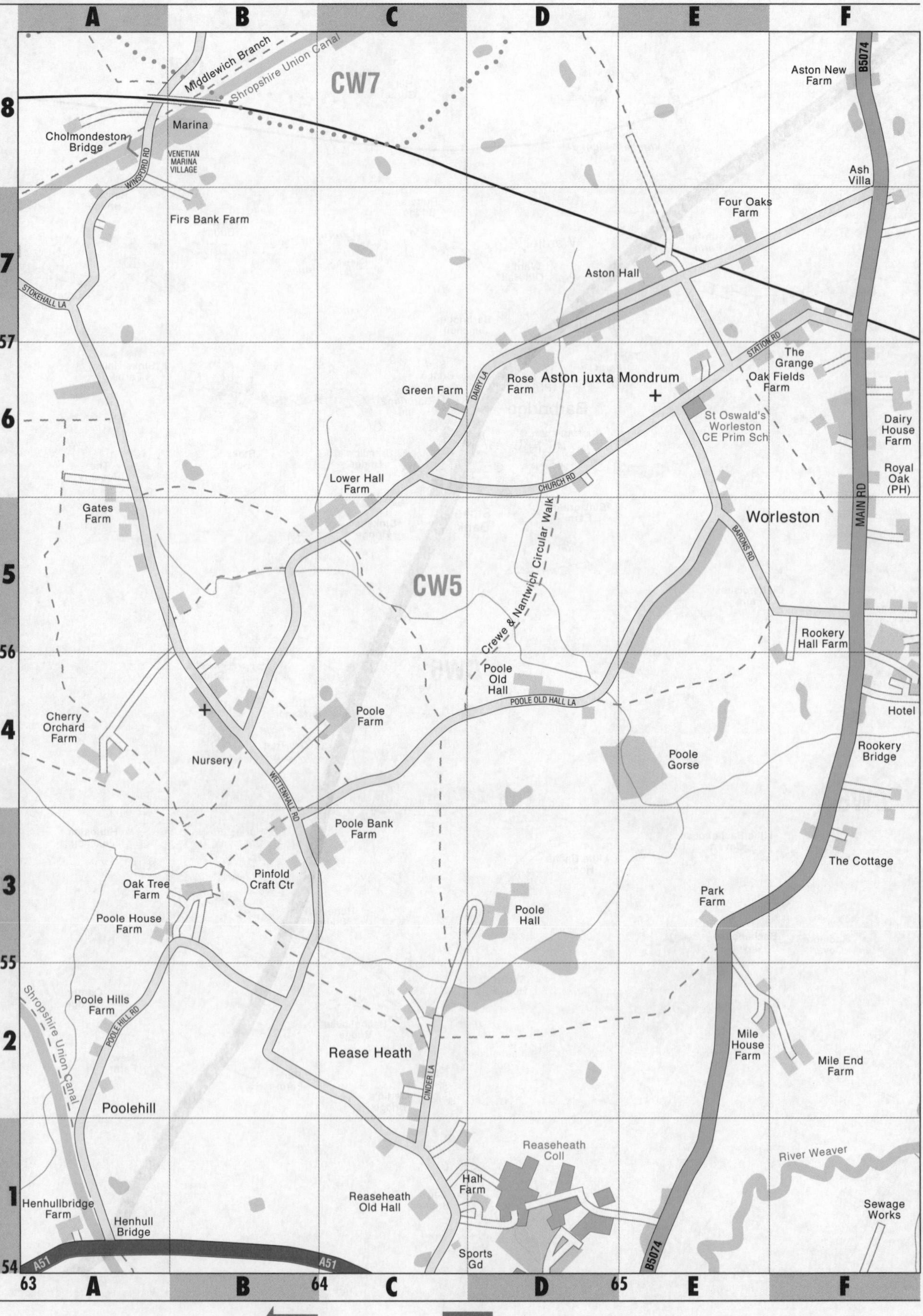
A
B
C
D
E
F
8
7
57
6
5
56
4
3
55
2
1
54
63
64
65
CW7
CW5
Middlewich Branch
Shropshire Union Canal
Marina
Cholmondeston Bridge
VENETIAN MARINA VILLAGE
WINSFORD RD
Firs Bank Farm
STOKEHALL LA
Aston New Farm
B5074
Ash Villa
Four Oaks Farm
Aston Hall
The Grange
Oak Fields Farm
STATION RD
Aston juxta Mondrum
Rose Farm
Green Farm
DAIRY LA
St Oswald's Worleston CE Prim Sch
Dairy House Farm
Royal Oak (PH)
CHURCH RD
Lower Hall Farm
Gates Farm
Worleston
BARONS RD
MAIN RD
Crewe & Nantwich Circular Walk
Rookery Hall Farm
Poole Old Hall
POOLE OLD HALL LA
Hotel
Cherry Orchard Farm
Poole Farm
Nursery
Poole Gorse
Rookery Bridge
WETTENHALL RD
Poole Bank Farm
The Cottage
Pinfold Craft Ctr
Oak Tree Farm
Poole House Farm
Poole Hall
Park Farm
Poole Hills Farm
Shropshire Union Canal
POOLE HILL RD
Rease Heath
CINDER LA
Mile House Farm
Mile End Farm
Poolehill
Reaseheath Coll
River Weaver
Henhullbridge Farm
Reaseheath Old Hall
Hall Farm
Sewage Works
Henhull Bridge
Sports Gd
A51
B5074

172
190

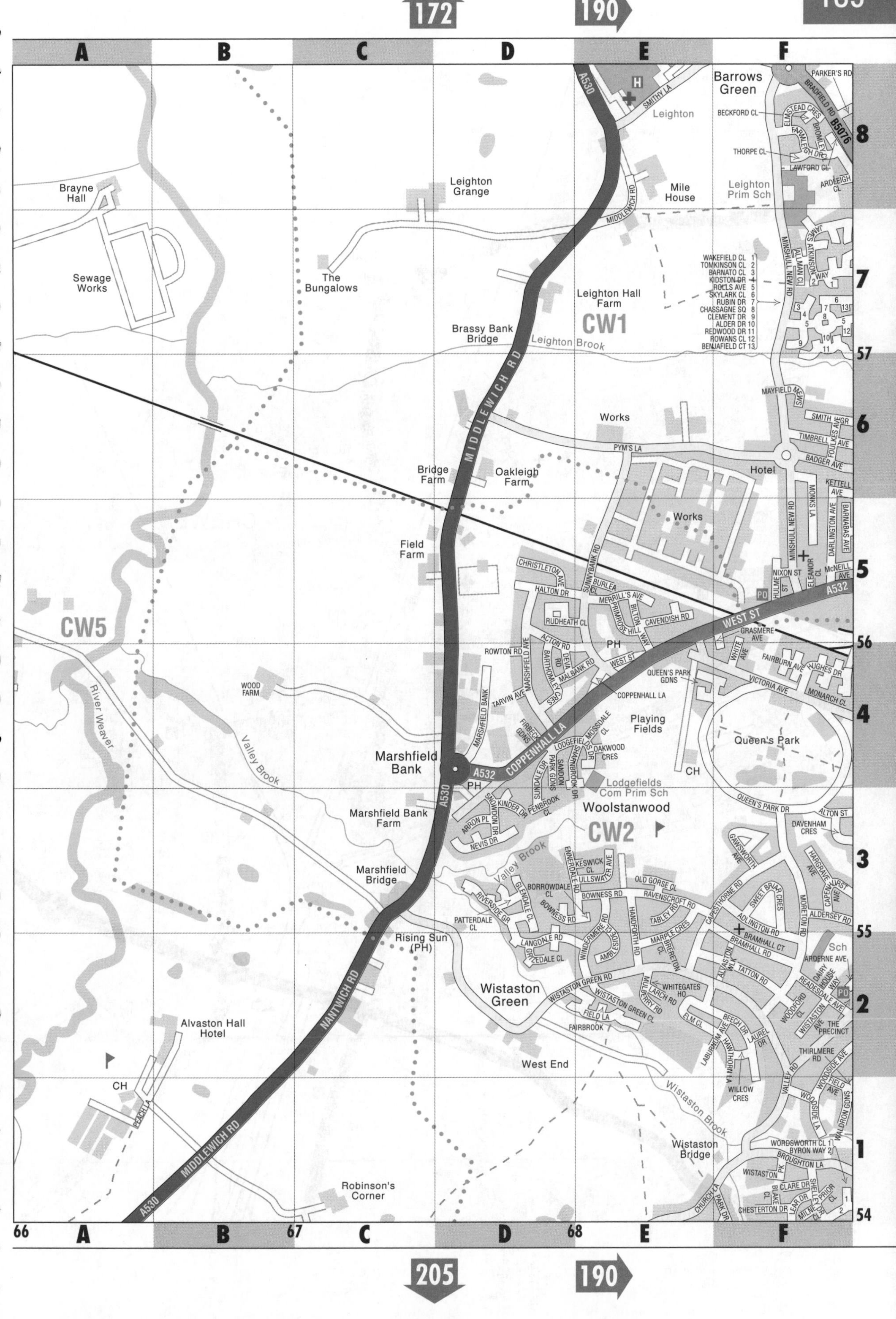

205
190

189
173

CREWE

CW1

CW2

Coppenhall

Maw Green

Sydney Bridge

The Valley

Tipkinder Park

Crewe Mill Bridge

Crewe

B5
1 PEEL SQ
2 RAMSBOTTOM ST
3 LINCOLN ST
4 SADE CT
5 RIGG ST
6 EARDLEY CT
7 PETER PL
8 COMBERMERE PL
9 OAKMERE PL
10 ELLESMERE PL
11 LEIGHTON ST
12 GROSVENOR CT
13 GODDARD CT
14 NOVA CT

C4
1 CASTLE ST
2 STANLEY ST
3 VICTORIA CT
4 CHARLES ST
5 ROYAL ARC
6 HIGHTOWN APPTS
7 DELAMERE CT

D2
1 WAVERLEY CT
2 ABBEYFIELD HO
3 ARTHUR ST
4 LONGFORD ST
5 BROADY CT

189
206

174
192

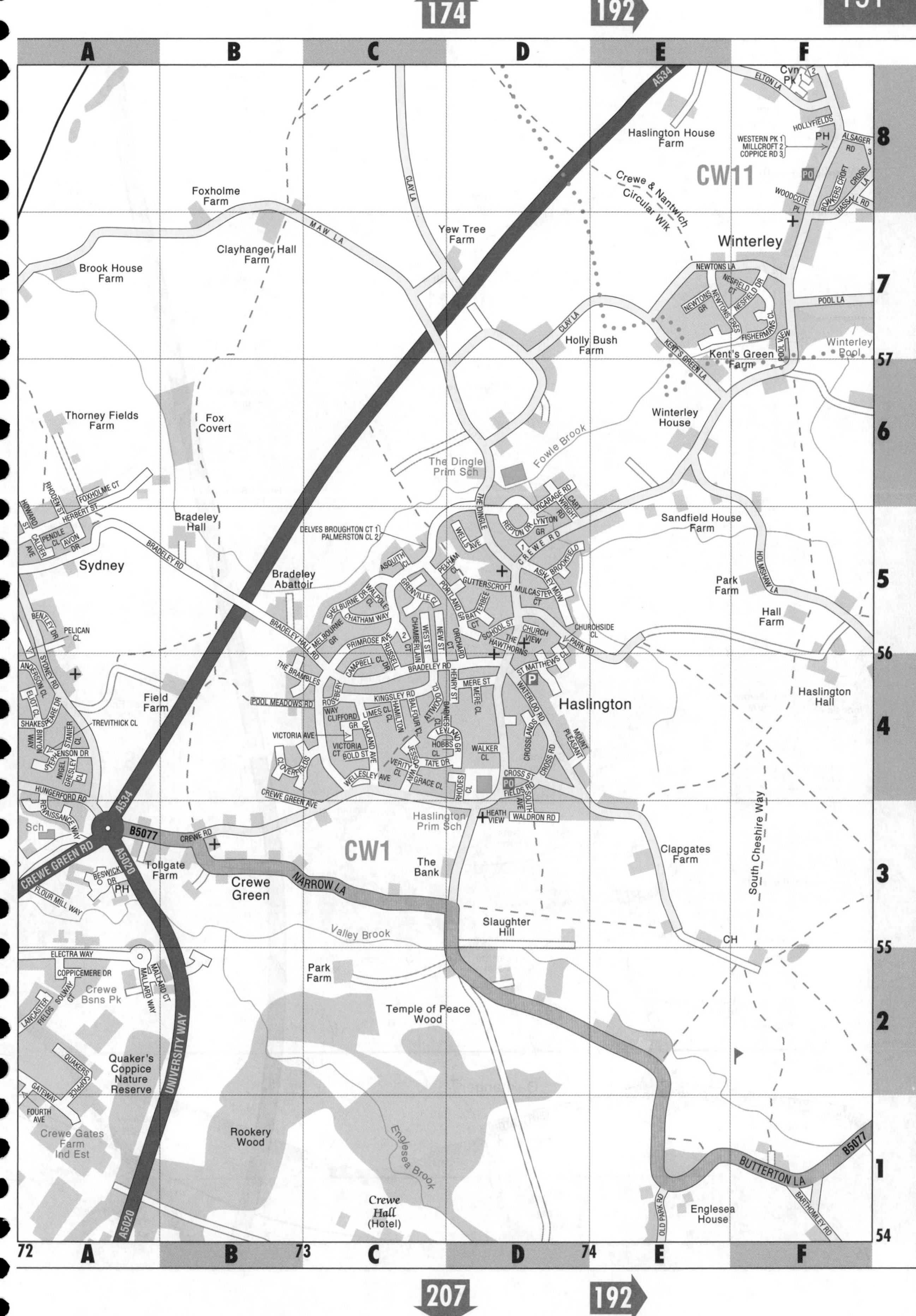

207
192

191
175

191
208

176
194

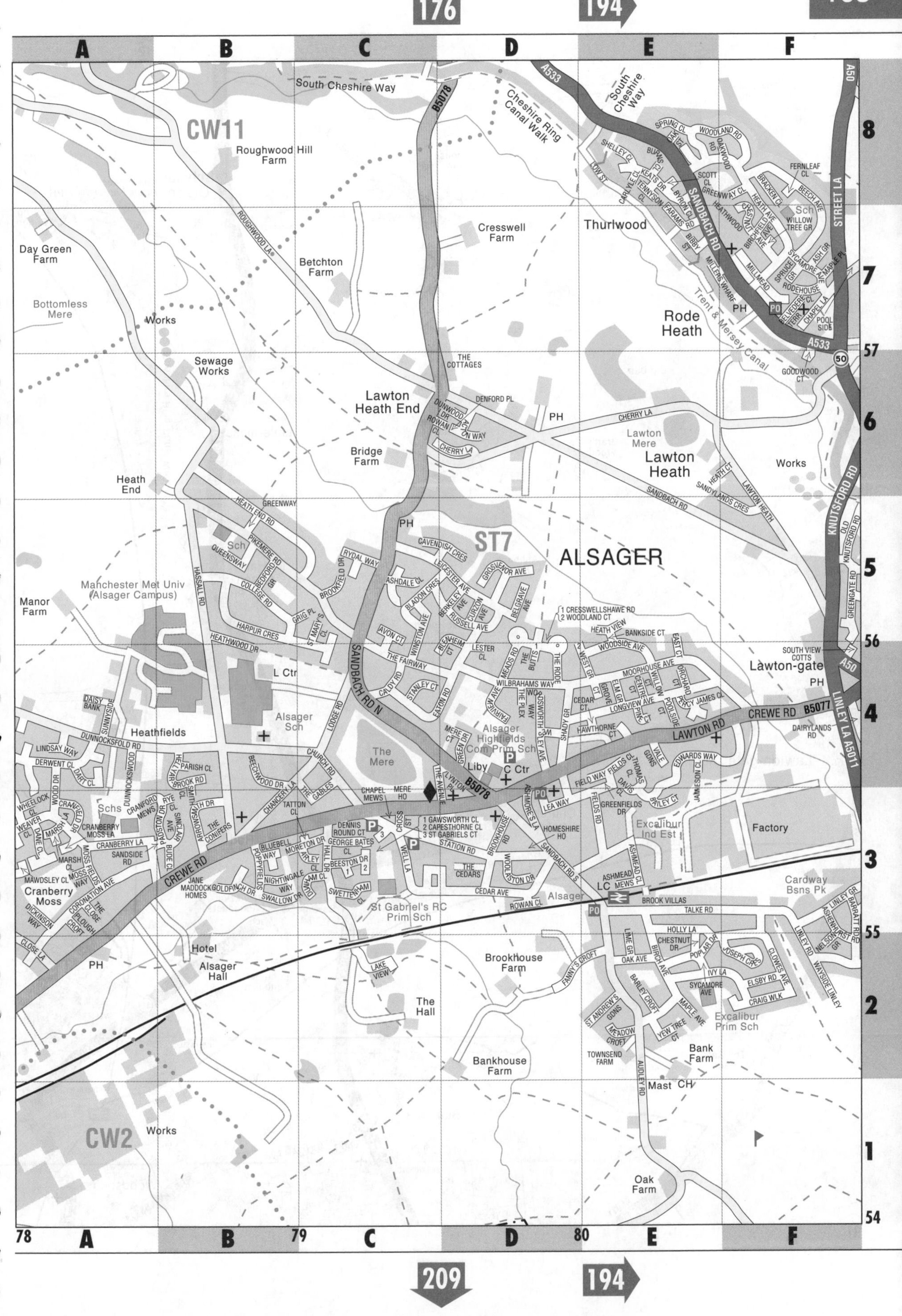
A
B
C
D
E
F
8
7
57
6
5
56
4
3
55
2
1
54
78
79
80
CW11
ST7
CW2
ALSAGER
South Cheshire Way
Cheshire Ring Canal Walk
Roughwood Hill Farm
Day Green Farm
Betchton Farm
Cresswell Farm
Thurlwood
Bottomless Mere
Works
Sewage Works
Rode Heath
Trent & Mersey Canal
Lawton Heath End
Bridge Farm
Lawton Mere
Lawton Heath
Heath End
Manor Farm
Manchester Met Univ (Alsager Campus)
Lawton-gate
L Ctr
Alsager Sch
Heathfields
The Mere
Alsager Highfields Com Prim Sch
Liby
C Ctr
Excalibur Ind Est
Factory
Cardway Bsns Pk
Cranberry Moss
St Gabriel's RC Prim Sch
Hotel
Alsager Hall
Brookhouse Farm
The Hall
Bankhouse Farm
Excalibur Prim Sch
Bank Farm
Mast
CH
Oak Farm
Townsend Farm
Alsager
LC
PH
Sch
Schs
THE COTTAGES
CREWE RD
SANDBACH RD N
LAWTON RD
KNUTSFORD RD
STREET LA
LINLEY LA A5011
A533
A50
B5078
B5077
1 CRESSWELLSHAWE RD
2 WOODLAND CT
1 GAWSWORTH CL
2 CAPESTHORNE CL
3 ST GABRIELS CT

193
177

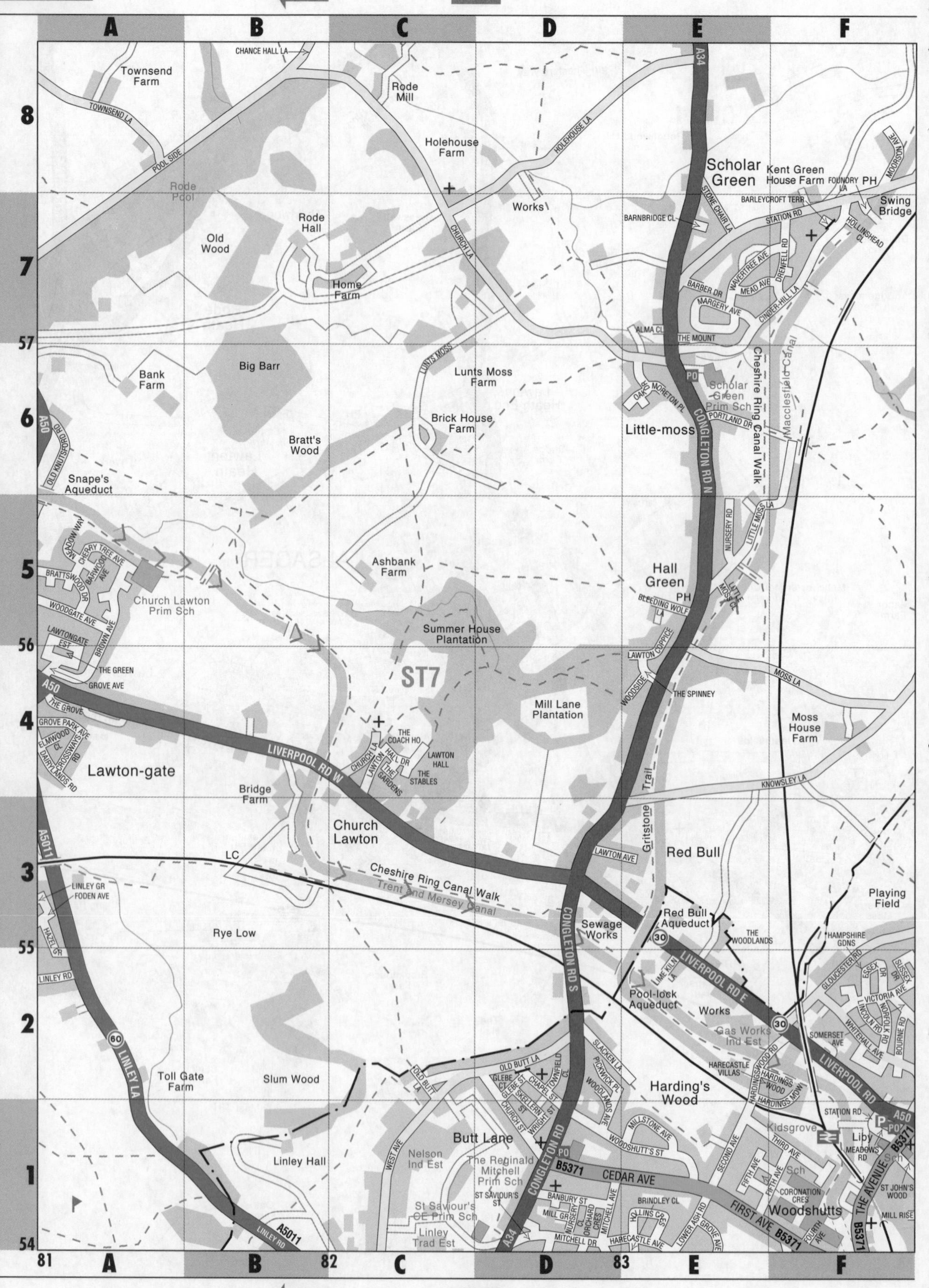

193
210

178

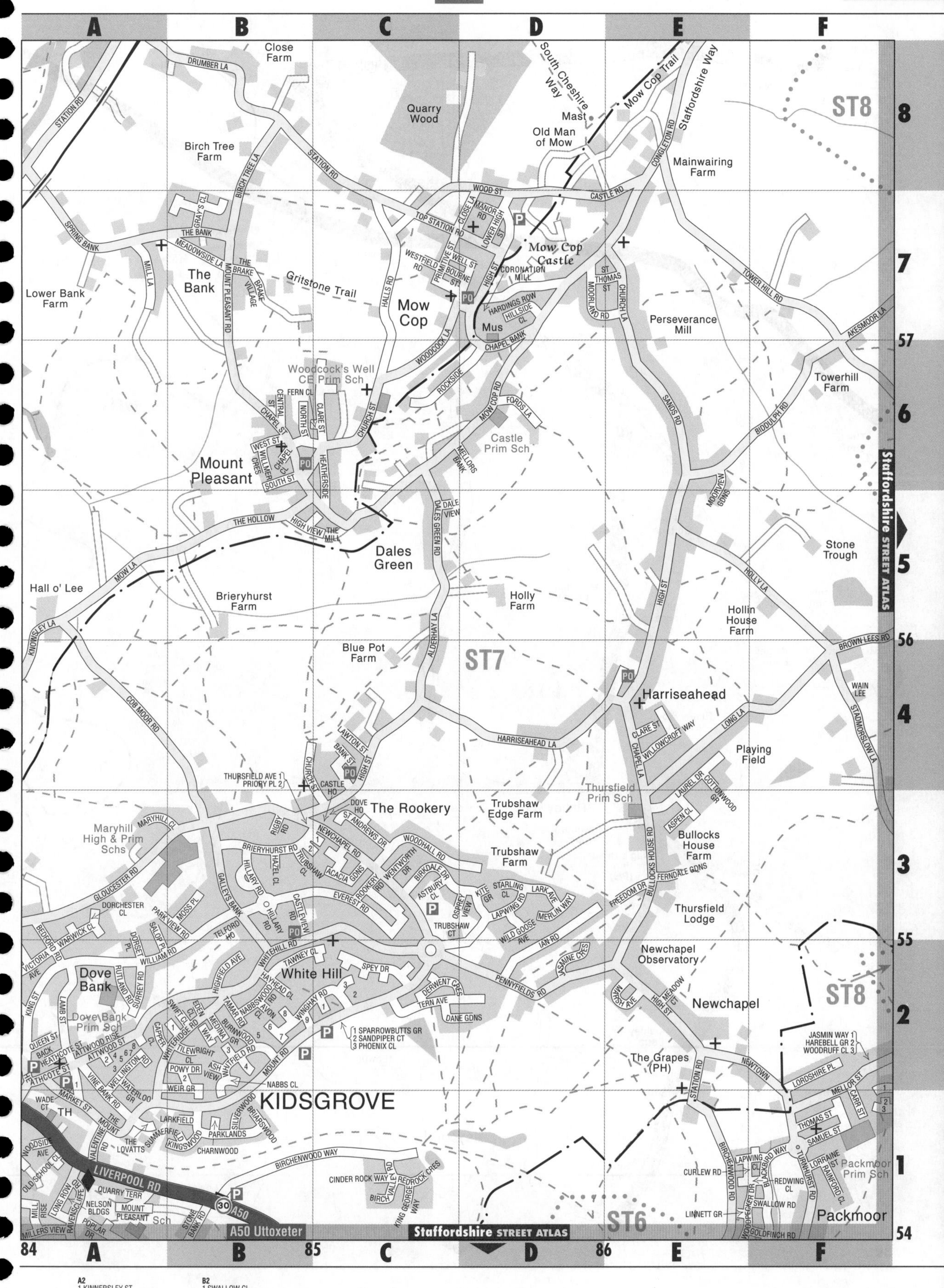

A2
1 KINNERSLEY ST
2 GILBERT CL
3 NAPIER GDNS
4 PEEL CT
5 BANK CT
6 HIGHERLAND CT
7 WESLEY GDNS
8 VICTORIA CT

B2
1 SWALLOW CL
2 WHEELOCK WAY
3 DIAMOND AVE
4 MOSSFIELD CRES
5 LITTLE ROW
6 BRIGHTS AVE
7 BIRCHES WAY
8 SILVERMINE CL
9 MAGPIE CRES

180

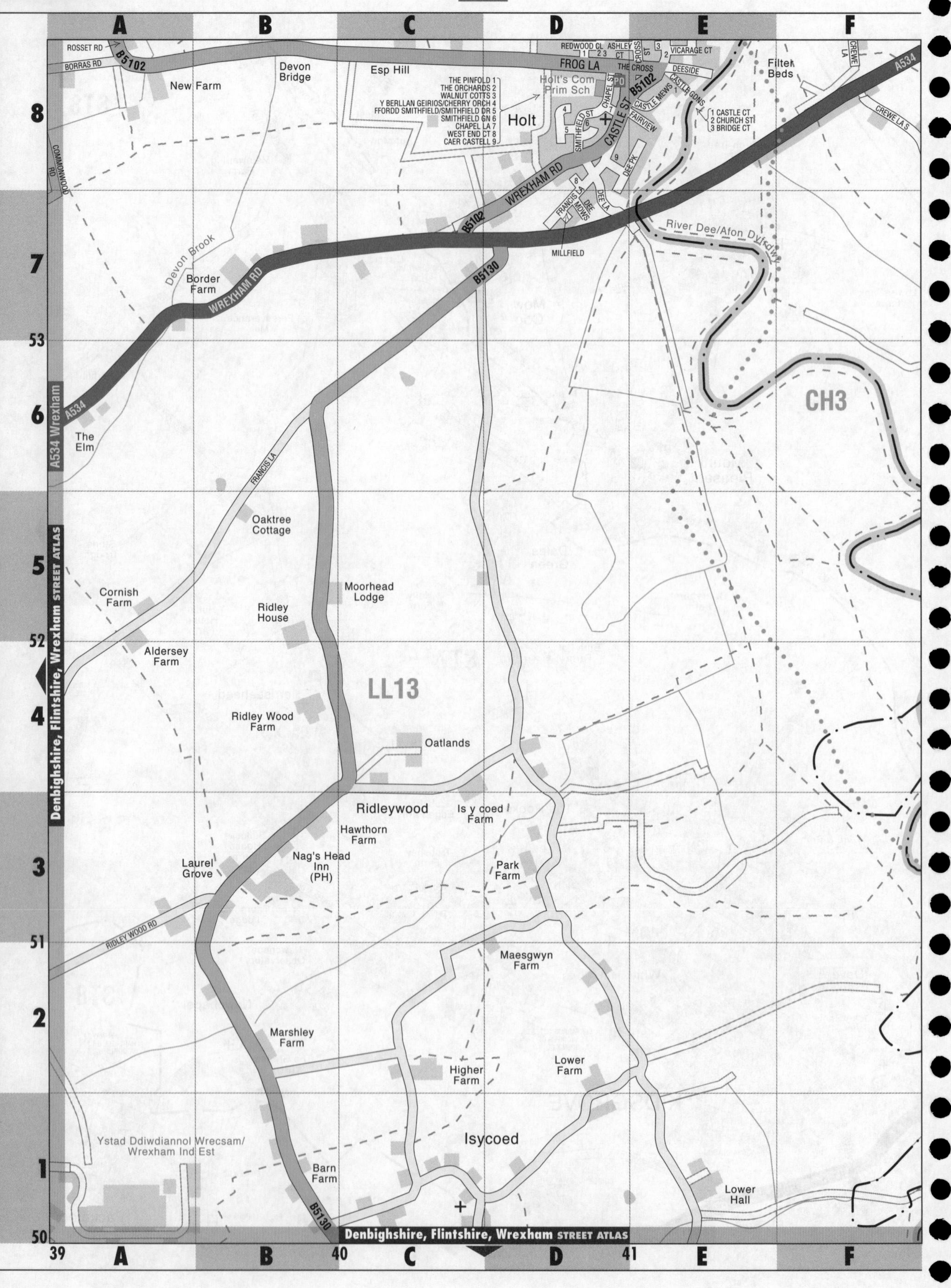

A
B
C
D
E
F
ROSSET RD
BORRAS RD
B5102
New Farm
Devon Bridge
Esp Hill
FROG LA
REDWOOD CL
ASHLEY CT
THE CROSS
VICARAGE CT
DEESIDE
Holt's Com Prim Sch
THE PINFOLD 1
THE ORCHARDS 2
WALNUT COTTS 3
Y BERLLAN GEIRIOS/CHERRY ORCH 4
FFORDD SMITHFIELD/SMITHFIELD DR 5
SMITHFIELD GN 6
CHAPEL LA 7
WEST END CT 8
CAER CASTELL 9
Holt
CHAPEL ST
SMITHFIELD ST
CASTLE ST
CASTLE MEWS
CASTLE GDNS
FAIRVIEW
DEE PK
1 CASTLE CT
2 CHURCH ST
3 BRIDGE CT
Filter Beds
CREWE LA
CREWE LA S
A534
COMMONWOOD RD
WREXHAM RD
B5102
FRANCIS LA
DEE MEWS
DEE LA
MILLFIELD
River Dee/Afon Dyfrdwy
Devon Brook
Border Farm
B5130
WREXHAM RD
A534 Wrexham
The Elm
CH3
FRANCIS LA
Oaktree Cottage
Cornish Farm
Moorhead Lodge
Ridley House
Aldersey Farm
LL13
Ridley Wood Farm
Oatlands
Ridleywood
Is y coed Farm
Hawthorn Farm
Laurel Grove
Nag's Head Inn (PH)
Park Farm
RIDLEY WOOD RD
Maesgwyn Farm
Marshley Farm
Lower Farm
Higher Farm
Ystad Ddiwdiannol Wrecsam/ Wrexham Ind Est
Isycoed
Barn Farm
Lower Hall
B5130
8
7
53
6
5
52
4
3
51
2
1
50
39
40
41

181
198

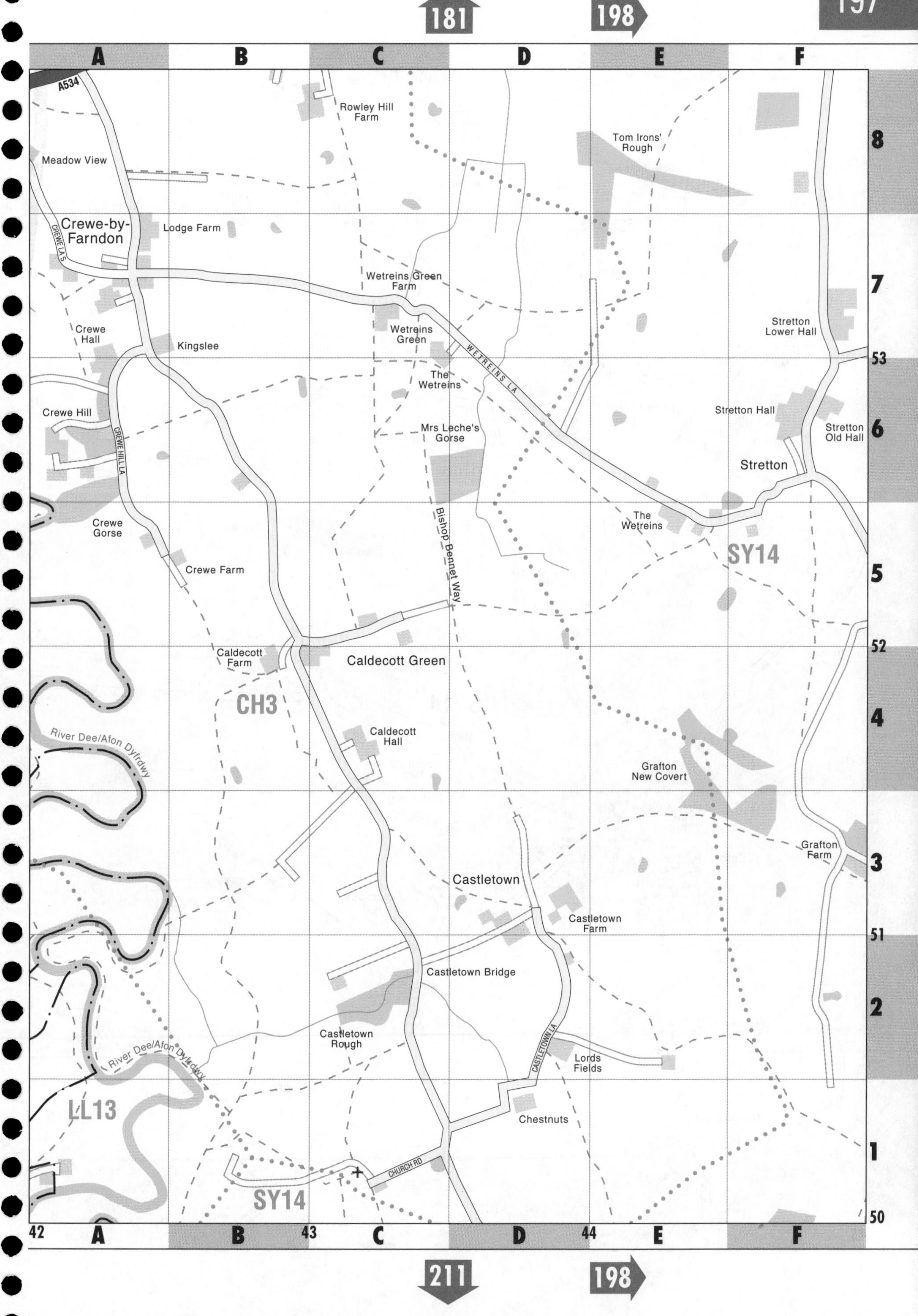

211
198

197
182

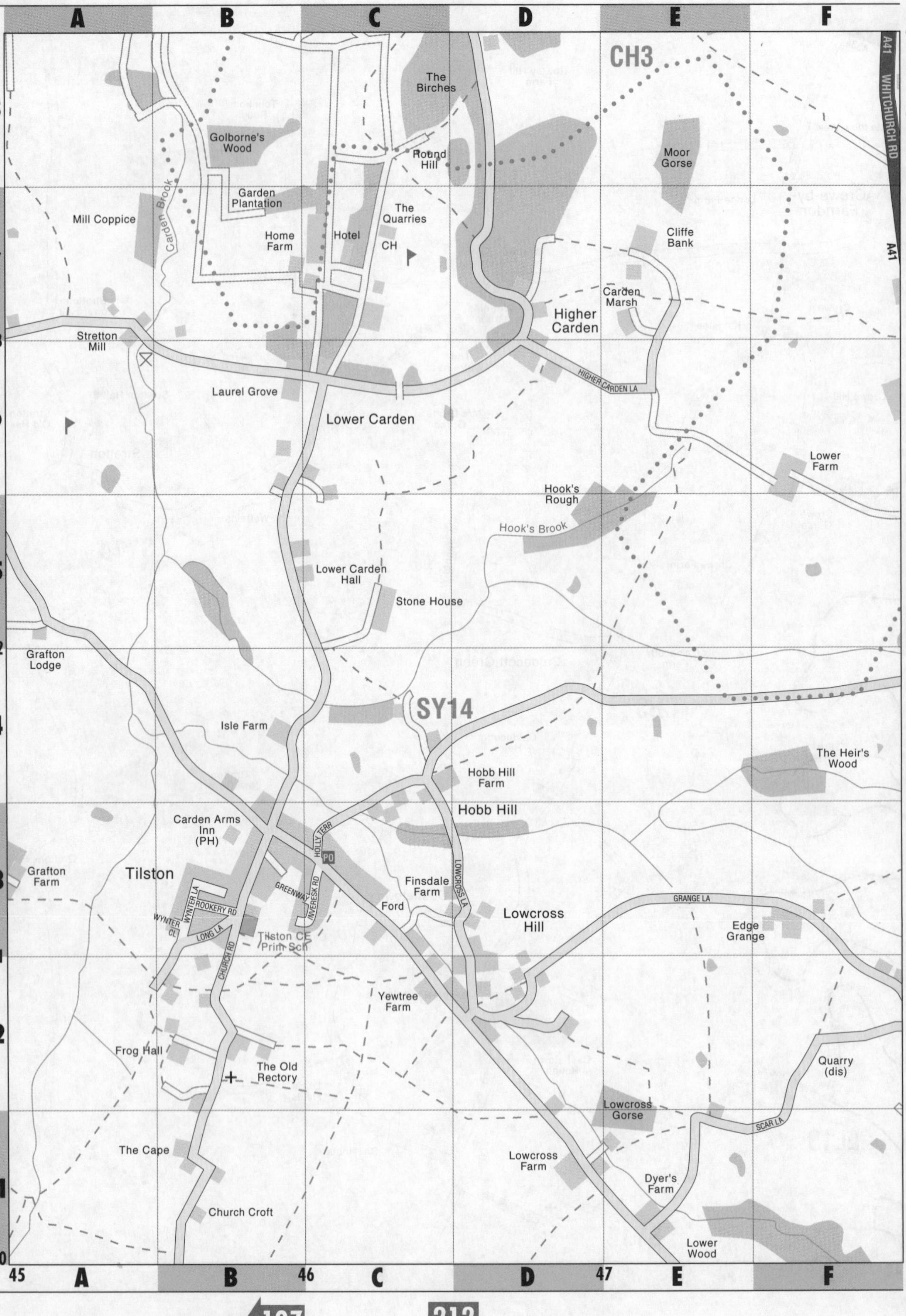

197
212

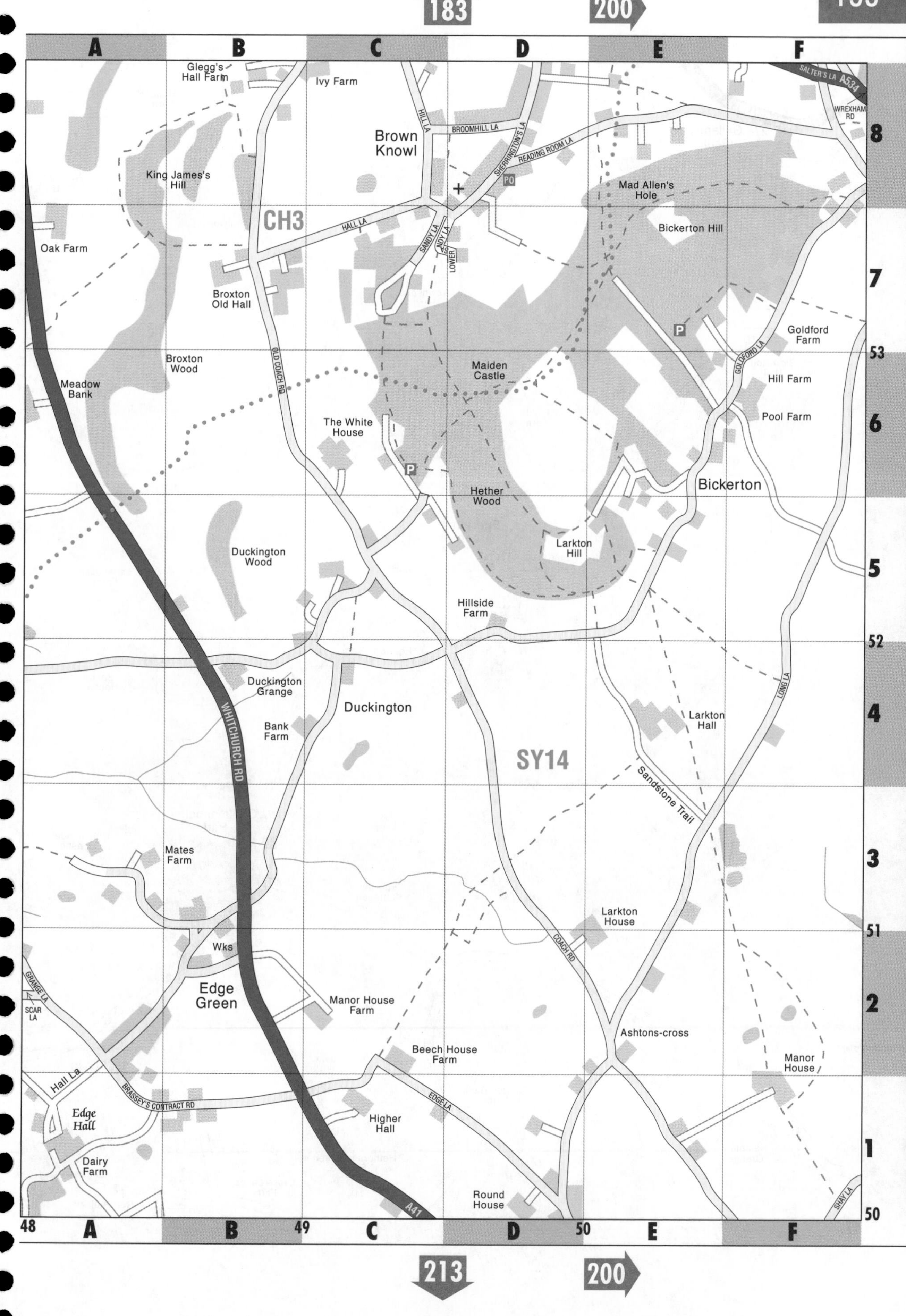
183
200
A
B
C
D
E
F
Glegg's Hall Farm
Ivy Farm
HILL LA
BROOMHILL LA
SHERRINGTON'S LA
READING ROOM LA
SALTER'S LA
A534
WREXHAM RD
Brown Knowl
King James's Hill
PO
Mad Allen's Hole
CH3
HALL LA
SANDY LA
LOWER
Bickerton Hill
Oak Farm
Broxton Old Hall
P
Goldford Farm
Broxton Wood
OLD COACH RD
Maiden Castle
GOLDFORD LA
Hill Farm
Meadow Bank
The White House
Pool Farm
P
Hether Wood
Bickerton
Larkton Hill
Duckington Wood
Hillside Farm
Duckington Grange
WHITCHURCH RD
Duckington
LONG LA
Larkton Hall
Bank Farm
SY14
Sandstone Trail
Mates Farm
Larkton House
COACH RD
Wks
GRANGE LA
SCAR LA
Edge Green
Manor House Farm
Ashtons-cross
Beech House Farm
Manor House
Hall La
BRASSEY'S CONTRACT RD
EDGE LA
Edge Hall
Higher Hall
Dairy Farm
Round House
A41
SHAY LA
8
7
53
6
5
52
4
3
51
2
1
50
48
49
50
213
200

199
184

A B C D E F

8 7 6 5 4 3 2 1

53 52 51 50

A534
WREXHAM RD
Gallantry Bank
Sandstone Trail
Bickerton Farm
COUNCIL HOS
LONG LA
CLAY LA
Gallantry-bank Farm
BULKELEY HALL LA
Bulkeley Hall
Yewtree Farm
Townsend Farm
Walnut Tree Farm
Manor Farm
CW6
CHOLMONDELEY LA
Bulkeleyhay
Bickerton Holy Trinity CE Prim Sch
Bickerton Hall
Fields Farm
Gate House Farm
Manor Farm
Egerton Green
Green Farm
Yew Tree Farm
Oak Tree Farm
Bankhouse Farm
SY14
Egerton Farm
Park House
Bickley Brook
Scotch Farm
Castle Hill
CASTLE FARM
Cholmondeley Park
PO
Cholmondeley Castle
Egerton Cottages
BICKERTON RD
Egerton Hall
Egerton Bank Farm
SHAY LA
Hampton Grange
Hetherson Green Farm
Cross Lanes Farm
GROTSWORTH LA
Red Hall

51 A B 52 C D 53 E F

199
214

185
202

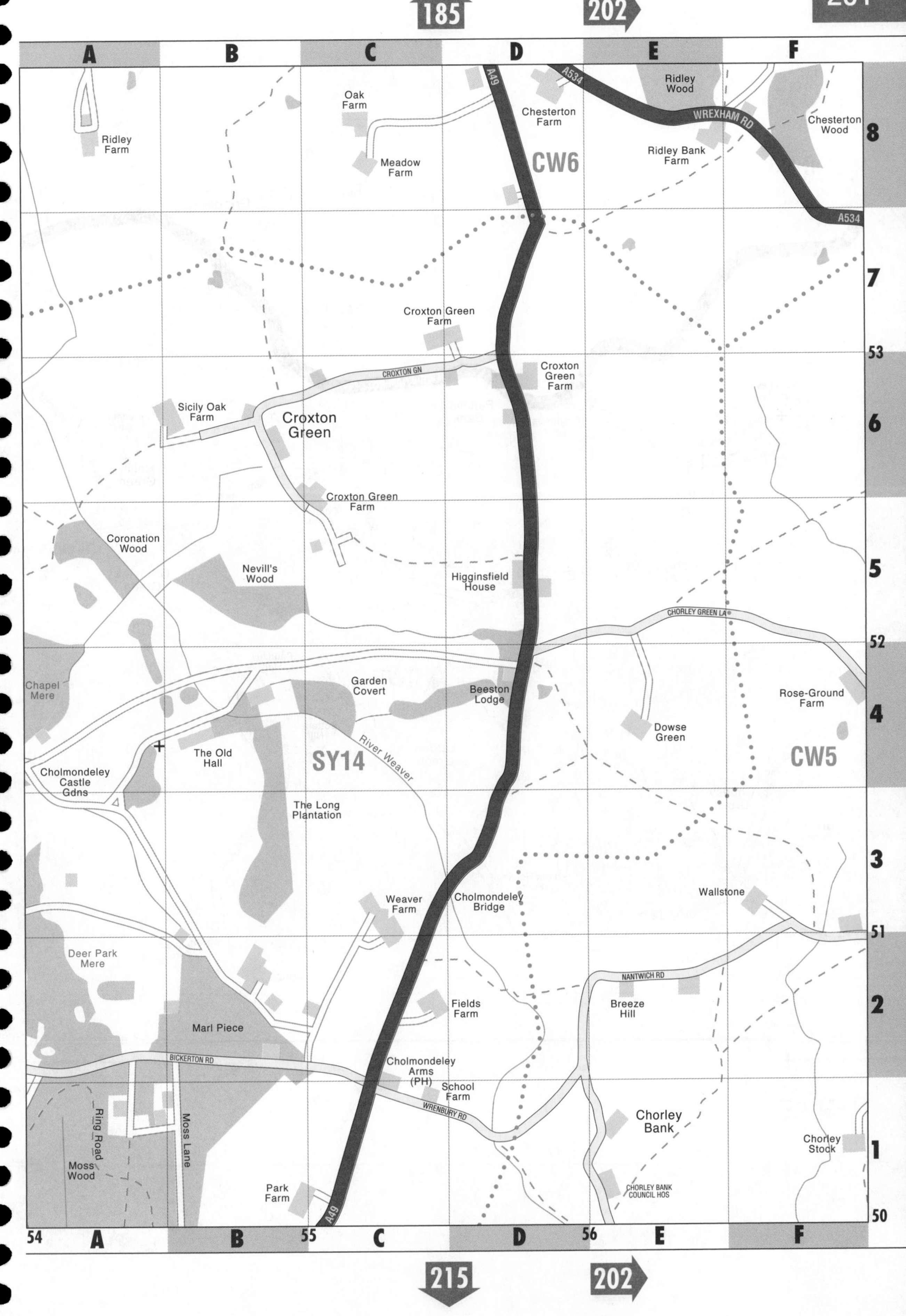

215
202

201
186

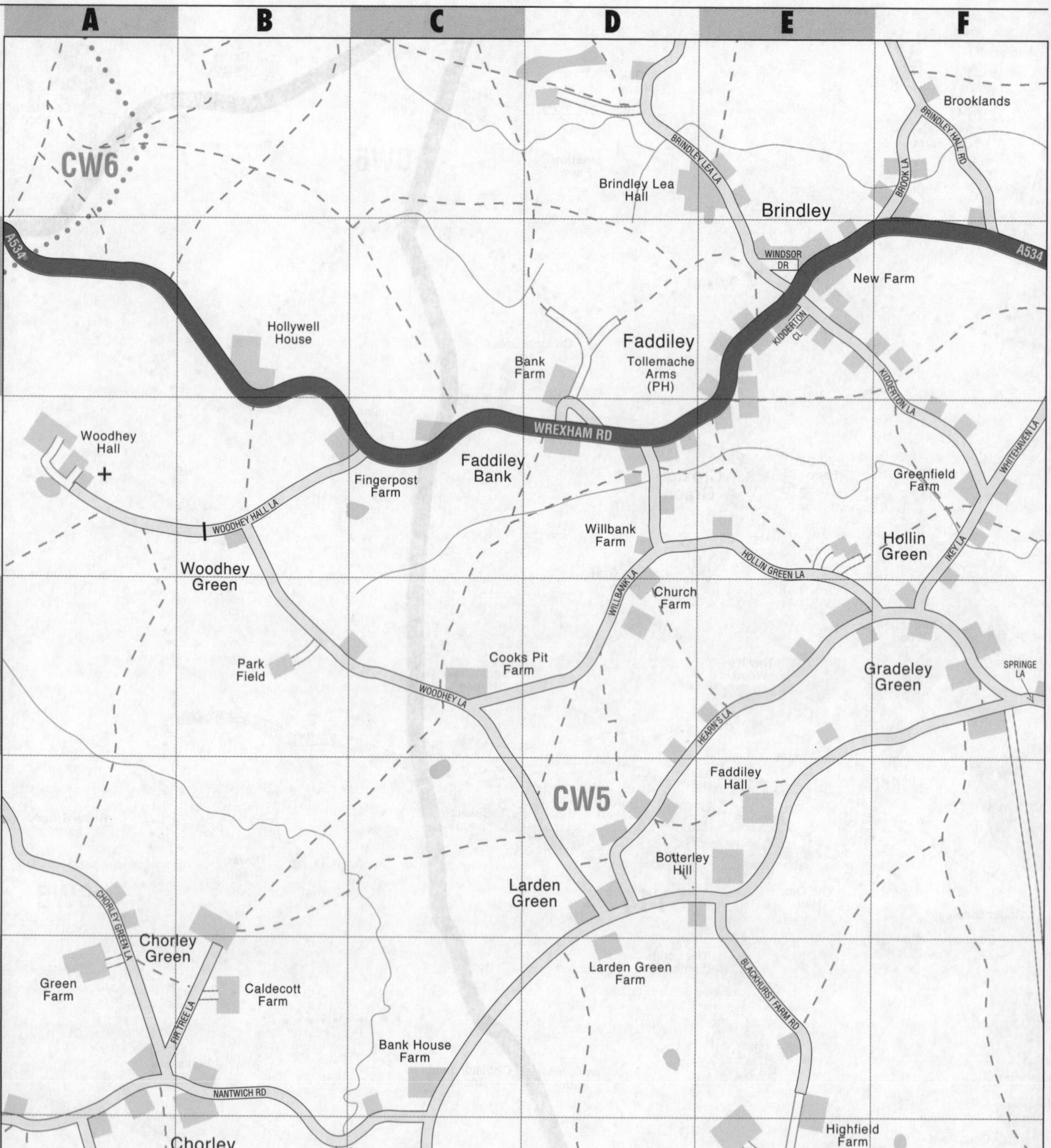

201
216

187
204

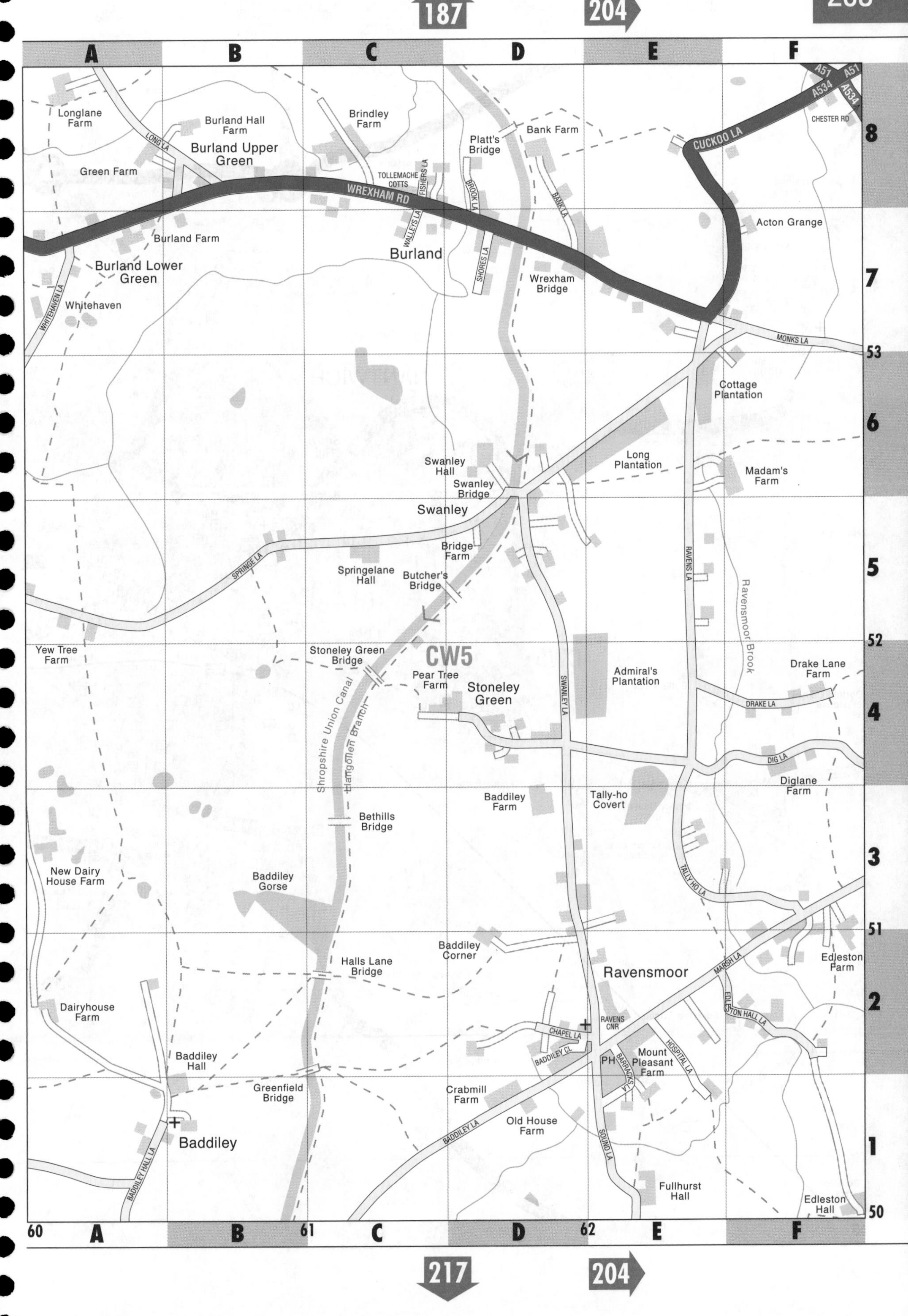

217
204

D5
1 THE OLD CONSTABULARY
2 CROSS WOOD ST
3 WHITEHALL CT

E5
1 CHAPEL MEWS
2 SWINE MARKET
3 OAT MARKET
4 BOWERS ROW
5 CASTLE ST
6 CROMWELL CT

E5
7 MAISTERSON CT
8 RECTORY CL
9 BOWLING GREEN CT
10 THE COCOA YD
11 COCOA GDNS
12 GROCOTTS ROW
13 PRIESTLY CT
14 BOLLANDS ROW
15 CHURCHE'S CT
16 CHATTERTON HO
17 CASTLE CT

E6
1 BARONY BLDGS
2 MANOR CT
3 GRESTY BLDGS
4 SCHOOL LA
5 GABLE CT
6 BOWYER AVE
7 VOLUNTEER AVE
8 THOMAS ROW
9 KENSINGTON CT
10 EAST VIEW
11 HAIGHTON CT

F5
1 ROOKERY CL
2 LABURNUM AVE
3 HAWTHORN AVE
4 NUTHURST GDNS
5 MANSION CT
6 WRIGHT LODGE
7 THE GATEHOUSE

203
188

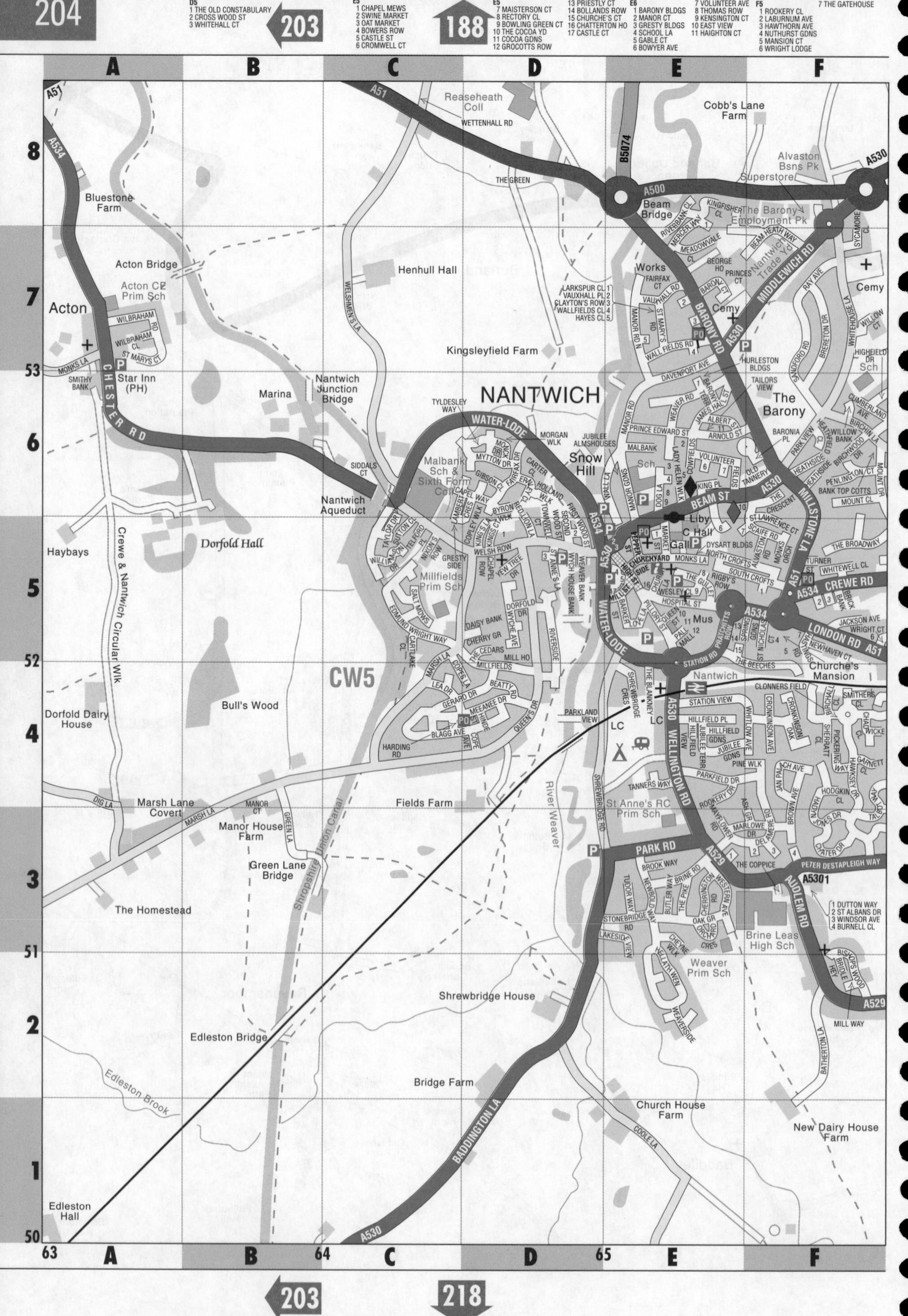

203
218

189
206

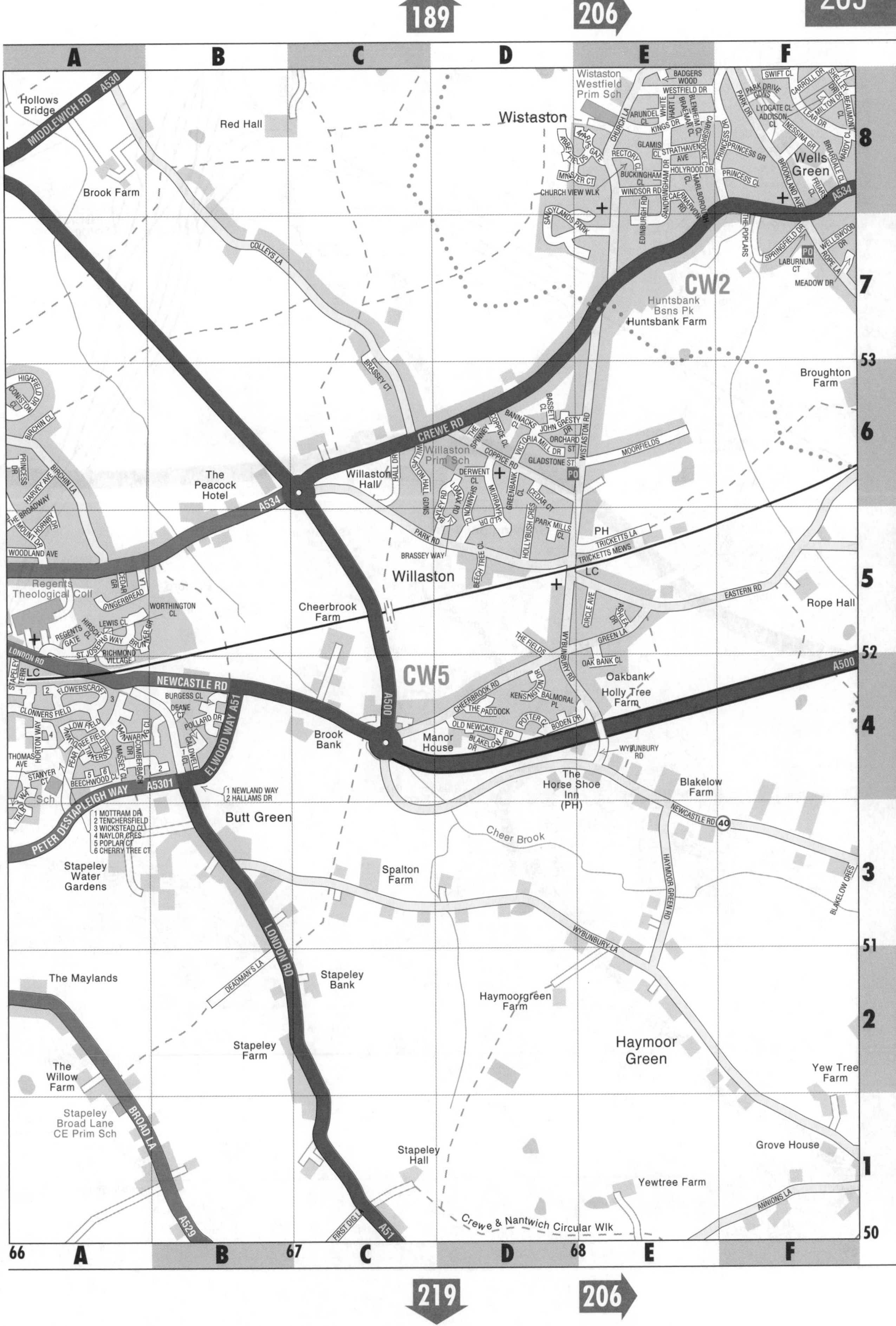

219
206

205 190

205 220

191
208

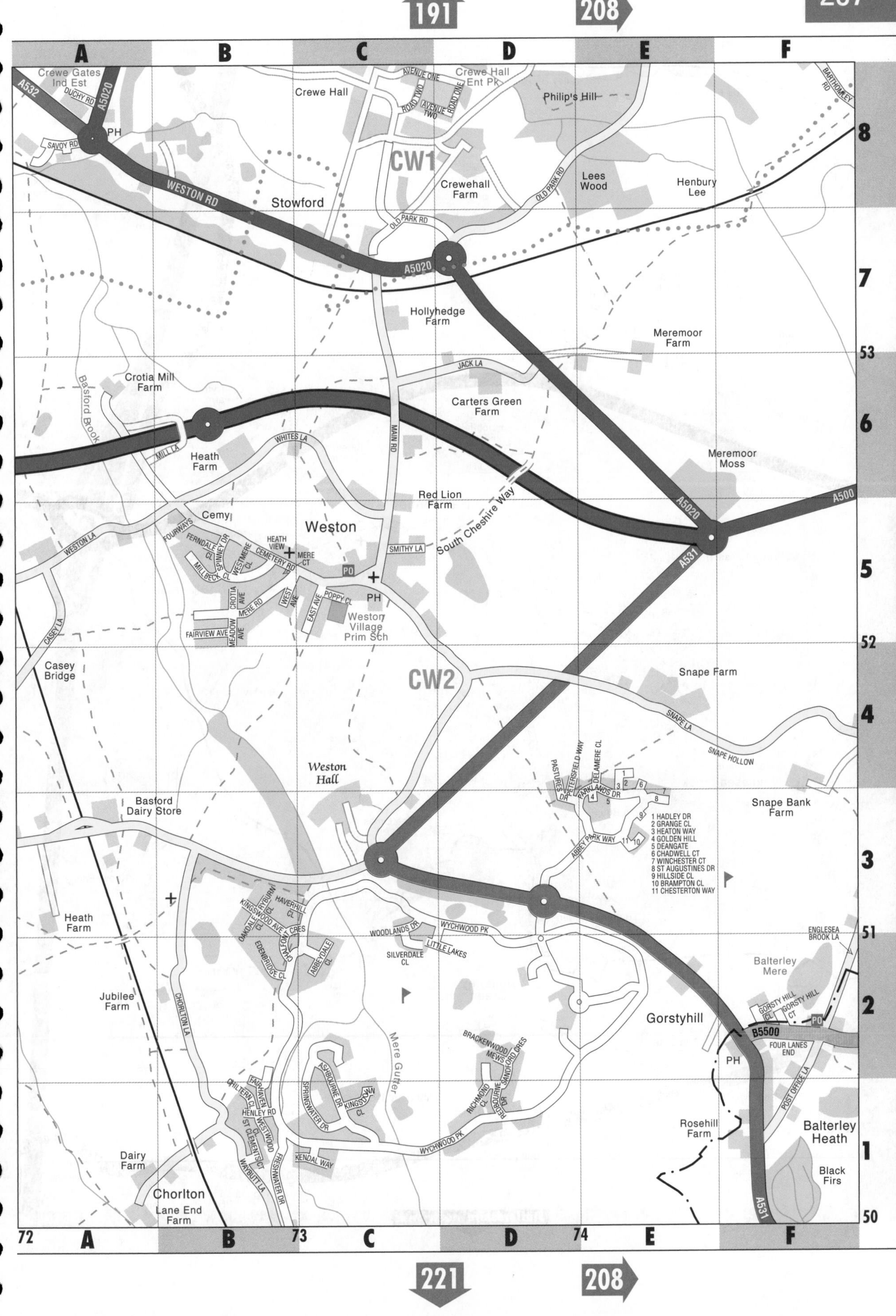

221
208

207
192

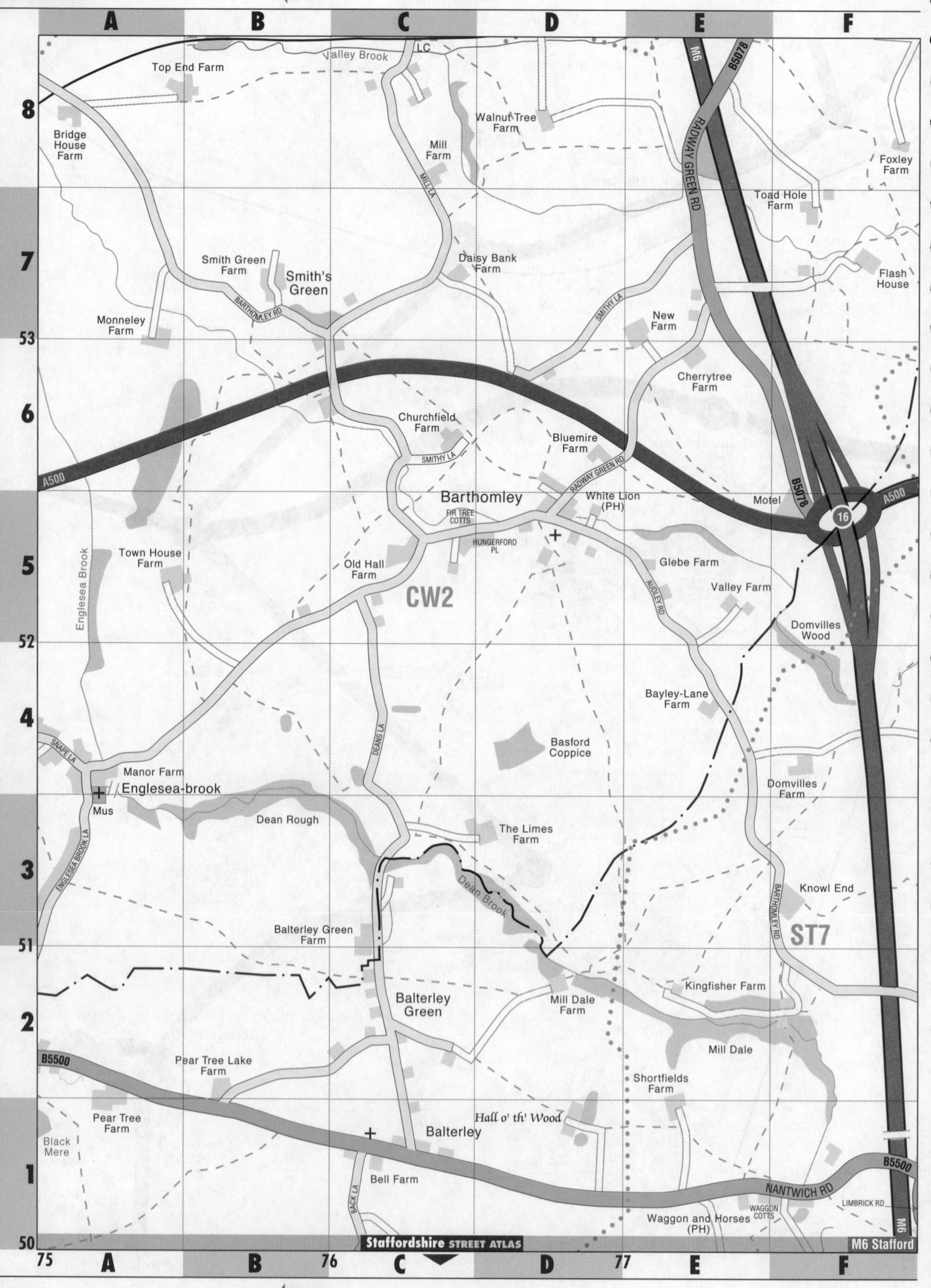
A
B
C
D
E
F
8
7
53
6
5
52
4
3
51
2
1
50
75
76
77
Valley Brook
LC
Top End Farm
Bridge House Farm
Walnut Tree Farm
Mill Farm
MILL LA
Foxley Farm
Toad Hole Farm
RADWAY GREEN RD
M6
B5078
Smith Green Farm
Smith's Green
Daisy Bank Farm
Flash House
BARTHOMLEY RD
Monneley Farm
SMITHY LA
New Farm
Cherrytree Farm
Churchfield Farm
Bluemire Farm
SMITHY LA
A500
Barthomley
RADWAY GREEN RD
White Lion (PH)
Motel
B5078
16
A500
FIR TREE COTTS
HUNGERFORD PL
Town House Farm
Old Hall Farm
Glebe Farm
Englesea Brook
CW2
AUDLEY RD
Valley Farm
Domvilles Wood
Bayley-Lane Farm
SNAPE LA
Basford Coppice
DEANS LA
Manor Farm
Englesea-brook
Mus
Domvilles Farm
Dean Rough
The Limes Farm
ENGLESEA BROOK LA
Dean Brook
Knowl End
BARTHOMLEY RD
Balterley Green Farm
ST7
Kingfisher Farm
Balterley Green
Mill Dale Farm
Mill Dale
B5500
Pear Tree Lake Farm
Shortfields Farm
Pear Tree Farm
Hall o' th' Wood
Black Mere
Balterley
B5500
Bell Farm
NANTWICH RD
BACK LA
LIMBRICK RD
WAGGON COTTS
Waggon and Horses (PH)
M6
Staffordshire STREET ATLAS
M6 Stafford

207

193
210

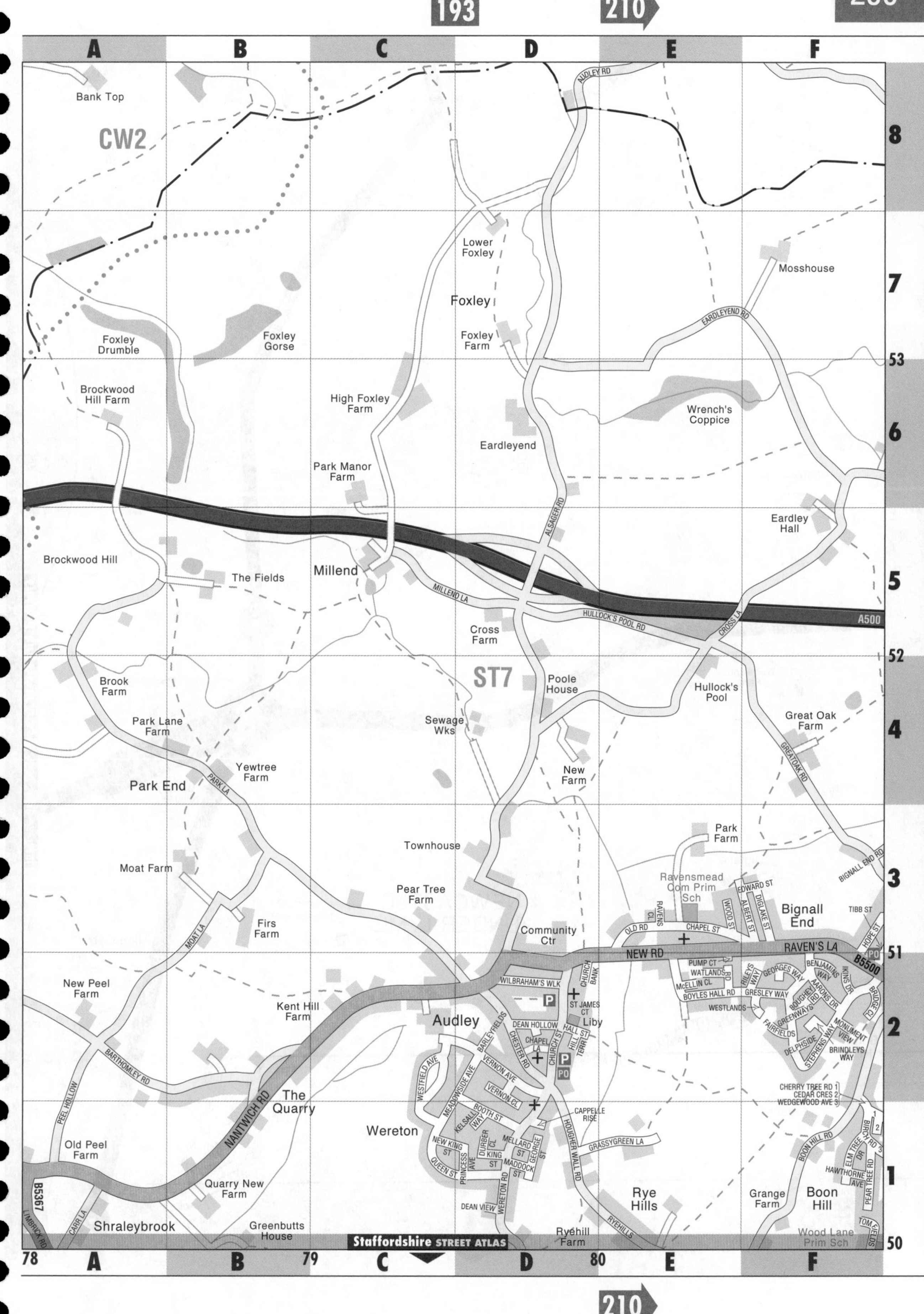
A
B
C
D
E
F
8
7
6
5
4
3
2
1
53
52
51
50
78
79
80
Bank Top
CW2
AUDLEY RD
Lower Foxley
Foxley
Mosshouse
EARDLEYEND RD
Foxley Drumble
Foxley Gorse
Foxley Farm
Brockwood Hill Farm
High Foxley Farm
Wrench's Coppice
Eardleyend
Park Manor Farm
ALSAGER RD
Eardley Hall
Brockwood Hill
The Fields
Millend
MILLEND LA
HULLOCK'S POOL RD
CROSS LA
A500
Cross Farm
ST7
Brook Farm
Poole House
Hullock's Pool
Great Oak Farm
Park Lane Farm
Sewage Wks
GREATOAK RD
Yewtree Farm
New Farm
Park End
PARK LA
Townhouse
Park Farm
Moat Farm
Ravensmead Com Prim Sch
BIGNALL END RD
Pear Tree Farm
EDWARD ST
Bignall End
TIBB ST
Firs Farm
Community Ctr
MOAT LA
OLD RD
CHAPEL ST
RAVEN'S LA
NEW RD
B5500
PO
New Peel Farm
Kent Hill Farm
Audley
WILBRAHAM'S WLK
ST JAMES CT
Liby
P
PUMP CT
WATLANDS
McELLIN CL
BOYLES HALL RD
GRESLEY WAY
WESTLANDS
BARTHOMLEY RD
NANTWICH RD
The Quarry
Wereton
PEEL HOLLOW
CAPPELLE RISE
GRASSYGREEN LA
CHERRY TREE RD 1
CEDAR CRES 2
WEDGEWOOD AVE 3
Old Peel Farm
B5367
Quarry New Farm
Rye Hills
Grange Farm
Boon Hill
BOON HILL RD
Shraleybrook
Greenbutts House
Ryehill Farm
RYEHILLS
Wood Lane Prim Sch

209
194

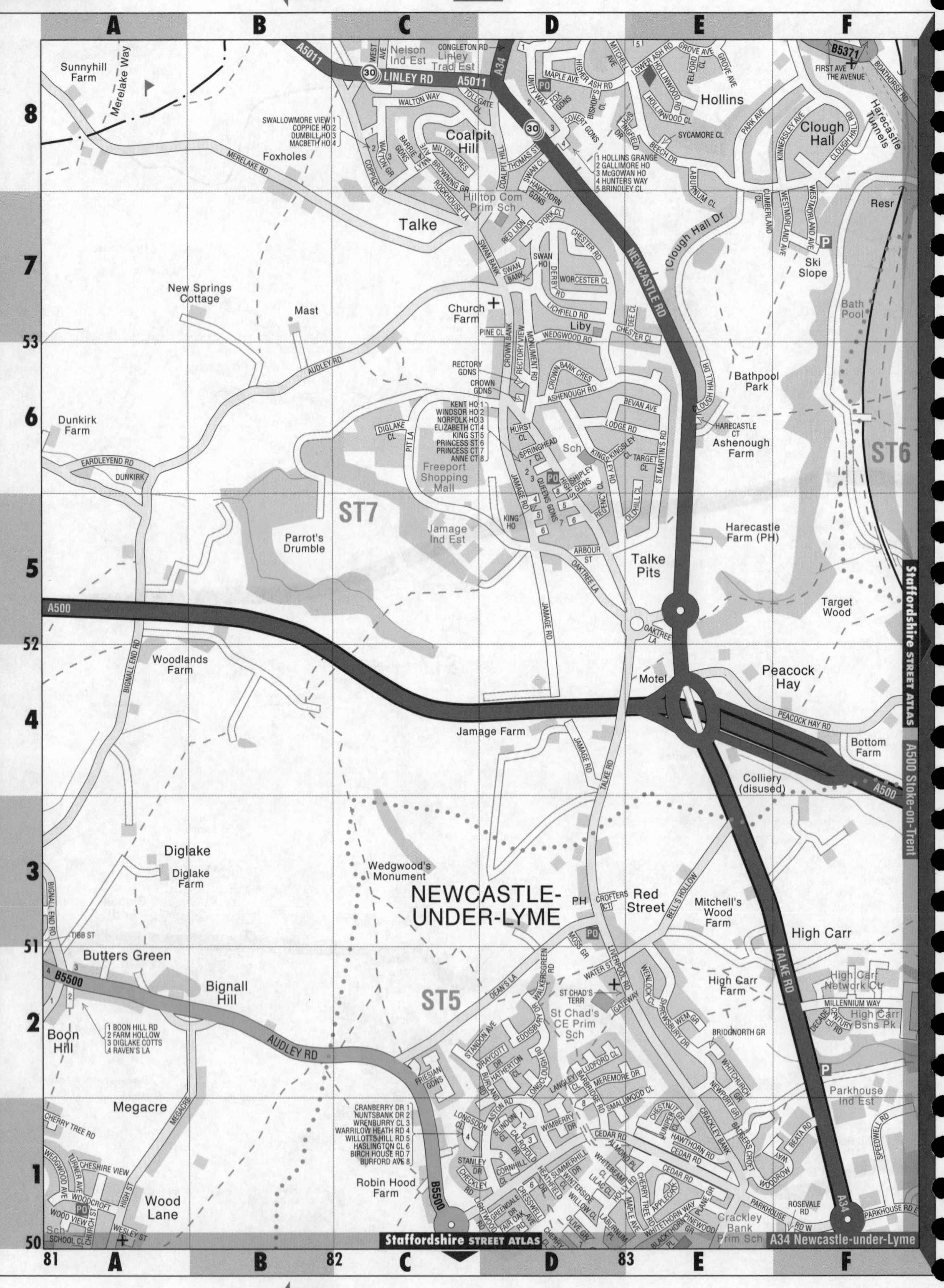
A
B
C
D
E
F
8
7
6
5
4
3
2
1
53
52
51
50
81
82
83
Sunnyhill Farm
Merelake Way
Nelson Ind Est
Linley Trad Est
CONGLETON RD
LINLEY RD
A5011
A34
Coalpit Hill
Foxholes
MERELAKE RD
Hollins
Clough Hall
Harecastle Tunnels
B5371
FIRST AVE
THE AVENUE
SWALLOWMORE VIEW 1
COPPICE HO 2
DUMBILL HO 3
MACBETH HO 4
1 HOLLINS GRANGE
2 GALLIMORE HO
3 McGOWAN HO
4 HUNTERS WAY
5 BRINDLEY CL
Hilltop Com Prim Sch
Talke
Resr
Clough Hall Dr
NEWCASTLE RD
Ski Slope
New Springs Cottage
Mast
Church Farm
Liby
Bath Pool
AUDLEY RD
Bathpool Park
Dunkirk Farm
EARDLEYEND RD
DUNKIRK
KENT HO 1
WINDSOR HO 2
NORFOLK HO 3
ELIZABETH CT 4
KING ST 5
PRINCESS ST 6
PRINCESS CT 7
ANNE CT 8
Freeport Shopping Mall
Sch
Ashenough Farm
HARECASTLE CT
ST6
ST7
Parrot's Drumble
Jamage Ind Est
Harecastle Farm (PH)
Talke Pits
Target Wood
A500
Woodlands Farm
BIGNALL END RD
Motel
Peacock Hay
PEACOCK HAY RD
Jamage Farm
Bottom Farm
Colliery (disused)
Staffordshire STREET ATLAS
A500 Stoke-on-Trent
Diglake
Diglake Farm
Wedgwood's Monument
NEWCASTLE-UNDER-LYME
PH
Red Street
Mitchell's Wood Farm
High Carr
Butters Green
Bignall Hill
B5500
ST5
St Chad's CE Prim Sch
High Carr Farm
High Carr Network Ctr
MILLENNIUM WAY
High Carr Bsns Pk
Boon Hill
1 BOON HILL RD
2 FARM HOLLOW
3 DIGLAKE COTTS
4 RAVEN'S LA
TALKE RD
Megacre
CRANBERRY DR 1
HUNTSBANK DR 2
WRENBURRY CL 3
WARRILOW HEATH RD 4
WILLOTTS HILL RD 5
HASLINGTON CL 6
BIRCH HOUSE RD 7
BURFORD AVE 8
Parkhouse Ind Est
Robin Hood Farm
Wood Lane
Crackley Bank Prim Sch
Sch
A34 Newcastle-under-Lyme

209

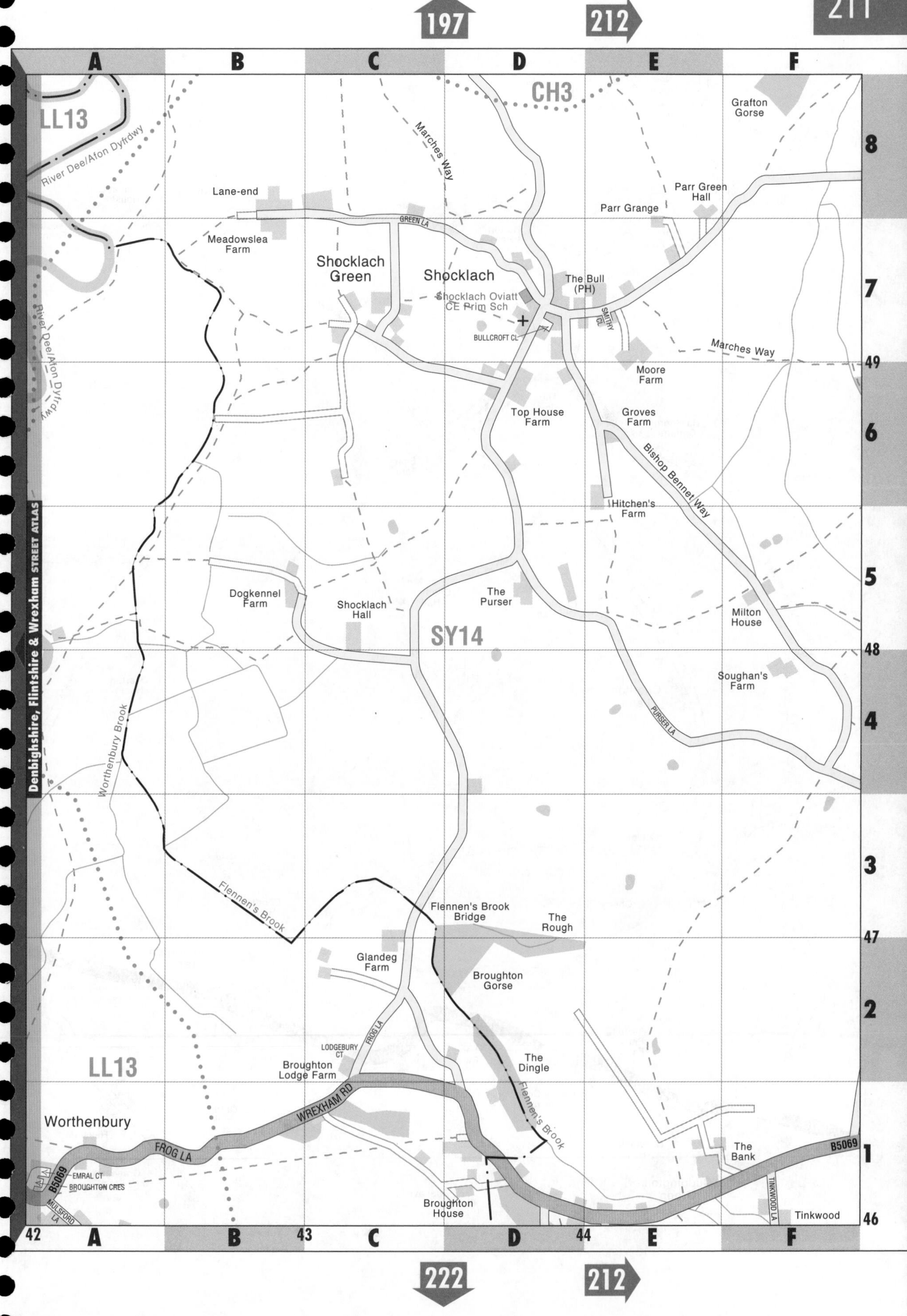
197
212
A
B
C
D
E
F
CH3
LL13
River Dee/Afon Dyfrdwy
Grafton Gorse
Marches Way
8
Lane-end
Parr Green Hall
Parr Grange
GREEN LA
Meadowslea Farm
Shocklach Green
Shocklach
The Bull (PH)
Shocklach Oviatt CE Prim Sch
SMITHY CL
7
BULLCROFT CL
Marches Way
49
Moore Farm
Top House Farm
Groves Farm
Bishop Bennet Way
6
Hitchen's Farm
Denbighshire, Flintshire & Wrexham STREET ATLAS
5
Dogkennel Farm
Shocklach Hall
The Purser
Milton House
SY14
48
Soughan's Farm
PURSER LA
Worthenbury Brook
4
3
Flennen's Brook
Flennen's Brook Bridge
The Rough
47
Glandeg Farm
Broughton Gorse
2
FROG LA
LODGEBURY CT
Broughton Lodge Farm
The Dingle
LL13
WREXHAM RD
Flennen's Brook
Worthenbury
FROG LA
The Bank
B5069
1
B5069
EMRAL CT
BROUGHTON CRES
MULSFORD LA
TINKWOOD LA
Broughton House
Tinkwood
46
42
43
44
222
212

211
198

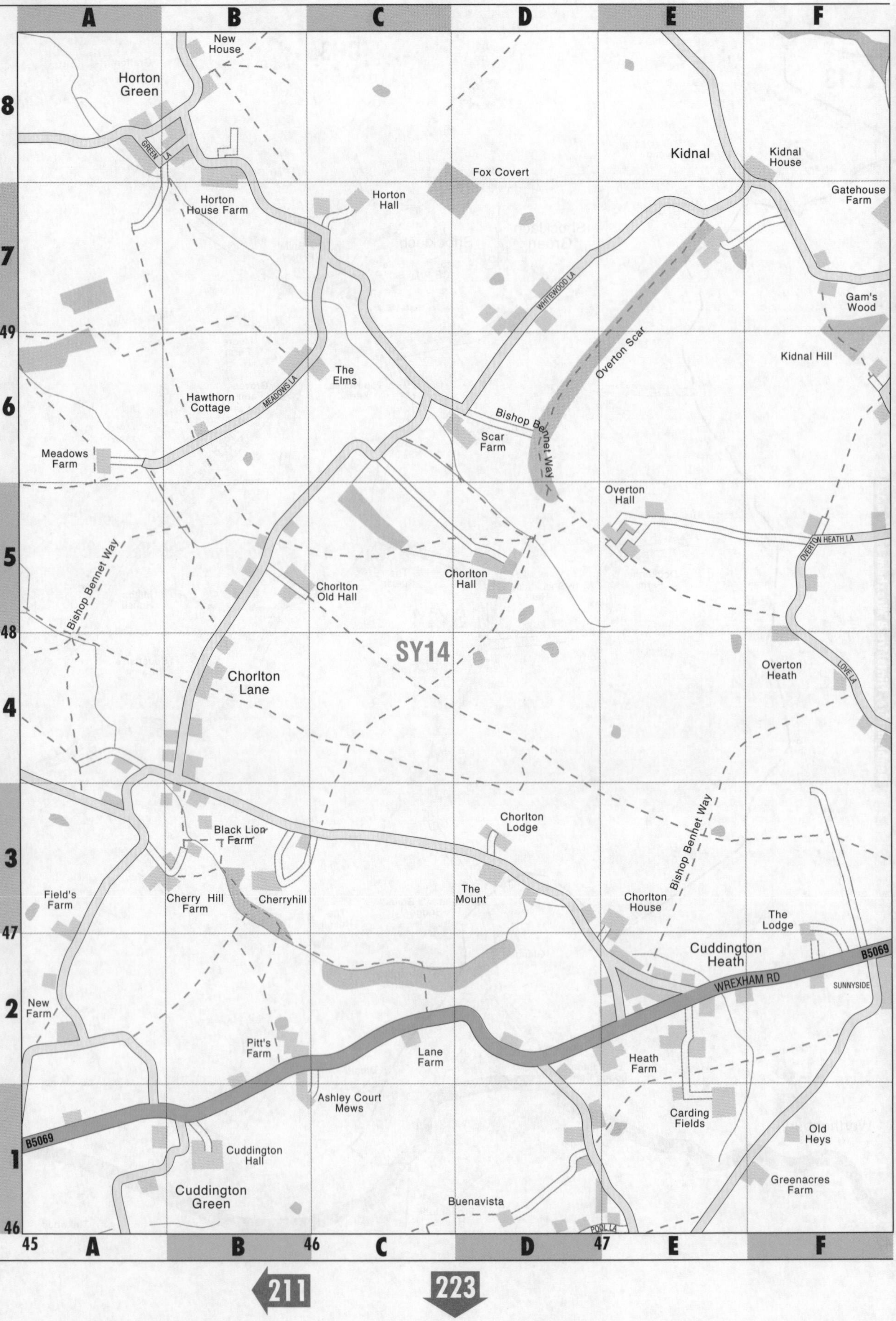

211
223

199
214

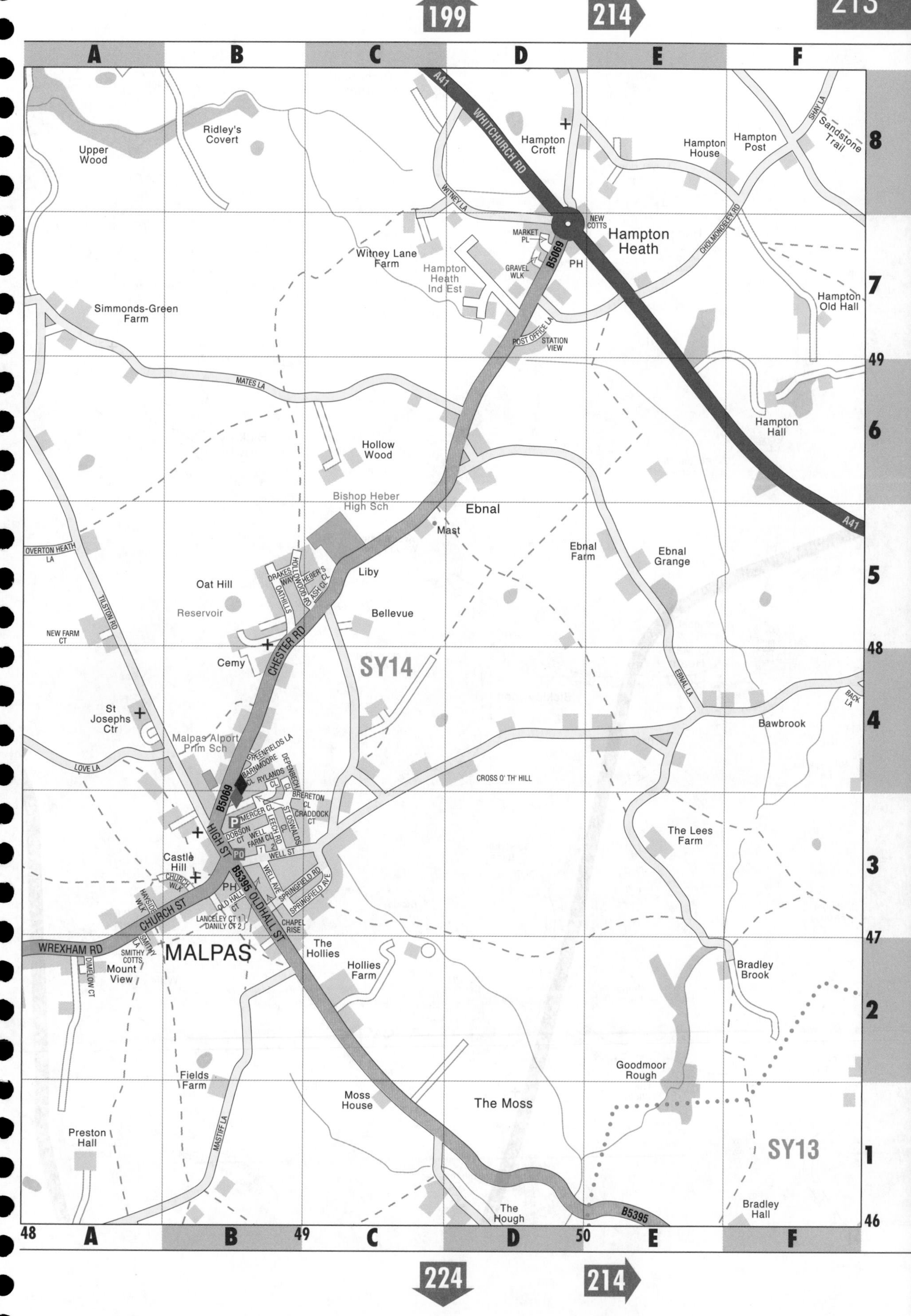

224
214

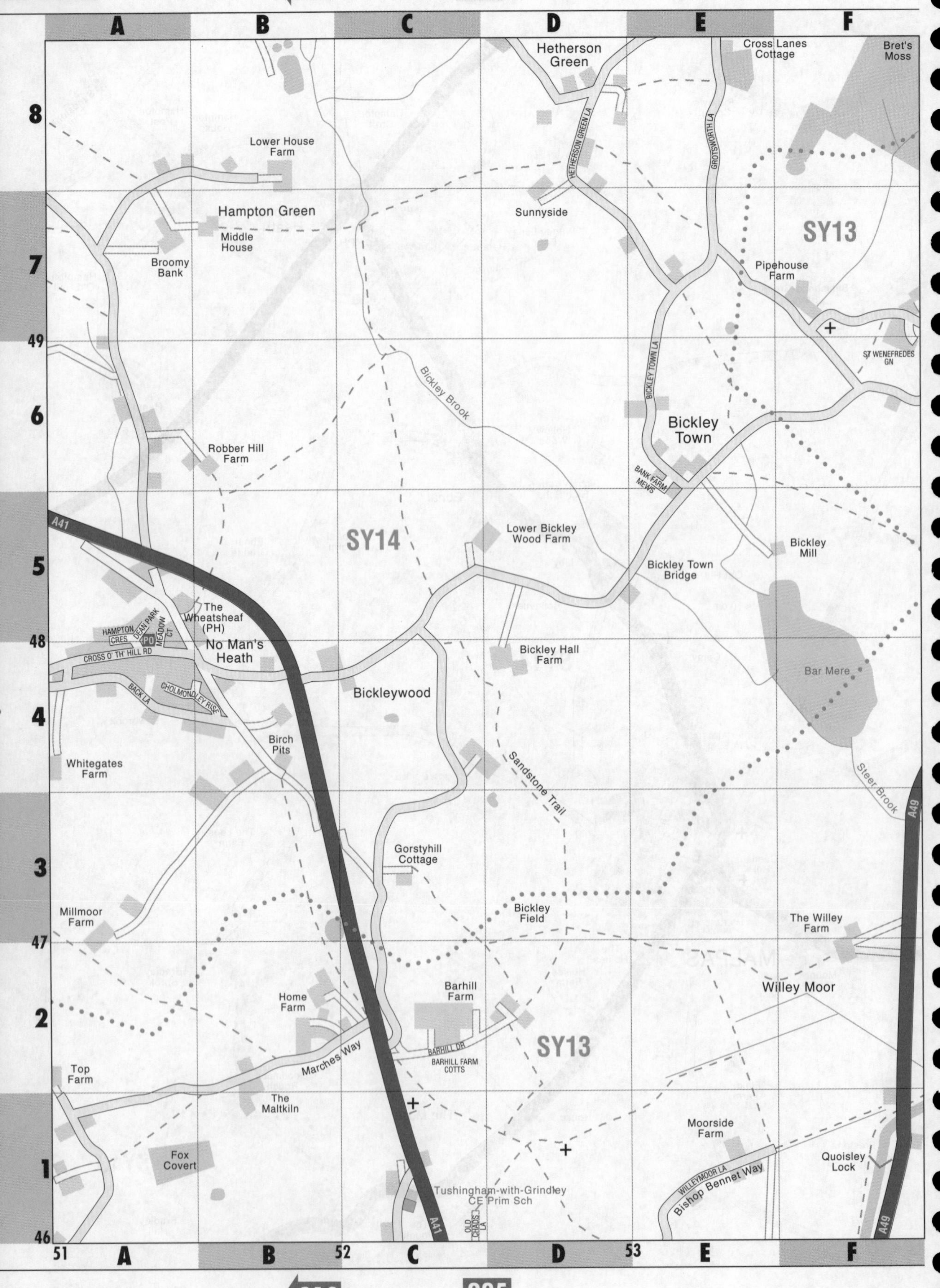
A
B
C
D
E
F
8
7
49
6
5
48
4
3
47
2
1
46
51
52
53
Hetherson Green
Cross Lanes Cottage
Bret's Moss
Lower House Farm
HETHERSON GREEN LA
GROTSWORTH LA
Hampton Green
Middle House
Sunnyside
SY13
Broomy Bank
Pipehouse Farm
ST WENEFREDES GN
Bickley Brook
BICKLEY TOWN LA
Bickley Town
Robber Hill Farm
BANK FARM MEWS
A41
SY14
Lower Bickley Wood Farm
Bickley Mill
Bickley Town Bridge
The Wheatsheaf (PH)
HAMPTON CRES
DEAN PARK
MEADOW CT
No Man's Heath
CROSS O' TH' HILL RD
Bickley Hall Farm
Bar Mere
BACK LA
CHOLMONDLEY RISE
Bickleywood
Birch Pits
Whitegates Farm
Sandstone Trail
Steer Brook
A49
Gorstyhill Cottage
Millmoor Farm
Bickley Field
The Willey Farm
Willey Moor
Home Farm
Barhill Farm
SY13
Marches Way
BARHILL DR
BARHILL FARM COTTS
Top Farm
The Maltkiln
Moorside Farm
Fox Covert
Quoisley Lock
WILLEYMOOR LA
Bishop Bennet Way
Tushingham-with-Grindley CE Prim Sch
OLD CHADS LA

201
216

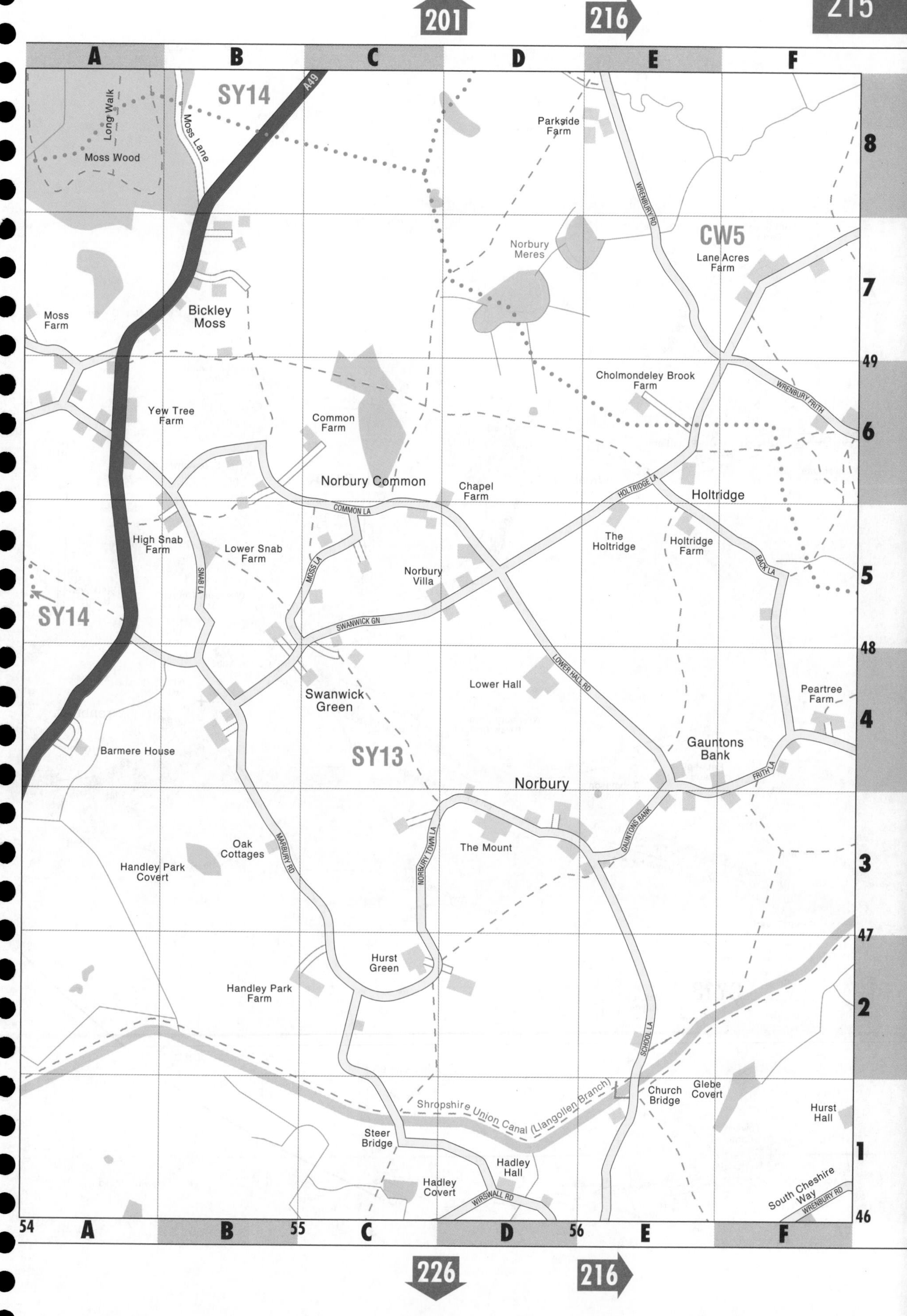

226
216

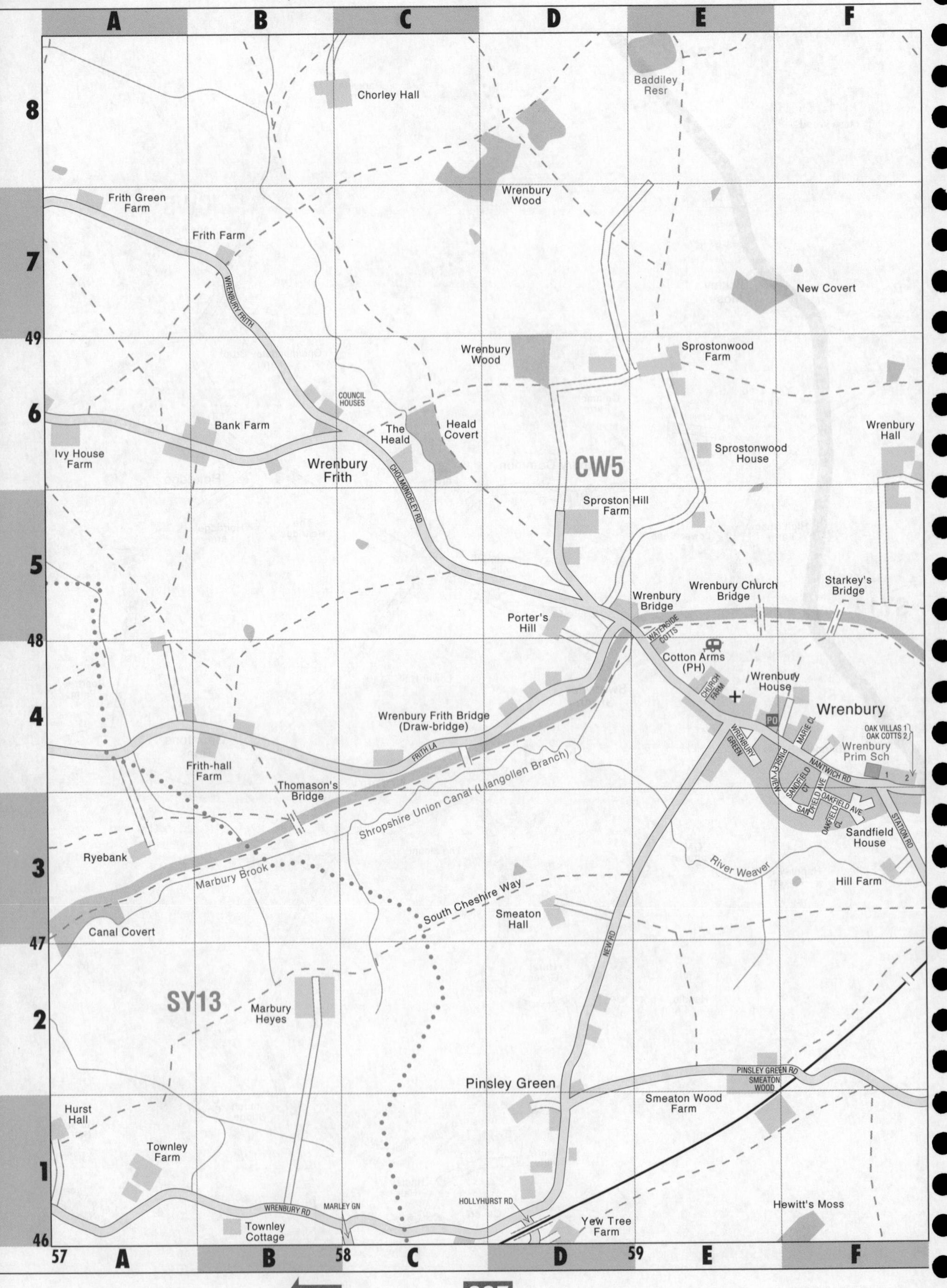
A
B
C
D
E
F
8
7
49
6
5
48
4
3
47
2
1
46
57
58
59
Chorley Hall
Baddiley Resr
Wrenbury Wood
Frith Green Farm
Frith Farm
WRENBURY FRITH
New Covert
Wrenbury Wood
Sprostonwood Farm
COUNCIL HOUSES
The Heald
Heald Covert
Bank Farm
Ivy House Farm
Wrenbury Frith
CHOLMONDELEY RD
CW5
Wrenbury Hall
Sprostonwood House
Sproston Hill Farm
Wrenbury Church Bridge
Starkey's Bridge
Wrenbury Bridge
Porter's Hill
WATERSIDE COTTS
Cotton Arms (PH)
CHURCH FARM
Wrenbury House
Wrenbury
PO
WRENBURY GREEN
MARIE CL
OAK VILLAS 1
OAK COTTS 2
Wrenbury Prim Sch
NANTWICH RD
PINSLEY VIEW
SANDFIELD CT
SANDFIELD AVE
OAKFIELD AVE
OAKFIELD CL
Sandfield House
STATION RD
Wrenbury Frith Bridge (Draw-bridge)
FRITH LA
Frith-hall Farm
Thomason's Bridge
Shropshire Union Canal (Llangollen Branch)
Ryebank
Marbury Brook
River Weaver
Hill Farm
South Cheshire Way
Smeaton Hall
Canal Covert
NEW RD
SY13
Marbury Heyes
Pinsley Green
PINSLEY GREEN RD
SMEATON WOOD
Smeaton Wood Farm
Hurst Hall
Townley Farm
WRENBURY RD
MARLEY GN
HOLLYHURST RD
Yew Tree Farm
Hewitt's Moss
Townley Cottage

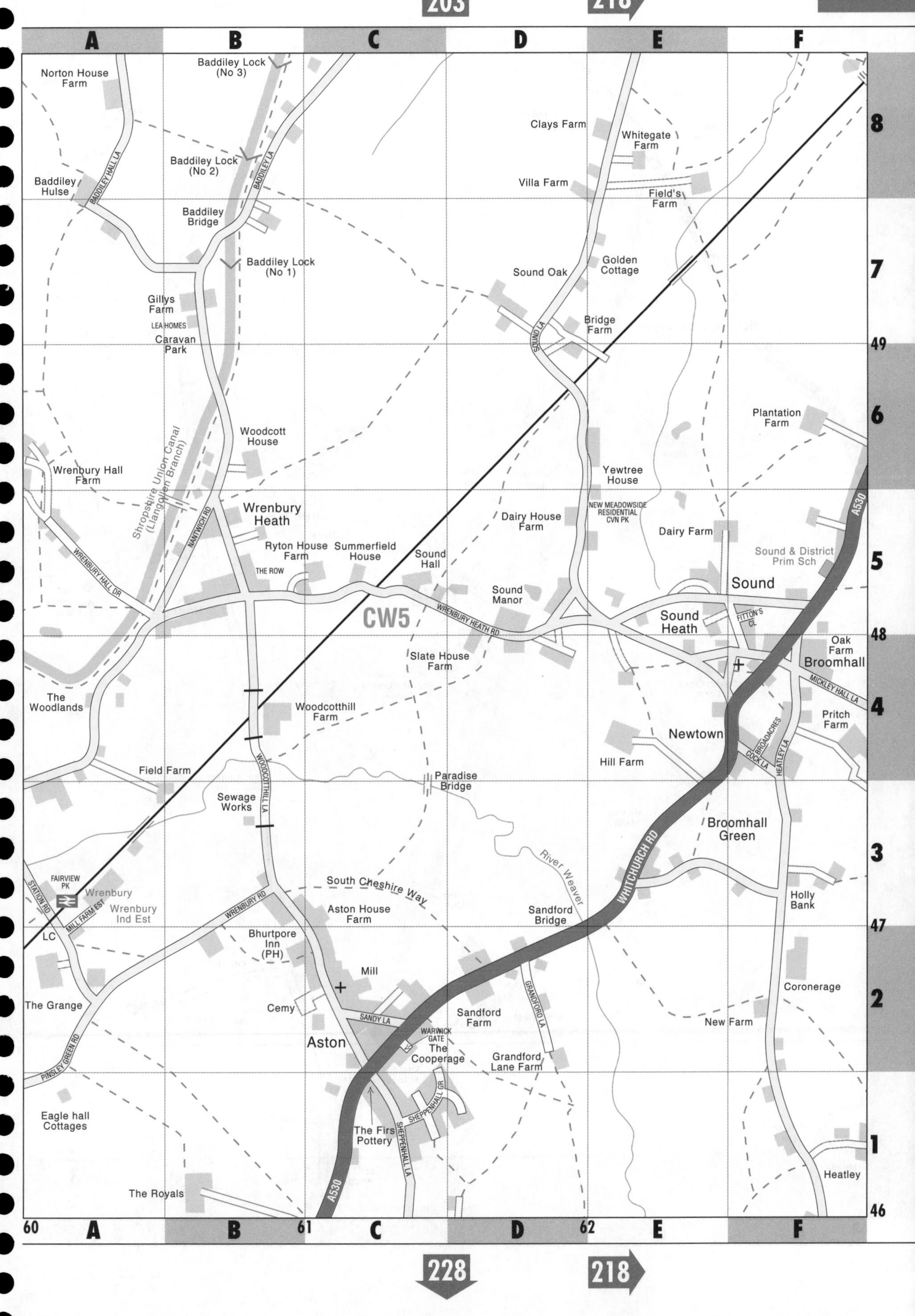
203
218
Norton House Farm
Baddiley Lock (No 3)
Baddiley Lock (No 2)
Baddiley Hulse
BADDILEY HALL LA
BADDILEY LA
Baddiley Bridge
Baddiley Lock (No 1)
Gillys Farm
LEA HOMES
Caravan Park
Woodcott House
Shropshire Union Canal (Llangollen Branch)
Wrenbury Hall Farm
Wrenbury Heath
NANTWICH RD
WRENBURY HALL DR
Ryton House Farm
Summerfield House
THE ROW
Sound Hall
CW5
WRENBURY HEATH RD
Clays Farm
Whitegate Farm
Villa Farm
Field's Farm
Sound Oak
Golden Cottage
Bridge Farm
SOUND LA
Plantation Farm
Yewtree House
NEW MEADOWSIDE RESIDENTIAL CVN PK
Dairy House Farm
Dairy Farm
Sound & District Prim Sch
A530
Sound
Sound Manor
Sound Heath
FITTON'S CL
Oak Farm
Broomhall
MICKLEY HALL LA
Slate House Farm
The Woodlands
Woodcotthill Farm
Newtown
Pritch Farm
BROADACRES
COCK LA
HEATLEY LA
Hill Farm
Field Farm
WOODCOTTHILL LA
Paradise Bridge
Sewage Works
Broomhall Green
WHITCHURCH RD
River Weaver
FAIRVIEW PK
STATION RD
Wrenbury
Wrenbury Ind Est
MILL FARM EST
LC
WRENBURY RD
South Cheshire Way
Aston House Farm
Sandford Bridge
Holly Bank
Bhurtpore Inn (PH)
Mill
The Grange
Cemy
SANDY LA
GRANDFORD LA
Coronerage
Sandford Farm
New Farm
WARWICK GATE
The Cooperage
Aston
Grandford Lane Farm
PINSLEY GREEN RD
SHEPPENHALL GR
Eagle hall Cottages
The Firs Pottery
SHEPPENHALL LA
A530
Heatley
The Royals
A B C D E F
8 7 49 6 5 48 4 3 47 2 1 46
60 61 62
228
218

217
204

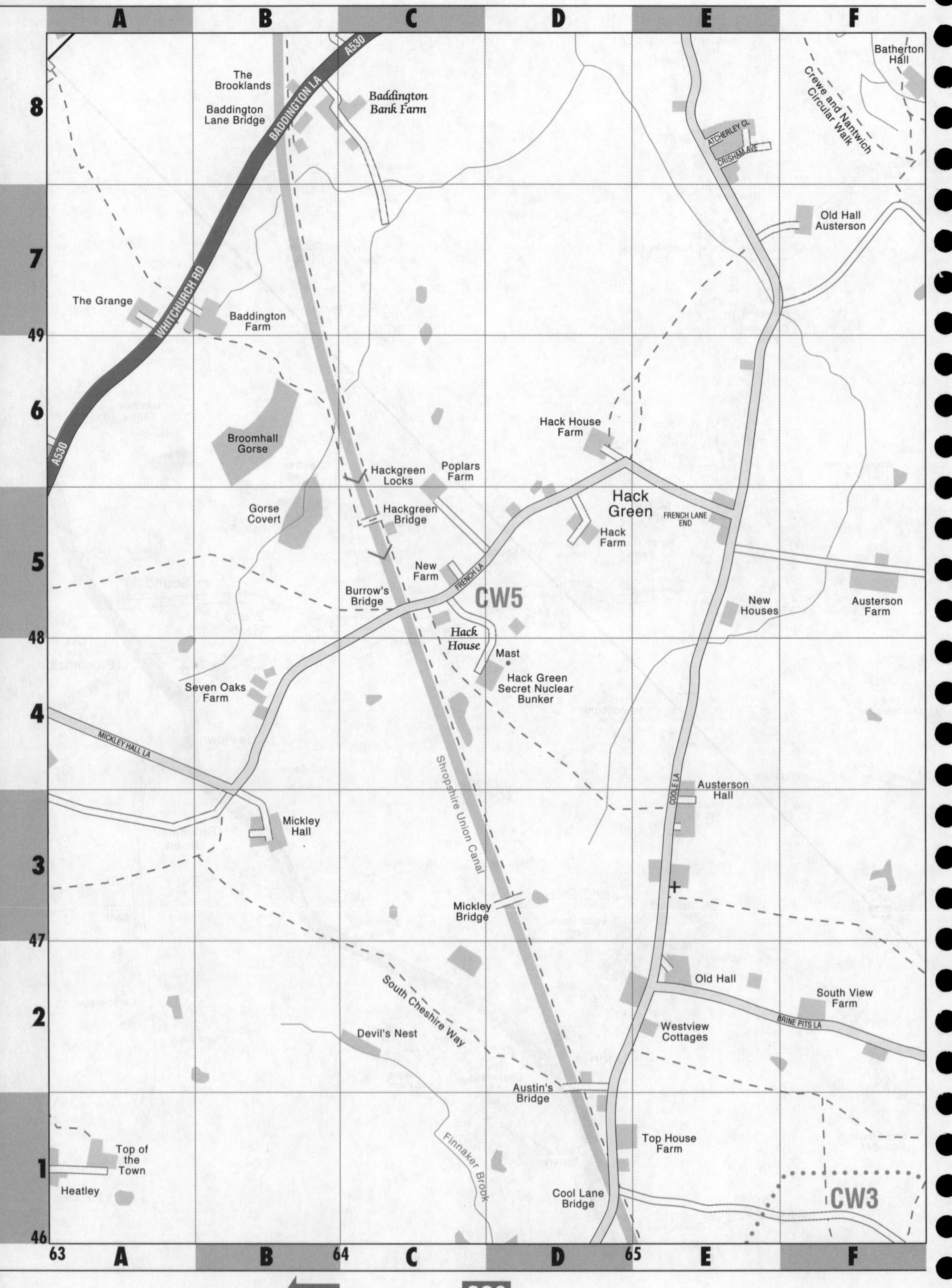

217
229

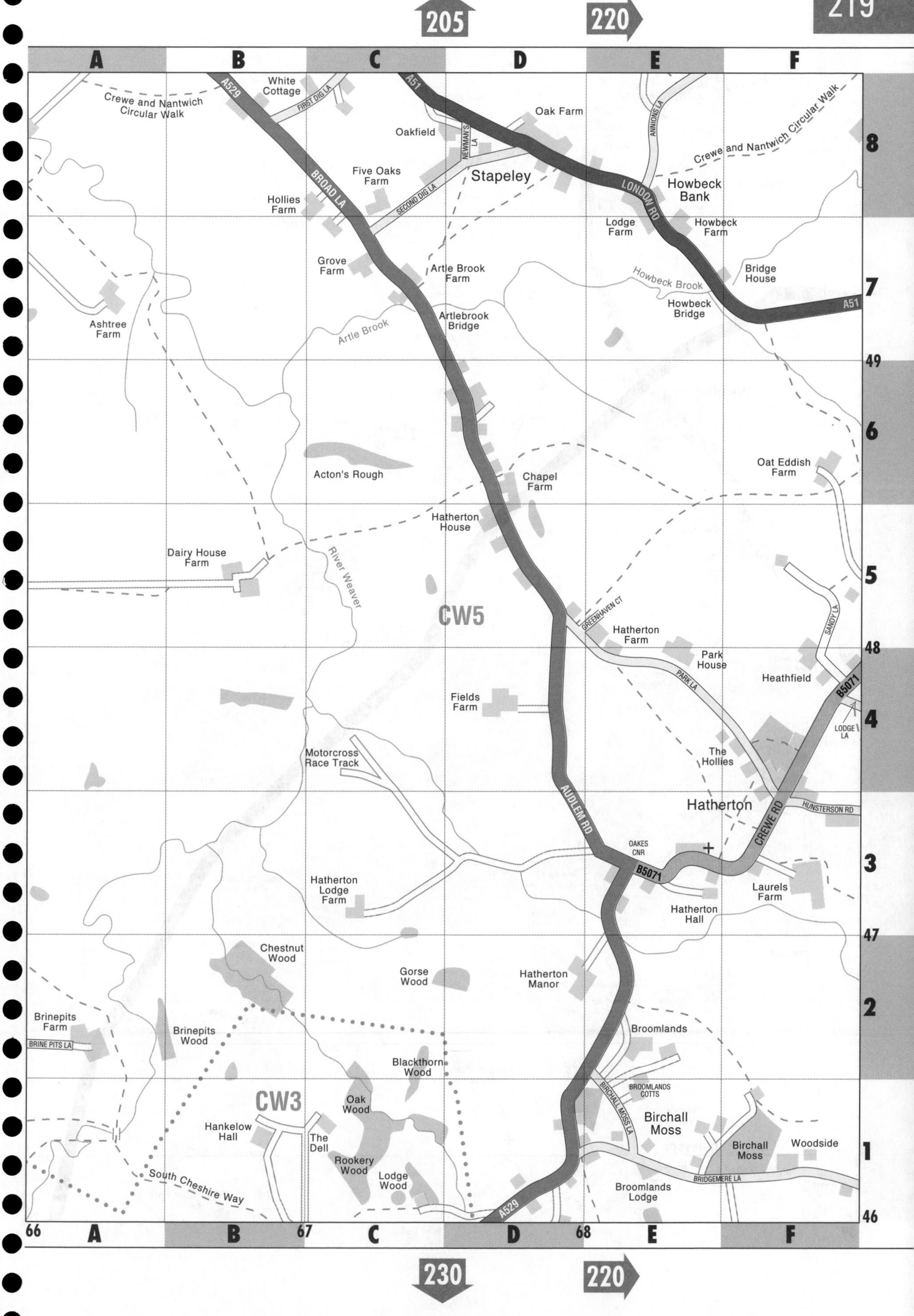
205
220
A
B
C
D
E
F
Crewe and Nantwich Circular Walk
White Cottage
FIRST DIG LA
A529
A51
Oak Farm
Oakfield
NEWMAN'S LA
ANNIONS LA
Crewe and Nantwich Circular Walk
Stapeley
Five Oaks Farm
Hollies Farm
BROAD LA
SECOND DIG LA
LONDON RD
Howbeck Bank
Lodge Farm
Howbeck Farm
Grove Farm
Artle Brook Farm
Howbeck Brook
Bridge House
Howbeck Bridge
A51
Ashtree Farm
Artle Brook
Artlebrook Bridge
Acton's Rough
Chapel Farm
Oat Eddish Farm
Hatherton House
Dairy House Farm
River Weaver
CW5
GREENHAVEN CT
Hatherton Farm
SANDY LA
Park House
PARK LA
Heathfield
B5071
Fields Farm
LODGE LA
The Hollies
Motorcross Race Track
Hatherton
HUNSTERSON RD
AUDLEM RD
CREWE RD
OAKES CNR
B5071
Hatherton Lodge Farm
Laurels Farm
Hatherton Hall
Chestnut Wood
Gorse Wood
Hatherton Manor
Brinepits Farm
BRINE PITS LA
Brinepits Wood
Broomlands
Blackthorn Wood
BROOMLANDS COTTS
BIRCHALL MOSS LA
CW3
Oak Wood
Birchall Moss
Hankelow Hall
The Dell
Rookery Wood
Birchall Moss
Woodside
BRIDGEMERE LA
Lodge Wood
South Cheshire Way
A529
Broomlands Lodge
8
7
49
6
5
48
4
3
47
2
1
46
66
67
68
230
220

219 206

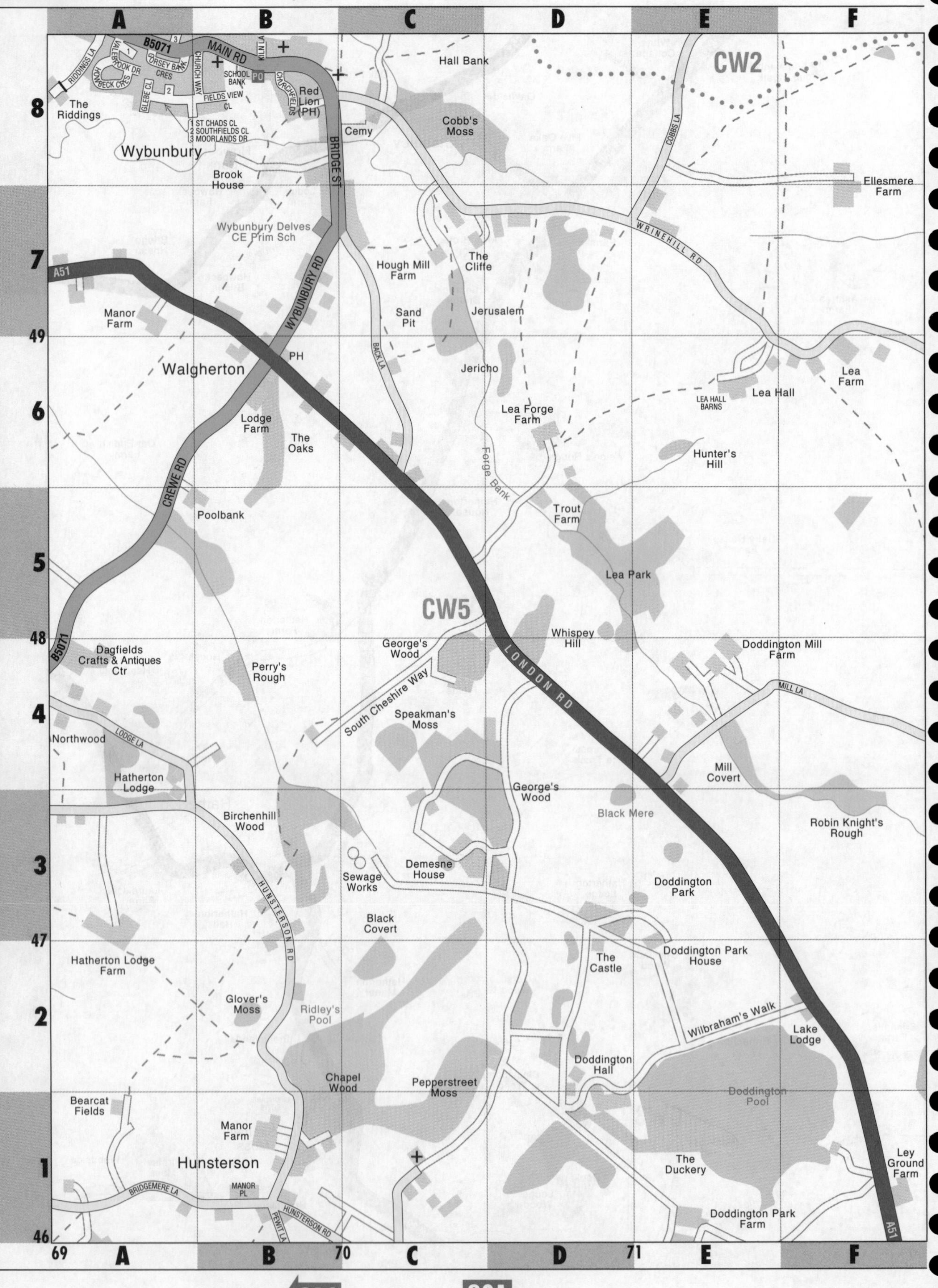

219 231

207

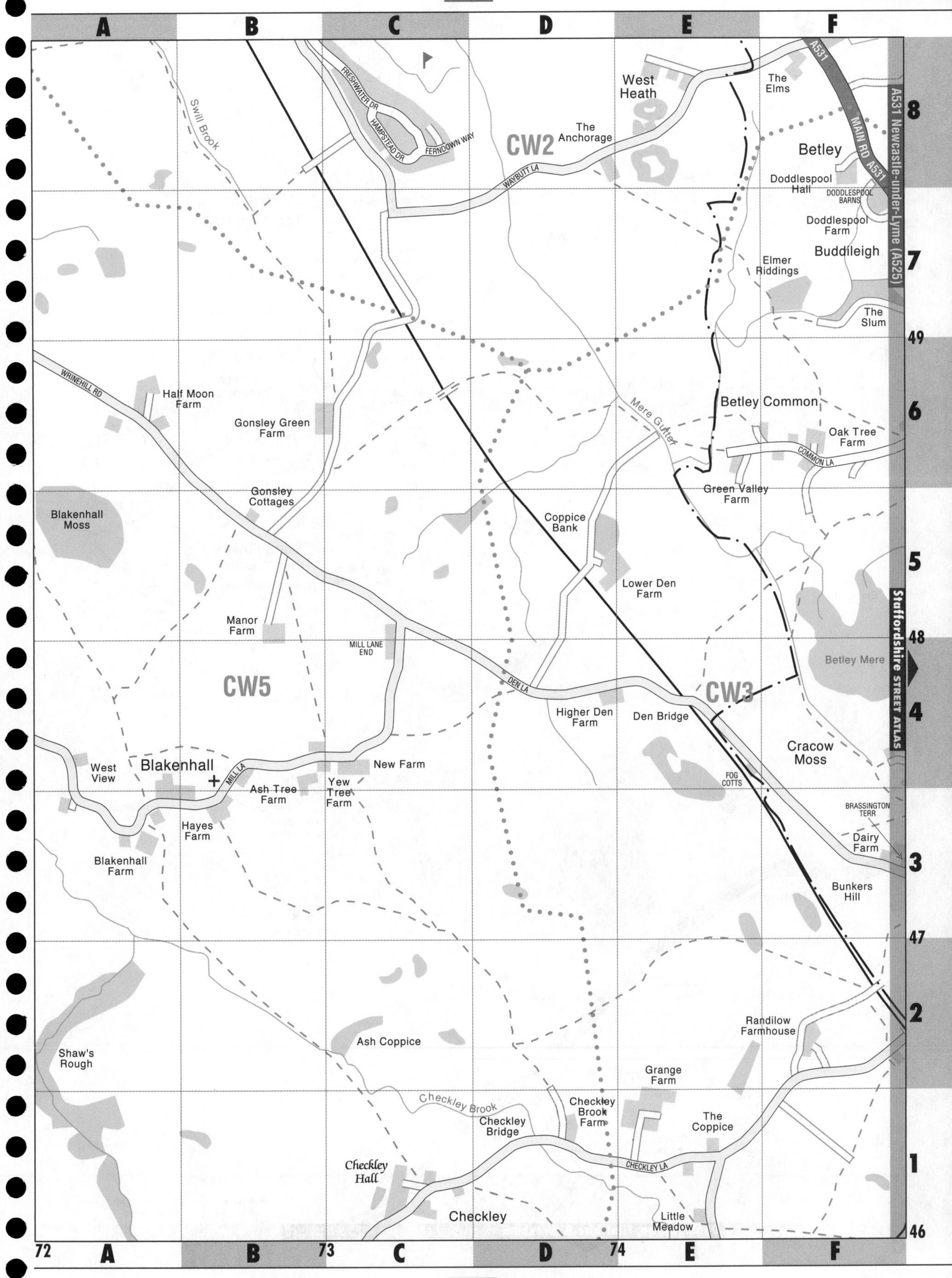

A
B
C
D
E
F
West Heath
The Elms
A531
FRESHWATER DR
HAMPSTEAD DR
FERNDOWN WAY
Swill Brook
CW2
The Anchorage
Betley
MAIN RD
Doddlespool Hall
DODDLESPOOL BARNS
WAYBUTT LA
Doddlespool Farm
Buddileigh
Elmer Riddings
The Slum
A531 Newcastle-under-Lyme (A525)
WRINEHILL RD
Half Moon Farm
Gonsley Green Farm
Mere Gutter
Betley Common
Oak Tree Farm
COMMON LA
Green Valley Farm
Gonsley Cottages
Blakenhall Moss
Coppice Bank
Lower Den Farm
Manor Farm
MILL LANE END
Betley Mere
Staffordshire STREET ATLAS
CW5
DEN LA
Higher Den Farm
Den Bridge
CW3
Cracow Moss
West View
Blakenhall
MILL LA
New Farm
Ash Tree Farm
Yew Tree Farm
FOG COTTS
Hayes Farm
BRASSINGTON TERR
Dairy Farm
Blakenhall Farm
Bunkers Hill
Randilow Farmhouse
Ash Coppice
Shaw's Rough
Grange Farm
Checkley Brook
Checkley Brook Farm
Checkley Bridge
The Coppice
Checkley Hall
CHECKLEY LA
Checkley
Little Meadow
8
7
49
6
5
48
4
3
47
2
1
46
72
73
74

232

211

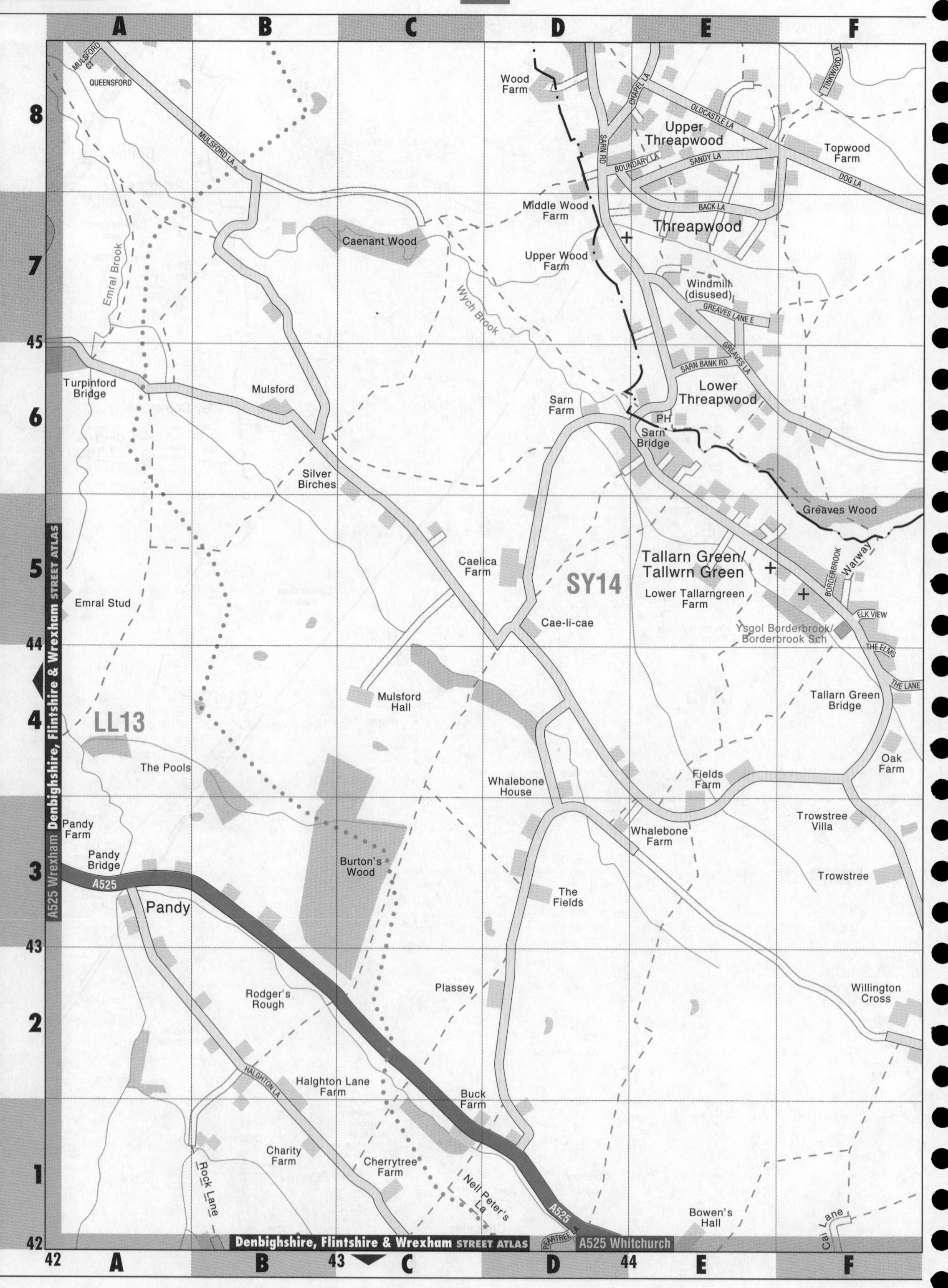

A
B
C
D
E
F
8
7
6
5
4
3
2
1
45
44
43
42
MULSFORD CT
QUEENSFORD
MULSFORD LA
Wood Farm
CHAPEL LA
OLDCASTLE LA
TINKWOOD LA
Upper Threapwood
SARN RD
BOUNDARY LA
SANDY LA
Topwood Farm
DOG LA
Middle Wood Farm
BACK LA
Threapwood
Caenant Wood
Upper Wood Farm
Emral Brook
Windmill (disused)
GREAVES LANE E
Wych Brook
GREAVES LA
SARN BANK RD
Turpinford Bridge
Mulsford
Sarn Farm
Lower Threapwood
PH
Sarn Bridge
Silver Birches
Greaves Wood
Caelica Farm
Tallarn Green/ Tallwrn Green
BORDERBROOK
Warway
SY14
Lower Tallarngreen Farm
Emral Stud
Cae-li-cae
ELK VIEW
Ysgol Borderbrook/ Borderbrook Sch
THE ELMS
THE LANE
Mulsford Hall
Tallarn Green Bridge
LL13
The Pools
Fields Farm
Oak Farm
Whalebone House
Pandy Farm
Whalebone Farm
Trowstree Villa
Pandy Bridge
Burton's Wood
Trowstree
A525
Pandy
The Fields
Rodger's Rough
Plassey
Willington Cross
HALGHTON LA
Halghton Lane Farm
Buck Farm
Charity Farm
Cherrytree Farm
Nell Peter's La
Rock Lane
A525
Bowen's Hall
Cai Lane
PEARTREE LA
A525 Whitchurch
A525 Wrexham
Denbighshire, Flintshire & Wrexham STREET ATLAS

212
224

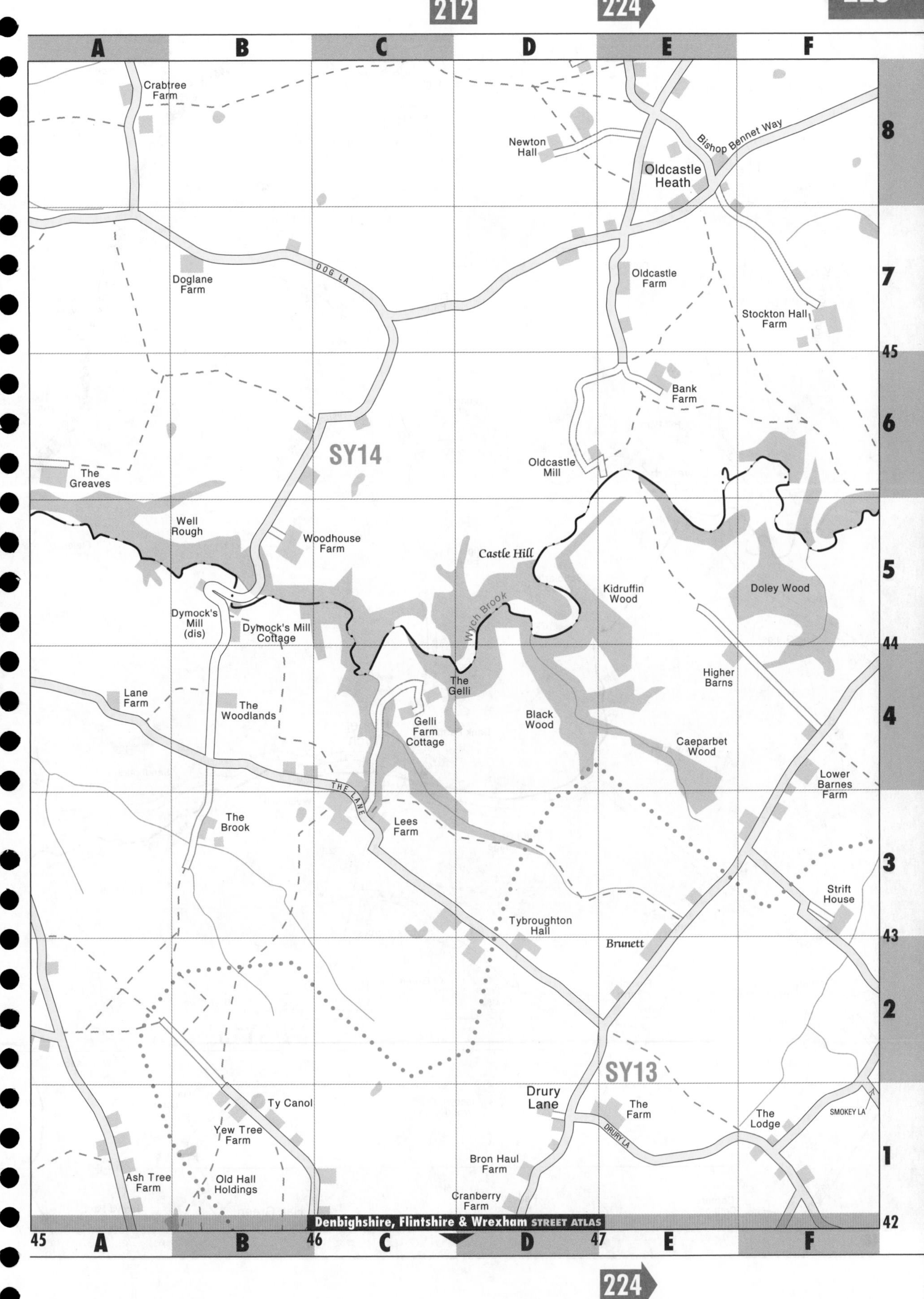
A
B
C
D
E
F
Crabtree Farm
Newton Hall
Bishop Bennet Way
Oldcastle Heath
8
Doglane Farm
DOG LA
Oldcastle Farm
7
Stockton Hall Farm
45
Bank Farm
6
SY14
Oldcastle Mill
The Greaves
Well Rough
Woodhouse Farm
Castle Hill
Kidruffin Wood
Doley Wood
5
Wych Brook
Dymock's Mill (dis)
Dymock's Mill Cottage
44
The Gelli
Higher Barns
Lane Farm
The Woodlands
Gelli Farm Cottage
Black Wood
4
Caeparbet Wood
THE LANE
Lower Barnes Farm
The Brook
Lees Farm
3
Strift House
Tybroughton Hall
Brunett
43
2
SY13
Drury Lane
Ty Canol
The Farm
The Lodge
SMOKEY LA
Yew Tree Farm
DRURY LA
1
Bron Haul Farm
Ash Tree Farm
Old Hall Holdings
Cranberry Farm
42
45
46
47

224

223
213

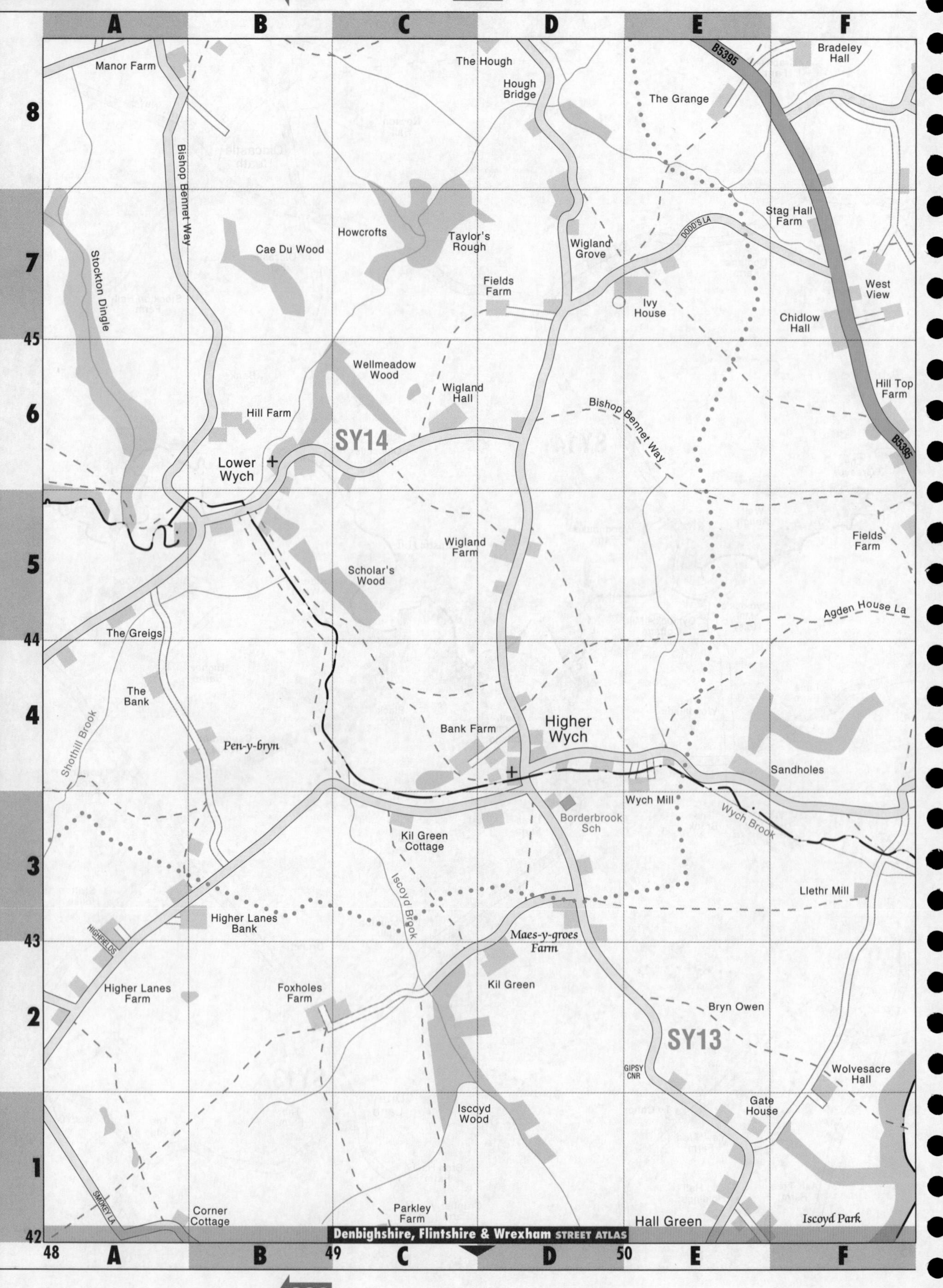
A
B
C
D
E
F
Manor Farm
The Hough
Hough Bridge
The Grange
Bradeley Hall
B5395
8
Bishop Bennet Way
7
Stockton Dingle
Cae Du Wood
Howcrofts
Taylor's Rough
Wigland Grove
DODD'S LA
Stag Hall Farm
West View
Fields Farm
Ivy House
Chidlow Hall
45
Wellmeadow Wood
Wigland Hall
Hill Top Farm
6
Hill Farm
Bishop Bennet Way
SY14
Lower Wych
5
Wigland Farm
Fields Farm
Scholar's Wood
Agden House La
44
The Greigs
The Bank
4
Shothill Brook
Pen-y-bryn
Bank Farm
Higher Wych
Sandholes
Wych Mill
Borderbrook Sch
Wych Brook
Kil Green Cottage
3
Iscoyd Brook
Llethr Mill
HIGHFIELDS
Higher Lanes Bank
Maes-y-groes Farm
43
Kil Green
Higher Lanes Farm
Foxholes Farm
Bryn Owen
2
SY13
GIPSY CNR
Wolvesacre Hall
Gate House
Iscoyd Wood
1
SMOKEY LA
Corner Cottage
Parkley Farm
Hall Green
Iscoyd Park
42
48
49
50

223

214
226

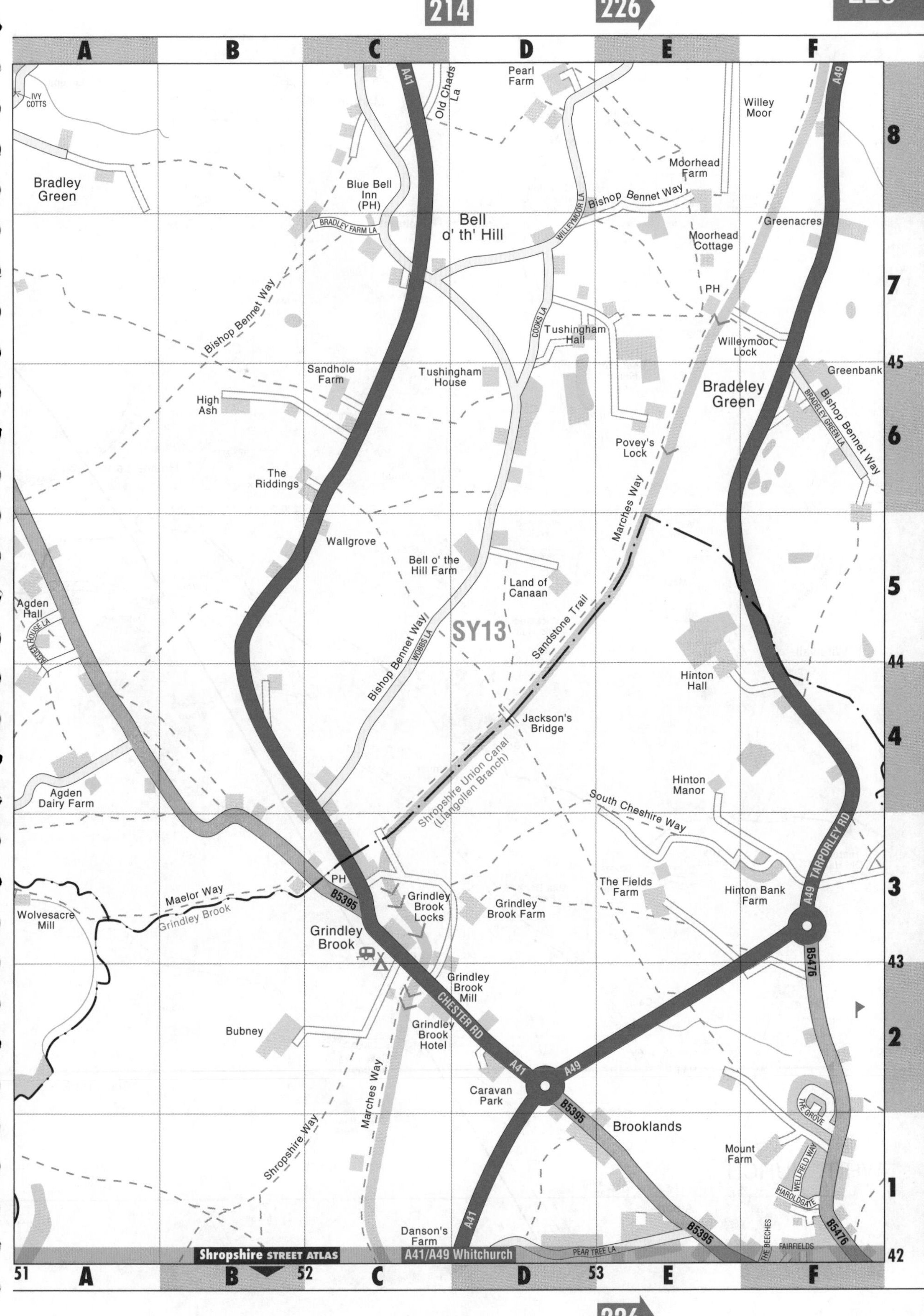

A
B
C
D
E
F
8
7
6
5
4
3
2
1
45
44
43
42
51
52
53
IVY COTTS
Bradley Green
Blue Bell Inn (PH)
BRADLEY FARM LA
Old Chads La
A41
Pearl Farm
Bell o' th' Hill
WILLEYMOOR LA
Bishop Bennet Way
Moorhead Farm
Willey Moor
A49
Greenacres
Moorhead Cottage
PH
COOKS LA
Tushingham Hall
Willeymoor Lock
Greenbank
Sandhole Farm
Tushingham House
High Ash
Bradeley Green
BRADELEY GREEN LA
Povey's Lock
The Riddings
Marches Way
Wallgrove
Bell o' the Hill Farm
Land of Canaan
Agden Hall
AGDEN HOUSE LA
SY13
Sandstone Trail
WOBBS LA
Hinton Hall
Jackson's Bridge
Shropshire Union Canal (Llangollen Branch)
Hinton Manor
Agden Dairy Farm
South Cheshire Way
TARPORLEY RD
The Fields Farm
Hinton Bank Farm
Maelor Way
PH
B5395
Grindley Brook Locks
Grindley Brook Farm
Wolvesacre Mill
Grindley Brook
Grindley Brook
B5476
Grindley Brook Mill
CHESTER RD
Bubney
Grindley Brook Hotel
Caravan Park
THE GROVE
Brooklands
Shropshire Way
Mount Farm
WELLFIELD WAY
HAROLDGATE
Danson's Farm
PEAR TREE LA
THE BEECHES
FAIRFIELDS

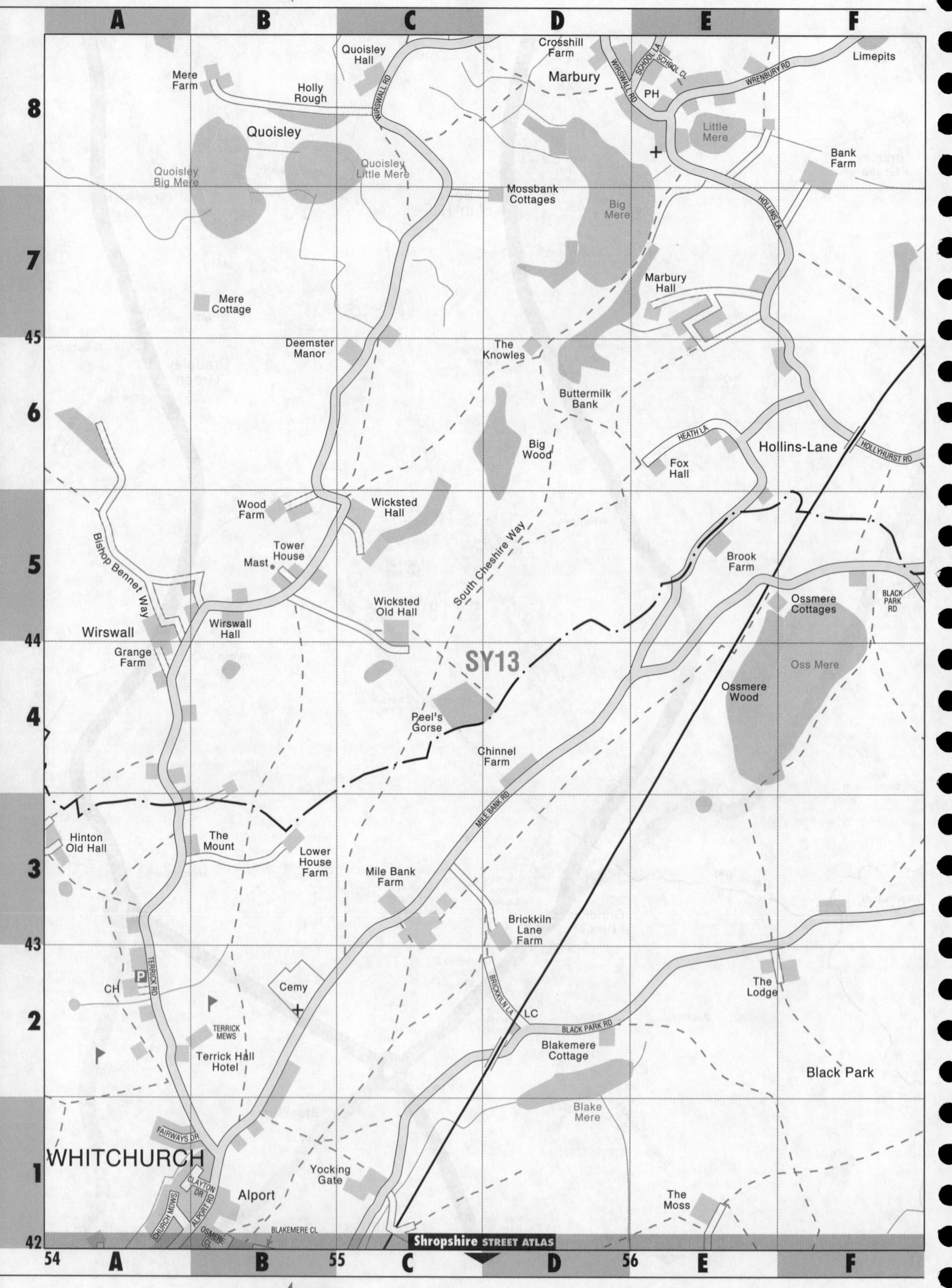
A
B
C
D
E
F
Quoisley Hall
Crosshill Farm
Limepits
Mere Farm
Holly Rough
Marbury
PH
Quoisley
Little Mere
Bank Farm
Quoisley Big Mere
Quoisley Little Mere
Mossbank Cottages
Big Mere
Marbury Hall
Mere Cottage
Deemster Manor
The Knowles
Buttermilk Bank
Big Wood
Hollins-Lane
Fox Hall
Wood Farm
Wicksted Hall
Brook Farm
Tower House
Mast
Bishop Bennet Way
South Cheshire Way
Wirswall
Wirswall Hall
Wicksted Old Hall
Ossmere Cottages
Black Park Rd
Grange Farm
SY13
Oss Mere
Ossmere Wood
Peel's Gorse
Chinnel Farm
Hinton Old Hall
The Mount
Lower House Farm
Mile Bank Farm
Brickkiln Lane Farm
CH
Cemy
The Lodge
Terrick Mews
LC
Terrick Hall Hotel
Blakemere Cottage
Black Park
Blake Mere
WHITCHURCH
Yocking Gate
Alport
The Moss
Wirswall Rd
School La
School Cl
Wrenbury Rd
Hollins La
Heath La
Hollyhurst Rd
Mile Bank Rd
Terrick Rd
Brickkiln La
Black Park Rd
Fairways Dr
Clayton Dr
Alport Rd
Church Mows
Osmere Cl
Blakemere Cl
8
7
45
6
5
44
4
3
43
2
1
42
54
55
56

216
228

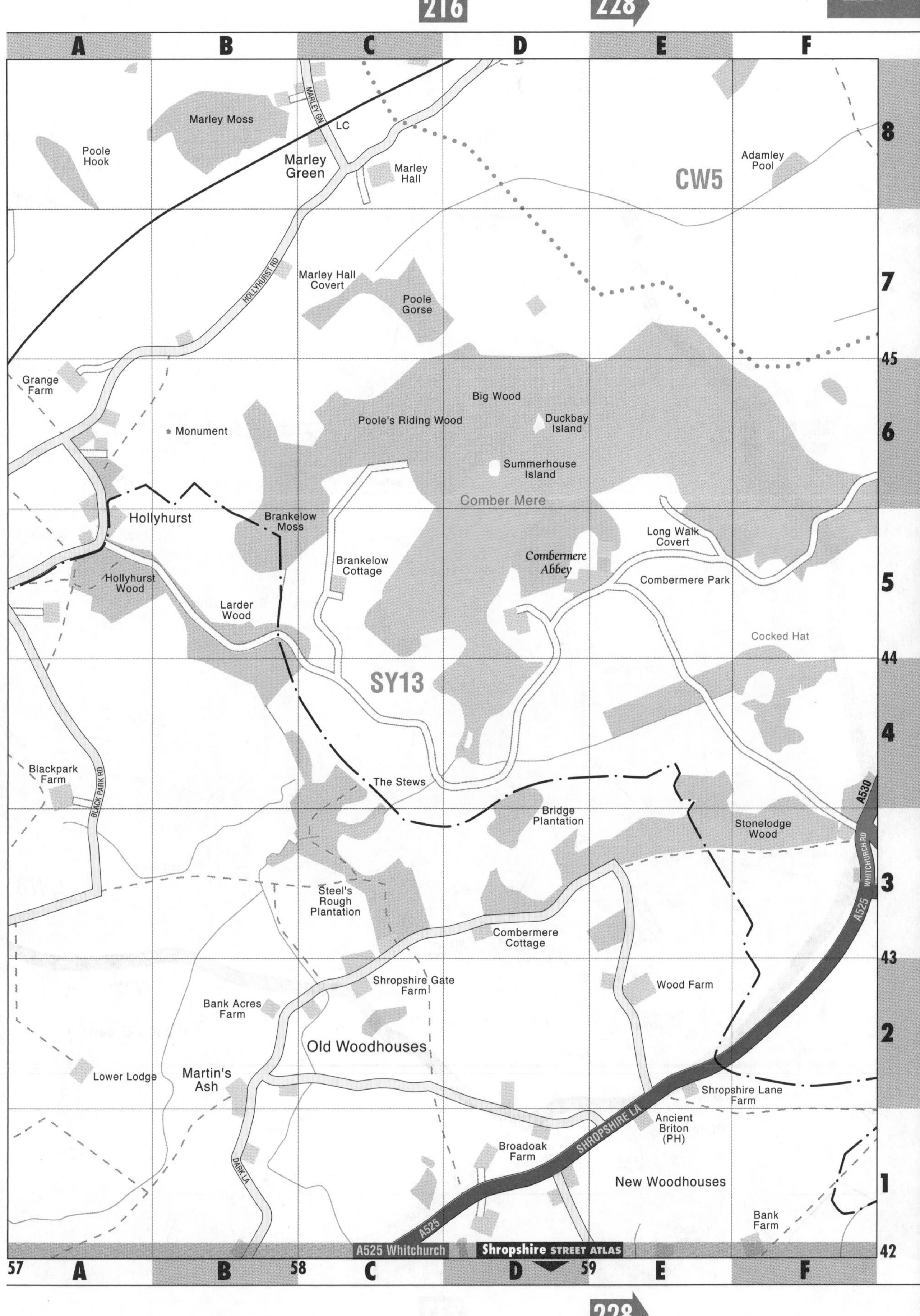

A
B
C
D
E
F
Marley Moss
Poole Hook
MARLEY GN
LC
Marley Green
Marley Hall
Adamley Pool
CW5
8
HOLLYHURST RD
Marley Hall Covert
Poole Gorse
7
45
Grange Farm
Big Wood
Poole's Riding Wood
Duckbay Island
Monument
6
Summerhouse Island
Comber Mere
Hollyhurst
Brankelow Moss
Long Walk Covert
Brankelow Cottage
Combermere Abbey
Hollyhurst Wood
Combermere Park
5
Larder Wood
Cocked Hat
44
SY13
4
Blackpark Farm
BLACK PARK RD
The Stews
A530
Bridge Plantation
Stonelodge Wood
WHITCHURCH RD
3
Steel's Rough Plantation
A525
Combermere Cottage
43
Shropshire Gate Farm
Wood Farm
Bank Acres Farm
2
Old Woodhouses
Lower Lodge
Martin's Ash
Shropshire Lane Farm
Ancient Briton (PH)
SHROPSHIRE LA
Broadoak Farm
DARK LA
New Woodhouses
1
A525
Bank Farm
A525 Whitchurch
Shropshire STREET ATLAS
42
57
58
59

228

227 217

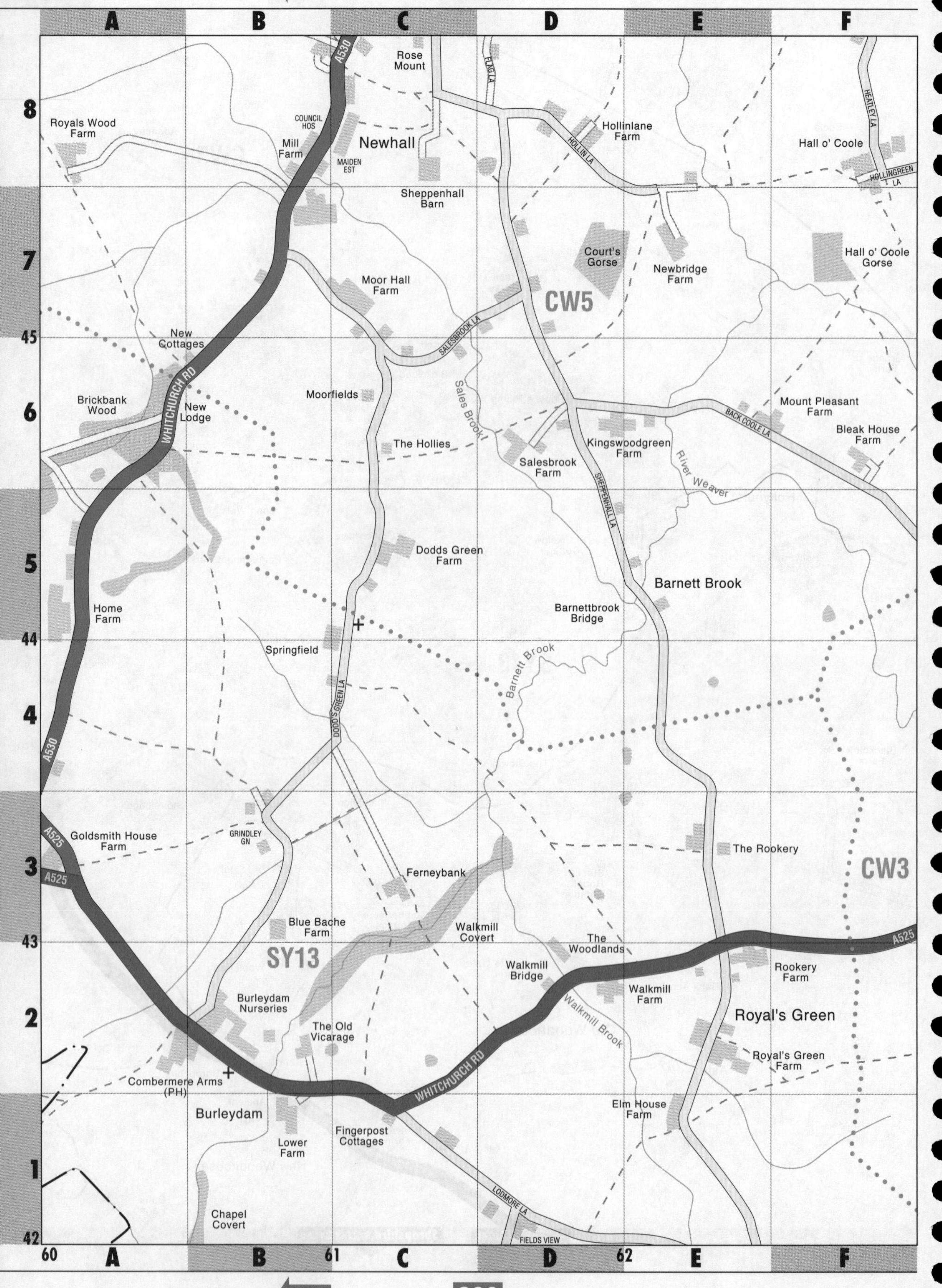

227 233

218
230

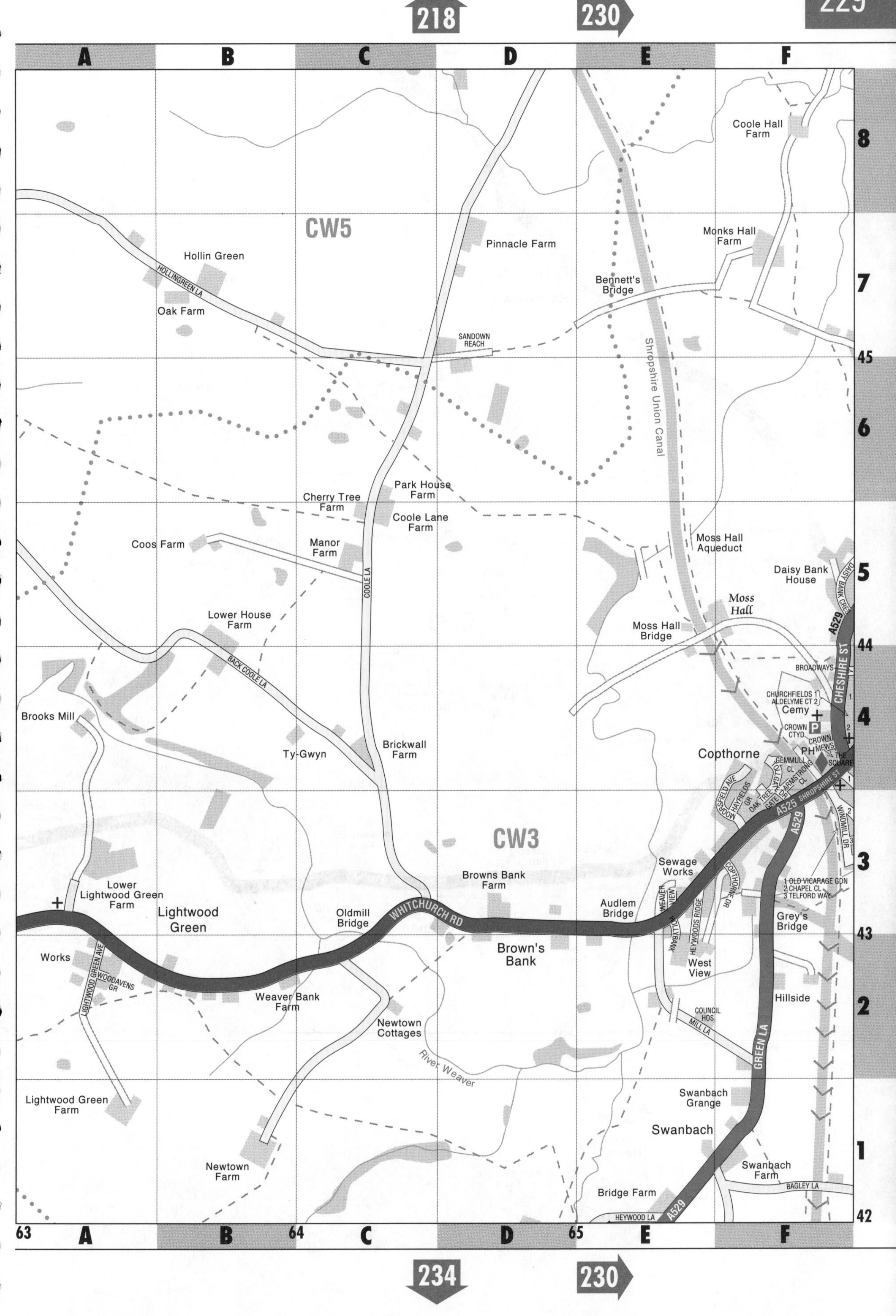

234
230

229
219

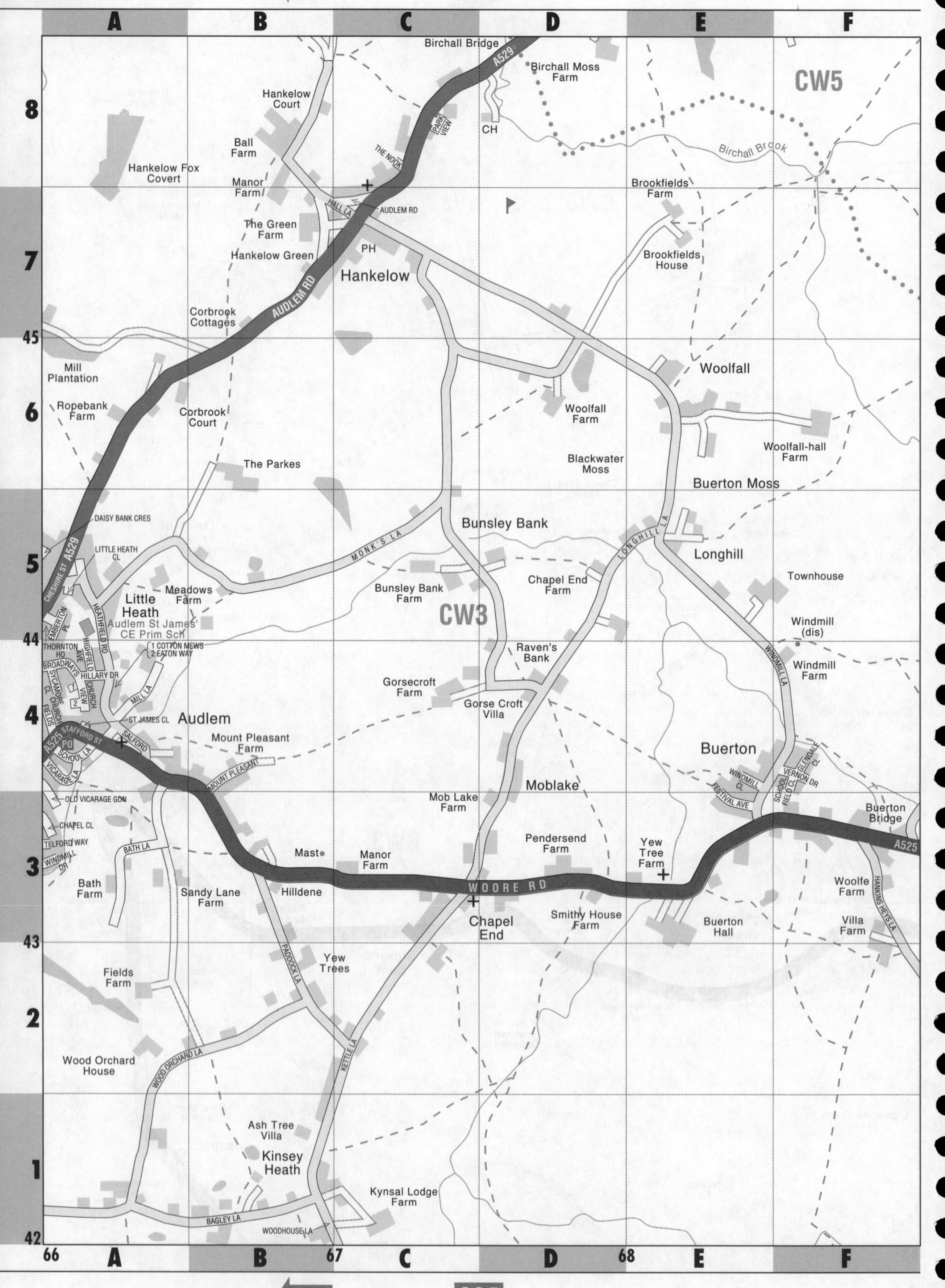

229
235

220
232

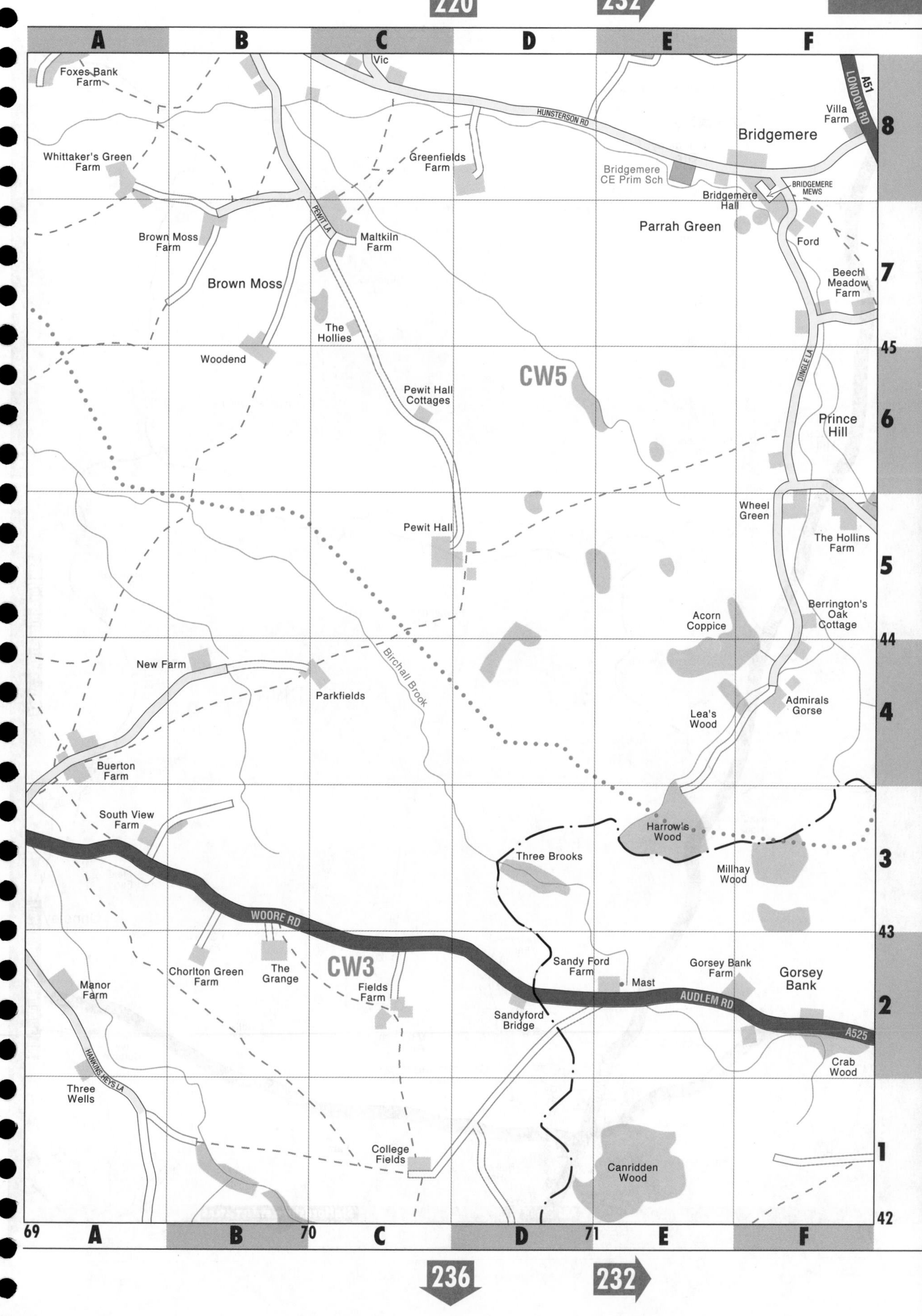

236
232

231
221

A
B
C
D
E
F
8
7
45
6
5
44
4
3
43
2
1
42
72
73
74
Checkley Lodge
Checkley Green
CHECKLEY LA
CHECKLEY ROW
Bank Farm
Ash Tree Farm
Checkleygreen Farm
Checkley Wood New Farm
Checkley Brook
Checkley Wood
Wrinehill Wood
CW5
Yew Tree Farm
Prince Hill
Bridgemere Farm
YEW TREE LA
Checkley Wood Farm
Threeper's Drumble
DINGLE LA
LONDON RD
Phynsons Hayes Farm
Blake Hall Farm
Bridgemere Garden World
The Gorse
Hollyhurst Farm
CW3
Newhouse Farm
HOLDINGS LA
SCHOOL LA
Flash Farm House
Field Farm
Onneley
Cherrytree Farm
The Greaves Farm
Syllenhurst Farm
A525
CHERRY TREE LA
Holly Villa
Ivy Cottage
CANDLE LA
AUDLEM RD
Moss Farm
Gravenhunger Moss
NANTWICH RD
AIZEFIELD CL
FARMFIELDS RISE
WESTFIELDS RISE
NEWCASTLE RD
The Old Crow
PH
PO
KENRICK CL
Woore Hall
Woore
THE GREEN
Bulkeley Hall
Bank Farm
GRAVENHUNGER LA
ASTON LA
TF9
Woore Prim Sch
NORTHLANDS
GROVE CRES
A51 Stone
Banktop
Staffordshire STREET ATLAS
A525 Newcastle-under-Lyme
A51

231

228
234

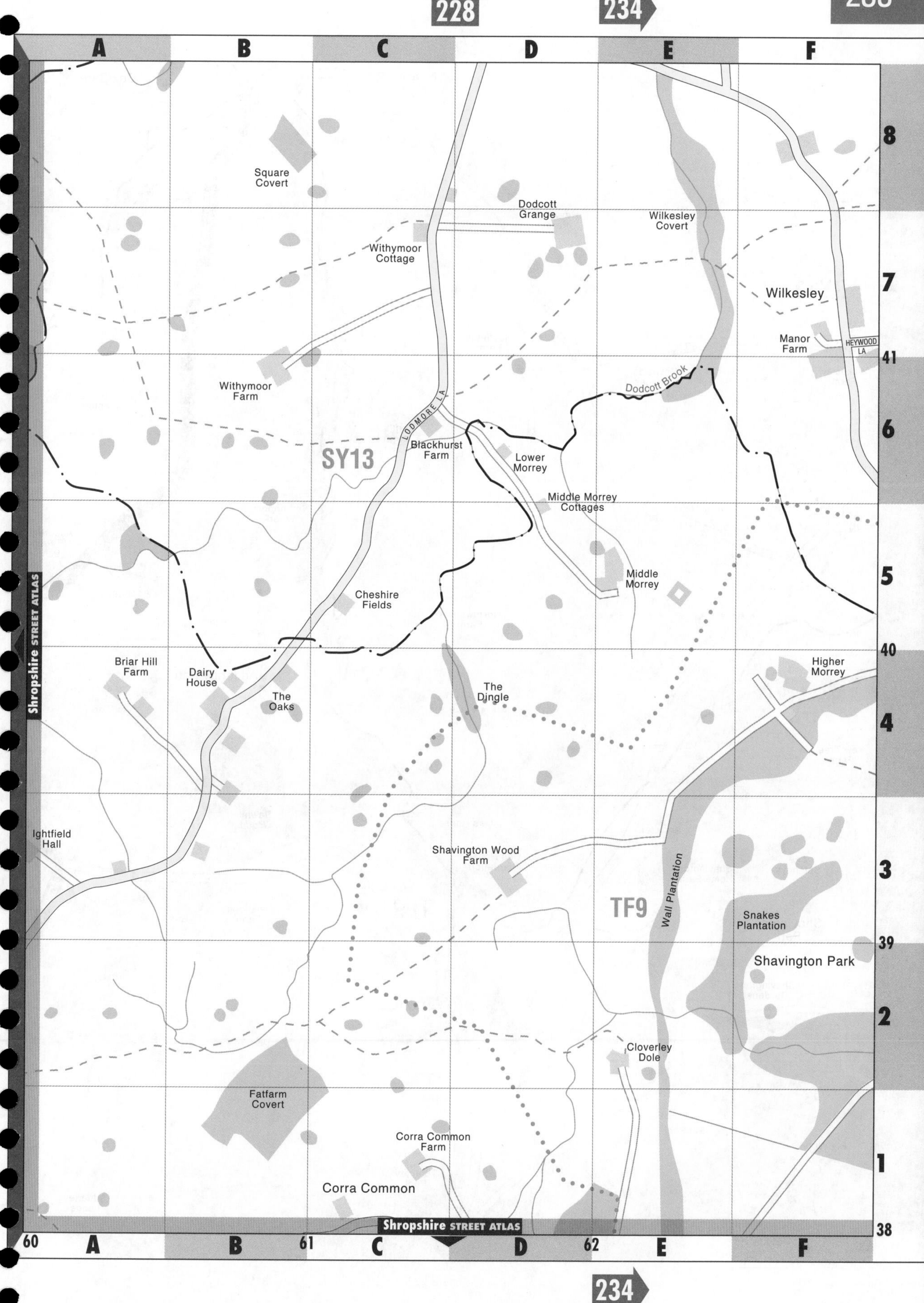
A
B
C
D
E
F
Square Covert
Dodcott Grange
Wilkesley Covert
Withymoor Cottage
Wilkesley
Manor Farm
HEYWOOD LA
Withymoor Farm
Dodcott Brook
LODMORE LA
Blackhurst Farm
SY13
Lower Morrey
Middle Morrey Cottages
Middle Morrey
Cheshire Fields
Briar Hill Farm
Dairy House
The Oaks
The Dingle
Higher Morrey
Ightfield Hall
Shavington Wood Farm
TF9
Wall Plantation
Snakes Plantation
Shavington Park
Cloverley Dole
Fatfarm Covert
Corra Common Farm
Corra Common
Shropshire STREET ATLAS
8
7
41
6
5
40
4
3
39
2
1
38
60
61
62

234

233
229

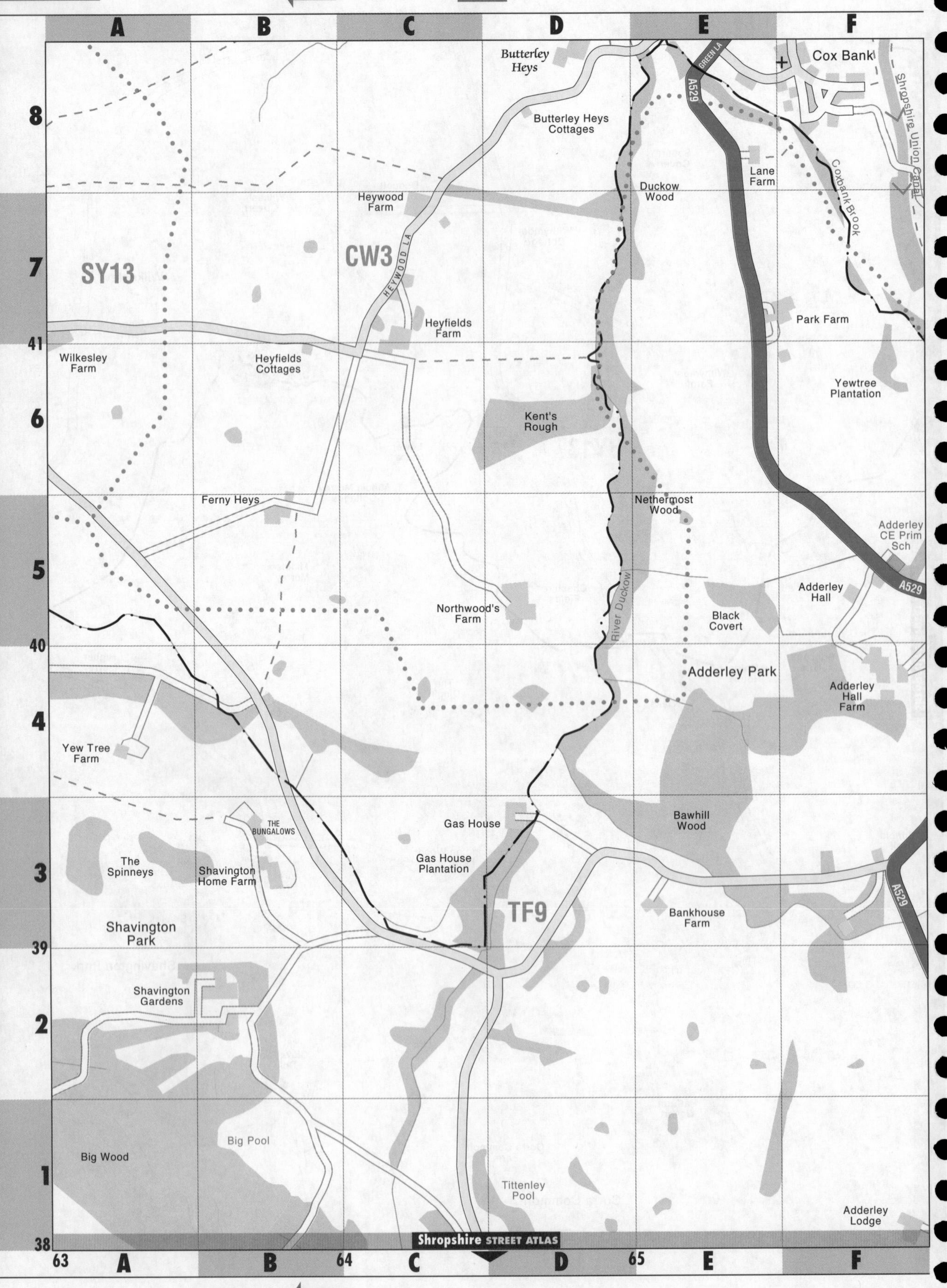
A
B
C
D
E
F
8
7
41
6
5
40
4
3
39
2
1
38
63
64
65
Butterley Heys
Butterley Heys Cottages
Cox Bank
GREEN LA
A529
Shropshire Union Canal
Coxbank Brook
Lane Farm
Duckow Wood
Heywood Farm
HEYWOOD LA
CW3
SY13
Heyfields Farm
Park Farm
Wilkesley Farm
Heyfields Cottages
Yewtree Plantation
Kent's Rough
Ferny Heys
Nethermost Wood
Adderley CE Prim Sch
Adderley Hall
River Duckow
Northwood's Farm
Black Covert
Adderley Park
Adderley Hall Farm
Yew Tree Farm
Gas House
Bawhill Wood
THE BUNGALOWS
The Spinneys
Shavington Home Farm
Gas House Plantation
TF9
Bankhouse Farm
Shavington Park
Shavington Gardens
Big Pool
Big Wood
Tittenley Pool
Adderley Lodge

233

230
236

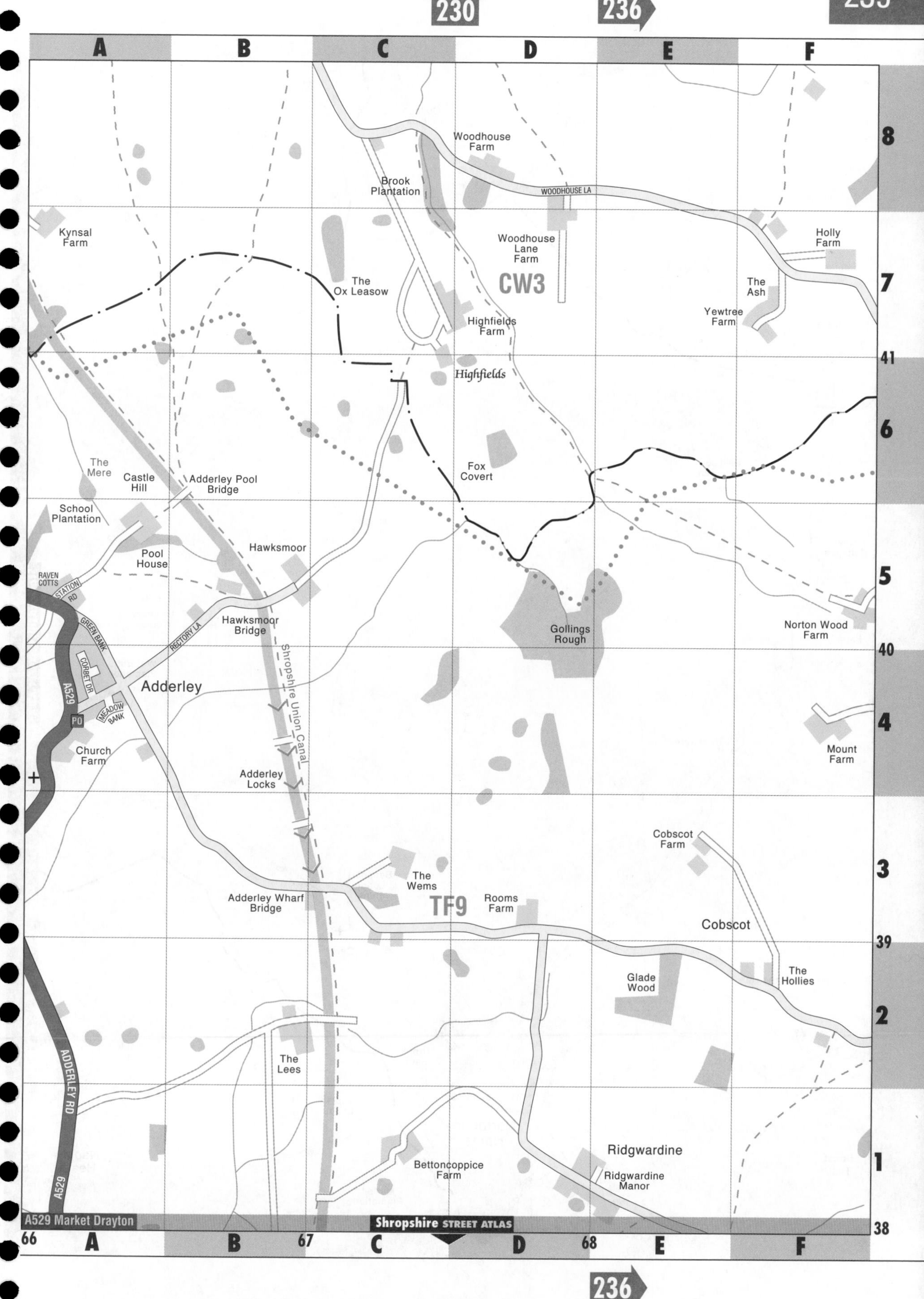
A
B
C
D
E
F
8
7
41
6
5
40
4
3
39
2
1
38
66
67
68
Woodhouse Farm
Brook Plantation
WOODHOUSE LA
Kynsal Farm
Woodhouse Lane Farm
Holly Farm
The Ox Leasow
CW3
The Ash
Yewtree Farm
Highfields Farm
Highfields
The Mere
Castle Hill
Adderley Pool Bridge
Fox Covert
School Plantation
Pool House
Hawksmoor
RAVEN COTTS
STATION RD
GREEN BANK
Hawksmoor Bridge
RECTORY LA
Gollings Rough
Norton Wood Farm
Shropshire Union Canal
CORBET DR
A529
Adderley
MEADOW BANK
PO
Church Farm
Mount Farm
Adderley Locks
Cobscot Farm
The Wems
Adderley Wharf Bridge
TF9
Rooms Farm
Cobscot
Glade Wood
The Hollies
The Lees
ADDERLEY RD
Ridgwardine
Bettoncoppice Farm
Ridgwardine Manor
A529 Market Drayton

236

235
231

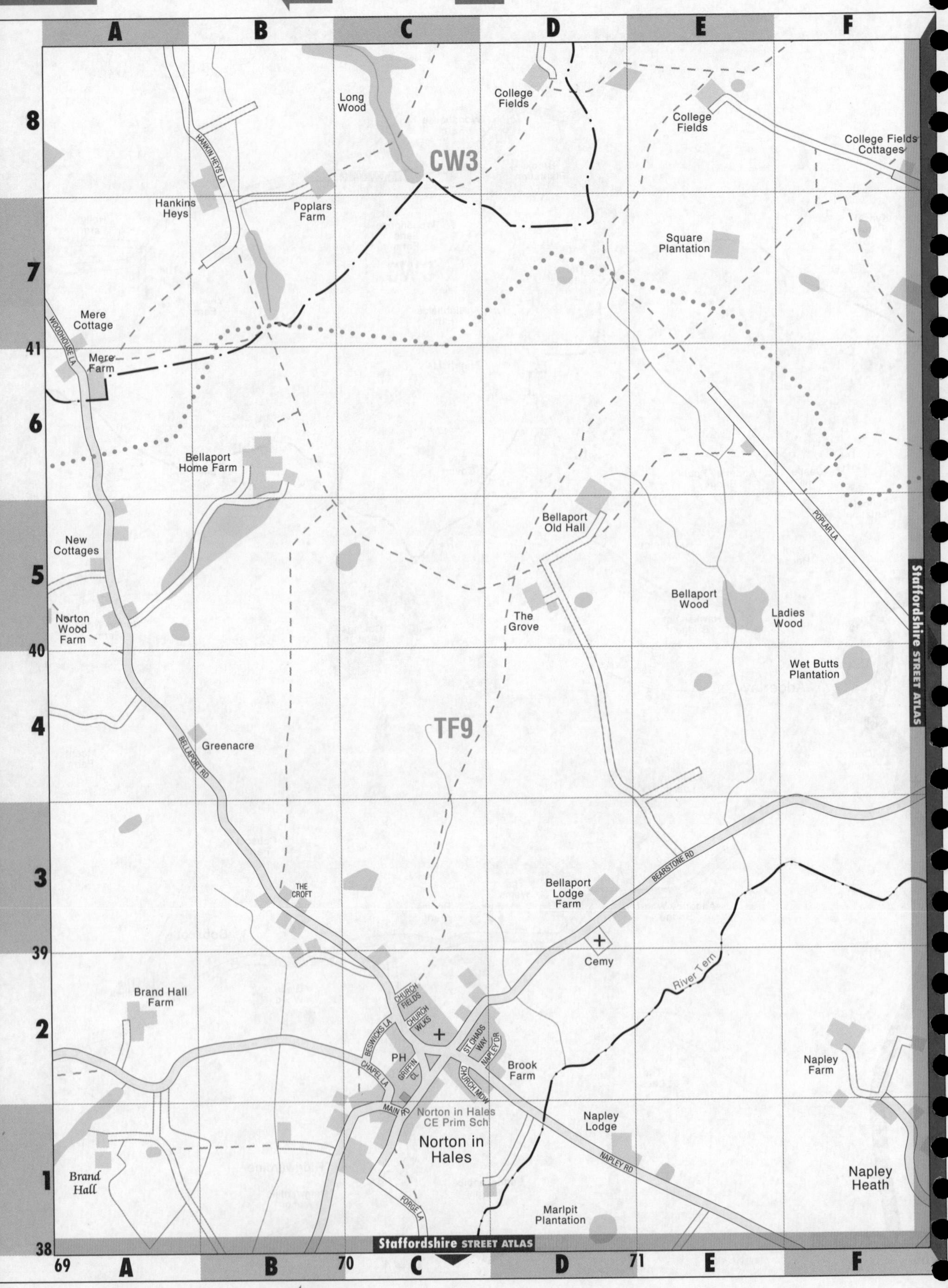
A
B
C
D
E
F
8
7
41
6
5
40
4
3
39
2
1
38
69
70
71
Long Wood
College Fields
College Fields
College Fields Cottages
CW3
Hankins Heys
Poplars Farm
HANKIN HEYS LA
Square Plantation
Mere Cottage
WOODHOUSE LA
Mere Farm
Bellaport Home Farm
New Cottages
Bellaport Old Hall
POPLAR LA
Norton Wood Farm
The Grove
Bellaport Wood
Ladies Wood
Wet Butts Plantation
TF9
Greenacre
BELLAPORT RD
THE CROFT
Bellaport Lodge Farm
BEARSTONE RD
Cemy
River Tern
Brand Hall Farm
CHURCH FIELDS
CHURCH WLKS
BESWICKS LA
ST CHADS WAY
NAPLEY DR
PH
GRIFFIN CL
CHAPEL LA
CHURCH MDW
Brook Farm
MAIN RD
Norton in Hales CE Prim Sch
Norton in Hales
Napley Lodge
Napley Farm
NAPLEY RD
Brand Hall
FORGE LA
Napley Heath
Marlpit Plantation
Staffordshire STREET ATLAS

235

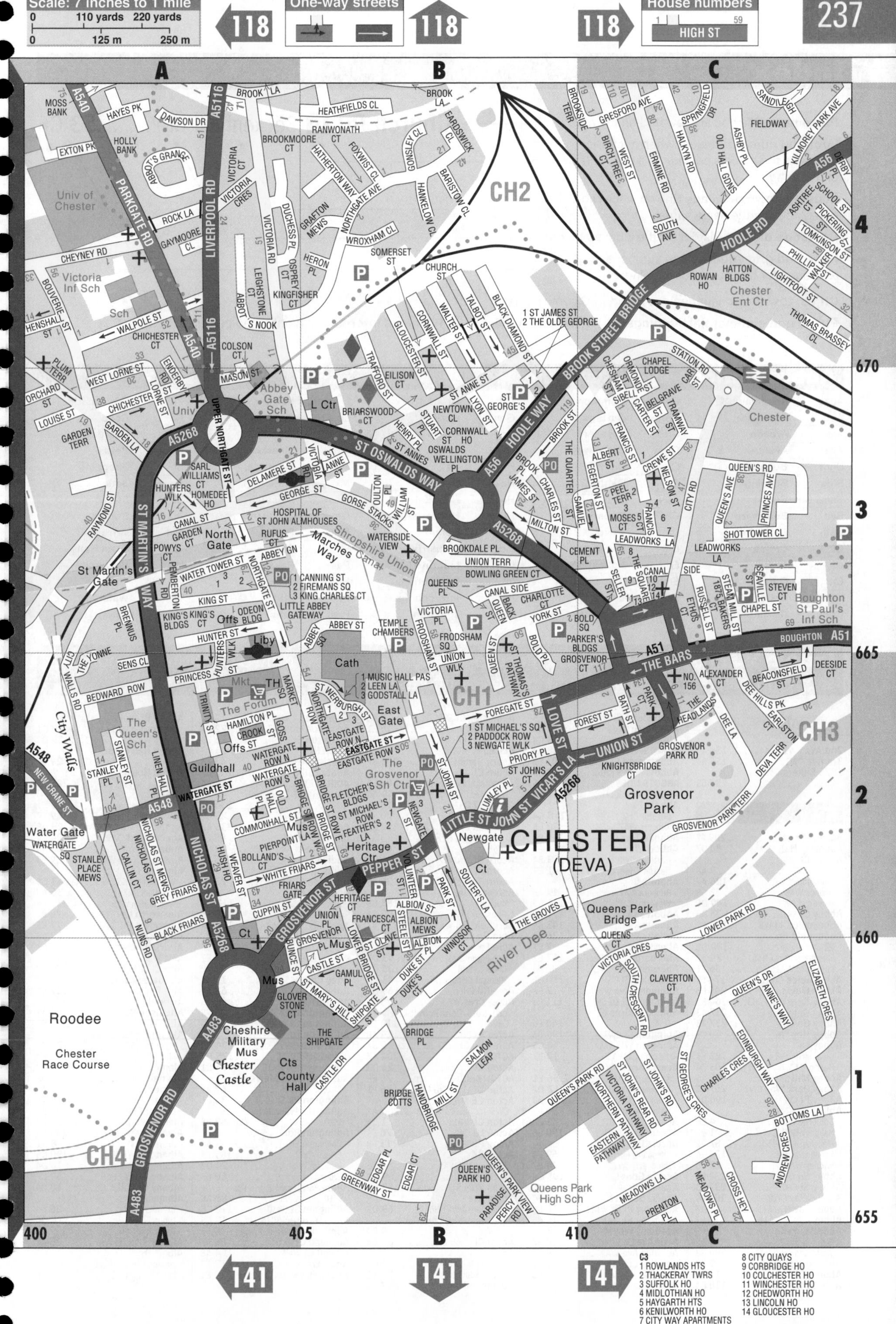
Scale: 7 inches to 1 mile
0 110 yards 220 yards
0 125 m 250 m
One-way streets
House numbers
1 59
HIGH ST
118
118
118
A
B
C
4
3
2
1
670
665
660
655
400
405
410
CHESTER
(DEVA)
CH1
CH2
CH3
CH4
Univ of Chester
Victoria Inf Sch
Sch
Abbey Gate Sch
L Ctr
North Gate
St Martin's Gate
Cath
East Gate
Offs
Liby
Mkt
TH
The Forum
The Queen's Sch
Guildhall
Mus
Heritage Ctr
The Grosvenor Sh Ctr
Newgate
Ct
Water Gate
City Walls
Roodee
Chester Race Course
Cheshire Military Mus
Chester Castle
Cts
County Hall
River Dee
Shropshire Union Canal
Marches Way
Grosvenor Park
Queens Park Bridge
Queens Park High Sch
Chester
Chester Ent Ctr
Boughton St Paul's Inf Sch
PARKGATE RD
LIVERPOOL RD
UPPER NORTHGATE ST
ST OSWALDS WAY
HOOLE WAY
BROOK STREET BRIDGE
HOOLE RD
ST MARTIN'S WAY
NICHOLAS ST
GROSVENOR RD
GROSVENOR ST
PEPPER ST
LITTLE ST JOHN ST
VICAR'S LA
LOVE ST
UNION ST
THE BARS
FOREGATE ST
EASTGATE ST
WATERGATE ST
NORTHGATE ST
BOUGHTON
CITY RD
NEW CRANE ST
A540
A5116
A5268
A56
A51
A548
A483
C3
1 ROWLANDS HTS
2 THACKERAY TWRS
3 SUFFOLK HO
4 MIDLOTHIAN HO
5 HAYGARTH HTS
6 KENILWORTH HO
7 CITY WAY APARTMENTS
8 CITY QUAYS
9 CORBRIDGE HO
10 COLCHESTER HO
11 WINCHESTER HO
12 CHEDWORTH HO
13 LINCOLN HO
14 GLOUCESTER HO
141
141
141

Index

Place name May be abbreviated on the map → **Church Rd** 6 Beckenham BR2..........**53** C6

Location number Present when a number indicates the place's position in a crowded area of mapping

Locality, town or village Shown when more than one place has the same name

Postcode district District for the indexed place

Page and grid square Page number and grid reference for the standard mapping

Cities, towns and villages are listed in Capital Letters

Public and commercial buildings are highlighted in magenta **Places of interest** are highlighted in blue with a star★

Abbreviations used in the index

Acad	**Academy**	Comm	**Common**	Gd	**Ground**	L	**Leisure**	Prom	**Promenade**
App	**Approach**	Cott	**Cottage**	Gdn	**Garden**	La	**Lane**	Rd	**Road**
Arc	**Arcade**	Cres	**Crescent**	Gn	**Green**	Liby	**Library**	Recn	**Recreation**
Ave	**Avenue**	Cswy	**Causeway**	Gr	**Grove**	Mdw	**Meadow**	Ret	**Retail**
Bglw	**Bungalow**	Ct	**Court**	H	**Hall**	Meml	**Memorial**	Sh	**Shopping**
Bldg	**Building**	Ctr	**Centre**	Ho	**House**	Mkt	**Market**	Sq	**Square**
Bsns, Bus	**Business**	Ctry	**Country**	Hospl	**Hospital**	Mus	**Museum**	St	**Street**
Bvd	**Boulevard**	Cty	**County**	HQ	**Headquarters**	Orch	**Orchard**	Sta	**Station**
Cath	**Cathedral**	Dr	**Drive**	Hts	**Heights**	Pal	**Palace**	Terr	**Terrace**
Cir	**Circus**	Dro	**Drove**	Ind	**Industrial**	Par	**Parade**	TH	**Town Hall**
Cl	**Close**	Ed	**Education**	Inst	**Institute**	Pas	**Passage**	Univ	**University**
Cnr	**Corner**	Emb	**Embankment**	Int	**International**	Pk	**Park**	Wk, Wlk	**Walk**
Coll	**College**	Est	**Estate**	Intc	**Interchange**	Pl	**Place**	Wr	**Water**
Com	**Community**	Ex	**Exhibition**	Junc	**Junction**	Prec	**Precinct**	Yd	**Yard**

Index of towns, villages, streets, hospitals, industrial estates, railway stations, schools, shopping centres, universities and places of interest

2nd–Alb

2nd Ave CW12 **156** A4
3rd Ave CW12 **156** A4
1875 Bakers Ct CH1, CH3 **237** C3

A

Aarons Dr ST7 **209** F2
Abberley Hall SK9 **84** D7
Abbey Cl
Croft WA3 **9** A8
Whitegate CW8 **126** A7
Widnes WA8 **22** C8
Winsford CW7 **149** D5
Abbey Ct SK12 **36** D3
Abbeydale Cl CW2 **207** C2
Abbeyfield Ho
2 Crewe CW2 **190** D2
Ellesmere Port CH65 **70** A3
Knutsford WA16 **56** F1
Abbeyfields CW11 **174** F5
Abbey Fields CW2 **205** E8
Abbey Gate Coll CH3 **164** E8
Abbey Gate Sch CH2 **237** A3
Abbey Gn CH1 **237** A3
Abbey Hey WA7 **50** C8
Abbey La
Delamere CW8 **123** E5
Hartford CW8 **103** B4
Abbey Mill SK10 **87** A6
Abbey Park Way CW2 **207** E3
Abbey Pl CW1 **190** D6
Abbey Rd
Golborne WA3 **4** C8
Haydock WA11 **1** E7
Macclesfield SK10 **87** B2
Sandbach CW11 **174** E6
Widnes WA8 **22** C8
Abbey Sq CH1 **237** B3
Abbey St CH1 **237** B3
Abbey Way CW8 **103** B4
Abbeyway N WA11 **2** A7
Abbeyway S WA11 **2** A7
Abbotsbury Cl
Poynton SK12 **36** D5
Wistaston CW2 **206** B8
Abbots Cl SK10 **87** B2
Abbots Ct CH2 **118** C4
Abbot's Dr CH2 **118** C4
Abbotsfield Cl WA4 **26** E6
Abbot's Grange CH2 **237** A4
Abbots Knoll CH2 **118** C4
ABBOT'S MEADS **118** A4
Abbotsmere Cl CW8 **101** F2
Abbots Mews CH65 **70** B6
ABBOTS MOSS **124** D5
Abbot's Nook CH2 **237** A4
Abbots Pk
Chester CH2 **118** C4
Runcorn WA7 **50** E5
Abbot's Terr CH1 **118** B5
Abbots Way
Hartford CW8 **103** B4
Neston CH64 **41** E1
Abbotts Cl
Runcorn WA7 **49** A8
Waverton CH3 **143** B5
Abbott's Cl CW12 **179** B8
Abbotts Rd CH3 **143** B5
Abbotts Way CW7 **126** B2
Aberdare Cl WA5 **7** E1
Aberdaron Dr CH1 **117** E3
Aberdeen Wlk SK10 **86** F3
Aberfeldy Cl CW4 **130** B2
Abingdon Ave WA1 **17** E7
Abingdon Cl 9 SK11 **111** F8
Abingdon Cres 4 CH4 **140** F6
Abington Cl CW1 **190** B6
Abington Wlk WA7 **50** C5
Abstone Cl WA1 **17** B7
Acacia Ave
Knutsford WA16 **56** E1
Warrington WA1 **17** D7
Widnes WA8 **13** B3
Wilmslow SK9 **59** F5
Acacia Cl CH2 **72** C3
Acacia Cres CW1 **190** E6
Acacia Dr
Ellesmere Port CH66 **69** F1
Sandbach CW11 **174** E7
Acacia Gdns ST7 **195** C3
Acacia Gr WA7 **49** C8
Acacia St WA12 **1** F4
Academy Pl 6 WA1 **16** B5
Academy St WA1 **16** B5
Academy Way WA1 **16** B5
Acer Ave CW1 **190** E7
Achilles Ave WA2 **8** B2
Achilles Ct WA7 **24** A2
Ackerley Cl WA2 **8** F3
Ackers La WA4 **16** E1
Ackersley Ct SK8 **35** B8
Ackers Rd WA4 **16** E1
Ack La E SK7 **35** D7
Ack La W SK8 **35** C7
Acorn Bank Cl CW2 **206** B7
Acorn Cl
Cuddington CW8 **101** F2
Winsford CW7 **150** A8
Acorn Ct CH2 **118** E8
Acorn Dr CH65 **70** B1
Acorn La CW12 **157** E3
Acorns Prim Sch The CH65 **69** F5
Acorn St WA12 **2** D3
Acorns The CH2 **118** E8
Acorn Terr SK22 **39** B6
Acreage The
Bunbury CW6 **185** E8
Goostrey CW4 **107** E1
Acrefield Rd WA8 **12** B1
Acre Gn L26 **21** A6
Acre La
Bebington CH62 **43** D8
Cheadle SK8 **35** C6
Heswall CH60 **41** C8
Acre Rd CH66 **69** D5
Acres Cres WA6 **75** B2
Acresfield Com Prim Sch CH2 **118** F8
Acres La CH2 **119** A8
Acreville Gr WA3 **5** C7
ACTON **204** A7
Acton Ave WA4 **26** D3
ACTON BRIDGE **76** E3
Acton Bridge Sta CW8 **76** F1
Acton CE Prim Sch CW5 **204** A7
Acton Cl WA11 **1** C6
Acton La CW8 **76** F4
Acton Pl SK11 **111** F8
Acton Rd
Burtonwood WA5 **6** E6
Crewe CW2 **189** D4
Acton Way ST7 **193** D6
Adam Ave
Ellesmere Port CH66 **69** D3
Ellesmere Port, Great Sutton CH66 **69** C4
Adam Cl CH66 **69** D4
Adams Cl
Newton-le-W WA12 **2** D2
Poynton SK12 **36** E2
Adams Hill WA16 **57** A1
Adamson Ct WA4 **17** B2
Adamson Ho WA7 **22** E3
Adamson St WA4 **16** B3
Adam St WA2 **16** C7
Adaston Ave CH62 **43** F4
Adder Hill CH3 **142** B7
ADDERLEY **235** A4
Adderley CE Prim Sch TF9 **234** F5
Adderley Cl WA7 **23** C1
Adderley Rd TF9 **235** A2
ADDER'S MOSS **85** F6
Addingham Ave WA8 **22** C7
Addison Cl CW2 **205** F8
Addison Sq WA8 **13** A1
Adelaide Ct 4 WA8 **23** A7
Adelaide Rd
Blacon CH1 **117** D4
Bramhall SK7 **35** F5
Adelaide Sch CW1 **190** C5
Adelaide St
Crewe CW1 **190** C5
Macclesfield SK10 **87** E1
Adela Rd WA7 **22** F2
Adey Rd WA13 **19** A5
Adfalent La CH64 **68** A7
ADLINGTON **62** D5
Adlington Cl SK12 **36** F2
Adlington Ct WA3 **9** F6
Adlington Dr
Northwich CW9 **104** A5
Sandbach CW11 **175** C7
Adlington Est SK10 **36** C1
Adlington Hall Mews SK10 **62** B5
Adlington Pk SK10 **36** C1
Adlington Prim Sch SK10 **62** E5
Adlington Rd
Bollington SK10 **63** A1
Crewe CW2 **189** F3
Runcorn WA7 **24** D2
Wilmslow SK9 **60** E7
Adlington Road Bsns Pk SK10 **88** A8
Adlington St SK10 **112** C8
Adlington Sta SK10 **62** C5
Admirals Rd WA3 **9** F3
Adshead Ct SK10 **88** B7
Adwell Cl WA3 **4** A8
Afton WA8 **12** A2
Agden Brow WA13 **19** E1
Agden Brow Pk
Broomedge WA13 **19** D1
Lymm WA13 **29** D8
Agden Hall Farm WA13 **29** E7
Agden House La SY13 **225** A5
Agden La
Broomedge WA13 **19** E1
Little Bollington WA13 **29** E7
Agden Park La WA13 **29** D8
Agecroft Rd CW9 **104** C7
Ainley Cl WA7 **50** A5
Ainscough Rd WA3 **9** E3
Ainsdale Cl
Bebington CH63 **43** C5
Bramhall SK7 **36** A7
Warrington WA5 **14** F4
Ainsworth La CW8 **76** B3
Ainsworth Rd CW8 **77** E1
Aintree Gr CH66 **69** D3
Airdrie Cl CH62 **43** D3
Aire WA8 **12** B2
Aire Cl CH65 **70** A7
Airedale Cl WA5 **14** F7
Aire Pl CW7 **127** B1
Airfield View CH5 **139** B6
Aitchison Rd CW9 **80** A2
Ajax Ave WA2 **8** B2
Akesmoor La
Biddulph ST8 **179** B1
Mow Cop ST7 **195** F7
Alamein Cres WA2 **16** C7
Alamein Dr CW7 **149** D8
Alamein Rd
Barnton CW8 **78** A4
Chester CH2 **95** B1
Alan Dr WA15 **32** A8
Alan St CW9 **104** B8
Alban Ret Pk WA2 **8** A1
Alban St CW1 **190** C5
Albany Cres WA13 **18** D4
Albany Gdns CH66 **69** C7
Albany Gr WA13 **18** C4
Albany Rd
Bramhall SK7 **35** F4
Lymm WA13 **18** D4
Wilmslow SK9 **59** F5
Albany Terr 15 WA7 **23** A2
Albert Dr
Neston CH64 **66** D8
Warrington WA5 **14** D6

Albert Pl
Congleton CW12 156 E2
16 Macclesfield SK11 112 D8
Northwich CW9 104 B8
Albert Rd
Bollington SK10 87 E8
Warrington WA4 17 A2
2 Widnes WA8 13 B1
Wilmslow SK9 60 A6
Albert Row WA6 49 B1
Albert Sq 1 WA8 23 B8
Albert St
Audley ST7 209 F3
Chester CH1 237 C3
Crewe CW1 190 C5
Irlam M44 11 E6
Knutsford WA16 56 F2
Macclesfield SK11 112 C8
Nantwich CW5 204 E6
6 Runcorn WA7 23 A2
Albert Terr WA5 1 E1
Albion Ct CW12 156 E2
Albion Mews
Chester CH1 237 B2
New Mills SK22 39 C7
Albion Pk WA3 5 C7
Albion Pl CH1 237 B1
Albion Rd
New Mills SK22 39 B6
Northwich CW9 79 A1
Albion St
Chester CH1 237 B2
Crewe CW2 190 A3
Albion Wlk CW9 79 A1
Albright Rd WA8 22 A6
Albury Cl WA11 1 D7
Alcock St 17 WA7 23 A3
Alconbury Cl WA5 15 B6
Alcott Pl WA2 8 A6
Aldcliffe WA3 3 F8
Aldelyme Ct CW3 229 F4
Alder Ave
Poynton SK12 36 F3
Widnes WA8 13 B3
Alderbank Rd WA5 15 A6
Alder Cl SK8 34 D8
Alder Cres WA2 16 C8
Alder Ct SK10 87 E5
Alderdale Dr SK6 37 E7
Alderdale Gr SK9 59 E5
Alder Dr
Crewe CW1 189 F7
Ellesmere Port CH66 69 F1
Alderfield Dr L24 21 A3
Alder Gr CH2 119 B4
Alderhay La ST7 195 C4
Alder La
Burtonwood WA2, WA5 7 C7
Cronton WA8, L35 12 A5
Frodsham WA6, WA7 48 D3
Warrington WA2 16 B8
Alderley Ave WA3 3 D7
Alderley Cl
Hazel Grove SK7 36 F8
Poynton SK12 36 F2
Sandbach CW11 175 D7
ALDERLEY EDGE 60 C2
Alderley Edge★ SK9, SK10 85 D8
Alderley Edge Prim Sch SK9 60 A2
Alderley Edge Sch for Girls SK9 60 A2
Alderley Edge Sta SK9 60 A2
Alderley Lo SK9 60 A5
Alderley Pl CH1 117 E6
Alderley Rd
Alderley Edge SK10, SK9 60 F2
Chelford SK10 84 C3
Northwich CW8 103 E8
Prestbury SK10 86 E3
Warrington WA4 17 D4
Wilmslow SK9 60 A6
Alderley Wlk 14 SK11 112 E7
Alderman Bolton Com Prim Sch WA4 16 F3
Alderney Cl
Ellesmere Port CH65 70 C1
4 Macclesfield SK11 111 F8
Alderney Ho CH2 119 B4
Alder Rd
Golborne WA3 3 F8
Warrington WA1 17 D7
Weaverham CW8 102 D8
Alder Rise SK23 65 D8
Alder Root La WA2 7 D7
Alders SK9 59 F6
Aldersey Cl
Runcorn WA7 24 D1
Saughall CH1 94 A1
ALDERSEY GREEN 182 C6
Aldersey La CH3 182 C5
Aldersey Rd CW2 190 A2
Aldersey Way CW6 185 E8
Aldersgate SK22 39 B8
Aldersgate Ave WA7 50 D7
Aldersgate Dr L26 21 A6
Aldersgate Rd SK8 35 C5
Alders Green Ave SK6 37 F7
Alders Rd SK12 38 A7
Alder St WA12 2 C3
Alders Way SK10 86 F6
Alderton Cl L26 21 A7
Alderton Gr CW7 127 A4
Alder Wood Ave L24 21 A3
Alderwood Ct WA8 12 E4
Alderwood Lo L24 21 A3
Aldewood Cl WA3 10 A6
ALDFORD 163 F3
Aldford Cl
Bebington CH63 43 B6
Hough CW2 206 E2
Aldford Pl SK9 59 F2
Aldford Rd CH2 118 F6
Aldford Sch CH3 163 F3
Aldford Way CW7 126 B2
Aldgate CH65 70 A5
Aldington Dr CW10 151 D5
Aldridge Dr WA5 6 F7
Aled Way CH4 140 D5
Alexander Ct CH3 237 C2
Alexander Dr WA8 22 D8
Alexandra Ct 1 M31 11 F3
Alexandra Gr
Irlam M44 11 F8
Runcorn WA7 23 C1
Alexandra Ind Est WA8 22 F7
Alexandra Mews WA6 49 B1
Alexandra Pl CW1 190 B5
Alexandra Rd
Middlewich CW10 151 D6
Warrington, Stockton Heath WA4 16 D1
Warrington WA4 16 F2
Alexandra Sq 6 CW7 149 A8
Alexandra St
Ellesmere Port CH65 70 C7
Warrington WA1 16 E7
Widnes WA8 23 A7
Winsford CW7 126 C1
Alexandria Way CW12 156 C4
Alford Ct 4 CW9 103 E5
Alforde St WA8 23 A7
Alfred Cl 12 WA8 23 B8
Alfred Rd
Golborne WA3 4 A8
Haydock WA11 1 F7
Alfred St
Irlam M44 11 E6
Newton-le-W WA12 2 E3
Northwich CW9 103 E6
Widnes WA8 23 B8
Algernon St
Runcorn WA7 22 F3
Warrington, Stockton Heath WA4 16 C1
Warrington WA1 16 D6
Alice Ct WA8 23 A4
Alison Dr
Goostrey CW4 130 D8
Macclesfield SK10 87 F1
Alistair Dr CH63 43 C6
Allans Cl CH64 66 E6
Allansford Ave CH3 143 A4
Allans Mdw CH64 66 E7
Allcard St WA5 15 F7
Allen Ave WA3 5 C4
Allenby Rd M44 11 D4
Allendale WA7 50 B6
Allen Dr CW9 103 F2
Allen Pl CW1 190 B5
Allen Rd WA7 48 D7
Allen St
Bollington SK10 88 B8
Macclesfield SK11 112 E7
Warrington WA2 16 A6
Allerby Way WA3 3 E8
Allerton Rd WA8 13 B1
ALLGREAVE 137 C3
Allgreave Cl CW10 151 C6
All Hallows RC High Sch SK11 112 B7
Allington Pl CH4 141 E7
Allman Cl CW1 189 F7
ALLOSTOCK 106 E3
Allotment Rd M44 11 D6
Allport La CH62 43 D8
Allport Rd CH62, CH63 43 D7
Allports The CH62 43 D7
All Saints Dr WA4 17 E3
All Saints RC Prim Sch WA3 3 B8
All Saints Upton CE Prim Sch WA8 12 B3
Allysum Ct WA7 49 F4
Alma Ave CW1 190 C6
Alma Cl
Macclesfield SK11 112 A7
Scholar Green ST7 194 E7
Alma La SK9 60 A7
Alma Rd SK7 37 A8
Alma St
Chester CH2 118 F2
Newton-le-W WA12 2 B3
Almeda Rd L24 21 A2
Almer Dr WA5 15 C5
Almond Ave
Crewe CW1 190 D6
Runcorn WA7 49 C8
Almond Dr WA5 6 F6
Almond Gr
Warrington WA1 17 B7
Weaverham CW8 102 E7
Widnes WA8 22 D8
Almond Pl ST5 210 E1
Almond Tree Cl L24 21 E1
Almond Wlk M31 11 D3
Almshouses CW11 175 C6
Alnwick Dr CH65 70 D2
Alpass Ave WA5 16 A8
Alpine St WA12 2 A3
ALPORT 226 B1
Alport Rd SY13 226 B1
ALPRAHAM 169 D4
Alpraham Cres CH2 118 E6
Alpraham Gn CW6 169 E5
ALPRAHAM GREEN 169 D5
Alric Wlk M22 33 E8
ALSAGER 193 E5
Alsager Highfields Com Prim Sch ST7 193 D4
Alsager Rd
Audley ST7 209 D5
Haslington CW11 192 C7
Sandbach CW11 175 E1
Alsager Sch ST7 193 B4
Alsager Sta ST7 193 E3
Alsfeld Way SK22 39 A8
Alt WA8 12 B2
Alton Dr SK10 87 F1
Alton Rd SK9 59 F7
Alton St CW2 190 B3
ALTRINCHAM 31 C8
Altrincham Priory Hospl WA15 32 A7
Altrincham Rd
Styal SK9 33 D4
Wilmslow SK9 33 C2
Alt Wlk CW7 127 A2
Alumbrook Ave CW4 130 C3
Alum Ct CW4 130 C2
Alun Cres CH4 141 A6
Alundale Rd CW7 126 C3
ALVANLEY 73 C1
Alvanley Dr WA6 73 C2
Alvanley Prim Sch WA6 73 D1
Alvanley Rd
Ellesmere Port CH66 69 E4
Helsby WA6 73 C2
Alvanley Rise CW9 104 A6
Alvanley Terr WA6 74 B8
Alvanley View CH2 72 B3
Alvanley Way CH66 69 E4
Alvaston Bsns Pk CW5 204 F8
Alvaston Rd CW5 204 F5
Alvaston Wlk CW2 189 F2
Alverstone Cl WA5 14 C7
Alverton Cl WA8 22 D8
Alveston Cl SK10 86 F1
Alveston Dr SK9 60 C8
Alvingham Cl 1 CW9 104 B8
Alvis Rd CH5 116 B3
Alwyn Gdns CH2 118 F8
Alyndale Rd CH4 140 D6
Alyn Rd CH2 96 F1
Amberleigh Cl WA4 27 B3
Amberley Dr WA15 32 B8
Amberley Rd SK11 112 A6
Ambleside CH2 119 A6
Ambleside Cl
Bebington CH62 43 E7
Crewe CW2 189 E2
Macclesfield SK11 111 F6
Runcorn WA7 49 E5
Winsford CW7 126 C3
Ambleside Cres WA2 8 C3
Ambleside Ct CW12 156 A2
Ambleside Rd CH65 70 C2
Ambrose Ct WA1 16 D6
Ambuscade Cl CW1 190 E5
Amelia Cl WA8 13 B4
Amelia St WA2 16 C7
Amersham Cl SK10 87 C3
Amis Gr WA3 3 E8
Ampleforth Ho 1 WA1 16 C5
Amusement Depot CW7 126 E2
Amy St CW2 190 C3
Anchorage The
1 Lymm WA13 18 D3
Neston CH64 66 C7
Waverton CH3 143 A5
Anchor Cl WA7 50 D6
Anchor Ct WA1 16 D6
Ancoats Rd WA16, SK9 83 F8
Anderson Cl
Crewe CW1 191 A4
Warrington WA2 9 B2
Anderson Ct CH62 43 D6
Andersons Ind Est WA8 23 A6
Anderson St 16 SK10 112 C8
ANDERTON 78 D4
Anderton Boat Lift & Nature Pk★ CW9 78 D3
Anderton Grange CW9 103 F7
Andertons La SK10, SK11 86 B1
Anderton Way SK9 34 D3
Andover Cl WA2 8 E1
Andover Rd WA11 1 E8
Andrew Cl WA8 22 C8
Andrew Cres CH4 237 C1
Andrew Gr SK10 113 A7
Andrew La SK6 37 F8
Andrew's Cl CH3 121 B2
Andrew's Wlk CH60 41 B8
Andromeda Way WA9 6 B7
Anemone Way WA9 6 A7
Angelina Cl CW11 174 D7
Anglers Rest M44 11 E5
Anglesey Cl 2 CH65 70 C1
Anglesey Dr SK12 36 F6
Anglesey Water SK12 36 E6
Angus Gr CW10 128 D2
Angus Rd CH63 43 C6
Angus Wlk SK10 86 F2
Ankers Knowl La SK11 114 D8
Ankers La SK11 114 D6
Annable Rd M44 11 F8
Annan Cl 2 CW12 157 A1
Ann Cl CH66 69 D7
Anne Ct ST7 210 D6
Anne's Way CH4 237 C1
Annette Ave WA12 2 A5
Annie St WA2 16 C6
Annions La CW5 205 F1
Annis Cl SK9 60 B2
Annis Rd SK9 60 B2
Ann St W WA8 23 B7
Ann St
Northwich CW9 79 D1
Runcorn WA7 23 B3
Ansdell Rd WA8 13 C2
Anson Cl SK7 35 F5
Anson Engine Mus The★ SK12 37 C4
Anson Rd
Handforth SK9 34 E1
Poynton SK12 37 B3
Anthony Dr CW9 126 F7
Anthony's Way CH60 41 A7
Antons Ct L26 21 A6
Antons Rd L26 21 A6
Antony Rd WA4 16 B1
Antrim Cl WA11 1 C6
Antrim Dr CH66 69 F2
Antrim Rd WA2 8 A2
ANTROBUS 53 C4
Antrobus St CW12 156 D3
Anvil Cl
Elton CH2 72 B4
Haslington CW11 174 F3
Saughall CH1 94 A1
Appleby Cl
Macclesfield SK11 111 F5
Widnes WA8 22 C8
Appleby Cres WA16 58 A4
Appleby Gr CH62 43 D6
Appleby Rd WA2 8 C3
Appleby Wlk 5 WA8 22 C8
Applecroft ST5 210 E1
Applecross Cl WA3 10 A6
Appledale Dr CH66 95 A8
Applefield CW8 103 D7
Appleford Cl WA4 26 E7
Apple Market St 10 CW9 103 F8
APPLETON 13 A2
Appleton Cl CW12 178 E8
Appleton Dr CH65 69 F3
Appleton Hall Gdns WA4 26 E5
Appleton Mews WA13 18 C4
APPLETON PARK 26 D5
Appleton Rd
Chester CH2 118 E6
Widnes WA8 13 B1
Appleton St
Widnes WA8 23 B7
Winnington CW8 78 D1
APPLETON THORN 27 B4
Appleton Thorn Prim Sch WA4 27 C4
Appleton Thorn Trad Est WA4 27 D5
Appleton Village WA8 13 B1
Appleton Wlk 8 SK9 34 E1
Apple Tree Cl L24 21 E1
Appletree Gr WA2 8 F2
Apple Tree Gr CH66 94 F8
Appleyards La CH4 141 E7
Apprentice La SK9 33 F3
April Rise SK10 87 A1
Arabis Gdns WA9 6 B7
Aragon Ct WA7 24 C3
Aragon Gn CH1 117 E6
Aran Cl L24 21 D1
Arbour Cl
Macclesfield SK10 87 D3
Northwich CW9 104 C8
Arbour Cres SK10 87 D3
Arbourhay St SK10 87 E1
Arbour Mews SK10 87 D3
Arbour St ST7 210 D5
Arbury La WA2 8 C6
Arcade The
Ellesmere Port CH65 70 A5
3 Northwich CW9 103 F8
Archer Ave WA4 16 E2
Archer Cl SK10 87 E7
Archers Gn CH62 43 E3
Archers Green Rd WA5 7 B3
Archers Way
Blacon CH1 118 A2
Ellesmere Port CH66 69 E1
Arches Com Prim Sch The CH1 117 E5
Archway Wlk WA12 2 E3
ARCLID 154 B1
Arclid Cl SK9 34 E1
Arclid Ct 10 CW12 156 F3
ARCLID GREEN 176 A8
Arclid Green Ind Est CW11 176 B8
Arden WA8 12 A2
Ardenbrook Rise SK10 86 F6
Arden Cl
Gatley SK8 34 C7
Tarvin CH3 121 C3
Warrington WA3 10 B6
Arden Ct CW12 179 B7
Arden Dr CH64 66 E6
Arden Est SK22 39 D7
Ardens Mdw CW6 168 C8
Arden St SK22 39 C7
Arderne Ave CW2 190 A2
Arderne Ho CH2 118 F7
Arderne Pl 12 SK9 60 A1
Ardern Lea WA6 73 D1
Ardleigh Cl CW1 189 F8
Arena Gdns WA2 16 D8
Argosy Dr M90 32 F7
Argyle Ct 10 WA16 57 A2
Argyll Ave
Bebington CH62 43 D4
Chester CH4 141 A7
Argyll Cl SK10 87 A1
Ariel Gdns WA3 5 A2
Ariel Wlk 4 WA3 3 E8
Arizona Cres WA5 15 B7
Arkenshaw Rd WA3 9 A7
Arkenstone Cl WA8 12 C2
Arkle Ave SK8, SK9 34 E4
Arkle Ct 1 CH3 119 B1
Arklow Dr L24 21 D2
Arkwright Cl CW7 149 A8
Arkwright Ct WA7 23 F3
Arkwright Rd WA7 23 F3
ARLEY 54 C7
Arley Ave WA4 26 D8
Arley Cl
Alsager ST7 193 C3
Chester CH2 118 F6
Macclesfield SK11 112 A7
Arley Ct CW9 103 E5
Arley Dr WA8 12 B2
Arley End WA16 29 C4
ARLEY GREEN 54 E6
Arley Hall & Gdns★ CW9 54 D6
Arley Mossend La CW9 54 D2
Arley Pl CW2 206 A8
Arley Rd
Antrobus CW9 54 B7
Appleton Thorn WA4 27 C3
Northwich CW9 104 C8
Arley Wlk CW11 174 D5
Arlington Cl CW2 206 C8
Arlington Cres SK9 59 E5
Arlington Dr
Golborne WN7 4 C8
Macclesfield SK11 112 A7
Poynton SK12 36 D3
Warrington WA5 14 E4
Arlington Way SK9 59 E5
Armistead Way CW4 130 A5
Armitstead Rd CW11 174 F4
Armitt St SK11 112 C7
Armour Ave WA2 8 B2
Armoury Court Mews 4 SK11 112 B6
Armoury Twrs 1 SK11 112 B6
Armstrong Cl
Audlem CW3 229 F4
Warrington WA3 9 D4
Armthorpe Dr CH66 69 C5
Arncliffe Dr WA5 6 F6
Arndale WA7 49 E5
Arnhem Cres WA2 16 C7
Arnhem Way CH3 142 B5
Arnold Pl WA8 22 C7
Arnold's Cres CH4 139 A3
Arnold St
Nantwich CW5 204 E6
Warrington WA1 16 D6
Arnside Ave
Congleton CW12 156 A2
Haydock WA11 1 B6
Arnside Cl
High Lane SK6 37 E8
Winsford CW7 126 D2
Arnside Gr WA4 16 B2
Arpley Rd WA1 16 B4
Arpley St WA1 16 A4
Arradon Ct CH2 118 E5
Arran Ave CH65 70 C1
Arran Cl
Holmes Chapel CW4 130 C2
Warrington WA2 9 A2
Arran Dr WA6 74 C6
Arrivals Way M90 33 B7
Arron Pl CW2 189 D3
Arrowcroft Rd CH3 119 F5
Arrowsmith Dr ST7 193 B3
Arrowsmith Rd WA11 1 F7
ARTHILL 30 B8
Arthill La
Little Bollington WA14 20 B1
Rostherne WA14 30 B8
Arthog Dr WA15 31 F8
Arthog Rd
Altrincham WA15 31 F8
Altrincham WA15 32 A8
Arthur Ave CH65 70 C5
Arthur St
Chester CH1 118 A2
3 Crewe CW2 190 D2
Lostock Gralam CW9 80 A2
12 Runcorn WA7 23 A2
Warrington WA2 16 A6
Artists La SK10 85 C7
Artle Rd CW2 206 C8
Arundel Ave SK7 36 D8
Arundel Cl
Knutsford WA16 82 A8
Macclesfield SK10 87 F2
Wistaston CW2 205 E8
Arundel Ct CH65 70 E3

Arundell Cl WA5 6 F6
Arundel Rd SK8 35 A6
Ascol Dr WA16 80 C3
Ascot Ave WA7 49 B6
Ascot Cl
Congleton CW12 156 D4
Macclesfield SK10 87 C3
Warrington, Martinscroft WA1 17 E7
Warrington WA4 17 C2
Ascot Ct CW9 104 C8
Ascot Dr CH66 69 E3
Ascot Ho CH1 118 B2
Ash Ave
Irlam M44 11 D5
Newton-le-W WA12 2 C2
Ashbank CW9 104 D7
Ashberry Cl SK9 60 D8
Ashberry Dr WA4 27 B5
Ashbourne Ave WA7 49 B6
Ashbourne Cl CH66 94 E8
Ashbourne Dr
Chorlton CW2 207 C1
High Lane SK6 37 F6
Ashbourne Mews 1 SK10 111 F8
Ashbourne Rd
Hazel Grove SK7 36 F8
Warrington WA5 15 B5
Ashbrook Ave WA7 49 F3
Ashbrook Cres WA2 16 D8
Ashbrook Dr SK10 87 A6
Ashbrook Rd
Bollington SK10 87 F7
Nether Alderley SK10 85 F6
Ashburton CH64 66 C8
Ashbury Cl WA7 24 D2
Ashbury Dr WA11 1 D7
Ashby Dr CW11 174 C5
Ashby Pl CH2 237 C4
Ash Cl
Ellesmere Port CH66 69 F1
Holmes Chapel CW4 130 D4
Malpas SY14 213 C5
Tarporley CW6 146 D2
Ashcroft Ave CW2 206 B3
Ashcroft Cl SK9 59 F5
Ashcroft Ct M44 11 D5
Ashcroft Rd WA13 19 B4
Ash Ct 15 WA16 57 A2
Ashdale Cl ST7 193 C5
Ashdene Prim Sch SK9 59 F5
Ashdene Rd SK9 59 F5
Ashdown Cl SK8 35 A6
Ashdown La WA3 10 B5
Ashdown Rd WA16 82 F6
Ashenhurst Rd ST7 193 F3
Ashenough Rd ST7 210 D6
Asher Ct WA4 27 D4
Ashfield Cl WA13 19 B4
Ashfield Cres
Bebington CH62 43 D8
Blacon CH1 117 D5
Ashfield Dr SK10 87 A2
Ashfield Gdns WA4 16 F3
Ashfield Gr M44 11 E6
Ashfield Ho 6 CH64 66 E8
Ashfield Rd
Bebington CH62 43 C8
Ellesmere Port CH65 70 C5
Ashfield Rd N 1 CH65 70 C5
Ashfield St CW10 151 D8
Ashford Cl SK9 34 C4
Ashford Dr WA4 26 E3
Ashford Rd SK9 60 A4
Ashford Way 1 WA8 13 D1
Ashgate La CW9 79 F6
Ash Gr
Chester CH4 141 B5
Congleton CW12 156 A3
Ellesmere Port CH66 69 C6
Gatley SK8 34 B8
Golborne WA3 3 B8
Handforth SK9 34 C3
Knutsford WA16 57 D1
Macclesfield SK11 112 C4
Middlewich CW10 151 D7
Nantwich CW5 204 F3
Rode Heath ST7 193 F7
Runcorn WA7 49 C8
Warrington WA4 16 D3
Weaverham CW8 102 E7
Widnes WA8 22 D8
Ashgrove CW7 149 D8
Ash Grove Prim Sch SK11 112 C4
Ash Hay La
Hoole Bank CH2 119 C8
Picton CH2 96 C2
Ash Ho
Chester CH2 118 C5
8 Sandbach CW11 175 B6
Ash House La CW8 77 D7
Ash La
Warrington WA4 26 E8
Widnes WA8 22 A8
Ashlands WA6 74 C7
Ash Lawn Ct CH2 118 C4
Ashlea Dr CW5 205 E5
Ashleigh Cl CH4 140 E6
ASHLEY 31 E5
Ashley CE Prim Sch WA15 31 F5
Ashley Cl WA4 17 C3
Ashley Ct
Frodsham WA6 74 A8
Holt LL13 196 D8
Warrington WA4 26 C6
Ashley Dr
Bramhall SK7 35 C6
Hartford CW8 103 A6
Ashley Gdns
Clutton CH3 182 C1
High Lane SK6 37 D8
Ashley Gn WA8 22 D8
Ashley Grange CW9 103 E3
ASHLEY HEATH 31 E8
Ashley Mdw CW1 191 D5
Ashleymill La WA14 31 D7
Ashley Mill La N WA14 31 E8
Ashley Rd
Ashley, Ashley Heath WA14, WA15 31 E7
Ashley WA14, WA15, WA16 31 C4
Handforth SK9 34 B1
Mere WA16 56 D8
Runcorn WA7 23 D2
Ashley Ret Pk WA8 23 B7
Ashley Sch WA8 12 D1
Ashley Sta WA15 31 E5
Ashley Way WA8 23 B7
Ashley Way W WA8 22 F7
Ash Lo SK12 36 D4
Ashmead Cl ST7 193 E3
Ashmead Mews ST7 193 E3
Ashmore Cl
Middlewich CW10 151 C6
Warrington WA3 10 A3
Ashmore's La ST7 193 D3
Ash Mount CW3 232 B1
Ashmuir Cl
Blacon CH1 117 E3
Crewe CW1 190 B6
Ashness Dr SK7 35 E8
Ash Priors WA8 12 D3
Ash Rd
Crewe CW1 190 D6
Cuddington CW8 101 F2
Elton CH2 72 C3
Haydock WA11 1 E7
Hollinfare WA3 11 A2
Lymm WA13 18 C3
Partington M31 11 D3
Poynton SK12 36 F3
Warrington WA5 14 F4
Winwick WA2 8 B6
Ash St CW9 79 A1
Ash Terr SK11 112 C4
Ashton Ave SK10 86 D1
Ashton Cl
Bebington CH62 43 E3
Congleton CW12 157 B1
Frodsham WA6 49 C1
Middlewich CW10 151 D5
Northwich CW9 103 E4
Runcorn WA7 48 F6
Ashton Ct WA6 49 C1
Ashton Dr WA6 49 C1
ASHTON HAYES 121 F7
Ashton Hayes Prim Sch CH3 121 F8
Ashton La CH3 121 E6
Ashton Rd
Manley WA6 99 E4
Newton-le-W WA12 2 C5
Norley WA6 100 B4
ASHTON'S GREEN 1 B3
Ashton St WA2 16 B6
Ashtree Cl
Neston CH64 67 A7
Prestbury SK10 87 C8
Ashtree Croft CH64 68 A7
Ashtree Ct CH2 237 C4
Ashtree Dr CH64 67 A7
Ashtree Farm Ct CH64 68 A7
Ash View ST7 195 B2
Ashville Ct CW2 206 B7
Ashville Ind Est WA7 49 E3
Ashville Way WA7 49 E3
Ash Way CH60 41 B6
Ashwood WA14 31 B8
Ashwood Ave
Golborne WA3 3 D8
Warrington WA1 16 E7
Ashwood Cl
Barnton CW8 78 B4
Ellesmere Port CH66 69 D1
Widnes WA8 22 A7
Ashwood Cres CW8 78 B3
Ashwood Ct CH2 119 A3
Ashwood Farm Ct CH2 96 B6
Ashwood La CH2 96 B5
Ashwood Rd SK12 38 D6
Ashworth Pk WA16 81 F8
Asiatic Cotts CH5 116 B3
Askerbank La SK11 159 A1
Askett Cl WA11 1 C7
Askrigg Ave CH66 69 B5
Aspen Cl
Ellesmere Port CH66 69 E1
Harriseahead ST7 195 E3
Heswall CH60 41 D8
Aspen Gr
Saughall CH1 117 B7
Warrington WA1 17 A7
Aspens The CW8 101 E5
Aspen Way
Chester CH2 119 B4
High Lane SK6 38 A7
Aspinall Cl WA2 9 A3
Aspull Cl WA3 9 C4
Asquith Cl CW1 191 C5
Assheton Cl WA12 2 B4
Assheton Wlk L24 21 E2
ASTBURY 178 B7
Astbury Cl
Crewe CW1 190 A7
Golborne WA3 4 B8
Kidsgrove ST7 195 C3
Astbury Dr CW8 78 A4
Astbury Lane Ends CW12 178 F8
ASTBURY MARSH 156 B1
Astbury Mere Ctry Pk★ CW12 156 B2
Astbury St Mary's CE Prim Sch CW12 178 B8
Astbury St CW12 156 C2
Aster Cres WA7 49 F5
Aster Rd WA11 1 F7
Aster Wlk M31 11 F2
ASTLE 109 D8
Astle Cl CW10 151 C7
Astle Ct SK11 84 A3
Astle La SK10 84 E1
Astley Cl
Knutsford WA16 82 C7
Warrington WA4 16 B3
Widnes WA8 12 C3
Astley Ct M44 11 E8
Astley Rd M44 11 E8
ASTMOOR 23 E3
Astmoor Bridge La WA7 23 F2
Astmoor East Intc WA7 24 A3
Astmoor Ind Est WA7 23 F3
Astmoor La WA7 23 F1
Astmoor Prim Sch WA7 23 F2
Astmoor Rd
Runcorn, Astmoor WA7 23 E3
Runcorn WA7 23 C3
ASTON
Nantwich 217 C2
Runcorn 50 D1
Aston Ave
Warrington WA3 9 F4
Winsford CW7 126 B2
Aston by Sutton Prim Sch WA7 50 C2
Aston Ct WA1 9 C1
Aston Fields Rd WA7 50 E4
Aston Forge WA7 50 F5
Aston Gn WA7 50 E6
ASTON HEATH 50 E2
ASTON JUXTA MONDRUM 188 D6
Aston La
Aston WA7 50 C2
Runcorn WA7 50 F5
Woore CW3 232 E1
Aston La N WA7 50 E4
Aston La S WA7 50 E3
Aston Rd ST5 210 D1
Aston Way
13 Handforth SK9 34 D5
Middlewich CW10 128 E1
Astor Dr WA4 26 F8
Atcherley Cl CW5 218 E8
Athelbrae Cl CW8 103 F7
Atherton La M44 11 E5
Atherton Rd CH65 69 F6
Athey St Mill 2 SK11 112 C7
Athey St SK11 112 C8
Athlone Rd WA2 8 A1
Athol Cl
Bebington CH62 43 E5
Newton-le-W WA12 1 F4
Athol Dr CH62 43 E5
Atholl Ave CW2 190 C1
Atholl Cl SK10 87 A1
Athol Rd SK7 35 D5
Atkin Cl CW12 156 A3
Atlanta Ave M90 33 A8
Atlanta Gdns WA5 15 B8
Atlantic Trad Pk CW7 126 E5
Atlas Way CH66 69 F7
Atterbury Cl WA8 12 C2
Attlee Ave WA3 5 C4
Attwood Cl CW1 191 C4
Attwood Rise ST7 195 A2
Attwood St ST7 195 A2
Atworth Terr CH64 67 F8
Aubourn Cl WA8 12 C3
Auckery Ave CH66 69 D3
Auckland Rd CH1 117 D4
AUDLEM 230 B4
Audlem Cl WA7 49 F4
Audlem Dr CW9 104 A6
Audlem Rd
Hankelow CW3 230 C7
Hatherton CW5 219 D3
Nantwich CW5 204 F3
Audlem St James' CE Prim Sch CW3 230 A5
AUDLEY 209 C2
Audley Cres CH4 141 E6
Audley Rd
Alsager ST7 193 E1
Barthomley CW2 208 E5
Newcastle-u-Lyme ST7, ST5 210 B2
Talke ST7 210 B6
Audley St W CW1 190 D5
Audley St CW1 190 D5
Audre Cl WA5 14 D6
Aughton Way CH4 139 D4
Augusta Dr SK10 87 B4
Augusta Ho CH1 117 F6
Austell Rd 3 M22 33 D8
Austen Cl 1 CW11 174 D6
Austen Dr WA2 8 A6
Austen Ho SK10 86 F1
Austin Cl CW7 149 C6
Austins Hill CH3 144 C8
Austin St CW9 79 D1
Austral Ave WA1 17 C7
Australia La WA4 17 C1
Autumn Ave WA16 57 C2
Avebury Cl
Golborne WA3 3 E8
Widnes WA8 13 F3
Aveley Cl WA1 17 B7
Avens Rd M31 11 F3
Avenue One CW1 207 C8
Avenue The
Alderley Edge SK9 60 A1
Alsager ST7 193 D4
Altrincham WA15 31 F8
Bebington CH62 43 C8
Comberbach CW9 78 D8
Great Barrow CH3 120 F7
High Legh WA16 29 C5
Kidsgrove ST7 194 F1
Lymm WA13 18 D1
Marston CW9 79 B3
Newton-le-W WA12 2 D4
Sandbach CW11 174 E8
Tarporley CW6 146 D1
Avenue Two CW1 207 C8
Avery Cl WA2 8 E2
Avery Cres WA11 1 C7
Avery Rd WA11 1 C7
Avery Sq WA11 1 C7
Aviemore Dr WA2 9 A3
Avocet Cl
Newton-le-W WA12 2 C4
Warrington WA2 8 D3
Avocet Dr CW7 149 D6
Avon WA8 12 A2
Avon Ave WA5 14 F4
Avon Cl
Kidsgrove ST7 195 B2
Macclesfield SK10 87 A2
Neston CH64 66 E6
Avon Ct ST7 193 C5
Avondale CH65 70 B2
Avondale Ave CH62 43 F5
Avondale Dr WA8 12 B1
Avondale Rd WA11 1 C7
Avondale Rise SK9 60 D6
Avon Dr
Congleton CW12 156 F1
Crewe CW1 191 A5
Avonlea Cl CH4 140 E4
Avon Rd
Altrincham WA15 31 E8
Culcheth WA3 5 A2
Gatley SK8 34 C7
Avonside Way SK11 112 C5
Avon Wlk CW7 127 A2
Avro Way M90 32 F7
Axminster Wlk SK7 35 E7
Aycliffe Wlk 6 WA8 22 C8
Aylesbury Cl
Ellesmere Port CH66 69 C3
Macclesfield SK10 87 D3
Aylesby Cl WA16 57 B1
Aylsham Cl WA8 12 C4
Ayrshire Cl CW10 128 D2
Ayrshire Way CW12 157 A1
Aysgarth Ave CW1 173 B1
Azalea Gdns WA9 6 A7
Azalea Gr WA7 49 F4

B

Babbacombe Rd WA5 14 E4
Babbage Rd CH5 116 A4
BACHE 118 B5
Bache Ave CH2 118 C5
Bache Dr CH2 118 D5
Bachefield Ave CH3 142 A6
Bache Hall Ct CH2 118 C5
Bache Hall Est CH2 118 C5
Bachelor's Ct CH3 142 A8
Bachelor's La CH3 142 A8
Bache Sta CH2 118 D5
Back Bridge St WA12 2 B3
Back Brook Pl WA4 16 E3
Back Coole La CW3 229 B4
Back Crosland Terr WA6 73 B2
Back Cross La
Congleton CW12 179 A8
Newton-le-W WA12 2 B4
Back Eastford Rd WA4 16 A1
Back Eddisbury Rd SK11 113 C7
BACKFORD 95 A4
Backford Cl WA7 50 C5
Backford Cross CH66 94 F7
Backford Gdns CH1 94 F7
Back Forshaw St WA2 16 C7
Back Heathcote St ST7 195 A2
Back High St 3 WA7 23 A2
Back Jodrell St SK22 39 B7
Back La
Alpraham CW6 169 D6
Altrincham WA15 32 B4
Bate Heath CW9 54 D7
Betley CW2 208 C1
Brereton Green CW11 153 D6
Back La *continued*
Burtonwood WA5 6 D7
Congleton CW12 156 A4
Duddon CW6 145 A6
Helsby WA6 73 D2
Higher Whitley WA4 52 E4
High Legh WA14 29 F5
Marton CW12, SK11 133 F2
No Man's Heath SY14 214 A4
Norbury SY13 215 F5
Partington WA14 20 C5
Plumley WA16 81 B1
Shavington CW2 206 E4
Smallwood CW11 176 D8
Swan Green WA16 106 B8
Tattenhall CH3 167 C2
Threapwood SY14 222 E7
Warrington WA5 14 A3
Wybunbury CW5 220 C6
Backlands CW1 190 C6
Back Lanes CW6 146 B2
Back Legh St WA12 2 A3
Back Market St WA12 2 A3
Back Paradise St 4 SK11 112 C7
Back Park St CW12 156 E2
Back Queen St CH1 237 B3
Back River St 1 CW12 156 D3
Back Union Rd 3 SK22 39 C7
Back Wallgate 13 SK11 112 D8
Badbury Cl WA11 1 D7
Badcock's La CW6 185 E4
BADDILEY 203 B1
Baddiley Cl CW5 203 D2
Baddiley Hall La CW5 217 A8
Baddiley La CW5 203 D1
Baddington La CW5 204 C1
Badger Ave CW1 190 B5
Badger Bait CH64 66 F6
Badger Cl WA7 50 A6
Badger Ho SK10 87 D2
Badger Rd
Macclesfield SK10 87 D2
Prestbury SK10 87 A7
Badgers Cl
Christleton CH3 142 E7
1 Ellesmere Port CH66 94 F8
1 Winsford CW7 126 A1
Badgers Croft ST5 210 E1
Badgers Pk CH64 66 F6
Badgersrake La CH66 68 D3
Badgers Set CW8 101 D5
Badgers Wlk CH2 95 E2
Badgers Wood CW2 205 E8
Bag La
Cuddington CW8, WA6 101 E7
Norley WA6 101 A6
Bagley La CW3 230 B1
Bagmere Cl
Brereton Green CW11 153 F4
Sandbach CW11 174 F7
Bagmere La CW11 154 B5
Bagnall Cl WA5 15 C5
Bagot Ave WA5 15 F8
Bagstock Ave SK12 36 E2
Baguley Ave WA8 22 A5
Bahama Cl WA11 1 D8
Bahama Rd WA11 1 D8
Baildon Gn CH66 69 B5
Bailey Ave CH65 69 F6
Bailey Bridge Cl CH2 118 D4
Bailey Bsns Pk SK10 87 F7
Bailey Cl CW1 190 C7
Bailey Cres
Congleton CW12 157 A4
Sandbach CW11 175 D6
Bailey Ct
Alsager ST7 193 E3
1 Macclesfield SK10 112 E7
Bailey La M31 11 F3
Bailey's Bank ST8 179 D3
Baileys Cl WA8 13 A5
Baileys La L26 21 A7
Bailey's La L24 21 A1
Bailey Wlk WA14 31 C8
Bainbridge Ave WA3 3 F8
Bainbridge Cres WA5 14 E8
Baines Ave M44 11 F8
Bakehurst Cl SK22 39 C7
Baker Cl CW2 190 A2
Baker Dr CH66 69 E3
Baker Rd WA7 48 D7
Baker's Cl CW7 126 E1
Baker's Ct CW7 126 E1
Baker's La
Swan Green WA16 106 D6
Winsford CW7 126 E1
Bakers Pl WA2 16 B7
Baker St 8 SK11 112 C7
Bakers Villas The CW12 156 D2
Bakestonedale Rd SK10 63 E4
Bakewell Cl CH66 94 E8
Bakewell Rd
Burtonwood WA5 7 A7
Hazel Grove SK7 36 E8
Bala Cl WA5 7 E2
BALDERTON 140 C1
Baldock Cl WA4 17 C3
Balfour Cl CW1 191 C4
Balfour St WA7 22 F1
Balham Cl WA8 13 A4

Balharry Ave WA11 . . . . 1 E7
Ballantyne Pl WA2 . . . . 8 A6
Ballantyne Way 5 WA3 . . . 3 E8
Ballater Cres CH3 . . . . 119 B2
Ballater Dr WA2 . . . . 8 E4
Ballerat Cl CH1 . . . . 117 D4
Balliol Cl SK11 . . . . 112 F3
Ball La
Bollington SK10 . . . . 87 D5
Kingsley WA6 . . . . 75 E4
BALL O' DITTON 12 E2
Ball Pathway WA8 . . . . 12 E1
Balmoral Ave
Crewe CW2 . . . . 190 B1
Northwich CW9 . . . . 104 A5
Balmoral Cl
Knutsford WA16 . . . . 57 B1
Winsford CW7 . . . . 126 C3
Balmoral Cres SK10 . . . . . . 87 F2
Balmoral Dr
Helsby WA6 . . . . 73 B4
High Lane SK6 . . . . 37 E7
Holmes Chapel CW4 . . . . . 130 B2
Poynton SK12 . . . . 36 D3
Balmoral Gdns
Congleton CW12 . . . . 156 F4
Ellesmere Port CH65 . . . . . 70 D3
Balmoral Pk CH1 . . . . 118 B3
Balmoral Pl CW5 . . . . 205 D4
Balmoral Rd
Warrington WA4 . . . . 16 F2
Widnes WA8 . . . . 13 A4
Balmoral Way SK9 . . . . 60 A6
BALTERLEY 208 C1
BALTERLEY GREEN 208 C2
BALTERLEY HEATH 207 F1
Baltimore Gdns WA5 . . . . . . 15 C7
Bamburgh Ct CH65 . . . . 70 E3
Bamford Cl
Bollington SK10 . . . . 88 A7
Gatley SK8 . . . . 34 D8
Runcorn WA7 . . . . 49 C7
Bamford St SK10 . . . . 87 E1
Banastre Dr WA12 . . . . 2 F3
Banbury Cl SK10 . . . . 87 E2
Banbury Dr WA5 . . . . 15 C5
Banbury St ST7 . . . . 194 D1
Bancroft CW8 . . . . 76 F4
Bancroft Rd WA8 . . . . 13 D2
Bandon Cl L24 . . . . 21 D2
Banff Ave CH63 . . . . 43 D5
Bangor Cl 11 CH66 . . . . 94 F8
Bank Cl
Chester CH2 . . . . 118 E5
Macclesfield SK11 . . . . 112 E7
Neston CH64 . . . . 67 A6
Bank Cott CW12 . . . . 156 E2
Bank Ct 5 ST7 . . . . 195 A2
Bankes' La
Runcorn, Weston Point
WA7 . . . . 48 E6
Runcorn, Weston WA7 . . . . . 48 F5
Bank Farm Mews
SY14 . . . . 214 E6
Bankfield Ave
Irlam M44 . . . . 11 D5
Wistaston CW2 . . . . 206 A7
Bankfield Rd WA8 . . . . 12 C1
Bankfield Sch The
WA8 . . . . 12 D1
Bankfields Dr CH62 . . . . . . 44 B5
Bank Gdns WA5 . . . . 14 E4
Bankhall La WA14,
WA15 . . . . 31 F8
Bankhall Pk WA1 . . . . 16 C4
BANK HEATH 3 A8
Bankhey CH64 . . . . 66 F5
Bank Ho CW7 . . . . 126 C1
Bankhouse Dr CW12 . . . . 157 A5
Bank House La
Helsby WA6 . . . . 73 C4
Smallwood CW11 . . . . 177 A6
Bank La
Burland CW5 . . . . 203 D8
Congleton CW12 . . . . 134 C1
Rainow SK10 . . . . 89 D6
Banklands Cl M44 . . . . 11 D5
Bank Mews WA6 . . . . 73 C4
Bank Pl SK9 . . . . 60 B7
BANK QUAY 15 F4
Bank Quay Trad Est
WA1 . . . . 15 F4
Bank Rd CH5 . . . . 91 D1
Banks Cl CW12 . . . . 156 C3
Banks Cres WA4 . . . . 16 F4
Bankside
Altrincham WA15 . . . . 32 D6
Runcorn WA7 . . . . 50 E7
Warrington WA1 . . . . 16 A5
Bank Side CW8 . . . . 77 C1
Bankside Cl
Barbridge CW5 . . . . 187 D6
Handforth SK9 . . . . 34 D1
Bankside Ct ST7 . . . . 193 E5
Bank Sq SK9 . . . . 60 B7
Banks Rd CH60 . . . . 40 D8
Bank St
Congleton CW12 . . . . 156 E2
Hollinfare WA3 . . . . 11 B5
Kidsgrove ST7 . . . . 195 C4
Macclesfield SK11 . . . . 112 E7
Newton-le-W WA12 . . . . 1 F3
8 Warrington WA1 . . . . 16 B5
Widnes WA8 . . . . 23 A4
Bank The ST7 . . . . 195 B7
Bank Top Cotts CW5 . . . . 204 F6
Bank View CW4 . . . . 107 E1
Banky Fields CW12 . . . . . . 156 C2
Banky Fields Cres
CW12 . . . . 156 C1
Bannacks Cl CW5 . . . . 205 D6
Bannister Ct CW7 . . . . 149 B7
Bannister Gr CW7 . . . . 149 B6
Barbauld St WA1 . . . . 16 B5
Barber Dr ST7 . . . . 194 E7
Barberry Wlk M31 . . . . 11 F3
Barber's La
Antrobus CW9 . . . . 53 D6
Northwich CW8 . . . . 103 E8
Barber St SK11 . . . . 112 E6
Barbondale Cl WA5 . . . . . . 14 F7
Barbour Sq CH3 . . . . 166 B1
BARBRIDGE 187 C6
Barbridge Mews
CW5 . . . . 187 D6
Barbridge Rd ST5 . . . . 210 D2
Barclay Hall WA16 . . . . 58 D4
Barclay Rd SK12 . . . . 36 E2
Bardell Cl SK12 . . . . 36 D2
Bardsey Cl 1 CH65 . . . . . . 70 C1
Bardsley Ave WA5 . . . . 7 F1
Barford Cl WA5 . . . . 7 B1
Barford Dr
Golborne WA3 . . . . 4 A8
Handforth SK9 . . . . 34 C1
Barford Grange CH64 . . . . 68 B8
Barham Ct WA3 . . . . 9 D4
Barhill Dr SY13 . . . . 214 C2
Barhill Farm Cotts
SY13 . . . . 214 C2
Barington Dr WA7 . . . . 50 E7
Baristow Cl CH2 . . . . 237 B4
Barker's Hollow Rd
WA4 . . . . 51 A5
Barker St
Crewe CW2 . . . . 190 D1
Nantwich CW5 . . . . 204 E5
Barkhill Rd CH3 . . . . 119 B3
Bark St CW12 . . . . 156 E2
Barley Castle Cl WA4 . . . . 27 B3
Barleycastle La WA4 . . . . . 27 D4
Barleycastle Trad Est
WA4 . . . . 27 D4
Barley Croft
Alsager ST7 . . . . 193 E2
Chester CH3 . . . . 142 A7
Barleycroft Terr ST7 . . . . 194 F7
Barley Dr SK7 . . . . 35 E7
Barleyfields ST7 . . . . 209 D2
Barley Mow Cl CH66 . . . . . 69 C2
Barley Rd WA4 . . . . 17 C3
Barleywood Cl CW2 . . . . . 206 B8
Barlow Dr CW7 . . . . 148 F8
Barlow Gr WA9 . . . . 1 A2
Barlow Hill SK11 . . . . 136 F2
Barlow Rd
Handforth SK9 . . . . 34 B1
Moulton CW9 . . . . 126 F7
Barlow Way CW11 . . . . . . 175 A8
Barmouth Cl WA5 . . . . 7 E2
Barnabas Ave CW1 . . . . . . 189 F5
Barnaby Chase CH3 . . . . . 182 C2
Barnaby Rd SK12 . . . . 36 D2
Barnack Cl WA1 . . . . 17 A8
Barnacre Dr CH64 . . . . 41 B2
Barnard Cl SK11 . . . . 111 F6
Barnard St WA5 . . . . 15 D3
Barnato Cl CW1 . . . . 189 F7
Barnbridge Cl ST7 . . . . . . 194 E7
Barnbrook Cl CW7 . . . . . . 126 A1
Barncroft WA7 . . . . 50 D7
Barn Croft WA6 . . . . 73 C4
Barncroft Cl SK11 . . . . 84 A3
Barn Croft Rd L26 . . . . 21 A7
Barn Ct CH3 . . . . 182 C2
Barnes Ave WA2 . . . . 9 B2
Barnes Cl
Blacon CH1 . . . . 117 F6
Haslington CW1 . . . . 191 C4
Warrington WA5 . . . . 15 A5
Widnes WA8 . . . . 13 D2
Barnes Rd WA8 . . . . 13 C2
Barneston Rd WA8 . . . . 13 E3
Barnett Ave WA12 . . . . 1 E3
BARNETT BROOK 228 E5
Barnett Gr CW12 . . . . 156 A3
Barnett St SK11 . . . . 112 B7
Barnett Wlk CW2 . . . . 206 C8
Barnfield CH3 . . . . 166 A2
Barnfield Ave WA7 . . . . 50 D7
Barnfield Cl CH66 . . . . 69 C2
Barnfield Rd
Bollington SK10 . . . . 87 F6
Warrington WA1 . . . . 17 C7
Barnham Cl WA3 . . . . 3 A8
BARNHILL 183 B1
Barnhill Grange CH3 . . . . 183 B3
Barnhill Rd CH3 . . . . 183 A1
Barnhouse La
Great Barrow CH3 . . . . 120 E7
Mouldsworth CH3 . . . . 98 A3
Barn La WA3 . . . . 2 F8
Barn Mdw CW8 . . . . 78 E1
Barnmoore Cl SY14 . . . . . 213 B4
Barn Rd CW12 . . . . 156 D4
Barnside Way
Macclesfield SK10 . . . . 87 C3
Moulton CW9 . . . . 126 F8
Barns La
Partington WA14 . . . . 20 A5
Partington WA14 . . . . 20 A6
Barns Pl WA15 . . . . 32 C8
Barn St WA8 . . . . 23 A6
Barnstaple Way WA5 . . . . . 14 E4
Barns The CW10 . . . . 127 D5
Barnston Ave CH65 . . . . . . 69 F5
Barnston Ct
Farndon CH3 . . . . 180 E2
Mickle Trafford CH2 . . . . . . 119 F8
Barnston Mews CH3 . . . . 180 E2
Barnston Prim Sch
CH60 . . . . 41 C7
Barnston Rd CH60 . . . . 41 C8
Barnston Towers Cl
CH60 . . . . 41 C8
Barnston Twrs CH60 . . . . . 41 C8
Barnswood Cl WA4 . . . . . . 17 C1
BARNTON 78 C4
Barnton Cl WA3 . . . . 3 D7
Barnton Prim Sch
CW8 . . . . 78 A4
Barn Way WA12 . . . . 2 B3
Barnwell Ave WA3 . . . . 4 D4
Barnwell Cl CW2 . . . . 206 B8
Barnwood Cl CH66 . . . . 68 F7
Baron Cl WA1 . . . . 17 D7
Baronet Mews WA4 . . . . . . 16 A1
Baronet Rd WA4 . . . . 16 A1
Baron Gn SK8 . . . . 34 D7
Baronia Pl CW5 . . . . 204 F6
Barons Cl WA7 . . . . 23 F1
Baron's Cl WA8 . . . . 22 C8
Barons Ct CH2 . . . . 118 C4
Barons Quay Rd CW9 . . . . 78 F1
Barons Rd
Shavington CW2 . . . . 206 B4
Worleston CW5 . . . . 188 E5
Barony Bldgs 1 CW5 . . . 204 E6
Barony Ct CW5 . . . . 204 E7
Barony Employment Pk
The CW5 . . . . 204 F8
Barony Rd CW5 . . . . 204 E7
Barony Terr CW5 . . . . 204 E6
Barony Way CH4 . . . . 140 E4
Barracks La
Burwardsley CH3 . . . . 184 C5
Macclesfield SK10 . . . . 112 F8
Ravensmoor CW5 . . . . 203 E2
Barracks Sq 3 SK11 . . . . 112 B6
Barrastitch La CW8 . . . . . 101 E6
Barratt Rd ST7 . . . . 193 F3
Barrel Well Hill CH2 . . . . 118 F1
BARRETS GREEN 169 D3
Barrie Gdns ST7 . . . . 210 C8
Barrie Gr CW1 . . . . 190 E4
Barrington Dr CW10 . . . . 151 C7
Barrow Ave WA2 . . . . 8 E2
Barrow CE Prim Sch
CH3 . . . . 120 D6
Barrowdale Rd WA3 . . . . . . 3 B8
Barrow Hall Com Prim Sch
WA5 . . . . 14 E7
Barrow Hall Farm
CH3 . . . . 120 E5
Barrow Hall La WA5 . . . . . 14 E7
Barrow La
Altrincham WA15 . . . . 32 B7
Golborne WA2 . . . . 3 C2
Great Barrow CH3 . . . . 120 C5
Tarvin CH3 . . . . 121 C4
Barrow Mdw SK8 . . . . 34 E8
Barrowmore Est CH3 . . . . 120 F7
Barrow's Brow WA16 . . . . 81 E1
Barrows Cl CW1 . . . . 190 A8
BARROWS GREEN 189 F8
BARROW'S GREEN 13 E4
Barrow's Green La
WA8 . . . . 13 E3
Barrow's Row WA8 . . . . 13 B4
Barrule Cl WA4 . . . . 26 D7
Barry Cl CH65 . . . . 95 C8
Barrymore Ave WA4 . . . . . 16 F4
Barrymore Cres CW9 . . . . 78 D8
Barrymore Ct WA4 . . . . . . 17 A1
Barrymore Rd
Runcorn WA7 . . . . 49 B7
Warrington WA4 . . . . 17 A1
Weaverham CW8 . . . . 77 E1
Barrymore Way CH63 . . . . 43 B6
Barry St WA4 . . . . 16 C4
Barsbank Cl WA13 . . . . 18 C3
Barsbank La WA13 . . . . . . 18 C3
Barshaw Gdns WA4 . . . . . . 26 E4
Bars The CH1, CH3 . . . . . 237 C2
Bartholomew Ct WA4 . . . . 17 B2
Bartholomew Way
CH4 . . . . 141 C6
BARTHOMLEY 208 C5
Barthomley Cres
CW2 . . . . 189 D4
Barthomley Rd
Barthomley CW2 . . . . 208 B7
Betley ST7 . . . . 208 F3
BARTINGTON 77 A5
Bartington Hall Pk
CW8 . . . . 77 A5
Bartlegate WA7 . . . . 50 B5
BARTON 181 F1
Barton Ave WA4 . . . . 17 A2
Barton Cl
Handforth SK9 . . . . 34 D2
Runcorn WA7 . . . . 50 D7
Barton Ct
Warrington WA2 . . . . 16 B6
Winsford CW7 . . . . 126 F1
Barton Rd
Barton CH3, SY14 . . . . 181 D1
Barton SY14 . . . . 181 F1
Congleton CW12 . . . . 156 F3
Farndon CH3 . . . . 180 F1
Barton's Pl CW9 . . . . 79 B1
Barton St SK11 . . . . 112 C7
Barton Stad CW7 . . . . 126 F1
Barwood Ave ST7 . . . . 194 A5
Barwoods Dr CH4 . . . . 140 F6
BASFORD 206 E5
Basford Rd CW2 . . . . 206 D8
Basford Way CW7 . . . . 126 B2
Baskervyle Cl CH60 . . . . . . 41 A6
Baskervyle Rd CH60 . . . . . 41 A6
Baslow Dr
Gatley SK8 . . . . 34 C8
Hazel Grove SK7 . . . . 36 F8
Bassett Cl CW5 . . . . 205 D6
Batchelors Wing The
CW10 . . . . 127 D5
BATE HEATH 54 F3
Bateman Almshouses
ST8 . . . . 179 E3
Bateman Cl CW1 . . . . 190 B4
Bateman Rd CW9 . . . . 80 B2
Batemans Ct CW2 . . . . . . 206 B8
Batemill Cl SK10 . . . . 86 F1
Batemill La WA16,
SK11 . . . . 108 E5
Bates La WA6 . . . . 73 D4
Bate's Mill La CW6 . . . . . 167 E5
Bath Cres SK8 . . . . 35 B6
Batherton Cl WA8 . . . . 23 B7
Batherton La CW5 . . . . . . 204 F2
Bath La CW3 . . . . 230 A3
Bath St
Chester CH1 . . . . 237 C2
Sandbach CW11 . . . . 175 C6
Warrington WA1 . . . . 16 A5
BATH VALE 157 A3
Bath Vale Cotts
CW12 . . . . 157 A3
Bathwood Dr CH64 . . . . . . 66 E5
Batterbee Ct CW1 . . . . . . 191 D5
Battersby La WA2 . . . . 16 C6
Battersea Ct WA8 . . . . 12 F3
Battery La
Warrington WA1 . . . . 17 F7
Wilmslow SK9 . . . . 59 D6
Bawtry Ct WA2 . . . . 8 E1
Baxter Cl WA7 . . . . 50 D7
Baxter Ho CW8 . . . . 78 E1
Baxter St WA5 . . . . 15 E5
Baycliffe WA13 . . . . 18 D2
Bayley Rd CW5 . . . . 205 D6
Bayswater Cl WA7 . . . . 24 F4
Baytree Cl CH66 . . . . 69 F1
Bayvil Cl WA7 . . . . 50 E7
Beach Gr CW8 . . . . 103 C6
Beachin La CH3 . . . . 182 A4
Beach Rd CW8 . . . . 103 B6
Beacon Ct 4 CH60 . . . . . . 41 A8
Beacon Hill View WA7 . . . 48 D7
Beacon La CH60 . . . . 41 A7
Beaconsfield Cres
WA8 . . . . 13 A4
Beaconsfield Gr WA8 . . . . 13 B4
Beaconsfield Rd
Runcorn WA7 . . . . 22 E1
Widnes WA8 . . . . 13 B4
Beaconsfield St CH3 . . . . 237 C2
Beacons The CH60 . . . . . . 41 A7
Beacons The WA3 . . . . 9 D5
Beadnell Dr WA5 . . . . 14 F3
Beagle Point CW7 . . . . . . 126 A1
Beagle Wlk M22 . . . . 33 E8
Beames Ho CW1 . . . . 190 B4
Beam Heath Way
CW5 . . . . 204 F7
Beamish Cl WA4 . . . . 26 D3
Beamont St WA8 . . . . 23 A4
Beam St CW5 . . . . 204 E6
Beard Cres SK22 . . . . 39 D8
Beardsmore Dr WA3 . . . . . . 3 E8
Bearhurst La SK11 . . . . . 111 A5
Bearstone Rd TF9 . . . . . . 236 E3
Beasley Cl CH66 . . . . 69 D3
Beata Rd ST5 . . . . 210 F1
Beatrice St WA4 . . . . 16 D3
Beatty Ave WA2 . . . . 8 C1
Beatty Dr CW12 . . . . 157 A4
Beatty Rd CW5 . . . . 204 D4
Beaufort Chase SK9 . . . . . 34 F1
Beaufort Cl
Alderley Edge SK9 . . . . 60 B2
Runcorn WA7 . . . . 49 B7
Warrington WA5 . . . . 15 A5
Widnes WA8 . . . . 22 A8
Beaufort St WA5 . . . . 15 E4
Beaulieu Ave CW7 . . . . . . 126 F2
Beaumaris Cres SK7 . . . . . 36 C8
Beaumaris Dr CH65 . . . . . . 70 D2
Beaumaris Way WA7 . . . . . 23 F2
Beaumont Cl
Biddulph ST8 . . . . 179 D3
Chester CH4 . . . . 140 E6
Wistaston CW2 . . . . 205 F8
Beaumont Com Inf & Jun
Schs WA2 . . . . 16 C7
Beaumont Ct
Handforth SK9 . . . . 34 C5
Warrington WA4 . . . . 16 C2
Beauty Bank
Whitegate CW7 . . . . 125 E5
Winsford CW7 . . . . 149 B3
Beauty Bank Cotts
CW7 . . . . 149 A3
Beaverbrook Ave WA3 . . . . 5 B4
Beaver Cl
Chester CH4 . . . . 140 E5
Pickmere WA16 . . . . 79 F7
Beaver Ctr The CW9 . . . . 103 F7
BEBINGTON 43 A7
Bebington Rd CH66 . . . . . . 69 D4
Becconsall Cl CW1 . . . . . . 190 A8
Becconsall Dr CW1 . . . . . 190 A8
Bechers WA8 . . . . 12 B3
Beckenham Cl WA8 . . . . . . 13 D4
Beckenham Gr 4
CW7 . . . . 126 A1
Beckett Ave CW7 . . . . 150 D8
Beckett Dr
Lymm WA13 . . . . 19 B8
Winwick WA2 . . . . 8 A5
Beckett's La CH3 . . . . 142 B8
Beckford Cl CW1 . . . . 189 F8
Becks La SK10 . . . . 86 F2
Bedells La SK9 . . . . 60 A6
Bedford Ave CH65 . . . . 70 A2
Bedford Ave E CH65 . . . . . 70 B2
Bedford Ct CW2 . . . . 190 D1
Bedford Gdns CW2 . . . . . . 190 C1
Bedford Gn M44 . . . . 11 B6
Bedford Gr ST7 . . . . 193 B5
Bedford Pl CW2 . . . . 190 C1
Bedford Rd
Kidsgrove ST7 . . . . 195 A3
Macclesfield SK11 . . . . 112 B7
Bedford Rise CW7 . . . . . . 149 C6
Bedford St
Crewe CW2 . . . . 190 C1
Warrington WA4 . . . . 26 C8
Bedward Row CH1 . . . . . . 237 A2
Beech Ave
Culcheth WA3 . . . . 5 A3
Frodsham WA6 . . . . 74 C8
Golborne WA3 . . . . 3 F7
Haydock WA11 . . . . 1 F7
Mobberley WA16 . . . . 57 E6
Rode Heath ST7 . . . . 193 F8
Warrington, Thelwall
WA4 . . . . 17 D3
Warrington WA5 . . . . 14 C3
Beech Bank SK10 . . . . 87 D1
Beech Cl
Alderley Edge SK9 . . . . 60 B3
Congleton CW12 . . . . 156 A4
Cuddington CW8 . . . . 101 F2
Holmes Chapel CW4 . . . . . 130 D4
Newton-le-W WA12 . . . . 2 C2
Ollerton WA16 . . . . 82 F6
4 Partington M31 . . . . 11 F3
Beech Cotts
Alderley Edge SK9 . . . . 85 A8
Stretton WA4 . . . . 26 E1
Beech Cres SK12 . . . . 36 E4
Beechcroft Ave CW2 . . . . 206 B7
Beechcroft Dr CH65 . . . . . 70 B2
Beech Ct WA8 . . . . 12 B3
Beech Dr
Crewe CW2 . . . . 189 F2
Knutsford WA16 . . . . 57 C2
Talke ST7 . . . . 210 E8
Beeches SK9 . . . . 59 F6
Beeches The
Chester CH2 . . . . 119 A6
Ellesmere Port CH66 . . . . . . 69 D4
Helsby WA6 . . . . 73 C4
Mobberley WA16 . . . . 58 E1
Nantwich CW5 . . . . 204 F5
3 Northwich CW9 . . . . . . 103 E6
Whitchurch SY13 . . . . 225 F1
Widnes WA8 . . . . 13 D4
Beech Farm Dr SK10 . . . . 87 D2
Beechfield
Moulton CW9 . . . . 126 E8
Wilmslow SK9 . . . . 60 A6
Beechfield Ave SK9 . . . . . 59 E5
Beechfield Cl CH60 . . . . . . 41 A7
Beechfield Dr CW10 . . . . 128 B2
Beechfield Gdns CW8 . . . 103 B6
Beechfield Rd
Alderley Edge SK9 . . . . 85 B8
Cheadle SK8 . . . . 35 B8
Ellesmere Port CH65 . . . . . 70 B5
Warrington WA4 . . . . 17 A2
Beechfields CW7 . . . . 150 B8
Beech Gdns 3 WA7 . . . . . 49 C8
Beech Gr
Chester CH2 . . . . 119 A3
Crewe CW1 . . . . 190 E5
Ellesmere Port CH66 . . . . . . 95 A8
Lymm WA13 . . . . 18 B2
Macclesfield SK11 . . . . 112 E5
Sandbach CW11 . . . . 175 D6
Warrington, Latchford
WA4 . . . . 16 D3
Warrington WA1 . . . . 17 A7
Weaverham CW8 . . . . 102 D8
Wilmslow SK9 . . . . 60 A6
Winsford CW7 . . . . 149 D8
Beech Hall Dr SK10 . . . . . 87 C2
Beech Hall Sch SK10 . . . . 87 C2
Beech Heyes Cl CW8 . . . . 102 E8
Beech Heyes Dr CW8 . . . 102 E8
Beech Hey La CH64 . . . . . 43 B1
Beech Hollows LL12 . . . . 162 C1
Beech La
Barnton CW8 . . . . 78 A3
Cotebrook CW6 . . . . 147 B6
Macclesfield SK10 . . . . 87 D1
Norley WA6 . . . . 75 E1
Wilmslow SK9 . . . . 60 A6
Beechlands Ave CH3 . . . . 119 A1
Beechmill Dr WA3 . . . . 4 E3
Beechmoore WA4 . . . . 25 B5
Beechmuir CH1 . . . . 117 E3
Beech Rd
Alderley Edge SK9 . . . . 60 B3
Aston WA7 . . . . 50 B4
Heswall CH60 . . . . 41 C8

Beech Rd continued
High Lane SK6 ... 37 F7
Little Budworth CW6 ... 124 D2
Paddockhill WA16 ... 59 B5
Runcorn WA7 ... 49 C8
Warrington WA4 ... 26 C8
Whaley Bridge SK23 ... 65 E7
Beech Rise
Crowton CW8 ... 76 B2
Horwich End SK23 ... 65 C5
Beech St W CW1 ... 190 C4
Beech St CW10 ... 128 C1
Beech Tree Cl CW5 ... 205 D5
Beechtree Farm Cl
WA16 ... 29 C7
Beechtree La WA13 ... 29 B7
Beech View Rd WA6 ... 75 C1
Beechway
Bollington SK10 ... 88 A7
Chester CH2 ... 118 C6
High Lane SK6 ... 37 F7
Neston CH64 ... 66 D7
Wilmslow SK9 ... 59 F5
Beechways WA4 ... 26 D5
Beechways Dr CH64 ... 66 D7
BEECHWOOD ... 49 E5
Beechwood
Knutsford, Cross Town
WA16 ... 57 C2
Knutsford WA16 ... 56 F3
Beechwood Ave
Hartford CW8 ... 103 A6
Newton-le-W WA12 ... 2 D4
Runcorn WA7 ... 49 E5
Warrington, Padgate
WA1 ... 16 E7
Warrington WA5 ... 14 F5
Beechwood Cl CW5 ... 205 A4
Beechwood Dr
Alsager ST7 ... 193 B4
Eaton (nr Congleton)
CW12 ... 156 F8
Ellesmere Port CH66 ... 69 D1
Higher Wincham CW9 ... 79 F6
Wilmslow SK9 ... 60 E8
Beechwood Gr SK8 ... 35 A8
Beechwood La WA3 ... 4 D4
Beechwood Mews
SK10 ... 87 C2
Beechwood Prim Sch
WA7 ... 49 E5
Beechwood Rd
Bebington CH62 ... 43 C8
Saltney CH4 ... 140 E5
Beechwood Sch CW1 ... 190 C5
Beecroft Cl WA5 ... 7 D1
Beehive La CW9 ... 126 F8
BEESTON ... 168 A2
BEESTON-BROOK ... 168 C5
Beeston Brow SK10 ... 88 B8
Beeston Castle★
CW6 ... 167 F3
Beeston Cl
Bollington SK10 ... 63 C1
Holmes Chapel CW4 ... 130 A3
Middlewich CW10 ... 151 D5
Warrington WA3 ... 9 D4
Beeston Ct WA7 ... 24 C4
Beeston Dr
Alsager ST7 ... 193 C3
Knutsford WA16 ... 82 A8
Winsford CW7 ... 149 C7
Beeston Gn CH66 ... 69 E5
Beeston Hall Mews
CW6 ... 168 B4
BEESTON MOSS ... 168 B1
Beeston Mount SK10 ... 63 C1
Beeston Pathway
CH4 ... 141 E7
Beeston Rd
Broughton CH4 ... 139 B3
Handforth SK9 ... 34 D5
Higher Kinnerton CH4 ... 161 A7
Beeston St CW8 ... 103 E7
Beeston Terr SK11 ... 111 E6
Beeston View CH4 ... 141 E7
Beggarman's La WA16 ... 82 A7
Begonia Gdns WA9 ... 6 A7
Beilby Rd WA11 ... 1 E7
Belfry Cl SK9 ... 60 D8
Belfry Dr SK10 ... 87 C4
BELGRAVE ... 162 E6
Belgrave App CH3 ... 163 C6
Belgrave Ave
Alsager ST7 ... 193 D5
Congleton CW12 ... 156 D3
Eccleston CH4 ... 162 F7
Saltney CH4 ... 140 E6
Warrington WA1 ... 16 F8
Belgrave Cl
Dodleston CH4 ... 162 A6
Golborne WN7 ... 4 C8
Widnes WA8 ... 13 E3
Belgrave Dr CH65 ... 69 F5
Belgrave Inf Sch CH4 ... 141 B5
Belgrave Rd
Chester CH3 ... 142 B8
Crewe CW2 ... 190 B2
Irlam M44 ... 11 D5
Macclesfield SK11 ... 112 C4
Northwich CW9 ... 104 A4
Belgrave St CH1 ... 237 C3
Belgravia Ct
Pulford CH4 ... 162 E5
Widnes WA8 ... 12 F3
Belgravia Gdns WA15 ... 31 E8
Bellaport Rd TF9 ... 236 A4
Bellard Dr CH2 ... 119 A4
Bell Ave SK11 ... 112 F3
Bellcast Cl WA4 ... 26 C5
Bellemonte Rd WA6 ... 74 C6
Belleville Ave M22 ... 33 E8
Bellevue La CH3 ... 119 E4
Belle Vue Terr CW11 ... 175 B6
Bell Farm Ct SK10 ... 87 C3
Bellflower Cl WA8 ... 12 E4
Bellhouse La
Higher Walton WA4 ... 25 D7
Warrington WA4 ... 17 C1
Bell House Rd WA8 ... 13 C1
Bellingham Cl WA16 ... 57 C2
Bellingham Dr WA7 ... 49 A8
Bell La
Smallwood CW11 ... 177 B7
Warrington WA4 ... 17 E3
Bell Meadow Bsns Pk
CH4 ... 162 E5
Bell Meadow Ct CW6 ... 146 C2
BELL O' TH' HILL ... 225 D7
Bellsfield Cl WA13 ... 18 F2
Bell's Hollow ST5 ... 210 E3
Belmont Ave
Macclesfield SK10 ... 86 C1
Sandbach CW11 ... 175 A7
Warrington WA4 ... 16 F3
Belmont Cres WA5 ... 15 A6
Belmont Dr CH4 ... 140 C6
Belmont Rd
Bramhall SK7 ... 35 F5
Great Budworth CW9 ... 53 F1
Northwich CW9 ... 104 C7
Widnes WA8 ... 13 E2
Belton Cl WA3 ... 3 A7
Beltony Dr CW1 ... 173 A1
Belvedere 9 WA7 ... 23 A3
Belvedere Cl 2 WA6 ... 49 C1
Belvedere Dr CH1 ... 117 E4
Belvedere Rd WA12 ... 2 B5
Belvedere Terr ST7 ... 193 F7
Belvoir Ave SK7 ... 36 E8
Belvoir Rd
Warrington WA4 ... 26 B8
Widnes WA8 ... 13 B1
Bembridge Cl
Warrington WA5 ... 14 C7
Widnes WA8 ... 12 F4
Bembridge Ct CW10 ... 151 C8
Bembridge Dr CW10 ... 151 C8
Benbrook Gr SK9 ... 34 E2
Benbrook Way SK11 ... 111 E1
Bendee Ave CH64 ... 67 A7
Bendee Rd CH64 ... 67 A7
Benjafield Ct CW1 ... 189 F7
Benjamins Way ST7 ... 209 F2
Bennet Cl CH64 ... 68 A8
Bennet Rd CW9 ... 104 D6
Bennett Ave WA1 ... 16 F6
Bennett Cl CW1 ... 190 E4
Bennett Ct CW7 ... 149 D5
Bennetts La SK11 ... 158 E7
Bennett's La
Higher Kinnerton CH4 ... 161 A7
Widnes WA8 ... 13 E1
Bennett St WA1 ... 16 B5
Ben Nevis Dr CH66 ... 68 F6
Benson Rd WA3 ... 9 D3
Benson Wlk 3 SK9 ... 34 D2
Bentham Ave WA2 ... 8 C3
Bentham Rd WA3 ... 5 A2
Bentinck St WA7 ... 22 F3
Bent La
Astbury CW12 ... 178 A8
Culcheth WA3 ... 5 A2
Lymm WA13 ... 19 C6
Norley CW8 ... 101 C8
Bentley Dr CW1 ... 191 A5
Bentley Gr CW7 ... 149 C6
Bentley's Farm La WA4 ... 52 E5
Benton Dr CH2 ... 118 C4
Bents Cotts CH2 ... 71 E2
Bentside Rd SK12 ... 38 D5
Benty Heath La CH64,
CH66 ... 43 B3
Beresford Ct 4 SK9 ... 60 A1
Beresford St WA1 ... 16 E7
Berisford Ho CW12 ... 156 E3
Berkeley Ave ST7 ... 193 D5
Berkeley Cl WN7 ... 4 C8
Berkeley Cres CW2 ... 206 A8
Berkeley Ct
Newton-le-W WA12 ... 1 F4
Runcorn WA7 ... 24 D4
Berkeley Prim Sch The
CW2 ... 206 B7
Berkeley Rise CW7 ... 149 A8
Berkley Ct SK23 ... 65 D6
Berkley Dr CH4 ... 141 D6
Berkshire Cl SK10 ... 86 E2
Berkshire Dr
Congleton CW12 ... 156 D4
Irlam M44 ... 11 C5
Warrington WA1 ... 17 E7
Bermondsey Gr WA8 ... 13 D4
Bernard Ave WA4 ... 26 D8
Bernisdale Rd WA16 ... 57 F4
Bernsdale Cl CH5 ... 116 A3
Bernsdale Ct/Llys
Bernsdale CH5 ... 116 A3
Berristall Rise SK10 ... 63 C1
Berristal Rd SK10 ... 88 E3
Berry Cl
Ellesmere Port CH66 ... 69 C3
Wilmslow SK9 ... 60 A5
Berry Dr CH66 ... 69 C3
Berry Rd WA8 ... 12 D1
Berrystead CW8 ... 103 B4
Bertram St WA12 ... 2 A4
Berwick Ave CH62 ... 43 E4
Berwick Cl
Macclesfield SK10 ... 86 F2
Warrington WA1 ... 17 E6
Berwick Ct CW4 ... 130 B2
Berwick Gdns CH66 ... 69 B6
Berwick Gr CH66 ... 69 B6
Berwick Rd CH66 ... 69 A6
Berwick Road W CH66 ... 69 A6
Berwyn Cl CH66 ... 69 A6
Bessancourt CW4 ... 130 C3
Bessemer Rd M44 ... 11 F6
Beswick Dr CW1 ... 191 A3
Beswicks La
Norton in Hales TF9 ... 236 C2
Row-of-Trees SK9 ... 59 C3
Beswicks Rd CW8 ... 78 E1
Beswick St SK11 ... 112 B7
Betchton Cl CW11 ... 175 C7
Betchton Ct 6 CW12 ... 156 F3
BETCHTON HEATH ... 175 E5
Betchton Rd CW11 ... 175 E3
Betchworth Cres WA7 ... 49 D6
Betchworth Way SK10 ... 87 C4
Bethany Cl WA11 ... 1 B7
Betjeman Cl WA4 ... 16 F4
Betjeman Way CW1 ... 190 F5
BETLEY ... 221 F8
Betley Cl CW9 ... 104 A5
Betley St CW1 ... 190 C4
Betsyfield Dr WA3 ... 9 A7
Bettisfield Ave CH62 ... 43 D6
Betty's La
Beeston CW6 ... 168 D1
Woore CW3 ... 232 C1
Bevan Ave ST7 ... 210 E6
Bevan Cl WA5 ... 15 D6
Bevan Ct WA4 ... 16 B3
Bevan View WA5 ... 15 F7
Beverley Ave WA4 ... 26 D8
Beverley Dr CH60 ... 41 B6
Beverley Rd WA5 ... 15 C6
Beverley Way
Ellesmere Port CH66 ... 69 B7
Macclesfield SK10 ... 87 C4
Bevin Ave WA3 ... 5 B4
Bevyl Rd CH64 ... 41 B2
Bewick Wlk WA16 ... 57 B3
Bewley Ct CH3 ... 142 A7
BEWSEY ... 15 F8
Bewsey Bsns Ctr WA5 ... 15 F6
Bewsey Farm Cl WA5 ... 15 D8
Bewsey Ind Est WA5 ... 16 A7
Bewsey Lodge Prim Sch
WA5 ... 15 F7
Bewsey Park Cl WA5 ... 15 F7
Bewsey Rd WA2, WA5 ... 16 A6
Bexhill Ave WA2 ... 8 B4
Bexington Dr CW1 ... 190 B8
Bexton Ave CW7 ... 126 A2
Bexton La WA16 ... 82 A8
Bexton Prim Sch WA16 ... 81 F7
Bexton Rd WA16 ... 56 F1
Bibby Ave WA1 ... 16 E6
Bibby's La SK10 ... 88 A1
Bibby St ST7 ... 193 E7
BICKERTON ... 199 E6
Bickerton Ave WA6 ... 74 D7
Bickerton Cl WA3 ... 9 D4
Bickerton Holy Trinity CE
Prim Sch SY14 ... 200 A7
Bickerton Rd SY14 ... 201 B2
Bickerton Way 1
CW9 ... 103 E4
Bickley Cl
Hough CW2 ... 206 E2
Northwich CW9 ... 103 E5
Runcorn WA7 ... 23 C1
Warrington WA2 ... 8 F3
BICKLEY MOSS ... 215 B7
BICKLEY TOWN ... 214 E6
Bickley Town La SY14 ... 214 E6
BICKLEYWOOD ... 214 C4
Bicknell Cl WA5 ... 15 B8
Bida La CW12 ... 179 B8
BIDDULPH ... 179 B2
Biddulph Common Rd
ST8 ... 179 F7
Biddulph Grange ST8 ... 179 E3
Biddulph Grange Ctry Pk★
ST8 ... 179 F3
Biddulph Grange Gdn★
ST8 ... 179 E3
Biddulph Park Rd
ST8 ... 179 F5
Biddulph Rd
Congleton CW12 ... 179 B8
Harriseahead ST7 ... 195 F6
Biddulph St CW12 ... 179 C7
Bideford Rd WA5 ... 14 E4
Bidston Cl CH2 ... 118 D5
Bidston Dr SK9 ... 34 E2
Bidston Gn CH66 ... 69 D4
Bidvale Way CW1 ... 190 D7
Big Field La CW6 ... 146 B7
Biggin Ct WA2 ... 8 E1
Biggs Way CW12 ... 156 E5
BIGNALL END ... 209 F3
Bignall End Rd
Audley ST7 ... 210 A3
Newcastle-u-Lyme ST7 ... 210 A4
Billington Ave WA12 ... 2 C5
Billington Cl
Barnton CW8 ... 77 F4
Billington Cl continued
Crewe CW2 ... 190 A2
Warrington WA5 ... 14 E8
Billington Rd WA8 ... 12 B3
Bilton Cl WA8 ... 13 E2
Bilton Way CW2 ... 189 E5
Bings Rd SK23 ... 65 F8
Bingswood Ave SK23 ... 65 E8
Bingswood Ind Est
SK23 ... 65 E8
Bingswood Rd SK23 ... 65 E7
Binney Rd CW9 ... 104 B8
Binyon Way CW1 ... 191 A4
Birchall Ave WA3 ... 4 E4
BIRCHALL MOSS ... 219 E1
Birchall Moss La
CW5 ... 219 E1
Birchall St WA3 ... 9 A7
Birchall Wlk CW2 ... 206 D8
Birch Ave
Alsager ST7 ... 193 E2
Crewe CW1 ... 190 F5
Irlam M44 ... 11 D5
Macclesfield SK10 ... 87 B1
Warrington WA2 ... 8 A4
Wilmslow SK9 ... 59 F6
Winsford CW7 ... 127 A1
Birch Brook Rd WA13 ... 19 C5
Birch Cl
Crewe CW1 ... 190 F5
Holmes Chapel CW4 ... 130 D3
Birch Cres WA12 ... 1 F4
Birch Ct CW12 ... 155 F3
Birchdale Cres WA4 ... 26 C8
Birchdale Ct WA4 ... 26 C8
Birchdale Rd
Warrington, Paddington
WA1 ... 17 A7
Warrington WA4 ... 26 C8
Birchencliff Cotts
SK10 ... 63 D6
Birchen Rd L26 ... 21 A7
Birchenwood Rd ST6,
ST7 ... 195 E1
Birchenwood Way
ST7 ... 195 B1
Birches Cl CH60 ... 41 A8
Birches Croft Dr SK10 ... 86 F1
Birches Ho 2 CH60 ... 41 A8
Birches La CW9 ... 105 B7
Birches The
Broughton CH4 ... 139 B3
Crewe CW2 ... 206 C8
Neston CH64 ... 41 F2
Birches Way 7 ST7 ... 195 B2
Birchfield Ave
Rode Heath ST7 ... 193 F7
Widnes WA8 ... 13 A2
Birchfield Rd
Lymm WA13 ... 19 B4
Warrington WA5 ... 15 B5
Widnes, Appleton WA8 ... 13 A1
Widnes, Farnworth WA8 ... 13 A3
Birch Fold CW4 ... 107 B1
Birchgate Cl SK10 ... 86 E1
Birch Gdns CW11 ... 175 C5
Birch Gr
Ellesmere Port CH66 ... 70 A1
Higher Wincham CW9 ... 79 F5
Knutsford WA16 ... 57 D2
Lostock Green CW9 ... 105 B7
Warrington, Bruche WA1 ... 16 F7
Warrington, Latchford
WA4 ... 16 D3
Birchhall Cl CW5 ... 204 F4
BIRCH HEATH ... 168 B8
Birch Heath La CH3 ... 142 F8
Birch Heath Rd CW6 ... 168 C8
Birch Hill WA6 ... 99 C8
Birch Ho CH2 ... 118 C5
Birch House Rd ST5 ... 210 D1
Birchinall Cl SK11 ... 112 A7
Birchin Cl CW5 ... 205 A6
Birchin La CW5 ... 205 A6
Birch La
Hough CW2 ... 206 F2
Winsford CW10 ... 127 F2
Birchmuir CH1 ... 117 E3
Birchmuir Cl CW1 ... 190 B6
Birch Rd
Audley ST7 ... 209 F1
Chester CH4 ... 140 F5
Congleton CW12 ... 155 F3
Haydock WA11 ... 1 E7
Hollinfare WA3 ... 11 B2
Partington M31 ... 11 D3
Poynton SK12 ... 36 F2
Runcorn WA7 ... 49 C8
Widnes WA8 ... 13 B3
Birch Rise CH2 ... 118 D6
Birch Tree Ave SK7 ... 37 A8
Birch Tree Ct CH2 ... 237 C4
Birch Tree La
Antrobus WA4 ... 53 A6
Goostrey CW4 ... 107 C1
The Bank ST7 ... 195 B8
Birch Tree Rd 6 WA3 ... 3 F8
Birchvale Cl SK12 ... 36 E3
Birch Valley Rd ST7 ... 195 C1
Birchway
Bollington SK10 ... 88 A8
Bramhall SK7 ... 35 D7
Heswall CH60 ... 41 C5
High Lane SK6 ... 37 F7
Birch Way SK10 ... 86 E6
Birchways WA4 ... 26 E5
BIRCHWOOD ... 9 E5
Birchwood Bvd WA3 ... 9 D2
Birchwood CE Prim Sch
WA3 ... 9 F3
Birchwood Cl
Ellesmere Port CH66 ... 69 D1
Elton CH2 ... 72 C3
Birchwood Com High Sch
WA3 ... 9 D3
Birchwood Dr
Nantwich CW5 ... 204 F6
Swan Green WA16 ... 106 D7
Wilmslow SK9 ... 60 D8
BIRCHWOOD FOREST
PARK ... 10 A5
Birchwood Office Pk
WA2 ... 9 B3
Birchwood One Bsns Pk
WA3 ... 9 E2
Birchwood Park Ave
WA3 ... 9 D5
Birchwood Pk WA3 ... 9 E5
Birchwood Sh Ctr WA3 ... 9 D2
Birchwood Sta WA3 ... 9 E2
Birchwood Way WA2,
WA3 ... 9 D3
Birds La
Tarporley CW6 ... 146 C1
Tattenhall CH3 ... 166 E1
Bird's La CW6 ... 186 B8
Birdwell Dr WA5 ... 15 A5
Birkdale Ave CH63 ... 43 C6
Birkdale Cl
Bramhall SK7 ... 36 A7
Macclesfield SK10 ... 87 C4
Birkdale Ct 3 CW9 ... 104 B8
Birkdale Dr ST7 ... 195 C3
Birkdale Gdns CW7 ... 126 A2
Birkdale Rd
Warrington WA5 ... 14 F4
Widnes WA8 ... 13 B5
Birkenhead Rd CH64 ... 42 E1
Birkenhead St CW9 ... 104 C8
Birkett Ave CH65 ... 70 C2
Birkin Cl WA16 ... 57 D4
Birkinheath La WA14 ... 31 B4
Birley St WA12 ... 2 D4
Birstall Ct WA7 ... 49 D7
Birtles Cl CW11 ... 175 C7
Birtles Hall SK10 ... 85 D2
Birtles La SK10 ... 85 E2
Birtles Rd
Macclesfield SK10 ... 86 D1
Warrington WA2 ... 8 D1
Birtles Way 4 SK9 ... 34 D5
Birtley Ct WA8 ... 12 B1
Birtwistle Rd CW9 ... 104 D6
Bisham Pk WA7 ... 24 D2
Bishopdale Cl WA5 ... 14 F7
Bishopgates Dr CW9 ... 103 E4
Bishop Heber High Sch
SY14 ... 213 C5
Bishop Rd SK10 ... 88 A7
Bishop Reeves Rd WA11 ... 1 E7
Bishops' Blue Coat CE
High Sch The CH3 ... 142 A8
Bishop's Cl ST7 ... 210 D8
Bishops Ct
Broughton CH4 ... 139 C4
Warrington WA2 ... 8 A4
Bishopsfield Ct CH2 ... 118 F3
Bishops Gate CH2 ... 119 A3
Bishops Gdns CH65 ... 70 A5
Bishop St CH2 ... 118 F3
Bishops Way WA8 ... 13 D3
Bishops Wood CW5 ... 204 F2
Bishopton Dr SK11 ... 111 F8
Bishop Wilson CE Prim
Sch CH64 ... 67 D1
Bispham Rd WA5 ... 15 B4
Bittern Cl
Poynton SK12 ... 36 A4
Runcorn WA7 ... 50 D8
Warrington WA2 ... 8 D3
Bittern Gr SK10 ... 87 A1
Blackacres Cl CW11 ... 174 F6
Blackbird Way ST7 ... 195 F1
Blackboards La CH66 ... 69 A8
BLACKBROOK
Haydock ... 1 A7
Warrington ... 8 E2
Blackbrook Ave WA2 ... 8 F2
Blackbrook Cl WA8 ... 12 C3
Blackburn Cl WA3 ... 3 E8
Blackburne Ave WA8 ... 22 B5
Blackburne Cl WA2 ... 9 C2
Blackburne Dr WA12 ... 2 A4
Blackcap Rd WA4 ... 27 A4
Blackcap Wlk WA3 ... 9 E3
Black Cat Ind Est WA8 ... 23 A6
Blackcroft Ave CW8 ... 78 A2
Blackden Firs CW4 ... 108 B2
Blackden La
Goostrey CW4 ... 108 A3
Siddington SK11 ... 132 F8
Black Denton's Pl WA8 ... 13 C1
Blackden Wlk SK9 ... 34 D1
Black Diamond St
CH1 ... 237 B4
Blackdown Cl CH66 ... 69 A5
Blackeys La CH64 ... 66 E8
Black Firs La CW12 ... 155 E4
Black Firs Prim Sch
CW12 ... 155 F4
Black Friars CH1 ... 237 A2
Blackheath La WA7 ... 24 F5
Blackhill La WA16 ... 81 F8
Blackhurst Brow SK10 ... 61 B2
Blackhurst Farm Rd
CW5 ... 202 E3

Blackhurst St WA1 16 B5
Black La SK10 87 E1
Blackledge Cl WA2 9 A3
Blackley Cl
Macclesfield SK10 87 B4
Warrington WA4 16 D3
Black Lion La CH66 69 C6
Black Moss Rd WA14 20 F7
BLACK PARK 226 F2
Black Park Rd SY13 226 D2
Black Rd SK11 112 F7
Blackshaw Cl CW12 157 B1
Blackshaw Dr WA5 7 B1
Blackshaw La SK9 59 F1
Blackshaw St 6
SK11 112 C7
Blackstairs Rd CH66 69 F7
Blackthorn Cl
Broughton CH4 139 B3
Huntington CH3 142 A5
Wistaston CW2 206 B8
Blackthorne Ave CH66 95 A8
Blackthorn Pl ST5 210 E1
Blackthorn Wlk 3
M31 11 E2
Blackwell Cl CW10 151 D6
BLACON 117 F3
Blacon Ave CH1 118 A5
Blacon Hall Rd CH1 117 F5
Blacon High Sch CH1 117 D4
Blacon Point Rd CH1 117 E3
Bladon Cres ST7 193 C5
Blagg Ave CW5 204 C4
Blair Cl SK7 36 C8
Blair Dr WA8 12 C3
Blairgowrie Dr SK10 87 B4
Blaizefield Cl CW3 232 C2
Blakeacre Rd L26 21 A6
Blake Cl
Blacon CH1 117 F6
Crewe CW2 189 F1
Blakeden La CW7 148 F8
Blake La CW8 102 A2
Blakeley Brow CH63 43 A6
Blakeley Ct CH63 43 A7
Blakeley Dell CH63 43 B6
Blakeley Dene CH63 43 B7
Blakeley La WA16 58 F8
Blakeley Rd CH63 43 A6
Blakelow Bank SK11 112 F6
Blakelow Cl CW10 151 B8
Blakelow Cres CW5 205 F3
Blakelow Dr CW5 205 D4
Blakelow Rd SK11 112 F6
Blakemere Cl SY13 226 B1
Blakemere Ct CH65 70 C7
Blakemere Dr CW9 103 E5
Blakemere La WA6 100 D4
Blakemere Way CW11 174 F8
BLAKENHALL 221 A4
Blake St CW12 156 C3
Blandford Dr
5 Macclesfield SK11 111 F8
Northwich CW9 103 E3
Blandford Rd WA5 15 B5
Blankney The CW5 204 E4
Blantern Rd CH4 161 A7
Blantyre St WA7 22 F3
Blaze Hill SK10 88 E8
Bleadale Cl SK9 34 D1
Bleasdale Rd
Crewe CW1 173 B1
Newton-le-W WA12 2 C4
Bleeding Wolf La ST7 194 E5
Blenheim Cl
Macclesfield SK10 87 A1
Northwich CW9 103 F4
Poynton SK12 36 F4
Warrington WA2 8 F2
Wilmslow SK9 60 D7
Wistaston CW2 205 E8
Blenheim Ct ST7 193 D5
Blenheim Gdns 5
CW7 149 C7
Blenheim Ho CH1 118 B3
Blenheim Pk CW11 175 A4
Bloomfield Cl SK8 34 E7
Bloomsbury Way WA8 12 D3
Blossom Hts CW8 103 D7
Blossom Rd M31 11 E2
Blossoms La SK7 35 B2
Blossom Way/Ffordd Y Blodau CH4 140 D5
Blount Cl CW1 190 B4
Blubell La CH64 42 C1
Bluebell Ave WA11 1 E7
Bluebell Cl
Huntington CH3 142 B6
Macclesfield SK10 87 D3
Winnington CW8 78 E1
Bluebell Ct WA7 49 F4
Bluebell La SK10 87 C3
Bluebell Mews 4
SK10 87 D3
Bluebell Way
Alsager ST7 193 B3
Handforth SK9 34 C1
Blue Bridge La WA6 73 C5
Bluecoat St WA2 16 B7
Blue Hatch WA6 74 C8
Blue Planet Aquarium★
CH65 70 D1
Blue Ridge Cl WA5 14 E7
Blundell Rd WA8 22 D8
Blunstone Cl CW2 190 A2
Blyth Cl
Macclesfield SK10 86 E1
Runcorn WA7 50 D5
Blythe Ave
Bramhall SK7 35 C6
Congleton CW12 156 A2
Widnes WA8 13 B5
Blythe Pl CW7 127 B2
Blythings The CW6 146 C3
Blyth Rd CH63 43 C7
Boardmans Pl CW9 104 A5
Boars Leigh Pk SK11 135 D1
Boathorse Rd ST7 210 F8
Boathouse La CH64 41 C3
Boat Mus The★ CH65 70 C7
Boat Stage WA13 18 E3
Boat Wlk WA4 16 A1
Bob's La M44 11 D4
Boddington Dr WA4 27 A7
Boden Dr CW5 205 D4
Boden St SK11 112 D8
Bodiam Ct CH65 70 E2
Bodmin Ave SK10 86 E1
Bodmin Cl WA7 50 B6
Bodmin Dr SK7 35 E7
Bodnant Cl CW1 190 A8
BOLD 6 B6
Bold Bsns Ctr WA9 6 B7
Bold Cross WA8 13 E7
BOLD HEATH 13 E7
Bold Ind Est WA8 13 C5
Bold Ind Park WA9 6 B6
Bold La WA5, WA9 6 C7
Bold Pl CH1 237 B3
Bold Sq CH1 237 C3
Bold St
Haslington CW1 191 C4
Runcorn WA7 23 B3
Sandbach CW11 175 B6
Warrington WA1 16 A5
Widnes WA8 23 A7
Bolesworth Hill Rd
CH3 183 C4
Bolesworth Rd
Chester CH2 118 F6
Tattenhall CH3 183 C7
Boleyn Cl CH1 117 E6
Boleyn Ct WA7 24 C3
Bolland's Ct CH1 237 A2
Bollands Rise 14 CW5 204 E5
Bolleyn Wood Ct SK9 34 B1
Bollin Ave
Altrincham WA14 31 B8
Winsford CW7 127 B2
Bollinbarn SK10 87 B2
Bollinbarn Dr SK10 87 A2
Bollinbrook CE Prim Sch
SK10 87 B2
Bollinbrook Rd SK10 87 B2
Bollin Cl
Alsager ST7 192 F3
Culcheth WA3 5 A2
Lymm WA13 19 A4
Sandbach CW11 174 E7
Winsford CW7 127 B2
Bollin Ct SK9 60 C6
Bollin Dr
Congleton CW12 156 F1
Lymm WA13 19 A4
Bollin Gr
Biddulph ST8 179 E1
Prestbury SK10 87 A7
BOLLINGTON 88 B7
Bollington Ave CW9 104 A5
BOLLINGTON CROSS 87 F7
Bollington Cross CE Prim Sch SK10 87 E7
Bollington Ho CW12 156 F1
Bollington La SK10 84 E2
Bollington Old Rd
SK10 87 D6
Bollington Rd SK10 87 E6
Bollinhead La SK11 113 D2
Bollin Hill
Prestbury SK10 87 A5
Wilmslow SK9 60 B8
Bollin Mews SK10 86 F7
Bollinway WA15 32 A8
Bollin Way SK10 87 A6
Bollin Wlk SK9 60 C7
Bollinwood Chase SK9 60 D7
Bolshaw Cl CW1 190 A7
Bolshaw Farm La SK8 34 C6
Bolshaw Prim Sch SK8 34 B7
Bolshaw Rd SK8 34 C6
Bolton Ave
Cheadle SK8 35 B6
Warrington WA4 16 F4
Bolton Cl
Golborne WA3 4 B8
Poynton SK12 36 D4
Bomish La CW4, SK11 108 C3
Bond Cl WA5 15 D4
Bond St
Macclesfield SK11 112 C7
Winnington CW8 78 D1
Bonis Hall La SK10 61 F4
BOON HILL 210 A2
Boon Hill Rd ST7 209 F1
Booth Ave
Ashton Hayes CH3 121 E7
Little Budworth CW6 147 F7
Sandbach CW11 175 C6
BOOTH BANK 30 B7
Boothbank La WA14 30 A6
Booth Bed La WA16,
CW4 107 B4
Boothby St 12 SK10 112 C8
Boothfields WA16 57 C2
BOOTH GREEN 62 F7
Booth La
Middlewich CW10 151 E6
Middlewich, Stud Green CW10, CW11 152 B3
Booth Rd
Handforth SK9 34 A1
Hartford CW8 103 A4
BOOTHSDALE 122 D3
Boothsdale CW6 122 D3
BOOTH'S HILL 18 C2
Booths Hill Cl WA13 18 C2
Booths Hill Ho 3
WA13 18 D3
Booth's Hill Rd WA13 18 C3
Booths La WA4 52 E6
Booth's La WA13 18 B1
Boothsmere Cl CW11 174 F8
Booth St
Audley ST7 209 D1
Congleton CW12 156 C2
Warrington WA5 15 E4
BOOTS GREEN 107 B5
Borderbrook SY14 222 F5
Borderbrook Sch
Higher Wych SY14 224 D3
Tallarn Green/Tallwrn Green
SY14 222 F5
Border Rd CH60 41 B8
Borders 2 Ind Pk CH4 140 C7
Borders Ind Pk The/Parc Ddiwydiannol Y Ffin
CH4 140 C7
Border Way CH3 119 C1
Borough Rd CW12 156 F3
Borras Rd LL13 196 A8
Borron Ct WA12 2 B4
Borron Rd WA12 2 B5
Borron Road Ind Est
WA12 2 C4
Borrowdale Ave WA2 8 C3
Borrowdale Cl
Crewe CW2 189 E3
Frodsham WA6 74 D8
Borrowdale Rd WA8 22 C8
Bosden Cl SK9 34 D5
BOSLEY 158 D8
Bosley Brook CW12 179 D5
Bosley Cl
Handforth SK9 34 D2
Middlewich CW10 151 C6
Bosley Dr SK12 37 A3
Bosley View CW12 157 B1
Bostock Gn
Bostock Green CW9 127 C7
Ellesmere Port CH65 69 F6
BOSTOCK GREEN 127 C7
BOSTOCK HALL 127 D5
Bostock Rd
Macclesfield SK11 111 E7
Winsford CW7 127 A4
Bostock St WA5 15 E6
Boston Ave WA7 23 D1
Boston Bvd
Warrington WA5 15 A7
Warrington WA5 15 B7
Boston Cl
Bramhall SK7 35 D7
Culcheth WA3 4 F4
Boswell Ave WA4 16 B2
Botany Bsns Pk SK23 65 D6
Botany Mews SK23 65 E6
Boteler Ave WA5 15 F7
Bottoms La CH4 141 F8
Boughey Rd ST7 209 F2
BOUGHTON 119 A2
Boughton CH2, CH3 118 F2
Boughton Hall Ave
CH3 119 A1
Boughton Hall Dr
CH3 119 B1
BOUGHTON HEATH 142 A8
Boughton Heath Prim Sch
CH3 142 B8
Boughton Lo 2 CH3 119 A1
Boughton St Paul's Inf Sch
CH3 237 C3
Boulevard The
Broughton CH4 139 C3
Ellesmere Port CH65 69 F4
Boulting Ave WA5 7 F1
Boulton Cl CW11 175 C3
Boundary Ct CH3 119 B1
Boundary La
Chester CH4 140 E5
Congleton CW12 179 B8
Heswall CH60 41 A8
Over Peover WA16,
SK11 108 D7
Siddington SK11 132 E8
Threapwood SY14 222 E8
Boundary Lane N
CW8 101 F2
Boundary Lane S
CW8 101 F2
Boundary Pk CH64 66 D7
Boundary St
Northwich CW9 79 E2
Warrington WA1 16 E7
Boundary Terr SK9 33 F6
Bourchier Way WA4 27 A8
Bourne Ave WA3 3 D8
Bourne Cl CW8 102 E7
Bournemouth Cl WA7 50 D6
Bourne Rd ST7 194 F2
Bourne St
Mow Cop ST7 195 C7
Wilmslow SK9 59 F6
Bouverie St CH1 237 A4
Boverton Cl WA5 7 E1
Bowden Cl
Congleton CW12 156 A3
Culcheth WA3 4 F4
Bowden Cres SK22 39 D8
Bowden Dr CW9 104 C8
Bowden House La SK9 61 A8
Bowden View La WA16 29 F2
Bowdon Cl WA1 16 F8
Bowen Cl
Bramhall SK7 35 F5
Widnes WA8 12 D4
Bowen Cooke Ave
CW1 190 A5
Bowen St CW2 190 A3
Bower Cres WA4 26 D2
Bowerfield Ave SK7 36 D8
Bowerfield Cres SK7 36 E8
Bower Rd CH60 41 C8
Bowers Bsns Pk WA8 23 B7
Bowers Row 4 CW5 204 E5
Bower St WA8 13 C1
Bowery Ave SK8 34 F6
Bowery The CH1 116 D4
Bowe's Gate Rd CW6 169 A1
Bowfell Cl CH62 43 D3
Bowfell Dr SK6 37 E8
Bow Green Rd WA14 20 F1
Bowkers Croft CW11 191 F8
Bow La WA14 31 B8
Bowland Cl
Runcorn WA7 49 E5
Warrington WA3 10 B5
Bowland Croft CW1 173 B1
Bowland Rise CW7 149 B7
Bowles Cl CW11 175 A6
Bowline Cl CW11 175 D3
Bowling Green Ct
Chester CH1 237 B3
9 Nantwich CW5 204 E5
Winnington CW8 78 E1
Bowman Ave WA4 17 A5
Bowmans The SK10 87 B1
Bowmere Cl
Biddulph ST8 179 C1
Tarporley CW6 146 D1
Bowmere Dr CW7 149 C8
Bowmere Rd CW6 146 D1
Bowness Ave
Bebington CH63 43 C5
Irlam M44 11 D4
Warrington WA2 8 C2
Winsford CW7 126 D2
Bowness Cl CW4 130 A3
Bowness Ct CW12 156 A1
Bowness Rd CW2 189 E3
Bowood Ct WA2 8 A4
Bowring Dr CH64 41 B1
Bowyer Ave 6 CW5 204 E6
Boxgrove Cl WA8 13 B3
Box La CW12 155 F3
Boxmoor Cl CH4 141 A5
Box Tree Mews SK11 112 A7
Box Wlk M31 11 E3
Boydell Ave
Warrington WA4 17 B2
Warrington, Westy WA4 16 F4
Boydell Way CH4 162 A6
Boyle Ave WA2 8 E1
Boyles Hall Rd ST7 209 E2
Bracken Cl
Broughton CH4 139 C3
Macclesfield SK10 86 F1
Rode Heath ST7 193 F8
Warrington WA3 9 C5
Brackendale
Elton CH2 72 B3
Runcorn WA7 49 D8
Brackenfield Way 11
CW7 149 A8
Bracken Rd CH66 69 E4
Brackens The
Daresbury WA4 25 A1
Higher Kinnerton CH4 161 A8
Bracken Way
Barnton CW8 78 B3
Comberbach CW9 78 C7
Frodsham WA6 74 C6
Knutsford WA16 82 A8
Wincham CW9 79 C3
Brackenwood Cl CW2 206 B8
Brackenwood Dr WA8 22 A8
Brackenwood Mews
Chorlton CW2 207 D2
Wilmslow SK9 60 E8
Brackley Ave M44 11 D6
Brackley St
Runcorn WA7 22 F3
Warrington WA4 16 C1
Bradburn Rd M44 11 E7
Bradburns La CW8 103 B6
Bradbury Gdns CW12 156 F1
Bradbury Rd CW7 127 B2
Braddon Cl CW9 103 F4
BRADELEY GREEN 225 E6
Bradeley Green La
SY13 225 F6
Bradeley Hall Rd
CW1 191 B5
Bradeley Rd CW1 191 C4
BRADFIELD GREEN 172 E3
Bradfield Rd CW1 190 B7
Bradford La SK10 85 C6
Bradford Pl CH4 141 D7
Bradford Rd CW7 126 E4
Bradford St CH4 141 D7
Bradgate SK8 34 D8
Bradgate Cl WA5 15 F6
Brading Wlk M22 33 E8
Bradlegh Rd WA12 2 B1
Bradley Cl CW10 151 B7
Bradley Farm La
SY13 225 C7
BRADLEY GREEN 225 A8
Bradley Hall Cotts
WA4 27 F6
Bradley La
Frodsham WA6 74 D7
Newton-le-W WA5, WA12 2 A1
BRADLEY MOUNT 87 B7
Bradley St SK11 112 E6
Bradley Way WA8 13 B1
Bradmoor Rd CH62 43 D8
Bradshaw Ave CH4 140 B7
Bradshaw Com Prim Sch
WA4 17 B2
Bradshaw Hall La
Cheadle SK8 34 E8
Gatley SK8 34 D8
Bradshaw La
Lymm WA13 19 D3
Warrington WA4 17 B3
Bradshaw Pl CW12 156 E2
Bradshaw St WA8 13 A2
BRADWALL GREEN 153 B3
Bradwall Rd CW11 175 B7
Bradwall St CW11 175 B7
Bradwell Cl CH65 70 A4
Bradwell Ct CW12 156 F2
Bradwell Dr SK8 34 C7
Bradwell Gr CW12 156 F2
Bradwell Rd
Golborne WA3 3 E7
Hazel Grove SK7 36 E8
Braemar Ave CW9 104 C7
Braemar Cl
Chester CH3 119 C3
Holmes Chapel CW4 130 C2
Warrington WA2 9 A3
Wistaston CW2 205 E8
Braemar Ct CH65 70 E3
Braeside Cl
6 Ellesmere Port CH66 69 C5
Macclesfield SK11 112 F6
Braidwood Ave WA16 57 C3
Brains La CW6 169 B6
Braintree Rd M22 33 E8
Braithwaite Cl WA7 49 D5
Braithwaite Rd WA3 3 D8
Brakeley La CW8 77 D4
Brakenwood Mews
WA4 17 C1
Brake The ST7 195 B7
Brake Village ST7 195 B7
Bramall Cl CW11 175 C7
Bramble Cl
Chester CH3 142 A7
Macclesfield SK10 87 B2
Middlewich CW10 128 E2
Warrington WA5 14 E3
Winsford CW7 126 C3
Brambles Chase CW8 101 F2
Brambles The
Burtonwood WA5 7 A7
Congleton CW12 178 F8
Haslington CW1 191 B4
Wincham CW9 79 C3
Bramble Way WA7 49 E4
Brambling Cl WA7 49 F5
Brambling Way WA3 3 E7
BRAMHALL 35 D8
Bramhall Cl CW7 126 B1
Bramhall Ct CW2 189 F2
Bramhall Ctr The SK7 35 E6
Bramhall Dr
Bebington CH62 43 F4
Holmes Chapel CW4 130 A3
Bramhall High Sch
SK7 35 F8
Bramhall La S SK7 35 E7
Bramhall Rd CW2 189 F2
Bramhalls Pk CW9 78 C3
Bramhall St WA5 15 E5
Bramhall Sta SK7 35 E6
Bramhall Way SK10 112 A8
Bramley Cl
Bramhall SK7 35 E6
2 Ellesmere Port CH66 94 F8
Wilmslow SK9 59 D4
Bramley Ct CW6 122 D5
Bramley Dr SK7 35 E6
Bramley Mews WA4 26 C8
Bramley Rd SK7 35 E6
Bramley Wlk WA6 73 A1
Brampton Ave SK10 87 A2
Brampton Cl CW2 207 E3
Brampton Ct WA9 1 B3
Bramshill Cl WA3 10 A6
Bramway
Bramhall SK7 35 C7
High Lane SK6 37 F7
Bramwood Ct SK7 35 E6
Brancaster Dr WA3 4 A7
Brancepeth Ct CH65 70 E3
Branch Way WA11 1 D6
Brancote Gdns CH62 43 D7
Branden Dr WA16 57 B1
Brandon WA8 12 B2
Brandon Cl SK9 34 D2
Brandwood Ave WA2 8 B2
Brandwood Ho 2
WA1 16 C5

Bransdale Cl WA5 14 F7
Bransdale Way SK11 111 F7
Brantfield Ct WA2 8 E2
Brassey Ct CW5 205 C6
BRASSEY GREEN 167 D6
Brassey's Contract Rd
SY14 199 A1
Brassey St CH3 118 F1
Brassey Way CW5 205 D5
Brassington Terr
CW3 221 F3
Brathay Cl WA2 8 C3
BRATT'S BANK 101 B5
Brattswood Dr ST7 194 A5
Bray Cl
Crewe CW1 190 E5
Runcorn WA7 49 D6
Bray Rd CH4 140 F6
Breach House La
WA16 32 A1
Bread St SK11 112 C7
Breck Rd WA8 13 B1
Breck The CH66 69 E7
Brecon Cl SK12 36 F4
Brecon Ct WA5 7 E2
Brecon Dr 1 CH66 69 E1
Breconway CW7 149 B8
Brecon Way CW2 206 A7
Bredon Cl CH66 69 A6
Breen Cl CH3 166 B1
Breezehill Cl CH64 66 F8
Breezehill Pk CH64 66 F8
Breezehill Rd CH64 66 F8
Brendon Ave WA2 8 A3
Brendon Gr WA9 1 A4
Brennus Pl CH1 237 A3
Brent Cl SK12 36 B4
Brentfield WA8 12 D2
Brentnall Cl WA5 15 C5
Brentwood Ave M44 11 D6
Brentwood Rd CH1 117 E5
Brereton CE Prim Sch
CW11 153 F5
Brereton Cl
Crewe CW2 189 E2
Malpas SY14 213 B3
Runcorn WA7 50 A8
Sandbach CW11 175 C7
Brereton Ct
Brereton Green
CW12 154 F6
1 Cheadle SK8 34 E8
Brereton Dr CW5 204 F7
Brereton Gr M44 11 E6
BRERETON GREEN 153 E5
BRERETON HEATH 154 F6
Brereton Heath Ctry Pk★
CW12 154 D7
Brereton Heath La CW11,
CW12 154 E6
Brereton Heath Local
Nature Reserve★
CW12 154 D6
Brereton La CW4 152 E8
Brereton Rd
Handforth SK9 34 E3
Hartford CW8 103 A4
Bretland Dr WA4 27 A7
Breton Cl CH2 118 E5
BRETTON 139 E4
Bretton Court Mews
CH4 139 E4
Bretton Dr CH4 139 B3
Bretton La CH4 139 F5
Bretton Rd CH4 139 E4
Bretton Wlk M22 33 D8
Brewery La CH3 180 E3
Brian Ave
Warrington, Stockton Heath
WA4 16 E1
Warrington WA2 16 D8
Brian Bevan Island
WA1 16 B4
Briar Ave WA3 11 B2
Briar Cl WA16 57 A3
Briardale Cl CW2 205 F8
Briardale Gdns 4
CH66 69 C6
Briardale Rd
Ellesmere Port CH66 69 C6
Willaston CH64 43 A1
Briar Dr CH60 41 A8
Briarfield Ave WA8 12 A1
Briarfield Rd
Ellesmere Port CH65 70 B5
Heswall CH60 41 B8
Briar La CW8 102 E7
Briarlands Cl SK7 35 D6
Briar Rd WA3 3 B8
Briarstead Cl SK7 35 D7
Briarswood
Biddulph ST8 179 D1
Kidsgrove ST7 195 B1
Briarswood Ct CH1 237 B3
Briar Wlk WA3 3 B8
Briarwood
Runcorn WA7 50 B8
Wilmslow SK9 60 C7
Briarwood Ave
Macclesfield SK11 112 D5
Warrington WA1 16 E7
Briarwood Ct CW7 149 C8
Brick Bank CW5 204 F5
Brick Bank La WA16,
CW4 107 B2
Brickfield Bsns Ctr
CW9 79 D1
Brickfield La CH3 119 F2
Brickhill La WA15 32 B4
Brickhurst Way WA1 17 B8
Brickkiln La
Little Bollington WA14 20 C3
Whitchurch SY13 226 D2
Brick Kiln La CW10 127 B7
Brickley Ct CW8 77 C1
Brick Rd CH4 139 D2
Brick St
Newton-le-W WA12 1 F3
Warrington WA1 16 C5
Bridestone Sh Ctr
CW12 156 D2
Bridewell Ct WA8 13 B3
Bridge Ave WA4 16 F4
Bridge Ave E WA4 16 F5
Bridge Bank Cl WA3 3 B7
Bridge Cl
Audley ST7 209 F2
Cuddington CW8 102 A3
Lymm WA13 19 B4
Wistaston CW2 206 A7
Bridge Cotts CH4 237 B1
Bridge Ct
Chester CH2 119 A2
Holt LL13 196 E8
Neston CH64 66 E7
Bridgedown CW6 146 C1
Bridge Dr
Christleton CH3 142 D7
Handforth SK9 34 D3
Bridge End Dr SK10 87 A7
Bridge End La SK10 87 A7
Bridge Farm Ct CW10 152 A4
Bridgefield Ave SK9 34 C1
Bridgefoot Ind Est
WA4 16 B4
Bridge Foyer The
CH1 118 B2
Bridge Gn SK10 87 A7
Bridge La
Cuddington CW8 101 F3
Frodsham WA6 49 D1
Goostrey CW4 108 C2
Warrington WA4 26 E7
Warrington WA4 26 E8
Warrington, Woolston
WA1 17 C7
Bridge Lane Mews
WA6 49 D1
Bridgeman Rd CH1 117 E3
Bridgeman St WA5 15 D4
Bridge Mdw CH66 69 F2
BRIDGEMERE 231 F8
Bridgemere CE Prim Sch
CW5 231 E8
Bridgemere Cl CW11 174 F8
Bridgemere Garden
World★ CW5 232 B4
Bridgemere La CW5 219 E1
Bridgemere Mews
CW5 231 F8
Bridgemere Way 4
CW9 103 E4
BRIDGEMONT 39 E2
Bridgend CH2 97 A1
Bridgend Cl WA8 12 D3
Bridge Pl CH1 237 B1
Bridge Rd WA1 17 C7
Bridge Row CW12 156 F4
Bridge St Row E CH1 237 B2
Bridge St Row W CH1 237 B2
Bridge Sh Ctr The
WA4 16 F3
Bridge Side Dr WA6 73 B4
Bridges Rd CH65 70 F5
Bridge St
Chester CH1 237 B2
Congleton CW12 156 D2
Golborne WA3 3 A7
Holt LL13 180 E1
Macclesfield SK11 112 C7
Neston CH64 66 E7
Newton-le-W WA12 2 B3
Northwich CW9 79 E2
Runcorn WA7 23 B2
Saltney CH4 140 D7
Warrington WA1 16 B4
Warrington WA1 16 B5
Whaley Bridge SK23 65 E7
Wybunbury CW5 220 B8
Bridge Terr CH3 119 B2
BRIDGE TRAFFORD 97 A3
Bridge View Cl WA8 23 A4
Bridgewater Ave WA4 16 F4
Bridgewater Cl
Congleton CW12 157 B1
6 Frodsham WA6 49 C1
Gatley SK8 34 D7
Bridgewater Ct
3 Lymm WA13 18 C3
6 Runcorn WA7 23 B2
Bridgewater Dr CH3 119 C2
Bridgewater Grange
WA7 50 F5
Bridgewater High Sch
(Lower Sch) WA4 26 D6
Bridgewater High Sch
(Upper Sch) WA4 26 D7
Bridgewater Mews
WA4 26 C8
Bridgewater Pl WA3 9 E4
Bridgewater St
4 Lymm WA13 18 E3
6 Runcorn WA7 23 A3
Bridgeway E WA7 24 C2
Bridgeway W WA7 24 C2
Bridge Wlk 7 WA7 49 F7
Bridgewood Dr CH66 69 C2
Bridgfield Cl SK6 37 E7
Bridgnorth Gr ST5 210 E2
Bridle Cl CH62 43 E7
Bridle Ct
Bramhall SK7 35 F2
Crewe CW2 190 B4
Bridle Hey CW5 204 F2
Bridle La CH1 94 E6
Bridlemere Ct WA1 16 E8
Bridle Pk CH62 43 E7
Bridle Rd
Bebington CH62 43 E6
Crewe CW2 190 B4
Woodford SK7 35 F2
Bridle Way
Ellesmere Port CH66 69 D3
Woodford SK7 36 A2
Briedden Way CH66 69 A6
Brierley Bsns Ctr
CW1 190 D4
Brierley Ct CW7 149 F8
Brierley Prim Sch
CW1 190 D4
Brierley Rd CW12 157 B1
Brierley St CW1 190 D4
Briers Cl WA2 8 F3
Brieryhurst Rd ST7 195 B3
Briggs Ave CW2 190 D1
Brighton Cres SK11 113 B3
Brighton St WA5 15 E6
Brights Ave 6 ST7 195 B2
Bright St CW1 190 B5
Brightwell Cl WA5 14 E5
Brimelow Cres WA5 14 E3
Brimstage Cl CH60 41 C8
Brimstage Gn CH60 41 D8
Brimstage Rd CH60 41 C7
BRINDLEY 186 E8
Brindley Ave
Warrington WA4 16 F4
Winsford CW7 126 C1
Brindley Cl
Kidsgrove ST7 194 E1
Talke ST7 210 E8
Brindley Ct WA4 26 D8
Brindley Gr SK9 34 E2
BRINDLEY GREEN 153 E2
Brindley Hall Rd CW5 186 E2
Brindley La CW11 153 C4
Brindley Lea La CW5 186 D1
Brindley Pk CW11 174 F3
Brindley Rd WA7 23 F3
Brindley St WA7 22 F3
Brindleys Way ST7 209 F2
Brindley Way
Congleton CW12 157 B1
Macclesfield SK11 112 C3
Brindley Wharf WA4 50 F6
Brine Leas High Sch
CW5 204 F3
Brinell Dr M44 11 F6
Brine Pits La CW5 218 F2
Brine Pump Cotts CW9 78 F4
Brine Rd CW5 204 E3
Brines Brow La CH3 99 C2
Brinley Cl CH62 43 D5
Brinton Cl WA8 22 E8
Brisbane Cl SK7 35 F5
Brisbane Rd CH1 117 C4
Bristol Ave WA7 50 E6
Bristol Cl
Blacon CH1 117 C4
Gatley SK8 34 C7
Bristol Dr 3 CH66 69 E1
Bristow Cl WA5 15 B8
Britannia Dr CW9 104 E7
Britannia Rd WA6 73 B2
Brittania Gdns WA6 73 B1
Brixham Ave SK8 34 F7
Brixham Wlk SK7 35 E7
Broadacre CW9 78 D6
Broadacre Pl SK9 59 D3
Broadacres CW5 217 F4
Broadbent Ave WA4 16 F4
Broadcar Rd SK11 113 C6
Broad Ct SK9 85 B8
Broadfields WA7 50 C8
Broadheath Terr WA8 12 D1
Broadheys La WA16 28 D6
Broadhurst Ave
Culcheth WA3 4 F2
3 Warrington WA5 15 D4
Broadhurst La CW12 156 C3
Broad La
Altrincham WA15 32 B8
Appleton Thorn WA4 27 C8
Burtonwood WA5 6 E8
Haydock WA5, WA9 1 C1
Heswall CH60 40 C8
Holmes Chapel CW4 129 F1
Stapeley CW5 205 A1
Broadlake CH64 67 F8
Broadland Gdns CH66 69 F2
Broadland Rd CH66 69 F2
Broadleigh Way CW2 206 C8
Broadley Ave WA3 3 C7
Broadmead
Chester CH3 119 C2
Heswall CH60 41 C7
BROADOAK 162 B1
Broad Oak Ave
Broughton CH4 139 A3
Haydock WA11 1 A6
Warrington WA5 14 E4
Broad Oak Com Prim Sch
WA9 1 A3
Broadoak La
High Legh WA16 29 D5
Mobberley WA16 57 E6
Broadoak Sch M31 11 F2
Broad St CW1 190 C6
Broadwalk SK10 87 A5
Broadway
Altrincham WA15 32 A8
Barnton CW8 78 B3
Widnes WA8 12 A1
Wilmslow SK9 60 B6
Broadway E CH2 118 E5
Broadways CW3 230 A4
Broadway The CW5 204 F5
Broadway W CH2 118 D5
Broad Wlk SK9 59 F8
Broadwood Cl SK6 37 F7
Broady Ct 5 CW2 190 D2
Brock Dr SK8 35 B8
Brock Gdns L24 21 E2
Brock Hollow CW11 174 F4
Brockhurst Mews
CW9 104 A6
Brockhurst St CW9 104 A8
Brockhurst Way CW9 104 A6
Brocklebank Dr CW8 103 E7
Brocklehurst Ave SK10 87 F2
Brocklehurst Ct 2
SK10 87 D3
Brocklehurst Dr SK10 87 A7
Brocklehurst Manor
SK10 87 E1
Brocklehurst Mews 3
SK10 87 D3
Brocklehurst Way
SK10 87 D3
Brock Rd WA3 9 D3
Brocks Croft Gdns
ST8 179 C1
Brock St
Macclesfield SK10 87 D1
Macclesfield SK10 112 D8
Brockton Ct WA4 26 C6
Brockway E CH3 166 A1
Brockway W CH3 166 A1
Brockwell Cl 2 CW7 149 A8
Brodie Cl CH2 95 C1
Brogden Ave WA3 4 E4
Broken Banks 10
SK11 112 D7
BROKEN CROSS 111 E8
Broken Cross SK11 111 F8
BROKEN CROSS 104 E7
Broken Cross Com Sch
SK11 111 E7
Brokencross Pl CW9 104 E7
Bromborough Rake Sta
CH62 43 C8
Bromborough Sta
CH63 43 C7
Bromborough Village Rd
CH62 43 E8
Bromley Ave WA3 3 D7
Bromley Cl
Crewe CW1 189 F8
Heswall CH60 40 E7
Warrington WA2 8 F3
Bromley Dr CW4 130 C2
Bromley Rd
Congleton CW12 156 F3
Macclesfield SK10 111 E8
Brompton Gdns WA5 15 E7
Brompton Way
Ellesmere Port CH66 69 E1
Handforth SK9 34 C5
Bronington Ave CH62 43 D6
Bronte Cl WA2 8 A6
Brook Acre Com Prim Sch
WA2 8 E1
Brookash Rd M22 34 A8
Brook Ave
Handforth SK9 34 D4
Shavington CW2 206 C5
Warrington, Stockton Heath
WA4 16 E1
Warrington, Westy WA4 16 F5
Brook Bank SK12 37 C2
Brook Bottom Rd SK22 39 A8
Brook Cl
Crewe CW1 190 F4
Cronton WA8 12 C6
Brook Ct
Chester CH1 118 B3
Sandbach CW11 175 B6
Brookdale WA8 12 A3
Brookdale Ave WA16 57 C2
Brookdale Ct CH3 143 D5
Brookdale Pk CW2 190 A3
Brookdale Pl CH1 237 B3
Brookdale Way CH3 143 B5
Brook Dr
Kelsall CW6 122 D4
Warrington WA5 15 A5
Brooke Ave CH2 118 F8
Brooke Ct SK9 34 E4
Brooke Dr SK9 34 D4
Brooke Ho SK10 86 F1
Brook End WA9 1 A1
Brookes Ave CH4 139 B3
Brooke Way SK9 34 D4
Brook Farm Cl M31 11 E2
Brookfield CW1 191 D5
Brookfield Ave
Poynton SK12 36 C3
Runcorn WA7 23 E2
Brookfield Cl
Lymm WA13 18 D3
Tarporley CW6 168 D8
Brookfield Cotts 2
WA13 18 D3
Brookfield Cres CW4 107 F1
Brookfield Ct CW1 190 B5
Brookfield Dr
Alsager ST7 193 C5
Chester CH2 118 E4
Holmes Chapel CW4 130 B3
Brookfield La SK11 112 F7
Brookfield Pk WA4 17 A2
Brookfield Rd
Comberbach CW9 78 D8
Culcheth WA3 4 D3
Lymm WA13 18 D3
Brookfields Sch WA8 13 D2
Brookfield St WA12 2 B3
Brook Furlong WA6 48 F2
Brook Gdns ST8 179 D1
Brook Hey CH64 41 B2
Brook Ho WA4 16 F3
BROOKHOUSE 88 D3
Brookhouse Cl SK10 86 F1
Brook House Ct WA13 18 D2
Brookhouse Dr CW2 206 C8
BROOKHOUSE GREEN
177 A7
Brookhouse La
Church Minshull CW1,
CW10 172 D7
Congleton CW12 157 C2
Duddon CH3 144 D6
Lower Whitley WA4 52 B2
Brookhouse Rd
Alsager ST7 193 D3
5 Sandbach CW11 175 B6
BROOKHURST 43 C5
Brookhurst Ave CH63 43 C5
Brookhurst Cl CH63 43 C5
Brookhurst Prim Sch
CH63 43 C6
Brookhurst Rd CH63 43 C5
Brook La
Alderley Edge SK9 59 F3
Astbury CW12 177 E5
Broughton CH5 139 C7
Burland CW5 203 D8
Chester CH2 118 E4
Faddiley CW5 202 F8
Knutsford WA16 57 B1
Neston CH64 41 C2
Northwich CW9 104 D7
Warrington WA3 18 A8
Brookland Ave CW2 205 F8
Brookland Dr CW11 175 E6
Brookland La WA9 1 A1
BROOKLANDS 225 E1
Brooklands Ave SK11 112 B7
Brooklands Dr
Goostrey CW4 107 F1
Northwich CW9 104 A4
Brooklands Gdns CH64 41 C1
Brooklands Gr CW1 190 A6
Brooklands Pk 1 WA8 13 C2
Brooklands Rd
Congleton CW12 155 F2
Neston CH64 41 C1
Brookland St WA1 16 E7
Brooklands The CW2 206 E3
Brookledge La SK10 62 E5
Brooklet Rd CH60 41 C8
Brooklyn Dr
Ellesmere Port CH65 69 F5
Lymm WA13 18 E4
Brooklyn St CW2 190 C2
Brookmere Cl CW11 174 E8
Brookmills Cotts ST8 179 C1
Brookmoore Ct CH2 237 A4
Brook Pl
Chester CH1 237 B3
Warrington WA4 16 E3
Brook Rd
Ellesmere Port CH66 69 D5
Lymm WA13 18 E4
Tarporley CW6 168 D8
Brooks Dr WA15 32 D8
Brookside
Ashton Hayes CH3 121 E7
Chester CH3 142 A8
Cuddington CW8 101 F3
Kelsall CW6 122 C4
Kingsley WA6 75 C2
Warrington WA4 16 E3
Brook Side CW8 102 C8
Brookside Ave
Lymm WA13 18 C4
Poynton SK12 36 E3
Sutton Lane Ends SK11 112 F2
Warrington, Stockton Heath
WA4 16 D1
Warrington WA5 15 A4
Brookside Cl WA11 1 B7
Brookside Cotts
CW11 176 A8
Brookside Ct SK10 87 A1
Brookside Gn CW2 206 C8
Brookside La SK6 37 E7
Brookside Mill 6
SK11 112 E7
Brookside Miniature Rly★
SK12 36 F7
Brookside Prim Sch
Ellesmere Port CH66 69 E4
High Lane SK6 37 E6
Brookside Rd
4 Congleton CW12 156 D3

Brookside Rd *continued*
Frodsham WA6 74 A8
Brookside Terr
Chester CH2 237 C4
Wilmslow SK9 59 E3
Brookside View WA11 1 B7
Brookside Way WA11 1 B7
Brooks La
Bosley SK11 135 E2
Middlewich CW10 128 D1
Brook Slack CW6 124 D1
Brooks Lane Ind Est
Middlewich CW10 128 D1
Middlewich CW10 151 D8
Brook St
Chester CH1 237 B3
Congleton CW12 156 F3
Crewe CW2 190 D3
Golborne, Bank Heath WA3 3 A8
Knutsford WA16 57 B1
Macclesfield SK11 112 E7
Neston CH64 66 E8
Northwich CW9 79 A1
Northwich, Lostock Gralam CW9 79 E2
2 Runcorn WA7 23 A2
3 Widnes WA8 13 B1
Brook Street Bridge CH1, CH2 237 C4
Brook Street Mill 19 SK11 112 E7
Brook Terr
Runcorn WA7 23 E1
Sandbach CW11 175 A3
BROOKVALE 50 B5
Brookvale Ave N WA7 50 B6
Brookvale Ave S WA7 50 B6
Brookvale Cl WA5 6 F6
Brookvale Prim Sch WA7 50 B5
Brook View
Alderley Edge SK9 60 A3
Allostock WA16 106 F3
Brookview Cl CW2 206 C8
Brook Villas ST7 193 E3
Brook Way
Hartford CW8 103 B4
Nantwich CW5 204 E3
Warrington WA5 15 A5
Brookway La WA9 1 A1
Brook Well CH64 66 F5
Brookwood Cl WA4 26 B8
Broom Ave WA4 26 E6
BROOM BANK 144 B8
Broom Cres CH3 121 B1
Broome Ct WA7 50 B5
BROOMEDGE 29 C8
Broomehouse Ave M44 11 E8
Broomfield CW12 154 F6
Broomfield Cl
Chelford SK11 84 A3
Wilmslow SK9 60 E8
13 Winsford CW7 149 A8
Broomfields WA4 26 E7
Broomfields Jun Sch WA4 26 E7
Broomfields La CW8 77 F4
Broomfields Rd WA4 26 D7
BROOMHALL 217 F4
BROOMHALL GREEN 217 F3
Broomheath La
Tarvin, Broom Bank CH3 144 C7
Tarvin CH3 121 C1
Broomhill La
Brown Knowl CH3 199 D8
Great Barrow CH3 120 E8
Broom La WA16 81 F2
Broomlands CH60 40 E8
Broomlands Cotts CW5 219 E1
Broom Rd M31 11 F2
Broomsfield La CW8 78 A4
Broom's La CW6 122 D6
Broom St CW1 190 A6
Broseley Ave WA3 4 D4
Broseley La WA3 4 D5
Brotherton Cl CH62 43 C8
Brotherton Way WA12 2 B4
Brough St W SK11 112 C7
BROUGHTON 139 A4
Broughton Ave WA3 3 D7
Broughton Cl WA4 26 F8
Broughton Cres SY14 211 A1
Broughton Hall Rd CH4 139 C4
Broughton Ind Est CH4 139 F6
Broughton Inf Sch CH4 139 C4
Broughton Jun Sch CH4 139 C4
Broughton La CW2 189 F1
Broughton Mills Rd CH4 139 F6
Broughton Rd
Adlington SK10 62 C5
Crewe CW1 190 C8
Broughton Sh Pk CH4 139 E4
Broughton Way WA8 22 B5
Brow Com Prim Sch The WA7 23 F1
Brow La
Antrobus CW9 53 D5
Heswall CH60 40 F7
Browmere Dr WA3 9 A7
Brown Ave
Lawton-gate ST7 194 A5
Nantwich CW5 204 F4
BROWNEDGE 154 A3
BROWN HEATH 143 B6
Brown Heath Rd CH3 143 B6
BROWNHILL 147 B6
Brownhill Dr WA1 16 F8
Brownhills Rd CW6 147 C6
Browning Ave WA8 22 F8
Browning Cl
Blacon CH1 117 F6
Sandbach CW11 174 D5
Browning Dr
Ellesmere Port CH65 69 F4
Winwick WA2 8 A6
Browning Gn CH65 69 F4
Browning Gr ST7 210 C8
Browning St CW1 190 C4
Browning Way CW7 149 A7
BROWN KNOWL 199 C8
Brown Lees Cl CW2 190 B1
Brown Lees Rd ST7 195 F4
BROWNLOW 177 E7
Brownlow Cl SK12 36 E2
Brownlow Hall Mews CW12 177 E5
BROWNLOW HEATH 177 D5
Brownlow Heath CW12 177 E5
Brownlow Heath La CW12 177 D6
BROWN MOSS 231 B7
BROWN'S BANK 229 D2
Brown's La
Chester CH4 141 C7
Wilmslow SK9 60 E8
Brown St
3 Alderley Edge SK9 60 A1
Congleton CW12 156 E3
Macclesfield SK11 112 C7
Widnes WA8 23 D7
Brow The WA6 75 C2
BROXTON 183 A1
Broxton Ave CW10 151 D6
Broxton Cl WA8 12 C3
Broxton Mews CH3 183 A1
Broxton Rd
Clutton CH3 182 D1
Ellesmere Port CH66 69 E5
Bruce Ave WA2 8 D1
Bruce Cres CH63 43 C6
Bruce Dr CH66 69 C4
BRUCHE 16 F7
Bruche Ave WA1 16 F8
Bruche Com Prim Sch WA1 17 A7
Bruche Dr WA1 16 F8
Bruche Heath Gdns WA1 17 A8
Bruen The CH3 121 C3
BRUERA 164 D6
Bruera Rd CH65 69 F4
Brunel Ct CW9 104 E5
Brunel Rd SK11 112 C3
Brunner Gr CW5 205 A5
Brunner Rd WA8 23 A8
Brunsborough Cl CH62 43 C6
Brunswick 11 WA7 23 A3
Brunswick Cres CH66 69 E3
Brunswick Ct 12 SK11 112 D7
Brunswick Hill SK10 112 D8
Brunswick Rd WA12 1 F4
Brunswick St
Congleton CW12 156 F3
5 Macclesfield SK10 112 D8
St Helens WA9 1 A3
Brunswick Terr SK10 112 D8
Bruntleigh Ave WA4 17 A3
Bryant Ave WA4 16 F5
Brymau Four Trad Est CH4 140 D7
Brymau One Trad Est CH4 140 E7
Brymau Three Trad Est CH4 140 D7
Brymau Two Trad Est CH4 140 E7
BRYN 102 A6
Brynlow Dr CW10 151 B8
Brynmore Dr SK11 112 F7
Brynn St WA8 23 B8
Brynton Cl SK10 87 C1
Brynton Rd SK10 87 C1
Buchanan Cl WA8 12 F3
Buchan Cl WA5 15 B8
Buchan Gr CW2 190 B3
Buckbean Way CW4 107 E1
Buckden Way 9 SK10 112 C8
Buckfast Ave WA11 2 A7
Buckfast Cl
Cheadle SK8 35 B6
Macclesfield SK10 87 C2
Poynton SK12 36 D5
Warrington WA5 14 E3
Buckfast Ct WA7 24 E3
Buckfast Way CW10 128 B1
Buckingham Ave
Chester CH3 119 B2
Widnes WA8 13 A4
Buckingham Cl
4 Congleton CW12 156 F4
Wistaston CW2 205 E8
Buckingham Dr
Knutsford WA16 57 B1
Macclesfield SK11 112 B5
Buckingham Dr *continued*
Northwich CW9 103 E4
Warrington WA5 15 C4
Winsford CW7 149 C7
Buckingham Gdns 1 CH65 70 D2
Buckingham Rd
Irlam M44 11 C6
Poynton SK12 36 D3
Wilmslow SK9 59 F6
Buckingham Rise SK11 112 B4
Buck La CW2 206 E3
Buckland Cl WA8 22 D7
Buckley Ave CW10 128 F7
Buckley Cl CW10 151 B8
Buckley Ct CH64 67 F8
Buckley St
Macclesfield SK11 112 D7
Warrington WA2 16 B6
Bucklow Ave
Mobberley WA16 58 A4
Partington M31 11 F3
Bucklow Gdns WA13 19 A4
BUCKLOW HILL 30 C3
Bucklowhill La WA16 30 B3
Bucklow Wlk 11 SK11 112 E7
BUCKOAK 99 A5
Buckton St WA1 16 D7
BUDDILEIGH 221 F7
Bude Cl
Alsager ST7 193 B3
Bramhall SK7 35 F7
Crewe CW1 190 B8
Bude Rd WA8 12 E2
Budworth Ave
Warrington WA4 16 F4
Widnes WA8 12 D2
Budworth Cl
Runcorn WA7 49 D7
Sandbach CW11 174 F7
BUDWORTH HEATH 54 A1
Budworth Heath La CW9 54 C1
Budworth La CW9 78 E7
Budworth Rd
Bate Heath CW9 54 E2
Ellesmere Port CH66 69 E2
Over Tabley WA16 55 C2
Budworth Wlk 1 SK9 34 E1
BUERTON 230 E4
Buerton App CH3 164 B6
BUERTON MOSS 230 E6
Buffs La CH60 41 B8
Buggen La CH64 66 D8
BUGLAWTON 157 A4
Buglawton Hall Sch CW12 157 D5
Buglawton Ind Est 5 CW12 156 F4
Buglawton Prim Sch CW12 157 A4
Buildwas Rd CH64 41 F2
BULKELEY 184 E2
Bulkeley Hall La SY14 200 C8
Bulkeley Rd
Handforth SK9 34 D3
Poynton SK12 36 E3
Bulkeley St
Chester CH3 119 A1
Crewe CW1 190 E3
Bullcroft Cl SY14 211 D7
Bull Hill CH64 66 F6
Bull-Hill-La SK10, SK11 88 D2
Bullocks House Rd ST7 195 E3
Bullocks La SK11 112 E3
Bull Ring CW9 103 F8
Bull Ring The CW10 128 C1
Bumper's La CH1 117 F1
BUNBURY 185 F8
Bunbury Aldersey CE Prim Sch CW6 185 E8
Bunbury Cl
Middlewich CW10 151 D5
Northwich CW9 104 A5
Stoak CH2 96 A7
Bunbury Comm CW6 168 E2
BUNBURY COMMONS 169 A2
Bunbury Ct CW6 146 D1
Bunbury Dr WA7 49 C6
Bunbury Gn CH65 70 D2
BUNBURY HEATH 185 D8
Bunbury La CW6 185 E8
Bunbury Mill★ CW6 169 A1
Bunbury Rd CW6 169 B3
Bunce La SK11 133 B4
Bunce St CH1 237 A1
Bungalow Rd WA12 2 E1
Bungalows The
Adderley TF9 234 B3
Dunham-on-t-H WA6 97 E6
Thornton Hough CH63 42 B6
BUNSLEY BANK 230 D5
Bunting Cl 6 WA3 3 E8
Buntingford Rd WA4 17 C3
Bunts La CW12 156 E1
Burdett Rd CH66 69 E2
Burfield Dr WA4 26 D7
Burford Ave
Bramhall SK7 35 D5
Newcastle-u-Lyme ST5 210 D1
Burford Cl SK9 59 E5
Burford Cres SK9 59 E5
Burford La WA13 19 C2
Burgamot La CW9 78 D8
Burganey Ct CH4 162 D2
Burgess Ave WA4 16 B2
Burgess Cl CW5 205 B4
Burgess Dr CH1 117 A5
Burgess La WA6 101 B6
Burgess Pl 5 CW8 103 E8
Burgess St SK10 112 F8
Burges St CH2 118 F3
Burjen Way CW1 190 B6
Burkhardt Dr WA12 2 E3
BURLAND 203 C7
Burland Cl WA7 22 F1
Burland Gr CW7 126 A2
BURLAND LOWER GREEN 203 A7
Burland Rd
Halewood L26 21 A6
Newcastle-u-Lyme ST5 210 D2
BURLAND UPPER GREEN 203 B8
Burlea Cl CW2 189 E5
Burlea Dr CW2 206 B5
BURLEYDAM 228 B1
Burleyhurst La SK9, WA16 59 B7
Burley La WA4 27 C4
Burnell Cl CW5 204 F3
Burnell Rd CH65 70 E4
Burnet Cl WA2 9 C2
Burnfell WA3 3 E7
Burnham Cl
Culcheth WA3 4 E4
Warrington WA5 14 F5
Widnes WA8 12 C3
Burnham Rd CH4 140 F6
Burnsall Ave WA3 3 F8
Burnsall Dr WA8 12 C3
Burns Cl
Ellesmere Port CH66 69 E4
Rode Heath ST7 193 E8
Burns Cres WA8 22 F8
Burns Dr CW1 190 F4
Burns Gr WA2 8 C2
Burnside WA15 32 D7
Burnside Ave WA4 16 D1
Burnside Cl SK9 60 C6
Burnside Way
Northwich CW8 103 D8
Winnington CW8 78 D1
Burns Rd CW12 157 A2
Burns Way CH1 117 E6
Burnt Acre SK11 84 B3
Burnt Mill La WA8 21 D5
Burnwood Gr ST7 195 B2
Burran Rd M22 33 D8
Burrough Cl WA3 9 F3
Burrows Hill CW8 103 B7
Burrows La WA6 73 F2
Burrows St WA11 1 A6
Burrows The CW8 101 D5
Bursar Cl WA12 2 D4
Burslam St CW12 156 E2
BURTON
Duddon 144 F4
Neston 67 D1
Burton Ave CW6 146 C3
Burton Cl
Culcheth WA3 4 F3
Widnes WA8 12 F3
Burton Dr SK12 36 D4
Burton Gn CH66 69 D4
Burton Gr CW1 173 B1
BURTON GREEN 161 D1
Burton Hall Rd LL12 161 E1
Burton La CW6 144 F6
Burton Manor Coll CH64 67 D1
Burton Rd
Blacon CH1 117 E5
Duddon CW6 144 E6
Neston CH64 66 F6
Warrington WA2 8 D1
Burton Sq CW6 146 C2
BURTONWOOD 6 E6
Burtonwood Com Prim Sch WA5 6 E7
Burtonwood Ind Ctr WA5 6 E7
Burtonwood Rd
Warrington, Great Sankey WA5 15 C6
Warrington, Kingswood WA5 7 A2
BURWARDSLEY 184 B5
Burwardsley Ct CH3 184 A6
Burwardsley Rd CH3 166 D1
Burwardsley Way CW9 103 E4
Bushell Cl CH64 66 F7
Bushell Rd CH64 66 F7
Bushells La WA6 99 B8
Bush Rd
Christleton CH3 142 E7
Widnes WA8 22 F5
Bush Way CH60 40 D8
Butler Way CW5 204 E3
Butley Cl
Macclesfield SK10 87 D3
Middlewich CW10 151 C7
Butley Hall SK10 87 A7
Butley Lanes SK10 61 F1
BUTLEY TOWN 87 C8
Butterbache Rd CH3 142 A6
Butterbur Cl CH3 142 A6
Buttercup Cl WA5 15 E3
Buttercup Way WA16 79 F6
Buttermarket St WA1 16 B5
Buttermere Ave
Ellesmere Port CH65 70 C3
Buttermere Ave *continued*
Warrington WA2 8 C3
Buttermere Cl WA6 74 D8
Buttermere Cres WA2 8 C3
Buttermere Ct CW12 156 A2
Buttermere Dr
Alderley Edge SK9 83 F7
Altrincham WA15 32 D6
Crewe CW1 173 B1
Buttermere Gr WA7 49 D5
Buttermere Rd
Partington M31 11 E3
Winsford CW7 126 C2
BUTTERS GREEN 210 A2
Butterton La
Oakhanger CW1 192 B2
Oakhanger CW1 192 C1
BUTT GREEN 205 B3
BUTT LANE 194 D1
Butts Gn WA5 7 A3
Butts The
Alsager ST7 193 D4
Runcorn WA7 23 F2
Buxton Ave CW1 190 E4
Buxton Cl WA5 15 A8
Buxton New Rd
Buxton SK11 115 A6
Macclesfield Forest SK11 114 D7
Macclesfield SK11 88 E1
Buxton Old Rd
Congleton CW12 157 A4
Disley SK12 38 E4
Macclesfield SK11 113 D7
Buxton Rd
Congleton CW12 157 C6
High Lane SK6, SK7, SK12 37 D8
Horwich End, New Horwich SK23 65 E6
Macclesfield SK10, SK11 113 A7
New Mills SK22, SK23 39 C4
Whaley Bridge SK23 39 E1
Buxton Rd W SK12 38 B5
Bye Pass The CH3 119 E2
Byland Ave SK8 35 B6
Byland Cl WA8 13 C5
Bylands Cl SK12 36 D4
BYLEY 129 A7
Byley La
Cranage CW4, CW10 129 C6
Middlewich CW10 128 E3
Byley Prim Sch CW10 129 B7
Byley Way CW7 126 B1
Byng Ave M44 11 D4
By-Pass Rd CH3 121 B3
Byron Cl
Blacon CH1 117 F6
Crewe CW1 190 F4
Middlewich CW10 151 D5
Rode Heath ST7 193 E7
Sandbach CW11 174 D6
Byron Ct WA2 8 C2
Byron's La SK11 112 E5
Byrons St SK11 112 D6
Byron St WA7 23 A1
Byron Way CW2 190 A1
Byron Wlk CW5 204 D6
Bythom Cl CH3 142 E7

C

Cabot Cl WA5 7 C1
Cabul Cl WA2 16 D7
CADISHEAD 11 E5
Cadishead Prim Sch M44 11 E6
Cadishead Way M44 11 F6
Cadnant Cl CH1 117 D3
Cadnant Ct/Llys Cadnant CH4 139 D5
Cadshaw Cl WA3 9 D5
Caer Castell LL13 196 D8
Caerleon Cl CW7 149 A8
Caerllew LL13 180 E1
Caernarvon Ave CW7 149 B7
Caernarvon Cl WA7 23 F2
Caernarvon Ct 4 CH65 70 D2
Caernarvon Rd CW2 205 E8
Caesars Cl WA7 23 E2
Cairn Brae WA12 2 C4
Cairns Cres CH1 117 D4
Cairo St WA1 16 B5
Caister Way CW7 149 C7
Caithness Ct 3 WA7 23 B2
Calamine St SK11 112 E6
Calday Gr WA11 1 A8
Caldbeck Ave WA2 8 D2
CALDECOTT GREEN 197 C4
Caldene Terr SK23 65 E7
Calder Ave CW1 191 A5
Calder Cl
Bollington SK10 87 F8
Poynton SK12 36 D2
Widnes WA8 13 F3
Calderfield Cl WA4 26 B8
Calder Way 2 CH66 69 C5
Caldicott Ave CH62 43 D7
Caldicott Cl 2 CW7 149 C7
Caldwell Ave WA5 7 F2
Caldwell Cl CW5 205 B4
Caldwell Rd WA8 23 A7

Caldwell's Gate La
CW9 54 B8
Caldy Cl CH2 118 D5
Caldy Dr CH66 69 D4
Caldy Rd
Alsager ST7 193 C4
Handforth SK9 34 D3
Caldy Valley Rd
Chester CH3 142 B7
Huntington CH3 142 A6
Caldy Way CW7 126 C1
Cale Rd SK22 39 D8
Calico La SK23 39 D4
California Cl WA5 15 C8
Callands Prim Sch WA5 7 E2
Callands Rd WA5 7 D2
Callender Gdns WA6 73 A2
Callin Ct CH1 237 A2
Calmington La WA7 24 F4
CALROFOLD 88 C2
Calrofold Dr ST5 210 D1
Calrofold La SK10 88 C2
Calstock Cl WA5 14 E3
CALVELEY 169 E2
Calveley Ave CH62 43 F4
Calveley Cl CW9 103 E5
Calveley Green La CW6,
CW7 170 C4
Calveley Hall La CW5,
CW6 170 A2
Calveley Prim Sch
CW6 170 B2
Calveley Rd
Halewood L26 21 A6
Macclesfield SK10 86 F1
Calveley Way CW7 126 B1
Calverley Cl 3 SK9 60 C8
Calverly Cl WA7 50 C5
Calver Rd WA2 8 A3
Calvers WA7 23 E1
Camberley Cl SK7 36 A7
Camberwell Park Rd
WA8 13 D4
Camborne Ave SK10 111 E8
Camborne Cl
Congleton CW12 178 E8
Runcorn WA7 50 C6
Cambourne Rd WA5 6 F6
Cambrai Ave WA4 16 C2
Cambrian Ave CH3 119 B2
Cambrian Cl CH66 69 A6
Cambrian Ct CH1 118 B2
Cambrian Rd CH1 118 B2
Cambrian Villas CH3 165 C2
Cambrian Way CW7 149 B8
Cambridge Ave
Macclesfield SK11 112 B7
Wilmslow SK9 59 F7
Winsford CW7 126 A1
Cambridge Cl
Biddulph ST8 179 C1
Warrington WA4 26 B7
Cambridge Ct 7 CH65 70 C5
Cambridge Gdns
Helsby WA6 73 D4
Warrington WA4 26 C6
Cambridge Rd
Bebington CH62 43 E8
Chester CH2 118 F5
Ellesmere Port CH65 70 D5
Macclesfield SK11 112 B7
Cambridge Road Com
Prim Sch CH65 70 C5
Cambridge St
Runcorn WA7 23 C2
Widnes WA8 23 B7
Camden Ct WA7 24 D1
Camden Rd CH65 70 A5
Camden St CW1 190 D4
Camellia Gdns WA9 6 B7
Camelot Cl WA12 1 F4
Camelot Gr CW2 206 C4
Camelot Way WA7 50 A8
Cameron Ave
Runcorn WA7 48 E8
Shavington CW2 206 B3
Cameron Ct WA2 8 A4
Cameron Rd WA8 23 A8
Camm St CW2 190 D2
Camomile Wlk 5 M31 11 F3
Campbell Ave WA7 49 A8
Campbell Cl
Congleton CW12 157 A4
Haslington CW1 191 C4
Macclesfield SK10 87 A1
Northwich CW9 103 F4
Campbell Cres WA5 14 F6
Campden Way SK9 34 D4
Campion Cl
Huntington CH3 142 A6
Warrington WA3 9 C4
Campsey Ash WA8 12 F4
Camrose Cl WA7 49 C6
Camsley La WA13 18 B3
Canaan WA3 4 C8
Canada Cl WA2 9 A2
Canadian Ave CH2 119 A3
Canal Bank WA13 18 D3
Canal Bridge Ent Pk
CH65 70 D6
Canal Cotts CW5 187 D6
Canal Rd CW12 156 F1
Canal Reach WA7 24 C2
Canalside CH65 70 D6
Canal Side
Barnton CW8 78 B2
Chester CH1 237 C3
Macclesfield SK11 112 F7
Moore WA4 25 C5
Runcorn WA7 48 D7
Warrington WA4 17 C1
Whaley Bridge SK23 39 F1
Canalside Cotts
CW11 175 C3
Canal Side Cotts WA7 50 F6
Canal St
Chester CH1 237 A3
Congleton CW12 156 E2
Macclesfield SK10 112 E8
Newton-le-W WA12 1 F3
Runcorn WA7 23 B2
Whaley Bridge SK23 65 E8
Canal Terr CW10 151 D8
Canberra Ave WA2 8 D3
Canberra Rd SK7 35 F5
Canberra Sq WA2 8 D2
Canberra Way CH1 117 D4
Candelan Way WA16 29 C4
Candle La CW3 232 B2
Candleston Cl WA5 7 E1
Candy La SK10 62 C8
Canford Cl
Crewe CW1 190 B8
Warrington WA5 15 C6
Cannell Ct WA7 50 A6
Cannell St 4 WA5 15 D4
Canning St CH1 237 A3
Canniswood Rd WA11 1 A6
Cann La CW9 55 A6
Cann La N WA4 26 E5
Cann La S WA4 26 F4
Cannock Cl CH66 94 E8
Cannonbury Cl WA7 50 A8
Cannon St CH65 70 A5
Cannon Way CH4 161 A7
Canon Dr WA14 31 B8
Canons Rd WA5 15 D6
Canon St WA7 22 F3
Canon Wilson Cl WA11 1 D6
Canterbury Cl CH66 94 E8
Canterbury Rd
Blacon CH1 117 F5
Widnes WA8 22 C8
Canterbury St WA4 16 C4
Cantilever Gdns WA4 16 E2
Cantley Cl WA7 49 D6
Canton Pl CW8 103 D7
Canton St SK11 112 D6
Canton Wlks SK11 112 D6
Canute Pl 12 WA16 57 A2
Capeland Cl CH4 140 E5
Capel Way CW5 204 D6
CAPENHURST 94 A8
Capenhurst Ave
Crewe CW2 190 A3
Warrington WA2 9 A2
Capenhurst CE Prim Sch
CH1 94 B8
Capenhurst Cl SK12 36 F4
Capenhurst Gdns
CH66 69 D1
Capenhurst Grange Sch
CH66 69 E2
Capenhurst La
Capenhurst CH1 94 B8
Ellesmere Port CH65 70 A3
Woodbank CH1 93 F7
Capenhurst Sta CH1 69 C1
Capenhurst Tech Pk
Capenhurst CH1 69 B1
Capenhurst CH1 94 B8
Capesthorne Cl
Alsager ST7 193 C3
Hazel Grove SK7 36 F8
Holmes Chapel CW4 130 B3
Northwich CW9 103 F4
Sandbach CW11 175 C7
Widnes WA8 22 E8
Capesthorne Hall★
SK11 110 A6
Capesthorne Rd
Crewe CW2 189 F3
Hazel Grove SK7 36 F8
High Lane SK6 37 E7
Warrington WA2 8 D2
Waverton CH3 143 B6
Wilmslow SK9 59 E5
Capesthorne Way 16
SK11 112 F7
Capitol Wlk CW12 156 D2
Cappelle Rise ST7 209 D1
Capper Cl ST7 195 A2
Cappers La CW11 176 C2
Capper's La CW5,
CW6 186 C3
Carden Ave CW7 126 B1
Cardenbrook Gr 4
SK9 34 D2
Carden Cl WA3 9 D4
Cardeston Cl WA7 49 F3
Cardiff Cl CH66 94 E8
Cardigan Cl
Macclesfield SK11 112 A8
Warrington WA5 7 D2
Cardinal Newman RC High
Sch WA4 16 F5
Cardway Bsns Pk ST7 193 F3
Carey St WA8 13 B1
Carisbrook Ave SK10 87 E2
Carisbrook Dr CW7 149 C7
Carisbrooke Cl CW2 205 E8
Carleton Rd SK12 37 C4
Carlett Bvd CH62 43 F5
Carlingford Rd WA4 26 B7
Carlisle Cl
Macclesfield SK11 111 F5
Mobberley WA16 58 A4
Winsford CW7 126 A1
Carlisle Rd CH1 117 E5
Carlisle St
13 Alderley Edge SK9 60 A1
Crewe CW2 190 B2
Warrington WA4 26 C8
Carlow Cl L24 21 D2
Carlton Ave
Bramhall SK7 35 D5
Handforth SK9 34 C2
Runcorn WA7 23 D2
Saltney CH4 140 D6
Carlton Cl
Mickle Trafford CH2 119 E8
Neston CH64 41 C2
Carlton Cres CH66 69 F8
Carlton Pl CH2 119 A4
Carlton Rd
Lymm WA13 19 B5
Northwich CW9 104 B7
Carlton St
Warrington WA4 26 C8
Widnes WA8 23 A8
Carlton Way M44 11 C5
Carlyle Cl ST7 193 E8
Carlyle Cres CH66 69 E4
Carmarthen Cl
Warrington WA5 7 D2
3 Winsford CW7 149 C7
Carmel Cl CH1 117 D3
Carmel Ct WA8 13 B4
Carmenna Dr SK7 35 F7
Carmichael Cl 6 M31 11 E3
Carnegie Cl SK10 87 A1
Carnoustie Cl
Wilmslow SK9 60 D8
Winsford CW7 126 B2
Carnoustie Dr SK10 87 D5
Carnoustie Gr WA11 1 A5
Carol Dr CH60 41 C8
Carolina Rd 2 WA5 15 B7
Caroline Ho CH1 117 F6
Caroline St
Irlam M44 11 F8
Widnes WA8 23 B7
Carol St WA4 16 D4
Carpenter Gr WA2 9 A1
Carpenters Ct SK9 60 A1
Carr Brook Cl SK23 65 E5
Carr Brow SK6 38 A7
Carrgreen La WA13 19 F6
Carriage Cl L24 21 D1
Carriage Dr
Biddulph ST8 179 E1
Frodsham WA6 74 A6
Carriage Ho CW1 190 A5
Carrick Dr CH65 70 B2
Carrick Rd CH4 141 B7
Carrington Cl WA3 9 C4
Carrington Way CW1 190 B8
Carrington Wlk WA1 16 C6
Carr La
Alderley Edge SK9 59 D2
Audley ST7 209 A1
Golborne WA3 4 A7
Golborne, Wash End WN7 4 E8
Hale L24, WA8 21 E4
Carr Mill Mews SK9 34 B1
Carroll Dr CW2 205 F8
Carrs Ct SK9 60 B7
Carrs La CH3 166 F1
Carr St ST7 195 F1
Carrwood
Altrincham WA15 32 B7
Knutsford WA16 57 C1
Carr Wood Ave SK7 35 E8
Carrwood Cl WA11 1 A6
Carrwood Rd SK9 59 F8
Carsdale Rd M22 33 E8
Car St CH1 237 C3
Carter Ave CW6 122 D4
Carter Bench Ho SK10 63 A1
Carter Cl CW5 204 D6
Carter La SK11 84 B4
Carter St CH1 237 C3
Cartier Cl
Warrington, Old Hall
WA5 7 C1
Warrington WA5 15 C8
Cartlake Cl CW5 204 C5
Cartledge Cl CW8 102 A3
Cartmel Ave WA2 8 C3
Cartmel Cl
Holmes Chapel CW4 130 A3
Macclesfield SK10 87 B2
Warrington WA5 7 E2
Winsford CW7 126 D2
Cartmel Dr CH66 69 F2
Cartmell Cl WA7 49 B6
Cartridge La WA4 27 E6
Cartwright Rd CW1 191 D5
Cartwright St
Runcorn WA7 23 C2
Warrington WA5 15 E6
Carver Ave CW4 130 A6
Carver Cl CW7 127 A4
Case Rd WA11 1 D6
Casey La CW2 206 F4
Cassia Green La CW7 125 D5
Cassia La CW7, CW8 125 E5
Cassley Rd L24 21 A3
Casson St CW1 190 B5
Castle Bank CW8 103 E7
Castle Cl
Broughton CH5 139 B6
Kelsall CW6 122 D4
Pulford CH4 162 D2
Castle Croft Rd CH4 141 B5
Castle Ct
Holt LL13 196 E8
17 Nantwich CW5 204 E5
Northwich CW8 103 E7
Castle Dr
Chester CH1 237 B1
Ellesmere Port CH65 70 A3
Heswall CH60 40 F8
Castle Farm SY14 200 E3
CASTLEFIELDS 23 F2
Castlefields CH3 166 C3
Castlefields Ave E
WA7 24 A2
Castlefields Ave N
WA7 23 F2
Castlefields Ave S
WA7 24 A1
Castleford Dr SK10 86 E6
Castlegate SK10 86 E6
Castlegate Mews SK10 86 F6
Castle Gdns LL13 196 E8
Castle Gn WA5 7 B2
Castlehill CH4 162 C2
Castle Hill
Newton-le-W WA12 2 E4
Prestbury SK10 86 E6
Castle Hill Ct SK10 86 F7
Castle Hill Farm 3
CW8 103 E8
Castle Ho ST7 195 C3
Castle Inn Rd CW12 179 C7
Castlemead Wlk CW9 103 E4
Castlemere Cl CH4 139 A3
Castlemere Dr CW1 190 C7
Castle Mews LL13 196 E8
Castle Mill La WA15 32 B5
Castle Park Arts Ctr
WA6 74 A8
Castle Prim Sch ST7 195 D6
Castle Rd
Mow Cop ST7 195 D7
Runcorn WA7 49 F8
Castle Rise
Prestbury SK10 86 F6
Runcorn WA7 23 D2
Castle St
Chester CH1 237 B1
1 Crewe CW1 190 C4
Holt LL13 196 D8
Macclesfield SK11 112 D8
5 Nantwich CW5 204 E5
Northwich CW8 103 F8
Widnes WA8 13 D1
Castleton Dr SK6 37 F6
CASTLETOWN 197 D3
Castletown Cl SK10 87 C4
Castletown La CH3 197 D2
Castle View Prim Sch
WA7 49 D8
Castleview Rd ST7 195 B3
Castleway WA15 32 C7
Castle Way CH4 162 A6
Castner Ave WA7 48 E7
Catalan Cl CW7 127 A1
Catalyst Mus★ WA8 23 A5
Catalyst Trade Pk WA8 23 A6
Catchpenny La SK11 108 F3
Catford Cl WA8 12 C2
Catfoss Cl WA2 8 E1
Cathcart Gn CH3 119 F5
Cathedral Church of
Christ & the Blessed
Virgin Mary★ CH1 237 B2
Catherine Ct/Llys Catrin
CH5 139 B6
Catherine St
Chester CH1 118 B2
Crewe CW2 190 D2
Macclesfield SK11 112 C8
Warrington WA5 15 F7
Warrington WA5 16 A7
Widnes WA8 23 A7
Catherine Way WA12 2 B2
Catholic High Sch The
CH4 141 D6
Catterall Ave WA2 8 D2
Caughall Rd CH2 95 E2
Caunce Ave
Golborne WA3 3 A7
Haydock WA11 1 B6
Newton-le-W WA12 2 C1
Causeway Ave WA4 16 C3
Causeway Pk WA4 16 C3
Cavalier Dr CH1 117 E6
Cavan Dr WA11 1 D7
Cavell Dr CH65 70 A4
Cavendish Ave WA3 9 F5
Cavendish Cl
5 Macclesfield SK10 87 D3
Warrington WA5 15 D7
Winsford CW7 149 A8
Cavendish Cres ST7 193 D5
Cavendish Ct
Chester CH4 141 A5
Widnes WA8 12 F1
Cavendish Farm Rd
WA7 49 A5
Cavendish Gdns CH65 70 A4
Cavendish Mews SK9 60 A6
Cavendish Pl WA3 9 F5
Cavendish Rd
Chester CH4 141 B6
Crewe CW2 189 E5
Cavendish Rd *continued*
Hazel Grove SK7 36 E8
Cavendish Sch WA7 49 C5
Cavendish St 7 WA7 22 F2
Cavendish Way CW4 130 A3
Caversham Cl WA4 26 E6
Cawdor Dr CH3 119 A2
Cawdor St
Runcorn WA7 22 F3
Warrington WA4 26 C8
Cawfield Ave WA8 12 D1
Cawley Ave WA3 4 E4
Cawley La SK10 62 E7
Cawley St
8 Macclesfield SK11 112 E7
Runcorn WA7 23 A1
Cawood Cl CH66 69 B5
Cawthorne Ave WA4 17 A2
Caxton Cl
Ellesmere Port CH66 69 E4
Widnes WA8 12 C3
Cecil Rd ST8 179 C2
Cecil Rigby Cl 1
CW11 175 B6
Cecil St CH3 119 A1
Cedab Rd CH65 70 C6
Cedar Ave
Alsager ST7 193 D3
Aston WA7 50 B4
Connah's Quay CH5 91 C1
Connah's Quay, Garden City
CH5 116 A7
Ellesmere Port CH66 69 D6
Golborne WA3 3 F7
Kidsgrove ST7 194 D1
Runcorn WA7 49 C7
Widnes WA8 13 B2
Cedar Cl
Connah's Quay CH5 116 A7
Holmes Chapel CW4 130 D4
Lostock Gralam CW9 80 A3
Middlewich CW10 151 E6
Poynton SK12 36 E3
Sandbach CW11 175 C5
Cedar Cres
Audley ST7 209 F1
Newton-le-W WA12 2 D2
Cedar Ct
Alsager ST7 193 E4
Congleton CW12 178 F8
Culcheth WA3 4 F1
Willaston CW5 205 D6
Cedardale Dr CH66 94 F8
Cedardale Pk WA8 13 E4
Cedar Dr
Barnton CW8 78 A4
Chester CH2 119 B4
Cedarfield Rd WA13 19 B4
Cedar Gr
Chester CH2 119 B4
Haydock WA11 1 E7
Macclesfield SK11 112 D5
Nantwich CW5 205 A5
Neston CH64 66 F8
Warrington, Latchford
WA4 16 D3
Warrington WA1 17 A7
Winsford CW7 127 A1
Cedar Ho CH3 142 B8
Cedar Lo SK7 35 F7
Cedar Mews CH1 117 E4
Cedar Pk CH3 119 C2
Cedar Rd
Newcastle-u-Lyme
ST5 210 D1
Partington M31 11 E3
Warrington WA5 14 F6
Weaverham CW8 102 C8
Cedars SK9 59 F6
Cedar St WA12 2 C2
Cedars The
Alsager ST7 193 D3
Mobberley WA16 58 E2
Nantwich CW5 204 D5
8 Northwich CW9 103 E6
Cedarway
Bollington SK10 88 A7
Heswall CH60 41 B5
Wilmslow SK9 59 F5
Cedar Way CW2 206 B7
Cedarways WA4 26 D5
Cedarwood CW8 101 D5
Cedarwood Ct CW6 146 C3
Celandine Cl CH3 142 A7
Celandine Way WA9 6 B7
Celyn Cres CH4 140 D5
Cement Pl CH1 237 B3
Cemetery Rd CW2 207 B5
Cemlyn Cl CH1 117 E3
Centenary Ho WA7 49 C8
Centenary Pl CW12 156 E3
Central Ave
Alsager CW2 192 F1
Ellesmere Port CH65 70 C4
Warrington, Latchford
WA4 16 B3
Warrington WA2 16 C8
Central Dr
Barnton CW8 78 A3
Gatley SK8 34 D8
Haydock WA11 1 B6
Central Expressway
WA7 49 D6
Central Gr CW9 104 D6
Central Pl SK9 60 B7
Central Rd
Northwich CW9 104 D7
Partington M31 11 F3

Central Rd *continued*
Warrington WA4 16 C3
Central St ST7 195 B6
Central Trad Pk CH4 140 E7
Central Way
Newton-le-W WA12 2 E2
Warrington WA2 16 B6
Centre Ct ST7 193 E4
Centre Park Sq WA1 16 A4
Centre Pk WA1 16 A4
Centurion Cl WA3 9 D4
Centurion Row WA7 23 F2
Centurion Way CW10 128 D2
Century Rd ST5 210 F2
Century Way SK10 87 F2
Cestria Cl CW11 174 D7
Chads Gn CW5 206 A1
Chadwell Ct CW2 207 E4
Chadwick Ave
Croft WA3 9 B7
Warrington WA4 16 E1
Chadwick Cl SK9 34 C1
Chadwick Ct CW10 151 D7
Chadwicke Cl CW5 204 F4
Chadwick Fields Orch
CW10 151 D6
Chadwick Pl WA3 9 E5
Chadwick Rd
Middlewich CW10 151 C6
Runcorn WA7 23 E3
Chadwick Terr SK10 87 E1
Chaffinch Cl
Congleton CW12 156 E1
Warrington WA3 9 F3
Chaffinch Way CW7 149 D6
Chaigeley Sch WA4 17 E4
Chailey Rise CH3 182 D1
Chain Maker's Row
CH4 140 E7
Chaise Mdw WA13 19 C5
Chalfield Ave CH66 69 C5
Chalfield Cl
1 Ellesmere Port
CH66 69 C5
Wistaston CW2 206 B7
Chalfont Cl WA4 26 E6
Chalfont Cres CW2 207 B2
Chalfont Ct WA16 57 C3
Chalgrave Cl WA8 13 F3
Chalkwell Dr CH60 41 C7
Challinor St CH3 119 A1
Chamber Brook La
WA6 75 D2
Chamberlain Ct CW1 191 C4
Chamberlain Dr SK9 34 D1
Chambers St CW2 190 D2
Chance Hall La CW12,
ST7 177 C3
Chancel La SK9 60 B8
Chancellor Rd WA7 24 D5
Chancery La
Alsager ST7 193 B3
Bollington SK10 88 B7
Chandlers Ct WA7 22 E1
Chandler Way WA3 3 E8
Chandos Cl CH4 141 E6
Change La CH64 68 B8
Channel The CH1 95 B4
Chantler Ave WA4 16 E4
Chantry Ave CW8 103 B4
Chantry Cl SK12 38 E5
Chantry Ct
Chester CH1 117 E2
Crewe CW1 190 D4
Macclesfield SK11 112 D5
Chantry Fold SK12 38 E6
Chantry Rd SK12 38 E6
Chantry The CW6 169 E2
Chantry Wlk CH60 41 A6
Chapel Ave WA6 75 C2
Chapel Bank ST7 195 D6
Chapel Cl
Audlem CW3 229 F3
Cholmondeston CW7 170 F4
Comberbach CW9 78 D7
Ellesmere Port CH65 70 C7
Mount Pleasant ST7 195 B6
Saughall CH1 94 A1
Waverton CH3 143 A5
Chapel Cotts CH3 143 A5
Chapel Croft SK11 84 B3
Chapel Cross Rd WA2 9 A2
Chapel Ct
Northwich CW9 103 F7
Wilmslow SK9 60 A6
Chapel Dr WA15 32 C7
Chapelfields WA6 74 A8
Chapel Gn CW6 122 C5
Chapel House La CH64 93 A7
Chapel La
Acton Bridge CW8 76 E4
Alford CH3 164 D5
Allostock WA16 106 E3
Altrincham WA15 32 C7
Appleton Thorn WA4 27 B4
Audley ST7 209 D2
Burtonwood WA5 6 F6
Chester CH3 119 A1
Crewe CW1 173 D1
Dutton WA4 77 B7
Hargrave CH3 144 A1
Harriseahead ST7 195 E4
Hollins Green WA3 10 F1
Holt LL13 196 D8
Kelsall CW6 122 E2
Kingsley WA6 75 C2
Ledsham CH66 68 F1
Manley WA6, CH3 98 F3

Chapel La *continued*
Mere WA16 30 B4
Milton Green CH3 165 B2
Moulton CW9 126 E8
Norton in Hales TF9 236 C2
Partington M31 11 F2
Rainow SK10 88 E5
Ravensmoor CW5 203 D2
Rode Heath ST7 193 F7
Saighton CH3 142 E1
Threapwood SY14 222 E8
Warrington WA4 26 C8
Widnes WA8 12 C4
Wilmslow SK9 60 A6
Windyharbour SK11 109 D2
Woodbank CH1 93 E8
Chapel Lo CH1 237 C3
Chapelmere Cl CW11 174 E7
Chapelmere Ct CW1 190 C7
Chapel Mews
Alsager ST7 193 C3
Ellesmere Port CH65 70 B4
Elton CH2 72 B3
1 Nantwich CW5 204 E5
Chapel Mus★ ST7 195 D7
Chapel Rd
Alderley Edge SK9 60 A1
Horwich End SK23 65 E5
Ollerton WA16 82 F6
Warrington WA5 14 E3
Wilmslow SK9 61 A8
Winsford CW7 126 F1
Chapel Rise SY14 213 B3
Chapel Row
Barbridge CW5 187 D6
Nantwich CW5 204 D5
Chapel St
7 Alderley Edge SK9 60 A1
Audley ST7 209 E3
Bollington SK10 88 B8
Chester CH3 237 C3
Congleton CW12 156 D2
Crewe CW2 190 D3
Haydock WA11 1 E6
Holt LL13 196 D8
Kidsgrove ST7 194 D2
Macclesfield SK11 112 D6
Moulton CW9 126 E8
Mount Pleasant ST7 195 B6
New Mills SK22 39 B6
Newton-le-W WA12 2 B3
Northwich CW8 103 E7
Sandbach CW11 175 B6
Sandbach, Wheelock
CW11 175 A3
Weaverham CW8 77 C1
Whaley Bridge SK23 65 E8
Widnes WA8 23 A7
Wincham CW9 79 C3
Chapel Terr WA3 4 B8
Chapel View
Bebington CH62 44 A6
Helsby WA6 73 B2
Chapel Wlk WA3 4 B8
Chapel Wlks
Broomedge WA13 19 D1
Cheadle SK8 35 B6
Chapel Yd WA2 16 A6
Chapman Cl WA8 12 D4
Chapterhouse Cl CH65 70 E5
Charcoal Rd WA14 20 F3
Charity La
Macclesfield Forest
SK11 114 B6
Macclesfield SK11 113 F8
Charlcote Cres CW2 206 C8
Charlecote Rd SK12 36 F4
Charles Ave
Davenham CW9 103 F2
Warrington WA5 14 F6
Charles Cres CH4 237 C1
Charles Ct CW2 190 C3
Charles Darwin Prim Sch
CW8 103 E7
Charles Forbes Ct 7
WA1 16 B5
Charles Price Gdns 8
CH65 70 C6
Charles Rd CH2 95 C1
Charles Sq CW11 175 F2
Charles St
Chester CH1 237 B3
Chester, Hoole Park
CH2 118 F3
4 Crewe CW1 190 C4
Irlam M44 11 E6
Widnes WA8 23 A8
Charleston Cl CH66 69 D2
Charleston Gr WA5 15 B6
Charlesworth Cl SK23 39 D3
Charlesworth Cres
SK23 39 D3
Charlesworth Ct
CW11 175 C6
Charlesworth Pl 1
CW12 156 F4
Charlesworth Rd SK23 39 D3
Charlesworth St CW1 190 D6
Charlock Wlk 6 M31 11 F3
Charlotte Ct CH1 237 B3
Charlotte Gr 6 WA5 15 C7
Charlotte St W 22
SK11 112 C8
Charlotte St
Chester CH1 118 B2
Macclesfield SK11 112 D7
Charlotte Wlk 2 WA8 23 B7
Charlton Cl WA7 50 A7

Charlton Ct CH2 119 A4
Charlton St
23 Macclesfield SK11 112 C8
Warrington WA4 16 F3
Charminster Cl WA5 15 B5
Charmouth Cl WA12 2 B4
Charnock Ave WA12 1 F3
Charnock Rd WA3 4 F3
Charnwood
High Lane SK6 37 F7
Kidsgrove ST7 195 B1
Charnwood Cl
Macclesfield SK10 87 A1
Warrington WA3 10 B5
Charnwood Cres SK7 36 D8
Charon Way WA5 7 B3
Charter Ave WA5 16 A8
Charter Cres CH66 69 E3
Charterhall Dr CH2 118 F2
Charter Rd SK10 88 A7
Charter Way SK10 87 F3
Chartley Gr CW10 128 D2
Chartwell Gdns WA4 26 F5
Chartwell Gr CW7 149 C5
Chartwell Pk CW11 175 A4
Chase Dr CH66 69 E2
Chaser Ct CH1 117 F3
Chase The
Bebington CH63 43 C5
5 Heswall CH60 41 A8
Chasewater WA7 24 F4
Chase Way CH66 69 E2
Chassagne Sq CW1 189 F7
Chatburn Ct WA3 4 F2
Chater Dr CW5 204 F3
Chatfield Dr WA3 9 E3
Chatham St 9 SK11 112 D8
Chatham Way CW1 191 C5
Chatsworth Ave
Culcheth WA3 4 F4
Macclesfield SK11 111 E6
Chatsworth Cl
Ellesmere Port CH66 69 C5
Northwich CW9 104 A5
Wistaston CW2 206 A7
Chatsworth Dr
Chester CH2 119 A5
Congleton CW12 155 F3
Widnes WA8 12 C3
Chatsworth Ho CH1 118 B3
Chatsworth Rd
Hazel Grove SK7 36 F8
High Lane SK6 37 F6
Wilmslow SK9 59 E4
Chatteris Pk WA7 24 E2
Chatterton Dr WA7 50 E8
Chatterton Ho 16
CW5 204 E5
Chaucer Cl CH1 117 E6
Chaucer Gr CW11 174 C5
Chaucer Pl WA4 16 F4
Chaucer St WA7 23 A1
CHEADLE HULME 35 A8
Cheadle Hulme High Sch
SK8 35 B7
Cheadle Hulme Sch
SK8 35 A8
Cheadle La WA16 81 A1
Cheadle Wood SK8 34 E8
CHECKLEY 221 C1
Checkley Dr ST8 179 D1
CHECKLEY GREEN 232 B8
Checkley La CW3,
CW5 221 E1
Checkley Rd ST5 210 C1
Checkley Row CW5 232 C8
Cheddar Gr WA5 6 F7
Cheddington Cl SK8 35 A7
Chedlee Dr SK8 34 E8
Chedworth Dr WA8 12 C4
Chedworth Ho 12
CH1 237 C3
Cheerbrook Rd CW5 205 D4
Cheese Hill La WA6,
CW8 101 B4
CHELFORD 84 B2
Chelford Ave WA3 3 D8
Chelford CE Prim Sch
SK11 84 A3
Chelford Cl
Chester CH1 117 F1
Warrington WA4 26 C8
Chelford Dr CW9 103 F5
Chelford La WA16 83 C1
Chelford Mews 2
CH3 119 B1
Chelford Rd
Chelford, Marthall WA16,
SK11 83 D4
Chelford SK10, SK11 84 D1
Congleton CW12 155 E6
Goostrey CW4 131 B7
Handforth SK9 34 D5
Macclesfield SK10,
SK11 111 C8
Monks Heath SK10 85 B1
Nether Alderley SK9 84 C7
Ollerton WA16 82 D7
Prestbury SK10 86 D5
Whisterfield SK11 109 F3
Chelford Rdbt SK11 84 B1
Chelford Sta SK11 84 A2
Chells Hill CW11 176 C1
Chell St CW1 190 B5
Chelsea Cl ST8 179 C1
Chelsea Gdns WA5 15 C4
Chelston Dr SK8 34 C6

Cheltenham Cl
2 Macclesfield SK10 87 C4
Warrington WA5 15 A8
Cheltenham Cres
Crewe CW1 190 B7
Runcorn WA7 49 B6
Cheltenham Dr WA12 2 C5
Cheltenham Rd CH65 70 D3
Chemical St WA12 2 B3
Cheney Wlk CW2 206 D8
Chepstow Cl
Biddulph ST8 179 C1
Macclesfield SK10 87 C4
Warrington WA5 7 E3
1 Winsford CW7 149 C7
Cherington Cl SK9 34 F3
Cherington Cres
SK11 112 B7
Cheriton Way CW2 206 A8
Cherrington Rd CW5 204 E3
Cherry Blossom Rd
WA7 49 F4
Cherry Brow Terr
CH64 67 F8
Cherry Cl
Newcastle-u-Lyme
ST5 210 D1
Newton-le-W WA12 1 F4
Willaston CH64 67 C8
Cherry Cnr WA13 28 A7
Cherry Cres CW7 149 C8
Cherry Dale Rd CH4 139 A3
Cherryfields Rd SK11 111 F8
Cherry Gdns CH3 119 A1
Cherry Gr
Ellesmere Port CH66 70 A1
Nantwich CW5 204 D5
Cherry Grove Prim Sch
CH3 119 A1
Cherry Grove Rd CH3 119 A1
Cherry La
Congleton CW12 179 E8
Cuddington CW8 101 F2
Lawton Heath ST7 193 E6
Lymm WA13 18 C1
Weaverham CW8 102 D8
Cherry Orch/Y Berllan
Geirios LL13 196 D8
Cherry Rd CH3 119 A1
Cherrysutton WA8 12 B3
Cherrysutton Mews
WA8 12 B4
Cherry Tree Ave
Barnton CW8 78 A4
Lawton-gate ST7 194 A5
Lymm WA13 18 D2
Poynton SK12 36 F3
Runcorn WA7 49 C8
Warrington WA5 14 F4
Cherry Tree Cl
Elton CH2 72 B4
Hale L24 21 E1
Haydock WA11 1 A5
Wilmslow SK9 60 E8
Cherry Tree Ct CW5 205 A4
Cherry Tree Dr
Hazel Grove SK7 37 A8
St Helens WA9 1 A2
Cherry Tree Ho SK9 85 C8
Cherry Tree La
Rostherne WA14 30 E6
Woore CW3 232 C2
Cherry Tree Mews 3
CH60 41 A8
Cherry Tree Prim Sch
WA13 18 C2
Cherry Tree Rd
Audley ST7 209 F1
Crewe CW1 190 E6
Golborne WA3 3 F8
Newcastle-u-Lyme ST5 210 E1
Cherry Tree Way
CW12 156 E2
Cherry Wlk
Cheadle SK8 35 C8
Partington M31 11 D2
Swan Green WA16 106 D7
Cherrywood Cres CW8 78 B4
Cherwell Cl
Cheadle SK8 35 A7
Warrington WA2 8 D2
Cheryl Ct CW8 102 A4
Cheryl Dr WA8 13 D1
Chesford Grange WA1 17 F7
Chesham Cl SK9 59 F4
Chesham Ct CH65 70 D4
Chesham Rd SK9 59 F4
Chesham St CH1 237 C3
Cheshire Acad CW1 190 E2
Cheshire Candle
Workshops★ CH3 184 C5
Cheshire Cl WA12 2 E3
Cheshire Farm Ice
Cream★ CH3 166 D4
Cheshire Military Mus★
CH1 237 A1
Cheshire Oaks High Sch
CH65 70 C2
Cheshire Oaks Outlet
Village CH65 70 E2
Cheshire Oaks Way
CH65 70 E2
Cheshire Pk WA6 97 D5
Cheshire Rd M31 11 D2
Cheshire Row WA16 108 B8
Cheshire St CW3 229 F4
Cheshire View
Audley ST7 210 A1

Cheshire View *continued*
Bollington SK10 88 B6
Chester CH4 141 E7
Cheshyre Dr WA7 23 F1
Cheshyre's La WA7 48 E7
Chessington Cl WA4 26 F6
CHESTER 237 B2
Chester Aerospace Pk
CH5 139 B6
Chester App
Aldford CH3 163 E7
Eccleston CH4 141 D2
Chester Ave WA3 3 D8
Chesterbank Bsns Pk
CH4 140 D7
Chester Bsns Pk CH4 141 B3
Chester Castle★ CH1 237 A1
Chester Cl
Handforth SK9 34 E2
Irlam M44 11 D5
Runcorn WA7 24 A2
Talke ST7 210 E7
Chester Ent Ctr CH2 237 C4
Chesterfield Cl CW7 125 F1
Chesterfield Rd CH62 43 D4
Chestergate SK10,
SK11 112 D8
Chester Heritage Ctr★
CH1 237 B2
Chester High Rd
Neston CH64 41 E4
Willaston CH64 67 D7
Chester La CW7 125 D2
Chester New Rd WA4 25 F7
Chester Race Course★
CH1 237 A1
Chester Rd
Acton CW5 204 A6
Aston WA7 50 B4
Audley ST7 209 D2
Barbridge CW5 187 D5
Broughton CH4 139 D5
Churton CH3 180 F6
Connah's Quay CH6 91 A3
Cuddington CW8 101 D1
Daresbury WA4 25 B1
Delamere CW6, CW8 123 C5
Dunham-on-t-H CH2,
WA6 97 D5
Ellesmere Port, Great Sutton
CH66 69 D4
Ellesmere Port, Whitby CH65,
CH66 70 A2
Frodsham WA6 74 A7
Gatesheath CH3 165 E5
Grappenhall WA4 17 B1
Hartford CW8 102 E3
Hartford, Greenbank
CW8 103 C6
Hazel Grove SK7 36 D8
Helsby WA6 73 C4
Heswall CH60, CH64 41 C6
Higher Walton WA4 25 D5
Holmes Chapel CW4 130 B2
Huntington CH3 142 A6
Kelsall CW6 122 D5
Lavister LL12 162 C1
Macclesfield SK11 112 B8
Malpas SY14 213 B4
Mere WA16 56 B6
Middlewich CW10 128 B2
Neston CH64 66 E7
Over Tabley WA16 56 A2
Plumley WA16 80 E5
Poynton SK12 36 B4
Rostherne WA14, WA16 30 C5
Runcorn WA7 50 E5
Saltney CH4 140 C6
Sandycroft CH5 116 A2
Talke ST7 210 D7
Warrington WA4 16 A2
Whitchurch SY13 225 D2
Winsford CW7 125 F2
Woodford SK7 35 E2
Chester Ret Pk CH1 118 A3
Chester Row WA12 7 D8
Chester's Croft Pk SK8 35 A5
Chester Sq CW1 190 C4
Chester St
Chester CH4 140 F7
Crewe CW1 190 C4
Warrington WA2 16 B6
Widnes WA8 13 B1
Chester Sta CH1 237 C3
Chesterton Cl CW10 151 E5
Chesterton Ct CH2 118 D4
Chesterton Dr
Crewe CW2 189 F1
Winwick WA2 8 A5
Chesterton Gr CW11 174 D5
Chesterton Way CW2 207 E3
Chester Toy & Doll Mus★
CH1 237 B2
Chester Trad Pk CH1 117 F2
Chester Way CW9 104 A8
Chester West Employment
Pk CH1 117 E2
Chester Zoo★ CH2 95 E1
Chester Zoological Gdns★
CH2 118 D8
Chestnut Ave
4 Ellesmere Port
CH66 69 F1
Irlam M44 11 D5
Macclesfield SK10 87 E2

Chestnut Ave *continued*
Rode Heath ST7 193 F7
Shavington CW2 206 C5
Warrington WA5 14 F6
Widnes WA8 13 B2
Chestnut Cl
Chester CH2 119 A3
Cuddington CW8 101 F2
Middlewich CW10 128 B2
Tarporley CW6 146 D2
Wilmslow SK9 60 E8
Chestnut Ct
Tarporley CW6 146 C2
Widnes WA8 12 D1
Chestnut Dr
Alsager ST7 193 E2
Congleton CW12 156 A4
Holmes Chapel CW4 130 D3
Poynton SK12 36 F3
Chestnut Gr
Barnton CW8 78 B4
Bebington CH62 43 C8
Crewe CW1 190 E5
Golborne WA3 3 F8
Newcastle-u-Lyme ST5 210 E1
Winsford CW7 149 C8
Chestnut Grange CH4 141 B7
Chestnut Ho 6 CW11 175 B6
Chestnut La WA6 73 E4
Chestnut Lodge Specl Sch WA8 12 E1
Chestnut Mews WA16 58 E1
Chestnuts The CH64 67 F8
Chestnut Wlk M31 11 D2
Chetham Ct WA2 8 A3
Chetton Dr WA7 50 E7
Chetwode Mews WA4 52 C2
Chetwode St CW1 190 C5
Chetwood Cl WA12 2 B5
Chetwood Dr WA8 12 F4
Cheveley Cl SK10 87 C2
Chevin Gdns SK7 36 A7
Cheviot Ave WA2 8 A3
Cheviot Cl CH66 69 A6
Cheviot Ct CW7 149 B7
Cheviot Sq CW7 149 B7
Chevron Cl CH1 117 E4
Chevron Hey CH1 117 E4
Cheyne Wlk CW5 204 E3
Cheyney Rd CH1 118 B3
Chicago Ave M90 33 B7
Chichester Cl
Grappenhall Heys WA4 27 A7
Runcorn WA7 50 D6
Chichester Ct CH1 237 A3
Chichester St CH1 237 A3
Chidlow Cl
Hough CW2 206 E2
Widnes WA8 23 A5
Childer Cres CH66 69 B7
Childer Gdns CH66 69 B7
CHILDER THORNTON 69 B8
Childer Thornton Prim Sch CH66 69 B8
Child's La CW12 177 E6
Childwall Ct CH66 69 F8
Childwall Gdns CH66 69 F8
Childwall Rd CH66 69 F8
Chilham Cl CW7 149 C7
Chilham Pl SK11 111 F6
Chilington Ave WA8 22 D8
Chillingham Cl CW10 128 D2
Chiltern Ave SK11 112 A7
Chiltern Cl
Chester CH4 141 B5
Chorlton CW2 207 B1
Cuddington CW8 102 A2
Chiltern Cres WA2 8 A3
Chiltern Ct SK10 87 D3
Chiltern Pl WA2 8 A3
Chiltern Rd
Culcheth WA3 4 E4
St Helens WA9 1 A3
Warrington WA2 8 A3
Chiltern Way CW7 149 B7
Chilton Dr CH66 69 F2
Chilwell Cl WA8 12 D4
Chilworth Cl CW2 206 C8
China La WA4 16 C2
Chines The CW8 101 D5
Chippingdall Cl WA5 15 C5
Chipstead Cl CW8 103 A4
Chirk Cl CH2 118 F6
Chirk Gdns CH65 70 D3
Chirk Pl CW7 126 A1
Chirton Cl WA11 1 D7
Chisledon Cl WA11 1 D7
Chislet Ct WA8 12 E4
Chiswick Cl WA7 50 D7
Chiswick Gdns WA4 26 F6
Chollerton Cl WA16 29 C4
Cholmley Dr WA12 2 E2
Cholmondeley Castle Gdns* SY14 201 A4
Cholmondeley La SY14 200 E7
Cholmondeley Rd
Ellesmere Port CH65 69 F4
Hampton Heath SY14 213 E7
Runcorn WA7 49 D4
Wrenbury CW5 216 C5
Cholmondeley St
Macclesfield SK11 112 D6
Widnes WA8 23 A4
CHOLMONDESTON 170 E4
Cholmondley Rise SY14 214 B4
Chorlegh Grange 8 SK9 60 A1
CHORLEY 202 B2
CHORLEY BANK 201 E1
Chorley Bank Council Hos CW5 201 E1
CHORLEY GREEN 202 A3
Chorley Green La CW5, SY14 201 E5
Chorley Hall Cl SK9 59 F1
Chorley Hall La
Alderley Edge SK9 60 A1
Faddiley CW5 202 C2
Chorley's La WA8 13 E3
Chorley St
Warrington WA2 16 B6
Warrington WA2 16 C6
Chorley Stock La CW5 202 A2
Chorleywood Cl SK10 87 B4
CHORLTON 207 B1
Chorlton Cl WA7 24 D1
Chorlton La CW2 207 B2
CHORLTON LANE 212 B4
CHOWLEY 182 F5
Chowley Oak La CH3 182 F6
Chrimes Dr CW8 123 F6
Christchurch Ave CW2 190 A1
Christ Church CE Prim Sch
Ellesmere Port CH65 70 B2
Warrington WA2 9 A1
Christ Church CE Sch CW8 76 B1
Christie Cl CH66 44 A2
Christie St WA8 13 D1
CHRISTLETON 142 E8
Christleton Ave
Crewe CW2 189 D5
Northwich CW9 104 A4
Christleton Ct WA7 24 C4
Christleton Dr CH66 69 E6
Christleton High Sch CH3 142 F7
Christleton Prim Sch CH3 142 E8
Christleton Rd CH3 119 A1
Christleton Sports Ctr CH3 142 F8
Christleton Way 15 SK9 34 D5
Christopher Dr CH62 44 A5
Christ The King RC Prim Sch CH62 43 E7
Church Ave SK9 34 A2
Church Bank
Audley ST7 209 D2
Goostrey CW4 107 F1
Kelsall CW6 122 D5
Tattenhall CH3 166 B2
Church Bk SK23 65 D7
Church Cl
Handforth SK9 34 D3
Weaverham CW8 77 D1
Church College Cl CH1 118 B3
Church Cotts
Astle SK11 109 B8
Rainow SK10 88 E5
Sealand CH1 116 E6
Waverton CH3 143 C3
Church Croft CH4 162 A6
Church Ct
Ashton Hayes CH3 121 F8
Farndon CH3 180 E2
Church Dr
Newton-le-W WA12 2 C1
Warrington WA2 9 A1
Church End L24 21 D1
Church End Mews L24 21 D1
Churche's Ct 15 CW5 204 E5
Churche's Mansion* CW5 204 F5
Church Farm CW5 216 E4
Church Farm Ct
Heswall CH60 40 F7
Willaston CH64 67 F8
Churchfield Rd WA6 74 C8
Churchfields
Audlem CW3 230 A4
Barnton CW8 78 B3
Croft WA3 9 B7
Cuddington CW8 102 B2
Helsby WA6 73 C4
Knutsford WA16 57 C2
Widnes WA8 13 B5
Wybunbury CW5 220 B8
Church Fields TF9 236 C2
Church Gn WA13 19 B8
CHURCH GREEN 18 E2
Church Hall Cl CH1 117 F4
CHURCH HILL 149 D6
Church Hill WA16 57 A2
Churchill Ave WA3 5 B4
Churchill Cl CW12 156 A3
Churchill Dr CW6 146 D1
Churchill Mans 10 WA7 23 A3
Churchill Parkway CW7 149 D8
Churchill Way
Macclesfield SK11 112 D8
Neston CH64 66 E8
Church La
Alderley Edge SK9 60 A2
Church La *continued*
Aldford CH3 163 F3
Backford CH1 95 B4
Bebington CH62 44 A4
Bramhall SK7 35 C2
Chester CH2 118 D7
Congleton CW12 134 E1
Culcheth WA3 4 F3
Ellesmere Port CH66 69 D3
Farndon CH3 180 E1
Golborne WA3 3 D7
Guilden Sutton CH3 119 F5
Hargrave CH3 144 B1
Henbury SK11 111 C8
Huxley CH3, CW6 167 C6
Lawton-gate ST7 194 C4
Mobberley WA16 58 C5
Mow Cop ST7 195 E7
Nantwich CW5 204 E5
Neston CH64 66 E7
New Mills SK22 39 C8
Rainow SK10 88 E5
Sandbach CW11 175 E7
Scholar Green ST7 194 C7
Smallwood CW11 176 E4
Stoak CH2 96 A7
Sutton Lane Ends SK11 112 F3
Warren SK11 134 D8
Warrington WA4 17 B1
Weaverham CW8 77 D1
Wistaston CW2 205 E8
CHURCH LAWTON 194 C3
Church Lawton Prim Sch ST7 194 A5
Church Mdw TF9 236 C2
Church Mdws
Little Leigh CW8 77 D5
Whitchurch SY13 226 A1
Church Mead CH3 181 A5
Church Meadow La CH60 40 F7
Church Meadow Wlk WA8 22 B5
Churchmere Cl CW1 190 C7
Church Mews
Bollington SK10 88 B8
Higher Wincham CW9 79 E5
Knutsford WA16 57 B2
6 Macclesfield SK11 112 D8
CHURCH MINSHULL 172 A6
Church Par 5 CH65 70 C6
Church Rd
Alsager ST7 193 C4
Ashton Hayes CH3 121 F8
Barnton CW8 78 B2
Broughton CH4 139 C4
Burwardsley CH3 184 A5
Cheadle SK8 35 B8
Dodleston CH4 162 B8
Eccleston CH4 141 E2
Frodsham WA6 74 C7
Hale L24 47 E8
Handforth SK9 34 D3
Haydock WA11 1 E7
Little Leigh CW8 77 D4
Lymm WA13 18 E2
Mouldsworth CH3 98 F1
New Mills SK22 39 C7
Northwich CW9 104 A8
Saughall CH1 94 A1
Shocklach CH3 197 C1
Thornton Hough CH63 42 B6
Tilston SY14 198 B2
Wilmslow SK9 59 E4
Worleston CW5 188 D6
Church Rise CW8 102 B2
Church Row CW6 168 F1
Church St N CW6 122 C5
Church St W SK11 112 C8
Churchside SK10 112 D8
Churchside Cl CW1 191 D5
Churchside Wlk CH4 140 F7
Church St
Audley ST7 209 D2
Audley, Wood Lane ST7 210 A1
Bollington SK10 88 B8
Chester CH1 237 B4
Connah's Quay CH5 91 D1
Davenham CW9 104 A3
Ellesmere Port CH65 70 C6
Farndon LL13 180 E2
Frodsham WA6 74 B8
Great Budworth CW9 79 A8
Higher Wincham CW9 79 E5
Kelsall CW6 122 D4
Kidsgrove, Butt Lane ST7 194 D1
Kidsgrove, The Rookery ST7 195 C4
Macclesfield SK10, SK11 112 D8
Malpas SY14 213 B3
Moulton CW9 126 F8
Mount Pleasant ST7 195 C6
Newton-le-W WA12 2 E4
Runcorn WA7 23 A3
Sandbach CW11 175 C6
Tarvin CH3 121 C2
Warrington WA1 16 C5
Weaverham CW8 77 D1
Widnes WA8 23 A5
Wilmslow SK9 60 B7
Winsford CW7 126 E1
Church Steadings CH3 143 C3
Church Terr SK9 34 D4
Church View
Audlem CW3 230 A4
Church View *continued*
Handforth SK9 34 A2
Haslington CW1 191 D5
Kingsley WA6 75 B2
16 Knutsford WA16 57 A2
Lymm WA13 19 B4
New Mills SK22 39 C8
Church View Terr SK11 112 F3
Church View Wlk CW2 205 E8
Churchward Cl CH2 118 D4
Churchway SK10 86 F2
Church Way
Alvanley WA6 73 A1
Blacon CH1 117 E5
Wybunbury CW5 220 B8
Churchway Rd L24 21 A2
Church Wlk
Broughton CH4 139 C5
Crowton CW8 76 C2
2 Ellesmere Port CH65 70 C6
Holmes Chapel CW4 130 C3
Knutsford WA16 57 A2
Lower Peover WA16 81 E1
Malpas SY14 213 B3
Northwich CW9 104 A8
Wilmslow SK9 59 F6
Winwick WA2 8 A6
Church Wlks
Christleton CH3 142 E8
Norton in Hales TF9 236 C2
Churchwood View WA13 18 F3
Churchyard Side CW5 204 E5
CHURTON 180 E5
Churton Cl
Hough CW2 206 E3
3 Northwich CW9 103 E4
Churton Rd
Chester CH3 119 A2
Farndon CH3 180 E2
Churton St CH3 119 A2
Cicely Mill La WA16 30 D3
Cinder Cl CH3 119 F5
Cinder Hill CW7 125 F6
Cinder-Hill La ST7 194 F7
Cinder La
Chelford SK11 83 E1
Guilden Sutton CH3 119 F5
Lostock Green CW9 105 A8
Nantwich CW5 188 C2
Over Peover WA16 108 C7
Warrington WA4 17 F1
Cinder Rock Way ST7 195 C1
CINNAMON BROW 8 F4
Cinnamon Brow CE Prim Sch WA2 8 F3
Cinnamon La WA2 8 F2
Cinnamon La N WA2 8 F3
Cinnamon Pk WA2 9 B3
Circle Ave CW5 205 E5
Circle The
Crewe CW2 190 D1
Mere WA16 30 C2
Circuit The
Alderley Edge SK9 60 B3
Cheadle SK8 35 A7
Wilmslow SK9 59 D5
Circular Dr CH4 140 F4
City Bank ST8 179 C2
City Quays 8 CH1 237 C3
City Rd CH1 237 C3
City Walls Rd CH1 237 A2
City Way Apartments 7 CH1 237 C3
Civic Way
Ellesmere Port CH65 70 B4
Middlewich CW10 128 C1
Clair Ave CH5 116 A3
Clamhunger La WA16 56 D7
Clamley Ct L24 21 A3
Clamley Gdns L24 21 E2
Clanbrook Ave WA13 19 A2
Clanfield Ave WA8 12 C3
Clap Gate Cres WA8 22 B5
Clap Gates Cres WA5 15 E7
Clap Gates Rd WA5 15 E7
Clare Ave
Chester CH2 119 A3
Handforth SK9 34 C3
Clare Dr
Crewe CW2 189 F1
Ellesmere Port CH65 70 B1
Macclesfield SK10 87 C3
Clare Ho CH1 117 F6
Claremont Ave WA8 13 C4
Claremont Cl CW9 103 F3
Claremont Dr WA8 13 B4
Claremont Rd
Cheadle SK8 35 A8
Crewe CW2 190 B2
Culcheth WA3 4 D4
Runcorn WA7 23 B2
Clarence Ave
Chester CH3 119 B2
Warrington WA5 14 D6
Widnes WA8 13 A4
Clarence Ct
Newton-le-W WA12 2 A4
Wilmslow SK9 60 A6
Clarence Gr CW1 190 B5
Clarence Mill Bsns Pk SK10 63 A1
Clarence Rd
Bollington SK10 63 A1
Warrington WA4 17 B2
Clarence St
Newton-le-W WA12 1 F4
Runcorn WA7 22 F3
Warrington WA1 16 E7
Clarence Terr
Bollington SK10 63 A1
7 Runcorn WA7 23 A3
Clarendon Cl
Chester CH4 141 E6
Runcorn WA7 50 D7
Clarendon Cotts SK9 34 A3
Clarendon Ct WA2 7 F4
Clarendon Dr SK10 88 A1
Clarendon Rd M44 11 F7
Clare Pl CW7 149 C7
Clares Farm Cl WA1 17 F7
Clare St
Harriseahead ST7 195 E4
Mount Pleasant ST7 195 C6
Clarke Ave
Culcheth WA3 5 A4
Warrington WA4 16 D2
Clarke Gdns 3 WA8 23 B7
Clarke La
Bollington SK10 87 E5
Langley SK11 113 D3
Clarke Terr SK11 112 D6
CLARK GREEN 63 A3
Clarks Terr WA7 48 D8
Clary Mdw CW8 78 E1
Clatterbridge Hospl CH63 42 D8
Clatterbridge Rd CH63 42 D8
Clatterwick La CW8 77 D7
Claude St WA1 16 C6
Claughton Ave CW2 190 C1
Claverton Cl WA7 49 B6
Claverton Ct CH4 237 C1
Claydon Gdns WA3 10 F1
Clay Heyes SK11 84 A3
Clayhill Gn CH66 69 D7
Clayhill Gr WA3 4 B8
Clayhill Light Ind Pk CH64 41 F2
Clay La
Bickerton SY14 200 B7
Burtonwood WA5 6 E5
Handforth SK9 34 C5
Haslington CW1, CW11 191 D7
Over Peover WA16 108 B8
Sandbach CW11, CW1 174 B2
Wilmslow SK9 59 C4
Winsford CW7 125 B4
Claypit Rd CH4 141 B5
Claypits La CH3 142 F5
Clayton Ave
Congleton CW12 157 A5
Golborne WA3 3 E8
Clayton-By-Pass CW12 156 C3
Clayton Cl CW1 190 A7
Clayton Cres
Runcorn WA7 22 F1
Widnes WA8 12 F1
Clayton Dr SY13 226 B1
Clayton Rd WA3 9 F6
Clayton's Row CW5 204 E7
Cleadon Way WA8 12 E4
Cleaver Mews SK11 112 C5
Cleaver Rd CH1 117 E4
Cledford Cres CW10 151 E6
Cledford Inf Sch CW10 151 C7
Cledford Jun Sch CW10 151 C7
Cledford La CW10 151 E7
Cledwen Rd/Ffordd Cledwen CH4 139 D5
Cleethorpes Rd WA7 50 C7
Cleeves Cl WA1 16 C5
Cleeve Way SK8 35 B6
Clegge St WA2 16 B7
Clelland St WA4 16 C3
Clement Dr CW1 189 F7
Clemley Cl CW6 122 D6
Clerewood Ave SK8 34 B7
Clevedon Cl SK11 112 A7
Cleveland Dr CH66 69 A6
Cleveland Rd WA2 8 B3
Cleveland Way CW7 149 B7
Cleveleys Ave WA8 13 D2
Cleveleys Rd WA5 15 B4
Cleves Cl CH1 117 D6
Cliffbrook Gr 2 SK9 34 D2
Cliffe Rd
Crewe CW1 190 B7
Neston CH64 66 F5
Warrington WA4 26 C7
Cliffe St 3 WA8 13 C1
Cliff La
Acton Bridge CW8 76 C4
Lymm WA13 28 B6
Macclesfield SK10, SK11 88 B1
Warrington WA4 17 D1
Clifford Dr CH4 140 F5
Clifford Gr CW1 191 C4
Clifford Pl 4 CW7 149 C7
Clifford Rd
Macclesfield SK11 112 A8
Poynton SK12 36 D3
Warrington WA5 15 A4
Wilmslow SK9 59 F6
Cliff Rd
Acton Bridge CW8 76 E4
Wilmslow SK9 60 B8
Cliff Side SK9 60 B8
Cliff View WA6 74 A8
CLIFTON 49 D4

Clifton Ave
Bebington CH62 43 E3
Crewe CW2 190 B3
Culcheth WA3 4 D3
Clifton Cl WA1 17 C7
Clifton Cres WA6 49 C1
Clifton Ct WA7 49 B6
Clifton Dr
Blacon CH1 117 E3
Northwich CW9 104 A5
Wilmslow SK9 59 E4
Clifton Gdns CH65 70 C3
Clifton La WA7 49 E3
Cliftonmill Mdws WA3 2 F8
Clifton Park Ave CH5 91 D1
Clifton Rd
Runcorn, Clifton WA7 49 E3
Runcorn, Heath WA7 49 B6
Sandbach CW11 174 D7
Clifton Rdbt WA7 49 E3
Clifton St
Alderley Edge SK9 60 A1
Crewe CW2 190 B3
Warrington WA4 16 C4
Cliftonville Rd WA1 17 D6
Clincton Cl WA8 22 A8
Clincton View WA8 22 A8
Clipsley Cres WA11 1 B7
Clipsley La WA11 1 C6
Clitheroe Rd CW8 77 E1
CLIVE 127 D1
Clive Ave WA2 8 C1
Clive Back La CW7 150 D7
Cliveden Rd CH4 140 F5
CLIVE GREEN 150 D6
Clivegreen La CW10 150 E7
Clive La CW7 150 C8
Clock Face Rd WA8 13 E8
Clocktower The CW4 130 D2
Clock Twr The WA4 16 C2
Cloister Way CH65 70 E5
Clonners Field CW5 205 A4
Closeburn Ave CH60 40 E6
Close La
Alsager ST7 192 F3
Mow Cop ST7 195 D7
Close The
Alsager ST7 193 A3
Hartford CW8 103 D6
Newton-le-W WA12 2 E1
Saughall CH1 94 A1
Tarporley CW6 146 C2
CLOTTON 145 D4
Cloudberry Wlk M31 11 F3
CLOUD SIDE 157 F4
Cloud The★ CW12 158 A4
Cloud View CW12 157 A2
Clough Ave
Handforth SK9 34 B2
Warrington WA2 8 B2
Clough Bank SK10 87 F7
Clough Field Cl SK23 65 D8
CLOUGH HALL 210 F8
Clough Hall Dr ST7 210 E6
Clough Hall Rd ST7 210 F8
Clough Hall Tech Sch
ST7 194 F1
Clough La CW8 103 D6
Clough Rd CW7 126 E1
Cloughside SK12 38 E6
Clough The WA7 23 F1
Clough Wlk CW2 206 D8
Cloughwood Sch
CW8 103 D5
Clovelly Ave WA5 14 E7
Clovelly Gr WA7 50 C5
Clover Ave WA6 74 D7
Clover Ct WA7 50 B5
Cloverdale CW8 103 C7
Cloverdale Rd SK11 112 B5
Clover Dr
Pickmere WA16 79 F7
Winsford CW7 126 D3
Cloverfield
Lymm WA13 18 F4
Runcorn WA7 50 C7
Cloverfield Gdns CH66 69 D7
Cloverfields CW1 191 B4
Clover La CH4 140 F5
Clover Pl CH4 140 F5
Clowes Ave ST7 193 F2
Clowes St SK11 112 B8
Clumber Cl SK12 36 E3
Clumber Rd SK12 36 E3
CLUTTON 182 D1
Clutton CE Prim Sch
CH3 182 D1
Clwyd Cl CH5 139 B6
Clwyd Way CH66 69 A6
Clyde Ave ST8 179 E1
Clyde Cres CW7 127 B1
Clyde Gr CW2 190 A3
Clydesdale CH65 70 B3
Clydesdale Ave CW2 190 B3
Clydesdale Rd WA4 26 D8
Coach Ho The ST7 194 C4
Coach Rd
Broxton CH3 183 A3
Edge Green SY14 199 D2
Little Budworth CW6 147 D8
Coachway SK10 86 F7
Coalbrookdale Rd
CH64 41 F2
COALPIT HILL 210 C8
Coalpit Hill ST7 210 D8
Coalpit La
Clive Green CW10 150 F7
Langley SK11 113 C5

Coalpit La *continued*
Mollington CH1 94 D4
Coalport Dr CW7 126 F3
Coare St SK10 87 D1
Coastguard La CH64 41 B1
Coatings By Pass Rd
CH5 91 F2
Coatings Two CH5 91 E2
Cobal Ct WA6 74 B8
Cobbett's Way SK9 59 F4
Cobblers Cross La
CW6 146 E2
Cobblers La / Lon Y
Cryddion LL12 161 B1
Cobbles The
Chester CH4 141 D7
Cuddington CW8 101 D4
Lower Peover WA16 81 E1
Cobblestone Ct CH2 119 E8
COBBS 26 E8
Cobbs Inf Sch The
WA4 26 E8
Cobbs La
Hough CW2 206 E2
Warrington WA4 26 E8
Cobden St
Newton-le-W WA12 2 D4
Warrington WA2 16 B6
Cob Hall La WA6 98 D5
Cob Moor Rd ST7 195 A4
COBSCOT 235 E3
Cock Hall La SK11 113 D3
Cockhedge La WA1 16 C5
Cockhedge Sh Ctr
WA1 16 B5
Cockhedge Way WA1 16 B5
Cockington Cl CW9 104 A4
Cock La
Great Budworth CW9 78 F8
Sound CW5 217 F4
Cocklade La L24 21 D1
Cock Lane Ends WA8 22 B4
Cockpit La CW8 102 B1
Cockshades farm
CW5 206 C2
Cocksheadhey Rd
SK10 63 C1
Cocksmoss La
Congleton SK11 134 A3
Marton SK11 133 D3
Cocoa Gdns [11] CW5 204 E5
Cocoa Yd The [10]
CW5 204 E5
CODDINGTON 182 A3
Coe La WA14 30 C7
Cogshall La
Anderton CW9 78 C5
Comberbach CW9 78 B7
Colchester Ho [10]
CH1 237 C3
Colchester Sq CH4 140 F5
COLDHARBOUR 164 F5
Coldmoss Dr CW11 175 C4
COLD MOSS HEATH 175 C5
Coldstream Cl WA2 8 E3
Coldstream Dr CH66 68 F5
Cole Ave WA12 2 C4
Colebrook Cl WA3 10 A4
Coleclough Pl WA3 4 F4
Coleg Glannau Dyfrdwy/
Deeside Coll CH5 91 B1
Colehill Bank CW12 156 E2
Colehill Pl CH5 91 D1
Colemere Cl WA1 17 A8
Colemere Ct CH65 70 C7
Coleridge Cl
Blacon CH1 118 A5
Sandbach CW11 174 C5
Coleridge Gr WA8 12 E1
Coleridge Way CW1 190 F5
Colinwood Ave CH4 139 B3
Coliseum Way CH65 70 D2
Collar House Dr SK10 86 E6
College Cl
Warrington, Fearnhead
WA2 9 B2
Warrington WA1 16 D5
Wilmslow SK9 59 F8
College Fields
Crewe CW2 190 A1
Widnes WA8 12 F5
College Gn CH4 141 D7
College La CW6 168 F1
College of Law
(Christleton Hall)
CH3 142 D8
College Rd ST7 193 B5
College View CH5 91 C1
Colley La CW11 175 D5
Colleys La CW5 205 B7
Colliers La CW9 54 E2
Collier's Row WA7 48 E7
Collier St WA7 22 F3
Colliery Green Cl CH64 66 E5
Colliery Green Ct CH64 66 E5
Colliery Green Dr
CH64 66 E5
Collinbrook Ave CW2 190 B1
Collingham Gn CH66 69 B5
Collingham Way CW7 126 D1
Collingtree Ave CW7 127 A3
Collingwood Cl
Macclesfield SK10 87 B2
Poynton SK12 37 A3
Collingwood Rd WA12 2 B3
COLLINS GREEN 1 E1
Collins Green La WA5 1 E1
Collinson Ct [2] WA6 74 B8

Collins St CW2 190 A3
Collin St WA5 15 F5
Colne Rd WA5 6 F6
Colorado Cl WA5 15 C7
Colshaw Dr SK9 34 D2
Colshaw Hall Cotts
WA16 82 F1
Colshaw La SK11 109 E1
Colson Ct CH2 237 A4
Coltsfoot Cl CH3 142 B5
Columbine Cl
Huntington CH3 142 A6
Widnes WA8 12 B4
Columbine Way WA9 6 B7
Columbine Wlk [8] M31 11 F3
Colville Ct WA2 8 A3
Colville Rd SK11 111 F8
Colwyn Cl
Ellesmere Port CH65 70 D3
Warrington WA5 7 E2
Colwyn Rd SK7 35 F8
COMBERBACH 78 C7
Comberbach Dr CW5 205 A4
Comberbach Prim Sch
CW9 78 C8
Combermere Pl [8]
CW1 190 B5
Comber Way WA16 82 A8
Comboy Dr CW9 104 C6
Combs Cl SK22 39 A8
Commercial Ave SK8 34 F5
Commercial Rd SK10 112 E8
Common Farm La
SK11 83 E1
Commongate SK10 112 E8
Commonhall St CH1 237 A2
Common La
Betley CW3 221 F6
Chelford SK11 83 E1
Culcheth WA3 4 E4
Duddon CW6 145 C7
Hapsford WA6 72 D1
Kelsall CW6 122 C3
Lach Dennis CW9 105 E5
Norbury SY13 215 C5
Stretton WA4 52 E8
Warrington WA4 16 E2
Waverton CH3 143 B4
Winsford CW7 125 B5
Common Rd WA12, WA5 1 E3
COMMONSIDE 100 B8
Commonside WA6 73 E1
COMMON SIDE 124 D3
Commons Mill CW11 175 B7
Common St WA12 1 E3
Commons The CW11 175 B6
Common The
Kelsall CW6 122 C3
Runcorn WA7 49 F8
Commonwealth Cl
CW7 149 D6
Commonwood Rd
LL13 196 A8
Company's Cl WA7 48 F6
Compass Cl WA7 50 D5
Compton Cl WA11 1 C7
Compton Pl
Chester CH4 141 A6
Ellesmere Port CH65 70 B5
Concorde Pl WA2 8 D2
Concourse Way WA9 1 A2
Condliffe Cl CW11 175 C5
Conery Cl WA6 73 C4
Coney Gr WA7 50 B5
CONGLETON 157 A4
Congleton Bsns Ctr
CW12 156 E3
Congleton Bsns Pk
CW12 156 C4
Congleton Cl SK9 85 A8
CONGLETON EDGE 179 B5
Congleton Edge Rd
CW12 179 B6
Congleton High Sch
CW12 155 F3
Congleton La SK11 109 D5
Congleton Mus★
CW12 156 E2
Congleton Rd
Alderley Edge SK9 60 A1
Biddulph ST8 179 D2
Broughton CH4 139 C4
Kidsgrove ST7 194 D1
Macclesfield SK11 112 B5
Marton SK11 133 B5
Mow Cop ST7 178 F1
North Rode SK11 134 C6
Sandbach, Arclid Green
CW11 175 E8
Sandbach CW11 175 B8
Scholar Green CW12,
ST7 177 E3
Siddington SK11 110 B5
Smallwood CW11 177 A6
Swettenham CW12 131 F4
Warren SK11 111 E2
Congleton Rd N ST7 194 E6
Congleton Rd S ST7 194 D3
Congleton Ret Pk
CW12 156 D4
Congleton Sta CW12 157 A1
Congleton War Meml
Hospl CW12 156 F1
Conifer Cl CH66 95 A8
Conifer Gr
Moore WA4 25 A7
Warrington WA5 14 F7
Conifers The ST7 193 B3

Conifer Wlk M31 11 E3
Coningsby Dr CW7 126 E1
Coningsby Gdns [13] WA3 3 E8
Coniston Ave
Bebington CH63 43 C4
Congleton CW12 155 F2
Warrington WA5 14 D4
Winsford CW7 126 C2
Coniston Cl
Alderley Edge SK9 84 A7
Hooton CH66 44 B2
Nantwich CW5 205 A6
Runcorn WA7 49 D6
Coniston Dr
Frodsham WA6 74 D8
Handforth SK9 34 C4
Holmes Chapel CW4 130 A3
Coniston Rd
Chester CH2 118 F5
High Lane SK6 37 D8
Neston CH64 66 E6
Partington M31 11 E4
Coniston Way SK11 111 F5
CONNAH'S QUAY 91 B1
Connah's Quay High Sch
CH5 91 C1
Connaught Ave WA1 16 E7
Connaught Cl SK9 60 C8
Connaught Dr WA12 2 C2
Conrad Cl CW1 190 E4
Conroy Way WA12 7 C8
Consort Cl SK10 87 E7
Constable Dr SK9 60 E8
Constables Cl WA7 24 A1
Constance Rd M31 11 F3
Constance Way WA8 23 A5
Convamore Rd SK7 35 D7
Conway Ave
Irlam M44 11 F8
Warrington WA5 7 F2
Winsford CW7 149 C7
Conway Cl
Crewe CW1 190 C8
Knutsford WA16 82 A8
Saltney CH4 140 D5
Warrington WA5 14 F6
Conway Cres SK10 87 F1
Conway Ct CH65 70 D3
Conway Dr WA12 2 E3
Conwy Ct WA7 24 A2
Coogee Ave WA5 14 E7
Cook Ave WA11 1 F7
Cookes Cl CH64 41 E1
Cookes Ct CH3 166 B1
Cooke's La CW9 104 F6
Cookesmere La
CW11 175 A8
Cooks Hill WA6 99 F8
Cooks La SY13 225 D7
COOKSONGREEN 76 A1
Cook St CH65 70 C6
Coole La
Hack Green CW5 218 E3
Newhall CW3 229 C5
Coombe Dr WA7 49 A8
Coombe Park Ct [1]
CH66 69 C6
Coombe Pk CH66 69 C6
Co-operative St SK12 38 D6
Cooper Ave
Newton-le-W WA12 1 F3
Warrington WA2 8 B2
Coope Rd SK10 87 E6
Cooper's Fold SK8 34 F6
Cooper La WA11 1 C6
Cooper's Croft CH3 142 A7
Cooper's La CH5 91 D1
Coopers Opening
CW11 175 B7
Coopers Pl WA4 16 C1
Cooper St
Congleton CW12 156 E3
Runcorn WA7 23 A3
Widnes WA8 13 B1
Cooper Terr CW6 146 D1
Cope Ave CW5 204 D4
Copeland Gr WA7 49 E5
Copeland Rd WA4 16 B2
Copes La CW5 204 C4
Copeswood Cl CH4 139 C3
Copgrove Wlk M22 33 E7
Copley Wlk CW5 204 D5
Cop Mdw SK11 112 F2
COPPENHALL 190 D7
Coppenhall Gr CW2 190 A4
Coppenhall Heyes
CW2 190 A4
Coppenhall La CW2 189 D4
COPPENHALL MOSS
173 D1
Copper Beech Cl CH4 139 C3
Copperfield Cl WA3 9 C5
Copperfield Rd
Cheadle SK8 35 B5
Poynton SK12 36 D2
Copperfields
Poynton SK12 36 D2
Tarporley CW6 146 D2
Wilmslow SK9 60 C8
Copperhill Rd CW12 179 B7
Coppermine La SY14 184 B2
Copper St SK11 112 E6
Copperwood WA7 24 C1
Copper Wood CW8 101 E5
Coppice Ave SK12 38 A6
Coppice Cl
High Lane SK12 38 A6
Runcorn WA7 24 A1

Coppice Cl *continued*
Willaston CW5 205 D6
Coppice Ct SK8 34 B8
Coppice Dr CW10 151 E6
Coppice Gn
Elton CH2 72 C4
Warrington WA5 7 A1
Coppice Gr WA16 57 A3
Coppice Ho
Poynton SK12 36 D2
Talke ST7 210 C8
Coppice La SK12 38 A5
Coppicemere Dr CW1 191 A2
Coppice Rd
Haslington CW11 192 A8
Poynton SK12 37 B3
Talke ST7 210 C8
Willaston CW5 205 D6
Coppice Rise SK11 112 D5
Coppice The
Altrincham WA15 32 B8
Cuddington CW8 101 D5
Horwich End SK23 65 F5
Nantwich CW5 204 F3
Sandbach CW11 174 E7
Wincham CW9 79 C3
Coppice Way SK9 34 E3
Coppins Cl
Chester CH3 119 A2
Helsby WA6 73 B4
Coppins The
Warrington WA2 8 C2
Wilmslow SK9 59 E4
Copse The
Altrincham WA15 32 D7
High Lane SK6 37 E7
Newton-le-W WA12 2 B4
Runcorn WA7 50 A6
COPTHORNE 229 F4
Copthorne Cl CW12 156 F2
Copthorne Dr CW3 229 F3
Copyhold CW8 102 D8
Corbet Ave WA2 16 B8
Corbet Dr TF9 235 A4
Corbet St WA2 16 B8
Corbridge Ho [9] CH1 237 C3
Corfe Way CW7 149 C7
Coriander Cl CW10 128 C3
Corks La SK12 38 E5
CORLTON 207 B1
Cormorant Cl CW1 190 F4
Cormorant Dr WA7 22 E2
Cornbrook Rd SK11 112 C4
Corner Croft SK9 60 A4
Cornerhouse La WA8 12 D3
Corners The CW8 102 E7
Cornfield Cl
Ellesmere Port CH66 69 F1
Macclesfield SK10 87 C3
Cornforth Way WA8 12 F3
Cornhill Cl ST5 210 D1
Cornish Cl M22 33 D8
Cornishway M22 33 D8
Cornishway Ind Est
M22 33 D8
Cornmill Cl CW11 173 D7
Cornmill Ct WA3 9 A8
Cornubia Rd WA8 23 D7
Cornwall Ave WA7 23 A2
Cornwall Cl
[3] Congleton CW12 157 A1
High Lane SK6 37 E7
Macclesfield SK10 86 E1
Runcorn WA7 23 F1
Cornwall Gr CW1 190 B5
Cornwall Ho CH1 237 B3
Cornwall Rd
Chester CH2 118 F7
Gatley SK8 34 B8
Irlam M44 11 D5
Widnes WA8 13 B3
Cornwall St
Chester CH1 237 B4
Warrington WA1 16 E7
Cornwell Cl SK9 60 D8
Coronation Ave
Alsager ST7 193 A3
Glazebury WA3 5 C7
Warrington WA4 17 C2
Winsford CW7 126 E1
Coronation Bldgs
SK10 88 A8
Coronation Cres
Crewe CW1 190 E6
Kidsgrove ST7 194 E1
Sandbach CW11 175 A5
Coronation Dr
Frodsham WA6 49 D1
Haydock WA11 2 A7
Newton-le-W WA12 2 E1
Warrington WA5 14 F4
Widnes WA8 22 C8
Coronation Gr CW8 78 A4
Coronation Ho WA7 49 C8
Coronation Mill ST7 195 D7
Coronation Rd
Broughton CH4 139 B3
Congleton CW12 156 F3
Ellesmere Port CH65 70 C4
Middlewich CW10 151 D6
Runcorn, Higher Runcorn
WA7 23 B1
Runcorn, Preston Brook
WA7 50 F6

Coronation Sq 19 WA16 . . . 57 A2
Coronation St
Chester CH4 . . . 140 F7
Crewe CW1 . . . 190 D5
Macclesfield SK11 . . . 112 D6
Coronation Terr CW6 . . . 146 D1
Coroner's La WA8 . . . 13 A4
Coronet Ave CW9 . . . 103 F3
Coronet Way WA8 . . . 22 B8
CORRA COMMON . . . 233 C1
Correction Brow SK12 . . . 37 C6
Corridor Rd CH65 . . . 71 B6
Corwen Cl WA5 . . . 7 E1
Cosgrove Bsns Pk CW9 . . . 78 D3
Cossack Ave WA2 . . . 8 C1
COTEBROOK . . . 147 A8
Cotebrook Dr CH2 . . . 118 E7
Cotebrook Rd CW9 . . . 104 C8
Cotebrook Shire Horse Ctr★ CW6 . . . 147 A7
Cote Lea Ct WA7 . . . 49 F6
Cotes Pl CH1 . . . 117 E3
Cotgreaves Cl CH4 . . . 141 B5
Cotswold Ave WA3 . . . 3 D6
Cotswold Cl
Chester CH2 . . . 118 F6
Cuddington CW8 . . . 102 A2
Macclesfield SK10 . . . 86 E1
Cotswold Ct 7 CH3 . . . 119 A1
Cotswold Gr WA9 . . . 1 A3
Cotswold Pl WA2 . . . 8 B4
Cotswold Rd WA2 . . . 8 B3
Cotswold Way CW7 . . . 149 B7
Cottage Cl
Bebington CH63 . . . 43 C5
Neston CH64 . . . 66 F7
Rudheath CW9 . . . 104 E8
Cottage Dr E CH60 . . . 40 F5
Cottage Dr W CH60 . . . 40 F5
Cottage Gr SK9 . . . 59 F5
Cottage La
Heswall CH60 . . . 40 F5
Macclesfield SK10 . . . 112 F7
Cottage Lawns SK9 . . . 60 B2
Cottage Rd CH4 . . . 141 B5
Cottage St SK11 . . . 112 B8
Cottages The
Lawton Heath ST7 . . . 193 D6
Sproston Green CW4 . . . 129 C2
Warrington WA4 . . . 17 F4
Cottam Dr WA2 . . . 9 A3
Cotterdale Cl WA5 . . . 14 F7
Cotterill WA7 . . . 49 D8
Cotterill Dr WA1 . . . 17 C7
Cotterill St CW2 . . . 190 D2
Cottesmore Dr CH60 . . . 41 D8
Cottesmore Gdns WA15 . . . 32 C8
Cotton La
Christleton CH3 . . . 120 D2
Runcorn WA7 . . . 49 D8
Sandbach CW11 . . . 175 A3
Cotton Mews CW3 . . . 230 A4
Cottons Bridge WA4 . . . 50 F5
Cottonwood Gr ST7 . . . 195 E4
Cottrell Rd WA15 . . . 32 D7
Coulton Rd WA8 . . . 13 F3
Council Hos
Audlem CW3 . . . 229 E2
Bickerton SY14 . . . 200 A8
Congleton CW12 . . . 156 F4
Newhall CW5 . . . 228 B8
Council Houses CW5 . . . 216 B6
Countess Ave SK8 . . . 34 E5
Countess Cl 7 SK11 . . . 111 F7
Countess Ct CH1 . . . 118 B5
Countess of Chester Health Pk CH2 . . . 118 B6
Countess of Chester Hospl CH2 . . . 118 B6
Countess Rd SK11 . . . 111 F7
Countess Way CH2 . . . 118 C5
Counting House Rd SK12 . . . 38 E5
Country Ctr The★ CH3 . . . 165 E5
County Terr WA16 . . . 56 F1
Courier Row SK10 . . . 87 F7
Court 2 SK10 . . . 87 F1
Court Ho The 9 CH65 . . . 70 C6
Courtney Gn SK9 . . . 34 D2
Courtney Rd CH4 . . . 140 E5
Court No 4 6 SK10 . . . 112 C8
Court The CH64 . . . 66 F6
Courtyard The
Bostock Green CW10 . . . 127 D5
Chester CH2 . . . 118 F6
Congleton CW12 . . . 156 B3
Cuddington CW8 . . . 101 E2
Elton CH2 . . . 72 B4
Haughton CW6 . . . 186 F4
Newton-le-W WA12 . . . 2 E4
Smallwood CW11 . . . 177 A7
4 Warrington WA1 . . . 16 B5
Weaverham CW8 . . . 102 A8
Willaston CH64 . . . 67 F8
Cousens Way CH1 . . . 118 B4
Covell Rd SK12 . . . 36 D5
Coventry Ave CH66 . . . 94 E8
Coverdale Cl WA5 . . . 14 F7
Coverdale Fold CW11 . . . 174 D5
Covert Cl CW7 . . . 149 B8
Covert Gdns ST7 . . . 210 D8
Covert Rise CH3 . . . 166 A2
Covington Pl SK9 . . . 60 B6
Cowanway WA8 . . . 12 F5
Cowbrook La SK11 . . . 135 B6
Cowdell St WA2 . . . 16 B7
Cowfields CW5 . . . 204 E6
Cowhey Cl CH4 . . . 141 B5
Cow Hey La WA6, WA7 . . . 49 A5
Cow La
Ashley WA15 . . . 31 F6
Bollington SK10 . . . 88 B7
Hargrave CH3 . . . 144 A2
Macclesfield SK11 . . . 112 D6
Norley WA6 . . . 101 A5
Rainow SK10 . . . 88 D4
Wilmslow SK9 . . . 60 C7
Winsford CW7 . . . 149 E8
Cowley Way CW1 . . . 190 E1
Cowper Cl CW2 . . . 206 A8
Cowthorne Dr CH3 . . . 143 A4
COX BANK . . . 234 F8
Crab La WA2 . . . 9 B3
Crabmill Dr CW11 . . . 174 E7
Crabmill La
Norley WA6 . . . 100 E6
Warmingham CW11 . . . 173 E7
Crabtree Ave
Altrincham WA15 . . . 32 D7
Disley SK12 . . . 38 E5
Crabtree Cl WA12 . . . 2 E3
Crab Tree Cl L24 . . . 21 E2
Crabtree Ct SK12 . . . 38 D6
Crabtree Fold WA7 . . . 50 C8
Crabtree Gr CW1 . . . 190 E6
CRABTREE GREEN . . . 101 C1
Crabtree Green Ct CW8 . . . 101 C2
Crabtree Green Pk CW8 . . . 124 C8
Crabtree La WA13 . . . 29 A7
Crabwall Pl CH1 . . . 117 F5
Crackley Bank ST5 . . . 210 E1
Crackley Bank Prim Sch ST5 . . . 210 E1
Craddock Ct SY14 . . . 213 B3
Cradley WA8 . . . 12 C2
Cragside Way SK9 . . . 60 C6
Craig Cl SK11 . . . 112 B5
Craig Dr SK23 . . . 65 E6
Craig Gdns CH66 . . . 69 E7
Craigleigh Gr CH62 . . . 43 F4
Craig Rd
Congleton CW12 . . . 156 F4
Macclesfield SK11 . . . 112 B5
Craigside ST8 . . . 179 C1
Craig Wlk ST7 . . . 193 F2
Craithie Rd CH3 . . . 119 A2
Crampton Dr WA15 . . . 32 C8
CRANAGE . . . 130 A6
Cranage Cl WA7 . . . 49 D7
Cranage Ct 3 CW12 . . . 156 F3
Cranage La CW9 . . . 79 D1
Cranage Rd CW2 . . . 190 A3
Cranage Way 16 SK9 . . . 34 D5
Cranberry Dr ST5 . . . 210 D1
Cranberry Inf Sch ST7 . . . 193 A3
Cranberry Jun Sch ST7 . . . 193 A3
Cranberry La ST7 . . . 193 A3
Cranberry Moss La ST7 . . . 193 A3
Cranberry Rd M31 . . . 11 F3
Cranborne Ave WA4 . . . 16 B1
Cranborne Rd CW1 . . . 190 D6
Cranebrook Cl CW1 . . . 190 A8
Crane Ho CH1 . . . 118 B1
Cranfield Dr ST7 . . . 193 A3
Cranford Ave
Knutsford WA16 . . . 56 F1
Macclesfield SK11 . . . 112 F7
Cranford Cl CH62 . . . 43 F4
Cranford Ct
Chester CH4 . . . 141 A5
Warrington WA1 . . . 17 E8
Cranford Mews ST7 . . . 193 A3
Cranford Rd SK9 . . . 34 A1
Cranford Sq WA16 . . . 56 F1
Cranham Ave WA3 . . . 3 E7
Cranleigh Cl WA4 . . . 26 B7
Cranleigh Cres CH1 . . . 118 B4
Cranleigh Dr SK7 . . . 37 A8
Cranmere Cl CW9 . . . 104 A4
Cranshaw La WA8 . . . 13 B6
Cransley Sch CW9 . . . 53 E1
Cranswick Gn CH66 . . . 69 C5
Crantock Dr SK8 . . . 34 C8
Cranwell Ave WA3 . . . 4 F4
Crauford Rd CW12 . . . 157 A8
Craven Ave WA3 . . . 3 E7
Craven Ct WA2 . . . 7 F4
Crawford Ave WA8 . . . 12 B1
Crawford Pl WA7 . . . 49 B6
Crawford's Wlk CH2 . . . 118 F3
Crawley Ave WA2 . . . 8 A3
Crayford Ave CW12 . . . 157 A5
Cresanne Cl CW10 . . . 151 C7
Crescent Dr
Furness Vale SK23 . . . 39 D2
Helsby WA6 . . . 73 B3
Crescent Rd
Alderley Edge SK9 . . . 60 B2
Congleton CW12 . . . 156 C2
Cranage CW4 . . . 129 F6
Ellesmere Port CH65 . . . 70 D6
Rostherne WA16 . . . 30 B3
Crescent The
Chester CH2 . . . 118 D4
Crescent The *continued*
Congleton CW12 . . . 156 C2
Ellesmere Port CH65 . . . 69 F5
Hartford CW8 . . . 103 A5
Heswall, Gayton CH60 . . . 41 B6
Lymm WA13 . . . 18 F2
Macclesfield SK10 . . . 87 E1
Middlewich CW10 . . . 128 B1
Mottram St Andrew SK10 . . . 61 A1
Nantwich CW5 . . . 204 F6
New Mills SK22 . . . 39 B8
Northwich CW9 . . . 103 F6
Rostherne WA16 . . . 30 B3
Utkinton CW6 . . . 146 B7
Weaverham CW8 . . . 77 E1
Cressbrook Rd 2 WA4 . . . 16 C1
Cressington Gdns 7 CH65 . . . 70 C6
Cresswell Ave
Newcastle-u-Lyme ST5 . . . 210 D1
New Mills SK22 . . . 39 C8
Cresswell Cl WA5 . . . 7 D2
Cresswellshawe Rd ST7 . . . 193 D4
Cresswell St SK22 . . . 39 C8
Cresta Dr WA7 . . . 48 F6
Crestwood Cl CW2 . . . 206 B7
Crew Ave SK10 . . . 87 E1
CREWE . . . 190 E5
Crewe Bsns Pk CW1 . . . 190 F2
CREWE-BY-FARNDON . . . 197 A7
Crewe Gates Farm Ind Est CW1 . . . 190 F2
Crewe Gates Ind Est CW1 . . . 207 A8
CREWE GREEN . . . 191 B3
Crewe Green Ave CW1 . . . 191 B4
Crewe Green Rd CW1 . . . 191 A3
Crewe Hall Ent Pk CW1 . . . 207 D8
Crewe Hill La CH3 . . . 197 A6
Crewe La CH3 . . . 180 F1
Crewe La S CH3 . . . 197 A7
Crewe Rd
Alsager ST7 . . . 193 B3
Crewe, Crewe Green CW1 . . . 191 B3
Crewe CW1 . . . 190 F2
Haslington CW1, CW11 . . . 191 D5
Hatherton CW5 . . . 219 F3
Lawton-gate ST7 . . . 193 F4
Nantwich CW2, CW5 . . . 205 D6
Sandbach CW11 . . . 175 A5
Shavington CW2 . . . 206 C6
Crewe St
Chester CH1 . . . 237 C3
Crewe CW1 . . . 190 D4
Crewe Sta CW1 . . . 190 E2
Crewood Common Rd CW8 . . . 76 A3
Crib La CW6 . . . 168 A8
Criccieth Ct CH65 . . . 70 D2
Criftin Cl CH66 . . . 69 C2
Crimes La CH3, CW6 . . . 167 D4
Crisham Ave CW5 . . . 218 E8
Crispin Rd M22 . . . 33 E8
Critchley Rd L24 . . . 21 A3
Croasdale Dr WA7 . . . 49 E5
Crocus Gdns WA9 . . . 6 A7
Crocus St CW8 . . . 78 B3
Croesmere Dr CH66 . . . 69 D2
CROFT . . . 9 B8
Croft Cl
Altrincham WA15 . . . 32 C6
Congleton CW12 . . . 156 F2
Utkinton CW6 . . . 146 B7
Waverton CH3 . . . 143 A5
Croft Cotts
Dunham-on-t-H WA6 . . . 97 E6
Ellesmere Port CH66 . . . 69 A8
Croft Ct CH65 . . . 70 E3
Croften Dr CH64 . . . 66 E5
Crofters Cl
6 Ellesmere Port CH66 . . . 69 E1
Pickmere WA16 . . . 80 A7
Wistaston CW2 . . . 206 B8
Crofters Ct
Holmes Chapel CW4 . . . 130 C3
Newcastle-u-Lyme ST5 . . . 210 D3
Crofters Gn SK9 . . . 59 F6
Crofters Heath CH66 . . . 69 E1
Crofters Lea CW8 . . . 103 D7
Crofters Pk CH5 . . . 116 A3
Crofters Way CH1 . . . 116 F8
Croft Gdns WA4 . . . 27 A7
Croft Heath Gdns WA3 . . . 9 A8
Croft Ho WA3 . . . 9 A7
Croft La
Dodleston CH4 . . . 162 A7
Knutsford WA16 . . . 82 B8
Crofton Cl WA4 . . . 27 C5
Crofton Cotts WA6 . . . 100 B8
Crofton Gdns WA3 . . . 4 E3
Crofton Rd WA7 . . . 22 E1
Croft Pk WA16 . . . 58 F5
Croft Prim Sch WA3 . . . 9 A8
Croft Rd SK9 . . . 59 E4
Croftside WA1 . . . 17 F7
Croftside Way SK9 . . . 60 C6
Croft St
Golborne WA3 . . . 3 A8
Widnes WA8 . . . 23 A6
Crofts The CH3 . . . 180 F1
Croftsway CH60 . . . 40 D8
Croft The
Chester CH2 . . . 118 D5
Norton in Hales TF9 . . . 236 B3
Runcorn WA7 . . . 23 F1
Croftwood Cl 10 CW7 . . . 149 A8
Cromdale Way WA5 . . . 14 E6
Cromer Dr CW1 . . . 190 B8
Cromford Ct SK23 . . . 65 E6
Cromford Mews SK23 . . . 65 E5
Cromley Rd SK6 . . . 37 E6
Crompton Cl CW12 . . . 157 A6
Crompton Dr WA2 . . . 8 A6
Crompton Rd SK11 . . . 112 C7
Crompton Way WA3 . . . 4 B8
Cromwell Ave WA5 . . . 15 D6
Cromwell Ave S WA5 . . . 15 D4
Cromwell Cl WA12 . . . 2 A4
Cromwell Ct
Irlam M44 . . . 11 E7
6 Nantwich CW5 . . . 204 E5
2 Warrington WA1 . . . 16 A5
Cromwell Dr CW2 . . . 206 C4
Cromwell Rd
Bramhall SK7 . . . 35 D6
Ellesmere Port CH65 . . . 70 D5
Irlam M44 . . . 11 E7
Northwich CW8 . . . 103 E8
Cromwell St WA8 . . . 23 A6
Cronkinson Ave CW5 . . . 204 F4
Cronkinson Oak CW5 . . . 204 F4
CRONTON . . . 12 D5
Cronton CE Prim Sch WA8 . . . 12 C6
Cronton Farm Ct WA8 . . . 12 E4
Cronton La
Cronton L35 . . . 12 B8
Widnes WA8 . . . 12 F5
Cronton Park Ave WA8 . . . 12 C6
Cronton Park Cl WA8 . . . 12 C6
Cronton Rd L35, WA8 . . . 12 C5
Cronulla Dr WA5 . . . 14 E7
Crooked La CH3, CW6 . . . 145 C4
Crookedyard Rd SK11 . . . 113 E7
Crookenden Cl CH2 . . . 95 C1
Crookenden Rd CH2 . . . 95 C1
Crook La CW7 . . . 127 A2
Crook St CH1 . . . 237 A2
Croppers Rd WA2 . . . 8 F3
Crosby Ave WA5 . . . 16 A8
Crosby Gr CH64 . . . 43 B1
Crosfield Ct WA5 . . . 15 A5
Crosfield St WA1 . . . 16 A5
Crossall St SK11 . . . 112 C7
Crossdale Rd CH62 . . . 43 D5
Cross Farm WA2 . . . 9 A2
Crossfield Ave
Culcheth WA3 . . . 4 F2
Lymm WA13 . . . 18 F3
Winsford CW7 . . . 149 D7
Crossfield Rd
Bollington SK10 . . . 87 E6
Handforth SK9 . . . 34 D4
Crossfields CH3 . . . 121 B2
Crossgates WA8 . . . 13 F3
Cross Gn CH2 . . . 118 E6
Cross Hey CH4 . . . 237 C1
Crossings Ho CW1 . . . 190 A5
Crossings The WA12 . . . 2 C3
Crosskeys Cl CW6 . . . 145 A6
Cross La
Audley ST7 . . . 209 E5
Church Minshull CW1, CW5 . . . 172 C6
Congleton CW12 . . . 157 A1
Croft WA3 . . . 9 D7
Haslington CW11 . . . 191 F8
Middlewich CW10 . . . 151 D6
Neston CH64 . . . 66 E5
Newton-le-W WA12 . . . 2 B4
Sandbach CW11 . . . 175 D5
Smallwood CW11 . . . 176 F5
Smallwood CW11 . . . 177 B5
Swettenham CW12 . . . 131 F4
Tarvin CH3 . . . 121 E2
Warrington WA4 . . . 17 A3
Wilmslow SK9 . . . 60 F8
Cross La E M31 . . . 11 F3
Crossland Mews WA13 . . . 18 C4
Crosslands
Congleton CW12 . . . 157 A1
Haslington CW1 . . . 191 D4
Crossland Terr WA6 . . . 73 B2
CROSS LANE . . . 172 D6
Cross Lanes CH3 . . . 144 C8
Cross Lane S WA3 . . . 9 E6
Cross La W M31 . . . 11 F2
Crossledge CW12 . . . 156 B3
Crossley Ave CH66 . . . 69 E6
Crossley Cres CH2 . . . 119 B5
Crossley Dr CH60 . . . 40 D8
Crossley Pk WA6 . . . 99 C7
Crossley St WA1 . . . 16 C5
Cross o' th' Hill SY14 . . . 213 D4
Cross O' Th' Hill Rd SY14 . . . 214 A4
Cross Rd
Gatley SK8 . . . 34 B7
Haslington CW1 . . . 191 D4
Cross St
Alsager ST7 . . . 193 C3
Barnton CW8 . . . 78 B3
Chester CH2 . . . 118 F2
Congleton CW12 . . . 156 D3
Crewe CW1 . . . 190 D3
Golborne WA3 . . . 3 A7
Haslington CW1 . . . 191 D4
Holt LL13 . . . 196 E8
Cross St *continued*
Macclesfield SK11 . . . 112 E6
Marston CW9 . . . 79 C3
Neston CH64 . . . 66 E8
New Mills SK22 . . . 39 C8
20 Runcorn WA7 . . . 23 A3
Warrington WA2 . . . 16 B7
Widnes WA8 . . . 13 C1
Cross The
Holt LL13 . . . 196 E8
Kingsley WA6 . . . 75 C2
Lymm WA13 . . . 18 E3
8 Neston CH64 . . . 66 E8
CROSS TOWN . . . 57 B2
Crossway
Bramhall SK7 . . . 35 E5
Crewe CW1 . . . 190 D6
Widnes WA8 . . . 22 D8
Crossways ST8 . . . 179 E1
Crossways Rd ST7 . . . 194 A4
Crossway The CH63 . . . 42 C4
Cross Wood St 2 CW5 . . . 204 D5
Crosthwaite Ave CH62 . . . 43 F4
Croston Cl
Alderley Edge SK9 . . . 60 C1
Widnes WA8 . . . 12 C3
Crotia Ave CW2 . . . 207 B5
Crouch La CW12 . . . 157 D4
Crouchley Hall Mews WA13 . . . 18 F1
Crouchley La WA13 . . . 18 F1
CROUGHTON . . . 95 F5
Croughton Ct CH66 . . . 69 F8
Croughton Rd
Ellesmere Port CH66 . . . 69 F8
Stoak CH2 . . . 96 A7
Stoak, Croughton CH2 . . . 95 F6
Crowbrook Gr 7 SK9 . . . 34 D1
Crowder's La CW9 . . . 105 B4
Crowe Ave WA2 . . . 8 B2
Crowland Gdns SK8 . . . 35 B6
Crow Lane E WA12 . . . 2 C4
Crow Lane W WA12 . . . 2 A4
Crowley La CW9, WA16 . . . 28 A3
Crowmere Cl CW8 . . . 102 A2
Crown Ave WA8 . . . 22 B8
Crown Bank
3 Sandbach CW11 . . . 175 B6
Talke ST7 . . . 210 D6
Crown Bank Cres ST7 . . . 210 D6
Crown Bldgs WA6 . . . 73 B1
Crown Cotts CW8 . . . 124 A7
Crown Ctr The 24 SK11 . . . 112 C8
Crown Ctyd CW3 . . . 229 F4
Crown Dr CW11 . . . 175 D3
Crownest La CW9 . . . 78 E8
Crown Fields Cl WA12 . . . 2 B5
Crown Gate WA7 . . . 49 F7
Crown Gdns
Newton-le-W WA12 . . . 2 B4
Talke ST7 . . . 210 D6
Crown Gn WA13 . . . 19 B4
Crown La WA16 . . . 106 D8
Crown Mews CW3 . . . 229 F4
Crown Park Dr WA12 . . . 2 B5
Crown St W SK11 . . . 112 C7
Crown St
Newton-le-W WA12 . . . 2 A3
8 Northwich CW8 . . . 103 F8
2 Warrington WA1 . . . 16 B5
Crow's Nest Cotts CH3 . . . 166 C6
CROWTON . . . 76 C1
Crowton Cotts CW7 . . . 170 F4
CROW WOOD . . . 13 D3
Crow Wood La WA8 . . . 13 D2
Crow Wood Pl WA8 . . . 13 D3
Croxton Gn SY14 . . . 201 C6
CROXTON GREEN . . . 201 C6
Croxton La CW10 . . . 128 A4
Croxton Way CW8 . . . 103 A4
Croyde Cl M22 . . . 33 F7
Croyde Rd L24 . . . 21 A3
Crum Hill 2 CW9 . . . 104 A8
Cryers La
Elton CH2 . . . 72 A2
Thornton-le-M CH2 . . . 96 F8
Cty High Sch Leftwich The CW9 . . . 104 A4
Cuckoo Clock Mus★ WA16 . . . 80 F8
Cuckoo La
Acton CW5 . . . 203 E8
Neston CH64 . . . 67 C7
CUCKOO'S NEST . . . 162 E5
Cuckstoolpit Hill SK10 . . . 112 E8
CUDDINGTON . . . 101 F4
CUDDINGTON GREEN . . . 212 B1
CUDDINGTON HEATH . . . 212 E2
Cuddington La
Cuddington CW8 . . . 101 D4
Sandiway CW8 . . . 102 A6
Cuddington Prim Sch CW8 . . . 101 F2
Cuddington Sta CW8 . . . 102 A4
Cuddington Way 7 SK9 . . . 34 D5
CUERDLEY CROSS . . . 13 A2
Cuerdley Gn WA5 . . . 14 A2
Cuerdley Rd WA5 . . . 14 C3
Cuerdon Dr WA4 . . . 17 D1
Culbin Cl WA3 . . . 10 A6

CULCHETH 4 E3
Culcheth Com Prim Sch WA3 5 A3
Culcheth Hall Dr WA3 4 F4
Culcheth Hall Farm Barns WA3 4 F4
Culcheth High Sch WA3 5 A3
Culford Cl WA7 24 D1
Culland St CW2 190 C2
Cullen Cl CH63 43 C4
Cullen Rd WA7 48 D7
Cumber Cl SK9 59 D4
Cumber Dr SK9 59 D4
Cumber La SK9 59 D4
Cumberland Ave
Irlam M44 11 C5
Nantwich CW5 204 F6
Cumberland Cl
Crewe CW1 190 D5
Talke ST7 210 E7
Cumberland Cres WA11 1 A6
Cumberland Dr
Altrincham WA14 31 B8
Bollington SK10 88 B8
Cumberland Gr CH66 69 C3
Cumberland Rd
Congleton CW12 156 A3
Partington M31 11 E2
Cumberland St
2 Macclesfield SK10 112 D8
Warrington WA4 16 C3
Cumbermere Dr CW11 174 E7
Cumbers Dr CH64 67 A5
Cumbers La CH64 67 A5
Cumbrae Dr 4 CH65 70 C1
Cumbria Cl 2 CH66 69 E1
Cundiff Cl SK11 112 E6
Cunliffe Ave WA12 2 B5
Cunliffe Cl WA7 50 A7
Cunningham Cl WA5 14 F5
Cunningham Dr
Bebington CH63 43 C7
Gatley M22 34 A8
Runcorn WA7 22 E1
Cunningham Ho WA7 48 E8
Cunningham Rd WA8 22 D8
Cuppin St CH1 237 A2
Curlender Way L24 21 E2
Curlew Cl
Golborne WA3 3 D8
Macclesfield SK10 87 C5
Winsford CW7 149 C5
Curlew Gr WA3 9 E3
Curlew Rd ST7 195 E1
Currans Rd WA2 8 B2
Curzon Ave ST7 193 D5
Curzon Cl CH4 141 B8
Curzon Ct CH4 140 F7
Curzon Dr WA4 27 A7
Curzon Gr CW7 126 F1
Curzon Mews SK9 60 A5
CURZON PARK 141 B7
Curzon Pk N CH4 141 B7
Curzon Pk S CH4 141 B7
Curzon Rd
Gatley SK8 34 B7
Poynton SK12 36 E2
Curzon St
Chester CH4 140 F7
5 Runcorn WA7 22 F1
Cwat Erwain CH4 140 E7
Cwrt Cwellyn CH5 139 B7
Cwrt Dinas CH5 139 B7
Cwrt Ogwen CH5 139 B7
Cygnet Cl CH66 69 D4
Cygnet Ct WA1 16 A3
Cyman Cl CH1 117 D3
Cynthia Ave WA1 17 B7
Cynthia Rd WA7 22 F1
Cypress Ave
Ellesmere Port CH66 69 F1
Widnes WA8 13 B2
Cypress Cl WA1 17 E7
Cypress Gr WA7 49 C7
Cypress Mews CW8 102 E7
Cypress Way SK6 38 A7
Cyril Bell Cl WA13 18 F3
Cyril St WA2 16 B7

D

Daffodil Cl WA8 13 E4
Daffodil Gdns WA9 6 A7
Dagfields Crafts & Antiques Ctr★ CW5 220 A4
Dagnall Ave WA5 7 F2
Dahlia Cl WA9 6 A7
Daintry St SK11 112 E7
Daintry Terr SK10 112 E8
Dairy Bank CH2 72 B4
Dairybrook Gr 7 SK9 34 E1
Dairy Farm Cl WA13 18 F4
Dairyground Rd SK7 35 F7
Dairy House La SK7 35 B4
Dairy House Rd SK7 35 B5
Dairy House Small Holdings SK7 35 B4
Dairy House Way CW2 189 F2
Dairy La CW5 188 D6
Dairylands Rd ST7 193 F4
Daisy Ave WA12 2 C2
Daisy Bank
Alsager ST7 193 A4
Nantwich CW5 204 D5
Daisy Bank Cres CW3 229 F5
Daisybank Dr
Congleton CW12 156 D4
Sandbach CW11 175 C6
Daisy Bank La CW9 78 C3
Daisy Bank Mill Cl WA3 4 E3
Daisy Bank Rd
Lymm WA13 18 C3
Warrington WA5 14 F4
Daisy Cl WA16 79 F6
Daisy Way SK6 37 F7
Dakota Dr WA5 15 C7
Dalby Cl WA3 10 B5
Dalby Ct CW9 104 E5
Dale Ave
Bebington CH62 43 D8
Bramhall SK7 35 F8
Ellesmere Port CH66 69 C6
Dale Cl
Warrington WA5 15 D4
Widnes WA8 22 A8
Dale Cres CW12 156 F2
Dalecroft WA6 72 E1
Dale Ct
Heswall CH60 40 F8
Middlewich CW10 151 D7
Dale Dr
Chester CH2 118 D8
Ellesmere Port CH65 69 F5
Daleford Manor CW8 125 B8
Daleford Manor Cvn Pk CW8 125 A8
Dalefords La
Cuddington CW8 102 A1
Whitegate CW8 125 D7
Dale Gdns CH65 70 B3
Dale Gr
Congleton CW12 157 A2
Irlam M44 11 E6
Dale Head Rd SK10 86 F4
Dale Hey CH66 43 E2
Dale House Fold SK12 37 A4
Dale La WA4 26 E7
Dale Pl CW12 156 F2
Dale Rd
Bebington CH62 43 D6
Golborne WA3 3 A7
New Mills SK22 39 C7
Dalesford Cl WN7 4 C8
Dalesford Cres SK10 111 E8
DALES GREEN 195 C5
Dales Green Rd ST7 195 C5
Daleside CH2 118 D8
Dale's Sq CW9 103 F6
Dale St
Chester CH3 119 A1
Macclesfield SK10 112 E8
Runcorn WA7 23 A1
Dalesway CH60 40 E8
Dale The
Neston CH64 66 E6
Tiverton CW6 168 C6
Warrington WA5 14 F5
Dale View
Kidsgrove ST7 195 C5
Newton-le-W WA12 2 E4
Dale Way CW1 190 A5
Dalewood Cl WA2 16 A6
Dalewood Cres CH2 72 A3
DALLAM 7 F2
Dallam Com Prim Sch WA5 7 F1
Dallam La WA2 16 A7
Dalmahoy Cl CW7 126 C2
Dalston Dr SK7 35 C5
Dalton Ave
Warrington, Birchwood WA3 9 E6
Warrington WA5 15 F7
Dalton Bank WA1 16 C6
Dalton Cl CH1 117 E3
Dalton Ct
Runcorn WA7 23 E3
Sandbach CW11 174 E7
Dalton St
Runcorn WA7 23 D2
Warrington WA3 9 E5
Dalton Way CW10 128 D1
Dalwood Cl WA7 50 E7
Dame Hollow SK8 34 D7
Damery Ct SK7 35 E8
Damery Rd SK7 35 E8
Damhead La CH64 67 E7
Dam Head La WA3 11 A5
Damian Dr WA12 2 A5
Dam La
Hollinfare WA3 11 A4
Mobberley WA16 58 C3
Warrington WA1 17 D7
Winwick WA3 8 F7
Dams La WA16 106 D5
Damson La WA16 58 C3
Damson Wlk M31 11 D3
Danby Cl
Runcorn WA7 49 D6
Warrington WA5 15 E7
Dane Ave M31 11 F4
DANEBANK 38 E5
Dane Bank Ave
Congleton CW12 156 E4
Crewe CW2 190 A2
Dane Bank Dr SK12 38 D6
Dane Bank Rd
Lymm WA13 18 E4
Northwich CW9 104 B7
Dane Bank Rd E WA13 18 E4
Dane Cl
Alsager ST7 193 A3
Chester CH4 140 F5
Dane Cl *continued*
Sandbach CW11 174 E7
Dane Dr
Biddulph ST8 179 E1
Wilmslow SK9 60 D6
Danefield Ct SK8 34 D8
Danefield Rd
Holmes Chapel CW4 130 C4
Northwich CW9 104 B7
Dane Gdns ST7 195 C2
Dane Gr CH2 119 F8
Dane Hill Cl SK12 38 D5
DANE IN SHAW 179 C8
Dane Mill Bsns Ctr CW12 156 C3
Dane Pl
Crewe CW1 190 D6
Winsford CW7 127 B1
Danescroft WA8 12 B3
Daneside Bsns Pk CW12 156 E4
Daneside County Pk CW12 155 B7
Danes Sq SK11 112 D5
Dane St
Congleton CW12 156 C3
Middlewich CW10 128 D2
Northwich CW9 103 F8
Daneswell Rd L24 21 A2
Daniel Adamson Ave M31 11 D3
Daniel Cl WA3 10 A4
Daniel Ct M31 11 F4
Daniell Way CH3 142 A7
Danily Ct SY14 213 B3
Dan's Rd WA8 13 E2
Dappleheath Rd CW2 190 A1
Darby Cl CH64 66 E4
D'Arcy Cotts CH63 42 B6
Darent Rd WA11 1 B7
DARESBURY 25 B2
Daresbury Cl
Holmes Chapel CW4 130 A3
4 Wilmslow SK9 60 C8
Daresbury Ct WA8 13 E3
DARESBURY DELPH 25 B1
Daresbury Expressway
Daresbury WA4 25 A3
Runcorn WA7 23 C2
Daresbury La WA4 25 D2
Daresbury Pk WA4 51 A8
Daresbury Prim Sch WA4 25 B2
Darian Ave M22 33 D8
Dario Gradi Dr CW2 190 D1
Dark Ark La CH3, WA6 99 B3
Darkie Mdw CW6 185 E8
Dark La
Henbury SK11 111 B8
Higher Whitley WA4 52 D6
Kingsley WA6 75 B1
Marston CW9 79 C6
Tattenhall CH3 183 E7
Warren SK11 111 C3
Whitchurch SY13 227 B1
Darland La LL12 162 C1
Darley Ave
Crewe CW2 190 A3
Warrington WA2 8 E3
Darley Cl WA8 12 B3
Darleydale Dr CH62 43 F5
Darley Rd SK7 36 F7
Darlington Ave CW1 189 F5
Darlington Cres CH1 94 A1
Darlington Ct 3 WA8 23 A7
Darlington St CW10 128 C1
Darnaway Cl WA3 10 B6
DARNHALL 149 A3
Darnhall Prim Sch CW7 149 D6
Darnhall School La CW7 149 C6
Dart Cl
Alsager ST7 193 A4
Biddulph ST8 179 D1
Dartnall Cl SK12 38 A6
Dart Wlk CW7 127 B2
Darwen Gdns WA2 8 E1
Darwin Gr SK7 35 E6
Darwin Rd CH1 117 C4
Darwin St CW8 103 E7
Daryl Rd CH60 41 A8
Dashwood Cl WA4 27 A7
Daten Ave WA3 9 E6
Daten Pk WA3 9 F6
Dauncey Cl CH2 95 C1
Davehall Ave SK9 60 A7
DAVENHAM 104 A2
Davenham Ave WA1 16 E8
Davenham CE Prim Sch CW9 103 F2
Davenham Cres CW2 190 A3
Davenham Ct CW9 104 A3
Davenham Mdws CW9 103 E3
Davenham Rd
Davenham CW9 104 E3
Handforth SK9 34 D4
Davenham Rdbt CW9 103 F3
Davenham Way CW10 151 D5
DAVENPORT 154 E7
Davenport Ave
Crewe CW2 206 D8
Nantwich CW5 204 E7
Warrington WA4 16 F5
Wilmslow SK9 59 E4
Davenport Cl CW11 175 D8
DAVENPORT GREEN 59 F3
Davenport La
Brereton Green CW11 154 C2
Marton SK11 132 F5
Mobberley WA16 58 D6
Davenport Park La CW12 131 D2
Davenport Rd CH60 40 E7
Davenport Row WA7 49 D8
Davenport St
Congleton CW12 156 C2
Crewe CW1 190 C6
Macclesfield SK10 112 E8
Daven Prim Sch CW12 156 E2
Daven Rd CW12 156 F1
Davey La SK9 60 B2
Daveylands SK9 60 D7
David Lewis Sch SK9 83 F6
David Rd WA13 18 C3
David's Ave WA5 15 B5
Davidson Ave CW12 157 A5
David St CW8 103 E7
Davies Ave
Gatley SK8 34 B6
Newton-le-W WA12 2 C4
Warrington WA4 16 F4
Davies Cl WA8 23 A4
Davies St SK10 112 E8
Davies Way WA13 18 E3
Davis Cl ST7 193 E3
Davy Ave WA3 9 E5
Davy Rd WA7 23 E3
Dawlish Ave SK8 34 F7
Dawlish Cl
Bramhall SK7 35 E7
Hollinfare WA3 11 B3
Dawn Cl CH64 67 A5
Dawn Gdns CH65 70 B4
Dawpool Cl CH2 118 D5
Dawpool Ct CH2 118 D5
Dawpool Dr CH62 43 C7
Dawson Cl 11 SK11 111 F7
Dawson Dr CH2 237 A4
Dawson Rd
Bollington SK10 88 A7
Gatley SK8 34 D8
Macclesfield SK11 111 F7
Dawstone Ct CH60 40 F8
Dawstone Rd CH60 41 A7
Dawstone Rise CH60 40 F7
DAY GREEN 192 F8
Deacon Rd WA8 13 B1
Deacons Cl WA3 9 A8
Deacon Trad Est WA12 2 A2
Deadman's La CW5 205 B2
Deakin's Rd
Winsford CW7 126 F4
Winsford, Wharton Green CW7 127 A4
Dean Bank CW6 168 C3
Dean Cl
Bollington SK10 88 A7
Handforth SK9 34 C1
Partington M31 11 F4
Sandbach CW11 174 E8
7 Widnes WA8 23 B8
Dean Cres WA2 8 B2
Dean Ct
Bollington SK10 88 B8
Golborne WA3 3 A7
Dean Dr SK9 34 D2
Deane Ct CW5 205 B4
Deanery Cl CH2 118 C4
Deangate CW2 207 E3
Dean Hollow ST7 209 D2
Dean La SK7 36 E8
Dean Mdw WA12 2 C4
Dean Pk SY14 214 A5
Dean Rd
Golborne WA3 3 A7
Handforth SK9 34 E3
Irlam M44 11 E6
DEAN ROW 60 F8
Dean Row Ct 9 SK9 34 D1
Dean Row Jun Sch SK9 34 E1
Dean Row Rd SK9 61 A8
Deans Cl
Chester CH2 118 D6
Tarvin CH3 121 B1
Deansfield Way CH2 72 A3
Deansgate CH65 70 A5
DEANSGREEN 29 A8
Deansgreen Ct WA13 29 A7
Deans La
Sandbach CW11 174 E6
Warrington WA4 17 F3
Dean's La
Barthomley CW2 208 C4
Newcastle-u-Lyme ST5 210 D2
Deans Rd CH65 70 F3
Dean St
Middlewich CW10 128 C2
Northwich CW9 104 C8
Widnes WA8 23 B8
Winsford CW7 126 D1
Deansway WA8 22 C8
Deans Way
Higher Kinnerton CH4 161 A7
Tarvin CH3 121 B2
Dean Valley Com Prim Sch SK10 87 E8
Dean View ST7 209 D1
Deanwater Cl WA3 9 D4
Deanwater Ct SK8 34 D7
Deanway SK9 34 C1
Deanway Trad Est SK9 34 D3
Dearnford Ave CH62 43 D6
Dearnford Cl CH62 43 D6
Debra Cl CH66 69 C4
Debra Rd CH66 69 C4
Decade Cl ST5 210 F2
Dee Banks
Chester CH3 142 A8
Huntington CH3 141 F7
Dee Banks Sch CH3 142 A7
Dee Cl
Biddulph ST8 179 E1
Sandbach CW11 174 E8
Talke ST7 210 E7
Dee Cres CH3 180 E2
Deefords CH3 118 F1
Dee Fords Ave CH3 119 A1
Dee Hills Pk CH3 237 C2
Dee La
Chester CH1, CH3 237 C2
Holt LL13 196 D7
Dee Mdws LL13 196 D7
Dee Park Cl CH60 41 B6
Dee Park Rd CH60 41 B5
Deepdale WA8 12 C3
Deep Dale WA5 14 F6
Dee Pk LL13 196 D8
Dee Point Prim Sch CH1 117 D3
Dee Rd CH2 96 F1
Deer Park Ct WA7 49 F6
Deerwood Cl
Ellesmere Port CH66 69 D7
Macclesfield SK10 86 F1
Deerwood Cres CH66 69 D7
Deeside
Ellesmere Port CH65 70 B2
Holt LL13 196 E8
Dee Side CH60 40 C8
Deeside Cl CH65 70 B2
Deeside Coll/Coleg Glannau Dyfrdwy CH5 91 B1
Deeside Cres CH1 116 E5
Deeside Ct
Chester CH3 237 C2
Neston CH64 41 B1
Deeside Ind Pk/Parc Ddiwydiannol Glannau Dyfrdwy CH5 92 E2
Deeside La CH1 116 D4
Dee Sq CW7 127 B2
Dee View CH3 180 E2
Dee View Cotts CH64 41 D1
Dee View Ct CH64 66 E6
Dee View Rd
Connah's Quay CH5 91 E1
Heswall CH60 40 F8
Dee Villas LL13 180 E1
Dee Way CW7 127 A2
Deirdre Ave WA8 13 A1
De Lacy Row WA7 24 A2
Delafield Cl WA2 8 F3
Delaisy Way CW7 127 A1
Delamare Pl 1 WA7 22 F1
DELAMERE 123 D6
Delamere Ave
Bebington CH62 43 E4
Ellesmere Port CH66 69 E5
Golborne WA3 3 E6
Widnes WA8 12 C1
Delamere CE Prim Sch CW6 123 C5
Delamere Cl
Barnton CW8 78 A3
Bebington CH62 43 E4
Chorlton CW2 207 E4
Sandbach CW11 174 F8
Delamere Ct
Alsager ST7 192 F4
Bebington CH62 43 E4
7 Crewe CW1 190 C4
Delamere Dr
Ellesmere Port CH66 69 E5
Macclesfield SK10 87 F2
Delamere Forest Sch WA6 100 C4
Delamere Forest Trail★ WA6 100 A4
Delamere Forest Visitor Ctr★ CW8 100 B2
Delamere Gn CH66 69 E5
Delamere Gr CW8 123 D7
Delamere Ho WA6 74 C7
Delamere La CH3 99 B2
DELAMERE PARK 101 C5
Delamere Park Way E CW8 101 D5
Delamere Park Way W CW8 101 D5
Delamere Rd
Congleton CW12 155 F3
Handforth SK9 34 E4
Nantwich CW5 204 F3
Norley WA6 100 B6
Delamere Rise CW7 126 B1
Delamere St
Chester CH1 237 A3
Crewe CW1 190 C4
Warrington WA5 15 E5
Winsford CW7 126 B1
Delamere Sta CW8 100 D1
Delamore's Acre CH64 68 A8
Delavor Cl CH60 40 E8
Delavor Rd CH60 40 E8

Delenty Dr WA3 9 E4
Delery Dr WA1 16 E8
Delfur Rd SK7 35 F7
Delhi Rd M44 11 F8
Dell Cl CH63 43 B6
Dell Dr WA2 9 A2
Dell La CH60 41 B7
Dell The
Cuddington CW8 101 D5
Guilden Sutton CH3 119 F5
Kelsall CW6 122 D5
Delmar Rd WA16 57 C1
Delphfields Rd WA4 26 C7
Delphield WA7 50 D8
Delph La
Daresbury WA4 25 A2
Warrington, Houghton Gn WA2 8 E6
Winwick WA2 8 A5
Delphside ST7 209 F2
Delta Cres WA5 7 C2
Delta Ct CH4 140 B6
Delves Ave WA5 15 F7
Delves Broughton Ct CW1 191 D5
Delves Cl CW2 206 B4
Delves Wlk CH3 142 B7
Delvine Dr CH2 118 D6
Demage Dr CH66 69 D3
Demage La
Backford CH1 94 F4
Chester CH2 118 D8
Demage La S CH2 118 D7
Denbigh Cl
Hazel Grove SK7 36 C8
Helsby WA6 73 A1
Denbigh Cres CW10 151 C7
Denbigh Ct CH65 70 D3
Denbigh Dr CW7 149 B7
Denbigh Gdns CH65 70 C3
Denbigh St CH1 118 B3
Denbury Ave WA4 16 F2
Dene Ave WA12 1 F4
Dene Dr CW7 149 D8
Denehurst Cl WA5 14 F4
Denehurst Park Way CW8 101 D5
Denesgate [1] CW7 149 D8
Deneside Ave CW1 190 C6
Deneway
Bramhall SK7 35 D7
High Lane SK6 37 F8
Denewood Ct [3] SK9 60 A6
Denford Cl CH4 139 C4
Denford Pl ST7 193 D6
Denhall Cl CH2 118 E5
Denhall La CH64 67 A3
Denham Ave WA5 15 B5
Denham Dr SK7 36 D8
Denise Ave WA5 14 E5
Denison Rd SK7 36 E8
Den La CW3, CW5 221 D4
Dennett Cl WA1 17 E6
Dennis Dr CH4 141 B6
Dennison Rd SK8 35 B8
Dennis Rd WA8 23 C7
Dennis Round Ct ST7 193 C3
Densham Ave WA2 8 B2
Denston Cl CW2 190 B1
Denstone Dr CH4 141 A4
Dentdale Wlk M22 33 C8
Dentith Dr CH1 117 E5
Denton Cl CW7 126 C1
Denton Dr CW9 79 C1
Denton Drive Ind Est CW9 79 C2
Denton St WA8 13 C1
Denver Ave CW2 190 B3
Denver Dr WA5 15 B7
Denver Rd WA4 17 A3
Denwall Ho [5] CH64 66 E8
Depenbech Cl SY14 213 B4
Depmore La WA6 75 A2
Derby Cl
Irlam M44 11 C5
Newton-le-W WA12 2 B3
Derby Dr WA1 16 F7
Derby Knoll SK23 39 F1
Derby Rd
Golborne WA3 3 C8
Talke ST7 210 D7
[4] Warrington WA4 16 C1
Widnes, Barrow's Green WA8 13 D4
Widnes, Lunts Heath WA8 13 B4
Derby Row WA12 7 D8
DERBYSHIRE HILL 1 A2
Derbyshire Hill Rd WA9 1 A2
Derbyshire Rd
Partington M31 11 E2
Poynton SK12 37 D5
Derby St
Congleton CW12 156 D3
Crewe CW1 190 B5
Newton-le-W WA12 2 B3
Dereham Way WA7 24 D3
Derek Ave WA2 8 E1
Derfel Terr [4] WA6 74 B8
Derrington Ave CW2 190 C3
Derwen Prim Sch CH4 161 A7
Derwent Ave CW7 127 B1
Derwent Cl
Alsager ST7 193 A4

Derwent Cl *continued*
Culcheth WA3 5 A2
Holmes Chapel CW4 130 A3
Macclesfield SK11 112 A6
Partington M31 11 F4
Willaston CW5 205 D6
Derwent Cres ST7 195 C2
Derwent Dr
Biddulph ST8 179 E1
Bramhall SK7 35 C5
Congleton CW12 156 F1
Handforth SK9 34 C5
Hooton CH66 44 B2
Derwent Rd
Chester CH2 119 A5
High Lane SK6 37 E8
Warrington WA4 16 B2
Widnes WA8 12 C1
Derwent Way
Alderley Edge SK9 83 F7
Neston CH64 66 F7
Desoto Rd WA8 22 E5
Desoto Rd E WA8 22 F6
Desoto Rd W WA8 22 F6
De Trafford Mews [9] SK9 34 D2
Deva Ave CH4 140 D6
Deva Bsns Pk CH5 116 A8
Deva Cl SK12 36 B4
Deva Ct CH2 118 F2
Deva Hts CH3 141 F7
Deva La CH2 118 C6
Deva Link CH1 118 B3
Deva Rd CW2 189 D4
Deva Ret Pk CH1 118 A3
Deva Roman Experience Mus★ CH1 237 B2
Deva Stad (Chester City FC) CH1 117 E1
Deva Terr CH3 237 C2
Devon Cl
Macclesfield SK10 86 F2
Middlewich CW10 128 D2
Devon Gr ST8 179 C1
Devon Pl
Congleton CW12 156 E4
Widnes WA8 13 B3
Devon Rd
Chester CH2 118 F5
Irlam M44 11 D5
Partington M31 11 E2
Devonshire Dr SK9 60 B2
Devonshire Gdns WA12 2 C2
Devonshire Pl CH4 141 E7
Devonshire Rd
Broughton CH4 139 C4
Hazel Grove SK7 36 F8
Warrington WA1 16 F8
Dewar Ct WA7 23 E3
Dewar St WA3 9 E5
Dewes St CW1 190 B5
Dewhurst Rd WA3 9 D2
Dexter Way CW10 128 D2
Dial Cotts CH64 67 A5
Dial La CW12, SK11 158 B1
Dial Rd WA15 32 C8
Dial St WA1 16 C5
Diamond Ave [3] ST7 195 B2
Dibbinsdale Rd CH63 43 B7
Dibbins Gn CH63 43 B7
Dickens Cl
Cheadle SK8 35 B5
Sandbach CW11 174 D6
Dickens La SK12 36 E2
Dickenson Ho CW10 128 C1
Dickenson St WA2 16 C7
Dickinson Cl WA11 1 A6
Dickinson Way ST7 193 A3
Dicklow Cob SK11 132 A8
Dickson Cl WA8 23 B8
Dicksons Dr CH2 118 D4
Dickson St
Widnes, Kingsway WA8 23 A8
[2] Widnes WA8 23 B8
Dierden St CW7 127 B1
Dierdens Terr [4] CW10 128 C1
Dig La
Acton CW5 203 F4
Frodsham WA6 74 A7
Shavington CW5 206 B2
Warrington WA2 9 B3
Diglake Cl ST7 210 C6
Diglake Cotts ST7 210 A2
Diglake St ST7 209 F3
Diglee Rd SK23 39 C3
Dillors Croft CW1 173 A1
Dimelow Ct SY14 213 A2
Dinas Cl CH1 117 D3
Dingle Ave
Newton-le-W WA12 1 F2
Row-of-Trees SK9 59 D3
Dingle Bank
Chester CH4 141 C7
Sandbach CW11 175 C6
Dingle Bank Cl WA13 18 E3
Dinglebrook Gr [5] SK9 34 D1
Dingle Cl SK10 87 B3
Dingle La
Bridgemere CW5 231 F6
Kelsall CW6 122 E6
Sandbach CW11 175 C6
Warrington WA4 26 F6
Winsford CW7 126 E1
Dingle Prim Sch The CW1 191 D6

Dingle The
Barnton CW8 78 B4
Haslington CW1 191 D5
Lymm WA13 18 E3
Dingleway WA4 26 D8
Dingle Way CW8 101 E5
Dingle Wlk [4] CW7 126 D1
Dinnington Ct WA8 12 E3
Diploma Dr CW10 128 C2
Dipping Brook Ave WA4 26 F4
DISLEY 38 C5
Disley Prim Sch SK12 38 D6
Disley Sta SK12 38 C6
Distaff Rd SK12 36 B4
District CE Prim Sch The WA12 2 A4
Ditchfield La WA16 29 D3
Ditchfield Pl WA8 22 B8
Ditchfield Rd
Warrington WA5 14 E3
Widnes WA8 22 B8
DITTON 22 C8
Ditton CE Prim Sch WA8 12 A1
Ditton Prim Sch WA8 12 E1
Ditton Rd WA8 22 D6
Dixon Ave WA12 2 C5
Dixon Cl WA11 2 A8
Dixon Ct SK11 84 A2
Dixon Dr SK11 84 B3
Dixon Rd CW12 157 A5
Dixon's Hos CH3 142 E8
Dixon St
Irlam M44 11 F8
Warrington WA1 16 A5
Dobb Hedge Cl WA15 32 C6
Dobell's Rd CW9 103 F5
Dobers La WA6 74 C4
Dobson Ct SY14 213 B3
Dock Rd
Northwich CW9 103 F7
Widnes WA8 22 F5
Widnes WA8 23 A5
Dock Road Edwardian Pumping Station The★ CW9 103 F7
Dock St
Ellesmere Port CH65 70 C7
Widnes WA8 23 A5
Dock Yard Rd CH65 70 E6
Doddington Dr CW11 175 C8
Doddington Rd CW2 190 A3
Doddlespool Barns CW3 221 F7
Dodd's Green La CW5, SY13 228 C4
Dodds La CW12 178 C6
Dodd's La SY13, SY14 224 E7
Doddswood Dr [2] CW12 156 F4
Dodgsley Dr WA6 75 C1
DODLESTON 162 B7
Dodleston CE Prim Sch CH4 162 A7
Dodleston La CH4 162 C3
Doeford Cl WA3 4 E5
Doe's Meadow Rd CH63 43 B7
Dog La
Brereton Green CW4, CW11 153 E7
Kelsall CW6 122 B5
Nantwich CW5 204 E6
Tattenhall CH3 182 D4
Threapwood SY14 223 C7
Dogmore La CW6 147 C4
Dolly La SK23 39 F3
Dolmans La [9] WA1 16 B5
Dolphin Cres CH66 69 E2
Dolphin Ct CH4 141 A7
Dombey Rd SK12 36 D2
Domestic App M90 33 C6
Domville Cl WA13 18 E3
Donagh Cl SK10 86 F2
DONES GREEN 77 B8
Donkey La SK9 60 A5
Donne Pl CH1 117 F6
Donnington Way CH4 140 F7
Don Wlk CH65 70 A7
Dood's La WA4 27 A5
Dooley's Grig SK11 108 F1
Dooley's La SK9 33 C2
Dorac Ave SK8 34 C7
Dorchester Cl
Kidsgrove ST7 195 A3
Wilmslow SK9 60 D8
Dorchester Pk WA7 24 E3
Dorchester Rd
Chester CH4 140 F5
Warrington WA5 15 C5
Dorchester Way
Burtonwood WA5 6 F6
Macclesfield SK10 87 C4
Doreen Ave CW12 179 B8
Dorfold Cl CW11 175 C7
Dorfold Dr CW5 204 D5
Dorfold Hall★ CW5 204 B5
Dorfold St CW1 190 C4
Dorfold Way CH2 118 E6
Doric Ave WA6 74 D7
Dorin Park Sch CH2 118 D6
Dormer Cl CH3 143 A5
Dorney Cl WA4 26 E6
Dornoch Ct CW4 130 B2
Dorothea St WA2 16 C7
Dorric Way CW1 190 C7
Dorrington Cl WA7 50 E8

Dorrit Cl SK12 36 E2
Dorset Cl CW12 156 E4
Dorset Dr ST8 179 C1
Dorset Gdns WA7 50 A6
Dorset Pl
Chester CH2 119 A5
Kidsgrove ST7 195 A2
Dorset Rd
Chester CH2 118 F7
Irlam M44 11 D5
Dorset Way WA1 17 B8
Dorset Wlk SK10 86 F2
Douglas Ave WA9 6 B6
Douglas Cl
Northwich CW8 103 C5
Widnes WA8 13 F3
Douglas La CW7 171 A6
Douglas Pl CH4 140 E6
Doulton Cl CW7 126 F3
Doune Ct CH65 70 D3
Dounrey Cl WA2 9 A2
DOVE BANK 195 A2
Dove Bank Prim Sch ST7 195 A2
Dove Cl
Ellesmere Port CH66 70 A8
Elton CH2 72 C4
Helsby WA6 73 C5
Sandbach CW11 175 A8
Warrington WA3 9 F4
Dovecote Cl CW2 206 B8
Dovecote Dr WA11 1 C7
Dovecote Gn WA5 7 A1
Dovedale Ave CH62 43 E5
Dovedale Cl
Congleton CW12 157 A4
High Lane SK6 37 E7
Warrington WA2 8 E3
Dovedale Ct WA8 12 B3
Dove Gr ST8 179 D1
Dove Ho ST7 195 C3
Dove Pl CW7 127 B2
Dover Cl WA7 50 E6
Dover Ct CH65 70 D2
Dover Ct WA4 16 F3
Dover Dr
Ellesmere Port CH65 70 D2
Winsford CW7 149 B6
Dover Rd
Chester CH4 141 A6
Macclesfield SK10 87 F2
Warrington WA4 17 A3
Dover St WA7 23 B3
Dovesmead Rd CH60 41 C7
Doward St WA8 13 C2
Downes Cl SK10 87 A1
Downesway SK9 59 F1
Downham Ave WA3 4 F2
Downham Ct [1] CH60 41 A8
Downham Dr CH60 41 A8
Downham Pl CH1 117 E4
Downham Road S CH60 41 A8
Downing Cl SK11 112 F3
Downs End WA16 57 C1
Downsfield Rd CH4 141 A6
Downside WA8 12 B3
Downs Rd WA7 23 A1
Downs The CW8 101 D5
Downswood Ct CH2 118 C4
Downswood Dr CH2 118 C4
Downway La WA9 1 A1
Dragon's La
Middlewich CW11 151 F1
Sandbach CW11 152 B1
Dragons Wharf CW11 152 C1
Dragon Yd WA8 13 B4
Drake Ave M44 11 E6
Drake Cl WA5 7 D1
Drake La CW5 203 F4
Drakelow La CW10 128 F8
Drake Rd CH64 41 E1
Drakes Way SY14 213 B5
Draycott Dr ST5 210 D2
Drayton Cl
[12] Handforth SK9 34 D1
Runcorn WA7 22 F1
Drayton Cres CW1 190 F5
Drayton Dr SK8 34 B7
Drenfell Rd ST7 194 F7
Drift Cotts LL12 162 C1
Drillfield Ct [20] CW9 103 F8
Drillfield Rd CW9 104 A8
Drill Field Rd CW9 103 F8
Drive A CH5 93 A2
Drive B CH5 93 A2
Drive C CH5 93 A2
Drive D CH5 93 A1
Drive The
Altrincham WA15 32 D8
Bollington SK10 87 F7
Broomedge WA13 19 D1
Holmes Chapel CW4 130 C2
Drome Rd CH5 93 A2
Drovers Way CW11 175 A5
Droxford Ct SK9 60 B6
Drumber La ST7 195 B8
Drumber The CW7 126 D1
Drumble Field SK11 84 A3
Drummond Ave CH66 69 C4
Drummond Ct WA8 13 D2
Drummond Way SK10 86 E1
Druridge Dr WA5 14 F4
Drury Cl CW1 190 F5
Drury La
Knutsford WA16 57 A2
Tallarn Green/Tallwrn Green SY13 223 E1

Drury La *continued*
Warmingham CW1 173 D4
DRURY LANE 223 D1
Dryden Cl CW2 190 A1
Dryden Pl WA2 8 C2
Dryersfield [5] CH3 142 A8
Dryhurst Dr SK12 38 D6
Dryhurst La SK12 38 D6
Dublin Croft CH66 69 E1
Duchess Pl CH2 237 A4
Duchy Rd CW1 207 A8
DUCKINGTON 199 C4
Duck La CH3 121 F7
Duckworth Gr WA2 9 A1
DUDDON 145 A6
Duddon Cl
Duddon CW6 145 B6
[3] Northwich CW9 103 F4
Duddon Hall Barns CW6 144 E8
DUDDON HEATH 144 E7
Duddon Hook La CW6 144 F6
Duddon Rd CW6 145 B5
Duddon St Peter's CE Prim Sch CW6 145 B6
Dudleston Rd CH66 69 B6
Dudley Ave WA7 23 D2
Dudley Cres CH65 44 B3
Dudley Rd
Ellesmere Port CH65 70 B5
Irlam M44 11 D4
Dudley St WA2 16 B7
Dudley Wlk [2] SK11 111 F7
Dudlow Green Rd WA4 26 E5
DUDLOW'S GREEN 26 E5
Dufton Wlk M22 33 E8
Duke Ave
Cheadle SK8 34 F6
Glazebury WA3 5 C7
Duke Cl WA7 22 F2
Dukesbridge Ct [7] WA13 18 E3
Duke's Cres CW11 175 A7
Dukes Ct [2] SK11 112 D7
Duke's Ct CH1 237 B1
DUKESFIELD 22 E3
Duke St
Alderley Edge SK9 60 B2
Chester CH1 237 B1
Congleton CW12 156 D2
Crewe CW2 190 C3
Macclesfield SK11 112 D7
Newton-le-W WA12 2 B3
Dukesway CH2 118 E7
Dukes Way CW9 103 E5
Dukes Wharf WA7 50 E6
Dulas Ct CH2 118 E8
Dulverton Ave CH3 119 C2
Dumbah La SK10 87 D6
Dumbers SK11 136 A2
Dumbill Ho ST7 210 C8
Dunbar Cl
Connah's Quay CH5 91 D1
Ellesmere Port CH66 69 C5
Holmes Chapel CW4 130 C2
Dunbar Ct CH66 69 C5
Duncan Ave
Newton-le-W WA12 2 C5
Runcorn WA7 23 C1
Duncansby Cres WA5 14 E6
Duncansby Dr CH63 43 C4
Duncan St WA2 16 C7
Dundalk Rd WA8 22 E8
Dundee Cl WA2 8 F4
Dundee Ct CH65 70 E3
Dundonald Ave [5] WA4 16 C1
Dundonald Rd SK8 35 A7
Dundrennan Cl SK12 36 D5
Dunge Valley Gdns★ SK23 89 F8
Dunham Cl
Alsager ST7 193 C3
Bebington CH62 43 F3
Sandbach CW11 175 C6
Dunham Cres CW2 206 B8
Dunham Ct
Dunham-on-t-H WA6 97 E6
Hartford CW8 102 F4
DUNHAM HEATH 98 A4
Dunham Hill Prim Sch WA6 97 E6
Dunham Massey Hall★ WA14 20 D3
DUNHAM-ON-THE-HILL 97 E5
Dunham Pk (Deer Pk)★ WA14 20 D3
Dunham Rd
Altrincham, Bowgreen WA14 20 F1
Handforth SK9 34 D5
Mossbrow WA13 19 E7
Northwich CW9 104 A4
Dunham Way CH2 118 F6
DUNHAM WOODHOUSES 20 B4
DUNKIRK 94 E6
Dunkirk ST7 210 A6
Dunkirk Ave CW7 149 D8
Dunkirk Dr CH65 70 B1
Dunkirk La
Capenhurst CH1 94 C7
Ellesmere Port CH65 70 A1
Dunkirk Trad Est CH1 94 D6
Dunley Cl WA3 10 A5
Dunlin Ave WA12 2 C4

Dunlin Cl
Poynton SK12 36 A4
Runcorn WA7 49 F5
Warrington WA2 8 E3
Dunlin Rise SK10 87 B5
Dunlop St WA4 16 B3
Dunmail Gr WA7 49 E5
Dunmore Cl CW10 151 C7
Dunmore Cres CH66 69 B6
Dunmore Rd CH66 69 B6
Dunmow Rd WA4 17 C3
Dunnillow Field CW5 205 A4
Dunnock Cl WA2 8 E3
Dunnock Gr WA3 9 E4
Dunnocksfold Rd ST7 193 A4
Dunnockswood ST7 193 A4
Dunn's Cotts CW1 192 C1
Dunn's La CH3 121 F7
Dunoon Cl CW4 130 B2
Dunraven Rd CH64 67 A7
Dunscar Cl WA3 9 D5
Dunsford WA8 12 B3
Dunsmore Cl WA11 1 C7
Dunstan La CH64 67 E3
Dunster Cl CW9 104 A4
Dunster Gr CH60 41 B7
Dunster Rd SK10 87 F1
Dunwood Dr ST7 193 D6
Dunwoody Way CW1, CW2 190 B4
Durban Ave CH3 142 D7
Durber Cl ST7 209 D1
Durham Cl
Macclesfield SK10 86 F2
Warrington WA1 17 E7
Durham Ct CH65 70 E3
Durham Dr CW7 149 C6
Durham Gr M44 11 C6
Durham Rd
Blacon CH1 117 F5
Widnes WA8 13 B3
Durlston Cl WA8 12 C2
Durrell Way WA3 3 E8
DUTTON 51 A4
Dutton Cl WA1 16 C5
Dutton Gn CH2 70 F3
Dutton Hall Ct WA4 76 E8
Dutton La CW8, WA6 101 B6
Duttons Bsns Ctr CW9 103 F7
Dutton's La CW6 122 C5
Dutton Way
Crewe CW1 190 B6
Nantwich CW5 204 E3
Duxford Ct WA2 8 E1
Dyar Terr CW8 78 D1
Dye House La SK22 39 C8
Dyers Cl WA13 19 A4
Dyers Ct SK10 88 B8
Dyers La WA13 19 A4
Dykin Cl WA8 13 E3
Dykin Rd WA8 13 E3
Dysart Bldgs CW5 204 E5
Dyserth Rd CH1 117 D3
Dystelegh Rd SK12 38 D6

E

Eadie Gr CW1 190 A7
Eaglais Way SK10 86 F2
Eagland Pl CW12 156 E4
Eagle Brow WA13 18 D3
Eagle La CH66 69 D7
Eagle Mount WA4 16 C2
Eagle Park Dr WA2 8 A1
Eaglesfield CW8 103 C4
Eagles Way WA7 49 E6
Ealing Cl WA7 24 D1
Ealing Rd WA5 15 B5
Eanleywood Farm Cl WA7 50 C7
Eanleywood La WA7 50 C7
Eardley Cres CW12 156 E4
Eardley Ct [6] CW1 190 B5
Eardleyend Rd ST7 209 E7
Eardswick Cl CH2 237 B4
Eardswick La CW1 172 D5
Eardswick Rd CW10 151 C6
Earle Cl WA12 1 F3
Earle Cres CH64 41 D1
Earle Dr CH64 41 D1
Earle Rd WA8 23 C7
Earles La CW9 79 E6
Earle's La CW6 122 C5
Earle St
Crewe CW1 190 D4
Newton-le-W WA12 2 A3
EARLESTOWN 2 B2
Earlestown Sta WA12 2 B3
Earl Rd SK8, SK9 34 E5
Earls Gdns CH65 70 B5
Earls Oak CH2 118 D7
Earl's Port CH1 118 B2
Earls Rd CW2 206 B4
Earl St WA2 16 B7
Earlston Ct CH3 237 C2
Earlsway
Chester CH4 141 A8
Macclesfield SK11 111 F7
Earls Way
Northwich CW9 103 E4
Runcorn WA7 49 E6
Earlswood Mews CW9 103 F3
Easby Cl
Cheadle SK8 35 B6
Poynton SK12 36 D4
Easby Cl *continued*
Runcorn WA7 23 C2
Easenhall Cl WA8 13 C5
East Ave
Bollington SK10 87 F7
Gatley SK8 34 D8
Northwich CW9 104 D6
Warrington, Great Sankey WA5 15 A4
Warrington, Stockton Heath WA4 16 D1
Warrington WA2 16 C8
Weston CW2 207 C5
Eastbury Cl WA8 13 C5
Eastcott Cl CW12 155 F4
East Ct ST7 193 E4
Eastdale WA15 31 F8
Eastdale Rd WA1 17 A7
East Dam Wood Rd L24 21 A2
East Dudley St CW7 126 F1
Easter Ct WA5 7 B2
Eastern Pathway CH4 237 C1
Eastern Rd CW5 205 F5
Eastfields Gr CH1 117 A8
Eastford Rd WA4 16 A1
Eastgate SK10 112 E8
Eastgate Rd
Holmes Chapel CW4 130 D3
Runcorn WA7 24 E5
Eastgate Row N CH1 237 B2
Eastgate Row S CH1 237 B2
Eastgate St CH1 237 B2
Eastgate Way WA7 24 D4
East Gn CH5 116 A6
EASTHAM 43 F5
Eastham Ctry Pk* CH62 44 A8
EASTHAM FERRY 44 B8
Eastham Ho CH62 44 A4
Eastham Mews CH62 44 A4
Eastham Rake CH62, CH64 43 D3
Eastham Rake Sta CH63 43 D3
Eastham Village Rd CH62 44 A5
Eastham Way [11] SK9 34 D5
East La
Cuddington CW8 102 A3
Runcorn WA7 49 F7
East Lancashire Rd WA11, WA12, WA3 2 C7
East Mains L24 21 A3
East Millwood Rd L24 21 A4
East Park Rd SK11 112 B5
East Rd
Halewood L24, L26 21 A5
Middlewich CW10 128 B1
Wythenshawe M90 33 C7
East St WA8 13 D1
East Terr WA16 56 F1
East View
[10] Nantwich CW5 204 E6
Warrington WA4 17 B2
Eastward Ave SK9 59 F6
Eastway
Ellesmere Port CH66 69 D7
Widnes WA8 12 D1
Eastwood WA7 24 C2
Eastwood Ave WA12 2 F3
Eastwood Ct CH5 139 B7
Eastwood Rd WA5 6 F7
EATON
Congleton 157 A8
Tarporley 147 A4
Eaton Ave CH4 141 D7
Eaton Bank CW12 156 F4
Eaton Bank Ind Est CW12 156 F4
Eaton Bank Sch CW12 156 F5
Eaton Cl
Broughton CH4 139 C4
Poynton SK12 37 A3
Sandbach CW11 175 C7
Eaton Cres CW9 103 E2
Eaton Ct
[1] Northwich CW9 103 E5
Wilmslow SK9 60 A6
Eaton Dr
Alderley Edge SK9 59 F2
Middlewich CW10 151 B8
Eaton Gr CH4 140 E6
Eaton La
Davenham CW9 103 E2
Eaton CW6 147 A5
Goostrey CW4 107 C1
Macclesfield SK11 112 D5
Tarporley CW6 168 E8
Eaton Mews CH4 141 D7
Eaton Pl CW8 102 F4
Eaton Prim Sch CW6 147 B3
Eaton Rd
Alsager ST7 193 D4
Chester CH4 141 E4
Tarporley CW6 146 D1
Wettenhall CW7 170 B8
Eaton St
Crewe CW2 190 C4
[13] Runcorn WA7 23 A2
Eaton View CW9 126 E8
Eaton Way CW3 230 A4
Eaves Brow Rd WA3 9 B7
Eaves Knoll Rd SK22 39 B8
EBNAL 213 D5
Ebnal La SY14 213 E4
Ebury Pl CH4 141 D7
Eccles Cl SK23 65 D8
Eccles Rd SK23 65 F6
ECCLESTON 141 E1
Eccleston Ave
Bebington CH62 43 C8
Chester CH4 141 D6
Ellesmere Port CH66 69 E5
Eccleston CE Prim Sch CH4 141 E2
Eccleston Cl WA3 9 C5
Eccleston Ct [5] CW9 103 E5
Eccleston Dr WA7 23 C1
Eccleston Rd CH4 161 A7
Eccleston Way [3] SK9 34 D4
Eccups La SK9 59 C8
Echo Cl CH4 140 E5
Ecton Ave SK10 113 A7
Ecton Cl CW7 127 A4
Edale Cl
Bebington CH62 43 E5
Gatley SK8 34 D7
Edale Dr CW6 122 D5
Edburton Ct WA3 3 A8
Eddisbury Cl SK11 112 F7
Eddisbury Dr ST5 210 D2
Eddisbury Hill CW6, CW8 123 D7
Eddisbury Hill Pk CW8 123 D7
Eddisbury Rd CH66 69 F1
Eddisbury Sq WA6 74 B8
Eddisbury Terr SK11 112 F7
Eddisbury Way CW9 103 E3
Eddisford Dr WA3 4 D4
Edelsten St WA5 15 F5
Eden Ave
Fowley Common WA3 5 C4
High Lane SK6 37 E7
Winsford CW7 126 F2
Edenbridge Cl CW2 207 B2
Edenbridge Gdns WA4 26 E3
Eden Cl
Biddulph ST8 179 E1
[5] Ellesmere Port CH66 69 C5
Kidsgrove ST7 195 B2
Wilmslow SK9 59 E5
Edendale WA8 12 B2
Eden Dr SK10 87 F1
Edenfield Cl WA16 58 A3
Edenfield Rd WA16 58 A4
Edenhall Cl CW4 130 A3
Eden Park Rd SK8 34 E8
Edgar Ct
Chester CH4 237 B1
[25] Macclesfield SK11 112 C8
Edgar Pl CH4 237 B1
Edgars Dr WA2 9 A1
Edgecroft CH3 166 A1
Edge Gr CH2 118 F2
EDGE GREEN 199 B2
Edgehill Chase SK9 60 E7
Edge La SY14 199 C1
Edgerley La CH3 181 B6
Edgerton Rd WA3 3 F8
Edge View La SK9 59 B2
Edgeview Rd CW12 179 B7
Edgeway
Henbury SK11 111 C8
Wilmslow SK9 60 B5
Edgewell La CW6 147 A3
Edgewood [3] CH3 142 A8
Edgewood Dr
Bebington CH62 43 D5
Wistaston CW2 206 A7
Edgworth St WA2 16 A6
Edinburgh Ct CH65 70 D3
Edinburgh Dr SK10 87 A1
Edinburgh Pl CW12 156 F2
Edinburgh Rd
Congleton CW12 156 F2
Widnes WA8 22 A8
Wistaston CW2 205 E8
Edinburgh Way CH4 237 C1
Edison Rd WA7 23 D3
Edith St WA7 22 F3
Edlestone Gr [2] SK9 34 E1
Edleston Hall La CW5 203 F2
Edleston Prim Sch CW2 190 C3
Edleston Rd CW2 190 D3
Edmund Wright Way CW5 204 C5
Edna St CH2 118 F3
Edward Gdns WA1 17 F6
Edward Rd WA5 14 D6
Edwards Ave CW2 206 C5
Edwards Cl CW2 206 C5
Edwards Rd CH4 141 A6
Edward St
Audley ST7 209 F3
Crewe CW2 190 D2
Ellesmere Port CH65 70 C7
Haydock WA11 1 A6
Macclesfield SK11 112 B7
Northwich CW9 104 C8
Widnes WA8 13 D1
Edwards Way
Alsager ST7 193 E4
Widnes WA8 22 C8
Edwin St WA8 13 C1
Egdon Cl WA8 13 E2
Egerton WA16 29 C5
Egerton Ave
Hartford CW8 103 A4
Partington WA13 19 C8
Warrington WA1 16 F7
Egerton Ct CW6 122 B5
Egerton Dr CH2 118 D5
EGERTON GREEN 200 C5
Egerton Mews [1] WA4 16 C1
Egerton Moss WA15 31 E5
Egerton Prim Sch WA16 56 F2
Egerton Rd
Blacon CH1 117 E5
Handforth SK9 34 B1
Lymm WA13 18 C2
Egerton Sq [7] WA16 57 A2
Egerton St
Chester CH1 237 C3
Congleton CW12 156 C2
Ellesmere Port CH65 70 C6
Runcorn WA7 22 F3
Warrington, Howley WA1 16 D5
Warrington, Stockton Heath WA4 16 C1
Egerton Terr CW9 105 D4
Egerton Wlk CH4 162 A7
Eggbridge La CH3 143 A5
Egremont Ct WA4 16 C3
Egypt St
[3] Warrington WA1 16 A5
Widnes WA8 22 F7
Eilison Ct CH1 237 B3
Elaine Cl
Ellesmere Port CH66 69 C4
Widnes WA8 13 C1
Elaine Price Ct [3] WA7 22 F1
Elaine St WA1 16 D7
Elanor Rd CW11 174 D7
Elcombe Ave WA3 3 E7
Elderberry Way SK9 60 E8
Elderberry Wlk M31 11 E3
Elder Dr CH4 140 E5
Eldon Rd SK10 111 F8
Eldon St WA1 16 C5
Eldon Terr CH64 66 E7
Eleanor Cl CW1 189 F5
Eleanor St
Ellesmere Port CH65 70 C6
[5] Widnes WA8 23 A7
Electra Way CW1 191 A2
Electricity St CW2 190 C3
Elgar Ave CH62 43 E5
Elgar Cl CH65 69 F3
Elgin Ave
Holmes Chapel CW4 130 B2
Macclesfield SK10 87 A2
Warrington WA4 16 A2
Elgin Cl CH3 119 B3
Eliot Cl CW1 191 A4
Elizabethan Way CW9 104 E6
Elizabeth Ave SK12 38 D5
Elizabeth Cl
Kelsall CW6 122 D5
Sandbach CW11 174 D7
Elizabeth Cres CH4 237 C1
Elizabeth Ct
Talke ST7 210 D5
Widnes WA8 23 B7
Elizabeth Dr WA1 17 A8
Elizabeth Gaskell Ct WA16 56 F2
Elizabeth Ho [15] SK11 112 E7
Elizabeth Rd
Haydock WA11 1 E7
Partington M31 11 F4
Elizabeth St
Congleton CW12 156 C2
Crewe CW1 190 B5
Macclesfield SK11 112 D7
Elizabeth Terr WA8 12 D1
Elkan Cl WA8 13 E2
Elkan Rd WA8 13 E2
Elk View SY14 222 F5
Ella Gr WA16 57 B2
Elland Dr CH66 69 C5
Ellen Brook Rd M22 33 D8
Ellen St WA5 15 F7
Ellerby Cl WA7 50 E7
Ellerton Ave CH66 69 C5
Ellerton Cl WA8 12 D3
Ellesmere Ave
Broughton CH4 139 D4
Chester CH2 118 D5
Ellesmere Cl CW11 174 F8
Ellesmere Pl [10] CW1 190 B5
ELLESMERE PORT 70 A7
Ellesmere Port Hospl CH65 70 A2
Ellesmere Port RC High Sch CH65 70 A3
Ellesmere Port Sch of Performing Arts CH66 69 E6
Ellesmere Port Sta CH65 70 C5
Ellesmere Port Stadium The CH65 70 E3
Ellesmere Rd
Culcheth WA3 4 E3
Northwich CW9 104 A4
Warrington WA4 16 B1
Ellesmere St
Runcorn WA7 23 B2
Warrington WA1 16 C5
[5] Warrington WA1 16 C5
Ellesworth Cl WA5 15 C8
Ellingham Way CW9 103 E3
Ellington Dr WA5 15 B5
Elliot Ho CH1 118 A5
Elliot St [9] WA8 23 B8
Elliott Ave WA1 16 E7
Ellis La WA6 49 D1
Ellison St
Warrington, Howley WA1 16 C5
Warrington, Stockton Heath WA4 16 D1
Ellis St
Crewe CW1 190 B6
Widnes WA8 22 F7
Elloway Rd L24 21 A3
Ellwood Cl L24 21 E2
Ellwood Gn CW2 206 E3
Elm Ave
Newton-le-W WA12 2 C2
Widnes WA8 13 B2
Elm Beds Rd SK12 37 C2
Elm Cl
Crewe CW2 189 E2
[2] Partington M31 11 F3
Poynton SK12 36 F3
Tarporley CW6 146 D2
Elm Cres SK9 60 B3
Elm Ct CW1 190 D6
Elm Dr
Crewe CW1 190 E6
Holmes Chapel CW4 130 D4
Macclesfield SK10 87 E2
Elmfield Cl SK9 60 B2
Elmfield Rd SK9 60 B2
Elm Gn CH64 67 F8
Elm Gr
Alderley Edge SK9 60 B2
Alsager ST7 193 E4
Ellesmere Port CH66 70 A1
Handforth SK9 34 C3
Saltney CH4 140 E5
Warrington WA1 16 F7
Widnes WA8 13 B1
Winsford CW7 127 A1
Elm Ho
Chester CH2 118 C5
[9] Sandbach CW11 175 B6
Elmore Cl
Holmes Chapel CW4 130 B3
Runcorn WA7 24 D1
Elm Rd
Congleton CW12 156 B3
Haydock WA11 1 E7
High Lane SK6 37 F7
Hollinfare WA3 11 A2
Middlewich CW10 151 D7
Runcorn WA7 49 C8
Warrington WA5 14 F4
Warrington, Winwick Quay WA2 8 B4
Weaverham CW8 102 D7
Willaston CH64 67 F8
Elmridge Ct WA3 3 F8
Elmridge Dr WA15 32 C8
Elmridge Prim Sch WA15 32 C8
Elmridge Way CW8 78 D1
Elm Rise
Frodsham WA6 74 C7
Prestbury SK10 86 E6
Elms SK9 59 F6
Elmsett Cl WA5 14 E5
Elm Sq CH4 140 F6
Elm St
Ellesmere Port CH65 70 C7
Northwich CW9 79 B1
Elmstead Cres CW1 189 F8
Elmstead Rd SK11 84 A3
Elms The
Golborne WA3 3 F7
Mobberley WA16 58 E2
[7] Northwich CW9 103 E6
Runcorn WA7 22 F1
Tallarn Green/Tallwrn Green SY14 222 F5
Elmsway
Altrincham WA15 32 B8
Bollington SK10 88 A8
Bramhall SK7 35 C7
High Lane SK6 37 E6
Elm Terr CW1 190 E6
Elm Tree Ave
Lymm WA13 18 D2
Warrington WA1 16 F8
Elm Tree Cotts CH3 167 A7
Elm Tree Ct CW6 147 A3
Elm Tree Dr ST7 209 F1
Elm Tree La CW11 174 D8
Elm Tree Rd
Golborne WA3 3 F8
Lymm WA13 18 D2
Elmuir CH1 117 E3
Elmwood WA7 24 C1
Elmwood Ave
Chester CH2 118 F4
Warrington WA1 16 E7
Elmwood Cl ST7 194 A4
Elmwood Gr CW7 149 F8
Elmwood Rd CW8 78 B4
Elnor Ave SK23 65 E5
Elnor La SK23 65 F4
Elphins Dr WA4 16 C2
Elsby Rd ST7 193 F2
Elston Ave WA12 2 C5
Elstree Ave CH3 119 B3
Elstree Ct WA8 13 D4
Elswick Ave SK7 35 E7
Eltham Cl WA8 13 E3
Eltham Wlk WA8 13 E3
ELTON 72 C3

Elton Cl
Bebington CH62. . . . . 43 E3
Golborne WA3 . . . . 3 E7
Handforth SK9. . . . . 34 E1
Warrington WA3 . . . . 9 C4
Elton Crossings Rd
CW11. . . . . 174 D6
Elton Dr SK7 . . . . 36 D8
ELTON GREEN 72 A3
Elton La
Elton CH2. . . . . 72 E4
Haslington CW11, CW1. . . 174 D1
Winterley CW11 . . . . 191 F8
Elton Lordship La WA6 . . . 73 B7
Elton Prim Sch CH2. . . . . . 72 B4
Elton Rd CW11. . . . . 174 D5
Elvington Cl
Congleton CW12 . . . . 156 E2
Runcorn WA7. . . . . 49 F4
Elwood Way CW5 . . . . 205 B4
ELWORTH 174 E6
Elworth Ave WA8 . . . . 13 A5
Elworth CE Prim Sch
CW11. . . . . 174 E7
Elworth Ct
12 Congleton CW12 . . . . . 156 F3
Sandbach CW11 . . . . 174 D7
Elworth Hall Prim Sch
CW11 . . . . 174 E7
Elworth Rd CW11 . . . . 174 E6
Elworth St CW11. . . . . 175 A7
Elworth Way 6 SK9. . . . . . 34 D4
Elwyn Dr L26 . . . . 21 A8
Ely Cl CH66. . . . . 94 E8
Ely Pk WA7. . . . . 24 E2
Embassy Cl CH1 . . . . 117 C4
Emberton Pl CW3. . . . . . . 230 A5
Embleton Ct WA7. . . . . 49 D5
Embridge Cswy SK10. . . . . 90 B5
Emerald Dr CW11. . . . . . . 175 C8
Emerald Rd M22 . . . . 33 F7
Emily St 7 WA8 . . . . 23 A7
Emmett St CW8. . . . . 78 A3
Empire Ct WA1 . . . . 16 A4
Empress Dr CW2. . . . . 190 B3
Emral Ct SY14 . . . . 211 A1
Emslie Ct CH64 . . . . 66 C7
Enderby Rd CH1 . . . . 237 A3
Endon Ave SK10 . . . . 88 A7
Endon Hall Mews SK10. . . 88 B5
Endsleigh Cl CH2 . . . . 118 E8
Endsleigh Gdns CH2 . . . . 118 E8
Enfield Cl CW2 . . . . 206 B3
Enfield Park Rd WA2. . . . . . 9 A3
Enfield Rd CH65 . . . . 70 B5
Engineer Pk CH5 . . . . 116 A4
Englefield Ave CH4 . . . . . 140 D6
Englefield Cl CW1 . . . . . . 190 A8
ENGLESEA-BROOK 208 A4
Englesea Brook La
CW2. . . . . 208 A3
Englesea Brook Mus of Primitive Methodism★
CW2 . . . . 208 A3
Englesea Gr CW2 . . . . 190 B1
Ennerdale
Chester CH2 . . . . 118 F5
Macclesfield SK11. . . . . . . 111 F5
Ennerdale Ave
Bebington CH62. . . . . 43 F4
Warrington WA2 . . . . 8 B3
Ennerdale Cl
Alderley Edge SK9. . . . . 83 F7
Winsford CW7. . . . . 126 D3
Ennerdale Dr
Congleton CW12 . . . . 156 B2
Frodsham WA6 . . . . 74 C8
Ennerdale Rd
Crewe CW2 . . . . 189 D3
Partington M31 . . . . 11 E3
Ennis Cl L24. . . . . 21 D2
Ensor Way SK22 . . . . 39 C7
Enterprise Ct CW11. . . . . . 174 D7
Enterprise Ctr The
CW12. . . . . 156 E3
Enterprise Way WA3. . . . . . 4 A7
Enticott Rd M44 . . . . 11 C5
Enville St WA4. . . . . 16 C4
Epping Dr WA1 . . . . 17 D8
Epsom Ave SK8, SK9. . . . . . 34 E4
Epsom Ct CH1 . . . . 118 B2
Epsom Gdns WA4. . . . . 26 E7
Epworth Cl WA5. . . . . 6 F7
ERF Way CW10 . . . . 151 E8
Eric Ave WA1. . . . . 16 E8
Eric Dr CW11. . . . . 174 D7
Eric Fountain Rd CH65 . . . 44 D3
Eric St WA8 . . . . 13 C2
Erindale Cres WA6. . . . . 74 A6
Ermine Rd CH2. . . . . 237 C4
Ernest St CW2. . . . . 190 C1
Ernley Cl CW5. . . . . 204 D6
Errington Ave CH65 . . . . . . 70 C6
Errwood Forest Walks★
SK17. . . . . 90 E2
Erskine Rd M31. . . . . 11 F3
Erwood St WA2. . . . . 16 B6
Eskdale CH65. . . . . 70 B3
Eskdale Ave
Bebington CH62. . . . . 43 E5
Bramhall SK7. . . . . 35 C5
Warrington WA2 . . . . 8 C3
Eskdale Cl WA7. . . . . 49 D5
Esk Dale Cl CW7 . . . . 126 C2
Esk Rd CW7 . . . . 127 A2
Essex Cl CW12. . . . . 156 E5
Essex Dr
Biddulph ST8. . . . . 179 D2
Kidsgrove ST7 . . . . 194 F2
Essex Gdns M44 . . . . 11 C4
Essex Rd CH2. . . . . 119 A5
Essex Wlk SK10. . . . . 86 F1
Esthers La CW8. . . . . 102 D8
Etchells Prim Sch SK8 . . . 34 C8
Ethelda Dr CH2 . . . . 119 A5
Etherow Cl CW11 . . . . 174 E7
Ethos Ct CH1 . . . . 237 C3
Eton Dr CH63 . . . . 41 F6
Eton Rd CH65. . . . . 70 D4
Ettiley Ave CW11. . . . . 174 C5
ETTILEY HEATH 174 C6
Ettrick Pk CH3. . . . . 119 A2
Euclid Ave WA4. . . . . 17 B2
Europa Bvd WA5. . . . . 7 D3
Europa Way CH65. . . . . 70 C6
Eustace St WA2. . . . . 16 A6
Evans Bsns Ctr CH5 . . . . . . 93 A1
Evans Cl WA11. . . . . 1 F7
Evansleigh Dr CH5 . . . . . . 116 A3
Evans Pl WA4. . . . . 16 D3
Evans St CW1. . . . . 190 C6
Eva St CW11. . . . . 174 D8
Evelyn St WA5. . . . . 15 D4
Evelyn Street Com Prim
Sch WA5. . . . . 15 E4
Evenwood Cl WA7 . . . . 24 E4
Everdon Cl CW7 . . . . 126 F4
Everest Cl CH66. . . . . 69 F3
Everest Rd ST7 . . . . 195 C3
Everglade Cl SK11 . . . . . . 112 B5
Evergreens The CW9. . . . . . 80 A3
Evergreen Way WA9 . . . . . . 6 A7
Everite Rd WA8. . . . . 22 B7
Everite Road Ind Est
WA8 . . . . 22 B7
Eversley WA8. . . . . 12 B2
Eversley Cl
Frodsham WA6 . . . . 74 C6
Warrington WA4 . . . . 26 F5
Eversley Ct CH2. . . . . 118 C4
Eversley Pk CH2 . . . . 118 C4
Evesham Cl
Macclesfield SK10. . . . . 87 E4
Warrington WA4 . . . . 26 C8
Evesham Dr SK9. . . . . 34 C2
Evington Ho 2 SK11 . . . . 112 B6
Ewart St CH4 . . . . 140 B7
Ewloe Ct CH65. . . . . 70 D2
Ewrin La SK10 . . . . 89 D5
Excalibur Ind Est ST7 . . . 193 E3
Excalibur Prim Sch
ST7. . . . . 193 E2
Excalibur Way M44 . . . . 11 F7
Exchange Cl 12 SK11 . . . . 112 D8
Exchange St SK11. . . . . . . 112 D8
Exeter Cl SK8. . . . . 34 F8
Exeter Pl CH1. . . . . 117 F5
Exeter Rd CH65 . . . . 70 C5
Exeter Wlk SK7 . . . . 35 F7
Exit Rd W M90. . . . . 33 B7
Exmouth Cres WA7 . . . . 50 E6
Exmouth Way WA5. . . . . 6 F6
Express Ind Est WA8 . . . . . 22 A7
Exton Pk CH1. . . . . 237 A4
Eyam Rd SK7 . . . . 36 E8
Eyebrook Rd WA14. . . . . . . 20 F2
Eyre Pl CH65 . . . . 70 B6
Eyston Cl CW9. . . . . 103 E5

F

Facit Glen Ind Est
CH4. . . . . 140 F7
Factory La
Warrington WA1, WA5. . . . 15 F4
Widnes WA8 . . . . 13 B3
Factory Rd CH5 . . . . 116 A3
FADDILEY 202 D7
FADDILEY BANK 202 C6
Fairacre Dr CW10. . . . . 151 E6
Fairacres Rd SK6 . . . . 37 E8
Fairbourne Ave
Alderley Edge SK9. . . . . 60 B3
Wilmslow SK9 . . . . 59 F4
Fairbourne Cl
Warrington WA5 . . . . 7 E3
Wilmslow SK9 . . . . 59 F4
Fairbourne Dr SK9. . . . . 59 F4
Fairbrook CW2 . . . . 189 E2
Fairbrother Cres WA2. . . . . . 8 D2
Fairburn Ave CW2 . . . . 189 F4
Fairburn Cl WA8. . . . . 13 E3
Fairclough Ave WA1 . . . . . . 16 C4
Fairclough Cres WA11 . . . . 1 A6
Fairclough St
Burtonwood WA5. . . . . 6 E6
Newton-le-W WA12. . . . . 2 B3
Fairfax Cl ST8 . . . . 179 C1
Fairfax Ct CW5 . . . . 204 E7
Fairfax Dr
Nantwich CW5. . . . . 204 D6
Runcorn WA7. . . . . 23 D2
Wilmslow SK9 . . . . 59 F4
Fairfield Ave
Bollington SK10. . . . . 88 A8
Ellesmere Port CH65. . . . . . 70 A2
Sandbach CW11 . . . . 175 B5
Fairfield Gdns WA4 . . . . . . 16 E2
Fairfield High Sch
WA8 . . . . 13 B3
Fairfield Inf Sch WA8 . . . . 13 B2
Fairfield Jun Sch WA8 . . . 13 B2
Fairfield Rd
Broughton CH4 . . . . 139 B4
Chester CH2 . . . . 119 A4
Irlam M44 . . . . 11 C5
Lymm WA13. . . . . 18 F3
Northwich CW9. . . . . 104 A4
Warrington WA4 . . . . 16 E2
Widnes WA8 . . . . 13 B2
Fairfields
Audley ST7. . . . . 209 F2
Whitchurch SY13. . . . . 225 F1
Fairfield St WA1 . . . . 16 D6
Fairford Cl WA5 . . . . 15 B6
Fairford Rd CH4 . . . . 140 F6
Fairford Way SK9. . . . . 60 D7
Fairhaven CW2 . . . . 207 B1
Fairhaven Cl
Bramhall SK7. . . . . 35 F8
Macclesfield SK10. . . . . 87 B4
Warrington WA5 . . . . 15 B4
Fairhaven Dr CH63. . . . . . . 43 C5
Fairhaven Rd WA8 . . . . 13 C2
Fair Haven's Ct WA8 . . . . . 23 B8
Fairhills Ind Est M44. . . . . 11 F8
Fairhills Rd M44 . . . . 11 F8
Fairholme Ave CH64 . . . . . 41 D1
Fairholme Cl CH1. . . . . 94 B1
Fairholme Pl 8 CH3 . . . . 119 A1
Fairholme Rd CW9. . . . . . 127 A8
Fair Isle Cl CH65. . . . . 70 C1
Fairlawn Cl CH63 . . . . 43 A6
Fair Mead WA16. . . . . 82 B8
Fairmeadow CH4 . . . . 162 D2
Fairoak Cl 12 CW7 . . . . . 149 A8
Fairoak Ct WA7. . . . . 50 F3
Fairoak La WA7. . . . . 50 F3
Fair Oak Rd ST5 . . . . 210 D1
Fairview LL13. . . . . 196 E8
Fairview Ave
Alsager ST7. . . . . 193 D4
Weston CW2. . . . . 207 B5
Fair View Cl CW8 . . . . 77 F3
Fairview Rd
Ellesmere Port CH65. . . . . . 70 A2
Macclesfield SK11. . . . . . . 112 A6
Fairway
Bramhall SK7. . . . . 35 D6
Sandycroft CH5 . . . . 116 A2
Fairways
Frodsham WA6 . . . . 74 D7
Warrington WA4 . . . . 26 D5
Fairways Dr
Ellesmere Port CH66. . . . . . 69 D7
Whitchurch SY13. . . . . 226 A1
Fairways The
Macclesfield SK10. . . . . 87 B4
Winsford CW7. . . . . 126 A2
Fairway The ST7. . . . . 193 C4
Fairway Trad Est WA8. . . . 22 E6
Fairywell Cl SK9 . . . . 34 D1
Falcon Cl
Middlewich CW10 . . . . 151 D5
New Mills SK22. . . . . 39 D8
Winsford CW7. . . . . 149 D6
Falcondale Rd WA2. . . . . . . 8 B6
Falcon Dr CW1 . . . . 190 B8
Falconers Gn WA5. . . . . 7 B2
Falcon Rd CH66. . . . . 69 F3
Falcons Way WA7. . . . . 49 E6
Falkirk Ave WA8. . . . . 12 F3
Fallibroome Cl SK10 . . . . 111 E8
Fallibroome High Sch
SK10. . . . . 86 E2
Fallibroome Rd SK10. . . . 111 E8
Fallon Ct CW10. . . . . 151 C7
Fallowfield WA7. . . . . 23 D1
Fallowfield Cl CW7 . . . . . 125 F1
Fallowfield Ct CW1 . . . . . 190 A6
Fallowfield Gr WA2 . . . . . . 9 B1
Falmouth Cl SK10. . . . . . . 111 E8
Falmouth Dr WA5. . . . . 14 E3
Falmouth Pl WA7 . . . . 50 E6
Falmouth Rd
Congleton CW12 . . . . 178 E8
Crewe CW1 . . . . 190 A6
Falstone Cl WA3. . . . . 10 B6
Falstone Dr WA7. . . . . 50 E7
Fanner's La WA16. . . . . 28 D5
Fanny's Croft ST7. . . . . . . 193 D2
FANSHAWE 110 C4
Fanshawe La SK11 . . . . . . 110 E5
Fanshawe Wlk CW2. . . . . 206 C8
Faraday Rd
Ellesmere Port CH65. . . . . . 70 A4
Runcorn WA7. . . . . 23 D3
Faraday St WA3 . . . . 9 E5
Farams Rd ST7 . . . . 193 E7
Farbailey Cl CH4. . . . . 141 B5
Farcroft Cl WA13 . . . . 19 C5
Farfields Cl SK11 . . . . 111 E1
Farley Cl CW10 . . . . 151 B8
Farm Cl CW8 . . . . 77 D1
Farmdale Dr CH2 . . . . 72 A3
Farm Dr CH5 . . . . 91 C1
Farmer Cl CW2 . . . . 190 A4
Farmers Heath CH66 . . . . . 69 D2
Farmer's La WA5 . . . . 7 A6
Farmfield Dr SK10 . . . . 87 C3
Farmfields Rise CW3. . . . 232 C1
Farmfold SK9. . . . . 33 F3
Farm Hollow ST7 . . . . 210 A2
Farm La
High Lane SK12. . . . . 38 A6
Warrington WA4 . . . . 26 E8
Withington Green SK11. . . 108 E1
Farmleigh Dr CW1 . . . . . . 189 F8
Farmleigh Gdns WA5 . . . . 15 C6
Farm Rd
Northwich CW9. . . . . 104 E7
Oakmere CW8. . . . . 124 A8
Weaverham CW8. . . . . 77 D1
Farmside Cl WA5 . . . . 15 F7
Farmstead Way CH66 . . . . 69 E1
Farm Way WA12 . . . . 2 E1
Farm Wlk WA14 . . . . 20 E1
Farndale WA8 . . . . 13 A5
Farndale Cl
Warrington WA5 . . . . 14 F7
Wistaston CW2. . . . . 206 A6
Farndale Wlk SK11. . . . . . 112 D6
FARNDON 180 F2
Farndon Cl
Broughton CH4 . . . . 139 C4
Cuddington CW8 . . . . 102 A3
Farndon Prim Sch
CH3. . . . . 180 E2
Farndon Rd CH66 . . . . 69 E6
Farne Cl CH65 . . . . 95 C8
Farnham Ave SK11. . . . . . 112 A6
Farnham Cl
Cheadle SK8 . . . . 35 A7
Warrington WA4 . . . . 26 E7
Farnhill Cl WA7. . . . . 50 D8
Farnley Cl WA7 . . . . 24 D1
FARNWORTH 13 A3
Farnworth CE Prim Sch
WA8 . . . . 13 A4
Farnworth Cl WA8 . . . . 13 B4
Farnworth Ct WA8 . . . . 13 B3
Farnworth Rd WA5 . . . . 14 C4
Farnworth St WA8 . . . . 13 B4
Farrant St WA8. . . . . 23 B8
Farrell Rd WA4 . . . . 26 C8
Farrell St WA1. . . . . 16 D5
Farr Hall Dr CH60. . . . . 40 E7
Farr Hall Rd CH60. . . . . 40 F8
Farrier Ct CW1 . . . . 190 D7
Farriers Way CW7 . . . . . . 126 A1
Farringdon Rd WA2. . . . . 8 B6
Farthing La CW9. . . . . 79 B8
Farthings The WA13 . . . . . 18 D4
Farwood Cl SK10 . . . . 86 F2
Faulkner Dr CW10 . . . . . . 151 E6
Faulkners Cl CH4 . . . . 161 A7
Faulkners La CH3. . . . . . . 142 D8
Faulkner's La WA16. . . . . . 58 E2
Faulkner St CH2 . . . . 118 F3
Fawns Keep SK9. . . . . 60 D7
Fawns Leap CW8 . . . . 101 E5
Fearndown Way SK10 . . . . 87 C4
FEARNHEAD 9 B2
Fearnhead Cross WA2 . . . . . 8 F2
Fearnhead La WA2. . . . . 9 A2
Fearnleigh CW8 . . . . 103 C7
Fearnley Way WA12. . . . . . . 2 C1
Feather La CH60. . . . . 40 F8
Feather's La CH1 . . . . 237 B2
Feilden Ct CH1 . . . . 94 F1
Felix Rd CW8 . . . . 103 E8
Felskirk Rd M22 . . . . 33 C8
Fence Ave SK10. . . . . 112 E8
Fence Ave Ind Est
SK10. . . . . 112 E8
Fence Ct SK10. . . . . 112 E8
Fence La CW12 . . . . 178 D4
Fenham Dr WA5 . . . . 14 F4
Fennel St WA1. . . . . 16 C5
Fenton Cl
Congleton CW12 . . . . 157 A1
Widnes WA8 . . . . 12 C3
Fenwick La WA7. . . . . 49 D6
Fenwick Rd CH66 . . . . 69 E2
Ferguson Ave CH66 . . . . . . 69 E6
Ferguson Dr WA2. . . . . 8 D1
Ferma La CH3 . . . . 120 D6
Fern Ave WA12 . . . . 2 D2
Fernbank Cl
Crewe CW1 . . . . 190 F3
Warrington WA3 . . . . 9 E4
Winsford CW7. . . . . 127 B1
Fernbank Rise SK10. . . . . . 88 B8
Fern Cl
Mount Pleasant ST7 . . . . . 195 C6
Warrington WA3 . . . . 9 D4
Fern Cres CW12 . . . . 157 A3
Fern Ct CW1. . . . . 190 E3
Ferndale Ave CH2. . . . . 72 A3
Ferndale Cl
Bold Heath WA8 . . . . 13 E7
Sandbach CW11 . . . . 175 C5
Warrington WA1 . . . . 17 C7
Weston CW2 . . . . 207 B5
Ferndale Cres SK11 . . . . . 111 E7
Ferndale Gdns ST7. . . . . . 195 E3
Ferndown Way CW2 . . . . . 221 C8
Fernhill Rd CH1. . . . . 117 E6
Fernhurst WA7 . . . . 49 D8
FERNILEE 65 E1
Fernilee Cotts SK23. . . . . . 65 E1
Fernlea Ct CH1 . . . . 116 F8
Fern Lea Dr SK11 . . . . 112 A8
Fernleaf Cl ST7. . . . . 193 F8
Fernlea Rd
Heswall CH60 . . . . 41 A8
Marston CW9. . . . . 79 B6
Fernleigh Cl
Middlewich CW10 . . . . 151 E6
Winsford CW7. . . . . 126 A1
Fern Rd CH65. . . . . 70 B2
Fernway CW7. . . . . 127 B1
Fern Way CW8. . . . . 77 C1
Fernwood WA7 . . . . 24 B1
Fernwood Gr SK9. . . . . 60 C8
Fernyess La CH64 . . . . 67 E7
Ferret Oak La CW6. . . . . . 186 B6
Ferrous Way M44. . . . . 11 F6
Ferry Cl CH5. . . . . 116 A6
Ferry La
Sealand CH1 . . . . 117 C1
Warrington WA4 . . . . 17 E4
Ferry Rd CH62 . . . . 44 A6
Festival Ave
Buerton CW3. . . . . 230 E3
Warrington WA2 . . . . 8 D2
Festival Cres WA2 . . . . 8 D2
Festival Dr SK10 . . . . 85 F6
Festival Hill CW12 . . . . . . 156 F2
Festival Rd CH65. . . . . 69 F5
Festival Terr 1 WA7. . . . . 49 C8
Festival Way WA7. . . . . 49 C8
Ffordd Cledwen/Cledwen
Rd CH4. . . . . 139 D5
Ffordd Smithfield/
Smithfield Dr LL13 . . . . . 196 D8
Ffordd Y Blodau/Blossom
Way CH4. . . . . 140 D5
Fiddlers Ferry Rd WA8 . . . 23 C8
Fiddler's Ferry Rd
WA8. . . . . 13 D1
Fiddlers La CH1. . . . . 94 C1
Field Ave CW2. . . . . 189 F1
Fieldbank Rd SK11. . . . . . 112 B8
Field Cl
Bollington SK10. . . . . 87 F7
Bramhall SK7. . . . . 35 D4
Northwich CW8 . . . . 103 C7
Tarvin CH3. . . . . 121 B2
Fieldfare CW7. . . . . 150 A8
Fieldfare Cl
Golborne WA3 . . . . 3 D8
Warrington WA3 . . . . 9 F4
Fieldgate WA8. . . . . 22 B6
Fieldhead Mews SK9. . . . . 60 E8
Fieldhead Rd SK9. . . . . 60 E8
Field Hey La CH64 . . . . 43 B1
Fieldhouse Row WA7. . . . . 49 D7
Fielding Ave SK12 . . . . 36 E2
Field La
Crewe CW2 . . . . 189 E2
Tarvin CH3. . . . . 121 B2
Tattenhall CH3. . . . . 166 B1
Warrington WA4 . . . . 26 C6
Fields Cl ST7 . . . . 193 E4
Fields Dr CW11 . . . . 175 A5
Fieldsend Dr WN7 . . . . 4 C8
Fieldside CW6. . . . . 145 B6
Fieldside Cl
Bramhall SK7. . . . . 35 D4
Goostrey CW4 . . . . 107 E1
Field Side Cl WA16. . . . . . . 58 A4
Fieldside Ct CH4. . . . . 139 B4
Fields Rd
Alsager ST7. . . . . 193 E3
Congleton CW12 . . . . 178 F8
Haslington CW1. . . . . 191 D4
Fields The CW5. . . . . 205 D5
Fields View SY13 . . . . 228 D1
Fields View Cl CW5 . . . . . 220 B8
Fieldsway WA7 . . . . 49 A6
Field View ST8 . . . . 179 D1
Fieldview Dr WA2. . . . . 8 C1
Field View Dr SK11 . . . . . 112 E5
Fieldway
Chester CH2 . . . . 118 E4
Ellesmere Port CH66. . . . . . 69 B7
Frodsham WA6 . . . . 74 C7
Saughall CH1. . . . . 94 A2
Weaverham CW8. . . . . 77 C1
Widnes WA8 . . . . 13 E2
Field Way ST7 . . . . 193 E4
Fieldways WA13 . . . . 18 C4
Field Wlk 7 M31 . . . . 11 E3
Fife Rd WA1. . . . . 16 E7
Fifth Ave
Kidsgrove ST7 . . . . 194 F1
2 Runcorn WA7. . . . . 49 F7
Fildes Cl WA5 . . . . 15 C5
Filkin's La CH3 . . . . 119 A1
Fillmore Gr WA8. . . . . 12 F3
Finchdale Gdns WA3. . . . . . . 4 B8
Finchett Ct CH1. . . . . 118 B3
Finchett Dr CH1 . . . . 118 B3
Finch La L26 . . . . 21 B7
Findlay Cl WA12 . . . . 2 C2
Finger Post La WA6. . . . . . 101 A4
Finlan Rd WA8. . . . . 22 F7
Finlay Ave WA5. . . . . 14 E3
Finlow Hill La SK10 . . . . . . 85 E6
Finney Cl SK9 . . . . 34 C2
Finney Dr SK9 . . . . 34 C2
Finney Gr WA11 . . . . 1 E6
FINNEY GREEN 34 E2
Finney La SK8 . . . . 34 B8
Finney's La CW10. . . . . . . 128 B2
Finningley Ct WA2. . . . . 8 E1
Finsbury Cl WA5. . . . . 15 C4
Finsbury Pk WA8 . . . . 13 C5
Finsbury Way SK9 . . . . 34 E2
Finsbury Wlk CW7 . . . . . . 149 A8
Fir Ave
Bramhall SK7. . . . . 35 E8
Halewood L26 . . . . 21 A8
Firbank CH2. . . . . 72 C3
Firbank Cl WA7 . . . . 24 D1
Firbeck Cl
Broughton CH4 . . . . 139 B3
Congleton CW12 . . . . 155 F3
Firbeck Gdns CW2. . . . . . 189 D4
Fir Cl
Halewood L26 . . . . 21 A8
Poynton SK12 . . . . 36 F3
Tarporley CW6. . . . . 146 D2
Fir Ct SK10 . . . . 86 F1

Firdale Rd CW8 .... 103 D7
Firecrest Ct WA1 .... 16 A3
Firemans Sq CH1 .... 237 A3
Fir Gr
Macclesfield SK11 .... 112 D5
Warrington WA1 .... 16 F7
Weaverham CW8 .... 102 E8
Fir La CW8 .... 102 A2
Firman Cl WA5 .... 15 B8
Fir Rd SK7 .... 35 E8
Firrview Pk CW5 .... 217 A3
Firs La WA4 .... 26 B6
Firs Pottery The★
CW5 .... 217 C1
Firs Sch CH2 .... 118 E5
Fir St
Irlam M44 .... 11 D6
Widnes WA8 .... 13 C2
First Ave
Connah's Quay CH5 .... 93 A2
Crewe CW1 .... 190 F2
Kidsgrove ST7 .... 194 E1
Poynton SK12 .... 36 D1
Sandbach CW11 .... 175 A5
First Dig La CW5 .... 219 C8
Firs The SK9 .... 60 A5
First Wood St CW5 ...... 204 D5
Firs View WA6 .... 73 D4
Firth Bvd WA2 .... 16 C7
Firth Cl CW11 .... 175 B7
Firth Fields CW9 .... 103 F2
Firthfields Cl CW9 ...... 103 F2
Firtree Ave WA1 .... 17 A8
Fir Tree Ave
Chester CH4 .... 141 B5
Golborne WA3 .... 3 F8
Knutsford WA16 .... 82 C8
Firtree Cl
Barnton CW8 .... 78 B4
Winsford CW7 .... 127 B1
Fir Tree Cl WA4 .... 26 D1
Fir Tree Cotts CW2 ..... 208 C5
Firtree Gr CH66 .... 95 A8
Fir Tree La
Burtonwood WA5 .... 7 A7
Chester CH3 .... 119 E2
Faddiley CW5 .... 202 B3
Fir Trees Holiday Pk
CH1 .... 117 C2
Fir Tree Wlk WA3 .... 3 F8
Fir Way CH60 .... 41 B5
Firwood Rd ST8 .... 179 E1
Firwood Wlk CW2 .... 190 C1
Fisher Ave WA2 .... 8 B2
Fisherfield Dr WA3 ...... 10 A6
Fishermans Cl CW11 ..... 191 F7
Fisher Rd CH1 .... 117 E4
Fishers Gn CW6 .... 146 B5
Fishers La CW5 .... 203 C8
Fisher St WA7 .... 23 B3
Fishpool Rd CW8 .... 123 F3
Fishwicks Ind Est WA11 .... 1 F8
Fistral Ave SK8 .... 34 C8
Fitton's Cl CW5 .... 217 F5
Fitton St CW9 .... 80 A2
Fitz Cl SK10 .... 87 D3
Fitz Cres SK10 .... 87 D3
Fitzherbert St WA2 ...... 16 C7
Fitzwalter Rd WA1 .... 17 D7
Fitzwilliam Ave SK11 .... 112 F3
Fiveashes Cotts SK10 .... 88 B5
Five Ashes Rd CH4 ...... 141 B5
FIVECROSSES 74 D5
Fivelanes End WA6 ...... 74 C6
Five Ways CH64 .... 41 F3
Fiveways Par SK7 .... 36 E8
Fiveways Pk CH64 .... 41 F3
Flacca Ct CH3 .... 166 B1
Flag La
Crewe CW1, CW2 .... 190 C4
Neston CH64 .... 66 F7
Newhall CW5 .... 228 D8
Flag La N CH2 .... 118 E8
Flag La S CH2 .... 118 E8
Flander Cl WA8 .... 12 C2
Flashes La CH64 .... 67 B5
Flash La
Antrobus CW9 .... 53 F5
Bollington SK10 .... 87 D7
Flat La
Kelsall CW6 .... 122 C4
Sandbach CW11 .... 175 B6
Flatt La CH65 .... 70 B5
Flatts La SK23 .... 64 F4
Flavian Cl CW10 .... 128 C2
Flavian Ct WA7 .... 23 E2
Flaxley Cl WA3 .... 10 A5
Flaxmere Dr CH3 .... 142 B8
Flaxyards CW6 .... 146 F2
Fleet La WA9 .... 1 A2
Fleet St CH65 .... 70 A5
Fleetwood Cl WA5 .... 15 B4
Fleetwood Dr WA12 .... 2 B4
Fleetwood Wlk WA7 ...... 50 C6
Fleming Dr WA2 .... 8 A6
Fleming St CH65 .... 70 C6
Flers Ave WA4 .... 16 C3
Fletcher Ct WA16 .... 56 F1
Fletcher Dr SK12 .... 37 F6
Fletcher Gr CW9 .... 104 C6
Fletcher's Bldgs
Chester CH1 .... 237 B2
6 Runcorn WA7 .... 23 F1
Fletchers La WA13 .... 18 F4
Fletcher's Row 5 WA7 ... 23 F1
Fletcher St
Crewe CW1 .... 190 B5
Warrington WA4 .... 16 B3
Fletsand Rd SK9 .... 60 D6
Flint Cl CH64 .... 66 E6
Flint Ct CH65 .... 70 D2
Flint Dr CH64 .... 66 E6
Flint Gr M44 .... 11 C6
Flint Mdw CH64 .... 66 E7
Flint St SK10 .... 112 E8
Flittogate La WA16 ...... 80 E8
Flixton Dr CW2 .... 190 A2
FLOOKERSBROOK 118 E4
Florence St WA4 .... 16 D3
Florida Cl WA5 .... 15 C7
Flour Mill Way CW1 ..... 191 A3
Flowcrete Bsns Pk
CW11 .... 152 C1
Flowerscroft CW5 ...... 205 A4
Flowers La CW1 .... 172 E1
Flower St CW8 .... 103 E7
Fluin La WA6 .... 74 C8
Flying Fields Dr SK11 ... 112 A5
Foden Ave ST7 .... 194 A3
Foden La
Alderley Edge SK9 .... 59 C1
Bramhall SK7 .... 35 D3
Foden St SK10 .... 87 D1
Fodens Terr CW11 ...... 175 A6
Foden Wlk 7 SK9 .... 34 D2
Fog Cotts CW3 .... 221 E4
Fogg's La CW9, WA4 ...... 53 A6
Fold La
Biddulph ST8 .... 179 E4
Bosley SK11 .... 135 D2
Folds La SK23 .... 65 F3
Folds The CH63 .... 42 A6
Fold The SK10 .... 87 A8
Foley Wlk M22 .... 33 E8
Fol Hollow CW12 .... 156 B1
Folkestone Cl SK10 ...... 87 B2
Folkstone Way WA7 ...... 50 C7
Folly La WA5 .... 15 F7
Forbes Cl WA3 .... 9 E3
Forbes Pk SK7 .... 35 D7
Ford Cl CW1 .... 190 B5
Ford Ct CW7 .... 149 C6
Fordington Rd WA5 ...... 15 B5
Ford La
Crewe CW1 .... 190 B6
Tattenhall CH3 .... 166 F4
Fords La ST7 .... 195 D6
Ford's La SK7 .... 35 D6
Ford St WA1 .... 16 D6
Foregate St CH1 .... 237 B2
Foreland Cl WA5 .... 14 C7
Forest Ave CW4 .... 107 C1
Forest Cl
Cuddington CW8 .... 101 F3
Rainow SK10 .... 88 E5
Forest Dr
Broughton CH4 .... 139 C3
Langley SK11 .... 113 C4
Forester Ave WA16 ...... 57 C2
Foresters Cl WA6 .... 101 A6
Forest Gate Com Prim Sch
M31 .... 11 D3
Forest Gate La CW6 ..... 122 E7
Forest Gdns M31 .... 11 D3
Forest Ho SK10 .... 87 F2
Forest La WA6 .... 100 C6
Forest Pl 3 CW9 .... 79 A1
Forest Rd
Cuddington CW8 .... 101 F2
Delamere CW6 .... 124 B1
Ellesmere Port CH66 ...... 69 E7
Heswall CH60 .... 41 A8
Macclesfield SK11 .... 113 E6
Tarporley CW6 .... 146 D3
Winsford CW7 .... 149 B8
Forest Road Pk CW8 ..... 101 E2
Forest St
Chester CH1 .... 237 C2
Weaverham CW8 .... 102 C8
Forest Wlk 5 WA7 .... 49 F7
Forge Cl
Cronton WA8 .... 12 C5
Warren SK11 .... 111 D2
Forge Fields CW11 ...... 174 F3
Forge La
Congleton CW12 .... 156 B3
Norton in Hales TF9 ..... 236 C1
Forge Mill La CW10 ..... 151 C1
Forge Rd
Ellesmere Port CH66 ...... 69 C6
Warrington WA5 .... 14 F5
Whaley Bridge SK23 ...... 65 E7
Forge Sh Ctr The WA4 .... 16 C1
Forge St CW1 .... 190 D4
Forge Way CH4 .... 140 F4
Formby Cl WA5 .... 14 F4
Formby Dr SK8 .... 34 B8
Forrest Way WA5 .... 15 D3
Forshaw's La WA5 .... 6 E8
Forshaw St WA2 .... 16 C7
Forster Ave CW8 .... 102 E8
Forster St WA2 .... 16 B7
Forsythia Wlk 2 M31 ..... 11 E2
Forty Acre La CW4,
CW12 .... 131 D6
Forum The CH1 .... 237 A2
Forwood Rd CH62 .... 43 D8
Fossa Cl CW10 .... 128 C2
Foster Rd CW12 .... 157 A5
Foster St WA8 .... 13 B1
Fothergill St WA1 .... 16 D7
Fotheringay Ct 3
CH65 .... 70 D2
Foulkes Ave CW1 .... 189 F6
Foundry Bank CW12 ..... 156 E3
Foundry Ct 1 SK22 .... 39 C7
Foundry Ind Est WA8 .... 23 B7
Foundry La
Sandbach CW11 .... 174 D7
Scholar Green ST7 ...... 194 F7
Widnes WA8 .... 22 C5
Foundry St
Bollington SK10 .... 88 B8
Newton-le-W WA12 .... 2 B3
Warrington WA2 .... 16 B6
Fountain Cl SK12 .... 36 D4
Fountain Ct
Biddulph ST8 .... 179 D1
Davenham CW9 .... 103 F2
2 Winsford CW7 .... 126 D1
Fountain Ho SK10 ...... 112 E8
Fountain La
Davenham CW9 .... 103 F2
Frodsham WA6 .... 74 B8
Fountain Pl SK12 .... 36 D4
Fountains Ave WA11 .... 1 F7
Fountains Cl
Middlewich CW10 .... 128 B1
Runcorn WA7 .... 50 C5
Fountain Sq SK12 .... 38 D6
Fountains Rd SK8 .... 35 C6
Fountain St
Congleton CW12 .... 156 D2
Macclesfield SK10 .... 112 E8
Fountains Wlk WA3 .... 4 B8
FOURLANE-ENDS 63 A8
FOUR LANE ENDS 168 D7
Four Lane Ends
Alvanley WA6 .... 74 B1
Warrington WA3 .... 9 D3
Four Lanes Ct 3
CW7 .... 149 B8
FOURLANES END 176 E4
Four Lanes End
Betley CW2 .... 207 F2
Thornton Hough CH63 ..... 42 D5
Fourseasons Cl CW2 .... 206 B8
Fourth Ave
Connah's Quay CH5 .... 92 E2
Crewe CW1 .... 190 F1
Kidsgrove ST7 .... 194 F1
1 Runcorn WA7 .... 49 F7
Fourways CW2 .... 207 B5
Fourways Tech Pk
CW11 .... 176 E4
Fowey Cl SK10 .... 86 D1
Fowler Rd CH1 .... 117 D4
Fowlers Bench La
CH3 .... 184 C5
Fowler St SK10 .... 87 D1
FOWLEY COMMON 5 B5
Fowley Common La
WA3 .... 5 C5
Foxall Way CH66 .... 69 D2
Fox Bank Cl WA8 .... 12 F4
Fox Bench Cl SK7 .... 35 C6
Foxcote WA8 .... 12 B2
Foxcote Cl CH1 .... 117 D5
Fox Cover CH3 .... 119 F5
Fox Cover Rd CH60 .... 41 D7
Fox Covert WA7 .... 50 C7
Foxcovert La WA16 ...... 106 E7
Fox Covert La
Hoole Bank CH2 .... 119 B8
Picton CH2 .... 96 A1
Fox Covert Way CW1 .... 173 A1
Foxdale Ct WA4 .... 26 C7
Foxdene CH66 .... 69 D5
Foxendale Cl CW8 ...... 103 D7
Foxes Fold CW8 .... 78 E1
Foxes Hey CW8 .... 101 D5
Foxes Hollow CW1 ...... 190 E7
Foxes Wlk CH3 .... 142 A7
Foxfield Cl WA2 .... 8 E3
Foxfield La CW7 .... 126 A1
Fox Gdns
Lymm WA13 .... 18 C4
Talke ST7 .... 210 D8
Foxglove Cl
Bollington SK10 .... 88 C8
2 Golborne WA3 .... 3 D8
Huntington CH3 .... 142 A6
Wistaston CW2 .... 206 B7
Foxglove Ct WA6 .... 74 C8
Foxglove Dell WA6 .... 73 D2
Foxglove Way CH64 .... 66 E5
Foxglove Wlk M31 .... 11 F2
Fox Gr WA16 .... 57 C1
Fox Hill CW6 .... 122 D4
Foxhill Cl CW8 .... 102 A2
Foxhill Ct CW6 .... 146 E1
Foxhill Gr WA6 .... 73 D4
Foxhills Cl WA4 .... 26 D3
Foxholme Ct CW1 .... 191 A6
Foxhunter Cl CH3 .... 121 F7
Fox La
Clutton CH3 .... 182 D1
Waverton CH3 .... 143 B5
Foxlea CW9 .... 78 C7
Fox Lea CH1 .... 117 A8
FOXLEY 209 D7
Foxley Cl WA13 .... 19 A2
Foxley Hall Mews
WA13 .... 19 A1
Foxley Heath WA8 .... 22 E8
Fox's Dr CH5 .... 116 A6
Fox St
Congleton CW12 .... 156 F3
Runcorn WA7 .... 23 A1
Warrington WA5 .... 15 E5
Foxwist Cl CH2 .... 237 B4
Foxwist Gn CW8 .... 125 E6
FOXWIST GREEN 125 F6
Foxwood Dr WA16 ...... 108 A8
Fox Wood Specl Sch
WA3 .... 9 E3
Francesca Ct CH1 .... 237 B2
Frances St
Crewe CW2 .... 190 D2
Irlam M44 .... 11 E5
Macclesfield SK11 .... 112 B8
Francis Cl WA8 .... 22 C8
Francis Ct CH1 .... 237 C3
Francis La
Holt LL13 .... 196 D7
Holt, Ridleywood LL13 ... 196 B6
Francis Rd
Frodsham WA6 .... 49 C1
Irlam M44 .... 11 F8
Warrington WA4 .... 16 B1
Francis St CH1 .... 237 C3
FRANDLEY 53 A3
Frank Bott Ave CW1 .... 190 A7
Franklin Cl
Macclesfield SK11 .... 112 B5
Warrington WA5 .... 15 C8
Franklyn Ave CW2 ...... 190 B3
Frank Perkins Way
M44 .... 11 F7
Frank St WA8 .... 13 C1
Frank Webb Ave CW1 ... 190 A6
Frappel Ct WA2 .... 16 B6
Fraser Ct CH4 .... 141 D7
Fraser Rd WA5 .... 14 D6
Frawley Ave WA12 .... 2 C5
Freckleton Cl WA5 .... 15 B4
Frederick St
Warrington WA4 .... 16 E3
Widnes WA8 .... 23 B8
Frederick Terr WA8 ...... 22 A4
Fredric Pl WA7 .... 23 B3
Freedom Dr ST7 .... 195 E3
Free Green La WA16 .... 107 A8
Freeport Shopping Mall
ST7 .... 210 C6
French La CW5 .... 218 C5
French Lane End
CW5 .... 218 E5
French St WA8 .... 13 D1
Freshfield SK8 .... 34 B8
Freshfield Dr SK10 .... 87 C3
Freshfields
Comberbach CW9 .... 78 C7
Knutsford WA16 .... 56 E3
Wistaston CW2 .... 206 A7
Freshfields Dr WA2 .... 9 C1
Freshmeadow La WA6 .... 73 B2
Freshwater Cl WA5 .... 14 D7
Freshwater Dr CW2 ..... 221 C8
Freshwater View
CW8 .... 103 F8
Friars Ave WA5 .... 14 E5
Friars Cl
Rainow SK10 .... 88 D5
Wistaston CW2 .... 205 F8
Friar's Cl SK9 .... 59 E8
Friars Ct 11 WA1 .... 16 B5
Friars Gate
Chester CH1 .... 237 B2
Warrington WA1 .... 16 B4
Friars La WA1 .... 16 B4
Friars Way SK10 .... 86 F2
Frida Cres CW9 .... 103 E6
Friends La WA5 .... 14 D6
Friesian Gdns ST5 ...... 210 C2
Frith Ave CW8 .... 123 D8
Frith La CW5 .... 216 C4
Frith Terr SK11 .... 112 D4
Frobisher Ct WA5 .... 15 D8
Frobisher Rd CH64 .... 66 E8
Froda Ave WA6 .... 74 B7
FRODSHAM 74 D7
Frodsham Bsns Ctr
WA6 .... 49 C1
Frodsham CE Prim Sch
WA6 .... 74 C7
Frodsham Manor House
Prim Sch WA6 .... 49 C1
FRODSHAM MARSH 48 E2
Frodsham Rd WA6 .... 73 D1
Frodsham Sch WA6 .... 74 B8
FRODSHAM SCORE 48 B2
Frodsham Sq CH1 .... 237 B3
Frodsham St CH1 .... 237 B3
Frodsham Sta WA6 .... 74 B8
Frodsham Way SK9 .... 34 E4
Frodsham Weaver Vale
Prim Sch WA6 .... 49 C2
Froghall La
High Legh WA16 .... 29 D7
High Legh WA16 .... 29 E6
Warrington WA2, WA5 .... 15 F5
Frog La
Holt LL13 .... 196 D8
Milton Green CH3 .... 165 E2
Pickmere WA16 .... 55 B1
Worthenbury LL13,
SY14 .... 211 B1
Worthenbury SY14 ...... 211 C2
Frome Ct CH65 .... 70 B7
Front St CW11 .... 175 C6
Frosts Mews CH65 .... 70 B6
Fryer Rd CW9 .... 80 A3
Fryer St 16 WA7 .... 23 A3
Fuchsia Cl CH66 .... 69 F1
Fulbeck WA8 .... 12 C2
Fulbeck Cl CW2 .... 206 B8
Fulbrook Dr SK8 .... 35 A6
Fuller Dr CW2 .... 206 B7
FULLER'S MOOR 183 D1
Fullerton Rd CW8 .... 103 A4
Fulmar Cl SK12 .... 36 A4
Fulmards Cl SK9 .... 60 C7
Fulshaw Ave SK9 .... 60 A6
Fulshaw Cross SK9 ...... 60 A5
Fulshaw Ct SK9 .... 60 A5
FULSHAW PARK 60 B5
Fulshaw Pk SK9 .... 60 A5
Fulshaw Pk S SK9 .... 60 A4
Fulton Gr CW9 .... 103 F2
Fulwood Gdns CH66 ...... 69 C6
Fulwood Mews CH66 ..... 69 C6
Fulwood Rd
Ellesmere Port CH66 ...... 69 C5
Golborne WA3 .... 3 E7
Furber St CW1 .... 190 C5
Furne Rd CH1 .... 117 E4
Furness Cl
Holmes Chapel CW4 ..... 130 A3
Poynton SK12 .... 36 D4
Winsford CW7 .... 149 B8
Furness Ct WA7 .... 24 F4
Furness Lodge Cl
SK23 .... 39 D4
Furness Rd SK8 .... 35 C6
FURNESS VALE 39 C3
Furness Vale Bsns Ctr
SK23 .... 39 D4
Furness Vale Prim Sch
SK23 .... 39 D3
Furness Vale Sta SK23 .... 39 D4
Furnivall St CW11 ...... 175 B7
Furnival St CW2 .... 190 C2
Furrocks Cl CH64 .... 66 F5
Furrocks La CH64 .... 66 F5
Furrocks Way CH64 ...... 66 F5
Furrows The CH66 .... 94 E8
Fylde Ave SK8 .... 34 C8
Fytton Cl SK11 .... 111 D1

G

Gable Ave SK9 .... 60 A7
Gable Ct 5 CW5 .... 204 E6
Gables Cl WA2 .... 8 F3
Gable St WA12 .... 2 B3
Gables The ST7 .... 193 C3
Gabriel Bank CW8 .... 76 A1
Gadbrook Bsns Ctr
CW9 .... 104 D5
Gadbrook Pk CW9 ...... 104 D5
Gadbrook Rd CW9 ...... 104 D6
Gail Cl SK9 .... 60 B2
Gainford Cl WA8 .... 12 C3
Gainsborough Cl SK9 .... 60 D8
Gainsborough Ct WA8 ... 12 B1
Gainsborough Prim Sch
CW2 .... 190 B2
Gainsborough Rd
Crewe CW2 .... 190 B3
Warrington WA4 .... 16 B2
Gairloch Cl WA2 .... 8 F4
Gaisgill Ct WA8 .... 12 C1
Gala Cl CH4 .... 139 C3
Galbraith Cl CW12 ...... 156 C2
Gale Ave WA5 .... 7 F1
Galion Way WA8 .... 12 F3
GALLANTRY BANK 200 B8
Galleys Bank ST7 .... 195 B3
Gallimore Ho ST7 ...... 210 D8
Galloway Cl
Holmes Chapel CW4 ..... 130 C2
Middlewich CW10 .... 128 E2
Galloway Gn CW12 ...... 156 E5
Gallowsclough La
WA6 .... 100 F4
Galway Ave WA8 .... 12 E3
Galway Gr CW2 .... 206 B4
Game St CW11 .... 175 A3
Gamul Pl CH1 .... 237 B1
Ganton Cl WA8 .... 13 B4
Garden Cl SK10 .... 87 E1
Garden Ct CH1 .... 237 A3
Garden La
Chester CH1 .... 237 A3
Harthill CH3 .... 183 E3
Garden Rd WA16 .... 56 F3
Garden St
Bollington SK10 .... 87 F8
Congleton CW12 .... 156 C3
Macclesfield SK10 .... 87 E1
Gardens The
Holt LL13 .... 180 E1
Lawton-gate ST7 .... 194 C4
Sandbach CW11 .... 175 B6
Garden Terr
Chester, Boughton
CH2 .... 118 F2
Chester CH1 .... 237 A3
Garden Wlk 8 M31 .... 11 E3
Gardiner Ave WA11 .... 1 C6
Garfit St CW10 .... 128 C2
Garner St WA2 .... 16 C7
Garnett Ave WA4 .... 17 A4
Garnett Cl CW5 .... 204 F4
Garnetts La WA8 .... 22 A3
Garrett Field WA3 .... 9 D5
Garrigill Cl WA8 .... 13 C5
Garsdale Cl WA5 .... 14 F7
Garside Ave WA3 .... 3 D7
Garth Dr CH2 .... 118 C5
Garth Hts SK9 .... 60 C7
Garth Rd CH65 .... 71 A5
Garton Dr WA3 .... 3 E8
Garven Pl WA1 .... 16 A5
Garwood Cl WA5 .... 15 C8

Gaskell Ave
Knutsford WA16 .... 56 F2
Warrington WA4 .... 17 A3
Gaskell St WA4 .... 16 C1
Gas Rd SK11 .... 112 D8
Gas Works Ind Est
ST7 .... 194 E2
Gatcombe Mews 1
SK9 .... 60 A6
Gateacre Ct CH66 .... 69 F8
Gatefield St CW1 .... 190 C4
Gatehouse The 7
CW5 .... 204 F5
Gateley Cl WA4 .... 17 E3
GATESHEATH 165 E5
Gatesheath Dr CH2 .... 118 E7
Gatesheath La CH3 .... 165 F5
Gatewarth Ind Est
WA5 .... 15 D3
Gate Warth St WA5 .... 15 D4
Gateway
Crewe CW1 .... 190 F2
Newcastle-u-Lyme ST5 .... 210 D2
Gateway Trad Pk WA5 .... 16 A7
Gathurst Ct WA8 .... 22 D8
Gauntlet Birds of Prey
Pk* WA16 .... 56 D5
GAUNTONS BANK 215 E4
Gauntons Bank SY13 .... 215 E3
Gaunts Way WA7 .... 49 E6
Gavin Rd WA8 .... 22 B7
Gaw End La SK11 .... 112 C2
Gawer Pk CH2 .... 118 C4
GAWSWORTH 135 E8
Gawsworth Ave CW2 .... 189 F3
Gawsworth Cl
Alsager ST7 .... 193 C3
Bramhall SK7 .... 35 E6
Holmes Chapel CW4 .... 130 B3
Northwich CW9 .... 104 A4
Poynton SK12 .... 36 F2
Gawsworth Ct WA3 .... 9 F5
Gawsworth Dr CW11 .... 175 C7
Gawsworth Hall*
SK11 .... 134 E8
Gawsworth Prim Sch
SK11 .... 111 D2
Gawsworth Rd
Ellesmere Port CH66 .... 69 E5
Macclesfield SK11 .... 111 D5
Gawsworth Way SK9 .... 34 E4
Gayhurst Ave WA2 .... 8 F2
Gaymoore Cl CH2 .... 237 A4
Gaynor Ave WA11 .... 1 F7
GAYTON 41 B6
Gayton Cl CH2 .... 118 E5
Gayton Farm Rd CH60 .... 41 A5
Gayton La CH60 .... 41 B6
Gayton Mill Cl CH60 .... 41 B7
Gayton Parkway CH60 .... 41 C5
Gayton Prim Sch CH60 .... 41 A6
Gayton Rd CH60 .... 41 A6
Gelli Dderw/Oak Gr
CH4 .... 140 D5
GEMINI 7 D3
Gemini Bsns Pk WA5 .... 7 E3
Gemmull Cl CW3 .... 229 F4
General St WA1 .... 16 C5
Genesis Ctr The WA3 .... 9 E5
Geneva Rd CW7 .... 126 C1
Geo Hampson's Bldgs
WA3 .... 5 C8
George Bates Cl ST7 .... 193 C3
George Cl WA6 .... 73 A2
George Ho CW5 .... 204 E7
George Kenyon Mews
CH4 .... 140 E6
George Rd WA5 .... 15 C4
George St W SK11 .... 112 C8
George's Cl SK12 .... 36 E3
Georges Cres WA4 .... 17 B2
Georges Ct 13 SK10 .... 112 C8
George's La CW9 .... 54 D1
George's Prec WA5 .... 14 D6
George's Rd E SK12 .... 36 E3
George's Rd W SK12 .... 36 E3
George St
Alderley Edge SK9 .... 60 A1
Audley ST7 .... 209 D1
Barnton CW8 .... 78 B3
Chester CH1 .... 237 A3
Ellesmere Port CH65 .... 70 C7
Knutsford WA16 .... 57 A2
Macclesfield SK11 .... 112 D7
Newton-le-W WA12 .... 2 A4
Sandbach CW11 .... 174 E8
Whaley Bridge SK23 .... 65 E7
Winsford CW7 .... 126 E1
Georges Way ST7 .... 209 F2
George's Wlk CW11 .... 175 B6
George VI Ave CW10 .... 151 D6
George VI Cl CW10 .... 151 D6
Georgia Pl WA5 .... 15 C7
Gerard Dr CW5 .... 204 C4
Gerosa Ave WA2 .... 8 B8
Gerrard Ave
Ellesmere Port CH66 .... 69 C4
Warrington WA5 .... 15 F7
Gerrard Dr CW8 .... 77 D1
Gerrard Rd WA3 .... 9 A7
Gerrards Ave CH3 .... 119 A1
Gerrard St WA8 .... 23 B8
Giantswood La
Congleton CW12 .... 156 C6
Marton CW12 .... 132 F1
GIBB HILL 53 D1
Gibb Hill CW9 .... 53 D1
Gibbon Dr SK9 .... 80 B3
Gibson Cl CW5 .... 204 D6
Gibson Cres CW11 .... 174 D6
Gibson Ct Trad Est
CH65 .... 70 C8
Gibson St
Warrington, Howley
WA1 .... 16 C5
Warrington, Stockton Heath
WA4 .... 16 D1
Gigg La
Moore WA4 .... 25 B5
Warrington WA4 .... 17 E3
Gig La WA1 .... 17 E8
Gilbert Cl 2 ST7 .... 195 A2
Gilbert Ct WA3 .... 4 F3
Gilbert Ho WA7 .... 22 E3
Gilchrist Ave SK11 .... 111 E7
Gilchrist Rd M44 .... 11 F6
Gilderdale Cl WA3 .... 10 B5
Gillan Cl WA7 .... 50 C5
GILLBENT 34 F6
Gillbent Rd SK8 .... 35 A7
Gillow Cl CW1 .... 190 A8
GILLOW HEATH 179 C2
Giltbrook Cl WA8 .... 12 F3
Gilwell Cl WA4 .... 17 C2
Gilwern Cl CH2 .... 118 C4
GINCLOUGH 88 F6
Gingerbread La CW5 .... 205 A5
Gipsy Cnr SY13 .... 224 E2
Girton Cl CH65 .... 70 D4
Girton Rd CH65 .... 70 D4
Girvin Dr CH64 .... 66 F6
Glade Dr CH66 .... 68 F6
Gladewood Cl 1 SK9 .... 60 C8
Gladstone Ave CH1 .... 118 B2
Gladstone Mews WA2 .... 16 A6
Gladstone Rd
Broughton CH4 .... 139 B3
Chester CH1 .... 118 B3
Neston CH64 .... 66 E8
Gladstone St
Crewe CW1 .... 190 C4
Northwich CW8 .... 103 E7
Warrington WA2 .... 16 A6
8 Widnes WA8 .... 23 B8
Willaston CW5 .... 205 D6
Winsford CW7 .... 149 D8
Gladstone Way WA12 .... 2 B4
Glaisdale Cl CW2 .... 206 A6
Glamis Cl
Chester CH3 .... 119 A2
Wistaston CW2 .... 205 E8
Glanaber Ct CH4 .... 141 A7
Glan Aber Dr CH4 .... 140 F7
Glan Aber Pk CH4 .... 141 A7
Glandon Dr SK8 .... 35 C8
Glastonbury Ave
Cheadle SK8 .... 35 C6
Chester CH2 .... 118 F7
Golborne WA3 .... 4 C8
Glastonbury Cl WA7 .... 24 F3
Glastonbury Dr
Middlewich CW10 .... 128 B1
Poynton SK12 .... 36 D5
Glastonbury Mews
WA4 .... 16 E2
GLAZEBROOK 11 B6
Glazebrook La WA3 .... 11 B5
Glazebrook St WA1 .... 16 D6
Glazebrook Sta WA3 .... 11 A5
GLAZEBURY 5 B7
Glazebury CE Prim Sch
WA3 .... 5 C7
Glaziers La WA3 .... 4 D2
Gleadmere WA8 .... 12 C2
GLEADSMOSS 132 B6
Gleaner Cl WA7 .... 22 F3
Gleave Ave SK10 .... 88 B8
Gleave Rd
Burtonwood WA5 .... 6 F6
Weaverham CW8 .... 77 D1
Glebe Ave WA4 .... 17 C1
Glebe Cl CW5 .... 220 A8
Glebecroft Ave CH2 .... 72 A3
Glebe Ct ST7 .... 194 D2
Glebe Farm Mews CH2 .... 71 E2
Glebe Green Dr CW7 .... 149 C6
Glebe La WA8 .... 13 B5
Glebeland WA3 .... 4 E2
Glebelands Rd WA16 .... 57 A1
Glebe Mdws CH2 .... 96 F1
Glebe Rd CW8 .... 102 A4
Glebe St ST7 .... 194 D2
Glebe The WA7 .... 23 E1
Glebeway Rd CH65 .... 70 F5
Gleggs Cl CH3 .... 142 B7
Glegg St SK11 .... 112 E7
Glenathol Rd CH66 .... 69 C4
Glenbourne Pk SK7 .... 35 D5
Glenburn Ave CH62 .... 43 E4
Glen Cl WA3 .... 11 B2
Glencoe Cl CW4 .... 130 C2
Glencoe Rd CH66 .... 69 C4
Glencourse Rd WA8 .... 13 A5
Glendale Ave
Elton CH2 .... 72 A3
Sandycroft CH5 .... 116 A3
Glendale Bsns Pk
CH5 .... 116 A3
Glendale Cl
Buerton CW3 .... 230 F4
Crewe CW2 .... 189 D3
Glendale Pk CH5 .... 116 A3
Glendene Ave SK7 .... 35 D5
Glendyke Rd CH66 .... 69 C4
Gleneagles Cl
Bramhall SK7 .... 36 A7
Chester CH3 .... 119 B3
Golborne WA3 .... 3 F7
Wilmslow SK9 .... 60 D8
Gleneagles Dr
Haydock WA11 .... 1 A5
Holmes Chapel CW4 .... 130 B2
Macclesfield SK10 .... 87 C4
Widnes WA8 .... 13 B5
Winsford CW7 .... 126 C2
Gleneagles Rd CH66 .... 69 C4
Glenesk Rd CH66 .... 69 C4
Glenfield Dr SK12 .... 36 D3
Glenholme Rd SK7 .... 35 D7
Glenmaye Rd CH66 .... 69 C4
Glenn Pl WA8 .... 12 E1
Glenorchy Cl CW4 .... 130 C2
Glen Rd CH66 .... 69 C4
Glenside Cl CH1 .... 117 D5
Glenside Dr SK9 .... 60 C6
Glen The
Blacon CH1 .... 117 E5
Runcorn WA7 .... 49 F5
Glenton Pk CH64 .... 66 F6
Glenville Cl WA7 .... 49 B6
Glenwood WA7 .... 24 C1
Glenwood Cl 3 CH66 .... 69 C6
Glenwood Gdns CH66 .... 69 C6
Glenwood Rd CH66 .... 69 C6
Gleyve WA16 .... 29 C5
Gloucester Ave WA3 .... 3 B8
Gloucester Cl
Ellesmere Port CH66 .... 94 E8
Macclesfield SK10 .... 87 E4
Warrington WA1 .... 17 D7
Gloucester Ho 14
CH1 .... 237 C3
Gloucester Rd
Gatley SK8 .... 34 C7
Kidsgrove ST7 .... 195 A3
Knutsford WA16 .... 81 F8
Poynton SK12 .... 36 D4
Widnes WA8 .... 13 B3
Gloucester St CH1 .... 237 B4
Glover Rd WA3 .... 9 C4
Glovers Loom CH3 .... 142 B7
Glover St
Crewe CW1 .... 190 A5
Newton-le-W WA12 .... 2 C3
Gloverstone Ct CH1 .... 237 B1
Glyn Ave CH62 .... 43 E7
Glyn Garth CH1 .... 117 D3
Go Ape Delamere*
CW8 .... 100 B2
Goathland Way SK11 .... 112 D6
Goddard Ct 13 CW1 .... 190 B5
Goddard Rd WA7 .... 23 E3
Goddard St CW1 .... 190 B5
Godfrey St WA2 .... 16 D7
Godscroft La WA6 .... 73 E6
Godshill Cl WA5 .... 14 D7
Godstall La CH1 .... 237 B2
Godstow WA7 .... 24 E4
Godward Rd SK22 .... 39 B8
GOLBORNE 3 B7
Golborne Dale Rd WA3,
WA12 .... 3 A5
Golborne Jun & Inf Sch
WA3 .... 3 A8
Golborne La WA16 .... 28 F3
Golborne Rd
Golborne WA3 .... 3 C8
Winwick WA12, WA2 .... 8 A7
Golborne St WA12 .... 2 E4
Goldcliff Cl WA5 .... 7 D3
Goldcrest Cl
Runcorn WA7 .... 49 F5
Winsford CW7 .... 149 C5
Golden Hill CW2 .... 207 E3
Golden Sq WA1 .... 16 B5
Goldfinch Cl CW12 .... 156 E1
Goldfinch Dr ST7 .... 193 B3
Goldfinch La WA3 .... 9 E4
Goldfinch Rd ST7 .... 195 F1
Goldford La SY14 .... 199 F6
Goldsmith Dr CW11 .... 174 D6
Gold Triangle Complex
WA8 .... 22 C5
Golftyn Dr CH5 .... 91 C1
Golftyn La CH5 .... 91 C1
GOLLY 161 B1
Gongar La
Ashton Hayes CH3 .... 121 E8
Mouldsworth CH3 .... 98 E1
Gonsley Cl CH2 .... 237 B4
Gonville Ave SK11 .... 112 F3
Gooch Dr WA12 .... 2 D2
Goodall's Cnr CW2 .... 206 C3
Goodall St SK11 .... 112 E7
Goode Way CW2 .... 190 D1
Goodier Ct WA7 .... 49 C7
Goodrington Rd SK9 .... 34 E3
Goodwin Cres CW2 .... 206 C4
Goodwood Cl
Barnton CW8 .... 78 B3
Chester CH1 .... 118 B2
Goodwood Ct ST7 .... 193 F6
Goodwood Gr CH66 .... 69 D3
Goodwood Rise
CW10 .... 128 A2
Gooseberry La
Kelsall CW6 .... 122 E3
Runcorn WA7 .... 24 D1
Goosebrook Cl CW9 .... 78 D8
Goosebrook La WA4,
CW9 .... 52 F2
Goose La WA4 .... 26 A2
Goosetrey Cl SK9 .... 34 E1
GOOSTREY 107 D1
Goostrey Com Prim Sch
CW4 .... 130 F8
Goostrey Com Prim Sch
(The Annexe) CW4 .... 107 F1
Goostrey Ct 4 CW12 .... 156 F3
Goostrey La
Goostrey CW4 .... 130 B8
Holmes Chapel CW4 .... 131 A6
Goostrey Sta CW4 .... 131 A8
Goostry La WA16 .... 108 A7
Gordale Cl
Congleton CW12 .... 157 A5
Northwich CW8 .... 103 D8
Warrington WA5 .... 14 F7
Winnington CW8 .... 78 D1
Gordon Ave
Bebington CH62 .... 43 E7
Haydock WA11 .... 1 F7
Warrington WA1 .... 17 B7
Gordon La CH1 .... 95 B5
Gore La SK9 .... 59 C3
Gorran Haven WA7 .... 50 C5
Gorse Bank Rd WA15 .... 32 C7
Gorse Cl WA6 .... 101 A6
GORSE COVERT 10 B5
Gorse Covert CW9 .... 79 C3
Gorse Covert Prim Sch
WA3 .... 10 B5
Gorse Covert Rd WA3 .... 10 B6
Gorsefield CH3 .... 166 A1
Gorsefield Ave CH62 .... 43 D5
Gorsefield Cl CH62 .... 43 D5
Gorsefield Hey SK9 .... 60 E8
Gorse Hill Hostel CH1 .... 117 E3
Gorse La CW12 .... 178 D5
Gorselands SK8 .... 35 B5
Gorse Sq M31 .... 11 D3
Gorse Stacks CH1 .... 237 B3
Gorse The WA14 .... 31 B8
Gorse Way CH3 .... 142 A5
Gorsewood Prim Sch
WA7 .... 50 D7
Gorsewood Rd WA7 .... 50 D6
GORSEY BANK 231 F2
Gorsey Bank Cres
CW5 .... 220 A8
Gorsey Bank Prim Sch
SK9 .... 59 F7
Gorsey La
Partington WA13 .... 20 B7
St Helens WA5, WA9 .... 6 C5
Warrington WA1, WA2 .... 16 D7
Widnes WA8 .... 13 E1
Gorsey Rd SK9 .... 59 F8
Gorseywell La WA7 .... 50 F6
Gorsley Cl CW10 .... 151 C6
GORSTAGE 102 C6
Gorstage La CW8 .... 102 C7
GORSTELLA 140 A1
Gorsthills Com Prim Sch
CH66 .... 69 C3
Gorstons La CH64 .... 67 A6
Gorston Wlk M22 .... 33 C8
GORSTYHILL 207 E2
Gorsty Hill Cl CW2 .... 207 F2
Gorsty Hill Ct CW2 .... 207 F2
Gosberryhole La
CW12 .... 158 A2
Gosforth Ct WA7 .... 49 E7
Gosforth Pl CH2 .... 118 F3
GOSLAND GREEN 169 B1
Gosling Cl WA4 .... 26 A1
Gosling Rd WA3 .... 9 B7
Gosling Way CW12 .... 156 A3
Gosport Cl WA2 .... 8 F1
Goss St CH1 .... 237 A2
Gough Ave WA2 .... 8 B2
Gough's La WA16 .... 82 C7
Goulden St
Crewe CW1 .... 190 A5
Warrington WA5 .... 15 E6
Goulders Ct WA7 .... 50 B5
GOWHOLE 39 E4
Gowy Cl
Alsager ST7 .... 192 F3
Handforth SK9 .... 34 E1
Sandbach CW11 .... 174 E8
Gowy Cres CH3 .... 121 B2
Gowy Ct
Calveley CW6 .... 169 E2
Ellesmere Port CH66 .... 69 E8
Gowy Rd CH2 .... 96 F1
Gowy Wlk CW7 .... 127 A3
Goyt Forest Walks*
SK11 .... 115 E7
Goyt Pl SK23 .... 65 E7
Goyt Rd
Disley SK12 .... 38 D5
Horwich End SK23 .... 65 E6
New Mills SK22 .... 39 D6
Goyt's La SK17 .... 90 F2
Goyt Valley Ind Est
SK23 .... 39 D4
Goyt View SK22 .... 39 B6
Grace Ave WA2 .... 16 B8
Grace Cl CW1 .... 191 C4
Grace Rd CH65 .... 70 C7
Gradbach Mill (YH)*
SK17 .... 138 A1
GRADELEY GREEN 202 F5
Grafton Mews CH2 .... 237 B4
Grafton Rd CH65 .... 70 C7
Grafton St
Newton-le-W WA12 .... 2 B3
Warrington WA5 .... 15 E6
Graham Ave CH66 .... 69 D5
Graham Cl WA8 .... 12 C1
Graham Cres M44 .... 11 C3
Graham Dr
Disley SK12 .... 38 C6
Halewood L26 .... 21 A8
Graham Rd
Blacon CH1 .... 117 F3
Widnes WA8 .... 22 C8
Grainger's Rd CW9 .... 103 F5
Grammar School Ct
WA4 .... 16 F3
Grammar School Rd
Lymm WA13 .... 18 F2
Warrington WA4 .... 16 F3
Grampian Way
Bebington CH62 .... 43 E4
Neston CH64 .... 66 E5
Winsford CW7 .... 149 A7
Granary Mews SK12 .... 36 E3
Granary Mill WA7 .... 50 F6
Granby Cl WA7 .... 50 C5
Granby Rd
Cheadle SK8 .... 35 B8
Warrington WA4 .... 26 B8
Grandford La CW5 .... 217 D2
Grand Junction Ret Pk
CW1 .... 190 D3
GRANGE
Runcorn 49 D7
Warrington 17 E8
Grange Ave
Barnton CW8 .... 78 A3
Warrington WA4 .... 16 E4
Grangebrook Dr CW7 .... 126 C3
Grange Cl
Chorlton CW2 .... 207 E4
Crewe CW1 .... 190 E3
Golborne WA3 .... 3 C6
Sandbach CW11 .... 174 F7
Grange Com Prim Sch
CW7 .... 126 B1
Grange Comp Sch
WA7 .... 23 C1
Grange Cres CH66 .... 44 A1
Grange Ct
Biddulph ST8 .... 179 D2
14 Knutsford WA16 .... 57 A2
Winsford CW7 .... 126 B2
Grange Dr
Hartford CW8 .... 103 A6
Thornton Hough CH63 .... 42 A7
Warrington WA5 .... 15 A4
Widnes WA8 .... 12 D1
Grange Farm Cl WA5 .... 15 D6
Grangefields ST8 .... 179 E4
Grange Green Manor
WA4 .... 25 E7
Grange Inf Sch The
WA7 .... 23 C1
Grange Jun Sch The
Hartford CW8 .... 103 A6
Runcorn WA7 .... 23 C1
Grange La
Tilston SY14 .... 198 E3
Weaverham CW8 .... 102 A7
Whitegate CW8 .... 125 F7
Winsford CW7 .... 126 B4
Grangelands SK10 .... 86 F2
Grange Lea CW10 .... 128 B1
Grangemoor WA7 .... 49 D8
Grange Park Ave
Runcorn WA7 .... 23 C2
Wilmslow SK9 .... 60 A8
Grange Park Dr ST8 .... 179 E3
Grange Pl M44 .... 11 E5
Grange Rd
Barnton CW8 .... 78 A3
Biddulph ST8 .... 179 E3
Chester CH2 .... 118 D4
Chester, Vicarscross
CH3 .... 119 C2
Cuddington CW8 .... 101 F3
Ellesmere Port CH65 .... 70 C4
Haydock WA11, WA12 .... 1 D5
Macclesfield SK11 .... 112 C6
Mouldsworth CH3 .... 99 B1
Northwich, Rudheath
CW9 .... 104 D6
Runcorn WA7 .... 23 C2
Grange Rd N WA7 .... 23 C2
Grange Rd W CH3 .... 119 C2
Grange Sch The CW8 .... 103 B6
Grangeside CH2 .... 118 D7
Grange The
Congleton CW12 .... 179 B8
Hartford CW8 .... 103 B5
Macclesfield SK11 .... 112 A6
Grange Valley WA11 .... 1 D6
Grange Valley Prim Sch
WA11 .... 1 D5
Grange Villas CH3 .... 142 F6
Grangeway
Handforth SK9 .... 34 D4
Runcorn WA7 .... 49 C8
Grange Way CW11 .... 174 F7
Grangeway Ct WA7 .... 49 C8
Grangewood Dr SK11 .... 83 F3
Granston Cl WA5 .... 7 E2
Grant Cl WA5 .... 7 D1
Grantham Ave
Warrington, Bruche
WA1 .... 16 E7
Warrington WA4 .... 26 B8
Grantham Cl CW9 .... 104 C7
Granville Dr CH66 .... 69 B7
Granville Rd
Chester CH1 .... 118 B3

Granville Rd *continued*
Northwich CW9 .... **104** A5
Wilmslow SK9 .... **59** F5
Granville Sq CW7 ...... **149** E8
Granville St
15 Runcorn WA7 .... **23** A3
Warrington WA1 .... **16** D6
Winsford CW7 .... **149** E8
Grapes St 9 SK11 ..... **112** D7
GRAPPENHALL **17** A1
Grappenhall Hall Sch
WA4 .... **17** B1
GRAPPENHALL HEYS **27** A8
Grappenhall Heys Com
Prim Sch WA4 .... **27** A7
Grappenhall La WA4 .... **27** E6
Grappenhall Rd
Ellesmere Port CH65 ..... **69** F3
Warrington WA4 .... **16** D1
Grappenhall St Wilfrid's
CE Prim Sch WA4 .... **17** B1
Grasmere SK11 .... **112** A6
Grasmere Ave
Congleton CW12 .... **155** F2
Crewe CW2 .... **189** F5
Warrington WA2 .... **8** E3
Grasmere Cl CW7 ...... **126** D2
Grasmere Cres
Bramhall SK7 .... **35** E8
High Lane SK12 .... **37** E8
Grasmere Dr
Holmes Chapel CW4 ..... **130** A3
Runcorn WA7 .... **49** D5
Grasmere Rd
Alderley Edge SK9 .... **60** A1
Chester CH2 .... **118** F5
Ellesmere Port CH65 ..... **70** C2
Frodsham WA6 .... **74** C8
Lymm WA13 .... **18** F4
Neston CH64 .... **66** E6
Partington M31 .... **11** E3
Grason Ave SK9 .... **34** C1
Grassfield Way WA16 .... **82** A8
Grassmoor Cl CH62 ..... **43** E8
Grassygreen La ST7 .... **209** E1
Gratrix Rd CH62 .... **43** D8
GRAVEL **127** A1
Gravel La SK9 .... **59** E5
Gravel Wlk SY14 ...... **213** D7
Gravenhunger La
CW3 .... **232** D1
GRAVENHUNGER MOSS
.... **232** D2
Graveyard La WA16 ..... **58** F5
Gray Ave WA11 .... **1** D6
Graylag Cl WA7 .... **49** F5
Graymarsh Dr SK12 ..... **36** E2
Gray's Cl ST7 .... **195** B7
Greasby Dr CH66 .... **69** E4
Great Ashfield WA8 ..... **12** D3
GREAT BARROW **120** E6
GREAT BUDWORTH **79** A7
Great Budworth CE Prim
Sch CW9 .... **79** B8
Great Delph WA11 .... **1** D7
Greater Grace Sch
CH1 .... **95** B4
Great King St SK11 .... **112** C8
Greatoak Rd ST7 ...... **209** F4
Great Oak Sq WA16 ..... **58** A4
Great Queen St SK11 ... **112** C8
Great Riding WA7 .... **50** C7
GREAT SANKEY **15** A6
Great Sankey High Sch
WA5 .... **14** E7
Great Sankey Prim Sch
WA5 .... **15** A5
GREAT SUTTON **69** D3
Greaves La SY14 .... **222** E6
Greaves La E SY14 ..... **222** E7
Greaves Rd SK9 .... **59** E7
Grebe Cl
Knutsford WA16 .... **57** B3
Poynton SK12 .... **36** B4
Greeba Ave WA4 .... **16** B3
Greek St WA7 .... **22** F3
Greenacre SK8 .... **34** C7
Green Acre Cl WA16 ..... **82** B8
Greenacre Dr CH63 ...... **43** C7
Greenacre Rd CH4 ..... **140** F4
Greenacres
Crewe CW1 .... **190** D6
Duddon CW6 .... **145** A6
Frodsham WA6 .... **74** C6
Sandbach CW11 .... **175** A7
Greenacres Cl WA3 .... **4** B8
Greenacres Ct CH2 ...... **95** F1
Greenacres Rd CW12 ... **155** F2
Greenacres The WA13 ... **19** A4
Greenall Ave WA5 .... **14** D4
Greenall Rd CW9 .... **104** B8
Greenall's Ave WA4 ...... **16** C2
Green Ave
Alpraham CW6 .... **169** D4
Barnton CW8 .... **78** A3
Davenham CW9 .... **103** F3
GREENBANK **103** C7
Greenbank
Chester CH4 .... **141** E6
Dunham-on-t-H WA6 ...... **97** E6
Green Bank
Adderley TF9 .... **235** A5
Chester CH4 .... **141** E6
Greenbank Ave CH66 ..... **69** C7
Greenbank Cl CW5 ..... **205** D6
Greenbank Dr SK10 ...... **88** A8
Greenbank Gdns WA4 .... **16** F2
Greenbank La CW8 ..... **103** D6
Greenbank Pk CW11 .... **175** A2
Greenbank Rd
Chester CH2 .... **119** A4
Warrington WA4 .... **16** F2
Greenbank Residential
Sch CW8 .... **103** D6
Greenbank St WA4 .... **16** C2
Greenbank Sta CW8 .... **103** D6
Green Bridge Cl WA7 .... **24** A2
Greenbridge Rd WA7 ..... **24** B2
Green Coppice WA7 ..... **50** C8
Greencourts Bsns Pk
M22 .... **34** A8
GREENDALE **86** E7
Greendale Dr
Middlewich CW10 ...... **151** B7
Newcastle-u-Lyme ST5 ... **210** D1
Greendale Gdns CW1 ... **190** E5
Greendale La SK10 ...... **86** D8
Green Dr
Alsager ST7 .... **193** D4
Handforth SK9 .... **34** D2
Green Farm CH4 .... **163** B2
Greenfield Ave CH4 .... **161** A7
Greenfield Cl SK22 ...... **39** A8
Greenfield Cres
Chester CH2 .... **119** B5
Waverton CH3 .... **143** B6
Greenfield Farm Ind Est
CW12 .... **156** B3
Greenfield Gdns CH2 ..... **72** B3
Greenfield La
Chester CH2 .... **119** B5
Frodsham WA6 .... **49** B1
Greenfield Rd
Bollington SK10 .... **88** A7
Broughton CH4 .... **139** C4
Congleton CW12 .... **156** B3
Ellesmere Port CH66 ..... **69** B7
Waverton CH3 .... **143** B6
Greenfields
Chester CH2 .... **95** F1
Winsford CW7 .... **127** B1
Greenfields Ave
Bebington CH62 .... **43** C7
Shavington CW2 .... **206** B4
Warrington WA4 .... **26** D8
Greenfields Cl
Neston CH64 .... **66** F5
Newton-le-W WA12 .... **2** C4
Warrington WA1 .... **17** C7
Greenfields Cres CH62 ... **43** C7
Greenfields Croft
CH64 .... **66** E5
Greenfields Dr
Alsager ST7 .... **193** E3
Neston CH64 .... **66** F5
Greenfields La
Malpas SY14 .... **213** B4
Rowton CH3 .... **142** F5
Greenfields Lo CH3 .... **120** D6
Greenfields Prim Sch
CW7 .... **126** A1
Greenfield Way CW8 .... **102** A4
Greengate WA15 .... **32** D7
Greengate Rd ST7 ..... **193** F5
Greengates Cres CH64 ... **66** E5
Green Hall Mews SK9 .... **60** B6
Greenhaven Ct CW5 .... **219** E5
Greenhill La WA4 .... **52** A5
Greenhills Cl SK11 ..... **112** E7
Greenhill Wlk SK12 ...... **38** D6
Greenhouse Farm Rd
WA7 .... **50** B6
Greenhythe Rd SK8 ..... **34** C6
Green Jones Brow WA5 .... **6** F6
Green La
Acton CW5 .... **204** B3
Alderley Edge SK9 .... **59** F1
Audlem CW3 .... **229** F2
Barbridge CW5 .... **187** A7
Bollington SK10 .... **63** B1
Burtonwood WA5 .... **6** E7
Chester CH4 .... **140** E4
Chester, Vicarscross
CH3 .... **119** B3
Christleton CH3 .... **120** C2
Davenham CW9 .... **103** F3
Disley SK12 .... **38** D4
Ellesmere Port, Great Sutton
CH66 .... **69** C4
Ellesmere Port, Great Sutton
CH66 .... **69** D4
Ellesmere Port, Wolverham
CH65 .... **70** C4
Higher Kinnerton CH4 ... **161** B6
Higher Wincham CW9 ..... **79** F4
Irlam M44 .... **11** E5
Kelsall CW6 .... **122** D4
Knutsford WA16 .... **56** D4
Lindow End SK9 .... **84** F8
Over Peover WA16 .... **83** D1
Picton CH2 .... **96** C3
Plumley WA16 .... **80** E6
Poynton SK12 .... **37** C4
Sandbach CW11 .... **173** F7
Saughall CH1 .... **117** C7
Shocklach SY14 .... **211** C7
Tattenhall CH3 .... **182** F5
Tilston SY14 .... **212** B8
Warrington, Dudlow's Green
WA4 .... **26** F5
Warrington, Paddington
WA1 .... **17** A8
Widnes WA8 .... **12** E1
Willaston CW5 .... **205** E5
Wilmslow SK9 .... **60** B7
Winwick WA2 .... **8** A7
Green Lake La CH3 ..... **163** F3
Greenland Cl CW6 ..... **146** D1
Greenlands CH3 .... **166** B3
Greenlands Cl 3 SK8 .... **34** E8
Green Lane Cl WA2 .... **8** A7
Green Lane Com Specl
Sch WA1 .... **17** B8
Green Lane E
Connah's Quay CH5 ...... **93** C1
Sealand CH5 .... **116** D7
Green Lane Est
Connah's Quay CH5 ...... **93** C1
Sealand CH5 .... **116** C8
Green Lane W CH5 .... **93** B3
Greenlaw Cl CW9 ...... **104** A5
Green Lawns Dr 8
CH66 .... **94** F8
Greenlea Cl CH65 .... **70** B2
GREENLOOMS **143** F4
Green Mdws
Golborne WA3 .... **3** E5
Macclesfield SK11 ...... **111** F6
Greenoaks Ctr WA8 ...... **23** B8
Greenoaks Farm Ind Est
WA8 .... **23** C8
Green Oaks Path WA8 .... **23** C8
Green Oaks Way WA8 .... **23** C8
Greenock Mews WA8 ..... **12** E3
Greenore Dr L24 .... **21** D2
Green Pk CW8 .... **102** E7
Green Rd M31 .... **11** E3
Greensbridge La L26 ..... **21** A8
Greenshall La SK12 ...... **38** F5
Greenshank Cl WA12 ...... **2** C4
Greenside Ave WA6 ...... **74** D7
Greenside Ct CW9 ..... **105** D5
Greenside Dr CW9 ..... **105** A8
Green St
5 Alderley Edge SK9 ..... **60** A1
Holt LL13 .... **180** E1
Knutsford WA16 .... **57** A2
Macclesfield SK10 ...... **112** E7
Sandbach CW11 .... **175** B6
Warrington WA5 .... **15** E5
Warrington WA5 .... **15** F5
Greens The WA15 .... **32** D7
Greensway CH4 .... **141** A7
Green The
Cheadle SK8 .... **34** F8
Congleton CW12 .... **156** C2
Ellesmere Port CH65 ..... **70** B2
Hale L24 .... **21** D1
Handforth SK9 .... **34** E3
Hartford CW8 .... **103** B5
Harthill CH3 .... **183** E3
Higher Kinnerton CH4 ... **161** B7
Lawton-gate ST7 .... **194** A4
Middlewich CW10 ...... **151** D6
Nantwich CW5 .... **204** D8
Neston CH64 .... **66** D8
Neston, Little Neston
CH64 .... **66** F6
Partington M31 .... **11** F4
4 Runcorn WA7 .... **23** F1
Saughall CH1 .... **94** A2
Tarvin CH3 .... **121** F2
Thornton Hough CH63 .... **42** C4
Woore CW3 .... **232** C1
Green View WA13 .... **19** B5
Green Villa Pk SK9 ...... **59** E4
Greenway
Alsager ST7 .... **193** B5
Bramhall SK7 .... **35** D6
Congleton CW12 .... **156** B3
Crewe CW1 .... **190** D7
Farndon CH3 .... **180** F1
Neston CH64 .... **41** B2
Saughall CH1 .... **94** A1
Tilston SY14 .... **198** C3
Warrington, Great Sankey
WA5 .... **14** E7
Warrington, Paddington
WA1 .... **16** F7
Warrington WA4 .... **26** D7
Wilmslow SK9 .... **60** B6
Greenway Cl
Helsby WA6 .... **73** B3
Rode Heath ST7 .... **193** F8
Greenway Dr CW9 ..... **104** C7
Greenway Rd
Biddulph ST8 .... **179** E2
Gatley SK8 .... **34** C6
Runcorn WA7 .... **23** A1
Speke L24 .... **21** A3
Widnes WA8 .... **13** B1
Greenways ST7 .... **209** F2
Greenways Ct CH62 ..... **43** C6
Greenway St CH4 ...... **237** B1
Greenway Wlk CW9 .... **104** C7
Greenwell Rd WA11 .... **1** C6
Greenwich Ave WA8 ..... **13** D4
Green Wlk
Cuddington CW8 .... **102** B4
Partington M31 .... **11** E3
Greenwood Ave
Chester CH4 .... **141** D7
Congleton CW12 .... **156** F3
Greenwood Cl CW8 ...... **77** D1
Greenwood Cres WA2 ...... **8** E2
Greenwood Ct WA3 .... **4** F1
Greenwood Dr
Newton-le-W WA12 .... **2** D2
Runcorn WA7 .... **24** F4
Wilmslow SK9 .... **60** D8
Greenwood Rd WA13 ..... **18** F2
Greenwood Terr WA16 ... **58** A4
Greenwood The CW6 ... **168** D8
Greg Ave SK10 .... **87** E8
Greg Mews SK9 .... **34** B2
Gregory Cl WA5 .... **15** C7
Gregorys Row WA3 .... **4** A8
Gregson Rd WA8 .... **13** C1
Grenfell Cl CH64 .... **41** C1
Grenfell Ct CH64 .... **66** C8
Grenfell Pk CH64 .... **41** C1
Grenfell St 11 WA8 .... **23** B8
Grenville Cl CW1 ...... **191** C5
Grenville Cres CH63 ..... **43** C7
Grenville Rd CH64 .... **41** F1
Gresford Ave CH2 ...... **237** C4
Gresford Cl WA5 .... **7** E1
Gresley Way ST7 .... **209** F2
Gresty Bldgs 3 CW5 .... **204** E6
Gresty Green Rd
CW2 .... **206** D7
Gresty La CW2 .... **206** B7
Gresty Rd CW2 .... **190** D1
Gresty Road Football Gd (
Crewe Alexandra FC)
CW2 .... **190** D2
Gresty Side CW5 .... **204** C5
Gresty Terr CW1 .... **190** E4
Greta Ave SK8 .... **34** C6
Greville Dr CW7 .... **127** A1
Grey Friars CH1 .... **237** A2
Greyfriars Cl WA2 .... **9** A3
Greyhound Park Rd
CH1 .... **118** A3
Greyhound Pk CH1 ..... **118** A3
Greyhound Rd SK10 ..... **86** B5
Greymist Ave WA1 .... **17** C7
Greys Ct WA1 .... **9** C1
Greysfield Flats CH3 ... **120** D6
Grey St WA1 .... **16** C6
Greystoke Dr SK9 .... **60** A2
Greystoke Rd SK10 ...... **87** F2
Greystone Pk CW1 ..... **190** D4
Greystone Rd WA5 ...... **14** F4
Greystones CH66 .... **69** D4
Greystones Rd CH3 .... **119** C1
Grice St WA4 .... **16** C1
Griffin Cl
Blacon CH1 .... **117** F6
New Mills SK22 .... **39** D6
Norton in Hales TF9 .... **236** C2
Griffin La SK8 .... **34** D7
Griffin Mews WA8 .... **13** B3
Griffith Ave WA3 .... **9** E5
Griffiths Dr CW9 ...... **104** D6
Griffiths Rd
Lostock Gralam CW9 ..... **79** F1
Northwich CW9 .... **104** E8
Griffiths St WA4 .... **16** F4
Grig Pl ST7 .... **193** C5
Grimsditch La WA4 ...... **52** B5
Grimshaw Ave SK10 ..... **88** A7
Grimshaw La SK10 ...... **88** A7
Grindley Bank CH2 ..... **119** F8
GRINDLEY BROOK **225** C3
Grindley Gdns CH65 ..... **70** C2
Grindley Gn SY13 ...... **228** B3
Grisedale Ave WA2 .... **8** B3
Grisedale Cl WA7 .... **49** E5
Grisedale Rd CH62 ...... **43** F8
Grisedale Way SK11 .... **112** A5
Gritstone Dr SK10 ..... **112** A8
Grizedale WA8 .... **12** B2
Grizedale Cl CW2 ...... **189** D2
Groarke Dr WA5 .... **14** D5
Groby Rd CW1 .... **190** E8
Grocotts Row 12 CW5 ... **204** E5
Grosvenor Ave
Alsager ST7 .... **193** D5
3 Golborne WA3 .... **3** D8
Hartford CW8 .... **103** A4
Warrington WA1 .... **16** F7
Grosvenor Cl
Warrington WA5 .... **15** C5
Wilmslow SK9 .... **60** A4
Grosvenor Cotts CH4 ... **141** D7
Grosvenor Ct
Chester CH1 .... **237** C2
12 Crewe CW1 .... **190** B5
Winsford CW7 .... **149** C7
Grosvenor Ctr SK11 .... **112** D8
Grosvenor Dr SK12 ...... **36** D3
Grosvenor Gdns WA12 .... **2** C2
Grosvenor Grange WA1 .... **9** B1
Grosvenor Mus*
CH1 .... **237** A1
Grosvenor Nuffield Hospl
CH4 .... **141** C6
Grosvenor Pk Rd CH1 ... **237** C2
Grosvenor Pk Terr CH1,
CH3 .... **237** C2
Grosvenor Pl CH1 ...... **237** B1
Grosvenor Rd
Chester CH4 .... **141** C7
Congleton CW12 .... **156** A3
Haydock WA11 .... **1** B7
Tarvin CH3 .... **121** A2
Widnes WA8 .... **13** B5
Grosvenor Sh Ctr The
CH1 .... **237** B2
Grosvenor St
Chester CH1 .... **237** A2
Crewe CW1 .... **190** B5
3 Macclesfield SK10 .... **112** C8
Runcorn WA7 .... **23** B3
Winsford CW7 .... **149** E8
Grotsworth La SY14 .... **214** E8
Grotto La WA16 .... **108** B7
Grounds St WA2 .... **16** B7
Grove Arc SK9 .... **60** A2
Grove Ave
Chester CH3 .... **119** B3
Grove Ave *continued*
Kidsgrove ST7 .... **194** E1
Lawton-gate ST7 .... **194** A4
Lostock Gralam CW9 ..... **80** A3
Lymm WA13 .... **18** C3
Wilmslow SK9 .... **60** B7
Grove Cl 1 CW7 .... **149** B8
Grove Cres CW3 .... **232** C1
Grove Ct
Alsager ST7 .... **193** E4
Lymm WA13 .... **18** C3
Grove Gdns CH3 .... **119** E2
Grove Ho SK8 .... **35** B6
Grove La SK8 .... **35** A6
Grovemount CW9 ...... **103** F2
Grove Park Ave ST7 .... **194** A4
Grove Pk WA16 .... **57** A1
Grove Rd CH1 .... **94** E4
Grove Rise WA13 .... **18** E3
Grove St
New Mills SK22 .... **39** B7
Runcorn WA7 .... **22** F3
Warrington WA4 .... **16** C4
Wilmslow SK9 .... **60** B7
Groves The
Chester CH1 .... **237** B2
Ellesmere Port CH66 ..... **95** A8
Grove Terr WA6 .... **73** C4
Grove The
Cheadle SK8 .... **35** A6
Knutsford WA16 .... **57** C4
Lawton-gate ST7 .... **194** A4
Lymm WA13 .... **18** E3
Tarporley CW6 .... **146** C2
Warrington WA5 .... **14** F4
Whitchurch SY13 .... **225** F1
Grove Way SK9 .... **60** B7
Grovewood Mews
SK11 .... **112** C6
Grub La CW6 .... **122** C5
Grundy Cl WA8 .... **12** F3
Grundy St WA3 .... **3** A7
Guardian St WA5 .... **15** F6
Guardian Street Ind Est
WA5 .... **15** F6
Guernsey Cl
Congleton CW12 .... **157** A2
Middlewich CW10 ...... **128** D2
Warrington WA4 .... **26** D8
Guernsey Dr CH65 .... **70** C1
Guernsey Ho CH2 ...... **119** B5
Guernsey Rd WA8 .... **13** E3
Guests Slack WA6 ...... **100** B8
Guest St WA8 .... **23** A7
Guilden Gn CH3 .... **119** E4
GUILDEN SUTTON **119** E5
Guilden Sutton CE Prim
Sch CH3 .... **119** F5
Guilden Sutton La
CH3 .... **119** D5
Guildford Ave SK8 .... **35** A6
Guildford Cl
1 Chester CH4 .... **140** F6
Warrington WA2 .... **9** A1
Guillemot Cl CW1 ...... **190** F5
Gullane Cl SK10 .... **87** B4
Gull Cl SK12 .... **36** B3
Gullet The CW5 .... **204** E5
Gullivers World Theme
Pk* WA5 .... **7** E1
Gulls Way CH60 .... **40** E7
Gunco La
Macclesfield SK11 ...... **112** E6
Prestbury SK10 .... **87** C8
Gunn Gr CH64 .... **66** F8
GURNETT **112** F4
Gutterscroft CW1 ...... **191** D5
Gutticar Rd WA8 .... **12** B1
Guy La CH3 .... **143** D5
Gypsy La CH1 .... **94** F2

H

Hacked Way La SK11 .... **113** F6
HACK GREEN **218** D5
Hack Green Secret
Nuclear Bunker*
CW5 .... **218** D4
Haddon Cl
Alderley Edge SK9 .... **59** F2
High Lane SK6 .... **37** E6
Holmes Chapel CW4 ..... **130** B3
Macclesfield SK11 ...... **112** B5
Wistaston CW2 .... **206** B7
Haddon Dr WA8 .... **12** C3
Haddon Ho 4 CH64 ...... **66** E8
Haddon La CH64 .... **67** C4
Haddon Rd
Burton CH64 .... **67** D2
Gatley SK8 .... **34** C7
Hadfield Cl WA8 .... **13** E2
Hadfield St CW9 .... **79** B1
Hadleigh Cl WA5 .... **14** E5
Hadley Ave CH62 .... **43** C8
Hadley Dr CW2 .... **207** E4
Hadlow La CH64 .... **67** F7
Hadlow Rd CH64 .... **67** F6
Hadlow Terr CH64 .... **67** F7
Hadrian Dr CH1 .... **117** E6
Hadrian Way
Cuddington CW8 .... **102** B2
Middlewich CW10 ...... **128** C2
Hadyn Jones Dr CW5 ... **204** F4

Hafod Cl
Blacon CH1 117 D3
Connah's Quay CH5 91 C1
Hag Bank La SK12 38 D7
HAGUE BAR 38 F8
Hague Bar Prim Sch
SK22 38 E8
Hague Bar Rd SK22 39 A7
Hague Fold Rd SK22 38 F8
Haig Ave
Irlam M44 11 C4
Warrington WA5 15 A5
Haig Ct WA16 57 C4
Haighton Ct 11 CW5 204 E6
Haig Rd
Knutsford WA16 57 C4
Widnes WA8 13 A1
Hailwood Ho SK10 88 B8
HALE
Altrincham 32 B8
Liverpool 21 D1
Hale Ave SK12 36 D2
HALE BANK 22 A4
Hale Bank CE Prim Sch
WA8 22 A5
Halebank Rd WA8 21 F5
Hale Bank Terr WA8 22 A4
HALE BARNS 32 D8
Hale CE Prim Sch L24 21 E1
Hale Ct WA8 22 A4
Hale Gate Rd
Hale WA8 21 F3
Widnes WA8 22 A3
Hale Gr WA5 15 A6
HALE HEATH 21 A1
Hale Rd
Hale L24 21 B2
Widnes WA8 22 C7
Hale Road Ind Est WA8 22 B4
Hale St WA2 16 B7
Hale View WA7 48 E8
Hale View Rd WA6 73 C4
HALEWOOD 21 B7
Halewood Lane Ends
L26 21 A8
HALEWOOD VILLAGE 21 A8
Haley Rd N WA5 6 E6
Haley Rd S WA5 6 E5
Halfacre La WA4 17 F2
Half St SK11 112 D6
Halghton La LL13 222 B2
Halifax Cl WA2 8 D2
Halkett Cl CH4 140 E5
Halkyn Rd CH2 237 C4
Hall Acres La SK8 34 E8
Hallams Dr CW5 205 B4
Hallastone Rd WA6 73 C4
Hall Ave WA8 12 A1
Halla-Way WA4 16 E3
Hall Bank WA16 58 C4
Hall Bank N WA16 58 C4
Hall Bank S WA16 58 C4
Hall Cl SK10 87 D4
Hallcroft M31 11 F4
Hallcroft Pl WA4 17 A2
Hall Dr
Alsager ST7 193 C3
Marston CW9 79 B6
Warrington WA4 26 D6
Willaston CW5 205 C6
Hallefield Cres 5
SK11 112 E7
Hallefield Dr 4 SK11 112 E7
Hallefield Rd SK10,
SK11 112 E7
Hall Farm CH62 44 A4
Hall Farm Cl SK23 65 D8
Hallfield Dr CH2 72 B3
Hallfield Pk CH66 69 D4
Hallfields Rd
Tarvin CH3 121 C2
Warrington WA2 8 D1
Hall Gr SK10 87 D3
HALL GREEN
Scholar Green 194 E5
Whitchurch 224 E1
Hallgreen La CW12 155 D8
Hall Hill SK10 87 E7
Halliday Cl WA3 9 F3
Halliwel Jones Stad
(Warrington Wolves
RLFC) The WA2 16 A6
Halliwell's Brow WA16 29 B3
Hall La
Appleton Thorn WA4 27 B8
Audlem CW3 230 C7
Brown Knowl CH3 199 C7
Cronton L35 12 C7
Daresbury WA4 25 D2
Haughton CW6 186 D5
Kelsall CW6 122 D6
Little Leigh CW9 77 F8
Lostock Gralam CW9 79 F3
Mobberley WA16 58 D4
Newton-le-W WA5 7 B8
Ollerton WA16 83 B5
Partington M31 11 F4
Pickmere WA16 55 B1
Sandbach CW11 174 B5
Shotwick CH1 93 B5
St Helens WA9 6 A4
Stretton WA4 52 D8
Sutton Lane Ends SK11 112 F3
Utkinton CW6 146 C6
Winsford CW7 149 B3
Hall La The CW6 147 D2
Hall Moss La SK7 35 C4
Hall Nook WA5 14 F3
Hall O'shaw St CW1 190 E4
Hallows Ave WA2 16 D8
Hallows Cl CW6 122 C4
Hallows Dr CW6 122 C4
HALLOWSGATE 122 C4
Hallowsgate Ct CW6 122 C4
Hall Rd
Handforth SK9 34 E3
Haydock WA11 1 E7
Warrington WA1 17 C7
Wilmslow SK9 60 A7
Hallsgreen La CH2 96 F7
Hallshaw Ave CW1 190 E5
Hallside Pk WA16 57 C1
Halls Rd
Biddulph ST8 179 C1
Mow Cop ST7 195 C7
Hall St
Audley ST7 209 D2
Macclesfield SK10 112 C8
New Mills SK22 39 B8
Warrington WA1 16 C5
Hall Terr WA5 14 E7
Hall View CH3 166 B1
Hall View Cl CW8 102 A7
Hall Wood Ave WA11 1 E8
Hallwood Cl WA7 49 B6
Hallwood Ct CH64 66 E7
Hallwood Dr CH66 68 D4
Hallwood Link Rd WA7 49 F6
HALLWOOD PARK 49 F6
Hallwood Park Ave
WA7 49 E6
Hallwood Park Prim Sch
WA7 49 E6
Hallwood Rd SK9 34 D2
Halsall Ave WA2 16 D8
Halsall Cl WA7 50 C5
Halsall's Cotts WA8 21 E5
Halstone Ave SK9 59 E4
HALTON BROOK 23 D1
Halton Brook Ave WA7 23 D1
Halton Brow WA7 23 E1
Halton Castle★ WA7 23 F1
Halton Cres CH66 69 F2
Halton Ct WA7 23 D2
Halton Dr CW2 189 D5
Halton General Hospl
WA7 49 F7
Halton High Sch WA7 50 C6
Halton Lea S Ctr WA7 49 E8
Halton Link Rd WA7 49 E8
HALTON LODGE 49 D7
Halton Lodge Ave
WA7 49 D7
Halton Lodge Prim Sch
WA7 49 D8
Halton Rd
Chester CH2 118 F6
Ellesmere Port CH66 69 E2
Runcorn WA7 23 D2
Warrington WA5 14 F6
Halton St WA11 1 E6
Halton Station Rd WA7 49 F3
HALTON VIEW 13 C1
Halton View Rd WA8 13 C1
HALTON VILLAGE 49 F8
Halton Way CH66 69 E1
Hambledon Cl CH66 69 A6
Hamble Dr WA5 14 F3
Hambleton Cl WA8 12 C3
Hambleton Rd SK8 34 C8
Hambleton Way CW7 149 A7
Hambletts Hollow
WA6 100 F6
Hamble Way SK10 86 E1
Hamilton Ave
Irlam M44 11 D4
Sandycroft CH5 116 A3
Hamilton Cl
Haslington CW1 191 C4
Macclesfield SK10 113 A8
Neston CH64 41 B2
Hamilton Ct CH64 66 F8
Hamilton Pl CH1 237 A2
Hamilton Rd CH5 91 D1
Hamilton St CH2 118 F3
Hamlin Cl WA7 49 A6
Hammersmith Way
WA8 13 D4
Hammond Sch CH2 119 B7
Hammond St CW2 190 C3
Hamnett Ct WA3 9 E3
Hampshire Cl CW12 156 D4
Hampshire Gdns ST7 194 F2
Hampshire Rd M31 11 D2
Hampshire Wlk SK10 86 F2
Hampson Ave WA3 4 F3
Hampson Cres SK9 34 C4
Hampstead Ct 7
CW7 149 A8
Hampstead Dr CW2 221 C8
Hampton Cl
Neston CH64 66 E6
Widnes WA8 13 E3
Hampton Court Way
WA8 13 D4
Hampton Cres
Neston CH64 66 E6
No Man's Heath SY14 214 A5
Hampton Ct
Gatley SK9 34 D5
Runcorn WA7 24 C4
Hampton Dr
Cronton WA8 12 C5
Hampton Dr *continued*
Warrington WA5 15 C4
Hampton Gdns CH65 70 A5
HAMPTON GREEN 214 B7
HAMPTON HEATH 213 E7
Hampton Heath Ind Est
SY14 213 D7
Hampton Rd
Chester CH4 140 F6
Irlam M44 11 D4
Hamson Dr SK10 63 B1
Hamsterley Cl WA3 10 B6
Hanbury Cl CW2 206 B7
Hancock Ct WA4 16 C4
Hancock Rd CW12 156 F4
Handa Dr CH65 95 B8
HANDBRIDGE 141 E7
Handbridge CH4 237 B1
Handford Ave CH62 43 F5
Handford Rd CH2 118 F6
HANDFORTH 34 C4
Handforth Cl WA4 17 C3
Handforth La WA7 49 D6
Handforth Rd
Crewe CW2 189 E3
Handforth SK9 34 E1
Handforth Sta SK9 34 D3
HAND GREEN 168 B6
HANDLEY 182 D8
Handley Dr WA2 8 E1
Handley Hill CW7 149 C8
Handley Hill Prim Sch
CW7 149 C8
Handley St WA7 22 F3
Hand St SK11 112 B8
Hangman's La
Lostock Green CW9 105 C7
Smallwood CW11 177 B5
HANKELOW 230 C7
Hankelow Cl
Chester CH2 237 B4
Middlewich CW10 151 C6
Hankey St 2 WA7 22 F2
Hankins Heys La CW3 231 A1
Hankinson Cl M31 11 E2
Hanley Cl
Disley SK12 38 D5
Widnes WA8 12 C1
Hanley Rd WA8 12 C1
Hannah's Wlk 2
CW10 151 C8
Hanns Hall Farm CH64 67 D8
Hanns Hall Rd CH64 67 D8
Hanover Ct WA7 50 A6
Hanover Dr 2 CW7 149 D6
Hanover Ho 6 CW8 103 C5
Hanover St WA1 16 A4
Hapsdale View WA6 72 E1
HAPSFORD 72 F1
Hapsford Cl WA3 9 C4
Hapsford La
Dunham-on-t-H WA6 97 E8
Elton CH2 72 D4
Hapsford Mews WA6 72 E2
Harbord St WA1 16 C4
Harbour Cl
Chester CH2 118 E7
Runcorn WA7 50 D6
Harbour La SK11 111 C1
Harburn Wlk M22 33 E8
Harcourt Cl WA3 9 E3
HARDEN PARK 60 A3
Harden Pk SK9 60 A3
Harding Ave
Tattenhall CH3 166 C2
Warrington WA2 8 E1
Harding Rd
Chester CH2 118 B8
Nantwich CW5 204 C4
Hardings Mdw ST7 194 F2
Hardings Row ST7 195 D7
Hardings Wood ST7 194 E2
HARDING'S WOOD 194 E2
Hardingswood Rd
ST7 194 E2
Hardknott Rd CH62 43 E8
Hardwick Cl SK6 37 F6
Hardwick Dr SK11 112 B5
Hardwicke Ct CW1 190 E4
Hardwicke Rd SK12 36 F4
Hardwick Grange WA1 17 E8
Hardwick Rd WA7 23 D3
Hardy Cl
Ellesmere Port CH66 69 F3
Wistaston CW2 205 F8
Hardy Dr SK7 35 D7
Hardy Rd WA13 18 C2
Hardy St WA2 16 B6
Harebell Cl
Huntington CH3 142 A6
Widnes WA8 12 E4
Harebell Gr ST7 195 F1
Harecastle Ave ST7 194 E1
Harecastle Ct ST7 210 E6
Harecastle Villas ST7 194 E2
Harefield Dr SK9 60 B5
Harefield Rd SK9 34 E4
Hare Hill Gdn★ SK10 86 B6
Hare La CH3 119 D3
Hare's La WA6 73 F7
Harewood Ave CH66 69 C4
Harewood Cl
Northwich CW9 103 F4
Winsford CW7 126 A1
Harewood Way SK11 112 B5
Harfield Gdns CH66 69 C5
Harford Cl WA5 14 F4
HARGRAVE 144 A1
Hargrave Ave CW2 189 F3
Hargrave Dr CH66 69 E5
Hargrave La
Bebington CH64 43 A4
Thornton Hough CH63,
CH64 42 F5
Hargreave Ho 7 CH64 66 E8
Hargreaves Ct WA8 13 D1
Hargreaves Ho 5
WA8 13 D1
Hargreaves Rd CW9 104 C8
Harington Cl CH2 118 C8
Harland Gn L24 21 A3
Harlech Cl WA5 7 E2
Harlech Ct CH65 70 D3
Harlech Gr 3 WA7 23 F1
Harlech Way CH65 70 D3
Harlow Cl WA4 17 C3
Harlyn Ave SK7 35 F7
Harlyn Gdns WA5 14 D3
Harn The CH66 69 C3
Haroldgate SY13 225 F1
Harold Rd WA11 1 F7
Harper Cl CH66 69 D4
Harper Gr CW12 156 E4
Harpers Rd WA2 9 B2
Harpur Cl SK11 112 D6
Harpur Cres ST7 193 B5
Harrier Rd WA2 8 F2
Harriet St M44 11 E5
Harrington Dr SK11 111 D1
Harris Cl CW1 173 B1
HARRISEAHEAD 195 E4
Harriseahead La ST7 195 D4
Harrison Cl WA1 16 C6
Harrison Dr
Crewe CW1 190 B4
Goostrey CW4 107 B1
Haydock WA11 1 A6
Harrison Gr CH5 116 A3
Harrisons Pl 4 CW8 103 E8
Harrison Sq WA5 7 F1
Harrison St WA8 22 B6
Harrisons Terr CH66 69 C6
Harrison Way WA12 2 C4
Harris Rd CW9 80 A2
Harris St WA8 13 C1
Harrogate Cl
Bebington CH62 43 D4
Warrington WA5 7 A1
Harrogate Rd CH62 43 D4
Harrop La SK10 62 E5
Harrop Rd
Bollington SK10 88 C8
Runcorn WA7 23 B1
Harrow Cl
Crewe CW2 190 A1
Warrington WA4 26 E6
Wilmslow SK9 60 D8
Harrow Dr WA7 23 E2
Harrow Gr CH62 43 E8
Harrow Rd CH65 70 D4
Harrow Way CW9 103 E3
HARTFORD 103 C4
Hartford Ave SK9 59 F5
HARTFORDBEACH 103 A6
Hartford Bsns Ctr
CW8 102 F4
Hartford Cl CW11 175 C7
Hartford Dr CH65 69 F4
Hartford High Sch
CW8 103 C5
Hartford Manor Com Prim
Sch CW8 103 C5
Hartford Mews 3
CH3 119 B1
Hartford Prim Sch
CW8 103 B4
Hartford Rd CW9 103 E3
Hartford Sta CW8 103 A4
Hartford Way CH1 118 A2
HARTHILL 183 E3
Harthill Cl CW9 103 E5
Harthill La CH3 183 E4
Harthill Prim Sch
CH3 183 E3
Harthill Rd
Blacon CH1 117 E6
Burwardsley CH3 184 A6
Hartington Dr SK7 36 E8
Hartington Rd
Bramhall SK7 35 E6
Gatley SK8 34 D8
High Lane SK12, SK6 37 F7
Hartington St CH4 141 E7
Hartland Cl
Poynton SK12 36 D5
Widnes WA8 13 A5
Hartley Cl WA13 18 F3
Hartley Gdns CW12 179 B8
Hartley Gn SK10 87 F8
Harton Cl WA8 12 E3
Hartswood Cl WA4 26 E3
Hartwell Gr CW7 126 F4
Harty Rd WA11 1 A5
Harvard Cl WA7 24 D2
Harvard Ct WA2 8 A3
Harvest Cl CW9 126 F8
Harvest Rd SK10 87 C3
Harvey Ave
Nantwich CW5 205 A6
Newton-le-W WA12 1 F3
Harvey Ct WA2 8 B3
Harvey La WA3 3 A8
Harvey Rd CW12 157 A5
Harwood Gdns WA4 17 A2
Haryngton Ave WA5 15 F7
Haseley Cl SK12 36 E5
Haslemere Ave WA15 32 C6
Haslemere Dr WA5 14 D4
Haslemere Way CW1 190 D6
Haslin Cres CH3 142 D7
HASLINGTON 191 D4
Haslington Cl ST5 210 D1
Haslington Gr L26 21 A6
Haslington Prim Sch
CW1 191 D4
HASSAL 192 C7
HASSALL GREEN 176 A2
Hassall Rd
Alsager ST7 193 B5
Haslington CW11 192 B7
Sandbach CW11 175 C4
Winterley CW11 191 F8
Hassall Way 7 SK9 34 E5
Hassals La CH2 96 F3
Hastings Ave WA2 8 B4
Hastings Rd CW5 204 F5
Hasty La
Altrincham WA15 32 E8
Hale WA15 32 E8
Wythenshawe WA15 32 F8
Hatchery Cl WA4 27 B4
Hatchings The WA13 18 E2
HATCHMERE 100 D4
Hatch Mere★ WA6 100 C4
Hatchmere Cl
Sandbach CW11 174 F7
Warrington WA5 15 E5
Hatchmere Dr CH3 142 B8
Hatchmere Pk WA6 100 C5
Hatfield Ct CW4 130 B3
Hatfield Gdns WA4 26 E4
Hathaway Cl SK8 34 B7
Hathaway Dr SK11 112 C5
HATHERTON 219 E3
Hatherton Cl
Newcastle-u-Lyme
ST5 210 D2
5 Northwich CW9 103 F4
Hatherton Gr L26 21 A6
Hatherton Way CH2 237 B4
Hatley La WA6 73 F7
Hatter St CW12 156 E3
HATTON 26 A2
Hatton Ave CH62 43 E3
Hatton Bldgs CH2 237 C4
Hatton Brow Terr
SK11 112 F4
HATTON HEATH 143 B1
Hatton La
Hartford CW8 103 D6
Stretton WA4 26 B1
Hatton Rd CH1 117 E6
Hatton St SK11 112 C7
HAUGHTON 186 C6
Haughton Cl SK10 86 F1
HAVANNAH 157 A6
Havannah Bsns Ctr 6
CW12 156 F4
Havannah La
Congleton CW12 156 F6
St Helens WA9 1 B3
Havannah Prim Sch
CW12 157 A5
Havannah St CW12 156 F4
Haven The
Crewe CW1 190 D7
Sandbach CW11 174 E7
Havergal St 4 WA7 22 F1
Haverhill Cl CW2 207 C3
Haverty Prec WA12 2 B1
Havisham Cl WA3 9 D5
Hawarde Cl WA12 2 A4
Hawarden Airport CH4,
CH5 139 D7
Hawarden Gdns CH65 70 D2
Hawarden Ind Pk
CH5 139 B6
Haweswater Ave
Crewe CW1 173 B1
Haydock WA11 1 A6
Haweswater Cl WA7 50 A5
Haweswater Dr CW7 126 D2
Hawick Cl CH66 69 A5
Hawker Cl CH4 139 C4
Hawkins La SK10 88 D4
Hawkins Rd CH64 41 F1
Hawkins View CH3 120 E6
Hawk Rd SK22 39 E8
Hawks Ct WA7 49 E6
Hawksey Dr CW5 204 F4
Hawkshaw Cl WA3 9 C4
Hawkshead Cl WA7 50 A4
Hawkshead Rd WA5 6 E6
Hawkshead Way CW7 126 D2
Hawk St CW11 175 B6
Hawkstone Gr WA6 73 C4
Hawks Way CH60 40 E8
Hawley Dr WA15 32 B8
Hawley La WA15 32 B8
Hawley's Cl WA5 7 F1
Hawley's La WA2, WA5 8 A1
Hawley's Lane Trad Pk
WA2 8 A1
Haworth Ave CW12 157 A5
Haworth Cl SK11 112 B5
Hawthorn Ave
3 Nantwich CW5 204 F5
Newton-le-W WA12 2 D3
Runcorn WA7 23 A1
1 Widnes WA8 13 B2
Wilmslow SK9 60 A7
Hawthorn Bank SK22 39 B6
Hawthorn Cl
Holmes Chapel CW4 130 D3

Hawthorn Cl *continued*
Winsford CW7 126 C3
Hawthorn Cotts CH60 40 F8
Hawthorn Dr M44 11 D5
Hawthorne Ave
Audley ST7 209 F1
Fowley Common WA3 5 C4
Warrington WA5 15 A6
Warrington, Woolston WA1 17 B7
Hawthorne Bsns Pk WA5 16 A8
Hawthorne Cl
Congleton CW12 156 A4
Haydock WA11 1 A5
Hawthorne Ct ST7 193 E4
Hawthorne Dr
Sandbach CW11 175 D6
Willaston CH64 43 B1
Hawthorne Gr
Barnton CW8 77 F4
Poynton SK12 37 C4
Warrington, Bruche WA1 16 F7
Warrington WA4 16 D3
Winsford CW7 127 A1
Hawthorne Rd
Frodsham WA6 49 B1
Warrington WA4 26 C8
Hawthorne St WA5 16 A8
Hawthorn Gdns ST7 210 D8
Hawthorn Gn SK9 60 A7
Hawthorn Gr
Bramhall SK7 35 C6
Crewe CW1 190 D7
Warrington WA4 16 D1
Wilmslow SK9 60 B7
Hawthorn La
Bebington CH62 43 D8
Congleton CW12 155 C6
Crewe CW2 189 F2
Wilmslow SK9 60 A7
Hawthorn Pk SK9 60 A7
Hawthorn Rd
Bollington SK10 87 F8
Chester CH4 141 A6
Christleton CH3 142 E7
Ellesmere Port CH66 69 D6
Lymm WA13 18 D3
Neston CH64 41 C1
Newcastle-u-Lyme ST5 210 E1
Plumley WA16 80 F3
Weaverham CW8 102 C8
Hawthorn Rise SK10 86 E6
Hawthorn St SK9 60 A6
Hawthorns The
Bunbury CW6 185 E8
Ellesmere Port CH66 69 F7
Haslington CW1 191 D5
Northwich CW8 103 C7
Tarporley CW6 146 D1
Hawthorn Terr SK9 60 A6
Hawthorn View
Connah's Quay CH5 116 A7
Lindow End WA16 59 B2
Wilmslow SK9 60 A7
Hawthorn Villas CW4 130 C3
Hawthorn Way SK10 87 E2
Hawthorn Wlk
3 Partington M31 11 E3
Wilmslow SK9 60 A7
Wincham CW9 79 C3
Haycroft SK8 34 E8
Haycroft Cl CH66 69 D2
Haydan Ct CH2 118 D4
Haydan Mews WA6 73 E6
Haydn Jones Dr CW5 204 F3
HAYDOCK 1 D6
Haydock Cl
Chester CH1 118 B2
Macclesfield SK10 87 C3
Haydock English Martyrs' RC Prim Sch WA11 1 E7
Haydock La WA11 1 C7
Haydock La Ind Est WA11 1 E8
Haydock Park Racecourse WA3 2 E8
Haydock Sports Coll WA11 1 C6
Haydock St
Newton-le-W WA12 2 A3
Warrington WA2 16 B6
Hayes Cl CW5 204 E7
Hayes Cres WA6 49 C1
Hayes Dr CW8 78 C3
Hayes Pk CH1 237 A4
Haye's Rd M44 11 E5
Hayfield Cl SK10 87 B3
Hayfield Rd
New Mills SK22 39 D8
Warrington WA1 17 C7
Hayfields WA16 57 C3
Hayfields Gr CW3 229 F3
Haygarth Hts 5 CH1 237 C3
Hayhead Cl ST7 195 B2
Hayhurst Ave CW10 151 C8
Hayhurst Cl CW9 103 F8
Hayle Cl SK10 86 D1
Hayling Cl CW1 190 B8
Haymakers Cl CH4 140 F4
Haymakers Way CH1 117 A8
HAYMOOR GREEN 205 E2
Haymoor Green Rd CW5 205 E3
Hayscastle Cl WA5 7 E1
Hayside Wlk SY14 213 A3
Hayton St WA16 56 F1
Haywood Cres WA7 24 D2

Hazel Ave
Macclesfield SK11 112 A5
Runcorn WA7 48 E8
Hazelbadge Cl SK12 36 C4
Hazelbadge Rd SK12 36 C4
Hazelbank CH65 69 F3
Hazelborough Cl WA3 10 B5
Hazel Cl
1 Ellesmere Port CH66 69 F1
Kidsgrove ST7 195 B3
Hazelcroft SK9 85 A8
Hazelcroft Gdns SK9 85 A8
Hazeldean Ct 17 SK9 34 E1
Hazel Dr
Gatley M22 34 A8
Lymm WA13 18 F2
Poynton SK12 36 F3
Weaverham CW8 102 D7
Winsford CW7 149 C8
Hazel Gr
Alsager ST7 194 A3
Crewe CW1 190 C7
Golborne WA3 3 B8
Warrington WA1 17 A8
Hazel Grove High Sch SK7 36 C8
Hazelhurst Dr SK10 88 A8
Hazelmere Cl CW8 103 C5
Hazel Rd CH4 140 F6
Hazel St WA1 16 D7
Hazel Wlk M31 11 E3
Hazelwood Cl WA8 22 A8
Hazelwood Mews WA4 17 C1
Hazelwood Rd
Barnton CW8 78 B4
Wilmslow SK9 60 D8
Wythenshawe M22 33 D8
Hazlehurst Rd WA6 74 D6
Hazlemere Ave SK11 112 A6
Headland Cl WA3 3 E6
Headlands The CH1, CH3 237 C2
Headworth Cl CW9 103 F4
HEALD GREEN 34 B8
Heald Green Sta M22 34 A8
Heald St WA12 1 F3
Healey Cl CW1 190 A8
Heapy St SK11 112 E6
Hearn's La CW5 202 E5
HEATH 49 A6
Heath Ave
Ellesmere Port CH65 70 A1
Rode Heath ST7 193 F7
Sandbach CW11 175 E6
Heath Bank CH3 119 D5
Heathbank Rd SK8 34 F8
Heathbrook Cotts CW9 104 E7
Heath Bsns & Technical Pk The WA7 49 A7
Heath Cl
Chester CH3 142 B8
Sandbach CW11 175 D6
Tarvin CH3 121 B1
Heathcote Cl CH2 118 C4
Heathcote Gdns CW9 104 D7
Heathcote St ST7 195 A2
Heath Ct
Alsager ST7 193 F6
Ellesmere Port CH66 69 B6
Heath Dr
Knutsford WA16 56 F2
Runcorn WA7 49 A7
Tarvin CH3 121 B1
Heath End Rd ST7 193 B5
Heather Ave M44 11 D6
Heather Brae WA12 2 A4
Heather Brae Mews CW12 156 A3
Heather Cl
Ellesmere Port CH66 69 E3
Macclesfield SK11 112 C3
Runcorn WA7 49 E4
Warrington WA3 9 D5
Heather Ct CH3 142 A8
Heather Falls SK22 39 B8
Heatherfield Ct SK9 60 E8
Heathergate Pl CW2 206 B8
Heatherside ST7 195 C6
Heatherways CW6 146 C3
Heather Wlk M31 11 E3
Heathfield SK9 60 A5
Heathfield Ave CW1 190 C4
Heathfield Cl
Congleton CW12 155 F3
Nantwich CW5 204 F6
Heathfield Ct
Ellesmere Port, Whitby CH65 70 B5
Ellesmere Port, Whitbyheath CH66 95 A8
Heathfield Dr ST5 210 D1
Heathfield Pk
Warrington WA4 17 A2
Widnes WA8 12 D3
Heathfield Rd
Audlem CW3 230 A5
Ellesmere Port CH65 70 B5
Heathfields Cl CH2 237 B4
Heathfield Sq WA16 56 F2
Heathgate Ave L24 21 A2
Heath Gn CW6 146 C4
Heath Gr CH66 69 B7
Heath La
Chester CH3 142 A8
Culcheth WA3 4 A1

Heath La *continued*
Ellesmere Port, Little Sutton CH66 69 B7
Golborne, Kenyon WA3 3 F2
Golborne WA3 3 D6
Great Barrow CH3 120 E6
Great Budworth CW9 54 A1
High Legh WA16 28 D5
Little Leigh WA4, CW8 77 B7
Marbury SY13 226 E6
Stoak CH2 95 E7
Stoak CH2 95 F7
Swan Green WA16 106 F6
Willaston CH64, CH66 68 D7
Wincham CW9 79 C3
Heathlands Ho WA16 56 F2
Heathlands Rd CH66 69 B7
Heathland Trail* CW6 147 E7
Heathmoor Ave WA3 3 D6
Heath Park Gr WA7 48 F8
Heath Rd
Bollington SK10 87 E6
Chester CH2 118 E7
Congleton CW12 156 A2
Runcorn WA7 23 B2
Sandbach CW11 175 D6
Warrington WA5 14 F5
Weaverham CW8 77 E1
Widnes WA8 12 D2
Heath Rd S WA7 48 F6
Heath Road Cres WA7 49 B8
Heath Sch The WA7 49 B7
Heathside CW5 204 F6
Heaths La CW6 123 D2
Heath St
Crewe CW1 190 D4
Golborne WA3 3 A8
Warrington WA4 26 C8
Heath Terr
Chester CH2 118 E8
Smallwood CW11 154 B1
Heathview CW1 191 D3
Heath View
Alsager ST7 193 E5
Weston CW2 207 B5
Heathview Cl WA8 22 A5
Heathview Rd WA8 22 A5
Heathway CH60 41 B7
Heath Way CW6 168 D8
Heathwood ST7 193 F7
Heathwood Dr ST7 193 B5
Heathwood Gr WA1 17 B7
HEATLEY 19 C5
Heatley Cl WA13 19 A4
Heatley La CW5 217 F3
Heatley Way 5 SK9 34 D4
HEATON 159 E2
Heaton Cl CW10 151 C6
Heaton Ct WA3 9 F6
Heaton Sq CW7 149 C8
Heaton Way CW2 207 E4
Heaward Cl CW2 206 B4
Hebden Ave WA3 5 B5
HEBDEN GREEN 148 F7
Hebden Green Com Sch CW7 149 A7
Heber's Cl SY14 213 C5
Heber Wlk CW9 104 A8
Hedge Hey WA7 24 A1
Hedge Row SK10 63 E1
Hedgerow Dr CW9 79 C3
Hedgerows The WA11 1 F7
Hedingham Cl 7 SK10 111 F8
Hefferston Grange Dr CW8 102 A7
Hefferston Rise CW8 102 A7
Heights The WA6 73 C4
Helena Cl WA16 57 C2
Hellath Wen CW5 204 E2
Hellyar-Brook Rd ST7 193 B4
Helmdon Cl CW7 127 A3
Helmsdale Cl CW1 190 B6
Helmsdale La WA5 15 C6
Helmsley Cl WA5 15 E7
HELSBY 73 C3
Helsby Ave CH62 43 F3
Helsby High Sch WA6 73 D5
Helsby Hillside Prim Sch WA6 73 D4
HELSBY MARSH 73 B5
Helsby Pk WA6 73 E5
Helsby Rd WA6 73 C1
Helsby St WA1 16 D6
Helsby Sta WA6 73 B4
Helsby Way 4 SK9 34 D4
Helston Cl
Bramhall SK7 35 F7
Runcorn WA7 50 B5
Warrington WA5 14 E5
Helston Gr SK8 34 C8
Helton Cl CW4 130 A3
Hemingford Cl CH66 69 D2
Hemlegh Vale WA6 73 B2
Hemmingshaw La CW11 176 B8
Hemming St CW8 78 D1
Hemswell Cl CW7 149 E8
Hemsworth Ave CH66 69 C5
HENBURY 111 B8
Henbury Cl CW10 151 C7
Henbury Gdns WA4 26 E3
Henbury High Sch SK10 111 E8
Henbury La SK8 34 F6
HENBURY MOSS 110 D5

Henbury Pl WA7 49 B6
Henbury Rd SK9 34 D4
Henbury Rise SK11 111 C8
Henderson Cl WA5 14 D6
Henderson Rd
Widnes, Lower House WA8 22 F8
2 Widnes WA8 13 A1
Henderson St SK11 112 C7
Hendon Cl CW1 190 F5
Henley Ave M44 11 E6
Henley Cl
Macclesfield SK10 87 B4
Neston CH64 66 E6
Warrington WA4 26 E6
Henley Ct WA7 23 D2
Henley Dr CW7 126 F1
Henley Rd
Chester CH4 140 F6
Chorlton CW2 207 B1
Neston CH64 66 E6
Henrietta St CW12 156 C3
Henry Pl CH1 237 B3
Henry St
Crewe CW1 190 D5
Haslington CW1 191 D4
2 Lymm WA13 18 E3
Tarporley CW6 146 C2
Warrington WA1 16 A5
4 Widnes WA8 13 C1
Henry Wood Ct CH4 140 E6
Henshall Ave WA4 16 F4
Henshall Dr CW11 175 D8
Henshall Hall Dr CW12 157 B1
Henshall La WA14 20 C6
Henshall Rd SK10 87 F7
Henshall St CH1 237 A4
Henshaw La SK11 110 E2
Hepherd St WA5 15 D4
Hepley Rd SK12 37 A3
Herald Dr CW1 190 E3
Herald Pk CW1 190 E3
Heralds Cl WA8 22 C8
Heralds Gn WA5 7 A2
Herberts La CH60 40 F8
Herbert St
Burtonwood WA5 6 E6
Congleton CW12 156 F3
Crewe CW1 191 A5
Lostock Gralam CW9 80 A2
Herbert Swindells Cl CW2 190 D1
Herdman St CW2 190 D2
Hereford Ave
Ellesmere Port CH66 94 E8
Golborne WA3 3 B8
Hereford Cl
Macclesfield SK10 86 F1
Warrington WA1 17 D7
Hereford Dr SK9 34 E3
Hereford Pl CH1 118 A5
Hereford Way CW10 128 E2
Hereward Rd CH3 119 B1
Heritage Ct CH1 237 B2
Hermitage Ct
Holmes Chapel CW4 130 D3
Saughall CH1 117 A8
Hermitage Dr CW4 130 D3
Hermitage Green La WA2, WA12 8 A8
Hermitage La CW4 130 C7
Hermitage Prim Sch CW4 130 D4
Hermitage Rd CH1 117 B7
Hermitage The CH60 40 F7
Heron Bsns Pk WA8 23 D8
Heron Cl
Broughton CH4 139 C4
Farndon CH3 180 F1
Knutsford WA16 57 B3
Runcorn WA7 50 D8
Winsford CW7 149 D5
Heron Cres CW1 190 F5
Heron Ct
Neston CH64 66 C7
Northwich CW9 79 C2
Heron Dr SK12 36 A3
Heron Pl CH2 237 B4
Herons Reach WA3 5 C6
Herons Way
Chester CH4 141 B2
Runcorn WA7 24 F4
Herrick Cl CW2 206 A8
Hertford Apartments WA2 9 A3
Hertford Cl
Congleton CW12 156 E4
Warrington WA1 17 E7
Hertford Gr M44 11 C6
Hesketh Cl WA5 14 F4
Hesketh Croft CW1 190 A8
Hesketh Dr CW9 80 A3
Hesketh Grange Cotts CH63 42 A7
Hesketh Meadow La WA3 3 F8
Hesketh Rd L24 21 E2
Hesketh St N WA5 15 D4
Hesketh St 5 WA5 15 D4
Hesnall Cl WA3 5 C8
Hessle Dr CH60 40 F7
HESWALL 40 D7
Heswall Ave WA3 4 E4
Heswall Point 7 CH60 41 A8
Heswall Rd CH66 69 D4
Heswall St Peter's CE Prim Sch CH60 40 F8

Heswall Sta CH60 41 D8
HETHERSON GREEN 214 D8
Hetherson Green La SY14 214 D8
Hewetson Cres SK11 111 E7
Hewitt Dr CW7 150 D8
Hewitt Gr CW9 79 F5
Hewitt St
Chester CH2 118 F3
Crewe CW2 190 D2
Northwich CW9 79 D2
Warrington WA4 16 C3
Hexham Ct CH1 118 B2
Hexham Way 4 SK10 87 C4
Heybridge La SK10 87 B6
Heydon Cl
Congleton CW12 156 C3
Halewood L26 21 A7
Heyes Ave WA11 1 D5
Heyes Dr WA13 18 C2
Heyes Farm Rd SK11 111 E8
Heyes Ho SK11 111 E8
Heyes La
Alderley Edge SK9 60 B3
Warrington WA4 26 E8
Heyes Pk CW8 102 F4
Heyes Rd WA8 22 C8
Heyeswood La CW8 103 A4
Heyfield Park Rd CH66 69 B7
Heygarth Prim Sch CH62 43 E5
Heygarth Rd CH62 43 E5
Hey Lock Cl WA12 7 C8
Heys Ave CH62 43 D8
Heysbank Rd SK12 38 D5
Heysham Cl WA7 50 D6
Hey Shoot La WA3 5 C5
Heysoms Ave CW8 103 D7
Heysoms Cl CW8 103 D7
Heys The
Bebington CH62 43 F5
Runcorn WA7 23 E1
Heythrop Dr CH60 41 D8
Heywood Cl SK9 60 B2
Hey Wood Cl WA12 7 C8
Heywood Gn CW2 206 C8
Heywood La CW3, SY13 234 C7
Heywood Rd
Alderley Edge SK9 60 B2
Ellesmere Port CH66 69 D5
Heywoods Ridge CW3 229 E3
Heywood St CW12 156 C2
Heywoods The CH2 118 C4
Hibbert St
New Mills SK22 39 B6
6 Widnes WA8 23 B8
Hibel Rd SK10 87 D1
Hickhurst La CW6 147 D3
Hickmore Heys CH3 119 F5
Hickory Cl WA1 17 E7
Hickson St CW8 78 B3
Hidcote Cl CW2 206 B8
HIDEBANK 39 C8
Hield Brow CW9 79 C7
Hield Gr CW9 79 C8
Hield La CW9 79 C8
Higginbotham Gn SK11 112 E6
Higginson Cl CW12 179 C8
Higham Ave WA5 7 F1
Highbank Cl CW8 78 B3
High Bank Cl M44 11 D6
Highbank Rd
Kingsley WA6 75 C2
Northwich CW8 103 D7
High Bent Ave SK8 35 A6
HIGH CARR 210 F3
High Carr Bsns Pk ST5 210 F2
High Carr Network Ctr ST5 210 F2
Highcliffe Ave CH1 118 B4
Highcroft Ave CW12 156 F2
High Cross La CH3 182 D1
High Ct SK10 88 B8
High Elm Dr WA15 32 C8
High Elm Rd WA15 32 D7
High Elms SK8 35 B5
Higher Ash Rd ST7 210 D8
Higher Ashton WA8 12 F3
HIGHER BUNBURY 168 F1
HIGHER BURWARDSLEY 184 C5
HIGHER CARDEN 198 D7
Higher Carden La SY14 198 D6
HIGHER DISLEY 38 E4
Higher Downs WA16 57 C2
HIGHERFENCE 113 A8
Higher Fence Rd SK10 87 F1
HIGHER FERRY 140 C8
Higher Heyes Dr WA6 75 C1
HIGHER HURDSFIELD 88 A2
HIGHER KINNERTON 161 B8
Higher Knutsford Rd WA4 16 F2
Higher La
Bollington SK10 88 B6
Disley SK12 38 E1
Dutton WA4 51 D4
Kettleshulme SK23 64 E6
Lymm WA13 19 B1

Higherland Ct 6 ST7 . . . 195 A2
HIGHER MARSTON 79 C6
HIGHER POYNTON 37 B2
Higher Rd L26, WA8 . . . . 21 C5
HIGHER RUNCORN 23 A1
HIGHER SHURLACH 104 E6
HIGHER WALTON 25 F7
HIGHER WHITLEY 52 D5
HIGHER WINCHAM 79 F4
Higher Works Cotts
SK11 . . . . 158 C6
HIGHER WYCH 224 D4
Highfield
Elton CH2. . . . . 72 B4
Prestbury SK10 . . . . 87 A5
High Field WA14. . . . . . . 20 B2
Highfield Ave
Audlem CW3 . . . . 230 A4
Golborne WA3 . . . . 2 F8
Kidsgrove ST7 . . . . 195 B2
Lostock Gralam CW9. . . . . . 80 A3
Warrington, Dudlow's Green
WA4 . . . . 26 D4
Warrington WA5 . . . . 15 A5
Highfield Cl CH64. . . . . . 66 E8
Highfield Com Prim Sch
CH1. . . . . 117 F4
Highfield Cres
Handforth SK9. . . . . 34 C1
Widnes WA8 . . . . 13 A2
Highfield Dr
Lymm WA13. . . . . 18 C2
Macclesfield SK10. . . . . . . 87 A1
Nantwich CW5. . . . . 205 A6
Highfield Est SK9 . . . . . . 34 C1
Highfield La
Coddington CH3. . . . . 181 E4
Golborne WA3 . . . . 3 C5
Winwick WA2. . . . . 8 C7
Highfield Parkway
SK7 . . . . 35 D4
Highfield Pl 1 CW8. . . . . 103 E8
Highfield Rd
Blacon CH1 . . . . 117 D5
Bollington SK10. . . . . 88 A8
Cheadle SK8 . . . . 34 F8
Congleton CW12 . . . . 156 E2
Ellesmere Port CH65. . . . . . 70 C5
Ellesmere Port, Little Sutton
CH66. . . . . 69 B6
Lymm WA13. . . . . 18 C2
Macclesfield SK11. . . . . . . 112 C7
Neston CH64 . . . . 66 F8
Northwich CW8 . . . . 103 F7
Poynton SK12 . . . . 36 A4
Widnes WA8 . . . . 13 A2
Highfield Rd N 11
CH65 . . . . 70 C6
Highfields SY13. . . . . 224 A2
Highfield Sch L26. . . . . . . 21 A7
Highfields Com Prim Sch
CW5 . . . . 204 F6
Highfield Terr SK22. . . . . . 39 D8
Highgate Cl
Crewe CW1 . . . . 190 A8
Runcorn WA7. . . . . 24 D1
High Gates Cl WA5. . . . . . . 15 E7
High Gates Lo WA5 . . . . . . 15 E7
Highgrove Mews 2
SK9 . . . . 60 A6
High Hill Rd SK22. . . . . . . 39 D8
Highlands Rd WA7. . . . . . . 48 F8
Highlands The CW6. . . . . 185 E8
Highland Way WA16 . . . . . 82 A7
HIGHLANE 134 C6
HIGH LANE 37 E8
High Lane Prim Sch
SK6. . . . . 37 F8
High Lea Rd SK22. . . . . . . 39 A8
HIGH LEGH 29 B5
High Legh Prim Sch
WA16 . . . . 29 C5
High Legh Rd WA13. . . . . . 29 C8
High Lowe Ave CW12 . . . 157 A4
Highmarsh Cres WA12 . . . . 2 B4
High Mdw 2 SK8 . . . . 34 E8
High Mount CH60. . . . . 40 F8
High St
Audley ST7. . . . . 210 A1
Bollington SK10. . . . . 88 B8
Clotton CW6 . . . . 145 D4
Congleton CW12 . . . . 156 D2
Crewe CW2 . . . . 190 D3
Farndon CH3 . . . . 180 E2
Frodsham WA6 . . . . 49 B1
Golborne WA3 . . . . 3 A8
Great Budworth CW9 . . . . . 79 A7
Hale L24 . . . . 21 D1
Harriseahead ST7 . . . . 195 E5
Kidsgrove, The Rookery
ST7 . . . . 195 C4
Macclesfield SK11. . . . . . . 112 D6
Malpas SY14 . . . . 213 B3
Mow Cop ST7. . . . . 195 D7
Nantwich CW5. . . . . 204 E5
Neston CH64 . . . . 66 E7
Newchapel ST7 . . . . 195 E2
New Mills SK22 . . . . 39 C8
Newton-le-W WA12. . . . . 2 D4
Norley WA6 . . . . 100 F5
Northwich CW9. . . . . 103 F8
Runcorn WA7. . . . . 23 A2
Saltney CH4 . . . . 140 E7
Sandbach CW11 . . . . 175 B6
Talke ST7. . . . . 210 D6

High St *continued*
Tarporley CW6. . . . . 146 C2
Tarvin CH3. . . . . 121 B2
Tattenhall CH3. . . . . 166 B1
Warrington WA1 . . . . 16 C5
Weaverham CW8. . . . . 77 C1
Winsford CW7. . . . . 126 D1
Hightown
Crewe CW1 . . . . 190 C4
Middlewich CW10 . . . . 128 C1
Sandbach CW11 . . . . 175 B6
Hightown Appts 6
CW1. . . . . 190 C4
Hightree Dr SK11 . . . . 111 C8
High View
Helsby WA6. . . . . 73 C4
Mount Pleasant ST7 . . . . . 195 B5
HIGH WARREN 26 C6
High Warren Cl WA4. . . . . . 26 C5
Highwood Rd WA4. . . . . . . 26 C7
Hignett Ave WA9 . . . . 1 B2
Hilary Ave SK8. . . . . 34 D8
Hilary Cl
Chester CH3 . . . . 119 B1
Warrington WA5 . . . . 14 D6
Widnes WA8 . . . . 13 E3
Hilbre Ave CH60 . . . . 40 E6
Hilbre Bank CW6 . . . . 169 D4
Hilbre Dr CH65 . . . . 70 C1
Hilden Pl WA2. . . . . 16 D8
Hilden Rd WA2 . . . . 8 E1
Hillary Ave CW12 . . . . . . 157 A2
Hillary Dr CW3 . . . . 230 A4
Hillary Rd
Bebington CH62. . . . . 43 E5
Kidsgrove ST7 . . . . 195 B3
Hillberry Cres WA4 . . . . . . 16 B3
Hillbre Way 1 SK9. . . . . . . 34 D4
Hillbrook Rd SK7 . . . . 35 D6
Hill Cl
Bunbury CW6. . . . . 185 E7
Neston CH64 . . . . 67 B5
HILLCLIFFE 26 C8
Hill Cliffe Rd WA4 . . . . . . 26 B8
Hill Cotts CH3 . . . . 164 A4
Hillcourt Rd SK6. . . . . 37 F7
Hillcrest WA7. . . . . 23 D1
Hillcrest Ave CW4 . . . . . . 130 B3
Hillcrest Dr CH66 . . . . 69 A6
Hillcrest Rd
Bollington SK10. . . . . 87 F7
Ellesmere Port CH66. . . . . . 69 B6
Kelsall CW6. . . . . 122 E6
Warren SK11. . . . . 112 A4
Hill Ct CH64 . . . . 67 B5
Hill Dr
Handforth SK9. . . . . 34 E3
Whaley Bridge SK23 . . . . . . 65 D8
Hillesden Rise CW12. . . . . 156 F2
Hillfield
Frodsham WA6 . . . . 74 B7
Runcorn WA7. . . . . 50 D8
Hillfield Gdns CW5. . . . . . 204 E4
Hillfield Pl CW5 . . . . 204 E4
Hillfield Rd CH66 . . . . 69 D7
Hillfields CW12 . . . . 156 D4
Hill Fields CW12 . . . . 156 D3
Hill Fields Cl CW12. . . . . . 156 D4
Hillfield View CW5. . . . . . 204 E4
Hillfoot Cres WA4. . . . . . . 26 B7
Hillfoot La WA6. . . . . 74 E3
Hilliards Ct CH4 . . . . 141 B3
Hillingden Ave L26. . . . . . . 21 A7
Hill La
Brown Knowl CH3 . . . . 199 C8
Peckforton CW6 . . . . 184 E6
Hillock La WA1 . . . . 17 C8
Hill Rd CH4. . . . . 141 E2
Hill Rd N WA6 . . . . 73 D3
Hill Rd S WA6 . . . . 73 C3
Hillsboro Ave WA6. . . . . . . 74 C7
Hillsdown Way CH66 . . . . . 69 C2
Hillside
Broomedge WA13 . . . . 19 E1
Northwich CW8 . . . . 103 C7
Hillside Ave
Newton-le-W WA12. . . . . 1 F2
Runcorn WA7. . . . . 48 E8
Hillside Cl
Bramhall SK7. . . . . 36 A7
Chorlton CW2 . . . . 207 E3
Helsby WA6. . . . . 73 D4
Mow Cop ST7. . . . . 195 D7
Hill Side Cl SK12. . . . . 38 E6
Hillside Ct
Macclesfield SK10. . . . . 88 A1
Warrington WA4 . . . . 26 D3
Hillside Dr
Crewe CW1 . . . . 190 E5
Ellesmere Port CH66. . . . . . 69 E7
Macclesfield SK10. . . . . 88 A1
Hillside Gr WA5. . . . . 14 F4
Hillside Ho 7 CW8. . . . . . 103 C5
Hillside La CW9. . . . . 126 E7
Hillside Rd
Blacon CH1 . . . . 117 E4
Frodsham WA6 . . . . 74 C7
Heswall CH60 . . . . 41 A7
Kelsall CW6. . . . . 122 D4
Knutsford WA16 . . . . 57 A2
Warrington WA4 . . . . 26 D3
Hillside View SK22. . . . . . . 39 A8
Hill St
Crewe CW1 . . . . 190 D4
Macclesfield SK11. . . . . . . 112 D6
Runcorn WA7. . . . . 23 A2
Sandbach CW11 . . . . 174 D7
Warrington WA1 . . . . 16 B5

Hill St *continued*
Winsford CW7 . . . . 126 F1
Hill Terr ST7 . . . . 209 D2
Hill The
Knutsford WA16 . . . . 82 B8
Sandbach CW11 . . . . 175 D5
HILLTOP 60 B8
Hilltop WA7 . . . . 50 C7
Hill Top
Altrincham WA15. . . . . 32 A8
Barnton CW8. . . . . 78 B2
Hill Top Ave
Cheadle SK8 . . . . 35 B8
Wilmslow SK9 . . . . 60 B8
Winsford CW7. . . . . 126 C1
Hilltop Com Prim Sch
ST7. . . . . 210 D7
Hill Top La
Heswall CH60 . . . . 41 B8
Neston CH64 . . . . 67 B5
Hilltop Pk WA16 . . . . 79 F7
Hilltop Rd
Guilden Sutton CH3. . . . . . 119 F5
Lymm WA13. . . . . 18 C2
Hill Top Rd
Acton Bridge CW8. . . . . 76 F2
Dutton WA4 . . . . 51 C1
Runcorn WA7. . . . . 50 F6
Warrington, Stockton Heath
WA4 . . . . 16 F2
Warrington, Woolston
WA1 . . . . 17 C7
Hill Top Rise SK23 . . . . . . 65 D8
Hill View
Bollington SK10. . . . . 87 F7
Whaley Bridge SK23 . . . . . . 65 C8
Widnes WA8 . . . . 12 F5
Hill View Ave WA6 . . . . 73 A1
Hillview Cl WA6 . . . . 74 C7
Hill View Prim Sch
WA7 . . . . 49 E4
Hillview Rise CW8 . . . . 78 E1
Hilton Ave WA5. . . . . 15 B5
Hilton Cl
9 Macclesfield SK11. . . . . 111 F7
Middlewich CW10 . . . . 151 B8
Hilton Dr M44 . . . . 11 C5
Hilton Gr SK12. . . . . 36 D4
Hilton Rd
Disley SK12 . . . . 38 B7
Poynton SK12 . . . . 37 C5
Himalayan Birch Cl
CH66 . . . . 69 E6
Hinchley Cl CW8. . . . . . . 103 A5
Hinckley Ct CW12. . . . . . . 156 A3
Hinderton Dr CH60. . . . . . . 40 F6
Hinderton Gn CH64 . . . . . . 66 F8
Hinderton La CH64. . . . . . . 67 A8
Hinderton Rd CH64 . . . . . . 66 F8
Hinderton Sch CH65 . . . . . 69 F3
Hinde St CW5 . . . . 204 D4
Hind Heath La CW11. . . . 174 F4
Hind Heath Rd CW11. . . . 174 E4
Hindle Ave WA5 . . . . 7 F1
Hindley Cres CW8 . . . . 78 A3
Hinton Cres WA4 . . . . 26 E8
Hinton Rd
Crewe CW2 . . . . 206 D8
Runcorn WA7. . . . . 23 A1
Hirsch Cl CW5. . . . . 205 A4
Hitchen's Cl WA7 . . . . 50 D7
Hitchens La SY14 . . . . . . 184 D1
Hitch Lowes SK11. . . . . 84 A3
Hobart Cl SK7 . . . . 35 F4
Hobart Way CH1 . . . . 117 D4
Hobb La WA4. . . . . 25 C5
Hobbs Cl CW1. . . . . 191 D4
Hobbs Hill La WA16. . . . . . 28 E1
Hobby Ct WA7. . . . . 49 E6
Hobcroft La WA16 . . . . 58 A7
Hob Hey La WA3. . . . . 4 D3
Hob La
Churton CH3 . . . . 180 F5
Dunham-on-t-H WA6 . . . . . . 97 C6
Hobson St SK11. . . . . 112 D6
Hockenhull Ave CH3 . . . . 121 B2
Hockenhull Cres CH3 . . . 121 B2
Hockenhull La
Tarvin, Broom Bank
CH3. . . . . 121 B1
Tarvin CH3. . . . . 121 B2
Hocker La
Adder's Moss SK10. . . . . . . 85 F4
Nether Alderley SK10 . . . . . 85 C4
Hockerley Ave SK23. . . . . . 65 D8
Hockerley Cl SK23 . . . . 65 D8
Hockerley La SK23. . . . . . . 65 D8
Hockerley New Rd
SK23 . . . . 65 D8
HOCKLEY 37 A2
Hockley Cl SK12 . . . . 37 A3
Hockley Paddock SK12. . . . 36 F3
Hockley Rd SK12. . . . . 37 A3
HODGEHILL 132 E8
Hodgehill La SK11 . . . . . . 132 E5
Hodge La
Hartford CW8 . . . . 103 A6
Weaverham CW8. . . . . 102 D5
Hodgkin Cl CW5 . . . . 204 F4
Hodgkinson Ave WA5 . . . . . . 7 F1
Hoghton Rd L24 . . . . 21 E2
Hogshead La CW8 . . . . . . 124 C7
Holbeck WA7. . . . . 50 C7
Holbein Cl CH4 . . . . 141 E6
Holborn Ct WA8 . . . . 12 F3
Holbrook Cl WA5 . . . . 14 E5
Holbury Cl CW1. . . . . 190 B8
Holcombe Ave WA3. . . . . . . 3 C8

Holcombe Dr SK10. . . . . . . 87 B3
Holcot Ct CW7. . . . . 127 A4
Holcroft La WA3 . . . . 5 D2
Holdings La CW3 . . . . 232 F4
Holehouse La
Langley SK11. . . . . 113 C4
Scholar Green ST7. . . . . . . 194 D8
Whiteley Green SK10. . . . . . 62 D2
Hole House La CW8 . . . . . . 77 E4
Hole La WA16 . . . . 106 E4
Holes La WA1 . . . . 17 B7
Holford Ave
Lostock Gralam CW9. . . . . . 80 A3
Warrington WA5 . . . . 15 F8
Holford Cres WA16 . . . . . . 57 B1
Holford Moss WA7. . . . . . . 24 D3
Holford St CW12. . . . . 156 D3
Holford Way WA12. . . . . 2 F3
Holgrave Cl WA16 . . . . 29 C4
Holkam Cl CW9. . . . . 103 F5
Holker Cl SK12 . . . . 36 F4
Holkham Cl WA8. . . . . 12 F1
Holkham The CH3 . . . . . . 119 B1
Holland Cl CW11. . . . . . . 175 C5
Holland Ct SK12 . . . . 36 E3
Holland Rd SK7. . . . . 35 E7
Hollands La CW6 . . . . 122 C5
Hollands Pl SK11 . . . . 112 F7
Hollands Rd CW9 . . . . 103 F7
Holland St
Crewe CW1 . . . . 190 B6
5 Macclesfield SK11 . . . . 112 C7
Holland Wlk CW5 . . . . . . 204 D6
Hollies La SK9 . . . . 60 F7
Hollies The
Moulton CW9. . . . . 126 E8
1 Northwich CW9 . . . . . . 103 E6
Runcorn WA7. . . . . 49 D8
Shavington CW2 . . . . 206 B4
HOLLINFARE 11 A3
Hollingford Pl WA16 . . . . . 82 A8
HOLLIN GREEN 202 F6
Hollingreen La CW5. . . . . 229 B7
Hollin Green La CW5. . . . . 202 E6
Hollinhey Prim Sch
SK11. . . . . 112 F3
Hollin La
Langley SK11. . . . . 113 A1
Newhall CW5. . . . . 228 D8
Styal SK9. . . . . 33 F5
Sutton Lane Ends SK11 . . . 136 C6
Hollin Rd SK10. . . . . 88 A7
HOLLINS 210 E8
Hollins Cres ST7. . . . . 194 E1
Hollins Dr WA2 . . . . 8 A6
Hollins Grange ST7 . . . . . 210 D8
HOLLINSGREEN 152 D4
HOLLINS GREEN 11 B2
Hollins Green St Helens CE Prim Sch WA3. . . . . 11 B2
Hollinshead Cl ST7 . . . . . 194 F7
Hollins Hill CW6. . . . . 146 F8
Hollins La
Antrobus CW9. . . . . 53 F4
Marbury SY13 . . . . 226 E7
Winwick WA2. . . . . 7 E6
HOLLINS-LANE 226 E6
Hollins Park Hospl WA2. . . . 7 F6
Hollins Rd SK11. . . . . 112 F6
Hollins Terr SK11 . . . . 112 F6
Hollins Way WA8 . . . . 22 B5
Hollinwood Cl ST7 . . . . . . 210 E8
Hollinwood Rd
Disley SK12 . . . . 38 D6
Talke ST7. . . . . 210 E8
Holloway WA7. . . . . 22 F1
Hollow Dr WA4 . . . . 16 E1
Hollow La
Kingsley WA6. . . . . 75 B3
Knutsford WA16 . . . . 57 B1
Hollowmoor Heath
CH3 . . . . 121 A6
Hollow Oak La CW8. . . . . . 101 D4
Hollowood Rd SY14 . . . . . 213 B5
Hollow The ST7. . . . . 195 B5
Holly Ave WA12. . . . . 2 D3
Hollybank
Audlem CW3 . . . . 229 E3
Moore WA4 . . . . 25 B5
Holly Bank
Chester CH1 . . . . 237 A4
Frodsham WA6 . . . . 74 C8
Helsby WA6. . . . . 73 D2
Lymm WA13. . . . . 18 D2
Hollybank Cl CW8. . . . . 78 D1
Hollybank Ct WA8 . . . . 12 F1
Holly Bank Cvn Pk
WA3. . . . . 11 A1
Hollybank Rd WA7 . . . . 49 F8
Holly Bank Rd SK9. . . . . . . 34 B1
Hollybush Cres CW5 . . . . 205 D5
Holly Bush La WA3. . . . . . . 10 C2
Holly Cl
Connah's Quay CH5. . . . . . . 91 C1
Hale L24 . . . . 21 D2
Mickle Trafford CH2. . . . . . 119 F8
Holly Cotts CW12 . . . . . . 132 C1
Holly Croft CW12 . . . . 154 F6
Holly Ct
Helsby WA6. . . . . 73 C5
Middlewich CW10 . . . . 128 B2
Holly Dr CW7 . . . . 149 D8
Holly Farm Ct WA8. . . . . . . 12 E4
Hollyfield Rd CH65 . . . . . . 70 B5
Hollyfields CW11 . . . . 191 F8
Holly Gr
Over Tabley WA16 . . . . 56 A3
Warrington WA1 . . . . 17 A7

Holly Heath Cl CW11. . . . 175 C5
Holly Hedge La WA4 . . . . . . 25 D6
Holly House Est
CW10 . . . . 129 C6
HOLLYHURST 227 A5
Hollyhurst Rd SY13 . . . . . 227 B7
Holly La
Alsager ST7. . . . . 193 E3
Harriseahead ST7 . . . . 195 F5
Wythenshawe SK9. . . . . 33 E5
Holly Mount CW2 . . . . 206 E5
Holly Rd
Bramhall SK7. . . . . 35 E5
Chester CH4 . . . . 140 F5
Ellesmere Port CH65. . . . . . 70 C5
Golborne WA3 . . . . 3 C8
Haydock WA11. . . . . 1 A6
High Lane SK6. . . . . 37 F7
Lymm WA13. . . . . 19 B5
Macclesfield SK11. . . . . . . 112 B7
Newcastle-u-Lyme ST5 . . . 210 D1
Poynton SK12 . . . . 36 E3
Warrington WA5 . . . . 14 E5
Weaverham CW8. . . . . 102 C8
Holly Rd N SK9 . . . . 60 B6
Holly Rd S SK9. . . . . 60 B5
Holly Terr
Tilston SY14. . . . . 198 C3
Warrington WA5 . . . . 14 F5
Hollythorn Ave SK8 . . . . . . 35 C7
Holly Tree Dr
Biddulph ST8 . . . . 179 C2
Swan Green WA16. . . . . . . 106 D7
Hollytree Rd WA16. . . . . . . 80 F3
Holly Wlk
Northwich CW8 . . . . 103 C7
Partington M31 . . . . 11 D3
Holm Dr CH2 . . . . 72 C3
HOLMES CHAPEL 130 C4
Holmes Chapel Bsns Pk
CW4 . . . . 130 D3
Holmes Chapel Comp Sch
CW4 . . . . 130 A2
Holmes Chapel Prim Sch
CW4 . . . . 130 B3
Holmes Chapel Rd
Allostock WA16 . . . . 106 B3
Brereton Green CW4,
CW12 . . . . 154 D8
Congleton CW12 . . . . 155 C4
Knutsford WA16 . . . . 82 C3
Lach Dennis CW9 . . . . 105 E4
Middlewich CW10 . . . . 128 E2
Sandbach CW11 . . . . 153 E1
Sproston Green CW4,
CW10 . . . . 129 B2
Withington Green SK11. . . 109 A7
Holmes Chapel Sta
CW4 . . . . 130 D2
Holmes Ct WA3. . . . . 9 C4
Holme St CH3 . . . . 120 F2
Holmesville Ave
CW12. . . . . 156 B3
Holmeswood Cl SK9 . . . . . 60 C8
Holmfield SK9. . . . . 85 A8
Holmfield Ave WA7 . . . . . . 23 C2
Holmfield Dr
Cheadle SK8 . . . . 35 B8
Ellesmere Port CH66. . . . . . 69 D3
Holmlea Dr CW1. . . . . 190 F3
Holmlee Way SK10. . . . . . . 86 D6
Holm Oak Way CH66 . . . . . 94 F8
Holmsfield Rd WA1 . . . . . . 16 D5
Holmshaw La CW1 . . . . . . 192 B3
Holmwood Dr CH65 . . . . . . 70 B2
HOLT 196 D8
Holt Gdns WA16 . . . . 58 E6
Holt Hey CH64 . . . . 67 A5
Holtís La SK9 . . . . 33 F3
Holt La WA7. . . . . 49 F8
HOLTRIDGE 215 E6
Holtridge La SY13. . . . . . . 215 E6
Holt's Com Prim Sch
LL13 . . . . 196 D8
Holt St CW1 . . . . 190 B4
Holy Family RC Prim Sch
WA8 . . . . 12 D5
Holyhead Cl WA5 . . . . 7 D3
Holyrood Ave WA8. . . . . 13 A4
Holyrood Dr CW2. . . . . . . 205 E8
Holyrood Way CH3. . . . . . 119 B2
Holy Spirit RC Prim Sch
WA9 . . . . 1 A3
Holy Spirit RC Prim Sch
The WA7. . . . . 49 D8
Holywell Cl CH64 . . . . 41 B1
Holywell Dr WA1 . . . . 16 C5
Holywell La CH3 . . . . 182 D2
Home Cl CH3 . . . . 142 E7
Homecrofts CH64. . . . . 66 E5
Homedee Ho CH1. . . . . . . 237 A3
Home Farm WA16 . . . . 56 B8
Home Farm Ave SK10 . . . . . 86 F1
Home Farm Pk CW5 . . . . . 172 A8
Home Pk CH1 . . . . 94 F1
Homeshire Ho ST7. . . . . . . 193 D3
Homestead Ave WA11. . . . . . 1 E6
Homestead Ct CW9 . . . . . 104 D7
Homestead Rd SK12 . . . . . 38 C6
Homesteads The
CW5. . . . . 172 A6
Homeway WA6 . . . . 73 B2
Homewood Cres CW8. . . . 103 B5
Honey Fields CW6 . . . . . . 146 C1
Honeysuckle Cl
Broughton CH4 . . . . 139 C3
Widnes WA8 . . . . 13 B4

Honey Suckle Cl 3
CH66 94 F8
Hong Kong Ave M90 33 A8
Honister Ave WA2 8 C2
Honister Gr WA7 49 E5
Honiton Way
Middlewich CW10 128 D2
Warrington WA5 14 E4
HONKLEY 161 C3
Hood La WA5 15 C4
Hood La N WA5 15 C6
HOOD MANOR 15 D5
Hood Rd WA8 12 F1
HOOFIELD 145 A2
Hoofield La CH3 145 A1
HOO GREEN 29 F2
Hoo Green La WA16 29 E1
Hooker St CW8 103 E7
Hook La CW6 145 A6
Hookstone Dr CH66 69 C6
HOOLE 119 A3
HOOLE BANK 119 C7
Hoole CE Prim Sch
CH2 119 A3
Hoole Gdns CH2 119 B3
Hoole Ho CH2 119 B4
Hoole La CH2 119 A3
HOOLE PARK 118 F3
Hoole Pk CH2 118 F2
Hoole Rd CH2 118 F3
Hoole Way CH1 237 B3
Hooleyhey La SK10,
SK11 89 D4
Hoolpool La WA6 72 F5
Hooten Hey CH66 69 D5
HOOTON 44 A1
Hooton Gn CH66 44 B2
Hooton La CH66 44 B1
Hooton Rd CH64, CH66 43 D1
Hooton Sta CH66 43 D1
Hooton Way
14 Handforth SK9 34 D5
Hooton CH66 44 A2
Hooton Works CH66 43 E1
Hope Ave SK9 34 C3
Hope Croft CH66 69 F2
Hope Farm Prec CH66 69 F2
Hope Farm Rd CH66 69 E2
Hopefield Rd WA13 19 B4
Hope Green Way SK10 36 D2
Hope La
Midway SK10 36 D1
Wardsend SK10 36 E1
Hope Rd CH4 139 B3
Hope St W SK10 112 C8
Hope St
Audley ST7 209 F3
Chester CH4 140 F7
Crewe CW2 190 D2
Macclesfield SK10 112 E8
Newton-le-W WA12 2 B3
Northwich CW8 103 E7
Sandbach CW11 175 B6
Hopkins Cl CW12 156 B3
Hopkinson Ct CH1 118 B1
Hopwood Cl 5 WA3 3 F8
Hopwood St WA1 16 C6
Horace Black Gdns
CH65 70 C6
Horace Lawton Ct 2
CW12 156 D3
Horbury Gdns CH66 69 C5
Hornbeam Ave CH66 69 F1
Hornbeam Cl
Chester CH2 119 B3
Runcorn WA7 24 C1
Hornbeam Dr CW8 102 E4
Hornbeam Rd L26 21 A7
Hornby Dr
Congleton CW12 156 A3
Nantwich CW5 205 A5
Hornby La WA2 8 A6
Horncastle Cl 4 WA3 3 F8
Horn's Mill Prim Sch
WA6 73 A1
Hornsmill Way WA6 73 A3
Horridge Ave WA12 2 C5
Horrocks La WA1 16 B5
Horrocks Rd CH2 118 E5
Horsemarket St WA1 16 B5
Horseshoe Cl WA6 75 B2
Horseshoe Cres WA2 8 E3
Horseshoe Dr SK11 112 B7
Horseshoe La SK9 60 A2
Horsley La CW6 167 E1
Horstone Cres CH66 69 F2
Horstone Gdns CH66 70 A2
Horstone Rd CH66 69 F2
HORTON GREEN 212 A8
Horton Way CW5 205 A4
HORWICH END 65 D5
Hoscar Ct WA8 22 D7
Hospital La CW5 203 E2
Hospital of St John
Almhouses CH1 237 A3
Hospital St
Crewe CW1 190 D6
Nantwich CW5 204 E5
Hospital Way WA7 49 F7
Hotel Rd M90 33 C7
Hotel St WA12 2 B3
Hothershall Cl CW1 173 B1
HOUGH
Alderley Edge 60 D1
Crewe 206 F3
Hough Cl SK10 88 D5
HOUGH COMMON 206 F2
Hough Cotts CW2 206 E3
Hougher Wall Rd ST7 209 D1
Hough Gn
Ashley WA15 31 E5
Chester CH4 141 B7
HOUGH GREEN 12 B2
Hough Green Rd WA8 12 B3
Hough Green Sta WA8 12 B2
Hough La
Alderley Edge SK9 60 D3
Barnton CW8, CW9 78 B4
Comberbach CW9 78 A7
Norley WA6 100 F5
Houghley Cl SK10 87 C2
Hough's La WA4 26 A6
Houghton Cl
Chester CH2 118 F3
Newton-le-W WA12 2 B3
9 Northwich CW9 103 F4
Widnes WA8 13 D2
Houghton Croft WA8 12 C5
HOUGHTON GREEN 8 E4
Houghton St
Newton-le-W WA12 2 B3
Warrington WA2 16 B6
Widnes WA8 13 D2
Houndings La CW11 175 B4
Hourd Way CH66 94 E8
Housesteads Dr CH2 118 F3
Housman Cl CH1 118 A5
Houston Gdns WA5 15 A8
Hove Cl CW1 190 B8
Hove The WA7 50 D6
Hovis Mill SK11 112 E7
Howard Ave
Bebington CH62 43 D8
Lymm WA13 19 B4
Howard Ct
Neston CH64 41 F1
Runcorn WA7 24 C4
Howard Rd
Culcheth WA3 5 A2
Saltney CH4 140 D6
Howard St CW1 191 A5
Howards Way CH64 67 A6
Howarth Ct 4 WA7 23 B2
HOWBECK BANK 219 E8
Howbeck Cres CW5 220 A8
Howbeck Wlk CW2 206 D8
Howells Ave CH66 69 D3
Howe Rd CH4 141 B7
Howe St SK10 87 F1
Howey Hill CW12 156 D1
Howey La
Congleton CW12 156 D2
Frodsham WA6 74 B7
Howey Rise WA6 74 B7
Howgill Cl CH66 68 F6
HOWLEY 16 D5
Howley La WA1 16 E5
Howley Quay Ind Est
WA1 16 D5
Howson Rd WA2 8 C3
Howty Cl SK9 34 D1
Hoylake Cl WA7 50 C6
Hoyle St WA5 15 F7
Hubert Dr CW10 151 C8
Hubert Worthington Ho 9
SK9 60 A1
Hudson Cl WA5 15 D8
Hudson Gr 9 WA3 3 E8
Hudson Rd WA2 8 E2
Hughes Ave WA2 8 D2
Hughes Dr CW2 189 F4
Hughes Pl WA2 8 D2
Hughes St WA4 16 C3
Hugh St CH4 141 D7
Hulley Pl SK10 87 F1
Hulley Rd SK10 87 F2
Hullock's Pool Rd
ST7 209 E5
HULME 8 B3
Hulme Hall Ave SK8 35 B8
Hulme Hall Cres SK8 35 A8
Hulme Hall Gram Sch
SK8 35 A8
Hulme Hall La WA16 106 B4
Hulme Hall Rd SK8 35 A8
Hulme La WA16 106 C7
Hulme Sq SK11 112 D5
Hulme St CW1 189 F5
HULME WALFIELD 156 B7
HULSEHEATH 30 A4
Hulseheath La WA16 30 A3
Hulse La CW9 105 D6
Hulton Cl CW12 157 B1
Humber Cl WA8 13 F3
Humber Dr ST8 179 E1
Humber Rd
Ellesmere Port CH66 69 F2
Warrington WA2 8 E2
Humble Bee Bank Cotts
CW5 187 C8
Hume St WA1 16 D6
Humphrey's Cl WA7 50 D7
Hungerford Ave CW1 190 E4
Hungerford Pl
Barthomley CW2 208 D5
Sandbach CW11 175 A5
Hungerford Prim Sch
CW1 190 E4
Hungerford Rd CW1 190 F4
Hungerford Terr CW1 190 F4
Hungerford Villas
CW1 190 F4
HUNSTERSON 220 B1
Hunsterson Rd
Bridgemere CW5 231 D8
Hatherton CW5 220 B3
Hunt Cl WA5 15 B8
Hunter Ave
Shavington CW2 206 D7
Warrington WA2 8 B3
Hunters Cl SK9 34 F1
Hunter's Cres CH3 121 C1
Hunters Ct
Helsby WA6 73 D4
Runcorn WA7 49 E6
Hunter's Dr CH3 121 C1
Huntersfield CW2 206 B3
Hunters Field CW8 103 D7
Hunters Hill
Kingsley WA6 75 C1
Weaverham CW8 77 C1
Hunters Lo SK9 34 F1
Hunters Mews SK9 60 C7
Hunters Pointe CW12 155 C6
Hunters Pool La SK10 86 C8
Hunters Rise CW7 126 C1
Hunter St CH1 237 A3
Hunter's View SK9 34 C3
Hunters Way
Neston CH64 66 C8
Talke ST7 210 D8
Hunters Wlk CH1 237 A2
Hunting Lodge Mews
CW8 102 A4
HUNTINGTON 142 A5
Huntington Com Prim Sch
CH3 142 A5
Huntley St WA5 15 C4
Huntly Chase SK9 60 C7
Hunt Rd WA11 1 E6
Huntsbank Bsns Pk
CW2 205 E7
Huntsbank Dr ST5 210 D1
Hunts Cl CH3 119 B1
Hunts Field Cl WA13 18 D2
Hunts La WA4 16 F2
Huntsman Dr M44 11 F7
HURDSFIELD 87 E2
Hurdsfield Cl CW10 151 C7
Hurdsfield Com Prim Sch
SK10 87 F2
Hurdsfield Gn SK10 87 E2
Hurdsfield Ind Est
SK10 87 E3
Hurdsfield Rd SK10 87 E1
Hurford Ave CH65 69 F3
Hurlbote Cl SK9 34 D5
Hurleston Bldgs CW5 204 E6
Hurlestone Cl CH2 96 F1
Hurley Cl WA5 15 C5
Hurn Cl CW1 190 B8
HURST 179 F3
Hurst Ave SK8 35 C6
Hurst Cl
Bunbury CW6 185 E8
Talke ST7 210 D6
Hurst Ct CW6 185 F8
Hursthead Inf Sch SK8 35 C6
Hursthead Jun Sch
SK8 35 C7
Hursthead Rd SK8 35 B7
Hurst La
Bollington SK10 88 A8
Glazebury WA3 5 C7
Hurst Lea Ct SK9 60 A2
Hurst Lea Rd SK22 39 C7
Hurst Mews WA6 75 C2
Hurst Mill La WA3 5 C8
Hurst Rd ST8 179 F4
Hurst St WA8 23 A4
Hurst The WA6 75 C2
Hurstwood CH3 143 A4
Hush Ho CH1 237 A2
Huskisson Way WA12 2 B4
Hutchins' Cl CW10 151 E6
Hutchinson St WA8 22 F6
Huttfield Rd L24 21 A4
Hutton Cl WA3 4 E5
Hutton Dr CW12 157 A2
HUXLEY 167 A8
Huxley CE Prim Sch
CH3 167 A7
Huxley Cl
Bramhall SK7 35 E7
Macclesfield SK10 87 B2
Huxley Ct CH66 69 F8
Huxley Dr SK7 35 E7
Huxley La CW6 168 B6
Huxley St CW8 103 E7
Hyacinth Cl WA11 1 F6
Hyde Bank Ct SK22 39 C7
Hyde Bank Mill SK22 39 C8
Hyde Bank Rd SK22 39 C8
Hyde Cl
Ellesmere Port CH65 69 F4
Runcorn WA7 49 D6
Hydrangea Way WA9 6 A7
Hylton Ct CH65 70 E2
Hylton Dr SK8 35 C8
Hythe Ave CW1 190 B8

I

Ian Rd ST7 195 D3
Iberis Gdns WA9 6 A7
Ibis Ct WA1 16 A3
Ikey La CW5 202 F6
Ikins Dr ST7 209 F2
Ilex Ave WA2 8 B7
Ilford Way WA16 58 A4
ILLIDGE GREEN 154 C4
Imperial Ave CH1 117 C4
Imperial Mews
Crewe CW2 190 D3
Ellesmere Port CH65 70 B6
INCE 71 F6
Ince Ave CH62 43 E3
Ince Dr CH3 180 F1
Ince & Elton Sta CH2 72 B4
Ince La
Elton CH2 72 B3
Wimbolds Trafford CH2 96 F5
Ince Orchards CH2 72 B4
Indigo Rd CH65 70 F6
Ingersley Ct SK10 88 B8
Ingersley Rd SK10 88 C8
Ingersley Vale SK10 88 B8
Ingham Ave WA12 2 C1
Ingham Cl CH3 119 A1
Ingham Rd WA8 12 F4
Inglegreen CH60 41 B8
Inglenook Rd WA5 14 F4
Ingleton Cl
Holmes Chapel CW4 130 A3
Newton-le-W WA12 2 B4
Ingleton Gr WA7 49 D5
Inglewood Ave CW10 151 D5
Inglewood Cl
Partington M31 11 F4
Warrington WA3 10 B6
Inglewood Cvn Pk M31 11 F4
Inman Ave WA9 1 B2
Inner Gosling Cl WA4 25 F1
Innisfree Cl 4 CH66 69 C5
Innovation Ho CW7 149 A7
Insall Rd WA2 8 F2
Intack La WA16 28 B3
Intake Cl CH64 68 A8
International App M90 33 C7
Int Peace Ctr WA5 15 D5
Inveresk Rd SY14 198 C3
Inward Way CH65 70 B7
Ion Path CW7 127 C1
Irby Cl CH66 69 E4
Ireland Blackburne Ho
WA1 16 E7
Ireland Rd
Hale L24 21 E1
Haydock WA11 1 C6
Ireland St
Warrington WA2 16 B8
Widnes WA8 13 D2
Iris Cl WA8 12 C2
Iris Wlk 7 M31 11 E2
Irlam & Cadishead Com
High Sch M44 11 E7
Irlam Ind Est M44 11 E7
Irlam Sta M44 11 E7
Ironbridge Dr CW4 130 C2
Irons La CH3 120 F7
Irvin Dr M22, SK8 34 A8
Irving's Cres CH4 140 E6
Irwell La WA7 23 B3
Irwell Rd WA4 16 B2
Irwell Rise SK10 87 F7
Irwell St WA8 23 A4
Irwin Dr SK9 34 C5
Isabella Ct CH4 140 E6
Isherwood Cl WA2 8 F3
Isis Cl CW12 156 F1
Islay Cl CH65 70 C1
Islington Gn WA8 13 D4
ISYCOED 196 C1
Iveagh Cl WA7 50 A7
Iver Cl
Chester CH2 118 E7
Cronton WA8 12 C6
Iver Rd CH2 118 E7
Ivy Ave WA12 2 C2
Ivy Bank Prim Sch
SK11 112 A5
Ivychurch Mews WA7 23 D2
Ivy Cotts SY13 225 A8
Ivy Ct CH4 162 D2
Ivy Dr CW8 102 A2
Ivy Farm Ct L24 21 D1
Ivy Farm Dr CH64 66 F6
Ivy Farm Gdns WA3 4 D4
Ivy Farm La CH3 183 C1
Ivy Gdns CW12 156 C2
Ivy Ho
Macclesfield SK11 112 A7
Nether Alderley SK9 84 C7
Ivy House Rd ST8 179 C2
Ivy La
Alsager ST7 193 E2
Macclesfield SK11 112 A6
Ivy Meade Cl 10 SK11 111 F7
Ivy Meade Rd SK11 111 F6
Ivy Mews CH2 119 A5
Ivy Rd
Golborne WA3 3 B8
Macclesfield SK11 112 A7
Poynton SK12 36 E3
Warrington WA1 17 E7
Ivy St WA7 23 A1
Ivy Wlk M31 11 D3

J

Jackie Stewart Bsns Ctr
CW6 147 D6
Jack La
Moulton CW9, CW10 127 A7
Weston CW2 207 D6
Jackson Ave
Culcheth WA3 4 E3
Nantwich CW5 204 F5
Warrington WA1 16 F6
Jackson Ct CH5 139 B7
Jackson La SK10 88 B7
Jackson Rd CW12 156 E5
Jacksons Cl SK10 88 B7
Jacksons Edge Rd
SK12 38 B6
Jackson's La SK7 36 C8
Jackson St
Burtonwood WA5 6 E6
Haydock WA11 1 A7
Macclesfield SK11 112 D6
Jacobs Way WA16 79 F7
Jamage Ind Est ST7 210 C5
Jamage Rd ST7 210 D5
James Atkinson Way
CW1 189 F7
James Ave CH66 69 C3
James Cl WA8 23 A4
James Hall St CW5 204 E6
James Pl CH2 118 F2
James Rd WA11 1 F7
James St
Chester CH1 237 B3
Macclesfield SK11 112 D6
Northwich CW9 104 C8
5 Warrington WA1 16 B5
Jamieson Cl
Alsager ST7 193 E4
Chester CH3 119 A2
Jane Maddock Homes
ST7 193 B3
Jan Palach Ave CW5 204 F4
Japonica Gdns WA9 6 A7
Jarman SK11 112 F4
Jasmine Cres ST7 195 D2
Jasmine Gdns WA9 6 A7
Jasmine Gr WA8 22 D8
Jasmine Wlk M31 11 F2
Jasmin Way ST7 195 F2
Jay Cl WA3 10 A4
Jays Cl WA7 50 E7
Jedburgh Ave CH66 69 A6
Jefferson Dr WA5 15 B7
Jefferson Gdns WA8 12 F3
Jellicoe Ave M44 11 E6
Jennet's La WA3 5 C8
Jenny La SK7 35 E4
Jensen Ct WA7 23 C3
Jersey Ave CH65 70 C1
Jersey Cl CW12 157 A2
Jersey Way CW10 128 D2
Jervis Cl WA2 9 A3
Jesmond Cres CW2 190 B2
Jesmond Gr SK8 35 B8
Jesmond Rd CH1 118 B2
Jessop Ho WA7 22 E3
Jessop Way CW1 191 C4
JH Godwin Prim Sch
CH1 117 D4
Jockey St WA2 16 B7
JODRELL BANK 108 D2
Jodrell Bank Obsy*
CW4 108 C3
Jodrell Bank Visitor Ctr*
SK11 108 D3
Jodrell Cl
Holmes Chapel CW4 130 A3
Macclesfield SK11 112 E7
Jodrell Dr WA4 27 A7
Jodrell Mdw SK23 65 E8
Jodrell Rd SK23 65 D8
Jodrell St
Macclesfield SK11 112 E7
New Mills SK22 39 B7
John Brunner Cres
CW9 103 E6
John Ford Way CW11 154 B1
John Fryer Ave CW9 80 A5
John Gresty Dr CW5 205 D6
John Lloyd Ct M44 11 F8
John May Ct SK10 87 B2
John Middleton Cl L24 21 E2
John Nicholas Cres
CH65 70 C6
John Rd WA13 18 C3
Johns Ave
Haydock WA11 1 E7
Runcorn WA7 48 F8
Johns Cl SK10 88 D5
Johnson Ave WA12 2 B5
Johnson Cl CW12 157 B1
Johnsons Cl CH4 141 B5
Johnson's La WA8 13 E1
Johnson St SK23 65 E8
John St
Bollington SK10 88 B8
Congleton CW12 156 C2
Crewe CW1 190 C5
Ellesmere Port CH65 70 B6
Golborne WA3 3 A8
Irlam M44 11 E5
Macclesfield SK11 112 D6
1 Northwich CW9 104 A8
Utkinton CW6 146 B7
Warrington WA2 16 B6
Winsford CW7 126 C1
John Street Com Prim Sch
CH65 70 B6
Jonathan's Way CH1 117 E5
Jones's La CW10 152 D6
Jonson Rd CH64 66 E8
Jordangate SK10 112 D8
Joseph Cres ST7 193 F2
Joseph Groome Twrs 10
CH65 70 C6

Joseph St WA8 . . . . . 13 C2
Joyce Ave CW7 . . . . . 126 C2
Joy La WA5 . . . . . 6 E4
Jubilee Almshouses CW5 . . . . . 204 E6
Jubilee Ave
Crewe CW2 . . . . . 190 B3
Warrington, Padgate WA1 . . . . . 16 F8
Warrington WA5 . . . . . 14 E4
Jubilee Cres WA11 . . . . . 1 F7
Jubilee Ct
2 Handforth SK9 . . . . . 34 E5
Holmes Chapel CW4 . . . . . 130 A3
Jubilee Gdns
Nantwich CW5 . . . . . 204 E4
New Mills SK22 . . . . . 39 C7
Jubilee Gn CH65 . . . . . 70 C4
Jubilee Gr WA13 . . . . . 18 C4
Jubilee Rd CW12 . . . . . 156 E2
Jubilee St SK22 . . . . . 39 C7
Jubilee Terr CW5 . . . . . 204 E4
Jubilee Villas CW11 . . . . . 175 C2
Jubilee Way
Widnes WA8 . . . . . 12 E1
5 Winsford CW7 . . . . . 126 D1
Jubits La WA8 . . . . . 13 A8
Juddfield St WA11 . . . . . 1 A7
Judy La SK11 . . . . . 113 A3
Julian Way WA8 . . . . . 12 F4
July Bglws CH4 . . . . . 141 E2
Jumper La SK10 . . . . . 88 F7
Junction Eight Bsns Ctr CH65 . . . . . 70 A7
Junction Ho CW1 . . . . . 190 A5
Junction La WA12 . . . . . 2 B3
June Ave CH62 . . . . . 43 E8
Juniper Cl ST5 . . . . . 210 E1
Juniper Ct CH2 . . . . . 119 B4
Juniper Dr CH66 . . . . . 69 E1
Juniper Gr CH66 . . . . . 69 F1
Juniper La WA3 . . . . . 18 A7
Juniper Rise SK10 . . . . . 86 E1
Jupiter Dr CH1 . . . . . 117 E2
Jurby Cl WA2 . . . . . 8 F1
Justice St SK10 . . . . . 87 D1

K

Kansas Pl WA5 . . . . . 15 B7
Karen Cl WA5 . . . . . 7 A6
Karen Way CH66 . . . . . 69 D3
Kaye Ave WA3 . . . . . 4 F3
Kay La WA13 . . . . . 29 B8
Keats Cl
Ellesmere Port CH66 . . . . . 94 E8
Widnes WA8 . . . . . 22 F8
Keats Dr
Macclesfield SK10 . . . . . 86 F1
Rode Heath ST7 . . . . . 193 E8
Wistaston CW2 . . . . . 206 A8
Keats Gr WA2 . . . . . 8 C2
Keats La CW9 . . . . . 80 A5
Keats Terr CH1 . . . . . 118 A5
Keble St WA8 . . . . . 23 B7
KECKWICK 25 A3
Keckwick La WA4 . . . . . 25 A3
Keele Cres SK11 . . . . . 112 B6
Keel Hey CH64 . . . . . 43 B1
Keepers Cl WA16 . . . . . 57 D3
Keepers La CW9 . . . . . 53 D4
Keeper's La CW8 . . . . . 102 E8
Keeper's Rd WA4 . . . . . 27 A7
Keepers Wlk WA7 . . . . . 23 F2
Keith Ave WA5 . . . . . 14 E6
Keith Dr CH63 . . . . . 43 D5
Kelburn Ct WA3 . . . . . 9 F6
Kelmscott Cl CH66 . . . . . 69 D2
KELSALL 122 C4
Kelsall Ave CH62 . . . . . 43 F3
Kelsall Cl
Bebington CH62 . . . . . 43 E3
Warrington WA3 . . . . . 9 C3
Widnes WA8 . . . . . 12 D1
Kelsall Com Prim Sch CW6 . . . . . 122 C4
Kelsall Rd CH3 . . . . . 121 C4
Kelsall St CW12 . . . . . 156 E3
Kelsall Way
Audley ST7 . . . . . 209 D1
6 Handforth SK9 . . . . . 34 D5
Kelsborrow Cl CW9 . . . . . 103 E3
Kelsborrow Way CW6 . . . . . 122 D4
Kelso Way SK10 . . . . . 87 C4
Kelstern Cl 2 CW9 . . . . . 104 B8
KELSTERTON 91 B2
Kelsterton Ct CH5 . . . . . 91 C1
Kelsterton La CH6 . . . . . 91 B1
Kelsterton Rd
Connah's Quay CH5, CH6 . . . . . 91 C2
Kelsterton CH6 . . . . . 91 A3
Kelvin Cl WA3 . . . . . 9 D6
Kelvin Gr CH2 . . . . . 118 E4
Kelvin St WA3 . . . . . 9 F5
Kemberton Dr WA8 . . . . . 13 A5
Kemble Cl CW2 . . . . . 206 B8
Kemmel Ave WA4 . . . . . 16 C3
Kempsell Way L26 . . . . . 21 A7
Kempsell Wlk L26 . . . . . 21 A7
Kempton Ave CW1 . . . . . 190 C7
Kempton Cl
Chester CH1 . . . . . 118 B2

Kempton Cl *continued*
Newton-le-W WA12 . . . . . 2 D5
Runcorn WA7 . . . . . 49 C6
Kempton Way SK10 . . . . . 87 C4
Kendal Ave WA2 . . . . . 8 C2
Kendal Cl
Chester CH2 . . . . . 119 A6
Ellesmere Port CH66 . . . . . 69 D2
Macclesfield SK11 . . . . . 111 E6
Kendal Ct CW12 . . . . . 156 A2
Kendal Dr
Bramhall SK7 . . . . . 35 C5
Ellesmere Port CH66 . . . . . 69 E2
Kendal Rd
Macclesfield SK11 . . . . . 111 F6
Widnes WA8 . . . . . 12 C1
Kendal Rise WA7 . . . . . 49 D5
Kendal Way CW2 . . . . . 207 C1
Kendrick Cl CW8 . . . . . 77 D1
Kendrick St WA1 . . . . . 16 A5
Kenilworth Ave
Handforth SK9 . . . . . 34 D3
Knutsford WA16 . . . . . 57 C2
Runcorn WA7 . . . . . 49 B8
Kenilworth Cl
Macclesfield SK11 . . . . . 111 F6
Wistaston CW2 . . . . . 206 A7
Kenilworth Ct CH65 . . . . . 70 E2
Kenilworth Dr
Hazel Grove SK7 . . . . . 36 D8
Warrington WA1 . . . . . 16 F8
Kenilworth Gdns WA12 . . . . . 2 C1
Kenilworth Gn SK11 . . . . . 111 F6
Kenilworth Ho 6 CH1 . . . . . 237 C3
Kenilworth Rd
Golborne WA3 . . . . . 3 E7
Macclesfield SK11 . . . . . 111 F6
Neston CH64 . . . . . 66 E5
Kenley Ave WA8 . . . . . 12 D5
Kenmare Bank CW9 . . . . . 104 A5
Kenmore Gr M44 . . . . . 11 D6
Kennedy Ave SK10 . . . . . 86 F2
Kennedy Cl CH2 . . . . . 119 A5
Kennedy Ct 4 WA5 . . . . . 15 B7
Kennel La
Cuddington CW8 . . . . . 102 A1
Little Budworth CW8 . . . . . 124 E7
Kennelwood Rd CW9 . . . . . 78 C7
Kennerley's Ct SK9 . . . . . 60 A7
Kennerley's La SK9 . . . . . 60 A7
Kennet Cl SK9 . . . . . 34 D2
Kennet Dr CW12 . . . . . 156 F1
Kenneth Rd WA8 . . . . . 22 C8
Kennet Rd WA11 . . . . . 1 C6
Kennet Way 10 SK11 . . . . . 111 F8
Kennington Pk WA8 . . . . . 12 E4
Kenrick Cl CW3 . . . . . 232 C1
Kensington Ave WA4 . . . . . 17 C2
Kensington Cl
Chester CH4 . . . . . 141 A6
Widnes WA8 . . . . . 13 D4
Kensington Ct
Alsager ST7 . . . . . 192 F3
9 Nantwich CW5 . . . . . 204 E6
Wilmslow SK9 . . . . . 60 A6
Winsford CW7 . . . . . 149 C7
Kensington Dr
Congleton CW12 . . . . . 156 F4
Willaston CW5 . . . . . 205 D4
Kensington Gn CH4 . . . . . 140 F6
Kensington Rd
Chester CH4 . . . . . 141 A6
Ellesmere Port CH65 . . . . . 70 A5
Kensington Sq 11 SK10 . . . . . 111 F8
Kensington Way CW9 . . . . . 103 E3
Kent Ave SK10 . . . . . 87 E6
Kent Cl CH63 . . . . . 43 B8
Kent Dr CW12 . . . . . 156 D4
Kent Gdns CH2 . . . . . 118 F5
Kent Gr WA7 . . . . . 23 B1
Kent Ho ST7 . . . . . 210 D6
Kentmere Ave CW7 . . . . . 126 D2
Kentmere Pl WA2 . . . . . 8 A3
Kenton Rd L26 . . . . . 21 A7
Kent Rd
Chester CH2 . . . . . 118 F5
Irlam M44 . . . . . 11 C5
Partington M31 . . . . . 11 E2
Warrington WA5 . . . . . 15 C4
Kentridge Dr CH66 . . . . . 69 D3
Kent's Green La CW1, CW11 . . . . . 191 E7
Kent's La CW1 . . . . . 173 C1
Kent St
Warrington WA4 . . . . . 16 C4
Widnes WA8 . . . . . 13 B1
Kent Way WA12 . . . . . 2 C1
Kentwell Dr SK10 . . . . . 87 C3
Kent Wlk SK10 . . . . . 86 F1
Kenview Cl WA8 . . . . . 22 A4
Kenwick Cl CH66 . . . . . 69 C3
Kenwood Ave SK7 . . . . . 35 D5
KENYON 3 F3
Kenyon Ave WA5 . . . . . 14 E5
Kenyon Ct WA8 . . . . . 23 A6
Kenyon La
Culcheth WA3 . . . . . 4 A4
Golborne, Kenyon WA3 . . . . . 3 F3
Golborne WA3 . . . . . 3 F5
Kenyons La N WA11 . . . . . 1 F8
Kenyon's La S WA11 . . . . . 1 F7
Kerfoot Bsns Pk WA2 . . . . . 16 A8
Kerfoot St WA2 . . . . . 16 A7
Keristal Ave CH3 . . . . . 142 A7
KERRIDGE 88 A6
Kerridge Cl CW10 . . . . . 151 B8

KERRIDGE-END 88 D3
Kerridge Rd SK10 . . . . . 88 B3
Kerry Croft CH66 . . . . . 69 E1
Kershaw Gr SK11 . . . . . 112 B8
Kershaw St WA8 . . . . . 12 D1
Kershaw Way WA12 . . . . . 2 C5
Kestrel Ave WA16 . . . . . 57 B3
Kestrel Cl
Congleton CW12 . . . . . 156 E1
Middlewich CW10 . . . . . 151 D6
Winsford CW7 . . . . . 149 D5
Kestrel Dr CW1 . . . . . 190 B8
Kestrel La WA3 . . . . . 9 E4
Kestrel Rd
Heswall CH60 . . . . . 41 C7
Northwich CW8 . . . . . 103 C7
Kestrels Way WA7 . . . . . 49 F6
Keswick Ave
Bebington CH63 . . . . . 43 C4
Macclesfield SK11 . . . . . 111 F5
Warrington WA2 . . . . . 8 C2
Keswick Cl
Chester CH2 . . . . . 119 A5
Crewe CW2 . . . . . 189 E3
Irlam M44 . . . . . 11 D4
Macclesfield SK11 . . . . . 111 F6
Widnes WA8 . . . . . 12 C1
Winsford CW7 . . . . . 126 D2
Keswick Cres WA2 . . . . . 8 C2
Keswick Ct CW12 . . . . . 156 A2
Keswick Dr
Bramhall SK7 . . . . . 35 C5
Frodsham WA6 . . . . . 74 D8
Keswick Gdns CH63 . . . . . 43 C5
Keswick Rd SK6 . . . . . 37 E8
Ketlan Ct CH4 . . . . . 140 E7
Kettell Ave CW1 . . . . . 190 A6
Kettle La CW3 . . . . . 230 C2
KETTLESHULME 64 F4
Kettleshulme St James CE Prim Sch SK23 . . . . . 64 F4
Kettleshulme Way SK12 . . . . . 37 A3
Kettleshulme Wlk 4 SK9 . . . . . 34 E1
Kew Gardens Cl WA8 . . . . . 13 D4
Keyes Cl WA3 . . . . . 9 F4
Keyes Gdn WA3 . . . . . 9 F4
KEY GREEN 157 E4
Keysbrook CH3 . . . . . 166 C2
Keysbrook Ave CH3 . . . . . 166 C2
Kidderton Cl CW5 . . . . . 202 E7
Kidderton La CW5 . . . . . 202 F7
KIDNAL 212 E8
KIDSGROVE 195 B1
Kidsgrove Sta ST7 . . . . . 194 F1
Kidston Dr CW1 . . . . . 189 F7
Kilbuck La WA11 . . . . . 2 A8
Kilburn Ave CH62 . . . . . 43 E6
Kilburn Cl SK8 . . . . . 34 B7
Kildare Cl L24 . . . . . 21 D2
Kildonan Rd WA4 . . . . . 17 A2
Kilford Cl WA5 . . . . . 7 E2
Killingworth La WA3 . . . . . 10 B5
Kilmorey Park Rd CH2 . . . . . 118 F3
Kilmorey Pk CH2 . . . . . 118 F4
Kilmorey Pk Ave CH2 . . . . . 237 C4
Kilncroft WA7 . . . . . 50 B5
Kiln Croft La SK9 . . . . . 34 E4
Kiln La CW5 . . . . . 220 B8
Kilsby Dr WA8 . . . . . 13 E2
Kilshaw Rd WA5 . . . . . 6 F6
Kilsyth Cl WA2 . . . . . 8 F4
Kimberley Dr WA4 . . . . . 16 C1
Kimberley St WA5 . . . . . 15 E5
Kimberley Terr CH2 . . . . . 118 F2
Kinder Dr CW2 . . . . . 189 D3
Kinderton Cl WA16 . . . . . 29 C4
Kinderton Mobile Home Pk CW10 . . . . . 152 A7
Kinderton St CW10 . . . . . 128 D1
Kinder View SK22 . . . . . 39 C7
King Arthur's Wlk WA7 . . . . . 24 A1
King Charles Ct CH1 . . . . . 237 A3
King Edward Bldgs 4 CH3 . . . . . 119 A1
King Edward Cl CW9 . . . . . 103 F5
King Edward Rd
Knutsford WA16 . . . . . 57 A2
3 Macclesfield SK10 . . . . . 112 D8
King Edward St
Macclesfield SK10 . . . . . 112 D8
Middlewich CW10 . . . . . 128 C1
Warrington WA1 . . . . . 16 E7
Kingfisher Cl
Congleton CW12 . . . . . 156 E1
Farndon CH3 . . . . . 180 F1
Nantwich CW5 . . . . . 204 E8
Runcorn WA7 . . . . . 49 F5
Warrington WA3 . . . . . 9 F4
Kingfisher Ct
Chester CH2 . . . . . 237 A4
Northwich CW9 . . . . . 79 C2
Kingfisher Dr 5 CW7 . . . . . 149 D6
Kingfisher Gr CW9 . . . . . 79 F5
King George Ave CW9 . . . . . 104 B8
King George Cres WA1 . . . . . 16 E7
King George Rd WA11 . . . . . 2 A7
King George Way ST7 . . . . . 195 C1
Kingham Cl 3 WA8 . . . . . 13 D1
King Ho ST7 . . . . . 210 D5
King James Ct WA7 . . . . . 49 E6
King Pl CW5 . . . . . 204 E6
King's Ave WA3 . . . . . 3 F7
King's Bldgs CH1 . . . . . 237 A3

Kingsbury Cl WA4 . . . . . 26 D3
Kingsbury Dr 14 SK9 . . . . . 34 D1
Kingsbury Rd WA8 . . . . . 13 D4
Kings Cl
Chester CH4 . . . . . 140 F5
Wilmslow SK9 . . . . . 60 A6
King's Cres CW10 . . . . . 128 C2
King's Cres E CH3 . . . . . 119 A1
King's Cres W CH3 . . . . . 119 A1
Kings Croft CH5 . . . . . 91 D1
Kings Ct
Nantwich CW5 . . . . . 204 D5
Runcorn WA7 . . . . . 24 D4
King's Ct
Chester CH1 . . . . . 237 A3
Middlewich CW10 . . . . . 128 D2
Kingsdale Rd WA5 . . . . . 14 F7
Kingsdown Cl CW2 . . . . . 207 C1
Kings Dr
Helsby WA6 . . . . . 73 B3
Wistaston CW2 . . . . . 205 E8
Kingsfield Ct CH4 . . . . . 141 C3
King's Gate CW8 . . . . . 102 A2
Kings Grove Sch CW2 . . . . . 190 A3
Kingshead Cl WA7 . . . . . 24 A2
Kings La CW6 . . . . . 147 D4
King's La
Allostock CW10, WA16 . . . . . 106 C1
Nantwich CW5 . . . . . 204 D5
Kingsland Grange WA1 . . . . . 9 D1
Kingslawn Cl 4 CW9 . . . . . 103 F5
Kings Lea Ho CH3 . . . . . 142 A8
KINGSLEY 75 C2
Kingsley Ave
Bebington CH62 . . . . . 43 E3
Handforth SK9 . . . . . 34 C2
Kingsley Cl
Northwich CW8 . . . . . 103 C5
Talke ST7 . . . . . 210 D6
Kingsley Com Prim Sch WA6 . . . . . 74 F2
Kingsley Cres WA7 . . . . . 23 A1
Kingsley Ct CW11 . . . . . 174 D8
Kingsley Dr
Northwich CW9 . . . . . 104 A6
Warrington WA4 . . . . . 26 C7
Kingsley Gdns CH3 . . . . . 142 B8
Kingsley Gn WA6 . . . . . 74 E5
Kingsley Rd
Chester CH3 . . . . . 142 B8
Congleton CW12 . . . . . 157 A3
Crowton CW8 . . . . . 76 B1
Ellesmere Port CH65 . . . . . 70 C5
Frodsham WA6 . . . . . 74 E4
Haslington CW1 . . . . . 191 C4
Runcorn WA7 . . . . . 23 A1
Talke ST7 . . . . . 210 D6
Kingsley St John's CE Prim Sch WA6 . . . . . 75 C2
Kingsley Wlk CW7 . . . . . 126 B2
Kings Mdw
Hough CW2 . . . . . 206 E2
Runcorn WA7 . . . . . 50 C8
KINGSMEAD 103 E5
Kingsmead
Chester CH2 . . . . . 118 C8
Northwich CW9 . . . . . 103 F5
Kingsmead Crossroads 10 CW9 . . . . . 103 F4
Kingsmead Ct WA3 . . . . . 9 A8
Kingsmead Prim Sch CW9 . . . . . 103 E5
Kingsmead Sq CW9 . . . . . 103 E4
Kings Mews CH66 . . . . . 69 C7
Kings Rd
Connah's Quay CH5 . . . . . 91 D1
Ellesmere Port CH66 . . . . . 69 C7
Golborne WA3 . . . . . 3 A7
Irlam M44 . . . . . 11 E6
Warrington WA2 . . . . . 9 A2
King's Rd SK9 . . . . . 59 E8
King's Sch The
Chester CH4 . . . . . 141 B4
Macclesfield SK10 . . . . . 87 C1
Macclesfield SK10 . . . . . 112 E8
King St
Audley ST7 . . . . . 209 D1
Chester CH1 . . . . . 237 A3
Congleton CW12 . . . . . 156 F4
Ellesmere Port CH65 . . . . . 70 C6
Hartford CW8 . . . . . 103 B5
Kidsgrove ST7 . . . . . 195 A2
Knutsford WA16 . . . . . 57 A2
Macclesfield SK10 . . . . . 112 E8
Middlewich CW10 . . . . . 128 B5
Newton-le-W WA12 . . . . . 2 B3
Northwich CW9 . . . . . 104 F6
Runcorn WA7 . . . . . 23 A3
Sandbach CW11 . . . . . 174 E8
Talke ST7 . . . . . 210 D5
Kingston Ave
Macclesfield SK11 . . . . . 112 F7
Warrington WA5 . . . . . 14 E6
Kingston Cl WA7 . . . . . 23 E2
Kingston Ct
14 Handforth SK9 . . . . . 34 E1
Saughall CH1 . . . . . 94 B2
Kingston Pl ST8 . . . . . 179 E2
Kingston Rd SK9 . . . . . 34 D5
Kingstreet SK7 . . . . . 35 B1
King Street Trad Est CW10 . . . . . 128 C2
KINGSWAY 23 A8
Kingsway
Bollington SK10 . . . . . 87 E7
Chester CH2 . . . . . 118 F5

Kingsway *continued*
Crewe CW2 . . . . . 190 B2
Frodsham WA6 . . . . . 74 B8
Heswall CH60 . . . . . 41 C6
Newton-le-W WA12 . . . . . 2 C2
Northwich CW9 . . . . . 104 B8
Widnes WA8 . . . . . 13 A1
Winsford CW7 . . . . . 126 F1
Kingsway Ho WA4 . . . . . 16 F4
Kingsway N WA1 . . . . . 16 F6
Kingsway S WA1, WA4 . . . . . 16 F4
Kingsway W CH2 . . . . . 118 E4
KINGSWOOD 74 C1
Kingswood ST7 . . . . . 195 B1
KINGSWOOD 7 B2
Kingswood WA5 . . . . . 7 B2
Kingswood Ave
Chorlton CW2 . . . . . 207 B3
Saughall CH1 . . . . . 94 C1
Kingswood Cres CW10 . . . . . 151 E5
Kingswood La CH1 . . . . . 94 C1
Kingswood Rd WA5 . . . . . 7 A2
Kings Wood Wlk CW6 . . . . . 122 D5
Kinloch Cl
Crewe CW1 . . . . . 190 B6
Halewood L26 . . . . . 21 A7
Kinnerley Rd CH65 . . . . . 70 A3
Kinnersley Ave ST7 . . . . . 210 F8
Kinnersley St 1 ST7 . . . . . 195 A2
Kinnerton Cl CH4 . . . . . 140 E5
KINNERTON GREEN 161 B7
Kinnerton Hts CH4 . . . . . 161 A7
Kinnerton La CH4 . . . . . 161 A8
Kinnerton Rd CH4 . . . . . 162 A7
Kinnington Way CH1 . . . . . 94 F7
Kinnock Pk WA5 . . . . . 6 E6
Kinross Cl WA2 . . . . . 8 F4
Kinsale Dr WA3 . . . . . 9 C4
KINSEY HEATH 230 B1
Kinsey Rd CH65 . . . . . 70 D1
Kinsey's La CH2 . . . . . 71 F6
Kinsey St CW12 . . . . . 156 E2
Kintore Cl
Bebington CH63 . . . . . 43 C4
Winsford CW7 . . . . . 127 A3
Kintore Dr WA5 . . . . . 14 D6
Kintyre Cl CH65 . . . . . 70 C1
Kipling Ave WA2 . . . . . 8 C1
Kipling Cres WA8 . . . . . 22 F8
Kipling Rd CH1 . . . . . 117 F5
Kipling Way CW1 . . . . . 190 F4
Kirby Cl CH2 . . . . . 118 D5
Kirkacre Ave WA12 . . . . . 7 C8
Kirkby Rd WA3 . . . . . 4 F3
Kirkcaldy Ave WA5 . . . . . 14 D6
Kirkfell Dr SK6 . . . . . 37 E8
Kirkham Ave WA3 . . . . . 3 E6
Kirkham Cl WA5 . . . . . 15 B4
Kirkham Rd
Gatley SK8 . . . . . 34 C8
Widnes WA8 . . . . . 13 C2
Kirkstall Cl
Macclesfield SK10 . . . . . 87 B2
Poynton SK12 . . . . . 36 D4
Kirkstead Rd SK8 . . . . . 35 C6
Kirkstead Way WA3 . . . . . 3 A8
Kirkstone Ave WA2 . . . . . 8 C2
Kirkstone Cres WA7 . . . . . 50 A4
Kirkstone Ct CW12 . . . . . 156 A1
Kirkwall Dr WA5 . . . . . 15 A3
Kirkwood Cl CH3 . . . . . 119 A2
Kishfield La SK23 . . . . . 65 A6
Kitchener Ave M44 . . . . . 11 C4
Kitchen St CH1 . . . . . 118 B1
Kite Gr ST7 . . . . . 195 D3
Kitfield Ave CW10 . . . . . 151 D7
KITT'S MOSS 35 D6
Kitt's Moss La SK7 . . . . . 35 D6
Knap The CH60 . . . . . 41 A6
Knebworth Ct CW12 . . . . . 179 B8
Knight Rd WA5 . . . . . 6 F6
Knightsbridge Ave
1 Northwich CW9 . . . . . 103 E3
Warrington WA4 . . . . . 17 C2
Knightsbridge Cl
13 Handforth SK9 . . . . . 34 D1
Widnes WA8 . . . . . 13 D4
Knightsbridge Ct
Chester CH4 . . . . . 237 C2
Warrington WA1 . . . . . 16 A5
Knight's Cl SK11 . . . . . 112 E7
Knight's Grange (Sports Complex) CW7 . . . . . 126 B3
Knights La CW6 . . . . . 123 E1
Knights Mdw CW7 . . . . . 126 C3
Knight St SK11 . . . . . 112 E7
Knights Way CW2 . . . . . 206 B3
Knightwake Rd SK22 . . . . . 39 A8
Knole Ave SK12 . . . . . 36 F4
KNOLLS GREEN 58 E3
Knoll St SK22 . . . . . 39 B8
Knoll The WA7 . . . . . 49 F7
KNOTBURY 138 F5
Knottingley Dr CH66 . . . . . 69 C5
Knott's Hos WN7 . . . . . 4 B8
Knotty La CW12 . . . . . 179 F8
Knowe The CH64 . . . . . 68 A8
Knowle Cl CH66 . . . . . 69 E3
Knowle Gn SK9 . . . . . 34 C3
Knowle Pk SK9 . . . . . 34 C3
Knowles Ind Est SK23 . . . . . 39 D3
Knowles St 2 WA8 . . . . . 13 C2
Knowl Hey Rd L26 . . . . . 21 A6
Knowl La CH3 . . . . . 180 E5
Knowl The CH3 . . . . . 180 F5
Knowsley Ave WA3 . . . . . 3 B8

Knowsley Ct CH2 118 F4
Knowsley Expressway L35,
WA8 21 F8
Knowsley La ST7 194 F4
Knowsley Rd
Chester CH2 118 F4
Hazel Grove SK7 36 F8
Macclesfield SK11 112 C5
KNUTSFORD 57 A3
Knutsford & Dist Hospl
WA16 56 F1
Knutsford High Sch
(Lower Sch) WA16 56 E1
Knutsford High Sch
(Upper Sch) WA16 56 F1
Knutsford Old Rd WA4 17 A2
Knutsford Rd
Alsager ST7 193 F6
Antrobus CW9 53 D4
Chelford SK11 84 A2
Grappenhall WA4 17 C1
Great Budworth CW9 54 A2
Holmes Chapel CW4 130 B5
Mobberley WA16 57 E4
Row-of-Trees SK9,
WA16 59 D3
Warrington WA4 16 D3
Knutsford Road Wlk 12
SK11 112 E7
Knutsford Sta WA16 57 A1
Knutsford View WA15 32 C8
Knutsford Way CH1 117 F2
Kohima Cres CH3 142 B5
Kronsbec Ave CH66 69 D6
KUS Ind Est CH5 139 A6
Kynaston Dr CH4 140 C7

L

Laburnum Ave
Crewe CW2 189 F2
2 Nantwich CW5 204 F5
Warrington WA1 17 C7
Laburnum Cl
Congleton CW12 156 A4
Talke ST7 210 E8
Laburnum Cres CW8 78 B3
Laburnum Ct
Lymm WA13 19 B4
Wistaston CW2 205 F7
Laburnum Farm Cl
CH64 67 A5
Laburnum Gr
Crewe CW1 190 D6
Ellesmere Port CH66 95 A8
Runcorn WA7 49 C7
Saltney CH4 140 E6
Weaverham CW8 102 D8
Laburnum La
Altrincham WA15 31 E8
Warrington WA5 14 C5
Laburnum Pl ST5 210 D1
Laburnum Rd
Davenham CW9 103 F3
Golborne WA3 3 F7
Irlam M44 11 D5
Macclesfield SK11 112 E5
Northwich CW9 104 C6
Laburnum Way LL13 180 D1
Lacey Ave SK9 34 B1
Lacey Ct
Handforth SK9 34 B1
Widnes WA8 23 B7
Lacey Gn SK9 34 B1
Lacey Gr SK9 34 C1
LACEY GREEN 34 B1
Lacey Green Prim Sch
SK9 34 B1
Lacey St WA8 23 A7
LACH DENNIS 105 D5
LACHE 140 F5
Lache Hall Cres CH4 140 F4
Lache La
Chester, Westminster Park
CH4 141 B5
Roughhill CH4 140 E3
Lache Park Ave CH4 141 A6
Lache Prim Sch CH4 141 A5
Lacy Ct CW12 156 F2
Ladies Mile WA16 56 F2
Ladies Wlk CH64 66 E8
Lady Acre Cl WA13 18 D2
Ladybarn Ave WA3 2 F7
Ladybarn Cres SK7 35 F6
Ladybarn Manor SK7 35 E8
Ladybrook Gr 6 SK9 34 D2
Ladybrook Prim Sch
SK7 35 F7
Ladycroft Cl WA1 17 E7
Ladyfield St SK9 60 B7
Ladyfield Terr SK9 60 C7
Lady Helen Wlk CW5 204 E6
Lady Heyes Craft &
Antique Restoration
Ctr* WA6 74 F4
Lady La
Croft WA3 9 C8
Culcheth WA3 4 C1
Mobberley WA16 58 C6
Lady Mary's Sq WA16 30 E3
Ladypit Rd SK23 39 E4
Ladypool L24 21 C2
Lady Richeld Cl WA7 24 D3
Ladys Cl SK12 36 E4
Ladythorn Cres SK7 35 F6
Ladythorn Gr SK7 35 F6
Ladythorn Rd SK7 35 E6
Ladywood Rd WA5 7 D1
Lagos Gr CW7 126 E2
Laidon Ave CW2 206 A7
Laira Ct WA2 16 C7
Laira St WA2 16 C7
Lake House Cl CW8 77 D1
Lake La WA4 52 F5
Lakelands Cl SK10 112 F7
Lakemore Ctry Pk*
CW1 174 C1
Lakeside
Bosley SK11 158 D8
Chester CH4 141 B2
Lakeside Cl
Chester CH2 118 F7
Widnes WA8 22 A8
Lakeside Cvn Pk CW7 149 F7
Lakeside Dr
Poynton SK12 36 E5
Warrington WA1 16 A3
Lakeside Rd WA13 18 D2
Lakeside View
Moulton CW7 126 F7
Nantwich CW5 204 E3
Lake View
Alsager ST7 193 C2
Congleton CW12 156 B2
Furness Vale SK23 39 D4
Lakewood CH4 141 B2
Laleston Cl WA8 22 E8
Lamb Cottage Cvn Pk
CW8 125 C7
Lambert Cres CW5 204 C6
Lambert's La CW12 156 E1
Lambert Way CW8 103 A4
Lamb La WA14 31 D4
Lambourn Ave WA8 12 C5
Lambourn Cl SK12 36 D4
Lambourn Dr CW1 173 B1
Lambourne Cl
4 Ellesmere Port
CH66 94 F8
Wythenshawe M22 33 D8
Lambourne Gr
1 Middlewich CW10 128 C1
St Helens WA9 1 A4
Lambs House Sch
CW12 156 F4
Lambsickle Cl WA7 48 F6
Lambsickle La WA7 49 A6
Lambs La
Warrington, Padgate
WA1 17 A8
Warrington WA1 17 A7
Lamb St ST7 195 A2
Lamerton Cl WA5 14 D4
Lamerton Way SK9 34 E2
Lampeter Cl WA5 7 E2
Lampits La CH3 120 E6
Lamport Cl WA8 13 E3
Lanark Gdns WA8 12 E3
Lanark Wlk SK10 86 F2
Lancashire Rd M31 11 E2
Lancaster Ave
Golborne WA3 3 C8
Runcorn WA7 48 E8
Widnes WA8 12 A2
Lancaster Cl
Hazel Grove SK7 36 D8
Newton-le-W WA12 1 F4
Warrington WA2 8 F2
Winsford CW7 149 D6
Lancaster Ct 3 WA4 16 E1
Lancaster Dr CH3 119 B2
Lancaster Fields CW1 191 A2
Lancaster Gdns CH65 70 D3
Lancaster Pk CH4 139 A3
Lancaster Rd
Handforth SK9 34 E1
Irlam M44 11 D5
Widnes WA8 13 B3
Lancaster St WA5 15 E5
Lanceley Ct SY14 213 B3
Lancelyn Dr SK9 60 D8
Lancer Ct WA7 23 E3
Lancers Croft CH66 69 E1
Lancing Ave WA2 8 A4
Lancing Rd CH65 70 D4
Land Cut La WA3 9 D3
Lander Cl WA5 15 D7
Land La SK9 60 C6
Landor Cl WA3 3 E8
Landscape Dene WA6 73 D4
Landseer Ave
Neston CH64 66 F7
Warrington WA4 16 B2
Landseer Dr SK10 111 E8
Landswood Pk CW8 103 B4
LANE ENDS 173 D3
Lane Ends WA8 21 D5
LANE HEAD 3 E6
Lane Head Ave WA3 3 F8
Lanehead Rd SK23 65 C5
Laneside Rd SK22 39 E7
Lane The SY13, SY14 223 C3
Langcliffe Cl WA3 4 E3
Langdale Ave WA13 18 F4
Langdale Cl
High Lane SK6 37 E8
Macclesfield SK11 111 F5
Warrington WA2 8 E2
Widnes WA8 22 C8
Winsford CW7 126 D2
Langdale Ct CW12 156 A1
Langdale Rd
Bramhall SK7 35 C5
Crewe CW2 189 D2
Partington M31 11 E3
Langdale Rd *continued*
Runcorn WA7 23 B1
Langdale Way WA6 49 C1
Langden Cl WA3 4 D4
Langdon Ho CH4 141 B7
Langfield WA3 3 E7
Langfield Gr CH62 43 D5
Langford L24 21 C2
Langford Ct CH3 121 C2
Langford Rd CW9 80 A3
Langford St 21 SK11 112 C8
Langford Way WA4 27 D4
Langland Cl WA5 7 E2
LANGLEY 113 C3
Langley Ave WA12 2 C1
Langley Cl
Newcastle-u-Lyme
ST5 210 D2
Sandbach CW11 175 C8
Langley Ct CH65 70 E3
Langley Dr
Crewe CW2 190 A2
Handforth SK9 34 E3
Macclesfield SK11 112 B4
Langley Hall Cl SK11 113 B4
Langley Hall Cotts
SK11 113 B4
Langley Rd
Langley SK11 113 A3
Northwich CW9 104 A6
Langport Dr CH3 119 C2
Langton Cl
Newton-le-W WA12 2 A4
Widnes WA8 12 B3
Langton Gn WA1 17 D7
Langwell Cl WA3 10 A5
Lanreath Cl SK10 86 D1
Lansbrook Ct WA7 23 C2
Lansdown Cl SK8 35 C7
Lansdowne
Culcheth WA3 4 E2
Frodsham WA6 74 D6
Lansdowne Gr CH4 141 A7
Lansdowne Rd
Connah's Quay CH5 91 D1
Crewe CW1 190 F5
Great Barrow CH3 120 D3
Lansdowne St SK10 87 E1
Lansdown Rd CH4 139 B4
Lanyard Way CW11 175 C3
Lapwing Cl
Golborne WA3 3 D8
Newton-le-W WA12 2 C3
Packmoor ST7 195 E1
Winsford CW7 149 C5
Lapwing Gr WA7 50 A6
Lapwing La
Moore WA4 25 A8
Whisterfield SK11 109 C4
Whisterfield SK11 109 C6
Lapwing Rd ST7 195 D3
Lapwing Rise CH60 40 F6
Larch Ave
Hough CW2 206 F5
Macclesfield SK11 112 A5
Newton-le-W WA12 2 C2
Warrington WA5 14 E5
Widnes WA8 13 B2
Larch Cl
Golborne WA3 3 F6
Poynton SK12 36 F3
Runcorn WA7 49 C7
Weaverham CW8 102 D7
Larchdale Cl CH66 94 F8
Larches The WA16 58 E2
Larchfields CH1 117 A8
Larch Rd
Crewe CW2 189 E2
Haydock WA11 1 E7
Partington M31 11 E3
Runcorn WA7 49 C7
Larch Rise SK10 86 D6
Larchtree Cl CW8 78 B4
Larchway
Bramhall SK7 35 C7
High Lane SK6 37 F7
Larch Way CH4 140 E6
Larchways WA4 26 D5
Larchwood Dr SK9 60 E8
LARDEN GREEN 202 D4
Lark Ave ST7 195 D3
Larkfield ST7 195 B1
Larkfield Ave WA1 17 A7
Lark Hall Cl SK10 113 A7
Lark Hall Cres SK10 113 A8
Lark Hall Rd SK10 113 A7
Lark Hill Cotts SK22 39 A8
Larkspur Cl
Chester CH4 140 F4
Nantwich CW5 204 E8
Runcorn WA7 49 F4
Larkspur Gr WA5 15 E3
Larkstoke Cl WA4 26 E6
Larksway CH60 41 B8
Larkwood Way SK10 87 E5
Larne Ct WA8 12 E2
Larne Dr CH4 139 D4
Laskey La WA4 17 F4
LATCHFORD 16 C3
Latchford CE Prim Sch
WA4 16 B4
Latchford Rd CH60 41 B6
Latchford St WA4 17 A3
Latham Ave
Helsby WA6 73 B1
Newton-le-W WA12 2 C4
Runcorn WA7 23 C1
Latham Ho WA12 2 B4
Latham Rd CW11 175 A5
Latham St CW7 126 C1
Lathom Ave WA2 16 B8
Lathom Rd M44 11 F8
Lathom Way SK10 87 F2
Latimer Dr CW2 190 A4
Launceston Cl
Runcorn WA7 50 C6
Winsford CW7 149 B7
Launceston Dr
Bramhall SK7 35 F7
Warrington WA5 14 E3
Laura St CW2 190 D1
Laurel Ave
Newton-le-W WA12 2 D3
Warrington WA1 17 D7
Laurel Bank
Warrington WA4 17 C1
Widnes WA8 13 A3
Winsford CW7 149 D8
Laurel Cl
Barnton CW8 78 A4
Middlewich CW10 128 B2
Sandbach CW11 175 C5
Laurel Dr
Crewe CW2 189 F2
Ellesmere Port CH65 70 B2
Harriseahead ST7 195 E4
Willaston CH64 43 B1
Laurel Gr
Chester CH2 119 A3
Golborne WA3 3 D8
Laurel Pk CW6 145 A6
Laurels Farm Ct CH2 72 B3
Laurels The
High Lane SK6 37 E8
Milton Green CH3 165 C2
Laurel Way SK8 35 C8
Laurel Wlk M31 11 E2
Laurelwood Dr 4
CH66 69 E1
Laureston Ave CW1 190 F4
Lavender Cl WA7 23 C1
Lavender Dr CW9 104 E7
Lavender Gdns WA9 6 A7
Lavender Wlk M31 11 E2
Lavenham Cl
Hazel Grove SK7 36 E8
Macclesfield SK10 87 C2
LAVISTER 162 C1
Lavister Cl 6 CW9 103 F4
Lavister Wlks LL12 162 C1
Lawford Cl CW1 189 F8
Lawford Dr CH60 41 C8
Lawn Ave WA1 16 F8
Lawn Dr CH2 118 D7
Lawns Ave CH63 43 B6
Lawnsdale CW8 101 D5
Lawns The SK9 59 E4
Lawnswood Gr CH2 72 B3
Lawrence Ave
3 Middlewich CW10 128 C1
Moulton CW9 126 E8
Lawrence Ave E 2
CW10 128 C1
Lawrence Cl
Cranage CW4 130 A5
3 Sandbach CW11 174 D6
Lawrence Pl SK12 36 D2
Lawrence St
Crewe CW1 190 C4
Sandycroft CH5 116 A3
Laws Gdns CH3 142 A8
Lawson Cl WA1 17 E7
Law St CH2 118 F3
Lawton Ave
Bramhall SK7 35 E8
Lawton-gate ST7 194 D3
Lawton Cl WA3 4 E3
Lawton Coppice ST7 194 E4
LAWTON-GATE 194 A4
Lawtongate Est ST7 194 A5
Lawton Hall ST7 194 C4
Lawton Hall Dr ST7 194 C4
LAWTON HEATH 193 E6
LAWTON HEATH END
193 C6
Lawton Heath Rd ST7 193 F5
Lawton Rd ST7 193 E4
Lawton St
Congleton CW12 156 E2
Crewe CW2 190 C3
Kidsgrove ST7 195 C4
Lawton Way CW11 174 E7
Laxey Ave WA1 17 D6
Laxton Cl CH66 94 F8
Laxton Way CW10 128 C2
Layland Ave WA3 4 E4
Layton Cl WA3 9 E3
Lea Ave
Crewe CW1 190 F4
Goostrey CW4 107 C1
Lea Bank Cl SK11 112 A8
Lea Cl CW11 175 C5
Leacroft Rd WA3 10 A7
Lea Cross Gr WA8 12 C3
Leadbeaters Cl SK11 112 F7
Leadbeaters Rd SK11 112 F7
Leadgate La CH3 144 F2
Lea Dr
Nantwich CW5 204 C4
Wimboldsley CW10 151 A4
Leadsmithy St CW10 128 C1
Leadworks La CH1 237 C3
Leaf Gr CW7 126 B1
Leafield Dr SK8 34 F6
Leafield Rd SK12 38 C6
Leaf La CW7 127 A2
Leaf Lane Inf Sch
CW7 127 A2
Leafy Way CW8 102 D7
LEA GREEN 172 A8
Lea Hall Barns CW5 220 E6
Lea Hall Pk CH1 95 A3
Lea Homes CW5 217 B7
Leahurst Cl CH2 118 F4
Lea La CH3 164 C3
Leamington Ave WA12 2 C1
Leamington Cl
Neston CH64 66 E6
Warrington WA5 15 A8
Leamington Rd
Congleton CW12 155 F3
Macclesfield SK10 86 F1
Lear Dr CW2 205 F8
Leas Cl 3 CH66 69 C5
Leaside WA7 23 D1
Leaside Rd CH1 117 E6
Leaside Way SK9 60 C6
Lea's Pas CW10 128 B1
Lea St SK22 39 A8
Leatham Cl WA3 9 E3
Leathers La L26 21 A7
Lea Way ST7 193 D3
Leawood Cl CW8 103 A6
Ledbury Dr CW2 206 A7
Ledge Ley SK8 34 E8
Ledger Rd WA11 1 A5
Ledley St SK10 87 F7
LEDSHAM 68 F2
Ledsham Cl WA3 9 C3
Ledsham Ct CH66 69 B6
Ledsham Hall La CH66 68 E4
Ledsham La CH66 68 F3
Ledsham Park Dr
CH66 69 A6
Ledsham Rd CH66 69 B6
Ledsham Village CH66 68 F2
Ledston Cl WA7 24 D1
Ledward St CW7 127 A1
Ledyard Cl WA5 15 D7
Leech Rd SY14 213 B3
Lee Cl WA16 56 F1
Lee Ct
Runcorn WA7 23 D2
Warrington WA2 8 C2
Lee Dr CW8 103 E7
Lee Green La CW5 150 A1
Leek Old Rd SK11 112 E2
Leek Rd CW12 179 A8
Leen La CH1 237 B2
Lee Rd WA5 15 B6
Lees La
Ellesmere Port CH65 70 E4
Mottram St Andrew
SK10 61 B7
Neston CH64 67 A7
Lees Mill 4 SK22 39 C7
Lees Rd SK7 35 D5
Lees The WA5 15 A8
LEFTWICH 104 B5
Leftwich Com Prim Sch
CW9 104 A4
Leftwich Warehouse
CW9 103 F7
Legh Cl SK12 36 E4
Legh Ct
Golborne WA3 3 A8
Knutsford WA16 57 D4
Legh Gdns WA16 57 B1
Legh Ho 2 WA16 57 B1
Legh Rd
Adlington SK10 62 C5
Haydock WA11 1 B6
High Lane SK12 38 A6
Knutsford WA16 82 B8
Prestbury SK10 87 A8
Legh St
Golborne WA3 3 A8
3 Lymm WA13 18 E3
Newton-le-W WA12 2 A3
Warrington WA1 16 A5
Legh Vale Prim Sch
WA11 1 B6
Leicester Ave ST7 193 D5
Leicester St
Northwich CW9 79 A1
Warrington WA5 15 F5
Leigh Ave
Knutsford WA16 57 C3
Widnes WA8 13 A1
Leigh Green Cl 4
WA8 22 C8
Leigh La CW8 77 C5
Leigh Rd
Congleton CW12 157 B5
Wilmslow SK9 59 D5
Leigh's Brow CW8 77 F3
Leigh St SK11 112 E7
Leighstone Ct CH2 237 A4
Leighton Chase CH64 41 D1
Leighton Cotts CH64 41 D5
Leighton Ct CH64 66 D8
Leighton Dr WN7 4 B8
Leighton Hospl CW1 172 E1
Leighton Pk CH64 66 D8
Leighton Prim Sch
CW1 189 F8
Leighton Rd CH64 41 D2
Leighton St 11 CW1 190 B5
Leightons The CH64 66 D8
Leighton View CW1 190 A8
Leigh Way CW8 77 C1

Leinster Gdns WA7 . . . . . . 22 F3
Leinster St WA7 . . . . 22 F3
Leiria Way WA7. . . . . 23 B2
Lenham Wlk M22 . . . . 33 D8
Lenthall Ave CW12 . . . . . . 178 F8
Leonard St
Chester CH1 . . . . 118 B3
Runcorn WA7. . . . . 48 D7
Warrington, Stockton Heath WA4 . . . . 16 C1
Warrington WA2 . . . . 16 C7
Leon Cl WA5 . . . . 14 D7
Leslie Rd CW7. . . . . 149 A7
Lessingham Rd WA8 . . . . . 12 F3
Lester Cl ST7. . . . . 193 D4
Leven Ave CW7 . . . . 126 F2
Levens Cl WA5. . . . . 15 F6
Levens Way 1 WA8. . . . . . . 22 C8
Leven Wlk CH66 . . . . 70 A7
Leveret Rd L24 . . . . 21 A3
Levisham Gdns WA5 . . . . . . 15 E7
Lewin St CW10 . . . . 128 C1
Lewis Ave WA5 . . . . 7 F2
Lewis Cl
Ellesmere Port CH65 . . . . . . 95 C8
Nantwich CW5. . . . . 205 A5
Lewis Cres WA8 . . . . 23 A7
Lewis Gr WA8 . . . . 12 D1
Lewis St CW1. . . . . 190 C3
Lexden St WA5 . . . . 15 E6
Lexington Wlk 2 WA5 . . . . 15 C7
Leycester Cl WA16 . . . . 82 C8
Leycester Dr WA16. . . . . . . 57 F7
Leycester Rd WA16 . . . . . . 82 B8
Leyfield Ct CH4 . . . . 140 F5
Leyland Dr CH4 . . . . 140 C6
Leyland Gr
Haslington CW1. . . . . 191 C4
Haydock WA11. . . . . 1 B6
Leyland Wlk CW7 . . . . 149 C6
Leyton Cl WA7. . . . . 49 B6
Libris Ho 1 WA16 . . . . 57 A1
Libris Pk 2 WA16. . . . . 57 A1
Libris Pl 3 WA16 . . . . 57 A1
Libson Cl WA2. . . . . 9 A3
Lichfield Ave
Golborne WA3 . . . . 3 D8
Grappenhall Heys WA4 . . . . 27 A7
Lichfield Cl WA16. . . . . 57 D2
Lichfield Ct CW7. . . . . 149 D7
Lichfield Dr CH66 . . . . 94 E8
Lichfield Rd
Blacon CH1 . . . . 117 F5
Talke ST7. . . . . 210 D7
Lichfield St CW10. . . . . . . 128 D2
Lidgetts La SK10. . . . . 88 C3
Lift La CW9. . . . . 78 D3
Light Alders La SK12. . . . . . 38 A6
Lightburn St 6 WA7 . . . . . . 22 F1
Lightfoot Cl CH60. . . . . 41 B7
Lightfoot La
Eaton CW6. . . . . 147 A4
Heswall CH60 . . . . 41 B7
Lightfoot St CH2. . . . . 118 F2
Lighthouse Rd L24. . . . . 47 E7
Lightley Cl CW11. . . . . 175 A4
Lightley Ct CW11 . . . . 175 A4
Light Oaks Rd WA3 . . . . 5 C6
LIGHTWOOD GREEN 229 B3
Lightwood Green Ave CW3. . . . . 229 A2
Lightwood Rd ST5 . . . . . . 210 D1
Lilac Ave
Knutsford WA16 . . . . 56 E1
Warrington WA5 . . . . 15 A5
Widnes WA8 . . . . 13 B2
Lilac Cl
Kelsall CW6. . . . . 122 E2
Newcastle-u-Lyme ST5 . . . 210 D1
Lilac Cres WA7. . . . . 49 C8
Lilac Ct CW12. . . . . 156 E2
Lilac Dr CW8 . . . . 103 D6
Lilac Gr
Ellesmere Port CH66. . . . . . 95 A8
Warrington WA4 . . . . 16 E1
Lilac Wlk M31 . . . . 11 E3
Lilford Ave WA5 . . . . 15 F8
Lilford Dr WA5 . . . . 14 F6
Lilford Sq SK11. . . . . 112 D5
Lilford St WA5. . . . . 15 F7
Lillyfield CH60. . . . . 40 F6
Lily Ave WA12 . . . . 2 D2
Lilybrook Dr WA16. . . . . 57 B1
Lily La CW10. . . . . 129 B6
Limbrick Rd ST7. . . . . 209 A1
Lime Ave
Frodsham WA6 . . . . 74 C8
Northwich CW9. . . . . 103 F5
Weaverham CW8. . . . . 102 D8
3 Widnes WA8. . . . . 13 B2
Lime Cl
Hollinfare WA3 . . . . 11 A2
Middlewich CW10 . . . . 128 B2
Sandbach CW11 . . . . 175 A7
Tarporley CW6. . . . . 146 D2
Lime Ct
Leftwich CW9 . . . . 104 A5
Northwich CW9. . . . . 103 F5
Limefield Ave WA13. . . . . . 18 F2
Lime Gr
Alsager ST7 . . . . 193 E2
Chester CH2 . . . . 119 A3
Elton CH2. . . . . 72 A3
Golborne WA3 . . . . 3 E6
Macclesfield SK10. . . . . . . 112 E8
Lime Gr *continued*
Runcorn WA7. . . . . 49 C8
Saltney CH4. . . . . 140 D6
Shavington CW2 . . . . 206 C4
Winsford CW7. . . . . 127 A1
Limehurst Gr CH62. . . . . 43 D6
Limekiln La WA5. . . . . 6 E3
Lime Kiln La ST7. . . . . 194 E2
Limekiln Row WA7. . . . . 50 A8
Limerick Cl WA8. . . . . 12 E3
Limes Cl CW1 . . . . 191 C4
Limes La WA4 . . . . 52 D6
Lime St
Congleton CW12 . . . . 156 D2
Crewe CW1 . . . . 190 C6
Ellesmere Port CH65. . . . . . 70 C7
Limes The
Culcheth WA3 . . . . 4 D4
Golborne WA3 . . . . 3 D6
Middlewich CW10 . . . . 128 B1
Limetree Ave
Warrington, Stockton Heath WA4 . . . . 16 E1
Warrington WA1 . . . . 17 A8
Lime Tree Ave
Congleton CW12 . . . . 156 B3
Crewe CW1 . . . . 190 E6
Lime Tree Cl
Ellesmere Port CH66. . . . . . 95 A8
Winsford CW7. . . . . 149 C8
Lime Tree Dr CH3. . . . . . . 180 F1
Lime Tree Gr CH60. . . . . . . 41 C8
Lime Tree La WA16 . . . . . . 29 D6
Limeways WA4 . . . . 26 E5
Lime Wlk
6 Handforth SK9. . . . . 34 D1
Partington M31 . . . . 11 D3
Lime Wood Cl CH2. . . . . . . 118 F4
Limewood Cres CW8. . . . . . 78 B4
Limewood Gr CW8. . . . . 78 B4
Linacre La WA8. . . . . 12 E5
Lincoln Ave
Gatley SK8. . . . . 34 B7
Irlam M44 . . . . 11 C4
Lincoln Cl
Golborne WN7. . . . . 4 C8
Macclesfield SK10. . . . . 86 F2
Rainow SK10. . . . . 88 E5
Runcorn WA7. . . . . 49 C6
Warrington WA1 . . . . 17 E6
Lincoln Ct
Helsby WA6. . . . . 73 B3
5 Warrington WA5 . . . . 15 B7
Lincoln Dr CH2 . . . . 119 A5
Lincoln Ho 13 CH1 . . . . . . 237 C3
Lincoln Pl SK10. . . . . 86 F2
Lincoln Rd
Blacon CH1 . . . . 117 F5
Ellesmere Port CH66. . . . . . 69 D3
Handforth SK9. . . . . 34 E1
Kidsgrove ST7 . . . . 194 F2
Lincoln Sq WA8. . . . . 13 B2
Lincoln St 3 CW1 . . . . 190 B5
Lincoln Wlk SK10. . . . . 86 F2
Lincombe Hey SK10. . . . . . . 87 C8
Lincombe Rd M22 . . . . 33 D8
Lindale Cl CW12 . . . . 157 A5
Linden Cl
Congleton CW12 . . . . 179 A8
Ellesmere Port CH66. . . . . . 94 F8
Lymm WA13. . . . . 19 A4
Warrington WA1 . . . . 17 D7
Linden Ct
Macclesfield SK10. . . . . 87 B2
Sandbach CW11 . . . . 174 F3
Widnes WA8 . . . . 12 F4
Linden Dr
Biddulph ST8. . . . . 179 C1
Crewe CW1 . . . . 190 F4
Helsby WA6. . . . . 73 B1
Mickle Trafford CH2. . . . . . . 96 F1
Linden Gr
Biddulph ST8. . . . . 179 C1
Bramhall SK7. . . . . 35 D4
Chester CH2 . . . . 119 A4
Saltney CH4. . . . . 140 D6
Linden Way
High Lane SK6. . . . . 38 A7
Widnes WA8 . . . . 12 F4
Lindfield Cl WA4. . . . . 25 A5
Lindfield Est N SK9 . . . . 60 A6
Lindfield Est S SK9. . . . . . . 59 F6
Lindfields CH4. . . . . 140 F6
Lindi Ave WA4. . . . . 17 C2
Lindisfarne Ave
Ellesmere Port CH65. . . . . . 70 C2
Golborne WA3 . . . . 4 C8
Lindisfarne Cl CW10 . . . . . 128 B1
Lindisfarne Ct WA8 . . . . . . 12 F6
Lindisfarne Dr SK12. . . . . . 36 D4
Lindley Ave WA4. . . . . 16 F4
Lindop Cl WA16. . . . . 57 C2
Lindow Com Prim Sch SK9. . . . . 59 D3
Lindow Court Pk WA16. . . . . 59 B5
Lindow Ct SK9. . . . . 59 E8
LINDOW END 59 B2
Lindow Fold Dr SK9. . . . . . . 59 D5
Lindow La SK9. . . . . 59 E6
Lindow Par SK9. . . . . 59 F6
Lindrick Cl SK10 . . . . 87 C4
Lindrum Ave SK11 . . . . 112 D2
Lindsay Way ST7. . . . . 193 A4
Lindsay Wlk CW8 . . . . 102 A4
Lindsworth Cl WA5 . . . . 15 C6
Linear View WA12 . . . . 2 C1
Linen Hall Pl CH1. . . . . . . 237 A2
Lines Rd M44. . . . . 11 F8
Lingdale Wlk SK11. . . . . . . 112 D5
Lingfield Cl SK10 . . . . 87 C4
Lingfield Dr CW1 . . . . 190 C7
Lingfield Ho WA7 . . . . 48 E8
Lingfield Rd WA7 . . . . 22 E1
LINGLEY GREEN 14 C7
Lingley Green Ave WA5. . . . . 14 D8
Lingley Mere Bsns Pk WA5 . . . . 14 D8
Lingley Rd WA5. . . . . 14 D6
Linglongs Ave SK23. . . . . . . 65 C5
Linglongs Rd SK23. . . . . . . 65 C5
Lingmell Gdns CW4. . . . . . 129 F3
Lingwell Ave WA8 . . . . 12 D2
Lingwell Pk WA8 . . . . 12 E2
Lingwood Rd WA5 . . . . 14 F6
Links Ave CH66. . . . . 69 C7
Links Cl CH63. . . . . 43 B6
Linkside Ave WA2. . . . . 8 B6
Linkside Way CH66. . . . . . . 94 F8
Links Rd SK9 . . . . 59 E4
Links View CH66. . . . . 69 C7
Linksway
Chester CH2 . . . . 118 C7
Congleton CW12 . . . . 178 E8
Linksway Cl CW12 . . . . . . 178 F8
Link The SK9 . . . . 34 D3
Linkway WA7. . . . . 49 C8
Link Wlk M31. . . . . 11 D2
Linley Gr ST7. . . . . 193 F3
Linley La ST7. . . . . 194 A2
Linley Rd
Alsager ST7 . . . . 193 F2
Cheadle SK8 . . . . 35 B8
Talke ST7. . . . . 210 C8
Linley Trad Est ST7. . . . . . 194 C1
Linnards La CW9, WA16. . . 80 B5
Linnet Cl
Newton-le-W WA12 . . . . 2 C3
Warrington WA2 . . . . 8 D3
Winsford CW7. . . . . 150 B8
Linnet Gr
Macclesfield SK10. . . . . 87 A1
Warrington WA3 . . . . 9 E4
Linnets Pk WA7. . . . . 23 C3
Linnets Way CH60. . . . . 40 E8
Linnett Cl CW1 . . . . 190 A7
Linnett Gr ST7. . . . . 195 E1
Linton Ct CW7. . . . . 127 A3
Linum Gdns WA9 . . . . 6 B7
Linwood CW7 . . . . 150 B8
Linwood Cl WA7. . . . . 50 C5
Lion Salt Works Mus★ CW9 . . . . 79 C3
Lion St CW12. . . . . 156 D2
Liskeard Cl WA7. . . . . 50 B6
Liskeard Dr SK7 . . . . 35 F7
Lismore Wlk M22. . . . . 33 E8
Lister Cl CW10. . . . . 151 D6
Lister Rd WA7 . . . . 23 C3
Little Abbey Gateway CH1 . . . . 237 A3
Little Aston Cl SK10. . . . . . 87 C4
LITTLE BOLLINGTON 20 B2
Little Bollington CE Prim Sch WA14 . . . . 20 B2
Littlebourne WA7. . . . . 50 E7
LITTLE BUDWORTH 147 F8
Little Budworth Ctry Pk★ CW6 . . . . 147 C8
Littlecote Gdns WA4 . . . . . . 26 D4
Littledale Rd WA5 . . . . 14 F7
Littledales La CW8. . . . . . . 102 E4
Little Delph WA11 . . . . 1 C7
Littlegate WA7 . . . . 49 E8
Little Gn CH66 . . . . 69 D3
LITTLE HEATH 230 A5
Little Heath Cl CW3. . . . . . 230 A5
Little Heath La WA14. . . . . . 20 D5
Little Heath Rd
Chester CH3 . . . . 119 E1
Christleton CH3. . . . . 142 E8
Little La CH64 . . . . 41 C1
Little Lakes CW2. . . . . 207 D2
LITTLE LEIGH 77 C4
Little Leigh Prim Sch CW8 . . . . 77 D5
Little Meadow Cl SK10 . . . 87 B7
Little Mere CH3. . . . . 142 E8
Little Moreton Hall★ CW12 . . . . 177 E2
LITTLE-MOSS 194 E6
Little Moss Cl ST7 . . . . . . 194 E5
Little Moss La ST7 . . . . . . 194 E5
LITTLE NESTON 66 D6
LITTLER 126 A2
Little Rake La CH2 . . . . 95 D5
Littler Grange Ct CW7. . . . . 126 A1
Littler La CW7 . . . . 125 F1
Little Roodee CH5 . . . . . . 139 B7
Little Row 5 ST7 . . . . 195 B2
Littler Rd WA11. . . . . 1 A5
Little St John St CH1. . . . . 237 B2
Little St
Congleton CW12 . . . . 156 D2
4 Macclesfield SK10 . . . . 112 D8
LITTLE STANNEY 70 E1
Little Stanney La CH2 . . . . . 95 F8
Littlestone Cl WA8. . . . . . . 13 A4
LITTLE SUTTON 69 B5
Little Sutton CE Prim Sch CH66. . . . . 69 A6
Little Sutton Sta CH66 . . . 69 C6
LITTLETON 119 E1
Littleton Cl
1 Northwich CW9 . . . . 103 F4
Littleton Cl *continued*
Warrington WA5 . . . . 15 D4
Littleton La CH3 . . . . 119 E2
LITTLE TOWN 4 C1
Little Wissage CH66. . . . . . . 69 F2
Littondale Cl CW12 . . . . . . 157 A5
Liverpool Pl WA8 . . . . 12 C1
Liverpool Rd
Backford CH1, CH2 . . . . 95 B4
Chester CH2 . . . . 118 C6
Haydock, Stanley Bank WA11 . . . . 1 A7
Haydock WA11. . . . . 1 B8
Irlam, Cadishead M44 . . . . . 11 D4
Kidsgrove ST7 . . . . 195 A1
Neston CH64 . . . . 41 F1
Newcastle-u-Lyme ST5 . . . 210 D2
Warrington, Great Sankey WA5 . . . . 14 E6
Warrington, Penketh WA5 . . . . 15 B4
Warrington WA5, WA1. . . . . 15 F5
Widnes WA8 . . . . 12 C1
Liverpool Rd E ST7. . . . . . 194 E2
Liverpool Rd W ST7. . . . . . 194 B4
Liverpool Row WA12 . . . . . . 7 D8
Liverpool St CW9 . . . . 104 C8
Livingstone Cl
Macclesfield SK10. . . . . . . 111 F8
Warrington WA5 . . . . 15 D7
Livingstone Rd CH65 . . . . . 70 C7
Livingstone Way CW10. . . . . 151 D6
Liz Kaye Ho SK11 . . . . 112 E7
Llandaff Cl CH66. . . . . 69 E1
Llandovery Cl CW7. . . . . . . 149 B7
Lloyd Cl CH3 . . . . 180 E2
Lloyd Cres WA12. . . . . 1 F3
Lloyd Dr CH65 . . . . 70 D1
Lloyd Pl CH1 . . . . 117 E4
Llyndir La LL12 . . . . 162 B1
Llys Bernsdale/Bernsdale Ct CH5. . . . . 116 A3
Llys Cadnant/Cadnant Ct CH4 . . . . 139 D5
Llys Caer CH4 . . . . 139 A3
Llys Catrin/Catherine Ct CH5 . . . . 139 B6
Llys Derwen CH4 . . . . 161 A8
Llys Maes Y Ffynnon / Springfield Ct CH4 . . . . 161 A8
Llys Perenna/Perenna Ct CH6. . . . . 91 B2
Llys Rhuddlan/Rhuddlan Ct 5 CH4. . . . . 140 F6
Llys Sant Iago/St James Ct CH5. . . . . 91 D1
Llys Y Faenol CH5 . . . . . . 139 B7
Loachbrook Ave CW12. . . . . 156 A2
Lobelia Gr WA7. . . . . 49 F4
Lobelia Wlk 6 M31 . . . . . . 11 E2
Lochinvar Ave CH66. . . . . . . 68 F6
Lochleven Rd CW2. . . . . . . 206 A7
Lochmaben Cl CW4 . . . . . . 130 B2
Loch St
4 Runcorn WA7. . . . . 23 A2
14 Runcorn WA7. . . . . 23 A3
Locke Ho CW1. . . . . 190 B4
Locker Ave WA2 . . . . 8 B2
Lockerbie Cl
Holmes Chapel CW4 . . . . . 130 C2
Warrington WA2 . . . . 8 E3
Lockett Rd WA8 . . . . 13 B3
Lockett St WA4. . . . . 16 F3
Lockgate E WA7 . . . . 24 C2
Lockgate W WA7 . . . . 24 C2
LOCKING STUMPS 9 C3
Locking Stumps Com Prim Sch WA3 . . . . 9 D4
Locking Stumps La WA3 . . . 9 B4
Lockitt St CW2 . . . . 190 D3
Lock La M31. . . . . 11 E3
Lock Rd
Bebington CH62. . . . . 44 A8
Warrington WA1 . . . . 16 F6
Locks The
Grappenhall WA4. . . . . 17 B3
Middlewich CW10 . . . . 151 D8
Lockton La WA5 . . . . 15 E7
Lockwood View WA7. . . . . . . 50 F5
Lodge Brow SK10. . . . . 63 A1
Lodgebury Ct SY14. . . . . . 211 C2
Lodge Cl WA13 . . . . 19 B4
Lodge Dr
Culcheth WA3 . . . . 4 F3
Moulton CW9. . . . . 126 F7
Winsford CW7. . . . . 127 A1
Lodgefields Com Prim Sch CW2 . . . . 189 E4
Lodgefields Dr CW2. . . . . . 189 E4
Lodge Gdns CH2. . . . . 118 D6
Lodge Hollow WA6 . . . . 73 B4
Lodge La
Antrobus CW9. . . . . 54 A6
Dutton WA4 . . . . 76 C8
Hartford CW8 . . . . 103 B4
Hatherton CW5 . . . . 220 A4
Haydock WA11, WA12, WN4 . . . . 2 B8
Lostock Gralam CW9. . . . . . 80 A2
Runcorn WA7. . . . . 49 F8
Saughall CH1. . . . . 94 A2
Warrington WA5 . . . . 15 F7
Widnes WA8 . . . . 12 B4
Lodge Rd
Alsager ST7. . . . . 193 C4
Knutsford WA16 . . . . 57 C3
Lodge Rd *continued*
Sandbach CW11 . . . . 174 E5
Talke ST7. . . . . 210 D6
Widnes WA8 . . . . 22 B8
Lodmore La SY13 . . . . 233 C6
Lofthouse Gate WA8 . . . . . . 12 F4
Lomas Sq SK11 . . . . 112 D5
Lomax Rd CW5 . . . . 205 D6
Lomond Gr CH66. . . . . 69 F3
London Rd
Adlington SK10 . . . . 62 C5
Alderley Edge SK9. . . . . 60 A1
Allostock WA16 . . . . 106 F3
Bridgemere CW5, CW3 . . . 232 A5
Davenham CW9. . . . . 104 A1
Frodsham WA6 . . . . 74 B8
Hatherton CW5 . . . . 220 D4
Holmes Chapel CW4 . . . . . 130 C2
Macclesfield SK11. . . . . . . 112 D3
Nantwich CW5. . . . . 204 F5
Northwich CW9 . . . . 103 F7
Northwich, Leftwich CW9 . . . . 104 A5
Sandbach CW11 . . . . 174 D8
Stapeley CW5 . . . . 205 B3
Warrington WA4 . . . . 26 D5
Woore CW3 . . . . 232 C1
London Rd N SK12 . . . . 36 E5
London Rd S SK12 . . . . 36 D3
London Road Terr SK11 . . . . 112 D5
London Row WA12. . . . . 7 D8
Loney St SK11 . . . . 112 C7
Long Acre
Cuddington CW8 . . . . 101 D4
Weaverham CW8. . . . . 77 C1
Longacres Rd WA15. . . . . . . 32 D7
Long Acres Rd CH64 . . . . . 41 E2
Longacre St SK10. . . . . . . 112 C8
LONGBARN 9 B1
Longbarn Bvd WA2 . . . . 9 C2
Longbarn Com Prim Sch WA2 . . . . 9 B1
Long Barn La
Warrington WA2 . . . . 9 B2
Warrington, Woolston WA1 . . . . 17 D8
Longbenton Way WA7 . . . 24 B4
Longburgh Cl CH2 . . . . . . 118 F3
Longbutt La WA13 . . . . 19 A2
Longbutts La SK11. . . . . . . 111 E2
Longclough Rd ST5. . . . . . 210 D2
Long Croft La SK8 . . . . 34 E8
Longcross Ct CW10 . . . . . 128 C1
Longdale Dr CH1 . . . . 117 C5
Longden Ct SK7 . . . . 35 E5
Longden La SK11 . . . . 113 A6
Longden St SK10 . . . . 112 E8
Longdin St WA4 . . . . 16 F3
Longdown Rd CW12. . . . . . 155 F4
Longfield Ave
Chester CH2 . . . . 118 E7
Gatley SK8. . . . . 34 C7
Longfield Rd WA2 . . . . 8 C1
LONGFORD 8 B1
Longford Dr WA8 . . . . 12 E2
Longford St
4 Crewe CW2 . . . . 190 D2
Warrington WA2 . . . . 16 B7
Long Gn CH3 . . . . 97 E1
LONG GREEN 97 F1
LONGHILL 230 E5
Long Hill SK23. . . . . 65 F2
Longhill La CW3 . . . . 230 E5
Longhorn Cl CW10. . . . . . . 128 D2
Long La
Alpraham CW6. . . . . 169 E4
Bickerton SY14 . . . . 199 F4
Bollington SK10. . . . . 63 B2
Burland CW5. . . . . 203 A8
Chester CH2 . . . . 118 F7
Hargrave CH3 . . . . 143 D2
Harriseahead ST7 . . . . 195 E4
Haughton CW6 . . . . 186 D4
Horwich End SK23. . . . . 65 F3
Huxley CH3 . . . . 166 C8
Middlewich CW10 . . . . 151 C7
Saughall CH1. . . . . 94 B2
Swan Green WA16. . . . . . . 107 D7
Swettenham CW12 . . . . . . 131 F5
Tilston SY14. . . . . 198 B3
Warrington WA2 . . . . 8 B1
Wettenhall CW6, CW7. . . . . 170 C6
Longlands Dr SK22. . . . . 39 B8
Longlands Rd SK22 . . . . . . 39 B8
Long La S CW10 . . . . 151 D7
Longley Ave CW6 . . . . 122 D6
Longley La CW6 . . . . 99 D1
Long Looms CH3. . . . . 120 D6
Longlooms Rd CH65 . . . . . . 70 D1
Long Marl Dr SK9. . . . . 34 F4
Long Mdw CH60 . . . . 40 F6
Longmeade Gdns SK9. . . . . 60 C6
Longmeadow
Cheadle SK8 . . . . 35 C7
Weaverham CW8. . . . . 102 C8
LONGMOSS 86 C1
Longmoss Cl CW10 . . . . . 151 B8
Longmynd Rise CW7 . . . . 149 B8
Longnor Rd
Gatley SK8. . . . . 34 D8
Hazel Grove SK7 . . . . 36 E7
Longridge WA16. . . . . 57 D3
Longridge Trad Est WA16. . . . . 57 D3
Long Row ST7. . . . . 195 A1
Longsdon Cl ST5. . . . . 210 C1

Longshaw St
Warrington, Bewsey
WA5 . . . . . 15 F8
Warrington, Dallam WA5 . . . . . 7 F1
Long Shoot CW4 . . . . . 130 D8
Long Shoot Rd SK11 . . . . . 108 E1
Longsides Rd WA15 . . . . . 32 C7
Longsight La SK8 . . . . . 34 F6
Long Spinney WA7 . . . . . 50 C8
Longster Cl WA6 . . . . . 73 B2
Longstone La CW6 . . . . . 124 E3
Longton Ave WA3 . . . . . 3 C7
Long Valley Rd ST8 . . . . . 179 C2
Longview Ave ST7 . . . . . 193 E4
Long Wlk M31 . . . . . 11 D3
Longwood Cl CW10 . . . . . 151 C7
Longwood Rd WA4 . . . . . 26 E5
Lonsdale Cl
Warrington WA5 . . . . . 14 F8
3 Widnes WA8 . . . . . 22 C8
Lonsdale Ct CH4 . . . . . 140 F4
Lon Y Cryddion / Cobblers
La LL12 . . . . . 161 B1
Lon yr Orsaf / Station App
CH1 . . . . . 116 F7
Lon yr Ywen / Yew Tree
Ave CH1 . . . . . 116 F7
Looe Cl WA8 . . . . . 12 E2
Looms The CH64 . . . . . 41 B2
Loont The CW7 . . . . . 149 C7
Lord Nelson St WA1 . . . . . 16 C5
Lordship La WA6 . . . . . 73 B7
Lordshire Pl ST7 . . . . . 195 F2
Lords La WA3 . . . . . 9 C4
Lords Mill Rd CW2 . . . . . 206 B4
Lord's St M44 . . . . . 11 C5
Lord St
Bollington SK10 . . . . . 88 B8
Chester CH3 . . . . . 118 F2
Crewe CW2 . . . . . 190 D3
Croft WA3 . . . . . 9 A8
Macclesfield SK11 . . . . . 112 D6
Macclesfield SK11 . . . . . 112 D7
Newton-le-W WA12 . . . . . 2 A3
Runcorn WA7 . . . . . 22 F3
Warrington WA4 . . . . . 16 B4
Lorne St CH1 . . . . . 237 A3
Lorraine St ST7 . . . . . 195 F1
Lostock Ave
Poynton SK12 . . . . . 36 B4
Warrington WA5 . . . . . 15 F8
Lostock Cl 2 CW9 . . . . . 103 E5
Lostock Gn CW9 . . . . . 80 A1
LOSTOCK GRALAM 80 A3
Lostock Gralam CE Prim
Sch CW9 . . . . . 80 A2
Lostock Gralam Sta
CW9 . . . . . 80 A2
LOSTOCK GREEN 105 B8
Lostock Hall Prim Sch
SK12 . . . . . 36 B3
Lostock Hall Rd SK12 . . . . . 36 B3
Lostock Hollow CW9 . . . . . 80 A2
Lostock Rd SK12 . . . . . 36 D2
Lostock Way SK9 . . . . . 34 D4
Lotus Gdns WA9 . . . . . 6 A7
Louise St CH1 . . . . . 237 A3
Loushers La WA4 . . . . . 16 D2
Lovage Cl WA2 . . . . . 9 C1
Lovat Dr WA16 . . . . . 82 B7
Lovatt Ct WA13 . . . . . 19 B4
Lovatts The ST7 . . . . . 195 A1
Love La
Hassall Green CW11 . . . . . 176 C3
Malpas SY14 . . . . . 213 A4
Nantwich CW5 . . . . . 204 E5
Lovell Ct CW4 . . . . . 130 C3
Lovel Terr WA8 . . . . . 22 B5
Lovely La WA5 . . . . . 15 E6
Love St CH1 . . . . . 237 B2
Lowcross La SY14 . . . . . 198 D3
Lowe Ave
Congleton CW12 . . . . . 156 E2
Warrington WA4 . . . . . 16 F4
Lowe Cres CW9 . . . . . 53 C4
Lowe Dr WA16 . . . . . 57 B2
Lower Appleton Rd
WA8 . . . . . 13 B1
Lower Ash Rd ST7 . . . . . 194 E1
Lower Bank St 10
SK11 . . . . . 112 E7
Lower Beech Cotts
SK10 . . . . . 87 D2
Lower Bridge St CH1 . . . . . 237 B1
Lower Brook St CH5 . . . . . 91 D1
LOWER BUNBURY 185 F8
LOWER CARDEN 198 C6
Lower Church St WA8 . . . . . 23 A5
Lower Cl L26 . . . . . 21 A8
Lower Darwin St
CW9 . . . . . 103 E6
Lower Exchange St 13
SK11 . . . . . 112 D7
Lower Farm Mews
CW6 . . . . . 147 B3
Lowerfield Rd SK10 . . . . . 87 E1
Lower Field Rd CH4 . . . . . 141 A5
Lower Fold Cott SK6 . . . . . 37 D7
Lower Greenshall La
SK12 . . . . . 38 F6
Lower Hague SK22 . . . . . 38 E8
Lower Haigh St 3
CW7 . . . . . 149 C8
Lower Hall La CH3 . . . . . 182 D2
Lower Hall Mews
CH3 . . . . . 182 C2
Lower Hall Rd SY13 . . . . . 215 D4
LOWER HEATH 156 E5
Lower Heath CW12 . . . . . 156 E4
Lower Heath Ave
CW12 . . . . . 156 E4
Lower Heath Terr
CW12 . . . . . 156 E4
Lower High St ST7 . . . . . 195 D7
LOWERHOUSE 87 E8
Lowerhouse SK10 . . . . . 87 E8
LOWER HOUSE 22 E8
Lower House La WA8 . . . . . 22 F8
LOWER KINNERTON 139 D1
Lower La
Aldford CH3 . . . . . 164 A2
Churton CH3 . . . . . 181 A7
Eaton CW6 . . . . . 147 A3
Lowerlea SK12 . . . . . 38 C6
Lower Macclesfield Rd
SK23 . . . . . 65 E6
Lower Meadow Dr
CW12 . . . . . 156 C3
Lower Meadow Rd
SK9 . . . . . 34 E4
Lower Mersey St CH65 . . . . . 70 C7
Lower Park Cres SK12 . . . . . 36 C6
Lower Park Prim Sch
SK12 . . . . . 36 C4
Lower Park Rd
Chester CH4 . . . . . 237 C2
Poynton SK12 . . . . . 36 B5
Lower Park St CW12 . . . . . 156 E3
LOWER PEOVER 81 E1
Lower Peover CE Prim
Sch WA16 . . . . . 81 E1
Lower Rake La WA6 . . . . . 73 B4
Lower Rd L26, WA8 . . . . . 21 C7
Lower Robin Hood La
WA6 . . . . . 73 B3
Lower Rock St 2 SK22 . . . . . 39 C7
Lower Sandy La CH3 . . . . . 199 C7
LOWER STRETTON 52 F8
LOWER THREAPWOOD
. . . . . 222 E6
LOWER WALTON 26 A8
Lower Wash La WA4 . . . . . 16 E3
LOWER WHITLEY 52 D3
LOWER WITHINGTON
. . . . . 132 A8
LOWER WYCH 224 B6
Lowes La SK11 . . . . . 111 F2
Lowe St
Golborne WA3 . . . . . 3 A8
Macclesfield SK11 . . . . . 112 D7
Loweswater Cl WA2 . . . . . 8 B3
Loweswater Cres WA11 . . . . . 1 A6
Lowfield Gdns WA3 . . . . . 5 C7
Lowfields Ave CH62 . . . . . 43 E3
Lowfields Cl CH62 . . . . . 43 E3
Low Hill WA6 . . . . . 97 D5
Lowlands Rd 6 WA7 . . . . . 22 F2
Lowland Way WA16 . . . . . 82 A8
LOW LEIGHTON 39 D8
Low Leighton Rd SK22 . . . . . 39 D8
Low Mdw SK23 . . . . . 65 D8
Lownorth Rd M22 . . . . . 33 E8
Lowry Cl WA5 . . . . . 15 D6
Low St ST7 . . . . . 193 E8
Lowther Ave WA3 . . . . . 4 F4
Lowther St SK10 . . . . . 88 C8
LOWTON 3 E8
Lowton Bsns Pk WA3 . . . . . 4 A7
LOWTON COMMON 4 A8
Lowton Com Sports Coll
WA3 . . . . . 4 B8
Lowton Gdns WA3 . . . . . 3 B5
LOWTON HEATH 3 C6
Lowton Jun & Inf Sch
WA3 . . . . . 4 A7
Lowton Rd WA3 . . . . . 3 C8
LOWTON ST MARY'S 3 F8
Lowton St Mary's CE Prim
Sch WA3 . . . . . 4 A8
Lowton West Prim Sch
WA3 . . . . . 3 D8
Loxdale Dr CH65 . . . . . 69 F4
Loxley Cl
Macclesfield SK11 . . . . . 112 B7
Warrington WA5 . . . . . 15 A8
Loyola Hey L35 . . . . . 12 E8
Lucerne Cl CH3 . . . . . 142 B6
Ludford Cl ST5 . . . . . 210 D2
Ludford St CW1 . . . . . 190 C5
Ludlow Ave CW1 . . . . . 190 F3
Ludlow Cl
Macclesfield SK10 . . . . . 87 E2
Warrington, Paddington
WA1 . . . . . 17 B8
Winsford CW7 . . . . . 149 B7
Ludlow Cres WA7 . . . . . 49 B8
Ludlow Dr CH65 . . . . . 70 E3
Ludlow Rd CH1 . . . . . 118 A5
Ludwell Cl CH4 . . . . . 141 B6
LUGSDALE 23 C7
Lugsdale Rd WA8 . . . . . 23 B7
Lulworth Cl CW7 . . . . . 149 B7
Lumb Brook Mews 5
WA4 . . . . . 16 E1
Lumb Brook Rd
Appleton Thorn WA4 . . . . . 27 A5
Warrington WA4 . . . . . 26 F8
Lumb Cl SK7 . . . . . 35 E6
Lumber La WA5 . . . . . 6 F8
Lumb La SK7 . . . . . 35 E6
Lumley Pl CH1 . . . . . 237 B2
Lumley Rd
Chester CH2 . . . . . 118 C4
Macclesfield SK11 . . . . . 111 F7
Lumley Wlk L24 . . . . . 21 E1
Lumpy St CW12 . . . . . 156 C3
Lundy Dr CH65 . . . . . 95 C8
Lune Cl 1 CW12 . . . . . 157 A1
Lunehurst 12 WA3 . . . . . 3 E8
Lune Way WA8 . . . . . 12 C1
Lunt Ave CW2 . . . . . 190 C2
LUNTS HEATH 13 A5
Lunts Heath Prim Sch
WA8 . . . . . 13 B5
Lunt's Heath Rd WA8 . . . . . 13 B5
Lunts Moss ST7 . . . . . 194 C6
Luntswood Gr WA12 . . . . . 2 A4
Lupin Dr
Haydock WA11 . . . . . 1 F6
Huntington CH3 . . . . . 142 B6
Lupus Way CH66 . . . . . 69 F3
Luscombe Cl L26 . . . . . 21 A8
Luther Gr WA9 . . . . . 1 B2
Luton Rd CH65 . . . . . 70 A5
Luton St WA8 . . . . . 23 A7
Lutyens Cl SK10 . . . . . 111 F8
Lyceum Cl CW1 . . . . . 190 A8
Lyceum Way CW1 . . . . . 190 A8
Lychgate WA4 . . . . . 25 F7
Lycroft Cl WA7 . . . . . 49 B6
Lydbury Cl WA5 . . . . . 7 D2
Lydden Rd CH65 . . . . . 70 B7
Lydgate Cl CW2 . . . . . 205 F8
Lydiate La
Runcorn WA7 . . . . . 48 D7
Willaston CH64 . . . . . 42 E1
Lydiate The
Heswall CH60 . . . . . 40 F7
Willaston CH64 . . . . . 42 D1
Lydiat La SK9 . . . . . 60 A1
Lydney Ave SK8 . . . . . 34 C7
Lydstep Ct WA5 . . . . . 7 E2
Lydyett La CW8 . . . . . 78 B3
Lymcote Dr CW8 . . . . . 103 A4
Lyme Ave
Handforth SK9 . . . . . 34 B1
Macclesfield SK11 . . . . . 112 D5
Lyme Com Prim Sch
WA12 . . . . . 1 F4
Lyme Gr WA13 . . . . . 18 C2
LYME GREEN 112 D2
Lyme Green Bsns Pk
SK11 . . . . . 112 C3
Lyme Green Settlement
SK11 . . . . . 112 D2
Lyme Lea Cl SK8 . . . . . 35 B8
Lyme Park Ctry Pk★
SK12 . . . . . 38 B2
Lyme Pk★ SK12 . . . . . 38 B1
Lyme Rd
High Lane SK12 . . . . . 38 A6
Poynton SK12 . . . . . 37 C3
Lyme St
Haydock WA11 . . . . . 1 E6
Newton-le-W WA12 . . . . . 1 F4
13 Warrington WA1 . . . . . 16 B5
Lyme View SK11 . . . . . 112 D2
Lymewood Dr
Disley SK12 . . . . . 38 C6
Wilmslow SK9 . . . . . 60 E8
LYMM 18 E4
Lymm Brook 1 WA13 . . . . . 18 E3
Lymm Hall WA13 . . . . . 18 E3
Lymmhay La WA13 . . . . . 18 E4
Lymm High Sch WA13 . . . . . 19 B3
Lymmington Ave
WA13 . . . . . 18 C3
Lymm Rd
Little Bollington WA14 . . . . . 20 B1
Warrington WA4 . . . . . 17 F3
Lynalls Cl CW12 . . . . . 155 F3
Lynbrook Rd CW1 . . . . . 190 F4
Lyncastle Rd WA4 . . . . . 27 D4
Lyncastle Way WA4 . . . . . 27 D4
Lyncombe Cl SK8 . . . . . 35 B6
Lyncroft Cl CW1 . . . . . 190 F3
Lyndale 2 WA7 . . . . . 49 C8
Lyndale Ave
Bebington CH62 . . . . . 43 E4
Warrington, Fearnhead
WA2 . . . . . 8 F2
Warrington WA2 . . . . . 16 D8
Lyndale Ct CW7 . . . . . 127 A3
Lyndale Sch The CH62 . . . . . 43 F5
Lyndhurst Cl SK9 . . . . . 59 D5
Lyndon Gr WA7 . . . . . 49 B8
Lyneal Ave CH66 . . . . . 69 C3
Lyngard Cl SK9 . . . . . 34 E1
Lynham Ave WA5 . . . . . 15 B5
Lynn Ave ST7 . . . . . 210 C8
Lynn Cl WA7 . . . . . 49 C7
Lynndene CH66 . . . . . 69 D7
Lynn Gr SK11 . . . . . 112 C6
Lynside Wlk M22 . . . . . 33 E8
Lynthorpe Ave M44 . . . . . 11 D6
Lynton Ave M44 . . . . . 11 E6
Lynton Cl
Chester CH4 . . . . . 140 F6
Heswall CH60 . . . . . 41 B6
Knutsford WA16 . . . . . 57 C1
Warrington WA5 . . . . . 14 E4
Lynton Cres WA8 . . . . . 12 E2
Lynton Dr SK6 . . . . . 37 E8
Lynton Gdns WA4 . . . . . 26 D4
Lynton Gr CW1 . . . . . 191 D5
Lynton La SK9 . . . . . 60 A2
Lynton Mews SK9 . . . . . 60 A2
Lynton Park Rd SK8 . . . . . 34 F8
Lynton Pl
Alsager ST7 . . . . . 193 D4
Broughton CH4 . . . . . 139 B4
Lynton Way CW2 . . . . . 206 A8
Lynwood
Altrincham WA15 . . . . . 32 A8
Lynwood *continued*
Wilmslow SK9 . . . . . 60 A6
Lynwood Ave
Golborne WA3 . . . . . 3 E6
Warrington WA4 . . . . . 26 C7
Lynwood Rd CH1 . . . . . 117 F5
Lyon Ct WA4 . . . . . 16 F3
Lyon's La WA4 . . . . . 26 E6
Lyons Rd WA5 . . . . . 15 A4
Lyon St
Chester CH1 . . . . . 237 B3
Crewe CW1 . . . . . 190 D4
Macclesfield SK11 . . . . . 112 C7
Warrington WA4 . . . . . 16 F3
Lysander Dr WA2 . . . . . 8 E2
Lyster Cl WA3 . . . . . 9 F3
Lytham Cl WA5 . . . . . 15 B3
Lytham Dr
Bramhall SK7 . . . . . 36 A7
Winsford CW7 . . . . . 126 C2
Lytham Rd WA8 . . . . . 13 C2
Lytherton Ave M44 . . . . . 11 D4
Lythgoes La WA2 . . . . . 16 B6

M

Mableden Cl SK8 . . . . . 34 D8
Mablins La CW1 . . . . . 190 B8
Mablins Lane Com Prim
Sch CW1 . . . . . 190 B8
Macbeth Ho ST7 . . . . . 210 C8
McCarthy Cl WA3 . . . . . 10 A3
Mc Clellan Pl WA8 . . . . . 13 B1
MACCLESFIELD 112 B4
Macclesfield Coll
SK11 . . . . . 112 B6
Macclesfield District
General Hospl SK10 . . . . . 112 B8
MACCLESFIELD FOREST
. . . . . 114 D5
Macclesfield Forest
Walks★ SK11 . . . . . 114 A3
Macclesfield Rd
Alderley Edge SK9 . . . . . 85 D7
Congleton CW12 . . . . . 156 F6
Eaton CW12 . . . . . 134 B2
Hazel Grove SK7 . . . . . 36 F8
Holmes Chapel CW4 . . . . . 130 E4
Kettleshulme SK23,
SK10 . . . . . 64 D3
Prestbury SK10 . . . . . 86 F4
Rainow SK10 . . . . . 89 B7
Wilmslow SK9 . . . . . 60 D6
Macclesfield Sta
SK11 . . . . . 112 D8
Macdermott Rd WA8 . . . . . 22 F5
Macdonald Rd M44 . . . . . 11 E8
McElin Cl ST7 . . . . . 209 E2
McGarva Way CH65 . . . . . 70 C4
McGowan Ho ST7 . . . . . 210 D8
McKeagney Gdns WA8 . . . . . 22 C7
McKee Ave WA2 . . . . . 8 B2
McKinley St WA5 . . . . . 15 A7
Mckinley Way WA8 . . . . . 12 F3
McLaren St CW1 . . . . . 190 C7
McMinnis Ave WA9 . . . . . 1 B2
McNeill Ave CW1 . . . . . 190 A5
Macon Ct CW1 . . . . . 190 E3
Macon Ind Pk CW1 . . . . . 190 E3
Macon Way CW1 . . . . . 190 E3
Maddocks Hill WA6 . . . . . 100 F5
Maddock St ST7 . . . . . 209 D1
Madeley Cl
Altrincham WA14 . . . . . 31 E8
Broughton CH4 . . . . . 139 C4
Madeley St CW2 . . . . . 190 C1
Madeline McKenna Ct
WA8 . . . . . 12 C3
Madron Ave SK10 . . . . . 86 D1
Maelor Cl CH63 . . . . . 43 C6
Maes-y-Coed CH4 . . . . . 140 E6
Magdala Pl CW9 . . . . . 104 C8
Magdalen Ct CW2 . . . . . 190 A1
Magecroft CW1 . . . . . 173 B1
Magenta Ave M44 . . . . . 11 E6
Maggoty La SK11 . . . . . 111 D1
Mag La WA13, WA16 . . . . . 28 F6
Magnolia Cl
3 Ellesmere Port
CH66 . . . . . 69 F1
5 Partington M31 . . . . . 11 E2
Warrington WA1 . . . . . 17 E7
Magnolia Dr WA7 . . . . . 49 F4
Magnolia Rise SK10 . . . . . 86 E6
Magpie Cres 9 ST7 . . . . . 195 B2
Maiden Est CW5 . . . . . 228 C8
Maiden Gdns CH65 . . . . . 70 D3
Maidenhills CW10 . . . . . 128 D1
Maidstone Cl SK10 . . . . . 87 B2
Maidwell Cl CW7 . . . . . 127 A4
Main Cl WA11 . . . . . 1 A6
Main Dr WA14 . . . . . 20 E3
Main La WA3 . . . . . 3 F3
Main Rd
Betley CW2, CW3 . . . . . 221 F8
Broughton CH4 . . . . . 139 B4
Goostrey CW4 . . . . . 107 E1
Higher Kinnerton CH4 . . . . . 161 A8
Langley SK11 . . . . . 113 C4
Moulton CW9 . . . . . 126 F8
Norton in Hales TF9 . . . . . 236 C1
Shavington CW2 . . . . . 206 B4
Weston CW2 . . . . . 207 C6
Worleston CW5 . . . . . 188 F5
Wybunbury CW5 . . . . . 220 B8
Main St
Frodsham WA6 . . . . . 74 B8
Main St *continued*
Great Barrow CH3 . . . . . 120 E5
Runcorn WA7 . . . . . 49 F8
Maintree Cres L24 . . . . . 21 A4
Mainwaring Cl CW5 . . . . . 205 A4
Mainwaring Dr
Saltney CH4 . . . . . 140 C7
Wilmslow SK9 . . . . . 60 D8
Mainwaring Rd
Bebington CH62 . . . . . 43 D8
Over Peover WA16 . . . . . 108 A8
Mairesfield Ave WA4 . . . . . 17 B2
Maisterson Ct 7
CW5 . . . . . 204 E5
Maitland Way CH1 . . . . . 117 D4
Maitland-Wood Cl
CW9 . . . . . 104 D7
Major Cross St 6 WA8 . . . . . 23 A7
Makepeace Cl CH3 . . . . . 119 C3
Makerfield Dr WA12 . . . . . 2 A5
Malaga Ave M90 . . . . . 33 B7
Malahide Ct WA8 . . . . . 12 E2
Malam Dr CW9 . . . . . 104 D6
Malbank CW5 . . . . . 204 E6
Malbank Rd CW2 . . . . . 189 E4
Malbank Sch & Sixth Form
Coll CW5 . . . . . 204 C6
Malcolm Ave WA2 . . . . . 8 D1
Malcolm Cres CH63 . . . . . 43 C6
Malcolm St WA7 . . . . . 23 B2
Malham Cl WA5 . . . . . 14 E8
Malhamdale Rd
CW12 . . . . . 157 A5
Malin Cl L24 . . . . . 21 D2
Maliston Rd WA5 . . . . . 15 B5
MALKINS BANK 175 C3
Mallaig Cl CW4 . . . . . 130 C2
Mallard Cl
Knutsford WA16 . . . . . 57 B3
Warrington WA2 . . . . . 8 D3
Mallard Cres SK12 . . . . . 36 A4
Mallard Ct
Chester CH2 . . . . . 118 F7
Crewe CW1 . . . . . 191 A2
Gatley SK8 . . . . . 34 B8
Mallard La WA3 . . . . . 9 F3
Mallard Way
Crewe CW1 . . . . . 191 A2
Winsford CW7 . . . . . 149 D6
Mallory Cl WA16 . . . . . 58 A4
Mallory Ct
Congleton CW12 . . . . . 155 F3
Mobberley WA16 . . . . . 58 A4
Mallory Rd CH65 . . . . . 70 A4
Mallory Wlk CH4 . . . . . 162 A7
Mallow Cl CH3 . . . . . 142 A6
Mallowdale Cl CH62 . . . . . 43 F5
Mallow Wlk M31 . . . . . 11 F2
Mall The WA1 . . . . . 16 A5
Malmesbury Cl
Middlewich CW10 . . . . . 128 B1
Poynton SK12 . . . . . 36 D4
Malmesbury Pk WA7 . . . . . 24 E2
Malmesbury Rd SK8 . . . . . 35 B6
Malory Cl CW1 . . . . . 190 F5
MALPAS 213 B2
Malpas Alport Prim Sch
SY14 . . . . . 213 B4
Malpas Cl
Handforth SK9 . . . . . 34 E1
Northwich CW9 . . . . . 104 B7
Malpas Dr WA5 . . . . . 15 C4
Malpas Rd
Ellesmere Port CH65 . . . . . 69 F4
Northwich CW9 . . . . . 104 C7
Runcorn WA7 . . . . . 49 C7
Malpas Way WA5 . . . . . 15 C4
Malta Rd CH2 . . . . . 95 B1
Malt Kiln Rd WA16 . . . . . 80 F4
Malt Kiln Way CW11 . . . . . 175 B7
Maltmans Rd WA13 . . . . . 18 D3
Malton Ave WA3 . . . . . 3 E7
Malton Cl WA8 . . . . . 12 C5
Malton Dr SK7 . . . . . 36 D7
Malt St WA16 . . . . . 57 A2
Malvern Ave CH65 . . . . . 70 D3
Malvern Cl
Congleton CW12 . . . . . 155 F3
Shavington CW2 . . . . . 206 B4
Warrington WA5 . . . . . 15 A8
Malvern Dr SK10 . . . . . 87 E4
Malvern Rd
Blacon CH1 . . . . . 118 A5
Haydock WA9 . . . . . 1 A4
Knutsford WA16 . . . . . 81 F8
Malvern Way CW7 . . . . . 149 B7
Manchester Airport Sta
M90 . . . . . 33 B7
Manchester Bridge
CW1 . . . . . 190 E4
Manchester Bsns Pk
M22 . . . . . 33 D8
Manchester International
Airport M90 . . . . . 33 A7
Manchester Met Univ
(Alsager Campus)
ST7 . . . . . 193 A5
Manchester New Rd
M31 . . . . . 11 F4
Manchester Rd
Congleton CW12 . . . . . 156 E5
Handforth SK9 . . . . . 34 C2
Hollinfare WA3 . . . . . 11 A2
Hollins Green WA3 . . . . . 11 B3
Knutsford WA16 . . . . . 56 E4

Manchester Rd *continued*
Macclesfield SK10 87 D4
Warrington, Bruche WA1 16 E6
Warrington WA3 18 D7
Warrington, Woolston WA1 17 C7
Wincham CW9 79 D1
Manchester Row WA12 7 D8
Mancroft Cl WA1 17 E7
Mandarin Ct WA1 16 A3
Manhattan Gdns 1 WA5 15 B7
Manifold Cl CW11 174 E8
Manifold Dr SK6 37 F6
MANLEY 99 A4
Manley Cl
Antrobus CW9 53 C4
Holmes Chapel CW4 130 A3
Northwich CW9 104 A5
MANLEY COMMON 99 C5
Manley Gdns WA5 15 F5
Manley Gr SK7 35 E6
Manley La
Dunham-on-t-H WA6 97 F5
Manley WA6 98 C4
Manley Mere* WA6 98 B5
Manley Rd
Frodsham WA6 74 B3
Manley WA6 98 E7
Warren SK11 112 A5
Manley View CH2 72 C3
Manley Village Sch WA6 99 A5
Manna Dr CH2 72 C3
Manners La CH60 40 E6
Mannings La CH2 119 B6
Mannings La S CH2 119 A5
Manning St CW2 190 D1
Manora Rd CW9 104 A8
Manor Ave
Crewe CW2 190 A1
Golborne WA3 3 C8
Goostrey CW4 107 F1
Marston CW9 79 B6
Newton-le-W WA12 1 F4
Manor Bsns Pk CW4 130 D3
Manor Cl
Broughton CH5 139 C7
Cheadle SK8 35 C8
Congleton CW12 157 A1
Great Barrow CH3 120 E6
Lymm WA13 18 E2
Neston CH64 66 C7
Warrington WA1 17 D7
Wilmslow SK9 59 F8
Manor Cres
Broughton CH4 139 C8
Knutsford WA16 57 B2
Macclesfield SK10 87 D3
Middlewich CW10 151 C7
Manor Ct
Acton CW5 204 B4
Crewe CW2 190 B1
Golborne WA3 3 C8
Knutsford WA16 57 B1
2 Nantwich CW5 204 E6
Manor Dr
Barnton CW8 78 B2
Chester CH3 119 C1
Northwich, Rudheath CW9 104 C7
Manor Farm Cl CH2 119 F8
Manor Farm Cres CH1 94 B8
Manor Farm Ct
Broughton CH5 139 B7
5 Frodsham WA6 49 C1
Manor Farm Mews WA7 24 D4
Manor Farm Rd WA7 24 D4
Manor Fell WA7 50 B7
Manorfield Cl CH1 69 A1
Manor Fields CW10 151 C7
Manor Gdns
Nantwich CW5 204 E6
Wilmslow SK9 60 D7
Manor Gr CW8 103 C6
Manor Ho
Bebington CH62 43 D8
Ellesmere Port CH66 69 D2
Row-of-Trees SK9 59 D3
Manorial Rd CH64 66 C8
Manorial Rd S CH64 66 C7
Manor Ind Est WA4 16 E4
Manor La
Broughton CH5 139 B7
Davenham CW9 104 D2
Ellesmere Port CH66 69 D3
Holmes Chapel CW4 130 D3
3 Middlewich CW10 151 C8
Ollerton WA16 82 E6
MANOR PARK
Middlewich 151 B7
Runcorn 24 B3
Manor Park Ave WA7 24 C4
Manor Park Dr CH66 69 D2
Manor Park N WA16 57 C2
Manor Park Prim Sch WA16 57 C2
Manor Park Rd CW12 134 D2
Manor Park S WA16 57 C1
Manor Pk CH5 139 B7
Manor Pk CH3 120 E6
Manor Pl
Hatherton CW5 220 B1
Widnes WA8 12 B1
Manor Rd
Bebington CH62 43 E6
Chester CH4 141 B5
Cuddington CW8 101 F2
Frodsham WA6 49 C1
Haydock WA11 1 E7
Horwich End SK23 65 E5
Lymm WA13 18 E2
Mow Cop ST7 195 D7
Nantwich CW5 204 E6
Runcorn WA7 23 D2
Sandbach CW11 175 D6
Sealand CH5 116 A6
Thornton Hough CH63 42 A7
Widnes WA8 12 B1
Wilmslow SK9 59 E8
Manor Rd N CW5 204 E7
Manor Sq CW7 149 A8
Manor St CW8 103 D6
Manor Terr SK11 113 B3
Manor The WA1 17 F7
Manor Way
Crewe CW2 190 C1
Sandbach CW11 175 E6
Manse Field Rd WA6 75 B1
Manse Gdns WA12 2 D4
Mansell Cl WA8 13 C5
Mansfield Apartments WA2 9 A3
Mansfield Cl WA3 10 A4
Mansfield Prim Sch CH65 69 F3
Mansfield Rd CH65 70 A2
Mansion Ct 5 CW5 204 F5
Mansion Dr WA16 57 B2
Manston Rd WA5 14 F3
Manuel Perez Rd WA5 15 B6
Manx Rd WA4 16 B3
Maori Dr WA6 74 A8
Maple Ave
Alsager ST7 193 E2
Aston WA7 50 A4
Disley SK12 39 A6
Ellesmere Port CH66 69 D6
Golborne WA3 3 F7
Haydock WA11 1 B7
Macclesfield SK11 112 D5
Newcastle-u-Lyme ST5 210 E1
Newton-le-W WA12 2 D2
Poynton SK12 36 F3
Runcorn WA7 49 C8
Talke ST7 210 D8
5 Widnes WA8 13 B2
Maple Cl
Brereton Green CW11 153 F5
Congleton CW12 155 F4
Holmes Chapel CW4 130 D4
Sandbach CW11 175 C6
Maple Cres WA5 14 F3
Maple Ct CW7 127 A3
Maple Gr
Barnton CW8 78 B4
Bebington CH62 43 C8
Chester CH2 119 B4
Crewe CW1 190 E6
Ellesmere Port CH66 95 A8
Northwich, Greenbank CW8 103 C7
Saltney CH4 140 D5
Warrington WA4 16 D3
Winsford CW7 127 A1
Maple La CW8 101 F2
Maple Pl ST7 193 F7
Maple Rd
Alderley Edge SK9 60 B3
Bramhall SK7 35 E6
Partington M31 11 E3
Warrington WA1 17 E7
Winwick WA2 8 B6
Maples SK9 59 F6
Maples The
Mobberley WA16 58 E1
Winsford CW7 127 A3
Mapleton Dr WA7 49 F3
Maplewood SK11 112 D5
Maplewood Cl WA8 22 A7
Maplewood Gr CH1 117 B8
Maplewood Rd SK9 60 E8
Mapplewell Cres WA5 15 A6
Marble Arch 5 WA16 57 A2
MARBURY 226 D8
Marbury Gdns CH65 69 F6
Marbury House Farm WA4 52 E5
Marbury La CW9 78 E5
Marbury Park Ctry Pk* CW9 78 E5
Marbury Rd
Chester CH3 119 C2
Comberbach CW9 78 D6
Handforth SK9 34 B1
Norbury SY13 215 B3
Marbury St WA4 16 C3
March St CW1 190 E4
Marchwiel Rd CH65 70 D4
Marcien Way WA8 12 F3
Marcliff Gr WA16 57 A1
Marcross Cl WA5 7 E1
Mardale Ave WA2 8 C3
Mardale Cl CW12 157 B5
Mardale Cres WA13 18 F3
Mardale Ct CW4 130 A2
Mardon Cl WA16 57 D3
Marfield Ave WA13 19 A2
Marford Cl CW9 103 E5
Marfords Ave CH63 43 C7
Margaret Ave WA1 17 B7
Margaret Ct WA8 23 B7
Margaret's La CH66 69 A7
Margery Ave ST7 194 E7
Marian Ave WA12 1 F3
Marian Dr CH3 142 B8
Marian Rd WA11 1 E7
Marie Cl CW5 216 F4
Marie Dr WA4 17 D2
Marigold Cl SK11 111 F8
Marigold Pl WA5 15 D3
Marigold Way WA9 6 A7
Marina Ave WA5 15 C4
Marina Cl SK9 34 D5
Marina Dr
Chester CH2 118 E7
Ellesmere Port CH65 70 B5
Warrington WA2 8 C1
Marina Flats CH3 142 E7
Marina Gr WA7 23 B1
Marina La WA7 50 E7
Marina Village WA7 50 E7
Marina Wlk CH65 70 B5
Marine App 19 CW9 103 F8
Marine Ave M31 11 D3
Marine Dr CH60 40 D6
Mariner Cl WA7 50 D6
Marion Dr
Mobberley WA16 58 A4
Runcorn WA7 48 F6
Maritime Cl WA12 2 C5
Mark Ave CH66 69 C4
Mark Cl CH2 118 F2
Market Cl CW1 190 D5
Market Ct CW6 146 C2
Market Ctr The CW1 190 D4
Market Gate WA1 16 B5
Market Pl
Bollington SK10 88 B8
Hampton Heath SY14 213 D7
Macclesfield SK10, SK11 112 D8
Winsford CW7 126 F1
Market Sq
Chester CH1 237 A2
Congleton CW12 156 D2
Crewe CW1 190 D4
4 Sandbach CW11 175 B6
Market St
Congleton CW12 156 D3
Crewe CW1 190 D4
Crewe CW1 190 D5
Disley SK12 38 D6
Kidsgrove ST7 195 A1
Nantwich CW5 204 E5
New Mills SK22 39 B7
Newton-le-W WA12 2 A3
9 Northwich CW9 103 F8
Whaley Bridge SK23 65 E7
Widnes WA8 23 A7
Market Way 7 CW9 103 F8
Marlborough Ave
Alderley Edge SK9 60 B2
Winsford CW7 126 C3
Marlborough Cl
Knutsford WA16 57 C4
Macclesfield SK10 87 D4
Wistaston CW2 205 E8
Marlborough Cres
Warrington WA4 16 F2
Widnes WA8 13 A5
Marlborough Ct
1 Chester CH3 119 B2
3 Macclesfield SK11 112 D7
Marlborough Dr
Helsby WA6 73 B2
Macclesfield SK10 87 D4
Sandbach CW11 175 B8
Marlborough Ho 8 SK11 111 F8
Marlborough Prim Sch The SK10 87 D4
Marlborough Rd CH65 70 D3
Marlborough Way WA11 1 E8
Marlborough Wlk CH65 70 C3
Marl Cl CW8 102 A4
Marl Croft CH3 142 B7
Marl Edge SK10 87 A5
Marley Ave CW1 190 B7
Marley Gn SY13 227 C8
MARLEY GREEN 227 C8
Marley Rd SK12 36 E2
Marley Way CH4 140 E7
Marlfield Rd
Altrincham WA15 32 D7
Warrington WA4 17 A2
Marlfields Prim Sch CW12 156 C2
Marl Heys CH2 118 E7
Marline Ave CH63 43 C6
Marling Cl WA6 74 D6
Marling Pk WA8 12 B1
Marlow Ave CH2 118 F7
Marlow Cl
Sandbach CW11 174 D5
Warrington WA3 9 C5
Marlow Dr
Altrincham WA14 20 F2
Handforth SK9 34 C5
Marlowe Cl
Blacon CH1 118 A5
Widnes WA8 12 F1
Wistaston CW2 206 A8
Marlowe Ct SK11 112 C5
Marlowe Dr CW5 204 F3
Marlowe Rd
1 Neston CH64 66 E8
Northwich CW9 104 C6
Marlston Ave CH4 141 A6
Marlston Ct CH4 140 E1
Marlston Pl WA7 49 B6
Marlwood Pl CH4 139 A3
Maroon Rd M22 33 F7
Marple Cres CW2 189 E2
Marple Rd CW9 104 C8
Marquis Dr SK8 34 D7
Marriott Rd CW11 174 F3
Marron Ave WA2 8 B2
Marryat Cl WA2 8 A6
Marsden Ave WA4 17 A4
Marsden Ct WA8 12 E4
Marsden Terr 3 SK11 112 C7
Marshall Ave WA5 7 F2
Marshall Gr CW12 179 B8
Marshall La CW8 103 D6
Marshall Rd WA1 17 D7
Marshalls Ct 2 CW8 103 C5
Marsh Ave ST7 195 E2
Marsh Brook Cl WA3 11 A2
Marsh Cl ST7 193 A3
Marshfield Ave CW2 189 D4
MARSHFIELD BANK 189 C4
Marshfield Bank CW2 189 D4
Marshfield La ST8 179 C2
Marshgate WA8 22 B6
Marshgate Pl WA6 49 D2
Marsh Gr ST8 179 C3
MARSH GREEN
Biddulph 179 D3
Frodsham 74 A8
Marsh Green Cl ST8 179 D2
Marshgreen Rd ST8 179 D3
Marsh Green Rd CW11 174 E8
Marsh Hall Pad WA8 13 B4
Marsh House La WA1, WA2 16 C7
Marsh La
Alsager ST7 193 A3
Barton CH3, SY14 181 E3
Churton CH3 181 B5
Dutton WA4 51 E3
Elton CH2 72 B4
Frodsham WA6 74 A8
Holmes Chapel CW4 130 E2
Ince CH2 72 D6
Mere WA16 30 F3
Nantwich CW5 204 C5
New Mills SK22, SK23 39 D6
Norley CW8, WA6 101 B7
Ravensmoor CW5 203 F2
Runcorn WA7 23 F3
Warrington, Penketh WA5 14 C2
Marshlands Rd CH64 66 E5
Marsh Lane Trad Est SK22 39 D7
Marsh Rd WA4 27 B4
Marsh St
Warrington WA1 16 D7
Widnes WA8 23 A6
Marshway Dr WA12 2 B5
Marson St WA2 16 A6
MARSTON 79 B4
Marston Cl CH62 43 E3
Marston Gdns CH65 69 F6
Marston La CW9 79 C6
Marten Ave CH63 43 C7
Martens Rd M44 11 E5
MARTHALL 83 E4
Marthall La WA16 83 B7
Marthall Way 8 SK9 34 E5
Martham Cl WA4 17 A3
Martin Ave
Newton-le-W WA12 2 C5
Warrington WA2 8 E1
Martin Cl
Chester CH2 118 C8
Runcorn WA7 50 A7
Martindale Gr WA7 49 D5
Martin Rd
Chester CH2 118 C8
Frodsham WA6 74 B8
MARTIN'S ASH 227 B2
MARTINSCROFT 17 F7
Martinscroft Gn WA1 17 F7
Martinsfields CW8 77 A5
Martin's La CH3 143 F3
Martins Mill CW12 179 C8
MARTIN'S MOSS 176 E6
Martland Ave WA3 3 E7
Martlet Ave SK12 38 C6
MARTON 133 B5
Marton Cl
Congleton CW12 156 E5
Culcheth WA3 4 E4
Hough CW2 206 E3
Macclesfield SK10 86 F1
Marton & District CE Prim Sch SK11 133 C5
MARTON GREEN 125 C4
Marton Hall La SK11 133 B3
Marton La
Marton SK11 133 D7
Warren SK11 111 B1
Marton Rd CH4 139 C3
MARTONSANDS 125 F4
Marton Way 5 SK9 34 E5
Martree Ct CW11 174 D8
Maryfield Cl WA3 3 A7
Maryhill Cl ST7 195 A3
Maryhill High Sch ST7 195 A3
Maryhill Prim Sch ST7 195 A3
Maryhill Rd WA7 49 A8
Maryland Cl WA5 15 C7
Marys Gate CW2 205 E8
Mary St
Crewe CW1 190 E5
Widnes WA8 23 D7
Maryville Cl 3 CH65 70 C6
Masefield Ave WA8 22 F8
Masefield Dr
Blacon CH1 117 E6
Crewe CW1 190 F4
Winwick WA2 8 A5
Masefield Way CW11 174 D5
Maskery Pl CW12 156 E4
Mason Ave
Warrington WA1 16 E8
Widnes WA8 13 B4
Mason Cl CH66 69 D2
Masons La SK10 87 F1
Mason's Row CW6 169 E2
Mason St
Chester CH2 237 A3
Runcorn WA7 23 C3
Warrington WA1 16 C5
Massey Ave
Hartford CW8 103 A4
Lymm WA13 18 B2
Warrington WA5 7 F2
Winsford CW7 126 F1
Massey Brook La WA13 18 B2
Massey Cl CW5 205 A4
Masseyfield Rd WA7 50 B5
Massey Hall Sch WA4 17 F2
Massey St 6 SK9 60 A1
Masters Ct WA16 56 F1
Mastiff La SY14 213 B1
Mates La SY14 213 B6
Mather Ave
Golborne WA3 3 E6
Runcorn WA7 48 D7
Mather Cl CW10 151 C8
Mather Dr
Comberbach CW9 78 C8
Northwich CW9 104 D7
Mathers Cl WA2 9 A4
Mathieson Rd WA8 22 E5
Matlock Cl WA5 15 A8
Matlock Dr SK7 36 E8
Matlock Rd SK8 34 C7
Matterdale Cl WA6 74 D7
Matthew Cl CH2 118 F2
Matthews Pl CW12 157 A2
Matthews St WA1 16 D7
Matty's La WA6 74 A7
Mavor Ct CW1 190 B4
Mawdsley Ave WA1 17 E7
Mawdsley Cl ST7 193 A3
MAW GREEN 190 E7
Maw Green Cl CW1 190 E7
Maw Green Rd CW1 190 F7
Maw La CW1 191 C7
Mawson Cl WA5 15 D8
Maxfield Cl SK11 111 F8
Maxwell Cl CH65 70 A2
Maxwell Rd CW12 179 A8
Maxwell St
Crewe CW2 190 C3
Warrington WA3 9 E6
May Ave SK8 35 B6
Mayberry Gr WA2 9 A1
Maybrook Pl WA4 16 F3
Maydor Ave CH4 140 C7
Mayfair Cl
Poynton SK12 36 E4
Warrington WA5 14 D7
Mayfair Ct CH4 162 E5
Mayfair Dr
Crewe CW1 190 F6
Northwich CW9 103 F3
Mayfair Gr WA8 12 D1
Mayfield Ave
Macclesfield SK11 112 C5
Widnes WA8 12 B1
Mayfield Cl CW4 130 D3
Mayfield Ct WA8 13 A2
Mayfield Dr
Bebington CH62 44 B6
Cuddington CW8 102 A4
Golborne WN7 4 C8
Winsford CW7 127 A3
Mayfield Gdns CH64 41 E1
Mayfield Gr
Cuddington CW8 102 A4
Wilmslow SK9 59 E5
Mayfield Mews CW1 189 F6
Mayfield Rd
Blacon CH1 117 D5
Bramhall SK7 35 E4
Mobberley WA16 57 F4
Northwich CW9 104 C8
Warrington WA4 17 A2
Mayfield Terr SK11 112 C5
Mayfield View WA13 18 F2
Mayflower Rd CW5 204 E3
May Rd
Cheadle SK8 35 B6
Heswall CH60 41 A8
Maythorn Ave WA3 9 A7
Maytree Ave CH3 119 B2
May Wlk 2 M31 11 E3
Mead Ave ST7 194 E7
Mead Cl WA16 56 F1
Meade The SK9 60 C8
Meadow Ave
Congleton CW12 156 C1

Meadow Ave *continued*
Goostrey CW4 .... **107** C1
Warrington WA4 .... **16** B2
Weston CW2 .... **207** B5
MEADOWBANK **126** D5
Meadow Bank
Adderley TF9 .... **235** A4
Kelsall CW6 .... **122** C4
Meadow Bank Cvn Pk
WA4 .... **25** C6
Meadowbank Dr CH66 ... **69** A6
Meadowbank Gdns
WA3 .... **5** C7
Meadow Brow SK9 .... **60** A2
Meadow Cl
Cuddington CW8 .... **102** A4
Farndon CH3 .... **180** F1
Goostrey CW4 .... **107** E1
Helsby WA6 .... **73** B3
High Lane SK6 .... **37** F8
Neston CH64 .... **66** E6
Newton-le-W WA12 .... **1** F3
Shavington CW2 .... **206** D5
Tarvin CH3 .... **121** B2
Whaley Bridge SK23 .... **65** C8
Widnes WA8 .... **12** D3
Willaston CH64 .... **67** F8
Wilmslow SK9 .... **59** E4
Winsford CW7 .... **126** C3
Meadow Com Prim Sch
CH66 .... **69** E2
Meadow Cotts [5]
CW12 .... **156** D3
Meadowcroft
Higher Kinnerton CH4 .... **161** A7
Saughall CH1 .... **94** B1
Meadow Croft
Alsager ST7 .... **193** E2
Willaston CH64 .... **67** E8
Meadowcroft Ct WA7 .... **50** A8
Meadow Ct
Frodsham WA6 .... **49** C1
Mollington CH1 .... **94** F1
Newchapel ST7 .... **195** E2
No Man's Heath SY14 .... **214** A5
Meadow Dr
Barnton CW8 .... **78** A3
Knutsford WA16 .... **81** F8
Prestbury SK10 .... **87** B7
Wistaston CW2 .... **205** F7
Meadowfield
Tarporley CW6 .... **146** C1
Whaley Bridge SK23 .... **65** D8
Meadow Field Rd
CH4 .... **141** A5
Meadow Gate CW9 .... **79** F5
Meadowgate Cl
CW11 .... **174** D5
Meadowgate Farm
WA7 .... **49** F2
Meadow Gr
Northwich CW9 .... **104** B5
Winsford CW7 .... **126** E5
Meadow Home Pk
CW7 .... **126** D6
Meadow House Pk
CW6 .... **185** D5
Meadow La
Comberbach CW9 .... **78** C7
Disley SK12 .... **38** D6
Ellesmere Port CH65 .... **70** D6
Huntington CH3 .... **142** A5
Moulton CW9 .... **126** F8
Warrington WA2 .... **9** A2
Willaston CH64 .... **67** F8
Meadow Lane Ind Pk
CH65 .... **70** D5
Meadow Mill Ct
CW12 .... **156** E3
Meadow Rd
Broughton CH4 .... **139** B4
Weaverham CW8 .... **102** E7
Meadow Rise
Clutton CH3 .... **182** D2
Winsford CW7 .... **126** A1
Meadow Row WA7 .... **24** A1
Meadowside
Disley SK12 .... **39** A6
Fourlane-ends SK10 .... **63** B8
Frodsham WA6 .... **74** A8
Northwich CW8 .... **103** D7
Whaley Bridge SK23 .... **65** D8
Meadowside Ave ST7 ... **209** D2
Meadowside Com Prim
Sch WA2 .... **8** B1
Meadowside La ST7 .... **195** B7
Meadowside Mews
CH1 .... **118** B4
Meadowside Rd CH62 .... **43** D8
Meadows La
Chester CH4 .... **237** C1
Saughall CH1 .... **117** A8
Tilston SY14 .... **212** B6
Meadows Pl CH4 .... **141** E7
Meadows Rd
Cheadle SK8 .... **34** F8
Kidsgrove ST7 .... **194** F1
Meadow St
New Mills SK22 .... **39** C8
[3] Northwich CW9 .... **104** A8
Meadows The
Ashton Hayes CH3 .... **121** E8
Bebington CH62 .... **43** D7
Congleton CW12 .... **156** E3
Irlam M44 .... **11** E6
Neston CH64 .... **66** F6
Meadowsway CH2 .... **118** D8
Meadowsweet Rd
WA16 .... **57** F3
Meadow The CW4 .... **130** D8
Meadowvale Cl CW5 .... **204** E7
Meadow View
Chester CH3 .... **118** F1
Ellesmere Port CH2 .... **70** E1
Elton CH2 .... **72** A3
Lymm WA13 .... **18** D4
Middlewich CW10 .... **128** B2
Sealand CH5 .... **116** A6
Meadow View Dr WA6 .... **74** A7
Meadow Way
Lawton-gate ST7 .... **194** A5
Macclesfield SK10 .... **87** E2
Wilmslow SK9 .... **59** E4
Meadow Wlk
Partington M31 .... **11** E3
[4] Runcorn WA7 .... **49** F7
Mead Rd WA1 .... **17** A8
Meadscroft Dr SK9 .... **59** F1
Meads Rd ST7 .... **193** D4
Meadway
Bramhall SK7 .... **35** E5
Ellesmere Port CH66 .... **69** B7
Golborne WA3 .... **3** D8
Heswall CH60 .... **40** F6
High Lane SK6 .... **37** F8
Poynton SK12 .... **36** B4
Prestbury SK10 .... **87** A5
Runcorn WA7 .... **49** E8
Widnes WA8 .... **12** A1
Meakin Cl CW12 .... **157** B1
Mealors New Cotts
CH64 .... **67** A4
Mealors Weint CH64 .... **41** B1
Meal St SK22 .... **39** C8
Meddings Cl SK9 .... **85** A8
Medina Ave CW7 .... **126** F2
Medina Way ST7 .... **195** B2
Medlar Cl CH4 .... **140** F5
Medway Cl
Golborne WN7 .... **4** C8
Handforth SK9 .... **34** D2
Warrington WA2 .... **8** E2
Medway Dr ST8 .... **179** D1
Medway Rd WA3 .... **5** A2
Meeanee Dr CW5 .... **204** D4
Mee St SK11 .... **112** E5
Meeting House La
WA6 .... **74** E2
Meeting La WA5 .... **14** E5
MEGACRE **210** A1
Megacre ST7 .... **210** A1
Meg La
Langley SK11 .... **113** D1
Macclesfield SK10 .... **111** E8
Megs La CW9 .... **53** B4
Melbourne Ave M90 .... **33** A8
Melbourne Gr CW1 .... **191** C5
Melbourne Rd
Blacon CH1 .... **117** D4
Bramhall SK7 .... **35** F5
Melbury Ct WA3 .... **9** F6
Melbury Rd SK8 .... **35** B6
Melchett Cres CW9 .... **104** D7
Melford Cl CW2 .... **206** C8
Melford Ct WA1 .... **17** D8
Melford Dr
Macclesfield SK10 .... **87** C2
Runcorn WA7 .... **23** C1
Meliden Gr WA6 .... **73** B1
Melkridge Cl CH2 .... **119** A3
Melksham Cl SK11 .... **112** A7
Mellard St ST7 .... **209** D1
Mellock Cl CH64 .... **66** F6
Mellock La CH64 .... **66** F7
Mellor Cl WA7 .... **24** D1
Mellor Cres WA16 .... **56** E1
Mellors Bank ST7 .... **195** D6
Mellor St
Crewe CW1 .... **190** D5
Packmoor ST7 .... **195** F2
Mellor View SK12 .... **38** E6
Melrose Ave
Burtonwood WA5 .... **6** F7
Chester CH3 .... **119** B2
Warrington WA4 .... **26** D8
Melrose Cres SK12 .... **37** D5
Melrose Ct [15] SK9 .... **34** E1
Melrose Dr
Crewe CW1 .... **190** B8
Ellesmere Port CH66 .... **94** F8
Melton Ave WA4 .... **26** B8
Melton Cl CW12 .... **155** F3
Melton Dr CW12 .... **155** F3
Melton Rd WA7 .... **49** C7
Melverly Dr CH1 .... **117** C4
Melville Cl
Warrington WA2 .... **16** B7
[2] Widnes WA8 .... **13** D1
Melville Rd M44 .... **11** C5
Mendell Cl CH62 .... **43** E8
Mendell Prim Sch
CH62 .... **43** E8
Mendip Ave WA2 .... **8** B3
Mendip Cl
Ellesmere Port CH66 .... **69** E3
Gatley SK8 .... **34** B7
Winsford CW7 .... **149** B8
Menin Ave WA4 .... **16** C3
Menlow Cl WA4 .... **17** C1
Mentmore Gdns WA4 .... **26** F5
Meols Cl
Ellesmere Port CH66 .... **69** E4
Hale L24 .... **21** E2
Mercer Cl SY14 .... **213** B3
Mercer Rd WA11 .... **1** D6
Mercer St
Burtonwood WA5 .... **6** E6
Newton-le-W WA12 .... **2** D4
Mercer Way
Chester CH4 .... **140** F6
Nantwich CW5 .... **204** E7
Mercer Wlk CH65 .... **70** C4
Merchants Ct CW1 .... **190** C7
Mercian Cl CW2 .... **206** B4
Mercury Ct CH1 .... **117** E2
MERE **56** B8
Mere Ave CH63 .... **43** B6
Mere Bank CW9 .... **127** A8
Merebank Rd CW2 .... **190** B1
Merebrook Cl SK11 .... **112** A8
Merebrook Rd SK11 .... **111** F8
Mere Brook Wlk CW2 .... **190** C1
Mere Cl
Ellesmere Port CH66 .... **69** D2
Haslington CW1 .... **191** D4
Pickmere WA16 .... **80** A7
Mere Cres CW8 .... **123** F6
Merecroft [1] CH3 .... **119** A1
Mere Ct
Alsager ST7 .... **193** D4
Chelford SK11 .... **83** F3
[6] Knutsford WA16 .... **57** A2
Weston CW2 .... **207** B5
Meredith Ave WA4 .... **17** B2
Meredith St CW1 .... **190** C5
Mere Hall WA16 .... **56** A8
Merehaven Cl WA16 .... **80** A7
MERE HEATH **127** A8
Mereheath La WA16 .... **56** E5
Mereheath Pk WA16 .... **56** F3
Mere Ho ST7 .... **193** C3
Mere La
Cuddington CW8 .... **102** A2
Pickmere WA16 .... **79** F7
Merelake Rd ST7 .... **210** B8
Meremore Dr ST5 .... **210** D2
Mere Rd
Marston CW9 .... **79** B6
Newton-le-W WA12 .... **2** F4
Warrington WA2 .... **9** A2
Weston CW2 .... **207** B5
Mereside Ave CW12 .... **156** B3
Mereside Cl SK10 .... **87** A1
Mereside Gdns SK23 .... **65** D6
Mereside Rd WA16 .... **30** C2
Mere St CW1 .... **191** D4
Merevale Cl WA7 .... **49** E6
Mere View WA6 .... **73** A2
Mere View Gdns WA4 .... **26** E5
Merewood Cl WA2 .... **8** D3
Mereworth Dr CW9 .... **103** F5
Meridian Ho CW7 .... **127** B3
Meriton Rd SK9 .... **34** D4
Merlin Ave WA16 .... **57** B3
Merlin Cl
Runcorn WA7 .... **24** A1
Winsford CW7 .... **150** A8
Merlin Way
Crewe CW1 .... **190** A8
Kidsgrove ST7 .... **195** D3
Merrick Cl WA2 .... **8** E3
Merridale The WA15 .... **32** A8
Merriden Rd SK10 .... **87** B2
Merrill's Ave CW2 .... **189** E5
Merriman Ave WA16 .... **57** C3
Merrivale Rd CW2 .... **206** B8
Merrydale Cl SK10 .... **86** F1
Merryman's La SK9 .... **84** B7
Mersey Pl CW7 .... **127** B1
Mersey Rd
Runcorn WA7 .... **23** A3
Widnes WA8 .... **23** A4
Mersey St
St Helens WA9 .... **1** A3
Warrington WA1 .... **16** B5
Merseyton Rd CH65 .... **70** B8
Merseyton Road
Workshops CH65 .... **70** C7
Mersey View WA7 .... **48** D7
Mersey View Rd WA8 .... **22** B4
Mersey Wlk WA4 .... **16** F5
Mersham Ct WA8 .... **12** F4
Merton Ave SK7 .... **36** F8
Merton Cl CH64 .... **66** E5
Merton Dr CH4 .... **141** A4
Merton House Sch
CH2 .... **118** C4
Merton Rd
Bebington CH65 .... **44** B3
Ellesmere Port CH66 .... **69** F3
Poynton SK12 .... **36** B4
Mertoun Rd WA4 .... **16** B1
Mervyn Rd CW8 .... **77** E1
Merwood Ave SK8 .... **34** D8
Messuage La CW12 .... **132** E4
Meteor Cres WA2 .... **8** D2
Mevagissey Rd WA7 .... **50** C5
Mevril Rd SK23 .... **65** E5
Mevril Springs Way
SK23 .... **65** E5
Mews The
Barnton CW8 .... **78** B2
Burtonwood WA5 .... **6** E6
Holmes Chapel CW4 .... **130** C3
New Mills SK22 .... **39** D8
Tarporley CW6 .... **168** C8
Willaston CH64 .... **68** A8
Wilmslow SK9 .... **33** D4
Meynell Cl CW2 .... **190** A1
Meynell Pl CH1 .... **118** A5
Meyrick Cl WA12 .... **2** A3
Miami Cl [9] WA5 .... **15** B7
Micawber Rd SK12 .... **36** E2
Micklegate
Mickle Trafford CH2 .... **119** E8
Runcorn WA7 .... **50** D7
MICKLE TRAFFORD **119** E8
Mickle Trafford Village
Sch CH2 .... **119** E8
Micklewright Ave
CW1 .... **190** D5
Mickley Hall La CW5 .... **218** A4
Mid-Cheshire Coll
(Hartford Campus)
CW8 .... **103** C6
Mid Cheshire Coll (London
Road Studios) CW9 .... **103** F6
Mid Cheshire Coll (Verdin
Ctr) CW7 .... **126** D1
Middlecroft CH3 .... **119** E5
Middlehills SK11 .... **113** A6
Middlehurst Ave CW8 ... **102** E8
Middlehurst Rd WA4 .... **17** A2
Middle La
Aldford CH3 .... **163** F3
Congleton CW12 .... **157** D4
Kingsley WA6 .... **74** F2
MIDDLEWICH **128** D3
Middlewich High Sch
CW10 .... **151** C8
Middlewich Prim Sch
CW10 .... **151** B8
Middlewich Rd
Allostock WA16 .... **106** D5
Church Minshull CW1,
CW10 .... **172** E5
Cranage CW4, CW10 .... **129** E6
Crewe CW1 .... **189** D6
Delamere CW6, CW8 .... **123** D5
Holmes Chapel CW4 .... **130** B3
Knutsford WA16 .... **82** A3
Lower Peover WA16 .... **81** F2
Nantwich CW5 .... **189** B1
Nantwich CW5 .... **204** F7
Northwich CW9 .... **104** D7
Sandbach CW11 .... **174** E7
Winsford CW7, CW10 .... **127** E1
Middlewich Road Ind Est
CW10 .... **129** A6
Middlewich St CW1 .... **190** D6
Middle Wlk
Frodsham WA6 .... **74** B7
Knutsford WA16 .... **57** B2
MIDDLEWOOD **37** C5
Middlewood WA3 .... **3** E8
Middlewood Rd
Hazel Grove SK7, SK12 .... **37** C7
High Lane SK6 .... **37** D7
Poynton SK12 .... **37** B4
Middlewood Sta SK12 .... **37** D6
Middlewood View SK6 ... **37** D7
Midfield Cl ST8 .... **179** C2
Midhurst Cl SK8 .... **34** F8
Midland St WA8 .... **13** B1
Midland Terr SK22 .... **39** C7
Midland Way WA1,
WA5 .... **16** B5
Midlothian Ho [4]
CH1 .... **237** C3
Midpoint 18 Motorway Ind
Est CW10 .... **128** E1
MIDWAY **36** D2
Midway SK8 .... **35** B5
Midway Dr SK12 .... **36** D2
Milborne Cl CH2 .... **118** E5
Mildenhall Cl WA5 .... **15** B6
Mile Bank Rd SY13 .... **226** D3
Miles Cl WA3 .... **9** F3
Milford Gdns WA4 .... **26** D4
Milk St CW12 .... **156** D3
Millar Cres WA8 .... **23** A7
Mill Ave WA5 .... **14** E7
Millbank WA13 .... **18** E3
Mill Bank CH64 .... **67** A5
Millbank Cl SK11 .... **84** A3
Millbank Cotts CH3 .... **166** C2
Millbank Ct WA6 .... **74** A8
Millbank Dr SK10 .... **86** F1
Millbeck Cl CW2 .... **207** B5
Mill Bridge Cl CW1 .... **190** F3
Millbridge Gdns WA12 .... **2** E3
Millbrook Cl
Fowley Common WA3 .... **5** C5
Winsford CW7 .... **148** F8
Millbrook Ct
Middlewich CW10 .... **128** D1
Warrington WA2 .... **8** B2
Millbrook End CH3 .... **166** A2
Millbrook Fold SK7 .... **36** F8
Millbrook Gr [1] SK9 .... **34** D1
Mill Brow WA8 .... **13** C1
Millbuck Pk CW11 .... **174** C5
Millbuck Way CW11 .... **174** C6
Mill Cl
Chester CH2 .... **118** D6
Knutsford WA16 .... **57** D4
Warrington WA2 .... **8** E4
Mill Cotts
Bollington SK10 .... **88** B8
Christleton CH3 .... **142** D8
Willaston CH64 .... **42** F1
Millcroft
Neston CH64 .... **41** E1
Sandbach, Wheelock
CW11 .... **191** F8
Mill Cross CH3 .... **143** B5
Mill Ct CH65 .... **69** F6
Milldale Rd WN7 .... **4** B8
MILLEND **209** C5
Millend La ST7 .... **209** C5
Millenium Way [8] WA5 ... **15** B7
Millennium Ct CH64 .... **41** E2
Millennium Way ST5 .... **210** F2
Millers Cl CH3 .... **143** A4
Millers Croft [8] SK10 .... **112** C8
Millers Ct [7] SK10 .... **112** C8
Millersdale Cl CH62 .... **43** F5
Millersdale Gr WA7 .... **49** D6
Millers La WA13 .... **19** B5
Millers Mdw SK10 .... **88** E5
Miller St WA4 .... **16** C4
Millers View ST7 .... **195** A1
Millers Wharf ST7 .... **193** E7
Milley La WA16 .... **80** C7
Mill Farm Cl WA2 .... **8** E3
Mill Farm Cotts CW7 .... **149** B3
Mill Farm Est CW5 .... **217** A3
Millfield
Holt LL13 .... **196** D7
Neston CH64 .... **41** E1
Millfield Bsns Ctr WA11 .... **1** E8
Mill Field Cl CH3 .... **180** F2
Millfield La
Haydock WA11 .... **1** E8
Saighton CH3 .... **142** F1
Tarporley CW6 .... **146** C2
Millfield Rd WA8 .... **13** C2
Millfields CW5 .... **204** D4
Millfields Prim Sch
Bebington CH62 .... **43** E4
Nantwich CW5 .... **204** C5
Millfield Terr CH66 .... **69** C7
Millgate CW8 .... **101** F4
Mill Gn
Congleton CW12 .... **156** D3
Willaston CH64 .... **67** F8
Mill Gr
Bulkeley SY14 .... **184** E2
Kidsgrove ST7 .... **194** D1
Mill Green La WA8 .... **13** E5
Mill Green Sch WA12 .... **2** E3
Mill Hill Ave SK12 .... **36** D7
Mill Hill Dr CW11 .... **175** A5
Mill Hill Hollow SK12 .... **36** D7
Mill Hill La CW11 .... **175** A4
Mill Ho CW5 .... **204** D5
Millhouse Ave WA4 .... **16** D1
Millhouse La WA3 .... **9** A6
Milling Field The
CW4 .... **130** C2
Millingford Ind Est WA3 ... **3** A8
Millington Cl
Runcorn WA7 .... **49** F3
Widnes WA8 .... **22** F8
Millington Hall La
WA14 .... **30** B5
Millington La
Rostherne WA14 .... **30** B6
Weaverham CW8 .... **102** B6
Mill La
Adlington SK10 .... **62** B6
Alford CH3 .... **163** F3
Alsager CW11 .... **192** E8
Altrincham WA15 .... **32** E4
Audlem, Little Heath
CW3 .... **230** A4
Audlem, Swanbach
CW3 .... **229** E2
Barthomley CW2 .... **208** C7
Blakenhall CW5 .... **221** B4
Bold Heath WA8 .... **13** D6
Bollington SK10 .... **88** C8
Brereton Green CW4 .... **153** E8
Bulkeley SY14 .... **184** E2
Burton CH64 .... **67** C1
Chester CH2 .... **118** D6
Christleton CH3 .... **120** D2
Congleton CW12 .... **179** C8
Cronton WA8 .... **12** D6
Cuddington CW8 .... **101** F4
Duddon CW6 .... **145** A7
Eaton CW6 .... **147** B2
Ellesmere Port CH66 .... **69** E5
Frodsham WA6 .... **49** E2
Goostrey CW4 .... **107** E2
Great Barrow CH3 .... **120** E5
Hazel Grove SK7 .... **36** F8
Heswall CH60 .... **41** B8
Higher Walton WA4 .... **25** E7
Holmes Chapel CW4 .... **154** A8
Huxley CH3 .... **144** C1
Kelsall CW6 .... **122** C1
Kingsley WA6 .... **75** E3
Lindow End SK9 .... **84** A7
Little Budworth CW6 .... **148** A8
Lymm WA13 .... **19** C4
Macclesfield SK11 .... **112** D7
Marton CW12 .... **132** F2
Middlewich CW10 .... **128** D1
Middlewich, Newtonia
CW10 .... **128** B1
Middlewich, Stud Green
CW11 .... **152** C1
Mobberley WA16 .... **58** B4
Mottram St Andrew
SK10 .... **61** C5
Neston CH64 .... **67** C5
Newton-le-W WA12 .... **2** E3
Over Peover WA16,
SK11 .... **108** D8
Prestbury SK10 .... **61** F6
Sandbach CW11 .... **174** C8
Sandbach, Wheelock
CW11 .... **175** B2
Siddington SK11 .... **109** F6
Smallwood CW11 .... **176** D7

Mill La *continued*
Tarvin CH3 . . . . . . 121 C4
The Bank ST7 . . . . . . 195 A7
Warrington, Houghton Gn WA2 . . . . . . 8 E4
Warrington, Stockton Heath WA4 . . . . . . 16 E1
Warrington WA2 . . . . . . 7 F4
Weston CW2 . . . . . . 207 B6
Whitegate CW7, CW8 . . . . 126 B6
Willaston CH64 . . . . . . 42 F1
Mill Lane Cotts CH3 . . . . 120 E5
Mill Lane End CW5 . . . . 221 C4
Mill Mdw WA12 . . . . . . 2 E3
Millmead ST7 . . . . . . 193 F7
Mill Park Dr CH62 . . . . . . 43 E3
Mill Pool La CW5 . . . . . . 187 C6
Millport Cl WA2 . . . . . . 9 A2
Millrace Dr CW2 . . . . . . 206 B8
Mill Rd
Macclesfield SK11 . . . . . . 112 D6
Wilmslow SK9 . . . . . . 60 B7
Mill Rise
Helsby WA6 . . . . . . 73 C4
Kidsgrove ST7 . . . . . . 195 A1
Mill Row CW11 . . . . . . 175 C6
Mill St
Chester CH4 . . . . . . 237 B1
Congleton, Buglawton CW12 . . . . . . 156 F4
Congleton CW12 . . . . . . 156 D3
Crewe CW2 . . . . . . 190 D3
Golborne WA3 . . . . . . 3 A8
Macclesfield SK11 . . . . . . 112 D7
Nantwich CW5 . . . . . . 204 E5
Neston CH64 . . . . . . 66 D8
Wilmslow SK9 . . . . . . 60 B7
Millstone Ave ST7 . . . . . . 194 E1
Millstone Cl SK12 . . . . . . 36 F5
Millstone La CW5 . . . . . . 204 F5
Millstone Pas SK11 . . . . . . 112 E6
Mill Stream Cl CW4 . . . . . . 107 E1
Mills Way CW1 . . . . . . 173 B1
Mill The ST7 . . . . . . 195 C5
Mill View Cl SY14 . . . . . . 184 E2
Mill View Prim Sch CH2 . . . . . . 118 E6
Millway
Altrincham WA15 . . . . . . 32 C7
Waverton CH3 . . . . . . 143 B5
Mill Way CW5 . . . . . . 204 F2
Millway Rd L24 . . . . . . 21 A4
Mill Wharf CH3 . . . . . . 143 B5
Millwood WA7 . . . . . . 24 C1
Millwood Cl 4 SK8 . . . . . . 34 E8
Millwood Ct L24 . . . . . . 21 A4
Millyard The CH4 . . . . . . 162 C1
Milne Cl CW2 . . . . . . 189 F1
Milner Cop CH60 . . . . . . 41 A8
Milner Rd
Heswall CH60 . . . . . . 41 A8
Northwich CW8 . . . . . . 103 C6
MILNERS GREEN 143 C2
Milner St WA5 . . . . . . 15 F5
Milnthorpe Rd WA5 . . . . . . 6 E6
Milton Ave
Irlam M44 . . . . . . 11 E6
Newton-le-W WA12 . . . . . . 2 B3
Widnes WA8 . . . . . . 22 F8
Milton Cl
Ellesmere Port CH65 . . . . . . 70 D4
Higher Wincham CW9 . . . . . . 80 A5
Middlewich CW10 . . . . . . 151 D5
Milton Cres ST7 . . . . . . 210 C8
Milton Ct SK7 . . . . . . 35 F6
Milton Dr
Poynton SK12 . . . . . . 36 D4
Wistaston CW2 . . . . . . 206 A8
Milton Gr
Helsby WA6 . . . . . . 73 A1
Warrington WA4 . . . . . . 16 D3
MILTON GREEN 165 C2
Milton Rd
Blacon CH1 . . . . . . 117 F6
Bramhall SK7 . . . . . . 35 E7
Ellesmere Port CH65 . . . . . . 70 D4
Golborne WA3 . . . . . . 3 D7
Widnes WA8 . . . . . . 23 A8
Milton Rough CW8 . . . . . . 76 E2
Milton St
Chester CH1 . . . . . . 237 B3
Widnes WA8 . . . . . . 23 A5
Milton Way CW11 . . . . . . 174 D6
Milvain Dr WA2 . . . . . . 8 C1
Milverton Dr SK7 . . . . . . 35 B5
Mimosa Cl CH2 . . . . . . 72 C4
Miners Way
Speke L24 . . . . . . 21 A3
Widnes WA8 . . . . . . 23 A7
Minerva Ave CH1 . . . . . . 117 E2
Minerva Cl WA4 . . . . . . 16 D2
Minerva Ct CH1 . . . . . . 117 E2
Mine Way WA11 . . . . . . 1 F7
Minn-End-La SK11 . . . . . . 159 B6
Minor Ave SK11 . . . . . . 112 D3
Minshull La CW5, CW7 . . . . . . 171 D4
Minshull New Rd CW1 . . . . . . 189 F7
Minshull St WA16 . . . . . . 57 A2
MINSHULL VERNON 172 E5
Minster Cl CW7 . . . . . . 149 D5
Minster Ct
Runcorn WA7 . . . . . . 48 E8
Wistaston CW2 . . . . . . 205 E8
Minster Dr WA14 . . . . . . 31 A8
Minton Cl CW12 . . . . . . 157 B1
Minton Way WA8 . . . . . . 13 B5
Mirfield Cl WA3 . . . . . . 3 D7
Mirion St CW1 . . . . . . 190 D4
Mission Mews CH2 . . . . . . 118 F2
Misty Cl WA8 . . . . . . 12 C2
Mitchell Ave
Burtonwood WA5 . . . . . . 6 E5
Kidsgrove ST7 . . . . . . 194 D1
Mitchell Dr ST7 . . . . . . 194 D1
Mitchell Fold
Fourlane-ends SK10 . . . . . . 63 D8
High Lane SK6 . . . . . . 37 D1
Mitchell St
Golborne WA3 . . . . . . 3 A8
Warrington WA4 . . . . . . 26 C8
Mithril Cl WA8 . . . . . . 13 E3
Mitton Cl WA3 . . . . . . 4 E5
MMU Cheshire (Crewe Campus) CW1 . . . . . . 190 F3
Moat Ho 17 CW8 . . . . . . 103 F8
Moat La
Audley ST7 . . . . . . 209 B3
Hollins Green WA3 . . . . . . 10 E2
MOBBERLEY 58 A4
Mobberley CE Prim Sch WA16 . . . . . . 58 C5
Mobberley Cl WA4 . . . . . . 17 D4
Mobberley Rd
Ashley WA14, WA15, WA16 . . . . . . 31 E3
Knutsford WA16 . . . . . . 57 B3
Wilmslow SK9 . . . . . . 33 D1
Mobberley Sta WA16 . . . . . . 57 F7
MOBLAKE 230 D4
Modyn CH2 . . . . . . 118 C4
Moelfre Dr SK8 . . . . . . 35 C7
Moggie La SK10 . . . . . . 36 F1
Mold Rd CH4 . . . . . . 139 A3
MOLLINGTON 94 E2
Mollington Ct CH1 . . . . . . 94 F2
Mollington Grange Bsns Pk CH1 . . . . . . 117 F8
Mollington Rd M22 . . . . . . 33 E8
Molly Potts Cl WA16 . . . . . . 82 B8
Molyneux Ave WA5 . . . . . . 15 F8
Monarch Cl
Crewe CW2 . . . . . . 189 F4
Irlam M44 . . . . . . 11 E6
Monarch Dr CW9 . . . . . . 103 E5
Monck Dr CW5 . . . . . . 204 D6
Mond Rd WA8 . . . . . . 23 A8
Mond St CW8 . . . . . . 78 B3
Monica Dr WA8 . . . . . . 13 A5
Monks Coppenhall Prim Sch CW1 . . . . . . 190 E7
Monks Gr CH65 . . . . . . 70 B6
MONKS HEATH 85 A1
Monk's Heath Crossroads SK10 . . . . . . 85 A1
Monks Heath Hall Wrkshps SK10 . . . . . . 85 B1
Monks La
Acton CW5 . . . . . . 203 F7
Crewe CW1 . . . . . . 189 F5
Nantwich CW5 . . . . . . 204 E5
Monk's La CW3 . . . . . . 230 C5
Monks Orch CW5 . . . . . . 204 F5
Monks Pl WA2 . . . . . . 16 C7
Monks St WA5 . . . . . . 15 E6
Monk St CW1 . . . . . . 190 A5
Monks Way CW8 . . . . . . 103 B4
Monkswood Cl WA5 . . . . . . 7 E2
Monmouth Cl WA1 . . . . . . 17 E7
Monroe Cl WA1 . . . . . . 17 B8
Monsall Cl SK11 . . . . . . 112 F7
Monsall Dr SK11 . . . . . . 112 F7
Montague Rd WA8 . . . . . . 22 A6
Montana Cl 3 WA5 . . . . . . 15 C7
Montclare Cres WA4 . . . . . . 16 F2
Montcliffe Cl WA3 . . . . . . 9 C5
Montgomery Cl
Knutsford WA16 . . . . . . 57 C4
Warrington WA5 . . . . . . 15 A8
Montgomery Rd WA8 . . . . . . 22 D8
Montgomery Way CW7 . . . . . . 149 B7
Montmorency Rd WA16 . . . . . . 57 D3
Montpelier Ave WA7 . . . . . . 48 F6
Montrose Cl
Macclesfield SK10 . . . . . . 87 A1
Shavington CW2 . . . . . . 206 B3
Warrington WA2 . . . . . . 8 F4
Montrose Ct
Chester CH4 . . . . . . 140 F7
Holmes Chapel CW4 . . . . . . 130 B2
Monument Rd ST7 . . . . . . 210 D6
Monument View ST7 . . . . . . 209 F2
Moody St CW12 . . . . . . 156 D2
Moor Cl ST8 . . . . . . 179 E1
Moor Cres CH4 . . . . . . 139 D1
Moorcroft WA16 . . . . . . 80 F3
Moorcroft Ave CH3 . . . . . . 119 B1
Moorcroft Cres CH3 . . . . . . 119 C4
Moorcroft Ct CH3 . . . . . . 119 B1
Moorcroft Mews CH4 . . . . . . 140 D6
Moordale Rd WA16 . . . . . . 57 B2
Moorditch La
Frodsham WA6 . . . . . . 48 D1
Frodsham WA6 . . . . . . 48 F1
MOORE 25 B6
Moore Ave
St Helens WA9 . . . . . . 1 B3
Warrington WA4 . . . . . . 17 D3
Moore Cl WA8 . . . . . . 13 D2
Moore Dr WA11 . . . . . . 1 F6
Moore Gr WA13 . . . . . . 19 B5
Moore La WA4 . . . . . . 25 C7
Moore Prim Sch WA4 . . . . . . 25 A5
Moorfield Cres WA3 . . . . . . 4 A7
Moorfield Dr
Neston CH64 . . . . . . 41 C1
Wilmslow SK9 . . . . . . 59 E5
Moorfield Prim Sch WA8 . . . . . . 13 D3
Moorfield Rd WA8 . . . . . . 13 D3
Moorfields CW5 . . . . . . 205 E6
Moorhead La CW11 . . . . . . 154 D3
Moorhill Rd SK11 . . . . . . 112 C4
Moor Ho WA6 . . . . . . 74 B8
Moorhouse Ave ST7 . . . . . . 193 E4
Moorhouse Cl CH2 . . . . . . 118 D5
Mooring Cl WA7 . . . . . . 50 D6
Moorings CW12 . . . . . . 156 E1
Moorings Cl CH64 . . . . . . 41 B1
Moorings The
Christleton CH3 . . . . . . 142 E7
Disley SK12 . . . . . . 38 E6
Heswall CH60 . . . . . . 40 C8
Middlewich CW10 . . . . . . 128 C1
Moor La
Bramhall SK7 . . . . . . 35 E3
Elton WA6 . . . . . . 72 E1
Frodsham WA6 . . . . . . 74 B8
Heswall CH60 . . . . . . 40 F8
Higher Kinnerton CH4 . . . . . . 161 D8
Lower Kinnerton CH4 . . . . . . 161 C6
Sandycroft CH5 . . . . . . 116 A2
Waverton CH3 . . . . . . 143 A5
Widnes WA8 . . . . . . 22 F7
Widnes WA8 . . . . . . 23 A7
Wilmslow SK9 . . . . . . 59 E5
Moorland Cl CH60 . . . . . . 41 A7
Moorland Dr
Cheadle SK8 . . . . . . 34 F8
Runcorn WA7 . . . . . . 50 E7
Moorland Pk CH60 . . . . . . 41 A7
Moorland Rd
Biddulph ST8 . . . . . . 179 D1
Ellesmere Port CH66 . . . . . . 69 E8
Mow Cop ST7 . . . . . . 195 D7
Moorlands Ave CW8 . . . . . . 102 A4
Moorlands Cl SK10 . . . . . . 87 C3
Moorlands Dr CW5 . . . . . . 206 A1
Moorlands Pk CW8 . . . . . . 102 A4
Moor Lane Bsns Ctr 9 WA8 . . . . . . 23 A7
Moor La S WA8 . . . . . . 22 F7
Moor-Park Way CW9 . . . . . . 103 F4
Moorsbrook Gr 9 SK9 . . . . . . 34 E1
Moorsfield Ave CW3 . . . . . . 229 F3
MOORSIDE 66 C7
Moorside
Knutsford WA16 . . . . . . 57 A2
Warrington WA4 . . . . . . 16 E4
Moorside Ave CH64 . . . . . . 66 C8
Moorside Ct WA8 . . . . . . 22 F7
Moorside La
Neston CH64 . . . . . . 66 D8
Pott Shrigley SK10 . . . . . . 63 E4
Moors La CW7 . . . . . . 149 D5
Moorson Ave ST7 . . . . . . 194 F8
Moor St CW12 . . . . . . 156 E2
Moorview Gdns ST7 . . . . . . 195 E6
Moorway CH60 . . . . . . 41 B8
Moran Cl SK9 . . . . . . 34 E2
Moran Cres SK11 . . . . . . 112 B7
Moran Dr WA5 . . . . . . 15 A6
Moran Rd SK11 . . . . . . 112 B7
Morcott La L24 . . . . . . 21 D2
Moresby Cl WA7 . . . . . . 50 E7
Moreton Ave SK7 . . . . . . 35 E5
Moreton Cl CW11 . . . . . . 175 C7
Moreton Dr
Alsager ST7 . . . . . . 193 C3
Handforth SK9 . . . . . . 34 E3
Holmes Chapel CW4 . . . . . . 130 B3
Poynton SK12 . . . . . . 36 F4
Moreton Pl ST7 . . . . . . 194 E6
Moreton Rd CW2 . . . . . . 189 F3
Moreton St CW8 . . . . . . 78 D1
Moreton Terr WA6 . . . . . . 74 A8
Moreville Cl CW9 . . . . . . 103 E3
Morgan Ave WA2 . . . . . . 8 C2
Morgan Cl
Blacon CH1 . . . . . . 117 F6
Crewe CW2 . . . . . . 190 A4
Morgans Way WA3 . . . . . . 4 A8
Morgan Wlk CW5 . . . . . . 204 D6
Morland Ave
Bebington CH62 . . . . . . 43 D6
Neston CH64 . . . . . . 66 F7
MORLEY 33 C2
Morley Cl CH2 . . . . . . 119 F8
MORLEY COMMON 15 F1
Morley Dr CW12 . . . . . . 157 A1
MORLEY GREEN 33 C1
Morley Green Rd SK9 . . . . . . 33 C1
Morley Rd
Runcorn WA7 . . . . . . 23 A1
Warrington WA4 . . . . . . 16 A1
Morley St WA1 . . . . . . 16 D6
Mornant Ave CW8 . . . . . . 103 A3
Mornington Ave CH65 . . . . . . 70 C5
Mornington Cl CW11 . . . . . . 174 D7
Morphany La WA4 . . . . . . 51 E6
Morreys La CW6 . . . . . . 122 F6
Morris Ave WA4 . . . . . . 16 F4
Morris Cl WA11 . . . . . . 1 A5
Morris Dr CW8 . . . . . . 77 D1
Morrison Cl WA5 . . . . . . 15 A5
Morris Pk CW8 . . . . . . 103 B4
Mort Ave WA4 . . . . . . 17 A5
Mortimer Ave WA2 . . . . . . 16 B8
Mortimer Dr CW11 . . . . . . 175 C5
Mortlake Cl WA8 . . . . . . 12 C3
Mortlake Cres CH3 . . . . . . 119 A1
Morton Ave WA6 . . . . . . 73 B1
Morton Cl WA5 . . . . . . 15 C8
Morton Dr SK11 . . . . . . 112 F3
Morton Gdns CH1 . . . . . . 117 E4
Morton Rd
Blacon CH1 . . . . . . 117 E4
Runcorn WA7 . . . . . . 50 D8
Morval Cres WA7 . . . . . . 23 D1
Morven Cl WA2 . . . . . . 8 E3
Mosedale Gr WA7 . . . . . . 49 E5
Moseley Ave WA4 . . . . . . 17 A3
Moses Ct CH1 . . . . . . 237 C3
MOSS BANK 23 D8
Moss Bank
Bramhall SK7 . . . . . . 35 C5
Chester CH2 . . . . . . 118 C4
Winsford CW7 . . . . . . 126 C1
Moss Bank Rd WA8 . . . . . . 23 D7
Moss Bower Rd SK11 . . . . . . 112 C4
MOSSBROW 19 E7
Moss Brow SK10 . . . . . . 87 E7
Moss Brow La WA16 . . . . . . 28 D4
Moss Cl
Warrington WA4 . . . . . . 16 E2
Willaston CH64 . . . . . . 68 A8
Moss Croft CW1 . . . . . . 190 A8
Mossdale Cl
Crewe CW2 . . . . . . 189 E4
Warrington WA5 . . . . . . 15 A7
Moss Dr
Manley WA6 . . . . . . 98 F4
Middlewich CW10 . . . . . . 151 D6
MOSSEND 154 E1
MOSS END 54 C2
Moss End La CW11 . . . . . . 176 E8
Moss Farm Barns CW8 . . . . . . 102 D4
Moss Farm Recn Ctr CW8 . . . . . . 103 D8
Mossfield Cres 4 ST7 . . . . . . 195 B2
Moss Fields
Alsager ST7 . . . . . . 193 A3
Crewe CW1 . . . . . . 173 A1
Mossford Ave CW1 . . . . . . 190 B7
Moss Gate WA3 . . . . . . 10 A5
Moss Gr
Lymm WA13 . . . . . . 19 B4
Newcastle-u-Lyme ST5 . . . . . . 210 D3
Saltney CH4 . . . . . . 140 D6
Moss Green Way WA9 . . . . . . 1 A1
Mosshall La WA4 . . . . . . 26 F1
Moss Hall La CW6 . . . . . . 147 C4
Moss Hey Prim Sch SK7 . . . . . . 35 C5
MOSS HOUSES 111 F2
Moss La
Alderley Edge SK9 . . . . . . 60 B1
Bollington SK10 . . . . . . 87 E8
Bramhall SK7 . . . . . . 35 D5
Brereton Green CW12 . . . . . . 154 F5
Byley CW10 . . . . . . 129 B7
Congleton CW12 . . . . . . 156 E6
Crewe CW1 . . . . . . 173 A2
Cuddington CW8 . . . . . . 102 A3
Dunham Woodhouses WA13 . . . . . . 20 B8
Fowley Common WA3 . . . . . . 5 D5
Golborne WA3 . . . . . . 3 B5
Higher Wincham CW9 . . . . . . 79 E6
High Legh, Sink Moss WA16 . . . . . . 28 D4
High Legh WA16 . . . . . . 29 E6
Hollins Green WA3 . . . . . . 10 E5
Irlam M44 . . . . . . 11 D5
Lawton-gate ST7 . . . . . . 194 F4
Lostock Green CW9 . . . . . . 105 D8
Macclesfield SK11 . . . . . . 112 C4
Manley WA6 . . . . . . 99 A4
Mere WA16 . . . . . . 56 C5
Mobberley WA16 . . . . . . 58 F4
Moore WA4 . . . . . . 25 A6
Mottram St Andrew SK10 . . . . . . 61 A2
Norbury SY13 . . . . . . 215 C5
Norley WA6 . . . . . . 101 B5
Northwich CW8 . . . . . . 103 D7
Over Peover WA16 . . . . . . 83 C3
Partington M31 . . . . . . 11 F3
Partington, Mossbrow WA13 . . . . . . 11 F1
Sandbach CW11 . . . . . . 174 C7
Siddington SK11 . . . . . . 109 E2
St Helens, Moss Nook WA9 . . . . . . 1 A1
Tarporley CW6 . . . . . . 146 B2
Warmingham CW1 . . . . . . 173 C3
Warrington WA3 . . . . . . 9 E1
Wybunbury CW5 . . . . . . 206 A1
Wythenshawe SK9 . . . . . . 33 E6
Mosslands Cl CH66 . . . . . . 69 E2
Moss Lane Bsns Ctr CW11 . . . . . . 174 D6
Moss Lane Ind Est CW11 . . . . . . 174 D7
MOSSLEY 179 A8
Mossley Ave CH62 . . . . . . 43 D8
Mossley CE Prim Sch CW12 . . . . . . 179 B8
Mossley Ct CW12 . . . . . . 178 F8
Mossley Garth Cl 4 CW12 . . . . . . 157 A1
Moss Mere CW11 . . . . . . 176 F7
MOSS NOOK 33 F7
Moss Pl ST7 . . . . . . 195 B3
Moss Rd
Alderley Edge SK9 . . . . . . 60 C2
Congleton CW12 . . . . . . 178 F7
Irlam M44 . . . . . . 11 C7
Northwich CW8 . . . . . . 103 D8
Warrington WA4 . . . . . . 17 A3
Moss Rose SK9 . . . . . . 60 B2
Moss Rose Football Gnd SK11 . . . . . . 112 D4
Moss Side La
Antrobus CW9 . . . . . . 53 D7
Hollins Green WA3 . . . . . . 10 F3
Moore WA4 . . . . . . 24 F7
Moss Side Rd M44 . . . . . . 11 E6
Moss Sq
Crewe CW1 . . . . . . 190 D4
Macclesfield SK11 . . . . . . 112 D4
Moss St
Weaverham CW8 . . . . . . 77 D1
Widnes WA8 . . . . . . 23 D7
Moss Terr
Warren SK11 . . . . . . 112 A5
Wilmslow SK9 . . . . . . 60 F8
Winnington CW8 . . . . . . 78 D1
Moss The CW9 . . . . . . 78 D7
Mossvale CH66 . . . . . . 69 D8
Moss View Rd SK11 . . . . . . 112 A4
Moss Way ST7 . . . . . . 193 A3
Mossways Pk SK9 . . . . . . 59 C7
Mosswood Rd SK9 . . . . . . 34 E1
MOSTON 95 C1
Moston Ct 5 CW12 . . . . . . 156 F3
Moston Gr WA13 . . . . . . 18 D3
MOSTON GREEN 174 B8
Moston Rd
Chester CH2 . . . . . . 118 D8
Sandbach CW11 . . . . . . 174 D6
Moston Way CH66 . . . . . . 69 F3
Mostyn Ave CH60 . . . . . . 40 C8
Mostyn Gdns CH64 . . . . . . 41 B1
Mostyn House Sch CH64 . . . . . . 66 C8
Mostyn Pl CH1 . . . . . . 117 E6
Mostyn Sq CH64 . . . . . . 41 B1
Mote Hill Ct WA1 . . . . . . 16 D6
Motherwell Cl WA8 . . . . . . 12 E3
Mottershead Cl 1 WA8 . . . . . . 23 A8
Mottershead Rd WA8 . . . . . . 23 A8
Mottram Cl
Middlewich CW10 . . . . . . 151 B7
Warrington WA4 . . . . . . 17 B3
Mottram Dr CW5 . . . . . . 205 A4
Mottram Rd SK9 . . . . . . 60 D1
MOTTRAM ST ANDREW 61 B2
Mottram St Andrew Prim Sch SK10 . . . . . . 61 B1
Mottram Way SK10 . . . . . . 87 E2
Moughland La WA7 . . . . . . 49 A8
Moulders La WA1 . . . . . . 16 B4
MOULDSWORTH 98 F2
Mouldsworth Cl 2 CW9 . . . . . . 103 E4
Mouldsworth Motor Mus★ CH3 . . . . . . 98 E1
Mouldsworth Sta CH3 . . . . . . 99 A2
MOULTON 126 E7
Moulton Cl
Knutsford WA16 . . . . . . 57 C1
Northwich CW9 . . . . . . 103 E4
Runcorn WA7 . . . . . . 49 F4
Moulton Sch CW9 . . . . . . 126 F8
Mountain View
Helsby WA6 . . . . . . 73 B3
Saltney CH4 . . . . . . 140 E6
Mount Ave CH60 . . . . . . 40 F8
Mount Barns CH2 . . . . . . 95 C6
Mountbatten Ct CW2 . . . . . . 190 A3
Mountbatten Way CW12 . . . . . . 156 E3
Mount Cl CW5 . . . . . . 204 F6
Mount Ct 3 CH60 . . . . . . 40 F8
Mount Dr CW5 . . . . . . 204 F6
Mount Farm Way CH66 . . . . . . 69 C2
Mountfield Rd SK7 . . . . . . 35 E5
Mount Mews CH60 . . . . . . 40 F8
Mount Pl CH2 . . . . . . 118 F2
Mount Pleasant
Audlem CW3 . . . . . . 230 B4
Chester CH4 . . . . . . 140 F7
Congleton CW12 . . . . . . 156 E2
Crewe CW1 . . . . . . 190 B6
Elton CH2 . . . . . . 72 A4
Haslington CW1 . . . . . . 191 D4
Kidsgrove ST7 . . . . . . 195 A1
Macclesfield SK10 . . . . . . 87 B1
MOUNT PLEASANT 195 B6
Mount Pleasant
Rainow SK10 . . . . . . 88 D3
Widnes WA8 . . . . . . 13 B2
Wilmslow SK9 . . . . . . 60 B8
MOUNT PLEASANT 149 A7
Mount Pleasant Ave WA9 . . . . . . 1 B3
Mount Pleasant Dr CW7 . . . . . . 149 A7
Mount Pleasant Rd
Davenham CW9 . . . . . . 103 F2
The Bank ST7 . . . . . . 195 B7
Mount Pleasant Residential Pk CW4 . . . 130 D8
Mount Rd
Kidsgrove ST7 . . . . . . 195 B2
Runcorn WA7 . . . . . . 49 F8
Mount St WA8 . . . . . . 13 B1
Mount Terr SK11 . . . . . . 112 F7

Mount The
Chester CH3 118 F1
Congleton CW12 156 A2
Great Budworth CW9 79 A7
Hale WA15 32 C8
Heswall CH60 40 F8
Kidsgrove ST7 195 A1
Scholar Green ST7 194 E7
Mount Way CH3 143 A4
Mourne Cl CH66 69 A6
MOW COP 195 C7
Mow Cop Rd ST7 195 D6
Mowcroft La WA5 14 B3
Mow La
Mount Pleasant ST7 195 A5
Mow Cop ST7 179 B2
Mowpen Brow WA16 29 B6
Moxon Ave WA4 16 F5
Moyles Cl WA8 12 D2
Mudhouse La CH64 67 F2
Mudhurst La SK12 38 E3
Muirfield Cl
Northwich CW9 104 A5
Warrington WA2 9 A3
Wilmslow SK9 60 D8
Muirfield Dr
Macclesfield SK10 87 D4
Winsford CW7 126 C2
Muirfield Mews CW7 126 C2
Muir Rd CH1 117 E3
Mulberry Ave WA3 3 F7
Mulberry Cl
Elton CH2 72 C3
Gatley SK8 34 C7
Warrington WA1 17 E7
Mulberry Ct
Macclesfield SK11 112 D4
Warrington WA4 16 D1
Mulberry Dr SK10 87 E1
Mulberry Gdns CW11 174 D7
Mulberry Rd CW2 189 E2
Mulberry Rise CW8 103 C7
Mulcaster Ct CW1 191 D5
Mull Cl CH65 70 C1
Mullein Cl WA3 3 D8
Mullen Cl WA5 7 F1
Mullins Ave WA12 2 C5
Mullion Cl WA7 50 B6
Mullion Gr WA2 9 A1
Mulsford Ct LL13 222 A8
Mulsford La LL13, SY14 222 B8
MURDISHAW 50 D7
Murdishaw Ave WA7 50 D6
Murdishaw West Com Prim Sch WA7 50 D6
Muriel Cl WA5 14 D6
Murray Cl SK10 87 A1
Murrayfield SK10 87 A5
Murrayfield Dr CW5 205 D5
Museum St WA1 16 A4
Music Hall Pass CH1 237 B2
Muslin Row CW5 172 A5
Mustard La WA3 4 B1
Myddleton La WA2 8 C6
Myrica Gr CH2 119 B3
Myrtle Ave
Haydock WA11 1 B7
Higher Kinnerton CH4 161 A7
Newton-le-W WA12 2 C2
Myrtle Gr
Warrington WA4 16 D3
Widnes WA8 22 D8
Myrtle Rd M31 11 D3
Myrtle St
Crewe CW2 190 C3
Ellesmere Port CH65 70 C7
Mytholme Ave M44 11 C3
Mytton Dr CW5 204 D6

N

Nabbs Cl ST7 195 B2
Nabbswood Rd ST7 195 B2
Nab Cl SK10 63 C1
Nab La SK10 63 C1
Nairn Ave CW4 130 B2
Nairn Cl
Bebington CH63 43 D4
Warrington WA2 9 B3
Nancy View SK10 88 B8
Nansen Cl WA5 15 D7
Nansmoss La SK9 33 D1
Nant Peris CH1 117 D3
NANTWICH 204 D6
Nantwich Mus★ CW5 204 E5
Nantwich Rd
Audley ST7 209 B1
Barbridge CW5 187 B8
Betley ST7 208 E1
Broxton CH3 183 C1
Chorley Bank CW5 201 E2
Crewe CW2 190 C2
Ellesmere Port CH66 69 F3
Middlewich CW10 151 A7
Sound CW5 217 B5
Tarporley CW6 168 D7
Wimboldsley CW10 150 F5
Wistaston CW2, CW5 189 C2
Woore CW3 232 B1
Nantwich Sta CW5 204 E4
Nantwich Trade Yd CW5 204 F7
Nantwich Way 6 SK9 34 E5
Naomi Cl CH1 117 D5
Napier Gdns 3 ST7 195 A2
Napier Rd CH2 118 C8
Napier St WA1 16 C5
Napley Dr TF9 236 C2
NAPLEY HEATH 236 F1
Napley Rd TF9 236 D1
Nares Cl WA5 7 C1
Narrow La
Crewe, Crewe Green CW1 191 C3
Wardsend SK10 37 A1
Naseby Rd CW12 156 A3
Nathan Dr WA11 1 E6
Nathans Mdw CW12 179 C7
Nat La CW7 126 F2
Nat Lane Ret Pk CW7 126 F2
Naughton Lea WA8 12 D3
Naughton Rd 3 WA8 23 A8
Navan Ct CW1 190 B5
Navigation Cl WA7 50 D6
Navigation Ho 16 CW9 103 F8
Navigation Rd CW8 103 F7
Navigation St WA1 16 D5
Naylor Ave WA3 3 B8
Naylor Cl CH66 69 F8
Naylor Cres
Ellesmere Port CH66 69 F8
Nantwich CW5 205 A4
Naylor Ct
Ellesmere Port CH66 69 E6
12 Northwich CW9 103 F8
Naylor Gn CH66 69 F8
Naylor Pl CH66 69 F8
Naylor Rd
Overpool CH66 69 F7
Widnes WA8 13 D1
Naylor St WA1 16 B5
Naylor Wlk CH66 69 F7
Nazareth House La WA8 22 C7
Neal Ave SK8 34 A8
Neath Cl SK12 36 D5
Needham Cl WA7 23 D2
Needham Dr
Cranage CW4 130 A5
Hartford CW8 103 A4
Needhams Bank CW11 174 C6
Needhams Wharf Cl SK10 88 A1
Neills Rd WA5 6 B6
Neil St WA8 13 C2
Nelson Ave SK12 37 A3
Nelson Bldgs ST7 195 A1
Nelson Cl SK12 37 A3
Nelson Dr M44 11 E6
Nelson Gr ST7 193 F2
Nelson Ind Est ST7 194 C1
Nelson Rd CH65 70 C7
Nelson St
Chester CH1 237 C3
Congleton CW12 156 D2
Crewe CW2 190 C2
Macclesfield SK11 112 D7
Newton-le-W WA12 2 A3
5 Runcorn WA7 23 A2
Widnes WA8 23 A6
Nemos Cl WA6 73 C2
Neptune Cl WA7 50 D7
Nesfield Ct CW11 191 F7
Nesfield Dr CW11 191 F7
NESS 67 B4
Ness Acre La CH64 67 E8
Ness Botanic Gdns★ CH64 67 A3
Nesse Ho CH64 66 D8
NESS HOLT 66 F5
Nessina Gr CW2 205 F8
NESTON 66 D7
Neston Dr CH2 118 E5
Neston Gn CH66 69 D4
Neston High Sch CH64 41 F1
Neston Prim Sch CH64 66 E7
Neston Rd
Heswall CH63, CH64 41 F5
Neston CH64 67 B3
Willaston CH64 67 F8
Neston Road Cotts CH63 42 A6
Neston Sta CH64 66 E8
Neston Way SK9 34 D3
NETHER ALDERLEY 85 A6
Nether Alderley Mill★ SK10 85 A5
Nether Alderley Prim Sch SK10 85 A6
Netherfield WA8 22 E8
Netherfields SK9 85 A8
Nether Fold SK10 87 A8
Nether Lea CW4 130 C8
Netherley Rd WA8 12 A2
Netherpool Rd CH66 69 F8
NETHER TABLEY 80 F8
NETHERTON 74 A6
Netherton Dr WA6 74 A7
Netherton Farm Cotts WA6 74 A7
Neumann St CW9 104 B8
Nevada Cl WA5 15 C8
Neville Ave
St Helens WA9 1 B2
Warrington WA2 8 D1
Neville Cres WA5 15 A3
Neville Dr CH3 119 B1
Neville Rd
Bebington CH62 43 E8
Chester CH3 119 B1
Neville St
Crewe CW2 190 D1
Neville St *continued*
Newton-le-W WA12 2 A3
Nevin Cl SK7 36 A7
Nevin Rd CH1 117 D3
Nevis Dr CW2 189 D3
New Albert Terr WA7 23 B3
Newall Ave CW11 175 A5
Newall Cl CH3 166 B1
Newall Cres CW7 127 A1
Newarth Dr WA13 19 A2
New Bank Pl WA8 12 B1
New Bank Rd WA8 12 B1
New Barnet WA8 12 F4
Newbiggin Way 10 SK10 112 C8
Newbold Ct 9 CW12 156 F3
New Bold Ct WA9 6 A7
Newbold Way CW5 204 E3
Newborough Cl WA5 7 E2
NEW BOSTON 1 E7
Newbridge Cl
Runcorn WA7 50 C6
Warrington WA5 7 D2
Newbridge Rd CH65 70 F4
New Bridge Rd CH65, CH2 70 F3
Newburgh Cl WA7 24 D1
Newbury Ave
Crewe CW1 190 C7
5 Winsford CW7 149 A8
Newbury Cl
Cheadle SK8 35 A6
Widnes WA8 13 A3
Newbury Ct SK9 60 A6
Newbury Rd
Chester CH4 140 F6
Gatley SK8 34 C7
Newby Ct CW12 156 A1
Newcastle Rd
Astbury CW12 178 A7
Brereton Green CW11 153 F4
Congleton CW12 156 A2
Hassall Green CW11 176 A3
Nantwich CW5 205 B4
Shavington CW2, CW5 206 C3
Smallwood CW11 176 D6
Talke ST7 210 E7
Willaston CW5 205 E4
Woore CW3 232 E1
Newcastle Rd N CW11 153 E5
Newcastle Rd S CW11 153 F5
Newcastle Road Cvn Pk CW11 175 E5
Newcastle St CW1 190 A5
NEWCASTLE-UNDER-LYME 210 D3
NEWCHAPEL 195 E2
Newchapel Obsy★ ST7 195 E2
Newchapel Rd ST7 195 C3
New Chester Rd CH62 43 E7
Newchurch Com Prim Sch WA3 4 E2
Newchurch La WA3 4 F2
Newcombe Ave WA2 16 E8
New Cotts
Hampton Heath SY14 213 E7
Manley WA6 99 C7
New Crane Bank CH1 118 B1
New Crane St CH1 118 B1
Newcroft CH1 94 B2
New Cut Ind Est WA1 17 C7
New Cut La WA1 17 B7
Newdigate St
Crewe CW1 190 C4
Crewe CW1 190 C5
New Farm Cotts WA3 11 A7
New Farm Ct
Great Barrow CH3 120 E5
Malpas SY14 213 A5
NEWFIELD 172 E8
Newfield Ct WA13 19 A5
Newfield Dr CW1 190 E5
Newfield Rd WA13 18 D3
Newfield St CW11 175 B7
Newfield Terr WA6 73 B2
Newgate
1 Macclesfield SK11 112 D7
Wilmslow SK9 59 E7
Newgate Rd SK9 59 D7
Newgate St CH1 237 B2
Newgate Wlk CH1 237 B2
New Grosvenor Rd CH65 70 B7
NEWHALL 228 C8
New Hall Ave SK8 34 B7
Newhall Ct CH2 118 E6
New Hall La
Culcheth WA3 5 A2
Culcheth, Wigshaw WA3 4 E1
New Hall Manor CH64 41 E6
Newhall Rd CH2 118 F6
New Hall St SK10 87 D1
Newham Cl SK11 112 F3
New Hampshire Cl 7 WA5 15 B7
Newhaven Ct CW5 204 F5
Newhaven Rd WA2 8 B4
New Heyes CH64 41 E1
New Hey La CH64 68 A6
New Home Farm Cotts CH64 93 A7
NEW HORWICH 65 E6
New Horwich Rd SK23 65 E7
New Hos CW5 187 D6
New Houses CH3 143 B7
New Inn Cotts WA16 108 C8
New Inn La CW11 176 A2
New King St
Audley ST7 209 C1
Middlewich CW10 128 C2
New La
Appleton Thorn WA4 27 B5
Churton CH3 180 F6
Croft WA3 9 B7
Harthill CH3 183 F3
Winsford CW7 149 F4
Newland Cl WA8 12 C3
Newland Mews WA3 4 E5
Newlands Ave
Bramhall SK7 35 F8
Cheadle SK8 35 A7
Newlands Cl
Cheadle SK8 35 A7
Frodsham WA6 74 C6
Newlands Dr
Golborne WA3 3 D8
Wilmslow SK9 59 E5
Newlands Rd
Macclesfield SK10 111 E7
Warrington WA4 16 F2
Newland Way CW5 205 B4
NEW LANE END 4 A2
New Lane End WA3 4 A2
Newlyn Ave
Congleton CW12 178 F8
Macclesfield SK10 86 D1
Newlyn Cl WA7 50 B6
Newlyn Gdns WA5 14 D3
New Manchester Rd WA1 17 A7
Newman Cl CW12 156 B3
New Manor Rd WA4 51 B6
Newman's La CW5 219 D8
Newman St WA4 16 F3
Newmarket Cl 1 SK10 87 C4
New Market Wlk 10 WA1 16 B5
New Meadowside Residential Cvn Pk CW5 217 E5
NEW MILLS 39 D7
New Mills Central Sta SK22 39 B7
New Mills Heritage Ctr★ SK22 39 B7
New Mills Newtown Sta SK22 39 B6
New Mills Prim Sch SK22 39 B8
New Mills Sch & Sixth Form Ctr SK22 39 C8
Newmoore La WA7 24 F4
New Moss Rd M44 11 D6
Newnham Dr CH65 70 C4
New Pale Rd WA6 99 C6
New Park Ct SK22 39 D7
New Platt La CW4 107 B1
Newport Gr ST5 210 E2
Newquay Cl WA7 50 B6
Newquay Ct CW12 178 E8
Newquay Dr
Bramhall SK7 35 F7
Macclesfield SK10 111 D8
New Rd
Anderton CW9 78 D4
Antrobus CW9 27 D1
Astbury CW12 178 B4
Audley ST7 209 E3
Duddon CW6 145 B6
Ellesmere Port CH66 69 A8
Horwich End SK23 65 E6
Lymm WA13 18 E3
Marton CW12 132 D1
Mossend CW11 154 F2
Prestbury SK10 87 A7
Rostherne WA16 30 E3
Warrington WA4 16 C4
Whaley Bridge, Bridgemont SK23 39 F1
Winsford CW7 126 E2
Wrenbury CW5 216 D3
New Road Bsns Ctr CW7 126 E2
New Russia Hall Craft Ctr★ CH3 165 E5
Newry Ct CH2 118 D4
Newry Pk CH2 118 D4
Newry Pk E CH2 118 D4
NEWSBANK 132 F1
New School La CH66 44 B1
Newsham Cl WA8 12 B4
Newsholme Cl WA3 4 F3
Newspaper Ho WA5 14 D3
New St
Congleton CW12 156 E2
Haslington CW1 191 C5
Neston CH64 66 E5
New Mills SK22 39 D7
9 Runcorn WA7 23 A2
Sandbach CW11 174 D7
Widnes WA8 23 B8
Wilmslow SK9 59 E5
Newstead Cl SK12 36 D5
Newstead Rd WA8 21 F6
New Street Cotts CW12 157 A6
Newtech Sq CH5 92 F2
NEWTON
Chester 118 F5
Frodsham 74 D3
Tattenhall 166 E4
Newton Ave WA3 9 E5
Newton Bank
Middlewich CW10 128 B1
Newton Bank *continued*
Preston on t H WA4 51 B8
Newton Bank Sch WA12 2 E4
Newton Com Hospl WA12 2 B2
Newton Cotts CH3 166 C4
Newton Gdns WA3 4 A8
Newton Gr WA2 8 F3
Newton Hall CH2 118 F5
Newton Hall Ct CH2 118 F5
Newton Hall Dr CH2 118 F5
Newton Hall La WA16 58 E5
Newton Hall Mews 1 CW10 151 C8
Newton Heath CW10 128 B1
Newton Ho CH2 118 F5
Newton Hollow WA6 74 D1
NEWTONIA 128 B1
Newton La
Chester CH2 118 F4
Daresbury WA4 51 C8
Daresbury WA4 51 E7
Golborne WA12 2 E6
Tattenhall CH3 166 D4
NEWTON-LE-WILLOWS 2 B2
Newton-le-Willows Com High Sch WA12 2 D5
Newton-le-Willows Prim Sch WA12 2 C3
Newton-le-Willows Sta WA12 2 E3
Newton Park Dr WA12 2 F3
Newton Park View CH2 118 D4
Newton Pl CW12 156 F2
Newton Prim Sch CH2 118 E4
Newton Rd
Ellesmere Port CH65 70 C5
Golborne, Lowton Common WA3, WN7 4 A8
Golborne, Town of Lowton WA12, WA3 3 D5
Handforth SK9 34 A1
St Helens WA9 1 A3
Winwick WA2 8 A5
Newtons Cres CW11 191 F7
Newtons Gr CW11 191 E7
Newtons La CW11 191 E7
Newton St
Crewe CW1 190 D5
Macclesfield SK11 112 C7
NEWTOWN
Burwardsley 183 E8
Frodsham 49 D1
Newtown
Neston CH64 66 F7
Newchapel ST7 195 F2
NEWTOWN
New Mills 39 B6
Poynton 37 A3
Sound 217 E4
Widnes 23 A6
Newtown Cl CH1 237 B3
Newtown Prim Sch SK22 39 B6
New Warrington Rd CW9 79 C2
New William Cl M31 11 F4
NEW WOODHOUSES 227 E1
New York Cotts WA16 29 F2
Nicholas Ave CW9 104 C6
Nicholas Ct CH1 237 A2
Nicholas Rd
Weaverham CW8 77 D1
Widnes WA8 22 C8
Nicholas St Mews CH1 237 A2
Nicholas St CH1 237 A2
Nicholls St WA4 17 B2
Nicholson Ave SK10 87 E1
Nicholson Cl SK10 87 E1
Nicholson St WA1 15 F5
NICK I' TH' HILL 179 B4
Nickleby Rd SK12 36 E3
Nickleford Hall Dr WA8 12 F6
Nickolson Cl CH2 119 F8
Nicol Ave WA1 17 F8
Nidderdale Cl CW12 157 A5
Niddries Ct CW9 126 F7
Niddries La CW9 126 F7
Nield Ct CH2 118 D7
Nigel Gresley Cl CW1 191 A4
Nigel Rd CH60 41 C8
Nightingale Cl
Farndon CH3 180 F1
Handforth SK9 34 B1
Middlewich CW10 151 D6
Runcorn WA7 49 F5
Warrington WA3 9 F4
Nightingale Ct 4 CW7 149 D6
Nightingale Way ST7 193 B3
Nile St CW2 190 C2
Nine Hos The CH3 166 B1
Nixon Dr CW7 126 B2
Nixon Rd CW8 101 F3
Nixon's Row CW5 204 C5
Nixon St
Crewe CW1 189 F5
Macclesfield SK11 112 B8
No 1 Road N CW2 192 F1
No 1 Road S CW2 192 F1

No 2 Road N CW2 192 F1
No 2 Road S CW2 192 F1
No 156 CH1 237 C2
Noahs Ark La WA16 58 F1
Noble Cl WA3 9 E3
NO MAN'S HEATH 214 B4
Nook La
Antrobus CW9 53 E6
Golborne WA3 3 B8
Warrington, Fearnhead WA2 9 B2
Warrington WA4 17 A3
Nook The
Backford CH1 95 B4
Bramhall SK7 35 D5
Chester CH2 118 E4
Guilden Sutton CH3 119 C4
Hankelow CW3 230 C8
Saltney CH4 140 E6
Noon Ct WA12 2 B1
Noonsun Farm WA16 58 E1
Nora St WA1 16 C5
Norbreck Ave CW2 190 B2
Norbreck Cl WA5 15 A4
NORBURY 215 D4
Norbury Ave WA2 16 D8
Norbury Cl
Hough CW2 206 E3
Knutsford WA16 57 C3
Widnes WA8 13 E1
NORBURY COMMON 215 C6
Norbury Dr
Congleton CW12 156 E4
Middlewich CW10 151 B8
Norbury Hollow Rd SK7 37 B8
Norbury St
Macclesfield SK11 112 C7
Northwich CW9 104 B8
Norbury Town La SY13 215 C3
Norbury Way 9 SK9 34 D5
Norcott Ave WA4 16 D2
NORCOTT BROOK 52 C6
Norcott Dr WA5 6 F6
Norden Cl WA3 9 C5
Norfolk Cl M44 11 C5
Norfolk Dr WA5 14 E6
Norfolk Gr ST8 179 C1
Norfolk Ho ST7 210 D6
Norfolk House Prep Sch CW11 175 B7
Norfolk Pl WA8 22 C8
Norfolk Rd
Chester CH2 118 F4
Congleton CW12 156 E4
Ellesmere Port CH65 70 C5
Kidsgrove ST7 194 F2
Norfolk St WA7 23 B3
Norfolk Wlk SK10 86 F2
Norgrove Cl WA7 50 E8
Norland's La L35, WA8 12 F7
Norlands Pk WA8 12 F6
Norland St WA8 13 D1
Norleane Cres WA7 49 B8
NORLEY 100 F6
Norley Ave
Bebington CH62 43 E3
Ellesmere Port CH65 69 F6
Norley CE Prim Sch WA6 100 F5
Norley Cl WA5 15 E6
Norley Dr CH3 119 C1
Norley La CW8 101 A8
Norley Pl CW9 103 E5
Norley Rd
Cuddington CW8, WA6 101 E4
Kingsley WA6 75 A1
Norley WA6 100 D7
Sandiway CW8 102 A3
Norman Ave
Haydock WA11 2 A7
Newton-le-W WA12 2 E3
Normanby Cl WA5 15 E7
Norman Cl CH66 94 F8
Norman Dr CW7 149 C6
Normandy Ave 2 CW7 149 D8
Normandy Rd CH2 95 C1
Norman Ho 3 CW8 103 C5
Norman Rd WA7 23 A1
Normans Cotts 1 CH64 66 F7
Norman's Hall Farm SK10 63 B5
Norman's La WA4 52 F4
Norman St WA2 16 B6
Norman Way CH1 117 E5
Norreys Ave WA5 15 F8
Norris Rd CH1 117 E5
Norris St WA2 16 D8
North Ave WA2 16 B8
Northbank Ind Pk M44 11 F6
Northbank Wlk CW2 206 C8
North Brook Rd CW6 146 B7
Northbury Rd CH66 69 E1
North Cheshire Coll (Museum St Ctr) WA1 16 A4
North Cheshire Hospl WA4 26 D1
Northcote Rd SK7 35 F7
North Crofts CW5 204 E5
Northdale Rd WA1 17 A8
North Downs WA16 57 D2
North Dr
Heswall CH60 41 A7
High Legh WA16 29 C4
Northwich CW9 104 E7
Northern La WA8 12 A3
Northern Pathway CH4 237 C1
Northern Rise CH66 69 E4
Northfield Dr
Biddulph ST8 179 E2
Wilmslow SK9 60 D8
Northfield Pl CW2 206 C5
Northfields WA16 57 C3
NORTH FLORIDA 1 D8
North Florida Rd WA11 1 D8
Northgate CW6 146 B7
Northgate Ave
Chester CH2 237 B4
Macclesfield SK10 87 C1
Northgate Row CH1 237 B2
Northgate St CH1 237 A3
North Gn CH5 116 A6
Northlands CW3 232 C1
Northmead SK10 87 A5
Northolt Ct WA2 8 E1
North Par CH64 41 B2
North Park Brook Rd WA5 7 E1
North Rd
Altrincham WA15 32 A8
Bebington CH65 44 E3
Connah's Quay CH5 91 F2
Ellesmere Port CH65 70 B8
Halewood L26 21 A5
NORTH RODE 134 E2
North St
Chester CH3 119 A1
Congleton CW12 156 D3
Crewe CW1 190 C7
Haydock WA11 1 E6
Mount Pleasant ST7 195 B6
Newton-le-W WA12 1 F4
Saltney CH4 140 B7
Sandycroft CH5 116 A3
North Stafford St CW1 190 D4
Northumberland Rd M31 11 E2
North View
Crewe CW1 190 A6
Ellesmere Port CH66 69 C7
Middlewich CW10 128 B2
Warrington WA5 14 E7
Northward Rd SK9 59 F6
Northway
Chester CH4 141 A7
Lymm WA13 18 D4
Runcorn WA7 49 F8
Warrington WA2 8 B2
Widnes WA8 12 D1
Winnington CW8 78 D1
North Way
Holmes Chapel CW4 130 C3
Shavington CW2 206 D5
NORTHWICH 103 D8
Northwich Rd
Allostock CW4, WA16 106 E1
Antrobus CW9 53 B2
Dutton WA4 51 B2
Great Budworth CW9 78 F8
Knutsford WA16 56 D1
Runcorn, Brookvale WA7 50 C5
Weaverham CW8 102 E7
Northwich Ret Pk CW9 79 C1
Northwich Sta CW9 104 B8
Northwood Ave
Middlewich CW10 151 E5
Newton-le-W WA12 2 F3
Northwood La WA16 28 F1
Northwood Rd WA7 23 E2
NORTON 24 C1
Norton Ave
Saltney CH4 140 D6
Warrington WA5 14 E5
Norton Cotts WA7 50 E7
Norton Gate WA7 50 C8
Norton Hill WA7 24 C2
NORTON IN HALES 236 C1
Norton in Hales CE Prim Sch TF9 236 C2
Norton La
Runcorn, Norton WA7 24 D1
Runcorn, Town Park WA7 50 A8
Runcorn WA7 50 B8
Norton Priory Mus* WA7 24 B3
Norton Priory Walled Gdn* WA7 24 B3
Norton Rd CH3 119 C2
Nortons La CW6 122 F7
Norton's La CH3 98 B2
Norton St SK10 112 E8
Norton Station Rd WA7 50 D8
Norton View WA7 50 A8
Norton Village WA7 24 D1
Norton Way CW11 174 D7
Nortonwood La WA7 24 C1
Norville CH66 69 D7
Norwich Ave WA3 3 D8
Norwich Dr CH66 94 E8
Norwood Ave
Bramhall SK7 35 D5
Golborne WA3 3 F7
High Lane SK6 37 D7
Norwood Dr CH4 141 B6
Nottingham Cl WA1 17 E6
Nova Ct 14 CW1 190 B5
NOVA SCOTIA 125 C6
Nun House Cl CW7 127 B2
Nun House Dr CW7 127 B2
Nunsmere Cl CW7 127 B1
Nuns Rd CH1 237 A1
Nursery Ave WA15 31 E8
Nursery Cl
Crewe CW2 190 A2
Kidsgrove ST7 194 D1
Shavington CW2 206 C3
Widnes WA8 13 D3
Nursery Dr
Biddulph ST8 179 C2
Poynton SK12 36 D4
Nursery Gr M31 11 F4
Nursery La
Congleton CW12 156 E2
Nether Alderley SK10 84 D5
Siddington SK11 110 A3
Wilmslow SK9 59 F5
Nursery Pk WA6 100 B7
Nursery Rd
Barnton CW8 78 B3
Bollington SK10 87 E7
Oakhanger CW1, ST7 192 D3
Scholar Green ST7 194 E5
Nursery The CW8 103 C6
Nutfield Ave CW1 190 B7
Nuthurst Gdns 4 CW5 204 F5
Nuttall Ct WA3 9 C4
Nuttall St M44 11 E6

O

Oak Ave
Alsager ST7 193 E2
Disley SK12 39 A6
Golborne WA3 3 B8
Haydock WA11 1 E7
Irlam M44 11 D5
Macclesfield SK11 112 A5
Newton-le-W WA12 2 D3
Wilmslow SK9 59 F5
Winsford CW7 149 D7
Oak Bank
Alderley Edge SK9 60 A2
Disley SK12 39 A6
Oak Bank Cl CW5 205 E4
Oak Bank Dr SK10 63 B1
Oak Bank La CH2 119 C6
Oak Brow Cotts SK9 33 E4
Oak Cl SK9 59 F6
Oak Cotts
Styal SK9 33 E4
Wrenbury CW5 216 F4
Oakdale Ave
Frodsham WA6 74 D6
Warrington WA4 16 D1
Oakdale Cl
Broughton CH4 139 B3
Chorlton CW2 207 B3
Oakdene Ave
Ellesmere Port CH66 69 C5
Gatley SK8 34 C7
Warrington WA1 17 C7
Oakdene Cl CH62 43 D5
Oakdene Ct SK9 34 B1
Oakdene Way CW6 168 D8
Oak Dr
Cheadle SK7 35 C7
Higher Kinnerton CH4 161 A7
Middlewich CW10 151 D7
Runcorn WA7 49 C7
Scholar Green ST7 194 E6
Oakenbank La SK10 88 D7
Oakenclough Cl SK9 34 D2
Oakes Cnr CW5 219 E3
Oak Farm CW6 186 C5
Oakfield Ave
Chester CH2 118 E8
Knutsford WA16 57 C3
Wrenbury CW5 216 F3
Oakfield Cl
Alderley Edge SK9 60 B3
Bramhall SK7 35 E4
Wrenbury CW5 216 F3
Oakfield Com Prim Sch WA8 22 B8
Oakfield Dr
Chester CH2 118 E8
Widnes WA8 22 A8
Oakfield Rd
Alderley Edge SK9 60 B2
Bebington CH62 43 C8
Blacon CH1 117 D4
Ellesmere Port CH66 68 E8
Plumley WA16 80 F3
Poynton SK12 36 F4
Oakfield Rise CW4 130 B3
Oakfield Terr CH66 68 E8
Oakfold SK10 88 A6
Oak Gr
Ellesmere Port CH65 70 A3
Nantwich CW5 204 E3
Poynton SK12 36 D4
Oak Gr/Gelli Dderw CH4 140 D5
OAKGROVE 135 D7
Oak Grove Sch SK8 34 C7
OAKHANGER 192 C2
Oakhill Cl SK10 87 B4
Oak Ho
Chester CH2 118 C5
Oak Ho *continued*
7 Sandbach CW11 175 B6
Oak House La CW7 149 B8
Oakhurst Chase SK9 60 A2
Oakhurst Dr CW2 206 B7
Oak La
Astbury CW12 178 B4
Cuddington CW8 101 F2
Kerridge SK10 88 A6
Marton SK11 133 C5
Wilmslow SK9 59 F6
Oakland Ave CW1 191 C4
Oakland Ct SK12 36 D4
Oakland Gdns WA1 16 E7
Oaklands
Bebington CH62 43 D6
Guilden Sutton CH3 119 F4
Oaklands Ave CH3 166 B2
Oaklands Cl SK9 34 E1
Oaklands Cres CH3 166 B2
Oaklands Dr WA13 18 D2
Oaklands Inf Sch SK9 34 E1
Oaklands Rd
Golborne WA3 3 F7
Ollerton WA16 82 F6
Oaklands Sch CW7 149 B7
Oakland St
Warrington WA1 16 E7
Widnes WA8 23 A4
Oaklea Ave CH2 118 F4
Oak Lea Ave SK9 60 A5
Oakleaf Lo SK11 112 D5
Oakleigh WA16 82 C7
Oakleigh Ct CW12 155 F3
Oakleigh Ho SK10 88 B8
Oakleigh Rd SK8 34 E8
Oakleigh Rise CW8 78 E1
Oakley Cl CW11 175 A8
Oakley Ct CH65 70 C4
Oakley St CW1 190 C5
Oak Lo SK7 35 F7
Oak Mdw CW8 102 E7
OAKMERE 124 A7
Oakmere Barns CW8 124 A7
Oakmere Cl CW11 174 F7
Oakmere Dr
Chester CH3 142 B8
Ellesmere Port CH66 69 F1
Warrington WA5 14 F3
Oakmere Hall CW8 101 E1
Oakmere Pl 9 CW1 190 B5
Oakmere Rd
Handforth SK9 34 D5
Winsford CW7 149 B8
Oakmere St 7 WA7 23 A2
Oak Mews SK9 34 C1
Oakmoore WA7 24 F4
Oak Rd
Chelford SK11 84 A3
Chester CH4 140 F6
Hooton CH66 43 E1
Lymm WA13 18 C3
Mottram St Andrew SK10 86 B7
Paddockhill WA16 59 B5
Partington M31 11 D2
Warrington WA5 14 F3
Oaks Com Prim Sch The CH65 70 D3
Oaks Dr The CH2 118 D7
Oaks Gdns WA5 14 E4
Oaks Pl WA8 23 A7
Oak St
Crewe CW2 190 D3
Croft WA3 9 A7
Ellesmere Port CH65 70 C7
Northwich CW9 79 A1
Rode Heath ST7 193 E8
Sandbach CW11 174 D8
Oaks The
Bebington CH62 43 C8
Goostrey CW4 130 D8
Mobberley WA16 58 E1
5 Northwich CW9 103 E6
Widnes WA8 13 D4
Oaksway CH60 41 C6
Oakthorn Gr WA11 1 C6
Oaktree Cl
Barnton CW8 78 B4
Tarporley CW6 146 D2
Oak Tree Cl CW1 190 F5
Oaktree Ct CH2 119 A3
Oak Tree Ct CW6 122 E2
Oak Tree Dr CW1 190 F5
Oak Tree Gate CW3 229 F3
Oaktree La ST7 210 D5
Oak Tree La CW10 129 E7
Oak View
Knutsford WA16 57 C1
Marton SK11 133 C5
Speke L24 21 A3
Oak Villas CW5 216 F4
Oakways WA4 26 D5
OAKWOOD 9 F4
Oakwood WA16 56 F3
Oakwood Ave
Warrington WA1 16 E7
Wilmslow SK9 59 E6
Oakwood Avenue Com Prim Sch WA1 16 D7
Oakwood Cl CH66 69 D1
Oakwood Cres
Crewe CW2 189 E4
Sandbach CW11 175 E6
Oakwood Ct WA14 31 B8
Oakwood Dr SK10 87 C6
Oakwood Gate WA3 9 D4
Oakwood Ho
Alderley Edge SK9 85 B8
Barnton CW8 78 A2
Oakwood La
Altrincham WA14 31 B8
Barnton CW8 78 A2
Sandbach CW11 174 B8
Oakwood Pk CH62 43 D5
Oakwood Rd
Disley SK12 38 D6
Rode Heath ST7 193 F8
Oak Wood Rd WA16 29 F2
Oakworth Cl CW12 156 C3
Oathills SY14 213 B5
Oathills Cl CW6 146 D1
Oathills Dr CW6 146 D1
Oathills Lea CW6 146 D1
Oatlands SK9 85 B8
Oat Market 3 CW5 204 E5
Oban Dr CH60 41 A8
Oban Gr WA2 9 A3
Obelisk Way CW12 156 C3
OCCLESTONE GREEN 151 B2
O'Connell Cl WA11 1 C6
Oddfellows Pas CW10 128 B1
Odeon Bldg CH1 237 A3
Offal Pit La WA6 74 F2
Offley Ave CW11 175 B7
Offley Prim Sch CW11 175 B7
Offley Rd CW11 175 B7
Off Spring Bank SK22 39 C8
Ogden Rd SK7 35 D5
Oglet La L24 45 C6
Oil Sites Rd CH65 71 C5
Okell St WA7 23 A2
Old Albert Terr WA7 23 B3
Old Alder La WA2, WA5 7 D5
Old Applecroft CW11 174 C5
OLD BOSTON 2 A8
Old Boston WA11 2 A7
Old Boston Trad Est WA11 2 B8
Old Brickworks Ind Est SK10 63 E4
Old Butt La ST7 194 D2
OLDCASTLE HEATH 223 E8
Oldcastle La SY14 222 E8
Old Cherry La WA13 28 A7
Old Chester Ct CW5 187 D6
Old Chester Rd
Barbridge CW5 187 D6
Ellesmere Port CH66 69 D4
Helsby WA6 73 C4
Higher Walton WA4 25 F7
Old Church Cl CH65 70 C7
Old Coach Rd
Brown Knowl SY14, CH3 199 B6
Kelsall CW6 122 D5
Runcorn WA7 22 F3
Old Constabulary The 1 CW5 204 D5
Old Court Ho The 9 WA16 57 A2
Olde George The CH1 237 B3
Old Farm Cl
Macclesfield SK10 87 A2
Willaston CH64 68 A8
Old Farm Cotts CH1 116 E3
Old Farm Mews SK8 35 C7
Oldfield Cres CH4 140 F5
Oldfield Dr
Chester CH3 119 C2
Mobberley WA16 58 A4
Oldfield La WA14 20 F4
Oldfield Prim Sch CH3 119 C3
Oldfield Rd
Ellesmere Port CH65 70 B5
Lymm WA13 18 C4
Sandbach CW11 174 F3
Oldgate WA8 22 C7
Old Gate Cl CW10 151 B7
Old Gorse Cl CW2 189 E3
OLD HALL 15 C8
Old Hall Cl WA4 26 A8
Oldhall Cres SK9 34 E3
Old Hall Ct
Ashton Hayes CH3 121 F7
Malpas SY14 213 B3
Old Hall Dr
Ellesmere Port CH65 70 B4
Horwich End SK23 65 E4
Old Hall Gdns CH2 237 C4
Old Hall La
Elton CH2 72 B3
Hargrave CH3 144 A1
Over Tabley WA16 55 E4
Woodford SK7 35 D1
Old Hall Pk CH3 119 F5
Old Hall Pl CH1 237 A2
Old Hall Rd
Northwich CW9 104 A5
Warrington WA5 15 D7
Oldhall St SY14 213 B3
Old Hall St SK10 87 D1
Oldhams Hill
Kingsmead CW8 103 F8
Winnington CW8 78 F1
Oldham's Rise SK10 87 D3
Oldham St
Bollington SK10 88 B8
Warrington WA4 16 D3
Old Hey Wlk WA12 2 C1
Old Higher Rd WA8 21 D5
Oldhill Cl ST7 210 E5

Old Hutte La L26........21 A6
Old Knutsford Rd
ST7..................194 A6
Old La
Acton Bridge CW8........76 F3
Antrobus CW9..........53 C3
Davenham CW9.........104 D2
Heswall CH60..........41 D8
Mouldsworth CH3........99 C2
Pulford CH4...........162 E2
Old Library The CW7....126 E1
Old Liverpool Rd WA5....15 E4
Old Man of Mow★
ST7..................195 D8
Old Market Pl
8 Knutsford WA16.......57 A2
12 Warrington WA1......16 B5
Old Marsh Farm Ho
CH5..................116 A8
Old Mill Cl
Heswall CH60..........41 B7
Lymm WA13.............19 C6
Old Mill Ct CH2........118 D6
Old Mill La
Hazel Grove SK7........37 A8
Higher Whitley WA4......52 F3
Macclesfield SK11......112 E6
Old Mill Pl CH3........166 B1
Old Mill Rd CW11.......175 C6
Old Mill The
Crowton CW8...........76 B2
Ellesmere Port CH66......69 C7
OLD MOSS.............144 D7
Old Moss La
Fowley Common WA3......5 E6
Tarvin CH3............144 D7
Old Newcastle Rd
CW5..................205 D4
Old Orch SK9...........60 A7
Old Orchard The
Antrobus CW9...........53 C4
Cuddington CW8........101 F4
Old Paddock The
CW4..................130 F8
Old Pale Cotts CW8.....123 C7
Old Pale Hts CW8.......123 C7
Old Park Rd CW1........207 D8
Old Pearl La CH3.......119 B1
Old Penny La WA11.......2 B8
Old Pewterspear La
WA4...................26 E4
Old Port Sq CH1........118 B2
Old Pump Ho The
CH66..................68 E8
Old Quay Cl CH64........66 C7
Old Quay La CH64........66 D7
Old Quay St WA7.........23 B3
Old Quays The WA4.......16 E3
Old Rd
Anderton CW9...........78 D3
Audley ST7............209 E3
Furness Vale SK23.......39 D4
Handforth SK9...........34 D3
Horwich End, New Horwich
SK23..................65 E6
Horwich End SK23........65 F3
Warrington WA4..........16 B4
Wilmslow SK9............60 B8
Old Ribbon Mill The
SK11.................112 D6
Old School Cl
Barnton CW8............78 B2
Farndon CH3...........180 E2
Kidsgrove ST7..........195 A1
Neston CH64.............66 F5
Old School House La
WA2.....................8 A7
Old School La SK8.......35 A8
Old Seals Way CH1......118 A3
Old Smithy La WA13......18 C2
Old Smithy Row SK22.....39 C7
Old Stack Yd CH3.......120 E6
Old Tannery CW5........204 F6
Old Upton La WA8........12 E4
Old Vicarage Gdn
CW3..................230 A3
Old Vicarage La CW8....103 C5
Old Vicarage Rd CH64....68 A8
Old Wargrave Rd WA12....2 C3
Old Warrington Rd
CW9....................79 A2
Old Wesleyan
Schoolhouse The
SK22...................39 B6
Old Whint Rd WA11.......1 A6
Old Woman's La CH3.....142 D7
OLD WOODHOUSES........227 C2
Old Wrexham Rd CH4.....141 C7
O'leary St WA2..........16 C7
Olive Dr CH64...........66 F8
Olive Gr ST5...........210 D1
Oliver Cl SK10..........87 F7
Olive Rd CH64...........66 E8
Oliver Ho CH66..........69 D4
Oliver La CH66..........69 D4
Oliver St WA2...........16 B6
Ollersett Ave SK22......39 D8
Ollersett Dr SK22.......39 D8
Ollersett Ho SK22.......39 D8
Ollershaw La CW9........79 C4
OLLERTON...............82 F6
Ollerton Cl WA4.........17 B3
Ollerton Pk WA5..........6 E7
Ollerton Rd SK9.........34 E5
Ollier St 1 WA8.........23 A7
Olympia Pl WA5..........15 B7
Omega Bvd WA5...........6 D1
One Oak La SK9..........60 F7
ONNELEY...............232 F3
Onslow Rd CH1..........117 D4
ONSTON..................76 E1
Onston La CW8..........101 E8
On The Air', The
Broadcasting Mus &
Vintage Sound Shop★
CH1...................237 B2
Openshaw La M44.........11 E6
Orange Gr WA2............8 E2
Orchard Ave
Acton Bridge CW8........76 E4
Lymm WA13..............18 F3
Partington M31..........11 F4
Whaley Bridge SK23......65 D7
Orchard Brow WA3........11 A2
Orchard Cl
Barnton CW8............78 B3
Bunbury CW6...........185 F8
Cheadle SK8.............35 C7
Chester CH2............118 D5
Ellesmere Port CH66......69 F1
Frodsham WA6...........74 A6
Goostrey CW4..........107 E1
Higher Wincham CW9......80 A6
Macclesfield SK11......112 B6
Middlewich CW10.......151 D7
Poynton SK12............36 E3
Weaverham CW8...........77 D1
Wilmslow SK9............59 F5
Winsford CW7...........149 D7
Orchard Cotts CW6......146 D1
Orchard Cres
Kidsgrove ST7..........194 D1
Nantwich CW5..........204 E3
Nether Alderley SK10.....84 F6
Orchard Croft CH3......119 E5
Orchard Ct
Alsager ST7............193 E4
3 Chester CH3..........119 A1
Croft WA3................9 A8
Frodsham WA6............74 A8
Haslington CW1.........191 D4
Orchard Dene CW8......101 D5
Orchard Dr
Handforth SK9...........34 E2
Little Leigh CW8........77 D5
Neston CH64.............66 E5
Orchard Gdns
Congleton CW12........156 A3
Tarporley CW6..........168 D8
Weaverham CW8...........77 B1
Orchard Gn SK9..........60 B1
Orchard Gr CH3.........180 F1
Orchard Haven CH66......69 E1
Orchard Ho SK10.........86 E1
Orchard La CH66.........69 A8
Orchard Park La CH2.....72 B4
Orchard Pk CH2..........72 B4
Orchard Pl
Helsby WA6..............73 C4
Poynton SK12............36 D4
Orchard Rd
Ellesmere Port CH65......70 B2
Lymm WA13..............19 B5
Whaley Bridge SK23......65 D7
Orchard Rise CW9.......126 E8
Orchard St
Chester CH1............237 A3
Crewe CW1..............190 C5
Northwich CW9..........104 B8
Warrington, Fearnhead
WA2.....................9 A2
Warrington, Stockton Heath
WA4....................26 C8
Warrington WA1..........16 C5
Willaston CW5..........205 D6
Orchards The
Holt LL13..............196 D8
Pickmere WA16...........79 F7
Saltney CH4............140 D6
Shavington CW2.........206 C4
Orchard The
Alderley Edge SK9.......85 B8
Chester CH3............142 A8
Disley SK12.............38 D6
Helsby WA6..............73 B2
Orchard Way
Congleton CW12........156 A3
Kelsall CW6............122 D5
Widnes WA8..............12 A3
Orchard Wlk
Neston CH64.............66 E8
3 Runcorn WA7...........49 F7
Orchid Cl
Huntington CH3.........142 A6
Irlam M44...............11 E8
Orchid Way WA9...........6 B7
Orchil Cl CH66..........69 A6
Ordnance Ave
Warrington, Birchwood
WA3....................10 A5
Warrington WA3...........9 F4
Ordsall Cl CW11........174 F3
ORFORD...................8 D2
Orford Ave
Disley SK12.............38 D6
Warrington WA1, WA2.....16 C7
Orford Cl
Golborne WA3.............3 A7
Hale L24................21 E2
High Lane SK6...........37 E7
Orford Gn WA2............8 D1
Orford La WA2...........16 B7
Orford Rd WA2...........16 E8
Orford St WA1...........16 B5
Organsdale Cotts
CW6...................123 B5
Oriel Ho CH2...........118 C4
Orion Bvd WA5............6 E1
Orkney Cl
3 Ellesmere Port
CH65...................70 C1
Widnes WA8..............13 E3
Orlando Dr WA5..........15 C7
Orme Cl
Macclesfield SK10.......87 D3
Prestbury SK10..........87 A8
Orme Cres SK10..........87 D3
Ormerod Cl CW11........175 C5
Ormesby Gr CH63.........43 B6
Orme St SK9.............60 A1
Ormond Cl WA8...........12 C2
Ormonde Rd CH2.........118 C4
Ormonde St CH1.........237 C3
Orrell Cl WA5...........15 A6
Orton Cl CW7...........127 A4
Orwell Cl SK9...........34 D2
Osborne Ave WA2..........8 D1
Osborne Cl CW11........174 D5
Osborne Gr CW2.........206 C5
Osborne Rd
Golborne WA3.............3 E7
Warrington WA4..........16 B1
Osbourne Cl
Bebington CH62..........43 E7
Wilmslow SK9............60 D6
OSCROFT................121 E2
Osier Cl CH2............72 C3
Osmere Cl SY13.........226 B1
Osnath Wks WA2..........16 B6
Osprey Ave CW7.........149 D5
Osprey Cl
Middlewich CW10.......151 D5
Runcorn WA7.............49 F5
Warrington WA2...........8 E3
Osprey Ct CH2..........237 A4
Osprey Dr SK9...........60 C8
Osprey View ST7........195 D3
Ossett Cl WA7...........50 D8
Ossmere Cl CW11........174 F8
Ostler's La WA16.........58 E7
Oteley Ave CH62.........43 D8
Otters Bank 2 CW7......126 A1
Ottersbank Mews
CW8...................123 F3
OUGHTRINGTON............19 C4
Oughtrington Com Prim
Sch WA13...............19 B4
Oughtrington Cres
WA13....................19 B4
Oughtrington La WA13....19 A2
Oughtrington View
WA13....................19 B4
Oulton Ave CH2.........118 E7
Oulton Ct WA4...........17 B2
Oulton Dr CH2..........155 F3
Oulton Mill La CW6.....147 B7
Oulton Pl CH1..........237 B3
Our Lady Mother of the
Saviour RC Prim Sch
WA7.....................50 A6
Our Lady of Lourdes RC
Prim Sch M31............11 E3
Our Lady of Perpetual
Succour RC Prim Sch
WA8.....................22 A8
Our Lady's RC Inf & Jun
Sch CH65...............70 A3
Our Lady's RC Prim Sch
WA4.....................16 E3
Ousel Nest CW8.........101 D4
Out La CH3.............184 C6
Outwood Dr SK8..........34 A8
Outwood La M90..........33 C7
Outwood La W M90........33 B8
Outwood Prim Sch
SK8.....................34 D7
Outwood Rd SK8..........34 B7
Oval The
Ellesmere Port CH65......70 C3
Gatley SK8...............34 B8
Ovenhouse La SK10.......87 E7
Oven La SK11...........114 D5
OVER...................149 B8
Overdale La CW8........101 D1
Overdale Rd
New Mills SK12...........38 F6
Willaston CH64...........43 A1
Overdene Rd CW7........149 D8
Overfields WA16..........57 D3
Over Hall Com Prim Sch
CW7....................149 B7
Over Hall Dr CW7.......149 C7
Overhill Dr SK9..........60 E7
Overhill La SK9..........60 E7
Overhill Rd SK9..........60 D7
OVER KNUTSFORD..........57 C1
OVER LEIGH..............65 F6
Overleigh Ct CH4.......141 D7
Overleigh Rd CH4.......141 C7
Overleigh St Mary's CE
Prim Sch CH4...........141 D6
Overleigh Terr CH4.....141 C7
OVER PEOVER.............83 A1
Over Pl WA16.............82 C8
OVERPOOL................69 F7
Overpool Gdns CH66......69 F3
Overpool Rd
Ellesmere Port CH66......70 A2
Ellesmere Port, Great Sutton
CH65, CH66..............69 F5
Overpool Sta CH66........69 E6
Over Rd
Church Minshull CW5....172 A7
Winsford CW7...........149 F1
Over St John's CE Prim
Sch CW7...............126 B1
OVER TABLEY.............56 A5
OVERTON.................74 C7
Overton Cl
Congleton CW12.........156 C3
Middlewich CW10........151 B8
Overton Dr WA6...........74 C6
Overton Heath La
SY14...................212 F5
Overton Rd ST8.........179 F6
Overton Way 2 SK9.......34 D5
Overway CW7............126 E1
Overwood Ave CH1.........94 E1
Overwood La
Blacon CH1.............117 C4
Mollington CH1...........94 E1
Ovington Cl WA7..........49 F3
Owen Cl CH1............117 E6
Owens Cnr WA4...........26 D3
Owen St
Crewe CW2..............190 C2
Northwich CW9..........104 B8
Warrington WA2...........16 A7
Owlers The SK23..........65 E6
Owley Wood Rd CW8.......77 E1
Owlhurst The SK10........88 B8
Owl Ind Est The CH5.....116 B6
Owlsfield WA12............2 E3
Oxborough Cl WA8.........12 F4
Oxenham Rd WA2............8 A3
Oxford Cl CH66...........94 E8
Oxford Ct WA1............16 D6
Oxford Dr
Halewood L26.............21 A8
Heswall CH63.............41 F6
Oxford Gr M44............11 C6
Oxford Rd
Chester CH4.............140 F6
Macclesfield SK11.......112 B7
Runcorn WA7..............49 A8
Oxford St
Crewe CW1..............190 B5
Newton-le-W WA12..........2 B3
Warrington WA4...........16 C4
Widnes WA8...............23 B7
Ox-Hey Cres ST8........179 D1
Ox-Hey Dr ST8..........179 D1
Oxhey Fst Sch ST8......179 E1
Oxheys WA7...............50 C8
Oxheys La CW6..........169 C8
Oxmead Cl WA2.............9 B1
Oxmoor Cl WA7............50 A5
Oxney Cl SK11...........111 F8
Oxton Cl WA8.............12 C4
Oxton Gn CH66............69 D4

P

PACKMOOR................195 F1
Packmoor Prim Sch
ST7....................195 F1
Packsaddle Pk SK10.......86 E5
Padarn Cl CH4...........140 D5
PADDINGTON...............17 A8
Paddington Bank WA1......16 F6
Paddock Brow SK10........87 A5
Paddock Chase SK12.......36 F6
Paddock Cl SK23..........64 F4
Paddock Dr CH64..........41 D2
PADDOCKHILL..............59 A4
Paddock Hill La WA16.....59 A3
Paddock La
Audlem CW3..............230 B2
Horwich End SK23.........65 F5
Kettleshulme SK23........64 F4
Lymm WA13................19 C7
Partington WA13, WA14....20 B5
Paddock Rd CH4..........141 E1
Paddock Rise WA7.........49 E4
Paddock Row CH1.........237 B2
Paddocks Gn CW12........178 F8
Paddocks The
Prestbury SK10...........87 A5
Whitegate CW8...........125 B6
Paddock The
Chester CH4.............141 B7
Ellesmere Port CH66......69 D3
Elton CH2................72 A3
Handforth SK9............34 D4
Hartford CW8............103 C3
Hassall Green CW11......175 F2
Helsby WA6...............73 C2
Heswall CH60.............41 C8
Horwich End SK23.........65 F6
Lymm WA13................19 C4
Sandbach CW11..........175 B7
Tarporley CW6...........146 D1
Willaston CW5...........205 D4
Paddock View CW10.......128 C2
Paddock Way CH4.........161 A7
Paddock Wlk CW8.........101 D5
PADGATE...................8 F1
Padgate Bsns Ctr WA1.....17 B8
Padgate Com High Sch
WA2.......................8 F2
Padgate La
Warrington, Padgate
WA1......................16 F8
Warrington WA1...........16 D7
Padgate Sta WA1...........9 A1
Padgbury Cl CW12........156 A1
Padgbury La CW12........156 A1
Padge La CH3............183 C2
Padmore Cl CW1..........190 A7
Padston Dr ST7..........193 B3
Padstow Cl
Crewe CW1..............190 C8
Macclesfield SK10.......111 E8
Warrington WA5...........14 E3
Padstow Dr SK7...........35 F7
Padstow Sq WA7...........50 B5
Padworth Pl CW1.........173 B1
Page Gr CW2.............206 B3
Page La WA8..............13 C1
Paignton Cl WA5..........14 E4
Painswick Rd CH66........69 E2
Paisley Ave CH62.........43 E4
PALACE FIELDS............50 A6
Palace Fields Ave WA7....50 A6
Palace Fields Local Ctr
WA7......................50 A6
Palace Fields Prim Sch
WA7......................50 A6
Palace Hey CH64..........67 A5
Palatine Cl CH1.........117 D6
Palatine Ind Est WA4.....16 C3
Palgrave Cl CH1.........118 A5
Palin Dr WA5.............14 F6
Palliser Cl WA3..........10 A3
Pall Mall CW5...........204 E5
Palma Ave M90............33 B8
Palmer Cl 3 CW9.........103 F5
Palmer Cres WA5..........15 D8
Palmer Rd CW11..........175 C5
Palmerston Cl CW1.......191 C5
Palmerstone Cl CH1......118 B4
Palmerston Rd SK11......112 A7
Palmerston St SK10.......88 B8
Palmerston Way ST8......179 D1
Palm Gr CH66.............70 A1
Palmyra Sq N WA1.........16 A5
Palmyra Sq S WA1.........16 A5
PANDY...................222 A3
Pangbourne Cl WA4........26 E6
Panton Pl CH2...........118 F3
Panton Rd CH2...........118 F3
Parade Rd M90............33 C7
Parade The
1 Alderley Edge SK9......60 A1
Blacon CH1..............117 E5
Culcheth WA3...............4 E3
Neston CH64..............41 B1
Paradise CH4............237 B1
PARADISE GREEN.........171 E6
Paradise La CW5.........171 E7
Paradise Mill Mus★
SK11....................112 D7
Paradise St SK11........112 C7
Paragon Cl WA8...........13 B5
Parbold Ct WA8...........22 D8
Parc Ddiwydiannol
Glannau Dyfrdwy/
Deeside Ind Pk CH5.......92 E2
Parc Ddiwydiannol Y Ffin/
Borders Ind Pk The
CH4.....................140 C7
Parchments The WA12.......2 D4
Parish Cl ST7...........193 B4
Park Ave
Bramhall SK7.............35 D5
Furness Vale SK23........39 D3
Haydock WA11..............1 A6
Poynton SK12.............36 E4
Saltney CH4.............140 E6
Saughall CH1..............94 A2
Talke ST7...............210 E8
Tattenhall CH3..........166 B2
Warrington WA4...........16 D3
Weaverham CW8............77 D1
Widnes WA8...............13 B1
Wilmslow SK9.............60 C8
Winsford CW7............127 A3
Park Ave N WA12...........2 C2
Park Ave S WA12...........2 C2
Park Bank CW12..........156 F2
Park Brook Rd SK11......112 A8
Park Bvd WA1.............16 B4
Park Cl CH3.............121 B2
Park Cres
Cuddington CW8..........101 F4
Furness Vale SK23........39 D3
Handforth SK9............34 B1
Warrington WA4...........26 D6
Park Ct
Chester CH1.............237 C2
Frodsham WA6.............74 A8
Runcorn WA7..............49 A8
1 Warrington WA1.........16 A5
Parkdale Ind Est WA1.....16 C4
Parkdale Rd WA1..........17 A7
Park Dr
Chester CH2.............119 A4
Ellesmere Port CH65......70 B3
Handforth SK9............34 B1
Wistaston CW2...........205 F8
Park Drive Gdns CW2.....205 F8
Park Dr S CH2...........119 A4
PARK END................209 A4
Parker Ave CW8..........103 A6
Parker Dr CH3...........180 E1
Parker Dr S CH3.........180 F1
Parker's Bldgs CH1......237 C3
Parkers Ct WA7...........49 E6
Parker's Rd CW1.........190 A8
Parker's Row CH3........180 F6
Parker St
Macclesfield SK11.......112 E7
Runcorn WA7..............23 B3
Warrington WA1...........16 A5
Parker Way CW12.........156 A3

Park Est CW2 ... 206 D5
Parkett Heyes Rd
SK11 ... 111 E7
Parkfield CW1 ... 173 A1
Parkfield Ave WA4 ... 17 A4
Parkfield Dr
Ellesmere Port CH65 ... 70 A3
Helsby WA6 ... 73 B3
Nantwich CW5 ... 204 E4
Parkfield Rd
Broughton CH4 ... 139 C3
Knutsford WA16 ... 82 B8
Northwich CW9 ... 104 C8
Parkfields La WA2 ... 8 F2
Parkgate WA16 ... 57 C3
PARKGATE
Neston ... 41 C1
Over Peover ... 108 B8
Parkgate Ave WA16 ... 108 B8
Parkgate Ct
Chester CH1 ... 118 B4
Warrington WA4 ... 16 C2
Parkgate Ho
Neston CH64 ... 41 B1
Neston CH64 ... 41 B2
Parkgate La
Heswall CH64 ... 41 F5
Knutsford WA16 ... 57 C3
Parkgate Prim Sch
CH64 ... 41 C1
Parkgate Rd
Blacon CH1 ... 118 A6
Macclesfield SK11 ... 112 C4
Neston CH64 ... 66 D8
Puddington CH66 ... 68 C2
Saughall CH1 ... 94 C3
Warrington WA4 ... 16 D1
Woodbank CH1 ... 93 E7
Parkgate Trad Est
WA16 ... 57 C4
Parkgate Way
7 Handforth SK9 ... 34 D4
Runcorn WA7 ... 50 D7
Park Gn SK11 ... 112 D7
Park Gr SK11 ... 112 C6
Parkhill Ct WA16 ... 57 B1
Park House Dr
Prestbury SK10 ... 87 A8
Sandbach CW11 ... 175 C8
Parkhouse Ind Est
ST5 ... 210 F1
Park House La SK10 ... 87 A8
Park House Mews
CW11 ... 175 D8
Parkhouse Rd E ST5 ... 210 F1
Parkhouse Rd W ST5 ... 210 E1
Park La
Audley ST7 ... 209 B4
Congleton CW12 ... 156 F2
Frodsham WA6 ... 74 B8
Hargrave CH3 ... 144 E3
Hartford CW8 ... 103 B4
Hatherton CW5 ... 219 E4
Higher Walton WA4 ... 25 F5
Little Bollington WA14 ... 20 B2
Littleton CH3 ... 119 F3
Macclesfield SK11 ... 112 C6
Macclesfield SK11 ... 112 D7
Moulton CW9 ... 126 F7
Pickmere CW9, WA16 ... 79 E8
Poynton SK12 ... 36 F3
Pulford CH4 ... 162 E5
Sandbach CW11 ... 174 F6
Parkland Cl WA4 ... 27 B4
Parkland Dr CH2 ... 72 B3
Parklands
Ellesmere Port CH66 ... 69 D6
Kidsgrove ST7 ... 195 B1
Widnes WA8 ... 12 C3
Parklands Com Prim Sch
CH66 ... 69 D5
Parklands Dr
Chorlton CW2 ... 207 E3
Heswall CH60 ... 41 C6
Parklands Gdns CH66 ... 69 D6
Parklands The
Congleton CW12 ... 157 A2
Middlewich CW10 ... 151 B7
Parklands View CH66 ... 69 D5
Parklands Way SK12 ... 36 E4
Parkland View CW5 ... 204 D4
Park Lane Sch SK11 ... 112 B6
Parklea CH66 ... 69 D6
Parkleigh CW12 ... 156 E2
Park Mills Cl CW5 ... 205 D5
Park Mount Cl SK11 ... 112 A6
Park Mount Dr SK11 ... 112 A6
Park Prim Sch The
WA7 ... 24 A1
Park Rd
Bebington, Eastham
CH62 ... 43 F6
Congleton CW12 ... 156 E3
Ellesmere Port CH65 ... 70 C4
Golborne WA3 ... 3 A7
Haslington CW1 ... 191 D5
Heswall CH60 ... 41 B8
High Lane SK12 ... 38 A6
Horwich End SK23 ... 65 D6
Little Budworth CW6 ... 124 F1
Lymm WA13 ... 29 D8
Middlewich CW10 ... 128 C1
Nantwich CW5 ... 204 E3
New Mills SK22 ... 39 C7
North Rode CW12 ... 134 F2
Park Rd *continued*
Partington, Warburton
WA13 ... 19 C8
Runcorn WA7 ... 49 A8
Tarporley CW6 ... 146 D2
Thornton-le-M CH2 ... 71 E1
Warrington, Orford WA2 ... 8 D1
Warrington WA5 ... 14 E6
Widnes WA8 ... 13 B1
Willaston CH64 ... 68 B8
Willaston(nr Nantwich)
CW5 ... 205 C5
Wilmslow SK9 ... 59 F7
Winnington CW8 ... 78 D1
Park Rd N WA12 ... 2 E4
Park Rd S WA12 ... 2 D2
Park Rd W CH4 ... 141 A7
Park Road Com Prim Sch
WA5 ... 14 E6
Parkroyal Com Sch
SK11 ... 112 C7
Parkside Bsns Pk WA3 ... 3 A8
Parkside Cl
High Lane SK6 ... 37 D8
Neston CH64 ... 66 D8
Parkside Ct WA8 ... 13 A2
Parkside Rd WA12, WA2 ... 3 B2
Park St
Bollington SK10 ... 88 B8
Chester CH1 ... 237 B2
Congleton CW12 ... 156 E2
Haydock WA11 ... 1 A6
Macclesfield SK11 ... 112 D7
Neston CH64 ... 66 E8
Northwich CW8 ... 103 E7
Parkstone Dr CW1 ... 190 B8
Parksway WA1 ... 17 D7
Park The
Christleton CH3 ... 142 E8
Warrington WA5 ... 14 D3
Park Vale Rd SK11 ... 112 C6
Park View
Audlem CW3 ... 230 C8
Bebington CH62 ... 43 C8
Congleton CW12 ... 156 E3
Hazel Grove SK7 ... 37 B8
Little Bollington WA14 ... 20 B2
Nantwich CW5 ... 204 F6
Newton-le-W WA12 ... 2 E3
Warrington WA2 ... 8 E3
Parkview Ct CH60 ... 40 F8
Park View Ct SK12 ... 36 E4
Parkview Pk WA13 ... 29 D8
Park View Rd ST7 ... 195 B3
Park W CH60 ... 40 E7
Parkway
Connah's Quay CH5 ... 92 E1
Holmes Chapel CW4 ... 130 C3
Wilmslow SK9 ... 60 B6
Park Way CH1 ... 94 A2
Parkway Bsns Ctr CH5 ... 92 E1
Park Wlk CH2 ... 118 E4
Parkwood Cl
Bebington CH62 ... 43 E8
Lymm WA13 ... 18 D2
Parliament St 4
CW8 ... 103 E7
Parliament Way 9
CH66 ... 94 F8
Parlington Cl WA8 ... 22 C7
Parnell Sq CW12 ... 157 A2
PARRAH GREEN ... 231 E7
Parr Gr WA11 ... 1 A6
Parr St
Macclesfield SK11 ... 112 C8
Warrington WA1 ... 16 C4
1 Widnes WA8 ... 13 C1
Parrs Wood View WA4 ... 17 B1
Parry Dr WA4 ... 17 E3
Parsonage Gn
Hale L24 ... 21 E1
Wilmslow SK9 ... 60 B7
Parsonage Rd WA8 ... 23 A4
Parsonage St SK11 ... 112 D7
Parsonage Way WA5 ... 15 A5
Parsons La CH2 ... 118 B7
Parson St CW12 ... 156 C2
PARTINGTON ... 11 F4
Partington Prim Sch
M31 ... 11 F3
Partington Sh Ctr M31 ... 11 F3
Partridge Cl
Congleton CW12 ... 156 E1
Warrington WA3 ... 9 E4
Winsford CW7 ... 149 D5
Partridge Way CW9 ... 79 F5
Parvey La SK11 ... 112 E2
Pasture Cl
Kelsall CW6 ... 122 C4
Macclesfield SK10 ... 87 C3
Pasture Dr WA3 ... 9 B7
Pasture La WA2 ... 9 B1
Pastures Dr CW2 ... 207 D3
Pastures The WA9 ... 6 A7
Patch La SK7 ... 35 D5
Patmos La WA16 ... 105 F8
Patrivale Cl WA1 ... 16 F6
Patten La WA1 ... 16 B5
Patterdale Ave WA2 ... 8 C2
Patterdale Cl CW2 ... 189 D3
Patterdale Rd M31 ... 11 E3
Patterson Cl WA3 ... 9 E3
Patterson St WA12 ... 2 B3
Patton Dr WA5 ... 15 B6
Paul Cl WA5 ... 14 D6
Paulden Rd CW9 ... 80 A2
Paul St WA2 ... 16 A6
Pavement La WA16 ... 57 F3
Pavilion Ct WA12 ... 2 A3
Pavilions The
Chester CH4 ... 141 B3
Davenham CW9 ... 103 E2
Pavilion Way
Congleton CW12 ... 156 C3
Macclesfield SK10 ... 86 F1
Paxford Pl SK9 ... 60 A5
Payne Cl WA5 ... 15 D6
Paythorne Cl WA3 ... 4 F3
Peace Dr WA5 ... 15 D5
Peach Field CH3 ... 142 B7
Peach Gr WA11 ... 1 E7
Peach La CW5 ... 189 A1
Peach Tree Cl L24 ... 21 E2
Peacock Ave
Warrington WA1 ... 16 E6
Winsford CW7 ... 149 C5
Peacock Dr SK8 ... 34 B6
Peacock Hay Rd ST7 ... 210 F4
Peacock La WA16 ... 29 E6
Peacock Way 5 SK9 ... 34 D5
Peak Rd SK22 ... 39 D8
Pearle St SK10 ... 87 D1
Pearlings The CH3 ... 119 B1
Pearl La
Chester CH3 ... 119 C1
Littleton CH3 ... 119 D1
Pearl St SK10 ... 87 A7
Pearson Ave WA4 ... 16 D2
Pearson St 9 SK11 ... 112 E7
Pear Tree Ave
Crewe CW1 ... 190 B7
Runcorn WA7 ... 49 C7
Pear Tree Bank CW12 ... 156 E2
Peartree Cl CW11 ... 175 E6
Pear Tree Cl
Frodsham WA6 ... 49 D1
Hale L24 ... 21 E1
Weaverham CW8 ... 77 C1
Winsford CW7 ... 149 D7
Pear Tree Dr CW9 ... 80 A6
Pear Tree Farm Cotts
CW9 ... 104 F4
Pear Tree Field CW5 ... 205 A4
Peartree La SY14 ... 222 D1
Pear Tree La
Acton Bridge CW8 ... 76 E4
Whitchurch SY13 ... 225 D1
Peartree Pl WA4 ... 16 C4
Pear Tree Rd ST7 ... 209 F1
Pear Tree Sch CW5 ... 205 A4
Pear Tree Way
Chester CH2 ... 118 F6
5 Ellesmere Port CH66 ... 69 E1
Pearwood Cl CW6 ... 146 D1
Peasley Cl WA2 ... 9 B1
Pebble Brook Prim Sch
CW2 ... 190 C1
Peckfield Cl WA7 ... 50 A5
PECKFORTON ... 184 F5
Peckforton Castle★
CW6 ... 167 E1
Peckforton Cl CW11 ... 174 E7
Peckforton Dr
Ellesmere Port CH66 ... 69 E3
Runcorn WA7 ... 49 F4
Peckforton Hall Farm
CW6 ... 185 A6
Peckforton Hall La
CW6 ... 185 B6
Peckforton Rd CW6 ... 168 A2
Peckforton Way
Chester CH2 ... 118 F6
2 Northwich CW8 ... 103 E7
Peckforton Wlk 11 SK9 ... 34 E1
Peckmill Cl SK9 ... 34 E2
Peck Mill La WA6 ... 98 A7
Peckmill Rdbt CW9 ... 127 B8
Pedley Hill
Booth Green SK10 ... 62 F7
Rainow SK10 ... 88 E4
Pedley House La WA16 ... 58 E1
Pedley La
Chelford WA16 ... 83 D8
Congleton CW12 ... 157 F4
Pedley St CW2 ... 190 D2
Peebles Cl
Ellesmere Port CH66 ... 68 F6
Holmes Chapel CW4 ... 130 B2
Peel Cl WA1 ... 17 D6
Peel Cres CH3 ... 121 E7
Peel Ct 4 ST7 ... 195 A2
Peel Dr CW12 ... 178 B7
Peel Hall La CH3 ... 121 E7
Peel Hall Pk CH3 ... 121 D8
Peel Hollow ST7 ... 209 A2
Peel House La WA8 ... 13 B2
Peel La CW12 ... 178 D7
Peel Sq 1 CW1 ... 190 B5
Peel St
Crewe CW1 ... 190 B5
Macclesfield SK11 ... 112 D6
Newton-le-W WA12 ... 2 A3
Runcorn WA7 ... 22 F3
Peel Terr CH1 ... 237 C3
Peerswood Ct CH64 ... 66 E5
Peewit Cl CW7 ... 149 D5
Peggie's La SK10 ... 62 D2
Pelham Cl CW1 ... 191 C5
Pelham Rd WA4 ... 17 C3
Pelican Cl CW1 ... 191 A5
Pemberton Cl CH64 ... 68 A8
Pemberton Rd CH1 ... 237 A3
Pembridge Ct CH65 ... 70 E3
Pembridge Gdns CH65 ... 70 E3
Pembroke Apartments
WA2 ... 9 A3
Pembroke Cl CH4 ... 141 E6
Pembroke Ct WA7 ... 24 D5
Pembroke Dr CH65 ... 70 A3
Pembroke Gdns WA4 ... 26 D4
Pembroke Gr M44 ... 11 C6
Pembroke Rd SK11 ... 111 F7
Pembroke Way CW7 ... 149 B7
Penare WA7 ... 50 C6
Penbrook Cl CW2 ... 189 D3
Penda Way CW11 ... 175 B6
Pendine Cl WA5 ... 7 C2
Pendlebury Gdns
SK11 ... 112 D2
Pendlebury St WA4 ... 17 A3
Pendle Cl
Crewe CW1 ... 191 A5
Ellesmere Port CH66 ... 68 F6
Pendle Gdns WA3 ... 4 E2
Penfold Cl CH1 ... 94 B8
Penfold Hey CH2 ... 118 D7
Penfolds WA7 ... 23 D1
Penfold Way CH4 ... 162 A7
Penhale Mews SK7 ... 35 F7
Peninsula Ho WA2 ... 16 C7
Penistone Dr CH66 ... 69 B5
PENKETH ... 14 D4
Penketh Ave WA5 ... 15 F8
Penketh Bsns Pk WA5 ... 15 B4
Penketh Com Prim Sch
WA5 ... 14 D4
Penketh Ct
1 Runcorn WA7 ... 23 B2
Warrington WA5 ... 14 D4
Penketh High Sch
WA5 ... 15 A5
Penketh Rd WA5 ... 15 A4
Penketh's La 19 WA7 ... 23 A3
Penketh South Com Prim
Sch WA5 ... 14 E3
Penkford La WA5 ... 1 D2
Penkford Sch WA12 ... 1 E2
Penkford St WA12 ... 1 E3
Penkmans La WA6 ... 74 C6
Penlington Ct CW5 ... 204 F6
Penmann Cres L26 ... 21 A7
Penmark Cl WA5 ... 7 C2
Penmon Cl CH1 ... 117 D3
Pennant Cl WA3 ... 10 A3
Penn Bridge SK11 ... 158 E6
Penn Gdns CH65 ... 70 B5
Penn House Cl SK7 ... 35 E8
Pennine Ct SK10 ... 87 E2
Pennine Rd WA2 ... 8 E2
Pennine Way
Biddulph ST8 ... 179 E1
Winsford CW7 ... 149 B8
Pennine Wlk CH66 ... 69 B6
Pennington Cl WA6 ... 49 D2
Pennington Dr WA12 ... 2 E3
Pennington Gn CH66 ... 69 C3
Pennington La WA5,
WA9 ... 1 D2
Penningtons La SK11 ... 111 F5
Penn La WA7 ... 22 F1
Penny Bank Cl CH4 ... 139 A3
Pennyfields Rd ST7 ... 195 D2
Penny La
Collins Green WA5 ... 1 D1
Cronton L35, WA8 ... 12 B6
Haydock WA11 ... 2 B7
Rainow SK10 ... 88 D3
Pennymoor Dr CW10 ... 128 D2
Pennypleck La CW9 ... 28 A2
Penny's La
Northwich CW9 ... 104 F7
Rudheath CW9 ... 105 B5
Penrhyn Cres
Hazel Grove SK7 ... 36 C8
Runcorn WA7 ... 49 B7
Penrhyn Rd CW8 ... 103 E8
Penrith Ave
Macclesfield SK11 ... 111 F5
Warrington WA2 ... 8 C2
Penrith Cl
Frodsham WA6 ... 49 D1
Partington M31 ... 11 E4
Penrith Ct CW12 ... 156 A2
Penrose Gdns WA5 ... 14 D3
Penry Ave M44 ... 11 E6
Penryn Cl WA5 ... 14 E3
Pensarn Gdns WA5 ... 7 D2
Pensby Ave CH2 ... 118 D5
Pensby Dr CH66 ... 69 D4
Pensby Rd CH60 ... 40 F8
Penshaw Ct WA7 ... 49 E7
Pentland Ave WA2 ... 8 B3
Pentland Cl
Chester CH3 ... 119 A2
Winsford CW7 ... 149 B8
Pentland Pl WA2 ... 8 B3
Pentre Cl CH3 ... 121 F7
Pentre La CH3 ... 121 F7
Penzance Cl SK10 ... 111 E8
Peony Gdns WA9 ... 6 B7
Peover Hall & Gdns★
WA16 ... 107 E8
PEOVER HEATH ... 108 C8
Peover La
Chelford SK11 ... 108 F8
Congleton CW12 ... 157 F6
Peover Prim Sch
WA16 ... 108 B8
Peover Rd SK9 ... 34 E5
Pepper Ct SK9 ... 60 A6
Pepper St
Appleton Thorn WA4 ... 27 B3
Ashley WA16 ... 31 F1
Chelford SK11 ... 83 E2
Pepper St *continued*
Chester CH1 ... 237 B2
Christleton CH3 ... 142 D8
Hale L24 ... 21 D1
Henbury SK11 ... 111 B8
Lymm WA13 ... 18 F3
Middlewich CW10 ... 128 C1
Nantwich CW5 ... 204 E5
Peppers The WA13 ... 18 F3
Percival Cl CH2 ... 118 C8
Percival La WA7 ... 22 E2
Percival Rd
Chester CH2 ... 118 C8
Ellesmere Port CH65 ... 70 B6
Percivals La WA16 ... 83 B3
Percival St WA1 ... 16 C5
Percy James Cl ST7 ... 193 E4
Percy Rd CH4 ... 141 D7
Percy St
Northwich CW9 ... 104 A8
Warrington WA5 ... 15 E5
Percyvale St SK10 ... 112 E8
Peregrine Cl CW7 ... 149 D5
Perenna Ct/Llys Perenna
CH6 ... 91 B2
Perimeter Rd CH2 ... 72 D5
Perrin Ave WA7 ... 48 E8
Perrins Rd WA5 ... 6 F6
Perry Fields CW1 ... 173 B1
Perry St WA7 ... 23 B2
Perth Cl
Bramhall SK7 ... 35 F5
Holmes Chapel CW4 ... 130 B2
Warrington WA2 ... 8 F3
Peterborough Cl
Ellesmere Port CH66 ... 94 F7
Macclesfield SK10 ... 87 A2
Peter Destapleigh Way
CW5 ... 205 A3
Peter Ellson Cl CW2 ... 190 D1
Peter House Rd SK11 ... 112 F3
Peter Pl 7 CW1 ... 190 B5
Peter St W 1 SK11 ... 112 C7
Peters Cl SK10 ... 87 A7
Petersfield Gdns WA3 ... 4 E4
Petersfield Way CW2 ... 207 D3
Petersgate WA7 ... 50 D7
Petersham Dr WA4 ... 26 E5
Peter St
Golborne WA3 ... 3 A8
Macclesfield SK11 ... 112 C7
Northwich CW9 ... 79 B1
Peterstone Cl WA5 ... 7 D2
Petham Ct WA8 ... 12 E4
Petrel Ave SK12 ... 36 B4
Petrel Cl CW7 ... 149 D5
Petunia Cl
Macclesfield SK11 ... 112 B5
St Helens WA9 ... 6 A7
Petworth Ave WA2 ... 8 B3
Petworth Cl CW2 ... 206 B8
Pevensey Dr WA16 ... 82 A8
Peveril Cl WA4 ... 26 D8
Peveril Dr SK7 ... 36 F8
Peveril Gdns SK12 ... 39 A6
Peveril Mews SK12 ... 39 A6
Peveril Wlk 3 SK11 ... 111 F7
Pewithall Prim Sch
WA7 ... 49 B7
Pewit La CW5 ... 231 C7
PEWTERSPEAR ... 26 E4
Pewterspear Green Rd
WA4 ... 26 E3
Pewterspear La WA4 ... 26 E4
Pexall Rd SK11 ... 134 C3
Pex Hill Ct WA8 ... 12 E5
Pexhill Dr SK10 ... 111 E7
Pexhill Rd SK11 ... 111 C5
Pex Hill Visitor Ctr★
WA8 ... 12 E6
Pheasant Cl WA3 ... 9 F4
Pheasant Dr CW9 ... 79 F5
Pheasant Field L24 ... 21 C2
Pheasant Way CW7 ... 149 D5
Pheasant Wlk WA16 ... 29 C4
Philip Rd WA8 ... 22 B8
Philips Dr WA5 ... 14 E7
Philips La CH66 ... 69 C4
Philip St CH5 ... 116 A2
Phillips Rd CH1 ... 117 D3
Phillip St CH2 ... 118 F3
Phillips Way CH60 ... 40 E8
Phipps' La WA5 ... 6 E7
Phoenix Ave WA5 ... 7 F2
Phoenix Cl ST7 ... 195 C2
Phoenix Ctr The CW7 ... 127 C1
Phoenix St CH5 ... 116 A3
Phythian Cres WA5 ... 14 F4
Pichael Nook WA4 ... 17 A4
Pickenham Cl SK11 ... 111 F6
Pickering Cres WA4 ... 17 D3
Pickerings Cl WA7 ... 49 C6
Pickerings Gdns WA3
Pickerings Lock Cvn PK
CW8 ... 76 A5
Pickerings O The Boat
CW8 ... 76 B5
Pickering's Pasture
(Nature Reserve)★
WA8 ... 22 B3
Pickerings Rd WA8 ... 22 B5
Pickering St CH2 ... 237 C4
Pickering Way CW5 ... 204 F4
Pickford St SK11 ... 112 D7
PICKMERE ... 80 A7
Pickmere Cl CW11 ... 174 F7
Pickmere Ct
Crewe CW1 ... 190 C5
10 Handforth SK9 ... 34 D5

Pickmere Dr
Bebington CH62 43 F3
Bebington CH62 43 F4
Chester CH3 142 B8
Runcorn WA7 50 C5
Pickmere La
Higher Wincham CW9 79 F6
Pickmere WA16 55 D2
Pickmere Rd SK9 34 D5
Pickmere St WA5 15 E5
Pickwick Cl CW11 175 C8
Pickwick Pl ST7 194 D2
Pickwick Rd SK12 36 D3
Picow Farm Rd WA7 22 E1
Picow St 2 WA7 22 F1
PICTON 96 C3
Picton Ave
Ellesmere Port CH65 70 C5
Runcorn WA7 23 B2
Picton Cl
Bebington CH62 43 E3
2 Northwich CW9 103 F4
Warrington WA3 9 C4
Picton Dr
Handforth SK9 34 E2
Winsford CW7 126 B2
Picton Gorse La CH2 119 B7
Picton La CH2 96 C4
Picton Sq CW4 130 C3
Piele Rd WA11 1 E8
Pierce St SK11 112 C8
Pierpoint La CH1 237 B2
Pierpoint St WA5 15 F7
Pigginshaw SK9 59 E8
Pigot Pl WA4 16 F5
Pike La WA6 75 A3
Pikemere Prim Sch ST7 193 B5
Pikemere Rd ST7 193 B5
Pikenall La CW8 76 D3
Pike Rd SK10 89 B6
Pike St WA4 16 D1
Pike The CW5 204 E3
Pilgrim Cl WA2 8 A6
Pilgrims Way WA7 24 D2
Pillar Box La CW11 153 B3
Pillmoss La WA4 52 B8
Pillory St CW5 204 E5
Pimblett Rd WA11 1 E7
Pimblett St WA3 3 A7
Pimlico Rd WA7 22 E2
Pinders Farm Dr WA1 16 C5
Pineapple Pk CW7 127 B2
Pine Ave
Newton-le-W WA12 2 D2
4 Widnes WA8 13 B2
Pine Cl
Haydock WA11 1 C6
Macclesfield SK10 87 F1
Talke ST7 210 D7
Pine Ct ST7 193 E4
Pinedale Cl CH66 95 A8
Pine Gdns CH2 118 C6
Pine Gr
Chester CH2 119 B4
Ellesmere Port CH66 70 A1
Golborne WA3 3 C8
Sandbach CW11 175 C6
Warrington WA1 17 A7
Winsford CW7 127 A1
Pinehey CH64 41 D1
Pine Ho CH2 118 C5
Pinehurst SK10 86 E6
Pinellas WA7 23 B3
Pine Lo SK7 35 F7
Pine Rd
Bramhall SK7 35 F8
Heswall CH60 41 C8
Macclesfield SK10 87 F1
Poynton SK12 36 F3
Runcorn WA7 49 C8
Pines The
Mobberley WA16 58 E1
6 Northwich CW9 103 E6
Widnes WA8 13 D4
Pinetree Cl
Barnton CW8 78 B4
Winsford CW7 127 A1
Pine Tree Cl CH4 139 C3
Pine Trees WA16 57 F8
Pineways WA4 26 D5
Pine Wlk
Nantwich CW5 204 F4
1 Partington M31 11 E3
Pinewood Ave WA1 16 E7
Pinewood Cl CH2 72 C3
Pinewood Ct CW2 206 B7
Pinewood Dr CH60 41 B8
Pinewood Gr ST5 210 E1
Pinewood Rd
Burtonwood WA5 6 F7
Wilmslow SK9 60 E8
Winsford CW7 126 B1
Pinfold Cl WA15 32 D7
Pinfold Craft Ctr★ CW5 188 B3
Pinfold Ct CH4 141 E6
Pinfold La
Alpraham CW6 169 D5
Chelford WA16 83 D6
Chester CH4 141 D6
Chester CH4 141 E7
Little Budworth CW6 147 E7
Middlewich CW10 128 B1
Plumley WA16 81 B4
Wythenshawe M90, WA15 32 F6
Pinfold St 18 SK11 112 C8
Pinfold The LL13 196 D8
Pinfold Way CW8 77 D1
Pingard's La CW8 101 C6
Pingate Dr SK8 35 A6
Pingate La SK8 35 A6
Pingate La S SK8 35 A6
Pingot Croft CH3 142 B7
Pingot La WA6 99 A5
Pingot Rd SK22 39 D8
Pinmill Brow WA6 74 B7
Pinmill Cl WA6 74 C7
Pinners Brow WA2 16 B6
Pinners Brow Ret Pk WA2 16 B6
Pinners Fold WA7 24 B1
PINSLEY GREEN 216 D2
Pinsley Green Rd CW5 216 E2
Pinsley View CW5 216 E4
Pintail Pl CW7 149 D6
Pinwood Ct 13 SK9 34 E1
Pipers Ash CW7 126 A1
PIPER'S ASH 119 D4
Piper's Cl CH60 40 D8
Pipers Ct CH2 119 B4
Piper's End CH60 40 D8
Pipers La
Chester CH2 119 B4
Puddington CH64 93 A8
Piper's La CH60 40 D8
Pipers The
Golborne WA3 3 F8
Heswall CH60 40 D8
Pipit Ave WA12 2 C3
Pipit La WA3 9 E3
Pippin Cl CW10 151 C7
Pippits Row WA7 49 E4
Pirie Cl CW12 157 A4
Pirie Rd CW12 157 A4
Pitcher La CW11 177 A8
Pit La
Hough CW2 206 E2
Talke ST7 210 C6
Widnes WA8 13 A4
Pitt La SK11 132 B8
Pitts Cl CH3 121 C2
Pitts Heath La WA7 24 E3
Pitt St
Macclesfield SK11 112 D6
Warrington WA5 15 F7
Widnes WA8 23 A5
Pitville Terr WA8 22 C7
Plaistow Ct WA7 49 E7
Plane Gr ST5 210 E1
Plane Tree Dr CW1 190 E6
Plane Tree Gr WA11 2 A7
Plane Tree Rd M31 11 D3
Plantagenet Cl 3 CW7 149 D6
Plantation Cl WA7 24 A1
Plantation Dr CH66 69 E7
Plant La CW11 174 B7
Plant St CW11 175 A7
Plas Dinas CH1 117 D3
Plas Newton La CH2 118 F5
Plas Newydd CH4 161 B6
Platt Ave CW11 175 A7
Platts La
Christleton CH3 143 D8
Duddon CH3, CW6 144 E7
Tarvin, Broom Bank CH3 144 B8
Tarvin CH3 121 B2
Tattenhall CH3 183 F7
Platt's La CH3 164 E5
Platts St WA11 1 A6
Pleasance Way WA12 2 D4
Pleasant St
Macclesfield SK10 87 F1
Northwich CW8 103 E7
Pleasant View SK10 111 C8
Pleasant Way SK8 35 C6
Pleck Rd CH65 70 A2
PLEMSTALL 97 B1
Plemstall Cl CH2 119 F8
Plemstall La CH2 97 A1
Plemstall Way CH2 96 F1
Plemston Ct CH66 69 F8
Plex The ST7 193 D4
Plinston Ave WA4 16 F4
Plough Croft ST7 193 A3
Plough Inn Pk The CW8 125 E5
Plough La CH3 143 B7
Ploughmans Cl CH66 94 E8
Ploughmans Way
Ellesmere Port CH66 94 E8
Macclesfield SK10 87 B3
Plover Ave CW7 149 D5
Plover Cl
Farndon CH3 180 F1
Macclesfield SK10 87 B4
Newton-le-W WA12 2 C3
Plover Dr WA7 50 D8
Plovers La WA6 73 C5
Plover Way WA3 3 E8
Plumbs Fold CW8 78 A2
PLUMLEY 80 F3
Plumley Cl
Chester CH3 119 C1
16 Macclesfield SK11 112 E7
Plumley Gdns WA8 12 A1
PLUMLEY MOOR 81 C2
Plumley Moor Rd WA16 81 C2
Plumley Rd SK9 34 D5
Plumley Sta WA16 81 A3
Plumpstons La WA6 49 B1
Plumpton Cross 6 WA8 13 B2
Plum Terr CH1 237 A3
Plumtree Ave WA5 15 F8
Plymouth Cl WA7 50 E6
Plymouth Dr SK7 35 F7
Plymyard Ave CH62 43 D5
Plymyard Cl CH62 43 D5
Plymyard Ct CH62 43 C6
Poachers' La WA4 16 F3
Pochard Ave CW7 149 D6
Pochard Dr SK12 36 A4
Pochard Rise WA7 50 D8
Pochin Way CW10 128 E1
Pocket Nook La WA3 4 B7
Pocklington Ct WA2 8 F1
Points Ho CW1 190 A5
Polden Cl CH66 69 A6
Poleacre Dr WA8 12 D2
Pole La CW9 53 E2
Pole Lane Ends CW9 53 C4
Pollard Ave WA6 74 D7
Pollard Dr CW5 205 B4
Polperro Cl
Macclesfield SK10 86 D1
Warrington WA5 14 E3
Pond Cotts CH2 72 A3
Pond St WA3 4 A8
Pond View Cl CH60 41 C8
Pond Wlk WA9 1 A1
Pool Bank Bsns Pk CH3 121 C3
Pool Bank Cotts CH3 121 C3
Poole Ave WA2 8 B2
Poole Cres WA2 8 B2
Poole Hall La CH66 69 E8
Poole Hall Rd CH66 69 F8
POOLEHILL 188 A2
Poole Hill Rd CW5 188 A2
Poole La CH2 71 E2
Pool End Cl SK10 87 D4
Pool End Rd SK10 87 D4
Poole Old Hall La CW5 188 D4
Pooles La CW11 177 A6
POOLFOLD 179 F4
Poolford La CW4 129 E2
Pool Hall Ind Est CH65, CH66 70 A8
Pool House Rd SK12 37 D5
Pool La
Cuddington CW8 102 B2
Haslington CW11 192 A7
Ince CH2 71 F4
Lymm WA13 18 B4
Malpas SY14 212 D1
Runcorn WA7 23 B3
Tarvin CH3 121 C4
Warrington WA4 16 A1
Pool Meadows Rd CW1 191 B4
Pool Rd WA3 11 A3
Pool Side ST7 194 A8
Poolside Ct ST7 193 E4
Poolside Rd WA7 23 B1
Pools Platt La CW9 53 E6
Pool St
Macclesfield SK11 112 E6
Widnes WA8 23 B7
Pooltown Rd CH65 69 F5
Pool View CW11 191 F7
Poplar Ave
Culcheth WA3 4 F3
Moulton CW9 126 F8
Newton-le-W WA12 2 D3
Runcorn WA7 49 C7
Warrington WA5 14 E3
Wilmslow SK9 59 F5
Poplar Cl
Congleton CW12 156 A4
Cuddington CW8 102 A3
Ellesmere Port CH65 70 B4
Runcorn WA7 49 C7
Winsford CW7 149 B8
Poplar Ct CW5 205 A4
Poplar Dr
Alsager ST7 193 E2
Kidsgrove ST7 195 A1
Middlewich CW10 151 D7
Poplar Gr
Bollington SK10 88 A8
Crewe CW1 190 E5
Elton CH2 72 A3
Haydock WA11 1 C6
Irlam M44 11 D6
Poplar Hall La CH2 95 C6
Poplar La TF9 236 F5
Poplar Rd
Chester CH4 140 F5
Haydock WA11 1 C6
Macclesfield SK11 112 D6
Weaverham CW8 102 D8
Poplars Ave
Warrington, Hulme WA2 8 C3
Warrington, Winwick Quay WA2 8 A4
Poplars Pl WA2 8 D2
Poplars The
Golborne, Wash End WN7 4 C8
Lymm WA13 18 D4
Wistaston CW2 205 F7
Poplar View WA4 25 A7
Poplar Way SK6 38 A7
Poplar Weint 2 CH64 66 E8
Poplar Wlk M31 11 D3
Poppy Cl CW2 207 C5
Poppyfields ST7 193 B3
Porlock Cl
Heswall CH60 41 B6
Warrington WA5 14 E4
Port Arcades The CH65 70 C5
Porter Ave WA12 2 C5
Porter Dr CW9 104 C6
Porters Croft CH3 119 F5
Porter St WA7 23 C2
Porter Way CW9 104 C6
Portford Cl SK10 86 F1
Porthcawl Cl WA8 12 C3
Porthleven Rd WA7 50 B5
Portland Dr
Biddulph ST8 179 D2
Scholar Green ST7 194 E6
Winsford CW7 149 B8
Portland Gr CW1 191 D5
Portland Pl WA6 73 C4
Portland Rd WA5 15 A8
Portland St
Newton-le-W WA12 1 F4
Runcorn WA7 22 F3
Portland Trad Pk WA2 16 A6
Portland Wlk 4 SK11 111 F7
Portloe Rd SK8 34 B7
Portman Pl 3 CW7 149 A8
Portmarnock Cl SK10 87 B3
Portola Cl WA4 17 C2
Portree Ave CH63 43 D5
Portree Dr CW4 130 B2
Portrush Cl
Macclesfield SK10 87 C4
Widnes WA8 12 E3
Portside WA7 50 E7
Portside Bsns Pk CH65 70 B8
Portsmouth Pl WA7 50 E6
Portway M22 33 E8
Postles Pl CW9 103 F6
Post Office La
Betley CW2 207 F1
Hampton Heath SY14 213 D7
Norley WA6 100 E5
Runcorn WA7 48 D7
Post Office Pl 1 CW9 79 A1
Potter Cl CW5 205 D4
Potters Barn The★ CW11 176 A1
Potters End ST8 179 C1
Potters La WA8 21 F5
Pott Hall SK10 63 D3
POTT SHRIGLEY 63 D3
Pott Shrigley Church Sch SK10 63 C3
POULTON 163 B2
Poulton Cres WA1 17 D8
Poulton Dr WA8 22 D8
Poulton Hall Rd CH63 43 A7
Poulton Rd CH63 43 A8
Pound Rd CH66 69 C7
Povey Rd WA2 8 D1
Powell's Orch CH4 141 C7
Powell St WA4 16 F3
Powey La CH1 94 B5
Pownall Ave SK7 35 F7
Pownall Ct SK9 59 E8
POWNALL GREEN 35 E6
Pownall Green Prim Sch SK7 35 E7
Pownall Hall Sch SK9 59 F8
POWNALL PARK 59 F7
Pownall Pl SK7 35 E7
Pownall Rd SK9 59 F8
Pownall Sq SK11 112 C8
Pownall St SK10 87 D1
Powy Dr ST7 195 B2
Powys Ct CH1 237 A3
Powys St WA5 15 F5
POYNTON 36 E4
Poynton Cl WA4 17 B3
Poynton High Sch SK12 36 F2
Poynton Ind Est SK12 36 D1
Poynton St 15 SK10 112 C8
Poynton Sta SK12 36 C4
Pratchitts Row CW5 204 E5
Precinct The CW2 189 F2
Preece Cl WA8 12 D4
Preece Ct CW1 190 B5
Preesall Ave SK8 34 B8
Premier Pk CW7 127 B3
Prenton Pl CH4 141 E7
Prescot Rd WA8 12 D2
Prescot St CH2 118 F3
Prescott Rd SK9 34 B1
Prescott St WA4 16 E3
PRESTBURY 87 B7
Prestbury CE Prim Sch SK10 86 F7
Prestbury Cl
8 Northwich CW9 103 F4
Widnes WA8 22 E8
Prestbury Ct SK10 86 F6
Prestbury Dr WA4 17 D4
Prestbury La SK10 87 B7
Prestbury Pk SK10 86 E6
Prestbury Rd
Adder's Moss SK10 85 F6
Macclesfield SK10 87 B1
Nether Alderley SK10 86 A5
Wilmslow SK9 60 E5
Prestbury Sta SK10 87 A7
Preston Ave M44 11 F7
PRESTON BROOK 50 F5
PRESTON ON THE HILL 51 A6
Preston St W SK11 112 B6
Prestwich Ave WA3 4 E3
Prestwick Cl
Macclesfield SK10 87 C5
Widnes WA8 12 F3
Winsford CW7 126 C2
Prestwood Ct WA3 10 A7
Pretoria St CH4 141 D7
Price Ave CW11 175 A5
Price Dr CW11 175 A5
Price Gr WA9 1 A2
Pride Cl WA12 2 E2
Priestfield Rd CH65 70 C5
Priest La SK10 61 B1
Priestley Bsns Ctr WA5 15 F5
Priestley Coll WA4 16 C3
Priestley Ct WA4 16 C2
Priestley St WA5 15 F5
Priestly Ct 13 CW5 204 E5
Priestner Dr WA6 73 B4
Priestway La CH64 67 E1
Priesty Ct CW12 156 D2
Priesty Fields CW12 156 D2
Primary Cl M44 11 D5
Primitive St ST7 195 C7
Primrose Ave
Haslington CW1 191 C5
Macclesfield SK11 112 B5
Primrose Chase CW4 130 D8
Primrose Cl
Huntington CH3 142 A6
Runcorn WA7 50 A8
Warrington WA2 8 D2
Widnes WA8 12 E1
Primrose Gr WA11 1 E7
PRIMROSE HILL 28 C6
Primrose Hill
Crewe CW2 189 E5
Cuddington CW8 101 F4
Kelsall CW6 122 E6
Primrose La WA6 73 B1
Primula Cl WA9 6 A7
Primula Dr WA3 3 D8
Prince Albert St CW1 190 D4
Prince Edward St CW5 204 E6
Prince Henry Sq 3 WA1 16 B5
PRINCE HILL 231 F6
Prince Rd SK12 37 C5
Princes Ave
Bebington CH62 43 E6
Chester CH1 237 C3
Northwich CW9 104 B8
Princes Cl WA7 23 F1
Princes Ct CW5 204 E7
Princes Pk CW8 78 A2
Princes Pl WA8 12 E1
Princes Rd CH65 70 B6
Princess Ave
Audley ST7 209 D1
Haydock WA11 2 A7
Warrington, Bruche WA1 16 F6
Warrington, Great Sankey WA5 14 E7
Warrington, Padgate WA1 17 A8
Princess Cl CW2 205 F8
Princess Cres
Middlewich CW10 151 D6
Warrington WA1 16 F6
Princess Ct ST7 210 D5
Princess Dr
Bollington SK10 87 E7
Nantwich CW5 205 A6
Sandbach CW11 175 A7
Wistaston CW2 205 F8
Princess Gr CW2 205 F8
Princess Rd
Allostock WA16 106 E3
Lymm WA13 18 C3
Wilmslow SK9 59 F5
Princess St
Bollington SK10 87 F7
Chester CH1 237 A2
Congleton CW12 156 D3
Crewe CW1 190 C6
Knutsford WA16 57 A2
Northwich CW9 79 E2
13 Runcorn WA7 23 A3
Talke ST7 210 D5
2 Warrington WA5 15 D4
Winsford CW7 127 A2
Princes St WA12 2 B3
Prince's St WA8 23 A8
Princess Wlk SK7 36 A7
Princes Way SK11 111 E7
Princeway WA6 74 B8
Prince William Ave CH5 116 B3
Prior Cl CW2 189 F1
Priory Ave CW9 103 F4
Priory Cl
Chester CH2 118 C4
Congleton CW12 179 B7
Crewe CW1 190 A8
Runcorn WA7 24 A1
Winsford CW7 126 C3
Priory Ct SK10 86 F1
Priory Dr SK10 86 E2
Priory La SK10 86 E2
Priory Pl
Chester CH1 237 B2
Kidsgrove ST7 195 B3
Priory Rd
Altrincham WA14 31 B8
Runcorn WA7 24 C2

Priory Rd *continued*
Wilmslow SK9 . . . . . 59 E8
Priory St
Northwich CW9 . . . . . 104 A8
Warrington WA4 . . . . . 16 B3
Priory The
Neston CH64 . . . . . 41 E1
Winwick WA2 . . . . . 8 A7
Priory Way CW8 . . . . . 103 B4
Pritchard Dr CW9 . . . . . 103 E2
Private Wlk CH3 . . . . . 142 A8
Probert Cl CW2 . . . . . 190 A4
Proctors Cl WA8 . . . . . 13 D2
Proctors La CW11 . . . . . 174 E5
Proffits La WA6 . . . . . 73 E4
Promenade Cvn Pk
WA4 . . . . . 25 B7
Promised Land La
CH3 . . . . . 142 E5
Prospect Ave M44 . . . . . 11 E6
Prospect Dr
Altrincham WA15 . . . . . 32 D8
Davenham CW9 . . . . . 103 E2
Prospect La WA3 . . . . . 10 D3
Prospect Rd M44 . . . . . 11 E6
Prospect Row WA7 . . . . . 48 F7
Prospect St CW12 . . . . . 156 C2
Prosperity Ct CW10 . . . . . 128 D1
Prosperity Way CW10 . . . 128 D1
Prosser Rd CH2 . . . . . 95 C1
Protector Way M44 . . . . . 11 F8
Provan Way CH1 . . . . . 117 D5
Provident St WA9 . . . . . 1 A3
Prunus Rd CW1 . . . . . 190 E6
Pryors The CH3 . . . . . 121 C3
Ptarmigan Pl CW7 . . . . . 149 D5
Public Hall St 18 WA7 . . . . 23 A3
Pudding La CW6 . . . . . 168 A7
PUDDINGLAKE 129 A8
PUDDINGTON 92 F8
Puddington La CH64 . . . . . 92 E8
Puddle Bank La CW12 . . . 178 F5
Puffin Ave SK12 . . . . . 36 B4
Puffin Cl CH65 . . . . . 95 C8
PULFORD 162 D3
Pulford App
Aldford CH3 . . . . . 163 D3
Pulford CH4 . . . . . 162 E2
Pulford Cl
Northwich CW9 . . . . . 103 E4
Runcorn WA7 . . . . . 49 E6
Pulford Ct CH4 . . . . . 162 D2
Pulford La CH4 . . . . . 162 A6
Pulford Rd
Blacon CH1 . . . . . 117 E5
Ellesmere Port CH65 . . . . . 69 F4
Winsford CW7 . . . . . 126 C1
Pullman Cl CH60 . . . . . 41 D8
Pullman Dr CW9 . . . . . 104 C8
Pump Ct ST7 . . . . . 209 E2
Pumping Station Hos
CW6 . . . . . 184 E3
Pump La
Churton CH3 . . . . . 181 A5
Runcorn WA7 . . . . . 49 F8
Tattenhall CH3 . . . . . 182 C6
Pumptree Mews
SK11 . . . . . 111 E7
Purdy Cl WA5 . . . . . 7 D1
Puritan Bldgs WA7 . . . . . 23 C2
Purley Dr M44 . . . . . 11 C5
Purser La SY14 . . . . . 211 E4
Puss Bank Sch SK10 . . . . 112 F8
Putney Ct WA7 . . . . . 49 F7
Pye Cl WA11 . . . . . 2 B8
Pyecroft Cl WA5 . . . . . 14 D6
Pyecroft Rd WA5 . . . . . 14 D6
Pyecroft St CH4 . . . . . 141 D7
Pye Rd CH60 . . . . . 41 A8
Pym's La CW1 . . . . . 189 E6
Pyrus Ave CW1 . . . . . 190 E6
Pyrus Gr WA6 . . . . . 73 C4
Pytcheley Hollow
WA6 . . . . . 100 F6

Q

Quadrant Cl WA7 . . . . . 50 D6
Quadrant The CH1 . . . . . 117 E2
Quadrant The WA3 . . . . . 9 F5
Quad The CH1 . . . . . 117 E2
Quail Cl WA2 . . . . . 8 D3
Quaintways CW8 . . . . . 103 C4
Quakers Coppice
CW1 . . . . . 191 A2
Quakers Way LL13 . . . . . 180 E1
Quantock Cl
Ellesmere Port CH66 . . . . . 69 A6
Winsford CW7 . . . . . 149 A7
Quarry Ave CH3 . . . . . 180 F1
QUARRYBANK 146 C8
Quarrybank CW6 . . . . . 184 F6
Quarry Bank CW6 . . . . . 146 C8
Quarry Bank Cotts
CW6 . . . . . 184 F6
Quarry Bank Mill★
SK9 . . . . . 33 F2
Quarry Bank Rd SK9 . . . . . 33 F3
Quarry Bank Rise
CW7 . . . . . 149 B8
Quarry Cl
Chester CH4 . . . . . 141 C7
Runcorn WA7 . . . . . 23 D1
Quarry Ct
Farndon CH3 . . . . . 180 F1
Widnes WA8 . . . . . 12 C1
Quarry Hill CH3 . . . . . 180 F1
Quarry La
Christleton CH3 . . . . . 142 E7
Kelsall CW6 . . . . . 122 D5
Warrington WA4 . . . . . 26 C6
Quarry Rd
Neston CH64 . . . . . 42 C1
New Mills SK22 . . . . . 39 D7
Quarry Terr ST7 . . . . . 195 A1
Quarter The CH1 . . . . . 237 B3
Quay Fold WA5 . . . . . 15 F4
Quayle Cl WA11 . . . . . 1 C6
Quay Pl WA7 . . . . . 50 E7
Quayside
Congleton CW12 . . . . . 156 E1
Neston CH64 . . . . . 66 E5
Quay Side WA6 . . . . . 49 D1
Quayside Mews WA13 . . . . 18 F3
Quayside Way SK11 . . . . . 112 E7
Quay The WA6 . . . . . 49 D2
Queastybirch La
Hatton WA4 . . . . . 25 F1
Hatton WA4 . . . . . 26 A1
Quebec Rd WA2 . . . . . 16 D7
Queen Anne Ct SK9 . . . . . 60 C6
Queen Annes Ct 5
SK11 . . . . . 112 B6
Queen Elizabeth Ho
CW9 . . . . . 79 A1
Queens Ave
Ellesmere Port CH65 . . . . . 70 A3
Warrington WA1 . . . . . 16 E7
Queen's Ave CH1 . . . . . 237 C3
Queen's Ave CH5 . . . . . 91 D1
Queen's Ave
Glazebury WA3 . . . . . 5 C7
Macclesfield SK10 . . . . . 87 E2
Sandycroft CH5 . . . . . 116 A3
Widnes WA8 . . . . . 22 B8
Queensbury Cl
15 Handforth SK9 . . . . . 34 D1
Wilmslow SK9 . . . . . 60 D8
Queensbury Way WA8 . . . . 12 E3
Queens Cl SK10 . . . . . 87 E6
Queen's Cl
Macclesfield SK10 . . . . . 87 E2
Runcorn WA7 . . . . . 22 F1
Queens Cres
Chester CH2 . . . . . 118 E7
Warrington WA1 . . . . . 17 A8
Queen's Cres CW1 . . . . . 172 E2
Queens Ct
Chester CH4 . . . . . 237 C1
Winsford CW7 . . . . . 126 D1
Queen's Ct CW10 . . . . . 128 D1
Queens Dr
Golborne WA3 . . . . . 3 C8
Helsby WA6 . . . . . 73 B3
Heswall CH60 . . . . . 40 E8
Newton-le-W WA12 . . . . . 2 C5
Warrington WA4 . . . . . 17 A2
Queen's Dr
Chester CH4 . . . . . 237 C1
Middlewich CW10 . . . . . 151 D7
Nantwich CW5 . . . . . 204 D4
Sandbach CW11 . . . . . 175 A8
Queensford LL13 . . . . . 222 A8
Queensgate
Bramhall SK7 . . . . . 35 E5
Northwich CW8 . . . . . 103 E8
Queensgate Prim Sch
SK7 . . . . . 35 E4
Queens Gdns
Ellesmere Port CH65 . . . . . 70 B5
Talke ST7 . . . . . 210 D5
Queen's Par 1 CW7 . . . . 126 D1
QUEEN'S PARK 141 F8
Queen's Park Dr CW1 . . . 189 F3
Queen's Park Gdns
CW2 . . . . . 189 E4
Queens Park High Sch
CH4 . . . . . 237 B1
Queen's Park Ho CH4 . . . 237 B1
Queen's Park Rd CH4 . . . 237 B1
Queen's Park View
CH4 . . . . . 237 B1
Queens Pk CH60 . . . . . 40 D8
Queens Pl CH1 . . . . . 237 B3
Queens Rd
Chester CH3 . . . . . 119 B3
Ellesmere Port CH66 . . . . . 69 C7
Haydock WA11 . . . . . 2 A7
Queen's Rd
Chester CH1 . . . . . 237 C3
Runcorn WA7 . . . . . 22 F1
Wilmslow SK9 . . . . . 60 A6
Queen's Sch (Lower) The
CH2 . . . . . 118 C4
Queen's Sch The CH1 . . . 237 A2
Queen St
Audley ST7 . . . . . 209 C1
Bollington SK10 . . . . . 88 B8
Bunbury CW6 . . . . . 185 E8
Chester CH1 . . . . . 237 B2
Congleton, Buglawton
CW12 . . . . . 156 F4
Congleton CW12 . . . . . 156 C2
Crewe CW1 . . . . . 190 E5
Ellesmere Port CH65 . . . . . 70 C7
Golborne WA3 . . . . . 3 B8
Kidsgrove ST7 . . . . . 195 A2
Knutsford WA16 . . . . . 56 F2
Macclesfield SK10 . . . . . 112 D8
Middlewich CW10 . . . . . 128 C1
Nantwich CW5 . . . . . 204 E5
Queen St *continued*
Newton-le-W WA12 . . . . . 2 B3
Northwich CW9 . . . . . 103 F7
8 Runcorn WA7 . . . . . 23 A3
Shavington CW2 . . . . . 206 C4
Queens Terr SK9 . . . . . 34 D3
Queensway
Alsager ST7 . . . . . 193 B5
Chester CH2 . . . . . 118 F5
Crewe CW1 . . . . . 190 C4
Frodsham WA6 . . . . . 74 B8
Gatley SK8 . . . . . 34 C8
Heswall CH60 . . . . . 41 C6
Knutsford WA16 . . . . . 56 E3
Partington M31 . . . . . 11 F4
Poynton SK12 . . . . . 36 D3
Runcorn WA7 . . . . . 22 F3
Widnes WA8 . . . . . 22 F6
Winsford CW7 . . . . . 149 D8
Queen's Way CH4 . . . . . 139 B4
Queensway Trad Est
WA8 . . . . . 23 A5
Queen Victoria St 14
SK11 . . . . . 112 D8
Quill Ct M44 . . . . . 11 E6
Quillet The CH64 . . . . . 66 F7
Quinn St WA8 . . . . . 23 B7
Quinta Prim Sch The
CW12 . . . . . 156 A2
Quinta Rd CW12 . . . . . 156 A3
QUOISLEY 226 B8

R

RABY 42 C4
Raby Ave CH63 . . . . . 43 B6
Raby Cl
Bebington CH63 . . . . . 43 A7
Heswall CH60 . . . . . 40 F7
Widnes WA8 . . . . . 13 E2
Raby Ct CH65 . . . . . 70 D3
Raby Dr CH63 . . . . . 43 A6
Raby Gdns CH64 . . . . . 66 E8
Raby Hall Rd CH63 . . . . . 43 A6
RABY MERE 43 B7
Raby Mere Rd CH63 . . . . . 42 D5
Raby Park Cl CH64 . . . . . 66 E8
Raby Park Rd CH64 . . . . . 41 F1
Raby Rd
Neston CH64 . . . . . 66 E8
Thornton Hough CH63 . . . . . 42 B5
Racecourse La CW6 . . . . . 124 A1
Racecourse Pk SK9 . . . . . 59 F6
Racecourse Rd SK9 . . . . . 59 E6
Racefield Cl WA13 . . . . . 18 F3
Racefield Rd WA16 . . . . . 56 F2
Race The SK9 . . . . . 34 D2
Radbroke Cl CW11 . . . . . 175 D8
Radcliffe Ave WA3 . . . . . 4 E3
Radcliffe Cl CH3 . . . . . 121 C3
Radcliffe Rd
Sandbach CW11 . . . . . 174 F3
Sutton Lane Ends SK11 . . . 135 D7
Winsford CW7 . . . . . 149 B6
Raddel La WA4 . . . . . 52 C5
Raddle Wharf CH65 . . . . . 70 C7
Raddon Pl WA4 . . . . . 16 E3
Radford Cl WA8 . . . . . 22 C7
Radlett Cl WA5 . . . . . 14 E3
Radley Dr CH63 . . . . . 41 F6
Radley La WA2 . . . . . 8 E4
RADMORE GREEN 186 E3
RADNOR 155 E6
Radnor Cl
Congleton CW12 . . . . . 156 B3
Sandbach CW11 . . . . . 174 E7
Radnor Dr
Chester CH4 . . . . . 141 A4
Widnes WA8 . . . . . 12 D2
Radnor Park Ind Ctr
CW12 . . . . . 156 A4
Radnor Park Trad Est
CW12 . . . . . 156 B4
Radnor St WA5 . . . . . 15 E6
Radway Gn CH66 . . . . . 69 E5
RADWAY GREEN 192 F1
Radway Green Bsns &
Tech Ctr CW2 . . . . . 192 F1
Radway Green Rd
Alsager CW2 . . . . . 208 E8
Barthomley CW2 . . . . . 208 D6
Raeburn Ave
Bebington CH62 . . . . . 43 E6
Neston CH64 . . . . . 66 F7
Raeburn Prim Sch
CH62 . . . . . 43 D6
Raglan Ct WA3 . . . . . 9 F6
Raglan Rd SK10 . . . . . 87 F2
Ragley Cl SK12 . . . . . 36 F4
Railbrook Ct CW2 . . . . . 190 D2
Railton Ave CW1 . . . . . 190 A7
Railway Age Mus The★
CW1 . . . . . 190 D3
Railway Cotts
Congleton CW12 . . . . . 157 A1
Hollinfare WA3 . . . . . 11 B5
Hooton CH66 . . . . . 43 E1
Wimboldsley CW10 . . . . . 150 F1
Railway St
Crewe CW2 . . . . . 190 D2
Newton-le-W WA12 . . . . . 2 B3
Railway Terr
Disley SK12 . . . . . 38 D6
Sandycroft CH5 . . . . . 116 B3
Railway View WA5 . . . . . 1 D1
Rainbow Cl WA8 . . . . . 12 C3
Rainbow St CW1 . . . . . 190 D4
Rainford Cl ST7 . . . . . 195 F1
RAINOW 88 D5
Rainow Cl CW10 . . . . . 151 B7
Rainow Dr SK12 . . . . . 37 A2
Rainow Prim Sch SK10 . . . 88 D4
Rainow Rd SK10 . . . . . 88 B2
Rainow View SK10 . . . . . 63 C1
Rainow Way 10 SK9 . . . . . 34 E1
Rajar Cotts WA16 . . . . . 57 F4
Rajar Wlk WA16 . . . . . 58 A4
Rake House Mews
WA6 . . . . . 73 B4
Rake La
Backford CH2 . . . . . 95 D6
Broughton CH5 . . . . . 139 A8
Christleton CH3 . . . . . 143 A7
Dunham-on-t-H WA6 . . . . . 97 B7
Dunham-on-t-H WA6 . . . . . 97 E7
Eccleston CH4 . . . . . 141 C1
Helsby, Helsby Marsh
WA6 . . . . . 73 A5
Helsby WA6 . . . . . 73 C4
Rake The
Bebington CH62 . . . . . 43 C8
Burton CH64 . . . . . 67 D1
Rake Way CH1 . . . . . 94 A1
Raleigh Cl WA5 . . . . . 7 D1
Raleigh Rd CH64 . . . . . 41 F1
Rampit Cl WA11 . . . . . 1 F7
Ramp Rd E M90 . . . . . 33 C7
Ramp Rd S M90 . . . . . 33 C7
Ramp Rd W M90 . . . . . 33 B7
Ramsay Cl WA3 . . . . . 9 E3
Ramsbottom St 2
CW1 . . . . . 190 B5
Ramsbrook La L24,
WA8 . . . . . 21 C3
Ramsdale Rd SK7 . . . . . 35 E8
Ramsden Ct CH4 . . . . . 140 F4
Ramsey Cl WA8 . . . . . 13 E3
Ramsey Rd CH65 . . . . . 70 C1
Ramsfield Rd L24 . . . . . 21 A4
Randal Cres SK23 . . . . . 65 E5
Randall Cl WA12 . . . . . 2 B4
Randle Bennett Cl
CW11 . . . . . 174 E7
Randle Mdw CH66 . . . . . 69 F1
Randle Meadow Ct
CH66 . . . . . 69 F2
Randle's View CW12 . . . . 179 C8
Range Ct SK10 . . . . . 87 E1
Rangemoor Cl WA3 . . . . . 10 A6
Rannoch Cl CH66 . . . . . 69 F3
Ranulph Ct WA6 . . . . . 74 C7
Ranwonath Ct CH2 . . . . . 237 B4
Ranworth Dr WA3 . . . . . 3 E7
Ranworth Rd WA5 . . . . . 14 E6
Rappax Rd WA15 . . . . . 32 A8
Raquets Ct The CW10 . . . 127 D5
Rathbone Pk CW6 . . . . . 146 D2
Rathlin Cl WA8 . . . . . 13 E3
Rathmell Cl WA3 . . . . . 4 E3
Rathvale Dr M22 . . . . . 33 C8
Ravenbank Com Prim Sch
WA13 . . . . . 18 F3
Raven Cl CW11 . . . . . 175 A8
Raven Cotts TF9 . . . . . 235 A5
Ravendale Cl CW7 . . . . . 149 E8
Ravenfield Dr WA8 . . . . . 12 C3
Ravenho La SK10 . . . . . 88 D4
Ravenhurst Ct WA3 . . . . . 9 F5
Ravenoak Park Rd SK8 . . . 35 B8
Ravenoak Rd SK8 . . . . . 35 B8
Ravenscar Cres M22 . . . . . 33 D8
Ravens Cl ST7 . . . . . 209 E3
Ravenscliffe Rd ST7 . . . . . 195 A1
RAVENSCLOUGH 101 E3
Ravens Cnr CW5 . . . . . 203 E2
Ravenscroft CW4 . . . . . 130 A3
Ravenscroft Cl CW11 . . . . 175 C7
Ravenscroft Rd CW2 . . . . 189 E3
Ravensdale Cl WA2 . . . . . 8 D3
Ravensfield CW8 . . . . . 101 D4
Ravensholme Ct CH3 . . . . 166 A2
Ravensholme La CH3 . . . . 166 A2
Ravens La CW5 . . . . . 203 E5
Raven's La ST7 . . . . . 209 F3
Ravensmead Com Prim
Sch ST7 . . . . . 209 E3
RAVENSMOOR 203 E2
Ravenswood CW8 . . . . . 103 B4
Ravenswood Dr SK8 . . . . . 35 B8
Ravenswood Rd SK9 . . . . . 59 E4
Ravenwood Dr WA15 . . . . . 32 D7
Rawcliffe Cl WA8 . . . . . 12 F4
Rawdon Cl WA7 . . . . . 50 A7
Rawlings Cl WA3 . . . . . 9 F3
Rawlinson Cres L26 . . . . . 21 B8
Rawson Rd CH1 . . . . . 117 E3
Ray Ave CW5 . . . . . 204 F7
Raycliffe Cl WA7 . . . . . 49 D5
Rayleigh Ave CW9 . . . . . 127 A8
Rayleigh Way SK10 . . . . . 86 E1
Raymond Ave WA4 . . . . . 16 D2
Raymond St CH1 . . . . . 237 A3
Raymond Way CH64 . . . . . 67 A7
Rays Brow CW8 . . . . . 78 B2
Readesdale Ave CW2 . . . . 189 F2
Reade's La CW12 . . . . . 179 D8
Reading Room La SY14,
CH3 . . . . . 199 D8
Rean Mdw CH3 . . . . . 166 B2
Reaper Cl WA5 . . . . . 15 D6
REASE HEATH 188 C2
Reaseheath Coll CW5 . . . 188 D1
Reay St WA8 . . . . . 13 C2
Rectory Ave WA3 . . . . . 3 C8
Rectory Cl
Farndon CH3 . . . . . 180 E1
Heswall CH60 . . . . . 40 F7
8 Nantwich CW5 . . . . . 204 E5
Winwick WA2 . . . . . 8 A6
Wistaston CW2 . . . . . 205 E8
Rectory Gdns
Lymm WA13 . . . . . 18 E3
Talke ST7 . . . . . 210 D6
Rectory La
Adderley TF9 . . . . . 235 B5
Capenhurst CH1 . . . . . 94 A8
Heswall CH60 . . . . . 40 E7
Lymm WA13 . . . . . 18 E3
Winwick WA2 . . . . . 8 A6
Rectory View ST7 . . . . . 210 D6
Redacre SK12 . . . . . 36 F6
Redacre Cl WA4 . . . . . 51 A3
Red Bank Ave WA12 . . . . . 2 F1
Redbourne Dr
Chorlton CW2 . . . . . 207 D1
Widnes WA8 . . . . . 12 B4
Redbrook Cl CH62 . . . . . 43 D6
Redbrook Gr 2 SK9 . . . . . 34 D1
Redbrook Rd M31 . . . . . 11 E2
Redbrook Way SK10 . . . . . 62 C5
Red Brow La WA7, WA4 . . . 50 F8
RED BULL 194 E3
Redcar Dr CH62 . . . . . 43 D5
Red Cow Yd 11 WA16 . . . . 57 A2
Reddish Ave SK23 . . . . . 65 D6
Reddish Cres WA13 . . . . . 18 F4
Reddish La
Horwich End SK23 . . . . . 65 D6
Lymm WA13 . . . . . 19 A5
Reddish Rd SK23 . . . . . 65 D6
Reddy La WA14 . . . . . 30 B8
Redesdale Cl WA2 . . . . . 8 E2
Redesmere Cl
Macclesfield SK10 . . . . . 87 A1
Northwich CW9 . . . . . 104 A5
Sandbach CW11 . . . . . 174 F7
Redesmere Dr SK9 . . . . . 60 A1
Redesmere La SK11 . . . . . 110 B3
Redesmere Rd SK9 . . . . . 34 D5
Redfern Ave CW12 . . . . . 156 F4
Red Gables WA4 . . . . . 27 B3
Redgate CW8 . . . . . 103 D7
Redhill Mews CH65 . . . . . 70 B6
Redhill Rd
Chester CH4 . . . . . 140 F6
Kelsall CW6 . . . . . 122 C5
Red Ho SK10 . . . . . 87 E1
Redhouse La SK12 . . . . . 38 E7
Red House La WA14 . . . . . 20 C8
Redhouses SK11 . . . . . 113 D3
Red La
Disley SK12 . . . . . 38 C5
Frodsham WA6 . . . . . 74 C7
Huxley CH3 . . . . . 166 D6
Lower Whitley WA4 . . . . . 52 C1
Sandbach CW11 . . . . . 174 C6
Warrington WA4 . . . . . 26 C7
Redland Cl CH4 . . . . . 141 A7
Redland Ho CH4 . . . . . 141 B7
Red Lion Cl ST7 . . . . . 210 D7
Red Lion La
Ellesmere Port CH66 . . . . . 69 C7
Nantwich CW5 . . . . . 204 D5
Red Lo SK12 . . . . . 38 A6
Redmain Gr WA3 . . . . . 3 E8
Redmayne Cl WA12 . . . . . 2 B4
Redmere Dr CH60 . . . . . 41 D8
Redmoor La
Disley SK12 . . . . . 39 A4
New Mills SK22 . . . . . 39 B6
Red Pike CH66 . . . . . 69 D8
Redpoll La WA3 . . . . . 9 E4
Redrock Cres ST7 . . . . . 195 C1
Red Row SK7 . . . . . 37 B8
Redruth Ave SK10 . . . . . 86 E1
Redruth Cl WA7 . . . . . 50 C6
Redshank Ave CW7 . . . . . 149 C5
Redshank Cl WA12 . . . . . 2 C4
Redshank Dr SK10 . . . . . 87 C5
Redshank La WA3 . . . . . 9 F4
Redshaw Cl CW10 . . . . . 151 C6
Redstart Cl 7 WA3 . . . . . 3 E8
Redstone Dr 3 CW7 . . . . . 126 A1
Red Stone Hill WA6 . . . . . 73 C4
RED STREET 210 E3
Redtail Cl WA7 . . . . . 22 F3
Redvales Ct WA3 . . . . . 9 C4
Redvers Ave CH66 . . . . . 44 A2
Redway La SK10 . . . . . 88 B7
Redwing Cl ST7 . . . . . 195 F1
Redwood Cl
Barnton CW8 . . . . . 78 B4
Holt LL13 . . . . . 196 D8
Saltney CH4 . . . . . 140 E6
Warrington WA1 . . . . . 17 E7
Redwood Ct SK10 . . . . . 87 E5
Redwood Dr
Crewe CW1 . . . . . 189 F7
Ellesmere Port CH66 . . . . . 69 F1
Elton CH2 . . . . . 72 C4
Reece Cl CH2 . . . . . 119 E8
Reedgate La CW9 . . . . . 27 F1
Reed La CW9 . . . . . 53 C6
Reedsmere Cl WA4 . . . . . 16 E2
Reedsmere Wlk CW9 . . . . . 78 D8
Reeman Ct SK9 . . . . . 34 B2
Rees Cres CW4 . . . . . 130 C3
Reeves Rd CH3 . . . . . 142 B8
Reeve St WA3 . . . . . 4 B8
Regal Cl
Ellesmere Port CH66 . . . . . 69 E3
Northwich CW9 . . . . . 103 E4

Regal Cres WA8 22 B8
Regency Cl ST7 210 D5
Regency Ct
Chester CH2 119 E8
Winsford CW7 149 C7
Regency Gdns SK8 34 E8
Regency Hospl SK11 112 B8
Regency Pk SK9 59 F5
Regency Sq WA5 15 F6
Regency Way CW9 103 E4
Regency Wlk CW10 128 D1
Regent Ave
Haydock WA11 1 B7
Macclesfield SK11 112 B6
Warrington WA1 17 A8
Regent Bank SK9 59 F5
Regent Cl
Bramhall SK7 35 D4
Shavington CW2 206 B3
Wilmslow SK9 59 F5
Regent St WA15 32 C8
Regent & Foundry Ct 19 SK11 112 C8
Regent Rd WA8 13 B1
Regents Cl CH3 119 B2
Regents Gate CW5 205 A5
Regent St
Ellesmere Port CH65 70 A5
Moulton CW9 126 F8
Newton-le-W WA12 2 A3
12 Runcorn WA7 23 A3
Warrington WA1 16 A5
Regents The SK9 60 C8
Regents Theological Coll CW5 205 A5
Regents Way 4 CW7 149 A8
Reginald Mitchell Prim Sch The ST7 194 D1
Registry Cl CW9 103 E4
Reid Ave WA5 15 F8
Reid Ct CH66 69 C7
Reid St CW1 190 C6
Reins Croft CH64 41 E1
Rembury Pl WA4 51 A3
Remer St CW1 190 D7
Renaissance Way CW1 191 A3
Rendel Cl WA12 2 D2
Rendlesham Cl WA3 10 B6
Renfrew Ave CH62 43 E5
Renfrew Cl SK10 86 F2
Renown Cl WA3 9 D4
Renshaw St CW9 79 D2
Rensherds Pl WA16 29 C5
Renton Ave WA7 23 D2
Repton Cl WA16 29 C4
Repton Dr CW1 191 D5
Repton Rd CH65 70 D4
Reservoir Rd SK23 65 D7
Reservoir Terr CH2 118 F2
Retreat The CW1 190 C6
Revesby Cl WA8 12 D2
Rex Bldgs SK9 60 B6
Reynolds Ave
St Helens WA9 1 B2
Warrington WA3 9 E5
Reynold's La CW11 175 F6
Reynolds Mews SK9 60 E8
Reynolds St WA4 16 F3
Rhoden St CW1 191 A6
Rhodes Cl CW1 191 D4
Rhodes St WA2 16 C7
Rhodesway CH60 41 B7
Rhona Cl CH63 43 C4
Rhona Dr WA5 14 E6
Rhone Ct CH3 142 A8
RHUDDALL HEATH 146 E1
Rhuddlan Ct CH65 70 D2
Rhuddlan Ct/Llys Rhuddlan 5 CH4 140 F6
Rhuddlan Rd CH1 117 D3
Rhum Cl CH65 70 C1
Rhyl St WA8 22 F7
Ribble Ave CW7 127 B1
Ribble Cl
Culcheth WA3 4 F2
Widnes WA8 13 F3
Ribble Dr ST8 179 E1
Ribble Pl CW7 127 B1
Ribblesdale CH65 70 B3
Ribblesdale Ave CW12 157 A5
Ribblesdale Cl CH62 43 F5
Ribchester Gdns WA3 5 A3
Richard Cl WA7 24 A2
Richard Moon St CW1 190 B4
Richard Reynolds Ct M44 11 E6
Richards Croft CH3 142 A7
Richards Gr CW12 156 A3
Richardson Cl
4 Sandbach CW11 174 D6
Shavington CW2 206 D5
Richardson St WA2 16 C8
Richard St
Crewe CW1 190 B5
Northwich CW9 104 C7
Richbell Cl M44 11 F7
Richmond Ave
Grappenhall WA4 17 C3
Handforth SK9 34 D4
Haydock WA11 1 B7
Runcorn WA7 23 E2
Warrington WA4 17 A4
Richmond Cl
Chorlton CW2 207 D1
Culcheth WA3 4 D4
Richmond Cl *continued*
Lymm WA13 19 B4
Sandbach CW11 174 E7
Richmond Cres CH3 119 C2
Richmond Ct
Chester CH3 118 F2
Ellesmere Port CH65 70 D3
Warrington WA4 17 A3
Widnes WA8 13 D4
Richmond Dr
Lymm WA13 19 B4
Northwich CW9 104 A4
Richmond Gdns WA12 2 C2
Richmond Gr SK7 35 F6
Richmond Hill
1 Knutsford WA16 57 B1
Macclesfield SK11 112 E6
Richmond Mews CH2 118 F2
Richmond Pl SK11 112 E6
Richmond Rd CW1 190 E5
Richmond St
Warrington WA4 17 A3
Widnes WA8 13 C1
Richmond Village CW5 205 A5
Rickaby Cl CH63 43 C8
Ridding La WA7 50 B5
Riddings Ct CW8 103 B4
Riddings La
Hartford CW8 103 B4
Wybunbury CW5 220 A8
Riddings The CH65 70 B4
Rides The WA11 1 D6
Ridge Ave WA15 32 D6
Ridgeborne Cl WA5 7 D2
Ridge Hill
Langley SK11 113 B2
Utkinton CW6 146 B5
Ridge Pk SK7 35 D6
Ridge The CW8 123 D7
Ridge View SK11 112 C5
Ridgeway
Golborne WA3 3 E7
Wilmslow SK9 60 F7
Ridgeway Cl CH66 69 C2
Ridgeway Ho CH3 121 C3
Ridgeway The
Alvanley WA6 74 A1
Cronton WA8 12 C6
Disley SK12 38 C6
Heswall CH60 41 B7
Runcorn WA7 50 D6
Tarvin CH3 121 C3
Ridgewell Ave 4 WA3 3 D8
Ridgmont Rd SK7 35 E5
RIDGWARDINE 235 E1
Ridgway Gdns WA13 18 D3
Ridgway St
Crewe CW1 190 D5
Warrington WA2 16 D8
Ridings Com Inf Sch The CH1 94 A1
Ridings The
Saughall CH1 117 B8
Wilmslow SK9 59 D4
Ridley Cl CW2 206 E2
Ridley Dr WA5 15 C4
Ridley Gn CW6 185 D1
Ridley Hill Farm CW6 185 C3
Ridley Rd SK10 87 E8
RIDLEYWOOD 196 C3
Ridley Wood Rd LL13 196 A3
Ridsdale 2 WA8 22 C8
Rigby Ave CW1 190 A7
Rigby Rd ST7 195 B3
Rigby's Row CW5 204 E5
Rigby St WA3 3 A8
Rigg St 5 CW1 190 B5
Riley Bank Mews WA6 74 B1
Riley Cl CW11 174 E5
Riley Dr WA7 49 A8
Rileys Way ST7 209 F2
Rilshaw La CW7 150 B8
Rilston Ave WA3 4 D3
Rimington Cl WA3 4 E3
Rimsdale Cl CW2 206 A7
Ring-o-Bells La SK12 38 D6
Ring Rd
Chester CH2, CH3 119 C3
Connah's Quay CH5 91 E2
Ringsfield Rd L24 21 A2
Ringstead Cl SK9 34 D1
Ringstead Dr SK9 34 D1
Ringstone Way SK23 65 D8
Ringway
Ellesmere Port CH66 69 E4
Neston CH64 41 E1
Waverton CH3 143 B5
Ringway Cl SK10 87 B4
Ringway Prim Sch M22 33 D8
Ringway Rd
Runcorn WA7 23 D2
Wythenshawe M22, M90 33 D7
Ringway Rd W M22, M90 33 D8
Ringway Trad Est M22 33 E8
Ringwood Cl WA3 10 B5
Ripley Ave SK8 35 B5
Ripley Cl SK7 36 E8
Ripley St WA5 15 E6
Ripon Ave
Ellesmere Port CH66 69 C5
Golborne WA3 3 D8
Ripon Cl
Macclesfield SK10 87 C3
Newton-le-W WA12 2 C5
Ripon Dr CW2 206 A7
Ripon Row WA7 49 D6
Riseley St SK10 112 C8
Rise The SK23 65 C6
Rising Sun Cl SK11 112 A5
Rising Sun Rd SK11 112 A4
RISLEY 9 E6
Risley Moss Local Nature Reserve Visitor Ctr★ WA3 10 B5
Risley Rd WA3 9 F6
Rivacre Brow CH66 69 E8
Rivacre Bsns Ctr CH66 69 E5
Rivacre Rd CH62, CH65, CH66 44 C2
Rivacre Valley Ctry Pk★ CH66 69 D8
Rivacre Valley Prim Sch CH66 69 E7
Riverbank Cl
Bollington SK10 87 F8
Heswall CH60 40 F6
Nantwich CW5 204 E8
Riverbank Rd CH60 40 E6
Riverdane Rd CW12 156 F4
River La
Chester CH4 141 C7
Farndon CH3 180 E2
Partington M31 11 F4
Saltney CH4 140 E7
Rivermead Ave WA15 32 C7
River Rd
Connah's Quay CH5 91 F1
Warrington, Latchford WA4 16 B3
Warrington, Wilderspool WA4 16 C2
Riversdale
Frodsham WA6 49 C1
Warrington WA1 17 F7
Riversdale Rd WA7 49 E8
Rivershill Gdns WA15 32 D6
Riverside
Nantwich CW5 204 D5
Northwich CW9 104 B5
Riverside Bsns Pk SK9 60 B7
Riverside Cl WA1 16 D4
Riverside Coll Halton (Kingsway Campus) WA8 23 A8
Riverside Coll Halton Runcorn Campus WA7 22 E3
Riverside Cres CW4 130 C4
Riverside Ct
Huntington CH3 141 F7
Langley SK11 113 C4
Riverside Dr SK10 87 A5
Riverside Gr CW2 189 D3
Riverside Pk CW9 103 E6
Riverside Ret Pk WA1 16 C4
Riverside Trad Est
Northwich CW8 103 F7
Warrington WA5 14 D1
Riverside Trad Pk CH4 140 E7
Riverside Wlk CH64 66 D5
Riversmead CH3 142 A6
River St
Congleton CW12 156 D3
Macclesfield SK11 112 E6
Wilmslow SK9 60 B8
River View CW7 126 E1
Riverview Rd CH64 66 F5
River Wlk 8 WA7 49 F7
Rivington Ct WA1 17 E8
Rivington Gr M44 11 D6
Rivington Rd
Ellesmere Port CH65 70 C5
Runcorn WA7 50 F3
Rixton Ave WA5 15 F8
Rixton Park Homes WA3 10 F2
Roaches The SK11 112 B5
Road Beta CW10 151 D8
Road Five CW7 127 C2
Road Four CW7 127 B2
Road One
Weston CW1 207 D8
Winsford CW7 127 B3
Roadside Ct WA3 3 C8
Road Three CW7 127 D1
Road Two
Anderton CW9 78 C3
Weston CW1 207 C8
Winsford CW7 127 B2
Roan Ct SK11 112 F7
Roan House Way SK11 112 F7
Roan Mews SK11 112 F7
Roan Way SK9 85 B8
Robert Moffat WA16 29 C5
Roberts Ave WA11 1 A5
Roberts Ct WA7 49 F6
Roberts Dr CW9 104 D6
Roberts Fold WA3 9 D4
Roberts Rd CW9 80 A2
Robert St
Northwich CW9 103 E6
Runcorn WA7 23 C2
Warrington WA5 15 F6
Widnes WA8 13 B1
Robert's Terr CH1 118 B1
Robin Cl
Chelford SK11 84 A2
Rainow SK10 88 E5
Runcorn WA7 50 D7
Sandbach CW11 175 A8
Robin Cres SK11 112 D2
Robin Hood Ave SK11 112 D5
Robin Hood La WA6 73 B2
Robin La
Chelford SK11 84 A3
Sutton Lane Ends SK11 112 D2
Robinsbay Rd M22 33 E8
Robins Cl SK7 35 E7
Robins Croft CH66 69 F2
Robins La WA3 4 D2
Robin's La SK7 35 E7
Robinsons Croft CH3 142 B7
Robins Way SK10 88 A7
Rob La WA12 2 E5
Robson St WA1 16 D6
Robson Way 3 WA3 3 F8
Roby Gr WA5 15 A6
Roche Gdns SK8 35 B6
Rochester Cl
Golborne WA3 3 A8
Warrington WA5 15 C5
Rochester Cres CW1 190 F6
Rochester Dr CH65 70 D3
Rochester Ho SK10 86 F1
Rock Bank SK23 65 E6
Rock Bank Rise SK10 63 A1
Rock Cotts CH5 91 D1
Rock Dr WA6 49 C1
Rock Farm Cl CH64 67 A6
Rock Farm Dr CH64 67 A6
Rock Farm Gr CH64 67 A6
Rockfield Cl WA8 12 D2
Rockfield Dr WA6 73 C2
Rockfield Mews WA4 16 F2
Rockford Gdns WA5 15 A8
Rockford Lo WA16 57 C1
Rockhouse La ST7 210 C7
Rockingham Cl WA3 10 C6
Rock La
Burwardsley CH3 184 C6
Chester CH2 237 A4
Widnes WA8 12 F4
Rocklands La CH63 42 C8
Rocklee Gdns CH64 67 A6
Rockliffe La CH6 91 A3
Rock Mill La SK22 39 B7
Rock Rd
Connah's Quay CH5 91 E1
Warrington WA4 16 E4
ROCKSAVAGE 49 B4
Rock Savage Rdbt WA7 49 E4
Rockside ST7 195 C6
Rock St SK22 39 C7
Rock The WA6 73 C2
Rock Villas LL13 180 E1
Rockwood Ave CW2 190 A3
Rockwood Cl CW2 190 A3
Rocky La
Heswall CH60 40 F8
Tattenhall CH3 182 F7
Rocky La S CH60 41 A8
Roddy La WA6 75 E2
Rode Ct 7 CW12 156 F3
Rode Hall★ ST7 194 B7
RODEHEATH 134 B3
RODE HEATH 193 E7
Rodeheath Cl SK9 60 D7
Rode Heath Prim Sch ST7 193 F7
Rodehouse Cl ST7 193 F7
Rodepool Cl SK9 34 D2
Rode St CW6 146 A3
Rode The ST7 193 D4
Rodgers Cl WA6 49 B1
Rodney St SK11 112 D7
Roebourne Rise CH1 117 D4
Roebuck St CW1 190 C5
Roeburn Way WA5 14 D3
Roedean Wlk CW1 190 D6
Roehampton Dr WA7 49 E7
Roehurst La CW7 126 D2
Roemarsh Ct WA7 49 E6
Roe Pk CW12 178 E1
Roe St
Congleton CW12 156 E2
Macclesfield SK11 112 D7
Roewood La
Higher Hurdsfield SK10 88 A1
Macclesfield SK10 113 A8
Roften Ind Est CH66 43 D1
Rokeby Ct WA7 24 D5
Rokeden WA12 2 D4
Roklis Grange 10 CH64 66 E8
Roland Ave WA7 22 F1
Rolands Wlk WA7 23 F2
Rolleston St WA2 16 A6
Rolls Ave CW1 190 A6
Rolt Cres CW10 151 C7
Roman Cl
Newton-le-W WA12 2 C2
Runcorn WA7 23 E2
Roman Ct CH64 66 F7
Roman Dr CH1 117 D6
Romanes St CW8 103 E7
Roman Rd WA4 16 C1
Roman Way CW11 174 E7
Romiley Rd CH66 69 E6
Romney Cl
Neston CH64 66 E7
Widnes WA8 13 E2
Romney Croft CH64 66 F7
Romney Way CH64 66 F7
Romsey Dr SK8 35 C6
Rona Ave CH65 70 C1
Ronald Dr WA2 9 B2
Ronaldshay WA8 13 E2
Ronaldsway
Halewood L26 21 A8
Heswall CH60 40 F6
Ronan Rd WA8 22 E5
ROODEE 237 A1
Rood Hill CW12 156 D3
Rood La CW12 156 E4
Rookery Cl
1 Nantwich CW5 204 F5
Sandbach CW11 174 C5
Rookery Ct CW11 174 C5
Rookery Dr
Nantwich CW5 204 E4
Tattenhall CH3 166 B2
Rookery Farm Rd CW6 169 A6
Rookery Gdns CW9 103 E3
Rookerypool Cl SK9 34 D2
Rookery Rd
Kidsgrove ST7 195 C3
Tilston SY14 198 B3
Rookery Rise CW7 150 A8
Rookery The
Broughton CH4 139 B3
Newton-le-W WA12 2 D4
Rook St CW2 190 C2
Rooks Way CH60 40 E8
Roome St WA2 16 C7
Rope Bank Ave CW2 206 A7
Rope La
Shavington CW2 206 A5
Wistaston CW2 205 F7
Ropewalk The CH64 66 C8
Rope Wlk CW12 156 D3
Ropeworks The CH1 118 B2
Rosam Ct WA7 49 E6
Roscoe Ave
Newton-le-W WA12 2 E3
Warrington WA2 16 D8
Roscoe Cres WA7 48 E7
Roscoe Rd M44 11 F8
Roscoes Yd 4 WA16 57 A2
Roscommon Way WA8 12 E3
Roscote Cl CH60 40 F7
Roscote The CH60 40 F7
Rose Ave WA11 1 E6
Rose Bank
Bollington SK10 87 F7
Lymm WA13 18 E3
Rosebank Cl CW7 149 F8
Rosebank Mews CW10 129 E5
Rosebank Rd M44 11 C4
Rosebank Sch CW8 78 A3
Rosebank Wlk CW8 78 A4
Rosebery Way CW1 191 C4
Rose Cl
Blacon CH1 117 D4
Halewood L26 21 A7
Runcorn WA7 50 D5
Rose Cnr CH3 166 A1
Rose Cotts CW12 154 F6
Rose Cres WA8 22 F7
Rosecroft CH62 43 C6
Rosedale Ave
Golborne WA3 3 C7
Warrington WA1 17 C7
Rosedene Cl CH2 118 E8
Rose Farm Ct CW9 79 E4
Rose Farm Mews WA6 73 B4
Rose Gdns CH64 66 F6
Roseheath Dr L26 21 A6
Rosehill Ave WA9 6 B5
Rosehill Rd CW2 190 B1
Roselands Ct LL12 162 C1
Rose Lea Cl WA8 13 A4
Rosemary Ave
Runcorn WA7 49 F4
Warrington WA4 16 E2
Rosemary Cl
Broughton CH4 139 C3
Warrington WA5 15 C6
Rosemary Dr WA12 2 F3
Rosemary La LL12 161 D1
Rosemary Row CH3 166 A1
Rosemary Wlk M31 11 F2
Rosemere Dr CH1 94 F7
Rosemoor Gdns WA4 26 F5
Rosemount CW10 128 C1
Rosemount Cotts WA2 8 B8
Rose St WA8 22 F7
Rose Terr
Blacon CH1 117 D4
Crewe CW1 190 C5
Rosetree Mdw CW9 80 A2
Rosevale Rd ST5 210 F1
Rose View Ave WA8 13 A2
Roseville Dr CW12 179 B8
Roseway SK11 112 D5
Rose Wharf SK11 112 E7
Rose Wlk 5 M31 11 E3
Rosewood Ave
Chester CH2 118 D5
Frodsham WA6 74 D7
Warrington WA1 16 E7
Rosewood Cl CW1 190 E6
Rosewood Dr CW7 126 A1
Rosewood Farm Ct WA8 12 E4
Rosewood Gr
Saughall CH1 117 B8
Widnes WA8 22 B8
Rosewood Ho CW12 156 A3
Rossall Cl L24 21 E2
Rossall Ct SK7 35 E6

Rossall Dr SK7 35 E6
Rossall Gr CH66 69 D6
Rossall Rd
Warrington WA5 15 B4
Widnes WA8 13 D2
Rossbank Rd CH65 70 A7
Ross Cl WA5 15 D7
Rosscliffe Rd CH65 70 A6
Ross Dr CH66 69 C5
Rossenclough Rd SK9 34 D1
Rossendale Dr WA3 10 A6
Rossendale Rd SK8 34 C8
Rossett Ave 1 M22 33 D8
Rossett Bsns Village LL12 162 B1
Rossett Cl
Northwich CW9 103 E4
Warrington WA5 7 E2
Rossett Pk LL12 162 C1
Rossett Rd LL13 180 A1
Rossfield Rd CH65 70 A6
Rossfield Rd N CH65 70 B7
Rosslyn Cl CH5 116 A2
Rosslyn La CW8 102 A3
Rosslyn Rd CH3 119 B3
Rossmill La WA15 32 B7
Rossmore Bsns Pk CH65 70 B7
Rossmore Ct CH66 69 E6
Rossmore Gdns CH66 69 D6
Rossmore Ind Est CH65 70 A6
Rossmore Rd E CH65 69 F7
Rossmore Rd W CH66 69 D7
Rossmore Sch CH66 69 C7
Rossmore Terraced Factories CH65 70 A6
Rossmount Rd CH65 70 A6
Ross Rd CH65 70 A6
Ross St WA8 13 B1
Rosswood Rd CH65 70 A6
ROSTHERNE 30 E4
Rostherne Ave
Ellesmere Port CH66 69 E4
Golborne WA3 3 D8
High Lane SK6 37 E8
Rostherne Cl 1 WA5 15 D4
Rostherne Cres WA8 12 D2
Rostherne La WA16 30 E4
Rostherne Rd SK9 34 F4
Rostherne Way CW11 174 F7
Rosyth Cl WA2 8 F3
Rothay Dr WA5 14 D3
Rothbury Cl WA7 49 D6
Rother Dr CH65 70 A7
Rother Dr Bsns Ctr CH65 70 A7
Rotherhead Dr SK11 112 B5
Rotherwood Rd SK9 59 D6
Rothesay Cl WA7 23 F2
Rothesay Dr CH62 43 E4
Rothesay Rd CH4 141 A7
Rough Bank CW12 179 E8
Rough Heys La SK11 111 A8
ROUGHHILL 140 E1
Roughlea Ave WA3 4 D4
Roughley Ave WA5 15 D4
Roughlyn Cres CH4 140 E1
Roughwood La
Alsager CW11, ST7 193 B7
Hassall Green CW11 176 A1
Roundabout The WA8 12 D6
Round Gdns SK10 88 A8
Roundhey SK8 34 C8
Round Hill Mdw CH3 142 B7
Round Mdw SK10 88 E5
Round Thorn WA3 9 A8
Roundway SK7 35 D6
Round Way SK22 39 D8
Roundy La SK10 62 F6
Routledge St WA8 13 B1
Rowan Ave WA3 3 F7
Rowan Cl
Alsager ST7 193 D3
Delamere CW8 123 D7
Lawton Heath ST7 193 D6
Middlewich CW10 151 E6
Runcorn WA7 49 C7
Sandbach CW11 174 F7
Warrington WA5 14 F6
Winsford CW7 126 D3
Rowan Ct SK9 60 B7
Rowan Dr SK8 35 C8
Rowan Gr CH5 91 C1
Rowan Ho CH2 237 C4
Rowan Lo SK7 35 F7
Rowan Pk CH3 142 E7
Rowan Pl CH2 119 B4
Rowan Rd CW8 102 D8
Rowan Rise CW8 78 A3
Rowans Cl CW1 189 F7
Rowanside SK10 86 E6
Rowanside Dr SK9 60 E8
Rowans The
Broughton CH4 139 B3
4 Northwich CW9 103 E6
Widnes WA8 13 D4
Rowan Tree Rd WA16 59 B5
Rowan Way SK10 87 E1
Rowan Wlk M31 11 E2
Rowcliffe Ave CH4 141 A4
Rowena Ct CH2 118 F3
Rowland Cl WA2 9 A3
Rowlands Hts 1 CH1 237 C3
Rowlands View CW6 146 B7
Rowley Bank La WA16 29 B1
ROWLEYHILL 181 B1
Rowley Rd SK7 36 E8
Rowley Way WA16 82 B7
ROWLINSON'S GREEN 28 C5
ROW-OF-TREES 59 D3
Rowson Dr M44 11 D6
Rowswood Ctyd WA4 25 E5
Rowswood Farm WA4 25 E5
Row The
3 Winsford CW7 126 D1
Wrenbury CW5 217 B5
Rowthorn Cl WA8 22 E8
ROWTON 142 E5
Rowton Bridge Rd CH3 142 E7
Rowton Cl 7 CW9 103 F4
Rowton La CH3 142 F6
Rowton Rd CW2 189 D4
Roxborough Cl WA5 7 A6
Roxburgh Cl SK10 87 A1
Roxburgh Rd CH66 68 F6
Roxby Way WA16 82 A7
Roxholme Wlk M22 33 C8
Royal Arc 5 CW1 190 C4
Royal Ave WA8 12 A1
Royal Ct 3 WA16 57 A2
Royal Gdns
Altrincham WA14 20 F2
Northwich CW9 103 E3
Royal La CW6 147 A3
Royal Mdws SK10 87 A1
Royal Mews CW9 104 D5
Royal Pl WA8 22 B8
Royal Rd SK12 38 D5
Royal Schools for The Deaf & Communication Disorders SK8 34 D6
ROYAL'S GREEN 228 E1
Royal Sh Arc The 9 CH64 66 E8
Royce Cl CW1 190 A7
Royce Cl WA16 56 F2
Royden Ave
Irlam M44 11 F8
Runcorn WA7 49 A8
Royds Cl CW8 103 B4
Royds Ct CW11 174 D5
Roylance Dr CW10 151 C8
Royleen Dr WA6 74 D6
Royle Pk CW12 156 D3
Royle's Pl CW8 103 D6
Royles Sq 2 SK9 60 A1
Royle St
Congleton CW12 156 D3
Northwich CW9 104 B8
Winsford CW7 126 E1
Royston Ave WA1 17 A7
Royston Cl
Ellesmere Port CH66 69 F3
2 Golborne WA3 3 E8
Rozel Cres WA5 15 B5
Rubin Dr CW1 189 F7
Rudd Ave WA9 1 A3
RUDHEATH 104 D6
Rudheath Cl CW2 189 D5
Rudheath Com High Sch CW9 104 D7
Rudheath Com Prim Sch CW9 104 D6
Rudheath La WA7 24 D3
Rudheath Way CW9 104 E5
Rudloe Ct WA2 8 F1
Rudstone Cl CH66 69 B5
Rudyard Cl SK11 112 B6
Rue De Bohars CW6 168 D8
Rufford Cl
Widnes WA8 12 C2
Wistaston CW2 206 B8
Rufford Ct WA1 17 E8
Rufus Ct CH1 237 A3
Rugby Cl SK10 87 E4
Rugby Dr SK10 87 E4
Rugby Ho SK10 87 D3
Rugby Rd CH65 70 D3
Rugby Wlk CH65 70 D3
Ruislip Ct WA2 8 F1
RULOE 101 D7
RUNCORN 23 C1
Runcorn All Saints CE Prim Sch WA7 23 A3
Runcorn Docks Rd WA7 22 E2
Runcorn East Sta WA7 50 D7
Runcorn Mkt WA7 23 A3
Runcorn Rd
Barnton CW8 78 B2
Higher Walton WA4 25 D6
Little Leigh CW8 77 D5
Runcorn Spur Rd WA7 23 B1
Runcorn Sta WA7 22 F2
Runger La M90, WA15 32 F8
Runnell The CH64 41 D4
Runnymede WA1 17 D7
Runnymede Ct 2 WA8 13 C1
Runnymede Dr WA11 1 A6
Runnymede Gdns 5 WA8 13 C1
Runnymede Wlk 3 WA8 13 C2
Rupert Row WA7 50 A8
Ruscoe Ave CW11 174 E6
Ruscolm Cl WA5 14 D7
Rushes Mdw WA13 19 B5
Rushey Cl WA15 32 D7
Rushfield Cres WA7 50 B5
Rushfield Rd
Cheadle SK8 35 A6
Chester CH4 141 B5
Rush Gdns WA13 19 A4
RUSHGREEN 19 A4
Rushgreen Rd WA13 19 A4
Rushmere Cl SK10 62 F2
Rushmere La CH3 163 F3
Rushmore Gr WA1 17 A7
Rusholme Cl L26 21 A6
Rushside Rd SK8 35 A6
RUSHTON 147 C5
Rushton Ave WA12 2 B4
Rushton CE Prim Sch SK11 159 B2
Rushton Cl
Burtonwood WA5 6 F7
Northwich CW9 104 C7
Widnes WA8 12 F3
Rushton Dr
Chester CH2 118 E7
Hough CW2 206 E2
Middlewich CW10 151 C7
Rushton Fold SK10 61 A2
Rushton La CW6 147 D6
Rushton Rd SK8 35 A6
RUSHTON SPENCER 159 B2
Rushy View WA12 2 A4
Ruskin Ave
Newton-le-W WA12 2 C4
Warrington WA2 8 C2
Ruskin Ct WA16 57 A2
Ruskin Dr CH65 70 D3
Ruskin Rd
Congleton CW12 156 C2
Crewe CW2 190 C2
Ruskin Sports Coll & Com High Sch CW2 190 C2
Ruskin Way WA16 57 A3
Russel Ct WA8 13 B4
Russell Ave
Alsager ST7 193 D5
High Lane SK6 37 E7
Russell Cl CW12 179 A8
Russell Dr CW1 191 C5
Russell Rd
Runcorn WA7 48 E8
Winsford CW7 149 C8
Russell St CH1, CH3 237 C3
Russet Cl CW10 128 B2
Russet Rd CW8 102 D8
Russett Sch & Cheshire MSI Unit The CW8 102 E8
Russet Way SK9 59 E3
Rutherford Dr WA16 82 C7
Ruthin Cl WA5 7 E3
Ruthin Ct CH65 70 D3
Ruthin Wlk WA6 73 A1
Rutland Ave
Golborne WA3 3 D7
Halewood L26 21 A8
Warrington WA4 26 B8
Rutland Cl
Congleton CW12 156 E4
Sandbach CW11 174 C5
Rutland Dr
Middlewich CW10 151 C7
Weaverham CW8 77 C1
Rutland Pl CH2 119 A5
Rutland Rd
Hazel Grove SK7 36 E8
Irlam M44 11 D5
Kidsgrove ST7 195 A2
Macclesfield SK11 112 D4
Partington M31 11 E2
Rutland St 1 WA7 22 F2
Rutter Ave WA5 7 F2
Ryburn Cl CW2 207 B3
Ryburn Rd SK11 112 A5
Rydal Ave
High Lane SK6 37 E8
Warrington WA4 16 A2
Rydal Cl
Ellesmere Port CH65 70 C2
Holmes Chapel CW4 130 B2
Neston CH64 66 F6
Winsford CW7 126 D3
Rydal Ct CW12 156 A2
Rydal Dr WA15 32 D8
Rydal Gr
Chester CH4 141 A6
Helsby WA6 73 B1
Runcorn WA7 49 B8
Rydal Mount CW1 173 B1
Rydal Pl SK11 112 A6
Rydal St WA12 2 C3
Rydal Way
Alsager ST7 193 C5
Widnes WA8 12 C1
Ryde Cl CW1 190 B8
Ryder Rd
Warrington WA1 17 C7
Widnes WA8 13 B4
Ryders St CW8 103 E8
Ryebank Ave CW1 190 B7
Ryebank Way SK10 87 C3
Rye Cl ST7 193 B3
Ryecroft CH2 72 B3
Ryecroft Cl CW10 151 B7
Ryecroft La
Duddon CH3, CW6 144 C6
Mobberley WA16 57 E4
Ryecroft Rd CH60 41 C7
Ryedale Way CW12 179 C8
Ryehills ST7 209 E1
RYE HILLS 209 E1
Rylands Cl SY14 213 B4
Rylands Dr WA2 16 C7
Rylands St
Warrington WA1 16 B5
5 Widnes WA8 23 B8
Ryles Cl SK11 112 C5
Ryles Cres SK11 112 C5
Ryles Ho SK11 112 C5
Ryle's Park Rd SK11 112 C6
Ryle St SK11 112 D6
Ryleys Farm SK9 59 F1
Ryleys La SK9 59 F1
Ryleys Sch The SK9 59 F1

S

Sabre Cl WA7 50 D7
Sack La CW9 54 F6
Sacred Heart RC Prim Sch WA5 15 E5
Saddleback Dr SK10 86 F7
Saddlers Rise WA7 50 C8
Saddlery Way CH1 118 B1
Sade Ct 4 CW1 190 B5
Sadler Cl CW7 126 D1
Sadler Rd CW7 126 D1
Sadler's Cl CW4 130 B3
Sadlers La CW6 124 A1
Sadler St WA8 13 C1
Sadlers Wells CW6 185 E8
Saffron Cl
Golborne WA3 3 E8
Warrington WA2 9 B1
Saffron Wlk M31 11 F2
Sagars Rd
Handforth SK9 34 C3
Styal SK9 34 B4
Sage Cl WA2 9 C2
SAIGHTON 142 E1
Saighton CE Prim Sch CH3 142 E1
Saighton La CH3 142 F2
St Aelred's RC Tech Coll WA12 2 D4
St Aidans Dr WA8 12 F6
St Alban Rd WA5 14 E5
St Albans Cl WA11 2 A7
St Albans Dr CW5 204 F3
St Alban's RC Prim Sch
Macclesfield SK10 86 F1
Warrington WA5 15 F6
St Albans St SK22 39 C8
St Ambrose Coll WA15 32 B8
St Ambrose Ct WA4 16 B2
St Ambrose RC Prim Sch L24 21 A2
St Ambrose Rd WA8 13 C1
St Andrew's Ave CW2 190 C1
St Andrew's CE Prim Sch WA2 8 C3
St Andrews Cl
Northwich CW9 104 E7
Warrington WA2 9 A4
St Andrews Ct
Crewe CW2 190 C1
Ellesmere Port CH65 70 E2
Macclesfield SK11 112 B7
St Andrews Dr
Holmes Chapel CW4 130 B2
Kidsgrove ST7 195 C3
St Andrew's Gdns ST7 193 E2
St Andrew's Rd
Ellesmere Port CH65 70 E3
Macclesfield SK11 112 B7
St Andrews Wlk
Mickle Trafford CH2 96 F1
New Mills SK22 39 D8
St Annes CH1 237 B3
St Annes Ave WA4 17 B2
St Anne's Ave CW10 151 D8
St Annes Ave E WA4 17 B2
St Anne's Fulshaw CE Prim Sch SK9 59 F6
St Anne's La CW5 204 D5
St Anne's RC Prim Sch CW5 204 E3
St Anne's Rd WA8 13 B2
St Anne St CH1 237 B3
St Ann's Rd CW10 151 C8
St Ann's Rd S SK8 34 C8
St Ann's Sq SK8 34 C8
St Anthony Pl WA2 8 B6
St Anthony's RC Prim Sch CH4 140 E6
St Asaph Dr WA5 7 E3
St Asaph Rd CH66 94 E8
St Augustine's Ave WA4 16 F4
St Augustines Dr CW2 207 E3
St Augustine's RC Prim Sch
Runcorn WA7 24 A2
Warrington WA4 16 F4
St Austel Cl WA5 14 E3
St Austell Ave SK10 86 E1
St Austell Cl
Macclesfield SK10 86 E1
Runcorn WA7 50 B6
St Austell Dr SK8 34 B8
St Austins La WA1 16 B4
St Barnabas CE Prim Sch
Macclesfield SK11 112 D6
Warrington WA5 15 F5
St Barnabas Ct SK11 112 D6
St Barnabas Pl WA5 15 E6
St Bartholomews Ct CH5 116 E6
St Basil's RC Prim Sch WA8 12 A2
St Bede's Ave CW8 77 D1
St Bede's RC Inf Sch WA8 13 A1
St Bede's RC Jun Sch WA8 13 A1
St Bede's RC Prim Sch CW8 102 F7
St Benedicts Cl WA2 16 B7
St Benedict's RC Prim Sch
Handforth SK9 34 E3
Warrington WA2 16 D7
St Bernard's RC Prim Sch CH65 70 D3
St Berteline's CE Prim Sch WA7 50 C8
St Brannocks Rd SK8 35 B7
St Brides Cl WA5 14 E3
St Bridgets Cl
Warrington WA2 8 F3
Widnes WA8 23 A5
St Bridgets Ct CH4 141 B6
St Bridget's RC Prim Sch WA2 8 E3
St Catherine Dr CW8 103 A4
St Catherine's RC Prim Sch WA3 3 E7
St Chad's CE Prim Sch
Newcastle-u-Lyme ST5 210 D2
Winsford CW7 149 E8
St Chads Cl CW5 220 A8
St Chad's Fields CW7 149 C5
St Chad's RC High Sch WA7 49 D7
St Chad's Rd CH1 117 F4
St Chad's Terr ST5 210 D2
St Chads Way TF9 236 C2
St Christophers Cl CH2 118 D8
St Clair St CW2 190 D1
St Clare's RC Prim Sch CH4 141 A5
St Clements Ct CW2 207 B1
St Clement's RC Prim Sch WA7 49 A8
St David Rd CH62 44 A6
St Davids Dr
12 Ellesmere Port CH66 94 F8
Warrington WA5 7 E2
St David's High Sch CH4 140 C6
St Davids' Ret Pk CH4 140 D7
St David's Terr CH4 140 C6
St Edwards Cl SK11 112 D6
St Edward's RC Prim Sch
Macclesfield SK11 112 C5
Runcorn WA7 23 B3
St Elmo Pk SK12 37 C4
St Elphins Cl WA1 16 C5
St Elphin's (Fairfield) CE Prim Sch WA1 16 D6
SS Peter & Paul RC High Sch WA8 12 F2
St Gabriels Ct ST7 193 C3
St Gabriel's RC Prim Sch ST7 193 C3
St George's Ch CH1 237 B3
St Georges Ave 13 CH66 94 F8
St George's CE Prim Sch SK22 39 C8
St Georges Cl WA4 26 E3
St George's Cl WA16 82 C8
St George's Cres
Chester CH4 237 C1
Waverton CH3 143 A5
St George's Ct WA8 22 D8
St George's Pl 11 SK11 112 D7
St Georges Rd SK22 39 C8
St George's Rd CW7 149 C8
St George's St SK11 112 D6
St George's Way
Northwich CW9 103 F5
Thornton Hough CH63 42 A7
St Gerard's RC Prim Sch WA8 23 B7
St Gregory's RC High Sch WA5 15 D5
St Gregory's RC Prim Sch SK10 87 F8
ST HELENS 1 A1
St Helens Cl WA3 11 B3
St Helens Coll Newton Campus WA12 2 B4
St Helens Rd
Golborne WN7 4 B8
5 Northwich CW9 104 A8
St Hilarys Pk SK9 85 A8
St Hilda's Dr WA6 49 C1
St Ives Cl SK10 86 E1
St Ives Pk CH5 116 A3
St Ives Way CH5 116 A3
St James Ave
Chester CH2 118 F7
Congleton CW12 156 C2
Warren SK11 111 E2
St James' CE Prim Sch WA11 1 E6
St James Cl
Audlem CW3 230 A4
1 Frodsham WA6 49 C1
St James Ct
Audley ST7 209 D2

St James Ct *continued*
Cheadle SK8 34 F6
Chester CH2 118 F3
St James' Ct
Biddulph ST8 179 E3
Warrington WA4 16 B3
St James Ct/Llys Sant Iago CH5 91 D1
St James' Dr SK9 60 A6
St James' RC High Sch SK8 34 F6
St James' Sq SK22 39 C8
St James St CH1 237 B3
St James Terr 9 CW7 149 A8
St James' Way SK8 34 F6
St James Wlk 1 CW8 103 E7
St John Ave WA4 16 B2
St John Fisher RC Prim Sch WA8 13 D1
St John's Ave
Knutsford WA16 56 F1
Lostock Gralam CW9 79 F3
St John's Brow WA7 23 B3
St John's CE Prim Sch
Bollington SK10 88 A7
Sandbach CW11 175 E6
St John's Cl CW9 104 E8
St Johns Ct
Chester CH1 237 B2
Winsford CW7 126 B1
St John's Ct
Knutsford WA16 57 C2
Warrington WA1 16 F7
St Johns Dr CW7 149 A8
St John's Rd
Bebington CH62 44 A5
Chester CH4 237 C1
Congleton CW12 157 A5
Knutsford WA16 57 A1
7 Macclesfield SK11 112 C7
Wilmslow SK9 59 E3
St John's Rear Rd CH4 237 C1
St John's St WA7 23 B3
St John St
Chester CH1 237 B2
Newton-le-W WA12 2 A3
St John's Way
Cuddington CW8 102 B2
Sandbach CW11 175 E6
St John's Wood ST7 194 F1
St John's Wood Com Sch WA16 57 D2
St John The Evangelist CE Prim Sch SK11 112 A7
St John The Evangelist RC Prim Sch ST7 194 F1
St Joseph's Cl WA5 14 E5
St Joseph's RC Prim Sch
Warrington WA5 14 E5
Winsford CW7 149 B8
St Josephs Way CW5 205 A5
St Katherines Way WA1 16 D5
St Kilda Cl CH65 70 C1
St Lawrence Ct CW5 204 F6
St Lawrence Rd WA6 74 B8
St Leonard's Way CW3 232 C1
St Lewis RC Prim Sch WA3 4 B1
St Luke's Ave WA3 3 D8
St Luke's CE Prim Sch WA3 3 E7
St Lukes Cl CW4 130 D3
St Luke's Cres WA8 13 B4
St Luke's Ho 3 SK10 111 F8
St Luke's RC Prim Sch WA6 74 C8
St Luke's Way WA6 49 B1
St Margaret's Ave WA2 8 D1
St Margaret's CE Prim Sch WA2 8 C1
St Mark's CE Prim Sch CW9 53 C4
St Marks Cres CH66 94 F8
St Mark's RC Prim Sch L26 21 A8
St Marks Rd CH4 140 F6
St Mark's St WA11 1 A6
St Martins Dr CH66 69 D2
St Martins La WA7 50 D7
St Martins RC Prim Sch WA7 50 D7
St Martin's Rd ST7 210 E6
St Martin's Way CH1 237 A3
St Mary of the Angels RC Prim Sch CH66 69 D6
St Mary's Ave CW8 77 D1
St Mary's CE Prim Sch
Bebington CH62 44 A5
Bosley SK11 158 D8
Irlam M44 11 C5
Runcorn WA7 50 A8
St Mary's Cl
Alsager ST7 193 C5
Hale L24 21 E2
Warrington WA4 26 C6
St Marys Ct CW5 204 A7
St Mary's Ct CW12 156 A2
St Mary's Ct
Golborne WA3 4 B8
Partington M31 11 F4
St Mary's Dr CW8 126 A8
St Mary's Hill CH1 237 B1
St Mary's Hospl The Phineas Gage Ctr WA2 8 B1
St Mary's RC Inf Sch WA12 2 C4
St Mary's RC Jun Sch WA12 2 B3
St Mary's RC Prim Sch
Congleton CW12 156 D3
Crewe CW2 190 A1
Middlewich CW10 151 C8
New Mills SK22 39 B8
St Mary's Rd
Disley SK12 38 D5
Dodleston CH4 162 A7
Nantwich CW5 204 E7
New Mills SK22 39 B8
Runcorn WA8 23 F1
Warrington WA5 14 F5
Widnes WA8 23 A4
St Mary's St
Crewe CW1 190 C4
Warrington WA4 16 D3
St Mary's Way CH4 139 C5
St Matthews CE Prim Sch WA4 26 E2
St Matthews Cl
Haslington CW1 191 D4
Warrington WA4 26 D7
St Mawes Cl WA8 12 E2
St Mawes Ct SK10 86 E1
St Mawgan Ct WA2 8 F2
St Michael's Ave SK7 35 E8
St Michael's Cl
Little Leigh CW8 77 D5
Widnes WA8 22 C7
St Michael's Cotts CW12 156 B7
St Michael's Ind Est WA8 22 C7
St Michael's RC Prim Sch WA8 22 C7
St Michael's Rd WA8 22 C7
St Michael's Row CH1 237 B2
St Michael's Sq CH1 237 B2
St Michaels Terr 10 SK11 112 D8
St Michael's View CW1 190 B5
St Michael's Way CW10 128 C1
St Monicas Cl WA4 26 D7
St Monica's RC Prim Sch WA4 26 D7
St Nicholas Ct CW5 204 F5
St Nicholas RC High Sch CW8 103 D6
St Nicholas Rd WA3 4 A8
St Olave St CH1 237 B1
St Oswalds CH1 237 B3
St Oswald's CE Prim Sch CH1 94 F2
St Oswalds Cl
Malpas SY14 213 B3
Winwick WA2 8 B6
St Oswald's Cres CW11 153 F5
St Oswald's RC Prim Sch WA1 16 F8
St Oswalds Way CH1, CH2 237 B3
St Oswald's Worleston CE Prim Sch CW5 188 E6
St Patricks Cl WA8 23 A5
St Paul of the Cross RC Prim Sch WA5 6 E6
St Paul's Cl CW1 190 C4
St Paul's Ct
2 Macclesfield SK11 112 E7
Warrington WA2 16 A6
St Pauls Gdns CH66 69 B7
St Paul's Pl 2 CW9 79 A1
St Paul's RC Prim Sch SK12 36 E2
St Paul's Rd
3 Macclesfield SK11 112 E7
Widnes WA8 23 A7
St Paul's St CW1 190 C4
St Peter's Ave WA16 56 F1
St Peter's CE Prim Sch WA12 2 E4
St Peter's Cl
Heswall CH60 40 F7
Lymm WA13 19 A4
St Peter's Ct WA2 16 C6
St Peter's Dr CW6 147 F7
St Peter's Ho SK11 112 E6
St Peter's RC Prim Sch WA1 17 C7
St Peters Rd CW12 156 E1
St Peter's Rise CW11 174 E7
St Peters Way CH2 119 F8
St Peter's Way WA2 16 B6
St Philip (Westbrook) CE Prim Sch WA5 7 B1
St Saviour's CE Prim Sch ST7 194 D1
St Saviour's RC Inf Sch CH66 69 E3
St Saviour's RC Jun Sch CH66 69 E3
St Saviour's St ST7 194 D1
St Stephen Rd WA5 14 F5
St Stephen's Ave WA2 8 B3
St Stephens Cl CH60 41 C6
St Stephens Ct
11 Congleton CW12 156 F3
Sandbach CW11 174 D7
St Stephen's RC Prim Sch WA2 8 B2
St Teresa's RC Prim Sch M44 11 E8
St Theresa's RC Prim Sch CH1 117 F5
St Thomas CE Prim Sch ST7 195 A1
St Thomas Ct WA8 12 E1
St Thomas More RC High Sch CW2 190 A2
St Thomas of Canterbury Blue Coat CE Jun Sch CH1 237 A4
St Thomas's CE Prim Sch WA4 16 D1
St Thomas's Pathway CH1 237 B2
St Thomas St ST7 195 E7
St Thomas Terr WA8 12 E1
St Thomas' View CH65 70 B4
St Vincent Dr CW8 102 F3
St Vincent Rd WA5 14 F5
St Vincent's RC Prim Sch
Knutsford WA16 57 C1
Warrington WA5 14 F3
St Wenefredes Gn SY13 214 F6
St Werburgh's & St Columba's RC Prim Sch CH2 118 F2
St Werburgh St CH1 237 B2
St Wilfrids Cl CW9 104 A3
St Wilfrid's Dr WA4 17 C1
St Wilfrid's RC Prim Sch CW8 103 D5
St Winefride's RC Prim Sch CH64 66 F7
Salander Cres CW2 206 A7
Salerno Rd CH2 95 B1
Salesbrook La CW5 228 C7
Salford CW3 230 A4
Salford Pl CW12 156 E3
Salisbury Ave
Crewe CW2 190 C1
Saltney CH4 140 E6
Salisbury Cl
Crewe CW2 190 C1
10 Ellesmere Port CH66 94 F8
Salisbury Pl SK10 87 E4
Salisbury Rd WA11 1 E8
Salisbury St
Chester CH1 118 B3
Golborne WA3 3 A8
Runcorn WA7 23 A1
Warrington WA1 16 D6
4 Widnes WA8 23 B8
Salkeld St 8 CW9 104 B8
Salmon Leap CH4 237 B1
Salop Pl ST7 195 A3
Salop Wlk SK10 86 F2
Saltash Cl WA7 50 B6
Saltersbrook Gr 12 SK9 34 E1
Salters Ford CW8 77 F3
Saltersford Cnr CW4 130 E3
Saltersgate CH66 69 F2
Salters La
Lower Withington SK11 132 B8
Windyharbour SK11 109 D1
Salter's La
Bickerton SY14 199 F8
Broxton CH3, SY14 183 E1
Hoole Bank CH2 119 C8
SALTERSWALL 125 F3
Salt Line Way CW11 174 D6
Salt Mdws CW5 204 C5
Salt Mus The★ CW9 103 F7
SALTNEY 140 D6
Saltney Bsns Ctr CH4 140 F7
Saltney Ferry Prim Sch CH4 140 B6
Saltney Ferry Rd CH4 140 B7
Saltney Terr CH4 140 B7
Salton Gdns WA5 15 E7
Saltwood Dr WA7 50 C5
Saltworks Cl WA6 49 D2
Samian Cl CW10 128 C2
Samphire Gdns WA9 6 B7
Samuel St
Chester CH1 237 C3
Crewe CW1 190 B5
Macclesfield SK11 112 D7
Packmoor ST7 195 F1
Warrington WA5 15 E4
Sanbec Gdns WA8 12 D5
Sandalwood WA7 24 C1
Sandalwood Cl WA2 8 D2
SANDBACH 175 B5
Sandbach Com Prim Sch CW11 175 A6
Sandbach Crosses★ CW11 175 B6
Sandbach Dr CW9 103 E6
SANDBACH HEATH 175 D6
Sandbach High Sch & Sixth Form Coll CW11 175 A7
Sandbach Rd
Congleton CW12 156 A3
Rode Heath ST7 193 E7
Sandbach Rd N ST7 193 C4
Sandbach Rd S ST7 193 D3
Sandbach Sch CW11 175 A6
Sandbach Sta CW11 174 D8
Sanderling Rd WA12 2 C4
Sanders Hey Cl WA7 50 B5
Sanderson Cl
Crewe CW2 206 C8
Sanderson Cl *continued*
Warrington WA5 14 D6
Sanderson Way CW10 128 E1
Sanders Sq SK11 112 D5
Sandfield Ave CW5 216 F3
Sandfield Cl 3 WA3 3 E8
Sandfield Cres WA3 5 C7
Sandfield Ct
3 Frodsham WA6 74 B8
Wrenbury CW5 216 F4
Sandfield Hall WA3 3 A4
Sandfield La
Acton Bridge CW8 76 E1
Hartford CW8 103 C4
Sandfield Pk CH60 40 D8
Sandfields WA6 74 B8
Sandfield Terr CW8 76 F1
Sandford Cres CW2 207 D2
Sandford Rd CW5 204 F7
Sandgate Rd SK10 87 F2
Sandham Gr CH60 41 D7
Sandham Rd L24 21 A4
Sandheys CH64 41 C1
Sandhill Terr WA4 16 E3
Sandhole Cotts 2 CW7 149 B8
Sandhole La
Chelford WA16 83 D4
Crowton CW8 101 B7
Sandhurst Ave CW2 190 A1
Sandhurst Dr 2 SK9 60 C8
Sandhurst Rd L26 21 A6
Sandhurst St WA4 16 F3
Sandicroft Cl WA3 9 C5
Sandiford Rd CW4 130 C3
Sandiford Sq CW9 104 A8
Sandileigh Ave WA16 56 F2
Sandington Dr CW8 101 F2
SANDIWAY 102 B3
Sandiway
Bebington CH63 43 C6
Knutsford WA16 57 B2
Sandiway Ave WA8 12 A1
Sandiway Cl CW8 102 A2
Sandiway La CW9 53 A2
Sandiway Pk CW8 102 E4
Sandiway Prim Sch CW8 102 B3
Sandiway Rd
Crewe CW1 190 A7
Handforth SK9 34 D5
Sand La SK10 84 F5
Sandlebridge Farm SK9 83 F6
Sandle Bridge La WA16, SK9 83 E5
Sandle Bridge Rise WA16 83 F6
SANDLOW GREEN 131 B1
Sandmoor Pl WA13 19 A2
Sandon Cres CH64 66 E5
Sandon Park Gdns CW2 189 D4
Sandon Pl WA8 13 D1
Sandon Rd CH2 118 E4
Sandon St CW1 190 D4
Sandown Cl
Culcheth WA3 4 F4
Middlewich CW10 151 C8
Runcorn WA7 49 C6
Wilmslow SK9 60 D8
Sandown Cres CW8 102 A3
Sandown Dr WA15 32 D6
Sandown Pl SK11 111 F7
Sandown Rd CW1 190 C7
Sandown Terr CW5 229 D7
Sandown Terr CH3 118 F1
Sandpiper Cl
Macclesfield SK10 87 B4
Newton-le-W WA12 2 C4
Sandpiper Ct
Chester CH4 141 B2
Kidsgrove ST7 195 C2
Sandpiper Way CH4 141 B3
Sandra Dr WA12 2 E3
Sandringham Ave
Chester CH3 119 A2
Helsby WA6 73 B4
Sandringham Cl
Altrincham WA14 20 F1
Northwich CW9 103 E4
Winsford CW7 126 C3
Sandringham Ct
Golborne WA3 3 E7
5 Wilmslow SK9 60 A6
Sandringham Dr
Poynton SK12 36 D3
Warrington WA5 15 C4
Wistaston CW2 205 E8
Sandringham Gdns 2 CH65 70 D2
Sandringham Rd
Congleton CW12 156 F4
Macclesfield SK10 87 F1
Widnes WA8 13 A4
Sandringham Way 4 SK9 60 A6
Sandrock Rd CH3 142 E7
Sandsdown Cl ST8 179 C1
Sandside Rd ST7 193 B3
Sands Rd ST7 195 E6
Sandstone Mews WA8 12 E4
Sandstone Wlk CH60 41 A7
Sandwich Dr SK10 87 C4
Sandwood Ave CH4 139 B3
Sandybank CW8 78 D1
Sandy Brow La WA3 3 E2
Sandy Cl SK10 87 F7
SANDYCROFT 116 B2
Sandyfield Ct ST8 179 C1
Sandyhill Pl 1 CW7 149 D6
Sandyhill Rd CW7 149 D6
Sandy La
Allostock CW4 106 E1
Astbury CW12 177 E6
Aston CW5 217 C2
Bold Heath WA8 14 B6
Brown Knowl CH3 199 C7
Bulkeley SY14 184 C1
Chester CH3 119 A1
Congleton, Astbury Marsh CW12 156 B2
Congleton CW12 155 D3
Croft WA3 9 A8
Cronton WA8 12 D5
Golborne, Lowton Common WA3 4 A8
Golborne WA3 2 F8
Goostrey CW4 107 D1
Haslington CW11 192 B7
Hatherton CW5 219 F5
Helsby WA6 73 B2
Higher Kinnerton CH4 161 A6
Huntington CH3 141 F8
Knutsford WA16 82 D3
Lymm WA13 19 B4
Macclesfield SK10 86 C2
Neston CH64 67 A7
Runcorn, Preston Brook WA7 50 F6
Runcorn WA7 48 E7
Saighton CH3 142 C3
Saltney CH4 140 D6
Sandbach CW11 174 D5
Swan Green WA16 106 E6
Swettenham CW12 131 F3
Tarvin CH3 121 C4
Threapwood SY14 222 E8
Warrington, Longford WA2 8 C2
Warrington, Penketh WA5 15 A4
Warrington, Stockton Heath WA4 26 D8
Weaverham CW8 77 C2
Whitegate CW8 125 D6
Wilmslow SK9 59 E8
Sandylands Cres ST7 193 F5
Sandylands Pk CW2 205 D7
Sandylane Mews CW12 156 C5
Sandy La W WA2 8 B3
Sandymere Ct CW7 126 B1
Sandymoor La WA7 24 D3
Sandy Moor La WA7 24 D3
Sandy Rd ST8 179 C2
Sandy Way CW7 149 B8
SANKEY BRIDGES 15 C4
Sankey Bridges Ind Est WA5 15 C4
Sankey for Penketh Sta WA5 14 F6
Sankey La WA4 25 F1
Sankey St
Golborne WA3 3 A8
Newton-le-W WA12 2 A3
Warrington WA1 16 A5
Widnes WA8 23 A6
Sankey Valley Ind Est WA12 2 A2
Sankey Valley Pk★
Newton-le-W WA5 1 D3
Warrington WA5 15 D5
Sankey Valley St James CE Prim Sch WA5 15 C6
Sankey Way WA5 15 D5
Santon Dr WA3 3 E8
Sapling La CW6 146 F3
Sark Ave CH65 95 B8
Sark Ho CH2 119 B4
Sarl Williams Ct CH1 237 A3
Sarn Bank Rd SY14 222 E6
Sarn Rd SY14 222 D8
Sarra La CH3 184 B5
Sarsfield Ave 1 WA3 3 D8
Sarus Ct WA7 24 B4
SAUGHALL 117 B8
Saughall Cl CW9 103 E4
Saughall Hey CH1 94 A1
Saughall Rd
Blacon, Abbot's Meads CH1 118 A4
Blacon CH1 117 E5
Saundersfoot Cl WA5 7 E2
Saunders St CW1 190 B4
Saunderton Cl WA11 1 C7
Saunton Cl CW7 126 A2
Savannah Pl 5 WA5 15 C7
Saville Ave WA5 15 F7
Saville St SK11 112 E7
Savoy Rd CW1 207 A8
Sawley Cl
Culcheth WA3 5 A2
Runcorn WA7 50 E7
Sawley Dr SK8 35 C6
Sawpit St WA13, WA14 20 A6
Sawyer Dr ST8 179 C1
Saxon Cl WA4 26 B5
Saxon Crossway CW7 126 B1
Saxon Rd WA7 23 C2
Saxons La CW8 103 D7
Saxon Terr 4 WA8 13 B1

Saxon Way
Blacon CH1 117 E6
6 Ellesmere Port CH66 94 F8
Sandbach CW11 175 C6
Sayce St WA8 13 B1
Scafell Ave WA2 8 C3
Scafell Cl
Bebington CH62 43 D3
High Lane SK6 37 E8
Scaife Rd CW5 204 F5
Scaliot Cl SK22 39 B8
Scar La SY14 198 F1
Sceptre Cl WA12 2 A3
SCHOLAR GREEN 194 E8
Scholar Green Prim Sch ST7 194 E6
Scholar Rise CW7 127 A2
Scholars Cl
Macclesfield SK10 111 D8
Saltney CH4 140 E6
Scholar's Ct 3 CH64 66 E8
Scholars Green La WA13 18 F2
School Ave CH64 66 F6
School Bank
Norley WA6 101 A6
Wybunbury CW5 220 B8
School Brow WA1 16 C6
School Cl
Audley ST7 210 A1
Knutsford WA16 56 E1
Marbury SY13 226 E8
Poynton SK12 36 F3
School Cotts
Bradwall Green CW11 153 B4
Wimboldsley CW10 150 F4
School Cres CW1 190 E4
School Dr
Barnton CW8 78 A3
Lymm WA13 19 C5
School Field Cl CW3 230 F4
Schoolfold La SK10 63 A7
School Gn CH3 182 C1
SCHOOL GREEN 149 C5
School Hill CH60 40 F7
School Hos SK11 109 A1
School House Cotts CH66 69 B6
School La
Aldford CH3 163 F2
Antrobus CW9 53 C3
Astbury CW12 178 B8
Audlem CW3 230 A4
Bold Heath WA8 13 E7
Brereton Green CW11 153 F5
Bunbury CW6 168 E1
Burwardsley CH3 184 B6
Cuddington CW8 102 A2
Eaton (nr Congleton) CW12 156 E8
Ellesmere Port CH66 69 A8
Elton CH2 72 B3
Frodsham WA6 74 C7
Great Budworth CW9 79 B8
Guilden Sutton CH3 119 E5
Hartford CW8 103 C4
Henbury SK11 111 B6
Higher Whitley WA4 52 E6
Hollinfare WA3 11 A2
Hooton CH66 43 F1
Irlam, Cadishead M44 11 D5
Lostock Gralam CW9 80 A2
Manley WA6 99 A5
Marton SK11 133 C5
Mickle Trafford CH2 119 E8
Moulton CW9 126 F8
4 Nantwich CW5 204 E6
Neston CH64 42 B2
Neston, Little Neston CH64 66 F6
Neston, Parkgate CH64 41 B1
Nether Alderley SK10 86 A6
Norbury SY13 215 E2
Norley WA6 100 D5
Ollerton WA16 83 B4
Onneley CW3 232 F3
Partington WA14 20 D5
Poynton SK12 36 F4
Runcorn WA7 49 F8
Sandbach CW11 174 D7
Sandbach Heath CW11 175 E6
Smallwood CW11 176 F5
Warmingham CW11 173 E7
Warrington WA3 10 D5
School Mews SK7 35 E7
School Rd
Ellesmere Port CH65 70 B5
Handforth SK9 34 D4
Higher Shurlach CW9 104 D5
Warrington WA2 8 C1
Winsford, Meadowbank CW7 126 E5
Winsford, Wharton CW7 127 A2
School Rd N CW9 104 E6
School Rd S CW9 104 E6
School St
Chester CH2 118 F3
Golborne WA3 3 A8
Haslington CW1 191 D5
Newton-le-W WA12 2 B3
Warrington WA4 16 B4
School Terr WA3 3 A8
School Way
Northwich CW9 104 A8
Widnes WA8 13 D3
Schooner Cl WA7 50 D6
Scilly Cl CH65 70 C1
Scope Ho CW1 190 E1
Scotch Hall La CW9 53 A3
Scotia Wlk 1 WA3 3 F8
Scotland Rd WA1 16 B5
Scott Ave
Crewe CW1 190 F4
Widnes WA8 22 F8
Scott Cl
Macclesfield SK10 113 A7
Rode Heath ST7 193 E8
2 Sandbach CW11 174 D6
Scott Ct WA2 16 B6
Scotthope Cl SK11 111 F6
Scotton Ave CH66 69 B5
Scott Rd SK10 87 A7
Scotts Ind Est WA5 16 A7
Scott St WA2 16 C6
Scott Wlk WA12 2 C1
Scroggins La M31 11 F4
Sea Bank CW10 128 D1
Seabank Rd CH60 40 E6
Seabury St WA4 17 A3
Seacombe Dr CH66 69 E3
Seafield Ave CH60 40 E6
Seaford Cl WA7 24 D1
Seaford Pl WA2 8 A4
Seagrave Cl CW9 103 F5
Seagull Cl CW1 190 F5
Seahill Rd CH1 116 F8
Sea La WA7 23 D2
SEALAND 116 E6
Sealand Cl WA2 8 E1
Sealand Ind Est CH1 117 F2
Sealand Rd
Blacon CH1 117 C3
Chester CH1 118 A2
Sealand CH1, CH5 116 D6
Sealand Trad Pk CH1 117 F2
Sealand Way 2 SK9 34 D4
Seal Rd SK7 36 A7
Seathwaite Cl WA7 49 E5
Seaton Cl CW1 190 B8
Seaton Pk WA7 24 E3
Seaton St CW7 127 D1
Seattle Cl 3 WA5 15 B7
Sea View CH64 66 E4
Seaview Ave CH62 44 B6
Seaville St CH3 237 C3
Secker Ave WA4 16 D2
Secker Cl WA4 16 D2
Second Ave
Connah's Quay CH5 92 F3
Crewe CW1 190 F2
Kidsgrove ST7 194 E1
Poynton SK12 36 D1
Runcorn WA7 49 F8
Sandbach CW11 175 A5
Second Dig La CW5 219 C8
Second Wood St CW5 204 D5
Sedbergh Cl CW4 130 A3
Sedbergh Gr WA7 49 E5
Seddon St CW10 128 C2
Sedgefield Cl 3 SK10 87 C4
Sedgefield Rd CH1 118 B2
Sedgeford Cl SK9 34 D1
Sedgewick Cres WA5 6 E6
Sedgmere Ave CW1 190 A8
Sedum Cl CH3 142 A6
Sefton Ave
Congleton CW12 157 A1
Widnes WA8 13 A3
Sefton Dr SK9 34 C2
Sefton Rd CH2 119 A4
Sefton St WA12 1 F3
Selby Cl
Poynton SK12 36 D5
Runcorn WA7 24 F4
Selby Gdns SK8 35 C6
Selby Gn CH66 69 B5
Selby St WA5 15 E5
Selkirk Ave
Bebington CH62 43 E4
Warrington WA4 17 A3
Selkirk Cl
Ellesmere Port CH66 68 F5
Macclesfield SK10 86 F2
Selkirk Dr
Chester CH4 141 A7
Holmes Chapel CW4 130 B2
Selkirk Rd CH4 141 A7
Seller St CH1 237 C3
Selsdon Ct CH4 141 C7
Selsey Cl CW1 190 B8
Selworthy Dr
Crewe CW1 190 B7
Warrington WA4 17 D3
Selwyn Cl
Newton-le-W WA12 2 B5
Widnes WA8 13 E3
Selwyn Dr
Cheadle SK8 35 C7
Sutton Lane Ends SK11 112 F3
Semper Cl CW12 157 A4
Seneschal Ct WA7 49 E6
Senna La CW9 78 C8
Sennen Cl WA7 50 C5
Sens Cl CH1 237 A2
Sephton Ave WA3 4 E3
Serin Cl WA12 2 C3
Serpentine The CH4 141 B7
Servite Cl CH65 69 F6
Servite Pl CH64 66 E7
Sett Cl SK22 39 B8
Sevenoaks Cl SK10 87 B2
Seven Row CH64 66 E5
Seven Sisters La WA16 82 E5
Severn Cl
Biddulph ST8 179 E1
Congleton CW12 156 F1
Macclesfield SK10 86 F2
Warrington WA2 8 E2
Widnes WA8 13 F3
Severn Dr SK7 35 C6
Severn Rd WA3 4 F2
Severnvale CH65 70 B3
Severn Wlk CW7 127 A2
Sewell St 7 WA7 23 B2
Sextant Cl WA7 50 D6
Sexton Ave WA9 1 B2
Seymour Chase WA16 82 A8
Seymour Ct WA7 24 C4
Seymour Dr
Ellesmere Port CH66 69 E6
Warrington WA1 17 A8
Seymour Ho 16 SK9 34 E1
Seymour Rd SK8 35 A8
Sgt York Loop WA5 15 B6
Shackleton Cl WA5 15 D8
Shade Terr SK6 37 F7
Shadewood Cres WA4 17 B2
Shadewood Rd SK11 112 A6
Shadowmoss Rd M22 33 E8
Shady Brook La CW8 77 C1
Shady Gr ST7 193 D4
Shaftesbury Ave
Chester CH3 119 C2
Warrington WA5 14 E2
Shaftesbury Way WA5 6 F7
Shaftway Cl WA11 1 F7
Shakerley Ave CW12 156 F3
Shakespeare Cl CW9 104 C7
Shakespeare Dr CW1 191 A4
Shakespeare Gr WA2 8 C2
Shakespeare Rd
Neston CH64 41 E1
Widnes WA8 13 A1
Shalcombe Cl L26 21 A7
Shallacres CH65 69 F7
Shallcross Ave SK23 65 F4
Shallcross Cres SK23 65 E4
Shallcross Hall Barns SK23 65 E4
Shallcross Mill Rd SK23 65 E5
Shallcross Rd SK23 65 E4
Shambles The WA16 57 B1
Shanklin Cl WA5 14 C6
Shannon Cl
Chester CH4 140 E5
Willaston CW5 205 D6
Shannon Gr WA8 12 E2
Shargate Cl SK9 34 C1
Sharnbrook Dr CW2 189 D4
Sharon Park Cl WA4 17 C1
Sharpley St 11 SK10 112 C8
Sharp St
Warrington WA2 16 C6
Widnes WA8 23 A8
Sharston Cres WA16 57 B1
SHAVINGTON 206 C5
Shavington Ave CH2 118 F4
Shavington High Sch CW2 206 A5
Shavington Prim Sch CW2 206 C4
Shavington Way CW9 103 F4
Shawbury Gr WA1 17 A8
Shaw Cl CH66 69 E4
Shaw Dr WA16 57 C3
Shawell Ct WA8 13 E2
Shaw Entry L35, WA8 12 A7
SHAW HEATH 57 D3
Shaw Heath View WA16 57 C3
Shaw's Ave WA2 16 C8
Shaws Fold SK9 33 F3
Shaws La
Winsford CW7 126 F4
Winsford, Wharton CW7 127 A3
Shaw St
Culcheth WA3 5 A3
Haydock WA11 1 E6
Macclesfield SK11 112 C8
Runcorn WA7 22 F2
Shay La
Ashton Hayes CH3 121 F7
Hampton Heath SY14 200 A1
Tarvin CH3 121 E3
Shay's La CW6 124 E4
Sheaf Cl CH3 121 C2
Shearbrook La CW4 107 E1
Sheardhall Ave SK12 38 E5
Sheath St CW9 104 A8
Shed La CH3 119 B2
Sheepfield Cl CH66 69 C7
Sheerwater Cl WA1 16 F7
Sheffield Cl WA5 15 C5
Sheffield Row WA12 7 D8
Sheilings The WA3 3 F8
Shelagh Ave WA8 13 A1
Shelbourne Mews 2 SK10 111 F8
Shelburne Dr CW1 191 C5
Sheldon Ave
Chester CH3 119 B2
Congleton CW12 157 A1
Sheldon Cl M31 11 F3
Sheldon Dr SK11 112 B4
Sheldon Pl SK10 88 B8
Sheldon Rd
Hazel Grove SK7 36 E8
Poynton SK12 37 C2
Sheldrake Gr CH64 66 E5
Shellbrook Gr 3 SK9 34 D1
Shelley Ave CW9 80 A5
Shelley Cl
Crewe CW1 190 F4
Middlewich CW10 151 E5
Rode Heath ST7 193 E8
Shelley Ct 5 CW11 174 D6
Shelley Dr CW2 189 F1
Shelley Gr WA4 16 F4
Shelley Rd
Blacon CH1 117 F6
Widnes WA8 13 A1
SHELL GREEN 13 E1
Shell Green Est WA8 23 E8
Shellow La CW12, SK11 134 C5
Shellway Rd CH2 71 A3
Shelton Cl WA8 13 F3
Shenhurst Cl SK9 59 E4
Shepcroft La WA4 26 C3
Shepherds Fold Dr CW7 126 C3
Shepherd's La CH2 118 D5
Shepherds Row WA7 23 F2
Shepherds View CW8 78 B2
Shepley Cl SK7 36 D8
Sheppard Cl CW1 190 D5
Sheppenhall Gr CW5 217 C1
Sheppenhall La CW5, SY13 228 D5
Shepperton Cl WA4 26 E6
Shepsides Cl CH66 69 C3
Shepton Rd CH66 69 E2
Sheraton Rd CH3 143 B5
Sherborne Cl WA7 24 F3
Sherborne Rd CW1 190 D6
Sherbourne Ave CH4 141 B5
Sherbourne Cl SK8 35 B6
Sherbourne Rd
Ellesmere Port CH65 70 D3
Macclesfield SK11 111 F7
Sherbourne Way WA5 6 F6
Sherbrooke Rd SK12 38 D6
Sherbrook Rise SK9 60 C6
Sheridan Ave WA3 3 D7
Sheridan Cl CW1 173 B1
Sheridan Pl WA2 8 A5
Sheridan Way WA7 24 D2
Sheri Dr WA12 2 E2
Sheringham Cl CH4 140 E5
Sheringham Dr CW1 190 B8
Sheringham Rd WA5 14 E6
Sherlock Ave WA11 1 E7
Sherratt Cl
Congleton CW12 156 E2
Nantwich CW5 204 F4
Sherrington's La CH3 199 D8
Sherwin St CW2 190 C1
Sherwood Cl WA8 12 C1
Sherwood Cres WA5 6 E6
Sherwood Gr WA6 73 A3
Sherwood Rd
Blacon CH1 117 E5
Macclesfield SK11 112 D5
Shetland Cl
Warrington WA2 8 E4
Widnes WA8 13 E3
Shetland Dr
Bebington CH62 43 E8
Ellesmere Port CH65 70 C1
Shevington Cl WA8 13 E3
Shevington Wlk WA8 13 E3
Shiggins Cl WA5 15 D6
Shillingford Cl WA4 26 E5
Shilton Cl CW10 151 E5
Shipbrook Rd
Chester CH2 118 F6
Davenham CW9 104 C3
Northwich CW9 104 C6
Shipgate St CH1 237 B1
Shipgate The CH1 237 B1
Shipley Gdns ST7 210 D6
Ship St WA6 49 C1
Shipton Cl
Warrington WA5 15 B8
Widnes WA8 12 D3
Shirley Ave SK8 34 C6
Shirley Dr WA4 17 A2
Shirleys Cl SK10 87 A6
Shirleys Dr SK10 87 A6
SHOCKLACH 211 D7
SHOCKLACH GREEN 211 C7
Shocklach Oviatt CE Prim Sch SY14 211 C7
Shocklach Rd CH2 118 F6
Shones Croft CH64 67 A5
Shop La
Congleton CW12 156 E1
Little Budworth CW6 124 F2
Shopping Precinct The CH2 72 B3
Shoreham Dr WA5 15 A3
Shores Green Dr CW9 79 F5
Shores La CW5 203 D7
Short Cl WA12 1 E3
Shorthorn Cl CW10 128 D2
Short St
Haydock WA11 1 E6
11 Macclesfield SK11 112 D8
Newton-le-W WA12 1 E3
Widnes WA8 23 A5
Shorwell Cl WA5 14 C7
Shot Tower Cl CH1 237 C3
SHOTWICK 93 B4
Shotwick La CH1 93 D6
Shotwick Rd CH5 92 F3
SHRALEYBROOK 209 A1
Shrewbridge Cres CW5 204 E4
Shrewbridge Rd CW5 204 D4
Shrewsbury Dr ST5 210 E2
Shrewsbury Gdns SK8 35 C6
Shrewsbury Rd 4 CH65 70 C5
Shrewsbury St WA4 16 D3
Shrewsbury Way CH4 140 F6
Shrigley Cl SK9 34 D1
Shrigley Ct SK10 88 B8
Shrigley Rd SK10 63 B5
Shrigley Rd N SK12 37 C3
Shrigley Rd S SK10, SK12 37 C2
Shrigley Rise SK10 63 C1
Shropshire Cl
Middlewich CW10 151 C8
Warrington WA1 17 E6
Shropshire La SY13 227 E2
Shropshire Rd CH2 70 F3
Shropshire St CW3 229 F4
Shuldham Cl WA16 29 C4
Shurlach Rd CW9 104 D6
Shutley La CW8 77 D6
Shutlingsloe Way SK10 112 A8
Sibbersfield La CH3 180 F4
Sibell St CH1 237 C3
Siddall St 7 CW9 104 B8
Siddals Ct CW5 204 C5
Siddeley Cl CH4 139 C4
Siddeley Dr WA12 1 F4
SIDDINGTON 110 A3
Siddington Ave CW9 104 A4
SIDDINGTON HEATH 109 E1
Siddington Rd
Handforth SK9 34 D5
Poynton SK12 36 F2
Siddorn St CW7 126 E1
Side End La SK23 64 F3
Side La CW6 144 E6
Sidings Ct WA1 16 C6
Sidings The SK23 65 E8
Sidlaw Cl CH66 69 A6
Sidmouth Cl WA5 14 E4
Sidmouth Gr SK8 34 F7
Sidney Cl CH64 41 F1
Sidney Rd CH64 41 F1
Siemens Rd M44 11 E5
Sienna Cl M44 11 E6
Signal Ct CH2 118 F2
Silk Hill SK23 65 F8
Silk Mill
Macclesfield SK11 112 D6
Poynton SK12 36 C4
Silk Mill St WA16 57 A2
Silk Mus Heritage Ctr* SK11 112 D7
Silk Rd The
Bollington SK10 87 E4
Macclesfield SK10 112 E7
Silk St CW12 156 C2
Silkstone Cres WA7 50 B7
Silsden Ave WA3 4 B8
Silvan Ct SK10 87 B1
Silver Ave WA11 1 A5
Silverbirch Croft CH4 139 B3
Silverbirch Way CH66 94 F8
Silverdale CW8 103 D7
Silverdale Cl
Chorlton CW2 207 C2
Frodsham WA6 74 C7
High Lane SK6 37 E8
Silverdale Dr SK9 60 A4
Silverdale Rd
Newton-le-W WA12 2 B4
Warrington WA4 16 B2
Silvergate Ct CW12 178 E8
Silver La
Croft WA3 9 F7
Warrington WA3 10 C6
Silvermine Cl 8 ST7 195 B2
Silvermuir CH1 117 E3
Silverne Dr CH65 70 A2
Silver St
Bollington SK10 88 B8
Congleton CW12 156 E2
Warrington WA2 16 B6
Silver Terr CW11 175 D6
Silverwood ST7 195 B1
Simkin Ave WA4 16 F4
Simmonds Cl CW9 103 E3
SIMM'S CROSS 23 B8
Simms Cross Prim Sch WA8 23 A8
Simonside WA8 12 C2
Simons La WA6 74 B5
Simonstone Rd CH4 139 D4
Simonswood Cl CW10 151 B8
Simpson Cl CH2 95 C1
Simpson Ct CW1 173 B1
Simpson La SK10 63 D7
Simpson Rd CH2 95 C1
Simpson's Ct 17 SK11 112 C8
Simpson St SK9 59 F6
Simpsons Way CH4 139 B3
Sinclair Ave
Alsager ST7 193 B3
Warrington WA2 8 B2
Widnes WA8 23 A8
Sinderland La
Partington WA13 20 B8
Partington WA13 20 E8

Singapore Ave M90 33 A8
Singleton Ave CW1 190 C6
Singleton Rd CH65 69 F4
SINK MOSS 28 D3
Sir John Deane's Coll CW9 103 F6
Sir Thomas Boteler CE High Sch WA4 16 E3
Siskin Cl WA12 2 C3
Six Acre Gdns WA4 25 A5
Six Acre La WA4 25 A5
Sixth Ave CH5 92 E1
Skeath Cl CW11 175 E6
Skellern St ST7 194 D2
SKELLORN GREEN 62 E8
Skellorn Green La SK10 62 F8
Skiddaw Cl WA7 50 A4
Skip's La CH3 142 F7
Skipton Cl
Hazel Grove SK7 36 C8
[2] Runcorn WA7 23 F1
Skipton Dr CH66 69 C5
Skye Cl
Ellesmere Port CH65 70 C1
Widnes WA8 13 E3
Skylark Cl CW1 189 F7
Sky Lark Rise WA9 1 A3
Slacken La ST7 194 D2
Slack St SK11 112 E6
Slade La
Mobberley WA16 58 A7
Nether Alderley SK10 85 E5
Slade St [5] CW9 104 B8
Slag La
Golborne WA3 3 D8
Haydock WA11 1 B7
Slater St
Macclesfield SK11 112 C6
Warrington WA4 16 D3
Slicks Bsns Ctr CW8 78 C2
Slindon Cl ST5 210 D1
Slutchers La WA1 16 A3
Small Ave WA2 8 C2
Smallbrook Wlk CW2 206 C8
Small Cres WA2 8 C2
Small La WA16 58 A8
Smallman Rd CW2 190 C1
SMALLWOOD 176 F5
Smallwood CE Prim Sch CW11 176 F5
Smallwood Cl
[4] Middlewich CW10 151 C8
Newcastle-u-Lyme ST5 210 D1
Smallwood Ct [1] CW12 156 F3
Smallwood Forge CW11 176 D5
Smeaton Wood CW5 216 E2
SMETHWICK GREEN 154 F4
Smethwick La CW11, CW12 154 E4
Smith Cl ST7 193 B4
Smith Cres WA2 16 D8
Smith Dr WA2 16 D8
Smithers Cl CW5 204 F4
Smithfield Dr/Ffordd Smithfield LL13 196 D8
Smithfield Gn LL13 196 D8
Smithfield La CW11 175 C6
Smithfields CH3 166 C2
Smithfield St LL13 196 D8
Smith Gr CW1 190 A6
Smithills Cl WA3 9 D5
Smith La
Mobberley WA16 57 F6
Rainow SK10 89 A5
Smith Rd WA8 22 F7
Smiths Cotts CH64 66 E5
SMITHS GREEN 109 A2
SMITH'S GREEN 208 B7
Smith's La CW8 77 C1
Smiths Lawn SK9 60 A5
Smith St
Macclesfield SK11 112 D6
Warrington WA1 16 B5
Smith's Terr SK11 112 E6
Smithy Bank
Acton CW5 204 A6
Winsford CW7 149 A3
Smithy Brow
Bollington SK10 88 C8
Winwick WA3 8 F7
Smithy Cl
Cronton WA8 12 C5
Neston CH64 67 A4
Saughall CH1 94 A1
Shocklach SY14 211 E7
Smithy Cotts SY14 213 A2
Smithy Ct
Christleton CH3 142 E7
Duddon CW6 145 C5
[5] Ellesmere Port CH66 69 C6
Smithy Dr WA14 20 D3
Smithy Gn
Cheadle SK8 35 A8
Gatesheath CH3 165 E5
Smithy Gr CW11 176 A2
SMITHY GREEN
Cheadle Hulme 35 B7
Lower Peover 81 E2
Smithy Hill CH63 42 A6
Smithy La
Alsager CW2 208 D7
Altrincham WA14 20 D3
Barthomley CW2 208 C6
Biddulph ST8 179 D2
Bosley SK11 158 E6

Smithy La *continued*
Broxton CH3 183 D1
Congleton CW12 156 C7
Crewe CW1 189 E8
Croft WA3 9 A7
Cronton WA8 12 C5
Cuddington CW8 102 A5
Ellesmere Port CH66 69 C6
Great Budworth CW9 79 A8
Helsby WA6 73 C5
Kingsley WA6 75 B2
Little Leigh CW8 77 B6
Lostock Gralam CW9 80 A2
Malpas SY14 213 A2
Mottram St Andrew SK10 61 C2
Mouldsworth CH3 98 F2
Partington M31 11 F3
Rainow SK10 88 E5
Utkinton CW6 146 C6
Weston CW2 207 C5
Willaston CH64 68 A7
Smithy Pathway CH4 140 F4
Smithy The CH2 118 E8
Smithy Wlk CW11 174 F3
Smokehall La CW7, CW9 126 F6
Smokehall Lane Ind Est CW7 127 A5
Smokey La SY13 224 A1
Smokies Way ST8 179 C1
Smyth Rd WA8 13 D2
Snab La
Neston CH64 66 F4
Norbury SY13 215 B5
Snabwood Cl CH64 66 E5
Snaefell Rise WA4 26 C7
Snapebrook Gr [6] SK9 34 E1
Snape Hollow CW2 207 F4
Snape La CW2 207 E4
Snape Rd
Crewe CW2 206 D8
Macclesfield SK10 87 E2
Snelson La
Chelford, Marthall WA16, SK9 83 D3
Chelford SK11 108 E7
Snipe Cl SK12 36 A4
Snowberry Cl WA8 13 E4
Snowberry Cres WA5 15 E3
Snowberry Way [5] CH66 94 F8
Snowberry Wlk M31 11 E3
Snowdon Cl
Ellesmere Port CH66 69 A6
Warrington WA5 14 E6
Snowdon Cres CH4 141 A5
Snowdon Dr CW2 189 D3
Snowdonia Way CW7 149 B7
Snowdon St CW8 77 F3
Snowdrop Cl WA7 49 F4
SNOW HILL 204 D6
Snow Hill SK11 112 E6
Solly Cres CW12 156 A2
Solvay Rd CW8 78 D1
Solway Cl WA2 8 F4
Solway Ct CW1 191 A2
Solway Gr WA7 49 D5
SOMERFORD 154 F7
Somerford Ave CW2 190 A3
Somerford Cl CW11 175 C8
Somerford Ct [2] CW12 156 F3
Somerford Ho SK12 36 E4
Somerford Rd CH4 139 C4
Somerford Way [3] SK9 34 E5
Somerford Wlk WA8 13 E3
Somerley Cl CW1 190 B8
Somerset Ave ST7 194 F2
Somerset Cl
Congleton CW12 156 D4
Irlam M44 11 D6
Somerset Rd CH2 118 F5
Somerset St CH1 237 B4
Somerset Way WA1 17 B8
Somerton Cl [5] SK11 111 F7
Somerton Rd SK11 111 F7
Somerville Cl
Bebington CH63 43 B6
High Legh WA16 29 C4
Neston CH64 66 E5
Somerville Cres CH65 70 C4
Somerville Rd WA8 22 D8
Somerville St CW2 190 B2
Soot Hill CW8, CW9 78 C3
Sorbus Cl CH2 72 C3
Sorbus Dr CW1 190 E6
Sorby Rd M44 11 F7
Sorrel Cl
Huntington CH3 142 A6
Warrington WA2 9 C2
Soss Moss Hospl (Mary Dendy Unit) SK10 84 C6
Sossmoss La SK10 84 D6
SOUND 217 F5
Sound & District Prim Sch CW5 217 F5
SOUND HEATH 217 E5
Sound La
Ravensmoor CW5 203 E1
Sound CW5 217 D7
Souter's La CH1 237 B2
South Acre Dr
Handforth SK9 34 D3
Macclesfield SK11 113 A7
Southampton Way WA7 50 E6

South Ave
Chester CH2 237 C4
Haslington CW1 191 D4
Warrington, Stockton Heath WA4 16 C1
Warrington WA2 16 B8
Southbank CW9 79 A7
South Bank CH2 118 C4
Southbank Ave CW2 206 C5
South Bank Cl SK9 60 B2
South Bank Gr CW12 156 F2
South Bank Terr WA7 22 F3
South Cheshire Coll CW2 190 B2
South Cheshire Private Hospl The CW1 172 E1
South Cl
Tarporley CW6 146 C2
Wilmslow SK9 59 F6
South Crescent Rd CH4 237 C1
South Croft CW6 185 D6
South Crofts CW5 204 F5
South Dale WA5 14 F5
Southdale Rd WA1 17 A7
Southdown Cl SK10 87 D4
Southdown Cres SK8 34 F8
South Downs WA16 57 C1
South Downs Dr WA14 31 D8
South Downs Rd WA14 31 E8
South Dr
Heswall CH60 41 A7
Northwich CW9 104 D6
Plumley WA16 80 F3
Wilmslow SK9 60 B6
Southern St WA4 16 C1
Southey Cl
[8] Sandbach CW11 174 D6
Widnes WA8 22 F8
Southfield SK10 87 A4
Southfield Cl SK9 34 C3
Southfield Rd CH66 69 C7
Southfields WA16 57 C3
Southfields Ave WA5 14 F6
Southfields Cl CW5 220 A8
South Gn CH5 116 A6
South Gr [10] SK9 60 A1
South La
Warrington WA5, WA8 14 E5
Widnes WA8 13 F4
Southlands CW4 130 C2
Southlands Ave WA5 14 F3
Southlands Ct
[9] Runcorn WA7 22 F1
Runcorn WA7 48 F8
Southlands Mews [8] WA7 22 F1
Southlands Rd CW12 157 A1
Southlands View CW4 107 E1
South Lane Entry WA8 13 F5
Southlawn SK9 60 A5
South Lo CW6 168 D8
South Mead SK12 36 B5
South Meadway SK6 37 F7
South Oak La SK9 59 F5
South Par WA7 48 D7
South Park Dr SK12 36 E5
South Park Rd SK11 112 C7
South Pier Rd CH65 70 D7
Southport St WA9 1 A3
South Rd
Altrincham, Ashley Heath WA14 31 E8
Ellesmere Port CH65 70 C3
Halewood L24 21 A4
Runcorn WA7 48 D7
Stanlow CH65 70 F4
South St
Alderley Edge SK9 60 A1
Chester CH3 119 A1
Congleton CW12 156 D3
Crewe CW2 190 D2
Mount Pleasant ST7 195 B6
[3] Widnes WA8 23 B8
South Terr [14] SK9 60 A1
South View
Chester CH4 141 D7
Christleton CH3 142 F7
Lower Withington SK11 132 A8
New Mills SK22 39 B8
South View Ave SK11 111 D2
South View Cotts ST7 193 F4
South View La CW7 170 F2
South View Rd CH1 118 B2
Southward Rd WA11 2 A7
Southwark Pl CW7 149 A8
Southway
Middlewich CW10 128 C1
Runcorn WA7 49 F7
Widnes WA8 22 D8
South Way CH1 117 F4
Southway Ave WA4 26 D7
Southwell Cl WA3 3 C8
South West Ave SK10 87 F6
South Wirral High Sch CH62 43 D4
Southwold Cres WA5 14 E5
Southwood Ave WA7 24 C2
Southworth Ave WA5 15 F8
Southworth La WA2, WA3 8 E7
Southworth Rd WA12 2 F4
Sovereign Cl
Golborne WA3 3 E7
Northwich CW9 104 F6
Runcorn WA7 50 D7
Sovereign Ct WA3 9 C4

Sovereign Way CH1 117 E2
Sowcar Way SK10 88 C8
Spark Hall Cl WA4 26 E1
Spark La
Runcorn WA7 23 F1
Smallwood CW11 154 C2
Sparks Cl CH3 142 B7
Sparrowbutts Gr ST7 195 C2
Sparrowhawk Cl WA7 50 A7
Sparrow La WA16 57 B1
Spath La SK8 34 F5
Spath La E SK8 35 B5
Spath Wlk SK8 35 B5
Spawell Cl WA3 3 E8
Speakman Ave WA12 2 C5
Speakman St WA7 22 F3
Speed's Way CH3 180 E2
Speedwell Cl
[11] Golborne WA3 3 E8
Heswall CH60 41 C8
Huntington CH3 142 A5
Speedwell Dr CH60 41 C8
Speedwell Rd ST5 210 F1
SPEKE 21 A3
Speke Bvd L24, L26, WA8 21 B5
Speke Ho L24 21 A2
Speke Rd WA8 22 C6
Spencer Brook SK10 86 F6
Spencer Cl
Alsager ST7 192 F4
Wistaston CW2 206 A8
Spencer Mews SK10 86 F6
Spencer St
Barnton CW8 78 B3
Northwich CW8 103 E7
SPEN GREEN 177 B6
Spenlow Cl SK12 36 E1
Spennymoor Ct WA7 49 E7
Spenser Cl WA8 12 F1
Spenser Rd CH64 41 E1
Spey Cl
Middlewich CW10 128 D3
Winsford CW7 126 F2
Spey Dr ST7 195 C2
Spike Island (Nature Reserve)★ WA8 23 A5
Spike Island Visitor Ctr★ WA8 23 A5
Spindle St CW12 156 E2
Spink La WA16 80 A6
Spinnaker Cl WA7 50 D5
Spinner Cres CW9 78 D7
Spinners La SK12 36 C4
Spinners Pl WA1 16 C6
Spinners Way SK10 87 F7
Spinney Ave
Goostrey CW4 107 F1
Widnes WA8 12 A1
Spinney Cl
Handforth SK9 34 C3
Winsford CW7 150 A8
Spinney Dr
Ellesmere Port CH66 69 D2
Weston CW2 207 B5
Spinney End CH3 166 A1
Spinney Gdns WA4 27 B4
Spinney La WA16 56 E3
Spinney Mead SK10 87 E2
Spinney The
Cuddington CW8 101 D5
Heswall CH60 41 C5
Lawton-gate ST7 194 E4
Neston CH64 41 D1
Norley WA6 100 E5
Sandbach CW11 175 C6
Willaston CW5 205 D6
Spinney Wlk WA7 24 A1
Spires Gdns WA2 8 A7
Spital Wlk CH2 118 F2
Spodegreen La WA14 30 C8
Spout La WA16 58 B4
Spragg St CW12 156 E3
Spring Ave [2] CH66 69 C6
Springbank SK10 87 F7
Spring Bank ST7 195 A7
Springbank Cl WA7 49 B6
Springbank Cres CW7 149 C8
Springbank Gdns
Lymm WA13 19 B5
New Mills SK22 39 B8
Spring Bank Rd SK22 39 C8
Springbourne WA6 74 D6
Springburn Gdns WA1 17 F7
Spring Cl ST7 193 E8
Springcroft CH64 41 C1
Spring Ct [2] WA7 23 B2
Springe La CW5 203 B5
Springfield Ave
Golborne WA3 2 F8
Grappenhall WA4 17 B3
Helsby WA6 73 B3
Lymm WA13 19 B5
Malpas SY14 213 C3
Warrington, Padgate WA1 17 A8
Springfield Cl CH4 161 A7
Springfield Cres CW8 77 F3
Springfield Ct / Llys Maes Y Ffynnon CH4 161 A8
Springfield Dr
Talke ST7 210 E8
Wilmslow SK9 59 D5
Wistaston CW2 205 F7
Springfield Pk WA11 1 C7
Springfield Rd
Macclesfield SK11 111 F8

Springfield Rd *continued*
Malpas SY14 213 B3
Mobberley WA16 57 F4
Widnes WA8 22 A8
Springfields
Cuddington CW8 101 D4
Helsby WA6 73 B3
Knutsford WA16 57 C3
Mickle Trafford CH2 119 E8
Prestbury SK10 87 A7
Springfield Sch CW1 191 A3
Springfields Dr CW12 156 D3
Springfield St WA1 16 A5
Spring Gdns
Crewe CW1 190 E5
Ellesmere Port CH66 69 C6
Macclesfield SK10 87 D1
Mobberley WA16 58 D5
Nantwich CW5 204 F5
Springhead Cl ST7 210 D6
Springhead Prim Sch ST7 210 D6
Springhill SK10 88 A1
Spring Hill CW6 168 C8
Springhill Ave CH62 43 D6
Springholm Dr WA4 26 D3
Spring La
Coddington CH3 181 E6
Croft WA3 9 B6
Lymm WA13 19 F3
Spring Mdw CW8 78 E1
Springmount WA3 3 E7
Spring Mount SK22 39 C8
Spring Rd SK12 36 F2
Spring St
Congleton CW12 156 E2
Widnes WA8 23 A6
Wilmslow SK9 60 A7
Springvale Bsns Ctr CW11 174 D6
Springvale Ct CW11 174 D6
Springvale Ind Pk CW11 174 C6
Springwater Dr CW2 207 C1
Springwell Cl CW2 206 C8
Springwood Ave WA16 57 C3
Springwood Cl
Blacon CH1 117 C4
Macclesfield SK10 87 D5
Springwood Way SK10 87 D5
Sprink La CW12 157 D5
SPROSTON GREEN 129 C2
Sproston Way CW9 103 E4
Spruce Ave CW8 102 B3
Spruce Cl
Golborne WA3 3 F7
Warrington WA1 17 E7
Spruce Gr ST7 193 F7
Spuley La SK10 63 D2
Spunhill Ave CH66 69 D2
Spurling Rd WA5 6 F6
Spurston Cl WA16 29 C4
SPURSTOW 185 D6
Spurstow Mews SK8 35 C8
Square St SK11 112 E6
Square The
Altrincham WA15 32 C8
Audlem CW3 229 F4
Chester CH1 237 C3
Christleton CH3 142 E8
Holmes Chapel CW4 130 C3
Ince CH2 71 F5
[6] Lymm WA13 18 E3
Woore CW3 232 C1
Squires Ave WA8 23 A8
Squires Cl WA11 1 B6
Squirrel Cl CW8 103 C7
Squirrels Chase SK10 86 F5
Squirrel's Jump SK9 60 C1
Stable La
Mouldsworth CH3 99 A3
Utkinton CW6 123 F1
Stables The
Bostock Green CW10 127 D5
Brereton Heath CW12 155 A7
Guilden Sutton CH3 119 F5
Lawton-gate ST7 194 C4
Stablings The SK9 60 A5
Stadium Way CH1 118 B3
Stadmorslow La ST7 195 F4
Staffin Ave CH65 95 B8
Stafford Cl SK10 86 F2
Stafford Gdns CH65 70 B5
Stafford Rd WA4 16 C2
Stafford St
Audlem CW3 230 A4
Crewe CW1 190 C5
Stafford Wlk SK10 86 F2
Stage La WA13 19 C4
Stainer Cl WA12 2 B5
Staines Cl WA4 26 E5
Stainforth Cl WA3 4 D4
Stainmore Cl WA3 10 B6
Staithes Rd M22 33 D8
Stalbridge Rd CW2 190 C2
Stallard Way CW10 151 C8
Stalmine Ave SK8 34 B8
Stamford Ave CW2 190 C3
STAMFORD BRIDGE 120 D4
Stamford Cl SK11 112 C4
Stamford Ct
Chester CH3 119 C2
Lymm WA13 18 F3
Macclesfield SK11 112 C5
Stamford La CH3 120 A1

Stamford Rd
Alderley Edge SK9 . . . . 60 B1
Blacon CH1 . . . . 117 E6
Handforth SK9 . . . . 34 A1
Little Bollington WA14 . . . . . 20 B2
Macclesfield SK11 . . . . . . 112 C4
Stamford St CH65 . . . . 70 A5
Stamp Ave CW1 . . . . 190 D6
Stamp Cl CW1 . . . . 190 D6
Standford Dr CW9 . . . . . . 104 A5
Standish Ct WA8 . . . . 22 D8
Standon Ave ST5 . . . . 210 C2
Stanford Cl 2 CW9 . . . . . . 103 F5
Stanhope Ave CW1 . . . . . . 190 E3
Stanhope Cl SK9 . . . . 60 D8
Stanier Cl
Crewe CW1 . . . . 191 A4
Sutton Lane Ends SK11 . . . 112 D2
Stanlaw Rd CH65 . . . . 70 C4
Stanley Ave
Warrington, Stockton Heath WA4 . . . . 16 F2
Warrington WA5 . . . . 14 D7
STANLEY BANK 1 A7
Stanley Bank Rd WA11 . . . . 1 A7
Stanley Bank Way WA11 . . . 1 A7
Stanley & Brocklehurst Ct 5 SK10 . . . . 112 C8
Stanley Cl
Hartford CW8 . . . . 103 A4
Widnes WA8 . . . . 13 C2
Stanley Ct ST7 . . . . 193 C4
Stanley Dr
Gatley SK8, SK9 . . . . 34 D6
Newcastle-u-Lyme ST5 . . . . 210 C1
Stanley Gr CW9 . . . . 79 E2
STANLEY GREEN 34 E6
Stanley Green Ind Est SK8 . . . . 34 E5
Stanley Green Ret Pk SK8 . . . . 34 F6
Stanley Hall La SK12 . . . . . . 38 C6
Stanley La CH62 . . . . 43 F4
Stanley Park Ct CH4 . . . . . 140 E5
Stanley Park Dr CH4 . . . . . 140 E5
Stanley Pl
Chester CH1 . . . . 237 A2
Warrington WA4 . . . . 16 F2
Stanley Place Mews CH1 . . . . 237 A2
Stanley Rd
Biddulph ST8 . . . . 179 C2
Ellesmere Port CH65 . . . . . . 70 C7
Handforth SK8, SK9 . . . . 34 E6
Knutsford WA16 . . . . 56 F2
Stanley Rd Ind Est WA16 . . . . 57 A1
Stanley St
Chester CH1 . . . . 237 A2
2 Crewe CW1 . . . . 190 C4
7 Macclesfield SK11 . . . . 112 D8
Newton-le-W WA12 . . . . 2 A3
Northwich CW9 . . . . 104 C8
Runcorn WA7 . . . . 23 B3
Warrington WA1 . . . . 16 B4
Stanley Villas 7 WA7 . . . . . 22 F1
STANLOW 71 B5
Stanlow Abbey Bsns Ctr CH65 . . . . 70 D2
Stanlow & Thornton Sta CH2 . . . . 71 D5
Stanmore Rd WA7 . . . . 23 D2
Stannage La CH3 . . . . 180 F5
Stanner Cl WA5 . . . . 7 D2
Stannerhouse La CW11 . . . . 175 E4
Stanneybrook Cl WA6 . . . . 101 A6
Stanney Cl
Bebington CH62 . . . . 43 E3
Neston CH64 . . . . 66 E7
Stanney Grange Sports Complex The CH65 . . . . . . 70 E3
Stanney La
Ellesmere Port CH65 . . . . . . 70 C3
Stoak CH2 . . . . 70 E1
Stanneylands Cl SK9 . . . . . 34 C2
Stanneylands Dr SK9 . . . . . 34 B2
Stanneylands Rd SK9 . . . . 34 B2
Stanney Mill Ind Est CH2 . . . . 70 F3
Stanney Mill La CH2 . . . . . 70 F2
Stanney Mill Rd CH2 . . . . . 70 F2
Stanney Ten Ind Est CH2 . . . . 70 F1
Stanney Woods Ave CH65 . . . . 70 C1
Stanney Woods Ctry Pk★ CH65 . . . . 70 B1
Stansfield Ave WA1 . . . . . . 16 F6
Stansfield Dr WA4 . . . . 27 A7
Stanstead Ave WA5 . . . . . . 14 F3
Stanthorne Ave CW2 . . . . 190 A3
Stanthorne Park Mews CW10 . . . . 150 E6
Stanton Cl WA11 . . . . 1 C6
Stanton Ct CH64 . . . . 66 E8
Stanton Dr CH2 . . . . 118 D5
Stanton Rd WA4 . . . . 17 D3
Stanyer Ct CW5 . . . . 205 A4
STAPELEY 219 D8
Stapeley Broad Lane CE Prim Sch CW5 . . . . 205 A1
Stapeley Cl CW9 . . . . 103 E4
Stapeley Ct CW1 . . . . 190 B5
Stapeley Gdns L26 . . . . 21 A6
Stapeley Terr CW5 . . . . . . 205 A4
Stapeley Water Gdns★ CW5 . . . . 205 A3
Stapleford Ct CH66 . . . . . . 69 F8
Stapleton Ave WA2 . . . . . . 16 D8
Stapleton Ct WA6 . . . . 74 C8
Stapleton Rd SK10 . . . . 87 B2
Stapleton Way WA8 . . . . . . 22 B5
Stapley Cl WA7 . . . . 22 F1
Starbeck Dr CH66 . . . . 69 B5
Starkey Gr WA4 . . . . 16 F4
Star La
Lymm WA13 . . . . 18 C4
Macclesfield SK11 . . . . 112 D4
Starling Cl
Farndon CH3 . . . . 180 F1
Kidsgrove ST7 . . . . 195 D3
Runcorn WA7 . . . . 50 D7
Start La SK23 . . . . 65 B7
STATHAM 18 C4
Statham Ave
Lymm WA13 . . . . 18 D3
Warrington WA2 . . . . 8 C2
Statham Cl WA13 . . . . 18 D3
Statham Com Prim Sch WA13 . . . . 18 C4
Statham Dr WA13 . . . . 18 D3
Statham La WA13 . . . . 18 B5
Statham St SK11 . . . . 112 D7
Station App / Lon yr Orsaf CH1 . . . . 116 F7
Station Ave
Ellesmere Port CH66 . . . . . . 69 C7
Helsby WA6 . . . . 73 B4
Station Cl CH64 . . . . 66 F7
Station Cotts
Mouldsworth CH3 . . . . 99 A2
Saughall CH1 . . . . 116 F7
Station Gn CH66 . . . . 69 C7
Station Hill CW8 . . . . 76 F2
Station La
Dunham-on-t-H CH3 . . . . . . 97 D3
Guilden Sutton CH2, CH3 . . . . 119 F7
Rushton Spencer SK11 . . . 159 B2
Station Rd
Adderley TF9 . . . . 235 A5
Alsager ST7 . . . . 193 D3
Astbury ST7, CW12 . . . . . . 178 B1
Aston WA7 . . . . 50 B4
Backford CH1 . . . . 95 A3
Biddulph ST8 . . . . 179 C1
Bosley CW12 . . . . 135 A2
Burton CH64 . . . . 67 B1
Calveley CW6 . . . . 169 E2
Chelford SK11 . . . . 84 A2
Chester CH1 . . . . 237 C4
Crowton CW8 . . . . 76 D2
Delamere CW8 . . . . 123 D8
Ellesmere Port CH65 . . . . . . 70 C6
Ellesmere Port, Little Sutton CH66 . . . . 69 C6
Elton CH2 . . . . 72 A5
Furness Vale SK23 . . . . 39 D4
Goostrey CW4 . . . . 131 A8
Handforth SK9 . . . . 34 D3
Haydock WA11 . . . . 1 C6
Heswall CH60 . . . . 40 F6
Holmes Chapel CW4 . . . . . 130 D2
Irlam M44 . . . . 11 E7
Kidsgrove ST7 . . . . 194 F1
Lostock Gralam CW9 . . . . . . 80 A2
Mobberley WA16 . . . . 57 F7
Mouldsworth CH3 . . . . 99 A2
Mow Cop ST7 . . . . 195 C8
Nantwich CW5 . . . . 204 E5
Neston CH64 . . . . 66 F7
Neston, Parkgate CH64 . . . . 66 C8
Newchapel ST7 . . . . 195 E2
New Mills SK22 . . . . 39 B7
Northwich CW9 . . . . 79 B1
Partington WA14 . . . . 20 B5
Runcorn WA7 . . . . 22 F2
Sandbach CW11 . . . . 174 D7
Sandycroft CH5 . . . . 116 A2
Scholar Green ST7 . . . . 194 F7
Styal SK9 . . . . 34 A4
Warrington, Fearnhead WA2 . . . . 9 A2
Warrington, Great Sankey WA5 . . . . 14 F6
Warrington, Penketh WA5 . . . . 14 E3
Warrington WA4 . . . . 16 E2
Weaverham CW8 . . . . 77 A1
Wilmslow SK9 . . . . 60 B7
Winsford CW7 . . . . 127 A1
Worleston CW5 . . . . 188 E6
Wrenbury CW5 . . . . 216 F3
Station Rd N WA2 . . . . 9 A1
Station Rd S WA2 . . . . 9 A1
Station St SK10 . . . . 87 D1
Station Terr WA7 . . . . 50 B4
Station View
Chester CH2 . . . . 118 F2
Hampton Heath SY14 . . . . . 213 D7
Nantwich CW5 . . . . 204 E4
Sandbach CW11 . . . . 174 D8
Station Yard Trad Est CW4 . . . . 130 D3
Staveley Dr CW7 . . . . 126 D2
Steadings Rise WA16 . . . . . 56 D6
Steadings The CH3 . . . . . 120 A4
Steam Mill St CH1, CH3 . . . . 237 C3
Stearns Cl CH1 . . . . 118 A5
Stearns Ho CH1 . . . . 118 A5
Steele Rd CW10 . . . . 151 D5
Steele St CH1 . . . . 237 B2
Steel St WA1 . . . . 16 D7
Steeple Ct CH64 . . . . 66 E7
Steeple St SK10 . . . . 87 E1
Stein Ave WA3 . . . . 3 E8
Stendall Rd CH1 . . . . 118 A3
Stenhills Cres WA7 . . . . . . 23 C2
Stephens Gdns CH66 . . . . . 69 B6
Stephen's Gr WA6 . . . . 73 B2
Stephenson Dr CW1 . . . . . 191 A4
Stephenson Rd WA12 . . . . . 2 D2
Stephenson Wlk CW7 . . . . 149 A8
Stephen St WA1 . . . . 16 D6
Stephens Terr CH66 . . . . . . 69 B6
Stephens Way ST7 . . . . . . 209 F2
Sterling Cl 1 CW9 . . . . . . 103 F5
Sterne Cl CW11 . . . . 174 D6
Stetchworth Rd WA4 . . . . . 16 B1
Stevenage Cl SK11 . . . . . . 112 B7
Stevenage Dr SK11 . . . . . 112 B7
Steven Ct CH3 . . . . 237 C3
Stevens Rd CH60 . . . . 41 C7
Stevens St SK9 . . . . 60 A1
Steventon WA7 . . . . 24 E4
Steward's Ave WA8 . . . . . . 22 F8
Stewart St CW2 . . . . 190 A3
Stile End CH2 . . . . 119 F8
Stiles The CW8 . . . . 101 D5
Stiperstones Cl CH66 . . . . 69 A6
Stirling Cl
Chester CH3 . . . . 119 A2
Congleton CW12 . . . . 156 C3
Macclesfield SK10 . . . . 86 F2
Warrington WA1 . . . . 17 E7
Winsford CW7 . . . . 127 A3
Stirling Ct
Ellesmere Port CH65 . . . . . . 70 D3
Holmes Chapel CW4 . . . . . 130 B2
Stirrup Cl WA2 . . . . 9 A3
STOAK 96 A7
Stoak Lo CH65 . . . . 70 C4
Stockdale Dr WA5 . . . . 14 E7
Stockham Cl WA7 . . . . 50 A8
Stockham La WA7 . . . . 50 B7
Stock La CW2, CW5 . . . . . . 206 B2
Stockley Farm★ CW9 . . . . . . 54 E7
Stockley La WA4 . . . . 52 F7
Stockport Rd WA4 . . . . 17 E3
Stocks Ave 5 CH3 . . . . . . 119 A1
Stocks Ct The WA3 . . . . 3 D8
Stocks Hill CW7 . . . . 149 F7
Stocks La
Chester CH3 . . . . 119 A1
Ollerton WA16 . . . . 82 E1
Rainow SK10 . . . . 88 E5
Warrington WA5 . . . . 14 D5
Stockswell Rd WA8 . . . . . . 12 A3
STOCKTON HEATH 16 D1
Stockton Heath Prim Sch WA4 . . . . 16 C1
Stockton La WA4 . . . . 16 F1
Stockton Rd SK9 . . . . 59 F4
Stockton View WA4 . . . . . . 16 B2
Stockwell Farm Ct WA8 . . . . 12 E4
Stoke Abbott Cl SK7 . . . . . 35 E7
Stoke Cl CH62 . . . . 43 E3
Stoke Gdns CH65 . . . . 70 C4
Stokehall La CW5 . . . . 187 E6
Stokesay Ct CH65 . . . . 70 E3
Stokes St WA3 . . . . 9 E5
Stoke Wlk CH65 . . . . 70 C4
Stoneacre Gdns WA4 . . . . . 26 E4
Stonebank Dr CH64 . . . . . . 67 A6
Stone Bank Rd ST7 . . . . . 195 B1
Stone Barn La WA7 . . . . . . 49 F6
Stonebridge Rd CW5 . . . . 204 E3
Stone Chair La ST7 . . . . . 194 E7
Stonechat Cl
10 Golborne WA3 . . . . 3 E8
Runcorn WA7 . . . . 49 E5
Stone Cotts CW12 . . . . . . 157 E2
Stone Croft
Chester CH3 . . . . 142 B7
Kingsmead CW9 . . . . 103 F5
Stonecrop Cl
Runcorn WA7 . . . . 49 F4
Warrington WA3 . . . . 9 C4
Stone Cross Dr WA8 . . . . . 12 E5
Stone Cross La N WA3 . . . . 3 C7
Stone Cross La S WA3 . . . . . 3 C6
Stone Cross Pk WA3 . . . . 3 B7
Stonehaven Dr WA2 . . . . 9 A3
Stoneheads SK23 . . . . 65 C8
Stoneheads Rise SK23 . . . . 65 D8
Stone Heyes La CW8, CW9 . . . . 77 F5
Stonehill Cl WA4 . . . . 26 D4
Stonehills Ct WA7 . . . . 23 C2
Stonehills La WA7 . . . . 23 C2
Stonehouse Gn 6 CW12 . . . . 156 D3
Stone House La CW6 . . . . 184 E4
Stonelea WA7 . . . . 24 B2
Stoneleigh Cl SK10 . . . . . . 87 C2
Stoneleigh Ct WA4 . . . . 17 D1
Stoneleigh Gdns WA4 . . . . 17 D1
Stoneley Ave CW1 . . . . . . 190 D7
STONELEY GREEN 203 D4
Stoneley Rd CW1 . . . . 190 D8
Stone Mead Ave WA15 . . . 32 C7
Stone Pit La WA3 . . . . 3 F2
Stone Pl CH2 . . . . 118 F3
Stones Manor La CW8 . . . . 103 C5
Stoneway Ct 1 CH60 . . . . . 40 F8
Stoneyfold La SK11 . . . . . 113 A6
Stoneyford La CW8 . . . . . 101 C2
Stoney Holt WA7 . . . . 50 C8
Stoney La
Delamere CW6 . . . . 123 C6
Wilmslow SK9 . . . . 59 F5
Stoneyland Dr SK22 . . . . . 39 B8
Stonyhurst Cres WA3 . . . . . 4 D5
Stony La CW12 . . . . 156 C1
Stopsley Cl CW12 . . . . . . 155 F4
Stores Rd M90 . . . . 33 A6
Store St SK10 . . . . 88 B8
Stour Ct CH65 . . . . 70 B7
STOWFORD 207 C8
Stradbroke Cl WA3 . . . . 4 A7
Straight Length WA6 . . . . . 73 E7
Straight Mile CH4 . . . . 162 F5
Straker Ave CH65 . . . . 69 F6
Stratford Gdns CH1 . . . . . 117 E4
Stratford Rd
Blacon CH1 . . . . 117 E4
Neston CH64 . . . . 66 D6
Stratford Sq SK8 . . . . 34 C7
Stratford Way SK11 . . . . . 112 C5
Strathaven Ave CW2 . . . . 205 E8
Strathearn Rd CH60 . . . . . . 40 F7
Strathmore Cl CW4 . . . . . 130 B2
Stratton Cl WA7 . . . . 50 B6
Stratton Pk WA8 . . . . 12 F5
Stratton Rd WA5 . . . . 15 B5
Strawberry Cl WA3 . . . . 9 C4
Strawberry Dr CH66 . . . . . . 95 A8
Strawberry Fields CH3 . . . . 142 B7
Strawberry Gn CH66 . . . . . 95 A8
Strawberry La
Acton Bridge CW8 . . . . 76 F3
Mollington CH1 . . . . 94 D4
Wilmslow SK9 . . . . 59 E6
Street Forest Walks The★ SK17 . . . . 90 E4
Street Hey La CH64 . . . . . . 43 B1
Street La
Lower Whitley WA4 . . . . 52 C3
Rode Heath ST7 . . . . 176 F2
Skellorn Green SK10 . . . . . . 62 D8
Street The
Mickle Trafford CH2 . . . . . . 119 D8
Whaley Bridge SK10, SK17 . . . . 90 C5
STRETTON
Farndon 197 F6
Warrington 26 E2
Stretton Ave WA3 . . . . 3 E7
Stretton Cl CH62 . . . . 43 E3
Stretton Hall Mews WA4 . . . . 52 E8
Stretton Mill★ SY14 . . . . . . 198 A7
Stretton Rd WA4 . . . . 26 E2
Stretton Way 3 SK9 . . . . . . 34 D5
Stretton Wlk CW9 . . . . 103 F4
Strickland Cl WA4 . . . . 27 A7
Strines Rd SK6 . . . . 38 D8
Stringer Ave CW11 . . . . . . 175 C5
Stringer Cres WA4 . . . . 16 E4
Stringer's La LL12, CH4 . . . . 161 B4
Stroma Ave CH65 . . . . 95 B8
Stromness Cl WA2 . . . . 9 B3
Stuart Cl
Chester CH3 . . . . 119 C3
Winsford CW7 . . . . 149 C5
Stuart Ct SK10 . . . . 87 B2
Stuart Dr WA4 . . . . 16 F2
Stuart Pl CH1 . . . . 237 B3
Stuart Rd WA7 . . . . 24 C4
Stubbs La
Lostock Gralam CW9 . . . . . . 80 A2
Mobberley WA16 . . . . 58 E4
Stubbs Pl CH1 . . . . 117 E3
Stubbs Terr 17 SK11 . . . . . 112 E7
Stubby La SK10 . . . . 84 E2
STUD GREEN 152 C1
Stud Green Ind Pk CW11 . . . . 152 C1
Sturgess St WA12 . . . . 1 F3
STYAL 33 F4
Styal Cl 4 CW9 . . . . 103 F4
Styal Cross SK9 . . . . 33 E4
Styal Ctry Pk★ SK9 . . . . 33 E3
Styal Gn SK9 . . . . 33 F3
STYAL GREEN 34 A3
Styal Prim Sch SK9 . . . . 33 E4
Styal Rd
Wilmslow SK9 . . . . 60 B8
Wythenshawe M22 . . . . 33 F7
Styal Sta SK9 . . . . 34 A4
Styal View SK9 . . . . 34 B2
Styperson Way SK12 . . . . . 36 E3
Sudbrook Cl WA3 . . . . 3 E8
Sudbury Dr SK8 . . . . 34 C8
Sudbury Rd SK7 . . . . 36 E8
Sudlow La
Knutsford WA16 . . . . 56 D1
Plumley WA16 . . . . 81 C7
Suez St
Newton-le-W WA12 . . . . 2 B3
Warrington WA1 . . . . 16 B5
Suffolk Ave CH65 . . . . 69 F5
Suffolk Cl
Congleton CW12 . . . . 156 D4
Macclesfield SK10 . . . . 86 F1
Warrington WA1 . . . . 17 E6
Suffolk Dr SK9 . . . . 34 C1
Suffolk Ho 3 CH1 . . . . 237 C3
Suffolk Pl WA8 . . . . 22 C7
Suffolk St WA7 . . . . 22 F3
Sugar La
Bollington SK10 . . . . 63 A3
Sugar La *continued*
Manley WA6 . . . . 98 E5
Rainow SK10 . . . . 88 D5
Sugar Pit La WA16 . . . . 56 E3
Sugar St SK11 . . . . 159 C2
Sulby Ave WA4 . . . . 16 B3
Sulgrave Ave SK12 . . . . 36 F4
Summer Cl 7 WA7 . . . . 23 F1
Summercroft Cl WA3 . . . . . 3 A7
Summer Dr CW11 . . . . 175 C6
Summerfield ST7 . . . . 195 B1
Summerfield Ave WA5 . . . . . 7 F2
Summerfield Cl CH4 . . . . . 139 A3
Summerfield Dr CW9 . . . . 126 F8
Summerfield Ho CH3 . . . . 119 F5
Summerfield Pl SK9 . . . . . 60 A5
Summerfield Rd
Guilden Sutton CH3 . . . . . . 119 F5
Mobberley WA16 . . . . 57 F4
Summerfields WA16 . . . . . 57 C3
Summerfields Ctr 10 SK9 . . . . 34 D1
Summerhill Dr ST5 . . . . . . 210 D1
Summerhill Rd SK10 . . . . . 86 F4
Summer La
Daresbury WA4 . . . . 51 D7
Hatton WA4 . . . . 25 F1
Runcorn WA7 . . . . 23 F1
Summerlea SK8 . . . . 35 B8
Summerlea Cl SK10 . . . . . . 87 D1
Summers Cl WA16 . . . . 82 A7
Summers Way WA16 . . . . . 82 A7
Summertrees Rd CH66 . . . 69 E3
Summerville Gdns WA4 . . . . 16 F1
Summerville Wlk 1 WA5 . . . . 15 C7
Summit Cl WA4 . . . . 26 E1
Sumner Rd CH1 . . . . 117 E4
Sumner St WA11 . . . . 1 A6
Sumpter Pathway CH2 . . . . 118 F3
Sunart Cl CW2 . . . . 206 B6
Sunbank La WA15 . . . . 32 E6
Sunbeam Cl WA7 . . . . 22 F3
Sunbeam St WA12 . . . . 2 C3
Sunbury Cl SK9 . . . . 34 E2
Sunbury Cres 3 CH4 . . . . 140 F6
Sunbury Gdns WA4 . . . . . . 26 E7
Suncroft Cl WA1 . . . . 17 E7
Suncroft Rd CH60 . . . . 41 C7
Sundale Dr CW2 . . . . 189 D4
Sunderland St SK11 . . . . . 112 D7
Sundial Ho WA3 . . . . 4 F3
Sundown Cl SK22 . . . . 39 A8
Sunfield Cl CH66 . . . . 69 D3
Sunflower Cl WA9 . . . . 6 A7
Sunflower Dr WA5 . . . . 15 D3
Sunningdale Ave WA8 . . . . 12 B1
Sunningdale Cl
Burtonwood WA5 . . . . 6 F6
Northwich CW9 . . . . 104 E7
Winsford CW7 . . . . 126 A2
Sunningdale Dr
Bebington CH63 . . . . 43 B6
Bramhall SK7 . . . . 36 A7
Sunningdale Rd
Cheadle SK8 . . . . 35 A7
Macclesfield SK11 . . . . 112 A6
Sunningdale Way CH64 . . . . 66 E4
Sunninghey Ct SK9 . . . . . . 59 F2
Sunnybank SK9 . . . . 60 B6
Sunny Bank SK11 . . . . 112 D5
Sunnybank Cl WA12 . . . . . . 2 C4
Sunny Bank Cl SK11 . . . . . 112 D5
Sunny Bank Cotts
Ashton Hayes CH3 . . . . 121 E7
Warrington WA8 . . . . 14 A4
Sunnybank Dr SK9 . . . . 59 D4
Sunnybank Rd CW1, CW2 . . . . 189 E5
Sunny Bank Rd WA14 . . . . . 31 C8
Sunny Lea Mews SK9 . . . . 60 A6
Sunnymill Dr CW11 . . . . . 175 A6
Sunnyside
Alsager ST7 . . . . 193 A4
4 Ellesmere Port CH65 . . . 70 C6
Malpas SY14 . . . . 212 F2
Warrington WA5 . . . . 14 E6
Sunnyside La WA7 . . . . 24 E4
Sunnyside Wlk CW11 . . . . 154 B1
Sunset Cotts CH64 . . . . 67 A4
Surrey Dr CW12 . . . . 156 E5
Surrey Rd
Chester CH2 . . . . 119 A5
Kidsgrove ST7 . . . . 195 A2
Warren SK11 . . . . 112 A4
Surrey St
Crewe CW1 . . . . 190 E4
8 Runcorn WA7 . . . . 23 A2
Warrington WA4 . . . . 16 D3
Surridge WA16 . . . . 29 C5
Susan Dr WA5 . . . . 14 D5
Susan St WA8 . . . . 13 C2
Sussex Ave SK11 . . . . 112 A5
Sussex Dr ST7 . . . . 194 F2
Sussex Pl CW12 . . . . 156 E5
Sussex Rd
Chester CH2 . . . . 118 F4
Irlam M44 . . . . 11 C6
Partington M31 . . . . 11 E2
Sussex St WA8 . . . . 13 D1
Sussex Way CH2 . . . . 118 F4
Sutch La WA13 . . . . 19 A3
Sutherland Ct 5 WA7 . . . . . 23 B2
Sutherland Dr
Bebington CH62 . . . . 43 D4

Sutherland Dr *continued*
Macclesfield SK10 87 A1
Sutherland Way CH3 119 B3
Sutton Ave
Culcheth WA3 4 F4
Neston CH64 66 E6
Sutton Cl
Bebington CH62 43 E3
Higher Wincham CW9 79 F6
Macclesfield SK11 112 D5
Mickle Trafford CH2 119 F8
Nantwich CW5 204 C5
Sutton Cswy WA6, WA7 49 E2
Sutton Dr CH2 118 E5
Sutton Field CW8 126 A7
SUTTON GREEN 69 C3
Sutton Green Prim Sch CH66 69 C5
Sutton Hall Dr CH66 69 A6
Sutton Hall Gdns CH66 69 A6
Sutton High Sch CH66 69 E6
Sutton La CW10 151 C7
SUTTON LANE ENDS 112 E2
Sutton Quays Bsns Pk WA7 49 E3
Sutton Rd
Alderley Edge SK9 59 F2
Poynton SK12 37 A2
Sutton's La 4 WA8 23 B7
Sutton St
Runcorn WA7 23 B2
Warrington WA1 16 C4
Sutton Way
Ellesmere Port CH66 69 E4
1 Handforth SK9 34 E5
SUTTON WEAVER 50 B3
Swale Cl SK9 34 E2
Swaledale Ave CW12 157 A5
Swaledale Cl
Bebington CH62 43 E5
Warrington WA5 14 F7
Swale Rd CH65 70 A7
Swallow Cl
1 Kidsgrove ST7 195 B2
Macclesfield SK10 113 A7
Warrington WA3 9 F4
Swallow Ct
Handforth SK9 34 B1
Winsford CW7 149 D5
Swallow Dr
Alsager ST7 193 B3
Kelsall CW6 122 D5
Sandbach CW11 175 A8
Swallowfield Cl CW2 206 A8
Swallowfield Gdns WA4 26 F5
Swallowfields CH3 180 E2
Swallowmore View ST7 210 C8
Swallow Rd ST7 195 F1
Swanage Cl WA4 16 E2
Swanage Ct 6 CW7 149 D6
Swan Ave WA9 1 A2
SWANBACH 229 E1
Swan Bank
Congleton CW12 156 D2
Talke ST7 210 D7
Swan Cl
Ellesmere Port, Great Sutton CH66 69 D2
Poynton SK12 36 B4
Talke ST7 210 D8
Swan Ct
Bunbury CW6 185 E8
Crowton CW8 101 E7
Swan Farm La CW3 232 B1
Swan Gr WA16 106 D7
SWAN GREEN 106 D8
Swan Ho ST7 210 D7
Swan La
Bunbury CW6 185 E8
Cheadle SK8 35 B8
SWANLEY 203 C5
Swanley La CW5 203 D4
Swanlow Ave CW7 149 D5
Swanlow Dr CW7 149 D6
Swanlow La CW7 149 E5
Swan Rd WA12 1 E4
Swanscoe Ave SK10 88 A7
Swanscoe Cl CW10 151 B8
Swanscoe La SK10 88 B3
Swan St
Congleton CW12 156 D2
Wilmslow SK9 60 B7
Swanwick Cl CW4 107 C1
Swanwick Gn SY13 215 C5
SWANWICK GREEN 215 C4
Swanwick Ho SK10 86 F6
Sweet Briar Cres CW2 189 F3
Sweet Brier Cl CW8 78 B4
Sweetfield Gdns CH66 69 D7
Sweetfield Rd CH66 69 D7
Sweettooth La CW11 175 A7
SWETTENHAM 131 E3
Swettenham Cl
Alsager ST7 193 C3
Sandbach CW11 175 D7
SWETTENHAM HEATH 132 B3
Swettenham La CW12 131 E3
Swettenham Rd
Handforth SK9 34 D5
Swettenham CW12 132 B2
Swettenham St SK11 112 E7
Swift Cl
Kidsgrove ST7 195 B2

Swift Cl *continued*
Warrington WA2 8 E3
Wistaston CW2 205 F8
Swinburne Dr CW1 190 F4
Swindale Ave WA2 8 B3
Swinden Cl WA7 24 D2
Swine Market 2 CW5 204 E5
Swineyard La WA16 28 C4
Swinford Ave WA8 13 E2
Swinhoe Pl WA3 4 D3
Swinley Chase SK9 34 F1
Swinleys Hey CH3 142 A7
Swinnerton St CW2 190 C2
Swinton Sq 18 WA16 57 A2
Swireford Rd WA6 73 B2
Swiss Cott
Alderley Edge SK9 60 C1
Macclesfield SK10 87 B2
Swiss Hill SK9 60 B1
Swithin Rd M22 33 E8
SWORTON HEATH 28 E5
Swynnerton Way WA8 13 B5
Sycamore Ave
Alsager ST7 193 E2
Congleton CW12 155 F4
Crewe CW1 190 D6
Haydock WA11 1 A5
Newton-le-W WA12 2 C3
Rode Heath ST7 193 F7
Widnes WA8 13 B2
Winsford CW7 149 D8
Sycamore Cl
Audlem CW3 230 A4
Biddulph ST8 179 E2
Handforth SK9 34 B2
Holmes Chapel CW4 130 D3
Nantwich CW5 204 F7
Talke ST7 210 E8
Sycamore Cres
Barnton CW8 78 B4
Hollinfare WA3 11 B2
Macclesfield SK11 112 A7
Sycamore Ct WA7 24 D5
Sycamore Dr
Aston WA7 50 B4
Chester CH4 140 F5
Ellesmere Port CH66 70 A1
Lymm WA13 18 D4
Middlewich CW10 151 E5
Sycamore Gr
Broughton CH4 139 B3
Sandbach CW11 175 A8
Sycamore La WA5 15 B6
Sycamore Lane Com Prim Sch WA5 15 B5
Sycamore Lo SK7 35 F7
Sycamore Rd
Paddockhill WA16 59 B5
Partington M31 11 E3
Runcorn WA7 49 D8
Sycamore Rise SK11 112 B6
Sycamores The WA16 58 E2
Syddal Cl SK7 35 D5
Syddal Cres SK7 35 D4
Syddal Gn SK7 35 D5
Syddall Ave SK8 34 D8
Syddal Rd SK7 35 D5
SYDNEY 191 A5
Sydney Ave M90 33 A8
Sydney Rd
Bramhall SK7 35 F5
Chester CH1 118 B3
Crewe CW1 190 F6
Sydney St
Northwich CW8 103 C7
Runcorn WA7 48 D7
Syers Ct WA1 16 E8
Sylvan Ave SK9 59 F5
Sylvan Cl CW8 103 C7
Sylvan Mews CH1 117 E6
Sylvia Cres WA2 8 D1
Symondley Rd SK11 112 F2
Synge St WA2 16 C7
Sytch Croft CH64 66 E8

T

Tabley Ave WA8 12 D2
Tabley Cl
Knutsford WA16 56 E3
Macclesfield SK10 112 A8
Sandbach CW11 174 E7
Tabley Ct WA16 56 B4
Tabley Gr WA16 56 E1
Tabley Hill La WA16 56 B2
Tabley Ho★ WA16 81 B8
Tabley Rd
Crewe CW2 189 E3
Handforth SK9 34 D5
Knutsford WA16 56 E3
Tabley St CW9 79 A1
Tabley Stables WA16 81 A8
Tabor St SK11 112 E6
Tadgers La WA6 73 D8
Tailors View CW5 204 E6
Talbot Ave CH64 66 F6
Talbot Cl
Neston CH64 66 F6
Shavington CW2 206 B4
Warrington WA3 9 E3
Talbot Gdns CH64 66 F6
Talbot Rd
Alderley Edge SK9 60 B1
Dunham-on-t-H WA6 97 E7
Ellesmere Port CH66 69 F3

Talbot St
Chester CH1 237 B4
Golborne WA3 3 A8
Talbot Way CW5 205 A3
Talfryn Cl CH5 91 D1
Talisman Cl WA7 50 D7
TALKE 210 C7
Talke Rd
Alsager ST7 193 E3
High Carr ST5 210 F2
Newcastle-u-Lyme ST7, ST5 210 D4
TALLARN GREEN/ TALLWRN GREEN 222 E5
Tall Ash Ave CW12 157 A4
Tall Chys CW11 175 D4
Tall Trees Cl CW8 103 C6
Tally Ho La CW5 203 E3
Tamar Cl
Congleton CW12 156 F1
Macclesfield SK10 86 E1
Tamar Rd
Haydock WA11 1 C6
Kidsgrove ST7 195 B2
Tamar Wlk CW7 127 A2
Tame Cl
Biddulph ST8 179 D1
Sandbach CW11 174 E8
Tame Wlk 8 SK9 34 D2
Tamworth Cl SK7 36 D8
Tamworth St WA12 2 A3
Tanhouse WA7 23 E1
Tanhouse Ind Est WA8 23 C7
Tan House La
Burtonwood WA5 7 A5
Widnes WA8 23 D8
Tankersley Gr WA5 15 B6
Tanners La WA2 16 A6
Tanner's La WA3 3 B8
Tanner St CW12 156 E2
Tanners Way CW5 204 E4
Tannery La
Neston CH64 66 E8
Warrington WA5 14 D3
Tanning Ct 3 WA1 16 C5
Tanyard Dr WA15 32 C6
Tanyard La WA15 32 A5
Tapley Ave SK12 36 E2
Taplow Cl WA4 26 E6
Taporley War Meml Hospl CW6 146 D2
Target Cl ST7 210 E6
Target Rd CH60 40 C8
Tarnbeck WA7 50 D8
Tarn Cl CW7 126 C3
Tarn Ct WA1 17 F7
Tarn Mount SK11 112 A5
Tarnway WA3 3 F7
TARPORLEY 146 C1
Tarporley Bsns Ctr CW6 168 C8
Tarporley CE Prim Sch CW6 146 D2
Tarporley Com High Sch CW6 146 D1
Tarporley Rd
Duddon CH3 144 E7
Ellesmere Port CH66 69 E4
Little Budworth CW6, CW8 124 C5
Lower Whitley WA4 52 C4
Tarvin CH3 121 C1
Utkinton CW6 146 E6
Whitchurch SY13 225 F3
Tarporley Wlk SK9 34 E2
Tarrant Ct CH1 94 F1
TARVIN 121 C3
Tarvin Ave CW2 189 D4
Tarvin Bridge CH3 119 A2
Tarvin Cl
Ellesmere Port CH65 70 C4
Golborne WA3 3 E7
Macclesfield SK11 112 E5
Middlewich CW10 151 D5
Northwich CW9 103 F5
Runcorn WA7 49 C6
Tarvin Prim Sch CH3 121 B1
Tarvin Rd
Alvanley WA6 73 F4
Bebington CH62 43 F3
Chester, Boughton CH3 119 A2
Chester, Vicarscross CH3 119 E2
Christleton CH3 120 C3
Manley WA6 99 A4
Tarvin Rdbt CH3 121 A2
TARVIN SANDS 121 D4
Tarvin Sands Industries CH3 121 B4
Tarvin Way
1 Handforth SK9 34 D5
Winsford CW7 126 C2
Tasman Cl WA5 15 C8
Tate Cl WA8 12 D2
Tate Dr CW1 191 C4
TATTENHALL 166 B1
Tattenhall La
Beeston CW6 167 F2
Tattenhall CH3 167 B3
Tattenhall Park Prim Sch CH3 166 B2
Tattenhall Rd CH3 166 C4
Tatton Cl
Alsager ST7 193 C3
Chester CH4 140 E5
Northwich CW9 103 F4
Winsford CW7 126 C1

Tatton Ct
4 Handforth SK9 34 E5
2 Knutsford WA16 57 A2
Warrington WA1 9 D1
TATTON DALE 30 E1
Tatton Dr CW11 175 C7
Tatton Lo 17 WA16 57 A2
Tatton Pk★ WA16 57 B7
Tatton Rd
Crewe CW2 189 F2
Handforth SK9 34 E5
Tatton St WA16 57 A2
Tatton Stile WA16 58 A4
Taurus Pk WA5 7 D3
Tavener Cl CH63 43 C5
Tavistock Rd WA5 14 E4
Tavlin Ave WA5 7 F1
Tawney Cl ST7 195 B2
Tawny Ct WA7 49 E7
TAXAL 65 D4
Taxal & Fernilee CE Prim Sch SK23 65 D6
Taxal Moor Rd SK23 65 C3
Taxi Rd M90 33 B7
Taxmere Cl CW11 174 F7
Tay Cl ST8 179 E1
Taylor Bsns Pk WA3 4 F1
Taylor Dr CW5 204 C5
Taylor Rd
Altrincham WA14 20 F5
Haydock WA11 1 F7
Taylor's La
Oakhanger CW1 192 C3
Warrington WA5 14 A2
Taylors Row WA7 23 C2
Taylor St
Warrington WA4 16 A1
Widnes WA8 13 C1
Teal Ave
Knutsford WA16 57 B2
Poynton SK12 36 A4
Tealby Cl CW9 104 B8
Teal Cl
Warrington WA2 8 E3
Winsford CW7 149 D5
Teal Gr WA3 9 F3
Teals Way CH60 40 E8
Tebay Rd CH62 43 E8
Technology Ctr The CH65 70 B7
Tedder Dr M22 33 F7
Tedder Sq WA8 22 D8
Teddington Cl WA4 26 E5
Tees Ct CH65 70 A7
Teesdale Cl WA5 14 F7
Teesdale Rd WA11 1 C7
Tegg's Nose Ctry Pk★ SK11 113 D6
Teggsnose La SK11 113 C6
Tegid Way CH4 140 D5
Tegsnose Mount SK11 113 C4
Telegraph Rd CH60 41 A7
Telfer Ct CW10 151 E6
Telford Cl
Congleton CW12 157 B2
Macclesfield SK10 88 A1
Talke ST7 210 E8
Widnes WA8 12 D4
Telford Ct CH1 94 D6
Telford Gdns CW11 174 F3
Telford Ho ST7 195 B3
Telford Pl CW5 204 C5
Telford Rd CH65 70 E4
Telford's Quay CH65 70 D7
Telford Way
Audlem CW3 230 A3
Chester CH4 140 F6
Middlewich CW10 128 E1
Tempest Rd SK9 60 C1
Templar Ct SK10 87 A1
Temple Chambers CH1 237 B3
Temple Ct WA3 9 E6
Templeton Dr WA2 9 A3
Tenbury Cl WA5 15 A8
Tenby Cl WA5 7 F2
Tenby Dr WA7 23 D2
Tenby Rd SK11 111 F6
Tenchersfield CW5 205 A4
Tennyson Ave CW1 190 F4
Tennyson Cl
Crewe CW2 190 A1
Macclesfield SK11 111 E6
Northwich CW9 104 C6
Rode Heath ST7 193 E8
Tennyson Dr WA2 8 C2
Tennyson Rd
Ellesmere Port CH65 70 A4
Widnes WA8 13 A1
Tennyson Wlk CH1 118 A5
Tensing Cl WA5 15 B8
Tenth Ave CH5 92 D3
Terence Ave WA1 16 F6
Terminal Rd N M90 33 B7
Terminal Rd S M90 33 B7
Tern Ave ST7 195 C2
Tern Cl WA8 13 B4
Tern Dr SK12 36 B4
Terrace Rd WA8 23 A5
Terra Nova Sch CW4 108 D1
Terrick Mews SY13 226 B2
Terrick Rd SY13 226 A2
Tetchill Cl
Ellesmere Port CH66 69 D2
Runcorn WA7 50 D8
Tetton Ct 8 CW12 156 F3
Tetton La CW10 151 E3

Tewkesbury Cl
Cheadle SK8 35 B6
Chester CH2 118 F7
Ellesmere Port CH66 94 E8
Middlewich CW10 128 B1
Poynton SK12 36 D4
Tewkesbury Dr SK10 87 E4
Tewkesbury Rd WA3 3 B8
Thackeray Dr CH3 119 C3
Thackeray Twrs 2 CH1 237 C3
Thackery Ct 6 CW11 174 D6
Thames Cl
Congleton CW12 156 F1
Warrington WA2 8 D2
Thamesdale CH65 70 B4
Thames Dr
Biddulph ST8 179 D1
Biddulph ST8 179 E1
Thames Gdns CH65 70 B3
Thames Pl CW7 127 B1
Thames Rd WA3 5 A2
Thames Side CH65 70 B3
Thames Trad Ctr M44 11 F7
Thatchers Mount WA5 1 D1
Thaxted Wlk M22 33 C8
Theatre Ct CW9 103 F8
THE BANK 195 B7
THE BARONY 204 F6
THELWALL 17 E3
Thelwall Com Inf Sch WA4 17 C3
Thelwall Com Jun Sch WA4 17 D3
Thelwall La
Warrington WA4 16 F3
Warrington WA4 17 B3
Thelwall New Rd WA4 17 C3
Thelwall New Rd Ind Est WA4 17 C3
Thelwall Rd CH66 69 E4
THE QUARRY 209 B1
THE ROOKERY 195 C3
Thetford Cl SK10 87 C3
Thetford Rd WA5 14 E6
THE VALLEY 190 A4
The Verdin High Sch CW7 126 C1
Thewlis St WA5 15 E5
Third Ave
Connah's Quay CH5 92 F1
Crewe CW1 190 F1
Kidsgrove ST7 194 F1
Poynton SK12 36 D1
Runcorn WA7 49 F8
Sandbach CW11 175 A5
Thirlmere
Macclesfield SK11 111 F5
Macclesfield SK11 112 A5
Thirlmere Ave WA2 8 C3
Thirlmere Cl
Alderley Edge SK9 59 F1
Frodsham WA6 49 D1
Holmes Chapel CW4 130 A3
Winsford CW7 126 F3
Thirlmere Ct CW12 156 A2
Thirlmere Dr WA13 18 F3
Thirlmere Lo 5 WA13 18 E3
Thirlmere Rd
Chester CH2 119 A5
Crewe CW2 190 A2
Ellesmere Port CH65 70 C2
Neston CH64 66 E6
Partington M31 11 E4
Thirlmere Way WA8 22 C8
Thirsk Cl WA7 49 C6
Thirsk Way SK10 87 C3
Thistle Cl WA16 79 F7
Thistle Sq M31 11 E2
Thistleton Cl SK11 112 D6
Thistle Wlk 4 M31 11 E2
Thistlewood Dr SK9 60 D8
Thomas Ave CW5 205 A3
Thomas Brassey Cl CH2 237 C4
Thomas Cl
Alsager ST7 193 E4
Blacon CH1 117 E6
Ellesmere Port CH65 70 B2
Mickle Trafford CH2 119 F8
Thomas Ct WA7 49 F7
Thomas Ho CH1 118 A5
Thomas Hodges Ct CW4 130 D3
Thomasons Bridge La WA4 25 E6
Thomas Row 8 CW5 204 E6
Thomas St
Biddulph ST8 179 D1
Congleton CW12 156 E3
Crewe CW1 190 D4
Golborne WA3 3 A8
Packmoor ST7 195 F1
Runcorn WA7 23 B3
Talke ST7 210 D8
2 Widnes WA8 23 A7
Thomas Wedge CE Jun Sch The CH1 94 A1
Thompson Ave WA3 4 E3
Thompson Cl WA12 2 C1
Thomson Gdns CW12 156 A3
Thomson St WA3 9 E5
Thoresway Rd SK9 59 F5
Thorlby Rd WA3 4 F3
Thorley Gr CW2 190 A1

- Thorley La
  - Wythenshawe M90 33 A8
  - Wythenshawe M90 33 B8
- Thorley Mews SK7 35 F7
- Thornberry Cl CH1 117 B8
- Thornbrook Way CW11 174 D5
- Thornbury Ave WA3 3 E7
- Thorn Cl
  - Runcorn WA7 49 C7
  - Warrington WA5 14 F3
- Thorn Dr M22 34 A8
- Thorne Cl SK10 87 A5
- Thorne Dr CH66 69 B4
- Thorneycroft Dr WA1 16 C6
- Thorney Dr SK8 35 C6
- Thorneyholme Dr WA16 57 B2
- Thornfield SK9 60 A4
- Thornfield Cl WA3 3 C8
- Thornfield Hey SK9 60 E8
- Thornfields CW1 173 B1
- Thorn Gr SK8 35 A7
- Thorngrove Dr SK9 60 C6
- Thorngrove Hill SK9 60 C6
- Thorn Grove Prim Sch SK8 35 A7
- Thorngrove Rd SK9 60 C6
- Thornhills WA8 12 A3
- Thorn Ho CH4 141 A5
- Thorn La CW8 103 C5
- Thornleigh Ave CH62 43 F3
- Thornleigh Dr CH66 69 E6
- Thornley Cl [1] WA13 18 C3
- Thornley Rd WA13 18 C3
- Thorn Rd
  - Bramhall SK7 35 E5
  - Runcorn WA7 49 C7
  - Warrington WA1 17 A8
- THORNS GREEN 32 C5
- Thornsgreen Rd M22 33 D8
- Thornton WA8 22 E8
- Thornton Ave SK11 112 A5
- Thornton Bank CW6 169 D4
- Thornton Cl CW7 127 A3
- Thornton Common Rd CH63 42 D7
- Thornton Cres CH60 41 B6
- Thorntondale Dr WA5 14 F7
- Thornton Dr
  - Chester CH2 118 D5
  - Handforth SK9 34 D3
  - Wistaston CW2 206 A7
- Thornton Green La CH2 71 E1
- Thornton Ho
  - Audlem CW3 230 A5
  - Thornton Hough CH63 42 B6
- THORNTON HOUGH 42 A7
- Thornton Hough Prim Sch CH63 42 B7
- THORNTON-LE-MOORS 71 F1
- Thornton Mews CH66 69 B8
- Thornton Rd
  - Ellesmere Port CH65 70 E3
  - Gatley SK8 34 C8
  - Warrington WA5 15 B4
- Thornton Sq SK11 112 A5
- Thorntree Bglws SK11 132 A8
- Thorn Tree Cl L24 21 E2
- Thorn Tree Dr CW1 173 A1
- Thorntree Gn WA4 27 B5
- Thornway
  - Bollington SK10 88 A7
  - Bramhall SK8 35 C7
  - High Lane SK6 37 F7
- Thorn Wlk M31 11 E2
- Thornwythe Gr CH66 69 E4
- Thornycroft CW7 126 A1
- Thornycroft Cl SK11 111 E1
- Thornycroft St [7] SK11 112 E7
- Thorpe Cl CW1 189 F8
- Thorp St SK10 112 D8
- Thowler La WA14 30 A5
- Threaphurst La SK12 37 C8
- THREAPWOOD 222 E7
- Three Acre La SK8 34 E7
- Three Fields Cl CW12 156 B3
- Threeways CW8 101 D4
- Thrush Way CW7 126 F4
- Thurlow WA3 3 E7
- THURLWOOD 193 E7
- Thursfield Ave ST7 195 C3
- Thursfield Ct CH1 118 B1
- Thursfield Prim Sch ST7 195 E3
- Thurstaston Rd CH60 40 F8
- Thurston Cl WA5 15 D6
- Thurston Gn SK9 60 A1
- Thurston Rd CH4 140 E5
- Thynne St WA1 16 A4
- Tibbs Cross La WA8 13 D8
- Tibb St ST7 209 F2
- Tidal La WA1 16 F8
- Tideswell Cl SK8 34 D8
- Tideswell Rd SK7 36 E8
- Tidnock Ave CW12 156 E5
- Tiffield Ct CW7 127 A4
- Tilbey Dr WA6 74 A8
- Tilbury Pl WA7 50 E6
- Tildsley Cres WA7 48 F6
- Tilewright Cl ST7 195 B2
- Tilley St WA1 16 C6
- Tilman Cl WA5 15 B8
- TILSTON 198 B3
- Tilston Ave WA4 17 A4
- Tilston CE Prim Sch SY14 198 B3
- TILSTONE BANK 168 F4
- Tilstone Cl
  - Hough CW2 206 E2
  - Northwich CW9 104 A5
- TILSTONE FEARNALL 168 F6
- Tilston Rd SY14 213 A5
- Tilston Wlk [5] SK9 34 E1
- Timberfields Rd CH1 117 A8
- Timber La [2] CW9 103 F8
- TIMBERSBROOK 157 E2
- Timbersbrook Gr [5] SK9 34 D2
- Timberscombe Gdns WA1 17 E6
- Timber St SK10 87 F1
- Timbrell Ave CW1 190 A6
- Timmis Cl WA2 9 A3
- Timmis Cres WA8 13 A1
- Timperley Ave WA4 17 A4
- Tinkersfield CW5 205 A4
- Tinkwood La SY14 211 F1
- Tinsley St WA4 16 F3
- Tintagel Cl
  - Macclesfield SK10 111 E8
  - Runcorn WA7 50 B6
- Tintern Ave CH2 118 F6
- Tintern Cl
  - Poynton SK12 36 D5
  - Warrington WA5 7 E2
- Tintern Rd SK8 35 B6
- Tipping Brow WA16 58 C4
- Tirley La CW6 123 A2
- Tithebarn Cl CH60 40 F7
- Tithebarn Dr CH64 41 B2
- Tithebarn Rd WA15 32 C8
- Tithings The WA7 23 E1
- TIVERTON 168 C6
- Tiverton Cl
  - Chester CH2 118 F5
  - Sandbach CW11 175 C7
  - Widnes WA8 12 C3
- Tiverton Ct [6] CW9 103 E5
- Tiverton Dr SK9 34 D1
- Tiverton Sq WA5 14 E4
- Tiveton Ct CW9 103 F5
- Tobermory Cl WA11 1 A5
- Todbrook Cl SK23 65 D6
- Todds Bldgs WA8 23 A6
- Toft Cl
  - Chester CH4 140 E5
  - Widnes WA8 12 F1
- Toft Rd WA16 82 B7
- Toft Way SK9 34 E4
- Tolland La WA15 31 F8
- Tollard Cl SK8 35 B6
- Toll Bar Ave SK11 112 F7
- Toll Bar Pl WA2 8 A4
- Toll Bar Rd
  - Chester CH3 142 C8
  - Macclesfield SK11 111 F8
  - Warrington WA2 8 A3
- Tollemache Cotts CW5 203 C8
- Tollemache Dr CW1 190 A8
- Tollemache Terr CH2 118 F2
- Tollgate Cl ST7 210 C8
- Tollgate Dr CW3 229 F4
- Tollitt St CW1 190 C4
- Tom Brads Croft SK23 65 E8
- Tom Fields ST7 209 F1
- Tomkinson Cl CW1 189 F7
- Tomkinson St CH2 237 C4
- Tom La WA14 30 E6
- Tomlinson Ave WA2 16 D8
- Tomlins Terr CH1 117 E5
- Tommy's La
  - Congleton CW12 156 F4
  - Crewe CW1 190 E2
- Tonbridge Cl SK10 87 B2
- Toogood Cl CH2 119 F8
- Top Farm La CW7 170 F2
- Topgate Cl CH60 41 B8
- Topping Ct WA3 9 B4
- Top Rd
  - Frodsham WA6 74 D5
  - Kingsley WA6 75 B1
- Top Station Rd ST7 195 C7
- Torbrook Gr [1] SK9 34 D2
- Torkington Rd SK9 60 D6
- Toronto Ave M90 33 B7
- Torr Dr CH62 44 A7
- Torridon Gr CH66 69 F3
- Torr Rd SK11 112 C4
- Torr Rise CW6 146 D1
- Torrs Valley SK22 39 C7
- TORR TOP 39 C8
- Torr Top St SK22 39 C7
- Torrvale Rd SK22 39 B7
- Totland Cl WA5 14 C7
- Totland Gr CH2 118 E4
- Tourney Gn WA5 7 A2
- Towergate CH1 118 B1
- TOWER HILL 88 D4
- Tower Hill SK10 88 D4
- Tower Hill Rd ST7 195 F7
- Tower Ho The [20] SK11 112 C8
- Tower La
  - Lymm WA13 18 F2
  - Runcorn WA7 50 D7
  - Weaverham CW8 77 B1
- Tower Rd CH1 118 B2
- Towers Cl
  - Poynton SK12 36 F5
  - Wistaston CW2 206 A7
- Towers Ct WA5 15 E7
- Towers La WA6 98 C7
- Towers Rd SK12 36 F5
- Towers The [6] SK10 111 F8
- Towers Yard Barns SK12 36 F5
- Tower Way CW1 190 C4
- Townbridge Ct [14] CW8 103 F8
- Towneley Ct WA8 13 A1
- TOWN END 12 C6
- Town Farm La WA6 100 E7
- Townfield Ave CH3 180 E2
- Townfield Cl ST7 194 D2
- Townfield Ct CW8 78 A3
- Townfield La
  - Barnton CW8 78 A3
  - Blacon CH1 117 F8
  - Farndon CH3 180 D2
  - Frodsham WA6 74 D7
  - Lymm WA13 19 B7
  - Mollington CH1 94 D2
  - Swan Green WA16 106 E5
  - Tarvin CH3 121 B2
  - Tiverton CW6 168 C6
- Townfield Rd
  - Mobberley WA16 58 A4
  - Runcorn WA7 24 C2
- Townfields WA16 57 C2
- TOWN FIELDS 149 D7
- Town Fields CW11 175 B5
- Townfields Cotts [6] CW7 149 C7
- Townfields Cres CW7 149 D7
- Townfields Dr CW7 149 C7
- Townfields Gdns CW7 149 D7
- Townfields Rd CW7 149 D7
- Townfield View WA7 24 C2
- Townfield Villas CH2 72 B3
- Towngate Bsns Ctr WA8 22 B7
- Town Gn The WA4 52 D5
- Town Hill WA1 16 B5
- Town La
  - Hale L24, WA8 21 E2
  - Mobberley WA16 58 B4
  - Neston CH64 66 F6
- Townley Mill [6] SK11 112 D7
- Townley Pl [5] SK11 112 D7
- Townley St [4] SK11 112 D7
- TOWN OF LOWTON 3 B5
- TOWN PARK 50 B8
- Townsend Farm ST7 193 E2
- Townsend La ST7 194 A8
- Townsend Rd CW12 156 E2
- Townsfield Dr CW6 147 F7
- Townsfield La WA2 8 A5
- Townshend Rd CW9 80 A3
- Township Cl CH3 182 C1
- Town Sq
  - [4] Northwich CW9 103 F8
  - [6] Runcorn WA7 49 F7
- Town Well WA6 75 C2
- Townwell Ct CW5 204 D5
- Town Wlk [9] WA7 49 F7
- Trackside Bsns Pk CW11 174 C6
- Tracy Dr WA12 2 E3
- Trafalgar Ave SK12 37 A3
- Trafalgar Cl
  - Northwich CW9 103 E3
  - Poynton SK12 37 A3
- Trafalgar Ct
  - [8] Macclesfield SK11 112 D7
  - Widnes WA8 23 A6
- Trafford Ave WA5 15 F7
- Trafford Cres WA7 49 C6
- Trafford Pl SK9 60 D6
- Trafford Rd
  - Alderley Edge SK9 60 B1
  - Handforth SK9 34 B1
- Trafford St CH1 237 B3
- Tragan Dr WA5 14 D3
- Tramway Rd M44 11 F7
- Tramway St CH1 237 C3
- Tranmere Dr SK9 34 E2
- Trap Rd CW12 132 C3
- Trap St SK11 132 B6
- TRAP STREET 132 C5
- Travellers Rest Cvn Pk CW7 150 C8
- Travers' Entry WA9 6 A7
- Travis St [10] WA8 23 B8
- Treborth Rd CH1 117 D3
- Tree Bank Cl WA7 49 A8
- Treen Cl SK10 86 D1
- Tree Tops CH64 66 E4
- Treetops Cl WA1 16 F7
- Tree Way WA16 82 A7
- Trefoil Cl
  - Huntington CH3 142 B6
  - Warrington WA3 9 C5
- Tregele Cl CH1 117 D3
- Trenance Cl WA7 50 C5
- Trenchard Dr M22 33 F7
- Trent Ave CW7 127 B1
- Trent Cl
  - Bramhall SK7 35 C6
  - Culcheth WA3 5 A2
  - Widnes WA8 13 B4
  - Winsford CW7 127 B1
- Trentdale CH65 70 B3
- Trentham Cl WA8 13 B4
- Trentham St WA7 22 F3
- Trent Way CH60 41 C6
- Tresham Dr WA4 27 A8
- Trevithick Cl CW1 191 A4
- Trevone Cl WA16 57 A1
- Trickett La CW8 102 A3
- Tricketts La CW5 205 E5
- Tricketts Mews CW5 205 E5
- Trident Ind Est WA3 9 E6
- Trident Ret Pk WA7 49 E7
- Trident Way SK11 112 A5
- Trinity Cl CW2 190 A1
- Trinity Ct
  - Congleton CW12 157 B1
  - [1] Knutsford WA16 57 A2
  - Warrington WA3 9 F5
- Trinity Gdns [4] WA6 49 C1
- Trinity Ho [3] WA6 49 C1
- Trinity La SK11 112 F3
- Trinity Pl
  - Congleton CW12 179 B8
  - [1] Widnes WA8 23 B7
- Trinity Sq SK10 87 F1
- Trinity St
  - Chester CH1 237 A2
  - Runcorn WA7 23 B3
- Trinity Terr [2] CW8 103 E8
- Troon Cl
  - Bebington CH63 43 C5
  - Bramhall SK7 36 A7
  - Haydock WA11 1 A5
  - Holmes Chapel CW4 130 C2
- Trossach Cl WA2 8 E2
- Troutbeck Ave
  - Congleton CW12 156 A2
  - Newton-le-W WA12 1 E4
  - Warrington WA5 15 F8
- Troutbeck Cl WA7 50 A5
- Troutbeck Gr CW7 126 D2
- Trouthall La WA16 81 A2
- Trubshaw Ct ST7 195 C3
- Trubshaw Pl ST7 195 B3
- Truman Cl WA8 12 F3
- Truman Ct [6] WA5 15 B7
- Trumans La CH66 69 C7
- Truro Cl
  - Bramhall SK7 35 F7
  - Congleton CW12 178 E8
  - Ellesmere Port CH66 94 F8
  - Macclesfield SK10 86 E1
  - Runcorn WA7 50 C6
  - Warrington WA1 17 B8
- Tudor Cl
  - Ellesmere Port CH66 94 F8
  - Middlewich CW10 128 D1
  - Northwich CW9 104 E6
  - Warrington WA4 17 A2
  - Winsford CW7 149 D6
- Tudor Ct
  - Congleton CW12 156 D2
  - [4] Warrington WA4 16 E1
- Tudor Dr SK10 86 D7
- Tudor Gn
  - Blacon CH1 117 E6
  - Handforth SK9 34 E1
- Tudor Rd
  - Handforth SK9 34 E1
  - Runcorn WA7 24 C3
- Tudorway CH60 41 B8
- Tudor Way
  - Chester CH3 142 A7
  - Congleton CW12 156 D1
  - Nantwich CW5 204 E3
- Tue La WA8 12 B6
- Tulip Gr WA5 15 E3
- Tulip Rd
  - Haydock WA11 1 F6
  - Partington M31 11 E2
- Tully Ave WA12 1 F3
- Tulworth Rd SK12 36 D4
- Tunbridge Cl
  - Warrington WA5 15 A8
  - Wistaston CW2 206 A8
- Tunnel Rd CW8 78 B2
- Tunnicliffe Rd SK11 112 F3
- Tunnicliffe St [1] SK10 112 D8
- Tunstall Rd
  - Biddulph CW12, SK11 158 C7
  - Congleton CW12 157 F2
- Turf La SK11 112 C3
- Turnall Rd WA8 22 B7
- Turnberry Cl
  - Lymm WA13 18 C4
  - Macclesfield SK10 87 C4
  - Northwich CW9 104 E7
  - Winsford CW7 126 C2
- Turnberry Dr SK9 60 D8
- Turner Ave ST7 210 A1
- Turner Cl
  - Crewe CW1 190 A8
  - Widnes WA8 12 D3
- Turner Rise SK10 88 C8
- Turner St
  - Bollington SK10 88 B8
  - Nantwich CW5 204 F5
- Turner's View CH64 41 D2
- Turnhurst Rd ST7 195 F1
- Turnock St SK11 112 E7
- Turnstone Ave WA12 2 C4
- Turret Hall Dr [1] WA3 3 E8
- Turriff Dr CH63 43 C4
- Turrocks Cl CH64 66 E5
- Turrocks Croft CH64 66 E5
- Turton Cl
  - Hale L24 21 E1
  - Warrington WA3 9 C5
- Turton St WA3 3 A8
- Turville Ho SK9 34 D2
- Tuscan Cl WA8 13 B5
- Tushingham Cl CH3 142 B7
- Tushingham-with-Grindley CE Prim Sch SY13 214 C1
- Tuson Dr WA8 12 F4
- Tutor Bank Dr WA12 2 D3
- Tweedsmuir CH3 119 A2
- Tweedsmuir Cl WA2 9 A4
- Twemlow Ave CW11 175 B7
- TWEMLOW GREEN 131 A5
- Twemlow La CW4 130 D6
- Twenty Acre Rd WA5 15 C8
- Twinnies Rd SK9 34 B1
- TWISS GREEN 4 E4
- Twiss Green Com Prim Sch WA3 4 E4
- Twiss Green Dr WA3 4 E4
- Twiss Green La WA3 4 E4
- Twist Ave WA3 3 C8
- Two Acre Gr CH66 69 F1
- TWO MILLS 93 E8
- Twyford Cl WA8 13 B5
- Twyford La WA8 13 D6
- Tyldesley Way CW5 204 D6
- Tyler St SK9 60 A1
- Tyne Cl WA2 8 E2
- Tynedale Ave CW2 190 C2
- Tynedale Cl SK11 112 C8
- Tynemouth Rd WA7 50 C6
- Tynesdale CH65 70 B3
- Tynwald Cres WA8 12 F5
- Tynwald Dr WA4 26 C7
- Tyrer Rd WA12 2 C1
- Tyrer Wlk [2] WA3 3 F8
- TYTHERINGTON 87 C3
- Tytherington Bsns Pk SK10 87 D5
- Tytherington Cl CW10 151 C6
- Tytherington Ct SK10 87 D3
- Tytherington Dr SK10 87 E4
- Tytherington Gn SK10 87 C4
- Tytherington High Sch SK10 87 D2
- Tytherington La SK10 87 D5
- Tytherington Park Rd SK10 87 D3
- Tytherington Sh Ctr [1] SK10 87 D3

U

- Ullapool Cl CH66 68 F6
- Ullswater SK11 111 F5
- Ullswater Ave
  - Crewe CW2 189 E3
  - Warrington WA2 8 D3
  - Winsford CW7 126 C2
- Ullswater Cres CH2 119 A6
- Ullswater Dr SK9 83 F7
- Ullswater Gr WA7 49 D5
- Ullswater Mans SK11 111 F6
- Ullswater Rd
  - Congleton CW12 156 A2
  - Ellesmere Port CH65 70 C2
  - Handforth SK9 34 C4
- Ulverston Ave WA2 8 B4
- Ulverston Cl WA11 1 A6
- Ulviet Gate WA16 29 C4
- Underbridge La WA4 25 E6
- Undercliffe Ho WA4 26 D8
- Under Rainow Rd CW12 157 E1
- Underway The WA7 49 F8
- Underwood Bsns Pk CW1 190 A6
- Underwood Cl SK10 86 F1
- Underwood Ct CW1 190 B6
- Underwood Dr CH65 70 C2
- Underwood La CW1 190 B6
- Underwood Rd SK9 60 C1
- Underwood West Prim Sch CW1 190 A5
- Unicorn Gateway [8] SK10 112 D8
- Union Cl CW12 156 D3
- Union Ind Est SK11 112 E7
- Union Pl CH1 237 A2
- Union Rd
  - Macclesfield SK11 112 E7
  - New Mills SK22 39 C7
- Union St
  - Chester CH1 237 C2
  - Congleton CW12 156 D3
  - Crewe CW2 190 D3
  - Macclesfield SK11 112 D7
  - Runcorn WA7 23 B2
  - Sandbach CW11 175 B6
  - Warrington WA1 16 B5
- Union Terr CH1 237 B3
- Union Wlk CH1 237 B2
- Unity Way ST7 210 D8
- University Way CW1 191 B2
- Univ of Chester CH1 237 A4
- Univ of Chester (Chichester House) CH1 237 A3
- Univ of Chester Warrington Campus WA2 9 B3
- Univ of Liverpool, Faculty of Veterinary Science (Leahurst) CH64 67 D8

Univ of Manchester School of Physics & Astronomy The SK11 108 D2
Unsworth Ct WA2 8 F1
Upcast La SK9 59 E3
Uplands CW8 101 D4
Uplands Rd CW9 78 E4
Uplands The
Biddulph ST8 179 E2
Macclesfield SK11 112 A8
Runcorn WA7 50 A7
Upper Cambrian Rd CH1 118 B2
Upper Haigh St CW7 149 C8
Upper Mersey Rd WA8 23 A5
Upper Mersey St CH65 70 C7
Upper Northgate St CH1 237 A3
Upper Raby Rd CH64 42 A2
UPPER THREAPWOOD 222 E7
UPTON
Chester 118 D6
Widnes 12 C4
Upton Ave SK8 35 A8
Upton Bridle Path WA8 12 F4
Upton-by-Chester High Sch CH2 118 F6
Upton Cl
Golborne WA3 3 D8
Winsford CW7 126 F4
Upton Dr
Chester CH2 118 C6
Warrington WA5 14 F5
Upton Grange WA8 12 D4
UPTON HEATH 118 F8
Upton Heath CE Prim Sch CH2 118 E8
Upton La
Chester CH2 118 D7
Widnes WA8 12 F4
Upton Mount SK10 87 A1
Upton Pk CH2 118 D6
Upton Priory Inf Sch SK10 86 F2
Upton Priory Jun Sch SK10 86 F2
Upton Rd CH66 69 D4
UPTON ROCKS 12 E4
Upton Rocks Ave WA8 12 E4
Upton Rocks Mews WA8 12 E4
Upton Way [12] SK9 34 D5
Upton Westlea Prim Sch CH2 118 E7
Upwood Rd WA3 3 D7
Ure Ct CH65 70 A7
Urmston Ave WA12 2 B5
Ursuline Way CW2 190 B1
UTKINTON 146 B7
Utkinton La CW6 146 E7
Utkinton Rd CW6 146 C5
Utkinton St Paul's CE Prim Sch CW6 146 B8

V

Vahler Terr WA7 23 C2
Vale Ave WA2 16 B8
Valebrook Dr CW5 220 A8
Vale Bsns Ctr CW12 156 D2
Vale Cl CH4 139 C3
Vale Ct WA4 51 A3
Vale Gdns
Alsager ST7 193 E4
Ellesmere Port CH65 70 B4
Helsby WA6 73 B4
Vale Head SK9 34 D2
Valentine Rd
Kidsgrove ST7 195 A1
Newton-le-W WA12 1 F3
Vale Owen Rd WA2 8 D1
Vale Rd
Alpraham CW6 169 A4
Ellesmere Port CH65 70 B4
Hartford CW8 103 C4
Marston CW9 79 B6
Wilmslow SK9 59 E8
Vale Royal Ctyd CW8 126 B8
Vale Royal Dr CW8 126 A8
Vale Royal River Park Cvn Site CW9 126 E6
Vale View CW9 79 D1
Vale Wlk CW12 156 D2
Valiant Cl WA2 8 F2
Valley Brook Bsns Ctr CW2 190 D3
Valley Cl
Alsager ST7 192 F3
Knutsford WA16 82 A7
Valley Ct
Crewe CW2 190 B3
Middlewich CW10 128 E1
Warrington WA2 8 F1
Valley Dr
Chester CH2 118 C5
Ellesmere Port CH66 69 D5
Handforth SK9 34 C3
Valley La
Cuddington CW8 101 F3
Sandiway CW8 102 A3
Valley Rd
Bebington CH62 43 D8
Bramhall SK7 35 F8
Crewe CW2 189 F1
Valley Rd *continued*
Macclesfield SK11 112 A6
Weaverham CW8 77 C1
Valley Sch SK7 35 C5
Valley View
Congleton CW12 156 C3
Ellesmere Port CH66 69 D5
Newton-le-W WA12 2 B1
Northwich CW9 104 C7
Valley Way WA16 82 A7
Vanguard Ct WA3 9 D4
Varden Rd SK12 36 E3
Varden Town Cotts SK10 86 A4
Vardon Dr SK9 60 D6
Varey Rd CW12 156 F4
Vaudrey Cres CW12 156 F3
Vaudrey Dr WA1 17 D7
Vaughan Rd SK23 65 E5
Vaughans La CH3 142 A8
Vauxhall Cl WA5 14 F4
Vauxhall Rd CW5 204 E7
Vauxhall Way CW7 149 C6
Vearows Pl CW8 103 F7
Venables Rd CW9 79 A1
Venable's Rd CH1 117 F4
Venables Way
High Legh WA16 29 C4
Middlewich CW10 151 E6
Venetian Marina Village CW5 188 B8
Venns Rd WA2 16 D7
Ventnor Cl
Middlewich CW10 151 C8
Warrington WA5 14 D7
Venture Ho SK11 112 D6
Venture Way SK12 36 F3
Verbena Cl
Partington M31 11 F3
Runcorn WA7 49 F4
Verdin Ave CW8 78 F1
Verdin Cl
Moulton CW9 126 F7
Winsford CW7 126 C2
Verdin Ct CW1 190 A8
Verdin St CW9 104 C8
Vere St CW1 190 C5
Verity Cl CW1 191 C4
Verity Ct CW10 128 E2
Vermont Cl WA5 15 C7
Vermont Gdns SK7 35 B5
Vernay Gn CH4 141 B5
Vernon Ave
Audley ST7 209 D2
Congleton CW12 178 F8
Hooton CH66 44 A2
Vernon Cl
Audley ST7 209 D2
Poynton SK12 36 D2
Saughall CH1 117 A8
Vernon Dr CW3 230 F4
Vernon Inf Sch SK12 36 E3
Vernon Jun Sch SK12 36 E3
Vernon Rd
Chester CH1 118 B2
Poynton SK12 36 E2
Vernon St
Crewe CW1 190 B5
Macclesfield SK10 112 F8
Warrington WA1 16 B4
Vernon Way CW1 190 D4
Veronica Mews WA8 12 D1
Veronica Way CH66 69 D7
Vetch Cl WA3 11 B5
Vetches The CH3 119 F5
Viaduct St WA12 2 A3
Vicarage Ave SK8 35 B7
Vicarage Cl
Guilden Sutton CH3 119 F5
Hale L24 21 E1
Vicarage Ct LL13 196 E8
Vicarage Dr WA11 1 B7
Vicarage Gdns CW11 174 E8
Vicarage Gr CW7 149 D5
Vicarage Hill WA6 73 C4
Vicarage La
Audlem CW3 230 A4
Bunbury CW6 168 F1
Burton CH64 67 D2
Frodsham WA6 74 C7
Helsby WA6 73 C4
Little Budworth CW6 147 F7
Poynton SK12 36 E5
Sandbach CW11 174 E8
Vicarage Rd
Chester CH2 118 F3
Haslington CW1 191 D6
Haydock WA11 1 A7
Northwich CW9 104 B8
Widnes WA8 23 A7
Vicarage Row CH62 44 A5
Vicarage Way [1] SK11 111 F7
Vicarage Wlk
Northwich CW9 104 B7
Warrington WA4 26 C8
Vicar's Cl CH3 121 F7
VICARSCROSS 119 E2
Vicars Cross Ct [2] CH3 119 B2
Vicars Cross Rd CH3 119 C2
Vicar's La CH1 237 B2
Vickers Rd WA8 22 F4
Vickers Way CW9 104 A7
Victoria Ave
Crewe CW2 190 A4
Grappenhall WA4 17 A2
Haslington CW1 191 C4
Victoria Ave *continued*
Heswall CH60 41 A6
Holmes Chapel CW4 130 C2
Kidsgrove ST7 194 F2
Warrington WA5 14 D6
Widnes WA8 13 A3
Victoria Cl SK7 35 D6
Victoria Com Tech Sch CW1 190 C5
Victoria Cres
Chester CH2 237 A4
Chester, Queen's Park CH4 237 C1
Victoria Ct
Chester CH2 237 A4
[3] Crewe CW1 190 C4
Haslington CW1 191 C4
[8] Kidsgrove ST7 195 A2
Knutsford WA16 56 F1
[2] Widnes WA8 23 A8
Victoria Gr WA8 13 A3
Victoria Infmy CW8 103 E8
Victoria Inf Sch CH1 237 A4
Victoria Mews CH65 70 B5
Victoria Mill Dr CW5 205 D6
Victoria Pathway CH4 237 C1
Victoria Pk CW8 78 F1
Victoria Pl
Chester CH1 237 B3
Warrington WA4 16 C1
Victoria Rd
Chester CH1, CH2 237 B3
Chester CH2 237 A4
Ellesmere Port CH65 70 C5
Macclesfield SK10 87 A1
Neston CH64 67 A6
Newton-le-W WA12 2 C3
Northwich CW9 104 B8
Runcorn WA7 23 A2
Runcorn WA7 23 B2
Saltney CH4 140 D5
Warrington, Great Sankey WA5 15 B4
Warrington, Penketh WA5 14 D4
Warrington, Stockton Heath WA4 16 D1
Warrington WA4 16 F2
Widnes WA8 23 A6
Wilmslow SK9 60 A6
Victoria Road Prim Sch
Northwich CW9 104 B8
Runcorn WA7 23 A2
Victoria Sq
Warrington WA4 16 C1
[8] Widnes WA8 23 A7
Winsford CW7 149 A8
Victoria St
Congleton CW12 156 D2
Crewe CW1 190 C4
Knutsford WA16 56 F2
New Mills SK22 39 B6
Northwich CW9 79 E2
Sandbach CW11 175 B7
Warrington WA1 16 C5
Widnes WA8 23 B7
Victoria Stadium (Northwich Victoria FC) CW9 79 D3
Victoria Trad Ctr WA8 23 A6
Victoria Way SK7 35 D6
Victoria Wlk SK10 112 E8
Victory Rd M44 11 C4
Viewlands Dr SK9 34 D2
Viking Way CW12 156 C4
Villa Farm CW11 176 B8
Village Cl
Lostock Green CW9 105 A8
Runcorn WA7 50 A8
Warrington WA4 17 E4
Village Ct [8] SK9 34 D1
Village Farm CW5 172 A5
Village La WA4 52 D4
Village Mews SK10 87 A6
Village Rd
Christleton CH3 142 E8
Great Barrow CH3 120 E6
Heswall CH60 40 F7
Waverton CH3 143 C4
Village St WA7 24 E2
Village Terr The [6] WA4 16 C1
Village The
Astbury CW12 178 B8
Burton CH64 67 D1
Prestbury SK10 86 F6
Village Way [11] SK9 34 D1
Villa Rd CH5 116 B7
Villars St WA1 16 C5
Villas The CW4 131 A8
Villiers Russell Cl CW1 190 D5
Vincent Cl WA5 15 C8
Vincent Dr CH4 141 C6
Vincent St
Crewe CW1 190 E4
Macclesfield SK11 112 D7
Vine Bank Rd ST7 195 A1
Vine Cl SK11 112 A6
Vine Cres WA5 14 F6
Vine Rd CH66 69 F1
Vine St
Bollington SK10 88 B8
[11] Runcorn WA7 23 A2
Widnes WA8 23 A7
Vine Terr WA8 12 A2
Vine Tree Ave
Crewe CW2 190 B1
Shavington CW2 206 B5
Vine Tree Prim Sch CW2 190 A1
Vineyard The CW2 206 B4
Violet Cl WA3 9 C5
Violet St WA8 23 A7
Virginia Chase SK8 34 F8
Virginia Dr CH1 117 C4
Virginia Gdns WA5 15 B8
Virginia Terr CH66 69 B8
Virtual Bsns Ctr CH1 117 E2
Viscount Dr
Gatley SK8 34 D7
Wythenshawe M90 32 F7
Viscount Rd WA2 8 E2
Vista Ave WA12 2 A4
Vista Rd
Newton-le-W WA11, WA12 2 A6
Runcorn WA7 49 A8
Vista The M44 11 C4
Vista Way WA12 2 A4
Vixen Gr WA8 12 F4
Volunteer Ave [7] CW5 204 E6
Volunteer Fields CW5 204 E6
Volunteer St
Chester CH1 237 B2
Frodsham WA6 49 D1
Vose Cl WA5 15 D6
Vulcan Cl
Newton-le-W WA12 2 C1
Warrington WA2 8 F2
Vulcan Ind Est WA12 2 D1
VULCAN VILLAGE 7 C8
Vyrnwy Rd CH4 140 D6

W

Waddington Cl
Golborne WA3 3 F8
Warrington WA2 8 F1
Wadebrook Gr [4] SK9 34 D1
Wadebrook Trad Est CW9 104 C8
Wade Cres CW8 78 A3
Wade Ct ST7 195 A1
Wade Deacon High Sch WA8 13 A2
WADES GREEN 171 F5
Wades La CW7 126 D3
Wadeson Way WA3 9 B7
Wade St CW9 79 B1
Wadsworth Cl SK9 34 E3
Waggon Cotts ST7 208 E1
Waggs Rd CW12 156 C1
Wagg St CW12 156 D2
Wagon La WA11 1 B6
Waine St CW1 190 D5
Wain Ho CH1 94 A1
Wain Lee ST7 195 F4
Wakefield Cl CW1 189 F7
Wakefield Ct CW9 104 A5
Wakefield Ho WA5 15 F6
Wakefield Rd CH66 69 E1
Wakefield St WA3 3 A7
Wakeham Chase [8] SK11 111 F7
Wakes Mdw CW6 185 E8
Walden Cl WA4 17 D3
Walden Dr CH1 93 D8
Waldon Rd SK11 112 A5
Waldron Gdns CW2 189 F1
Waldron Rd CW1 191 D3
Waldron's La CW1 173 D1
Walfield Ave CW12 156 D5
Walford Ave CW2 190 B3
WALGHERTON 220 B6
Walgrave Cl CW12 156 A3
Walker Cl CW1 191 D4
Walker Dr CW10 151 C8
Walker La SK11 112 E2
WALKER'S GREEN 152 D7
Walkersgreen Rd ST5 210 D2
Walkers La
Ellesmere Port CH66 69 C6
Farndon CH3 180 F2
Scholar Green ST7 177 B2
Tarporley CW6 146 D1
Warrington WA5 14 E3
Walker St
Chester CH2 237 C4
Crewe CW1 190 B5
[2] Macclesfield SK10 112 C8
Warrington WA2 16 A6
Wallace Ct CW7 127 D1
Wallace St
Northwich CW8 103 E7
Widnes WA8 23 A8
Wallcroft CH64 68 A7
Wallcroft Gdns CW10 128 C1
Walled Gdn The CW10 127 D5
Wallerscote Cl CW8 102 E8
Wallerscote Com Sch CW8 102 E8
Wallerscote Rd CW8 102 E8
Waller St SK11 112 E6
WALLEY'S GREEN 172 E7
Walleys La CW5 203 C7
Wallfields Cl CW5 204 E7
Wall Fields Rd CW5 204 E7
Wallhill La CW11 177 D7
Wall Hill Way CW8 76 F3
Wallingford Rd SK9 34 C5
Wallis St
Crewe CW1 190 D4
Warrington WA4 16 B3
Wall La CW5 204 E6
Wallrake CH60 40 F7
Walls Ave CH1 118 B1
Wallsend Ct WA8 12 F3
Wallworth's Bank CW12 156 E2
Wallworth Terr SK9 59 E8
Walmer Pl CW7 149 C6
Walmoor Pk CH3 119 A1
Walmsley St
Newton-le-W WA12 2 D4
Widnes WA8 23 C8
Walnut Ave CW8 102 D7
Walnut Cl
Chester CH2 118 D7
Warrington WA1 17 E7
Wilmslow SK9 60 E8
Walnut Cotts LL13 196 D8
Walnut Croft CH3 180 F6
Walnut Dr CW7 127 A1
Walnut Gr CH66 70 A1
Walnut La CW8 103 A5
Walnut Rd M31 11 D3
Walnut Rise CW12 156 B2
Walnut Tree La
Bradwall Green CW11 153 A4
Warrington WA4 26 F4
Walpole Cl CW1 191 C5
Walpole Gr WA2 8 C2
Walpole Rd WA7 49 C6
Walpole St CH1 237 A4
Walsh Cl WA12 2 C5
Walsingham Dr WA7 24 D2
Walsingham Rd WA5 14 F5
Walter St
Chester CH1 237 B4
Warrington WA1 16 E7
Widnes WA8 13 D1
Walters Wood SK23 65 F5
Walthall St CW2 190 C2
Waltham Ave WA3 5 C7
Waltham Ct WA7 24 E4
Waltham Dr SK8 35 B6
Waltham Pl CH4 141 A6
Walton Ave WA5 14 E5
Walton Gr ST7 210 C8
Walton Hall* WA4 25 F7
Walton Hall Gdns* WA4 25 F6
Walton Heath Dr SK10 87 B4
Walton Heath Rd WA4 16 B1
Walton La WA3 9 E5
Walton Lea Rd WA4 26 A7
Walton New Rd WA4 26 B8
Walton Pl CH1 117 E4
Walton Rd
Culcheth WA3 4 F3
Warrington WA4 26 C8
Walton St [14] WA7 23 A2
Waltons The CH4 141 E6
Walton Way ST7 210 C8
Wandsworth Way WA8 22 F5
Wansfell Pl WA2 8 A3
WARBURTON 19 C8
Warburton Bridge Rd WA13, WA3 11 A1
Warburton Cl
Altrincham WA15 32 D6
Barnton CW8 77 F4
Lymm WA13 19 A4
Warburton Dr WA15 32 D6
WARBURTON GREEN 32 D6
Warburton La
Partington M31 11 F4
Partington M31, WA13 11 E2
Warburton Rd SK9 34 D4
Warburton St WA4 16 D1
Warburton View WA3 11 A2
Ward Ave SK10 88 A8
Ward Cl WA5 7 B1
Ward La SK12 38 F4
Wardle Ave CW5 187 C7
Wardle Cotts CW5 187 C7
Wardle Cres SK11 111 E1
Wardle Ind Est CW5 187 A7
Wardle Mews CW10 151 D8
Wardle St [7] SK11 112 D7
Wardley Rd WA4 16 B1
Wardour Cl [6] SK11 111 F7
Wardour St WA5 15 E6
WARDSEND 37 A1
Wards La CW12 179 C8
Ward's La CW11 153 C5
Ward's Terr CH2 118 F3
Wareham Cl
Haydock WA11 1 C7
Warrington WA1 17 C8
Wareham Dr CW1 190 B8
Wareham St SK9 60 B7
Warford Ave SK12 37 A2
Warford Cres SK9 84 B7
Warford Hall Dr SK9 84 B6
Warford La WA16 59 B1
WARFORD PARK 58 E1
Warford Terr WA16 59 B2
WARGRAVE 2 D3
Wargrave CE Prim Sch WA12 2 C1
Wargrave House Sch WA12 2 C1

Wargrave Mews WA12 2 C1
Wargrave Rd WA12 2 C2
Waring Ave
St Helens WA9 1 B2
Warrington WA4 16 F5
Warkworth Cl WA8 12 C3
Warkworth Ct CH65 70 E3
WARMINGHAM 173 D7
Warmingham CE Prim Sch CW11 173 E8
Warmingham Ct CW10 151 D7
Warmingham La
Middlewich CW10 151 D5
Sandbach CW11 174 B8
Warmingham Rd CW1 173 D4
Warnley Cl WA8 12 D3
WARREN 111 D1
Warren Ave
Knutsford WA16 56 E2
Lostock Gralam CW9 80 A3
Warren Cl
Knutsford WA16 56 F2
Middlewich CW10 151 B7
Poynton SK12 36 B4
Warren Croft WA7 50 D7
Warren Ct
Ellesmere Port CH66 69 D3
Frodsham WA6 74 D6
Warren Dr
Altrincham WA15 32 D7
Broughton CH4 139 A3
Ellesmere Port CH66 69 E7
Newton-le-W WA12 2 F4
Warren SK11 111 D1
Warrington WA4 26 D8
Warren Gr SK11 111 D1
Warren Hey SK9 60 E8
Warren La
Hartford CW8 103 A4
Warrington WA1 17 D8
Warren Lea SK12 36 E5
Warren Rd
Warrington, Orford WA2 8 D1
Warrington WA4 26 C7
Warren The
Cuddington CW8 101 D5
Newton-le-W WA12 2 A3
Warren Way CW6 168 D8
Warrilow Heath Rd ST5 210 C1
WARRINGTON 16 E6
Warrington Ave
Crewe CW1 190 C6
Ellesmere Port CH65 70 B2
Warrington Bank Quay Sta WA1 15 F4
Warrington Bsns Ctr
14 Warrington WA1 16 B5
Warrington WA2 16 A6
Warrington Bsns Pk WA2 8 C1
Warrington Central Sta WA2 16 B6
Warrington Central Trad Est WA2 16 A6
Warrington Collegiate WA2 8 B1
Warrington Hospl WA5 15 F6
Warrington La WA13 19 E2
Warrington Mus & Art Gallery★ WA1 16 A4
Warrington Rd
Bold Heath L35, WA8 13 D7
Comberbach CW9 78 D7
Cronton L35 12 E8
Cronton L35 12 F8
Cuddington CW8 102 A5
Fowley Common WA3, WN7 5 C5
Golborne WA3, WA12 3 A6
Hatton WA4 25 F4
Little Leigh CW8 77 A5
Lymm WA13 18 B4
Mere WA16 56 B7
Mickle Trafford CH2 119 E7
Runcorn, Castlefields WA7 23 E2
Runcorn, Manor Park WA7 24 B4
Warrington, Risley WA3 9 E7
Warrington WA5 14 F4
Widnes WA8 13 D1
Warrington St Ann's CE Prim Sch WA2 16 C8
Warton Cl
Bramhall SK7 36 A7
Warrington WA5 15 A3
Warwick Ave
Newton-le-W WA12 2 E2
Warrington, Bewsey WA5 15 F7
Warrington, Great Sankey WA5 14 D7
Warwick Cl
Kidsgrove ST7 195 A3
Knutsford WA16 57 C1
Macclesfield SK11 111 F6
Neston CH64 66 E5
Warwick Ct
Ellesmere Port CH65 70 E2
Warrington WA1 16 E7
Warwick Dr SK7 36 D8
Warwick Gate CW5 217 C2
Warwick Gr 1 WA7 23 F1
Warwick Mews SK11 111 F6
Warwick Pl CW7 149 C6
Warwick Rd
Blacon CH1 117 F5
Irlam M44 11 D5
Macclesfield SK11 111 E6
Warwick Wlk SK11 111 F6
Wasdale Gr CW1 173 B1
WASH END 4 C8
Washington Cl
Biddulph ST8 179 C2
Cheadle SK8 34 F8
Widnes WA8 12 F3
Wash La
Allostock WA16 106 E3
Warrington WA4 16 E3
Wasley Cl WA2 8 F3
Waste La
Cuddington CW8 101 E3
Delamere CW8 123 F6
Kelsall CW6 122 F4
Watch La CW11 174 A6
Waterbank Row CW9 103 F7
Waterbridge Ct
2 Lymm WA13 18 C3
Warrington WA4 26 D8
Waterbridge Mews WA7 24 A2
Waterfoot La SK23 65 D6
Waterford Dr CH64 67 A7
Waterford Pl SK8 34 B8
Waterford Way WA7 50 C6
Waterfront WA4 50 F6
Watergate Row N CH1 237 A2
Watergate Row S CH1 237 A2
Watergate Sq CH1 237 A2
Watergate St CH1 237 A2
Waterhouse Ave SK10 87 F8
Water La SK9 60 A7
Water-Lode CW5 204 E5
Waterloo Cl 5 CH65 70 C5
Waterloo Cotts WA6 99 F8
Waterloo Gr ST7 195 A2
Waterloo Ho 15 CW8 103 F8
Waterloo La WA6 74 F1
Waterloo Rd
Bramhall SK7 35 F8
Chester CH2 118 C4
Haslington CW1 191 D4
Northwich CW8 103 E7
Poynton SK12 37 A2
3 Runcorn WA7 22 F2
Runcorn WA7 22 F3
Widnes WA8 23 A5
Waterloo St W SK11 112 C8
Watermead Dr WA7 50 F5
Watermill Dr SK11 112 F7
Watersedge WA6 49 D2
Waters Edge
Anderton CW9 78 D3
Chester CH1 118 B2
Waters Edge Mews CW10 151 C8
Watersfield Cl SK8 34 F8
Waters Gn SK11 112 D8
Waterside
Disley SK12 38 E7
Furness Vale SK23 39 E3
Macclesfield SK11 112 E7
Warrington WA4 26 D8
Waterside Cotts CW5 216 E5
Waterside Ct WA7 22 E3
Waterside Dr WA6 49 D2
Waterside La WA8 22 C5
Waterside Mews CW11 174 F3
Waterside Rd SK12, SK22 38 E7
Waterside View
Chester CH1 237 B3
Northwich CW9 104 E6
Waterside Way CW10 128 B2
Waters Reach SK12 36 F5
Water's Reach SK6 37 E7
Waters Reams CH3 142 B8
Water St
Bollington SK10 88 B8
Macclesfield SK11 112 C8
Newcastle-u-Lyme ST5 210 D2
Newton-le-W WA12 2 C4
Northwich CW9 104 A7
Runcorn WA7 23 A3
Widnes WA8 23 A6
Watertower View CH2 118 F2
Waterway CH3 143 B5
Waterways WA5 15 D6
Waterworks Dr WA12 2 F4
Waterworks La
Ellesmere Port CH66 68 E8
Hooton CH66 43 E1
Winwick WA2 8 B7
Watery La
Astbury CW12 178 C5
Frodsham WA6 74 E6
Winwick WA2 7 E6
Watkins Ave WA12 1 F3
Watkinson Way WA8 13 C5
Watkin St
Sandycroft CH5 116 A3
Warrington WA2 16 B7
Watlands Rd ST7 209 E2
Watling Cres CH4 141 E7
Watling Ct
Chester CH3 119 C2
Watling Ct *continued*
Cuddington CW8 102 B2
Watling Dr CW6 123 C6
Watling St CW9 103 F8
Watson's Cl CH4 139 C3
Watton Cl WA4 17 C3
Wavell Ave WA8 22 D8
Wavells Way CH3 142 B5
Waveney Dr SK9 34 D2
Waverley Ave WA4 26 D8
Waverley Cl SK10 113 A8
Waverley Ct 1 CW2 190 D2
Waverley Dr SK8 35 B7
Waverley Terr CH2 118 E4
WAVERTON 143 B4
Waverton App CH3 164 E6
Waverton Bsns Pk CH3 142 F4
Waverton Cl
Hough CW2 206 E2
Northwich CW9 103 E4
Waverton Com Prim Sch CH3 143 A5
Waverton Mill Quays CH3 143 B5
Waverton Pk CH3 143 B5
Waverton Rd CH66 69 E5
Wavertree Ave
Scholar Green ST7 194 E7
Widnes WA8 23 A8
Wavertree Ct CH66 69 F7
Wavertree Dr CW10 151 B7
Wavertree Rd CH1 117 C5
Waybutt La CW2 221 D8
Wayfarers Ct CW9 79 F7
Wayfarers Dr WA12 2 E2
Wayford Cl WA6 49 B1
Wayford Mews WA7 49 B1
Way's Gn CW7 149 E8
WAY'S GREEN 149 E8
Wayside Cl WA13 18 D2
Wayside Ct CH2 119 F8
Wayside Dr SK12 36 C4
Wayside Linley ST7 193 F2
Wayside Rd SK10 112 F8
Waystead Cl CW9 103 F4
Waywell Cl WA2 8 F3
Weald Dr CH66 69 A6
Wealstone Ct CH2 118 E5
Weal Stone La CH2 118 E6
Wearhead Cl WA3 2 F7
Weaste La WA4 17 E2
Weates Cl WA8 13 F3
Weathercock La CW12 157 E3
Weatherstones Cotts CH64 67 D8
Weatherstones Mews CH64 67 C8
Weaver Bank CW5 204 D5
Weaver Cl
Alsager ST7 193 A3
Biddulph ST8 179 D1
Sandbach CW11 174 E7
Weaver Cres WA6 49 D1
Weaver Ct
Macclesfield SK11 112 C7
Northwich CW9 103 F8
Weaver Gr
Mickle Trafford CH2 119 F8
St Helens WA9 1 A3
Weaver Grange CW9 126 E8
Weaverhall La CW7 150 B5
WEAVERHAM 77 C2
Weaverham Forest Prim Sch CW8 77 C1
Weaverham High Sch CW8 102 C8
Weaverham Rd CW8 102 B4
Weaverham Way SK9 34 E4
Weaver Ho 18 CW8 103 F8
Weaver La WA6 49 B2
Weaver Park Ind Est WA6 49 D2
Weaver Prim Sch CW5 204 E3
Weaver Rd
Culcheth WA3 5 A2
Ellesmere Port CH65 70 C2
Frodsham WA6 49 D1
Moulton CW9 126 E7
Nantwich CW5 204 E6
Northwich CW8 103 E7
Runcorn, Heath WA7 49 A6
Weavers Cotts 3 CW12 156 D3
Weaverside CW5 204 E2
Weaverside Ave WA7 49 F4
Weavers La SK7 35 D6
Weaver St
Chester CH1 237 A2
Winsford CW7 126 E1
Weavervale Pk CW8 77 A6
Weaver Valley Rd CW7 126 F3
Weaver View
Audlem CW3 229 E3
Church Minshull CW5 172 A6
Northwich CW8 103 F7
Weaverham CW8 77 D1
Weaver Way CW9 78 F1
Webb Dr WA5 6 F6
Webb's Ct CW9 103 F7
Webb's La CW10 128 C2
Webbs Orch SK23 65 D8
Webster Cl CH4 139 C3
Websters La CH66 69 F2
Weddell Cl WA5 15 D7
Wedge Ave WA11 1 A5
Wedgwood Ave ST7 210 A1
Wedgwood Dr WA8 13 B4
Wedgwood La ST8 179 C2
Wedgwood Rd ST7 210 D7
Wednesbury Dr WA5 14 F6
Weedon Ave WA12 2 B5
WEETWOOD COMMON 122 C2
Weighbridge Rd
Connah's Quay CH5 92 B4
Connah's Quay CH5 92 C5
Weint The WA3 11 B3
Weir Gr ST7 195 B2
Weir La WA1 17 E6
Weir St
Northwich CW9 103 F7
Warrington WA4 16 A1
Welbeck Ave WA12 2 D2
Welbeck Cl CW10 128 B1
Welford Ave WA3 3 C7
Welford Cl SK9 60 E8
Welland Cl CW11 174 C5
Welland Rd SK9 34 E2
Well Ave SY14 213 B3
Well Bank CW11 175 B6
Well Bank Cotts WA16 108 C8
Wellbank Ct CW12 156 E2
Well Bank La WA16, SK11 108 C7
Wellbrook Cl WA7 50 C5
Well Cl CH64 67 A4
Wellcroft Cl CW2 206 B7
Wellcroft Gdns WA13 19 A2
Weller Ave SK12 36 D2
Weller Cl SK12 36 D2
Wellesbourne Cl
Macclesfield SK10 86 F1
Neston CH64 66 D6
Wellesley Ave
Ellesmere Port CH65 70 C5
Haslington CW1 191 C4
Wellesley Cl WA12 2 B5
Wellesley Wlk 6 CH65 70 C5
Welles St CW11 175 B6
Well Farm Cl
Malpas SY14 213 B3
Warrington WA1 17 D8
Wellfield
Runcorn WA7 50 E5
Widnes WA8 13 A3
Winsford CW7 127 A2
Wellfield Cl WA16 80 A7
Wellfield Rd WA3 4 F4
Wellfield St
Warrington, Bank Quay WA5 15 E5
Warrington, Whitecross WA5 15 E6
Wellfield Way SY13 225 F1
Wellington Cir SK10 112 E8
Wellington Cl
Congleton CW12 156 D4
3 Ellesmere Port CH65 70 C5
Knutsford WA16 57 C4
Newton-le-W WA12 2 A3
Warrington WA2 8 F2
Wellington Gate L24 21 E2
Wellington Gdns WA12 2 A3
Wellington Pl CH1 237 B3
Wellington Rd
Bollington SK10 87 F8
Broughton CH4 139 B4
Ellesmere Port CH65 70 B4
Hazel Grove SK7 37 B8
Kidsgrove ST7 195 A2
Nantwich CW5 204 E4
Wellington Rd N CH65 70 C5
Wellington St Wrkshps 4 WA1 16 C5
Wellington St
15 Macclesfield SK11 112 D8
Newton-le-W WA12 2 A3
Northwich CW8 103 E7
3 Runcorn WA7 23 A3
Warrington WA1 16 C5
Widnes WA8 23 A6
Wellington Street Ind Est WA8 23 A6
Well La
Alsager ST7 193 C3
Antrobus CW9 53 A4
Biddulph ST8 179 D3
Chester CH2 118 E5
Heswall CH60 41 B6
Kingsley WA6 75 C2
Little Budworth CW6 147 F7
Macclesfield SK10 88 B2
Manley WA6 98 F3
Mollington CH1 94 F2
Neston CH64 66 F5
Prestbury SK10 87 C8
Stretton WA4 52 E8
Warrington WA5 14 F3
Weaverham CW8 77 C1
Wells Ave CW1 191 D5
Wells Cl
Ellesmere Port CH66 94 E8
Gatley SK8 34 C7
Mickle Trafford CH2 119 F8
Warrington WA1 17 B8
WELLS GREEN 205 F8
Well St
Malpas SY14 213 B3
Mow Cop ST7 195 D7
New Mills SK22 39 B8
Winsford CW7 126 C1
Wellswood Dr CW2 205 F7
Wellswood Rd CH66 69 E7
Welsby Cl WA2 8 F3
Welshampton Cl CH66 69 D2
Welsh La CW7 149 D6
Welshmen's La CW5 204 C7
Welshpool Cl WA5 7 D2
Welsh Rd
Connah's Quay CH5 116 A7
Ellesmere Port CH66 68 E4
Woodbank CH1 93 C6
Welsh Road Cotts CH1 93 D8
Welsh Row
Nantwich CW5 204 D5
Nether Alderley SK10 84 F6
Welton Cl SK9 59 F4
Welton Dr SK9 59 E4
Welton Gr SK9 59 E4
Welwyn Cl WA4 17 C3
Wem Gr ST5 210 E2
Wemyss Rd CH1 117 D4
Wendover Cl WA11 1 D7
Wenger Rd WA8 13 B5
Wenlock Cl
Macclesfield SK10 87 B2
Newcastle-u-Lyme ST5 210 E2
Warrington WA1 17 A8
Wenlock Gdns CH66 69 F2
Wenlock La CH66 69 F2
Wenlock Rd WA7 50 A4
Wenlock Way CH4 140 F6
Wensleydale Ave
Bebington CH62 43 E5
Congleton CW12 157 A5
Wensleydale Cl WA5 14 F8
Wensley Dr SK7 36 D7
Wensley Rd WA3 3 E7
Wentworth Ave
Macclesfield SK11 111 F6
Warrington WA1 17 B7
Wentworth Cl
Northwich CW9 104 E7
Widnes WA8 13 A5
Wentworth Dr
Bebington CH63 43 C5
Bramhall SK7 36 A7
Kidsgrove ST7 195 C3
Wentworth Gr CW7 126 A2
Werburgh Cl WA13 19 C8
WERETON 209 C1
Wereton Rd ST7 209 D1
WERVIN 96 A4
Wervin Rd CH2 96 A3
Wesley Ave
Alsager ST7 193 D4
Haydock WA11 1 F7
2 Sandbach CW11 175 B6
Wesley Cl
Nantwich CW5 204 E5
Neston CH64 66 D8
Wesley Ct
Congleton CW12 156 D2
Winsford CW7 126 F1
Wesley Gdns 7 ST7 195 A2
Wesley Pl
Crewe CW2 190 D2
4 Northwich CW9 104 A8
Wesley St ST7 210 A1
Wessex Cl
Shavington CW2 206 C3
Warrington WA1 17 E7
Wessex Dr CW9 104 C6
Westage La CW9 79 B8
West Ave
Crewe CW1 190 B4
Kidsgrove ST7 194 C1
Middlewich CW10 128 C2
Northwich CW9 104 D7
Warrington, Stockton Heath WA4 16 C1
Warrington WA2 16 B8
Weston CW2 207 B5
WEST BANK 23 A4
West Bank
Alderley Edge SK9 85 A8
Chester CH2 118 C4
West Bank Dock Est WA8 22 E5
West Bank Prim Sch WA8 23 A4
West Bank Rd SK10 87 B1
West Bank St WA8 23 A5
West Bond St SK11 112 C7
Westbourne Ave CW1 190 A6
Westbourne Dr 16 SK9 34 D1
Westbourne Ho CW12 156 B2
Westbourne Mews CW12 156 B2
Westbourne Rd
Blacon CH1 118 A4
Warrington WA4 26 B7
Westbrook Ave WA4 16 D2
WESTBROOK CENTRE 7 B1
Westbrook Cres WA5 7 B2
Westbrook Ctr WA5 7 C1
Westbrook Dr SK10 87 C1
Westbrook Old Hall Prim Sch WA5 15 D8
Westbrook Rd WA6 75 B2
Westbrook Way WA5 7 B1
Westbury Cl
Crewe CW2 206 C7
Middlewich CW10 151 B8
Warrington WA1 17 A8
Westbury Ct SK11 112 A7
Westbury Dr SK11 112 A7
Westbury Way CH4 140 F6

Westby Cl SK7 36 A7
West Cheshire Coll CH65 70 B5
West Cheshire Coll (Greenbank Ctr) CH4 141 D6
West Cheshire Coll (Handbridge Ctr) CH4 141 D7
West Cl SK10 87 F7
Westcliffe Ct WA8 13 B4
Westcliff Gdns WA4 26 E3
Westdale Rd WA1 17 A7
West Dr
Heswall CH60 41 A7
Neston CH64 66 E6
Warrington WA5 15 B4
Winsford CW7 127 A2
West Dudley St CW7 126 F1
West End CH3 121 E7
West End Cotts CW12 156 C2
West End Ct LL13 196 D8
West End Gr WA11 1 A6
West End Rd WA11 1 A6
Westenra Ave CH65 69 F6
Westerham Cl SK10 87 B2
Westerhope Way WA8 12 F3
Westerings The CH62 43 C6
Western App CH2 118 E4
Western Ave
Blacon CH1 117 D4
Macclesfield SK11 112 C5
Macclesfield SK11 112 D5
Milton Green CH3 165 C2
Nantwich CW5 204 E3
Western Ct CH2 118 E4
Western Dr SK11 112 C5
Western Pk CW11 191 F8
Westfield Ave ST7 209 C2
Westfield Cl
Chester CH4 141 B7
Winsford CW7 149 C5
Westfield Cres WA7 22 E1
Westfield Dr
Knutsford WA16 56 E1
Willaston CW2 205 E8
Westfield Gr CW8 77 F4
Westfield Mews WA7 22 F1
Westfield Prim Sch WA7 22 E1
Westfield Rd
Cheadle SK8 34 F8
Mow Cop ST7 195 C7
Northwich CW9 104 B7
Runcorn WA7 22 E1
Westfields WA15 31 F8
Westfields Ave SK10 87 B1
Westfields Rise CW3 232 C1
Westford Rd WA4 16 A1
Westgate
Widnes WA8 22 B7
Wilmslow SK9 60 A5
Westgate Ave CW7 126 A1
Westgate Pk CW2 206 E2
West Gn CH5 116 A6
West Gr
Alsager ST7 193 E4
Heswall CH60 40 F8
West Hall Ct WA16 29 C5
West Halton Hospl WA7 49 F6
Westhay Cres WA3 10 A5
WEST HEATH
Congleton 156 A4
Crewe 221 E8
West Heath Gr WA13 18 C4
West Heath Sh Ctr CW12 156 A3
Westholme Cl
Congleton CW12 156 C3
Crewe CW2 206 C8
Westholme Ct SK9 60 A2
Westhouse Cl CH63 43 C5
West House Ct SK10 86 E1
West Hyde WA13 18 C3
West La
Cuddington CW8 101 F3
High Legh WA16 29 C6
Runcorn WA7 49 F8
Westland Ct CW12 156 C2
Westland Dr WA2 8 E2
Westlands ST7 209 F2
Westlands Cl CH64 41 F1
Westlands Rd CW10 128 B1
Westlands The CW12 156 C2
West Lorne St CH1 237 A3
West Mains L24 21 A3
Westmere Cl CW2 207 B5
Westmere Dr CW1 190 F2
Westminster Ave CH4 141 B7
Westminster Cl
Middlewich CW10 128 B1
Warrington WA4 17 C2
Widnes WA8 22 B8
Westminster Ct CH2 118 F2
Westminster Dr
Bebington CH62 43 D7
Cheadle SK8 35 B6
Haydock WA11 1 F7
Wilmslow SK9 60 A4
Westminster Gn CH4 141 D7
Westminster Gr
Ellesmere Port CH65 70 C6
8 Winsford CW7 149 A8
Westminster Ind Pk CH65 69 F6
WESTMINSTER PARK 141 B6
Westminster Pl 1 WA1 16 B5
Westminster Rd
Broughton CH4 139 B3
Chester CH2 118 F3
Ellesmere Port CH65 70 C6
Macclesfield SK10 87 C1
4 Macclesfield SK10 112 C8
Westminster St
Crewe CW2 190 C2
14 Macclesfield SK10 112 C8
Westminster Terr CH4 141 C7
Westmoreland Cl WA14 31 B8
Westmorland Ave
Talke ST7 210 F7
Widnes WA8 13 B1
Westmorland Cl SK10 86 F2
Westmorland Rd M31 11 E2
Westmorland Terr CW4 130 B3
WESTON
Crewe 207 C5
Macclesfield 111 F8
Weston Cl
Middlewich CW10 151 C7
Northwich CW9 103 F5
Weston Cres WA7 49 A6
Weston Ct
Runcorn WA7 48 F7
Shavington CW2 206 C5
Weston Ctr The CW1 190 E1
Weston Gr
Chester CH2 118 E7
Halewood L26 21 A6
Weston La CW2 206 E5
WESTON POINT 48 D7
Weston Point Com Prim Sch WA7 48 E7
Weston Point Expressway
Runcorn, Rocksavage WA7 49 B5
Runcorn WA7 22 E2
Runcorn, Weston WA7 48 E6
Weston Prim Sch WA7 49 A6
Weston Rd
Crewe CW1 190 F1
Runcorn WA7 48 E7
Weston CW1, CW2 207 B7
Wilmslow SK9 60 E6
Weston Sq SK11 111 F7
Weston View WA7 49 D4
WESTON VILLAGE 48 F6
Weston Village Prim Sch CW2 207 C5
Westover Rd WA1 16 F8
West Park Ave SK12 36 A4
West Park Dr 7 CH66 94 F8
West Park Mus* SK10 87 C1
West Quay Rd WA2 7 F3
West Rd
Congleton CW12 156 C3
Ellesmere Port CH65 70 C3
Runcorn WA7 48 D7
Weaverham CW8 77 B1
Westrees CW8 101 D5
West Side Ave WA11 1 A6
West St
Alderley Edge SK9 60 A1
Chester CH2 237 C4
Congleton CW12 156 D3
Crewe CW1 190 B5
Haslington CW1 191 C5
Macclesfield SK11 112 B8
Middlewich CW10 128 C1
Mount Pleasant ST7 195 B6
Warrington WA2 16 B7
West Vale CH64 66 E6
West View
Antrobus WA4 53 A5
Ellesmere Port CH66 69 A8
Northwich CW9 104 B8
Warrington WA2 9 A1
West View Rd WA6 101 A6
Westville Dr CW12 156 A2
Westward Rd
Chester CH3 142 B8
Wilmslow SK9 59 F6
Westway CH60 40 F6
West Way
Holmes Chapel CW4 130 B3
Sandbach CW11 174 F4
Shavington CW2 206 D5
West Wing The CW10 127 D5
Westwood WA7 24 C1
Westwood Cl CW2 207 B1
Westwood Ct CH64 41 E2
Westwood Rd SK8 34 B8
WESTY 16 F5
Westy La WA4 16 F4
Wet Gate La WA13 19 E4
Wetheral Rd SK10 87 B2
Wetherby Cl
Chester CH1 118 B2
Newton-le-W WA12 2 C5
Wetherby Way CH66 69 B5
Wetreins La SY14, CH3 197 D6
WETTENHALL 170 F7
WETTENHALL GREEN 170 F6
Wettenhall Rd CW5 188 B4
Wetton La CW8 76 E4
Wetton Way SK11 113 D2
Wexford Ave L24 21 D2
Wexford Cl WA11 1 D7
Weybourne Cl CH4 140 E5
Weybridge Cl WA4 26 E7
Weybridge Dr SK10 87 B3
Weygates Dr WA15 32 C7
Weymouth Cl WA7 50 E6
Weymouth Rd WA5 6 F6
Whaddon Dr CH4 140 F4
WHALEY BRIDGE 65 D7
Whaley Bridge Prim Sch SK23 65 E7
Whaley Bridge Sta SK23 65 E8
Whaley Ct CH1 117 A8
Whaley La SK23 65 C8
Whalley Ave WA3 5 C7
Whalley Dr CW6 147 B3
Whalley Gr WA8 13 D3
Whalley Hayes SK10 112 C8
Whalley Rd CW9 104 A8
Whalley St WA1 16 C6
Wharams Bank CW11 176 F5
Wharburton Cl CW8 101 F2
Wharf Ct SK23 65 E7
Wharfdale Ave CW1 173 B1
Wharfdale Cl WA5 15 A7
Wharfe Cl CW12 156 F1
Wharfedale WA7 50 B6
Wharfedale Dr CH62 43 F5
Wharfedale Rd CW12 157 A5
Wharfe La CH65 70 A7
Wharf La CW12 178 B3
Wharf Mill CW12 156 F1
Wharford La WA7 24 E3
Wharf Rd
Collins Green WA12 1 E2
Whaley Bridge SK23 65 E7
Wharfside Ct 6 WA4 16 E1
Wharf St WA1 16 C4
Wharf The
Chester CH1 118 B1
Runcorn WA7 50 F6
Wharmby Rd WA11 1 E6
WHARTON 127 A2
Wharton CE Jun Sch CW7 126 F1
Wharton Ct CH2 118 F2
Wharton Gdns CW7 127 A3
Wharton Gn CW7 127 A4
WHARTON GREEN 127 B4
Wharton Hall CW7 127 A3
Wharton Ind Est CW7 126 F2
Wharton Park Rd CW7 126 F2
Wharton Rd CW7 127 A2
Wharton Ret Pk CW7 126 F3
Whatcroft Cl WA7 49 D6
Whatcroft Hall La CW9 104 F1
Wheatcroft Cl WA5 15 C6
Wheatfield Cl
Barnton CW8 78 A3
Ellesmere Port CH66 69 C3
Macclesfield SK10 87 C3
Wheatfield Rd WA8 12 C5
Wheatland Rd CH60 41 C7
Wheatlands WA7 23 E1
Wheatley Ave WA12 2 C5
Wheatley Rd CW1 190 E6
Wheat Moss SK11 84 B3
Wheatsheaf Cl SK23 65 E6
Wheatsheaf La CW9 53 B3
Wheatsheaf Rd SK23 65 E6
Wheelman Rd CW1 190 A7
WHEELOCK 174 F4
Wheelock Cl
Alsager ST7 193 A3
Handforth SK9 34 D1
Kingsmead CW9 103 F6
Wheelock Ct CW11 175 A2
Wheelock Dr CW7 127 B1
WHEELOCK HEATH 192 A8
Wheelock Prim Sch CW11 175 A4
Wheelock St CW10 128 C1
Wheelock Way 2 ST7 195 B2
Wheldon Cl CH2 118 E8
Wheldon Rd WA8 21 F7
Wheldrake Cl CH66 69 B5
Whernside WA8 12 C3
Whetstone Hey CH66 69 D5
Whetstone Rd ST8 179 C2
Wheycroft Mews CW1 190 C5
Whickham Cl WA8 12 F3
Whimbrel Ave WA12 2 C3
Whimbrel Cl WA7 49 F5
Whinchat Ave WA12 2 C4
Whinchat Cl WA3 3 E7
Whinchat Dr WA3 9 F3
Whinfell Gr WA7 49 E5
Whipcord La CH1 118 B2
Whirley Cl CW10 151 C7
WHIRLEY GROVE 86 D3
Whirley La SK10 85 F1
Whirley Prim Sch SK10 86 D1
Whirley Rd SK10 86 C1
Whirlow Rd CW2 206 B7
WHISTERFIELD 109 D3
Whisterfield La SK11 109 E3
Whiston Cl
Macclesfield SK11 112 B4
Winsford CW7 127 A4
Whiston Mews SK11 113 B4
Whiston St SK11 112 C7
Whitbarrow Rd WA13 18 D4
WHITBY 70 A4
Whitby Ave
Chester CH2 118 D5
Warrington WA2 8 D2
Whitby Cl
Crewe CW1 190 B8
Poynton SK12 36 D4
WHITBYHEATH 70 B1
Whitby Heath Prim Sch CH65 70 B3
Whitby High Sch The CH66 70 A2
Whitby La CH1 95 B6
Whitby Rd
Ellesmere Port CH65 70 C5
Runcorn WA7 23 A1
Whitby's La CW7 126 B1
WHITCHURCH 226 A1
Whitchurch Cl WA1 17 A8
Whitchurch Gr ST5 210 E2
Whitchurch Rd
Audlem CW3 229 C3
Broxton CH3 183 A3
Chester CH3 119 B1
Christleton CH3 142 E7
Edge Green SY14, CH3 199 B4
Handley CH3 182 D8
Milton Green CH3 165 C4
Newhall CW5, SY13 228 A6
Royal's Green CW3, SY13 228 C2
Sound CW5 217 E3
Waverton CH3 143 A3
Whitchurch Way WA7 49 D7
White Ave CW2 189 F4
Whitebarn Rd SK9 85 B8
Whitebeam Ave 5 CH66 69 F1
Whitebeam Cl
Newcastle-u-Lyme ST5 210 D1
Runcorn WA7 24 C1
Whitebeam Row CW8 102 E7
White Bear Yd 13 WA16 57 A2
White Broom WA13 19 B4
White Clover Sq WA13 19 A2
Whitecroft Ct SK10 87 E2
Whitecroft Heath Rd SK11 109 B3
Whitecroft Rd CH66 69 E2
Whitecroft Villas M31 11 E2
WHITECROSS 15 E6
Whitecross Rd WA5 15 E5
Whitefield WA13 19 A4
Whitefield Ave WA12 2 E2
Whitefield Cl
Golborne WA3 3 A8
Lymm WA13 19 A5
Whitefield Ct WA3 4 F2
Whitefield Gr WA13 19 A4
Whitefield Rd WA4 26 B8
Whitefields CH2 72 B3
White Friars CH1 237 A2
Whitefriars Wlk 2 M22 33 D8
WHITEGATE 126 A7
Whitegate Ave WA3 4 F2
Whitegate CE Prim Sch CW8 125 F7
Whitegate Cl CW10 151 C6
Whitegate Fields LL13 180 D1
Whitegate La CH3 121 E7
Whitegate Rd CW7 125 F3
Whitegates CW12 179 D4
Whitegates Cl CH64 42 E1
Whitegates Cres CH64 42 E1
Whitegates Ho CW2 189 E2
Whitehall Ave ST7 194 F2
Whitehall Cl
Barnton CW8 78 A4
Wilmslow SK9 60 A5
Whitehall Ct 3 CW5 204 D5
Whitehall Dr CW8 103 C5
Whitehall La CW6 124 E1
White Hall La CW11 151 E1
Whitehall Pl 5 WA6 74 B8
White Hart Gdns CW8 102 F4
White Hart La CW2 205 E8
Whitehaven La CW5 203 A7
Whitehaven Rd SK7 35 C5
WHITE HILL 195 B2
Whitehill Rd ST7 195 B2
White House Cl WA11 1 B6
Whitehouse Dr WA15 32 B8
White House Dr WA1 17 E7
Whitehouse Expressway WA7 50 B5
Whitehouse Ind Est WA7 50 E4
Whitehouse La
Nantwich CW5 204 F7
Partington WA14 20 D8
Plumley WA16 80 F5
Whitehouse Rd WA16 30 B3
White La CH3 142 D8
Whiteleas Rd SK23 65 D3
Whiteleggs La WA13 19 B1
WHITELEY GREEN 62 E2
White Lodge Cl CH62 43 D5
White Lodge Mews CW8 102 A3
Whitemere Ct CH65 70 C7
WHITEMOOR 179 D6
Whitemore Rd CW10 151 C6
White Park Cl CW10 128 D2
Whiteridge Rd ST7 195 B2
Whitesands Rd WA13 18 C4
Whiteside Rd WA11 1 B6
Whites La CW2 207 B6
Whites Mdw CH3 142 A7
Whitesmead Cl SK12 38 D5
White St
Macclesfield SK11 112 D6
Warrington, Stockton Heath WA4 16 C1
Warrington WA1 16 A5
Widnes WA8 23 A5
Whitethorn Ave WA5 14 F5
Whitethorn Way ST5 210 E1
Whitethroat Wlk WA3 9 F3
Whitewell Cl CW5 204 F5
Whitewood La SY14 212 D7
Whitfield Ave WA1 16 F7
Whitfield Dr SK11 112 B4
Whitfield Gr WA11 1 A6
Whitfield Rd ST7 195 B2
Whitfields The SK10 87 A1
Whitley Ave
Barnton CW8 78 B3
Warrington WA4 17 A4
Whitley Cl
Middlewich CW10 151 B7
Runcorn WA7 48 F8
Whitley Dr CW8 103 A4
Whitley La WA16 55 B8
WHITLEY REED 53 D8
Whitley Village Sch WA4 52 D4
Whitlow Ave CW5 204 F4
Whitlow La CW9 126 F8
Whitney Croft SK10 113 A8
Whitson Cl WA16 29 C4
Whitstable Pk WA8 12 E4
Whittaker Ave WA2 8 D2
Whittaker Cl CW1 190 A7
Whittington Gdns CW9 104 A2
Whittle Ave
Haydock WA11 1 A5
Warrington WA5 15 A7
Whittle Cl CH5 116 A3
Whittle Hall La WA5 14 F6
Whittlewood Cl WA3 10 A5
Whitton Dr CH2 118 E5
Whitwell Cl WA5 14 D7
Whitworth Cl WA3 9 E3
Wicker La
Altrincham WA15 32 C8
Guilden Sutton CH3 120 A4
Wicklow Cl CH66 69 A6
Wickson La CH3, CW6 167 D3
Wickstead Cl CW5 205 A4
Wicksten Dr WA7 23 C2
Widdale Cl WA5 14 F7
Widgeon Cl SK12 36 B4
Widgeons Covert CH63 41 F5
WIDNES 22 E7
Widnes Rd
Cuerdley Cross WA5, WA8 13 F2
Warrington WA5 14 C3
Widnes WA8 23 B8
Widnes Sta WA8 13 A3
Wiend The CH2 118 D4
Wight Cl CH65 70 C1
Wightman Ave WA12 2 C5
Wigmore Cl WA3 10 A6
Wigsey La WA13 19 A7
WIGSHAW 4 D2
Wigshaw La WA3 4 D2
Wigwam Cl SK12 36 C4
Wilbraham Cl
Acton CW5 204 A7
Mickle Trafford CH2 119 F8
Wilbraham Rd
Acton CW5 204 A7
Congleton CW12 156 F3
Weaverham CW8 77 E1
Wilbrahams Way ST7 193 D4
Wilbraham's Wlk ST7 209 D2
Wilcock Rd WA11 2 B8
Wilcote Cl WA8 13 C4
Wilcott Dr SK9 59 F4
Wild Arum Cl 8 WA3 3 E8
WILDBOARCLOUGH 137 E6
Wilderhope Cl CW2 206 C7
WILDERSPOOL 16 C2
Wilderspool Cres WA4 16 B1
Wilderspool Cswy WA4 16 C3
Wild Goose Ave ST7 195 D3
Wilding Ave 8 WA7 23 B2
Wilding Bsns Pk CH3 119 C4
Wildings Old La WA3 9 A8
Wilding St CW1 190 E4
Wildmoor La CH3 97 D1
Wildwood Gr WA1 17 B7
WILKESLEY 233 F7
Wilkins La SK9 33 E5
Wilkinson Ave WA1 16 F6
Wilkinson Cl WA8 23 A5
Wilkinson Ct CW7 149 B6
Wilkinson St N CH65 70 C6
Wilkinson St
Ellesmere Port CH65 70 C6
Warrington WA2 16 C7
Wilkinson Street Mews 1 CH65 70 C6
Wilkinson Way CW7 149 B7
Willan Rd CH1 117 D4
WILLASTON
Ellesmere Port 68 A8

WILLASTON *continued*
Nantwich 205 D8
Willaston CE Prim Sch CH64 . . . . 67 F8
Willaston Dr L26 . . . . 21 A6
Willaston Farm CH64 . . . . 67 F8
Willaston Green Mews CH64 . . . . 67 F8
Willaston Hall Gdns CW5 . . . . 205 C6
Willaston Prim Sch CW5 . . . . 205 D6
Willaston Rd CH63, CH64 . . . . 42 D4
Willaston Way 8 SK9 . . . . 34 D5
Willbank La CW5 . . . . 202 D5
Willerby Cl 1 SK10 . . . . 112 C8
Willeymoor La SY13 . . . . 225 D8
William Barker Ct 10 CW11 . . . . 175 B6
William Beamont Com High Sch WA2 . . . . 8 C1
William Ct CH64 . . . . 41 F2
William Foden Cl CW11 . . . . 174 D7
William Johnson Gdns CH65 . . . . 70 C6
William Penn Cl WA5 . . . . 14 E5
William Rd ST7 . . . . 195 A2
Williams Ave WA12 . . . . 2 C5
Williams Cl CH2 . . . . 118 C4
Williamson Cres SK23 . . . . 65 D8
Williamson Dr CW5 . . . . 204 C5
Williamson Rd SK23 . . . . 65 D8
William St
Chester CH1 . . . . 237 B3
Chester, Hoole Park CH2 . . . . 118 F3
Congleton CW12 . . . . 157 A4
Macclesfield SK10 . . . . 112 F8
6 Northwich CW9 . . . . 104 B8
Widnes WA8 . . . . 13 C1
Winsford CW7 . . . . 126 E1
William Stockton Com Sch CH65 . . . . 70 B5
Williams Way
Frodsham WA6 . . . . 74 A8
Henbury SK11 . . . . 111 C8
Willington Ave CH62 . . . . 43 E3
Willington Cnr CW6 . . . . 122 E2
Willington La
Duddon CW6 . . . . 145 E7
Kelsall CW6 . . . . 122 D4
Willington Rd
Duddon CW6 . . . . 145 B7
Kelsall CW6 . . . . 122 C2
Willis St WA1 . . . . 16 D6
Willmer Cres ST7 . . . . 195 B6
Willotts Hill Rd ST5 . . . . 210 D1
Willoughby Cl WA5 . . . . 7 C1
Willow Ave
Newton-le-W WA12 . . . . 2 E4
2 Widnes WA8 . . . . 13 B2
Willoway Rd CH3 . . . . 119 B2
Willow Bank
Cheadle SK8 . . . . 35 A6
Helsby WA6 . . . . 73 D2
Nantwich CW5 . . . . 204 F6
Willowbank Dr SK10 . . . . 88 C8
Willow Bank Est WA12 . . . . 2 F4
Willowbrook CH5 . . . . 116 B4
Willowbrow Rd CH63, CH64 . . . . 42 D3
Willow Cl
Chester CH2 . . . . 118 D8
Lymm WA13 . . . . 18 E4
Newcastle-u-Lyme ST5 . . . . 210 D1
Paddockhill WA16 . . . . 59 B5
Poynton SK12 . . . . 36 E3
Runcorn WA7 . . . . 49 C7
Winsford CW7 . . . . 126 D3
Willow Cres
Chester CH2 . . . . 119 A4
Crewe CW2 . . . . 189 F2
Moore WA4 . . . . 25 A7
Warrington WA1 . . . . 17 B8
Willowcroft Way ST7 . . . . 195 E4
Willow Ct
Alsager ST7 . . . . 193 E4
Connah's Quay CH5 . . . . 91 D1
Higher Kinnerton CH4 . . . . 161 A7
Macclesfield SK10 . . . . 87 B2
Middlewich CW10 . . . . 128 C2
Nantwich CW5 . . . . 204 F7
Newton-le-W WA12 . . . . 2 D4
Warrington WA2 . . . . 7 F3
Winsford CW7 . . . . 127 B2
Willowdale WA12 . . . . 2 E3
Willowdale Way CH66 . . . . 94 F8
Willow Dr
Blacon CH1 . . . . 117 D5
Bunbury CW6 . . . . 185 E8
Handforth SK9 . . . . 34 D3
Sandbach CW11 . . . . 175 E7
Warrington WA4 . . . . 16 E1
Willow Gn
Knutsford WA16 . . . . 56 F3
Weaverham CW8 . . . . 102 D8
Willow Gr
Barnton CW8 . . . . 78 B4
Chester CH2 . . . . 119 B4
Ellesmere Port CH66 . . . . 95 A8
Elton CH2 . . . . 72 A3
WILLOW GREEN 77 B5
Willow Green La CW8 . . . . 77 B5
Willow Hayes CH3 . . . . 121 F7
Willowherb Cl CH3 . . . . 142 A6
Willow La
Goostrey CW4 . . . . 107 E1
Thornton Hough CH63, CH64 . . . . 42 D3
Warrington WA4 . . . . 26 E4
Willow Lea CH1 . . . . 94 F2
Willowmead Dr SK10 . . . . 87 A5
Willow Rd
Chester CH4 . . . . 140 F6
Haydock WA11 . . . . 1 E7
High Lane SK6 . . . . 37 F7
Newton-le-W WA12 . . . . 2 E4
Partington M31 . . . . 11 E2
Willows SK9 . . . . 59 F6
Willows Cl CW2 . . . . 206 B7
Willow Sq CW7 . . . . 127 A2
Willow St CW12 . . . . 156 E3
Willows The
Frodsham WA6 . . . . 74 C8
Higher Wincham CW9 . . . . 79 F6
Newton-le-W WA12 . . . . 2 D4
2 Northwich CW9 . . . . 103 E6
Partington M31 . . . . 11 F3
Sandbach CW11 . . . . 175 B7
Warrington WA5 . . . . 14 F5
Willow Tree Ct WA8 . . . . 13 D2
Willow Tree Gr ST7 . . . . 193 F7
Willow Way
Bramhall SK7 . . . . 35 D7
Broughton CH4 . . . . 139 B3
Prestbury SK10 . . . . 87 A5
Willow Wood Com Jun Sch CW7 . . . . 127 B2
Willow Wood Inf Sch CW7 . . . . 127 A2
Wilmere La WA8 . . . . 13 A6
Wilmot Ave WA5 . . . . 14 F6
Wilmot Dr WA3 . . . . 2 F7
WILMSLOW 60 C5
Wilmslow Ave CH66 . . . . 69 E5
Wilmslow Cres WA4 . . . . 17 D4
Wilmslow Ct SK9 . . . . 34 D3
Wilmslow Dr CH66 . . . . 69 E5
Wilmslow Grange Prim Sch SK9 . . . . 34 C4
Wilmslow High Sch SK9 . . . . 60 B6
Wilmslow Old Rd
Mottram St Andrew SK10 . . . . 61 A2
Wythenshawe M90 . . . . 33 A6
WILMSLOW PARK 60 D7
Wilmslow Pk N SK9 . . . . 60 D7
Wilmslow Pk S SK9 . . . . 60 C7
Wilmslow Prep Sch SK9 . . . . 60 B7
Wilmslow Rd
Adlington SK10 . . . . 61 D6
Alderley Edge SK9 . . . . 60 A2
Gatley SK8 . . . . 34 D7
Gatley SK8, SK9 . . . . 34 C6
Handforth SK9 . . . . 34 D4
Mottram St Andrew, Greendale SK10 . . . . 86 D8
Mottram St Andrew SK10 . . . . 61 A3
Woodford SK7 . . . . 35 C1
Wythenshawe M90, SK9, WA15 . . . . 32 F5
Wilmslow Sta SK9 . . . . 60 C7
Wilmslow Wlk 13 SK11 . . . . 112 E7
Wilsbury Grange CW8 . . . . 103 A5
Wilsden Rd WA8 . . . . 12 B1
Wilshaw Terr CH63 . . . . 42 B6
Wilson Cl
Warrington WA4 . . . . 17 D3
4 Widnes WA8 . . . . 13 D1
Wilson Cres CW9 . . . . 80 B3
Wilson Dr CW9 . . . . 126 F7
Wilson Patten St WA1 . . . . 16 A4
Wilsons La CH65 . . . . 70 A3
Wilson St
Warrington, Bewsey WA5 . . . . 16 A7
Warrington, Birchwood WA3 . . . . 9 E5
Wilton Ave SK8 . . . . 34 C7
Wilton Cl CW9 . . . . 103 E4
Wilton Cres
Alderley Edge SK9 . . . . 59 F2
Macclesfield SK11 . . . . 111 E6
Wilton Dr WA15 . . . . 32 C8
Wilton La WA3 . . . . 4 B5
Wiltshire Cl
Macclesfield SK10 . . . . 86 E2
Warrington WA1 . . . . 17 D6
Wiltshire Dr CW12 . . . . 156 E4
Wiltshire Rd M31 . . . . 11 E2
Wiltshire Wlk SK10 . . . . 86 F2
Wilwick La SK11 . . . . 111 F7
Wimberry Dr ST5 . . . . 210 D1
WIMBOLDSLEY 150 F4
Wimboldsley Com Prim Sch CW10 . . . . 150 F4
WIMBOLDS TRAFFORD 96 F6
WINCHAM 79 C3
Wincham Ave CW9 . . . . 79 D3
Wincham Bsns Pk CW9 . . . . 79 D3
Wincham Com Prim Sch CW9 . . . . 79 F5
Wincham La CW9 . . . . 79 D3
Wincham Park (Witton Albion FC) CW9 . . . . 79 C2
Winchester Ave
Ellesmere Port CH65 . . . . 70 D4
Warrington WA5 . . . . 15 C5
Winchester Cl
Shavington CW2 . . . . 206 B3
Wilmslow SK9 . . . . 59 E5
Winchester Ct CW2 . . . . 207 E3
Winchester Dr SK10 . . . . 111 F8
Winchester Ho
11 Chester CH1 . . . . 237 C3
12 Macclesfield SK10 . . . . 111 F8
Winchester Pl WA8 . . . . 22 C8
Winchester Sq CH4 . . . . 140 F5
WINCLE 160 A7
Wincle Ave SK12 . . . . 36 F2
Wincle CE Prim Sch SK11 . . . . 136 F1
Windermere Ave
Chester CH2 . . . . 119 A6
Warrington WA2 . . . . 8 D3
Widnes WA8 . . . . 13 B4
Windermere Cl CH64 . . . . 66 F7
Windermere Dr
Alderley Edge SK9 . . . . 59 F1
Congleton CW12 . . . . 156 A2
Windermere Rd
Crewe CW2 . . . . 189 E2
Ellesmere Port CH65 . . . . 70 C2
Handforth SK9 . . . . 34 C4
Haydock WA11 . . . . 1 B6
High Lane SK6 . . . . 37 E8
Winsford CW7 . . . . 126 C2
Windermere St WA8 . . . . 13 B4
Windfield Gdns CH66 . . . . 69 D7
Windings The CW10 . . . . 128 B2
Windle Ct
Neston CH64 . . . . 41 E2
Warrington WA3 . . . . 9 C4
WINDLE HILL 67 C7
Windlehurst Ct SK6 . . . . 37 D7
Windlehurst Rd SK12 . . . . 37 D8
Windmill Cl
Buerton CW3 . . . . 230 E4
Warrington WA4 . . . . 26 C6
Windmill Ctr The WA8 . . . . 23 B8
Windmill Dr CW3 . . . . 229 F3
WINDMILL HILL 24 C1
Windmill Hill Ave WA7 . . . . 24 D2
Windmill Hill Ave E WA7 . . . . 24 D1
Windmill Hill Ave N WA7 . . . . 24 D3
Windmill Hill Ave S WA7 . . . . 24 D2
Windmill Hill Ave W WA7 . . . . 24 C2
Windmill Hill Prim Sch WA7 . . . . 24 C2
Windmill La
Bollington SK10 . . . . 88 B6
Christleton CH3 . . . . 142 D8
Hankelow CW3 . . . . 230 F4
Preston on t H WA4 . . . . 51 A6
Warrington, Penketh WA5 . . . . 14 E5
Warrington WA4 . . . . 26 C6
Windmill Rise CH2 . . . . 118 D7
Windmill St
Macclesfield SK11 . . . . 112 E6
Runcorn WA7 . . . . 23 B2
Windscale Rd WA2 . . . . 9 A2
Windsor Ave
Crewe CW1 . . . . 190 B6
Nantwich CW5 . . . . 204 F3
Newton-le-W WA12 . . . . 2 D2
Tarporley CW6 . . . . 146 D1
Wilmslow SK9 . . . . 59 F7
Windsor Cl
Bollington SK10 . . . . 87 E6
Cuddington CW8 . . . . 101 F4
Poynton SK12 . . . . 36 D4
Windsor Ct
Chester CH1 . . . . 237 B1
1 Warrington WA4 . . . . 16 E1
Windsor Dr
Alsager ST7 . . . . 192 F4
Altrincham, Bowdon WA14 . . . . 20 F1
Broughton CH4 . . . . 139 A3
Ellesmere Port CH65 . . . . 70 A3
Faddiley CW5 . . . . 202 E7
Haydock WA11 . . . . 2 A7
Helsby WA6 . . . . 73 B2
Warrington WA4 . . . . 17 B2
Winsford CW7 . . . . 149 C5
Windsor Gr
Cheadle SK8 . . . . 34 F8
Runcorn WA7 . . . . 49 B8
Windsor Ho
5 Northwich CW8 . . . . 103 C5
Talke ST7 . . . . 210 D6
Windsor Pl CW12 . . . . 156 F2
Windsor Rd
Chester CH4 . . . . 140 F6
Golborne WA3 . . . . 3 C8
Widnes WA8 . . . . 13 A4
Wistaston CW2 . . . . 205 E8
Windsor Sq SK11 . . . . 112 D4
Windsor St WA5 . . . . 15 E6
Windsor Way WA16 . . . . 56 F2
Windways CH66 . . . . 69 D7
Windy Bank Ave WA3 . . . . 3 E8
WINDYHARBOUR 109 C1
Winfield Way WA8 . . . . 23 B8
Winfrith Rd WA2 . . . . 9 A2
Wingate Rd CH62 . . . . 43 E5
Wingfield Ave SK9 . . . . 59 E6
Wingfield Dr SK9 . . . . 59 E6
Wingfield Pl CW7 . . . . 149 B6
Winghay Rd ST7 . . . . 195 B2
Winifred St WA2 . . . . 16 C7
Winkwell Dr CH4 . . . . 141 A5
Winlowe 18 SK11 . . . . 112 E7
Winmarith Dr WA15 . . . . 32 D7
Winmarleigh St WA1 . . . . 16 A4
WINNINGTON 78 D1
Winnington Ave CW8 . . . . 103 C8
Winnington Ct 13 CW8 . . . . 103 F8
Winnington Hill CW8 . . . . 103 F8
Winnington La CW8 . . . . 78 D1
Winnington Park Com Prim Sch CW8 . . . . 103 D7
Winnington St
Northwich CW8 . . . . 103 F8
Winsford CW7 . . . . 126 E1
Winnows The WA7 . . . . 23 D1
Winscombe Dr CH3 . . . . 119 C2
Winsfield Rd SK7 . . . . 36 E8
WINSFORD 126 E2
Winsford Cl WA11 . . . . 1 F7
Winsford Cross Sh Ctr CW7 . . . . 126 D1
Winsford Dr WA5 . . . . 6 E7
Winsford Gr CH66 . . . . 69 C3
Winsford High Street Com Sch CW7 . . . . 126 D1
Winsford Ind Est CW7 . . . . 127 C3
Winsford Rd CW7 . . . . 170 F6
Winsford Sta CW7 . . . . 127 C1
Winsford Way CH1 . . . . 117 F2
Winslow Cl WA7 . . . . 50 D8
Winstanley Cl WA5 . . . . 15 C5
Winstanley Ho WA16 . . . . 56 F2
Winstanley Ind Est WA2 . . . . 8 B1
Winstanley Rd CH64 . . . . 66 E5
Winston Ave
Alsager ST7 . . . . 193 C5
Newton-le-W WA12 . . . . 2 C3
St Helens WA9 . . . . 1 B2
Winston Ct CH2 . . . . 119 A5
Winterbottom La WA16 . . . . 55 E8
Winterford La CW6 . . . . 147 B2
Winter Gr WA9 . . . . 1 B3
Wintergreen Wlk 3 M31 . . . . 11 F3
Winterlea Dr L26 . . . . 21 A6
WINTERLEY 191 F7
Winterside Cl ST5 . . . . 210 D1
Winterton Way SK11 . . . . 112 D3
Winton Gr WA7 . . . . 24 D1
Winton Rd WA3 . . . . 3 E6
WINWICK 8 A6
Winwick CE Prim Sch WA2 . . . . 8 B6
Winwick La WA3 . . . . 3 E3
Winwick Link Rd WA2, WA3 . . . . 8 C6
Winwick Park Ave WA2 . . . . 8 A5
WINWICK QUAY 8 A3
Winwick Rd
Newton-le-W WA12 . . . . 2 F1
Warrington WA2 . . . . 8 A2
Winwick St WA2 . . . . 16 B6
Winwick View WA5 . . . . 1 D1
Wirksmoor Rd SK22 . . . . 39 B7
Wirral Cl WA3 . . . . 4 E4
Wirral Cres CH64 . . . . 66 F5
Wirral Ctry Pk* CH64 . . . . 67 C7
Wirral Metropolitan Coll CH62 . . . . 44 A7
WIRSWALL 226 A5
Wirswall Rd SY13 . . . . 226 C8
Wisdom Wlk CW11 . . . . 174 D7
Wisenholme Cl WA7 . . . . 49 E5
WISTASTON 205 D8
Wistaston Ave CW2 . . . . 189 F2
WISTASTON GREEN 189 D2
Wistaston Green Cl CW2 . . . . 189 E2
Wistaston Green Prim Sch CW2 . . . . 189 F2
Wistaston Green Rd CW2 . . . . 189 E2
Wistaston Pk CW2 . . . . 189 F1
Wistaston Rd
Crewe CW2 . . . . 190 C3
Wistaston CW5 . . . . 205 E6
Wistaston Road Bsns Ctr CW2 . . . . 190 B4
Wistaston Westfield Prim Sch CW2 . . . . 205 E8
Wisterdale Cl CW2 . . . . 206 A7
Wisteria Way WA9 . . . . 6 A7
Witham Cl CW2 . . . . 206 A8
Witham Way ST8 . . . . 179 E1
Withens Cl CW8 . . . . 102 D8
Withenshaw La SK11 . . . . 136 E5
Withens La CW8 . . . . 102 D8
Withers Ave WA2 . . . . 16 D8
Wither's La
High Legh, Primrose Hill WA16 . . . . 28 C6
High Legh, Rowlinson's Green WA16 . . . . 28 B4
Witherwin Ave WA4 . . . . 26 F7
Withington Ave WA3 . . . . 5 A3
Withington Cl
Northwich CW9 . . . . 104 A6
Sandbach CW11 . . . . 175 C7
WITHINGTON GREEN 108 E3
Withinlee Rd SK10 . . . . 86 D6
Withins Rd
Culcheth WA3 . . . . 4 F3
Haydock WA11 . . . . 1 F8
Within Way L24 . . . . 21 E1
Withnall Dr CW2 . . . . 206 B4
Withy Cl WA6 . . . . 74 C8
Withycombe Rd WA5 . . . . 14 E4
Withy Croft CH3 . . . . 142 B7
Withyfold Dr SK10 . . . . 87 E1
Witney Gdns WA4 . . . . 26 E6
Witney La SY14 . . . . 213 D8
Wittenham Ho SK9 . . . . 34 D2
Wittering La CH60 . . . . 40 D7
Witterings The CH64 . . . . 41 E1
Witton Church Walk CE Prim Sch CW9 . . . . 104 A8
Witton St CW9 . . . . 79 A1
Witton Wlk 5 CW9 . . . . 103 F8
Witt Rd WA8 . . . . 23 A7
Wivern Pl WA7 . . . . 23 B3
Wizard Country Pk SK10 . . . . 85 D6
Wobbs La SY13 . . . . 225 C5
Woburn Ave WA12 . . . . 2 D2
Woburn Cl
Haydock WA11 . . . . 1 F7
Macclesfield SK10 . . . . 87 C2
Northwich CW9 . . . . 103 E5
Woburn Ct SK12 . . . . 36 F4
Woburn Dr
Chester CH2 . . . . 118 F7
Congleton CW12 . . . . 179 B8
Cronton WA8 . . . . 12 D6
Woburn Rd WA2 . . . . 8 A4
Woking Rd SK8 . . . . 35 A7
Wolfe Cl
Grappenhall Heys WA4 . . . . 27 A8
Knutsford WA16 . . . . 57 C3
Wolstanholme Cl CW12 . . . . 156 F1
WOLVERHAM 70 D4
Wolverham Prim Sch CH65 . . . . 70 D4
Wolverham Rd CH65 . . . . 70 D3
Wolverton Dr
Handforth SK9 . . . . 34 D1
Runcorn WA7 . . . . 24 D1
Wolverton Ho 11 SK9 . . . . 60 A1
Wolvesey Pl CW7 . . . . 149 B6
Woodacre Gr CH66 . . . . 69 F8
Woodacre Rd CH66 . . . . 69 F8
Woodacres Ct SK9 . . . . 59 F6
Woodale Cl WA5 . . . . 14 E7
Woodall Ave CH4 . . . . 140 E6
Woodall Dr WA7 . . . . 23 B1
Woodavens Gr CW3 . . . . 229 A2
WOODBANK 93 F6
Woodbank SK9 . . . . 60 A2
Woodbank Cl CW2 . . . . 206 A7
Woodbank La CH1 . . . . 93 D5
Woodbank Rd
Ellesmere Port CH65 . . . . 70 B2
Warrington WA5 . . . . 15 A4
Woodbine Ave M44 . . . . 11 D4
Woodbine Rd WA13 . . . . 19 B4
Woodbourne Rd SK22 . . . . 39 A5
Woodbridge Cl WA4 . . . . 26 E4
Woodbrook SK23 . . . . 65 E8
Woodbrook Ct SK23 . . . . 65 E7
Woodbrook Rd SK9 . . . . 60 C1
Woodburn Dr CH60 . . . . 40 F6
Woodchurch La CH66 . . . . 69 E6
Woodclose CH66 . . . . 44 A1
Woodcock La ST7 . . . . 195 C6
Woodcock's Well CE Prim Sch ST7 . . . . 195 C6
Woodcote Ave CH65 . . . . 70 B1
Woodcote Cl WA2 . . . . 8 D1
Woodcote Pl CW11 . . . . 191 F8
Woodcotes The CH62 . . . . 43 D6
Woodcote View SK9 . . . . 34 F1
Woodcott Ave CW7 . . . . 126 B1
Woodcott Cl CW2 . . . . 206 E2
Woodcott Gr 3 SK9 . . . . 34 E1
Woodcotthill La CW5 . . . . 217 B3
Woodcroft ST7 . . . . 210 A1
Wood Croft CH3 . . . . 119 F4
Woodcroft Gdns WA4 . . . . 26 E6
Wood Dr ST7 . . . . 193 A4
WOODEND 38 E8
Woodend WA7 . . . . 50 E7
Woodend Cl CW10 . . . . 151 C6
Wood End Ct WA8 . . . . 13 D2
Woodend La
Hollins Green WA3 . . . . 10 D2
Mobberley WA16 . . . . 58 E8
Wood End La CH64 . . . . 67 E4
Woodend Rd CH65 . . . . 69 F6
Woodfall Cl CH64 . . . . 67 A6
Woodfall Gr CH64 . . . . 67 A6
Woodfall La CH64 . . . . 67 B6
Woodfall Prim Sch CH64 . . . . 67 A6
Wood Farm CW2 . . . . 189 B4
Woodfield Cl CH4 . . . . 139 A3
Woodfield Gr CH2 . . . . 119 B5
Woodfield Ho CH2 . . . . 119 A5
Woodfield Prim Sch CH2 . . . . 119 A5
Woodfield Rd
Cheadle SK8 . . . . 35 B7
Ellesmere Port CH65 . . . . 70 C5
Woodfield Rd N 2 CH65 . . . . 70 C5
Woodfields CH3 . . . . 142 E7
Woodfin Croft SK11 . . . . 84 A3
WOODFORD 35 E2

Woodford Aerodrome SK7 36 A1
Woodford Ave WA3 3 D7
Woodford Cl
 Crewe CW2 189 F2
 Helsby WA6 73 B2
 Runcorn WA7 49 B6
 Warrington WA4 17 C3
Woodford Court Ind Est CW7 149 A8
Woodford Ct CW7 149 A7
Woodford La
 Prestbury SK10 61 D7
 Winsford CW7 149 B8
Woodford La W CW7 149 A7
Woodford Lo SK12 36 C4
Woodford Lodge High Sch CW7 149 A7
Woodford Mews SK9 34 D4
Woodford Park Ind Est CW7 148 F8
Woodford Rd
 Bramhall SK7 35 E4
 Poynton SK12 36 B6
 Wilmslow SK9 61 B8
Woodgate Ave ST7 194 A5
Wood Gdns SK9 60 B2
Woodgreen La CW5 171 D5
Woodhall Cl
 Bramhall SK7 35 E3
 Warrington WA5 15 A8
Woodhall Rd ST7 195 C3
Woodham Cl CW8 103 C5
Woodham Gr CH64 66 F5
Woodhatch Rd WA7 50 B5
Wood Heath Way CH62 44 A7
WOODHEY GREEN 202 B6
Woodhey Hall La CW5 202 B6
Woodhey La CW5 202 C5
Woodhouse Cl WA3 9 F3
WOODHOUSE-END 135 C8
Woodhouse End Rd SK11 135 C8
WOODHOUSE GREEN 158 D2
Woodhouse La
 Biddulph ST8 179 F2
 Buerton CW3 235 D8
 Partington WA14 20 C4
 Warren SK11 111 E1
 Wythenshawe M90 33 D7
Woodhouse Mid Sch ST8 179 E2
Woodhouse Rd M22 33 D8
WOODHOUSES 73 E4
Woodhouses Pk WA6 73 F5
Wood La
 Bradwall Green CW10, CW11 152 E3
 Broughton CH4 139 B4
 Burton CH64 67 C2
 Duddon CW6 145 E7
 Goostrey CW4 107 C1
 Neston CH64 41 D2
 Partington M31 11 D3
 Runcorn, Brookvale WA7 50 C6
 Runcorn WA7 49 F5
 Sutton Weaver WA7 49 F4
 Tattenhall CH3 167 A1
 Warrington WA4 26 E8
 Weaverham CW8 102 E8
 Wilmslow WA16 32 D1
Wood La E SK10 63 B8
Wood La N
 Fourlane-ends SK10 63 B8
 Wardsend SK10 37 B1
Woodlan Ct CW6 146 B6
Woodland Ave
 Crewe CW1 190 F4
 Lymm WA13 19 A2
 Nantwich CW5 205 A5
 Newton-le-W WA12 2 F3
 Widnes WA8 12 F1
Woodland Bank CH2 96 F1
Woodland Cl SK11 84 A3
Woodland Ct ST7 193 D4
Woodland Dr WA13 19 A2
Woodland End SK11 84 A3
Woodland Gdns CW1 190 D6
Woodland Rd
 Ellesmere Port CH65 70 B2
 Rode Heath ST7 193 E8
Woodlands CW8 103 B5
Woodlands Ave
 Chester CH1 118 B4
 Congleton CW12 156 D4
 Kidsgrove ST7 194 D1
Woodlands Cl
 Cheadle SK8 35 A8
 Cotebrook CW6 147 A8
 Neston CH64 66 D8
Woodlands Cres WA16 29 C4
Woodlands Ct
 Alderley Edge SK9 85 A8
 18 Knutsford WA16 57 B2
Woodlands Cvn Pk WA16 106 E3
Woodlands Dr
 Chester CH2 118 E4
 Chorlton CW2 207 C3
 Goostrey CW4 107 E1
 Knutsford WA16 57 B2
 Warrington WA4 17 D3
Woodlands Gr CW8 77 F3
Woodlands Ind Est WA12 2 C6
Woodlands Inf Sch CH66 69 F2
Woodlands Jun Sch CH66 69 F2
Woodlands La CH3 119 A2
Woodlands Pk
 Congleton CW12 156 C3
 Newton-le-W WA12 2 C6
Woodlands Rd
 Chester CH4 141 A7
 Handforth SK9 34 E3
 High Lane SK12 38 A6
 Huntington CH3 142 A6
 Macclesfield SK11 112 C6
 Neston CH64 66 D8
 New Mills SK22 39 A8
 Northwich CW8 103 C5
 Wilmslow SK9 33 F1
Woodlands Rd E 1 CW8 103 C5
Woodlands The
 Higher Wincham CW9 80 A6
 Kidsgrove ST7 194 E3
 Winnington CW8 78 E1
Woodlands Way CW6 146 D2
Woodland View
 Ellesmere Port CH66 69 B8
 Horwich End SK23 65 F2
Woodland Wlk
 Bebington CH62 43 C8
 Runcorn WA7 24 A1
WOOD LANE 210 A1
Wood Lane Prim Sch ST7 210 A1
Woodlark Cl CW7 150 A8
Wood La S SK10 63 B7
Wood La W SK10 63 A8
Woodlea Ave CH2 118 F7
Woodlea Cl CH62 43 D5
Woodlea Ct CW8 103 D7
Woodlea Dr SK10 87 E8
Woodleigh Ct SK9 60 A2
Woodley Fold WA5 14 F4
Wood Meml Prim Sch CH4 140 F6
Woodnoth Dr CW2 206 C5
Wood Orchard La CW3 230 A2
Woodpecker Cl WA3 9 F4
Woodpecker Dr
 Northwich CW9 103 F4
 Packmoor ST7 195 E1
Woodridge WA7 24 C1
Woodrow Ct 4 WA5 15 C7
Woodrow Way
 Irlam M44 11 F8
 Newcastle-u-Lyme ST5 210 F1
Woodruff Cl ST7 195 F1
Woodruff Wlk 7 M31 11 F3
Wood's Cl WA16 82 F6
Woods Ct WA12 2 A3
Woodsfin La CH3 183 F7
Woods Gr SK8 35 B7
WOODSHUTTS 194 F1
Woodshutt's St ST7 194 E1
WOODSIDE 99 C2
Woodside
 Ellesmere Port CH65 70 C2
 Knutsford WA16 57 B1
 Lawton-gate ST7 194 E4
 Poynton SK12 36 F4
 Siddington SK11 110 A3
Woodside Ave
 Alsager ST7 193 E4
 Crewe CW2 189 F2
 Frodsham WA6 74 D7
 Kidsgrove ST7 195 A1
Woodside Ct CH2 118 C4
Woodside Dr
 High Lane SK6 37 F7
 Sandbach CW11 175 C6
Woodside La
 Crewe CW2 189 F1
 Lymm WA13 19 B1
 Poynton SK12 36 E4
Woodside Prim Sch WA7 49 D7
Woodside Rd
 Blacon CH1 117 C5
 Haydock WA11 1 E7
 Warrington WA5 14 F6
Woodside St SK22 39 B6
Woodside Terr CW9 104 B4
Woods La SK8 35 B7
Wood's La CW8 101 C5
Woodsome Cl CH65 70 B1
Woodsome Dr CH65 70 B1
Wood Sorrel Way WA3 3 E8
Woods Rd M44 11 F8
Wood St
 Audley ST7 209 E3
 Congleton CW12 156 D3
 Crewe CW2 190 D2
 Golborne WA3 3 B8
 Macclesfield SK11 112 D7
 Mow Cop ST7 195 D7
 New Mills SK22 39 B7
 Sandycroft CH5 116 A2
 Warrington WA1 16 D6
 Widnes WA8 13 C1
Woodstock Ave
 Cheadle SK8 35 A7
 Newton-le-W WA12 2 D2
Woodstock Cl SK10 87 A2
Woodstock Dr CW10 151 E5
Woodstock Gdns WA4 26 F6
Woodstock Gr WA8 12 D2
Woodthorn Cl WA4 24 F4
Woodvale Cl WA2 8 E1
Woodvale Rd
 Ellesmere Port CH66 69 D6
 Knutsford WA16 82 A8
Wood View ST7 210 A1
Woodview Cres WA8 22 A8
Woodview Rd WA8 22 A8
Woodville Pl WA8 12 D1
Woodwards Cotts CH64 66 E7
Woodward St CW8 77 D1
Woodward Wlk CH3 121 C3
WOODWORTH GREEN 186 B8
Woodyear Rd CH62 43 E7
Woolacombe Cl WA4 16 D2
Woolaston Dr ST7 193 D3
Woolden Rd M44, WA3 11 B8
WOOLFALL 230 E6
Woollam Dr CH66 69 D7
Woolley Ave SK12 36 D2
Woolley Cl WA6 49 D2
Woolmer Cl WA3 10 B6
WOOLSTANWOOD 189 E3
WOOLSTON 17 C8
Woolston Ave CW12 157 A2
Woolston CE Prim Sch WA1 17 D8
Woolston Com High Sch WA1 17 B7
Woolston Com Prim Sch WA1 17 C7
Woolston Dr CW2 206 E2
Woolston Grange Ave
 Warrington WA1 9 D1
 Warrington, Woolston WA1 17 F8
Woolston Hall WA1 17 D7
Woolston Rd WA11 1 C7
Woolton Ct CH66 69 F8
WOORE 232 B1
Woore Prim Sch CW3 232 C1
Woore Rd CW3 230 D3
Worcester Ave WA3 3 B8
Worcester Cl
 Talke ST7 210 D7
 Warrington WA5 15 C5
Worcester Pl CH1 118 A4
Worcester St CH65 70 C6
Worcester Wlk 6 CH65 70 C6
Wordsworth Ave
 Warrington WA4 16 B2
 Widnes WA8 22 F8
Wordsworth Cl
 Crewe CW2 189 F1
 7 Sandbach CW11 174 D6
Wordsworth Cres CH1 118 A5
Wordsworth Dr CW1 190 F4
Wordsworth Ho SK10 86 F1
Wordsworth Mews CH1 118 A5
Wordsworth Sq CH1 118 A5
Wordsworth Way
 Alsager ST7 193 D4
 Ellesmere Port CH66 69 E1
Works Cotts WA7 49 E3
Works La CW9 79 E1
World Freight Terminal M90 32 F7
World Way M90 33 B8
WORLESTON 188 F5
Worleston Cl CW10 151 C6
Worley Ct CH3 183 A8
Worrall St CW12 156 E3
Worsborough Ave WA5 15 B5
Worsley Ave
 Saughall CH1 117 A8
 Warrington WA4 16 F4
Worsley Dr CW12 157 B1
Worsley Rd WA4 16 B1
Worsley St
 Golborne WA3 3 A8
 Warrington WA5 15 F7
Worth Ct SK12 36 D2
WORTHENBURY 211 A1
Worthing St CW9 104 C8
Worthington Ave 9 M31 11 F3
Worthington Cl
 Henbury SK11 111 C8
 Nantwich CW5 205 A5
 Runcorn WA7 50 A7
Worthington Ct CH2 118 D4
Worth Prim Sch SK12 36 F2
Wrekin Ho 8 CW8 103 C5
Wrekin Way CH4 140 F6
Wren Ave CW4 129 C2
Wrenbury Cl ST5 210 D1
WRENBURY 216 F4
Wrenbury Dr 3 CW9 103 E5
WRENBURY FRITH 216 C6
Wrenbury Frith CW5 216 B7
Wrenbury Gn CW5 216 E4
Wrenbury Hall Dr CW5 217 A5
WRENBURY HEATH 217 B5
Wrenbury Heath Rd CW5 217 D5
Wrenbury Ind Est CW5 217 A3
Wrenbury Prim Sch CW5 216 F4
Wrenbury Rd
 Aston CW5 217 B3
 Chorley Bank SY14 201 D1
 Marbury SY13 226 E8
 Wrenbury SY13, CW5 216 B1
Wrenbury Sta CW5 217 A3
Wren Cl
 Macclesfield SK10 87 A1
 Runcorn WA7 50 A6
 Warrington WA3 9 F4
Wrenmere Cl CW11 174 E8
Wrenshot La WA16 29 D4
Wrexham Cl
 Biddulph ST8 179 D1
 Warrington WA5 7 E1
Wrexham Ind Est/Ystad Ddiwdiannol Wrecsam LL13 196 A1
Wrexham Rd
 Bickerton SY14 200 A8
 Bulkeley SY14, CW6 184 E1
 Burland CW5 203 C8
 Chester CH4 141 B4
 Faddiley CW5, CW6 202 D6
 Holt LL13 196 B7
 Malpas SY14 212 E2
 Pulford CH4 162 E5
 Roughhill CH4 140 F1
 Worthenbury SY14 211 C1
Wright Ave CW9 104 D6
Wright Cres WA8 23 A5
Wright Ct CW5 204 F5
Wright Lo 6 CW5 204 F5
WRIGHT'S GREEN 27 A6
Wrights La WA5 13 F2
Wright's La
 Burtonwood WA5 6 F3
 Sandbach CW11 175 D6
Wright St ST7 194 D1
Wright Tree Villas M44 11 D5
Wrigley La SK10 86 B3
Wrigley Rd WA11 1 E6
Wrinehill Rd CW5 220 E7
Wroxham Cl
 Chester CH2 237 B4
 Helsby WA6 73 B4
Wroxham Rd WA5 14 E6
Wr Twr (Mus)★ CH1 118 B2
Wr Twr Rd CH64 41 E1
Wr Twr St CH1 237 A3
Wrynose Rd CH62 43 E8
Wybersley Rd SK6 38 A8
WYBUNBURY 220 A8
Wybunbury Delves CE Prim Sch CW5 220 B7
Wybunbury La CW5 205 E3
Wybunbury Rd
 Willaston CW5 205 D4
 Wybunbury CW5 220 B7
Wyche Ave CW5 204 D5
Wyche Cl CW9 104 E6
Wyche La CW6 185 F8
Wychelm Rd M31 11 F3
Wyche Prim Sch CW5 204 E6
Wyche Rd CW6 185 F8
Wych House Bank CW5 204 D5
Wych-House La CW10 128 C1
Wych La SK10 62 D5
Wychwood Ave WA13 18 C3
Wychwood Pk CW2 207 C1
Wycliffe Ave SK9 60 A7
Wycliffe Ct CH2 119 A2
Wycliffe Rd
 Ellesmere Port CH65 69 F3
 Haydock WA11 1 E7
Wyedale CH65 70 B3
Wyedale Rd WA11 1 C6
Wyncroft Cl
 Ellesmere Port CH65 70 B3
 Widnes WA8 22 C7
Wyncroft Ct CW8 77 C1
Wyncroft Rd WA8 22 C7
Wyndham Cl
 Bramhall SK7 35 E7
 Northwich CW9 103 F5
Wyndham Cres CH66 69 E2
Wyndham Rd CH1 117 C4
Wynd The CW6 122 C4
Wynfield Ave M22 33 F7
Wyngate Rd WA15 31 F8
Wynnstay Rd CH4 139 C4
Wynter Cl SY14 198 B3
Wynter La SY14 198 B3
Wythburn Gr WA7 49 E5
Wythens Rd SK8 34 B8
Wythin St CW6 168 D1

Y

Yardley Ave WA5 15 F8
Yarmouth Rd WA5 14 E6
Yarrow Cl CH4 139 C3
Yarwood Cl CW8 103 F7
Yarwoodheath La WA14 30 E7
YATEHOUSE GREEN 128 D6
Yatehouse La CW10 128 D7
Yates Cl WA5 15 C5
Yates Rd
 New Mills SK22 39 C7
 Thornton-le-M CH2 71 E1
Yates St CW2 190 C2
Y Berllan Geirios/Cherry Orch LL13 196 D8
Yeald Brow WA13 18 B3
Yeardsley Ave SK23 39 D3
Yeardsley Gn SK23 65 D8
Yeardsley La SK23 39 D3
Yearsleys La WA6 101 A5
Yeld La CW6 122 E8
Yeoman Way CH66 69 F1
Yeovil Cl WA1 17 C8
Yerburgh St CH2 118 D4
Yewdale Dr CH66 69 F1
Yewlands CW8 101 D5
Yewlands Dr WA16 57 C2
Yew Tree Ave WA12 2 A4
Yew Tree Ave / Lon yr Ywen CH1 116 F7
Yew Tree Bank CW6 145 B5
Yewtree Cl CH64 66 F7
Yew Tree Cl
 Broughton CH4 139 C3
 Bulkeley SY14 184 D2
 Little Budworth CW6 147 F7
 Lymm WA13 18 E4
 Macclesfield SK11 112 A6
 Middlewich CW10 128 B2
 Prestbury SK10 87 B7
 Thornton-le-M CH2 71 E1
 Wilmslow SK9 60 D7
Yew Tree Ct
 Alsager ST7 193 E2
 6 Heswall CH60 41 A8
 Wimboldsley CW10 150 F3
Yew Tree Dr
 Barnton CW8 78 B3
 Nantwich CW5 204 D5
Yew Tree Farm Trad Est WA11 2 A8
Yew Tree La
 Appleton Thorn WA4 27 C5
 Astbury CW12 178 C3
 Bridgemere CW5 232 A6
 Poynton SK12 36 F3
Yew Tree Park Rd SK8 35 B6
Yewtree Rd WA16 80 F3
Yew Tree Rd
 Wardsend SK10 37 B1
 Wistaston CW2 206 A8
Yew Tree Way
 Golborne WA3 3 B7
 Prestbury SK10 87 C6
Yew Wlk 1 M31 11 E2
Yonne The CH1 237 A2
York Ave
 Culcheth WA3 4 F2
 Warrington WA5 14 E7
York Cl
 Biddulph ST8 179 C2
 Talke ST7 210 D7
York Cres SK9 60 D8
York Ct 2 WA4 16 E1
York Dr
 Mickle Trafford CH2 119 E8
 Warrington WA4 17 A2
 Winsford CW7 149 D6
 Wythenshawe M90 32 F7
York Ho 4 CW8 103 C5
York Pl WA7 23 A2
York Rd
 Connah's Quay CH5 91 C1
 Ellesmere Port CH65 70 C5
 Irlam M44 11 D5
 Warrington WA4 17 A2
 Widnes WA8 22 C8
Yorkshire Rd M31 11 E2
York St
 Chester CH1 237 B3
 Macclesfield SK10 112 E8
 Runcorn WA7 23 A2
 Warrington WA4 16 C4
Yorston Lodge Sch WA16 56 F1
Ysgol Borderbrook SY14 222 F5
Ystad Ddiwdiannol Wrecsam/Wrexham Ind Est LL13 196 A1

Z

Zan Dr CW11 175 A3
Zan Ind Pk CW11 175 A3
Zara Ct WA11 1 C7
Zinnia Dr M44 11 E8
Zion St 3 CW8 103 E7

PHILIP'S MAPS

the Gold Standard for drivers

◆ **Philip's street atlases cover every county in England, Wales, Northern Ireland and much of Scotland**

◆ Every named street is shown, including alleys, lanes and walkways

◆ Thousands of additional features marked: stations, public buildings, car parks, places of interest

◆ Route-planning maps to get you close to your destination

◆ Postcodes on the maps and in the index

◆ Widely used by the emergency services, transport companies and local authorities

BEST BUY • BEST BUY • Auto EXPRESS

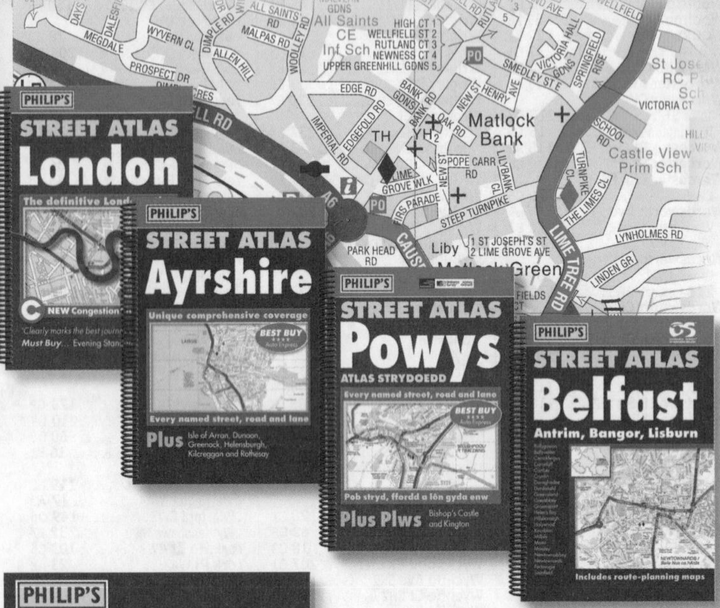

PHILIP'S

NAVIGATOR Britain

New speed camera sites, now with speed limits

Major roads named as well as numbered

Thousands of farms, houses, tracks and footpaths

'The ultimate in UK mapping'
The Sunday Times

For national mapping, choose **Philip's Navigator Britain** the most detailed road atlas available of England, Wales and Scotland. Hailed by Auto Express as 'the ultimate road atlas', the atlas shows every road and lane in Britain.

Street atlases currently available

England

- Bedfordshire
- Berkshire
- Birmingham and West Midlands
- Bristol and Bath
- Buckinghamshire
- Cambridgeshire
- Cheshire
- Cornwall
- Cumbria
- Derbyshire
- Devon
- Dorset
- County Durham and Teesside
- Essex
- North Essex
- South Essex
- Gloucestershire
- Hampshire
- North Hampshire
- South Hampshire
- Herefordshire Monmouthshire
- Hertfordshire
- Isle of Wight
- Kent
- East Kent
- West Kent
- Lancashire
- Leicestershire and Rutland
- Lincolnshire
- London
- Greater Manchester
- Merseyside
- Norfolk
- Northamptonshire
- Northumberland
- Nottinghamshire
- Oxfordshire
- Shropshire
- Somerset
- Staffordshire
- Suffolk
- Surrey
- East Sussex
- West Sussex
- Tyne and Wear
- Warwickshire
- Birmingham and West Midlands
- Wiltshire and Swindon
- Worcestershire
- East Yorkshire Northern Lincolnshire
- North Yorkshire
- South Yorkshire
- West Yorkshire

Wales

- Anglesey, Conwy and Gwynedd
- Cardiff, Swansea and The Valleys
- Carmarthenshire, Pembrokeshire and Swansea
- Ceredigion and South Gwynedd
- Denbighshire, Flintshire, Wrexham
- Herefordshire Monmouthshire
- Powys

Scotland

- Aberdeenshire
- Ayrshire
- Dumfries and Galloway
- Edinburgh and East Central Scotland
- Fife and Tayside
- Glasgow and West Central Scotland
- Inverness and Moray
- Lanarkshire
- Scottish Borders

Northern Ireland

- County Antrim and County Londonderry
- County Armagh and County Down
- Belfast
- County Tyrone and County Fermanagh

How to order

Philip's maps and atlases are available from bookshops, motorway services and petrol stations. You can order direct from the publisher by phoning **0207 531 8473** or online at **www.philips-maps.co.uk**
For bulk orders only, e-mail philips@philips-maps.co.uk